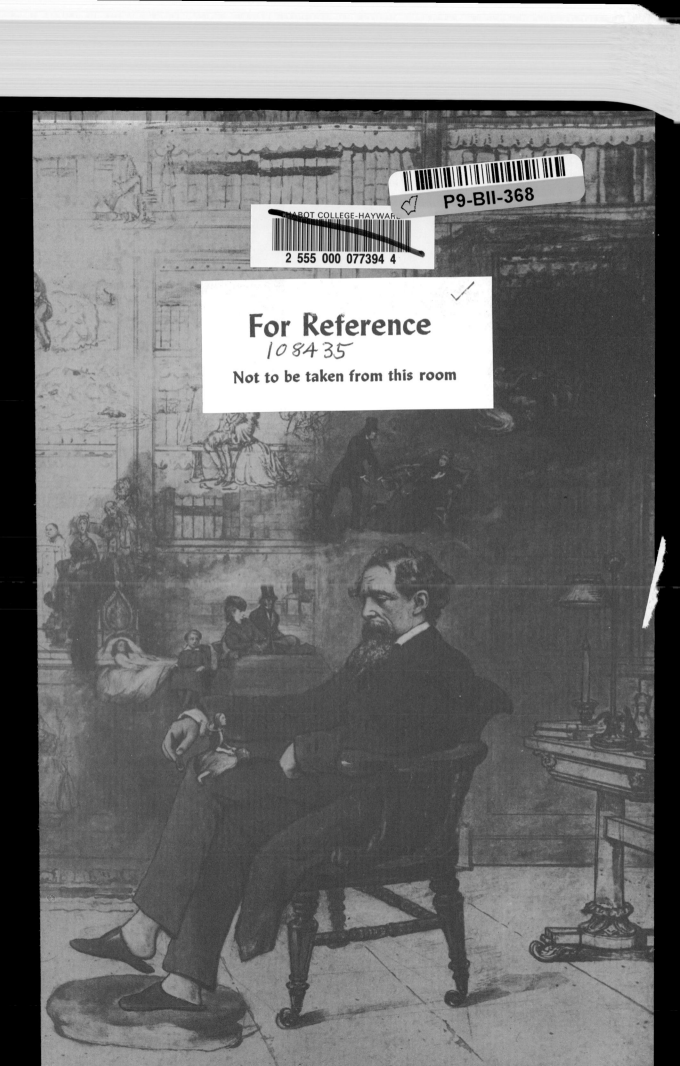

THE CHARLES DICKENS ENCYCLOPEDIA

THE
CHARLES DICKENS
ENCYCLOPEDIA

COMPILED BY
MICHAEL AND MOLLIE
HARDWICK

CHARLES SCRIBNER'S SONS · NEW YORK

Copyright © 1973 Michael and Mollie Hardwick
Copyright under the Berne Convention
All rights reserved. No part of this book
may be reproduced in any form without the
permission of Charles Scribner's Sons.

Book designed by Frederick Price

Printed in Great Britain
Library of Congress Catalog Card Number 73–7212
SBN 684–13562–0

First published in Great Britain in 1973 by
Osprey Publishing Limited, 707 Oxford Road, Reading, Berkshire
© Copyright 1973 Michael and Mollie Hardwick
All rights reserved

PREFACE

SOME day, inevitably, someone will produce a complete concordance to the works of Charles Dickens. One hears already of an American computer test-run on one of the novels which, at a cost of tens of thousands of dollars, has counted the commas. Our aim has been more modest and, we believe, more realistic: to provide the most comprehensive 'companion' to the works that has yet been attempted, but to include in it only the sort of information that we can imagine being of use or entertainment to someone.

Dickens, with Shakespeare and Dr. Johnson, is probably the most quoted of all English writers, and certainly one of the most quotable. He is therefore one of the most drawn-upon by other writers, teachers, speakers, competition compilers, quiz-masters, and producers of entertainments of many kinds. In setting out to serve all these, not to mention the ordinary reader, the difficulty has been to determine not what to include, but what to leave out. The ideal, perhaps, is simply to reprint the entire works, with a colossal index; but that takes us close to that computer. We have made our selection, based on a lifetime's savouring of Dickens's writings and frequent plundering of them for work in most of the media of entertainment and instruction. Rather than attempt to categorise the quotations, which would have necessitated scores of divisions, hundreds of cross-references, and some very forced classifications, we present them work by work with a large index of key words, which we believe should satisfy almost all the needs of the work's users, practical and pleasurable. Many of the quotations are of fair length, the intention being that this section can be read, not just referred to, and will convey more of the essence of Dickens's writing and outlook than could be demonstrated by thousands of brief snippets.

The other most substantial part of the work, 'The People', we can claim is virtually exhaustive. There are more than 2,000 entries and they cover every named character in the stories, with the exception of some to whom mere allusion is made by, say, Mrs. Nickleby casting about for a memory. Nearly all are accompanied by a quotation illustrative of appearance, character, habit, manner of speaking, and so forth, which has been selected to be of genuine value to those who use the book as a tool, as well as to amuse.

It will be seen that we have confined ourselves to those works which are to be found in the usual 'complete' sets of Charles Dickens's writings: in other words, mostly the work of his imagination, as opposed to the straight reporting, critical essays, and campaigning pamphleteering. This has meant taking in those pieces from periodicals such as *Household Words* that are familiar in volume form as *Reprinted Pieces*, comprising both imaginative sketches and straight journalism; but we have glanced only in passing at *Miscellaneous Papers, American Notes* and *Pictures from Italy* which include no made-up stories, and have ignored the *Memoirs of Joseph Grimaldi*, which Dickens and his father merely edited and added to. We have touched upon the poetry briefly – the less said about Dickens as poet, the better – but have included the plays, for all their inferiority, since they appear in some full editions.

Both the sections dealing with Dickens's circle and the places associated with his life and works are selective, and the selection is ours, based on our notion of what will prove useful or entertaining. Someone, somewhere, will deplore an omission. We can only answer that, even with half a million words at our disposal, some things had to go; and Dickens wrote over five million words.

We have dealt with Dickens's own life in the form of a Time Chart, in the belief that to have written exhaustively about it in essay form would not have shown up the sequence of related dates and facts in the quick-reference way this book requires. A chart of dates and events, however, can offer only a conjectural picture of the man as personality and character; and while a good deal more about him can be deduced from a study of what he wrote, we believe that this preface might be no bad place in which to add an impression or two of Charles Dickens which will summon him from behind the scenes.

His childhood nurse, for instance, remembered him as 'a lively boy of a good, genial, open disposition . . . a terrible boy to read'. The latter was perhaps due in part to his physical delicacy and slightness of frame, though his schoolmaster's sister thought him 'a very handsome boy, with long curly hair of a light colour'. A schoolfellow at Wellington House saw him as 'full of animation and animal spirits'. All these descriptions add up to that given by his friend and biographer, John Forster, of Dickens the young man on the brink of fame.

A look of youthfulness first attracted you, and then a candour and openness of expression which made you sure of the qualities within. The features were very good. He had a capital forehead, a firm nose with full wide nostrils, eyes wonderfully beaming with intellect and running over with humour and cheerfulness, and a rather prominent mouth strongly marked with sensibility . . . the hair so scant and grizzled in later days was then of a rich brown and luxurious abundance, and the bearded face of his last two decades had hardly a vestige of hair or whisker; but there was that in the face as I first recollect it which no time could change, and which remained implanted on it unalterably to the last. This was the quickness, keenness and practical power, the eager, restless, energetic outlook on each several feature, and so much of a man of action and business in the world. Light and motion flashed from every part of it. *It was as if made of steel*, was said of it ... by a most original and delicate observer, the late Mrs. Carlyle. 'What a face is his to meet in a drawing-room!' wrote Leigh Hunt to me, the morning after I made them known to each other. 'It has the life and soul in it of fifty human beings.'

Such, for many years, was the outward man. At first a dandy, with a taste for bright clothes and jewellery, he became with prosperity more sober in appearance, and, as middle age came on and troubles increased, the thick hair receded and the smooth face took on premature lines and wrinkles, while the beard and moustache added apparent years to his age. Within, he never varied. With a terrifying, daemonic energy which compelled him to wear himself out, he had the capacity for work and play of fifty human beings, as Hunt might have added. When he was not writing novels he was engaged in journalism, or in dashing off long vivacious letters, or walking huge distances, or playing with his children, or producing and acting in amateur theatricals, or travelling on a reading tour. The two latter activities were necessary to him as release for that part of him which yearned to act rather than write; and yet he was no Bohemian in spirit. His meticulous passion for tidiness and order was the bane of his family. A byword for generosity, he yet had a streak in him which made a perceptive

woman friend remark that while Thackeray was the gentlest-hearted, most generous, most loving of men, 'Dickens, whose whole mind went to almost morbid tenderness and sympathy, was infinitely less plastic, less self-giving, less personally sympathetic.'

From this trait, perhaps, came the failures of his personal life in connection with his wife, his family and other women. 'My father never understood women,' said the daughter who married the wrong man to get away from home; and it is a truism to add that it is only the comic women in his stories who spring to real life. Nor did he understand as young men the sons he had idolised when they were babies. One after another, as they failed to come up to his high ideals, they were sent as far away as possible to work out their destinies. It was a contradiction as strange as that which compelled him to write of London as if he loved it, to yearn for it in foreign places, and yet to loathe its squalor while mentally wallowing in it. He was in no way a countryman, yet it was in a country house in Kent, the dream-house of his boyhood, that he spent the last portion of his life.

'Whatever the word "great" means,' said G. K. Chesterton, 'Dickens was what it means.' Our personal tribute to him, if one may be permitted, is that after all the time and labour expended on preparing this book, a seemingly endless task of selection, checking, revision, re-checking, proof-reading, and all the rest of it, we can still sit down to read Charles Dickens's works with a certainty of enjoyment greater than any other writer can give us.

Michael and Mollie Hardwick

ACKNOWLEDGEMENTS

WE acknowledge with gratitude the help of the following people in preparing this book: Mr. John Greaves, Hon. Secretary of the Dickens Fellowship and Miss Marjorie Pillers, Curator of the Dickens House, London, for providing information and helping to settle debatable points of 'fact'; Miss Alison Hodgson, for her admirably relentless editing of the MS and assistance with the proof-reading; Miss Ann Hoffmann, for compiling the demanding Indexes; Mrs. Margaret Morton, for typing well over half a million words with less than a dozen mistakes, and Mr. Roger Cleeve of Osprey Publishing, on whose initiative this work was undertaken, and whose co-operation and understanding have been all that the authors could have desired.

The jacket portrait of Charles Dickens aged 47 is from the painting by William Powell Frith, reproduced by permission of the Trustees of the Dickens House, and the endpapers are reproduced from the painting *Dickens's Dream* by Robert William Buss, in the possession of the Dickens Fellowship.

CONTENTS

A NOTE ON TYPOGRAPHY
AND ABBREVIATIONS

TYPOGRAPHY

ALL references to titles of books and plays are given in italic script, and to magazine articles, book chapters, short stories, essays, poems and songs, in quotation marks. Thus 'No Thoroughfare' refers to the short story, *No Thoroughfare* to the play based upon it.

ABBREVIATIONS

The following abbreviations are used in this work

'At Dusk'	'To be Read at Dusk'
Boz	*Sketches by Boz*
Chuzzlewit	*The Life and Adventures of Martin Chuzzlewit*
Copperfield	*The Personal History of David Copperfield*
Curiosity Shop	*The Old Curiosity Shop*
Dombey	*Dealings with the Firm of Dombey and Son*
Dorrit	*Little Dorrit*
Drood	*The Mystery of Edwin Drood*
Expectations	*Great Expectations*
Humphrey	*Master Humphrey's Clock*
Mudfog	*The Mudfog and other Sketches*
Mutual Friend	*Our Mutual Friend*
Nickleby	*The Life and Adventures of Nicholas Nickleby*
Nightingale's Diary	*Mr. Nightingale's Diary*
Pickwick	*The Posthumous Papers of the Pickwick Club*
Reprinted	*Reprinted Pieces*
Rudge	*Barnaby Rudge*
'Silverman'	'George Silverman's Explanation'
Twist	*The Adventures of Oliver Twist*
Two Apprentices	*The Lazy Tour of Two Idle Apprentices*
Two Cities	*A Tale of Two Cities*
Uncommercial	*The Uncommercial Traveller*
Young Couples	*Sketches of Young Couples*
Young Gentlemen	*Sketches of Young Gentlemen*

ALPHABETICAL LIST OF WORKS
COVERED BY THIS ENCYCLOPEDIA

This list gives all the writings of Dickens covered by this encyclopedia, each followed by the date(s) of journal or serial publication (if applicable) and of first known bound publication. Short stories and articles are posted up to the titles of the collections in which they appear. More detailed publishing history will be found in 'The Works' section.

'Aboard Ship' 5 Dec. 1868; 1875 in *Uncommercial*

American Notes 1842

'Arcadian London' 29 Sept. 1860; 1860 in *Uncommercial*

'Astley's' 9 May 1835; 1836 in *Boz*

'Barbox Brothers', a chapter of 'Mugby Junction' q.v., below

Barnaby Rudge 13 Feb. – 27 Nov. 1841; 1841

'Bashful Young Gentleman, The' 1838 in *Young Gentlemen*

'Battle of Life, The' Dec. 1846; 1852 in *Christmas Books*

'Beadle, The. The Parish Engine. The Schoolmaster' 28 Feb 1835; 1836 in *Boz*

'Begging-letter Writer, The' 18 May 1850; 1858 in *Reprinted*

'Bill-sticking' 22 Mar. 1851; 1858 in *Reprinted*

'Birthday Celebrations' 6 June 1863; 1865 in *Uncommercial*

' "Births. Mrs. Meek, of a Son" ' 22 Feb. 1851; 1858 in *Reprinted*

'Black Veil, The' 1836 in *Boz*

Bleak House Mar. 1852–Sept. 1853; 1853

'Bloomsbury Christening, The' Apr. 1834; 1836 in *Boz*

'Boarding-house, The' May and Aug. 1834; 1836 in *Boz*

'Boiled Beef of New England, The' 15 Aug. 1863; 1865 in *Uncommercial*

'Bound for the Great Salt Lake' 4 July 1863; 1865 in *Uncommercial*

'Boy at Mugby, The', a chapter of 'Mugby Junction' q.v., below

'Brokers' and Marine-store Shops' 15 Dec. 1834; 1836 in *Boz*

'Broker's Man, The' 28 July 1835; 1836 in *Boz*

'Calais Night Mail, The' 2 May 1863; 1865 in *Uncommercial*

'Censorious Young Gentleman, The' 1838 in *Young Gentlemen*

'Chambers' 18 Aug. 1860; 1860 in *Uncommercial*

'Chatham Dockyard' 29 Aug. 1863; 1865 in *Uncommercial*

'Child's Dream of a Star, A' 6 Apr. 1850; 1858 in *Reprinted*

Child's History of England, A 25 Jan. 1851–10 Dec. 1853; 1852–4

'Child's Story, The' Dec. 1852; 1858 in *Reprinted*, 1871 in *Christmas Stories*

'Chimes, The' Dec. 1844; 1852 in *Christmas Books*

Christmas Books Dec. 1843–Dec. 1848; 1852

'Christmas Carol, A' Dec. 1843; 1852 in *Christmas Books*

'Christmas Dinner, A' 27 Dec. 1835; 1836 in *Boz*

Christmas Stories Dec. 1850–Dec. 1867; 1871

'Christmas Tree, A' Dec. 1850; 1858 in *Reprinted*, 1871 in *Christmas Stories*

'City of London Churches' 5 May 1860; 1860 in *Uncommercial*

'City of the Absent, The' 18 July 1863; 1865 in *Uncommercial*

'Contradictory Couple, The' 1840 in *Young Couples*

'Cool Couple, The' 1840 in *Young Couples*

'Couple Who Coddle Themselves, The' 1840 in *Young Couples*

'Couple Who Dote Upon Their Children, The' 1840 in *Young Couples*

'Cricket on the Hearth, The' Dec. 1845; 1852 in *Christmas Books*

'Criminal Courts' 23 Oct. 1834; 1836 in *Boz*

'Curate, The. The Old Lady. The Half-pay Captain' 19 May 1835; 1836 in *Boz*

'Dancing Academy, The' 11 Oct. 1835; 1836 in *Boz*

David Copperfield, The Personal History of May 1849–Nov. 1850; 1850

'Detective Police, The' 27 July and 10 Aug. 1850; 1858 in *Reprinted*

'Dinner at Poplar Walk, A' see 'Mr. Minns and his Cousin' below

'Doctor Marigold' Dec. 1865; 1871 in *Christmas Stories*

'Doctors' Commons' 11 Oct. 1836; 1836 in *Boz*

Dombey and Son, Dealings with the Firm of Oct. 1846–Apr. 1848; 1848

'Domestic Young Gentleman, The' 1838 in *Young Gentlemen*

'Down with the Tide' 5 Feb. 1853; 1858 in *Reprinted*

'Drunkard's Death, The' 1836 in *Boz*

'Dullborough Town' 30 June 1860; 1860 in *Uncommercial*

'Early Coaches 19 Feb. 1835; 1836 in *Boz*

'Egotistical Couple, The' 1840 in *Young Couples*

'Election for Beadle, The' 14 July 1835; 1836 in *Boz*

'Familiar Epistle from a Parent to a Child' Feb. 1839; post-1880 editions of *Mudfog*

'First of May, The' 31 May 1836; 1836 in *Boz*

'Flight, A' 30 Aug. 1851; 1858 in *Reprinted*

'Fly-leaf in a Life, A' 22 May 1869; 1890 in *Uncommercial*

'Formal Couple, The' 1840 in *Young Couples*

'Four Sisters, The' 18 June 1835; 1836 in *Boz*

'Full Report of the First Meeting of the Mudfog Association' Oct. 1837; 1880 in *Mudfog*

'Full Report of the Second Meeting of the Mudfog Association' Sept. 1838; 1880 in *Mudfog*

THE WORKS

LISTED IN ORDER OF FIRST

APPEARANCE IN ANY FORM: SERIALS BY FIRST

INSTALMENT, COLLECTIONS BY EARLIEST

INDIVIDUAL PIECE

CONTENTS OF 'THE WORKS'

THE WORKS

SKETCHES BY BOZ

Dickens's first published writings, beginning with 'A Dinner at Poplar Walk' (later re-titled 'Mr. Minns and his Cousin') which appeared in the *Monthly Magazine* in December 1833. Other sketches subsequently appeared in this magazine and in the *Morning Chronicle, Evening Chronicle,* and *Bell's Life in London.* Dickens's pseudonym in the latter publication was Tibbs. The 'Boz' used elsewhere derived from the adenoidal pronunciation of the name Moses by which his young brother Augustus was known in the family. The first collected series of *Sketches by Boz* appeared in February 1836 and the second in December, both published by Macrone. The first complete edition, embodying further pieces, was published in 1839 by Chapman & Hall. Published in the U.S.A. in two volumes, 1837 (Carey, Lea & Blanchard, Philadelphia).

The *Sketches* are a mixture of descriptive pieces of journalism, whose titles generally convey their subject, fictional portraits, and short stories, of varying quality but replete with hints of the Dickens-to-come, and valuable in their reflection of contemporary manners and conditions. Looking back in 1850, Dickens wrote in a Preface to the first cheap edition: 'They comprise my first attempts at authorship – with the exception of certain tragedies achieved at the mature age of eight or ten, and represented with great applause to overflowing nurseries. I am conscious of their often being extremely crude and ill-considered, and bearing obvious marks of haste and inexperience.'

OUR PARISH

A series of character sketches: 'The Beadle. The Parish Engine. The Schoolmaster'; 'The Curate. The Old Lady. The Half-pay Captain'; 'The Four Sisters'; 'The Election for Beadle'; 'The Broker's Man'; 'The Ladies' Societies'; 'Our Next-door Neighbour'.

SCENES

Portrayals of London life, owing much to Dickens's habit of tramping the streets at all hours of the night: 'The Streets – Morning'; 'The Streets – Night'; 'Shops and their Tenants'; 'Scotland-yard'; 'Seven Dials'; 'Meditations in Monmouth-street'; 'Hackney-coach Stands'; 'Doctors' Commons'; 'London Recreations'; 'The River'; 'Astley's'; 'Greenwich Fair'; 'Private Theatres'; 'Vauxhall-gardens by Day'; 'Early Coaches'; 'Omnibuses'; 'The Last Cab-driver, and the First Omnibus Cad'; 'A Parliamentary Sketch'; 'Public Dinners'; 'The First of May'; 'Brokers' and Marine-store Shops'; 'Gin-shops'; 'The Pawnbroker's Shop'; 'Criminal Courts'; 'A Visit to Newgate'.

CHARACTERS

Reflections about types, some of them in the form of short stories: 'Thoughts about People' – Dickens considers a humble clerk, rich bachelors, carefree apprentices; 'A Christmas Dinner' – a typical family gathering; 'The New Year' – Tupple, the perfect guest, attends a quadrille party given by Dobble, a fellow clerk in a government office; 'Miss Evans and the Eagle' – Samuel Wilkins takes J'mima Ivins to the Eagle Pleasure Gardens in the City Road and gets into a fight; 'The Parlour Orator' – a public-house know-all; 'The Hospital Patient' – a dying girl refuses to accuse her lover of beating her; 'The Misplaced Attachment of Mr. John Dounce' – a well-to-do widower is attracted by a pretty young oyster-bar keeper, is cut by his friends and relatives and refused by his young woman, and ends up married to his cook; 'The Mistaken Milliner. A Tale of Ambition' – Miss Amelia Martin disastrously fancies herself as a concert singer; 'The Dancing Academy' – Augustus Cooper takes a course of dancing lessons with Signor Billsmethi and finds himself sued for breach of promise by Miss Billsmethi; 'Shabby-genteel People' – an old reader in the British Museum typifies his kind; 'Making a Night of it' – two City clerks, Potter and Smithers, spend their quarter's salary on a one-night spree; 'The Prisoners' Van' – two young prostitute sisters are seen leaving Bow Street for Cold Bath Fields prison.

TALES

Twelve short stories: 'The Boarding-house' – the arrival of Mrs. and the Misses Maplesone at Mrs. Tibbs's boarding-house brings upheaval to the lives of the gentlemen boarders; 'Mr. Minns and his Cousin' – Augustus Minns, a fastidious bachelor, is pestered into visiting his deplorable cousin, Octavius Budden, and wishes he had stayed at home; 'Sentiment' – Lavinia Brook Dingwall is sent to the Misses Crumpton's educational establishment to remove her from the attentions of Theodosius Butler, who turns out to be the Misses Crumpton's cousin and a guest at their half-yearly ball; 'The Tuggses at Ramsgate' – the newly-rich Tuggs family are fleeced by two confidence tricksters, Captain and Belinda Waters; 'Horatio Sparkins' – the snobbish Malderton family bask in the acquaintance of the mysteriously aristocratic Horatio Sparkins, who proves to be a draper's assistant named Smith; 'The Black Veil' – a surgeon is pressed by a woman to visit a dying man, but finds himself confronted with the corpse of an executed criminal, her son; 'The Steam Excursion' – Percy Noakes organises a steam-packet excursion on the Thames, which is a great success until the weather turns rough; 'The Great Winglebury Duel' – Alexander Trott, trying to get himself arrested in order to avoid having to fight a duel with Horace Hunter, his rival for Emily Brown, is mistaken for Lord Peter, who has an assignation with the wealthy Julia Manners, and she finds him agreeable enough to marry instead; 'Mrs. Joseph Porter' – the Gattletons' private theatricals are ruined by their rival Mrs. Joseph Porter, who eggs on Mrs. Gattleton's erudite brother Thomas to keep correcting the players; 'A Passage in the Life of Mr. Watkins Tottle' – in return for the payment of his debts by Gabriel Parsons, Watkins Tottle agrees to marry Miss Lillerton and let Parsons share the advantage of her private income, but it emerges that she is engaged to the Revd. Charles Timson, who Tottle thinks is going to conduct the ceremony, and Tottle drowns himself in the Regent's Canal; 'The Bloomsbury Christening' – Nicodemus Dumps, a misanthropic bachelor, gets his own back for having to attend the christening of the baby of his nephew, Charles Kitterbell, by making a speech full of baleful prophecies about the child's future and sending Mrs. Kitterbell into hysterics; 'The Drunkard's Death' – Warden, whose drunkenness has caused his wife's death from grief and driven his sons from home, unintentionally betrays one of them to the police to face execution for murder, is deserted at long last by his loyal daughter, and drowns himself in the Thames.

THE POSTHUMOUS PAPERS OF THE PICKWICK CLUB

Dickens's first novel. Writing began in London in February 1836, at 15 Furnival's Inn, and continued at 48 Doughty Street; completed October 1837. First publication in England in monthly numbers, 31 March 1836 to 30 October 1837. Issued complete by Chapman & Hall, November 1837. First American publication 1836-7 by Carey, Lea & Blanchard, Philadelphia, in five volumes, each including four of the original parts.

In 1836 Chapman & Hall invited Dickens to provide the text for a series of 'Cockney sporting-plates of a superior sort' by the artist Robert Seymour. Dickens objected to their proposal for sketches concerning the activities of a 'Nimrod Club' on the grounds that he was no sportsman and that the idea was an old one. 'My views being deferred to, I thought of Mr. Pickwick, and wrote the first number.' The appearance and some characteristics of Pickwick himself were based on a 'fat old beau', John Foster, of Richmond. The early numbers were received quietly, but soon reviews became warm and the public enthusiastic as the original scrappy form gave place to a continuous

story with developing characters and a humour previously unknown in English literature. The appearance of Sam Weller sealed the triumph of the book. Traces of the influence of Smollett, Fielding, and Defoe are noticeable in the writing, and the plot bears evidence of Dickens's wide travels as a parliamentary reporter and of his early experience of a debtors' prison, while Jingle, the actor, is an aspect of Dickens the actor *manqué*.

The Pickwick Club as a body makes an early and brief appearance, at one of its London meetings. Thereafter the central figures of the book are its President, the middle-aged, stout, jovial, and naïf Samuel Pickwick, a retired gentleman who sets out on a tour of investigation of scientific and cultural matters, and the three friends who accompany him: Nathaniel Winkle, who fancies himself as a sportsman but fails dismally to justify his pretensions; Augustus Snodgrass, melancholy and romantic in the fashionable Byronic manner (the period of the story is 1827-31); and the somewhat older Tracy Tupman, a plump bachelor amorist.

Their first adventure occurs at Rochester, where the cowardly Winkle is mistakenly challenged to a duel, the real offending party being Alfred Jingle, a strolling player. Jingle joins the party; it is the first of his mischievous appearances in Mr. Pickwick's life.

At a military review in Chatham the Pickwickians meet Mr. Wardle, a country squire, his daughters Bella and Emily, his spinster sister Rachael, and their servant Joe, an immensely fat and greedy youth with a tendency to sleep on his feet. An invitation from Wardle takes the party down to his Kentish manor at Dingley Dell, where the unfortunate Winkle, taken out shooting, misses his bird and shoots Tupman in the arm. Rachael Wardle, on the lookout for a husband, evinces great emotion at the incident, and a romantic association springs up between her and Tupman. But Jingle, who has again come on the scene, cuts out Tupman and elopes with Rachael to London, where Wardle and Pickwick find the pair about to marry by special licence. Jingle is bribed to abandon Rachael.

At the White Hart Inn, Borough, where the couple are staying, Pickwick meets the lively young Cockney Sam Weller, self-taught, voluble, and irrepressible, who is working as Boots. Pickwick decides to take Sam into his service as valet and servant; but his attempts to announce this to his landlady, the widowed Mrs. Bardell, are interpreted by that lady as a proposal of marriage to herself, and the other three Pickwickians arrive to see her fainting in the horrified Pickwick's arms.

They travel on to Eatanswill and witness the humours of an election. Once more Jingle appears, this time masquerading as a captain. Pickwick follows him to Bury St. Edmunds, proposing to unmask him. With the aid of his servant, the lugubrious Job Trotter, Jingle entices Pickwick into the grounds of a girls' boarding-school by night. Pickwick's intentions are gravely misunderstood by the teachers and pupils.

After a pleasant visit to Dingley Dell, the Pickwickians return to London and Pickwick is disturbed to learn that Mrs. Bardell, under the influence of the rascally lawyers Dodson and Fogg, has instituted an action for breach of promise against him. He journeys to Ipswich, where at the Great White Horse he finds himself by mistake in the bedroom of a lady just about to become engaged to the jealous Mr. Peter Magnus, who challenges him to a duel. The lady reports them to the magistrate Nupkins, but Pickwick clears his name and incidentally finds that Jingle is in Ipswich attempting to marry Miss Nupkins under false pretences. Pickwick unmasks him, and with his friends returns for a happy visit to Dingley Dell, enjoying country sports and pastimes and attending the wedding of Bella Wardle to Mr. Trundle.

Other romantic affairs are on hand: Winkle is in love with Arabella Allen, a friend of Emily Wardle, with whom Snodgrass is infatuated. Arabella's brother Ben, a medical student, turns up at Dingley Dell with his friend Bob Sawyer, also a suitor for Emily's hand.

There follows the hearing of the Bardell and Pickwick breach of promise case. Pickwick's defence is shattered by the inept testimony of Winkle and the eloquence of Mrs. Bardell's counsel, Serjeant Buzfuz. Mrs. Bardell is awarded £750 damages, which Pickwick refuses to pay. He takes refuge from his troubles at Bath, where he experiences the niceties of spa society, Sam attends a 'swarry' of snobbish footmen, and Mr. Winkle is seriously compromised by being found at midnight, clad only in his nightshirt, with the pretty Mrs. Dowler in her sedan-chair. Pickwick and Sam rescue him, and he meets Arabella Allen once again in Bristol. Sam Weller falls in love with Mary, a pretty housemaid.

Again in London, Pickwick is imprisoned in the Fleet for non-payment of damages. Sam gets himself imprisoned to remain in company with his master by a trick worked with his father, Tony Weller, a stout coachman who has married a widow addicted to piety and tea-drinking in the company of the Reverend Mr. Stiggins, a hypocritical drunken parson.

In the Fleet Pickwick meets again Jingle and Job Trotter, penniless, starving, and distressed. He befriends them generously and obtains their release and a passage to Australia where they may start a new life. Mrs. Bardell arrives in the Fleet, sent there by Dodson and Fogg for non-payment of costs. Pickwick pays the costs for her on condition that she agrees to forgo his damages.

His final adventures are all connected with romance. Winkle has secretly married Arabella, and Pickwick reconciles both Winkle's father and Ben Allen to the match. Snodgrass and Emily Wardle are bent on elopement, because of Wardle's attitude to their engagement, but Pickwick brings father and daughter together and all misunderstandings are sorted out.

The Pickwick Club is dissolved. Pickwick retires to a neat villa in Dulwich, with Sam and Mary as his servants; they, too, marry. Tony Weller is now a widower, and has at last taken his revenge upon the Reverend Mr. Stiggins by ducking him in a horse-trough.

SUNDAY UNDER THREE HEADS

Sub-titled 'As it is: As Sabbath Bills would make it: As it might be made', this pamphlet was written for Chapman & Hall to publish in 1836, with three illustrations by Hablôt K. Browne. It is a sharp and early attack on advocates of more rigid observance of the Sabbath.

THE VILLAGE COQUETTES

Written in 1836 at Furnival's Inn, London, it was produced on 6 December 1836. It played in repertory for nineteen performances, afterwards transferring to Edinburgh. First published in 1836 by Richard Bentley, and in 1837 by Bradbury & Evans.

It had been suggested to Dickens by John Hullah, a young composer, that they should combine their talents. The resulting comic opera in two acts was accepted by Braham, lessee of the St. James's Theatre. The audience's reception was enthusiastic, but the press in general criticised the libretto.

Two village maidens, Lucy Benson and her cousin Rose, are respectively betrothed to George Edmunds and John Maddox. But at Harvest Home time the two girls transfer their attentions to Squire Norton and his friend the Honourable Sparkins Flam. The Squire tries to persuade Lucy to elope with him, and her father overhears him and banishes him from his farm, but later relents. Flam's proposed abduction of Rose is likewise foiled, and the rustic sweethearts are finally reconciled.

THE STRANGE GENTLEMAN

Written in 1836 at Furnival's Inn, London, and produced at the St. James's Theatre on 29 September the same year, it ran for sixty nights. First published in 1836 or 1837 by Chapman & Hall. It is based on the *Boz* tale, 'The Great Winglebury Duel'.

The Strange Gentleman arrives at a posting-house on the way to Gretna Green and demands a private room. He has been challenged to a duel by Horatio Tinkles, his rival for the hand of Emily Brown; but Tinkles does not know that the Strange Gentleman, in reality Walter Trott, has never set eyes on Emily, their betrothal having been arranged by his father. Two young ladies, Fanny and Mary, arrive, on the way to Gretna Green. They imagine that Trott is Fanny's admirer, disguised. Miss Julia Dobbs is also en route for Gretna to marry a young lord, and in her turn mistakes Trott for him. Complications follow, Julia loses her lord and Trott his Emily, but they console each other and depart for Gretna together.

IS SHE HIS WIFE? OR, SOMETHING SINGULAR

Written early in 1837, at Furnival's Inn, London, this comic burletta was produced at the St. James's

Theatre on 6 March in the same year. No author's name appeared on the playbill, but a later playbill attributed it to 'Boz'. No English publication date is known, nor does Forster mention it. But in 1876 James R. Osgood, a publisher of Boston, Mass., bought a printed copy from an English collector, who had in turn bought it from the stock of the theatrical bookseller T. H. Lacy. He paid £6 for the thirty-page pamphlet, and reprinted it in Boston in 1877. In 1879 the business premises of Osgood & Co. were destroyed by fire, and the original copy with them.

The newly-married Mr. Lovetown becomes indifferent to his wife who, to provoke his jealousy, pretends to a passion for Felix Tapkins, a bachelor neighbour. Overhearing her amorous soliloquy in which she regrets that an unnamed 'he' is not married, Tapkins assumes she is not really Lovetown's wife. Another couple, the Limburys, come on the scene. Lovetown flirts with the vain Mrs. Limbury, rousing the rage of her jealous husband, and a farrago of misunderstandings ensues.

THE MUDFOG AND OTHER SKETCHES

Three papers from *Bentley's Miscellany*, 1837–38.

The first, 'The Public Life of Mr. Tulrumble', January 1837, concerns the débâcle which ensues when the vain new mayor of Mudfog, Nicholas Tulrumble, persuades 'Bottle-nosed' Ned Twigger, the town drunkard, to grace his electoral procession in a full suit of brass armour. The other two are 'Full Report of the First Meeting of the Mudfog Association for the Advancement of Everything', October 1837, satirising the earnest scientists, sociologists, and statisticians who delivered papers at the annual meetings of the British Association for the Advancement of Science, founded in 1831, and a similar report, 'Full Report of the Second Meeting of the Mudfog Association for the Advancement of Everything', published September 1838.

Three further pieces are included with the *Mudfog Sketches*: 'The Pantomime of Life', March 1837, drawing parallels between everyday life and that of the stage; 'Some Particulars Concerning a Lion', May 1837, about the antics of a literary lion at a party; and 'Mr. Robert Bolton', August 1838, about a 'gentleman connected with the press' who regales an admiring audience in the Green Dragon, near Westminster Bridge, with an anecdote about a baker who assaults his wife and boils his protesting son in the wash-house copper.

All the above pieces were collected together for the first time in book form by Richard Bentley & Son in 1880 under the title *The Mudfog Papers, etc.*

'Familiar Epistle from a Parent to a Child', Dickens's valedictory to the *Miscellany*, was added in later editions.

THE ADVENTURES OF OLIVER TWIST
or, The Parish Boy's Progress

Dickens's second novel, written in part concurrently with *Pickwick*. First publication in monthly numbers in the new *Bentley's Miscellany*, published by Richard Bentley, 31 January (February issue) 1837 to March 1839; written mainly at 48 Doughty Street, London. Published in three volumes, 1838, with illustrations by Cruikshank. The third edition, with Preface dated Devonshire Terrace, March 1841, published by Chapman & Hall. First publication in America 1837: first and second chapters only, included in the second volume of *Tales and Sketches from Bentley's Miscellany* (these included various other writings of Dickens, including 'Public Life of Mr. Tulrumble', 'Mudfog Association', etc.), published by Carey, Lea & Blanchard. The entire work was published in 1838 in the American reprint of *Bentley's Miscellany*, published in New York by William and Jemima Walker.

In *Oliver Twist* Dickens embarked upon a straightforward storyline after the multi-plots of *Pickwick*. It is the first work in which he directly attacks social institutions, in this case the workhouse system of which Oliver is a victim. Dickens's travels as a reporter had shown him much of this particular evil, and he was able at the same time to dwell on the criminal world of London which he delighted to explore. The book is full of youthful melodrama: the villains are incredibly black and the good people improbably white, but the figure of Fagin is one of Dickens's immortals, touched with a strange sympathy, perhaps because he fascinated his author more than he repelled him. 'The Jew,' he wrote to Forster, '. . . is such an out and outer that I don't know what to make of him.'

Oliver Twist was in general liked, though it did not command the adulation given to *Pickwick*. There were comments on the 'lowness' of the subject, and some Jewish readers thought Fagin a libel upon their race.

In the workhouse of a provincial town seventy-five miles north of London a young woman who has arrived in an exhausted condition gives birth to a boy, and dies. The child is named Oliver Twist and put into the workhouse orphanage, presided over by the ill-natured Mrs. Corney. When he is nine, the beadle, Bumble, transfers him to the workhouse itself and he is set to picking oakum. When Oliver is chosen as the speaker for the other half-starved boys and asks for more of the gruel which is their staple fare, the authorities decide it is time to put him to a trade.

He becomes apprenticed to Sowerberry, an undertaker, his small frame and delicate appearance making him suitable for acting as a mute at children's funerals. But when Noah Claypole, another apprentice, insults his dead mother, Oliver attacks him and is cruelly punished by the Sowerberrys. He runs away to London, and in Barnet meets with a boy thief, Jack Dawkins, 'The Artful Dodger', a member of a pickpocket gang run by Fagin, a Jew. Fagin decides to use the uncomprehending Oliver, whom he instructs in the picking of pockets, and sends him out with the Dodger and another boy, Charley Bates. Oliver is horrified to see them pick the pocket of an old gentleman at a bookstall, runs away, and is captured and taken before a magistrate; but the old gentleman, Mr. Brownlow, has seen the true robbers and exculpates Oliver.

Oliver is taken to Mr. Brownlow's house in Pentonville, where the housekeeper, Mrs. Bedwin, nurses him through an illness. He is treated with kindness and affection for the first time in his life, and is happy. But Fagin plots to recapture him, for while the boy is free his secrets are in danger. He engages Bill Sikes, a brutal robber, and Nancy, his mistress, also a member of the gang, to bring Oliver back.

Their stratagem is successful, and Sikes takes Oliver by night to Chertsey to carry out a robbery on the house of a Mrs. Maylie. When the alarm is given Sikes takes fright and escapes, and Oliver is shot and wounded. Mrs. Maylie and her adopted niece, Rose, take him in, listen to his story, and believe it. He settles with them, becoming a household favourite.

Rose is suddenly stricken with a serious illness. Mrs. Maylie's son, Harry, arrives, and on her recovery begs her to marry him. She refuses because she is nameless, having been adopted from a baby-farm by Mrs. Maylie. During his idyllic life with the Maylies Oliver catches glimpses of Monks, a sinister man who is in league with Fagin to recapture him. In Fagin's den they lay plots to do this; but Nancy, overhearing them and feeling compassion for the child, tells Rose about the conspiracy, without giving away the gang. Rose and her adviser, Dr. Losberne, promise Nancy that if Monks is brought to justice Fagin and Sikes shall not be in any danger of arrest.

Fagin has set Noah Claypole, now his tool, to follow Nancy and spy on her as she meets Rose and Dr. Losberne on the steps of London Bridge. He reports the conversation to Fagin, who repeats it to Sikes. Sikes, maddened by Nancy's supposed treachery, rushes back to his own room, awakens her from sleep and clubs her to death.

He takes flight into the country north of London, driven from place to place by fear and conscience. Then, feeling that London is after all the safest place in which to conceal himself, he returns to his old haunts. He has been followed by his ill-treated but faithful dog, Bullseye, and has attempted to drown it, but it has escaped and returns to the gang's headquarters. Sikes arrives there to be greeted with horror and loathing by those of the gang who have escaped a police raid in which Fagin and Noah Claypole have been arrested. Charley Bates gives the alarm; Sikes attempts to escape across the roofs in order to drop into Folly Ditch below, but falls with a rope round his neck, and hangs himself. The dog, which has followed its brutal master even to this point, leaps for the dead man's shoulders and falls to death below.

Fagin is executed, appealing to Oliver in the condemned cell to save him. The Dodger is transported, Charley Bates sees the error of his ways and becomes a reformed character, and Noah Claypole escapes justice by turning King's evidence.

The plot against Oliver is unravelled by Mr. Brownlow, to whom Oliver has now been restored. Monks, otherwise Edward Leeford, is Oliver's half-brother, their father having seduced and promised marriage to Agnes, Oliver's mother, while still married to Leeford's mother. The provisions of the father's will leave money to Oliver on condition that he maintains a spotless reputation, and for this reason Monks has tried to keep the boy in Fagin's gang in order to discredit him and

inherit the full sum himself. It is now discovered that Oliver's dead mother and Rose Maylie were sisters, and that Rose is, after all, legitimate.

Monks receives his share of the legacy, goes to America, and dies there in prison. Mr. and Mrs. Bumble (for the pompous beadle has married the orphanage matron) are proved to have been in the plot against Oliver, lose their positions of trust, and become workhouse inmates. Oliver is adopted by Mr. Brownlow, and Rose marries Harry Maylie, who for her sake has given up a promising political career to become a country clergyman, in whose church a memorial is raised to Oliver's mother, Agnes.

SKETCHES OF YOUNG GENTLEMEN

Twelve character sketches of types, written in 1838 for publication that year in volume form by Chapman & Hall: 'The Bashful Young Gentleman'; 'The Out-and-out Young Gentleman'; 'The Very Friendly Young Gentleman'; 'The Military Young Gentleman'; 'The Political Young Gentleman'; 'The Domestic Young Gentleman'; 'The Censorious Young Gentleman'; 'The Funny Young Gentleman'; 'The Theatrical Young Gentleman'; 'The Poetical Young Gentleman'; 'The "Throwing-off" Young Gentleman'; 'The Young Ladies' Young Gentleman'.

THE LIFE AND ADVENTURES OF
NICHOLAS NICKLEBY

Dickens's third novel. He began it at 48 Doughty Street, London, in February 1838, and finished it during the family summer holiday at 40 Albion Street, Broadstairs in September 1839. It was published by Chapman & Hall in twenty monthly parts, the first appearing on 31 March 1838 (dated April). Issued complete in October 1839. First American publication begun 1838, in parts, by Carey, Lea & Blanchard, Philadelphia; completed in 1839 by Lea & Blanchard, successors of the old firm. Also published by James Turney of New York.

As a child, Dickens had heard of the notorious Yorkshire boarding schools, to which unwanted boys were sent to be out of the way, and where they were terribly ill-treated; an account of the trial of a Yorkshire schoolmaster for the death of such a boy remained in his mind. In 1838 he and Hablôt K. Browne ('Phiz', who illustrated *Nickleby*) travelled to Yorkshire to investigate the schools at first-hand, and met Shaw, the original of Mr. Squeers. Dickens subsequently stated that 'Mr. Squeers and his school are faint and feeble pictures of an existing reality'.

At the time when he had first heard of them, he says that his head was 'full of Partridge, Strap, Tom Pipes, and Sancho Panza'; and *Nickleby*, intended to be mainly propagandist, turned out, in fact, to be a picaresque, lively, humorous novel with a hero whose adventures echo those of Dickens's own childhood heroes. As in *Pickwick*, there are evidences of the influence of Fielding, Defoe, and Smollett. The

Crummles family are an exuberant outburst of Dickens's love for, and knowledge of, the theatre, especially the provincial theatre, and he sets their headquarters in his birthplace, Portsmouth. The novel contains entertaining satires on snobbery and greed.

The widowed Mrs. Nickleby comes up to London from Devon to seek financial help from her brother-in-law, Ralph Nickleby, a money-lender, for herself and her children, Nicholas, aged nineteen, and his younger sister Kate. The miserly Ralph takes an immediate dislike to Nicholas, though he feels a grudging affection for Kate. He finds the two women a lodging in a decrepit house in Thames Street, settles Kate as an assistant to Madame Mantalini, a dress-maker in the West End, and dispatches Nicholas to Yorkshire to teach at Mr. Wackford Squeers's 'Academy', Dotheboys Hall.

Squeers is a coarse, brutal man with a wife and son to match, and a daughter, Fanny, as ugly as himself, who develops a sentimental passion for the handsome Nicholas, and is jealous of his polite attentions to her pretty friend, Matilda Price, who is engaged to a big, bluff Yorkshireman, John Browdie. Nicholas remains impervious to Fanny's charms. His anger is awakened by the cruelty and starvation imposed upon Squeers's miserable pupils, and particularly upon Smike, a poor drudge whose wits have become enfeebled by deprivation. Smike runs away, is caught, and is rescued by Nicholas from receiving a savage beating. The beating is, instead, administered by Nicholas to Squeers, after which Nicholas leaves for London. Smike catches up with him and begs to be his companion.

In London, Nicholas and Smike are befriended by Ralph's clerk, Newman Noggs, an eccentric, kindly alcoholic, who has come down in the world and dis-approves of his hard master. Nicholas becomes tutor to the daughters of one of Newman's neighbours, Mr. Kenwigs, a turner in ivory, who aspires to gentility.

Kate is unhappy at Madame Mantalini's establishment. Her youthful beauty has attracted the jealousy of Miss Knag, a senior assistant, and the attentions of the flamboyant Mr. Mantalini, to the annoyance of his wife. Ralph tries to sell Kate as mistress to one of his noble clients, introducing her at a dinner party to Sir Mulberry Hawk and Lord Frederick Verisopht. He removes her from Madame Mantalini's and finds her a situation as companion to the snobbish and hypochondriacal Mrs. Wititterley.

Nicholas quarrels with Ralph and decides to turn his back on London. Travelling coastwards with Smike, he meets the actor-manager of the Theatre Royal, Portsmouth, Vincent Crummles, who persuades Nicholas to join his company as actor and dramatist, but Nicholas returns to London in response to a letter from Newman Noggs. He overhears a conversation between Hawk and Verisopht in which Kate's name is mentioned insultingly, and beats Hawk, injuring him seriously. Hawk later kills Verisopht in a duel, fought over Kate's reputation. Nicholas, his mother and Kate go to lodge with Miss La Creevy, a miniature-painter. In search of work at a registry office, Nicholas meets the elderly twin brothers Cheeryble, a philanthropic pair who engage him as a clerk and place the Nickleby family in a rural cottage at Bow, at a low rent.

Nicholas calls upon the Kenwigses, his one-time employers, to break the news that his Portsmouth friend, the actress Henrietta Petowker, has married Mr. Lillyvick, uncle of Mrs. Kenwigs. The Kenwigs family had expectations from Lillyvick, and are devastated by the news.

Smike is recaptured in the street by Squeers and imprisoned at Squeers's lodging, from which he is rescued by John Browdie, who is honeymooning with Matilda in London. Squeers then conspires with Ralph to pass off a man named Snawley as Smike's long-lost father, but they are foiled by Nicholas and John.

Nicholas falls in love with Madeline Bray, daughter of an ailing debtor in the Rules of the King's Bench. Ralph Nickleby is planning to marry her off to Arthur Gride, an old money-lender who possesses a deed concerning some property due to Madeline. Madeline promises to marry Gride in return for the payment of her father's debts. But on the wedding morning Bray dies of heart failure, and Nicholas takes Madeline home to Bow, where Mrs. Nickleby and Kate nurse her through an illness.

The Cheerybles discover that Madeline is heiress to a fortune. Nicholas finds this a barrier between himself and Madeline, just as Kate, proposed to by the Cheerybles' nephew Frank, refuses him because he is so much wealthier than herself. Smike, who has never recovered from the privations of Dotheboys Hall, dies, confessing at the last to Nicholas his hopeless love for Kate.

The old brothers sort out the financial difficulties of the two young couples, and they are married on the same day. A few weeks later the Cheerybles' old clerk, Tim Linkinwater, marries Miss La Creevy.

Ralph receives a terrible shock in the news that Smike was his own son, the result of a secret marriage. At the same time his plotting with Gride is brought to light. From remorse and rage that Nicholas, his hated nephew, has rescued and befriended his son, and the desire to thwart his enemies, he hangs himself from a hook in the attic which had been one of Smike's only memories of childhood.

Squeers is transported. At Dotheboys Hall a riot breaks out at the news, and the school disbands in confusion.

SKETCHES OF YOUNG COUPLES

Eleven sketches of marital relationships, inspired by Queen Victoria's impending marriage, written in 1840 for publication as a book that year by Chapman & Hall: 'The Young Couple'; 'The Formal Couple'; 'The Loving Couple'; 'The Contradictory Couple'; 'The Couple Who Dote Upon Their Children'; 'The Cool Couple'; 'The Plausible Couple'; 'The Nice Little Couple'; 'The Egotistical Couple'; 'The Couple Who Coddle Themselves'; 'The Old Couple'.

MASTER HUMPHREY'S CLOCK

Written at 1 Devonshire Terrace, Marylebone, Broadstairs, Brighton and Windsor, it was published in 88 weekly numbers, beginning in April 1840, and ending in December 1841. Published in three single volumes by Chapman & Hall on 15 October 1840, 12/15 April 1841, and 15 December 1841. First American publication simultaneously with British edition by Lea & Blanchard, Philadelphia, in monthly parts.

Dickens designed *Master Humphrey's Clock* as a work on original lines: 'the best general idea of the plan of the work might be given perhaps by reference to the *Tatler*, the *Spectator*, and Goldsmith's *Bee*; but it would be far more popular both in the subjects of which it treats and its mode of treating them.' The work was to introduce a little club or knot of characters whose stories were to run throughout, to reintroduce Pickwick and Sam Weller, and to contain humorous essays and contemporary comments, satires on administration in imaginary countries, and papers on old London.

In fact, the plan proved unsatisfactory. The story of *The Old Curiosity Shop*, at first intended to be merely an episode, took over Dickens's imagination and became a full-length novel serialised within the *Master Humphrey* frame. *Barnaby Rudge* followed later, and at the conclusion of it *Master Humphrey* was abandoned.

The linked tales of Master Humphrey, a crippled old man who addresses his readers from the chimney-corner beside his beloved grandfather clock, are supposedly derived from 'a pile of dusty papers' stored in the clock itself. They include stories told to Joe Toddyhigh in the Guildhall by the giants Gog and Magog, Jack Redburn's tale of a murderer's confession, the story of John Podgers told by Mr. Pickwick, an anecdote of Bill Binder, told by Sam Weller, Tony Weller's account of his grandson, the hairdresser's story, another of Sam's tales, and miscellaneous anecdotes.

THE OLD CURIOSITY SHOP

Dickens's fourth novel. Begun in March 1840, finished in January 1841, and written at 1 Devonshire Terrace, Marylebone, and at Broadstairs. Published in *Master Humphrey's Clock*, 25 April 1840 to 6 February 1841, and as a single volume on 15 December 1841. First American publication simultaneously with British publication, in monthly parts, by Lea & Blanchard, Philadelphia.

Dickens's first idea was that it should be a 'little child-story' to be included among the 'Personal Adventures of Master Humphrey', and an early form of the title was *The Curiosity Dealer and the Child*. It was to have finished the *Master Humphrey* sequence of stories, but grew in importance until it became a full-length novel which, with *Barnaby Rudge*, dwarfed the other stories into mere anecdotes. Forster says that it was conceived 'with less direct consciousness of design on his own part than I can remember in any other instance throughout his career,' and that it was, in his opinion, 'a story which was to add largely to his popularity, more than any other of his works to make the bond between himself and his readers one of personal attachment.'

The character of Little Nell took hold of the public's imagination as none of Dickens's creations had yet done, and obsessed the author. 'All night I have been pursued by the child,' he wrote, 'and this morning I am unrefreshed and miserable.' His final killing-off of Nell (who was probably an idealised version of Mary Hogarth) reduced him to tears and drew protests from his distressed public.

Master Humphrey begins as the narrator of the story, but fades out after chapter 3. He is walking at dusk in Covent Garden when a child asks him the way to her home. He leads her there, and finds that she is Nelly Trent, who keeps house for her grandfather, the keeper of an old curiosity shop. Nell's profligate brother, Fred, is jealous of her closeness to their grandfather and fears that she may inherit all his money, in spite of the old man's repeated assurances that he is poor. Fred plans to marry Nelly to his dissipated friend, Dick Swiveller, so that he may share in the fortune.

The old man is, in fact, a compulsive gambler whose obsessional desire is to win a fortune for Nell. By borrowing money he falls into the clutches of the sinister dwarf, Daniel Quilp, who lives on Tower Hill with his pretty young wife and inimical mother-in-law, Mrs. Jiniwin. Quilp's legal adviser is Sampson Brass, a shady lawyer who shares his practice in Bevis Marks with his hard-favoured sister Sally. Quilp persuades the ailing old Trent that his shop-boy, Kit Nubbles, whom Quilp hates, had been spying on him, to reveal his gambling habits, and Kit is summarily dismissed, to his distress, for he is devoted to Nell. The old man's furniture and possessions are sold up by Quilp to regain the money borrowed from him. Terrified of Quilp and Brass, and on the verge of senility since his recent illness, Trent persuades Nelly to leave the house secretly with him by night and go as far away as they can from Quilp.

Their long journey from London into the Midlands forms the main thread of the story. They meet two travelling showmen, Codlin and Short, and for a time accompany them and their Punch and Judy show, but begin to sense that Codlin suspects there may be a reward offered for the revelation of their whereabouts. The old man and the child move on.

Their next encounter is with Mrs. Jarley and her travelling waxworks show. She takes a fancy to Nell, and trains her to deliver little lectures on the waxworks to the public. But Trent's gambling mania once again overcomes him; he falls into the hands of card-sharpers, and steals money from Nell. To save him, she makes him resume their wanderings.

The journey now becomes rougher and more exhausting. They travel part of the way along a canal in a barge, with drunken bargees. They arrive at an industrial town in the Midlands, where an eccentric furnace-keeper takes pity on them and lets them sleep on warm ashes by the furnace. As they wander on through the Black Country Nell feels the effects of their privations, but remains brave and cheerful, guiding her grandfather through ugly scenes, including a Chartist riot. By now they are at the point of starvation. Suddenly they encounter an old friend – a schoolmaster whom they met earlier in their travels, who had then lost a favourite pupil by death, and welcomed Nell as a replacement for him. He takes them to a village where he has been appointed clerk and schoolmaster, and establishes them in a peaceful home, a curious little house near the ancient church.

In London, Quilp is trying to track down the pair, as is (for benevolent reasons) the brother of old Trent, who has, without revealing his name, taken a lodging at Sampson Brass's house. Also at Brass's is Dick Swiveller, employed as a clerk. He is highly suspicious of Sampson's and Sally's activities with Quilp. He befriends the twelve-year-old servant of the Brasses, a down-trodden drudge whom he calls 'The Marchioness' and introduces to the pleasures of beer, bread, and cribbage. (The little girl is, in fact, the illegitimate child of Quilp and Sally, but Dickens merely hints at this.) The lodger Trent gets to know Kit Nubbles, and through him finds a clue to Nell's whereabouts. Kit is now employed by Mr. and Mrs. Garland at Finchley, where he is becoming enamoured of their pretty young maid, Barbara, and is able to support his widowed mother and small brothers. Quilp still hates him, and through Brass fakes a theft-charge against him and has him imprisoned. Dick Swiveller gives evidence on Kit's behalf and looks after the boy's distressed mother, for which Brass dismisses him. Dick is taken suddenly and seriously ill, and remains in danger and delirium for three weeks before returning to consciousness to find that the Marchioness has established herself in his lodgings and has nursed him through his fever. In gratitude and affection he promises to bring her up and educate her, for an aunt has died and left him a comfortable annuity.

Quilp, who has already teased his wife and mother-in-law by pretending to be dead, dies in reality while flying from justice; for the Marchioness has overheard the plotting of Brass, Sally, and Quilp to incriminate Kit, and Brass has been arrested. Quilp is drowned in the marshes near his riverside lair.

Nell's great-uncle and Kit follow up the clues they have obtained, and with Mr. Garland arrive at the village where Nell and her grandfather have been staying – but they are too late. Nell's health has been declining steadily, and just before they arrive she has died, peacefully and happily. Her grandfather, driven crazy with sorrow, cannot believe in her death, and is unable to recognise his brother. Shortly afterwards he dies on her grave.

Sampson Brass is struck off the Rolls, and finishes up a convict. Sally sinks into poverty and oblivion. Quilp's widow marries again. The Marchioness's education proceeds so well that when she is nineteen, 'good-looking, clever, and good-humoured', Dick marries her. Because of her mysterious origins he has given her the name of Sophronia Sphynx. Kit marries Barbara, and Nell's great-uncle travels in the steps of the two dead wanderers, rewarding those who had been kind to them.

BARNABY RUDGE

A Tale of the Riots of 'Eighty

Dickens's fifth novel. Begun at 48 Doughty Street in January 1839, and finished at Windsor in November 1841. The novel was commissioned by the publisher Richard Bentley, to follow *Oliver Twist* in *Bentley's Miscellany*. In May 1840 the contract was transferred to Chapman & Hall. The first number was published in *Master Humphrey's Clock* in February 1841, the last in November 1841. Published in book form in December, with illustrations by 'Phiz' and others. First American publication 1841–2 in monthly parts by Lea & Blanchard, Philadelphia.

This was Dickens's first historical novel, the only other being *A Tale of Two Cities*. Intended to centre on the anti-Catholic riots instigated by Lord George Gordon in 1780, and to show the brutality of the capital punishment system of the time, the book was largely taken over by its lighter characters, Grip the raven (based on Dickens's own pet bird), the Varden family, and the two Willets. Gordon and the riots are dutifully dealt with, but other scenes remain more vividly in the reader's mind.

On a March night of 1775, at the Maypole Inn, Chigwell, Essex, a story is told by Solomon Daisy, parish clerk and bell-ringer, of the events of twenty-two years earlier, to the very night. Reuben Haredale, owner of The Warren, the local manor-house, had been found murdered in his bedroom, with a cash-box missing. The steward, Rudge, and the gardener were not to be found, but later in the year the body of Rudge was discovered, with a knife-wound in the breast. The corpse was recognisable only by its clothes and belongings.

The day after the murder a child was born to Mrs. Rudge. This is Barnaby Rudge, who has grown up a gentle, slightly dim-witted boy, whose imagination is as fantastic as his appearance. His companion and confidant is a talking raven, Grip. His mother is menaced and shadowed by a mysterious stranger, who has heard the story told at the Maypole, and on the same night has committed a highway robbery, wounding and taking the purse of Edward Chester, a young gentleman in love with Emma Haredale, niece of the murdered man. Edward is rescued by Gabriel Varden, a Clerkenwell locksmith.

Edward's father, John Chester, is the lifelong enemy of Geoffrey Haredale, Emma's uncle and brother to the murdered man. Chester, 'a man without heart and without principle', wishes Edward to marry a rich heiress, and opposes the Haredale match, as does Geoffrey Haredale. Apart from his hatred of Chester, Haredale is a Roman Catholic, and does not wish his niece to marry a Protestant.

We are introduced at length to the Varden household. Bluff, cheerful Gabriel has a wife whose sole interest in life seems to be the Protestant Manual, a tome which she reads constantly. It is her disposition to be jolly when other people are miserable, and miserable when other people are jolly, and she is supported in this as in all things by her maid, the vinegary spinster Miggs. Dolly, the Vardens' only child, is a pretty coquette, much eyed by Gabriel's apprentice, Sim Tappertit, a conceited youth with revolutionary notions. But Dolly is being seriously courted by Joe Willet, son of the landlord at the

Maypole. Dolly's father approves of Joe, but her mother affects to disdain him, and Chester, for his own purposes, succeeds in coming between the two young people. Joe decides to join the army, and comes to say goodbye to Dolly, who pretends to be unaffected by the parting. After Joe has left for America, Dolly becomes companion to Emma Haredale, whose friend she has been from childhood.

Five years pass. Lord George Gordon, the Protestant fanatic, begins his 'No Popery' movement and incites a mob to riot in London. The Rudges are now in London, where Mrs. Rudge hopes to hide from her persecutor. Barnaby and Hugh, the wild, gipsy-like ostler of The Maypole, join the rioters. The mob surges out to Chigwell, and The Warren is burnt because the Haredales are Catholics. Emma and Dolly are kidnapped, taken to London, and kept as prisoners. Hugh and Sim Tappertit both covet Dolly, and Gashford, Lord George's secretary, has designs on Emma. Dennis, the hangman of Newgate, and Stagg, a blind man, are also concerned in the affair.

Barnaby is captured and imprisoned in Newgate. He is joined there by a man who proves to be his own father, Rudge, who twenty-eight years before had murdered Reuben Haredale and his gardener, and has since been in hiding, sometimes supplied with money by his wife. The rioters break into Newgate and release the prisoners. Barnaby and his father are recaptured and sentenced to death. Meanwhile, Emma and Dolly have been rescued by Geoffrey Haredale, Edward Chester, and Joe Willet – Joe less one arm, lost while fighting in the Savannahs.

Barnaby is pardoned, by the intercession of Gabriel Varden, but his father is hanged, as are Maypole Hugh and Dennis, the hangman of Newgate, who has been one of the rioters and has constantly gloated over the prospect of hanging others. John Chester (now knighted) discovers that Hugh was his bastard son. Chester and Haredale fight a duel: Chester is killed and Haredale goes abroad.

Dolly tells Joe that she repents the foolish pride which kept her from telling him that she loved him, five years before. They marry, and Joe takes over the Maypole, which has been pillaged by the rioters. The shock has left old Willet in a state of stupefaction, in which he remains for the rest of his life.

Emma and Edward marry and go to the West Indies. Barnaby and his mother go to live on the farm of the Maypole, and Barnaby's wits improve in these happy conditions. Miggs, disappointed that the now reformed Mrs. Varden no longer requires her services, becomes a female turnkey at Bridewell. Sim Tappertit's pride and glory, his legs, were crushed in the riots; he becomes a shoe-black, and marries the widow of a rag-and-bone merchant.

THE LAMPLIGHTER'S STORY

First published in 1841 in *The Pic Nic Papers*, a work in three volumes edited by Dickens and illustrated by George Cruikshank and 'Phiz' for the benefit of the widow and children of John Macrone, publisher of *Sketches by Boz*. The story was adapted from an unacted farce by Dickens, *The Lamplighter*.

Tom Grig, a lamplighter, is persuaded by an eccentric astrologer that he is destined to marry the old man's niece. Mooney, another scientist, predicts that Tom will die in two months' time, and the lamplighter resigns himself to the marriage. Just in time, a mistake is found in the calculations and it emerges that Tom will live to a ripe old age. He refuses the niece and the astrologer takes a mystical revenge.

AMERICAN NOTES
for *General Circulation*

Written mainly at Broadstairs between August and October 1842. Published in October 1842 in two volumes by Chapman & Hall. First publication in America 1842, by Wilson & Co., New York, as an extra number of *Brother Jonathan*.

The outcome of Dickens's visit to America in the first half of 1842, the *Notes* were based largely on the letters written by him to John Forster describing his American experiences. In the Preface he claimed that they were 'a record of the impressions I received from day to day . . . and sometimes (but not always) of the conclusions to which they, and after-reflection on them, have led me.' He proposed to tell the truth, at the risk of offending persons who thought their country perfect, while acknowledging the hospitality he had received in America and the friends he had made.

Four editions were sold in England before the end of the year, but feeling in America ran high at Dickens's adverse comments on such matters as prison systems, the prevalence of pigs on Broadway, the corruption of the House of Representatives, and the universal habit of spitting. His views on international copyright had been highly unpopular, and his opinions on slavery even more so. In *American Notes* he reinforced them by the reproduction of actual advertisements, gruesome to a degree, about missing slaves.

THE LIFE AND ADVENTURES OF
MARTIN CHUZZLEWIT

Dickens's sixth novel. Begun December 1842 or early January 1843, at Devonshire Terrace, London; written there and at Broadstairs; finished June 1844. Commissioned by Chapman & Hall after the termination of *Master Humphrey's Clock*, the first number was published in January 1843, the last in July 1844. Published in one volume, July 1844, by Chapman & Hall. First American publication 1844 (Harper & Bros., New York) in seven parts.

Dickens first conceived this as *The Life and Adventures of Martin Chuzzlewig, his family, friends and enemies. Comprising all his wills and his ways. With an historical record of what he did and what he didn't. The whole forming a complete key to the house of Chuzzlewig.* It was to have opened in Cornwall, which

Dickens had just visited. Title, setting, and scheme for the book changed as Dickens was taken over by the character of Pecksniff from the moment he appeared in chapter 2. Forster says that 'the notion of taking Pecksniff for a type of character was really the origin of the book; the design being to show, more or less by every person introduced, the number and variety of humours and vices that have their root in selfishness.' In November 1843 Dickens wrote to Forster that 'I think *Chuzzlewit* in a hundred points immeasurably the best of my stories.' Early sales were disappointing, but later they became next to those of *Pickwick* and *Copperfield*. The American scenes, the fruit of his visit in 1842, provoked considerable anger and criticism across the Atlantic: 'made them all stark staring raving mad across the water,' said Dickens.

The novel's popularity rests largely on the more-than-lifesize figures of Pecksniff and Sairey Gamp, the Chuzzlewit interest being comparatively pale.

The story begins at the house of Mr. Pecksniff, a Salisbury architect. His monumental hypocrisy is revealed to the reader at once. His moralising is admired and echoed by his daughters, Charity and Mercy, playfully known as Cherry and Merry. Charity, the elder, is plain and vinegary; Mercy, a pretty frivolous giggler. Both are on the look-out for husbands, possibly from the ranks of their father's apprentices, who in fact are responsible for all the designs for which he takes the credit.

One, John Westlock, has been dismissed for speaking his mind. Still with Pecksniff, and blindly devoted to him, is Tom Pinch, a simple, young-old creature. A new apprentice is expected – young Martin Chuzzlewit. Martin is the grandson of another Martin, rich and eccentric, at this time lying ill in the local inn, the Blue Dragon, with the orphaned Mary Graham as his companion. Mary and young Martin are in love, to the displeasure of old Martin, who wanted to bring the match about his own way, and feels thwarted that his grandson has taken the initiative. Tom Pinch, seeing Mary in the church, falls in love with her.

Mr. Pecksniff takes his daughters to London, to stay at Mrs. Todgers's boarding-house. They encounter old Martin and his cousin, Anthony Chuzzlewit, and Anthony's son Jonas, a cold-hearted villain. At Todgers's, Merry is a great success with the gentlemen boarders. Jonas makes overtures to both sisters, raising Cherry's matrimonial hopes. Old Martin asks Pecksniff to dismiss his grandson, telling him of the young man's forbidden engagement to Mary. Pecksniff, hoping to profit by old Martin's wealth, agrees. When they return to Salisbury, Martin is dismissed summarily. He decides to emigrate to America, a country which must be in need of young architects, and takes with him Mark Tapley, the cheerful ostler of the Blue Dragon. Mark is an optimist who feels that his life is altogether too comfortable at the Dragon, and wants to experience circumstances in which his ability to be 'jolly' will be severely tested. When Martin leaves, Tom Pinch gives him his last half-sovereign and Mary sends him her diamond ring. He pays no particular regard to either present.

Anthony Chuzzlewit dies, in circumstances suggesting poison. Jonas, to Cherry's fury, proposes to Merry, who accepts him in a spirit of wilful coquetry. Jonas becomes a director of the Anglo-Bengalee Disinterested Loan and Life Insurance Company, a swindle organised and run by one Tigg Montague, alias Montague Tigg, a sharper. Tigg sees possibilities of blackmail in Jonas, and unearths details which suggest that Jonas has killed his father by poison. Jonas, who has by this time turned the laughing Merry into a bullied, beaten wife, is fear-ridden.

Pecksniff has now apparently ingratiated himself with old Martin, who, with Mary, is living in his house. But when Pecksniff makes advances to Mary she turns for help to Tom Pinch, and for the first time Tom sees his master clearly. Pecksniff accuses Tom of having made improper proposals to Mary himself, and dismisses him. Tom goes to London, renews acquaintance with John Westlock, removes his sister Ruth from a disagreeable situation as governess, and settles with her in an Islington lodging.

Meanwhile Mrs. Sairey Gamp, nurse and midwife, has entered the story. Lewsome, a doctor's assistant who has sold poison to Jonas, falls seriously ill and is nursed by Mrs. Gamp and her friend Betsey Prig, who annoys her greatly by casting doubts upon the existence of Sairey's much-quoted friend Mrs. Harris.

In America, young Martin finds that the rosy picture he had had of the place was a false one. At first welcomed into New York society, he is coldly treated when he admits that he travelled over as a steerage passenger. The 'thriving city' of Eden, for which he had hoped to design fine municipal buildings, is no more than a fever-ridden swamp. He becomes seriously ill, and Mark, having nursed him for weeks, falls ill himself. Martin's selfishness begins to leave him under the influence of Mark's devotion. They return to England, and see the laying of the corner-stone of a new building, with Pecksniff, the supposed architect, present. Martin recognises the design for one of his own. They go to call on Tom and Ruth Pinch in Islington, and hear how Tom has been given a situation as secretary and librarian by a mysterious employer. They visit Salisbury, where Martin tries to see his grandfather, but is foiled by Pecksniff.

Jonas, still hounded by Tigg, who has set Nadgett, a private detective, to watch him, travels to Wiltshire, leaving Merry to cover up for him during his absence. He waylays Tigg, murders him, and buries him in a wood. Back in London, he is visited by old Martin, John Westlock, Mark Tapley, and the now recovered Lewsome. Lewsome accuses Jonas of the murder of his father; but Anthony Chuzzlewit's old clerk, Chuffey, reveals that he discovered Jonas's intentions, and that Anthony died of a broken heart on learning the truth of his son's wickedness.

Jonas, relieved, orders them all out; but Nadgett appears with a band of officers and arrests him for the murder of Tigg. The chief officer is Chevy Slyme, a relative of the Chuzzlewits and a friend of Tigg. Jonas tries to bribe him for time in which to commit suicide. Slyme refuses, but Jonas manages to poison himself in the coach on the way to gaol.

The story ends happily for most parties. Young Martin's selfishness is cured, as well as old Martin's pride: 'the curse of our house has been the love of self,' he says. The two are reconciled, and Martin is openly betrothed to Mary. John Westlock and Ruth Pinch follow their example, as do Mark and Mrs. Lupin, the widowed landlady of the Blue Dragon. Cherry Pecksniff is less fortunate. At the point of marriage to her, Augustus Moddle, a young gentleman of Todgers's, finds he cannot face it, for he was desperately in love with her sister; and he leaves her on the wedding morning.

Pecksniff is exposed and struck down by old Martin. He deteriorates into a 'drunken, squalid, begging-letter-writing man', with his shrewish daughter beside him. Old Martin (who is revealed to have been Tom's mysterious employer) takes Merry under his wing. Tom Pinch goes to live with Ruth and John after their marriage, remaining a life-long bachelor who is a particular favourite with Mary's small daughter.

CHRISTMAS BOOKS

Five of Dickens's long stories with a Christmas theme, collected in one volume in 1852. The *Christmas Books* were reprinted in so many forms in the U.S.A. that it is impossible to ascribe all the first publications. 'A Christmas Carol' was first published by Carey & Hart, Philadelphia, in 1844, and 'The Chimes' by Lea & Blanchard, Philadelphia, in 1845.

Dickens stated in the Preface, 'My purpose was, in a whimsical kind of masque, which the good humour of the season justified, to awaken some loving and for-bearing thoughts, never out of season in a Christian land.' 'A Christmas Carol' has always been the most popular of the *Christmas Books*, followed by 'The Cricket on the Hearth' and 'The Chimes'. 'The Haunted Man' and 'The Battle of Life' are generally considered to be inferior to his normal standards. Of 'The Battle of Life' *Tait's Edinburgh Magazine* for January 1847 said: 'If Mr. Dickens really believes that a modest and discreet young lady could leave a ball-room on a winter night; make off with the greatest rake in the parish . . .': then follows a string of im-probabilities in the plot, concluding with the re-viewer's observation that he has nothing to say to any credulous readers 'except that the engravings of the volume are well executed'.

A CHRISTMAS CAROL
IN PROSE
BEING
A Ghost Story of Christmas

Begun in October 1843, written at Devonshire Terrace, London, and finished before the end of November. It was published in December in one volume by Chapman & Hall, with eight illustrations by John Leech.

Ebenezer Scrooge, a curmudgeonly miser, survivor of the partnership of Scrooge and Marley, spends a surly Christmas Eve reviling the institution of Christ-mas and all its merriment. That night he is visited by the ghost of his old partner, Marley, who tells him that three Spirits will visit him in turn so that he may have the chance of escaping Marley's own fate, to wander round the world in chains. The Spirits of Christmas Past, Christmas Present, and Christmas Yet to Come duly visit Scrooge, showing him the happiness he might have enjoyed, the happiness poor folk such as his own clerk Bob Cratchit do enjoy at Christmas, and what the future will be unless he mends his ways. He awakes a reformed character on Christmas morning.

THE CHIMES
A Goblin Story
OF SOME BELLS
THAT RANG AN OLD YEAR OUT
AND A NEW YEAR IN

First published in one volume in December 1844 by Chapman & Hall, with illustrations by Maclise, Leech, Doyle, and Stanfield. One of Dickens's own favourites, it was designed as 'a plea for the poor'. It was written in 1844 at the Palazzo Peschiere, Genoa, in October and the beginning of November.

Toby Veck, a poor ticket-porter, whose daughter Meg is engaged to marry Richard, a young blacksmith, falls asleep on New Year's Eve while reading a news-paper, and dreams that the chimes in the church bell-tower above him summon him to join them. They blame him for his own shortcomings, and show him what man's callousness, pride, and hypocrisy can do to poor people such as himself. He sees the little niece of a Chartist, Lilian Fern, turn prostitute through poverty, and his own daughter prepare to drown herself and her baby in her despair. He awakes to find morning and the New Year Bells ringing a message of hope.

THE CRICKET ON THE HEARTH
A Fairy Tale of Home

Written in October 1845 and first published in one volume in December, by Bradbury & Evans, with illustrations by Maclise, Stanfield, Landseer, Doyle, and Leech. Its sales at first were double those of 'A Christmas Carol' and 'The Chimes': Dickens had succeeded in his design to 'put everybody in a good temper, and make such a dash at people's fenders and arm-chairs as hasn't been made for many a long day.'

John Peerybingle, the slow, sturdy carrier, is much older than his little wife Dot, but she is devoted to him. She has 'a very doll' of a baby tended by the nurse Tilly Slowboy. Their neighbours are Caleb Plummer, a poor toymaker, and his blind daughter Bertha, whom he has amiably deceived in letting her think that they are rich, and that their ill-tempered landlord and employer, Tackleton, is a model of charm. Another neighbour is May Fielding, forced by her snobbish mother into an engagement to Tackleton, though her heart is with Caleb's son Edward, long vanished overseas. A deaf old stranger arrives and misunderstandings ensue when

Dot is seen alone with him, minus his white wig; but the Cricket on the Hearth, the little household god, reassures John that Dot is faithful and all will be well. The disguised man is Edward Plummer; he and May are reunited, Bertha is happy to know the truth at last, and all ends with a dance.

THE BATTLE OF LIFE
A Love Story

Written in Lausanne, Switzerland, in September–October 1846. Published in one volume in December 1846, with illustrations by Maclise, Stanfield, Doyle, and Leech.

Doctor Jeddler, a philosopher, has two daughters, Marion and Grace. He regards life as a great joke. On the eve of her wedding to Alfred Heathfield, the Doctor's ward, Marion runs away, supposedly with a spendthrift young man, Michael Warden. When she has been gone some time her sister Grace marries Alfred. Marion returns, and reveals that she ran away because she knew that Grace loved Alfred, and sacrificed her own happiness for her sister's. But she has not been with Warden, having spent the intervening years with an aunt in the country. There is a sub-plot concerning the servant Clemency Newcome and her future husband Benjamin Britain.

THE HAUNTED MAN
AND
THE GHOST'S BARGAIN
A fancy for Christmas Time

Begun at Broadstairs in the autumn of 1847 and completed at Brighton in the winter of 1848. Published by Bradbury & Evans in December 1848. Illustrated by Stanfield, Tenniel, Frank Stone and Leech.

Redlaw, a chemist and lecturer, lives at an ancient institution for students. One night he is brooding over the past when the Swidgers, who keep the Lodge, enter to decorate his room for Christmas. They point out a brighter side of life to him. When they depart he is visited by an awful ghostly likeness of himself. It offers him the power to forget his sorrows without cancelling his knowledge and mental powers; and the power also to communicate this to others. He does so, with shocking results, depriving those he meets of their past. At last he prays the phantom to return; it does so, accompanied by the shade of Milly Swidger, a great influence for good, who tells him that it is a good thing to remember wrong 'that we may forgive it'.

PICTURES FROM ITALY

Written from December 1845 to February 1846 at 1 Devonshire Terrace, London. First published in the *Daily News*, January to March 1846, with the title *Travelling Letters written on the Road.* Originally illustrated by Samuel Palmer. Published, with five additional chapters, by Bradbury & Evans 'for the Author' in 1846 as *Pictures from Italy.* First American publication 1846, under the title *Travelling Letters written on the Road,* by Wiley & Putnam, New York. Issued later as *Pictures from Italy* in Wiley & Putnam's Library of Choice Reading.

Dickens's impressions of his Italian tour of 1844–5, largely based on letters written home to John Forster. Full of enjoyment and considerably less critical of Italian institutions than he had been of American ones, Dickens deals many swingeing blows at the Catholicism he found everywhere; as when, touring the Vatican, he remarks, 'I freely acknowledge that when I see a Jolly Young Waterman representing a cherubim (sic) or a Barclay and Perkins's drayman depicted as an Evangelist, I see nothing to commend or admire in the performance.'
Places visited include Rome, Naples, Carrara, Pisa, Florence, and Genoa.

Dealings with the Firm
of
DOMBEY AND SON,
Wholesale, Retail and for Exportation

Dickens's seventh novel, begun on 27 June 1846 at the Villa Rosemont, Lausanne, and continued in London, Paris, and Broadstairs. Completed in March 1848. First published in monthly numbers, October 1846 to April 1848. Issued complete by Bradbury & Evans, 1848. Illustrated by 'Phiz'. First American publication begun in parts in 1846 by Wiley & Putnam, New York, seventeen parts bearing their imprint, and the last two, in 1848, that of John Wiley.

Dickens's first notion was that *Dombey* was to do with pride what its predecessor, *Chuzzlewit*, had done with selfishness; but, says his biographer, John Forster, 'this limit he soon overpassed'. As the characters took over the thesis slipped behind. After writing the first four chapters, Dickens told Forster 'I design to show Mr. Dombey with that one idea of the Son taking firmer and firmer possession of him, and swelling and bloating his pride to a prodigious extent.' His professed plan for the book seems to have worked out almost precisely, except that he originally thought it a good idea to ruin the career of Walter Gay 'to show how the good turns into bad by degrees'. He was persuaded to reserve Walter for a happier future. He was particularly nervous that Dombey might be caricatured in the illustrations, and tried hard to get 'Phiz', the artist, to meet Dombey's living physical prototype, an unidentifiable 'Mr. A.'
Though he had decided from the first to 'slaughter' little Paul, in order to bring about the later workings of the plot, the actual death harrowed Dickens as the deaths of his child-angels usually did. 'There was but one small chapter more to write,' says Forster, 'in which he and his little friend were to part company for ever; and the greater part of the night of the day on which it was written, Thursday the 14th, he was wandering desolate and sad about the streets of Paris.' Dickens's readers were similarly affected, Lord Jeffrey writing to him from Edinburgh 'I have so cried and sobbed over it last night, and again this morning.'

The first number of *Dombey* outstripped the sale of the first *Chuzzlewit* by more than twelve thousand copies, and it continued to sell in large numbers.

Paul Dombey, senior, is the proud, stiff-necked head of a large London mercantile firm. He is gratified when his meek wife presents him with a son, Paul, six years after the birth of their only other child, Florence. Mrs. Dombey dies, unable to obey the advice of her brisk sister-in-law Mrs. Chick to Make an Effort. Dombey dedicates himself to the upbringing of little Paul as inheritor of and partner in the firm. A wet-nurse is hired, Polly Toodle, wife of a railway employee in Camden Town. Her maternal influence upon the orphaned children is a good one; sensing Florence's loneliness, she brings the child as much into contact with her baby brother as possible. Dombey insists that Polly be known as Richards, and that while in his employ she shall be separated from her own five children and her husband. But seeing the beneficial effect of Polly's nursing on Paul, he condescends to find her eldest son Robin, known as Biler, a place in the Charitable Grinders' school.

Paul is christened, his godmother being Miss Lucretia Tox, a timid, genteel spinster who hopes to capture her neighbour Major Joey Bagstock as a husband.

Polly and Florence's sharp-tongued maid, Susan Nipper, take Florence and Paul to Camden Town for an outing, as Polly is suffering from separation from her family. Returning home, the party is scattered by an alarm of 'Mad Bull!' and Florence, lost in the streets, is captured by an evil old woman calling herself Good Mrs. Brown, who robs her of her clothes and sends her out in rags. Florence wanders the City in search of her father's business premises, and is rescued by Walter Gay, a boy employed by Dombey's. Walter is struck by her childish beauty. He restores her to her father, who thanks him coldly. Polly is dismissed for taking Paul into the contaminating airs and society of Camden Town.

Miss Tox begins to hope that Dombey, in his solitary condition, will consider her as his second wife.

Paul has never recovered from the loss of Polly in infancy, and at five is a delicate child. He is sent with Florence to Brighton, where they lodge with the formidable Mrs. Pipchin.

Walter Gay, now a young man, lives with his uncle, Solomon Gills, a ships' instrument dealer, whose shop is known as the Wooden Midshipman from the wooden effigy above the door. His great friend is Captain Ned Cuttle, a one-armed retired seaman lodging with the widowed Mrs. MacStinger, who keeps a matrimonial eye upon him, as Miss Tox does upon Mr. Dombey. Sol Gills gets into debt and has his stock seized by a broker; Walter and Captain Cuttle seek a loan from Dombey, and receive it, Dombey pointing out to Paul how good it is to be rich and to be able to bestow charity. Paul is sent to school at Dr. Blimber's, a forcing-house where he is the youngest boy and the pet of the staff and his fellow-pupils. His particular friend is Mr. Toots, the eldest pupil, a young gentleman whose mental powers have become somewhat atrophied by over-study. Toots becomes the adorer of Florence. Paul is unable to cope with the arduous lessons imposed on him, becomes more and more frail, and faints at an end-of-term party. He is taken home to London.

Meanwhile the Carker brothers have appeared in the story. John is a junior clerk at Dombey's, who once robbed the firm, escaped dismissal, but was demoted to a minor post. James Carker, Dombey's manager, is a smiling villain who hates his brother and is secretly contemptuous of Dombey. Anxious to get Walter Gay out of his way, he finds him a position in Barbados. Before sailing in the *Son and Heir* Walter is summoned to Paul's bedside, where he is joined by Polly Toodle and Florence. Paul dies in Florence's arms. Walter and Florence take an affectionate leave of each other and Walter sails for Barbados.

Dombey, broken by the death of his son, becomes more and more cold and indifferent towards Florence. She leads a lonely life, her only companions Susan Nipper and Diogenes, a dog Paul was fond of at Blimber's, brought to her by Toots.

Dombey goes to Leamington with Major Bagstock, who introduces him to Edith Granger, a beautiful young widow who matches him in coldness. She is accompanied by her vain, coquettish old mother, 'Cleopatra' Skewton, who urges Edith to accept the proposal from Dombey which is certainly imminent. Edith does so, cold-bloodedly bartering her beauty and accomplishments for wealth and position. Miss Tox is devastated by Dombey's marriage. An affectionate friendship springs up between Edith and Florence, discouraged by Dombey, who goads Edith in vain to neglect the girl as he does.

The *Son and Heir* is missing. Sol Gills disappears from his shop, gone to seek news of his nephew. Captain Cuttle furtively leaves Mrs. MacStinger's, and moves into the Wooden Midshipman to take charge in his friend's absence. He is hampered by the presence of Rob Toodle, whom James Carker has set as a spy upon Sol Gills. Mrs. MacStinger discovers Captain Cuttle, but is pacified by his friend Jack Bunsby, whom she ultimately marries.

'Good Mrs. Brown' reappears on the scene. She had told an ominous fortune for Edith before her marriage. She proves to be the mother of Alice Brown, or Marwood, a handsome woman of Edith's type who returns home after years as a convict. Alice is the cast-off mistress of James Carker; befriended by James's sister Harriet and his brother John, she throws their charity in their faces with curses. Alice and her mother keep a close watch on James.

James Carker and Edith elope. Through the spying of Mrs. Brown and Rob, Dombey discovers that they have fled to Dijon. Florence attempts to console him, but he strikes her down with an angry blow. She rushes from the house and takes refuge with Captain Cuttle, who cares for her tenderly. He seems in a strangely disturbed state of mind, and throws out a series of hints leading to the telling of a story about a lost ship from which one passenger was saved: Walter appears at the door, and she flies into his arms, to the joy of Captain Cuttle.

In Dijon, Edith is alone at the hotel. Carker appears; she rejects his advances, telling him that she has eloped with him to be revenged upon him and her husband for the insults they have put upon her. Dombey arrives, Edith escapes, and Carker flies. Dombey pursues him back to England, catches up with him at a country railway station, and sees him cut to pieces by a train in an attempt to avoid his pursuer.

Sol Gills returns to the Midshipman in time for the wedding of Florence and Walter, who then go abroad. Toots is consoled by Susan Nipper, and marries her. The House of Dombey fails. Dombey, a lonely, broken man, sits in his darkened house and meditates suicide. He is saved by the sudden appearance of Florence, returned from abroad, to offer him the love he once rejected and to tell him that she has a son – another Paul. At last her father's reserve is broken. He allows Florence to take him home with her, and spends the rest of his life in quiet happiness with Florence and her family.

THE PERSONAL HISTORY OF DAVID COPPERFIELD

Dickens's eighth novel. Begun at Devonshire Terrace, London, in February 1849, continued at Bonchurch, Isle of Wight, and Broadstairs, and completed at Devonshire Terrace in October 1850. It was the last of his books to be written there. First number published May 1849, last number November 1850. A dinner in honour of it was given at the Star and Garter, Richmond, in June 1850. Published by Bradbury & Evans. First published as a single volume, November 1850. First published in America 1849–50 (Lea & Blanchard, Philadelphia) in twenty parts.

'Whether I shall turn out to be the hero of my own life, or whether that station will be held by anybody else, these pages must show.' The opening words of the novel are indicative of its autobiographical quality. Dickens had at one time contemplated an autobiography, but chose instead to incorporate much of himself in fictional form.

John Forster is careful to state in his biography that 'too much has been assumed . . . of the full identity of Dickens with his hero;' but certainly a good deal of Dickens's character and experience went into the book. In it he was able to write out of his heart the bitterness of his childhood servitude in the blacking warehouse, only slightly disguised, and his youthful adoration for Maria Beadnell, here presented as Dora. Dora's unsatisfactoriness as a housekeeper, and Agnes's efficient perfection, are probably an allegory of Dickens's irritation with his wife, and his admiration of her sister, Georgina Hogarth. His own career as law reporter and successful writer is faithfully reproduced. 'The story carried him along,' says Forster. The strength of the author's feeling and his close self-identification with the narrator make *Copperfield* the least involved and most convincing of his novels. There are fewer caricatures than in previous books: the character of Micawber, over which Dickens dwelt with obvious enjoyment, was so close to his own father in personality that, overdrawn as he appears to be, he never becomes one of the great grotesques, like Mrs. Gamp or Pecksniff. When writing the final chapter Dickens wrote to Forster: 'Oh, my dear Forster, if I were to say half of what *Copperfield* makes me feel tonight, how strangely, even to you, I should be turned inside out! I seem to be sending some part of myself into the Shadowy World.'

The book surpassed in popularity, though not in sales, all its predecessors except *Pickwick*.

Awaiting the birth of her child at the Rookery, Blunderstone, Suffolk, the widowed young Mrs. Copperfield receives a surprise visit from her dead husband's aunt, the eccentric Betsey Trotwood. When the child is born, and proves to be a boy, Miss Trotwood departs in dudgeon, for she does not approve of the male sex. David's early childhood is happy; he is the pet of his gay, pretty young mother and her devoted servant Clara Peggotty. Then Mrs. Copperfield begins to receive attentions from Edward Murdstone, a saturnine bachelor. David is sent with Peggotty to her brother Daniel, at Great Yarmouth.

Daniel, a bluff, genial fisherman, lives with his niece Emily (known as Little Em'ly), her cousin Ham, and the gloomy Mrs. Gummidge in an upturned boat which David finds the most fascinating dwelling possible. He feels a childish love for Em'ly.

When David returns home he finds his mother and Murdstone married. His life darkens. Murdstone is a harsh stepfather, and his sister Jane equally unsympathetic; she takes over the running of the household from David's mother. Failing to satisfy Murdstone in the learning of his lessons, David is beaten, bites Murdstone's hand, and is imprisoned in his room before being sent away to boarding school at Blackheath. The carrier who conveys him, Mr. Barkis, is struck by Peggotty's charms, and sends her the message 'Barkis is willin'' by David.

Salem House's headmaster is the sadistic Mr. Creakle, a flogger. Through innocent betrayal by David an assistant master, Mr. Mell, is dismissed. David becomes the protégé of James Steerforth, an older boy, handsome and arrogant.

In the next term, David hears that his mother has died after the birth of her child, also dead. Peggotty is dismissed by the Murdstones and accepts Barkis's proposal of marriage. David is taken away from school and sent to work in a warehouse, washing and labelling wine-bottles. He is humiliated and wretched, his troubles being slightly alleviated by the family with whom he lodges, the Micawbers. Mr. Micawber is a hopelessly improvident optimist, always confident that something will turn up; his devoted wife supports him in everything and avers that she will never desert him.

When conditions at the warehouse become intolerable, and the Micawbers leave London, David runs away to take refuge at Dover with Miss Trotwood, his great-aunt whom he has never met but who is the only relative he knows of. At the beginning of the journey he is robbed of his luggage and money, and has to travel to Dover on foot, selling his clothes to buy food: he arrives exhausted. Miss Trotwood, who is astonished to see him, soon reveals a kind heart under a forbidding exterior. She takes counsel with Mr. Dick, her slightly simple lodger, and decides to fight for the custody of the boy. The Murdstones arrive to claim David back, but Miss Trotwood routs them.

David's life now takes a turn for the better. He is sent to Canterbury, to a well-run school with a benevolent headmaster, Dr. Strong; he lodges there with Mr. Wickfield, a solicitor, and his young daughter Agnes. Wickfield's clerk is Uriah Heep, a sly, hypocritical youth, who frequently affirms himself to be 'very 'umble'. Heep gradually gains influence over the weak, bottle-addicted Wickfield. There is a shadow in Dr. Strong's life, too: his young wife Annie may be too fond of her cousin Jack Maldon.

David leaves school and in London meets Steerforth again. He visits Steerforth's mother at her home in Highgate, where she lives with her companion, the sharp-tongued Rosa Dartle. David and Steerforth go to Yarmouth, where they find celebrations in progress for the engagement of Ham and Little Em'ly. Steerforth becomes instantly popular, using all his charm on people whom he secretly despises as peasants, though he is impressed with Em'ly's beauty.

Agnes warns David against Steerforth, but he takes no notice of her. By now he has met another old schoolfellow, the comic Tommy Traddles, who is reading for the Bar. David himself now has to choose a profession, decides to become a proctor, a species of solicitor, and is articled to the firm of Spenlow and Jorkins. He falls in love at first sight with Spenlow's daughter, Dora. Dora's chaperone is Miss Murdstone.

Hearing that Barkis is seriously ill, David goes to Yarmouth. Barkis dies; and on Daniel Peggotty's home a worse sorrow falls, for Little Em'ly elopes with Steerforth. Daniel vows to find her, and sets out on their trail. When David calls upon Mrs. Steerforth, taking Daniel with him, he finds her adamant that she will never encourage Steerforth to marry Em'ly, and that if he does not get rid of the girl she will forbid him her house. Rosa Dartle reveals depths of jealous rage.

David becomes secretary to Dr. Strong, now living in Highgate; and Mr. Micawber takes up a clerk's post at Canterbury in the firm of Wickfield and Heep – for Uriah has now wormed his way into a partnership. He is also meddling in the affairs of the Strong household, and has ambitions to marry Agnes.

Dora's father dies suddenly, and after a decent interval Dora and David become officially engaged. Their marriage is idyllic at first, until Dora's deficiencies as a housekeeper become apparent. She is delightful but quite incompetent. Daniel Peggotty and David discover Em'ly in London, through the agency of a prostitute, Martha Endell. Steerforth, tiring of Em'ly, has tried to pass her on to his servant Littimer, and she has found her way back to England alone. Daniel plans to take her to Australia.

At Canterbury, Uriah Heep's villainy is exposed, and he is firmly dealt with by Traddles, in his legal capacity. Micawber's affairs are put in order: Miss Trotwood reveals that the death of the husband who long ago deserted her and has since sponged on her relieves her of a great burden, and she also discovers that she has not, after all, lost the bulk of her property through Mr. Wickfield. She offers to finance the emigration of the Micawbers.

After the birth of a still-born child, Dora dies. In a great storm at sea, off Yarmouth, Ham loses his life trying to save a passenger, who proves to be Steerforth, also drowned. David, stricken and sorrowful, goes abroad for three years. He returns with the realisation that he has always loved Agnes. Miss Trotwood leads him to believe that Agnes has 'an attachment', and the resultant questioning precipitates a mutual confession of love. The impecunious Traddles marries his sweetheart, Sophy Wackles; Littimer and Heep are found in a model prison, both model prisoners.

David and Agnes are married. Years later, they are visited by Daniel Peggotty, with good news of the Australian emigrants.

MISCELLANEOUS PAPERS FROM HOUSEHOLD WORDS

A posthumous selection of non-fiction pieces by Dickens published in *The Examiner*, *Household Words* and *All the Year Round* between 1838 and 1869, collected by B. W. Matz and first published in volume form in the National Edition of Dickens's works by Chapman & Hall in 1908.

REPRINTED PIECES

Thirty-one of Dickens's essays from *Household Words*, the weekly journal founded and edited by him which first appeared on 30 March 1850, and was last published on 28 May 1859, upon its absorption by *All the Year Round*, were published by Chapman & Hall as a collection entitled *Reprinted Pieces* in 1858. Five of the pieces – 'A Christmas Tree', 'The Poor Relation's Story', 'The Child's Story', 'The Schoolboy's Story' and 'Nobody's Story' – were subsequently incorporated in *Christmas Stories*. The twenty-six remaining *Reprinted Pieces* are:

'The Long Voyage' – the wreck of the *Halsewell* East Indiaman; 'The Begging-letter Writer'; 'A Child's Dream of a Star' – a dead child, become an angel, waits for her brother to join her; 'Our English Watering-place' – Broadstairs; 'Our French Watering-place' – Boulogne; 'Bill-sticking'; ' "Births: Mrs. Meek, of a Son" '; 'Lying Awake'; 'The Ghost of Art' – a meeting with a male model; 'Out of Town' – impressions of Pavilionstone (Folkestone); 'Out of the Season' – staying at (presumably) Broadstairs, author walks to (presumably) Deal; 'A Poor Man's Tale of a Patent' – a smith's difficulties in getting his invention patented; 'The Noble Savage' – author debunks the delusion that savage peoples are virtuous, happy, and noble; 'A Flight' – by rail and steam-packet from London to Paris; 'The Detective Police' – author visits criminal establishments, escorted by Scotland Yard detectives under 'Inspector Wield', a pseudonym for Inspector Charles F. Field; 'Three "Detective" Anecdotes' – again involving Inspector Field, these are: 1. 'The Pair of Gloves'; 2. 'The Artful Touch'; 3. 'The Sofa'; 'On Duty with Inspector Field' – a night tour of unsavoury London; 'Down with the Tide' – a visit to the Thames Police; 'A Walk in a Workhouse'; 'Prince Bull. A Fairy Tale' – an allegory on British inefficiency and humiliation in the Crimean War; 'A Plated Article' – conditions in the Staffordshire potteries; 'Our Honourable Friend' – the hypocrisy of Members of Parliament; 'Our School' – Wellington House Academy, Hampstead Road, London; 'Our Vestry' – playing at parish politics; 'Our Bore'; 'A Monument of French Folly' – English slaughter-houses ironically compared with French abbatoirs.

CHRISTMAS STORIES

A posthumous collection, first published by Chapman & Hall in 1871 as part of the Charles Dickens Edition of his works, commenced 1867, under the editorship of his son Charley. It comprises some of the stories which Dickens habitually wrote each Christmas for *Household Words* and *All the Year Round* over the period 1850–67. Five of them – 'A Christmas Tree', 'The Poor Relation's Story', 'The Child's Story', 'The Schoolboy's Story' and 'Nobody's Story' – had originally been included in *Reprinted Pieces*. There were no illustrations. They were republished in America in so many forms that it is not possible to define first publication there.

'A Christmas Tree' – reflections upon the delights and macabre fantasies engendered by the Christmas tree and its decorations; 'What Christmas is as we grow Older'; 'The Poor Relation's Story' – Michael, the Poor Relation, tells of his happiness with his wife and children in his Castle, but admits finally that it is all a Castle in the Air; 'The Child's Story' – a grandfather's journey through life; 'The Schoolboy's Story' – Old Cheeseman, a Latin master despised by pupils and fellow masters at a boarding-school, acquires a fortune and marries his only friend, an assistant matron; 'Nobody's Story' – a parable of the life and death of an unknown working man; 'The Seven Poor Travellers' – a story told by the narrator to the Six Poor Travellers who inhabit Watts's Charity, Rochester, one Christmas Eve, about Richard Doubledick who joins the army hoping to get killed, but finds redemption from despair and dissipation through the death of his officer, Captain Taunton, and regains his lost love; 'The Holly-Tree' – a traveller detained at the Holly-Tree inn when his coach becomes snowbound ruminates upon types of inn he has known, is told by the Boots of two children's attempt to elope to Gretna Green, and finds that the love whom he had thought had left him for his friend is his after all; 'The Wreck of the Golden Mary' – the sailing ship *Golden Mary*, California-bound, strikes an iceberg and founders, and the survivors endure twenty-seven days in small boats, during which several, including the child 'Golden Lucy', die; 'The Perils of Certain English Prisoners' – Gill Davis, former private of the Royal Marines, tells how the small English community on Silver-Store Island, off the Mosquito Coast, held out against pirate attack; 'Going into Society' – Chops, a fairground dwarf, achieves his ambition of entering society upon winning

a lottery, is fleeced of his money, returns to his showman employer, Toby Magsman, and dies; 'The Haunted House' – the narrator and a group of friends spend several nights investigating the haunting of a house, but he discovers that the ghost of Master B. is that of his own childhood; 'A Message from the Sea' – Captain Jorgan brings a message about an inheritance from one of his sailors who is believed drowned, and helps to rid the man's family of a long-standing suspicion of guilt; 'Tom Tiddler's Ground' – a traveller tries to persuade a filthy hermit to reform, without success; 'Somebody's Luggage' – a head waiter passes off two manuscripts to *All the Year Round* as his own work: the story of how 'Monsieur the Englishman' befriends an orphan child in France, and the story of a pavement artist; 'Mrs. Lirriper's Lodgings' – Mrs. Lirriper, a lodging-house keeper, tells how she takes in an unmarried couple, and after the man absconds and the woman dies she brings up their boy, Jemmy, herself; 'Mrs. Lirriper's Legacy' – Mrs. Lirriper goes to France to find Jemmy's father dying, and allows Jemmy to believe his own romanticised version of his background; 'Doctor Marigold' – a travelling showman loses his wife and daughter and adopts a deaf-and-dumb girl, who marries a deaf-and-dumb husband but produces a perfect child (see also 'No. 1 Branch Line: The Signalman' below); 'Mugby Junction' – a traveller known as Barbox Brothers arrives at Mugby: he is moved by the fortitude of Phoebe, invalid daughter of Lamps, the porter; in a nearby town he meets the child of his old love; the Boy at Mugby Junction recounts the grim secrets of railway refreshment-room practices; and the narrator hears the ghost story of 'No. 1 Branch Line: The Signal-man' which, together with 'Doctor Marigold' (see above) was later republished under the title 'Two Ghost Stories'; 'No Thoroughfare', written with Wilkie Collins, and subsequently dramatised by him – the quest for the true identity of Walter Wilding, a London vintner, leads to his death and the attempted murder of his partner, George Vendale, by Jules Obenreizer, with whose niece Vendale is in love. The girl saves Vendale, who proves to be the real Wilding, and Obenreizer is killed. 'No Thoroughfare' was dramatised by Collins alone in 1867, but is often included in collections of Dickens's plays.

A CHILD'S HISTORY OF ENGLAND

Begun at 1 Devonshire Terrace, London, in October 1850 and finished at Boulogne in September 1853. Published as a serial in *Household Words* between January 1851 and December 1853. Published by Bradbury & Evans in three volumes in 1852, 1853, 1854, with frontispieces by F. W. Topham, and in complete form, with dedication to his own children, in 1854.

Told in language which for that period was easy reading for children, the *History* covers the centuries between 55 B.C. and 1689, when William and Mary were established on the throne, the Protestant religion was established in England, and 'England's great and glorious Revolution was complete'. The years from then up to the date of writing are crisply summarised in one chapter, ending with 'GOD SAVE THE QUEEN!' Dickens's view of history is highly individual and violently prejudiced, with a strong Protestant bias throughout. Henry VIII is described as 'one of the most detestable villains that ever drew breath,' and James I referred to as His Sowship.

MR. NIGHTINGALE'S DIARY

This farce was privately printed in 1851, no author or publisher being given. First published in America in 1877 by James R. Osgood & Co., late Ticknor & Fields, Boston.

In one act, it was written for the Guild of Literature and Art founded by Dickens and Bulwer-Lytton for the benefit of impoverished authors and artists. The first charity performance of it was given at Devonshire House on 27 May 1851. Though generally thought of as being solely the work of Dickens, it had started out as a farce by Mark Lemon, but Dickens contributed so much humour to it that it came to be looked upon as his own. He acted in it, playing five characters, one of them (a version of Mrs. Gamp) Mr. Gabblewig of the Middle Temple, who arrives at a Malvern inn disconsolate because his future father-in-law, Mr. Nightingale, does not approve of his verbosity. Nightingale, a hypochondriac, arrives at Malvern with his daughter Rosina to take the cure. In order to get round Nightingale, Gabblewig, working against an impoverished actor, Slap, Nightingale's brother-in-law, assumes a variety of comic disguises, aided by Rosina, and wins her in the end.

BLEAK HOUSE

Dickens's ninth novel. Begun November 1851 at Tavistock House, London, and completed at Boulogne in August 1853. Published March 1852 to September 1853 by Bradbury & Evans. Illustrated by 'Phiz'. Published as a single volume, September 1853. First publication in America 1852-3 (Harper & Bros., New York) in twenty parts; also in *Harper's Magazine*.

The idea of the story came to Dickens in August 1851 at Broadstairs, while staying at the seaside villa then known as Fort House, now Bleak House. It nagged at him until he felt 'a torment of desire to be anywhere but where I am,' and longed to rush off to Switzerland. But removal from Devonshire Terrace to Tavistock House prevented the writing of the first words until November. The book was intended to illustrate the evils caused by long-drawn-out suits in the Courts of Chancery, known to Dickens from his youthful days in association with the law; and to point out the terrible condition of the uneducated poor, as exemplified in the person of Jo the crossing-sweeper. Various titles combining the two themes were proposed: *The Solitary House that was always shut up. Tom-all-Alone's. The Ruined (House, Building,*

Factory, Mill) that got into Chancery and never got out. These and others were abandoned, and the Jo thread occupies a lesser part of the story than Dickens had at first intended. The book is full of allegory. The pervading London fog represents the miasma surrounding the victims of Chancery and the terrible London slums and graveyards.

Bleak House is the only full-length novel in which Dickens uses a woman as first-person narrator, a device not wholly successful because of the aura of mock-modesty with which Esther Summerson surrounds herself: 'the too conscious unconsciousness of Esther,' as Forster says, and he comments fairly enough on the dark humours of the lesser characters, 'The Guppys, Weevles, Snagsbys, Chadbands, Krooks, and Smallweeds, even the Kenges, Vholeses, and Tulkinghorns, are much too real to be pleasant.' *Bleak House*, in fact, marked the end of Dickens's great comic inventions.

A hearing of the suit of Jarndyce and Jarndyce, in the High Court of Chancery before the Lord Chancellor, begins the story. Mr. Tulkinghorn, the Dedlock family's lawyer, visits Sir Leicester and Lady Dedlock at their town house and reports some new developments in the case, producing an affidavit at the sight of which Lady Dedlock becomes faint; she recognises the writing as that of her one-time lover.

Esther Summerson begins her own story. Illegitimate, brought up by a stern aunt, she is educated at the cost of her guardian, John Jarndyce, and after six years is summoned by his lawyers, Kenge and Carboy, to become companion to his ward, Ada Clare. In London she meets Ada, a pretty, winning girl, and her young cousin, Richard Carstone, who are obviously in love. Jarndyce has taken the young people into his home while the case is being heard in Chancery; it has dragged on for years. Jarndyce is sceptical of its success, but the optimistic Richard believes that it will make his fortune. The two wards and Esther meet Miss Flite, a whimsically mad old lady, also a victim of Chancery; and spend the night at the house of Mrs. Jellyby, who neglects her family and devotes all her time and energy to the cause of African natives. Miss Flite introduces them to her landlord, Krook, a drunken and eccentric old rag and bottle merchant.

Esther soon becomes the efficient housekeeper ('Dame Durden' is Jarndyce's affectionate name for her) of Bleak House, near St. Albans, and the close friend of Ada and Richard. Her advice is sought by both and by Jarndyce. She meets Harold Skimpole, delightful, artistic, irresponsible, 'a mere child', as he is fond of saying, in money matters. Richard unwisely pays a debt for which Skimpole has been arrested.

The link between Lady Dedlock and Esther is now made apparent. Mr. Guppy, a lawyer's clerk from Kenge and Carboy's, has become infatuated with Esther. Visiting the Dedlocks' country house, Chesney Wold, in Lincolnshire, he is struck by the familiar appearance of Lady Dedlock in her portrait, though he cannot pin-point the resemblance. He visits Esther, proposes to her, and is refused.

Tulkinghorn makes inquiries about the writer of the affidavit which had such a marked effect on Lady

Dedlock. He discovers the man, a law-writer calling himself Nemo, to be a lodger at Krook's; but calling there, finds Nemo dead of poison. No papers of his are to be found. Jo, a young crossing-sweeper, gives evidence at the inquest, for Nemo had been his only friend. Tulkinghorn reports to the Dedlocks what has happened, and Lady Dedlock affects indifference.

Richard decides to become a surgeon, is soon bored, and chooses first the Law, then the Army, confident all the time that when the suit in Chancery is settled he will be rich and able to marry Ada. Esther falls in love with Allan Woodcourt, a young doctor whom she meets through Miss Flite. Jo reports to Tulkinghorn how a veiled lady has given him money for showing her the grave of Nemo; shown a similarly dressed woman in Tulkinghorn's chambers, he identifies the dress but does not recognise the wearer. She is, in fact, Hortense, Lady Dedlock's French maid, who has turned against her because she is jealous of her lady's preference for another maid, Rosa. Tulkinghorn is using her, and George Rouncewell, son of the housekeeper at Chesney Wold, to obtain information about Nemo with which to blackmail Lady Dedlock.

Guppy calls on Lady Dedlock and tells her that he has deduced that Esther is her daughter; that Esther's name is really Hawdon, and that Nemo was a pseudonym for Captain Hawdon.

Esther and her little maid Charley visit Jenny, a brickmaker's wife, and find Jo there, suffering with a feverish illness. They take him back to Bleak House, but he runs away in the night. Charley has caught smallpox from him. Esther nurses her, catches the disease herself, and emerges from it badly scarred. She renounces all thought of Allan Woodcourt. For the first time she meets Lady Dedlock, who tells her, after a tender interview, that they must never again meet for fear of their relationship being revealed. Guppy, on seeing Esther's changed face, loses interest in her.

The pursuit of Hawdon's papers goes on. Guppy and a friend, expecting a packet of them to be handed over by Krook, find him dead of spontaneous combustion. Tulkinghorn obtains from George Rouncewell a specimen of Hawdon's writing; he promises Lady Dedlock that he will not expose her without previous warning, provided that she does not leave Chesney Wold, as she proposes. He himself is being harried by Hortense, who insists that he finds her a new post in exchange for the help she has given him. After another interview with Lady Dedlock, Tulkinghorn is found the next morning shot dead in his chambers. George Rouncewell is arrested for his murder, but Mr. Bucket, a detective, discovers that it has been committed by Hortense, and arrests her.

Lady Dedlock disappears. She has been told by Guppy that not only he but several other people incidental to the story (Smallweed, Chadband, Mrs. Snagsby) know her secret. Bucket, with Esther, sets out in pursuit of her, but they are misled because she has changed clothes with Jenny. At last they find her, dead on the step of the sordid burial-ground where Hawdon lies.

The suit in Chancery has dragged to its close; costs have swallowed up the whole of the estate. Richard Carstone has drifted out of the Army and is lodging, ill and restive, at Symond's Inn. He has unfairly blamed John Jarndyce for all his troubles. Ada secretly marries him, and only tells Esther her secret when she knows herself pregnant. Richard is reconciled to Jarndyce, and dies.

Jarndyce, who proposed to Esther after the loss of her beauty, and was accepted, now sees that she loves Allan Woodcourt, who has attended Jo in his last illness and befriended the dying Richard. Allan declares his love to Esther, but she refuses him. Jarndyce takes her to see Allan's future home, which he has called Bleak House, and tells her that this is the Bleak House of which she is to be mistress. He gives her, cheerfully and nobly, to Allan, relinquishing his own claims.

The story has also followed the fortunes of Caddy, Mrs. Jellyby's daughter, her dancing-master husband Prince Turveydrop and his pompous, selfish father; of Snagsby the law-stationer and his jealous wife; of Charley Neckett, the orphan who becomes Esther's maid; of the soldier Bagnet and his family; of Boythorn, Jarndyce's temperamental friend; and of the maid Rosa and the Rouncewell family.

TO BE READ AT DUSK

First published in 1852 in *The Keepsake*, an annual formerly edited by Lady Blessington. It was reprinted as an individual pamphlet in 1852.

There are two sombre stories in one: the tragedy of an English bride, narrated by a Genoese courier, and a ghostly legend recounted by his German counterpart.

HARD TIMES
for These Times

Dickens's tenth novel. Begun January 1854 at Tavistock House, written there and at Boulogne, where it was finished at about the end of July 1854. It was the first of his novels to be serialised in *Household Words,* between April and August 1854, but without illustrations. Published as an illustrated complete novel in August 1854, with a dedication to Thomas Carlyle, by Bradbury & Evans. The first cheap edition, 1865, had a frontispiece by A. Boyd Houghton. Fred Walker contributed four drawings to the Library Edition. First published in America 1854–5, by Harper & Bros., New York.

The shortest of Dickens's novels, it was the most difficult to write because of the limited space at his disposal in *Household Words*; but it more than doubled the circulation of his journal. It was meant to be, he said, a satire 'against those who see figures and averages, and nothing else – the representatives of the wickedest and most enormous vice of this time; the men who, through long years to come, will do more to damage the really useful truths of political economy than I could do (if I tried) in my whole life.' Because of its brevity it contained none of the embellishments, humorous or sentimental, of his earlier novels, and hardly any grotesquerie. Even the circus scenes appear perfunctory. It has the air of being a tract against materialism rather than a story told for its own sake, and Dickens's extremely poor ear for local dialect makes the dialogue of the Lancashire characters hard reading. There is a general dryness about it which suggests overwork and exhaustion in its author.

Thomas Gradgrind's family is ruled by Fact, and the school in Coketown, a northern industrial town, over which he presides is also dominated by it. He is displeased with Sissy Jupe, a circus clown's daughter, because of her unrealistic upbringing; and appalled when he finds his own children, Louisa and Tom, trying to see something of Sleary's Circus, where Jupe works. He and Josiah Bounderby, proud self-made man, banker, merchant, and owner of the Coketown mills, decide that Sissy had better be removed from the school, and are about to tell her so when they find that her father is missing. Gradgrind offers her a home, on condition that she holds no further communication with the circus people.

Tom is a weak, easily influenced boy, Louisa a dreamy, dissatisfied girl. Sensing Louisa's attraction for Bounderby, Tom decides to get at that powerful man through her.

Stephen Blackpool, a mill-hand married to a drunken, dissolute wife, is in love with Rachael, a fellow-worker. He consults Bounderby about the possibility of divorcing his wife, and finds it impossible under the existing laws. He meets a strange old woman outside Bounderby's house, who asks searching questions about its owner. Rachael nurses Stephen's wife and prevents her from taking poison. They are resigned to a life apart so long as his wife lives.

Gradgrind tells Louisa that Bounderby has asked for her in marriage. In spite of the disparity of their years and characters, she accepts. Bounderby shocks his aristocratically-related housekeeper, Mrs. Sparsit, with the news.

Louisa's marriage is unhappy. She tolerates the attentions of James Harthouse, a languid man of the world who has political business with Bounderby. He sees Louisa's love for her brother, and pretends an interest in Tom, whom he influences in turn.

Bounderby's Bank is robbed, and Stephen Blackpool suspected. He has been discharged from Bounderby's mill for failing to support a strike of operatives, and is generally in bad odour. Bitzer, clerk at the Bank, gives evidence against him. Louisa suspects Tom's guilt, and maintains her suspicions in spite of Harthouse's persuasions to the contrary. Mrs. Sparsit spies upon Louisa and Harthouse; when she discovers that they are meeting alone at Bounderby's country house she follows them, and overhears Harthouse's attempted seduction of Louisa. Louisa hurries back to Coketown, followed by Mrs. Sparsit, hopeful of collecting more evidence. But Louisa has gone to her father, to confess her temptation and take refuge with him. Her confession moves him to the point of realising his mistakes in her upbringing. Bounderby follows her to Gradgrind's, and decides that they would be better apart. Sissy Jupe goes to Harthouse's hotel, and tells him to have no further hope of Louisa.

B

Stephen has left Coketown in search of work, and Bounderby offers a reward for his capture. Sissy and Rachael find Stephen's hat near a disused mine-shaft, and Stephen himself at the bottom of the shaft, seriously injured. Dying, he asks Gradgrind to clear his name, hinting that Tom, his son, can tell him how.

Mrs. Sparsit, intent on malice, finds the so-called Mrs. Pegler, whom Stephen has met outside Bounderby's house. She proves to be Bounderby's unacknowledged mother, whose very existence contradicts all his fabrications about his hard, sordid childhood, deserted and thrown on the world by his mother as a baby. Bounderby is deflated.

Gradgrind learns from Louisa and Sissy that Tom was the bank-robber, and that he is hiding with Sleary's Circus. They find him there, and Sleary disguises him as a circus performer. His escape is nearly foiled by the spying of Bitzer, but Sleary and his accomplished horse and dog effect Tom's flight.

Tom dies abroad, sending a loving and penitent message to Louisa from his death-bed. Louisa does not re-marry, but matures into the woman she might have been earlier but for her harsh rearing. Rachael remains single and faithful to Stephen's memory, but Sissy marries. Gradgrind lives into old age, 'making his facts and figures subservient to Faith, Hope and Charity'.

LITTLE DORRIT

Dickens's eleventh novel. Begun at Tavistock House, London, May 1855, and written there, at Folkestone, Boulogne and Paris. Finished in May or June 1857 in London. Published by Bradbury & Evans in monthly parts between December 1855 and June 1857. Published complete in June 1857. Illustrated by 'Phiz'. First publication in America 1855–7 by Harper & Bros., New York, in *Harper's Magazine*.

The first title Dickens chose was *Nobody's Fault*, as his original idea had been to weave the story round a man 'who should bring about all the mischief in it, lay it all on Providence, and say at every fresh calamity, "Well, it's a mercy, however, nobody was to blame you know!"' He abandoned this for a plot in which the characters 'came together, in a chance way, as fellow-travellers' and later were connected. He was, in fact, less sure of the outline of *Dorrit* than he had been about any previous book. It is a dark novel, with a preponderance of characters who are failures in life. There is little light relief beyond Flora Finching, Mr. F's Aunt and young John Chivery, who is in the main a pathetic figure. Arthur Clennam and Little Dorrit are stock figures from Dickens's cupboard: Little Dorrit might be Little Nell risen from the tomb. The core of the story is the Marshalsea Prison, the scene of Dickens's early humiliation when his father was imprisoned there.

The public bought the book with enthusiasm, but *Blackwood's Magazine* condemned it as 'twaddle', and the *Edinburgh Review* complained of Dickens's lack of originality in basing fictional events upon real ones, and criticised him for slandering real people in his descriptions of the Circumlocution Office.

In a Marseilles prison the villainous Rigaud tells his companion, Cavalletto, that he is there for murdering his wife for her money. He is sent for trial. Also in Marseilles is Arthur Clennam, who has been in business with his father in the East for twenty years, and is now returning to England, his father having died. He is in quarantine with the Meagles family: Mr. Meagles, a retired banker, his cheerful wife, his pretty daughter known as 'Pet', and her maid, nicknamed 'Tattycoram'. Tattycoram is wildly jealous of the attentions paid by everyone to Pet, and finds a sympathiser in Miss Wade, a coldly detached fellow-passenger.

Back in London, Arthur receives a chilly welcome from his mother, Mrs. Clennam, an invalid obsessed by her gloomy religion, who lives alone but for two old servants, Jeremiah Flintwinch and his wife Affery. Arthur tells his mother that he feels his father has been guilty of dishonesty in business, and she replies that she will cast him out with her curse if he speaks of the matter again. He hands over his share of the business to Flintwinch.

Arthur meets the girl who sews for Mrs. Clennam. Christened Amy, she is known as Little Dorrit, and is the younger daughter of William Dorrit, 'The Father of the Marshalsea'. Little Dorrit was born in the prison and has grown up there. Precociously mature, she supports her father, her brother Edward, known as 'Tip', and her sister Fanny, keeping her work a secret from the old man. Through William Dorrit's brother Frederick, Arthur is introduced to the family; because of his interest in the girl he seeks a way of releasing Dorrit. But his inquiries at the Circumlocution Office about Dorrit's creditors meet with no success. He meets Daniel Doyce, an engineer and inventor, who is to become his partner, and the Plornishes of Bleeding Heart Yard. Rigaud, now free, reappears in the story.

Arthur meets Flora Finching, once Flora Casby, his early love. She is now middle-aged, fat, voluble, and silly. Disillusioned, Arthur visits the Meagles family and wonders whether or not to allow himself to fall in love with Pet, but decides against it. Fanny Dorrit is pursued by Edmund Sparkler, son of the chill, fashionable Mrs. Merdle, and stepson of her banker husband, but she is too proud to encourage him in view of his mother's opposition. Besides, she tells her sister, 'he is almost an idiot'. Little Dorrit herself is in love with Arthur, but does not let him suspect it. Pet Meagles has formed an attachment to Henry Gowan, an artist of independent means, and marries him. Rigaud arrives at Mrs. Clennam's house, calling himself Blandois.

Pancks, a rent-collector, discovers that William Dorrit is heir-at-law to a great unclaimed estate, and is free to leave the Marshalsea, a rich man. With his family Dorrit sets out on foreign travels. In Switzerland they meet the newly-married Gowans. Later in the journey they are joined by Fanny's suitor, Sparkler, and his mother, and by Blandois. They are also accompanied by the formidable Mrs. General,

chaperone to the Misses Dorrit, who has matrimonial designs on William. Fanny marries Sparkler. Merdle offers to assist William to invest his wealth, and the offer is accepted. Dorrit's failing mind reverts to his Marshalsea years, with embarrassing results when he addresses the guests at Mrs. Merdle's party; ten days later he dies, his brother Frederick dying at his bedside.

Arthur Clennam goes to Calais to interview Miss Wade, who is accompanied by Tattycoram, who has run away to her. She refuses to give him any information about Blandois, with whom he saw her in London, but hands him a written explanation of her own background. Back in London, he encounters Cavalletto, who tells him all he knows of the criminal past of Rigaud, alias Blandois, and Arthur passes this on to Mrs. Clennam, but she refuses to accept the truth. Arthur hears from Affery of the strange noises she hears at night in the house: 'rustlings and stealings about, tremblings. . . .'

The banker Merdle commits suicide, his bank fails, and Arthur finds himself ruined. Arrested for debt and taken to the Marshalsea, he is conducted to Little Dorrit's old room by young John Chivery, son of the Turnkey and the adorer of Little Dorrit. She visits Arthur in prison, and offers him all her wealth, which he refuses.

Blandois reveals to Mrs. Clennam that he knows her secret: Arthur is not her child, but the son of a woman whom her husband loved, but was forced to give up by family pressure. Mrs. Clennam removed the baby from his mother and brought him up as her own, in a spirit of revenge upon his parents, 'that the child might work out his release in bondage and hardship'. She has, Blandois knows, suppressed the codicil of a will by which Little Dorrit would inherit two thousand guineas. He threatens that if she will not accept his terms he will deliver the papers to Arthur. Mrs. Clennam is shocked out of her invalid chair. She rushes from the house to the Marshalsea, where Little Dorrit is watching over Arthur in an illness. Little Dorrit promises to return with her to plead with Blandois; but as they approach the house, it crumbles and disintegrates, burying Blandois in its debris. The strange noises heard by Affery had been intimations of the rot and decay which were to bring the house down at last.

Mr. Meagles calls on Miss Wade in France, to beg her to give up important papers left with her by Blandois. She refuses, but when he returns to England Tattycoram appears with the papers. She has followed him, and now confesses how much she has grown to fear Miss Wade's power over her, and that she has come to realise that she is being trained to become what Miss Wade is – a self-destroyer and a destroyer of others. She begs to come back to the Meagles family, who accept her joyfully.

Arthur, recovered, is released from the Marshalsea by the agency of Daniel Doyce and Meagles. Little Dorrit tells him that she has no fortune to offer him: she knows now that the Dorrit fortunes were dissipated, like his own, by the fraudulent Merdle. Nothing any longer stands in the way of their marriage, which takes place in the church next to the Marshalsea, where Little Dorrit had been christened.

A strong sub-theme in the novel concerns the Circumlocution Office, satirising red-tape administration: 'The most important department under Government ... the Circumlocution Office was beforehand with all the public departments in the art of perceiving – How Not to Do It.' The family of Barnacle helps to administer it, Lord Decimus Barnacle being a master of the afore-named art; other members are Clarence, 'the born idiot of the family', Tite, Ferdinand, and William. A figure of hypocrisy is Christopher Casby, Flora Finching's father. Flora's aunt-in-law, 'Mr. F's Aunt', is the chief eccentric of the book, given to the utterance of startling irrelevancies. The Merdles and their pretensions are the target Dickens sets up for his attack on snobbery.

THE LAZY TOUR OF TWO IDLE APPRENTICES

First published in *Household Words* in October 1857, and written jointly by Dickens and Wilkie Collins, it is an account of a trip made by them to the North of England in the autumn of 1857. They call themselves respectively Thomas Idle and Francis Goodchild, after the characters in Hogarth's series of pictures. Its first appearance in book form was in 1890 when Chapman & Hall printed it with 'No Thoroughfare' and 'The Perils of Certain English Prisoners' in a single volume, illustrated by Arthur Layard. The most notable episodes of the *Tour* are the ghost story told of a Lancaster inn, and a lively account of a race-meeting at Doncaster.

A TALE OF TWO CITIES

Dickens's twelfth novel. Written at Tavistock House, London, and Gad's Hill from March 1859. The first instalment appeared on 30 April 1859 in the first number of *All the Year Round*, the new weekly journal published by Chapman & Hall and conducted by Dickens which superseded and absorbed *Household Words*. The last instalment was on 26 November, and the story was published by Chapman & Hall in the same month as a complete novel, illustrated by 'Phiz'. First published in America 1859 by Harper & Bros., New York, in *Harper's Weekly*.

The idea occurred to Dickens when acting in *The Frozen Deep* with his amateur company in the summer of 1857. He had difficulty in getting down to the writing, and in finding a title. Among those he suggested to John Forster were *One of these Days, The Doctor of Beauvais*, and *Buried Alive*. He did not start writing it until March 1859. He was scrupulous in getting his historical details right and making a thorough study of the background to the French Revolution, and perhaps this very thoroughness led to the curiously un-Dickensian remoteness about the book, and a woodenness in its characters. There are only three strong themes: the imprisonment and recurrent amnesia of Doctor Manette; the heartless behaviour of the women spectators at the guillotine, linked with the revenge of the peasantry for their wrongs; and the self-sacrifice of Sydney Carton, the dominant figure of the book.

There is little humour, Jerry Cruncher's anathematising of his praying wife being repetitive and inferior to any of the 'humours' of comic characters in previous books, and Miss Pross being used in the end as an instrument of drama. The *Saturday Review* anatomised the book scathingly, remarking that 'whenever Mr. Dickens writes a novel, he makes two or three comic characters just as he might cut a pig out of a piece of orange peel.'

The book was popularised by a dramatisation, *The Only Way*, produced at the Lyceum Theatre in 1899, starring John Martin Harvey.

The story opens in 1775. The states of England and France are described and compared, and the scene set for the French Revolution.

Jarvis Lorry, agent for Tellson's Bank in London, receives on his way to Paris a mysterious message, to which he sends back the answer RECALLED TO LIFE. At a Dover inn he meets by appointment Lucie Manette, French-born but brought up in England. Lorry tells her that her father, the physician Dr. Alexandre Manette, is not dead, as she supposed, but has been for many years a prisoner, for a State offence, in the Bastille, from where he has now been released. He takes her to the house in Paris where her father has been lodged. Defarge, a wine-shop keeper with a handsome, dominant wife, leads them to him: he is sitting at a bench, making shoes, a vacant-faced, prematurely white-haired man whose voice is unused to speaking and whose memory has apparently gone. Lucie tries to make him recognise her, with little success. She and Lorry take him back to England.

Five years later, in London, Jerry Cruncher, odd-jobber at Tellson's and 'resurrectionist' by night of dead bodies for medical purposes, is sent to the Old Bailey with a note for Lorry, grumbling as he departs about his pious wife's habit of 'flopping', as he describes her frequent bouts of prayer for his soul. The Court is trying a treason case: a young Frenchman, Charles Darnay (whose true name is St. Evrémonde), is accused of spying. He is acquitted after his counsel, Mr. Stryver, has pointed out that identification is unreliable evidence when one man can resemble another as much as the prisoner resembles another lawyer present in court, Sydney Carton. Lorry and the Manettes, who have been witnesses at the trial, congratulate Charles.

Carton is a dissolute, irresponsible character, who could have been a brilliant lawyer, but who aspires no higher than to do hack work for the more pushing Stryver. Carton and Charles visit the Manettes at their Soho home. Dr. Manette is now restored to health and sanity and lives happily with Lucie and her eccentric companion, Miss Pross.

The action moves to France. Driving in his carriage, the Marquis St. Evrémonde, Charles's uncle, runs over and kills the child of a peasant. That evening Charles visits him; the next morning the Marquis is found murdered, an act of vengeance by the child's father.

In England again, Charles, Carton, and Stryver all hope to marry Lucie Manette. Lorry advises Stryver not to propose to her. Charles speaks to Dr. Manette, who gives him his blessing. Carton tells Lucie of his love for her, but says that he knows she cannot return it, and that he is not worthy of her. He gives her a solemn assurance that for her, or anybody dear to her, he would do anything; that he is 'a man who would give his life, to keep a life you love beside you!'

In Paris, an English spy calling himself John Barsad arrives at the wine-shop and tells Monsieur and Madame Defarge that Charles Darnay is to marry Lucie Manette; and in England, on the evening before the wedding, Dr. Manette tells Lucie that he is entirely happy in the outcome. But after the couple have left for their honeymoon, a prison story about the discovery of a hidden paper, once told to him by Charles, comes back to his mind, and with it his amnesia. He goes back to his old employment of making shoes, to the distress of Lorry and Miss Pross who, when he returns to his senses, destroy his bench, tools, and leather.

In Paris the Revolution has broken out, the people of St. Antoine rise, and Defarge is their leader in the siege of the Bastille. The governor is captured and decapitated by Madame Defarge, herself a leader of the revolutionary women. The mob burns the castle of the late Marquis St. Evrémonde and Gabelle, his tax and rent collector, is imprisoned in L'Abbaye, Paris. He writes to Charles begging for help. Charles leaves for Paris, as does Lorry, who is on business for Tellson's. Lorry warns Charles that he will be in danger when he reaches France, which proves to be the case. He has barely reached Paris when he is flung into the prison of La Force. Defarge, who befriended Dr. Manette after his release from the Bastille, refuses to help him.

Lucie, with her baby daughter, Miss Pross, and her father, follows him to Paris, full of apprehension, having heard of his imprisonment. When they arrive at Tellson's Lorry is shocked, both by their news and their presence there. Dr. Manette assures him that by virtue of his once having been a Bastille prisoner he can help Charles. The revolutionaries accept him and lead him to La Force, while Lorry places Lucie, little Lucie and Miss Pross in lodgings. They receive a note from the Doctor saying that Charles is safe. Madame Defarge does not respond to Lucie's gratitude for the note, and the aggressively British Miss Pross takes an instant dislike to the Frenchwoman.

Dr. Manette does not return for four days, during which time eleven hundred prisoners have been killed. Charles has been spared, but all Dr. Manette's efforts to get him released are fruitless. Every day, for a year and three months, Lucie fears to hear that her husband is to go to the guillotine. Her father tells her that there is a window in the prison from which Charles can see her if she stands at a certain point in the street. From that time she goes there every day, often with her child, horrified to see the fearful Carmagnole, expressing bloodthirsty hatred of aristocrats, danced in the streets.

Charles is called before the Tribunal, and on the testimony of Dr. Manette, Gabelle, and Lorry is acquitted and carried home in triumph; but he is almost immediately re-arrested at the instigation of the Defarges, and by the denunciation of 'one other', he is told.

Miss Pross, shopping with Jerry Cruncher, meets her brother Solomon, known as John Barsad in France and Roger Cly in England, where he has staged a mock funeral and is supposed dead. Once a spy for the British Government, he is now a turnkey at the Conciergerie. Jerry, who knows that Cly is not dead because he opened the coffin supposed to contain Cly's body during one of his resurrectionist excursions, recognises him. Sydney Carton arrives on the scene, also recognises Pross as Cly, and persuades him that he knows enough about him to get him into trouble unless he allows Charles's family and friends access to him if sentence should be passed upon him. Cly agrees.

Once again before the Tribunal, Charles hears the identity of the 'one other' accuser. A paper has been found beneath the floor of Dr. Manette's old prison cell, setting out how he came to be imprisoned. In 1757 he had been summoned to a country house outside Paris to attend a young woman raving in delirium of 'my husband, my father, and my brother', and counting repeatedly up to twelve. Another patient was a young man who, in the hearing of the Marquis St. Evrémonde and his brother, told them that the girl was his sister, who as a bride was coveted by the younger St. Evrémonde. Her husband refusing to 'lend' her, the nobles literally worked him to death, and then St. Evrémonde took her away and raped her. Her brother challenged the rapist to a duel, and was fatally wounded, cursing the Marquis and his brother with a cross marked in blood. Some days later the girl died.

Manette had been visited at home by the wife of the Marquis St. Evrémonde, with her son, young Charles. She wished to make reparation for the wrongs done to the dead girl's family; she believed there was a young sister. Later Dr. Manette had been abducted and imprisoned at the behest of the Marquis. He wrote down his story and buried it beneath the floor.

Charles, as a St. Evrémonde, is condemned on this evidence to die in two days. Carton, drinking in Defarge's wine-shop, overhears Madame Defarge and other conspirators plotting the complete extermination of the St. Evrémonde family, and Madame's revelation that she herself was the little sister of the girl and boy attended by Dr. Manette. This has been her motivation in the pursuit of Charles and all who bear his name. Dr. Manette, distracted at having been the innocent cause of Charles's condemnation, returns to his old illusion that he is still making shoes in the Bastille.

Carton gives Lorry his own passport enabling him to leave Paris, and another allowing Lucie and the child to leave, telling him to get her, the Doctor and himself out of the city as soon as possible. Lorry obeys.

In the prison, during the early hours of the morning of his execution, Charles is visited by Carton, who commands him to change clothes with him and write a note referring to an old promise. Charles does not understand him, but obeys. Carton drugs him, puts on his discarded clothes, and orders Solomon Pross to carry Carton away, telling the guards that St. Evrémonde's visitor has fainted. He takes Charles's place and because of the great likeness between the two is not detected.

Madame Defarge and her fellow-revolutionaries decide to have Lucie and the child denounced. Madame goes to Lucie's lodging, to be confronted by Miss Pross, determined to play for time and cover Lucie's retreat. Neither she nor Madame can understand a word the other says, yet a fierce battle of wills takes place between them. Madame Defarge draws a pistol, struggles with Miss Pross and is shot. Miss Pross, deafened for ever by the noise of the pistol, hurries from the house and sets out with Jerry Cruncher for England.

Sydney Carton's last day has come. Still in the character of Charles, he is taken to the guillotine in a tumbril, comforting a little sempstress who is to die with him. For the first time Madame Defarge is not there with her knitting, to watch the executions.

In his last moments Carton sees vengeance falling on the revolutionaries, and his sacrifice justified by the safety and happiness of Darnay and his family: for he has kept his old promise to Lucie to save a life dear to her. 'It is a far, far better thing that I do, than I have ever done; it is a far, far better rest that I go to than I have ever known.'

HUNTED DOWN

First published in the *New York Ledger*, 20 and 27 August and 3 September 1859, and in *All the Year Round* 4 and 11 August 1860. The American version was illustrated with seven woodcuts. The first publication in separate form in England was as an 89-page pamphlet issued by John Camden Hotten, London, 1870, and including an account of the Wainewright poisoning case on which Dickens had founded the story. An earlier edition appeared in America in 1861.

Julius Slinkton is suspected of having poisoned one of his nieces for her insurance money. Meltham, an actuary of the insurance company, who had been in love with the girl, determines to trap Slinkton into betraying himself. 'Disappearing' as Meltham and reappearing as Alfred Beckwith, a seemingly excessive drinker, he strikes up a friendship with Slinkton and persuades the latter to insure him heavily, anticipating that he will attempt to dispose of him too. Slinkton is meanwhile working on his other niece, Margaret Niner, but she is saved from her sister's fate and Slinkton, unmasked, poisons himself. Miss Niner marries a nephew of Sampson, chief manager of the insurance company. Meltham, his task achieved, dies of his broken heart.

THE UNCOMMERCIAL TRAVELLER

A series of essays and sketches from life, written as articles for *All the Year Round* between 1860 and 1869. The first edition in volume form was published by Chapman & Hall in December 1860, comprising seventeen pieces. A subsequent edition, in 1865, added eleven more papers, and the posthumous edition of 1875 was enlarged by eight more. All these, with one final addition, make up the volume which is part of any 'complete' edition of Dickens's works.

The Uncommercial Traveller introduces himself as a faceless representative of what he might term 'the great house of Human Interest Brothers', setting forth from his rooms in Covent Garden to wander in city and country, observing 'many little things, and some great things, which, because they interest me, I think may interest others.' Most of his titles are self-explanatory: 'His General Line of Business'; 'The Shipwreck'; 'Wapping Workhouse'; 'Two Views of a Cheap Theatre'; 'Poor Mercantile Jack' – seamen's haunts in Liverpool; 'Refreshments for Travellers' – the difficulty of getting a good cheap meal in England; 'Travelling Abroad' – Paris, Strasbourg, Switzerland; 'The Great Tasmania's Cargo' – the Uncommercial Traveller is appalled by the condition of soldiers returned from the Crimea; 'City of London Churches'; 'Shy Neighbourhoods' – ruminations chiefly about birds and dogs; 'Tramps'; 'Dullborough Town' – the Uncommercial Traveller revisits his boyhood home (Chatham); 'Night Walks'; 'Chambers' – impressions of the Inns of Court; 'Nurse's Stories' – macabre tales recalled from childhood; 'Arcadian London' – the West End; 'The Italian Prisoner' – the Uncommercial Traveller transports an immense bottle of wine from Italy, a released prisoner's debt of gratitude to an English benefactor; 'The Calais Night Mail' – by train and night packet from London to Paris; 'Some Recollections of Mortality' – the Uncommercial Traveller visits the Paris morgue and recalls a drowning in the Regent's Canal and his experience as a Coroner's juror; 'Birthday Celebrations'; 'The Short-Timers' – he sees demonstrated the Half-Time system of educating the children of the poor; 'Bound for the Great Salt Lake' – a visit to a Mormon emigrant ship; 'The City of the Absent' – weekend wanderings in the City of London; 'An Old Stage-coaching House' – the effect of the railway upon an old coaching inn; 'The Boiled Beef of New England' – a 'Cooking Depot' for the working classes of Whitechapel; 'Chatham Dockyard'; 'In the French-Flemish Country' – mainly describing a visit to a Fair; 'Medicine Men of Civilisation' – funerals and other absurd ceremonies of western society; 'Titbull's Alms-Houses' – the Uncommercial Traveller visits some almshouses in the East End of London, probably the Vintners' Almshouses, Mile End Road; 'The Ruffian' – the Uncommercial Traveller calls for harsher sentences for ruffianly behaviour, and tries to enforce a clause of the Police Act for himself; 'Aboard Ship' – travelling to New York in the Cunard steamship *Russia*; 'A Small Star in the East' – visits to poor workers' homes and to the East London Children's Hospital, Ratcliff; 'A Little Dinner in an Hour' – the Uncommercial Traveller and a friend dine disastrously at a seaside inn; 'Mr. Barlow' – thoughts about the pedantic tutor in the well-known children's book *The History of Sandford and Merton* by Thomas Day, published in parts 1783–9; 'On an Amateur Beat' – wanderings amongst London's deprived areas, a further visit to the East London Children's Hospital, and an investigation of lead-mills; 'A Fly-leaf in a Life' – overwork and its consequences; 'A Plea for Total Abstinence' – those who advocate abstinence from drink should abstain from other, generally accepted, excesses.

GREAT EXPECTATIONS

Dickens's thirteenth novel. Begun at Gad's Hill Place, October 1860, continued at 3 Hanover Terrace, Regent's Park, and finished at Gad's Hill in June 1861. The first instalment appeared in *All the Year Round* on 1 December 1860, and it was published weekly until 3 August 1861. In August it was published by Chapman & Hall in three volumes, and in 1862 in one volume, the latter illustrated by Marcus Stone. First published in America in 1861 by Harper & Bros., New York, in *Harper's Weekly*.

Dickens got his 'very fine, new, and grotesque idea' for the book while working on *The Uncommercial Traveller*. He could see 'the whole of a serial revolving on it, in a most singular and comic manner'. He had, apparently, a clear scheme for the plot in his head before he began it, and went so far as to re-read *David Copperfield* to make sure he was not repeating himself in his autobiographical vein; for the new book was to be highly subjective without reproducing actual details of its author's youth, other than geographical ones. It is a greater novel than *Copperfield* by reason of its close integration, and lack of sub-plot and 'orange-peel-pig' comics; it bears every sign of Dickens's own outlook on life and intense feeling for his characters. The folly of pretended gentility, the impossibility of manipulating a human being into becoming a different personality for one's own pleasure (Magwitch and Pip, Miss Havisham and Estella), the ease with which wealth can corrupt, and the essential goodness of simplicity (Joe Gargery), all bear witness to Dickens's own state of mind and reveal much about him. Estella has been much praised as Dickens's first real young woman character, but in fact she lacks the life of his next two feminine juveniles, Bella Wilfer and Rosa Bud, and serves mainly to illustrate Miss Havisham's tragic mistake. Pip's sufferings from her coldheartedness may have been Dickens's own at Ellen Ternan's failure to reciprocate his autumn passion. Pip is the first 'hero' to have a real personality; to know himself as Nickleby, Chuzzlewit, Clennam, and even Copperfield do not. The lighter characters, Herbert Pocket, Wemmick, the Wopsles, and Uncle Pumblechook, are wholly credible as well as amusing.

Little Philip Pirrip, known as Pip, lives in the Kent marshes with his shrewish sister and her husband, the simply, kindly blacksmith, Joe Gargery. The story opens in a country churchyard, where Pip is terrified by the appearance of an escaped convict who threatens him with awful vengeance unless some food and a file for his fetters are obtained smartly. Pip manages to hide some of his own supper, steals more food from the pantry and, after an encounter with a different,

younger convict, finds the original one and leaves him filing off his irons.

The convicts are later captured by soldiers. Pip's convict chivalrously says it was he who stole the food, and Pip is too afraid to confess the truth. Pip is sent for by Miss Havisham, of Satis House in the local market town, taken there by his Uncle Pumblechook, a corn-chandler, and conducted to Miss Havisham by her companion, Estella, a proud, beautiful young girl. Miss Havisham is a middle-aged woman whose whim it is to live perpetually in the bridal dress she wore on the day she was jilted by her lover, surrounded by the debris of the wedding-feast. She hates all the male sex, and has sent for Pip to enjoy the sight of him being tormented by Estella. On another visit he meets a 'pale young gentleman', Herbert Pocket, one of Miss Havisham's many relations, with whom he has a fight.

When Pip is old enough to become an apprentice blacksmith, Miss Havisham gives Joe twenty-five guineas as a premium for him. Mrs. Gargery is attacked and severely injured by an unknown hand. Pip is sure that her attacker was Orlick, an uncouth journeyman of Joe's. Mrs. Gargery's injuries have left her an invalid, and Joe takes a young orphan, Biddy, as his housekeeper. Pip tells Biddy of his longing to be a gentleman. He is disgusted and unhappy at the smithy, he says, without telling her that his ambitions are centred on Estella; but Biddy guesses as much.

Jaggers, a lawyer from London whom Pip has seen at Miss Havisham's, informs Joe and Pip that Pip has Great Expectations from an unknown benefactor, whose name he must never try to find out. He is always to be known as Pip, and will be brought up as a gentleman. His indentures are cancelled, he buys new clothes, says farewell to Miss Havisham, and goes to London, where he calls on Jaggers at his office in Little Britain. Wemmick, Jaggers's clerk, takes Pip to Barnard's Inn, where he meets Herbert, the son of Matthew Pocket, Miss Havisham's cousin, who is to be his tutor. Pip recognises Herbert as the boy he once fought at Satis House. They become close friends, and are to share chambers at the Inn. Pip is also friendly with Wemmick, who takes him to tea at his home, a curious little residence known as the Castle, at Walworth, presided over by his Aged Parent, almost totally deaf but cheerful and contented.

Herbert tells Pip Miss Havisham's story, mentioning that the man who jilted her had extracted from her large sums of money, in which her half-brother was thought to have shared; and that Estella's origins are unknown. Pip becomes increasingly sure that his Expectations are from Miss Havisham. Jaggers invites him to dinner: Wemmick advises him to look closely at Jaggers's housekeeper, 'a wild beast tamed'. She proves to be about forty, with a striking face, and Jaggers draws the company's attention to her remarkably strong wrists. Pip takes a dislike to a boorish young man called Bentley Drummle, who is present.

Miss Havisham summons Pip to the old town. Orlick, he finds, is now her porter. He is reunited with Estella, home from being educated in France, grown up and more beautiful than ever. Pip is puzzled by a resemblance to somebody he cannot identify. Miss Havisham begs him, with wild insistence, to love

Estella, however much she may hurt him. Soon after, Pip receives a note from Estella saying that she is coming to London. He meets her and escorts her to Richmond. She is friendly but cool, leaving Pip with the realisation that he is unhappy both with and without her.

Pip's sister dies just before Pip comes of age. He receives from Jaggers five hundred pounds, the gift of his anonymous benefactor. He visits Estella several times, and reproaches her for encouraging the attentions of Bentley Drummle.

One night Pip has a visitor; he is horrified to recognise the convict from his childhood. The man announces himself as Abel Magwitch, alias Provis, and shocks Pip by revealing that he, not Miss Havisham, is the founder of Pip's fortunes, in gratitude for the help given him long ago. He has got rich sheep-farming in Australia, and devoted all his wealth to Pip: 'Yes, Pip, dear boy, I've made a gentleman of you!' If his return to England were known, it would be death to him, he tells Pip and Herbert. They agree to hide him. He tells them the story of his life and association with a man called Compeyson, the other convict seen by the child Pip, and with Arthur Havisham, Miss Havisham's half-brother. When Magwitch and Compeyson were jointly tried for felony, Compeyson was let off with a seven-year sentence because of his gentlemanly appearance and speech, Magwitch receiving fourteen years.

Pip visits Miss Havisham and tells of his discovery, asking her to continue to help Herbert, whom he has set up in business. Confessing his love to Estella, he hears that she is to marry Drummle. With a final protestation of love, he rushes away and back to London.

Magwitch and he have been watched. Magwitch has been taken to a safer place, at the house where Herbert's fiancée, Clara Barley, lives with her father, near the Pool of London. A plan is arranged for Magwitch to escape by boat to a foreign vessel. Pip visits Miss Havisham, who is deeply distressed at the realisation of what she has done to him and to Estella. What she tells him of Estella's first coming to her confirms his belief that Jaggers's housekeeper is Estella's mother; he later learns that this is true, that she is a murderess whom Jaggers has saved, and that Magwitch is Estella's father. Miss Havisham's clothes catch fire; Pip saves her from burning, but she soon dies of her injuries.

Pip is summoned to a night appointment at the old lime-kiln on the marshes. He finds Orlick there, lying in wait for the man he deludedly imagines to be his old enemy, his rival for Biddy's affections and the favourite of the forge. He admits to attacking Pip's sister out of hatred for Pip, and threatens to kill Pip and burn his body in the lime-kiln. It is he who has tracked down Magwitch in Pip's chambers, and he is in league with Compeyson to prevent Magwitch's escape. But Pip is rescued in the nick of time.

The operation of rescuing Magwitch is begun. The boat in which Pip and Herbert are taking Magwitch down the river to board a foreign steamer is commanded to stop by an officer's boat, in which is Compeyson. The steamer runs them down, Compeyson is drowned, and Magwitch is severely hurt. He is brought to trial, and convicted, but is too ill for imprisonment. Pip visits him in the prison hospital; a new relationship springs up between them. Pip now feels for him tenderness and gratitude, and shame at his own former attitude. Magwitch dies, Pip giving him at the last news that his daughter, whom he thought dead, lives.

Pip becomes seriously ill. He rouses from delirium to find that Joe has been nursing him for weeks. As with Magwitch, his feelings change to remorse, for since becoming a 'gentleman' he has viewed poor Joe snobbishly, and been ashamed of him in public. His Great Expectations have done him no good; he is glad to be rid of them. After Joe has left, not waiting for thanks, Pip decides to go down to the country and ask Biddy to marry him, for long ago she seemed fond of him. He arrives to find that it is the wedding-day of Biddy and Joe.

He sells up, pays his many creditors, and leaves England to join Herbert Pocket in business in the East. Returning eleven years later, he pays a nostalgic evening visit to the site of Satis House. Walking in the garden is Estella. She is a widow, after an unhappy married life, from which she has learnt understanding and sympathy at last. She asks Pip to be her friend, and leave her. But as the evening mists rise and the light grows, he can see no shadow of another parting from her.

OUR MUTUAL FRIEND

Dickens's fourteenth novel. Begun in November 1863 at Gad's Hill; written there, at 57 Gloucester Place, Marylebone, and at 16 Somers Place, Hyde Park; finished at Gad's Hill about October 1865. First number published by Chapman & Hall on 1 May 1864; last number November 1865; the complete work in two volumes published in the same month. Illustrated by Marcus Stone. First American publication 1864–5 by Harper & Bros., New York, in *Harper's Magazine*.

Dickens chose the title for the book four years before he began to write it. He wrote to Forster of the leading themes. The many handbills he had seen describing persons drowned in the river suggested the 'ghastly calling' of the long-shore men Hexam and Riderhood. The idea of the 'living dead', which he perhaps intended to use again in *Drood*, provided the character of Rokesmith, supposed dead and 'retaining the singular view of life and character so imparted'. The Lammles were suggested by the notion of two people marrying each other for their money and finding out their mistake after marriage. The Veneerings exemplified his idea of 'new' people, 'bran new, like the furniture and the carriages – shining with varnish, and just home from the manufacturers'. An uneducated father with an educated son, whom Leech had he had seen, became Charley Hexam and his father; and Riah, the impossibly saintly old Jew, was a sop to those who had objected to Fagin as a disgrace to Judaism. The taxidermist's shop of Mr. Venus was found for him by Marcus Stone in Monmouth Street, St. Giles's.

The writing was slow, delayed by personal worries and by the illness which was beginning to trouble him. He was carrying some of the manuscript when involved in the Staplehurst railway disaster, and wrote a humorous 'postscript in lieu of preface' about the experiences of his characters in the accident.

Our Mutual Friend is, like *Little Dorrit*, a novel of failures and a parable of the corruption money brings. The society in which his middle-class characters move is a hollow one, superficially flittering; boredom, pretence, and pride invest it. The pretended greed of Boffin is painfully like the real thing. Venus's profession is grisly, Silas Wegg is mutilated. The recovery of corpses is the trade of Riderhood and Hexam. Abbey Potterson is the least genial of Dickens's innkeepers, Pleasant Riderhood that rarity in his novels, a thoroughly ugly young woman. Yet among the pessimism and satire there are fine things: the unforgettable figure of the pretty, psychic dwarf, Jenny Wren, the savagely jealous Bradley Headstone, the astonishing reality of the heroine with refreshing weaknesses, Bella Wilfer.

Jesse Hexam, called 'Gaffer', lives by retrieving dead bodies from the Thames. His partner is Roger 'Rogue' Riderhood. Hexam and his daughter Lizzie find the body of a man in the river, and he refuses to share any reward he may get from it with Riderhood.

At the 'bran-new house in a bran-new quarter of London' live the Veneerings, a parvenu couple. At a dinner given by them, Mortimer Lightwood, a young solicitor, tells the story of John Harmon, a 'dust contractor' who made his fortune from the mountains of ordure piled up at Battle Bridge in north London. He turned his young son, John, out of doors after the boy had protested against his father's treatment of his sister, and the boy went abroad to make his own living. Harmon died, making the condition of his son's inheritance that he should marry Bella Wilfer, daughter of a clerk. Lightwood receives a note to say that the dead body of young John Harmon has been found in the Thames, and goes with his friend Eugene Wrayburn to Hexam's, encountering a young man calling himself Julius Handford, on the same errand.

Julius Handford is, in fact (though this is not revealed until half way through the novel), young John Harmon himself. On his way back from the Cape he had found himself so mistrustful of the destiny that awaited him that he arranged with the ship's third mate, who resembled him physically, to exchange clothes and identities. By this means he would be able to inspect Bella Wilfer from a distance and decide whether or not he would claim his inheritance and marry her. Should he not claim, the money would go to Mr. Nicodemus 'Noddy' Boffin, a confidential servant of his father's. Boffin and his wife befriended John in his unhappy childhood, and he is reluctant to deprive them of the legacy.

When they reached England the third mate drugged and robbed Harmon, but was himself attacked by other men at the lodging-house. Both he and Harmon were thrown into the river. The third mate drowned; his body was recovered and mistaken for Harmon's, but Harmon dragged himself out and recovered.

Now officially dead, he decides to go through with his plan to live under an alias. Calling himself John Rokesmith, he goes to lodge with 'Rumty' Wilfer, a clerk in Veneering's employ, who lives with his temperamental wife, and his daughters, Bella and Lavinia. He finds Bella pretty, but vain, spoilt, and over-fond of money.

Mr. Boffin is now manager of the Harmon Estates. He and his wife, far from rejoicing in their legacy, are grieved by the discovery of the body of the supposed John, and offer a reward of £10,000 for the arrest of his murderer. Mrs. Boffin decides to adopt an orphan, to take the place of the little John Harmon she loved, who shall in turn be given John's name. They also decide to ask Bella Wilfer to come and live with them, which she does with alacrity, delighted to leave her family, though she is deeply attached to her put-upon little father. At the Wilfers' they meet John 'Rokesmith', to whom Boffin refers as Our Mutual Friend. John becomes Boffin's secretary. Mrs. Boffin, when John enters their house, is haunted by the faces of old Harmon and his son and daughter.

The Boffins propose to adopt Johnny, the small grandson of Betty Higden, a child-minder, but he dies in the Children's Hospital. Betty is afraid of being taken to the workhouse, leaves home, and dies of exhaustion.

In parallel with the story of John and Bella runs that of Lizzie, Hexam's daughter. Handsome and intelligent, she attracts the attention of Wrayburn, and also of Bradley Headstone, her young brother's schoolmaster. When her father is accidentally drowned, after being accused of the murder of the supposed John Harmon, Lizzie goes to live in Westminster with a little crippled girl, Fanny Cleaver, known as Jenny Wren, who supports her drunken father by making dolls' dresses. Jenny is a whimsical, precocious child, and something of a visionary. When Headstone's importunities become too much for her Lizzie seeks the help of Riah, a kindly old Jew, who finds her a job at a paper-mill outside London.

In the world of fashion, John Harmon is being discussed by the Veneerings. They tell Boffin that his secretary is an adventurer. John proposes marriage to Bella, but she scornfully tells him that she intends to marry money. Boffin has secretly recognised his secretary as John Harmon, and in order to change Bella's worldly point of view he pretends to persecute John. He also pretends to become a miser, and abuses John for his supposed neglect of the Estate. Finally John is dismissed. Bella, in sympathy, goes with him. They are married, in the name of Rokesmith, for Bella still does not know her lover's identity, and after an idyllic wedding-breakfast at Greenwich, shared by Bella's father, settle down in a cottage at Blackheath.

Wrayburn has sought and found Lizzie. But he has been followed by Headstone, who considers Wrayburn to be the cause of Lizzie's rejection of him, and is madly jealous. He tracks down Wrayburn, and watches him keep an appointment with Lizzie on the river-bank, during which Lizzie refuses to marry Wrayburn on account of the difference in their social status. Headstone imagines the interview to be an amorous one, and after Lizzie and Wrayburn have parted he attacks Wrayburn, wounds him severely, and throws him into the river. Lizzie rescues him and nurses him, and when he appears to be dying promises to marry him. Headstone, who thinks him dead, hears the news of the forthcoming wedding from the clergyman who is to perform it, and falls into a fit. Later he encounters Riderhood, who is blackmailing him. They struggle by the river and are both drowned.

John 'Rokesmith' meets Mortimer Lightwood, whom he has so far managed to avoid, as being the one person who would recognise him. He does so, and the secret is out. John takes Bella and their baby to their new home in London. Mrs. Wilfer tells Bella how she came to recognise John, and why Boffin pretended to be harsh and miserly.

A will is found which appears to leave old Harmon's wealth to the Crown, and a later one naming the Boffins. Boffin generously makes over the money to John and Bella, retaining only 'Harmon's Jail', the home of his old employer, now renamed 'Boffin's Bower' by Mrs. Boffin.

Into the main plots are woven many other threads: the loveless marriage for money of the Lammles; the humours of Silas Wegg the one-legged ballad-monger and Mr. Venus the taxidermist; the pompous Podsnap, his equine-faced wife, and their gauche daughter Georgiana; Miss Emma Peecher, a little teacher at Headstone's school and his devoted adorer; Miss Abbey Potterson, formidable hostess of the Six Jolly Fellowship Porters, a Thames-side tavern, Pleasant Riderhood the pawnbroker; Sloppy the orphan; Betty Higden's mangle-turner; Twemlow, the Veneerings' humble friend and hanger-on; Fascination Fledgeby the money-broker. All their stories are interdependent.

GEORGE SILVERMAN'S EXPLANATION

First published in the American *Atlantic Monthly* in January, February, and March 1868 and in England in *All the Year Round* in February the same year.

George Silverman, an orphan, is brought up by Brother Hawkyard and other fanatical Nonconformists in Lancashire. He becomes a clergyman and secretary to Lady Fareway, with whose daughter Adelina, his pupil, he falls in love. When he self-sacrificingly contrives Adelina's marriage to another pupil, Granville Wharton, Lady Fareway believes Silverman has acted out of self-interest, dismisses him, and pursues him vengefully for some years before he finds peace.

HOLIDAY ROMANCE

Written for an American children's magazine, *Our Young Folks*, and first published there January–May 1868, and in England, in *All the Year Round*, in January–April 1868. The American edition had four illustrations by John (later Sir John) Gilbert.

Purportedly edited by William Tinkling, aged eight, it is in four parts, each supposedly written by a small child. William Tinkling, the eight-year-old editor, tells of his 'marriage' to Nettie Ashford, aged seven. He and Lieutenant-Colonel Robin Redforth, aged nine, try to rescue Nettie and Robin's bride, Alice Rainbird, aged seven, from imprisonment in the school of the Misses Drowvey and Grimmer. The plan fails and Tinkling is court-martialled. Alice Rainbird's story is of the Princess Alicia, eldest child of King Watkins the First. Her godmother, the Fairy Grandmarina, gives her a Magic Fishbone, which will bring her anything she wants. Alicia uses the wish to save her father's fortunes and is rewarded by her fairy godmother with a magnificent wedding to Prince Certainpersonio. Robin Redforth's romance concerns Captain Boldheart, intrepid master of the schooner *Beauty*, and his tussles with the Latin-grammar master, the treacherous commander of the *Scorpion*. The final romance, by Nettie Ashford, tells of Mrs. Orange and Mrs. Lemon, children in charge of grown-ups who 'are never allowed to sit up to supper, except on their birthdays.'

THE MYSTERY OF EDWIN DROOD

Dickens's fifteenth novel, left unfinished at his death. Begun at Gad's Hill in October 1869, and written there and at 5 Hyde Park Place, London; the last words written at Gad's Hill on 8 June 1870. First instalment published on 1 April 1870, and the sixth in September 1870, by Chapman & Hall, with illustrations by Luke Fildes (the 'Green Cover' designed, and some unused drawings made, by Charles Collins). First published in America, April to October 1870, as a serial in a monthly Dickens Supplement to *Harper's Weekly*. Also published by Fields, Osgood & Co., Boston, April–September 1870. It first appeared in book form in England in August 1870.

Dickens outlined to Forster several ideas for what he little realised was to be his last novel. 'Two people – boy or girl, or very young, going apart from one another, pledged to be married after many years – at the end of the book. The interest to arise out of the tracing of their separate ways, and the impossibility of telling what will be done with that impending fate.' This he discarded for a 'very curious and new idea' about the murder of a nephew by an uncle, who would review his own career in the condemned cell as though it were somebody else's. The murderer was to discover the utter needlessness of the murder soon after its commission, and was to be discovered by means of a gold ring found uncorroded in quicklime.

Exactly half the numbers of the book had been written when Dickens died. It is impossible to deduce with any certainty what the outcome of the mystery was to be; whether he had changed the scheme mentioned to Forster or not. What exists seems to make Jasper so inescapably the murderer that there is not much interest in the plot. 'If Edwin Drood is dead, there is not much mystery about him,' commented G. K. Chesterton. Many volumes have been devoted to conjecture, but no completely satisfactory solution has ever been suggested.

The writing is unlike anything Dickens had done before, as though, in his last year of life, he had slipped into a new, fresh style, in complete contrast to the heaviness and complexity of the preceding novel, *Our Mutual Friend*. It might be described as the literary equivalent of architectural High Gothic, with many passages of poetic prose and the most vivid scenic descriptions Dickens had yet produced. It is as though he were writing the narrative to accompany a film as it unrolled itself in his mind. He had never conveyed so clearly the essence of his beloved Rochester before. The Cathedral dominates the story as no building has previously done in his works. London has receded to a 'gritty' place; but the Law and its practice are no longer portrayed with Dickens's usual contempt. Mr. Grewgious is a man with a heart and (it seems) some detective ability; Staple Inn has flowers and birds instead of the cats and bugs of early disgusted descriptions of the Inns of Court. Crisparkle is his first likeable clergyman, Rosa his most real and living girl, more vital even than Bella Wilfer. When the book suddenly stops, the reader is left with a feeling of disappointment and loss. 'It is certainly one of his most beautiful works, if not the most beautiful of all,' said Longfellow.

In the Prologue, written like the telling of a dream, a man lies on a squalid broken bed in an opium den, lost in a vision of eastern pageantry. As he wakes from his stupor, the bedpost becomes the tower of an English cathedral: the cathedral of Cloisterham.

The dreamer is John Jasper, music-master and choirmaster of the cathedral. He is a dark, pale man of sombre manner. He welcomes to his rooms in the cathedral gatehouse his nephew Edwin Drood, only a few years younger than himself, a cheerful youth with whom he seems on the best and most affectionate of terms. Edwin, a student engineer, has been engaged since childhood to Rosa Bud, his father having expressed the dying wish that his son should marry the daughter of his old friend. Both are now orphans. Edwin's guardian is Jasper, Rosa's is Mr. Hiram Grewgious, a lawyer of Staple Inn.

Edwin has come down to see Rosa on her birthday. She is a pupil at Miss Twinkleton's Academy, where she receives Edwin somewhat pettishly, telling him how it irks her to be so teased about their engagement. They quarrel. Edwin treats her casually and calls her 'Pussy'. But Jasper has other and deeper feelings. As though trying to tell Edwin something without words, he confesses that he is unhappy, unfulfilled, in his cathedral work – that 'even a poor monotonous chorister and grinder of music – in his niche – may be troubled with some stray sort of ambition, aspiration´ . . .' – and bids Edwin take it as a warning. Edwin obviously fails to understand him.

Canon Crisparkle, a brisk, sporting young bachelor clergyman, receives visitors at his mother's house in Minor Canon Corner. They are Neville and Helena Landless, twins from Ceylon, dark, handsome, and with an untamed air. Neville is to be Crisparkle's pupil, Helena to attend Miss Twinkleton's. She becomes friendly with Rosa. A musical party is held at which Rosa sings to Jasper's accompaniment, wavers

under his passionate, hypnotic gaze, and faints. Neville is attracted to Rosa and antagonistic to Edwin, who treats her far too lightly, he thinks; and Edwin seems more attracted to Helena than to Rosa. On the way home the two young men quarrel, a quarrel subtly fed by Jasper as he entertains them later. Neville's fiery temper is roused, and Jasper dwells on its violence to Crisparkle.

Grewgious visits Rosa to discuss the marriage settlement, and she asks him if her engagement could be broken without any forfeit on either side. He replies that it was 'merely a wish' on the part of Edwin's father and hers, and is not a binding contract. But he does not sense the feeling behind her query.

Edwin calls on Grewgious in London, and receives from him a tactfully veiled lecture on his light-minded attitude towards Rosa, whom he does not seem to value enough: Grewgious was in love with her dead mother, whom he sees again in Rosa. He gives Edwin a ring taken from her dead finger, charging him to give it to Rosa on the day their betrothal is finally and solemnly settled; but if Edwin has doubts, or if there is anything wrong between them, Edwin is to bring the ring back to him.

Edwin goes down to Cloisterham for Christmas, having been invited by Jasper to become reconciled with Neville at his rooms. When he meets Rosa, they walk by the river, and she tells him that she feels they should only be friends, not lovers, for they have not voluntarily chosen each other and will never be happy. Edwin, touched and saddened, agrees; but they decide not to tell Jasper yet, for his heart (Edwin believes) is set on the union. Rosa looks strangely at him. Their parting kiss is seen by Jasper.

Jasper goes on a night tour of the cathedral with Durdles, the sexton, plying him with strong drink as they go, until Durdles falls into a stupor and seems to hear the clink of keys and footsteps going away from him. Jasper seems deeply interested in Durdles's ability to detect, by tapping the masonry, bodies, or other objects lying within ancient tombs. He is angered by the attentions of an urchin, Deputy, whose job it is to stone Durdles if he catches him out after ten o'clock and drive him home.

On Christmas Eve, Neville prepares for a walking-tour he intends to make next day. He leaves the house with his bundle and a stout, heavy stick. Edwin wanders about the town until it is time to go to Jasper's, calls at a jeweller's to have his watch repaired, and mentions to the man that he wears no jewellery but his watch, chain, and shirt-pin. He meets the old woman who is the proprietress of the opium den in London frequented by Jasper. She asks him for money and warns him that if his name is Eddy he is in grave danger. John Jasper goes to the rendezvous singing, with a great black scarf wound in a loop over his arm.

That night a terrible gale of wind blows, tearing off the hands of the cathedral clock and damaging the tower. Jasper rushes among the spectators of the damage exclaiming that Edwin has vanished after walking down to the river with Neville the previous night. Neville is pursued, brought back, and taken before the Mayor. He angrily declares his innocence. A day and night search is instituted for Edwin, and Crisparkle, bathing early in the river, finds his watch and shirt-pin, seeming drawn to them by a kind of magnetism. Grewgious visits Jasper, finds him exhausted after hours of futile search, and apparently deeply despondent. Grewgious's manner to him is notably abrupt. He informs Jasper that the engagement between Edwin and Rosa had been broken off before Edwin's disappearance. Jasper swoons. Days afterwards, when no trace other than the jewellery has yet been found of Edwin, Jasper shows Crisparkle an entry in his diary vowing to track down the murderer of his 'dear dead boy'.

Six months later, Neville Landless is living in chambers in Staple Inn, near Grewgious, driven away from Cloisterham by suspicion and rumour. He is ill and worried. Crisparkle visits him and Grewgious, who points out that Jasper is lurking outside, possibly keeping a watch on Neville. Neville receives a visit from a neighbour, Mr. Tartar, a handsome, lively young man who has resigned from the Royal Navy on coming into property. Tartar befriends him.

After the end of the summer term, Rosa has been left alone at Miss Twinkleton's. Jasper joins her in the garden, and makes a wild declaration of love to her, swearing to hound Neville to his death if she will not love him. Rosa is terrified. That night she goes up to London and tells Grewgious her story. He finds a temporary lodging for her at Furnival's Inn. Next morning Crisparkle arrives, and Helena, who is now staying with Neville. Tartar calls, and Crisparkle and he greet each other as once master and fag in schooldays. Tartar and Rosa are instantly attracted to one another, and he gallantly offers her the use of his chambers. From Tartar's, Rosa goes to lodge with Mrs. Billickin, and Miss Twinkleton comes up to chaperone her, though she and Mrs. Billickin are natural enemies. Tartar disappears from the scene, and Rosa pines.

A new face appears in Cloisterham: Dick Datchery, a sturdy man of indeterminate age with somewhat odd-looking white hair. He takes the lodgings beneath Jasper's, and appears very inquisitive about all the recent doings in Cloisterham. He enlists Deputy as spy or reporter, and questions people, including Jasper, notching up successes in chalk on his cupboard door. The opium woman arrives on the track of Jasper; Datchery directs her to the cathedral.

Jasper, meanwhile, has visited her in London and in an opium trance has related an apparently symbolical journey he has made repeatedly, in imagination, always in the same way and with the same companion; but when it was made in fact, it was 'the poorest of all. No struggle, no consciousness of peril, no entreaty – and yet I never saw *that* before. . . .'

The story breaks off as Datchery, having seen the opium woman into the cathedral, falls to his breakfast with an appetite.

Minor characters are Mr. Honeythunder, the pompous and bigoted District Philanthropist, who is the Landlesses' guardian; Mr. Sapsea, the equally pompous Mayor of Cloisterham; and Bazzard, Grewgious's mysterious clerk, thought by many Dickensians to be the disguised Datchery.

THE LAMPLIGHTER

On the crest of his *Pickwick* fame, Dickens was invited in 1838 by William Macready to write a play for him. The result was *The Lamplighter*, a farce, which Dickens completed in November and read to the actor-manager and his company. The piece was rehearsed, but never performed, as Macready, pressed by his actors, asked Dickens to withdraw it. The text is included in volumes of Dickens's plays. He made use of the plot in the story entitled 'The Lamplighter's Story'.

THE LIFE OF OUR LORD

Written in 1846 at the Villa Rosemont, Lausanne. Never intended for publication, it was however published in 1934, by Associated Newspapers.

John Forster describes this as 'an abstract, in plain language for the use of his children, of the narrative in the Four Gospels. . . . Allusion was made, shortly after his death, to the existence of such a manuscript, with expression of a wish that it might be published; but nothing would have shocked himself so much as any suggestion of that kind. The little piece was of a peculiarly private character; written for his children, and exclusively and strictly for their use only.'

THE PEOPLE

AN ALPHABETICAL LIST
OF ALL THE NAMED CHARACTERS IN
DICKENS'S WORKS

THE PEOPLE

'Aaron': Wrayburn's slighting name for Riah. *'If Mr. Aaron,' said Eugene . . . 'will be good enough to relinquish his charge to me, he will be quite free for any engagement he may have at the Synagogue'* (Mutual Friend).

Adams: Head-boy at Dr. Strong's. *He looked like a young clergyman, in his white cravat, but he was very affable and good-humoured* (Copperfield).

Adams: Sampson's clerk ('Hunted Down').

Adams, Captain, and **Westwood:** Seconds to Verisopht and Hawk in their duel. *Both utterly heartless, both men upon town, both thoroughly initiated in its worst vices, both deeply in debt, both fallen from some higher estate, both addicted to every depravity for which society can find some genteel name and plead its most depraving conventionalities as an excuse, they were, naturally, gentlemen of unblemished honour themselves, and of great nicety concerning the honour of other people* (Nickleby).

Adams, Jack: Subject of one of Cousin Feenix's anecdotes. *'Jack – little Jack – man with a cast in his eye, and slight impediment in his speech – man who sat for somebody's borough. We used to call him in my parliamentary time W. P. Adams, in consequence of his being Warming Pan for a young fellow who was in his minority'* (Dombey).

Adams, Jane: The Fieldings' housemaid who takes her friend Anne in to see the wedding preparations. *Comes all out of breath to redeem a solemn promise of taking her in, under cover of the confusion, to see the breakfast table spread forth in state, and – sight of sights! – her young mistress ready dressed for church* (Young Couples – 'Young Couple'). She appears again, widowed and living in an alms-house, in *Young Couples – 'Old Couple'*.

Admiralty: Naval magnate, guest at Merdle's (Dorrit).

Affery: Maiden name of Mrs. Jeremiah Flintwinch, by which she is still known in Mrs. Clennam's service. *Lived in terror of her husband and Mrs. Clennam, the clever ones* (Dorrit).

African Knife-Swallower, The: Member of the Crummleses' theatrical company. *Looked and spoke remarkably like an Irishman* (Nickleby).

'Aged, The': Wemmick's father. *A very old man in a flannel coat: clean, cheerful, comfortable, and very well cared for, but intensely deaf* (Expectations).

'Aggerawayter': See **Cruncher, Mrs.** *(Two Cities)*.

Agnes: Mrs. Bloss's maid, admired by Tibbs. *In a cherry-coloured merino dress, open-work stockings, and shoes with sandals: like a disguised Columbine* (Boz – 'Boarding-House').

Akerman: Head jailer at Newgate at the time of the Gordon Riots. He was a real character, of humane disposition. *'I have a good many people in my custody.' He glanced downward, as he spoke, into the jail: and the feeling that he could see into the different yards, and that he overlooked everything which was hidden from their view by the rugged walls, so lashed and goaded the mob, that they howled like wolves* (Rudge).

Akershem, Sophronia: A predatory friend of the Veneerings. She marries Lammle, believing him to be wealthy. *Mature young lady; raven locks, and complexion that lights up well when well-powdered – as it is – carrying on considerably in the captivation of mature young gentleman* (Mutual Friend).

Alice: Youngest of the Five Sisters of York (q.v.). *If the four elder sisters were lovely, how beautiful was the youngest, a fair creature of sixteen! The blushing tints in the soft bloom on the fruit, or the delicate painting on the flower, are not more exquisite than was the blending of the rose and lily in her gentle face, or the deep blue of her eye. The vine, in all its elegant luxuriance, is not more graceful than were the clusters of rich brown hair that sported round her brow* (Nickleby).

Alice, Mistress: A sixteenth century bowyer's daughter, heroine of Magog's tale. *Mistress Alice, his only daughter, was the richest heiress in all his wealthy ward. Young Hugh had often maintained with staff and cudgel that she was the handsomest. To do him justice, I believe she was* (Humphrey).

Alicia, Princess: Eldest child of King Watkins the First and god-daughter of the Fairy Grandmarina in Alice Rainbird's romantic tale. She marries Prince Certainpersonio ('Holiday Romance').

Alick: Young passenger who dances on the Gravesend steam packet. *Alick, who is a damp earthy child in red worsted socks, takes certain small jumps upon the deck, to the unspeakable satisfaction of his family circle* (Boz – 'The River').

Alicumpaine, Mrs.: A juvenile friend of the Oranges in Nettie Ashford's romantic tale ('Holiday Romance').

Allen, Arabella: Ben's sister who secretly marries Winkle. *A young lady with black eyes, an arch smile, and a pair of remarkably nice boots with fur round the top (Pickwick).*

Allen, Benjamin: Arabella's brother, drinking companion of Bob Sawyer, his fellow medical student. *A coarse, stout, thick-set young man, with black hair cut rather short, and a white face cut rather long. He was embellished with spectacles, and wore a white neckerchief. Below his single-breasted black surtout, which was buttoned up to his chin, appeared the usual number of pepper-and-salt coloured legs, terminating in a pair of imperfectly polished boots. Although his coat was short in the sleeves, it disclosed no vestige of a linen wristband; and although there was quite enough of his face to admit of the encroachment of a shirt collar, it was not graced by the smallest approach to that appendage. He presented, altogether, rather a mildewy appearance, and emitted a fragrant odour of full-flavoured Cubas (Pickwick).*

Alphonse: The Wittiterlys' page. *A little page; so little, indeed, that his body would not hold, in ordinary array, the number of small buttons which are indispensable to a page's costume, and they were consequently obliged to be stuck on four abreast. . . . If ever an Alphonse carried plain Bill in his face and figure, that page was the boy (Nickleby).*

'Altro': Pancks's nickname for Cavaletto, from his habit of frequently using the Italian word, meaning 'certainly' *(Dorrit).*

Amelia: Sister of Jane, two marriageable girls displayed by their mamma at the Ramsgate library gambling tables. *'Nice figure, Amelia,' whispered the stout lady to a thin youth beside her (Boz – 'Tuggses at Ramsgate').*

Amelia: Wife of Bill, a criminal, and supplicant to Jaggers for him *(Expectations).*

America Junior: Of Messrs. Hancock & Floby, Dry Goods Store, No. 47, Bunker Hill Street. Name and address to which Putnam Smif wishes Martin Chuzzlewit to address his letter of reply *(Chuzzlewit).*

'Analytical Chemist': Simile for the Veneerings' butler. *The retainer goes round, like a gloomy Analytical Chemist; always seeming to say, after 'Chablis, sir?' – 'You wouldn't if you knew what it's made of' (Mutual Friend).*

Anderson, John and Mrs. John: A couple of self-respecting tramps. *Monarchs could not deprive him of his hard-earned character. Accordingly, as you come up with this spectacle of virtue in distress, Mrs. Anderson rises, and with a decent curtsey presents for your consideration a certificate from a Doctor of Divinity, the reverend the Vicar of Upper Dodgington, who informs his Christian friends and all whom it may concern that the bearers, John Anderson and his lawful wife, are persons to whom you cannot be too liberal (Uncommercial – 'Tramps').*

Angelica: A former sweetheart of the Uncommercial Traveller. *O, Angelica, what has become of you, this present Sunday morning when I can't attend to the sermon; and, more difficult question than that, what has become. of Me as I was when I sat by your side? (Uncommercial – 'City of London Churches').*

Anglo-Bengalee Disinterested Loan and Life Assurance Company: Fraudulent company promoted by Montague Tigg, with David Crimple as secretary. *'What,' asked the secretary . . . 'will be the paid-up capital, according to the next prospectus?' 'A figure of two, and as many oughts after it as the printer can get into the same line,' replied his friend. 'Ha, ha!' (Chuzzlewit).*

Anne: A housemaid at Dombey's. Marries Towlinson, the footman *(Dombey).*

Anne: Housemaid friend of Jane Adams, who takes her in to see Emma Fielding's wedding preparations. *Heaven alone can tell in what bright colours this marriage is painted upon the mind of the little housemaid at number six, who has hardly slept a wink all night with thinking of it, and now stands on the unswept door-steps leaning upon her broom, and looking wistfully towards the enchanted house. Nothing short of omniscience can divine what visions of the baker, or the greengrocer, or the smart and most insinuating butterman, are flitting across her mind – what thoughts of how she would dress on such an occasion, if she were a lady – of how she would dress, if she were only a bride (Young Couples – 'Young Couple').* She is referred to again in *Young Couples – 'Old Couple'* as having married a man who ill-treated her and having died in Lambeth workhouse.

Anny: One of the old paupers attending Agnes Fleming's deathbed *(Twist).*

Antonio: Spanish guitarist in a London sailors' lodging-house. *The look of the young man and the tinkling of the instrument so change the place in a moment to a leaf out of Don Quixote, that I wonder where his mule is stabled (Uncommercial – 'Poor Mercantile Jack').*

'Archbishop of Greenwich': Simile for the head waiter at Rokesmith's and Bella Wilfer's wedding breakfast. *A solemn gentleman in black clothes and a white cravat, who looked much more like a clergyman than the clergyman, and seemed to have mounted a great deal higher in the church: not to say, scaled the steeple. This dignitary, conferring in secrecy with John Rokesmith on the subject of punch and wines, bent his head as though stooping to the Papistical practice of receiving auricular confession. Likewise, on John's offering a suggestion which didn't meet his views, his face became overcast and reproachful, as enjoining penance (Mutual Friend).*

'Artful Dodger, The': See **Dawkins, John** *(Twist).*

Ashford, Nettie: William Tinkling's 'bride', aged 'half-past six', and author of the romantic tale of the Oranges and Mrs. Alicumpaine. *We were married in the right-hand closet in the corner of the dancing-school, where first we met, with a ring (a green one) from Wilkingwater's toy-shop ('Holiday Romance').*

Atherfield, Mrs.; Passenger in the *Golden Mary* with her daughter Lucy. *A bright-eyed, blooming young wife who was going out to join her husband in California, taking with her their only child, a little girl of three years old, whom he had never seen* (Christmas Stories – 'Golden Mary').

Atherfield, Lucy: Mrs. Atherfield's daughter. She dies in the long-boat after the wreck. *As the child had a quantity of shining fair hair, clustering in curls all about her face, and as her name was Lucy, Steadiman gave her the name of the Golden Lucy* (Christmas Stories – 'Golden Mary').

Augustus: The pet dog dissected by Professors Muff and Nogo in their hotel room. *The deceased was named, in affectionate remembrance of a former lover of his mistress, to whom he bore a striking personal resemblance, which renders the circumstances additionally affecting* (Mudfog).

Aunt, Mr. F's: See **Mr. F's Aunt** (Dorrit).

'Avenger, The': See **Pepper** (Expectations).

Ayresleigh: A debtor whom Pickwick meets while under arrest at Namby's. *A middle-aged man in a very old suit of black, who looked pale and haggard, and paced up and down the room incessantly* (Pickwick).

B., Master: The ghost of the haunted house, really a manifestation of the lost youth of John, the narrator. *The young spectre was dressed in an obsolete fashion: or rather, was not so much dressed as put into a case of inferior pepper-and-salt cloth, made horrible by means of shining buttons. I observed that these buttons went, in a double row, over each shoulder of the young ghost, and appeared to descend his back. He wore a frill round his neck. His right hand (which I distinctly noticed to be inky) was laid upon his stomach; connecting this action with some feeble pimples on his countenance, and his general air of nausea, I concluded this ghost to be the ghost of a boy who had habitually taken a great deal too much medicine* (Christmas Stories - 'Haunted House').

Babley, Richard: See **Dick, Mr.** (Copperfield).

Bachelor, The: An old gentleman who is kind to Little Nell and her grandfather at a village they visit in their wanderings. He proves to be brother to Abel Garland's father. *The little old gentleman was the active spirit of the place, the adjuster of all differences, the promoter of all merrymakings, the dispenser of his friend's bounty, and of no small charity of his own besides; the universal mediator, comforter, and friend. None of the simple villagers had cared to ask his name, or, when they knew it, to store it in their memory. Perhaps from some vague rumour of his college honours which had been whispered abroad on his first arrival, perhaps because he was an unmarried, unencumbered gentleman, he had been called the bachelor* (Curiosity Shop).

Badger, Bayham: A doctor cousin of Kenge, practising at Chelsea, to whom Richard Carstone is articled. *A pink, fresh-faced, crisp-looking gentleman, with a weak voice, white teeth, light hair, and surprised eyes: some years younger, I should say, than Mrs. Bayham Badger. He admired her exceedingly, but principally, and to begin with, on the curious ground (as it seemed to us) of her having had three husbands. We had barely taken our seats, when he said to Mr. Jarndyce quite triumphantly, 'You would hardly suppose that I am Mrs. Bayham Badger's third!'* (Bleak House).

Badger, Mrs. Bayham: Badger's wife, widow of Captain Swosser, R.N., and of Professor Dingo. *She was surrounded in the drawing-room by various objects, indicative of her painting a little, playing the piano a little, playing the guitar a little, playing the harp a little, singing a little, working a little, reading a little, writing poetry a little, and botanising a little. She was a lady of about fifty, I should think, youthfully dressed, and of a very fine complexion. If I add, to the little list of her accomplishments, that she rouged a little, I do not mean that there was any harm in it* (Bleak House).

Bagman, The: Narrator of 'The Bagman's Story' and 'The Bagman's Uncle' at the Peacock, Eatanswill. *A stout, hale personage of about forty, with only one eye – a very bright black eye, which twinkled with a roguish expression of fun and good humour* (Pickwick).

Bagman's Uncle, The: See **Martin, Jack** (Pickwick).

Bagnet, Malta and **Quebec:** The Bagnets' elder and younger small daughters, sisters of Woolwich. *Not supposed to have been actually christened by the names applied to them, though always so called in the family, from the places of their birth in barracks* (Bleak House).

Bagnet, Matthew ('Lignum Vitae'): Bassoon player in a theatre orchestra and proprietor of a musical instrument shop in London. He helps George Rouncewell in his financial and other difficulties. *An ex-artilleryman, tall and upright, with shaggy eyebrows, and whiskers like the fibres of a cocoa-nut, not a hair upon his head, and a torrid complexion. His voice, short, deep, and resonant, is not at all unlike the tones of the instrument to which he is devoted. Indeed, there may be generally observed in him an unbending, unyielding, brass-bound air, as if he were himself the bassoon of the human orchestra* (Bleak House).

Bagnet, Mrs. Matthew: Bagnet's strong-minded wife. She reunites Mrs. Rouncewell with George. *Not at all an ill-looking woman. Rather large-boned, a little coarse in the grain, and freckled by the sun and wind which have tanned her hair upon the forehead; but healthy, wholesome, and bright-eyed. A strong, busy, active, honest-faced woman of from forty-five to fifty. Clean, hardy, and so economically dressed (though substantially), that the only article of ornament of which she stands possessed appears to be her wedding-ring; around which her finger has grown to be so large since it was put on, that it will never come off again until it shall mingle with Mrs. Bagnet's dust* (Bleak House).

Bagnet, Woolwich: The Bagnets' young son, brother of Malta and Quebec. *Young Woolwich is the type and model of a young drummer* (Bleak House).

Bagstock, Major Joseph: Neighbour to Miss Tox and toady to Dombey. *A wooden-featured, blue-faced major, with his eyes starting out of his head, in whom Miss Tox recognised, as she herself expressed it, 'something so truly military.' // 'Joey B., sir,' the major would say, with a flourish of his walking-stick, 'is worth a dozen of you. If you had a few more of the Bagstock breed among you, sir, you'd be none the worse for it. Old Joe, sir, needn't look far for a wife even now, if he was on the look-out; but he's hard-hearted, sir, is Joe – he's tough, sir, tough, and de-vilish sly!' After such a declaration wheezing sounds would be heard; and the major's blue would deepen into purple, while his eyes strained and started convulsively (Dombey).*

Bailey, Captain: David Copperfield's rival at the Larkinses' ball. *I take Miss Larkins out. I take her sternly from the side of Captain Bailey. He is wretched, I have no doubt; but he is nothing to me. I have been wretched, too (Copperfield).*

Bailey, Benjamin: A small boy, page at Todgers's, later taken into partnership by Sweedlepipe. Also known as Uncle Ben, Uncle, Barnwell and other nicknames. *The gentlemen at Todgers's had a merry habit, too, of bestowing upon him, for the time being, the name of any notorious malefactor or minister; and sometimes when current events were flat, they even sought the pages of history for these distinctions; as Mr. Pitt, Young Brownrigg, and the like. // A small boy with a large red head, and no nose to speak of (Chuzzlewit).*

Balderstone, Thomas (Uncle Tom): Mrs. Gattleton's rich brother. *He was one of the best-hearted men in existence: always in a good temper, and always talking. It was his boast that he wore top-boots on all occasions, and had never worn a black silk neckerchief; and it was his pride that he remembered all the principal plays of Shakespeare from beginning to end – and so he did. The result of this parrot-like accomplishment was, that he was not only perpetually quoting himself, but that he could never sit by, and hear a misquotation from the 'Swan of Avon' without setting the unfortunate delinquent right (Boz – 'Mrs. Joseph Porter').*

Balim: A young ladies' young gentleman. *Seated upon the ground, at the feet of a few young ladies who were reclining on a bank; he was so profusely decked with scarfs, ribands, flowers, and other pretty spoils, that he looked like a lamb – or perhaps a calf would be a better simile – adorned for the sacrifice. One young lady supported a parasol over his interesting head, another held his hat, and a third his neckcloth, which in romantic fashion, he had thrown off; the young gentleman himself, with his hand upon his breast, and his face moulded into an expression of the most honeyed sweetness, was warbling forth some choice specimens of vocal music in praise of female loveliness, in a style so exquisitely perfect, that we burst into an involuntary shout of laughter, and made a hasty retreat (Young Gentlemen – 'Young Ladies' Young Gentleman').*

Bamber, Jack: Narrator of the 'Tale of the Queer Client'. *A little yellow high-shouldered man. . . . There was a fixed grim smile perpetually on his countenance; he leant his chin on a long skinny hand, with nails of extraordinary length; and as he inclined his head to one side, and looked keenly out from beneath his ragged grey eyebrows, there was a strange, wild slyness in his leer, quite repulsive to behold (Pickwick).* He reappears in *Humphrey.*

Banger, Captain: Vestryman, of Wilderness Walk (*Reprinted* – 'Our Vestry').

Bangham, Mrs.: Attendant at Amy Dorrit's birth in the Marshalsea. *Mrs. Bangham, charwoman and messenger, who was not a prisoner (though she had been once), but was the popular medium of communication with the outer world, had volunteered her services as fly-catcher and general attendant. The walls and ceiling were blackened with flies. Mrs. Bangham, expert in sudden device, with one hand fanned the patient with a cabbage leaf, and with the other set traps of vinegar and sugar in gallipots; at the same time enunciating sentiments of an encouraging and congratulatory nature, adapted to the occasion (Dorrit).*

Banks, Major: Retired East India Director: a disguise assumed by Meltham to outwit Julius Slinkton. *An old man, whose head was sunk on his breast, and who was enveloped in a variety of wrappers* ('Hunted Down').

Bantam, Angelo Cyrus: Master of the Ceremonies at Bath. *A charming young man of not much more than fifty, dressed in a very bright blue coat with resplendent buttons, black trousers, and the thinnest possible pair of highly-polished boots. A gold eye-glass was suspended from his neck by a short broad black ribbon; a gold snuff-box was lightly clasped in his left hand; gold rings innumerable glittered on his fingers; and a large diamond pin set in gold glistened in his shirt frill. He had a gold watch, and a gold curb-chain with large gold seals; and he carried a pliant ebony cane with a heavy gold top. His linen was of the very whitest, finest, and stiffest; his wig of the glossiest, blackest, and curliest. His snuff was prince's mixture; his scent bouquet du roi. His features were contracted into a perpetual smile; and his teeth were in such perfect order that it was difficult at a small distance to tell the real from the false (Pickwick).*

Baps: Dancing-master at Dr. Blimber's school. *A very grave gentleman, with a slow and measured manner of speaking (Dombey).*

Baps, Mrs.: Baps's wife *(Dombey).*

Baptista, Giovanni: Genoese courier who narrates the story of Clara and Signor Dellombra ('At Dusk').

Baptiste: Soldier billeted on the water-carrier in the French town where Langley lodges. *Sitting on the pavement in the sunlight, with his martial legs asunder, and one of the Water-carrier's spare pails between them, which (to the delight and glory of the heart of the Water-carrier coming across the Place from the fountain, yoked and burdened) he was painting bright-green outside and bright-red within (Christmas Stories – 'Somebody's Luggage').*

Bar: Legal magnate, guest at Merdle's. *With his little insinuating Jury droop, and fingering his persuasive double eye-glass (Dorrit).*

Barbara: The Garlands' housemaid. She marries Kit Nubbles. *Very tidy, modest and demure, but very pretty too (Curiosity Shop).*

Barbara's Mother: Mother of the Garlands' servant. *Didn't she look genteel, standing there with her gloves on (Curiosity Shop).*

Barbary, Miss: Esther Summerson's stern aunt at Windsor who brings her up in childhood. Sister to Lady Dedlock. *She was a good, good woman! She went to church three times every Sunday, and to morning prayers on Wednesdays and Fridays, and to lectures whenever there were lectures; and never missed. She was handsome; and if she had ever smiled, would have been (I used to think) like an angel – but she never smiled. She was always grave and strict. She was so very good herself, I thought, that the badness of other people made her frown all her life (Bleak House).*

Barbary, Mrs. Captain, of Cheltenham: Horse-owner who sells her mount for spite, through Captain Maroon, because it had run away with her *(Dorrit).*

Barbox Brothers: A financial house off Lombard Street taken over and closed down by Jackson (q.v.). *The firm of Barbox Brothers had been some offshoot or irregular branch of the Public Notary and bill-broking tree. It had gained for itself a griping reputation before the days of Young Jackson, and the reputation had stuck to it and to him. . . . But he did at last effect one great release. . . . With enough to live on (though, after all, with not too much), he obliterated the firm of Barbox Brothers from the pages of the Post-Office Directory and the face of the earth, leaving nothing of it but its name on two portmanteaus (Christmas Stories – 'Mugby Junction').*

Bardell, Mrs. Martha: Pickwick's landlady in Goswell Street and his opponent in the celebrated lawsuit for breach of promise. Mother of Tommy. *Mrs. Bardell – the relict and sole executrix of a deceased custom-house officer – was a comely woman of bustling manners and agreeable appearance, with a natural genius for cooking, improved by study and long practice, into an exquisite talent (Pickwick).*

Bardell, Tommy: Mrs. Bardell's small son. *Clad in a tight suit of corduroy, spangled with brass buttons of a very considerable size (Pickwick).*

Bark: Lodging-house keeper and receiver of stolen goods in Wentworth Street, Whitechapel, visited by the narrator and Inspector Field. *Bark is a red villain and a wrathful, with a sanguine throat that looks very much as if it were expressly made for hanging, as he stretches it out, in pale defiance, over the half-door of his hutch. Bark's parts of speech are of an awful sort – principally adjectives. I won't, says Bark, have no adjective police and adjective strangers in my adjective premises! I won't, by adjective and substantive! Give me my trousers, and I'll send the whole adjective police to adjective and substantive! Give me, says*

Bark, my adjective trousers! I'll put an adjective knife in the whole bileing of 'em (Reprinted – 'On Duty with Inspector Field').

Barker, Mrs.: A lady of whom the censorious young gentleman's opinion is sought. *It is forthwith whispered about, that Mr. Fairfax (who, though he is a little prejudiced, must be admitted to be a very excellent judge) has observed something exceedingly odd in Mrs. Barker's manner (Young Gentlemen – 'Censorious Young Gentleman').*

Barker, Fanny: See **Brown, Fanny** ('Lamplighter's Story').

Barker, Phil: A thieving frequenter of the Three Cripples. *'I've got Phil Barker here: so drunk, that a boy might take him' (Twist).*

Barker, William (also Bill Boorker or **Aggera-watin' Bill):** The first London omnibus cad, or conductor. *When the appearance of the first omnibus caused the public mind to go in a new direction, and prevented a great many hackney-coaches from going in any direction at all . . . his active mind at once perceived how much might be done in the way of enticing the youthful and unwary, and shoving the old and helpless, into the wrong buss, and carrying them off, until, reduced by despair, they ransomed themselves by the payment of sixpence a-head, or, to adopt his own figurative expression in all its native beauty, 'till they was rig'larly done over, and forked out the stumpy' (Boz – 'First Omnibus Cad').*

Barkis: The Yarmouth carrier. Suitor, and eventually husband, of Clara Peggotty. *The carrier had a way of keeping his head down, like his horse, and of drooping sleepily forward as he drove, with one of his arms on each of his knees. I say 'drove', but it struck me that the cart would have gone to Yarmouth quite as well without him, for the horse did all that; and as to conversation, he had no idea of it but whistling. // 'Barkis is willin' ' (Copperfield).*

Barley, Clara: Old Bill Barley's daughter. Herbert Pocket's fiancée, later wife, who arranges for Magwitch, under the name of Campbell, to wait in her father's house near London Bridge until he can be smuggled abroad. *A very pretty, slight, dark-eyed girl of twenty or so. . . . She really was a most charming girl, and might have passed for a captive fairy, whom that truculent Ogre, Old Barley, had pressed into his service (Expectations).*

Barley, Old Bill ('Gruff and Grim'): Clara's father, a retired ship's purser. *'I am afraid he is a sad old rascal,' said Herbert, smiling, 'but I have never seen him. Don't you smell rum? He is always at it.' . . . As we passed Mr. Barley's door, he was heard hoarsely muttering within, in a strain that rose and fell like the wind, the following Refrain; in which I substitute good wishes for something quite the reverse. 'Ahoy! Bless your eyes, here's old Bill Barley, bless your eyes. Here's old Bill Barley on the flat of his back, by the Lord. Lying on the flat of his back, like a drifting old dead flounder, here's your old Bill Barley, bless your eyes. Ahoy! Bless you' (Expectations).*

Barnacle, Lady: Wife of Lord Decimus Tite Barnacle. See **Bilberry, Lady Jemima** (*Dorrit*).

Barnacle, Clarence (Barnacle, Junior): Tite Barnacle's empty-headed son, employed in the Circumlocution Office. *Had a youthful aspect, and the fluffiest little whisker, perhaps, that ever was seen. Such a downy tip was on his callow chin, that he seemed half fledged like a young bird; and a compassionate observer might have urged, that if he had not singed the calves of his legs, he would have died of cold. He had a superior eye-glass dangling round his neck, but unfortunately had such flat orbits to his eyes, and such limp little eyelids, that it wouldn't stick in when he put it up, but kept tumbling out against his waistcoat buttons with a click that discomposed him very much* (*Dorrit*).

Barnacle, Lord Decimus Tite: Tite Barnacle's uncle, Minister of Circumlocution. *Had risen to official heights on the wings of one indignant idea, and that was, My Lords, that I am yet to be told that it behoves a Minister of this free country to set bounds to the philanthropy, to cramp the charity, to fetter the public spirit, to contract the enterprise, to damp the independent self-reliance, of its people. That was, in other words, that this great statesman was always yet to be told that it behoved the Pilot of the ship to do anything but prosper in the private loaf and fish trade ashore, the crew being able, by dint of hard pumping, to keep the ship above water without him. On this sublime discovery, in the great art How not to do it, Lord Decimus had long sustained the highest glory of the Barnacle family; and let any ill-advised member of either House but try How to do it, by bringing in a Bill to do it, that Bill was as good as dead and buried when Lord Decimus Tite Barnacle rose up in his place* (*Dorrit*).

Barnacle, Ferdinand: Private secretary to Lord Decimus Tite Barnacle. *A vivacious, well-looking, well-dressed, agreeable young fellow – he was a Barnacle, but on the more sprightly side of the family. . . . This touch and go young Barnacle had 'got up' the Department in a private secretaryship, that he might be ready for any little bit of fat that came to hand; and he fully understood the Department to be a politico-diplomatic hocus pocus piece of machinery, for the assistance of the nobs in keeping off the snobs. This dashing young Barnacle, in a word, was likely to become a statesman, and to make a figure* (*Dorrit*).

Barnacle, Tite: Nephew to Lord Decimus Tite Barnacle and one of his senior officials in the Circumlocution Office. *Mr. Barnacle dated from a better time, when the country was not so parsimonious, and the Circumlocution Office was not so badgered. He wound and wound folds of white cravat round his neck, as he wound and wound folds of tape and paper round the neck of the country. His wristbands and collar were oppressive, his voice and manner were oppressive. He had a large watch-chain and bunch of seals, a coat buttoned up to inconvenience, a waistcoat buttoned up to inconvenience, an unwrinkled pair of trousers, a stiff pair of boots. He was altogether splendid, massive, overpowering, and impracticable.*

He seemed to have been sitting for his portrait to Sir Thomas Lawrence all the days of his life (*Dorrit*).

Barnacle, William, M.P.: One of the parliamentary Barnacles present at the wedding of Henry Gowan and Minnie Meagles. *Who had made the ever-famous coalition with Tudor Stiltstalking, and who always kept ready his own particular recipe for How not to do it; sometimes tapping the Speaker, and drawing it fresh out of him, with a 'First, I will beg you, sir, to inform the House what Precedent we have for the course into which the honourable gentleman would precipitate us'* (*Dorrit*).

Barney: Jewish waiter at the Three Cripples, Saffron Hill. *Younger than Fagin, but nearly as vile and repulsive in appearance . . . whose words: whether they came from the heart or not: made their way through the nose* (*Twist*).

Barroneau, Madame Henri: An innkeeper's widow, beautiful and wealthy, married by Rigaud. He is charged with her murder, which he represents as suicide, but is acquitted. *'Even when I wanted any little sum of money for my personal expenses, I could not obtain it without collision – and I, too, a man whose character it is to govern! One night, Madame Rigaud and myself were walking amicably – I may say like lovers – on a height overhanging the sea. An evil star occasioned Madame Rigaud to advert to her relations; I reasoned with her on that subject, and remonstrated on the want of duty and devotion manifested in her allowing herself to be influenced by their jealous animosity towards her husband. Madame Rigaud retorted; I retorted. Madame Rigaud grew warm; I grew warm and provoked her. . . . At length, Madame Rigaud, in an access of fury that I must ever deplore, threw herself upon me with screams of passion (no doubt those that were overheard at some distance), tore my clothes, tore my hair, lacerated my hands, trampled and trod the dust, and finally leaped over, dashing herself to death upon the rocks below'* (*Dorrit*).

Barsad, John: See **Pross, Solomon** (*Two Cities*).

Barton, Jacob: Mrs. Malderton's brother, a social embarrassment to the *nouveau riche* family. *A large grocer; so vulgar, and so lost to all sense of feeling, that he actually never scrupled to avow that he wasn't above his business: 'he'd made his money by it, and he didn't care who know'd it'* (*Boz* – 'Horatio Sparkins').

Bates, Belinda: Close friend of the sister of John, the narrator, and a member of the party visiting the haunted house. *A most intellectual, amiable, and delightful girl. . . . She has a fine genius for poetry, combined with real business earnestness, and 'goes in' – to use an expression of Alfred's – for Woman's mission, Woman's rights, Woman's wrongs, and everything that is woman's with a capital W, or is not and ought to be, or is and ought not to be* (*Christmas Stories* – 'Haunted House').

Bates, Charley: Member of Fagin's gang. *Charley Bates exhibited some very loose notions concerning the rights of property, by pilfering divers apples and onions from the stalls at the kennel sides, and thrust-*

ing them into pockets which were so surprisingly capacious, that they seemed to undermine his whole suit of clothes in every direction (Twist).

Battens: A Titbull's pensioner. *A virulent old man ... who had a working mouth which seemed to be trying to masticate his anger and to find that it was too hard and there was too much of it (Uncommercial – 'Titbull's Alms-Houses').*

Bayton: A poor man whose wife is buried by Bumble's parish *(Twist).*

Bayton, Mrs.: Bayton's wife, a victim of starvation *(Twist).*

Bazzard: Grewgious's clerk, and an aspiring playwright. *A pale, puffy-faced, dark-haired person of thirty with big dark eyes that wholly wanted lustre, and a dissatisfied doughy complexion, that seemed to ask to be sent to the baker's, this attendant was a mysterious being, possessed of some strange power over Mr. Grewgious. As though he had been called into existence, like a fabulous Familiar, by a magic spell which had failed when required to dismiss him, he stuck tight to Mr. Grewgious's stool, although Mr. Grewgious's comfort and convenience would manifestly have been advanced by dispossessing him. A gloomy person with tangled locks, and a general air of having been reared under the shadow of that baleful tree of Java which has given shelter to more lies than the whole botanical kingdom, Mr. Grewgious, nevertheless, treated him with unaccountable consideration (Drood).*

Beadle, Harriet ('Tattycoram'): Taken from the Foundling Hospital to become Pet Meagles's maid, she is influenced by Miss Wade to run away and join her, but returns penitently. *A sullen, passionate girl! Her rich black hair was all about her face, her face was flushed and hot, and as she sobbed and raged, she plucked at her lips with an unsparing hand.* // *'She was called in the Institution, Harriet Beadle – an arbitrary name, of course. Now, Harriet, we changed into Hattey, and then into Tatty, because, as practical people, we thought even a playful name might be a new thing to her, and might have a softening and affectionate kind of effect, don't you see? As to Beadle, that I needn't say was wholly out of the question. If there is anything that is not to be tolerated on any terms, anything that is a type of Jack-in-office insolence and absurdity, anything that represents in coats, waistcoats, and big sticks, our English holding-on by nonsense, after every one has found it out, it is a beadle. . . . The name of Beadle being out of the question, and the originator of the Institution for these poor foundlings having been a blessed creature of the name of Coram, we gave that name to Pet's little maid. At one time she was Tatty, and at one time she was Coram, until we got into a way of mixing the two names together, and now she is always Tattycoram' (Dorrit).*

Beadwood, Ned: One of Miss Mowcher's allusions. *'Have I got all my traps? It seems so. It won't do to be like long Ned Beadwood, when they took him to*

church *"to marry him to somebody," as he says, and left the bride behind' (Copperfield).*

Bear, Prince: Prince Bull's adversary, symbolising Russia in the Crimean War *(Reprinted – 'Prince Bull').*

Beatrice: See **Tresham, Beatrice** *(Christmas Stories – 'Mugby Junction').*

Beaver, Nat: Captain of a merchantman, an old shipmate of Jack Governor, who brings him on his visit to the haunted house. *A thick-set, wooden face and figure, and apparently as hard as a block all over, proved to be an intelligent man, with a world of watery experiences in him, and great practical knowledge (Christmas Stories – 'Haunted House').*

Bebelle: Pet name of Gabrielle, the orphan baby befriended by Corporal Théophile and adopted by Langley. *A mere baby, one might call her, dressed in the close white linen cap which small French country children wear (like the children in Dutch pictures), and in a frock of homespun blue, that had no shape except where it was tied round her little fat throat. So that, being naturally short and round all over, she looked behind, as if she had been cut off at her natural waist, and had had her head neatly fitted on it (Christmas Stories – 'Somebody's Luggage').*

Beckwith, Alfred: Identity assumed by Meltham after he has circulated reports of his death, so as to be able to hunt down Julius Slinkton. *A man with all the appearances of the worst kind of drunkard, very far advanced upon his shameful way to death* ('Hunted Down').

Becky: Barmaid at the Red Lion, Hampton, where Bill Sikes and Oliver Twist pause on their way to burgle Mrs. Maylie's *(Twist).*

Bedwin, Mrs.: Brownlow's housekeeper. *A motherly old lady, very neatly and precisely dressed (Twist).*

Begs, Mrs. Ridger: See **Micawber, Emma** *(Copperfield).*

Belinda: A love-sick young woman who writes to Master Humphrey for help in tracing her elusive swain. *Heavens! into what an indiscretion do I suffer myself to be betrayed! To address these faltering lines to a total stranger, and that stranger one of conflicting sex! – and yet I am precipitated into the abyss, and have no power of self-snatchation (forgive me if I coin that phrase) from the yawning gulf before me (Humphrey).*

Bell, Knight, M.R.C.S.: Speaker at the anatomy and medicine session at the first meeting of the Mudfog Association. *Exhibited a wax preparation of the interior of a gentleman who in early life had inadvertently swallowed a door-key. It was a curious fact that a medical student of dissipated habits, being present at the post mortem examination, found means to escape unobserved from the room, with that portion of the coats of the stomach upon which an exact model of the instrument was distinctly impressed, with which he hastened to a locksmith of doubtful character, who made a new key from the pattern so shown to him.*

With this key the medical student entered the house of the deceased gentleman, and committed a burglary to a large amount, for which he was subsequently tried and executed (Mudfog).

Bella: Miss Pupford's housemaid (*Christmas Stories* – 'Tom Tiddler's Ground').

Bella and **Emily:** Young prostitutes observed entering the prisoners' van at Bow Street. *The elder could not be more than sixteen, and the younger of whom had certainly not attained her fourteenth year. That they were sisters, was evident, for the resemblance which still subsisted between them, though two additional years of depravity had fixed their brand upon the elder girl's features, as legibly as if a red-hot iron had seared them. They were both gaudily dressed, the younger one especially; and, although there was a strong similarity between them in both respects, which was rendered the more obvious by their being handcuffed together, it is impossible to conceive a greater contrast than the demeanour of the two presented. The younger girl was weeping bitterly – not for display, or in the hope of producing effect, but for very shame; her face was buried in her handkerchief; and her whole manner was but too expressive of bitter and unavailing sorrow (Boz – 'Prisoners' Van').*

Belle: Scrooge's former sweetheart. *A fair young girl in a mourning-dress: in whose eyes there were tears* (*Christmas Books* – 'Christmas Carol').

Beller, Henry: Convert reported to the committee of the Brick Lane Branch of the United Grand Junction Ebenezer Temperance Association. *For many years toast-master at various corporation dinners, during which time he drank a great deal of foreign wine; may sometimes have carried a bottle or two home with him; is not quite certain of that, but is sure if he did, that he drank the contents. Feels very low and melancholy, is very feverish, and has a constant thirst upon him; thinks it must be the wine he used to drink (cheers). Is out of employ now; and never touches a drop of foreign wine by any chance (tremendous plaudits) (Pickwick).*

Belling: Pupil at Dotheboys Hall. *On the trunk was perched – his lace-up half-boots and corduroy trousers dangling in the air – a diminutive boy, with his shoulders drawn up to his ears (Nickleby).*

Bellows, Brother: Legal magnate, guest at Merdle's (*Dorrit*).

'Belltott': See **Tott, Mrs. Isabella** (*Christmas Stories* – 'English Prisoners').

Belvawney, Miss: Member of the Crummleses' theatrical company. *Seldom aspired to speaking parts, and usually went on as a page in white silk hose, to stand with one leg bent, and contemplate the audience, or to go in and out after Mr. Crummles in stately tragedy (Nickleby).*

Ben: A waiter at Rochester. *I would trust Ben, the waiter, with untold gold; but there are strings in the human heart which must never be sounded by another, and drinks that I make myself are those strings in mine* (*Christmas Stories* – 'Seven Poor Travellers').

Ben: Mail-coach guard at Hatfield whom Bill Sikes overhears tell of Nancy's murder (*Twist*).

Bench: Magisterial magnate, guest at Merdle's (*Dorrit*).

Benjamin: Officer of the Prentice Knights (*Rudge*).

Benjamin, Thomas: Plaintiff in a divorce suit successfully conducted by Spenlow and David Copperfield. *Had taken out his marriage licence as Thomas only; suppressing the Benjamin, in case he should not find himself as comfortable as he expected. Not finding himself as comfortable as he expected, or being a little fatigued with his wife, poor fellow, he now came forward, by a friend, after being married a year or two, and declared that his name was Thomas Benjamin, and therefore he was not married at all. Which the Court confirmed, to his great satisfaction (Copperfield).*

Benson, Lucy: Old Benson's daughter, Young Benson's sister. She flirts with Squire Norton, but recognises the dangers in time and returns to her humble sweetheart, George Edmunds (*Village Coquettes*).

Benson, Old: Father of Lucy and Young Benson. A small farmer (*Village Coquettes*).

Benson, Young: Old Benson's son, Lucy's brother (*Village Coquettes*).

Benton, Miss: Master Humphrey's housekeeper, briefly loved by Tony Weller. She marries Slithers. *Miss Benton, hurrying into her own room and shutting herself up, in order that she might preserve that appearance of being taken by surprise which is so essential to the polite reception of visitors (Humphrey).*

Berinthia (Berry): Miss Pipchin's middle-aged niece and drudge. *Possessing a gaunt and iron-bound aspect, and much afflicted with boils on her nose (Dombey).*

Berry: See **Berinthia** (*Dombey*).

Bet, or **Betsy:** Prostitute and friend to Nancy. She is driven mad by the ordeal of identifying Nancy's body. *Gaily, not to say gorgeously attired, in a red gown, green boots, and yellow curl-papers (Twist).*

Betley: One of Mrs. Lirriper's first lodgers. *Which at that time had the parlours and loved his joke* (*Christmas Stories* – 'Mrs. Lirriper's Lodgings').

Betsey: Nurse to the two Master Britains (*Christmas Books* – 'Battle of Life').

Betsey Jane: Mrs. Wickam's cousin, whom she cites in warning Berry not to allow little Paul Dombey to attach himself too closely to her. *'She took fancies to people; whimsical fancies, some of them; others, affections that one might expect to see – only stronger than common. They all died' (Dombey).*

Betsy: Mrs. Raddle's maid. *A dirty slipshod girl in black cotton stockings, who might have passed for the neglected daughter of a superannuated dustman in very reduced circumstances (Pickwick).*

Bevan: A kind man from Massachusetts whom

Martin Chuzzlewit meets at Pawkins's Boarding-House, New York. He subsequently lends Martin money to enable him and Mark Tapley to return to England. *A middle-aged man with a dark eye and a sunburnt face, who had attracted Martin's attention by having something very engaging and honest in the expression of his features (Chuzzlewit).*

Bevan, Mrs.: Former neighbour of Mrs. Nickleby. *'I recollect dining once at Mrs. Bevan's, in that broad street round the corner by the coachmaker's, where the tipsy man fell through the cellar-flap of an empty house nearly a week before the quarter-day, and wasn't found till the new tenants went in – and we had roast pig there. It must be that, I think, that reminds me of it, especially as there was a little bird in the room that would keep on singing all the time of dinner – at least, not a little bird, for it was a parrot, and he didn't sing exactly, for he talked and swore dreadfully'* (Nickleby).

Beverley: See **Loggins** (*Boz* – 'Private Theatres').

Bib, Julius Washington Merryweather: A boarder at the National Hotel in America where Martin Chuzzlewit stays before embarking for Eden. *'A gentleman in the lumber line, sir, and much esteemed'* (Chuzzlewit).

Biddy: Wopsle's great-aunt's granddaughter. She is devoted to Pip, but he is blind to her affection and does not decide to ask her to marry him until too late – her wedding day to Joe Gargery. *She was an orphan like myself; like me, too, had been brought up by hand. She was most noticeable, I thought, in respect of her extremities; for, her hair always wanted brushing, her hands always wanted washing, and her shoes always wanted mending and pulling up at heel. This description must be received with a week-day limitation. On Sundays she went to church elaborated* (Expectations).

Bigby, Mrs.: Mrs. Meek's mother. *In my opinion she would storm a town, single-handed, with a hearth-broom, and carry it. I have never known her to yield any point whatever, to mortal man. She is calculated to terrify the stoutest heart* (Reprinted – 'Births. Mrs. Meek, of a Son').

Bigwig Family: A large and wealthy family devoted to directing the destinies of their inferiors. *Composed of all the stateliest people thereabouts, and all the noisiest* (Christmas Stories – 'Nobody's Story').

Bilberry, Lady Jemina: First daughter by the second marriage of the fifteenth Earl of Stiltstalking with the Honourable Clementina Toozellem. Married, in 1797, to Lord Decimus Tite Barnacle (Dorrit).

'Biler': See **Toodle, Robin** (Dombey).

Bilkins: The 'only' authority on taste. *Never took any notice that we can find out, of our French watering-place. Bilkins never wrote about it, never pointed out anything to be seen in it, never measured anything in it, always left it alone. For which relief, Heaven bless the town and the memory of the immortal Bilkins likewise!* (Reprinted – 'Our French Watering-place').

Bill: Criminal being defended by Jaggers. Husband of Amelia (Expectations).

Bill: Former turnkey at the Fleet Prison who figures in Sam Weller's tale of the little dirty-faced man in the brown coat (Pickwick).

Bill: Grave-digger who buries Mrs. Bayton (Twist).

Bill, Aggerawatin': See **Barker, William** (Boz – 'First Omnibus Cad').

Bill, Black: Prisoner in Newgate visited by Pip and Wemmick (Expectations).

Bill, Uncle: Life and soul of a party at a public tea-garden. *Observe the inexpressible delight of the old grandmother, at Uncle Bill's splendid joke of 'tea for four: bread-and-butter for forty.' . . . The young man is evidently 'keeping company' with Uncle Bill's niece: and Uncle Bill's hints – such as 'Don't forget me at the dinner, you know,' 'I shall look out for the cake, Sally,' 'I'll be godfather to your first – wager it's a boy,' and so forth, are equally embarrassing to the young people, and delightful to the elder ones* (Boz – 'London Recreations').

Billickin, Mrs.: Widowed cousin of Grewgious with whom Rosa Bud lodges in Bloomsbury after fleeing from Jasper's attentions. *Personal faintness, and an overpowering personal candour, were distinguishing features of Mrs. Billickin's organisation. She came languishing out of her own exclusive back parlour, with the air of having been expressly brought-to for the purpose, from an accumulation of several swoons* (Drood).

Billsmethi, Master: Billsmethi's son. *When everybody else was breathless, danced a hornpipe, with a cane in his hand, and a cheese-plate on his head, to the unqualified admiration of the whole company* (Boz – 'Dancing Academy').

Billsmethi, Miss: Billsmethi's daughter. She partners Augustus Cooper in his dancing lessons, courts him, and finally sues him for breach of promise. *A young lady, with her hair curled in a crop all over her head, and her shoes tied in sandals all over her ankles* (Boz – 'Dancing Academy').

Billsmethi, Signor: of the 'King's Theatre'. Proprietor of a dancing academy near Gray's Inn Lane. *The Signor was at home, and what was still more gratifying, he was an Englishman! Such a nice man – and so polite!* (Boz – 'Dancing Academy').

Bilson and Slum: Commercial house, of Cateaton Street, City of London, employing Tom Smart as traveller (Pickwick).

Bintrey: Walter Wilding's solicitor. He helps to expose Obenreizer and prove Vendale's identity. *A cautious man, with twinkling beads of eyes in a large overhanging bald head, who inwardly but intensely enjoyed the comicality of openness of speech, or hand, or heart* (Christmas Stories – 'No Thoroughfare').

Bishop: Ecclesiastical magnate, guest at Merdle's. *Jauntily stepping out a little with his well-shaped right* leg, *as though he said to Mr. Merdle 'don't mind the apron; a mere form!' (Dorrit).*

Bit, Charley: A theatre-going Boots, one of the characters assumed by Mr. Gabblewig (q.v.) in order to unmask Slap *(Nightingale's Diary).*

Bitherstone, Master: A boarder at Mrs. Pipchin's. *Master Bitherstone, whose relatives were all in India, and who was required to sit, between the services, in an erect position with his head against the parlour wall neither moving hand nor foot, suffered so acutely in his young spirits that he once asked Florence on a Sunday night, if she could give him any idea of the way back to Bengal (Dombey).*

Bitzer: A pupil at Gradgrind's, later a porter at Bounderby's Bank. *He held the respectable office of general spy and informer in the establishment. // His cold eyes would hardly have been eyes, but for the short ends of lashes which, by bringing them into immediate contrast with something paler than themselves, expressed their form. His short-cropped hair might have been a mere continuation of the sandy freckles on his forehead and face. His skin was so unwholesomely deficient in the natural tinge, that he looked as though, if he were cut, he would bleed white (Hard Times).*

Black, Mrs.: A pert and flouncing pupil of Mrs. Lemon in Nettie Ashford's romantic tale ('Holiday Romance').

Black and **Green:** Police constables who accompany the narrator and Inspector Field to thieves' lodgings in Wentworth Street, Whitechapel. *Imperturbable Black opens the cab-door; Imperturbable Green takes a mental note of the driver (Reprinted – 'On Duty with Inspector Field').*

'Black Lion, The': Landlord of a Whitechapel inn frequented by Joe Willet. *This Lion or landlord, – for he was called both man and beast, by reason of his having instructed the artist who painted his sign, to convey into the features of the lordly brute whose effigy it bore, as near a counterpart of his own face as his skill could compass and devise . . . stood indebted, in no small amount, to beer; of which he swigged such copious draughts, that most of his faculties were utterly drowned and washed away, except the one great faculty of sleep, which he retained in surprising perfection (Rudge).*

Blackey: A beggar lodging in the Old Farm House, Borough, visited by the narrator and Inspector Field. *Has stood near London bridge these five-and-twenty years, with a painted skin to represent disease (Reprinted – 'On Duty with Inspector Field').*

Blackpool, Stephen: A power-loom weaver in Bounderby's mill. Unable to divorce his drunken wife and marry Rachael, hounded by his workmates for refusing to join a union, and suspected of bank robbery, he falls down a disused pit shaft and is killed. *It is said that every life has its roses and thorns; there seemed, however, to have been a misadventure or mistake in Stephen's case, whereby somebody else had become possessed of his roses, and he had become* possessed of the same somebody else's thorns in addition to his own. He had known, to use his words, a peck of trouble. He was usually called Old Stephen, in a kind of rough homage to the fact (Hard Times).*

Blackpool, Mrs. Stephen: Stephen's wife. *A disabled, drunken creature, barely able to preserve her sitting posture by steadying herself with one begrimed hand on the floor, while the other was so purposeless in trying to push away her tangled hair from her face, that it only blinded her the more with the dirt upon it. A creature so foul to look at, in her tatters, stains and splashes, but so much fouler than that in her moral infamy, that it was a shameful thing even to see her (Hard Times).*

Bladud, Prince: Mythical founder of Bath, whose legend Pickwick reads while visiting that city *(Pickwick).*

Blake, 'Warmint': An out-and-out young gentleman. *Upon divers occasions has distinguished himself in a manner that would not have disgraced the fighting man (Young Gentlemen – 'Out-and-out Young Gentleman').*

Blandois: See **Rigaud** *(Dorrit).*

Blank: Exhibitor in the display of models and mechanical science at the second meeting of the Mudfog Association. *Exhibited a model of a fashionable annual, composed of copper-plates, gold leaf, and silk boards, and worked entirely by milk and water (Mudfog).*

Blanquo, Pierre: Swiss guide accompanying Our Bore. *Pierre Blanquo: whom you may know, perhaps? – our bore is sorry you don't, because he's the only guide deserving of the name (Reprinted – 'Our Bore').*

Blathers: Bow Street officer investigating the burglary at Mrs. Maylie's. *A stout personage of middle height, aged about fifty: with shiny black hair, cropped pretty close; half-whiskers, a round face, and sharp eyes (Twist).*

Blaze and Sparkle: Fashionable London jewellers. *'If you want to address our people, sir,' say Blaze and Sparkle the jewellers – meaning by our people, Lady Dedlock and the rest – 'you must remember that you are not dealing with the general public' (Bleak House).*

Blazo, Colonel Sir Thomas: Jingle's opponent in a single-wicket cricket match in the West Indies. *'Won the toss – first innings – seven o'clock A.M. – six natives to look out – went in; kept in – heat intense – natives all fainted – taken away – fresh half-dozen ordered – fainted also – Blazo bowling – supported by two natives – couldn't bowl me out – fainted too – cleared away the Colonel – wouldn't give in – faithful attendant – Quanko Samba – last man left – sun so hot, bat in blisters – ball scorched brown – five hundred and seventy runs – rather exhausted – Quanko mustered up last remaining strength – bowled me out – had a bath, and went out to dinner' (Pickwick).*

Blight: Lightwood's office factotum. *A dismal boy . . . the managing clerk, junior clerk, common-law clerk,* *conveyancing clerk, chancery clerk, every refinement and department of clerk (Mutual Friend).*

Blimber, Dr.: Principal of the Brighton boarding-school attended by Paul Dombey. *A portly gentleman in a suit of black, with strings at his knees, and stockings below them. He had a bald head, highly polished; a deep voice; and a chin so very double, that it was a wonder how he ever managed to shave into the creases. He had likewise a pair of little eyes that were always half shut up, and a mouth that was always half expanded into a grin, as if he had, that moment, posed a boy, and were waiting to convict him from his own lips. Insomuch that when the Doctor put his right hand into the breast of his coat; and with his other hand behind him, and a scarcely perceptible wag of his head, made the commonest observation to a nervous stranger, it was like a sentiment from the sphinx, and settled his business (Dombey).*

Blimber, Mrs: Dr. Blimber's wife. *Not learned herself, but she pretended to be, and that did quite as well. She said at evening parties, that if she could have known Cicero, she thought she could have died contented. It was the steady joy of her life to see the Doctor's young gentlemen go out walking, unlike all other young gentlemen, in the largest possible shirt-collars, and the stiffest possible cravats. It was so classical, she said (Dombey).*

Blimber, Cornelia: Dr. Blimber's daughter and a teacher in his school. *Miss Blimber, too, although a slim and graceful maid, did no soft violence to the gravity of the house. There was no light nonsense about Miss Blimber. She was dry and sandy with working in the graves of deceased languages. None of your live languages for Miss Blimber. They must be dead – stone dead – and then Miss Blimber dug them up like a ghoul (Dombey).*

Blinder, Mrs.: The Necketts' neighbour who looks after their children. *A good-natured-looking old woman, with a dropsy, or an asthma, or perhaps both (Bleak House).*

Blinder, Bill: Deceased ostler who left Tony Weller his lantern. *'The hostler as had charge o' them two vell-known piebald leaders that run in the Bristol fast coach, and vould never go to no other tune but a sutherly vind and a cloudy sky, which wos consekvently played incessant, by the guard, wenever they wos on duty' (Humphrey).*

Blinkins: Latin master at Our School. *A colourless doubled-up near-sighted man with a crutch, who was always cold, and always putting onions into his ears for deafness, and always disclosing ends of flannel under all his garments, and almost always applying a ball of pocket-handkerchief to some part of his face with a screwing action round and round. He was a very good scholar, and took great pains where he saw intelligence and a desire to learn; otherwise, perhaps not. Our memory presents him (unless teased into a passion) with as little energy as colour – as having been worried and tormented into monotonous feebleness – as having had the best part of his life ground out of him in a Mill of boys (Reprinted – 'Our School').*

Blockitt, Mrs.: Nurse to the first Mrs. Dombey. *A simpering piece of faded gentility, who did not presume to state her name as a fact, but merely offered it as a mild suggestion (Dombey).*

Blockson, Mrs.: The Knags' charwoman. *'As I had two twin children the day before yesterday was only seven weeks, and my little Charley fell down an airy and put his elber out, last Monday, I shall take it as a favior if you'll send nine shillings, for one week's work, to my house, afore the clock strikes ten to-morrow' (Nickleby).*

Blogg: Parish beadle who arranged Betty Higden's adoption of Sloppy *(Mutual Friend).*

Bloss, Mrs.: The wealthy widow of (and formerly cook to) a cork-cutter. She imagines herself an invalid, eats prodigiously, and marries her fellow hypochondriac and boarder at Mrs. Tibbs's, Gobler. *There arrived a single lady with a double-knock, in a pelisse the colour of the interior of a damson-pie; a bonnet of the same, with a regular conservatory of artificial flowers; a white veil, and a green parasol, with a cobweb border. The visitor (who was very fat and red-faced) was shown into the drawing-room (Boz – 'Boarding-House').*

Blotton: A member of the Pickwick Club whose calling Pickwick 'humbug' occasions a debate upon the meaningful use of abuse *(Pickwick).*

Blower, Captain, R.N.: An ancient invalid, one of the characters assumed by Gabblewig in order to unmask Slap *(Nightingale's Diary).*

Blowers: Counsel appearing before the former Lord Chancellor. *The last Lord Chancellor handled it neatly, when, correcting Mr. Blowers the eminent silk gown who said that such a thing might happen when the sky rained potatoes, he observed, 'or when we get through Jarndyce and Jarndyce, Mr. Blowers'; – a pleasantry that particularly tickled the maces, bags, and purses (Bleak House).*

Blubb: Lecturer at the umbugology and ditchwaterisics session of the second meeting of the Mudfog Association. His subject is the skull of Greenacre, the murderer, but it proves to be a carved coconut. *Delivered a lecture upon the cranium before him, clearly showing that Mr. Greenacre possessed the organ of destructiveness to a most unusual extent, with a most remarkable development of the organ of carveativeness (Mudfog).*

Blumb, R.A.: Royal Academician taken by Our Bore to see 'the finest picture in Italy'. *And you never saw a man so affected in your life as Blumb was. He cried like a child! (Reprinted – 'Our Bore').*

Blunderbore, Captain: Officer of the Horse Marines who makes the profound observation that a one-eyed pony winks his eye and whisks his tail simultaneously *(Mudfog).*

Blunderum: Speaker at the zoology and botany session of the first meeting of the Mudfog Association. *Delighted the section with a most interesting and valuable paper 'on the last moments of the learned* pig,' which produced a very strong impression on the assembly (Mudfog).

Bob: Turnkey at the Marshalsea who befriends William Dorrit and becomes godfather to Amy. *Time went on, and the turnkey began to fail. His chest swelled, and his legs got weak, and he was short of breath. The well-worn wooden stool was 'beyond him,' he complained. He sat in an arm-chair with a cushion, and sometimes wheezed so, for minutes together, that he couldn't turn the key. When he was overpowered by these fits, the debtor often turned it for him (Dorrit).*

Bobbo: Schoolfellow of the hero of Jemmy Lirriper's tale. *'The cleverest and bravest and best-looking and most generous of all the friends that ever were'* (Christmas Stories – 'Mrs. Lirriper's Lodgings').

Bobby, Lord: See **Mizzler, Marquis of** (Curiosity Shop).

Bobster: Cecilia Bobster's father. *Of a violent and brutal temper* (Nickleby).

Bobster, Cecilia: The girl whom Newman Noggs mistakes for Madeline Bray and arranges for Nicholas to meet clandestinely (Nickleby).

Bocker, Tom: Orphan suggested by Milvey for adoption by the Boffins. *'I doubt, Frank,' Mrs. Milvey hinted, after a little hesitation, 'if Mrs. Boffin wants an orphan* quite *nineteen, who drives a cart and waters the roads'* (Mutual Friend).

Boffer: Ruined stockbroker whose probable suicide is the subject of a bet between Flasher and Simmery. *'I'm very sorry he has failed,' said Wilkins Flasher, Esquire. 'Capital dinners he gave.' 'Fine port he had too,' remarked Mr. Simmery* (Pickwick).

Boffin, Nicodemus ('Noddy' or 'The Golden Dustman'): Former confidential servant and foreman to John Harmon's father, who left him a fortune on his death. He and his wife are Bella Wilfer's benefactors and enable John Harmon to marry her. *A broad, round-shouldered, one-sided old fellow in mourning, coming comically ambling towards the corner, dressed in a pea overcoat, and carrying a large stick. He wore thick shoes, and thick leather gaiters, and thick gloves like a hedger's. Both as to his dress and to himself, he was of an overlapping rhinoceros build, with folds in his cheeks, and his forehead, and his eyelids, and his lips, and his ears; but with bright, eager, childishly-inquiring grey eyes, under his ragged eyebrows, and broad-brimmed hat. A very odd-looking old fellow altogether* (Mutual Friend).

Boffin, Mrs. Nicodemus (Henrietta): Boffin's wife who befriends Bella Wilfer. *A stout lady of rubicund and cheerful aspect, dressed (to Mr. Wegg's consternation) in a low evening dress of sable satin, and a large velvet hat and feathers. 'Mrs. Boffin, Wegg,' said Boffin, 'is a high-flyer at Fashion. And her make is such, that she does it credit'* (Mutual Friend).

Bogles, Mrs.: A former landlady of the Uncommercial Traveller, who recalls a party given at her boarding-house. *On which occasion Mrs. Bogles was taken in execution by a branch of the legal profession who got in as the harp, and was removed (with the keys and subscribed capital) to a place of durance, half an hour prior to the commencement of the festivities* (Uncommercial – 'Refreshments for Travellers').

Bogsby, James George: Landlord of the Sol's Arms, Chancery Lane. *A highly respectable landlord* (Bleak House).

Boiler, The Revd. Boanerges: A boring preacher whose services the Uncommercial Traveller was compelled to attend as a child. *I have sat under Boanerges when he has specifically addressed himself to us – us, the infants – and at this present writing I hear his lumbering jocularity (which never amused us, though we basely pretended that it did), and I behold his big round face, and I look up the inside of his outstretched coat-sleeve as if it were a telescope with the stopper on, and I hate him with an unwholesome hatred for two hours* (Uncommercial – 'City of London Churches').

Bokum, Mrs.: Friend and bridesmaid to Mrs. MacStinger. *He learnt from this lady that she was the widow of a Mr. Bokum, who had held an employment in the Custom House; that she was the dearest friend of Mrs. MacStinger, whom she considered a pattern for her sex* (Dombey).

Bolder: Pupil at Dotheboys Hall. *An unhealthy-looking boy, with warts all over his hands* (Nickleby).

Boldheart, Captain: Piratical captain of the schooner *Beauty* and hero of Robin Redforth's romantic tale. *Considering himself spited by a Latin-grammar master, demanded the satisfaction due from one man of honour to another. Not getting it, he privately withdrew his haughty spirit from such low company, bought a second-hand pocket pistol, folded up some sandwiches in a paper bag, and made a bottle of Spanish liquorice-water, and entered on a career of valour* ('Holiday Romance').

Boldwig, Captain: Landowner near Dingley Dell who finds Pickwick sleeping off the effects of punch on his land and consigns him in a wheelbarrow to the pound. *A little fierce man in a stiff black neckerchief and blue surtout, who, when he did condescend to walk about his property, did it in company with a thick rattan stick with a brass ferrule, and a gardener and sub-gardener with meek faces, to whom (the gardeners, not the stick) Captain Boldwig gave his orders with all due grandeur and ferocity: for Captain Boldwig's wife's sister had married a Marquis, and the Captain's house was a villa, and his land 'grounds,' and it was all very high, and mighty, and great* (Pickwick).

Bolo, Miss: Pickwick's card partner at Bath Assembly Rooms. *If he played a wrong card, Miss Bolo looked a small armoury of daggers* (Pickwick).

Bolter, Mrs.: See **Charlotte** (Twist).

Bolter, Morris: See **Claypole, Noah** (Twist).

Bolton, Robert: The 'gentleman connected with the press' who tells tall stories to admiring listeners at the Green Dragon, Westminster Bridge. *An individual who defines himself as 'a gentleman connected with* the press,' which is a definition of peculiar indefiniteness (Mudfog – 'Mr. Robert Bolton').

Bones, Banjo and **Mrs. Banjo:** Entertainers in a sailors' 'singing-house'. *The celebrated comic favourite, Mr. Banjo Bones, looking very hideous with his blackened face and limp sugar-loaf hat; beside him, sipping rum-and-water, Mrs. Banjo Bones, in her natural colours – a little heightened (Uncommercial – 'Poor Mercantile Jack').*

Bonney: Promoter of the United Metropolitan Improved Hot Muffin and Crumpet Baking and Punctual Delivery Company. *A pale gentleman in a violent hurry, who, with his hair standing up in great disorder all over his head, and a very narrow white cravat tied loosely round his throat, looked as if he had been knocked up in the night and had not dressed himself since (Nickleby).*

Boodle, Lord: A friend of Dedlock. *Of considerable reputation with his party, who has known what office is, and who tells Sir Leicester Dedlock with much gravity, after dinner, that he really does not see to what the present age is tending (Bleak House).*

Boorker, Bill: See **Barker, William** (Boz – 'First Omnibus Cad').

Boots: See **Cobbs** (Christmas Stories – 'Holly-Tree').

Boots: Frequent guest, with Brewer, at the Veneerings', and one of Veneering's election campaign workers (Mutual Friend).

Boorey, William: Captain of the foretop in the schooner *Beauty*, commanded by Captain Boldheart, who saves him from drowning ('Holiday Romance').

Boozle: Actor approached to take over from Flimkins at the Surrey Theatre, but declines (Young Gentlemen – 'Theatrical Young Gentleman').

Borum, Mrs.: Patron of Crummles's productions and mother of six children, including **Augustus, Charlotte** and **Emma** (Nickleby).

'Bottle-Nosed Ned': See **Twigger, Edward** (Mudfog).

Bottles: Deaf stable-man employed by John. *I kept him in my service, and still keep him, as a phenomenon of moroseness not to be matched in England (Christmas Stories – 'Haunted House').*

Bouclet, Madame: Langley's landlady in France. *A compact little woman of thirty-five or so (Christmas Stories – 'Somebody's Luggage').*

Bounderby, Josiah: Coketown banker and manufacturer, son of Mrs. Pegler. He marries Louisa Gradgrind. *A big, loud man, with a stare, and a metallic laugh. A man made out of a coarse material, which seemed to have been stretched to make so much of him. A man with a great puffed head and forehead, swelled veins in his temples, and such a strained skin to his face that it seemed to hold his eyes open, and lift his eyebrows up. A man with a pervading appearance on him of being inflated like a balloon, and ready to start. A man who could never sufficiently vaunt himself a self-made man. A man who was always proclaiming, through that brassy speaking-trumpet of a voice of his, his old ignorance and his old poverty. A man who was the Bully of humility (Hard Times).*

Bounderby, Mrs. Josiah (Louisa): See **Gradgrind, Louisa** (Hard Times).

Bowley, Lady: Sir Joseph's wife. *A stately lady in a bonnet (Christmas Books – 'Chimes').*

Bowley, Master: The Bowleys' son, aged twelve. *'Sweet boy! We shall have this little gentleman in Parliament now . . . before we know where we are. We shall hear of his successes at the poll; his speeches in the House; his overtures from Governments; his brilliant achievements of all kinds; ah! we shall make our little orations about him in the Common Council, I'll be bound' (Christmas Books – 'Chimes').*

Bowley, Sir Joseph, M.P.: An elderly Member of Parliament, father of Master Bowley. *'I do my duty as the Poor Man's Friend and Father; and I endeavour to educate his mind, by inculcating on all occasions the one great moral lesson which that class requires. That is, entire Dependence on myself. They have no business whatever with – with themselves. If wicked and designing persons tell them otherwise, and they become impatient and discontented, and are guilty of insubordinate conduct and black-hearted ingratitude; which is undoubtedly the case; I am their Friend and Father still. It is so Ordained. It is in the nature of things' (Christmas Books – 'Chimes').*

Bowyer, The: Mistress Alice's father and Hugh Graham's master in Magog's story. *An honest Bowyer who dwelt in the ward of Cheype, and was rumoured to possess great wealth. Rumour was quite as infallible in those days as at the present time, but it happened then as now to be sometimes right by accident. It stumbled upon the truth when it gave the old Bowyer a mint of money (Humphrey).*

Boxer: John Peerybingle's dog. *Everybody knew him, all along the road – especially the fowls and pigs, who when they saw him approaching, with his body all on one side, and his ears pricked up inquisitively, and that knob of a tail making the most of itself in the air, immediately withdrew into remote back settlements, without waiting for the honour of a nearer acquaintance. He had business everywhere; going down all the turnings, looking into the wells, bolting in and out of all the cottages, dashing into the midst of all the Dame-schools, fluttering all the pigeons, magnifying the tails of all the cats, and trotting into the public-houses like a regular customer. Wherever he went, somebody or other might have been heard to cry, 'Halloa! Here's Boxer!' (Christmas Books – 'Cricket').*

'Boy at Mugby, The': See **Ezekiel** (Christmas Stories – 'Mugby Junction').

Boythorn, Lawrence: An old friend of Jarndyce and litigating neighbour of Dedlock. *There was a sterling quality in this laugh, and in his vigorous healthy voice, and in the roundness and fulness with which he uttered every word he spoke, and in the very fury of his superlatives, which seemed to go off like blank* *cannons and hurt nothing. . . . He was not only a very handsome old gentleman – upright and stalwart as he had been described to us – with a massive grey head, a fine composure of face when silent, a figure that might have become corpulent but for his being so continually in earnest that he gave it no rest, and a chin that might have subsided into a double chin but for the vehement emphasis in which it was constantly required to assist; but he was such a true gentleman in his manner, so chivalrously polite, his face was lighted by a smile of so much sweetness and tenderness, and it seemed so plain that he had nothing to hide, but showed himself exactly as he was (Bleak House).*

Brandley, Mrs.: A widow with whom Estella lodges at Richmond. *The lady with whom Estella was placed, Mrs. Brandley by name, was a widow, with one daughter several years older than Estella. The mother looked young and the daughter looked old; the mother's complexion was pink, and the daughter's was yellow; the mother set up for frivolity, and the daughter for theology (Expectations).*

Brass, Sally: Sampson Brass's sister and partner, probably mother of 'The Marchioness' (q.v.) by Quilp. *His clerk, assistant, housekeeper, secretary, confidential plotter, adviser, intriguer, and bill of cost increaser, Miss Brass – a kind of amazon at common law. . . . A lady of thirty-five or thereabouts, of a gaunt and bony figure, and a resolute bearing, which if it repressed the softer emotions of love, and kept admirers at a distance, certainly inspired a feeling akin to awe in the breasts of those male strangers who had the happiness to approach her. . . . In complexion Miss Brass was sallow – rather a dirty sallow, so to speak – but this hue was agreeably relieved by the healthy glow which mantled in the extreme tip of her laughing nose. Her voice was exceedingly impressive – deep and rich in quality, and, once heard, not easily forgotten. . . . In mind she was of a strong and vigorous turn, having from her earliest youth devoted herself with uncommon ardour to the study of the law; not wasting her speculation upon its eagle flights, which are rare, but tracing it attentively through all the slippery and eel-like crawlings in which it commonly pursues its way (Curiosity Shop).*

Brass, Sampson: Quilp's legal adviser, who eventually turns evidence against him, but is jailed for his part in the plot against Kit Nubbles. *An attorney of no very good repute, from Bevis Marks in the City of London; he was a tall, meagre man, with a nose like a wen, a protruding forehead, retreating eyes, and hair of a deep red. He wore a long black surtout reaching nearly to his ankles, short black trousers, high shoes, and cotton stockings of a bluish-grey. He had a cringing manner, but a very harsh voice; and his blandest smiles were so extremely forbidding, that to have had his company under the least repulsive circumstances, one would have wished him to be out of temper that he might only scowl (Curiosity Shop).*

Bravassa, Miss: Member of the Crummleses' theatrical company. *The beautiful Miss Bravassa, who had once had her likeness taken 'in character' by an engraver's apprentice, whereof impressions were hung*

up for sale in the pastry-cook's window, and the greengrocer's, and at the circulating library, and the box-office, whenever the announce bills came out for her annual night (Nickleby).

Bray, Madeline: Slave to her misanthropic father, she is rescued by his death from having to marry Gride, and eventually marries Nicholas Nickleby. *A young lady who could be scarcely eighteen, of very slight and delicate figure, but exquisitely shaped. . . . She raised her veil, for an instant, while she preferred the inquiry, and disclosed a countenance of most uncommon beauty, though shaded by a cloud of sadness, which, in one so young, was doubly remarkable (Nickleby).*

Bray, Walter: A bankrupt widower, embittered and selfish, father to Madeline whom he tries to marry off to Gride, one of his principal creditors. *He was scarce fifty, perhaps, but so emaciated as to appear much older. His features presented the remains of a handsome countenance, but one in which the embers of strong and impetuous passions were easier to be traced than any expression which would have rendered a far plainer face much more prepossessing. His looks were very haggard, and his limbs and body literally worn to the bone, but there was something of the old fire in the large sunken eye notwithstanding, and it seemed to kindle afresh as he struck a thick stick, with which he seemed to have supported himself in his seat, impatiently on the floor twice or thrice, and called his daughter by her name (Nickleby).*

Brewer: Frequent guest, with Boots, at the Veneerings', and one of Veneering's election campaign workers *(Mutual Friend).*

Brick, Jefferson: War correspondent of the New York Rowdy Journal. *A small young gentleman of very juvenile appearance, and unwholesomely pale in the face; partly, perhaps, from intense thought, but partly, there is no doubt, from the excessive use of tobacco, which he was at that moment chewing vigorously. He wore his shirt-collar turned down over a black ribbon; and his lank hair, a fragile crop, was not only smoothed and parted back from his brow, that none of the Poetry of his aspect might be lost, but had, here and there, been grubbed up by the roots: which accounted for his loftiest developments being somewhat pimply (Chuzzlewit).*

Brick, Mrs. Jefferson: Brick's wife. *'Pray,' said Martin, 'who is that sickly little girl opposite, with the tight round eyes?' (Chuzzlewit).*

Briggs: Paul Dombey's room-mate at Dr. Blimber's school. *Sat looking at his task in stony stupefaction and despair – which it seemed had been his condition ever since breakfast-time (Dombey).*

Briggs, Mr. and **Mrs.:** Friends of the egotistical couple *(Young Couples – 'Egotistical Couple').*

Briggs, Mrs.: Mother of two sons, **Samuel,** an attorney, and **Alexander,** articled to his brother, and three daughters, **Julia, Kate,** and another. Their chief preoccupation is trying to gain ascendancy over the **Tauntons** (q.v.). *Between the Briggses and the*

Tauntons there existed a degree of implacable hatred, quite unprecedented. The animosity between the Montagues and Capulets, was nothing to that which prevailed between these two illustrious houses. . . . If the Miss Briggses appeared in smart bonnets, the Miss Tauntons eclipsed them with smarter. If Mrs. Taunton appeared in a cap of all the hues of the rainbow, Mrs. Briggs forthwith mounted a toque, with all the patterns of the kaleidoscope. If Miss Sophia Taunton learnt a new song, two of the Miss Briggses came out with a new duet. The Tauntons had once gained a temporary triumph with the assistance of a harp, but the Briggses brought three guitars into the field, and effectually routed the enemy. There was no end to the rivalry between them (Boz – 'Steam Excursion').

Britain, Benjamin (Little Britain): Dr. Jeddler's manservant, later husband of Clemency Newcome, father of two sons, and landlord of the Nutmeg Grater inn. *A small man, with an uncommonly sour and discontented face. // 'I was hid for the best part of two years behind a bookstall, ready to fly out if anybody pocketed a volume: and after that, I was light porter to a stay and mantua-maker, in which capacity I was employed to carry about, in oilskin baskets, nothing but deceptions – which soured my spirits and disturbed my confidence in human nature* (Christmas Books – 'Battle of Life').

Brittles: Servant at Mrs. Maylie's. *A lad of all-work: who, having entered her service a mere child, was treated as a promising young boy still, though he was something past thirty* (Twist).

Brobity, Miss: See **Sapsea, Mrs. Ethelinda** (Drood).

Brogley: Secondhand dealer and broker who takes possession of Sol Gills's business in execution of a debt. *A moist-eyed, pink-complexioned, crisp-haired man, of a bulky figure and an even temper – for that class of Caius Marius who sits upon the ruins of other people's Carthages, can keep up his spirits well enough* (Dombey).

Brogson: Dinner guest at the Buddens'. *An elderly gentleman in a black coat, drab knee-breeches, and long gaiters* (Boz – 'Mr. Minns and his Cousin').

Brook Dingwall, Cornelius, M.P.: Father of Lavinia and Frederick. *Very haughty, solemn, and portentous. He had, naturally, a somewhat spasmodic expression of countenance, which was not rendered the less remarkable by his wearing an extremely stiff cravat. He was wonderfully proud of the M.P. attached to his name, and never lost an opportunity of reminding people of his dignity. He had a great idea of his own abilities, which must have been a great comfort to him, as no one else had* (Boz – 'Sentiment').

Brook Dingwall, Mrs. Cornelius: Brook Dingwall's wife, mother of Lavinia and Frederick (Boz – 'Sentiment').

Brook Dingwall, Frederick: The Brook Dingwalls' infant son, brother of Lavinia. *One of those public nuisances, a spoiled child, was playing about the room, dressed after the most approved fashion – in a blue tunic with a black belt a quarter of a yard wide, fastened with an immense buckle – looking like a robber in a melodrama, seen through a diminishing glass* (Boz – 'Sentiment').

Brook Dingwall, Lavinia: Daughter of the Brook Dingwalls and sister to Frederick. She is sent to the Misses Crumpton's establishment to quench her ardour for Edward M'Neville Walter (see **Butler, Theodosius**). *One of that numerous class of young ladies, who, like adverbs, may be known by their answering to a commonplace question, and doing nothing else* (Boz – 'Sentiment').

Brooker: Ralph Nickleby's former clerk, turned criminal. He knows that Nickleby is the father of Smike, and tries to blackmail him, but fails. *A spare, dark, withered man . . . with a stooping body, and a very sinister face rendered more ill-favoured by hollow and hungry cheeks deeply sunburnt, and thick black eyebrows, blacker in contrast with the perfect whiteness of his hair; roughly clothed in shabby garments, of a strange and uncouth make; and having about him an indefinable manner of depression and degradation* (Nickleby).

Brooks: One of five occupants of a bed at Dotheboys Hall (Nickleby).

Brooks: Former fellow-lodger of Sam Weller. A pieman. *'Wery nice man he was – reg'lar clever chap, too – make pies out o' anything, he could. "What a number o' cats you keep, Mr. Brooks," says I, when I'd got intimate with him. "Ah," says he, "I do – a good many," says he. "You must be wery fond o' cats," says I. "Other people is," says he, a winkin' at me; "they an't in season till the winter, though," says he. "Not in season!" says I. "No," says he, "fruits is in, cats is out"'* (Pickwick).

Browdie, John: A blunt Yorkshire corn factor who becomes friends with Nicholas Nickleby while he is at Dotheboys Hall. He marries Matilda Price. *The expected swain arrived, with his hair very damp from recent washing, and a clean shirt, whereof the collar might have belonged to some giant ancestor, forming, together with a white waistcoat of similar dimensions, the chief ornament of his person . . . something over six feet high, with a face and body rather above the due proportion than below it* (Nickleby).

Brown: Performer on the violoncello at the Gattletons' private theatricals (Boz – 'Mrs. Joseph Porter').

Brown: Friend of Mrs. Nubbles, whom she offers as testifier to her statements. *Supposed to be then a corporal in the East Indies, and who could of course be found with very little trouble* (Curiosity Shop).

Brown: Greedy, gout-ridden pupil of Mrs. Lemon in Nettie Ashford's romantic tale ('Holiday Romance').

Brown: Member of the Mudfog Association (Mudfog).

Brown, the three Misses: Three spinster sisters in 'our parish' whose admiration for the young curate spurs them to charitable works. *The curate preached a charity sermon on behalf of the charity school, and in the charity sermon aforesaid, expatiated in glowing terms on the praiseworthy and indefatigable exertions of certain estimable individuals. Sobs were heard to issue from the three Miss Browns' pew; the pew-opener of the division was seen to hurry down the centre aisle to the vestry door, and to return immediately, bearing a glass of water in her hand. A low moaning ensued; two more pew-openers rushed to the spot, and the three Miss Browns, each supported by a pew-opener, were led out of the church, and led in again after the lapse of five minutes with white pocket-handkerchiefs to their eyes, as if they had been attending a funeral in the churchyard adjoining* (Boz – 'Our Parish', 'Ladies' Societies').

Brown, Mrs. ('Good Mrs. Brown'): Mother of Alice Marwood. She briefly abducts Florence Dombey and steals her clothes. *A very ugly old woman, with red rims round her eyes, and a mouth that mumbled and chattered of itself when she was not speaking. She was miserably dressed, and carried some skins over her arm. She seemed to have followed Florence some little way at all events, for she had lost her breath; and this made her uglier still, as she stood trying to regain it: working her shrivelled yellow face and throat into all sorts of contortions* (Dombey).

Brown, Mrs: Hostess of the party at which Griggins's antics offend everyone. *They were surprised at Mrs. Brown's allowing it* (Young Gentlemen – 'Funny Young Gentleman').

Brown, Alice: See **Marwood, Alice** (Dombey).

Brown, Conversation: Colleague of Lord Feenix's Parliamentary days. *Four bottle man at the Treasury Board* (Dombey).

Brown, Fanny: Stargazer's niece whom he wishes to marry Tom Grig (Lamplighter). In 'The Lamplighter's Story', the subsequent prose version of this farce, she is renamed Fanny Barker.

Brown of Muggleton: Maker of Rachael Wardle's shoes, through which Jingle is tracked down in the nick of time *(Pickwick)*.

Brown and **O'Brien:** Passengers on the Gravesend steam packet with an eye for the young ladies. *Mr. Brown or Mr. O'Brien, as the case may be, remarks in a low voice that he has been quite insensible of late to the beauties of nature – that his whole thoughts and wishes have centred in one object alone – whereupon the young lady looks up, and failing in her attempt to appear unconscious, looks down again* (Boz – 'The River').

Browndock, Miss: One of Mrs. Nickleby vaguely-recalled connections. *'Your poor dear papa's cousin's sister-in-law – a Miss Browndock – was taken into partnership by a lady that kept a school at Hammersmith, and made her fortune in no time at all. I forget, by the bye, whether that Miss Browndock was the same lady that got the ten thousand pounds prize in the lottery, but I think she was'* (Nickleby).

Brownlow: Gentleman who befriends Oliver Twist, who has been accused of picking his pocket. He establishes his true identity and eventually adopts him as his son. *A very respectable-looking personage, with a powdered head and gold spectacles. He was dressed in a bottle-green coat with a black velvet collar; wore white trousers; and carried a smart bamboo cane under his arm* (Twist).

Bucket, Inspector: The detective officer employed by Tulkinghorn and later by Dedlock. He is instrumental in clearing up the prolonged case of Jarndyce and Jarndyce. *Mr. Snagsby is dismayed to see . . . a person with a hat and stick in his hand, who was not there when he himself came in, and has not since entered by the door or by either of the windows. There is a press in the room, but its hinges have not creaked, nor has a step been audible upon the floor. Yet this third person stands there, with his attentive face, and his hat and stick in his hands, and his hands behind him, a composed and quiet listener. He is a stoutly built, steady-looking, sharp-eyed man in black, of about the middle-age* (Bleak House).

Bucket, Mrs.: Bucket's wife. She helps her husband find Tulkinghorn's murderer. *A lady of a natural detective genius, which if it had been improved by professional exercise, might have done great things, but which has paused at the level of a clever amateur* (Bleak House).

Bud, Rosa: Also known as **Rosebud** and **Pussy.** A pupil at Miss Twinkleton's, betrothed to Drood at their fathers' wish. *A blooming schoolgirl . . . her flowing brown hair tied with a blue riband, and her beauty remarkable for a quite childish, almost baby-ish, touch of saucy discontent, comically conscious of itself. // 'You're very welcome, Eddy. . . . No, I can't kiss you, because I've got an acidulated drop in my mouth'* (Drood).

Budden, Alexander Augustus: Small son of Octavius and Amelia and godson by proxy of Augustus Minns. *Habited in a sky-blue suit with silver buttons; and possessing hair of nearly the same colour as the metal* (Boz – 'Mr. Minns and his Cousin').

Budden, Octavius: Father of Alexander Augustus and cousin to Augustus Minns. A wealthy retired corn-chandler living near Stamford Hill. *He always spoke at the top of his voice, and always said the same thing half a dozen times* (Boz – 'Mr. Minns and his Cousin').

Budden, Mrs. Octavius (Amelia): Budden's wife, mother of Alexander Augustus (Boz – 'Mr. Minns and his Cousin').

Budger, Mrs.: Tupman's partner in a quadrille at the Bull, Rochester. *A little old widow, whose rich dress and profusion of ornament bespoke her a most desirable addition to a limited income* (Pickwick).

Buffer, Dr.: Member of the Mudfog Association (Mudfog).

Buffle: Father of Robina. Tax-collector resented by Mrs. Lirriper and Major Jackman. They become friends with the Buffles after taking them in when their house burns down. *Mr. Buffle's manners when engaged in his business were not agreeable. To collect is one thing, and to look about as if suspicious of the goods being gradually removing in the dead of the night by a back door is another, over taxing you have no control but suspecting is voluntary* (Christmas Stories – 'Mrs. Lirriper's Legacy.').

Buffle, Mrs.: Buffle's wife, Robina's mother, whose superior air is resented by Mrs. Lirriper *It was considered besides that a one-horse pheayton ought not to have elevated Mrs. Buffle to that height* (Christmas Stories – 'Mrs. Lirriper's Legacy').

Buffle, Robina: The Buffles' daughter, in love with George. *It was whispered that Miss Buffle would go either into a consumption or a convent she being so very thin and off her appetite* (Christmas Stories – 'Mrs. Lirriper's Legacy').

Buffum, Oscar: A boarder at the National Hotel, in America, where Martin Chuzzlewit stays before embarking for Eden *(Chuzzlewit)*.

Buffy, The Right Hon. William, M.P.: A friend of Dedlock. *Contends across the table with some one else, that the shipwreck of the country – about which there is no doubt; it is only the manner of it that is in question – is attributable to Cuffy* (Bleak House).

Bulder, Colonel: Officer commanding the Rochester garrison. *Colonel Bulder, in full military uniform, on horseback, galloping first to one place and then to another, and backing his horse among the people, and prancing, and curvetting, and shouting in a most alarming manner, and making himself very hoarse in the voice, and very red in the face, without any assignable cause or reason whatever* (Pickwick).

Bulder, Mrs. and Miss: Colonel Bulder's wife and daughter, present at the charity ball at the Bull, Rochester *(Pickwick)*.

Bule, Miss: Leader of society, though aged only eight or nine, at Miss Griffin's school. *Struggling with the diffidence so natural to, and charming in, her adorable sex* (Christmas Stories – 'Haunted House').

Bull, Prince: A mighty prince – symbolising England at the time of the Crimean War – hampered by a tyrannical godmother and the Civil Service Establishment. *He had gone through a great deal of fighting, in his time, about all sorts of things, including nothing; but, had gradually settled down to be a steady, peaceable, good-natured, corpulent, rather sleepy Prince. . . . This good Prince had two sharp thorns in his pillow, two hard knobs in his crown, two heavy loads on his mind, two unbridled nightmares in his sleep, two rocks ahead in his course. He could not by any means get servants to suit him, and he had a tyrannical old godmother, whose name was Tape* (Reprinted – 'Prince Bull').

Bullamy: Porter at the Anglo-Bengalee Disinterested Loan and Life Assurance Company's offices. *A wonderful creature, in a vast red waistcoat and a short-tailed pepper-and-salt coat – who carried more conviction to the minds of sceptics than the whole establishment without him. . . . People had been known to apply to effect an insurance on their lives for a thousand pounds, and looking at him, to beg, before the form of proposal was filled up, that it might be made two* (Chuzzlewit).

Bull-Dogs, The United: Name adopted by the Prentice Knights (q.v.) when older members' indentures expired *(Rudge)*.

Bullfinch: Friend of the Uncommercial Traveller who makes the disastrous suggestion that they dine at the Temeraire, at the seaside resort of Namelesston. *An excellent man of business* (Uncommercial – 'A Little Dinner in an Hour').

Bullman: Plaintiff in Bullman and Ramsey, the case discussed at length by Dodson and Fogg's clerks while Pickwick awaits attention *(Pickwick)*.

Bullock: See **Tipkins against Bullock** *(Copperfield)*.

Bull's Eye: Bill Sikes's dog. *A white shaggy dog, with his face scratched and torn in twenty different places* (Twist).

Bulph: A pilot with whom Crummles lodges in Portsmouth *(Nickleby)*.

Bumble: Beadle of the parish workhouse where Oliver Twist is born. He marries the matron, Mrs. Corney, but they are eventually dismissed and end their days as workhouse inmates. *A fat man, and a choleric . . . Mr. Bumble had a great idea of his oratorical powers and his importance* (Twist).

Bumble, Mrs.: See **Corney, Mrs.** *(Twist)*.

Bumple, Michael: Complainant against Sludberry for brawling *(Boz – 'Doctors' Commons')*.

Bung: A broker's assistant who defeats Spruggins in election for beadle of 'Our Parish'. *There was a serenity in the open countenance of Bung – a kind of moral dignity in his confident air – an 'I wish you may get it' sort of expression in his eye – which infused animation into his supporters, and evidently dispirited his opponents* (Boz – 'Election for Beadle'. See also *Boz* – 'Broker's Man').

Bunkin, Mrs.: Neighbour quoted by Mrs. Sanders as having told her that Pickwick was engaged to Mrs. Bardell. *Mrs. Bunkin which clear-starched* (Pickwick).

Bunsby, Captain Jack: Master of the *Cautious Clara*, much admired by Captain Cuttle whom he rescues from the matrimonial designs of Mrs. MacStinger; though at sacrifice of himself, for she carries him off in forcible marriage. *Immediately there appeared, coming slowly up above the bulk-head of the cabin, another bulk-head – human, and very large – with one stationary eye in the mahogany face, and one revolving one, on the principle of some lighthouses. This head was decorated with shaggy hair, like oakum, which had no governing inclination towards the north, east, west, or south, but inclined to all four quarters of the compass, and to every point upon it. The head was followed by a perfect desert of chin, and by a shirt-collar and neckerchief, and by a dread-*

nought pilot-coat, and by a pair of dreadnought pilot-trousers, whereof the waistband was so very broad and high, that it became a succedaneum for a waistcoat: being ornamented near the wearer's breast-bone with some massive wooden buttons, like back-gammon men. As the lower portions of these panta-loons became revealed, Bunsby stood confessed (Dombey).

Burton, Thomas: Convert reported to the committee of the Brick Lane Branch of the United Grand Junction Ebenezer Temperance Association. *Purveyor of cat's meat to the Lord Mayor and Sheriffs, and several members of the Common Council (the announcement of this gentleman's name was received with breathless interest). Has a wooden leg; finds a wooden leg expensive, going over the stones; used to wear second-hand wooden legs, and drink a glass of hot gin-and-water regularly every night – sometimes two (deep sighs). Found the second-hand wooden legs split and rot very quickly; is firmly persuaded that their constitution was undermined by the gin-and-water (prolonged cheering). Buys new wooden legs now, and drinks nothing but water and weak tea. The new legs last twice as long as the others used to do, and he attributes this solely to his temperate habits (triumphant cheers) (Pickwick).*

Butcher, William: John's friend, who advises him to patent his invention. *A Chartist. Moderate. He is a good speaker. He is very animated (Reprinted – 'Poor Man's Tale of a Patent').*

Butcher, The Young: David Copperfield's adversary in Canterbury. *He is the terror of the youth of Canterbury. There is a vague belief abroad, that the beef suet with which he anoints his hair gives him unnatural strength, and that he is a match for a man. He is a broad-faced, bull-necked young butcher, with rough red cheeks, an ill-conditioned mind, and an injurious tongue. His main use of this tongue, is, to disparage Doctor Strong's young gentlemen. He says, publicly, that if they want anything he'll give it 'em (Copperfield).*

Butler, Theodosius: Author, under the pseudonym Edward M'Neville Walter, of the pamphlet 'Considerations on the Policy of Removing the Duty on Bees'-wax', with which he gains the favour of Cornelius Brook Dingwall, M.P., and the heart of his daughter Lavinia. *One of those immortal geniuses who are to be met with in almost every circle. They have, usually, very deep, monotonous voices. They always persuade themselves that they are wonderful persons, and that they ought to be very miserable, though they don't precisely know why. They are very conceited, and usually possess half an idea; but, with enthusiastic young ladies, and silly young gentlemen, they are very wonderful persons. The individual in person, Mr. Theodosius, had written a pamphlet containing some very weighty considerations on the expediency of doing something or other; and as every sentence contained a good many words of four syllables, his admirers took it for granted that he meant a good deal (Boz – 'Sentiment').*

Buxom Widow, The: Landlady of an inn on the Marlborough Downs wooed by Tom Smart and Jinkins in 'The Bagman's Story'. (See **Bagman, The**). *A buxom widow of somewhere about eight and forty or thereabouts, with a face as comfortable as the bar (Pickwick).*

Buzfuz, Serjeant: Mrs. Bardell's counsel in the trial of Bardell and Pickwick. *Serjeant Buzfuz then rose with all the majesty and dignity which the grave nature of the proceedings demanded ... pulled his gown over his shoulders, settled his wig, and addressed the jury (Pickwick).*

Callow: One of many doctors consulted by Our Bore. *Said, 'Liver!' and prescribed rhubarb and calomel, low diet, and moderate exercise (Reprinted – 'Our Bore').*

Calton: Boarder at Mrs. Tibbs's. He courts Mrs. Maplesone, but when he fails to marry her is successfully sued for breach of promise. *A superannuated beau – an old boy. He used to say of himself that although his features were not regularly handsome, they were striking. They certainly were. It was impossible to look at his face without being reminded of a chubby street-door knocker, half-lion half-monkey; and the comparison might be extended to his whole character and conversation.... He had never been married; but he was still on the look-out for a wife with money. He had a life interest worth about 300l. a year – he was exceedingly vain, and inordinately selfish. He acquired the reputation of being the very pink of politeness, and he walked round the Park, and up Regent Street, every day (Boz – 'Boarding-House').*

Camilla: Raymond's wife, Matthew Pocket's sister. *Very much reminded me of my sister, with the difference that she was older, and (as I found when I caught sight of her) of a blunter cast of features. Indeed, when I knew her better I began to think it was a Mercy she had any features at all, so very blank and high was the dead wall of her face (Expectations).*

Campbell: See **Magwitch, Abel** (*Expectations*).

Cape: Performer on the violin at the Gattletons' private theatricals (*Boz – 'Mrs. Joseph Porter'*).

Capper: The narrator's friend who introduces him to Mincin. (*Young Gentlemen – 'Very Friendly Young Gentleman'*).

Captain, The: A Member of Parliament. *The spare, squeaking old man, who sits at the same table, and who, elevating a little cracked bantam sort of voice to its highest pitch, invokes damnation upon his own eyes or somebody else's at the commencement of every sentence he utters. 'The Captain', as they call him, is a very old frequenter of Bellamy's, much addicted to stopping 'after the House is up' (an inexpiable crime in Jane's eyes), and a complete walking reservoir of spirits and water (Boz – 'Parliamentary Sketch').*

Captain, The Half-pay: A neighbour of the Old Lady. *He is an old naval officer on half-pay, and his bluff and unceremonious behaviour disturbs the old lady's domestic economy, not a little (Boz – 'Half-pay Captain').*

Carker, Harriet: Sister of John and James Carker and later wife to Morfin. She is Alice Marwood's only friend and tends her at death. *On her beauty there has fallen a heavier shade than Time of his unassisted self can cast, all-potent as he is – the shadow of anxiety and sorrow, and the daily struggle of a poor existence. But it is beauty still; and still a gentle, quiet, and retiring beauty that must be sought out, for it cannot vaunt itself; if it could, it would be what it is, no more (Dombey).*

Carker, James: Brother of John and Harriet. Manager and confidential assistant to Dombey, with whose second wife he elopes to France. Tracked down through the agency of Mrs. Brown, whose daughter had been his mistress, he is pursued back to England by Dombey and is killed by a train. *Thirty-eight or forty years old, of a florid complexion, and with two unbroken rows of glistening teeth, whose regularity and whiteness were quite distressing. It was impossible to escape the observation of them, for he showed them whenever he spoke; and bore so wide a smile upon his countenance (a smile, however, very rarely, indeed, extending beyond his mouth), that there was something in it like the snarl of a cat. He affected a stiff white cravat, after the example of his principal, and was always closely buttoned up and tightly dressed. His manner towards Mr. Dombey was deeply conceived and perfectly expressed. He was familiar with him, in the very extremity of his sense of the distance between them. 'Mr. Dombey, to a man in your position from a man in mine, there is no show of subservience compatible with the transaction of business between us, that I should think sufficient. I frankly tell you, sir, I give it up altogether' (Dombey).*

Carker, John: Brother of James and Harriet. Junior clerk at Dombey and Son's and known as Mr. Carker the Junior, though he is James's elder. He had been tempted into embezzlement when young but kept on by Dombey, whom he helps financially after inheriting James's fortune on his death. *He was not old, but his hair was white; his body was bent, or bowed as if by the weight of some great trouble: and there were deep lines in his worn and melancholy face. The fire of his eyes, the expression of his features, the very voice in which he spoke, were all subdued and quenched, as if the spirit within him lay in ashes. He was respectably, though very plainly dressed, in black; but his clothes, moulded to the general character of his figure, seemed to shrink and abase themselves upon him, and to join in the sorrowful solicitation which the whole man from head to foot expressed, to be left unnoticed, and alone in his humility (Dombey).*

Carlavero, Giovanni: Wine-shopkeeper on the Mediterranean coast of Italy, who persuades the Uncommercial Traveller to convey a huge bottle of wine to a friend in England who has helped him. *A well-favoured man of good stature and military bearing, in a great cloak.... As his striking face is pale, and his action is evidently that of an enfeebled man, I remark that I fear he has been ill. It is not much, he courteously and gravely answers, though bad while it lasts: the fever (Uncommercial – 'Italian Prisoner').*

C

Carlo: One of Jerry's performing dogs. *The lucky individual whose name was called, snapped up the morsel thrown towards him, but none of the others moved a muscle (Curiosity Shop).*

Carolina: Clara's maid, admired by Baptista. *La belle Carolina, whose heart was gay with laughter: who was young and rosy ('At Dusk').*

Caroline: Wife of one of Scrooge's debtors (*Christmas Books* – 'Christmas Carol').

Carstone, Richard: Ward in Chancery under John Jarndyce's guardianship. He secretly marries his cousin and fellow ward, Ada Clare, but his involvement in the case of Jarndyce and Jarndyce undermines his health and causes his death. *A handsome youth, with an ingenuous face, and a most engaging laugh. . . . He was very young; not more than nineteen then, if quite so much (Bleak House).*

Carter: President of the mechanical science session at the first meeting of the Mudfog Association (*Mudfog*).

Carton, Captain George (later Admiral Sir George Carton, Bart.): Officer commanding the expedition against the pirates at Silver-Store Island. He marries Marion Maryon. *With his bright eyes, brown face, and easy figure (Christmas Stories – 'English Prisoners').*

Carton, Sydney: Dissolute barrister who prepares Stryver's law cases for him. He falls in love with Lucie Manette but sacrifices his life to save Charles Darnay by means of their physical resemblance. *Sydney Carton, idlest and most unpromising of men, was Stryver's great ally. What the two drank together between Hilary Term and Michaelmas, might have floated a king's ship. . . . They prolonged their usual orgies late into the night, and Carton was rumoured to be seen at broad day, going home stealthily and unsteadily to his lodgings, like a dissipated cat. At last, it began to get about, among such as were interested in the matter, that although Sydney Carton would never be a lion, he was an amazingly good jackal (Two Cities).*

Casby, Christopher: Flora Finching's father. An apparently benign, but grasping landlord of slum properties, including Bleeding Heart Yard, whose extortionate methods are exposed by his employee, Pancks. *Patriarch was the name which many people delighted to give him. Various old ladies in the neighbourhood spoke of him as The Last of the Patriarchs. So grey, so slow, so quiet, so impassionate, so very bumpy in the head, Patriarch was the word for him. He had been accosted in the streets, and respectfully solicited to become a Patriarch for painters and for sculptors (Dorrit).*

Cavalletto, John Baptist ('Altro'): Italian refugee imprisoned with Rigaud, whom he later helps to track down in London. *A sunburnt, quick, lithe, little man, though rather thick-set. Earrings in his brown ears, white teeth lighting up his grotesque brown face, intensely black hair clustering about his brown throat, a ragged red shirt open at his brown breast. Loose, seamanlike trousers, decent shoes, a long red cap, a red sash round his waist, and a knife in it (Dorrit).*

Caveton: A 'throwing off' young gentleman. *Sometimes the throwing-off young gentleman happens to look in upon a little family circle of young ladies who are quietly spending the evening together, and then indeed he is at the very height and summit of his glory; for it is to be observed that he by no means shines to equal advantage in the presence of men as in the society of over-credulous young ladies, which is his proper element (Young Gentlemen – ' "Throwing-off" Young Gentleman').*

Celia: See **Joseph** and **Celia** (*Uncommercial* – 'City of the Absent').

Certainpersonio, Prince: Alicia's bridegroom in Alice Rainbird's romantic tale ('Holiday Romance').

Chadband, The Revd. Mr.: A hypocritical clergyman who is drawn into the Smallweeds' scheme for blackmailing Dedlock. Marries Mrs. Rachael. *A large yellow man, with a fat smile, and a general appearance of having a good deal of train oil in his system. . . . Mr. Chadband moves softly and cumbrously, not unlike a bear who has been taught to walk upright. He is very much embarrassed about the arms, as if they were inconvenient to him, and he wanted to grovel; is very much in a perspiration about the head; and never speaks without first putting up his great hand, as delivering a token to his hearers that he is going to edify them (Bleak House).*

Chadband, Mrs.: Chadband's wife, formerly Mrs. Rachael, Esther Summerson's nurse. *A stern, severe-looking silent woman (Bleak House).*

Chancery Prisoner, The: A wretched debtor whose death Pickwick witnesses in the Fleet. *A tall, gaunt, cadaverous man, in an old great-coat and slippers: with sunken cheeks, and a restless, eager eye. His lips were bloodless, and his bones sharp and thin. God help him! the iron teeth of confinement and privation had been slowly filing him down for twenty years (Pickwick).*

Chaplain, Drunken: A fellow prisoner of Pickwick in the Fleet. *Fastened his coat all the way up to his chin by means of a pin and a button alternately, had a very coarse red face, and looked like a drunken chaplain; which, indeed, he was (Pickwick).*

Charker, Corporal Harry: Gill Davis's comrade in the Royal Marines, killed in the fight with pirates. *Besides being able to read and write like a Quartermaster, he had always one most excellent idea in his mind. That was, Duty (Christmas Stories – 'English Prisoners').*

Charles and **Louisa:** A cool couple. *The cool couple are seldom alone together, and when they are, nothing can exceed their apathy and dulness: the gentleman being for the most part drowsy, and the lady silent. If they enter into conversation, it is usually of an ironical or recriminatory nature (Young Couples – 'Cool Couple').*

Charles, Old: A highly respected waiter, believed to have made a fortune at it, but found at his death to possess nothing. *Long eminent at the West Country Hotel, and by some considered the Father of the Waitering (Christmas Stories – 'Somebody's Luggage').*

Charley: Pot-boy at the Magpie and Stump. *A shambling pot-boy, with a red head (Pickwick).*

Charley: Narrator of the story. Supposing himself jilted by Angela Leath, he sets off for America, is snowed-up at the Holly-Tree Inn in Yorkshire, and discovers in time that his love is true to him, after all. *I am a bashful man. Nobody would suppose it, nobody ever does suppose it, nobody ever did suppose it, but I am naturally a bashful man (Christmas Stories – 'Holly-Tree').*

Charley: Chatham marine-store dealer to whom David offers his jacket for half-a-crown during his tramp from London to Dover. *'Oh, my lungs and liver,' cried the old man, 'no! Oh, my eyes, no! Oh, my limbs, no! Eighteenpence. Goroo!' (Copperfield).*

Charley: See **Neckett, Charlotte** (*Bleak House*).

Charlotte: Schoolfellow of Miss Wade who makes her jealously infatuated with her. *I loved that stupid mite in a passionate way that she could no more deserve, than I can remember without feeling ashamed of, though I was but a child. She had what they called an amiable temper, an affectionate temper. She could distribute, and did distribute, pretty looks and smiles to every one among them. I believe there was not a soul in the place, except myself, who knew that she did it purposely to wound and gall me! (Dorrit).*

Charlotte: One of the two daughters of John, the narrator. *Her husband run away from her in the basest manner, and she and her three children live with us (Reprinted – 'Poor Man's Tale of a Patent').*

Charlotte: Sowerberry's maidservant, later, as 'Mrs. Bolter', Noah Claypole's mistress and associate in crime. *A slatternly girl, in shoes down at heel, and blue worsted stockings very much out of repair (Twist).*

Charlotte: Edward's wife and mother of James and Charlotte. *She now lets down her back hair, and proceeds to brush it; preserving at the same time an air of conscious rectitude and suffering virtue, which is intended to exasperate the gentleman – and does so (Young Couples – 'Contradictory Couple').*

Charlotte, Miss: See **James** and **Charlotte** (*Young Couples* – 'Contradictory Couple').

Cheeryble, Charles: First of the twin brothers to meet Nicholas Nickleby, whose benefactors they become. Self-made merchants, they are models of benevolence, notably to the Nicklebys, Madeline Bray, and their nephew Frank. *A sturdy old fellow in a broad-skirted blue coat, made pretty large, to fit easily, and with no particular waist; his bulky legs clothed in drab breeches and high gaiters, and his head protected by a low-crowned broad-brimmed white hat, such as a wealthy grazier might wear. He wore his coat buttoned; and his dimpled double-chin rested in the folds of a white neckerchief – not one of your stiff-starched apoplectic cravats, but a good, easy, old-*

fashioned white neckcloth that a man might go to bed in and be none the worse for. But what principally attracted the attention of Nicholas, was the old gentleman's eye, – never was such a clear, twinkling, honest, merry, happy eye, as that. And there he stood, looking a little upward, with one hand thrust into the breast of his coat, and the other playing with his old-fashioned gold watch-chain; his head thrown a little on one side, and his hat a little more on one side than his head (but that was evidently accident; not his ordinary way of wearing it), with such a pleasant smile playing about his mouth, and such a comical expression of mingled slyness, simplicity, kind-heartedness, and good-humour, lighting up his jolly old face, that Nicholas would have been content to have stood there, and looked at him until evening, and to have forgotten, meanwhile, that there was such a thing as a soured mind or a crabbed countenance to be met with in the whole wide world (Nickleby).

Cheeryble, Edwin: Twin brother of Charles. *Something stouter than his brother; this, and a slight additional shade of clumsiness in his gait and stature, formed the only perceptible difference between them (Nickleby).*

Cheeryble, Frank: Nephew of Charles and Edwin. Marries Kate Nickleby and becomes a partner, with Nicholas, in the brothers' firm. *A sprightly, good-humoured, pleasant fellow, with much both in his countenance and disposition that reminded Nicholas very strongly of the kind-hearted brothers. His manner was as unaffected as theirs, and his demeanour full of that heartiness which, to most people who have anything generous in their composition, is peculiarly prepossessing. Add to this, that he was good-looking and intelligent, had a plentiful share of vivacity, was extremely cheerful (Nickleby).*

Cheeseman, Old: Pupil, then second Latin master, at the school, where he is always the butt of the boys. He marries his only friend there, Jane Pitts, a matron. *Old Cheeseman used to be called by the names of all sorts of cheeses – Double Glo'sterman. Family Cheshireman, Dutchman, North Wiltshireman, and all that. But he never minded it. And I don't mean to say he was old in point of years – because he wasn't – only he was called from the first, Old Cheeseman (Christmas Stories – 'Schoolboy's Story').*

Cheggs, Miss: Cheggs's sister *(Curiosity Shop).*

Cheggs, Alick: The market gardener who wins the hand of Sophy Wackles from Dick Swiveller *(Curiosity Shop).*

'Cherub, The': See **Wilfer, Reginald** *(Mutual Friend).*

Chester, Edward: Son of Sir John Chester, by whom he is disowned for persisting in courting Emma Haredale, whom he later saves from Gashford and marries. *A young man of about eight-and-twenty, rather above the middle height, and though of a somewhat slight figure, gracefully and strongly made. He wore his own dark hair, and was accoutred in a riding-dress, which together with his large boots (re-*

sembling in shape and fashion those worn by our Life Guardsmen at the present day), showed indisputable traces of the bad condition of the roads. But travel-stained though he was, he was well and even richly attired, and without being over-dressed looked a gallant gentleman (Rudge).

Chester, Sir John: A suave but ruthless gentleman, father of Edward, whose marriage to Emma Haredale, daughter of his lifelong enemy, he tries unsuccessfully to thwart. Natural father of Hugh, the Maypole ostler. He is killed in a duel by Geoffrey Haredale. *He was a staid, grave, placid gentleman, something past the prime of life, yet upright in his carriage, for all that, and slim as a greyhound. He was well-mounted upon a sturdy chestnut cob, and had the graceful seat of an experienced horseman; while his riding gear, though free from such fopperies as were then in vogue, was handsome and well chosen. He wore a riding-coat of a somewhat brighter green than might have been expected to suit the taste of a gentleman of his years, with a short, black velvet cape, and laced pocket-holes and cuffs, all of a jaunty fashion; his linen, too, was of the finest kind, worked in a rich pattern at the wrists and throat, and scrupulously white (Rudge).*

Chestle: Kentish hop-grower who marries the eldest Miss Larkins *(Copperfield).*

Chib: Of Tucket's Terrace, father of the Vestry. *A remarkably hale old gentleman of eighty-two (Reprinted – 'Our Vestry').*

Chick, John: Dombey's brother-in-law. *A stout bald gentleman, with a very large face, and his hands continually in his pockets, and who had a tendency in his nature to whistle and hum tunes, which, sensible of the indecorum of such sounds in a house of grief, he was at some pains to repress at present. 'Don't you over-exert yourself, Loo,' said Mr. Chick, 'or you'll be laid up with spasms, I see. Right tol loor rul! Bless my soul, I forgot! We're here one day and gone the next!' (Dombey).*

Chick, Mrs. John (Louisa): Wife of John Chick, sister to Dombey, and friend of Miss Tox until she becomes aware that the latter aspires to be the second Mrs. Dombey. *A lady rather past the middle age than otherwise, but dressed in a very juvenile manner, particularly as to the tightness of her bodice (Dombey).*

Chickenstalker, Mrs. Anne: General shopkeeper. She marries Tugby. *A good-humoured comely woman of some fifty years of age, or thereabouts (Christmas Books – 'Chimes').*

Chicksey, Veneering and Stobbles: Firm of drug dealers near Mincing Lane, City of London, where Reginald Wilfer is clerk and Hamilton Veneering is sole surviving partner. *Chicksey and Stobbles, his former masters, had both become absorbed in Veneering, once their traveller or commission agent: who had signalised his accession to supreme power by bringing into the business a quantity of plate-glass window and French-polished mahogany partition, and a gleaming and enormous door-plate (Mutual Friend).*

Chickweed, Conkey: Landlord of a public-house near Battle Bridge who, according to Blathers, faked the theft of all his money in order to raise more from sympathetic public benefits and subscriptions *(Twist)*.

Chiggle: Renowned American sculptor of Elijah Pogram. *'Our own immortal Chiggle, sir, is said to have observed, when he made the celebrated Pogram statter in marble, which rose so much con-test and preju-dice in Europe, that the brow was more than mortal' (Chuzzlewit)*.

Childers, jun. ('The Little Wonder of Scholastic Equitation'): Son of E. W. B. Childers and Josephine Sleary *(Hard Times)*.

Childers, E. W. B.: Equestrian with Sleary's Circus who helps Tom Gradgrind escape arrest and leave the country. Married to Josephine Sleary. *His face, close-shaven, thin, and sallow, was shaded by a great quantity of dark hair, brushed into a roll all round his head, and parted up the centre. His legs were very robust, but shorter than legs of good proportion should have been. His chest and back were as much too broad, as his legs were too short. He was dressed in a Newmarket coat and tight-fitting trousers; wore a shawl round his neck; smelt of lamp-oil, straw, orange-peel, horses' provender, and sawdust; and looked a most remarkable sort of Centaur, compounded of the stable and the play-house. Where the one began, and the other ended, nobody could have told with any precision. This gentleman was mentioned in the bills of the day as Mr. E. W. B. Childers, so justly celebrated for his daring vaulting act as the Wild Huntsman of the North American Prairies (Hard Times)*.

Chill, Uncle: Uncle of Michael, the Poor Relation. *Avarice was, unhappily, my uncle Chill's master-vice. Though he was rich, he pinched, and scraped, and clutched, and lived miserably (Christmas Stories –'Poor Relation')*.

Chillip, Dr.: Mrs. Copperfield's medical attendant at David's birth. *He was the meekest of his sex, the mildest of little men. He sidled in and out of a room, to take up the less space. He walked as softly as the Ghost in Hamlet, and more slowly. He carried his head on one side, partly in modest depreciation of himself, partly in modest propitiation of everybody else. It is nothing to say that he hadn't a word to throw at a dog. He couldn't have thrown a word at a mad dog. He might have offered him one gently, or half a one, or a fragment of one; for he spoke as slowly as he walked; but he wouldn't have been rude to him, and he couldn't have been quick with him, for any earthly consideration (Copperfield)*.

Chinaman, Jack: Princess Puffer's rival opium-den keeper. *'Nobody but me (and Jack Chinaman t'other side the court; but he can't do it as well as me) has the true secret of mixing it' (Drood)*.

Chips: Family of shipyard carpenters involved in a bargain with the Devil in a story told to the Uncommercial Traveller in his childhood by his nurse Mercy. *Chips the father had sold himself to the Devil for an iron pot and a bushel of tenpenny nails and half a ton of copper and a rat that could speak; and Chips the grandfather had sold himself to the Devil for an iron pot and a bushel of tenpenny nails and half a ton of copper and a rat that could speak; and Chips the great-grandfather had disposed of himself in the same direction on the same terms; and the bargain had run in the family for a long, long time. So, one day, when young Chips was at work in the Dock Slip all alone, down in the dark hold of an old Seventy-four that was haled up for repairs, the Devil presented himself (Uncommercial – 'Nurse's Stories')*.

Chirrup, Mr. and **Mrs.:** The nice little couple. *Mr. Chirrup has the smartness, and something of the brisk, quick manner of a small bird. Mrs. Chirrup is the prettiest of all little women, and has the prettiest little figure conceivable. She has the neatest little foot, and the softest little voice, and the pleasantest little smile, and the tidiest little curls, and the brightest little eyes, and the quietest little manner, and is, in short, altogether one of the most engaging of all little women, dead or alive. . . . Nobody knows all this better than Mr. Chirrup, though he rather takes on that he don't. Accordingly he is very proud of his better-half, and evidently considers himself as all other people consider him, rather fortunate in having her to wife (Young Couples – 'Nice Little Couple')*.

Chitling, Tom: Member of Fagin's gang, recently out of prison. *He had small twinkling eyes, and a pock-marked face; wore a fur cap, a dark corduroy jacket, greasy fustian trousers, and an apron. His wardrobe was, in truth, rather out of repair; but he excused himself to the company by stating that his 'time' was only out an hour before; and that, in consequence of having worn the regimentals for six weeks past, he had not been able to bestow any affection on his private clothes (Twist)*.

Chivery, John: Kindly but laconic non-resident turnkey at the Marshalsea. Father of Young John. *He had imbibed a professional habit of locking everything up. He locked himself up as carefully as he locked up the Marshalsea debtors. Even his custom of bolting his meals may have been a part of an uniform whole; but there is no question, that, as to all other purposes, he kept his mouth as he kept the Marshalsea door. He never opened it without occasion. When it was necessary to let anything out, he opened it a little way, held it open just as long as sufficed for the purpose, and locked it again (Dorrit)*.

Chivery, Mrs. John: Chivery's wife and mother of Young John. Keeper of a tobacco-shop near the Marshalsea. *A comfortable looking woman, much respected about Horsemonger Lane for her feelings and her conversation (Dorrit)*.

Chivery, Young John: John Chivery's son, in love with Amy Dorrit and Pancks's associate in restoring her family's fortunes. *Small of stature, with rather weak legs and very weak light hair. One of his eyes (perhaps the eye that used to peep through the key-hole) was also weak, and looked larger than the other, as if it couldn't collect itself. Young John was gentle* *likewise. But he was great of soul. Poetical, expansive, faithful (Dorrit).*

Choke, General Cyrus: American Militia officer, member of the Watertoast Association of United Sympathisers and of the Eden Land Corporation, in which he advises Martin Chuzzlewit to invest. *One very lank gentleman, in a loose limp white cravat, a long white waistcoat, and a black great-coat, who seemed to be in authority (Chuzzlewit).*

Chollop, Major Hannibal: Caller upon Martin Chuzzlewit at Eden. *A lean person in a blue frock and a straw hat, with a short black pipe in his mouth, and a great hickory stick, studded all over with knots, in his hand; who smoking and chewing as he came along, and spitting frequently, recorded his progress by a train of decomposed tobacco on the ground (Chuzzlewit).*

Chopper, Great-uncle: William Tinkling's great-uncle, present at the christening of his baby brother. *I said that ma had said afterwards (and so she had), that Great-uncle Chopper's gift was a shabby one ... electrotyped, second-hand, and below his income ('Holiday Romance').*

Chopper, Mrs.: Mrs. Merrywinkle's mother, who fosters her hypochondria. *A mysterious old lady who lurks behind a pair of spectacles, and is afflicted with a chronic disease, respecting which she has taken a vast deal of medical advice, and referred to a vast number of medical books, without meeting any definition of symptoms that at all suits her, or enables her to say, 'That's my complaint' (Young Couples – 'Couple who Coddle Themselves').*

Chops (real name **Stakes,** but also known as **Major Tpschoffki, of the Imperial Bulgraderian Brigade,** contracted to **Chopski):** Dwarf in Magsman's Amusements who wins a fortune and goes into society with disastrous results. *He was an un-common small man, he really was. Certainly not so small as he was made out to be, but where is your Dwarf as is? He was a most uncommon small man, with a most uncommon large Ed. ... The kindest little man as never growed! Spirited, but not proud (Christmas Stories – 'Going into Society').*

'Chowley': See **MacStinger, Charles** *(Dombey).*

Chowser, Colonel: A dinner guest of Ralph Nickleby *(Nickleby).*

Christiana: Former sweetheart and imagined wife of Michael, the Poor Relation. *She was very beautiful, and very winning in all respects. ... I never had loved any one but Christiana, and she had been all the world, and O far more than all the world, to me, from our childhood! (Christmas Stories – 'Poor Relation').*

Christina, Donna: One of Jingle's boasted thousands of conquests in Spain. Daughter of Don Bolaro Fizzgig (q.v.). *'Splendid creature – loved me to distraction – jealous father – high-souled daughter – handsome Englishman – Donna Christina in despair – prussic acid – stomach pump in my portmanteau – operation performed – old Bolaro in ecstasies – consent to our*

union – join hands and floods of tears – romantic story – very.' 'Is the lady in England now, sir?' inquired Mr. Tupman, on whom the description of her charms had produced a powerful impression. 'Dead, sir,' said the stranger, applying to his right eye the brief remnant of a very old cambric handkerchief. 'Never recovered the stomach pump – undermined constitution – fell a victim' (Pickwick).

Christopher: Head-waiter at a London hotel coffee-house, 'author' and narrator of this collection of stories. *Having come of a family of Waiters, and owning at the present time five brothers who are all Waiters, and likewise an only sister who is a Waitress (Christmas Stories – 'Somebody's Luggage').*

Chuckster: Witherden's clerk and friend of Swiveller. *Being a gentleman of cultivated taste and refined spirit, was one of that Lodge of Glorious Apollos whereof Mr. Swiveller was perpetual Grand (Curiosity Shop).*

Chuffey: Clerk to Anthony Chuzzlewit and Son. *A little blear-eyed, weazen-faced, ancient man came creeping out. He was of a remote fashion, and dusty, like the rest of the furniture; he was dressed in a decayed suit of black; with breeches garnished at the knees with rusty wisps of ribbon, the very paupers of shoe-strings; on the lower portion of his spindle legs were dingy worsted stockings of the same colour. He looked as if he had been put away and forgotten half-a-century before, and somebody had just found him in a lumber-closet (Chuzzlewit).*

Chuzzlewit, Anthony: Old Martin's brother and father of Jonas. A Manchester warehouseman. *The face of the old man so sharpened by the wariness and cunning of his life, that it seemed to cut him a passage through the crowded room (Chuzzlewit).*

Chuzzlewit, Diggory: A Chuzzlewit ancestor. *In the habit of perpetually dining with Duke Humphrey (i.e. going without his lunch) (Chuzzlewit).*

Chuzzlewit, George: A gay bachelor cousin of old Martin. *Claimed to be young but had been younger, and was inclined to corpulency, and rather overfed himself: to that extent, indeed, that his eyes were strained in their sockets, as if with constant surprise (Chuzzlewit).*

Chuzzlewit, Jonas: Cruel and scheming son of Anthony, whose death he causes, and nephew of old Martin. He marries Mercy Pecksniff and ill-treats her, murders Tigg, and poisons himself after arrest. *The education of Mr. Jonas had been conducted from his cradle on the strictest principles of the main chance. The very first word he learnt to spell was 'gain', and the second (when he got into two syllables), 'money'. ... From his early habits of considering everything as a question of property, he had gradually come to look, with impatience, on his parent as a certain amount of personal estate, which had no right whatever to be going at large, but ought to be secured in that particular description of iron safe which is commonly called a coffin, and banked in the grave (Chuzzlewit).*

Chuzzlewit, Martin, jun.: The central character, grandson of old Martin, who has brought him up expecting to become his heir, but turns him out for loving Mary Graham. After experiencing hardships – which temper his unlikeable nature – in London and America, in company with Mark Tapley, Martin returns to favour and marries Mary. *He was young – one-and-twenty, perhaps – and handsome; with a keen dark eye, and a quickness of look and manner (Chuzzlewit).*

Chuzzlewit, Martin, sen.: The rich old family head, brother of Anthony, cousin of George and grandfather of Martin jun. He manipulates those with designs upon his money, breaks Pecksniff, and eventually gives Martin jun. the hand of Mary Graham, old Martin's adopted daughter and constant companion. *He was, beyond all question, very ill, and suffered exceedingly; not the less, perhaps, because he was a strong and vigorous old man, with a will of iron, and a voice of brass (Chuzzlewit).*

Chuzzlewit, Mrs. Ned, and the **Misses:** Widow of a brother of old Martin. *Being almost supernaturally disagreeable, and having a dreary face and a bony figure and a masculine voice, was, in right of these qualities, what is commonly called a strong-minded woman. . . . Beside her sat her spinster daughters, three in number, and of gentlemanly deportment, who had so mortified themselves with tight stays, that their tempers were reduced to something less than their waists, and sharp lacing was expressed in their very noses (Chuzzlewit).*

Chuzzlewit, Toby: A Chuzzlewit ancestor whose deathbed reply that his father was 'The Lord No Zoo' is regarded as evidence in the family's claims to noble connections *(Chuzzlewit).*

Cicero: A negro truckman, formerly a slave, encountered by Mark Tapley and Martin Chuzzlewit in New York. *'Ah!' said Mark in the same tone. 'Nothing else. A slave. Why, when that there man was young – don't look at him, while I'm a telling it – he was shot in the leg; gashed in the arm; scored in his live limbs, like crimped fish; beaten out of shape; had his neck galled with an iron collar, and wore iron rings upon his wrists and ankles. The marks are on him to this day. When I was having my dinner just now, he stripped off his coat, and took away my appetite' (Chuzzlewit).*

Clara: The English bride, mistress of Carolina, haunted by Dellombra. *Brooding in a manner very strange; in a frightened manner; in an unhappy manner; with a cloudy, uncertain alarm upon her ('At Dusk').*

Clare, Ada: Ward in Chancery under John Jarndyce's guardianship, and close friend to Esther Summerson. Left a pregnant widow by the death of her cousin, Richard Carstone, after their secret marriage, she returns to Jarndyce's care. *I saw in the young lady, with the fire shining upon her, such a beautiful girl! With such rich golden hair, such soft blue eyes, and such a bright, innocent, trusting face! (Bleak House).*

Clark: A clerk at Dombey and Son's. *A stout man stood whistling, with his pen behind his ear, and his hands in his pockets, as if the day's work were nearly done (Dombey).*

Clark, Mrs.: Employer to whom the agency sends Madeline Bray. *'She'll have a nice life of it, if she goes there,' observed the fat lady (Nickleby).*

Clark, Betsy: Servant-girl in the Covent Garden district. *The servant of all work, who, under the plea of sleeping very soundly, has utterly disregarded 'Missis'' ringing for half an hour previously . . . awakes all of a sudden, with well-feigned astonishment, and goes downstairs very sulkily, wishing, while she strikes a light, that the principle of spontaneous combustion would extend itself to coals and kitchen range (Boz – 'The Streets – Morning').*

Clarke, Mrs. Susan: Widowed landlady of the Marquis of Granby, Dorking, whom Tony Weller marries. See **Weller, Mrs. Tony, sen.** *(Pickwick).*

Clarkson: Counsel for Shepherdson and other criminals arrested by Sergeant Mith *(Reprinted – 'Detective Police').*

Clarriker: Shipping broker in whose firm Pip secretly buys an interest for Herbert Pocket. He himself obtains work in the firm after the loss of his fortunes. *A worthy young merchant or shipping-broker, not long established in business, who wanted intelligent help, and who wanted capital, and who in due course of time and receipt would want a partner (Expectations).*

Clatter: One of many doctors consulted by Our Bore. *The moment Clatter saw our bore, he said, 'Accumulation of fat about the heart!' (Reprinted – 'Our Bore').*

Claypole, Noah: Sowerberry's apprentice, later a criminal under the name **Morris Bolter.** It is after a fight with him that Oliver Twist runs away and falls into criminal company. Claypole, too, enters Fagin's service, spies on Nancy, and brings about her murder. *It is difficult for a large-headed, small-eyed youth, of lumbering make and heavy countenance, to look dignified under any circumstances; but it is more especially so, when superadded to these attractions are a red nose and yellow smalls. . . . Noah was a charity-boy, but not a workhouse orphan. No chance-child was he, for he could trace his genealogy all the way back to his parents, who lived hard by; his mother being a washerwoman, and his father a drunken soldier (Twist).*

Cleaver ('Mr. Dolls'): Fanny Cleaver's drunken father, known as 'Mr. Dolls' after the trade by which she supports him. *'Like his own father, a weak wretched trembling creature, falling to pieces, never sober. But a good workman too, at the work he does' (Mutual Friend).*

Cleaver, Fanny ('Jenny Wren'): A crippled child, who supports her drunken father by making dolls' dresses. She becomes Lizzie Hexam's faithful friend. *A child – a dwarf – a girl – a something. . . . The queer little figure, and the queer but not ugly little face, with its bright grey eyes, were so sharp, that the sharpness of* the manner seemed unavoidable. *As if, being turned out of that mould, it must be sharp (Mutual Friend).*

Clennam, Mrs.: Adoptive mother of Arthur Clennam, the son of her husband and his mistress. She conducts all her affairs from the confinement of her room. *On a black bier-like sofa in this hollow, propped up behind with one great angular black bolster, like the block at a state execution in the good old times, sat his mother in a widow's dress. She and his father had been at variance from his earliest remembrance. To sit speechless himself in the midst of rigid silence, glancing in dread from the one averted face to the other, had been the peacefullest occupation of his childhood. She gave him one glassy kiss, and four stiff fingers muffled in worsted (Dorrit).*

Clennam, Arthur: Mrs. Clennam's adopted son. Becoming Doyce's partner, he speculates with Merdle, and is bankrupted and imprisoned in the Marshalsea, where he is tended by Amy Dorrit, whom he subsequently marries. *A grave dark man of forty. // 'I am the son, Mr. Meagles, of a hard father and mother. I am the only child of parents who weighed, measured, and priced everything; for whom what could not be weighed, measured, and priced, had no existence. Strict people as the phrase is, professors of a stern religion, their very religion was a gloomy sacrifice of tastes and sympathies that were never their own, offered up as a part of a bargain for the security of their possessions. Austere faces, inexorable discipline, penance in this world and terror in the next – nothing graceful or gentle anywhere, and the void in my cowed heart everywhere – this was my childhood, if I may so misuse the word as to apply it to such a beginning of life' (Dorrit).*

Clennam, Gilbert: Uncle of Mrs. Clennam's late husband. He leaves Frederick Dorrit or his niece £1,000 in his own will. Mrs. Clennam suppresses the information and Rigaud attempts to blackmail her in consequence *(Dorrit)*.

'Cleopatra': See **Skewton, The Hon. Mrs.** *(Dombey)*.

Clergyman, The: Clergyman of a village visited by Little Nell and her grandfather. *A simple-hearted old gentleman, of a shrinking, subdued spirit, accustomed to retirement, and very little acquainted with the world (Curiosity Shop).*

Clergyman, The: Guest at Dingley Dell who sings 'The Ivy Green' and narrates 'The Convict's Return'. *A bald-headed old gentleman, with a good-humoured benevolent face. His* **Wife**, *also a guest, was a stout blooming old lady, who looked as if she were well skilled, not only in the art and mystery of manufacturing home-made cordials greatly to other people's satisfaction, but of tasting them occasionally very much to her own (Pickwick).*

Cleverly, William and **Susannah:** Brother and sister, Mormon recruits aboard the emigrant ship *Amazon (Uncommercial – 'Bound for the Great Salt Lake').*

Click: Fellow lodger and friend of Tom. *In the gas-fitting way of life. He is very good company,*

having worked at the theatres, and, indeed, he has a theatrical turn himself, and wishes to be brought out in the character of Othello; but whether on account of his regular work always blacking his face and hands more or less, I cannot say (Christmas Stories – 'Somebody's Luggage').*

Click: A villain encountered by Inspector Field's party in Saint Giles's *(Reprinted – 'On Duty with Inspector Field').*

Clickett ('The Orfling'): The Micawbers' servant. *A dark-complexioned young woman, with a habit of snorting, who was servant to the family, and informed me, before half an hour had expired, that she was 'a Orfling', and came from St. Luke's workhouse, in the neighbourhood (Copperfield).*

Clickit, Mr. and **Mrs.:** Subjects of the Bobtail Widgers' praise. *The plausible lady immediately launches out in their praise. She quite loves the Clickits. Were there ever such true-hearted, hospitable, excellent people – such a gentle, interesting little woman as Mrs. Clickit, or such a frank, unaffected creature as Mr. Clickit? (Young Couples – 'Plausible Couple').*

Clip: A hairdresser, one of the admiring audience of the gentleman connected with the press at the Green Dragon, Westminster Bridge *(Mudfog – 'Mr. Robert Bolton').*

Clissold, Lawrence: Clerk with Dringworth Bros. who stole £500 and laid the blame upon Tregarthen, a crime uncovered by the message from the sea *(Christmas Stories – 'Message from the Sea').*

Clive: Official at the Circumlocution Office, to whom Wobbler refers Arthur Clennam *(Dorrit)*.

Clocker: A grocer referred to in a story told to the narrator in a Kent coastal inn *(Reprinted – 'Out of the Season').*

Clubber, Sir Thomas, Lady and the **Misses:** Commissioner of Chatham Dockyard and his family, present at the charity ball at the Bull, Rochester. *A great sensation was created throughout the room by the entrance of a tall gentleman in a blue coat and bright buttons, a large lady in blue satin, and two young ladies, on a similar scale, in fashionably-made dresses of the same hue (Pickwick).*

Cluppins, Mrs. Elizabeth: Mrs. Bardell's neighbour and friend, who testifies on her behalf at the trial. *A little brisk, busy-looking woman (Pickwick).*

Cly, Roger: Formerly servant to Charles Darnay, whom he betrays. Associate of Solomon Pross, and spy, who shams death and is given a mock burial to escape the revolutionary mob. *The virtuous servant, Roger Cly. . . . He had never been suspected of stealing a silver tea-pot; he had been maligned respecting a mustard-pot, but it turned out to be only a plated one (Two Cities).*

Coavinses: Skimpole refers to Neckett (q.v.) as Coavinses *(Bleak House).*

Cobb, Tom: General chandler and post-office keeper at Chigwell and *habitué* of the Maypole. *Beyond all question the dullest dog of the party (Rudge).*

Cobbey: Pupil at Dotheboys Hall. *'Oh!' said Squeers: 'Cobbey's grandmother is dead, and his uncle John has took to drinking, which is all the news his sister sends, except eighteenpence, which will just pay for that broken square of glass' (Nickleby).*

Cobbler, The: Prisoner in the Fleet for twelve years who rents Sam Weller a bed in his room. *He was a sallow man – all cobblers are; and had a strong bristly beard – all cobblers have. His face was a queer, good-tempered, crooked-featured piece of workmanship, ornamented with a couple of eyes that must have worn a very joyous expression at one time, for they sparkled yet. The man was sixty, by years, and Heaven knows how old by imprisonment, so that his having any look approaching to mirth or contentment, was singular enough. He was a little man, and, being half doubled up as he lay in bed, he looked about as long as he ought to have been without his legs. He had a great red pipe in his mouth, and was smoking, and staring at the rushlight, in a state of enviable placidity (Pickwick).*

Cobbs: Boots at the Holly-Tree Inn, Yorkshire. Former under-gardener to Walmers. *Where had he been in his time? he repeated, when I asked him the question. Lord, he had been everywhere! And what had he been? Bless you, he had been everything you could mention a'most! (Christmas Stories – 'Holly-Tree').*

Cobby: Gigantic tramp observed by the Uncommercial Traveller eating meat-pie in a hedgerow with a lady. *It was on an evening in August, that I chanced upon this ravishing spectacle, and I noticed that, whereas the Giant reclined half concealed beneath the overhanging boughs and seemed indifferent to Nature, the white hair of the gracious Lady streamed free in the breath of the evening, and her pink eyes found pleasure in the landscape (Uncommercial – 'Tramps').*

Cocker, Indignation: A disgruntled patron of the Temeraire, Namelesston. *A severe diner, lately finished, perusing his bill fiercely through his eye-glass (Uncommercial – 'A Little Dinner in an Hour').*

Codger, Miss: An American literary celebrity at Pogram's levee at the National Hotel. *'To be presented to a Pogram,' said Miss Codger, 'by a Hominy, indeed, a thrilling moment is it in its impressiveness on what we call our feelings. But why we call them so, or why impressed they are, or if impressed they are at all, or if at all we are, or if there really is, oh gasping one! a Pogram or a Hominy, or any active principle to which we give those titles, is a topic, Spirit searching, light abandoned, much too vast to enter on, at this unlooked-for crisis' (Chuzzlewit).*

Codlin, Thomas: Partner of Short (alias Harris) in the Punch-and-Judy show which Little Nell and her grandfather accompany briefly. *He who took the money – had rather a careful and cautious look, which was perhaps inseparable from his occupation (Curiosity Shop).*

Coiler, Mrs.: The Matthew Pockets' neighbour. *A widow lady of that highly sympathetic nature that she agreed with everybody, blessed everybody, and shed smiles and tears on everybody, according to circumstances (Expectations).*

Coleshaw, Miss: Passenger in the Golden Mary. *A sedate young woman in black, some five years older (about thirty as I should say), who was going out to join a brother (Christmas Stories – 'Golden Mary').*

Compact Enchantress, The: A French actress sharing a railway compartment with the narrator. *Twenty minutes' pause, by Folkestone clock, for looking at Enchantress while she eats a sandwich (Reprinted – 'A Flight').*

Compeyson: Miss Havisham's absconded fiancé. A criminal who drew Magwitch into crime. He informs about the attempt by Pip and Herbert Pocket to get Magwitch out of the country, and takes part in his arrest, but is drowned by Magwitch in the struggle. *'He set up fur a gentleman, this Compeyson, and he'd been to a public boarding-school and had learning. He was a smooth one to talk, and was a dab at the ways of gentlefolks. He was good-looking, too. . . . He'd no more heart than an iron file, he was as cold as death, and he had the head of the Devil afore mentioned' (Expectations).*

Compeyson, Mrs. (Sally): Compeyson's wife. *'Which Compeyson kicked mostly' (Expectations).*

Conway, General: A political opponent of Lord George Gordon. *(Rudge).*

Cooper, Augustus: Young man in the oil and colour business who takes dancing lessons at Billsmethi's academy, is pursued by Miss Billsmethi and finally sued by her for breach of promise, having to buy himself off. *With a little money, a little business, and a little mother, who, having managed her husband and his business in his lifetime, took to managing her son and his business after his decease; and so, somehow or other, he had been cooped up in the little back-parlour behind the shop of week-days, and in a little deal box without a lid (called by courtesy a pew) at Bethel Chapel, on Sundays, and had seen no more of the world than if he had been an infant all his days (Boz – 'Dancing Academy').*

Copperfield, Mrs. Clara: David's young mother. Widowed a year after his birth, she marries Murdstone but is separated from David and ill-used by her husband and his sister, and dies of a broken heart. *When my mother is out of breath and rests herself in an elbow-chair, I watch her winding her bright curls round her fingers, and straightening her waist, and nobody knows better than I do that she likes to look so well, and is proud of being so pretty (Copperfield).*

Copperfield, David: The central figure and narrator of the story, the most nearly autobiographical of Dickens's novels. *Whether I shall turn out to be the hero of my own life, or whether that station will be held by anybody else, these pages must show . . . . It was declared by the nurse, and by some sage women in the neighbourhood who had taken a lively interest in*

60

me several months before there was any possibility of our becoming personally acquainted, first, that I was destined to be unlucky in life; and secondly, that I was privileged to see ghosts and spirits; both these gifts inevitably attaching, as they believed, to all unlucky infants of either gender, born towards the small hours on a Friday night (Copperfield).

Copperfield, Mrs. David the First: See **Spenlow, Dora** *(Copperfield)*.

Copperfield, Mrs. David the Second: See **Wickfield, Agnes** *(Copperfield)*.

Coppernose: Exhibitor in the display of models and mechanical science at the second meeting of the Mudfog Association. He proposes creating an enclosed area, ten miles by four, for the exclusive use of young noblemen. *This delightful retreat would be fitted up with most commodious and extensive stables, for the convenience of such of the nobility and gentry as had a taste for ostlering, and with houses of entertainment furnished in the most expensive and handsome style. It would be further provided with whole streets of door-knockers and bell-handles of extra size, so constructed that they could be easily wrenched off at night, and regularly screwed on again, by attendants provided for the purpose, every day. There would also be gas lamps of real glass, which could be broken at a comparatively small expense per dozen, and a broad and handsome pavement for gentlemen to drive their cabriolets upon when they were humorously disposed – for the full enjoyment of which feat live pedestrians would be procured from the workhouse at a very small charge per head (Mudfog).*

Cornberry: Former fiancé of Julia Manners. *'Who was to have married you, and didn't, because he died first; and who left you his property unencumbered with the addition of himself,' suggested the mayor (Boz – 'Great Winglebury Duel').*

Corney, Mrs.: Matron of the workhouse where Oliver Twist was born, later married to Bumble and dismissed with him. *'It's no part of my duty to see all the old women in the house die, and I won't – that's more. Mind that, you impudent old harridans' (Twist).*

'Countess, The': See **Grimwood, Eliza** *(Reprinted – 'Three "Detective" Anecdotes').*

Cower: The Tuggses' solicitor whose clerk brings them the news that they are rich *(Boz – 'Tuggses at Ramsgate').*

Crackit, Toby ('Flash Toby'): Housebreaker, partner of Bill Sikes, who is hunted down to Crackit's house on Jacob's Island, Bermondsey, after murdering Nancy. *He was dressed in a smartly-cut snuff-coloured coat, with large brass buttons; an orange neckerchief; a coarse, staring shawl-pattern waistcoat; and drab breeches. Mr. Crackit (for he it was) had no very great quantity of hair, either upon his head or face; but what he had, was of a reddish dye, and tortured into long corkscrew curls, through which he occasionally thrust some very dirty fingers, ornamented with large common rings (Twist).*

Craddock, Mrs.: Pickwick's landlady at Royal Crescent, Bath *(Pickwick).*

Craggs, Thomas: Partner in Snitchey and Craggs, Dr. Jeddler's lawyers. *A cold, hard, dry man, dressed in grey and white, like a flint; with small twinkles in his eyes, as if something struck sparks out of them (Christmas Books – 'Battle of Life').*

Craggs, Mrs. Thomas: Craggs's wife and friend of Mrs. Snitchey. *Snitchey and Craggs had each, in private life as in professional existence, a partner of his own. Snitchey and Craggs were the best friends in the world, and had real confidence in one another; but, Mrs. Snitchey, by a dispensation not uncommon in the affairs of life, was on principle suspicious of Mr. Craggs; and Mrs. Craggs was on principle suspicious of Mr. Snitchey (Christmas Books – 'Battle of Life').*

Cratchit, Bob: Scrooge's clerk, father of Tiny Tim, Martha, Belinda and Peter. *His clerk, who in a dismal little cell beyond, a sort of tank, was copying letters. Scrooge had a very small fire, but the clerk's fire was so very much smaller that it looked like one coal. But he couldn't replenish it, for Scrooge kept the coal-box in his own room; and so surely as the clerk came in with the shovel, the master predicted that it would be necessary for them to part. Wherefore the clerk put on his white comforter, and tried to warm himself at the candle; in which effort, not being a man of a strong imagination, he failed (Christmas Books – 'Christmas Carol').*

Cratchit, Mrs. Bob: Bob's wife, mother of Martha, Belinda, Peter, and Tim (q.v.). *Dressed out but poorly in a twice-turned gown, but brave in ribbons, which are cheap and make a goodly show for sixpence (Christmas Books – 'Christmas Carol').*

Cratchit, Tim (Tiny Tim): The Cratchits' youngest son; brother of Martha, Belinda and Peter. Speaker of the celebrated line, 'God bless us every one!' *Alas for Tiny Tim, he bore a little crutch, and had his limbs supported by an iron frame! (Christmas Books – 'Christmas Carol').*

Creakle: Proprietor and headmaster of Salem House school, near Blackheath, attended by David Copperfield and Steerforth. *Mr. Creakle's face was fiery, and his eyes were small, and deep in his head; he had thick veins in his forehead, a little nose, and a large chin. He was bald on the top of his head; and had some thin wet-looking hair that was just turning grey, brushed across each temple, so that the two sides interlaced on his forehead. But the circumstance about him which impressed me most, was, that he had no voice, but spoke in a whisper. . . . I should think there never can have been a man who enjoyed his profession more than Mr. Creakle did. He had a delight in cutting at the boys, which was like the satisfaction of a craving appetite. I am confident that he couldn't resist a chubby boy, especially; that there was a fascination in such a subject, which made him restless in his mind, until he had scored and marked him for the day. I was chubby myself, and ought to know (Copperfield).*

Creakle, Miss: The Creakles' daughter, widely believed by the pupils at Salem House to be in love with

Steerforth. *I didn't think Miss Creakle equal to little Em'ly in point of beauty, and I didn't love her (I didn't dare); but I thought her a young lady of extraordinary attractions, and in point of gentility not to be surpassed. When Steerforth, in white trousers, carried her parasol for her, I felt proud to know him (Copperfield).*

Creakle, Mrs.: Creakle's wife. She breaks the news to David Copperfield of his mother's death. *Thin and quiet. . . . She was very kind to me (Copperfield).*

Crewler, Caroline, Sarah, Louisa, Margaret, and **Lucy:** Daughters of the Revd. and Mrs. Crewler, and sisters to Sophy and four other girls. *They were a perfect nest of roses; they looked so wholesome and fresh. They were all pretty (Copperfield).*

Crewler, The Revd. Horace: A penurious Devonshire curate, father of Sophy and nine other daughters. *'An excellent man, most exemplary in every way' (Copperfield).*

Crewler, Mrs. Horace: Crewler's wife, mother of 'ten, down in Devonshire', including Sophy, Caroline, Sarah, Louisa, Margaret, and Lucy. *'She is a very superior woman, but has lost the use of her limbs. Whatever occurs to harass her, usually settles in her legs' (Copperfield).*

Crewler, Sophy: The Crewlers' fourth daughter, sister to Caroline, Sarah, Louisa, Margaret, Lucy, and four others. She cares for them all and Traddles finds some difficulty in getting consent to marry her, but succeeds. *'It was rather a painful transaction, Copperfield, in my case. You see, Sophy being of so much use in the family, none of them could endure the thought of her ever being married. Indeed, they had quite settled among themselves that she never was to be married, and they called her the old maid' (Copperfield).*

Crimp: See **Crimple, David** *(Chuzzlewit).*

Crimple, David: A pawnbroker's clerk named Crimp, who changes his name upon becoming secretary of the Anglo-Bengalee Disinterested Loan and Life Assurance Company. *A smiling gentleman, of less pretensions and of business looks, whom he addressed as David. Surely not David of the – how shall it be phrased? – the triumvirate of golden balls? (Chuzzlewit).*

Crinkles: Exhibitor in the display of models and mechanical science at the second meeting of the Mudfog Association. *Exhibited a most beautiful and delicate machine, of little larger size than an ordinary snuff-box, manufactured entirely by himself, and composed exclusively of steel, by the aid of which more pockets could be picked in one hour than by the present slow and tedious process in four-and-twenty (Mudfog).*

Cripples: Proprietor of an academy for evening tuition in the building where Frederick and Fanny Dorrit lodge *(Dorrit).*

Cripples, Master: Cripples's son. *A little white-faced boy, with a slice of bread-and-butter, and a battledore (Dorrit).*

Cripps, Tom: Boy employed by Bob Sawyer to advertise the medical practice of Sawyer's, late Nockemorf's, by delivering the wrong medicines, thereby causing patients to send round to, and thus notice, the surgery. *In a sober grey livery and a gold-laced hat, with a small covered basket under his arm (Pickwick).*

Crisparkle, Mrs.: Crisparkle's mother. *What is prettier than an old lady – except a young lady – when her eyes are bright, when her figure is trim and compact, when her face is cheerful and calm, when her dress is as the dress of a china shepherdess: so dainty in its colours, so individually assorted to herself, so neatly moulded on her? Nothing is prettier, thought the good Minor Canon frequently, when taking his seat at table opposite his long-widowed mother. Her thought at such times may be condensed into the two words that oftenest did duty together in all her conversations: 'My Sept!' (Drood).*

Crisparkle, Canon Septimus: Minor Canon at Cloisterham Cathedral. Mentor of Neville Landless. *Mr. Crisparkle, Minor Canon, fair and rosy, and perpetually pitching himself head-foremost into all the deep running water in the surrounding country; Mr. Crisparkle, Minor Canon, early riser, musical, classical, cheerful, kind, good-natured, social, contented, and boy-like; Mr. Crisparkle, Minor Canon and good man, lately 'Coach' upon the chief Pagan high roads, but since promoted by a patron (grateful for a well-taught son) to his present Christian beat (Drood).*

Crofts: Harvey's barber *(Young Couples – 'Old Couple').*

Crookey: Attendant at Namby's lock-up. *In dress and general appearance looked something between a bankrupt grazier, and a drover in a state of insolvency (Pickwick).*

Cropley, Miss: Friend of Mrs. Nickleby at Exeter, whose brother had a place at court. *'It was the chief part of his duty to wear silk stockings, and a bag wig like a black watch-pocket' (Nickleby).*

Crowl: Fellow lodger of Newman Noggs. *A hard-featured square-faced man, elderly and shabby (Nickleby).*

Crummles, Ninetta ('The Infant Phenomenon'): The Crummleses' daughter, sister to Percy and Charles. *The infant phenomenon, though of short stature, had a comparatively aged countenance, and had moreover been precisely the same age – not perhaps to the full extent of the memory of the oldest inhabitant, but certainly for five good years. But she had been kept up late every night, and put upon an unlimited allowance of gin-and-water from infancy, to prevent her growing tall, and perhaps this system of training had produced in the infant phenomenon these additional phenomena (Nickleby).*

Crummles, Percy and **Charles:** The Crummleses' sons, brothers of Ninetta. *A couple of boys, one of them very tall and the other very short, both dressed as sailors – or at least as theatrical sailors, with belts, buckles, pigtails, and pistols complete –*

fighting what is called in playbills a terrific combat, with two of those short broad-swords with basket hilts which are commonly used at our minor theatres (Nickleby).

Crummles, Vincent: A touring actor-manager who employs and befriends Nicholas Nickleby and Smike. *He saluted Nicholas, who then observed that the face of Mr. Crummles was quite proportionate in size to his body; that he had a very full under-lip, a hoarse voice, as though he were in the habit of shouting very much, and very short black hair, shaved off nearly to the crown of his head – to admit (as we afterwards learnt) of his more easily wearing character wigs of any shape or pattern. . . . He was very talkative and communicative, stimulated perhaps, not only by his natural disposition, but by the spirits and water he sipped very plentifully, or the snuff he took in large quantities from a piece of whitey-brown paper in his waistcoat pocket (Nickleby).*

Crummles, Mrs. Vincent: Crummles's wife. *A stout, portly female, apparently between forty and fifty, in a tarnished silk cloak, with her bonnet dangling by the strings in her hand, and her hair (of which she had a great quantity) braided in a large festoon over each temple (Nickleby).*

Crumpton, Amelia and **Maria:** Spinster sisters who conduct Minerva House, a 'finishing establishment for young ladies'. *Two unusually tall, particularly thin, and exceedingly skinny personages: very upright, and very yellow. Miss Amelia Crumpton owned to thirty-eight, and Miss Maria Crumpton admitted she was forty; an admission which was rendered perfectly unnecessary by the self-evident fact of her being at least fifty. They dressed in the most interesting manner – like twins! and looked as happy and comfortable as a couple of marigolds run to seed. They were very precise, had the strictest possible ideas of propriety, wore false hair, and always smelt very strongly of lavender (Boz – 'Sentiment').*

Cruncher, Jerry, sen.: Father of Young Jerry. Tellson's Bank messenger and resurrectionist. He accompanies Jarvis Lorry and Miss Pross to Paris, where the horrors of the Revolution put an end to his fascination with death. *He had eyes . . . of a surface black, with no depth in the colour or form, and much too near together – as if they were afraid of being found out in something, singly, if they kept too far apart. They had a sinister expression, under an old cocked hat like a three-cornered spittoon, and over a great muffler for the chin and throat, which descended nearly to the wearer's knees (Two Cities).*

Cruncher, Mrs. Jerry, sen.: Jerry Cruncher's wife, mother of Young Jerry. A devout woman whose predilection for prayer irritates her husband into naming her 'Aggerawayter'. *A woman of orderly and industrious appearance rose from her knees in a corner, with sufficient haste and trepidation to show that she was the person referred to (Two Cities).*

Cruncher, Young Jerry: The Crunchers' son. *A grisly urchin of twelve, who was his express image (Two Cities).*

Crupp, Mrs.: David Copperfield's plump landlady at Buckingham Street, Adelphi, when he becomes an articled clerk. *Mrs. Crupp was a martyr to a curious disorder called 'the spazzums', which was generally accompanied with inflammation of the nose, and required to be constantly treated with peppermint. . . . She came up to me one evening, when I was very low, to ask . . . if I could oblige her with a little tincture of cardamums mixed with rhubarb, and flavoured with seven drops of the essence of cloves, which was the best remedy for her complaint; – or, if I had not such a thing by me, with a little brandy, which was the next best (Copperfield).*

Crushton, The Hon. Mr.: Obsequious companion of Lord Mutanhed at Bath (Pickwick).

Curdle, Mr. and **Mrs.:** Patrons of Miss Snevellici's dramatic 'bespeak' in Portsmouth. *Mrs. Curdle was supposed, by those who were best informed on such points, to possess quite the London taste in matters relating to literature and the drama; and as to Mr. Curdle, he had written a pamphlet of sixty-four pages, post octavo, on the character of the Nurse's deceased husband in Romeo and Juliet, with an inquiry whether he really had been a 'merry man' in his life-time, or whether it was merely his widow's affectionate partiality that induced her so to report him. He had likewise proved, that by altering the received mode of punctuation, any one of Shakespeare's plays could be made quite different, and the sense completely changed; it is needless to say, therefore, that he was a great critic, and a very profound and most original thinker (Nickleby).*

Cute, Alderman: A pompous worthy, determined to 'put down' all talk of poverty and sickness. *Coming out of the house at that kind of light-heavy pace – that peculiar compromise between a walk and a jog-trot – with which a gentleman upon the smooth down-hill of life, wearing creaking boots, a watch-chain, and clean linen, may come out of his house: not only without any abatement of his dignity, but with an expression of having important and wealthy engagements elsewhere. . . . He was a merry fellow, Alderman Cute. Oh, and a sly fellow too! A knowing fellow. Up to everything. Not to be imposed upon. Deep in the people's hearts! He knew them, Cute did (Christmas Books – 'Chimes').*

Cutler, Mr. and **Mrs.:** Friends of the Kenwigses (Nickleby).

Cuttle, Captain Edward: An old seafaring friend of Sol Gills, whose shop he cares for during Sol's disappearance, eventually becoming his partner. Lodger with Mrs. MacStinger, whose matrimonial advances he narrowly evades. *A gentleman in a wide suit of blue, with a hook instead of a hand attached to his right wrist; very bushy black eyebrows; and a thick stick in his left hand, covered all over (like his nose) with knobs. He wore a loose black silk handkerchief round his neck, and such a very large coarse shirt collar, that it looked like a small sail. He was evidently the person for whom the spare wine-glass was intended, and evidently knew it; for having taken off his rough outer coat and hung* up, on a particular peg behind the door, such a hard glazed hat as a sympathetic person's head might ache at the sight of, and which left a red rim round his own forehead as if he had been wearing a tight basin, he brought a chair to where the clean glass was, and sat himself down behind it. He was usually addressed as Captain, this visitor; and had been a pilot, or a skipper, or a privateer's-man, or all three perhaps; and was a very salt-looking man indeed. // 'When found, make a note of' (Dombey).

Dabber, Sir Dingleby: Portraitist, imagined by Mrs. Nickleby as the painter of Kate's portrait to be reproduced in annuals on her marriage to Sir Mulberry Hawk. *Perhaps some one annual, of more comprehensive design than its fellows, might even contain a portrait of the mother of Lady Mulberry Hawk, with lines by the father of Sir Dingleby Dabber. More unlikely things had come to pass. Less interesting portraits had appeared. As this thought occurred to the good lady, her countenance unconsciously assumed that compound expression of simpering and sleepiness which, being common to all such portraits, is perhaps one reason why they are always so charming and agreeable* (Nickleby).

Dadson, Mr. and **Mrs.:** Writing-master at the Misses Crumpton's and his wife. *The wife in green silk, with shoes and cap-trimmings to correspond: the writing-master in a white waistcoat, black knee-shorts, and ditto silk stockings, displaying a leg large enough for two writing-masters* (Boz – 'Sentiment').

Daisy, Solomon: Parish clerk and bellringer of Chigwell, Essex, and *habitué* of the village inn, the Maypole. *The little man . . . had little round black shiny eyes like beads; moreover this little man wore at the knees of his rusty black breeches, and on his rusty black coat, little queer buttons like nothing except his eyes; but so like them, that as they twinkled and glistened in the light of the fire, which shone too in his bright shoe-buckles, he seemed all eyes from head to foot* (Rudge).

'Dame Durden': See **Summerson, Esther** (Bleak House).

Dando: Head boatman at Searle's yard on the Thames. *Watch him, as taking a few minutes' respite from his toils, he negligently seats himself on the edge of a boat, and fans his broad bushy chest with a cap scarcely half so furry. Look at his magnificent, though reddish whiskers, and mark the somewhat native humour with which he 'chaffs' the boys and 'prentices, or cunningly gammons the gen'l'm'n into the gift of a glass of gin, of which we verily believe he swallows in one day as much as any six ordinary men, without ever being one atom the worse for it* (Boz – 'The River').

Danton: Friend of Kitterbell, introduced to Dumps at the christening party. *A young man of about five-and-twenty, with a considerable stock of impudence, and a very small share of ideas: he was a great favourite, especially with young ladies of from sixteen to twenty-six years of age, both inclusive. He could imitate the French-horn to admiration, sang comic*

songs most inimitably, and had the most insinuating way of saying impertinent nothings to his doting female admirers. He had acquired, somehow or other, the reputation of being a great wit, and accordingly, whenever he opened his mouth, everybody who knew him laughed very heartily* (Boz – 'Bloomsbury Christening').

Darby: Police constable who goes with Bucket and Snagsby to Tom-all-Alone's (Bleak House).

Darby, Mr. and **Mrs.:** Keepers of an unregistered lodging-house in the Liverpool dock area (Uncommercial – 'Poor Mercantile Jack').

Darnay, Charles: English identity of the exiled French aristocrat Charles St. Evrémonde. He marries Lucie Manette; later Sydney Carton saves him from the guillotine. *A young man of about five-and-twenty, well-grown and well-looking, with a sunburnt cheek and a dark eye. His condition was that of a young gentleman. He was plainly dressed in black, or very dark grey, and his hair, which was long and dark, was gathered in a ribbon at the back of his neck; more to be out of his way than for ornament. As an emotion of the mind will express itself through any covering of the body, so the paleness which his situation engendered came through the brown upon his cheek, showing the soul to be stronger than the sun* (Two Cities).

Dartle, Rosa: Mrs. Steerforth's companion. Jealously in love with Steerforth, she exacts bitter revenge on Little Em'ly for eloping with him. *She had black hair and eager black eyes, and was thin, and had a scar upon her lip. . . . I concluded in my own mind that she was about thirty years of age, and that she wished to be married. She was a little dilapidated – like a house – with having been so long to let* (Copperfield).

Datchery, Dick: The unidentified investigator who visits Cloisterham after Edwin Drood's disappearance to observe John Jasper. *A white-haired personage, with black eyebrows. Being buttoned up in a tightish blue surtout, with a buff waistcoat and grey trousers, he had something of a military air; but he announced himself at the Crozier (the orthodox hotel, where he put up with a portmanteau) as an idle dog who lived upon his means* (Drood).

David: The Cheeryble brothers' butler. *An ancient butler of apoplectic appearance, and with very short legs* (Nickleby).

David, Old: Assistant sexton at the village where Little Nell dies (Curiosity Shop).

Davis, Gill: Narrator of the story. *There I was, a-leaning over the bulwarks of the sloop Christopher Columbus, in the South American waters off the Mosquito shore: a subject of his Gracious Majesty King George of England, and a private in the Royal Marines* (Christmas Stories – 'English Prisoners').

Dawes, Miss: The nurse who goaded Miss Wade into leaving the noble family in which she was governess. *A rosy-faced woman always making an obtrusive pretence of being gay and good-humoured, who had* *nursed them both, and who had secured their affections before I saw them. I could almost have settled down to my fate but for this woman (Dorrit).*

Dawkins, John ('The Artful Dodger'): Member of Fagin's gang who enlists Oliver Twist. He is transported for life for picking pockets. *He was a snub-nosed, flat-browed, common-faced boy enough; and as dirty a juvenile as one would wish to see; but he had about him all the airs and manners of a man. He was short of his age: with rather bow-legs, and little, sharp, ugly eyes. His hat was stuck on the top of his head so lightly, that it threatened to fall off every moment – and would have done so, very often, if the wearer had not had a knack of every now and then giving his head a sudden twitch, which brought it back to its old place again. He wore a man's coat, which reached nearly to his heels. He had turned the cuffs back, half-way up his arm, to get his hands out of the sleeves: apparently with the ultimate view of thrusting them into the pockets of his corduroy trousers; for there he kept them. He was, altogether, as roystering and swaggering a young gentleman as ever stood four feet six, or something less, in his bluchers (Twist).*

Daws, Mary: Kitchenmaid at Dombey's *(Dombey).*

Dawson: Surgeon who attends Mrs. Robinson's confinement. *Mr. Dawson, the surgeon, etc., who displays a large lamp with a different colour in every pane of glass, at the corner of the row (Boz – 'Four Sisters').*

Deaf Gentleman, The: A close companion of Master Humphrey, who never discovers his name or his story. *Whatever sorrow my dear friend has known, and whatever grief may linger in some secret corner of his heart, he is now a cheerful, placid, happy creature. Misfortune can never have fallen upon such a man but for some good purpose (Humphrey).*

Dean of Cloisterham: *With a pleasant air of patronage, the Dean as nearly cocks his quaint hat as a Dean in good spirits may, and directs his comely gaiters towards the ruddy dining-room of the snug old red-brick house where he is at present, 'in residence' with Mrs. Dean and Miss Dean (Drood).*

Dedlock, Lady (Honoria): Sir Leicester's wife and natural mother of Esther Summerson by Captain Hawdon. She flies from home when her secret threatens to emerge and dies near Hawdon's grave in a squalid London burial-ground. *He married her for love. A whisper still goes about, that she had not even family; howbeit, Sir Leicester had so much family that perhaps he had enough, and could dispense with any more. But she had beauty, pride, ambition, insolent resolve, and sense enough to portion out a legion of fine ladies. Wealth and station, added to these, soon floated her upward; and for years, now, my Lady Dedlock has been at the centre of the fashionable intelligence, and at the top of the fashionable tree. How Alexander wept when he had no more worlds to conquer, everybody knows – or has some reason to know by this time, the matter having been rather frequently mentioned. My Lady Dedlock, having conquered her world, fell, not into the melting, but rather into the freezing mood. An exhausted composure, a worn-out placidity, an equanimity of fatigue not to be ruffled by interest or satisfaction, are the trophies of her victory. She is perfectly well-bred. If she could be translated to Heaven to-morrow, she might be expected to ascend without any rapture (Bleak House).*

Dedlock, Sir Leicester, Bart.: Owner of Chesney Wold. *Sir Leicester is twenty years, full measure, older than my Lady. He will never see sixty-five again, nor perhaps sixty-six, nor yet sixty-seven. He has a twist of the gout now and then, and walks a little stiffly. He is of a worthy presence, with his light grey hair and whiskers, his fine shirt-frill, his pure white waistcoat, and his blue coat with bright buttons always buttoned. He is ceremonious, stately, most polite on every occasion to my Lady, and holds her personal attractions in the highest estimation. His gallantry to my Lady, which has never changed since he courted her, is the only little touch of romantic fancy in him (Bleak House).*

Dedlock, Volumnia: Dedlock's cousin and beneficiary, living at Bath, who keeps house for him after his wife's death. *A young lady (of sixty), who is doubly highly related; having the honour to be a poor relation, by the mother's side, to another great family. Miss Volumnia, displaying in early life a pretty talent for cutting ornaments out of coloured paper, and also for singing to the guitar in the Spanish tongue, and propounding French conundrums in country houses, passed the twenty years of her existence between twenty and forty in a sufficiently agreeable manner. Lapsing then out of date, and being considered to bore mankind by her vocal performances in the Spanish language, she retired to Bath. . . . She has an extensive acquaintance at Bath among appalling old gentlemen with thin legs and nankeen trousers, and is of high standing in that dreary city. But she is a little dreaded elsewhere, in consequence of an indiscreet profusion in the article of rouge, and persistency in an obsolete pearl necklace like a rosary of little bird's-eggs (Bleak House).*

Deedles: Eminent banker (Deedles Brothers) and high officer of the Goldsmiths' Company who commits suicide in his counting-house, to the consternation of Alderman Cute. *'It's almost enough to make one think, if one didn't know better,' said Alderman Cute, 'that at times some motion of a capsizing nature was going on in things, which affected the general economy of the social fabric. Deedles Brothers!'* (Christmas Books – 'Chimes').

Defarge, Ernest: Parisian wine-shop keeper and revolutionary, custodian of Dr. Manette after his release from the Bastille. He produces the evidence which condemns Darnay. *A bull-necked, martial-looking man of thirty. . . . He was a dark man altogether, with good eyes and a good bold breadth between them. Good-humoured looking on the whole, but implacable-looking, too; evidently a man of a strong resolution and a set purpose; a man not desirable to be met, rushing down a narrow pass with a gulf on either side, for nothing would turn the man (Two Cities).*

Defarge, Madame Ernest (Thérèse): Defarge's wife and a leader of women revolutionaries. Killed in a struggle with Miss Pross. *A stout woman ... with a watchful eye that seldom seemed to look at anything, a large hand heavily ringed, a steady face, strong features, and great composure of manner. ... Madame Defarge being sensitive to cold, was wrapped in fur, and had a quantity of bright shawls twined about her head, though not to the concealment of her large earrings. Her knitting was before her, but she had laid it down to pick her teeth with a toothpick (Two Cities).*

Defresnier et Cie: Swiss wine exporters employing Obenreizer as their London agent (*Christmas Stories – 'No Thoroughfare'*).

Dellombra, Signor: Mysterious acquaintance of Clara's husband, whose face haunts her. *He was dressed in black, and had a reserved and secret air, and he was a dark, remarkable-looking man, with black hair and a grey moustache* ('At Dusk').

Demented Traveller: One of the narrator's companions on a journey to France. *Demented Traveller, who has been for two or three minutes watchful, clutches his great-coats, plunges at the door, rattles it, cries 'Hi!' eager to embark on board of impossible packets, far inland (Reprinted – 'A Flight').*

Demple, George: A doctor's son, pupil at Salem House (*Copperfield*).

Denham, Edmund: Assumed name of the Tetterbys' student lodger, Edmund Longford. He is evilly influenced by Redlaw, and temporarily loses his gratitude for Milly's kindness in his illness (*Christmas Books – 'Haunted Man'*).

Dennis, Ned: Hangman and a ringleader of the Gordon rioters, for which he is executed. *A squat, thickset personage, with a low, retreating forehead, a coarse shock head of hair, and eyes so small and near together, that his broken nose alone seemed to prevent their meeting and fusing into one of the usual size. A dingy handkerchief twisted like a cord about his neck, left its great veins exposed to view, and they were swoln and starting, as though with gulping down strong passions, malice, and ill-will. His dress was of threadbare velveteen – a faded, rusty, whitened black, like the ashes of a pipe or a coal fire after a day's extinction; discoloured with the soils of many a stale debauch, and reeking yet with pot-house odours. In lieu of buckles at his knees, he wore unequal loops of packthread; and in his grimy hands he held a knotted stick, the knob of which was carved into a rough likeness of his own vile face (Rudge).*

Deputy: Boy employed at the Travellers' lodging-house, Cloisterham. Paid tormentor of Durdles and ally of Datchery. Also known as 'Winks'. *A hideous small boy in rags flinging stones at him as a well-defined mark in the moonlight. // 'I'm man-servant up at the Travellers' Twopenny in Gas Works Garding,' this thing explains. 'All us man-servants at Travellers' Lodgings is named Deputy' (Drood).*

Derrick, John: The narrator's servant in the interpolated tale 'To be Taken with a Grain of Salt' (*Christmas Stories – 'Doctor Marigold'*).

Despair: One of Miss Flite's birds (*Bleak House*).

Dibabs, Jane: Lady whose example is instanced by Mrs. Nickleby in arguing that Madeline Bray might reasonably marry Gride. *'Jane Dibabs – the Dibabses lived in the beautiful little thatched white house one storey high, covered all over with ivy and creeping plants, with an exquisite little porch with twining honeysuckles and all sorts of things: where the earwigs used to fall into one's tea on a summer evening, and always fell upon their backs and kicked dreadfully, and where the frogs used to get into the rushlight shades when one stopped all night, and sit up and look through the little holes like Christians – Jane Dibabs, she married a man who was a great deal older than herself, and would marry him, notwithstanding all that could be said to the contrary, and she was so fond of him that nothing was ever equal to it' (Nickleby).*

Dibble, Sampson and **Dorothy:** A very old couple of Mormon recruits, the man quite blind, aboard the emigrant ship *Amazon* (*Uncommercial – 'Bound for the Great Salt Lake'*).

Dick: Sweetheart of Sally (**Sarah Goldstraw**) (*Christmas Stories – 'No Thoroughfare'*).

Dick: Ostler at the Salisbury inn where Tom Pinch and Martin Chuzzlewit jun. meet (*Chuzzlewit*).

Dick: Guard of the coach taking Nicholas Nickleby and Squeers to Yorkshire (*Nickleby*).

Dick: Tim Linkinwater's blind blackbird. *There was not a bird of such methodical and business-like habits in all the world, as the blind blackbird, who dreamed and dozed away his days in a large snug cage, and had lost his voice, from old age, years before Tim first bought him. There was not such an eventful story in the whole range of anecdote, as Tim could tell concerning the acquisition of that very bird; how, compassionating his starved and suffering condition, he had purchased him, with the view of humanely terminating his wretched life; how he determined to wait three days and see whether the bird revived; how, before half the time was out, the bird did revive; and how he went on reviving and picking up his appetite and good looks until he gradually became what – 'what you see him now, sir!' – Tim would say, glancing proudly at the cage (Nickleby).*

Dick: Child workhouse inmate with Oliver Twist. *Pale and thin; his cheeks were sunken; and his eyes large and bright. The scanty parish dress, the livery of his misery, hung loosely on his feeble body; and his young limbs had wasted away, like those of an old man (Twist).*

Dick, Mr.: The name by which Richard Babley, Betsey Trotwood's lodger and protégé, insists upon being known. A mild eccentric, having had his mind disturbed by his sister's ill-treatment by her husband, he is a kind friend to David Copperfield and reconciles Dr. Strong and his wife with one another. *Grey-headed and florid: I should have said all about him in saying so, had not his head been curiously bowed – not by age; it reminded me of one of Mr. Creakle's boys' heads after a beating – and his grey eyes prominent and large, with a strange kind of watery brightness in them that made me, in combination with his vacant manner, his submission to my aunt, and his childish delight when she praised him, suspect him of being a little mad. . . . He was dressed like any other ordinary gentleman, in a loose grey morning coat and waistcoat, and white trousers; and had his watch in his fob, and his money in his pockets: which he rattled as if he were very proud of it (Copperfield).*

Diego, Don: *Don Diego de – I forget his name – the inventor of the last new Flying Machines (Reprinted – 'A Flight').*

Digby: See **Smike** (*Nickleby*).

Dilber, Mrs.: A laundress shown to Scrooge by the Ghost of Christmas Yet to Come (*Christmas Books – 'Christmas Carol'*).

Dingo, Professor: Mrs. Bayham Badger's deceased second husband. *The Professor was yet dying by inches in the most dismal manner, and Mrs. Badger was giving us imitations of his way of saying, with great difficulty, 'Where is Laura? Let Laura give me my toast and water!' when the entrance of the gentlemen consigned him to the tomb (Bleak House).*

Dingwall: See **Brook Dingwall** (*Boz – 'Sentiment'*).

Diogenes: Florence Dombey's dog, a present from Toots. *Diogenes was as ridiculous a dog as one would meet with on a summer's day; a blundering, ill-favoured, clumsy, bullet-headed dog, continually acting on a wrong idea that there was an enemy in the neighbourhood, whom it was meritorious to bark at (Dombey).*

'Dismal Jemmy': See **Hutley, Jemmy** (*Pickwick*).

Diver, Colonel: Editor of the New York Rowdy Journal who introduces Martin Chuzzlewit to the Pawkins Boarding-House. *A sallow gentleman, with sunken cheeks, black hair, small twinkling eyes, and a singular expression hovering about that region of his face, which was not a frown, nor a leer, and yet might have been mistaken at the first glance for either. Indeed it would have been difficult, on a much closer acquaintance, to describe it in any more satisfactory terms than as a mixed expression of vulgar cunning and deceit (Chuzzlewit).*

Dobble Family: A clerk, his wife, son, and daughter, hosts at a New Year's Eve party. *The master of the house with the green blinds is in a public office; we know the fact by the cut of his coat, the tie of his neckcloth, and the self-satisfaction of his gait – the very green blinds themselves have a Somerset House air about them (Boz – 'New Year').*

Dobbs, Julia: See **Manners, Julia** (*Strange Gentleman*).

Dodger, The Hon. Ananias: A millionaire, the story of whose acquisition of wealth at first bores and then relieves the narrator ('At Dusk').

Dodson: Dominant partner of Dodson and Fogg, Mrs. Bardell's attorneys. *A plump, portly, stern-looking man, with a loud voice (Pickwick).*

Do'em: Livery servant and accomplice in crime of Captain the Hon. Fitz-Whisker Fiercy (q.v.). *A most respectable servant to look at, who has grown grey in the service of the captain's family (Mudfog – 'Pantomime of Life').*

Dogginson: Vestryman. *Regarded in our Vestry as 'a regular John Bull' (Reprinted – 'Our Vestry').*

Dolloby: Kent Road old-clothes dealer who buys David Copperfield's waistcoat for ninepence during his walk to Dover. *He looked like a man of a revengeful disposition, who had hung all his enemies, and was enjoying himself (Copperfield).*

'Dolls, Mr.': See **Cleaver** (*Mutual Friend*).

Dombey, Florence (Floy): Dombey's unwanted daughter by his first wife. She becomes close friends with his second, is turned out of his house and taken in by Captain Cuttle. She marries Walter Gay and eventually persuades her broken father to accept the love she has always cherished for him. *If a book were read aloud, and there were anything in the story that pointed at an unkind father, she was in pain for their application of it to him; not for herself. So with any trifle of an interlude that was acted, or picture that was shown, or game that was played, among them. . . . How few who saw sweet Florence, in her spring of womanhood, the modest little queen of those small revels, imagined what a load of sacred care lay heavy in her breast! (Dombey).*

Dombey, Little Paul: The awaited son upon whom Dombey's hopes for the posterity of his firm and fortune are centred. Left motherless at birth, cared for by Polly Toodle and his sister Florence and doted upon by all who encounter him, the sickly child dies aged six. *He was a pretty little fellow; though there was something wan and wistful in his small face, that gave occasion to many significant shakes of Mrs. Wickam's head, and many long-drawn inspirations of Mrs. Wickam's breath. His temper gave abundant promise of being imperious in after-life; and he had as hopeful an apprehension of his own importance, and the rightful subservience of all other things and persons to it, as heart could desire. He was childish and sportive enough at times, and not of a sullen disposition; but he had a strange, old-fashioned, thoughtful way, at other times, of sitting brooding in his miniature arm-chair, when he looked (and talked) like one of those terrible beings in the fairy tales, who, at a hundred and fifty or two hundred years of age, fantastically represent the children for whom they have been substituted (Dombey).*

Dombey, Paul: Father of Florence and Little Paul by his first wife, Fanny. Later married to Edith Granger. A wealthy London merchant, head of the firm of Dombey and Son. *Dombey was about eight-and-forty* *years of age ... rather bald, rather red, and though a handsome well-made man, too stern and pompous in appearance to be prepossessing.... On the brow of Dombey, Time and his brother Care had set some marks, as on a tree that was to come down in good time – remorseless twins they are for striding through their human forests, notching as they go (Dombey).*

Dombey, Mrs. Paul the First (Fanny): Dombey's first wife, mother of Florence and of Paul, at whose birth she dies. *Mr. Dombey would have reasoned: That a matrimonial alliance with himself must, in the nature of things, be gratifying and honourable to any woman of common sense. That the hope of giving birth to a new partner in such a house, could not fail to awaken a glorious and stirring ambition in the breast of the least ambitious of her sex. That Mrs. Dombey had entered on that social contract of matrimony: almost necessarily part of a genteel and wealthy station, even without reference to the perpetuation of family firms: with her eyes fully open to these advantages. That Mrs. Dombey had had daily practical knowledge of his position in society. That Mrs. Dombey had always sat at the head of his table, and done the honours of his house in a remarkably lady-like and becoming manner. That Mrs. Dombey must have been happy. That she couldn't help it (Dombey).*

Dombey, Mrs. Paul the Second (Edith): Dombey's second wife, widow of Colonel Granger and daughter of the Hon. Mrs. Skewton. She elopes briefly with James Carker and after his death makes her home with her Cousin Feenix. *Very handsome, very haughty, very wilful, who tossed her head and drooped her eyelids, as though, if there were anything in all the world worth looking into, save a mirror, it certainly was not the earth or sky (Dombey).*

Donny, the **Misses:** Twin sisters, proprietors of Greenleaf, the boarding school near Reading attended by Esther Summerson *(Bleak House).*

Dor, Madame: Obenreizer's housekeeper and ally of Marguerite. *She was a true Swiss impersonation ... from the breadth of her cushion-like back, and the ponderosity of her respectable legs (if the word be admissible), to the black velvet band tied tightly round her throat for the represssion of a rising tendency to goître; or, higher still, to her great copper-coloured gold ear-rings; or, higher still, to her head-dress of black gauze stretched on wire (Christmas Stories – 'No Thoroughfare').*

Dorker: Pupil who died at Dotheboys Hall. *'I remember very well, sir,' rejoined Squeers. 'Ah! Mrs. Squeers, sir, was as partial to that lad as if he had been her own; the attention, sir, that was bestowed upon that boy in his illness! Dry toast and warm tea offered him every night and morning when he couldn't swallow anything – a candle in his bed-room on the very night he died – the best dictionary sent up for him to lay his head upon – I don't regret it though. It is a pleasant thing to reflect that one did one's duty by him' (Nickleby).*

Dornton, Sergeant: One of the Detective Force officers of Scotland Yard. *About fifty years of age, with a ruddy face and a high sunburnt forehead, has the air of one who has been a Sergeant in the army – he might have sat to Wilkie for the Soldier in the Reading of the Will. He is famous for steadily pursuing the inductive process, and, from small beginnings, working on from clue to clue until he bags his man (Reprinted – 'Detective Police').*

Dorrit, Amy (Little Dorrit): Daughter of William Dorrit, sister of Edward and Fanny. Born in the Marshalsea, she tends her father there, directs her brother's and sister's destinies, and succours Clennam, when he is a Marshalsea prisoner, eventually marrying him. *A pale, transparent face, quick in expression, though not beautiful in feature, its soft hazel eyes excepted. A delicately bent head, a tiny form, a quick little pair of busy hands, and a shabby dress. // She took the place of eldest of the three, in all things but precedence; was the head of the fallen family; and bore, in her own heart, its anxieties and shames. At thirteen, she could read and keep accounts – that is, could put down in words and figures how much the bare necessaries that they wanted would cost, and how much less they had to buy them with. She had been, by snatches of a few weeks at a time, to an evening school outside, and got her sister and brother sent to day schools.... She knew well – no one better – that a man so broken as to be the Father of the Marshalsea, could be no father to his own children (Dorrit).*

Dorrit, Edward ('Tip'): William Dorrit's son, brother to Amy and Fanny, an unstable character who ruins his health with drink. *Tip tired of everything.... His small second mother, aided by her trusty friend, got him into a warehouse, into a market garden, into the hop trade, into the law again, into an auctioneer's, into a brewery, into a stockbroker's, into the law again, into a coach office, into a waggon office, into the law again, into a general dealer's, into a distillery, into the law again, into a wool house, into a dry goods house, into the Billingsgate trade, into the foreign fruit trade, and into the docks. But whatever Tip went into, he came out of tired, announcing that he had cut it (Dorrit).*

Dorrit, Fanny: Sister to Amy and Edward. A ballet dancer who marries Edmund Merdle, proves heartless and neglects her children, who are cared for by Amy. *A pretty girl of a far better figure and much more developed than Little Dorrit, though looking much younger in the face when the two were observed together (Dorrit).*

Dorrit, Frederick: William's brother, uncle of Fanny, Edward and Amy. Ruined along with William, he is kept from the knowledge of a legacy under Gilbert Clennam's will and lives an outcast from the family, save Little Dorrit. *Naturally a retired and simple man, he had shown no particular sense of being ruined, at the time when that calamity fell upon him, further than that he left off washing himself when the shock was announced, and never took to that luxury any more. He had been a very indifferent musical amateur in his better days; and when he fell with his brother, resorted for support to playing a clarionet as dirty as himself in a small Theatre Orchestra. It was the* theatre in which his niece became a dancer; he had been a fixture there a long time when she took her poor station in it; and he accepted the task of serving as her escort and guardian, just as he would have accepted an illness, a legacy, a feast, starvation – anything but soap *(Dorrit)*.

Dorrit, William ('Father of the Marshalsea'): Father of Amy, Edward and Fanny. A debtor in the Marshalsea Prison for twenty-five years, he is found to be heir to a fortune, but loses it and ruins his family afresh through speculating with Merdle. *A very amiable and very helpless middle-aged gentleman, who was going out again directly. Necessarily, he was going out again directly, because the Marshalsea lock never turned upon a debtor who was not. He brought in a portmanteau with him, which he doubted its being worth while to unpack; he was so perfectly clear – like all the rest of them, the turnkey on the lock said – that he was going out again directly. He was a shy, retiring man; well-looking, though in an effeminate style; with a mild voice, curling hair, and irresolute hands – rings upon the fingers in those days – which nervously wandered to his trembling lip a hundred times, in the first half-hour of his acquaintance with the jail (Dorrit).*

Doubledick, Richard: Hero of the story with which the narrator entertains the Six Poor Travellers, a tale of Doubledick's adventurous rise from dissolute private to reformed captain. He marries Mary Marshall. *His object was to get shot; but he thought he might as well ride to death as be at the trouble of walking.... He was passed as Richard Doubledick; age, twenty-two; height, five foot ten; native place, Exmouth, which he had never been near in his life. There was no cavalry in Chatham when he limped over the bridge here with half a shoe to his dusty feet, so he enlisted into a regiment of the line, and was glad to get drunk and forget all about it (Christmas Stories – 'Seven Poor Travellers').*

Dounce, John: An 'old boy' who becomes infatuated with a barmaid in an oyster saloon, is first encouraged, then spurned by her, and in desperation offers marriage to several ladies. He eventually marries his own cook, who henpecks him. *A retired glove and braces maker, a widower, resident with three daughters – all grown up and all unmarried – in Cursitor Street, Chancery Lane. He was a short, round, large-faced, tubbish sort of man, with a broad-brimmed hat, and a square coat; and had that grave, but confident, kind of roll, peculiar to old boys in general. Regular as clockwork – breakfast at nine – dress and tittivate a little – down to the Sir Somebody's Head – a glass of ale and the paper – come back again, and take daughters out for a walk – dinner at three – glass of grog and pipe – nap – tea – little walk – Sir Somebody's Head again – capital house – delightful evenings (Boz – 'Misplaced Attachment').*

Dowdles, the two Misses: Proprietresses (or fellow pupils) of Kate Nickleby's school in Devonshire. *'Twenty-five young ladies, fifty guineas a-year without the et-ceteras, both the Miss Dowdles, the most accomplished, elegant, fascinating creatures' (Nickleby).*

Dowler, Captain: A bombastic ex-army officer who becomes involved with Pickwick and his friends at Bath and quarrels violently with Winkle over Mrs. Dowler. *A stern-eyed man of about five-and-forty, who had a bald and glossy forehead, with a good deal of black hair at the sides and back of his head, and large black whiskers.... He looked up from his breakfast as Mr. Pickwick entered, with a fierce and peremptory air, which was very dignified; and having scrutinised that gentleman and his companions to his entire satisfaction, hummed a tune, in a manner which seemed to say that he rather suspected somebody wanted to take advantage of him, but it wouldn't do (Pickwick).*

Dowler, Mrs.: Dowler's wife, involved with Winkle in the misunderstanding over the sedan chair at Bath. *A rather pretty face in a bright blue bonnet (Pickwick).*

Doyce, Daniel: A neglected inventor whose partner Arthur Clennam becomes. Clennam speculates the firm's money with Merdle and loses everything, but Doyce sells his invention abroad and returns to reclaim Clennam. *He was not much to look at, either in point of size or in point of dress; being merely a short, square, practical looking man, whose hair had turned grey, and in whose face and forehead there were deep lines of cogitation, which looked as though they were carved in hard wood. He was dressed in decent black, a little rusty, and had the appearance of a sagacious master in some handicraft. He had a spectacle-case in his hand, which he turned over and over while he was thus in question, with a certain free use of the thumb that is never seen but in a hand accustomed to tools (Dorrit).*

Doylance, Old: Former schoolmaster of John, the narrator *(Christmas Stories – 'Haunted House').*

Doze, Professor: A vice-president of the zoology and botany session at the first meeting of the Mudfog Association *(Mudfog).*

Drawley: A vice-president of the zoology and botany session at the second meeting of the Mudfog Association *(Mudfog).*

Dringworth Bros.: Of America Square, London. Employers of Clissold and Tregarthen *(Christmas Stories – 'Message from the Sea').*

Droce, Sergeant: Sergeant of Royal Marines in the sloop *Christopher Columbus*. *The most tyrannical non-commissioned officer in His Majesty's service (Christmas Stories – 'English Prisoners').*

Drood, Edwin: John Jasper's nephew, betrothed to Rosa Bud under his father's will, whose disappearance is the Mystery of the novel. *'I am afraid I am but a shallow, surface kind of fellow, Jack, and that my headpiece is none of the best. But I needn't say I am young; and perhaps I shall not grow worse as I grow older. At all events, I hope I have something impressible within me, which feels – deeply feels – the disinterestedness of your painfully laying yourself bare, as a warning to me' (Drood).*

Drowvey, Miss: Partner in Miss Grimmer's school in William Tinkling's romantic tale ('Holiday Romance').

Drummle, Bentley ('The Spider'): Fellow boarder with Pip at Matthew Pocket's. Marries Estella, whom he ill-treats, and is killed by a horse which he has also used cruelly. 'The Spider' is Jaggers's nickname for him. *Bentley Drummle, who was so sulky a fellow that he even took up a book as if its writer had done him an injury, did not take up an acquaintance in a more agreeable spirit. Heavy in figure, movement, and comprehension – in the sluggish complexion of his face, and in the large awkward tongue that seemed to loll about in his mouth as he himself lolled about in a room – he was idle, proud, niggardly, reserved, and suspicious. He came of rich people down in Somersetshire, who had nursed this combination of qualities until they made the discovery that it was just of age and a blockhead (Expectations).*

Dubbley: Constable's assistant at Ipswich. *A dirty-faced man, something over six feet high, and stout in proportion (Pickwick).*

Duff: Bow Street officer investigating the burglary at Mrs. Maylie's. *A red-headed, bony man, in top boots; with a rather ill-favoured countenance, and a turned-up sinister-looking nose (Twist).*

Dull: A vice-president of the umbugology and ditchwaterisics session at the second meeting of the Mudfog Association *(Mudfog).*

Dumbledon: A favoured pupil at Our School. *An idiotic goggle-eyed boy, with a big head and half-crowns without end, who suddenly appeared as a parlour-boarder, and was rumoured to have come by sea from some mysterious part of the earth where his parents rolled in gold. He was usually called 'Mr.' by the Chief, and was said to feed in the parlour on steaks and gravy; likewise to drink currant wine. And he openly stated that if rolls and coffee were ever denied him at breakfast, he would write home to that unknown part of the globe from which he had come, and cause himself to be recalled to the regions of gold. He was put into no form or class, but learnt alone, as little as he liked – and he liked very little – and there was a belief among us that this was because he was too wealthy to be 'taken down' (Reprinted – 'Our School').*

Dumkins: Renowned batsman of the All-Muggleton Cricket Club. *The redoubtable Dumkins (Pickwick).*

Dummins: An out-and-out young gentleman, friend of Blake. *'Both Mr. Blake and Mr. Dummins are very nice sort of young men in their way, only they are eccentric persons, and unfortunately rather too wild!'* (Young Gentlemen – 'Out-and-out Young Gentleman').

Dummy: A vice-president of the umbugology and ditchwaterisics session at the second meeting of the Mudfog Association *(Mudfog).*

Dumps, Nicodemus: Charles Kitterbell's uncle and reluctant godfather to the Kitterbells' first baby. He solaces himself by throwing the christening party into dismay with a speech full of gloomy prophecies. *Mr. Nicodemus Dumps, or, as his acquaintance called him, 'long Dumps', was a bachelor, six feet high, and fifty years old: cross, cadaverous, odd, and ill-natured. He was never happy but when he was miserable; and always miserable when he had the best reason to be happy. The only real comfort of his existence was to make everybody about him wretched – then he might be truly said to enjoy life. He was afflicted with a situation in the Bank worth five hundred a year, and he rented a 'first-floor furnished', at Pentonville, which he originally took because it commanded a dismal prospect of an adjacent churchyard. He was familiar with the face of every tombstone, and the burial service seemed to excite his strongest sympathy. . . . He adored King Herod for his massacre of the innocents; and if he hated one thing more than another, it was a child. . . . He subscribed to the 'Society for the Suppression of Vice' for the pleasure of putting a stop to any harmless amusements; and he contributed largely towards the support of two itinerant Methodist parsons, in the amiable hope that if circumstances rendered any people happy in this world, they might perchance be rendered miserable by fears for the next (Boz – 'Bloomsbury Christening').*

Dundey, Dr.: Robber of a bank in Ireland, tracked down in America by Sergeant Dornton *(Reprinted – 'Detective Police').*

Dunkle, Dr. Ginery: Spokesman of the deputation of boarders waiting on the Hon. Elijah Pogram at the National Hotel in America where Martin Chuzzlewit stays before embarking for Eden. *A very shrill boy (Chuzzlewit).*

Dunstable: Village butcher whose name is invoked by Pumblechook to persuade Pip that he is lucky not to have been born a pig. *'Dunstable the butcher would have come up to you as you lay in your straw, and he would have whipped you under his left arm, and with his right he would have tucked up his frock to get a penknife from out of his waistcoat-pocket, and he would have shed your blood and had your life. No bringing up by hand then. Not a bit of it!' (Expectations).*

Durdles: Cloisterham stonemason made drunk by John Jasper, who abstracts his keys to the burial vaults. *In a suit of coarse flannel with horn buttons, a yellow neckerchief with draggled ends, an old hat more russet-coloured than black, and laced boots of the hue of his stony calling, Durdles leads a hazy, gipsy sort of life, carrying his dinner about with him in a small bundle, and sitting on all manner of tombstones to dine. This dinner of Durdles's has become quite a Cloisterham institution: not only because of his never appearing in public without it, but because of its having been, on certain renowned occasions, taken into custody along with Durdles (as drunk and incapable), and exhibited before the Bench of Justices at the townhall (Drood).*

Dust: One of Miss Flite's birds *(Bleak House).*

Edkins: Loquacious member of Percy Noakes's committee for organising the steam excursion. *A pale young gentleman, in a green stock and spectacles of the same, a member of the Honourable Society of the Inner Temple (Boz – 'Steam Excursion').*

Edmunds: John Edmunds's father in the story of 'The Convict's Return'. *'A morose, savage-hearted, bad man: idle and dissolute in his habits; cruel and ferocious in his disposition. Beyond the few lazy and reckless vagabonds with whom he sauntered away his time in the fields, or sotted in the alehouse, he had not a single friend or acquaintance; no one cared to speak to the man whom many feared, and every one detested' (Pickwick).*

Edmunds, Mrs.: John Edmunds's mother in the story of 'The Convict's Return', killed by grief for her son and by her husband's ill-usage. *'Brute as he was, and cruelly as he had treated her, she had loved him once; and the recollection of what he had been to her, awakened feelings of forebearance and meekness under suffering in her bosom, to which all God's creatures, but women, are strangers' (Pickwick).*

Edmunds, George: A farm labourer, sweetheart of Lucy Benson. She is temporarily enticed away from him by Squire Norton, but finally returns *(Village Coquettes).*

Edmunds, John: Central figure in the story of 'The Convict's Return', told by the clergyman at Dingley Dell. *'Many a look was turned towards him, and many a doubtful glance he cast on either side to see whether any knew and shunned him. There were strange faces in almost every house; in some he recognised the burly form of some old schoolfellow – a boy when he last saw him – surrounded by a troop of merry children; in others he saw, seated in an easy-chair at a cottage door, a feeble and infirm old man, whom he only remembered as a hale and hearty labourer; but they had all forgotten him, and he passed on unknown' (Pickwick).*

Edson, Mr. and 'Mrs.' (Peggy): A young couple who take lodgings with Mrs. Lirriper. Edson abandons Peggy. Mrs. Lirriper prevents her drowning herself, but she dies giving birth to Jeremy Jackman Lirriper (q.v.). Years later Mrs. Lirriper is summoned to Edson's death-bed in France. *I did not quite take to the face of the gentleman though he was good-looking too but the lady was a very pretty young thing and delicate (Christmas Stories – 'Mrs. Lirriper's Lodgings' and 'Mrs. Lirriper's Legacy').*

Edward: Charlotte's husband, whose pleasure is in contradicting her. Father of James and Charlotte. *They return home from Mrs. Bluebottle's dinner-party, each in an opposite corner of the coach, and do not exchange a syllable until they have been seated for at least twenty minutes by the fireside at home, when the gentleman, raising his eyes from the stove, all at once breaks silence: 'What a very extraordinary thing it is,' says he, 'that you will contradict me, Charlotte!' (Young Couples – 'Contradictory Couple').*

Edward ('Eddard'): Donkey who responds to his owner's mentioning the name of Boffin by taking Wegg straight to Boffin's Bower. *The effect of the name was so very alarming, in respect of causing a temporary disappearance of Edward's head, casting his hind hoofs in the air, greatly accelerating the pace and increasing the jolting, that Mr. Wegg was fain to* devote his attention exclusively to holding on, and to relinquish his desire of ascertaining whether this homage to Boffin was to be considered complimentary or the reverse (Mutual Friend).*

Edwards, Miss: Pupil-teacher at Miss Monflathers's school. *This young lady, being motherless and poor, was apprenticed at the school – taught for nothing – teaching others what she learnt, for nothing – boarded for nothing – lodged for nothing – and set down and rated as something immeasurably less than nothing, by all the dwellers in the house (Curiosity Shop).*

Edwin: Charley's supposed rival for Angela Leath. He proves to be engaged to her cousin Emmeline. *A bright-eyed fellow, muffled in a mantle (Christmas Stories – 'Holly-Tree').*

Eight Club: Club founded at Cloisterham by Sapsea. *We were eight in number; we met at eight o'clock during eight months of the year; we played eight games of four-handed cribbage, at eightpence the game; our frugal supper was composed of eight rolls, eight mutton chops, eight pork sausages, eight baked potatoes, eight marrow-bones with eight toasts, and eight bottles of ale. There may, or may not, be a certain harmony of colour in the ruling idea of this (to adopt a phrase of our lively neighbours) reunion (Drood fragment).*

Ellis: Admirer of Rogers's oratory. *A sharp-nosed, light-haired man in a brown surtout reaching nearly to his heels, who took a whiff at his pipe, and an admiring glance at the red-faced man, alternately (Boz – 'Parlour Orator').*

Emile: Soldier billeted at the clock-maker's in the French town where Langley lodges. *Perpetually turning to of an evening, with his coat off, winding up the stock (Christmas Stories – 'Somebody's Luggage').*

Emilia: Mrs. Orange's baby in Nettie Ashford's romantic tale. *Mrs. Orange's baby was a very fine one, and real wax all over ('Holiday Romance').*

Emily: See **Bella** and **Emily** (Boz – 'Prisoners' Van').

Em'ly, Little: Daniel Peggotty's orphan niece and adopted daughter. On the eve of her marriage to Ham she elopes with Steerforth, who before long deserts her. She is eventually found by Daniel Peggotty and emigrates to Australia with him, Mrs. Gummidge and Martha Endell. *A most beautiful little girl . . . who wouldn't let me kiss her when I offered to, but ran away and hid herself (Copperfield).*

Emma: Waitress at an anglers' inn, gratefully recalled by Charley, the narrator. *The peerless Emma with the bright eyes and the pretty smile, who waited, bless her! with a natural grace that would have converted Blue-Beard (Christmas Stories – 'Holly-Tree').*

Emma: A maidservant at Dingley Dell. *Mr. Weller, not being particular at being under the mistletoe, kissed Emma and the other female servants, just as he caught them (Pickwick).*

Emmeline: Angela Leath's cousin, engaged to Edwin (*Christmas Stories* – 'Holly-Tree').

Endell, Martha: A former schoolmate of Little Em'ly, turned prostitute. She is saved and emigrates to Australia with the Peggottys. *'It's a poor wurem, Mas'r Davy,' said Ham, 'as is trod underfoot by all the town. Up street and down street. The mowld o' the churchyard don't hold any that the folk shrink away from, more' (Copperfield).*

'Englishman, Mr. The': See **Langley** (*Christmas Stories* – 'Somebody's Luggage').

Estella: Daughter of Magwitch and Molly, adopted by Miss Havisham who teaches her to hate and tantalise men. She marries Drummle, who ill-treats her, and separates from him. *'You must know,' said Estella, condescending to me as a brilliant and beautiful woman might, 'that I have no heart, . . . Oh! I have a heart to be stabbed in, or shot in, I have no doubt,' said Estella, 'and, of course, if it ceased to beat I should cease to be. But you know what I mean. I have no softness there, no – sympathy – sentiment – nonsense' (Expectations).*

Etc. Etc.: Applicant for a place in Master Humphrey's circle of friends. *'I am considered a devilish gentlemanly fellow, and I act up to the character. If you want a reference, ask any of the men at our club. Ask any fellow who goes there to write his letters, what sort of conversation mine is. Ask him if he thinks I have the sort of voice that will suit your deaf friend and make him hear, if he can hear anything at all. Ask the servants what they think of me. There's not a rascal among 'em, sir, but will tremble to hear my name' (Humphrey).*

Eugène: Soldier billeted at the tinman's in the French town where Langley lodges. *Cultivating, pipe in mouth, a garden four feet square, for the Tinman, in the little court behind the shop, and extorting the fruits of the earth from the same, on his knees, with the sweat of his brow (Christmas Stories – 'Somebody's Luggage').*

Evans: Plays the role of Roderigo in the Gattletons' private production of *Othello*. *Pronounced by all his lady friends to be 'quite a dear'. He looked so interesting, and had such lovely whiskers: to say nothing of his talent for writing verses in albums and playing the flute!* (*Boz* – 'Mrs. Joseph Porter').

Evans, Mrs., and **Tilly:** Jemima's mother and sister (*Boz* – 'Miss Evans and the Eagle').

Evans, Jemima ('J'mima Ivins'): Shoe-binder and straw-bonnet maker, courted by Samuel Wilkins. *In a white muslin gown carefully hooked and eyed, a little red shawl, plentifully pinned, a white straw bonnet trimmed with red ribbons, a small necklace, a large pair of bracelets, Denmark satin shoes, and open-worked stockings; white cotton gloves on her fingers, and a cambric pocket-handkerchief, carefully folded up, in her hand – all quite genteel and ladylike (Boz – 'Miss Evans and the Eagle').*

Evans, Richard: A pupil at Marton's village school.

'An amazing boy to learn, blessed with a good memory, and a ready understanding, and moreover with a good voice and ear for psalm-singing, in which he is the best among us. Yet, sir, that boy will come to a bad end; he'll never die in his bed; he's always falling asleep in sermon-time' (Curiosity Shop).

Evenson, John: Boarder at Mrs. Tibb's. *A stern-looking man, of about fifty, with very little hair on his head. . . . He was very morose and discontented. He was a thorough Radical, and used to attend a great variety of public meetings, for the express purpose of finding fault with everything that was proposed (Boz – 'Boarding-House').*

'Exchange or Barter': Pupil at Salem House. *I heard that one boy, who was a coal-merchant's son, came as a set-off against the coal-bill, and was called, on that account, 'Exchange or Barter' – a name selected from the arithmetic-book as expressing this arrangement (Copperfield).*

Ezekiel: 'The boy at Mugby', narrator of the third chapter. *I am the boy at what is called The Refreshment Room at Mugby Junction, and what's proudest boast is, that it never yet refreshed a mortal being (Christmas Stories – 'Mugby Junction').*

F, Mr.: Abbreviation used by Flora Finching to refer to her late husband. See also **Mr. F's Aunt** (*Dorrit*).

Face-Maker, Monsieur The: Performer at a Flemish country fair. *'Messieurs et Mesdames, with no other assistance than this mirror and this wig, I shall have the honour of showing you a thousand characters' (Uncommercial – 'In the French-Flemish Country').*

Fagin: Receiver of stolen goods and leader of the gang of young thieves in London into which Oliver Twist is introduced. He informs Bill Sikes of Nancy's treachery, bringing about her murder, is in turn informed against by Noah Claypole, and hanged. *A very old shrivelled Jew, whose villainous-looking and repulsive face was obscured by a quantity of matted red hair. He was dressed in a greasy flannel gown, with his throat bare. // 'We are very glad to see you, Oliver, very,' said the Jew. 'Dodger, take off the sausages; and draw a tub near the fire for Oliver. Ah, you're a staring at the pocket-handkerchiefs! eh, my dear! There are a good many of 'em, ain't there? We've just looked 'em out, ready for the wash; that's all, Oliver; that's all. Ha! ha! ha!' (Twist).*

Fair Freedom: Prince Bull's lovely wife. *She had brought him a large fortune, and had borne him an immense number of children, and had set them to spinning, and farming, and engineering, and soldiering, and sailoring, and doctoring, and lawyering, and preaching, and all kinds of trades (Reprinted – 'Prince Bull').*

Fairfax: A censorious young gentleman. *Of music, pictures, books, and poetry, the censorious young gentleman has an equally fine conception. As to men and women, he can tell all about them at a glance (Young Gentlemen – 'Censorious Young Gentleman').*

Family Pet: Nickname of a criminal to whom Duff attributes the theft at Conkey Chickweed's (q.v.) (*Twist*).

Fan: Scrooge's sister, mother of Fred (*Christmas Books* – 'Christmas Carol').

Fanchette: Daughter of a Swiss innkeeper who nurses Our Bore (*Reprinted* – 'Our Bore').

Fang: Magistrate who sentences Oliver Twist to three months' hard labour on the unproven charge of picking Brownlow's pocket. *A lean, long-backed, stiff-necked, middle-sized man, with no great quantity of hair, and what he had, growing on the back and sides of his head. His face was stern, and much flushed. If he were really not in the habit of drinking rather more than was exactly good for him, he might have brought an action against his countenance for libel, and have recovered heavy damages* (*Twist*).

Fanny: A pretty girl, presumably the narrator's sweetheart. *One of the prettiest girls that ever was seen – just like Fanny in the corner there* (*Christmas Stories* – 'Child's Story').

Fareway: Lady Fareway's second son and Adelina's brother; no Christian name is given. George Silverman is his college tutor for a time and through him meets Lady Fareway, with unhappy consequences ('Silverman').

Fareway, Lady: Adelina's mother, widow of Gaston Fareway, Bart. She presents George Silverman to a living and appoints him Adelina's tutor, but dismisses him upon learning that he has married Adelina to Granville Wharton ('Silverman').

Fareway, Adelina: Pupil of George Silverman and daughter of his benefactor. She reciprocates his love, but allows him to ally her with Granville Wharton, whom she marries ('Silverman').

Fat Boy, The: See **Joe** (*Pickwick*).

'Father of the Marshalsea': See **Dorrit, William** (*Dorrit*).

Fee, Dr. W. R.: Member of the Mudfog Association (*Mudfog*).

Feeder, Mr., B.A.: Dr. Blimber's assistant and subsequent successor. Marries Cornelia Blimber. *A kind of human barrel-organ, with a little list of tunes at which he was continually working, over and over again, without any variation. He might have been fitted up with a change of barrels, perhaps, in early life, if his destiny had been favourable; but it had not been; and he had only one, with which, in a monotonous round, it was his occupation to bewilder the young ideas of Dr. Blimber's young gentlemen* (*Dombey*).

Feeder, The Revd. Alfred, M.A.: Brother of Feeder, B.A., whose marriage ceremony he conducts (*Dombey*).

Feenix, Lord (Cousin Feenix): Man-about-town cousin to Edith Dombey, whom he shelters after her flight from Dombey. *Cousin Feenix was a man about town, forty years ago; but he is still so juvenile in figure and in manner, and so well got up, that strangers are amazed when they discover latent wrinkles in his lordship's face, and crows' feet in his eyes; and first observe him, not exactly certain when he walks across a room, of going quite straight to where he wants to go* (*Dombey*).

Fendall, Sergeant: One of the Detective Force officers of Scotland Yard. *A light-haired, well-spoken, polite person, is a prodigious hand at pursuing private inquiries of a delicate nature* (*Reprinted* – 'Detective Police').

Ferdinand, Miss: Inattentive fellow pupil of Rosa Bud at Miss Twinkleton's. *Miss Ferdinand, being apparently incorrigible, will have the kindness to write out this evening, in the original language, the first four fables of our vivacious neighbour, Monsieur La Fontaine* (*Drood*).

Fern, Lilian: Will Fern's orphan niece. *'She's my brother's child: an orphan. Nine year old, though you'd hardly think it; but she's tired and worn out now'* (*Christmas Books* – 'Chimes').

Fern, Will: Uncle of Lilian, an unemployed countryman befriended by Toby Veck after being taken before the magistrates for sleeping rough in London. He turns out to be an old friend of Mrs. Chickenstalker. *A sun-browned, sinewy, country-looking man, with grizzled hair, and a rough chin* (*Christmas Books* – 'Chimes').

Féroce, Monsieur: Proprietor of bathing machines at the narrator's French watering-place. *How he ever came by his name we cannot imagine. He is as gentle and polite a man as M. Loyal Devasseur himself; immensely stout withal; and of a beaming aspect. M. Féroce has saved so many people from drowning, and has been decorated with so many medals in consequence, that his stoutness seems a special dispensation of Providence to enable him to wear them* (*Reprinted* – 'Our French Watering-place').

Fezziwig: Scrooge's master in his apprentice days. *An old gentleman in a Welsh wig, sitting behind such a high desk, that if he had been two inches taller he must have knocked his head against the ceiling* (*Christmas Books* – 'Christmas Carol').

Fezziwig, Mrs. and the Misses: Fezziwig's wife and daughters. *In came Mrs. Fezziwig, one vast substantial smile. In came the three Miss Fezziwigs, beaming and loveable* (*Christmas Books* – 'Christmas Carol').

Fibbitson, Mrs.: Fellow resident of Mrs. Mell in a Blackheath almshouse. *Another old woman in a large chair by the fire, who was such a bundle of clothes that I feel grateful to this hour for not having sat upon her by mistake* (*Copperfield*).

Field, Inspector: Central figure of 'On Duty with Inspector Field'. He is based on a real-life figure, Inspector Charles F. Field, on whom Dickens also modelled Inspector Wield of 'Detective Police' and 'Three "Detective" Anecdotes' (*Reprinted*).

Fielding, Mrs.: May's mother. *A little querulous chip of an old lady with a peevish face, who, in right of having preserved a waist like a bedpost, was supposed to be a most transcendent figure; and who, in consequence of having once been better off, or of labour-*

ing under an impression that she might have been, if something had happened which never did happen, and seemed to have never been particularly likely to come to pass – but it's all the same – was very genteel and patronising indeed (*Christmas Books* – 'Cricket').

Fielding, Emma: The bride. *'Looking like the sweetest picter,' in a white chip bonnet and orange flower, and all other elegancies becoming a bride* (*Young Couples* – 'Young Couple'). She appears again in old age in 'Old Couple': *One or two dresses from the bridal wardrobe are yet preserved. They are of a quaint and antique fashion, and seldom seen except in pictures. White has turned yellow, and brighter hues have faded. Do you wonder, child? The wrinkled face was once as smooth as yours, the eyes as bright, the shrivelled skin as fair and delicate.*

Fielding, May: Friend of Dot Peerybingle. Persuaded to marry Tackleton, she jilts him on the wedding morning for her long-lost Edward Plummer. *May was very pretty. You know sometimes, when you are used to a pretty face, how, when it comes into contact and comparison with another pretty face, it seems for the moment to be homely and faded, and hardly to deserve the high opinion you have had of it. Now, this was not at all the case, either with Dot or May; for May's face set off Dot's, and Dot's face set off May's, so naturally and agreeably, that, as John Peerybingle was very near saying when he came into the room, they ought to have been born sisters – which was the only improvement you could have suggested* (*Christmas Books* – 'Cricket').

Fiercy, Captain the Hon. Fitz-Whisker: Confidence trickster who buys goods on credit and disposes of them for cash through his 'servant', Do'em. *Struts and swaggers about with that compound air of conscious superiority and general blood-thirstiness which a military captain should always, and does most times, wear, to the admiration and terror of plebeian men. But the tradesmen's backs are no sooner turned, than the captain, with all the eccentricity of a mighty mind, and assisted by the faithful Do'em, whose devoted fidelity is not the least touching part of his character, disposes of everything to great advantage; for, although the articles fetch small sums, still they are sold considerably above cost price, the cost to the captain having been nothing at all* (*Mudfog* – 'Pantomime of Life').

Fikey: Secondhand carriage dealer and forger of South-Western Railway debentures, taken by Inspector Wield (*Reprinted* – 'Detective Police').

Filer: Friend of Alderman Cute, preoccupied with statistics. *A low-spirited gentleman of middle age, of a meagre habit, and a disconsolate face; who kept his hands continually in the pockets of his scanty pepper-and-salt trousers, very large and dog's-eared from that custom; and was not particularly well brushed or washed* (*Christmas Books* – 'Chimes').

Filletoville: The Marquis of Filletoville's heir, from whose abduction the Bagman's Uncle rescues the beautiful lady. *A young gentleman in a powdered wig, and a sky-blue coat trimmed with silver, made very*

full and broad in the skirts, which were lined with buckram. . . . *He wore knee breeches, and a kind of leggings rolled up over his silk stockings, and shoes with buckles; he had ruffles at his wrists, a three-cornered hat on his head, and a long taper sword by his side. The flaps of his waistcoat came half-way down his thighs, and the ends of his cravat reached to his waist* (*Pickwick*).

Finchbury, Lady Jane: Something of an artist. *'There's an uncommon good church in the village,'* says cousin Feenix, thoughtfully; *'pure specimen of the Anglo-Norman style, and admirably well sketched too by Lady Jane Finchbury – woman with tight stays'* (*Dombey*).

Finches of the Grove: Club joined by Pip and Herbert Pocket, also frequented by Startop and Drummle. *The object of which institution I have never divined, if it were not that the members should dine expensively once a fortnight, to quarrel among themselves as much as possible after dinner, and to cause six waiters to get drunk on the stairs* (*Expectations*).

Finching, Mrs.: Friend of the plausible couple, the Widgers. *'Oh dear!'* cries the plausible lady, *'you can-not think how often Bobtail and I have talked about poor Mrs. Finching – she is such a dear soul, and was so anxious that the baby should be a fine child – and very naturally, because she was very much here at one time, and there is, you know, a natural emulation among mothers* (*Young Couples* – 'Plausible Couple').

Finching, Mrs. Flora: Christopher Casby's widowed daughter, once loved by Arthur Clennam, for whose sake she befriends Amy Dorrit. *Flora, always tall, had grown to be very broad too, and short of breath; but that was not much. Flora, whom he had left a lily, had become a peony; but that was not much. Flora, who had seemed enchanting in all she said and thought, was diffuse and silly. That was much. Flora, who had been spoiled and artless long ago, was determined to be spoiled and artless now. That was a fatal blow* (*Dorrit*).

Fips: Solicitor of Austin Friars, City of London, retained by old Martin Chuzzlewit to employ Tom Pinch as his librarian. *Small and spare, and looked peaceable, and wore black shorts and powder* (*Chuzzlewit*).

Fish: Sir Joseph Bowley's confidential secretary. *A not very stately gentleman in black* (*Christmas Books* – 'Chimes').

Fisher, Fanny: Mrs. Venning's daughter, living with her husband on Silver-Store Island. *Quite a child she looked, with a little copy of herself holding to her dress* (*Christmas Stories* – 'English Prisoners').

Fithers: See **Slummery** and **Fithers** (*Young Couples* – 'Plausible Couple').

Fitz Binkle, Lord and **Lady:** Chairman at a dinner of the Indigent Orphans' Friends' Benevolent Institution, and his wife. *'Lord Fitz Binkle, the chairman of the day, in addition to an annual donation of fifteen pound – thirty guineas [prolonged knocking: several* *gentlemen knock the stems off their wine-glasses, in the vehemence of their approbation*]. *Lady Fitz Binkle, in addition to an annual donation of ten pound – twenty pound'* [*protracted knocking and shouts of 'Bravo!'*] (*Boz* – 'Public Dinners').

Fitz-Marshall, Captain Charles: An alias used by Jingle (q.v.) at Eatanswill and Ipswich (*Pickwick*).

Fitz-Osborne, The Hon. Augustus Fitz-Edward Fitz-John: Suggested by Flamwell to be the true identity of Horatio Sparkins (*Boz* – 'Horatio Sparkins').

Fitz-Sordust, Colonel: The garrison commander (*Young Gentlemen* – 'Military Young Gentleman').

Five Sisters of York, The: Subjects of a tale told by a passenger of a broken-down coach in which Squeers and Nicholas Nickleby are travelling to Yorkshire (*Nickleby*).

Fixem: A broker, master of Bung. He uses the alias of Smith. *'Fixem (as we always did in that profession), without waiting to be announced, walks in'* (*Boz* – 'Broker's Man').

Fizkin, Horatio: Defeated Parliamentary candidate at Eatanswill. *The speeches of the two candidates, though differing in every other respect, afforded a beautiful tribute to the merit and high worth of the electors of Eatanswill. . . . Fizkin expressed his readiness to do anything he was wanted* (*Pickwick*).

Fizzgig, Don Bolaro: Spanish grandee, father of Jingle's conquest, Donna Christina (q.v.), who consents to the match too late, causing her death. *'And her father?' inquired the poetic Snodgrass. 'Remorse and misery,' replied the stranger. 'Sudden disappearance – talk of the whole city – search made everywhere – without success – public fountain in the great square suddenly ceased playing – weeks elapsed – still a stoppage – workmen employed to clean it – water drawn off – father-in-law discovered sticking head first in the main pipe, with a full confession in his right boot – took him out, and the fountain played away again, as well as ever'* (*Pickwick*).

Flabella, Lady: Heroine of a romantic novel read by Kate Nickleby to Mrs. Wititterly. *'The Lady Flabella, with an agitation she could not repress, hastily tore off the envelope and broke the scented seal. It was from Befillaire – the young, the slim, the low-voiced – her own Befillaire'* (*Nickleby*).

Fladdock, General. American Militia officer introduced to Martin Chuzzlewit at the Norrises' in New York. *The general, attired in full uniform for a ball, came darting in with such precipitancy, that, hitching his boot in the carpet, and getting his sword between his legs, he came down headlong, and presented a curious little bald place on the crown of his head to the eyes of the astonished company. Nor was this the worst of it; for being rather corpulent and very tight, the general, being down, could not get up again, but lay there writhing and doing such things with his boots, as there is no other instance of in military history* (*Chuzzlewit*).

Flam, The Hon. Sparkins: Wastrel man-about-town, friend of Squire Norton. He plans to abduct Rose, but is thwarted by Martin Stokes (*Village Coquettes*).

Flamwell: Toadying friend to the Maldertons. *One of those gentlemen of remarkably extensive information whom one occasionally meets in society, who pretend to know everybody, but in reality know nobody. At Malderton's, where any stories about great people were received with a greedy ear, he was an especial favourite; and, knowing the kind of people he had to deal with, he carried his passion of claiming acquaintance with everybody, to the most immoderate length. He had rather a singular way of telling his greatest lies in a parenthesis, and with an air of self-denial, as if he feared being thought egotistical* (*Boz* – 'Horatio Sparkins').

Flanders, Sally: Formerly the Uncommercial Traveller's nurse. He attends the funeral of her late husband, a small master builder. *The moment I saw her I knew that she was not in her own real natural state. She formed a sort of Coat of Arms, grouped with a smelling-bottle, a handkerchief, an orange, a bottle of vinegar, Flanders's sister, her own sister, Flanders's brother's wife, and two neighbouring gossips – all in mourning, and all ready to hold her whenever she fainted* (*Uncommercial* – 'Medicine Men of Civilisation').

'Flash Toby': See **Crackit, Toby** (*Twist*).

Flasher, Wilkins: Stockbroker who assists Tony Weller with his late wife's estate. *Wilkins Flasher, Esquire, was balancing himself on two legs of an office stool, spearing a wafer-box with a pen-knife, which he dropped every now and then with great dexterity into the very centre of a small red wafer that was stuck outside* (*Pickwick*).

Fledgeby ('Fascination Fledgeby'): Owner of the moneylending business of Pubsey and Co., run for him by Riah as a front for financial sharp practices. He has a hold upon Lammle, Wrayburn, Twemlow, and others, but is eventually thwarted by Lightwood. *Young Fledgeby had a peachy cheek, or a cheek compounded of the peach and the red red red wall on which it grows, and was an awkward, sandy-haired, small-eyed youth, exceeding slim (his enemies would have said lanky), and prone to self-examination in the articles of whisker and moustache. While feeling for the whisker that he anxiously expected, Fledgeby underwent remarkable fluctuations of spirits, ranging along the whole scale from confidence to despair. There were times when he started, as exclaiming, 'By Jupiter, here it is at last!' There were other times when, being equally depressed, he would be seen to shake his head, and give up hope* (*Mutual Friend*).

Fleetwood, Mr. and Mrs.: Participants in the steam excursion with their small son Alexander. *The latter was attired for the occasion in a nankeen frock, between the bottom of which and the top of his plaid socks, a considerable portion of two small mottled legs was discernible. He had a light blue cap with a gold band and tassel on his head, and a damp piece of gingerbread in his hand, with which he had slightly embossed his countenance* (*Boz* – 'Steam Excursion').

75

Fleming, Agnes: Oliver Twist's mother, Rose Maylie's sister. Having been seduced by Leeford, she dies giving birth to Oliver in a workhouse. *The pale face of a young woman was raised feebly from the pillow; and a faint voice imperfectly articulated the words, 'Let me see the child, and die' (Twist).*

Fleming, Rose: See **Maylie, Rose** *(Twist)*.

Flimkins, Mr. and **Mrs.:** An acting couple at the Surrey Theatre *(Young Gentlemen – 'Theatrical Young Gentleman')*.

Flintwinch, Ephraim: Jeremiah's brother and double, entrusted by Jeremiah with getting the Dorrit legacy documents out of England *(Dorrit)*.

Flintwinch, Jeremiah: Mrs. Clennam's confidential clerk and later partner. *A short, bald old man, in a high-shouldered black coat and waistcoat, drab breeches, and long drab gaiters. He might, from his dress, have been either clerk or servant, and in fact had long been both. There was nothing about him in the way of decoration but a watch, which was lowered into the depths of its proper pocket by an old black ribbon, and had a tarnished copper key moored above it, to show where it was sunk. His head was awry, and he had a one-sided, crab-like way with him, as if his foundations had yielded at about the same time as those of the house, and he ought to have been propped up in a similar manner (Dorrit).*

Flintwinch, Mrs. Jeremiah: Jeremiah's wife. See **Affery** *(Dorrit)*.

Flipfield: Friend of the Uncommercial Traveller, notable for his successful birthday parties. *There had been nothing set or formal about them; Flipfield having been accustomed merely to say, two or three days before, 'Don't forget to come and dine, old boy, according to custom'; – I don't know what he said to the ladies he invited, but I may safely assume it not to have been 'old girl' (Uncommercial – 'Birthday Celebrations').*

Flipfield, Miss: Sister of Flipfield and Tom Flipfield. *Held her pocket-handkerchief to her bosom in a majestic manner, and spoke to all of us (none of us had ever seen her before), in pious and condoning tones, of all the quarrels that had taken place in the family, from her infancy – which must have been a long time ago – down to that hour (Uncommercial – 'Birthday Celebrations').*

Flipfield, Mrs.: Flipfield's, Tom Flipfield's, and Miss Flipfield's mother. *With a blue-veined miniature of the late Mr. Flipfield round her neck, in an oval, resembling a tart from the pastrycook's (Uncommercial – 'Birthday Celebrations').*

Flipfield, Tom ('The Long Lost'): Brother of Miss Flipfield and of Flipfield, whose birthday party he wrecks by returning from 'the banks of the Ganges'. *He was an antipathetical being, with a peculiar power and gift of treading on everybody's tenderest place. They talk in America of a man's 'Platform'. I should describe the Platform of the Long-lost as a Platform composed of other people's corns, on which he had stumped his way, with all his might and main, to his present position (Uncommercial – 'Birthday Celebrations').*

Flite, Miss: A veteran suitor in Chancery who haunts the Law Courts. She is a tenant of Krooks and makes friends with Esther Summerson and her companions. *A curious little old woman in a squeezed bonnet, and carrying a reticule, came curtseying and smiling up to us, with an air of great ceremony.... 'I was a ward myself. I was not mad at that time,' curtseying low, and smiling between every little sentence. 'I had youth and hope. I believe, beauty. It matters very little now. Neither of the three served, or saved me. I have the honour to attend Court regularly. With my documents. I expect a judgment. Shortly. On the Day of Judgment.'* She keeps a score of larks, linnets, and goldfinches in cages in her room. *'I began to keep the little creatures,' she said ... 'with the intention of restoring them to liberty. When my judgment should be given. Ye-es! They die in prison, though' (Bleak House).*

Flopson: One of the Matthew Pockets' nursemaids *(Expectations)*.

Flowers: Mrs. Skewton's maid. *At night, she should have been a skeleton, with dart and hour-glass, rather than a woman, this attendant; for her touch was as the touch of Death. The painted object shrivelled underneath her hand; the form collapsed, the hair dropped off, the arched dark eyebrows changed to scanty tufts of grey; the pale lips shrunk, the skin became cadaverous and loose; an old, worn, yellow nodding woman, with red eyes, alone remained in Cleopatra's place, huddled up, like a slovenly bundle, in a greasy flannel gown (Dombey).*

Fluggers: Member of Crummles's theatrical company. *'Old Fluggers, who does the heavy business you know' (Nickleby).*

Flummery: Speaker at the zoology and botany session of the second meeting of the Mudfog Association. *Exhibited a twig, claiming to be a veritable branch of that noble tree known to naturalists as the* SHAKESPEARE, *which has taken root in every land and climate, and gathered under the shade of its broad green boughs the great family of mankind (Mudfog).*

Fogg: Partner in Dodson and Fogg, Mrs. Bardell's attorneys. *An elderly, pimply-faced, vegetable-diet sort of man, in a black coat, dark mixture trousers, and small black gaiters: a kind of being who seemed to be an essential part of the desk at which he was writing, and to have as much thought or sentiment (Pickwick).*

Folair: Dancer and actor with Crummles's theatrical company. *A shabby gentleman in an old pair of buff slippers came in at one powerful slide (Nickleby).*

Foley: One of Feenix's numerous acquaintances *(Dombey)*.

Folly: One of Miss Flite's birds *(Bleak House)*.

Foreign Gentleman: Guest at the Podsnaps'. *There was a droll disposition, not only on the part of Mr. Podsnap, but of everybody else, to treat him as if he were a child who was hard of hearing (Mutual Friend).*

GARGERY

Formiville: See **Slap** (*Nightingale's Diary*).

Foxey, Dr.: Member of the Mudfog Association. *Nothing unpleasant occurred until noon, with the exception of Doctor Foxey's brown silk umbrella and white hat becoming entangled in the machinery while he was explaining to a knot of ladies the construction of the steam-engine (Mudfog).*

Francis, Father: See **Voigt, Maître** (*No Thoroughfare*).

François: A waiter attending Carker and Edith Dombey at Dijon. *'François has flown over to the Golden Head for supper. He flies on these occasions like an angel or a bird' (Dombey).*

Frank, Little: Child cousin and friend of Michael, the Poor Relation. *He is a diffident boy by nature; and in a crowd he is soon run over, as I may say, and forgotten. He and I, however, get on exceedingly well. I have a fancy that the poor child will in time succeed to my peculiar position in the family. We talk but little; still, we understand each other (Christmas Stories – 'Poor Relation').*

Fred: Scrooge's nephew, son of Fan. *He had so heated himself with rapid walking in the fog and frost, this nephew of Scrooge's, that he was all in a glow: his face was ruddy and handsome; his eyes sparkled, and his breath smoked again (Christmas Books – 'Christmas Carol').*

Frost, Miss: A girl at Our School. *Why a something in mourning, called 'Miss Frost,' should still connect itself with our preparatory school, we are unable to say. We retain no impression of the beauty of Miss Frost – if she were beautiful; or of the mental fascinations of Miss Frost – if she were accomplished; yet her name and her black dress hold an enduring place in our remembrance (Reprinted – 'Our School').*

G: The gentleman believed by Miss Pupford's pupils to be in love with her. *It is suspected by the pupil-mind that G is a short, chubby old gentleman, with little black sealing-wax boots up to his knees (Christmas Stories – 'Tom Tiddler's Ground').*

Gabblewig: Lawyer suitor of Rosina Nightingale. Her uncle disapproves, thinking him a weak character, so he proves his strength by saving Mr. Nightingale from Slap's planned extortion, in the course of which he assumes disguises as Charley Bit, Mr. Poulter, Captain Blower, R.N., and a deaf sexton (*Nightingale's Diary*).

Gabelle, Théophile: Postmaster and official on the St. Evrémonde estate. Denouncer of Charles Darnay. *A small Southern man of retaliative temperament (Two Cities).*

Gabrielle: See **Bebelle** (*Christmas Stories – 'Somebody's Luggage'*).

Gallanbile, M.P.: Client of the General Agency Office. *'Fifteen guineas, tea and sugar, and servants allowed to see male cousins, if godly. Note. Cold dinner in the kitchen on the Sabbath, Mr. Gallanbile being devoted to the Observance question. No victuals whatever, cooked on the Lord's Day, with the exception of dinner for Mr. and Mrs. Gallanbile, which, being a work of piety and necessity, is exempted. Mr. Gallanbile dines late on the day of rest, in order to prevent the sinfulness of the cook's dressing herself' (Nickleby).*

'Game Chicken, The': Pugilist who tutors Toots in the noble art. *Always to be heard of at the bar of the Black Badger, wore a shaggy white great-coat in the warmest weather, and knocked Mr. Toots about the head three times a week, for the small consideration of ten and six per visit (Dombey).*

Gamfield: Chimney sweep who wishes to take Oliver Twist for his apprentice. *Whose villainous countenance was a regular stamped receipt for cruelty ('Twist).*

Gammon: One of Miss Flite's birds (*Bleak House*).

Gamp, Mrs. Sarah (Sairey): Midwife and nurse who attends Anthony Chuzzlewit, Lewsome, and Chuffey, and is one of the causes of Jonas Chuzzlewit's exposure. *She was a fat old woman, this Mrs. Gamp, with a husky voice and a moist eye, which she had a remarkable power of turning up, and only showing the white of it. Having very little neck, it cost her some trouble to look over herself, if one may say so, at those to whom she talked. She wore a very rusty black gown, rather the worse for snuff, and a shawl and bonnet to correspond. . . . The face of Mrs. Gamp – the nose in particular – was somewhat red and swollen, and it was difficult to enjoy her society without becoming conscious of a smell of spirits. Like most persons who have attained to great eminence in their profession, she took to hers very kindly; insomuch, that setting aside her natural predilections as a woman, she went to a lying-in or a laying-out with equal zest and relish (Chuzzlewit).* See also **Harris, Mrs.**

Gander: A boarder at Todgers's. *Gander was of a witty turn (Chuzzlewit).*

Ganz, Dr.: Physician practising at Neuchâtel, whose testimony helps to prove George Vendale's identity (*Christmas Stories – 'No Thoroughfare'*).

Gargery, Joe: Pip's blacksmith brother-in-law married to Pip's sister Georgiana Mary. He remains Pip's loyal friend, even after Pip, turning gentleman, comes to despise his unsophisticated ways. After his wife's death Joe marries Biddy and finds happiness. *A fair man, with curls of flaxen hair on each side of his smooth face, and with eyes of such a very undecided blue that they seemed to have somehow got mixed with their own whites. He was a mild, good-natured, sweet-tempered, easy-going, foolish, dear fellow – a sort of Hercules in strength, and also in weakness (Expectations).*

Gargery, Mrs. Joe (Georgiana Mary): Pip's sister, Joe's first wife. A neurotic shrew, she bullies the uncomplaining Joe and Pip. She is paralysed in an assault by Orlick, and dies. *My sister, Mrs. Joe, with black hair and eyes, had such a prevailing redness of skin, that I sometimes used to wonder whether it was possible she washed herself with a nutmeg-grater instead of soap. She was tall and bony, and almost* *always wore a coarse apron, fastened over her figure behind with two loops, and having a square impregnable bib in front, that was stuck full of pins and needles. She made it a powerful merit in herself, and a strong reproach against Joe, that she wore this apron so much (Expectations).*

Garland: Father of Abel and brother of 'The Bachelor' (q.v.). Friend and defender of Kit Nubbles. *A little fat placid-faced old gentleman (Curiosity Shop).*

Garland, Mrs.: Garland's wife. Mother of Abel. *A little old lady, plump and placid (Curiosity Shop).*

Garland, Abel: The Garlands' son, articled to Witherden and later his partner. *Had a quaint old-fashioned air about him, looked nearly of the same age as his father, and bore a wonderful resemblance to him in face and figure, though wanting something of his full, round cheerfulness, and substituting in its place, a timid reserve. In all other respects, in the neatness of the dress, and even in the club-foot, he and the old gentleman were precisely alike (Curiosity Shop).*

Gashford: Lord George Gordon's secretary. Would-be possessor of Emma Haredale. He eventually poisons himself. *Angularly made, high-shouldered, bony, and ungraceful. His dress, in imitation of his superior, was demure and staid in the extreme; his manner, formal and constrained. This gentleman had an overhanging brow, great hands and feet and ears, and a pair of eyes that seemed to have made an unnatural retreat into his head, and to have dug themselves a cave to hide in. His manner was smooth and humble, but very sly and slinking. He wore the aspect of a man who was always lying in wait for something that wouldn't come to pass; but he looked patient – very patient – and fawned like a spaniel dog (Rudge).*

Gaspard: Parisian labourer, murderer of Marquis St. Evrémonde, whose carriage had killed his child. *One tall joker . . . his head more out of a long squalid bag of a nightcap than in it, scrawled upon a wall with his finger dipped in muddy wine-lees – BLOOD (Two Cities).*

Gattleton: Of Rose Villa, Clapham Rise; head of a family 'infected with the mania for Private Theatricals'. He acts as prompter for their production of *Othello. A stock-broker in especially comfortable circumstances (Boz – 'Mrs. Joseph Porter').*

Gattleton, the Misses: The Gattletons' three daughters, sisters to Sempronius. Caroline plays Fenella and Lucina Desdemona in the family's private theatricals (*Boz – 'Mrs. Joseph Porter').*

Gattleton, Mrs.: Gattleton's wife, mother of Sempronius, Caroline, Lucina, and another daughter. *A kind, good-tempered, vulgar soul, exceedingly fond of her husband and children, and entertaining only three dislikes. In the first place, she had a natural antipathy to anybody else's unmarried daughters; in the second, she was in bodily fear of anything in the shape of ridicule; lastly – almost a necessary consequence of this feeling – she regarded, with feelings of the utmost horror, one Mrs. Joseph Porter over the way (Boz – 'Mrs. Joseph Porter').*

Gattleton, Sempronius: The Gattletons' son, brother to Caroline, Lucina, and another sister. He produces, and plays the title role in, their private presentation of *Othello. In consideration of his sustaining the trifling inconvenience of bearing all the expenses of the play, Mr. Sempronius had been, in the most handsome manner, unanimously elected stage-manager (Boz – 'Mrs. Joseph Porter').*

Gay, Walter: Nephew of Solomon Gills. A junior clerk employed by Dombey, who sends him abroad at James Carker's instigation, and he is thought lost in a shipwreck; but he returns and marries Florence Dombey. *A cheerful-looking, merry boy, fresh with running home in the rain; fair-faced, bright-eyed, and curly-haired (Dombey).*

Gazingi, Miss: Member of Crummles's theatrical company. *With an imitation ermine boa tied in a loose knot round her neck (Nickleby).*

General, Mrs.: A middle-aged widow engaged to impart gentility to the Dorrit girls. *In person, Mrs. General, including her skirts which had much to do with it, was of a dignified and imposing appearance; ample, rustling, gravely voluminous; always upright behind the proprieties. She might have been taken – had been taken – to the top of the Alps and the bottom of Herculaneum, without disarranging a fold in her dress, or displacing a pin. If her countenance and hair had rather a floury appearance, as though from living in some transcendently genteel Mill, it was rather because she was a chalky creation altogether, than because she mended her complexion with violet powder, or had turned grey. If her eyes had no expression, it was probably because they had nothing to express. If she had few wrinkles, it was because her mind had never traced its name or any other inscription on her face. A cool, waxy, blown-out woman, who had never lighted well (Dorrit).*

Gentleman in Small-clothes, The: A deranged old gentleman who woos Mrs. Nickleby over the garden wall. *The apparition of an old black velvet cap, which, by slow degrees, as if its wearer were ascending a ladder or pair of steps, rose above the wall dividing their garden from that of the next cottage . . . and was gradually followed by a very large head, and an old face in which were a pair of most extraordinary grey eyes: very wild, very wide open, and rolling in their sockets, with a dull languishing leering look, most ugly to behold (Nickleby).*

George: Member of a typical audience at Astley's. *The eldest son, a boy of fourteen years old, who was evidently trying to look as if he did not belong to the family (Boz – 'Astley's').*

George: Guard of the snowbound coach taking Charley to Liverpool. *The coachman had already replied, 'Yes, he'd take her through it,' – meaning by Her the coach, – 'if so be as George would stand by him.' George was the guard, and he had already sworn that he would stand by him (Christmas Stories – 'Holly-Tree').*

George: Buffle's articled clerk, in love with Robina (*Christmas Stories – 'Mrs. Lirriper's Legacy').*

George: Guard of the Yarmouth mailcoach taking David Copperfield to school. *'Take care of that child, George, or he'll burst!'* (*Copperfield*).

George: Mrs. Jarley's caravan driver, later her husband (*Curiosity Shop*).

George: A friend of the Kenwigses. *A young man, who had known Mr. Kenwigs when he was a bachelor, and was much esteemed by the ladies, as bearing the reputation of a rake* (*Nickleby*).

George, Aunt and **Uncle:** Hosts at Christmas dinner. *Aunt George at home dusting decanters and filling castors, and uncle George carrying bottles into the dining-parlour, and calling for corkscrews, and getting into everybody's way* (*Boz* – 'Christmas Dinner').

George, Mrs.: Friend and neighbour of Mrs. Quilp (*Curiosity Shop*).

George, Trooper or **Mr.:** See **Rouncewell, George** (*Bleak House*).

Georgiana: Cousin of Miss Havisham and one of the toadies surrounding her. *An indigestive single woman, who called her rigidity religion, and her liver love* (*Expectations*).

Ghost of Christmas Past: An apparition which shows Scrooge scenes and characters from his past life. *It was a strange figure – like a child: yet not so like a child as like an old man, viewed through some supernatural medium, which gave him the appearance of having receded from the view, and being diminished to a child's proportions. Its hair, which hung about its neck and down its back, was white as if with age; and yet the face had not a wrinkle in it, and the tenderest bloom was on the skin. The arms were very long and muscular; the hands the same, as if its hold were of uncommon strength. Its legs and feet, most delicately formed, were, like those upper members, bare. It wore a tunic of the purest white; and round its waist was bound a lustrous belt, the sheen of which was beautiful. It held a branch of fresh green holly in its hand; and, in singular contradiction of that wintry emblem, had its dress trimmed with summer flowers. But the strangest thing about it was, that from the crown of its head there sprung a bright clear jet of light, by which all this was visible; and which was doubtless the occasion of its using, in its duller moments, a great extinguisher for a cap, which it now held under its arm* (*Christmas Books* – 'Christmas Carol').

Ghost of Christmas Present: An apparition which shows Scrooge present scenes, including the Cratchits' Christmas Day. *It was clothed in one simple green robe, or mantle, bordered with white fur. This garment hung so loosely on the figure, that its capacious breast was bare, as if disdaining to be warded or concealed by any artifice. Its feet, observable beneath the ample folds of the garment, were also bare; and on its head it wore no other covering than a holly wreath, set here and there with shining icicles. Its dark brown curls were long and free; free as its genial face, its sparkling eye, its open hand, its cheery voice, its unconstrained demeanour, and its joyful air. Girded round its middle was an antique scabbard; but no sword was in it, and the ancient sheath was eaten up with rust* (*Christmas Books* – 'Christmas Carol').

Ghost of Christmas Yet to Come: An apparition which shows Scrooge prophetic scenes. *It was shrouded in a deep black garment, which concealed its head, its face, its form, and left nothing of it visible save one outstretched hand. But for this it would have been difficult to detach its figure from the night, and separate it from the darkness by which it was surrounded. He felt that it was tall and stately when it came beside him, and that its mysterious presence filled him with a solemn dread. He knew no more, for the Spirit neither spoke nor moved* (*Christmas Books* – 'Christmas Carol').

Gibbs, Villiam. A young hairdresser, obsessed with the beauty of one of the dummy figures in his shop window, in a tale told by Sam Weller. *' "I never vill enter into the bonds of vedlock," he says, "until I meet vith a young 'ooman as realises my idea o' that 'ere fairest dummy vith the light hair. Then, and not till then," he says, "I vill approach the altar." All the young ladies he know'd as had got dark hair told him this wos very sinful, and that he wos wurshippin' a idle; but them as wos at all near the same shade as the dummy coloured up wery much, and wos observed to think him a wery nice young man'* (*Humphrey*).

Giggles, Miss: Inattentive fellow pupil of Rosa Bud at Miss Twinkleton's. *Responsible inquiries having assured us that it was but one of those 'airy nothings' pointed at by the Poet (whose name and date of birth Miss Giggles will supply within half an hour), we would now discard the subject* (*Drood*).

Gilbert, Mark: A London apprentice, initiate to the Prentice Knights, or United Bull-Dogs, and later close associate of Sim Tappertit. *'Mark Gilbert. Age, nineteen. Bound to Thomas Curzon, hosier, Golden Fleece, Aldgate. Loves Curzon's daughter. Cannot say that Curzon's daughter loves him. Should think it probable. Curzon pulled his ears last Tuesday week'* (*Rudge*).

Giles: Mrs. Maylie's butler at Chertsey. He wounds Oliver Twist with a pistol shot during the attempted burglary. *He had taken his station some half-way between the sideboard and the breakfast-table; and, with his body drawn up to its full height, his head thrown back, and inclined the merest trifle on one side, his left leg advanced, and his right hand thrust into his waistcoat, while his left hung down by his side, grasping a waiter, looked like one who laboured under a very agreeable sense of his own merits and importance* (*Twist*).

Gill, Mrs.: Frequent client of Mrs. Gamp in her capacity as midwife. *' "Often and often have I heerd him say," I says to Mrs. Harris, meaning Mr. Gill, "that he would back his wife agen Moore's almanack, to name the very day and hour, for ninepence farden" '* (*Chuzzlewit*).

Gills, Solomon (Old Sol): Walter Gay's uncle. Ship's instrument-maker and proprietor of a shop in the City of London, The Wooden Midshipman (q.v.). He goes searching for Walter when he disappears at sea and returns to make Captain Cuttle his partner. *Solomon Gills himself (more generally called Old Sol) was far from having a maritime appearance. To say nothing of his Welsh wig, which was as plain and stubborn a Welsh wig as ever was worn, and in which he looked like anything but a Rover, he was a slow, quiet-spoken, thoughtful old fellow, with eyes as red as if they had been small suns looking at you through a fog; and a newly-awakened manner, such as he might have acquired by having stared for three or four days successively through every optical instrument in his shop, and suddenly come back to the world again, to find it green. The only change ever known in his outward man, was from a complete suit of coffee-colour cut very square, and ornamented with glaring buttons, to the same suit of coffee-colour minus the inexpressibles, which were then of a pale nankeen. He wore a very precise shirt-frill, and carried a pair of first-rate spectacles on his forehead, and a tremendous chronometer in his fob, rather than doubt which precious possession, he would have believed in a conspiracy against it on the part of all the clocks and watches in the City, and even of the very sun itself* (Dombey).*

Gimblet, Brother: An elderly drysalter who acts as chorus to the preaching of Verity Hawkyard ('Silverman').

Glamour, Bob: Regular drinker at the Six Jolly Fellowship Porters *(Mutual Friend)*.

Glavormelly: A deceased fellow actor of Mr. Snevellici. *'You never saw my friend Glavormelly, sir!' said Miss Snevellici's papa. 'Then you have never seen acting yet'* (Nickleby).*

Glibbery: See **Gliddery, Bob** *(Mutual Friend)*.

Gliddery, Bob: Potboy at the Six Jolly Fellowship Porters. (He is referred to as **Glibbery** early in the story, **Gliddery** later) *(Mutual Friend)*.

Globson, Bully: Schoolmate of the Uncommercial Traveller. *A big fat boy, with a big fat head and a big fat fist, and at the beginning of that Half had raised such a bump on my forehead that I couldn't get my hat of state on, to go to church* (Uncommercial – 'Birthday Celebrations').*

Glogwog, Sir Chipkins: One of the aristocratic acquaintances claimed by the egotistical couple *(Young Couples – 'Egotistical Couple')*.

Glorious Apollos: A 'select convivial circle' of which Dick Swiveller is Perpetual Grand *(Curiosity Shop)*.

Glubb, Old: An old man who wheeled Paul Dombey along the parade at Brighton. *'He used to draw my couch. He knows all about the deep sea, and the fish that are in it, and the great monsters that come and lie on rocks in the sun, and dive into the water again when they're startled, blowing and splashing so, that they can be heard for miles'* (Dombey).*

Gobler: Boarder at Mrs. Tibbs's. He marries his fellow boarder and hypochondriac, Mrs. Bloss, who admires his symptoms. *A lazy, selfish hypochondriac;*

always complaining and never ill.... He was tall, thin, and pale; he always fancied he had a severe pain somewhere or other, and his face invariably wore a pinched, screwed-up expression; he looked, indeed, like a man who had got his feet in a tub of exceedingly hot water, against his will (Boz – 'Boarding-House').*

Gog and **Magog:** Two giant figures in the Guildhall, City of London, which come to life and converse, overheard by Joe Toddyhigh. *These guardian genii of the City had quitted their pedestals, and reclined in easy attitudes in the great stained glass window. Between them was an ancient cask, which seemed to be full of wine; for the younger Giant, clapping his huge hand upon it, and throwing up his mighty leg, burst into an exulting laugh, which reverberated through the hall like thunder* (Humphrey).* The figures, commemorating two survivors of a brood of giants, who had been made to serve as porters at the medieval palace formerly on the Guildhall site, were destroyed in the Great Fire and replaced by new ones over 14 ft. high (those of Dickens's time), which were in turn destroyed in an air raid in 1940. New figures replaced them in 1953.

'Golden Dustman, The': See **Boffin, Nicodemus** *(Mutual Friend)*.

'Golden Lucy': See **Atherfield, Lucy** *(Christmas Stories – 'Golden Mary')*.

Goldstraw, Mrs. Sarah: Wilding's new housekeeper, a widow, formerly a nurse at the Foundling Hospital known as Sally. She reveals the mistake in his identity. *A woman, perhaps fifty, but looking younger, with a face remarkable for placid cheerfulness, and a manner no less remarkable for its quiet expression of equability and temper. Nothing in her dress could have been changed to her advantage. Nothing in the noiseless self-possession of her manner could have been changed to her advantage* (Christmas Stories – 'No Thoroughfare' and dramatised version of 'No Thoroughfare').*

Goodchild, Francis: One of the two apprentices. *Goodchild was laboriously idle and would take upon himself any amount of pains and labour to assure himself that he was idle; in short, had no better idea of idleness than that it was useless industry* (Two Apprentices).*

Goodwin: Mrs. Pott's maid. *Attached to Mrs. Pott's person was a body-guard of one, a young lady whose ostensible employment was to preside over her toilet, but who rendered herself useful in a variety of ways, and in none more so than in the particular department of constantly aiding and abetting her mistress in every wish and inclination opposed to the desires of the unhappy Pott* (Pickwick).*

Goody, Mrs.: An old parishioner whose grandchild, the Rev. Mr. Milvey suggests, might suit the Boffins for adoption. *I don't think,' said Mrs. Milvey, glancing at the Reverend Frank – 'and I believe my husband will agree with me when he considers it again – that you could possibly keep that orphan clean from snuff. Because his grandmother takes so many ounces, and drops it over him.... And she is an inconvenient* woman. *I hope it's not uncharitable to remember that last Christmas Eve she drank eleven cups of tea, and grumbled all the time' (Mutual Friend).*

Gordon, Colonel: Kinsman and political opponent of Lord George Gordon *(Rudge).*

Gordon, Emma: Member of Sleary's Circus, subsequently married to a cheesemonger who admired her from the audience. *The most accomplished tight-rope lady (Hard Times).*

Gordon, Lord George: President of the Protestant Association and leader of the anti-Popery 'Gordon Riots' of 1780. Arrested for high treason but acquitted. He died during imprisonment for libel in 1793. *About the middle height, of a slender make, and sallow complexion, with an aquiline nose, and long hair of reddish brown, combed perfectly straight and smooth about his ears, and slightly powdered, but without the slightest vestige of a curl. He was attired, under his great-coat, in a full suit of black, quite free from any ornament, and of the most precise and sober cut. The gravity of his dress, together with a certain lankness of cheek and stiffness of deportment, added nearly ten years to his age, but his figure was that of one not yet past thirty. As he stood musing in the red glow of the fire, it was striking to observe his very bright large eye, which betrayed a restlessness of thought and purpose, singularly at variance with the studied composure and sobriety of his mien, and with his quaint and sad apparel. It had nothing harsh or cruel in its expression; neither had his face, which was thin and mild, and wore an air of melancholy; but it was suggestive of an air of indefinable uneasiness, which infected those who looked upon him, and filled them with a kind of pity for the man: though why it did so, they would have had some trouble to explain (Rudge).*

Governor, Jack: Old friend of John, the narrator, and one of the party visiting the haunted house. *I have always regarded Jack as the finest-looking sailor that ever sailed. He is grey now, but as handsome as he was a quarter of a century ago – nay, handsomer. A portly, cheery, well-built figure of a broad-shouldered man, with a frank smile, a brilliant dark eye, and a rich dark eyebrow. I remember those under darker hair, and they look all the better for their silver setting. He has been wherever his Union namesake flies, has Jack (Christmas Stories – 'Haunted House').*

Gowan, Mrs.: Gowan's mother, widow of a 'Commissioner of nothing particular somewhere or other'. *A courtly old lady, formerly a Beauty, and still sufficiently well-favoured to have dispensed with the powder on her nose, and a certain impossible bloom under each eye. She was a little lofty (Dorrit).*

Gowan, Henry: A feckless artist who marries Minnie Meagles. *This gentleman looked barely thirty. He was well dressed, of a sprightly and gay appearance, a well-knit figure, and a rich dark complexion. . . . Mr. Henry Gowan, inheriting from his father, the Commissioner, that very questionable help in life, a small independence, had been difficult to settle; the rather, as public appointments chanced to be scarce, and his*

genius, *during his earlier manhood, was of that exclusively agricultural character which applies itself to the cultivation of wild oats. At last he had decided that he would become a Painter (Dorrit).*

Gradgrind, Adam Smith: A younger son of Gradgrind *(Hard Times).*

Gradgrind, Jane: Gradgrind's younger daughter. *Little Jane, after manufacturing a good deal of moist pipe-clay on her face with slate-pencil and tears, had fallen asleep over vulgar fractions (Hard Times).*

Gradgrind, Louisa: Gradgrind's eldest child. She is married off to Bounderby, but runs home to her father after Harthouse's attempted seduction and, refusing to return to Bounderby, is disowned by him. *There was an air of jaded sullenness . . . particularly in the girl: yet, struggling through the dissatisfaction of her face, there was a light with nothing to rest upon, a fire with nothing to burn, a starved imagination keeping life in itself somehow, which brightened its expression. Not with the brightness natural to cheerful youth, but with uncertain, eager, doubtful flashes, which had something painful in them, analogous to the changes on a blind face groping its way. She was a child now, of fifteen or sixteen; but at no distant day would seem to become a woman all at once. Her father thought so as he looked at her. She was pretty. Would have been self-willed (he thought in his eminently practical way) but for her bringing-up (Hard Times).*

Gradgrind, Malthus: A younger son of Gradgrind *(Hard Times).*

Gradgrind, Thomas: Retired merchant of Coketown, father of Louisa, Tom, Adam Smith, Malthus and Jane. He blighted their youth by his emphasis of the superiority of fact to imagination. *The emphasis was helped by the speaker's square wall of a forehead, which had his eyebrows for its base, while his eyes found commodious cellarage in two dark caves, overshadowed by the wall. The emphasis was helped by the speaker's mouth, which was wide, thin, and hard set. The emphasis was helped by the speaker's voice, which was inflexible, dry, and dictatorial. The emphasis was helped by the speaker's hair, which bristled on the skirts of his bald head, a plantation of firs to keep the wind from its shining surface, all covered with knobs, like the crust of a plum pie, as if the head had scarcely warehouse-room for the hard facts stored inside. The speaker's obstinate carriage, square coat, square legs, square shoulders – nay, his very neckcloth, trained to take him by the throat with an unaccommodating grasp, like a stubborn fact, as it was, – all helped the emphasis (Hard Times).*

Gradgrind, Mrs. Thomas: Gradgrind's wife. *A little, thin, white, pink-eyed bundle of shawls, of surpassing feebleness, mental and bodily; who was always taking physic without any effect, and who, whenever she showed a symptom of coming to life, was invariably stunned by some weighty piece of fact tumbling on her (Hard Times).*

Gradgrind, Tom ('The Whelp'): Gradgrind's eldest son. Feckless and dishonest as a result of his repressive upbringing, he robs Bounderby's Bank and throws the blame on Blackpool, but is found out and flees the country to escape arrest. *It was very remarkable that a young gentleman who had been brought up under one continuous system of unnatural restraint, should be a hypocrite; but it was certainly the case with Tom. It was very strange that a young gentleman who had never been left to his own guidance for five consecutive minutes, should be incapable at last of governing himself; but so it was with Tom. It was altogether unaccountable that a young gentleman whose imagination had been strangled in his cradle, should be still inconvenienced by its ghost in the form of grovelling sensualities; but such a monster, beyond all doubt, was Tom (Hard Times).*

Graham, Hugh: A sixteenth-century bowyer's apprentice in love with his master's daughter, Mistress Alice, in Magog's tale. *A bold young 'prentice who loved his master's daughter. There were no doubt within the walls a great many 'prentices in this condition, but I speak of only one (Humphrey).*

Graham, Mary: Companion to old Martin Chuzzlewit and eventual wife to young Martin. *She was very young; apparently no more than seventeen; timid and shrinking in her manner, and yet with a greater share of self-possession and control over her emotions than usually belongs to a far more advanced period of female life. . . . She was short in stature; and her figure was slight, as became her years; but all the charms of youth and maidenhood set it off, and clustered on her gentle brow. Her face was very pale, in part no doubt from recent agitation. Her dark brown hair, disordered from the same cause, had fallen negligently from its bonds, and hung upon her neck: for which instance of its waywardness, no male observer would have had the heart to blame it (Chuzzlewit).*

Grainger: Friend of Steerforth. Guest at David Copperfield's first bachelor dinner at Adelphi. *Very gay and lively (Copperfield).*

Gran, Mrs.: Jemmy Lirriper's name for Mrs. Lirriper in the story he makes up (*Christmas Stories* – 'Mrs. Lirriper's Legacy').

Grandfather, Little Nell's: See **Trent** (*Curiosity Shop*).

Grandmarina, Fairy: Princess Alicia's godmother in Alice Rainbird's romantic tale ('Holiday Romance').

Grandpapa and **Grandmamma:** Senior guests at Christmas dinner. *Grandpapa produces a small sprig of mistletoe from his pocket, and tempts the boys to kiss their little cousins under it – a proceeding which affords both the boys and the old gentleman unlimited satisfaction, but which rather outrages grandmamma's ideas of decorum, until grandpapa says, that when he was just thirteen years and three months old, he kissed grandmamma under a mistletoe too, on which the children clap their hands, and laugh very heartily, as do aunt George and uncle George; and grandmamma looks pleased, and says, with a benevolent smile, that grandpapa was an impudent young dog, on which the children laugh very heartily again, and grandpapa more heartily than any of them (Boz – 'Christmas Dinner').*

Granger, Edith: See **Dombey, Mrs. Paul the Second** (*Dombey*).

Grannett: Workhouse overseer admired by Bumble and Mrs. Corney for his treatment of a dying pauper. *'As he wouldn't go away, and shocked the company very much, our overseer sent him out a pound of potatoes and half a pint of oatmeal. "My heart!" says the ungrateful villain, "what's the use of this to me? You might as well give me a pair of iron spectacles!" "Very good," says our overseer, taking 'em away again, "you won't get anything else here." "Then I'll die in the streets!" says the vagrant . . . and he did die in the streets. There's a obstinate pauper for you' (Twist).*

Graymarsh: Pupil at Dotheboys Hall. *'Graymarsh's maternal aunt,' said Squeers . . . 'is very glad to hear he's so well and happy, and sends her respectful compliments to Mrs. Squeers, and thinks she must be an angel. She likewise thinks Mr. Squeers is too good for this world; but hopes he may long be spared to carry on the business. Would have sent the two pair of stockings as desired, but is short of money, so forwards a tract instead' (Nickleby).*

Grayper, Mr. and **Mrs.:** Mrs. Copperfield's neighbours at Blunderstone, at whose house she meets Murdstone (*Copperfield*).

Grazinglands, Mr. and **Mrs. (Arabella):** A wealthy Midlands couple in search of a meal in London. *Over the whole, a young lady presided, whose gloomy haughtiness as she surveyed the street, announced a deep-seated grievance against society, and an implacable determination to be avenged. From a beetle-haunted kitchen below this institution, fumes arose, suggestive of a class of soup which Mr. Grazinglands knew, from painful experience, enfeebles the mind, distends the stomach, forces itself into the complexion, and tries to ooze out at the eyes (Uncommercial – 'Refreshments for Travellers').*

Green: A law writer said to have known the deceased Nemo better than anybody. *Which son of Mrs. Green's appears, on inquiry, to be at the present time aboard a vessel bound for China, three months out, but considered accessible by telegraph, on application to the Lords of the Admiralty (Bleak House).*

Green, Miss: Friend of the Kenwigses (*Nickleby*).

Green, Police Constable: See **Black** and **Green** (*Reprinted* – 'On Duty with Inspector Field').

Green, Lucy: See **Specks, Mrs. Joe** (*Uncommercial* – 'Dullborough Town').

Green, Tom: The name taken by Joe Willet as a soldier. *He was a gallant, manly, handsome fellow, but he had lost his left arm (Rudge).*

Greenwood (also **Joby**): One-eyed tramp said to have encountered the hooded woman (*Christmas Stories* – 'Haunted House').

Greenwood, the Misses: Acquaintances of Fairfax (*Young Gentlemen* – 'Censorious Young Gentleman').

Gregory: Foreman packer at Murdstone and Grinby's warehouse (*Copperfield*).

Gregsbury, M. P.: A Member of Parliament to whom Nicholas Nickleby applies for work. *A tough, burly, thick-headed gentleman, with a loud voice, a pompous manner, a tolerable command of sentences with no meaning in them, and, in short, every requisite for a very good member indeed (Nickleby).*

Grewgious, Hiram: Lawyer of Staple Inn. Guardian of Rosa Bud, with whose late mother he had been in love. Ardent defender of Neville Landless when he is suspected of Drood's murder. *He was an arid, sandy man, who, if he had been put into a grinding-mill, looked as if he would have ground immediately into high-dried snuff. He had a scanty flat crop of hair, in colour and consistency like some very mangy yellow fur tippet; it was so unlike hair, that it must have been a wig, but for the stupendous improbability of anybody's voluntarily sporting such a head. The little play of feature that his face presented, was cut deep into it, in a few hard curves that made it more like work; and he had certain notches in his forehead, which looked as though Nature had been about to touch them into sensibility or refinement, when she had impatiently thrown away the chisel, and said: 'I really cannot be worried to finish off this man; let him go as he is.' With too great length of throat at his upper end, and too much ankle-bone and heel at his lower; with an awkward and hesitating manner; with a shambling walk; and with what is called a near sight – which perhaps prevented his observing how much white cotton stocking he displayed to the public eye, in contrast with his black suit – Mr. Grewgious still had some strange capacity in him of making on the whole an agreeable impression (Drood).*

Grey, the Misses: Amelia and her sister, friends of Felix Nixon (*Young Gentlemen* – 'Domestic Young Gentleman').

Gride, Arthur: Co-creditor, with Ralph Nickleby, of Walter Bray, whose daughter Madeline he proposes to marry. Bray's death prevents it, Gride's housekeeper, Peg Sliderskew, makes off with the documents which give him power over many people, and he is eventually murdered by burglars. *A little old man of about seventy or seventy-five years of age, of a very lean figure, much bent, and slightly twisted. . . . His nose and chin were sharp and prominent, his jaws had fallen inwards from loss of teeth, his face was shrivelled and yellow, save where the cheeks were streaked with the colour of a dry winter apple; and where his beard had been, there lingered yet a few grey tufts, which seemed, like the ragged eyebrows, to denote the badness of the soil from which they sprung. The whole air and attitude of the form, was one of stealthy cat-like obsequiousness; the whole expression of the face was concentrated in a wrinkled leer, compounded of cunning, lecherousness, slyness, and avarice (Nickleby).*

Gridley ('The Man from Shropshire'): A ruined Chancery suitor constantly attempting to address the Lord Chancellor and being imprisoned for contempt.

He dies evading arrest. *A tall sallow man with a careworn head, on which but little hair remained, a deeply lined face, and prominent eyes. He had a combative look; and a chafing, irritable manner, which, associated with his figure – still large and powerful, though evidently in its decline – rather alarmed me (Bleak House).*

Griffin, Miss: Principal of the school attended by Master B. *We knew Miss Griffin to be bereft of human sympathies (Christmas Stories* – 'Haunted House').

Grig, Tom: The lamplighter, believed by Stargazer to have been sent by destiny to fulfil a prediction of his. Thinking the old man will make him rich by his discovery of the philosopher's stone, Grig agrees to marry Stargazer's niece, Fanny Brown, but declines when the stone fails to materialise. Led to believe he has only weeks to live, he accepts the servant, Betsy Martin, recanting in the nick of time when he learns that he is actually destined for a ripe old age *(The Lamplighter).* The ending of 'The Lamplighter's Story', the subsequent prose version of this farce, is different, and Tom Grig does not escape entirely unscathed.

Griggins: Life and soul of Mrs. Brown's party. *Presented himself, amidst another shout of laughter and a loud clapping of hands from the younger branches. This welcome he acknowledged by sundry contortions of countenance, imitative of the clown in one of the new pantomimes, which were so extremely successful, that one stout gentleman rolled upon an ottoman in a paroxysm of delight, protesting, with many gasps, that if somebody didn't make that fellow Griggins leave off, he would be the death of him, he knew (Young Gentlemen* – 'Funny Young Gentleman').

Griggs: See **Porkenham, Griggs,** and **Slummintowken Families** (*Pickwick*).

Grimble, Sir Thomas: Wealthy Yorkshire landowner with whom Mrs. Nickleby supposes Smike might have dined while at Dotheboys Hall. *'A very proud man, Sir Thomas Grimble, with six grown-up and most lovely daughters, and the finest park in the county.' 'My dear mother!' reasoned Nicholas, 'do you suppose that the unfortunate outcast of a Yorkshire school was likely to receive many cards of invitation from the nobility and gentry in the neighbourhood?' 'Really, my dear, I don't know why it should be so very extraordinary,' said Mrs. Nickleby. 'I know that when I was at school, I always went at least twice every half-year to the Hawkinses at Taunton Vale, and they are much richer than the Grimbles, and connected with them in marriage; so you see it's not so very unlikely, after all' (Nickleby).*

Grime, Professor: Member of the Mudfog Association. *Professor Grime having lost several teeth, is unable, I observe, to eat his crusts without previously soaking them in his bottled porter (Mudfog).*

Grimmer, Miss: School proprietress, with Miss Drowvey, in William Tinkling's romantic tale ('Holiday Romance').

Grimwig: Brownlow's friend, a lawyer, who tries in vain to persuade Brownlow that Oliver Twist is not to be trusted. *A stout old gentleman, rather lame in one leg, who was dressed in a blue coat, striped waistcoat, nankeen breeches and gaiters, and a broad-brimmed white hat, with the sides turned up with green. A very small-plaited shirt frill stuck out from his waistcoat; and a very long steel watch-chain, with nothing but a key at the end, dangled loosely below it. The ends of his white neckerchief were twisted into a ball about the size of an orange; the variety of shapes into which his countenance was twisted, defy description. He had a manner of screwing his head on one side when spoke; and of looking out of the corners of his eyes at the same time: which irresistibly reminded the beholder of a parrot (Twist).*

Grimwood, Liza ('The Countess'): Young woman whose murder in her bedroom in the Waterloo Road was investigated by Inspector Wield. *'She was commonly called The Countess, because of her handsome appearance and her proud way of carrying of herself' (Reprinted – 'Three "Detective" Anecdotes').*

Grinder: Proprietor of a travelling stilt-act encountered by Little Nell and her grandfather. *Used his natural legs for pedestrian purposes and carried at his back a drum (Curiosity Shop).*

Grip: The ancient raven who constantly accompanies Barnaby Rudge. *After a short survey of the ground, and a few sidelong looks at the ceiling and at everybody present in turn, he fluttered to the floor, and went to Barnaby – not in a hop, or walk, or run, but in a pace like that of a very particular gentleman with exceedingly tight boots on, trying to walk fast over loose pebbles. Then, stepping into his extended hand, and condescending to be held out at arm's-length, he gave vent to a succession of sounds, not unlike the drawing of some eight or ten dozen of long corks, and again asserted his brimstone birth and parentage with great distinction (Rudge).*

Groffin, Thomas: Chemist, who tries in vain to be excused jury service in Bardell and Pickwick. *'I've left nobody but an errand-boy in my shop. He is a very nice boy, my Lord, but he is not acquainted with drugs; and I know that the prevailing impression on his mind is, that Epsom salts means oxalic acid; and syrup of senna, laudanum. That's all, my Lord' (Pickwick).*

Grogzwig: See **Koëldwethout** *(Nickleby).*

Grompus: Partner of an unwilling Georgiana Podsnap in a set of dances at her birthday party. *That complacent monster, believing that he was giving Miss Podsnap a treat, prolonged to the utmost stretch of possibility a peripatetic account of an archery meeting; while his victim, heading the procession of sixteen as it slowly circled about, like a revolving funeral, never raised her eyes except once to steal a glance at Mrs. Lammle, expressive of intense despair (Mutual Friend).*

Groper, Colonel: A boarder at the National Hotel, in America, where Martin Chuzzlewit stays before embarking for Eden *(Chuzzlewit).*

Groves, James: Rascally landlord of the Valiant Soldier inn. *'Honest Jem Groves, as is a man of unblemished moral character, and has a good dry skittle-ground. If any man has got anything to say again Jem Groves, let him say it to Jem Groves, and Jem Groves can accommodate him with a customer on any terms from four pound a side to forty' (Curiosity Shop).*

Grub: President of the umbugology and ditchwater-isics session at the second meeting of the Mudfog Association *(Mudfog).*

Grub, Gabriel: The sexton stolen by goblins in Wardle's Christmas Eve story at Dingley Dell. *'An ill-conditioned, cross-grained, surly fellow – a morose and lonely man, who consorted with nobody but himself, and an old wicker bottle which fitted into his large deep waistcoat pocket – and who eyed each merry face, as it passed him by, with such a deep scowl of malice and ill-humour, as it was difficult to meet, without feeling something the worse for' (Pickwick).*

Grubble, W.: Landlord of the Dedlock Arms, Chesney Wold. *A pleasant-looking, stoutish, middle-aged man, who never seemed to consider himself cosily dressed for his own fireside without his hat and top-boots, but who never wore a coat except at church (Bleak House).*

Grudden, Mrs.: Member of Crummles's theatrical company. *Assisted Mrs. Crummles in her domestic affairs, and took money at the doors, and dressed the ladies, and swept the house, and held the prompt book when everybody else was on for the last scene, and acted any kind of part on any emergency without ever learning it, and was put down in the bills under any name or names whatever, that occurred to Mr. Crummles as looking well in print (Nickleby).*

Grueby, John: Lord George Gordon's manservant, who tries to save his wayward master from himself and his provokers. *He was a square-built, strong-made, bull-necked fellow, of the true English breed.... He was much older than the Maypole man, being to all appearance five-and-forty; but was one of those self-possessed, hard-headed, imperturbable fellows, who, if they are ever beaten at fisticuffs, or other kind of warfare, never know it, and go on coolly till they win (Rudge).*

'Gruff and Glum': Old Greenwich pensioner enchanted by Bella Wilfer as she arrives to marry John Rokesmith. *Two wooden legs had this gruff and glum old pensioner, and, a minute before Bella stepped out of the boat, and drew that confiding little arm of hers through Rokesmith's, he had had no object in life but tobacco, and not enough of that (Mutual Friend).*

'Gruff and Grim': Herbert Pocket's nickname for Old Bill Barley (q.v.) *(Expectations).*

Gruff and Tackleton: See **Tackleton** *(Christmas Books – 'Cricket').*

Grummer, Daniel: Constable at Ipswich who arrests Pickwick and Tupman. *The elderly gentleman in the top-boots, who was chiefly remarkable for a bottle-*

nose, a horse voice, a snuff-coloured surtout, and a wandering eye (Pickwick).

Grummidge, Dr.: Speaker at the anatomy and medicine session of the second meeting of the Mudfog Association. *Stated to the section a most interesting case of monomania, and described the course of treatment he had pursued with perfect success. The patient was a married lady in the middle rank of life, who, having seen another lady at an evening party in a full suit of pearls, was suddenly seized with a desire to possess a similar equipment, although her husband's finances were by no means equal to the necessary outlay (Mudfog).*

Grundy: Fellow law clerk, and drinker, of Lowten (Pickwick).

Guard, The: The railway guard who sets Jackson down at Mugby Junction. *Glistening with drops of wet, and looking at the tearful face of his watch by the light of his lantern (Christmas Stories – 'Mugby Junction').*

Gubbins: Ex-churchwarden of Our Parish who presents an engraved silver inkstand to the curate. *Acknowledged by the curate in terms which drew tears into the eyes of all present – the very waiters were melted (Boz – 'Curate').*

Gulpidge, Mr. and Mrs.: Fellow dinner guests with David Copperfield at the Waterbrooks' (Copperfield).

Gummidge, Mrs.: Widow of Daniel Peggotty's partner and now his housekeeper. She emigrates to Australia with him, Martha Endell, and Little Em'ly. *'I an't what I could wish myself to be. . . . I had better go into the house and die. I am a lone lorn creetur', and had much better not make myself contrairy here' (Copperfield).*

Gunter: Medical student present at Bob Sawyer's party. *A gentleman in a shirt emblazoned with pink anchors (Pickwick).*

Guppy, Mrs.: Guppy's mother. *An old lady in a large cap, with rather a red nose and rather an unsteady eye, but smiling all over (Bleak House).*

Guppy, William: Clerk to Kenge and Carboy. He falls in love with Esther Summerson and 'files a declaration' to her, which, rejected at the time, he subsequently regrets ever having made. *A young gentleman who had inked himself by accident. // I scarcely knew him again, he was so uncommonly smart. He had an entirely new suit of glossy clothes on, a shining hat, lilac-kid gloves, a neckerchief of a variety of colours, a large hot-house flower in his button-hole, and a thick gold ring on his little finger. Besides which, he quite scented the dining-room with bear's-grease and other perfumery (Bleak House).*

Gusher: A missionary friend of Mrs. Pardiggle. *A flabby gentleman with a moist surface, and eyes so much too small for his moon of a face that they seemed to have been originally made for somebody else (Bleak House).*

Guster: The Snagsbys' maidservant. *A lean young woman from a workhouse (by some supposed to have* D

been christened Augusta); *who, although she was farmed or contracted for, during her growing time, by an amiable benefactor of the species resident at Tooting, and cannot fail to have been developed under the most favourable circumstances, 'has fits' – which the parish can't account for (Bleak House).*

Gwynn, Miss: Writing and ciphering governess at Westgate House school, Bury St. Edmunds (Pickwick).

Haggage, Dr.: A Marshalsea prisoner who brings Amy Dorrit into the world there. *The doctor was amazingly shabby, in a torn and darned rough-weather sea-jacket, out at elbows and eminently short of buttons (he had been in his time the experienced surgeon carried by a passenger ship), the dirtiest white trousers conceivable by mortal man, carpet slippers, and no visible linen (Dorrit).*

'Hamlet's Aunt': See **Spiker, Mrs. Henry** (Copperfield).

'Handel': Herbert Pocket's nickname for Pip. *'We are so harmonious, and you have been a blacksmith. . . . Would you mind Handel for a familiar name? There's a charming piece of music by Handel called the Harmonious Blacksmith' (Expectations).*

Handford, Julius: Alias used by John Harmon when viewing his own supposed corpse (Mutual Friend).

Hannah: Miss La Creevy's servant (Nickleby).

Hardy: Percy Noakes's great friend and fellow organiser of the steam excursion. *A stout gentleman of about forty . . . a practical joker, immensely popular with married ladies, and a general favourite with young men. He was always engaged in some pleasure excursion or other, and delighted in getting somebody into a scrape on such occasions. He could sing comic songs, imitate hackney-coachmen and fowls, play airs on his chin, and execute concertos on the Jew's-harp. He always eat and drank most immoderately, and was the bosom-friend of Mr. Percy Noakes. He had a red face, a somewhat husky voice, and a tremendous laugh (Boz – 'Steam Excursion').*

Haredale, Emma: Daughter of the murdered Reuben, niece of Geoffrey, who tries to discourage her suitor, Edward Chester. Edward rescues her from Gashford's clutches after the Gordon Riots, and they eventually marry. *A lovely girl (Rudge).*

Haredale, Geoffrey: A Roman Catholic gentleman living at 'The Warren', near the Maypole Inn, Chigwell. Uncle of Emma. He is widely suspected of having murdered his brother Reuben, but the burning of his house by the Gordon Rioters leads to his innocence being established. He kills his lifelong rival, Sir John Chester, in a duel and retires to a religious establishment abroad. *A burly square-built man, negligently dressed, rough and abrupt in manner, stern, and, in his present mood, forbidding both in look and speech (Rudge).*

Harker: Officer in charge of the jury in the interpolated tale 'To be taken with a Grain of Salt' (Christmas Stories – 'Dr. Marigold').

Harker, The Revd. John: Vicar of Groombridge Wells, martyred abroad for his faith, who provided a reference for Mrs. Miller to adopt Walter Wilding (*Christmas Stories* – 'No Thoroughfare').

Harleigh: Principal singer in the Gattletons' private production of the musical play *Masaniello*. *Mr. Harleigh smiled and looked foolish – not an unusual thing with him – hummed 'Behold how brightly breaks the morning,' and blushed as red as the fisherman's night-cap he was trying on* (*Boz* – 'Mrs. Joseph Porter').

Harmon: John Harmon's deceased father, a garbage contractor. *'He grew rich as a Dust Contractor, and lived in a hollow in a hilly country entirely composed of Dust. On his own small estate the growling old vagabond threw up his own mountain range, like an old volcano, and its geological formation was Dust. Coal-dust, vegetable-dust, bone-dust, crockery-dust, rough dust, and sifted dust – all manner of Dust'* (*Mutual Friend*).

Harmon, John (alias **Julius Handford**, alias **John Rokesmith**): The central character of the story, who assumes other identities after his supposed murder, works for his late father's servant, Boffin, and lodges with the Wilfers, whose daughter Bella was to have become his bride under his father's will. He marries Bella, the Boffins discover his true identity, and he takes up his father's legacy. *A dark gentleman. Thirty at the utmost. An expressive, one might say handsome, face. A very bad manner. In the last degree constrained, reserved, diffident, troubled* (*Mutual Friend*).

Harmon, Mrs. John: See **Wilfer, Bella** (*Mutual Friend*).

Harriet: See **Hopkins** and **Harriet**: (*Young Gentlemen* – 'Bashful Young Gentleman').

Harris: Law stationer friend of Dounce (*Boz* – 'Misplaced Attachment').

Harris: Greengrocer at Bath in whose house the footmen's soirée is held (*Pickwick*).

Harris ('Short Trotters', 'Short', or 'Trotters'): Partner of Codlin in the Punch-and-Judy show which Little Nell and her grandfather accompany briefly. *A little merry-faced man with a twinkling eye and a red nose, who seemed to have unconsciously imbibed something of his hero's character* (*Curiosity Shop*).

Harris, Mrs.: Mrs. Gamp's imaginary friend, with whom she holds conversations upon all sorts of subjects. Betsey Prig's declaration that she does not believe Mrs. Harris exists is her culminating insult to Mrs. Gamp. *A fearful mystery surrounded this lady of the name of Harris, whom no one in the circle of Mrs. Gamp's acquaintance had ever seen; neither did any human being know her place of residence, though Mrs. Gamp appeared on her own showing to be in constant communication with her. There were conflicting rumours on the subject; but the prevalent opinion was that she was a phantom of Mrs. Gamp's brain – as Messrs Doe and Roe are fictions of the law – created for the express purpose of holding visionary*

dialogues with her on all manner of subjects, and invariably winding up with a compliment to the excellence of her nature (*Chuzzlewit*).

Harrison: Orphan suggested by Milvey for adoption by the Boffins. *'Oh, Frank!' remonstrated his emphatic wife. . . . 'I don't think Mrs. Boffin would like an orphan who squints so much'* (*Mutual Friend*).

Harry: Marton's favourite pupil. *A very young boy; quite a little child. His hair still hung in curls about his face, and his eyes were very bright; but their light was of Heaven, not earth* (*Curiosity Shop*).

Harry: Pedlar who offers to remove a bloodstain from Bill Sikes's hat. *This was an antic fellow, half pedlar and half mountebank, who travelled about the country on foot to vend hones, strops, razors, washballs, harness-paste, medicine for dogs and horses, cheap perfumery, cosmetics, and such-like wares, which he carried in a case slung to his back* (*Twist*).

Harry and **Kate:** A debtor in Solomon Jacobs's sponging-house and his wife. *A genteel-looking young man was talking earnestly, and in a low tone, to a young female, whose face was concealed by a thick veil* (*Boz* – 'Watkins Tottle').

Harthouse, James: A friend of Gradgrind's who, visiting Coketown as a Parliamentary candidate, attempts to seduce Louisa Bounderby. *'Five-and-thirty, good-looking, good figure, good teeth, good voice, good breeding, well-dressed, dark hair, bold eyes.' // Had tried life as a Cornet of Dragoons, and found it a bore; and had afterwards tried it in the train of an English minister abroad, and found it a bore; and had then strolled to Jerusalem, and got bored there; and had then gone yachting about the world, and got bored everywhere* (*Hard Times*).

Harvey: Emma Fielding's bridegroom. *There are two points on which Anne expatiates over and over again, without the smallest appearance of fatigue or intending to leave off; one is, that she 'never see in all her life such a – oh such an angel of a gentleman as Mr. Harvey'* (*Young Couples* – 'Young Couple'). He appears again, in old age, in 'Old Couple': *How the old gentleman chuckles over boyish feats and roguish tricks, and tells long stories of a 'barring-out' achieved at the school he went to: which was very wrong, he tells the boys, and never to be imitated of course, but which he cannot help letting them know was very pleasant too – especially when he kissed the master's niece.*

Havisham, Miss: Once a beautiful heiress, she had been jilted by Compeyson and has lived ever since in her bridal dress amongst the decaying ruins of her wedding feast at Satis House, Rochester, where she has brought up her protégée Estella to despise men. She pays for Pip's apprenticeship and he believes her his secret benefactor. He rescues her from nearly burning to death; but when she later dies she leaves almost all her fortune to Estella. *She was dressed in rich materials – satins, and lace, and silks – all of white. Her shoes were white. And she had a long white veil dependent from her hair, but her hair was white.*

Some bright jewels sparkled on her neck and on her hands. . . . But, I saw that everything within my view which ought to be white, had been white long ago, and had lost its lustre, and was faded and yellow. I saw that the bride within the bridal dress had withered like the dress, and like the flowers, and had no brightness left but the brightness of her sunken eyes. I saw that the dress had been put upon the rounded figure of a young woman, and that the figure upon which it now hung loose, had shrunk to skin and bone. Once, I had been taken to see some ghastly waxwork at the Fair, representing I know not what impossible personage lying in state. Once, I had been taken to one of our old marsh churches to see a skeleton in the ashes of a rich dress, that had been dug out of a vault under the church pavement. Now, waxwork, and skeleton seemed to have dark eyes that moved and looked at me (Expectations).

Havisham, Arthur: Miss Havisham's deceased brother, who had been drawn into crime by Compeyson *(Expectations)*.

Hawdon, Captain ('Nemo'): Penurious law-writer lodging at Krook's, where he dies. As a rakish young officer he had been Lady Dedlock's lover before her marriage, and is the father by her of Esther Summerson. *He lies there, dressed in shirt and trousers, with bare feet. He has a yellow look in the spectral darkness of a candle that has guttered down, until the whole length of its wick (still burning) has doubled over, and left a tower of winding-sheet above it. His hair is ragged, mingling with his whiskers and his beard – the latter, ragged too, and grown, like the scum and mist around him, in neglect. Foul and filthy as the room is, foul and filthy as the air is, it is not easy to perceive what fumes those are which most oppress the senses in it; but through the general sickliness and faintness, and the odour of stale tobacco, there comes into the lawyer's mouth the bitter, vapid taste of opium (Bleak House).*

Hawk, Sir Mulberry: Man-about-town and would-be seducer of Kate Nickleby. He kills Verisopht in a duel and flees the country. *Remarkable for his tact in ruining, by himself and his creatures, young gentlemen of fortune – a genteel and elegant profession, of which he had undoubtedly gained the head. With all the boldness of an original genius, he had struck out on an entirely new course of treatment quite opposed to the usual method; his custom being, when he had gained the ascendancy over those he took in hand, rather to keep them down than to give them their own way; and to exercise his vivacity upon them, openly, and without reserve. Thus, he made them butts, in a double sense, and while he emptied them with great address, caused them to ring with sundry well-administered taps, for the diversion of society (Nickleby).*

Hawkins: Middle-aged baker successfully sued for breach of promise by Anastasia Rugg *(Mutual Friend)*.

Hawkins, M.P.: A new Member of Parliament. *When they praise the good looks of Mr. Hawkins, the new member, [the political young gentleman] says he's*

very well for a representative, all things considered, but he wants a little calling to account, and he is more than half afraid it will be necessary to bring him down on his knees for that vote on the miscellaneous estimates (Young Gentlemen – 'Political Young Gentleman').

Hawkinson, Aunt: An aunt of Georgiana Podsnap who left her a necklace which Georgiana gives to Mrs. Lammle to help her in financial difficulty *(Mutual Friend)*.

Hawkyard, Brother Verity: George Silverman's self-appointed guardian. Preacher to an obscure Nonconformist congregation at West Bromwich ('Silverman').

Headstone, Bradley: Charley Hexam's headmaster. Loving Lizzie Hexam passionately, he tries to murder his rival, Wrayburn, is blackmailed by Riderhood and drowns with him in a struggle. *Bradley Headstone, in his decent black coat and waistcoat, and decent white shirt, and decent formal black tie, and decent pantaloons of pepper and salt, with his decent silver watch in his pocket and its decent hair-guard round his neck, looked a thoroughly decent young man of six-and-twenty. He was never seen in any other dress, and yet there was a certain stiffness in his manner of wearing this, as if there were a want of adaptation between him and it, recalling some mechanics in their holiday clothes. . . . There was a kind of settled trouble in the face. It was the face belonging to a naturally slow or inattentive intellect that had toiled hard to get what it had won, and that had to hold it now that it was gotten. He always seemed to be uneasy lest anything should be missing from his mental warehouse, and taking stock to assure himself (Mutual Friend).*

Heathfield, Alfred: Medical student and ward of Dr. Jeddler, to whose daughter, Marion, he is engaged. She sacrifices him to her sister Grace. *The active figure of a handsome young man (Christmas Books – 'Battle of Life').*

Heep, Mrs.: Uriah's mother. *The dead image of Uriah, only short. She received me with the utmost humility, and apologised to me for giving her son a kiss, observing that, lowly as they were, they had their natural affections, which they hoped would give no offence to any one (Copperfield).*

Heep, Uriah: Wickfield's hypocritical clerk, later partner, who designs to marry Agnes Wickfield. He defrauds Wickfield, is unmasked by Micawber and sentenced to transportation for life. *Hardly any eyebrows, and no eyelashes, and eyes of a red-brown, so unsheltered and unshaded, that I remember wondering how he went to sleep. He was high-shouldered and bony; dressed in decent black, with a white wisp of a neckcloth; buttoned up to the throat; and had a long, lank, skeleton hand, which particularly attracted my attention. . . . It was no fancy of mine about his hands, I observed; for he frequently ground the palms against each other as if to squeeze them dry and warm, besides often wiping them, in a stealthy way, on his pocket-handkerchief. // '"Be umble, Uriah," says father to* me, *"and you'll get on. It was what was always being dinned into you and me at school; it's what goes down best. Be umble,"* says father, *"and you'll do!"* And really it ain't done bad!' *(Copperfield).*

Helves, Captain: A specious military type, met by the Tauntons on a Gravesend packet (and therefore considered respectable), whom they bring with them on the steam excursion. His courtship of Julia Briggs is cut short by his arrest for embezzlement. *A lion – a gentleman with a bass voice and an incipient red moustache (Boz – 'Steam Excursion').*

Henrietta: Tom's sweetheart until she jilts him for another pavement-artist. *To say that Henrietta was volatile is but to say that she was woman. . . . She consented to walk with me. Let me do her the justice to say that she did so upon trial. 'I am not,' said Henrietta, 'as yet prepared to regard you, Thomas, in any other light than as a friend; but as a friend I am willing to walk with you, on the understanding that softer sentiments may flow.' We walked (Christmas Stories – 'Somebody's Luggage').*

Henry: Pawnbroker's assistant. *The gentleman behind the counter, with the curly black hair, diamond ring, and double silver watch-guard (Boz – 'Pawnbroker's Shop').*

Henry: Cousin and eventual husband of Maria Lobbs in Sam Weller's tale of 'The Parish Clerk'. *'The only eye-sore in the whole place' (Pickwick).*

Herbert, M.P.: Member of the House of Commons who points out that Lord George Gordon is present in the House with a blue cockade, signal of rebellion, in his hat, during the debate on the Catholic Emancipation question *(Rudge).*

Herschel, Mr. and **Mrs. John:** First cousin of John, the narrator, and his wife, who visit the haunted house with him. *So called after the great astronomer: than whom I suppose a better man at a telescope does not breathe. With him, was his wife: a charming creature to whom he had been married in the previous spring (Christmas Stories – 'Haunted House').*

Hexam, Charley: Son of Jesse, brother to Lizzie. He is obsessed with becoming 'respectable', which aim he pursues through the schoolmastering profession. *There was a curious mixture in the boy, of uncompleted savagery, and uncompleted civilisation. His voice was hoarse and coarse, and his face was coarse, and his stunted figure was coarse; but he was cleaner than other boys of his type; and his writing, though large and round, was good; and he glanced at the backs of the books, with an awakened curiosity that went below the binding. No one who can read, ever looks at a book, even unopened on a shelf, like one who cannot (Mutual Friend).*

Hexam, Jesse (Gaffer): Father of Charley and Lizzie, a seeker for, and robber of, corpses in the Thames. He eventually becomes one himself when about to be arrested on suspicion of murdering John Harmon. *A strong man with ragged grizzled hair and a sun-browned face . . . with no covering on his matted head, with his brown arms bare to between the elbow and the shoulder, with the loose knot of a looser kerchief lying low on his bare breast in a wilderness of beard and whisker, with such dress as he wore seeming to be made out of the mud that begrimed his boat, still there was business-like usage in his steady gaze (Mutual Friend).*

Hexam, Lizzie: Daugher of Jesse, sister to Charley. Her father's unwilling helper until his death, she is educated by Wrayburn. She refuses Headstone's passionate proposal, precipitating his attempted murder of Wrayburn, whom Lizzie at length marries. *A dark girl of nineteen or twenty (Mutual Friend).*

Heyling, George: The revengeful central figure of 'The Old Man's Tale About the Queer Client', told to Pickwick at the Magpie and Stump. *'The deepest despair, and passion scarcely human, had made such fierce ravages on his face and form, in that one night, that his companions in misfortune shrunk affrighted from him as he passed by. His eyes were bloodshot and heavy, his face a deadly white, and his body bent as if with age. He had bitten his under-lip nearly through in the violence of his mental suffering, and the blood which had flowed from the wound had trickled down his chin, and stained his shirt and neckerchief. No tear, or sound of complaint escaped him: but the unsettled look, and disordered haste with which he paced up and down the yard, denoted the fever which was burning within' (Pickwick).*

Heyling, Mrs. George (Mary): George Heyling's wife, whose death he devotes himself to avenging. *'The slight and delicate young woman was sinking beneath the combined effects of bodily and mental illness' (Pickwick).*

Hicks, Septimus: Boarder at Mrs. Tibbs's. He marries, but deserts, Matilda Maplesone. *A tallish, white-faced young man, with spectacles, and a black ribbon round his neck instead of a neckerchief – a most interesting person; a poetical walker of the hospitals, and a 'very talented young man.' He was fond of 'lugging' into conversation all sorts of quotations from Don Juan, without fettering himself by the propriety of their application (Boz – 'Boarding-House').*

Higden, Mrs. Betty: A poor child-minder and laundress from whom Mrs. Boffin wishes to adopt Johnny. *She was one of those old women, was Mrs. Betty Higden, who by dint of an indomitable purpose and a strong constitution fight out many years, though each year has come with its new knock-down blows fresh to the fight against her, wearied by it; an active old woman, with a bright dark eye and a resolute face, yet quite a tender creature too; not a logically-reasoning woman, but God is good, and hearts may count in Heaven as high as heads (Mutual Friend).*

Hilton: Master of the ceremonies at the Misses Crumpton's ball. *The popular Mr. Hilton (Boz – 'Sentiment').*

Holliday, Arthur: The fictitious name given by Dr. Speddie to the racegoer central figure in his story of the corpse in the hotel bed. *One of those reckless,* *rattle-pated, open-hearted, and open-mouthed young gentlemen, who possess the gift of familiarity in its highest perfection, and who scramble carelessly along the journey of life making friends, as the phrase is, wherever they go (Two Apprentices).*

Hominy, Mrs. Major: An American literary celebrity imposed upon Martin Chuzzlewit at the National Hotel where he stays before embarking for Eden. *A lady who certainly could not be considered young – that was matter of fact; and probably could not be considered handsome – but that was matter of opinion. She was very straight, very tall, and not at all flexible in face or figure. On her head she wore a great straw-bonnet, with trimmings of the same, in which she looked as if she had been thatched by an unskilful labourer (Chuzzlewit).*

Honeythunder, The Revd. Luke: Professional philanthropist. Mrs. Crisparkle's brother-in-law, guardian of the Landless twins. *Always something in the nature of a Boil upon the face of society, Mr. Honeythunder expanded into an inflammatory Wen in Minor Canon Corner. Though it was not literally true, as was facetiously charged against him by public unbelievers, that he called aloud to his fellow-creatures: 'Curse your souls and bodies, come here and be blessed!' still his philanthropy was of that gunpowderous sort that the difference between it and animosity was hard to determine (Drood).*

Hope: One of Miss Flite's birds *(Bleak House).*

Hopkins: Candidate for election for beadle of 'Our Parish'. *'Hopkins for Beadle. Seven small children!!'* *(Boz – 'Election for Beadle').*

Hopkins, Captain: Fellow prisoner of Micawber in the King's Bench. *In the last extremity of shabbiness (Copperfield).*

Hopkins, Jack: A medical student present at Bob Sawyer's party. *He wore a black velvet waistcoat, with thunder-and-lightning buttons; and a blue striped shirt, with a white false collar (Pickwick).*

Hopkins and Harriet: The bashful young gentleman and his sister. *The bashful young gentleman then observes it is very fine weather, and being reminded that it has only just left off raining for the first time these three days, he blushes very much, and smiles as if he had said a very good thing. The young lady who was most anxious to speak, here inquires, with an air of great commiseration, how his dear sister Harriet is to-day; to which the young gentleman, without the slightest consideration, replies with many thanks, that she is remarkably well. 'Well, Mr. Hopkins!' cries the young lady, 'why, we heard she was bled yesterday evening, and have been perfectly miserable about her.' 'Oh, ah,' says the young gentleman, 'so she was. Oh, she's very ill, very ill indeed' (Young Gentlemen – 'Bashful Young Gentleman').*

Horse Guards: Military magnate, guest at Merdle's *(Dorrit).*

Hortense: Lady Dedlock's maid, supplanted by Rosa and dismissed. Failing to extort money from Tulkinghorn she murders him, but is brought to justice by Inspector and Mrs. Bucket. *My Lady's maid is a Frenchwoman of two-and-thirty, from somewhere in the southern country about Avignon and Marseilles – a large-eyed brown woman with black hair: who would be handsome, but for a certain feline mouth, and general uncomfortable tightness of face, rendering the jaws too eager, and the skull too prominent. There is something indefinably keen and wan about her anatomy; and she has a watchful way of looking out of the corners of her eyes without turning her head, which could be pleasantly dispensed with – especially when she is in an ill-humour and near knives. Through all the good taste of her dress and little adornments, these objections so express themselves, that she seems to go about like a very neat She-Wolf imperfectly tamed (Bleak House).*

Howler, The Revd. Melchisedech: Evangelical preacher who conducts Mrs. MacStinger's marriage to Captain Bunsby. *Having been one day discharged from the West India Docks on a false suspicion (got up expressly against him by the general enemy) of screwing gimlets into puncheons, and applying his lips to the orifice, had announced the destruction of the world for that day two years, at ten in the morning, and opened a front-parlour for the reception of ladies and gentlemen of the Ranting persuasion, upon whom, on the first occasion of their assemblage, the admonitions of the Reverend Melchisedech had produced so powerful an effect, that, in their rapturous performance of a sacred jig, which closed the service, the whole flock broke through into a kitchen below, and disabled a mangle belonging to one of the fold (Dombey).*

Hubble: Wheelwright friend of the Gargerys. *A tough high-shouldered stooping old man, of a sawdusty fragrance, with his legs extraordinarily wide apart: so that in my short days I always saw some miles of open country between them when I met him coming up the lane (Expectations).*

Hubble, Mrs.: Hubble's wife. *A little curly sharp-edged person in sky-blue, who held a conventionally juvenile position, because she had married Mr. Hubble – I don't know at what remote period – when she was much younger than he (Expectations).*

Hugh: Ostler at the Maypole Inn, later a leader of the Gordon Riots, for which he is executed after his natural father, Sir John Chester, has refused to appeal for him. *A young man, of a hale athletic figure, and a giant's strength, whose sunburnt face and swarthy throat, overgrown with jet black hair, might have served a painter for a model. Loosely attired, in the coarsest and roughest garb, with scraps of straw and hay – his usual bed – clinging here and there, and mingling with his uncombed locks, he had fallen asleep in a posture as careless as his dress. The negligence and disorder of the whole man, with something fierce and sullen in his features, gave him a picturesque appearance (Rudge).*

Humm, Anthony: President of the Brick Lane Branch of the United Grand Junction Ebenezer Temperance Association. *A converted fireman, now a schoolmaster, and occasionally an itinerant preacher (Pickwick).*

Humphrey, Master: An amiable, deformed old semi-recluse, whose small circle of friends, romantics all, gather in his rooms each week to chat and read their compositions which they store in the case of his old clock. *I am not a churlish old man. Friendless I can never be, for all mankind are my kindred, and I am on ill terms with no one member of my great family. But for many years I have led a lonely, solitary life; – what wound I sought to heal, what sorrow to forget, originally, matters not now; it is sufficient that retirement has become a habit with me, and that I am unwilling to break the spell which for so long a time has shed its quiet influence upon my home and heart* (*Humphrey*). See also **Single Gentleman, The** (*Curiosity Shop*).

Hunt: Boldwig's head gardener (*Pickwick*).

Hunter, Horace: Alexander Trott's rival – and intended duelling opponent – for Emily Brown, whom he eventually marries. *'I've seen him hit the man at the Pall Mall shooting-gallery, in the second button-hole of the waistcoat, five times out of every six, and when he didn't hit him there, he hit him in the head'* (*Boz* – 'Great Winglebury Duel'). In the dramatised version, *The Strange Gentleman*, he is renamed Horatio Tinkles.

Hunter, Leo: Mrs. Hunter's husband. *A grave man* (*Pickwick*).

Hunter, Mrs. Leo: The Eatanswill poetess. *'She doats on poetry, sir. She adores it; I may say that her whole soul and mind are wound up, and entwined with it. She has produced some delightful pieces herself, sir. You may have met her "Ode to an Expiring Frog," sir. . . . It created an immense sensation. It was signed with an "L" and eight stars, and appeared originally in a Lady's Magazine. It commenced*

> *"Can I view thee panting, lying*
> *On thy stomach, without sighing;*
> *Can I unmoved see thee dying*
> *On a log,*
> *Expiring frog!"'*
> (*Pickwick*).

Hutley, Jemmy ('Dismal Jemmy'): Job Trotter's brother and Jingle's actor friend, who recounts 'The Stroller's Tale' at The Bull, Rochester. *A careworn looking man, whose sallow face, and deeply sunken eyes, were rendered still more striking than nature had made them, by the straight black hair which hung in matted disorder half way down his face. His eyes were almost unnaturally bright and piercing; his cheek-bones were high and prominent; and his jaws were so long and lank, that an observer would have supposed that he was drawing the flesh of his face in, for a moment, by some contraction of the muscles, if his half-opened mouth and immovable expression had not announced that it was his ordinary expression* (*Pickwick*).

Hyppolite, Private: Soldier billeted at the perfumer's in the French town where Langley lodges. *When not on duty, volunteered to keep shop while the fair Perfumeress stepped out to speak to a neighbour or so,* *and laughingly sold soap with his war-sword girded on him* (*Christmas Stories* – 'Somebody's Luggage').

Idle, Thomas: One of the two apprentices. *An idler of the unmixed Irish or Neapolitan type; a passive idler, a born-and-bred idler, a consistent idler, who practised what he would have preached if he had not been too idle to preach; a one entire and perfect chrysolite of idleness* (*Two Apprentices*).

Ikey: Assistant bailiff to Solomon Jacobs. *A man in a coarse Petersham great-coat, whity-brown necker-chief, faded black suit, gamboge-coloured top-boots, and one of those large-crowned hats, formerly seldom met with, but now very generally patronised by gentlemen and costermongers* (*Boz* – 'Watkins Tottle').

Ikey: Stable-boy at the inn near the haunted house. *A high-shouldered young fellow, with a round red face, a short crop of sandy hair, a very broad humorous mouth, a turned-up nose, and a great sleeved waistcoat of purple bars, with mother-of-pearl buttons, that seemed to be growing upon him, and to be in a fair way – if it were not pruned – of covering his head and overrunning his boots* (*Christmas Stories* – 'Haunted House').

'Infant Phenomenon, The': See **Crummles, Ninetta** (*Nickleby*).

Inspector: The police officer investigating John Harmon's supposed murder. *His elbows leaning on his desk, and the fingers and thumb of his right hand fitting themselves to the fingers and thumb of his left. Mr. Inspector moved nothing but his eyes* (*Mutual Friend*).

Isaac: Associate of Jackson in apprehending Mrs. Bardell. *A shabby man in black leggings* (*Pickwick*).

'Ivins, J'mima': See **Evans, Jemima** (*Boz* – 'Miss Evans and the Eagle').

Izzard: A boarder at the National Hotel, in America, where Martin Chuzzlewit stays before embarking for Eden (*Chuzzlewit*).

Jack: Prisoner for an assault, which proves fatal, on his mistress. *A powerful, ill-looking young fellow* (*Boz* – 'Hospital Patient').

Jack: Driver of the London-Salisbury coach. *Of all the swells that ever flourished a whip, professionally, he might have been elected emperor* (*Chuzzlewit*).

Jack: Mrs. Lupin's manservant (*Chuzzlewit*).

Jack: Police officer assisting at the arrest of Jonas Chuzzlewit (*Chuzzlewit*).

'Jack', The: Thames-side boatmen's helper, concerned in the attempt to smuggle Magwitch out of England. *A grizzled male creature, the 'Jack' of the little causeway, who was as slimy and smeary as if he had been low water-mark too* (*Expectations*).

Jack, Dark: The species of coloured sailorman. *I should be very slow to interfere oppressively with Dark Jack, for, whenever I have had to do with him I have found him a simple and a gentle fellow* (*Uncommercial* – 'Poor Mercantile Jack').

Jack, Mercantile: The species of merchant sailorman. *Is the sweet little cherub who sits smiling aloft and keeps watch on the life of poor Jack, commissioned to take charge of Mercantile Jack, as well as Jack of the national navy? If not, who is? What is the cherub about, and what are we all about, when poor Mercantile Jack is having his brains slowly knocked out by penny-weights, aboard the brig Beelzebub, or the barque Bowie-knife – when he looks his last at the infernal craft, with the first officer's iron boot-heel in his remaining eye, or with his dying body towed overboard in the ship's wake, while the cruel wounds in it do 'the multitudinous seas incarnadine'? (Uncommercial – 'Poor Mercantile Jack').*

Jackman, Major Jemmy: Permanent lodger and friend of Mrs. Lirriper. He joins with her in adopting Jemmy Jackman Lirriper (q.v.). *A most obliging Lodger and punctual in all respects except one irregular which I need not particularly specify. . . . So much the gentleman that though he is far from tall he seems almost so when he has his shirt-frill out and his frock coat on and his hat with the curly brims, and in what service he was I cannot truly tell you my dear whether Militia or Foreign, for I never heard him even name himself as Major but always simple 'Jemmy Jackman'* (Christmas Stories – 'Mrs. Lirriper's Lodgings' and 'Mrs. Lirriper's Legacy').

Jackson: Also termed 'Young Jackson' and 'Barbox Brothers' (the firm he had come to control and closed down). Visiting Mugby Junction, he rediscovers his lost love, Beatrice Tresham, and hears the Signalman's story. *A man within five years of fifty either way, who had turned grey too soon, like a neglected fire; a man of pondering habit, brooding carriage of the head, and suppressed internal voice; a man with many indications on him of having been too much alone* (Christmas Stories – 'Mugby Junction').

Jackson: Former turnkey at the Marshalsea, whose brother's courting of the daughter of a prisoner, Captain Martin, William Dorrit cites as an example to Amy to encourage Young John Chivery's attentions *(Dorrit).*

Jackson: Chief clerk to Dodson and Fogg. *An individual in a brown coat and brass buttons, whose long hair was scrupulously twisted round the rim of his napless hat, and whose soiled drab trousers were so tightly strapped over his Blucher boots, that his knees threatened every moment to start from their concealment (Pickwick).*

Jackson, Mr. and **Mrs.:** Friends of the Plausible Couple *(Young Couples – 'Plausible Couple').*

Jackson, Michael: Inspector Bucket's imaginary informant about Lady Dedlock's visit to the brickmakers' cottage. *'A person of the name of Michael Jackson, with a blue welveteen waistcoat with a double row of mother of pearl buttons' (Bleak House).*

Jacobs, Solomon: A bailiff, to whose sponging-house in Cursitor Street Watkins Tottle is taken by Jacobs's assistant, Ikey, and from which he is released by Gabriel Parsons. *The two friends soon found themselves on that side of Mr. Solomon Jacobs's establishment, on which most of his visitors were very happy when they found themselves once again – to wit, the outside (Boz – 'Watkins Tottle').*

Jacques One, Two, Three, Four, and **Five:** Revolutionary associates whose ringleader, Jacques Four, is Defarge. *The looks of all of them were dark, repressed, and revengeful. . . . They had the air of a rough tribunal (Two Cities).*

Jaggers: Lawyer employed by both Miss Havisham and Magwitch. Employer of Molly (q.v.). *He was a burly man of an exceedingly dark complexion, with an exceedingly large head and a corresponding large hand. He took my chin in his large hand and turned up my face to have a look at me by the light of the candle. He was prematurely bald on the top of his head, and had bushy black eyebrows that wouldn't lie down, but stood up bristling. His eyes were set very deep in his head, and were disagreeably sharp and suspicious (Expectations).*

James: Twin brother of John, whose phantasm he sees ('At Dusk').

James: The Bayham Badgers' butler *(Bleak House).*

James: Mrs. Tibbs's male servant *(Boz – 'Boarding-House').*

James: Servant to Brook Dingwall. *A red-hot looking footman in bright livery (Boz – 'Sentiment').*

James: Son of John, the narrator. *Went wild and for a soldier, where he was shot in India, living six weeks in hospital with a musket-ball lodged in his shoulder-blade (Reprinted – 'Poor Man's Tale of a Patent').*

James, Henry: Commander of the barque *Defiance* which found the wreckage of the brig *Son and Heir* *(Dombey).*

James and **Charlotte, Master** and **Miss:** Children of Edward and Charlotte. *Present themselves after dinner, and being in perfect good humour, and finding their parents in the same amiable state, augur from these appearances half a glass of wine a-piece and other extraordinary indulgences (Young Couples – 'Contradictory Couple').*

Jane: The Kitterbells' maidservant *(Boz – 'Bloomsbury Christening').*

Jane: Barmaid at Bellamy's restaurant in the Houses of Parliament. *The Hebe of Bellamy's. . . . Her leading features are a thorough contempt for the great majority of her visitors; her predominant quality, love of admiration, as you cannot fail to observe, if you mark the glee with which she listens to something the young Member near her mutters somewhat unintelligibly in her ear (for his speech is rather thick from some cause or other), and how playfully she digs the handle of a fork into the arm with which he detains her, by way of reply (Boz – 'Parliamentary Sketch').*

Jane: Sister of Amelia. Both are marriageable girls displayed by their mamma at the Ramsgate library gambling tables. *'Throw, Jane, my dear,' said the stout lady. An interesting display of bashfulness – a* *little blushing in a cambric handkerchief (Boz – 'Tuggses at Ramsgate').*

Jane: Miss Wozenham's maidservant (*Christmas Stories* – 'Mrs. Lirriper's Lodgings').

Jane: Pecksniff's maidservant (*Chuzzlewit*).

Jane: Mrs. Orange's maidservant ('Holiday Romance').

Jane: Sister of the fiancée of the old lord who admires Kate Nickleby at Madame Mantalini's *salon* (*Nickleby*).

Jane: The Potts' maidservant (*Pickwick*).

Jane: One of Wardle's maidservants (*Pickwick*).

Jane, Aunt: See **Robert, Uncle** (*Boz* – 'Christmas Dinner').

Janet: Betsey Trotwood's maidservant. Despite her professed aversion to matrimony she marries a tavern-keeper. *A pretty, blooming girl, of about nineteen or twenty, and a perfect picture of neatness. . . . She was one of a series of protégées whom my aunt had taken into her service expressly to educate in a renouncement of mankind, and who had generally completed their abjuration by marrying the baker (Copperfield).*

Jarber: Reader of the manuscript of this story (*Christmas Stories* – 'Going into Society').

Jargon: One of Miss Flite's birds (*Bleak House*).

Jarley, Mrs.: Proprietress of a travelling waxworks who befriends and employs Little Nell. Marries her driver, George. *A Christian lady, stout and comfortable to look upon, who wore a large bonnet trembling with bows (Curiosity Shop).*

Jarndyce, John: Bachelor guardian of his cousins Richard Carstone and Ada Clare, for whose companion he employs Esther Summerson. He proposes marriage to her, and is accepted, but when she is married it is to Allan Woodcourt. *It was a handsome, lively, quick face, full of change and motion; and his hair was a silvered iron-grey. I took him to be nearer sixty than fifty, but he was upright, hearty, and robust. // I felt that if we had been at all demonstrative, he would have run away in a moment (Bleak House).*

Jarndyce, Tom: See **Jarndyce and Jarndyce** (*Bleak House*).

Jarndyce and Jarndyce: The interminable Chancery suit which hangs over the whole story and those involved in it. *Jarndyce and Jarndyce drones on. This scarecrow of a suit has, in course of time, become so complicated, that no man alive knows what it means. The parties to it understand it least; but it has been observed that no two Chancery lawyers can talk about it for five minutes, without coming to a total disagreement as to all the premises. Innumerable children have been born into the cause; innumerable young people have married into it; innumerable old people have died out of it. Scores of persons have deliriously found themselves made parties in Jarndyce and Jarndyce, without knowing how or why; whole families have inherited legendary hatreds with the suit. The little*

plaintiff or defendant, who was promised a new rocking-horse when Jarndyce and Jarndyce should be settled, has grown up, possessed himself of a real horse, and trotted away into the other world. Fair wards of court have faded into mothers and grandmothers; a long procession of Chancellors has come in and gone out; the legion of bills in the suit have been transformed into mere bills of mortality; there are not three Jarndyces left upon the earth, perhaps, since old Tom Jarndyce in despair blew his brains out at a coffee-house in Chancery Lane; but Jarndyce and Jarndyce still drags its weary length before the Court, perenially hopeless (Bleak House).

Jarvis: Wilding's clerk (*Christmas Stories* – 'No Thoroughfare', but not in the dramatised version).

Jasper, John: Lay Precentor at Cloisterham Cathedral and secret opium smoker. Uncle to Edwin Drood and jealously in love with Rosa Bud. At the point where the novel ends, unfinished, Jasper seems the likeliest candidate for Drood's supposed murderer. *Mr. Jasper is a dark man of some six-and-twenty, with thick, lustrous, well-arranged black hair and whiskers. He looks older than he is, as dark men often do. His voice is deep and good, his face and figure are good, his manner is a little sombre. His room is a little sombre, and may have had its influence in forming his manner. It is mostly in shadow (Drood).*

Jean Marie: An Alpine guide appearing in the dramatic version, but not the printed story (*No Thoroughfare*).

Jean Paul: An Alpine guide appearing in the dramatic version, but not the printed story (*No Thoroughfare*).

Jeddler, Dr. Anthony: Philosopher and widower father of Grace and Marion, and brother of Martha. *Doctor Jeddler was, as I have said, a great philosopher, and the heart and mystery of his philosophy was, to look upon the world as a gigantic practical joke; as something too absurd to be considered seriously, by any rational man (Christmas Books – 'Battle of Life').*

Jeddler, Grace and **Marion:** Elder and younger daughters of Dr. Jeddler. Marion is engaged to Alfred Heathfield, but pretends to elope with Warden, in reality taking refuge with Aunt Martha in order to enable Grace, whose love for Heathfield she has recognised, to marry him, which she does. *It was agreeable to see the graceful figures of the blooming sisters, twined together, lingering among the trees, conversing thus, with earnestness opposed to lightness, yet, with love responding tenderly to love. . . . The difference between them, in respect of age, could not exceed four years at most; but, Grace, as often happens in such cases, when no mother watches over both (the Doctor's wife was dead), seemed, in her gentle care of her young sister, and in the steadiness of her devotion to her, older than she was; and more removed, in course of nature, from all competition with her, or participation, otherwise than through her sympathy and true affection, in her wayward fancies, than their ages seemed to warrant (Christmas Books – 'Battle of Life').*

Jellyby: Mrs. Jellyby's husband. *I was a little curious to know who a mild bald gentleman in spectacles was, who dropped into a vacant chair . . . and seemed passively to submit himself to Borrioboola-Gha, but not to be actively interested in that settlement (Bleak House).*

Jellyby, Mrs.: A devotee of public causes, especially concerning Africa and the natives of Borrioboola-Gha, preoccupations which cause her to neglect herself and her family. *She was a pretty, very diminutive, plump woman, of from forty to fifty, with handsome eyes, though they had a curious habit of seeming to look a long way off. As if – I am quoting Richard again – they could see nothing nearer than Africa! . . . Mrs. Jellyby had very good hair, but was too much occupied with her African duties to brush it. The shawl in which she had been loosely muffled, dropped on to her chair when she advanced to us; and as she turned to resume her seat, we could not help noticing that her dress didn't nearly meet up the back, and that the open space was railed across with a lattice-work of stay-lace – like a summer-house (Bleak House).*

Jellyby, Caroline ('Caddy'): The Jellybys' eldest daughter and her mother's overworked amanuensis. Sister of 'Peepy'. She makes a happy marriage with Prince Turveydrop and has a deaf and dumb daughter. *A jaded and unhealthy-looking, though by no means plain girl, at the writing-table, who sat biting the feather of her pen, and staring at us. I suppose nobody ever was in such a state of ink. And, from her tumbled hair to her pretty feet, which were disfigured with frayed and broken satin slippers trodden down at heel, she really seemed to have no article of dress upon her, from a pin upwards, that was in its proper condition or its right place (Bleak House).*

Jellyby, 'Peepy': The Jellybys' neglected small son, brother of Caddy. *Everything the dear child wore, was either too large for him or too small. Among his other contradictory decorations he had the hat of a Bishop, and the little gloves of a baby. His boots were, on a small scale, the boots of a ploughman: while his legs, so crossed and recrossed with scratches that they looked like maps, were bare, below a very short pair of plaid drawers finished off with two frills of perfectly different patterns. The deficient buttons on his plaid frock had evidently been supplied from one of Mr. Jellyby's coats, they were extremely brazen and so much too large. Most extraordinary specimens of needlework appeared on several parts of his dress, where it had been hastily mended (Bleak House).*

Jem: Doorkeeper of Solomon Jacobs's sponging-house. *A sallow-faced red-haired sulky boy (Boz – 'Watkins Tottle').*

Jem: One of Wardle's farm hands *(Pickwick).*

Jemima: Polly Toodle's unmarried sister who cares for her children while she is in Dombey's service. *A younger woman not so plump, but apple-faced also, who led a plump and apple-faced child in each hand (Dombey).*

Jenkins: Sir Mulberry Hawk's manservant *(Nickleby).*

Jenkins: Acquaintance of the Contradictory Couple and the subject of one of their arguments. *'I appealed to Mr. Jenkins who sat next to me on the sofa in the drawing-room during tea – ' 'Morgan, you mean,' interrupts the gentleman. 'I do not mean anything of the kind,' answers the lady (Young Couples – 'Contradictory Couple').*

Jenkins, Miss: Pianist at the Gattletons' private theatricals. *Miss Jenkins's talent for the piano was too well known to be doubted for an instant (Boz – 'Mrs. Joseph Porter').*

Jenkinson: A messenger for the Circumlocution Office. *Was eating mushed potatoes and gravy behind a partition by the hall fire (Dorrit).*

Jennings: Robe-maker friend of Dounce *(Boz – 'Misplaced Attachment').*

Jennings: Tulrumble's secretary. *Just imported from London, with a pale face and light whiskers (Mudfog).*

Jennings: One of five occupants of a bed at Dotheboys Hall *(Nickleby).*

Jennings, Miss: Fellow pupil of Rosa Bud at Miss Twinkleton's *(Drood).*

Jenny: Wife of a drunken brickmaker visited by Mrs. Pardiggle. She helps Lady Dedlock in her flight from home. *A woman with a black eye, nursing a poor little gasping baby (Bleak House).*

Jerry: Proprietor of a troupe of performing dogs, encountered by Little Nell and her grandfather in their travels. *A tall black-whiskered man in a velveteen coat (Curiosity Shop).*

Jilkins: Last of the many doctors consulted by Our Bore. *Jilkins then got up, walked across the room, came back, and sat down. His words were these. 'You have been humbugged. This is a case of indigestion, occasioned by deficiency of power in the Stomach. Take a mutton chop in half an hour, with a glass of the finest old sherry that can be got for money. Take two mutton chops to-morrow, and two glasses of finest old sherry. Next day, I'll come again.' In a week our bore was on his legs, and Jilkins's success dates from that period! (Reprinted – 'Our Bore').*

Jingle, Alfred: An irresponsible strolling actor who throws in his lot with the Pickwickians, succeeds in embarrassing them extremely by eloping with Rachael Wardle, masquerades as a Captain Fitz-Marshall, and becomes a prisoner in the Fleet, from where he is rescued by Pickwick, who sends him to Demerara to turn over a new leaf. *He was about the middle height, but the thinness of his body, and the length of his legs, gave him the appearance of being much taller. The green coat had been a smart dress garment in the days of swallow-tails, but had evidently in those times adorned a much shorter man than the stranger, for the soiled and faded sleeves scarcely reached to his wrists. It was buttoned closely up to his chin, at the imminent hazard of splitting the back; and an old stock, without a vestige of shirt collar, ornamented his neck. His scanty black trousers displayed here and there those shiny patches which bespeak long service, and were* *strapped very tightly over a pair of patched and mended shoes, as if to conceal the dirty white stockings, which were nevertheless distinctly visible. His long black hair escaped in negligent waves from beneath each side of his old pinched-up hat; and glimpses of his bare wrists might be observed between the tops of his gloves, and the cuffs of his coat sleeves. His face was thin and haggard; but an indescribable air of jaunty impudence and perfect self-possession pervaded the whole man (Pickwick).*

Jiniwin, Mrs.: Betsey Quilp's mother. *Resided with the couple and waged perpetual war with Daniel; of whom, notwithstanding, she stood in no slight dread (Curiosity Shop).*

Jinkins: Pawnbroker's customer. *An unshaven, dirty, sottish-looking fellow, whose tarnished paper-cap, stuck negligently over one eye, communicates an additionally repulsive expression to his very uninviting countenance (Boz – 'Pawnbroker's Shop').*

Jinkins: Senior boarder at Todgers's; a fish-salesman's book-keeper. *Of a fashionable turn, being a regular frequenter of the Parks on Sundays, and knowing a great many carriages by sight. He spoke mysteriously, too, of splendid women, and was suspected of having once committed himself with a countess (Chuzzlewit).*

Jinkins: Tom Smart's rival for the buxom widow in 'The Bagman's Story'. (See **Bagman, The.**) *'A tall man – a very tall man – in a brown coat and bright basket buttons, and black whiskers, and wavy black hair, who was seated at tea with the widow, and who it required no great penetration to discover was in a fair way of persuading her to be a widow no longer' (Pickwick).*

Jinkins, Mrs.: Jinkins's wife. *A wretched worn-out woman, apparently in the last stage of consumption, whose face bears evident marks of recent ill-usage, and whose strength seems hardly equal to the burden – light enough, God knows! – of the thin, sickly child she carries (Boz – 'Pawnbroker's Shop').*

Jinkinson: Barber and bear-keeper in a tale of Sam Weller's. *'Easy shavin' was his natur', and cuttin' and curlin' was his pride and glory. His whole delight wos in his trade. He spent all his money on bears' (Humphrey).*

Jinks: Clerk to the magistrates at Ipswich. *A pale, sharp-nosed, half-fed, shabbily-clad clerk, of middle-age (Pickwick).*

Jip (short for **Gypsy**): Dora Spenlow's little dog. *I approached him tenderly, for I loved even him; but he showed his whole set of teeth, got under a chair expressly to snarl, and wouldn't hear of the least familiarity (Copperfield).*

Jo ('Toughey'): A boy crossing-sweeper. He is Hawdon's only mourner and shows Lady Dedlock her former lover's haunts, for which he is hounded by Tulkinghorn. He dies in George's Shooting-gallery. *Name, Jo. Nothing else that he knows on. Don't know that everybody has two names. Never heerd of sich a think. Don't know that Jo is short for a longer name.*

Thinks it long enough for him. He don't find no fault with it. Spell it? No. He can't spell it. No father, no mother, no friends. Never been to school. What's home? (Bleak House).

Jobba: Speaker at the mechanical science session of the first meeting of the Mudfog Association. *Produced a forcing-machine on a novel-plan, for bringing joint-stock railway shares prematurely to a premium. The instrument was in the form of an elegant gilt weather-glass, of most dazzling appearance, and was worked behind, by strings, after the manner of a pantomime trick, the strings being always pulled by the directors of the company to which the machine belonged (Mud-fog).*

Jobling, Dr. John: Medical attendant to Anthony Chuzzlewit and Lewsome, later medical officer of the Anglo-Bengalee Disinterested Loan and Life Assurance Company. *He had a portentously sagacious chin, and a pompous voice, with a rich huskiness in some of its tones that went directly to the heart, like a ray of light shining through the ruddy medium of choice old burgundy.... Perhaps he could shake his head, rub his hands, or warm himself before a fire, better than any man alive; and he had a peculiar way of smacking his lips and saying, 'Ah!' at intervals while patients detailed their symptoms, which inspired great confidence. It seemed to express, 'I know what you're going to say better than you do; but go on, go on' (Chuzzlewit).*

Jobling, Tony ('Weevle'): Snagsby's law writer and close friend of Guppy. *Mr. Jobling is buttoned up closer than mere adornment might require. His hat presents at the rims a peculiar appearance of a glistening nature, as if it had been a favourite snail-promenade. The same phenomenon is visible on some parts of his coat, and particularly at the seams. He has the faded appearance of a gentleman in embarrassed circumstances; even his light whiskers droop with something of a shabby air (Bleak House).*

Jobson, Jessie, Sophronia, Jessie Number Two, Matilda, William, Jane, Matilda Number Two, Brigham, Leonardo, and **Orson:** Mormon emigrants aboard the *Amazon* (*Uncommercial* – 'Bound for the Great Salt Lake').

Joby (also **Greenwood**): One-eyed tramp said to have encountered the hooded woman (*Christmas Stories* – 'Haunted House').

Jock: Boy at the little Cumberland inn where Idle's sprained ankle is treated. *A white-headed boy, who, under pretence of stirring up some bay salt in a basin of water for the laving of this unfortunate ankle, had greatly enjoyed himself for the last ten minutes in splashing the carpet (Two Apprentices).*

Jodd: A boarder at the National Hotel, in America, where Martin Chuzzlewit stays before embarking for Eden (*Chuzzlewit*).

Joe: Receiver of stolen goods, shown to Scrooge by the Ghost of Christmas Yet to Come. *A grey-haired rascal, nearly seventy years of age (Christmas Books – 'Christmas Carol').*

Joe: A labourer at the wharf where Florence Dombey meets Walter Gay after her ordeal with Good Mrs. Brown *(Dombey)*.

Joe: Driver of the Cloisterham omnibus *(Drood)*.

Joe: The fat boy, servant to Wardle. *The fat boy rose, opened his eyes, swallowed the huge piece of pie he had been in the act of masticating when he last fell asleep, and slowly obeyed his master's orders – gloating languidly over the remains of the feast, as he removed the plates, and deposited them in the hamper (Pickwick).*

Joe: Waiter at the hotel where Rose Maylie stays near Hyde Park *(Twist)*.

Joe: Guard of the Dover mailcoach. *He stood on his own particular perch behind the mail, beating his feet, and keeping an eye and a hand on the arm-chest before him, where a loaded blunderbuss lay at the top of six or eight loaded horse-pistols, deposited on a substratum of cutlass (Two Cities).*

Joey: One of Miss Flite's birds *(Bleak House)*.

Joey, Captain: Regular drinker at the Six Jolly Fellowship Porters *(Mutual Friend)*.

John: Twin brother of James, to whom his phantasm appears as he lies dying ('At Dusk').

John: The Maldertons' multi-purpose manservant. *A man who, on ordinary occasions, acted as half-groom, half-gardener; but who, as it was important to make an impression on Mr. Sparkins, had been forced into a white neckerchief and shoes, and touched up, and brushed, to look like a second footman (Boz – 'Horatio Sparkins').*

John: The Parsonses' manservant *(Boz – 'Watkins Tottle')*.

John: Narrator of the story and tenant of the haunted house. *I find the early morning to be my most ghostly time. Any house would be more or less haunted, to me, in the early morning; and a haunted house could scarcely address me to greater advantage than then (Christmas Stories – 'Haunted House').*

John: A riverside labourer on whom Florence Dombey takes pity when she is visiting the Skettles. Father of Martha. *A very poor man, who seemed to have no regular employment, but now went roaming about the banks of the river when the tide was low, looking out for bits and scraps in the mud (Dombey).*

John: The Lovetowns' servant *(Is She His Wife?)*.

John: A bibulous pantomime clown whose death is the subject of 'The Stroller's Tale' told by Jem Hutley. *'Never shall I forget the repulsive sight that met my eye when I turned round. He was dressed for the pantomime, in all the absurdity of a clown's costume. The spectral figures in the Dance of Death, the most frightful shapes that the ablest painter ever portrayed on canvas, never presented an appearance half so ghastly. His bloated body and shrunken legs – their deformity enhanced a hundred fold by the fantastic dress – the glassy eyes, contrasting fearfully with the thick white paint with which the face was besmeared;*

the grotesquely ornamented head, trembling with paralysis, and the long, skinny hands, rubbed with white chalk – all gave him a hideous and unnatural appearance' (Pickwick).

John: Waiter at the Saracen's Head, Towcester *(Pickwick)*.

John: The narrator, a working-man who has to spend almost all his life-savings in various officials' fees in order to patent an invention. Father of James, Mary, Charlotte, and others. *I am a smith by trade. My name is John. I have been called 'Old John' ever since I was nineteen year of age, on account of not having much hair. I am fifty-six year of age at the present time, and I don't find myself with more hair, nor yet with less, to signify, than at nineteen year of age aforesaid (Reprinted – 'Poor Man's Tale of a Patent').*

John: Waiter at the St. James's Arms *(Strange Gentleman)*.

John: Unemployed boilermaker in east London, visited by the Uncommercial Traveller. *It soon appeared that he was rather deaf. He was a slow, simple fellow of about thirty (Uncommercial – 'Small Star in the East').*

John: The Fieldings' manservant who finds Jane Adams showing Anne the wedding preparations, and claims a forfeit: *Mr. John, who has waxed bolder by degrees, pleads the usage at weddings, and claims the privilege of a kiss, which he obtains after a great scuffle (Young Couples – 'Young Couple').*

Johnny: Betty Higden's child grandson, whom the Boffins wish to adopt. He dies before they can succeed *(Mutual Friend)*.

Johnson: Pupil at Dr. Blimber's. *Every young gentleman fastened his gaze upon the Doctor, with an assumption of the deepest interest. One of the number who happened to be drinking, and who caught the Doctor's eye glaring at him through the side of his tumbler, left off so hastily that he was convulsed for some moments, and in the sequel ruined Doctor Blimber's point (Dombey).*

Johnson: Nicholas Nickleby's stage name *(Nickleby)*.

Johnson, John: Traveller to Gretna Green, with his intended bride Mary Wilson. He is detained at the St. James's Arms by lack of funds to pay his bill *(Strange Gentleman)*.

Johnson, Tom: One of Feenix's numerous acquaintance. *Cousin Feenix, sitting in the mourning-coach, recognises innumerable acquaintances on the road, but takes no other notice of them, in decorum, than checking them off aloud as they go by, for Mr. Dombey's information, as 'Tom Johnson. Man with cork leg from White's. What are you here, Tommy? Foley on a blood mare. The Smalder girls –' and so forth (Dombey).*

Jollson, Mrs.: Mrs. MacStinger's predecessor at 9, Brig Place, India Docks *(Dombey)*.

Joltered, Sir William: President of the zoology and botany session at the second meeting of the Mudfog Association *(Mudfog)*.

Jonathan: Regular drinker at the Six Jolly Fellowship Porters (*Mutual Friend*).

Jones: Employee of Blaze and Sparkle's. *'Our people, Mr. Jones,' said Blaze and Sparkle to the hand in question on engaging him, 'our people, sir, are sheep – mere sheep. Where two or three marked ones go, all the rest follow. Keep those two or three in your eye, Mr. Jones, and you have the flock' (Bleak House).*

Jones: Barrister's clerk friend of Dounce. *Rum fellow that Jones – capital company – full of anecdote! (Boz – 'Misplaced Attachment').*

Jones: Dinner guest at the Buddens'. *A little smirking man with red whiskers, sitting at the bottom of the table, who during the whole of dinner had been endeavouring to obtain a listener to some stories about Sheridan (Boz – 'Mr. Minns and his Cousin').*

Jones, George: Regular drinker at the Six Jolly Fellowship Porters (*Mutual Friend*).

Jones, Mary: A victim of Ned Dennis, the hangman. *'A young woman of nineteen who come up to Tyburn with a infant at her breast, and was worked off for taking a piece of cloth off the counter of a shop in Ludgate Hill, and putting it down again when the shopman see her; and who had never done any harm before, and only tried to do that, in consequence of her husband having been pressed three weeks previous, and she being left to beg, with two young children – as was proved at the trial. Ha ha! – Well! That being the law and the practice of England, is the glory of England, an't it, Muster Gashford?' (Rudge).*

Jones, Spruggins, and Smith's: Of Tottenham-court Road. The cut-price drapery of which Samuel Smith, alias Horatio Sparkins, is junior partner (*Boz – 'Horatio Sparkins'*).

Joper, Billy: Fellow member of Brooks's with Feenix. *'Man with a glass in his eye' (Dombey).*

Joram: Omer's assistant, later partner. He marries Minnie Omer, and becomes father of Joe and Minnie. *A good-looking young fellow (Copperfield).*

Joram, Mrs.: See **Omer, Minnie** (*Copperfield*).

Joram, Joe and **Minnie:** The Jorams' children (*Copperfield*).

Jorgan, Captain Silas Jonas: Native of Salem, Massachusetts, finder of Hugh Raybrock's message. *He had seen many things and places, and had stowed them all away in a shrewd intellect and a vigorous memory. He was an American born . . . but he was a citizen of the world, and a combination of most of the best qualities of most of its best countries (Christmas Stories – 'Message from the Sea').*

Jorkins: Junior partner in the law practice of Spenlow and Jorkins. *A mild man of a heavy temperament, whose place in the business was to keep himself in the background, and be constantly exhibited by name as the most obdurate and ruthless of men. // A large, mild, smooth-faced man of sixty, who took so much snuff that there was a tradition in the Commons that he lived principally on that stimulant, having little* room in his system for any other article of diet (*Copperfield*).

Joseph: Much respected head waiter at the Slamjam Coffee-house, London, E.C., to whom Christopher dedicates his essays. *Than which a individual more eminently deserving of the name of man, or a more amenable honour to his own head and heart, whether considered in the light of a Waiter or regarded as a human being, do not exist (Christmas Stories – 'Somebody's Luggage').*

Joseph and **Celia:** Charity children observed in a City churchyard. *They were making love – a tremendous proof of the vigour of that immortal article, for they were in the graceful uniform under which English Charity delights to hide herself (Uncommercial – 'City of the Absent').*

Jowl, Joe: A gambler under whose influence little Nell's grandfather falls. *A burly fellow of middle age, with large black whiskers, broad cheeks, a coarse wide mouth, and bull neck, which was pretty freely displayed as his shirt-collar was only confined by a loose red handkerchief (Curiosity Shop).*

Joy, Thomas: Friend of William Butcher with whom John lodges in London, and who helps him with his patent application. *A carpenter, six foot four in height, and plays quoits well (Reprinted – 'Poor Man's Tale of a Patent').*

Julia: The narrator's beloved (*Reprinted – 'Ghost of Art'*).

Jupe, Signor: Sissy's father, a clown in Sleary's Circus. Thinking himself finished, he disappears with his dog, Merrylegs, and is never seen again. *Signor Jupe was that afternoon to 'elucidate the diverting accomplishments of his highly trained performing dog Merrylegs'. He was also to exhibit 'his astounding feat of throwing seventy-five hundred-weight in rapid succession backhanded over his head, thus forming a fountain of solid iron in mid-air, a feat never before attempted in this or any other country, and which having elicited such rapturous plaudits from enthusiastic throngs it cannot be withdrawn.' The same Signor Jupe was to 'enliven the varied performances at frequent intervals with his chaste Shakespearean quips and retorts' (Hard Times).*

Jupe, Cecilia (Sissy): Jupe's deserted daughter. Taken into Gradgrind's household, she proves a ministering angel and helps its members in their varying troubles. *So dark-eyed and dark-haired, that she seemed to receive a deeper and more lustrous colour from the sun, when it shone upon her (Hard Times).*

Kags: A wanted man hiding at Toby Crackit's on Jacob's Island, Bermondsey, when Bill Sikes takes refuge there. *A robber of fifty years, whose nose had been almost beaten in, in some old scuffle, and whose face bore a frightful scar which might probably be traced to the same occasion. (Twist).*

Kate: See **Harry** and **Kate** (*Boz – 'Watkins Tottle'*).

Kate: An orphan child whom Florence Dombey meets at Skettles's. *There came among the other visitors,* soon after Florence, one beautiful girl, three or four years younger than she, who was an orphan child, and who was accompanied by her aunt (Dombey).

Kate: Sister of Henry and cousin to Maria Lobbs in Sam Weller's story of 'The Parish Clerk'. *'An arch, impudent-looking, bewitching little person'* (Pickwick).

Kedgick, Captain: Landlord of the National Hotel in America where Martin Chuzzlewit stays before embarking for Eden *(Chuzzlewit)*.

Kenge ('Conversation Kenge'): Solicitor, of Kenge and Carboy, employed by Jarndyce. Richard Carstone becomes articled to the firm. *A portly important-looking gentleman, dressed all in black, with a white cravat, large gold watch seals, a pair of gold eye-glasses, and a large seal-ring upon his little finger. . . . He appeared to enjoy beyond everything the sound of his own voice. I couldn't wonder at that, for it was mellow and full, and gave great importance to every word he uttered. He listened to himself with obvious satisfaction, and sometimes gently beat time to his own music with his head, or rounded a sentence with his hand. I was very much impressed by him – even then, before I knew that he formed himself on the model of a great lord who was his client, and that he was generally called Conversation Kenge (Bleak House).*

Kenwigs: Fellow lodger, with his family, of Noggs. Nicholas Nickleby is engaged to teach the Kenwigs children. *A turner in ivory, who was looked upon as a person of some consideration on the premises, inasmuch as he occupied the whole of the first floor, comprising a suite of two rooms (Nickleby).*

Kenwigs, Mrs. (Susan): Kenwigs's wife. *Quite a lady in her manners, and of a very genteel family, having an uncle who collected a water-rate; besides which distinction, the two eldest of her little girls went twice a week to a dancing-school in the neighbourhood, and had flaxen hair, tied with blue ribands, hanging in luxuriant pigtails down their backs; and wore little white trousers with frills round the ankles – for all of which reasons, and many more equally valid but too numerous to mention, Mrs. Kenwigs was considered a very desirable person to know, and was the constant theme of all the gossips in the street, and even three or four doors round the corner at both ends (Nickleby).*

Kenwigs, Morleena: The Kenwigses' eldest daughter. *Regarding whose uncommon Christian name it may be here remarked that it had been invented and composed by Mrs. Kenwigs previous to her first lying-in, for the special distinction of her eldest child, in case it should prove a daughter (Nickleby).*

Ketch, Professor John: Exhibitor of the skull of Greenacre at the umbugology and ditchwaterisics session at the second meeting of the Mudfog Association. *Remarking, on being invited to make any observations that occurred to him, 'that he'd pound it as that 'ere 'spectable section had never seed a more gamerer cove nor he vos' (Mudfog).*

Kettle, La Fayette: Secretary of the Watertoast Association of United Sympathisers whom Martin Chuzzlewit meets while travelling in America. *He was as languid and listless in his looks, as most of the gentlemen they had seen; his cheeks were so hollow that he seemed to be always sucking them in; and the sun had burnt him, not a wholesome red or brown, but dirty yellow. He had bright dark eyes, which he kept half closed; only peeping out of the corners, and even then with a glance that seemed to say, 'Now you won't overreach me: you want to, but you won't' (Chuzzlewit).*

Kibble, Jacob: Fellow-passenger of John Harmon from Cape Colony to England who gives evidence at the inquest on him. *An unctuous broad man of few words and many mouthfuls (Mutual Friend).*

Kidderminster: Childers's assistant in his riding act in Sleary's Circus. *A diminutive boy with an old face, who now accompanied him, assisted as his infant son: being carried upside down over his father's shoulder, by one foot, and held by the crown of his head, heels upwards, in the palm of his father's hand, according to the violent paternal manner in which wild huntsmen may be observed to fondle their offspring. Made up with curls, wreaths, wings, white bismuth, and carmine, this hopeful young person soared into so pleasing a Cupid as to constitute the chief delight of the maternal part of the spectators; but in private, where his characteristics were a precocious cutaway coat and an extremely gruff voice, he became of the Turf, turfy (Hard Times).*

Kidgerbury, Mrs.: One of David and Dora Copperfield's domestic trials. *The oldest inhabitant of Kentish town, I believe, who went out charing, but was too feeble to execute her conceptions of that art (Copperfield).*

Kimber: Dancing-master. A member of the Eight Club (q.v.) at Cloisterham. *A commonplace, hopeful sort of man, wholly destitute of dignity or knowledge of the world (Drood fragment).*

Kimmeens, Kitty: Pupil of Miss Pupford, whom Mr. Traveller takes to visit Tom Tiddler's Ground. *A self-helpful, steady little child is Miss Kitty Kimmeens: a dimpled child too, and a loving (Christmas Stories – 'Tom Tiddler's Ground').*

Kinch, Horace: Prisoner in the King's Bench, where he dies. *He was a likely man to look at, in the prime of life, well to do, as clever as he needed to be, and popular among many friends. He was suitably married, and had healthy and pretty children. But, like some fair-looking houses or fair-looking ships, he took the Dry Rot. The first strong external revelation of the Dry Rot in men, is a tendency to lurk and lounge; to be at street-corners without intelligible reason; to be going anywhere when met; to be about many places rather than at any; to do nothing tangible, but to have an intention of performing a variety of intangible duties to-morrow or the day after (Uncommercial – 'Night Walks').*

Kindheart: The Uncommercial Traveller's companion during a period of residence in Italy. *An*

Englishman of an amiable nature, great enthusiasm, and no discretion (*Uncommercial* – 'Medicine Men of Civilisation').

King, Christian George: Pilot of the sloop *Christopher Columbus* on her arrival at Silver-Store Island, and her betrayer to the pirates. He is shot by Captain Carton. *I confess, for myself, that on that first day, if I had been captain of the Christopher Columbus, instead of private in the Royal Marines, I should have kicked Christian George King – who was no more a Christian than he was a King or a George – over the side, without exactly knowing why, except that it was the right thing to do* (*Christmas Stories* – 'English Prisoners').

Kitt, Miss: Girl with whom David Copperfield flirts at Dora Spenlow's birthday picnic when Red Whisker makes him jealous of Dora. *A young creature in pink, with little eyes* (*Copperfield*).

Kitten: Pordage's Vice-commissioner at Silver-Store Island. *A small, youngish, bald, botanical and mineral-ogical gentleman* (*Christmas Stories* – 'English Prisoners').

Kitterbell, Charles: Husband of Jemima and father of Frederick Charles William. Nephew of Nicodemus Dumps, whom he persuades, against his better judgement, to stand godfather to the child. *A small, sharp, spare man, with a very large head, and a broad, good-humoured countenance. He looked like a faded giant, with his head and face partially restored; and he had a cast in his eye which rendered it quite impossible for any one with whom he conversed to know where he was looking. His eyes appeared fixed on the wall, and he was staring you out of countenance. . . . In addition to these characteristics, it may be added that Mr. Charles Kitterbell was one of the most credulous and matter-of-fact little personages that ever took to himself a wife, and for himself a house in Great Russell Street, Bedford Square* (*Boz* – 'Bloomsbury Christening').

Kitterbell, Mrs. Charles (Jemima): Kitterbell's wife, mother of Frederick Charles William. *A tall, thin young lady, with very light hair, and a particularly white face – one of those young women who almost invariably, though one hardly knows why, recall to one's mind the idea of a cold fillet of veal* (*Boz* – 'Bloomsbury Christening').

Kitterbell, Frederick Charles William: The Kitterbells' first baby, subject of the gloomy prognostications of his godfather, Nicodemus Dumps. *A remarkably small parcel . . . packed up in a blue mantle trimmed with white fur* (*Boz* – 'Bloomsbury Christening').

Klem, Miss: The Klems' daughter. *Apparently ten years older than either of them* (*Uncommercial* – 'Arcadian London').

Klem, Mr. and Mrs.: The woman who waits on the Uncommercial Traveller while he lodges with a Bond Street hatter, and her husband. Parents of Miss Klem. *An elderly woman labouring under a chronic sniff, who, at the shadowy hour of half-past nine o'clock of every evening, gives admittance at the street door to a*

meagre and mouldy old man whom I have never yet seen detached from a flat pint of beer in a pewter pot (*Uncommercial* – 'Arcadian London').

Knag, Miss: Sister of Mortimer Knag. Forewoman and successor to Madame Mantalini. *A short, bustling, over-dressed female, full of importance. . . . Every now and then, she was accustomed, in the torrent of her discourse, to introduce a loud, shrill, clear, 'hem!' the import and meaning of which, was variously interpreted by her acquaintance; some holding that Miss Knag dealt in exaggeration, and introduced the mono-syllable, when any fresh invention was in course of coinage in her brain; others, that when she wanted a word, she threw it in to gain time, and prevent anybody else from striking into the conversation. It may be further remarked, that Miss Knag still aimed at youth, although she had shot beyond it, years ago; and that she was weak and vain, and one of those people who are best described by the axiom, that you may trust them as far as you can see them, and no farther* (*Nickleby*).

Knag, Mortimer: Miss Knag's brother. A stationer and keeper of a circulating library off Tottenham Court Road. *A tall lank gentleman of solemn features, wearing spectacles, and garnished with much less hair than a gentleman bordering on forty, or thereabouts, usually boasts* (*Nickleby*).

Koëldwethout, Baron von, of Grogzwig: Hero of a tale told by a passenger of a broken-down coach in which Squeers and Nicholas Nickleby are travelling to Yorkshire. *A fine swarthy fellow, with dark hair and large moustachios, who rode a-hunting in clothes of Lincoln green, with russet boots on his feet, and a bugle slung over his shoulder, like the guard of a long stage* (*Nickleby*).

Koëldwethout, Baroness von: Koëldwethout's wife, daughter of Baron von Swillenhausen (*Nickleby*).

Krook, ('Lord Chancellor'): Rag-and-bone dealer and landlord to Miss Flite and Hawdon. Brother to Mrs. Smallweed. On the night that he is due to hand over to Jobling papers relating to Hawdon he disappears, leaving a room full of smoke and some ashes. He is assumed to have died by spontaneous combustion, about the possibility of which there has been much controversy since this story appeared. *He was short, cadaverous, and withered; with his head sunk sideways between his shoulders, and the breath issuing in visible smoke from his mouth, as if he were on fire within. His throat, chin and eyebrows were so frosted with white hairs, and so gnarled with veins and puckered skin, that he looked from his breast upward, like some old root in a fall of snow* (*Bleak House*).

Kutankumagen, Dr.: Of Moscow. Speaker at the anatomy and medicine session of the first meeting of the Mudfog Association, who describes his treatment of a patient 'labouring under symptoms peculiarly alarming to any medical man' – perfect health and heartiness. *By dint of powerful medicine, low diet, and bleeding, the symptoms in the course of three days perceptibly decreased. . . . At the present moment he was restored so far as to walk about, with the slight* assistance of a crutch and a boy. *It would perhaps be gratifying to the section to learn that he ate little, drank little, slept little, and was never heard to laugh by any accident whatever (Mudfog).*

Kwakley: Speaker at the statistics session of the second meeting of the Mudfog Association. *Stated the result of some most ingenious statistical inquiries relative to the difference between the value of the qualification of several members of Parliament as published to the world, and its real nature and amount (Mudfog).*

La Cour, Capitaine de: Officer billeted at Madame Bouclet's (*Christmas Stories* – 'Somebody's Luggage').

La Creevy, Miss: A miniature painter, landlady and friend to the Nicklebys in London. She marries Tim Linkinwater. *The wearer of the yellow head-dress, who had a gown to correspond, and was of much the same colour herself. Miss Lu Creevy was a mincing young lady of fifty (Nickleby).*

Ladle, Joey: Head cellarman of Wilding and Co. He goes to Switzerland with Marguerite Obenreizer and they rescue Vendale. *A slow and ponderous man, of the drayman order of human architecture, dressed in a corrugated suit and bibbed apron, apparently a composite of door-mat and rhinoceros-hide (Christmas Stories* – 'No Thoroughfare' and dramatised version).

Lady Jane: Krook's cat. *A large grey cat leaped from some neighbouring shelf . . . and ripped at a bundle of rags with her tigerish claws, with a sound that it set my teeth on edge to hear. 'She'd do as much for any one I was to set her on,' said the old man. 'I deal in cat-skins among other general matters, and hers was offered to me. It's a very fine skin, as you may see, but I didn't have it stripped off!' (Bleak House).*

Lagnier: See **Rigaud** (*Dorrit*).

Lambert, Miss: A partner of Hopkins in the quadrille. *The young lady, after several inspections of her bouquet, all made in the expectation that the bashful young gentleman is going to talk, whispers her mamma, who is sitting next her, which whisper the bashful young gentleman immediately suspects (and possibly with very good reason) must be about him. (Young Gentlemen* – 'Bashful Young Gentleman').

Lammle, Alfred: A fortune-hunter inveigled by Veneering into marrying Sophronia Akershem in the belief that she is rich. *Too much nose in his face, too much ginger in his whiskers, too much torso in his waistcoat, too much sparkle in his studs, his eyes, his buttons, his talk, and his teeth (Mutual Friend).*

Lammle, Mrs. Alfred: See **Akershem, Sophronia** (*Mutual Friend*).

'Lamps': Phoebe's father, employed at Mugby Junction. *'On Porter's wages, sir. But I am Lamps.' // He was a spare man of about the Barbox Brothers time of life, with his features whimsically drawn upward as if they were attracted by the roots of his hair. He had a peculiarly shining, transparent complexion, probably occasioned by constant oleaginous application; and his attractive hair, being cut short, and being grizzled,* and standing straight up on end as if it in its turn were attracted by some invisible magnet above it, the top of his head was not very unlike a lamp-wick (Christmas Stories* – 'Mugby Junction').

Landless, Neville and **Helena:** Orphan twins from Ceylon, wards of Luke Honeythunder. Neville is coached by Crisparkle at Cloisterham, while Helena attends Miss Twinkleton's. Neville is attracted by Rosa and incurs Drood's hostility. He is arrested as Drood's suspected murderer. *An unusually handsome lithe young fellow, and an unusually handsome lithe girl; much alike; both very dark, and very rich in colour; she of almost the gypsy type; something untamed about them both; a certain air upon them of hunter and huntress; yet withal a certain air of being the objects of the chase, rather than the followers. Slender, supple, quick of eye and limb; half shy, half defiant; fierce of look; an indefinable kind of pause coming and going on their whole expression, both of face and form, which might be equally likened to the pause before a crouch or a bound (Drood).*

Landlord: Landlord of the Peal of Bells village inn who tells Mr. Traveller about Mopes. *With an asphyxiated appearance on him as one unaccustomed to definition (Christmas Stories* – 'Tom Tiddler's Ground').

Lane, Miss: Governess to the Borum children (*Nickleby*).

Langdale: Distiller and vintner who shelters Haredale from the Gordon Rioters and has his premises ransacked and burnt. *The vintner – whose place of business was down in some deep cellars hard by Thames Street, and who was as purple-faced an old gentleman as if he had all his life supported their arched roof on his head (Rudge).*

Langley ('Mr. The Englishman'): Living misanthropically in France after disowning his daughter in England, he meets Corporal Théophile and Bebelle, and after the soldier's death adopts the child and returns to reconciliation with his daughter. *Now the Englishman, in taking his Appartement, – or, as one might say on our side of the Channel, his set of chambers, – had given his name, correct to the letter,* LANGLEY. *But as he had a British way of not opening his mouth very wide on foreign soil, except at meals, the Brewery had been able to make nothing of it but L'Anglais. So Mr. The Englishman he had become and he remained (Christmas Stories* – 'Somebody's Luggage').

'Larkey Boy, The': Prizefighter who gives the 'Game Chicken' a beating. *The Chicken himself attributed this punishment to his having had the misfortune to get into Chancery early in the proceedings, when he was severely fibbed by the Larkey One, and heavily grassed. But it appeared from the published records of that great contest that the Larkey Boy had had it all his own way from the beginning, and that the Chicken had been tapped, and bunged, and had received pepper, and had been made groggy, and had come up piping, and had endured a complication of similar* *strange inconveniences, until he had been gone into and finished (Dombey).*

Larkins: The eldest Miss Larkins's father. *A gruff old gentleman with a double chin, and one of his eyes immoveable in his head (Copperfield).*

Larkins, the eldest **Miss:** An object of David Copperfield's youthful infatuation. She marries Chestle. *The eldest Miss Larkins is not a little girl. She is a tall, dark, black-eyed, fine figure of a woman. The eldest Miss Larkins is not a chicken; for the youngest Miss Larkins is not that, and the eldest must be three or four years older. Perhaps the eldest Miss Larkins may be about thirty. . . . I picture Miss Larkins sinking her head upon my shoulder, and saying, 'Oh, Mr. Copperfield, can I believe my ears!' I picture Mr. Larkins waiting on me next morning, and saying, 'My dear Copperfield, my daughter has told me all. Youth is no objection. Here are twenty thousand pounds. Be happy!' (Copperfield).*

Larkins, Jem: Amateur actor, known as Horatio St. Julien. *That gentleman in the white hat and checked shirt, brown coat and brass buttons, lounging behind the stage-box on the O.P. side. . . . His line is genteel comedy – his father's coal and potato (Boz – 'Private Theatres').*

Latin-Grammar Master, The: Captain Boldheart's adversary, captain of the *Scorpion*, in Robin Redforth's romantic tale ('Holiday Romance').

Lazarus: Brother of 'Habraham Latharuth', an arrested thief. He tries in vain to persuade Jaggers to defend the case. *I remarked this Jew, who was of a highly excitable temperament, performing a jig of anxiety under a lamp-post, and accompanying himself, in a kind of frenzy, with the words, 'Oh Jaggerth, Jaggerth, Jaggerth! all otherth ith Cag-Maggerth, give me Jaggerth!' (Expectations).*

Leath, Angela: Charley's sweetheart, and subsequent wife. *It happened in the memorable year when I parted for ever from Angela Leath, whom I was shortly to have married, on making the discovery that she preferred my bosom friend (Christmas Stories – 'Holly-Tree').*

Leaver: A vice-president of the display of models and mechanical science session at the second meeting of the Mudfog Association *(Mudfog).*

Leaver, Augustus and **Augusta:** A loving couple. *Mr. and Mrs. Leaver are pronounced by Mrs. Starling . . . to be a perfect model of wedded felicity. 'You would suppose,' says the romantic lady, 'that they were lovers only just engaged. Never was such happiness! They are so tender, so affectionate, so attached to each other, so enamoured, that positively nothing can be more charming!' (Young Couples – 'Loving Couple').*

Ledbrain, X.: Vice-president of the statistics session at the first meeting of the Mudfog Association. *Read a very ingenious communication, from which it appeared that the total number of legs belonging to the manufacturing population of one great town in*

Yorkshire was, in round numbers, forty thousand, while the total number of chair and stool legs in their houses was only thirty thousand, which, upon the very favourable average of three legs to a seat, yielded only ten thousand seats in all. From this calculation it would appear . . . that ten thousand individuals (one half of the whole population) were either destitute of any rest for their legs at all, or passed the whole of their leisure time in sitting upon boxes (Mudfog).*

Ledrook, Miss: Member of Crummles's theatrical company *(Nickleby).*

Leeford, Edward (alias **Monks**): Oliver Twist's villainous half-brother, son of Edwin Leeford. *The man who was seated there, was tall and dark, and wore a large cloak. . . . Mr. Bumble felt, every now and then, a powerful inducement, which he could not resist, to steal a look at the stranger: and that, whenever he did so, he withdrew his eyes, in some confusion, to find that the stranger was at that moment stealing a look at him. Mr. Bumble's awkwardness was enhanced by the very remarkable expression of the stranger's eye, which was keen and bright, but shadowed by a scowl of distrust and suspicion, unlike anything he had ever observed before, and repulsive to behold (Twist).*

Leeford, Edwin: Seducer of Agnes Fleming and father of Oliver Twist and Edward Leeford (alias Monks) *(Twist).*

Lemon, Mrs.: Proprietress of a preparatory school for grown-ups in Nettie Ashford's romantic tale ('Holiday Romance').

Lenville, Thomas: Member of Crummles's theatrical company. *A dark-complexioned man, inclining indeed to sallow, with long thick black hair, and very evident indications (although he was close shaved) of a stiff beard, and whiskers of the same deep shade. His age did not appear to exceed thirty, though many at first sight would have considered him much older, as his face was long, and very pale, from the constant application of stage paint (Nickleby).*

Lenville, Mrs. Thomas: Lenville's wife, also a member of Crummles's theatrical company. *In a very limp bonnet and veil, decidedly in that way in which she would wish to be if she truly loved Mr. Lenville (Nickleby).*

Lewsome: A physician's young assistant induced by Jonas Chuzzlewit to supply poison for the attempted murder of Anthony Chuzzlewit. Mrs. Gamp, attending him in subsequent sickness, hears his delirious confession. *He was so wasted, that it seemed as if his bones would rattle when they moved him. His cheeks were sunken, and his eyes unnaturally large. He lay back in the easy-chair like one more dead than living; and rolled his languid eyes towards the door when Mrs. Gamp appeared, as painfully as if their weight alone were burdensome to move (Chuzzlewit).*

Licensed Victualler, Mr.: Proprietor of a Liverpool sailors' 'singing-house'. *A sharp and watchful man, Mr. Licensed Victualler, the host, with tight lips and a* complete edition of Cocker's arithmetic in each eye (*Uncommercial* – 'Poor Mercantle Jack').

Life: One of Miss Flite's birds *(Bleak House).*

Lightwood, Mortimer: Boffin's lawyer, much connected with the Harmon mystery. *A certain 'Mortimer', another of Veneering's oldest friends; who never was in the house before, and appears not to want to come again, who sits disconsolate on Mrs. Veneering's left, and who was inveigled by Lady Tippins (a friend of his boyhood) to come to these people's and talk, and who won't talk (Mutual Friend).*

'Lignum Vitae': See **Bagnet, Matthew** *(Bleak House).*

Lillerton, Miss: The spinster to whom Gabriel Parsons tries to marry off Watkins Tottle, for his own pecuniary advantage. She is already engaged to the Revd. Charles Timson, and marries him. *A lady of very prim appearance, and remarkably inanimate. She was one of those persons at whose age it is impossible to make any reasonable guess; her features might have been remarkably pretty when she was younger, and they might always have presented the same appearance. Her complexion – with a slight trace of powder here and there – was as clear as that of a well-made wax-doll, and her face as expressive (Boz – 'Watkins Tottle').*

Lillyvick: Mrs. Kenwigs's uncle, a collector of water-rates. He marries Henrietta Petowker. *'The kindest-hearted man as ever was,' said Kenwigs. 'It goes to his heart, I believe, to be forced to cut the water off, when the people don't pay,' observed the bachelor friend (Nickleby).*

Lillyvick, Mrs.,: See **Petowker, Henrietta** *(Nickleby).*

Limbkins: Chairman of the authorities of the parish in whose workhouse Oliver Twist is born. *At the top of the table, seated in an arm-chair rather higher than the rest, was a particularly fat gentleman with a very round, red face (Twist).*

Limbury, Peter and **Mrs. Peter:** Friends of the Lovetowns. Alfred Lovetown's flirtation with Mrs. Limbury infuriates Limbury but helps to restore his own wife's affection for him *(Is She His Wife?).*

Linderwood, Lieutenant: Officer commanding the Royal Marines in the sloop *Christopher Columbus* (*Christmas Stories* – 'English Prisoners').

Linkinwater, Miss: Tim Linkinwater's sister *(Nickleby).*

Linkinwater, Tim: The Cheeryble brothers' faithful old clerk, whom Nicholas Nickleby assists for some time. He befriends the Nickleby family and marries Miss La Creevy. *A fat, elderly, large-faced clerk, with silver spectacles and a powdered head (Nickleby).*

Linseed, Duke of: Writer of a begging letter to Boffin *(Mutual Friend).*

Linx, Miss: One of Miss Pupford's pupils who notes gentlemen's advances to her teacher at Tunbridge Wells. *A sharply observant pupil (Christmas Stories – 'Tom Tiddler's Ground').*

Lion: Henry Gowan's dog, poisoned by Rigaud. *A fine Newfoundland dog (Dorrit).*

Lirriper, Mrs. Emma: Narrator of the two stories. Keeper of a lodging-house at 81, Norfolk Street, Strand, London. She adopts, with Major Jackman, the child of Peggy Edson, who dies at her lodgings. *It was about the Lodgings that I was intending to hold forth and certainly I ought to know something of the business having been in it so long, for it was early in the second year of my married life that I lost my poor Lirriper and I set up at Islington directly afterwards and afterwards came here, being two houses and eight-and-thirty years and some losses and a deal of experience (Christmas Stories – 'Mrs. Lirriper's Lodgings' and 'Mrs. Lirriper's Legacy').* See also **Gran, Mrs.**

Lirriper, Jemmy Jackman: Peggy Edson's child, adopted by Mrs. Lirriper and Major Jackman after his mother's death following Edson's desertion. *We called him Jemmy, being after the Major his own godfather with Lirriper for a surname being after myself, and never was a dear child such a brightening thing in a Lodgings or such a playmate to his grandmother as Jemmy to this house and me, and always good and minding what he was told (upon the whole) (Christmas Stories – 'Mrs. Lirriper's Lodgings' and 'Mrs. Lirriper's Legacy').*

Lirriper, Dr. Joshua: Youngest brother of Mrs. Lirriper's deceased husband. *Doctor of what I am sure it would be hard to say unless Liquor, for neither Physic nor Music nor yet Law does Joshua Lirriper know a morsel of except continually being summoned to the County Court and having orders made upon him which he runs away from, and once was taken in the passage of this very house with an umbrella up and the Major's hat on, giving his name with the doormat round him as Sir Johnson Jones, K.C.B. in spectacles residing at the Horse Guards (Christmas Stories – 'Mrs. Lirriper's Legacy').*

List, Isaac: A gambler who fleeces Little Nell's grandfather and then induces him to rob Mrs. Jarley. *Stooping, and high in the shoulders – with a very ill-favoured face, and a most sinister and villainous squint (Curiosity Shop).*

Lithers, Thomas: Landlord of the Water-Lily Hotel at Malvern, the setting of the farce *(Nightingale's Diary).*

Littimer: Steerforth's manservant. He assists his master to elope with Little Em'ly and is offered her when Steerforth tires of her. Miss Mowcher reveals him to be a thief and he is transported. *He was taciturn, soft-footed, very quiet in his manner, deferential, observant, always at hand when wanted, and never near when not wanted; but his great claim to consideration was his respectability.... Nobody could have thought of putting him in a livery, he was so highly respectable. To have imposed any derogatory work upon him, would have been to inflict a wanton insult on the feelings of a*

101

most respectable man. And of this, I noticed the women-servants in the household were so intuitively conscious, that they always did such work themselves, and generally while he read the paper by the pantry fire (Copperfield).

Little Dorrit: See **Dorrit, Amy** (Dorrit).

Little Em'ly: See **Em'ly, Little** (Copperfield).

Little Nell: See **Trent, Nell** (Curiosity Shop).

Lively: Receiver of stolen goods on Saffron Hill, from whom Fagin inquires Bill Sikes's whereabouts. A salesman of small stature, who had squeezed as much of his person into a child's chair as the chair would hold (Twist).

Liz: A brickmaker's wife, friend of Jenny (Bleak House).

Lobbs, Maria: The object of Nathaniel Pipkin's affections in Sam Weller's tale of 'The Parish Clerk'. She is cousin to Kate and also to Henry, whom she marries. 'A prettier foot, a gayer heart, a more dimpled face, or a smarter form, never bounded so lightly over the earth they graced, as did those of Maria Lobbs, the old saddler's daughter. There was a roguish twinkle in her sparkling eyes ... and there was such a joyous sound in her merry laugh, that the sternest misanthrope must have smiled to hear it' (Pickwick).

Lobbs, Old: The fiery father of Maria. 'Old Lobbs the great saddler, who could have bought up the whole village at one stroke of his pen, and never felt the outlay ... old Lobbs, who it was well known, on festive occasions garnished his board with a real silver tea-pot, cream-ewer, and sugar-basin, which he was wont, in the pride of his heart, to boast should be his daughter's property when she found a man to her mind' (Pickwick).

Lobley: Ex-seaman. Tartar's man and boatman. A jolly-favoured man, with tawny hair and whiskers, and a big red face. He was the dead image of the sun in old woodcuts, his hair and whiskers answering for rays all around him (Drood).

Lobskini, Signor: Singing-master at the Misses Crumpton's. The splendid tenor of the inimitable Lobskini (Boz – 'Sentiment').

Loggins: Amateur actor, known as Beverley, who plays Macbeth (Boz – 'Private Theatres').

Long Eers, The Hon. and Revd.: Member of the Mudfog Association (Mudfog).

Longford, Edmund: See **Denham, Edmund** (Christmas Books – 'Haunted Man').

'Lord Chancellor': Krook's neighbours' nickname for him. His shop is called the Court of Chancery (Bleak House).

Lord Mayor, The: Lord Mayor of London during the Gordon Riots. The real-life incumbent of the office was the incompetent Alderman Kennet, a waiter turned vintner. 'I'm sure I don't know what's to be done. – There are great people at the bottom of these riots. – Oh dear me, what a thing it is to be a public character!' (Rudge).

Lord Mayor Elect, The: Wholesale fruiterer, alderman, Sheriff, member of the worshipful Company of Patten-makers, and subject of the Deaf Gentleman's narrative. He was a very substantial citizen indeed. His face was like the full moon in a fog, with two little holes punched out for his eyes, a very ripe pear stuck on for his nose, and a wide gash to serve for a mouth. The girth of his waistcoat was hung up and lettered in his tailor's shop as an extraordinary curiosity. He breathed like a heavy snorer, and his voice in speaking came thickly forth, as if it were oppressed and stifled by feather-beds. He trod the ground like an elephant, and eat and drank like – like nothing but an alderman, as he was (Humphrey).

Lorn: Dr. Speddie's assistant, who may have been the revived 'corpse' from the story told by Speddie to Goodchild. He was at least two-and-fifty; but, that was nothing. What was startling in him was his remarkable paleness. His large black eyes, his sunken cheeks, his long and heavy iron-grey hair, his wasted hands, and even the attenuation of his figure, were at first forgotten in his extraordinary pallor. There was no vestige of colour in the man (Two Apprentices).

Lorry, Jarvis: Confidential clerk at Tellson's Bank who brings Dr. Manette back to England after his long imprisonment in the Bastille. He wore an odd little sleek crisp flaxen wig, setting very close to his head: which wig, it is to be presumed, was made of hair, but which looked far more as though it were spun from filaments of silk or glass. ... A face habitually suppressed and quieted, was still lighted up under the quaint wig by a pair of moist bright eyes that it must have cost their owner, in years gone by, some pains to drill to the composed and reserved expression of Tellson's Bank. He had a healthy colour in his cheeks, and his face, though lined, bore few traces of anxiety (Two Cities).

Losberne, Mr.: Surgeon, friend to the Maylies, who treats the shot Oliver Twist and helps save him from arrest. Known throughout a circuit of ten miles round as 'the doctor', had grown fat, more from good-humour than from good living; and was as kind and hearty, and withal as eccentric an old bachelor, as will be found in five times that space, by any explorer alive (Twist).

Louis: Murderer whose arrest was witnessed by the narrator at a Swiss inn (Christmas Stories – 'Holly-Tree').

Louis: A servant of the Uncommercial Traveller while visiting France. A bright face looked in at the window (Uncommercial – 'Travelling Abroad').

Louisa: See **Charles** and **Louisa** (Young Couples – 'Cool Couple').

Lovetown, Alfred and **Mrs. Alfred:** A young married couple who re-stimulate affection for one another by arousing mutual jealousy, Alfred flirting with Mrs. Limbury and his wife with Felix Tapkins (Is She His Wife?).

Lowfield, Miss: An admirer of Caveton. *A young lady who, truth to tell, is rather smitten with the throwing-off young gentleman* (*Young Gentlemen* – ' "Throwing-off" Young Gentleman').

Lowten: Perker's clerk, and *habitué* of the Magpie and Stump. *A puffy-faced young man* (*Pickwick*).

Loyal Devasseur, Monsieur: The narrator's landlord during his sojourns in France. *We doubt if there is, ever was, or ever will be, a man so universally pleasant in the minds of people as M. Loyal is in the minds of the citizens of our French watering-place. They rub their hands and laugh when they speak of him. Ah, but he is such a good child, such a brave boy, such a generous spirit, that Monsieur Loyal!* . . . *A portly, upright, broad-shouldered, brown-faced man, whose soldierly bearing gives him the appearance of being taller than he is, look into the bright eye of M. Loyal, standing before you in his working-blouse and cap, not particularly well shaved, and, it may be, very earthy, and you shall discern in M. Loyal a gentleman whose true politeness is ingrain, and confirmation of whose word by his bond you would blush to think of* (Reprinted – 'Our French Watering-place').

Lucas, Solomon: Jewish theatrical costumier patronised by the Pickwickians for Mrs. Leo Hunter's fancy-dress breakfast at Eatanswill. *His wardrobe was extensive – very extensive – not strictly classical perhaps, nor quite new, nor did it contain any one garment made precisely after the fashion of any age or time, but everything was more or less spangled; and what can be prettier than spangles!* (*Pickwick*).

Luffey: Leading player of Dingley Dell Cricket Club. *The highest ornament of Dingley Dell* (*Pickwick*).

Lumbey, Dr.: Mrs. Kenwigs's attendant at her last confinement. *Doctor Lumbey was popular, and the neighbourhood was prolific; and there had been no less than three other knockers muffled, one after the other, within the last forty-eight hours* (*Nickleby*).

Lummy Ned: Former guard of the Light Salisbury coach whose example in emigrating to America, recounted by William Simmons, inspires young Martin Chuzzlewit to follow suit (*Chuzzlewit*).

Lupin, Mrs.: Landlady of the Blue Dragon, near Salisbury, where Mark Tapley is ostler before joining Martin Chuzzlewit on his travels. When Mark returns he marries her and the inn is renamed The Jolly Tapley. *Just what a landlady should be: broad, buxom, comfortable, and good-looking, with a face of clear red and white, which, by its jovial aspect, at once bore testimony to her hearty participation in the good things of the larder and cellar, and to their thriving and healthful influences. She was a widow, but years ago had passed through her state of weeds, and burst into flower again* (*Chuzzlewit*).

Mac Coorts of Mac Coort: Great Highland family from which Mrs. Woodcourt states her late husband was descended (*Bleak House*).

Macey, Mr. and **Mrs.:** Marion Maryon's sister and her husband, residents of Silver-Store Island (*Christmas Stories* – 'English Prisoners').

M'Choakumchild: Teacher in Gradgrind's school. *He and some one hundred and forty other schoolmasters, had been lately turned at the same time, in the same factory, on the same principles, like so many pianoforte legs. He had been put through an immense variety of paces, and had answered volumes of head-breaking questions. Orthography, etymology, syntax, and prosody, biography, astronomy, geography, and general cosmography, the sciences of compound proportion, algebra, land-surveying and levelling, vocal music, and drawing from models, were all at the ends of his ten chilled fingers.* . . . *If only he had learnt a little less, how infinitely better he might have taught much more* (*Hard Times*).

Mackin, Mrs.: Pawnbroker's customer. *A slipshod woman, with two flat-irons in a little basket* (*Boz* – 'Pawnbroker's Shop').

Macklin, Walker, and **Peplow, Mesdames:** London suburban housewives. *In the suburbs, the muffin-boy rings his way down the little street, much more slowly than he is wont to do; for Mrs. Macklin, of No. 4, has no sooner opened her little street-door, and screamed out 'Muffins!' with all her might, than Mrs. Walker, at No. 5, puts her head out of the parlour-window, and screams 'Muffins!' too; and Mrs. Walker has scarcely got the words out of her lips, than Mrs. Peplow, over the way, lets loose Master Peplow, who darts down the street, with a velocity which nothing but buttered muffins in perspective could possibly inspire, and drags the boy back by main force* (*Boz* – 'The Streets – Night').

MacStinger, Mrs.: Captain Cuttle's domineering landlady at 9 Brig Place, India Docks. When her matrimonial intentions become too apparent he escapes, but she tracks him down and he is only rescued when Captain Bunsby makes himself her ultimate sacrifice. *A widow lady, with her sleeves rolled up to her shoulders, and her arms frothy with soap-suds and smoking with hot water* (*Dombey*).

MacStinger, Alexander: Mrs. MacStinger's younger son. *Alexander being black in the face with holding his breath after punishment, and a cool paving-stone being usually found to act as a powerful restorative in such cases* (*Dombey*).

MacStinger, Charles: Mrs. MacStinger's elder son. *Popularly known about the scenes of his youthful sports, as Chowley* (*Dombey*).

MacStinger, Juliana: Mrs. MacStinger's daughter. *One of the most frightful circumstances of the ceremony to the captain, was the deadly interest exhibited therein by Juliana MacStinger; and the fatal concentration of her faculties, with which that promising child, already the image of her parent, observed the whole proceedings. The captain saw in this a succession of man-traps stretching out infinitely; a series of ages of oppression and coercion, through which the seafaring line was doomed* (*Dombey*).

Maddox, John: Farm labourer, sweetheart of Rose (*Village Coquettes*).

Madgers, Winifred: One of Mrs. Lirriper's succession of maids. *She was what is termed a Plymouth*

Sister, and the Plymouth Brother that made away with her was quite right, for a tidier young woman for a wife never came into a house and afterwards called with the beautifullest Plymouth Twins (Christmas Stories – 'Mrs. Lirriper's Legacy').

Madman, The: Author of the manuscript, lent to Pickwick by the clergyman at Dingley Dell, which frightens him when he reads it alone in his bedroom. *'I knew that madness was mixed up with my very blood, and the marrow of my bones; that one generation had passed away without the pestilence appearing among them, and that I was the first in whom it would revive. I knew it must be so: that so it always had been, and so it ever would be: and when I cowered in some obscure corner of a crowded room, and saw men whisper, and point, and turn their eyes towards me, I knew they were telling each other of the doomed madman; and I slunk away again to mope in solitude'* (Pickwick).

Madness: One of Miss Flite's birds *(Bleak House).*

Magg: Vestryman, of Little Winkling Street. *One of our first orators (Reprinted – 'Our Vestry').*

Maggy: Mrs. Bangham's granddaughter, befriended by Amy Dorrit and later employed by Mrs. Plornish. *She was about eight-and-twenty, with large bones, large features, large feet and hands, large eyes and no hair. Her large eyes were limpid and almost colourless; they seemed to be very little affected by light, and to stand unnaturally still. There was also that attentive listening expression in her face, which is seen in the faces of the blind; but she was not blind, having one tolerably serviceable eye. Her face was not exceedingly ugly, though it was only redeemed from being so by a smile; a good-humoured smile, and pleasant in itself, but rendered pitiable by being constantly there. A great white cap, with a quantity of opaque frilling that was always flapping about, apologised for Maggy's baldness, and made it so very difficult for her old black bonnet to retain its place upon her head that it held on round her neck like a gipsy's baby. A commission of haberdashers could alone have reported what the rest of her poor dress was made of; but it had a strong general resemblance to seaweed, with here and there a gigantic tea-leaf. Her shawl looked particularly like a tea-leaf, after long infusion (Dorrit).*

Magnus, Peter: Traveller with Pickwick in a coach to Ipswich, where Magnus is to propose to Miss Witherfield. Pickwick enters her bedroom by mistake that night and he and his friends are denounced by Magnus next day and arrested. *A red-haired man with an inquisitive nose and blue spectacles ... who was an important-looking, sharp-nosed, mysterious-spoken personage, with a bird-like habit of giving his head a jerk every time he said anything (Pickwick).*

Magog: See **Gog** and **Magog** *(Humphrey).*

Magsman, Robert (Toby): Narrator of the story, a showman. *A Grizzled Personage in velveteen, with a face so cut up by varieties of weather that he looked as if he had been tattooed (Christmas Stories – 'Going into Society').*

Magwitch, Abel (alias **Provis**, alias **Campbell**): An escaped convict; grateful to Pip for befriending him, he returns secretly from Australia, a rich man, to reveal himself as Pip's secret benefactor. It emerges that he is the father of Estella by Molly. Trying to escape the country again, he drowns his betrayer, Compeyson, is sentenced to death, but dies in prison. The fortune he had intended for Pip goes to the Crown. *A fearful man, all in coarse grey, with a great iron on his leg. A man with no hat, and with broken shoes, and with an old rag tied round his head. A man who had been soaked in water, and smothered in mud, and lamed by stones, and cut by flints, and stung by nettles, and torn by briars; who limped and shivered, and glared and growled; and whose teeth chattered in his head as he seized me by the chin (Expectations).*

Malderton: Father of Thomas, Frederick, Teresa and Marianne. A *nouveau riche* City man who entertains Horatio Sparkins at his Camberwell home, believing him to be a notability. *A man whose whole scope of ideas was limited to Lloyd's, the Exchange, the India House, and the Bank. A few successful speculations had raised him from a situation of obscurity and comparative poverty, to a state of affluence. As frequently happens in such cases, the ideas of himself and his family became elevated to an extraordinary pitch as their means increased; they affected fashion, taste, and many other fooleries, in imitation of their betters, and had a very decided and becoming horror of anything which could, by possibility, be considered low. He was hospitable from ostentation, illiberal from ignorance, and prejudiced from conceit. Egotism and the love of display induced him to keep an excellent table: convenience, and a love of good things of this life, ensured him plenty of guests. He liked to have clever men, or what he considered such, at his table, because it was a great thing to talk about (Boz – 'Horatio Sparkins').*

Malderton, Mrs.: Malderton's wife, mother of Thomas, Frederick, Teresa, and Marianne. Sister of Jacob Barton. *A little fat woman (Boz – 'Horatio Sparkins').*

Malderton, Frederick: The Maldertons' elder son, brother of Thomas, Teresa, and Marianne. *In full-dress costume, was the very* beau ideal *of a smart waiter (Boz – 'Horatio Sparkins').*

Malderton, Marianne: The Maldertons' younger daughter, sister to Teresa, Frederick, and Thomas. *Engaged in netting a purse, and looking sentimental (Boz – 'Horatio Sparkins').*

Malderton, Teresa: The Maldertons' elder daughter, sister to Marianne, Frederick, and Thomas. *A very little girl, rather fat, with vermilion cheeks, but good-humoured, and still disengaged, although, to do her justice, the misfortune arose from no lack of perseverance on her part. In vain had she flirted for ten years; in vain had Mr. and Mrs. Malderton assiduously kept up an extensive acquaintance among the young eligible bachelors of Camberwell, and even of Wandsworth and Brixton; to say nothing of those who 'dropped in' from town (Boz – 'Horatio Sparkins').*

Malderton, Thomas: The Maldertons' younger son, brother to Frederick, Teresa, and Marianne. *With his white dress-stock, blue coat, bright buttons, and red watch-ribbon, strongly resembled the portrait of that interesting, but rash young gentleman, George Barnwell (Boz – 'Horatio Sparkins').*

Maldon, Jack: Mrs. Strong's cousin and admirer, who precipitates her temporary estrangement from her husband. *Mr. Jack Maldon shook hands with me; but not very warmly, I believed; and with an air of languid patronage, at which I secretly took great umbrage. But his languor altogether was quite a wonderful sight; except when he addressed himself to his cousin Annie (Copperfield).*

Mallard: Serjeant Snubbin's clerk. *An elderly clerk, whose sleek appearance, and heavy gold watch-chain, presented imposing indications of the extensive and lucrative practice of Mr. Serjeant Snubbin (Pickwick).*

Mallet: President of the display of models and mechanical science session at the second meeting of the Mudfog Association *(Mudfog).*

'Man from Shropshire, The': See **Gridley** *(Bleak House).*

Manette, Dr. Alexandre: Father of Lucie. Confined in the Bastille for eighteen years before the Revolution, then reunited with his daughter in London. The unwitting instrument of Darnay's condemnation to death. *He had a white beard, raggedly cut, but not very long, a hollow face, and exceedingly bright eyes. The hollowness and thinness of his face would have caused them to look large, under his yet dark eyebrows and his confused white hair, though they had been really otherwise; but, they were naturally large, and looked unnaturally so. His yellow rags of shirt lay open at the throat, and showed his body to be withered and worn. He, and his old canvas frock, and his loose stockings, and all his poor tatters of clothes, had, in a long seclusion from direct light and air, faded down to such a dull uniformity of parchment-yellow, that it would have been hard to say which was which (Two Cities).*

Manette, Lucie: Dr. Manette's daughter, loved by Sydney Carton; but she marries Charles Darnay, who is later saved from execution by Carton. *His eyes rested on a short, slight, pretty figure, a quantity of golden hair, and pair of blue eyes that met his own with an inquiring look, and a forehead with a singular capacity (remembering how young and smooth it was), of lifting and knitting itself into an expression that was not quite one of perplexity, or wonder, or alarm, or merely of a bright fixed attention, though it included all the four expressions (Two Cities).*

Mann, Mrs.: Matron of the branch workhouse where Oliver Twist lives until he is nine. *The elderly female was a woman of wisdom and experience; she knew what was good for children; and she had a very accurate perception of what was good for herself. So, she appropriated the greater part of the weekly stipend to her own use, and consigned the rising parochial generation to even a shorter allowance than was* originally provided for them. Thereby finding in the lowest depth a deeper still; and proving herself a very great experimental philosopher (Twist).*

Manners, Julia: A wealthy spinster who elopes with Alexander Trott, mistaking him for her suitor, Lord Peter, and likes him enough to marry him. *A buxom richly-dressed female of about forty (Boz – 'Great Winglebury Duel').* In the dramatised version, *The Strange Gentleman,* she is renamed Julia Dobbs.

Manning, Sir Geoffrey: One of Wardle's neighbouring landowners, on whose ground the shooting party takes place *(Pickwick).*

Mantalini, Alfred: An idler, philanderer and spendthrift, constantly sponging upon his wife, whom he bankrupts. *His name was originally Muntle; but it had been converted, by an easy transition, into Mantalini: the lady rightly considering that an English appellation would be of serious injury to the business. He had married on his whiskers; upon which property he had previously subsisted, in a genteel manner, for some years; and which he had recently improved, after patient cultivation, by the addition of a moustache, which promised to secure him an easy independence: his share in the labours of the business being at present confined to spending the money (Nickleby).*

Mantalini, Madame Alfred: A fashionable dressmaker in the West End of London, married to Mantalini, whose extravagance bankrupts her. *A buxom person, handsomely dressed and rather good-looking, but much older than the gentleman in the Turkish trousers, whom she had wedded some six months before (Nickleby).*

Maplesone, Mrs.: Mother of Matilda and Julia. She and her daughters come to board at Mrs. Tibbs's, where all are courted by the male boarders. Mrs. Maplesone successfully sues her beau, Calton, for a thousand pounds for breach of promise. *An enterprising widow of about fifty; shrewd, scheming, and good-looking. She was amiably anxious on behalf of her daughters; in proof whereof she used to remark, that she would have no objection to marry again, if it would benefit her dear girls – she could have no other motive (Boz – 'Boarding-House').*

Maplesone, Matilda and **Julia:** Elder and younger daughters of Mrs. Maplesone. Matilda marries Septimus Hicks, but is deserted by him; Julia marries Simpson, and deserts him. *The 'dear girls' themselves were not at all insensible to the merits of 'a good establishment'. One of them was twenty-five; the other, three years younger. They had been at different watering-places, for four seasons; they had gambled at libraries, read books in balconies, sold at fancy fairs, danced at assemblies, talked sentiment – in short, they had done all that industrious girls could do – but, as yet, to no purpose (Boz – 'Boarding-House').*

'Marchioness, The': The Brass family's ill-treated maidservant. Since she has no given name, Dick Swiveller calls her Sophronia Sphynx. He educates her, and eventually marries her. *A small slipshod girl in a dirty coarse apron and bib, which left nothing of* *her visible but her face and feet. She might as well have been dressed in a violin-case (Curiosity Shop).*

Margaret: Winkle senior's maidservant *(Pickwick).*

Margaret, Aunt: Guest at Christmas dinner. *Grandmamma draws herself up, rather stiff and stately; for Margaret married a poor man without her consent, and poverty not being a sufficiently weighty punishment for her offence, has been discarded by her friends, and debarred the society of her dearest relatives (Boz – 'Christmas Dinner').*

Marigold, Dr.: The narrator, a cheap-jack showman. After the death of his daughter Sophy he adopts another Sophy (q.v.), who is deaf and dumb, and teaches her to help him. *I am at present a middle-aged man of a broadish build, in cords, leggings, and a sleeved waistcoat the strings of which is always gone behind. . . . I am partial to a white hat, and I like a shawl round my neck wore loose and easy, Sitting down is my favourite posture. If I have a taste in point of personal jewelry, it is mother-of-pearl buttons (Christmas Stories – 'Doctor Marigold').*

Marigold, Mrs.: Marigold's Suffolk-born wife, mother of Sophy, whom she ill-treats. She drowns herself. *She wasn't a bad wife, but she had a temper. If she could have parted with that one article at a sacrifice, I wouldn't have swopped her away in exchange for any other woman in England. Not that I ever did swop her away, for we lived together till she died, and that was thirteen year (Christmas Stories – 'Doctor Marigold').*

Marigold, Little Sophy: Marigold's own daughter, ill-treated by his wife. She dies of fever, still a child. *She had a wonderful quantity of shining dark hair, all curling natural about her. It is quite astonishing to me now, that I didn't go tearing mad when I used to see her run from her mother before the cart, and her mother catch her by this hair, and pull her down by it, and beat her. . . . Yet in other respects her mother took great care of her. Her clothes were always clean and neat, and her mother was never tired of working at 'em. Such is the inconsistency in things (Christmas Stories – 'Doctor Marigold').*

Marigold, Willum: Dr. Marigold's late father. *Had been a lovely one in his time at the Cheap Jack work (Christmas Stories – 'Doctor Marigold').*

Marker, Mrs.: Client of the General Agency Office. *' "Mrs. Marker," ' said Tom, reading, ' "Russell Place, Russell Square; offers eighteen guineas; tea and sugar found. Two in family, and see very little company. Five servants kept. No man. No followers" ' (Nickleby).*

Markham: Friend of Steerforth; guest at David Copperfield's first bachelor dinner at Adelphi. *He said it was no derogation from a man's dignity to confess that I was a devilish good fellow (Copperfield).*

Markleham, Mrs. ('The Old Soldier'): Annie Strong's mother. *Our boys used to call her the Old Soldier, on account of her generalship, and the skill with which she marshalled great forces of relations*

against the Doctor. She was a little, sharp-eyed woman, who used to wear, when she was dressed, one unchangeable cap, ornamented with some artificial flowers, and two artificial butterflies supposed to be hovering above the flowers (Copperfield).

Marks, Will: John Podgers's nephew, hero of the dangerous adventures of Mr. Pickwick's tale. *A wild, roving young fellow of twenty who had been brought up in his uncle's house and lived there still, – that is to say, when he was at home, which was not as often as it might have been (Humphrey).*

Marley, Jacob: Scrooge's deceased partner, whose ghost visits him on Christmas Eve to warn him of the consequences of misanthropy. *Marley in his pigtail, usual waistcoat, tights and boots; the tassels on the latter bristling, like his pig-tail, and his coat-skirts, and the hair upon his head. The chain he drew was clasped about his middle. It was long, and wound about him like a tail; and it was made (for Scrooge observed it closely) of cash boxes, keys, padlocks, ledgers, deeds, and heavy purses wrought in steel. His body was transparent; so that Scrooge, observing him, and looking through his waistcoat, could see the two buttons on his coat behind (Christmas Books – 'Christmas Carol').*

Maroon, Captain: Creditor of Edward Dorrit. *A gentleman with tight drab legs, a rather old hat, a little hooked stick, and a blue neckerchief (Dorrit).*

Marshall, the Misses: Acquaintances of Fairfax *(Young Gentlemen – 'Censorious Young Gentleman').*

Marshall, Mary: Richard Doubledick's fiancée, eventually wife. *Slowly labouring, at last, through a long, heavy dream of confused time and place, presenting faint glimpses of army surgeons whom he knew, and of faces that had been familiar to his youth, – dearest and kindest among them, Mary Marshall's, with a solicitude upon it more like reality than anything he could discern, – Lieutenant Richard Doubledick came back to life (Christmas Stories – 'Seven Poor Travellers').*

Martha: The Parsonses' servant who had helped bring her master and mistress together *(Boz – 'Watkins Tottle').*

Martha: Daughter of John, the riverside labourer. *Ugly, misshapen, peevish, ill-conditioned, ragged, dirty – but beloved! (Dombey).*

Martha: Workhouse inmate who attends Agnes Fleming in giving birth to Oliver Twist. *Her body was bent by age; her limbs trembled with palsy; her face, distorted into a mumbling leer, resembled more the grotesque shaping of some wild pencil, than the work of Nature's hand (Twist).*

Martha, Aunt: Dr. Jeddler's sister, with whom Marion takes refuge when she pretends to have eloped *(Christmas Books – 'Battle of Life').*

Martin: A gamekeeper at Dingley Dell. *A tall raw-boned gamekeeper (Pickwick).*

Martin: Ben Allen's aunt's coachman. *A surly-looking man with his legs dressed like the legs of a groom, and his body attired in the coat of a coachman (Pickwick).*

Martin, Captain: Former prisoner in the Marshalsea, who had encouraged his sister to accept attentions from the son of Jackson, a turnkey, an invented example held up by William Dorrit to Amy to influence her in favour of young John Chivery. *'Captain Martin (highly respected in the army) then unhesitatingly said, that it appeared to him that his – hem! – sister was not called upon to understand the young man too distinctly, and that she might lead him on . . . on her father's – I should say, brother's – account'* (*Dorrit*).

Martin, Miss: Cashier at the coffee-house where Christopher works. *Miss Martin is the young lady at the bar as makes out our bills; and though higher than I could wish considering her station, is perfectly well-behaved* (*Christmas Stories* – 'Somebody's Luggage').

Martin, Amelia: Milliner and dressmaker with misplaced ambitions as a singer. *Pale, tallish, thin, and two-and-thirty – what ill-natured people would call plain, and police reports interesting* (*Boz* – 'Mistaken Milliner').

Martin, Betsy: The Stargazer family's servant. Believing he has only weeks to live, Tom Grig agrees to marry her, but hastily changes his mind on learning that he will live to a ripe old age (*Lamplighter*, and its short story version).

Martin, Betsy: Convert reported to the committee of the Brick Lane Branch of the United Grand Junction Ebenezer Temperance Association. *Widow, one child, and one eye. Goes out charing and washing, by the day; never had more than one eye, but knows her mother drank bottled stout, and shouldn't wonder if that caused it (immense cheering). Thinks it not impossible that if she had always abstained from spirits, she might have had two eyes by this time (tremendous applause)* (*Pickwick*).

Martin, Jack: The Bagman's uncle, central figure of the story of that name. *'In personal appearance, my uncle was a trifle shorter than the middle size; he was a thought stouter too, than the ordinary run of people, and perhaps his face might be a shade redder. He had the jolliest face you ever saw, gentlemen: something like Punch, with a handsomer nose and chin; his eyes were always twinkling and sparkling with good humour; and a smile – not one of your unmeaning wooden grins, but a real, merry, hearty, good-tempered smile – was perpetually on his countenance. He was pitched out of his gig once, and knocked, head first, against a mile-stone. . . . I have heard my uncle say, many a time, that the man said who picked him up that he was smiling as merrily as if he had tumbled out for a treat, and that after they had bled him, the first faint glimmerings of returning animation, were, his jumping up in bed, bursting out into a loud laugh, kissing the young woman who held the basin, and demanding a mutton chop and a pickled walnut. He was very fond of pickled walnuts, gentlemen. He said he always found that, taken without vinegar, they relished the beer'* (*Pickwick*).

Martin, Tom: A fellow prisoner of Pickwick in the Fleet. *A gentleman prematurely broad for his years: clothed in a professional blue jean frock, and top-boots with circular toes* (*Pickwick*).

Martin Family: Friends of Mincin (*Young Gentlemen* – 'Very Friendly Young Gentleman').

Marton: A village schoolmaster who befriends Little Nell and her grandfather during their wanderings. *He had a kind face. In his plain old suit of black, he looked pale and meagre. They fancied, too, a lonely air about him and his house, but perhaps that was because the other people formed a merry company upon the green, and he seemed the only solitary man in all the place* (*Curiosity Shop*).

Marwood, Alice: Alias of Alice Brown, daughter of 'Good Mrs. Brown' and discarded mistress of James Carker. She returns to England from transportation for theft, bent on revenge. *A solitary woman of some thirty years of age; tall; well-formed; handsome; miserably dressed. . . . As her hands, parting on her sun-burnt forehead, swept across her face, and threw aside the hindrances that encroached upon it, there was a reckless and regardless beauty in it: a dauntless and depraved indifference to more than weather: a carelessness of what was cast upon her bare head from heaven or earth* (*Dombey*).

Mary: Nupkins's housemaid, with whom Sam Weller falls in love on sight. She helps bring Winkle and Arabella Allen together and enters their service, but is eventually married to Sam and made Pickwick's housekeeper. *'Your master's a knowin' hand, and has just sent me to the right place,' said Mr. Weller, with a glance of admiration at Mary. 'If I wos master o' this here house, I should always find the materials for comfort vere Mary was'* (*Pickwick*).

Mary: One of the two daughters of John, the narrator. *Comfortable in her circumstances, but water on the chest* (*Reprinted* – 'Poor Man's Tale of a Patent').

Mary Anne: A young woman presiding over the gambling at Ramsgate library (*Boz* – 'Tuggses at Ramsgate').

Mary Anne: Wemmick's maidservant. *A neat little girl* (*Expectations*).

Mary Anne: Miss Peecher's favourite pupil and household assistant. *The pupil had been, in her state of pupilage, so imbued with the class-custom of stretching out an arm, as if to hail a cab or omnibus, whenever she found she had an observation on hand to offer to Miss Peecher, that she often did it in their domestic relations* (*Mutual Friend*).

Mary and **Sarah:** Residents of Seven Dials who fight in the street. *A little crowd has collected round a couple of ladies, who having imbibed the contents of various 'three-outs' of gin-and-bitters in the course of the morning, have at length differed on some point of domestic arrangement, and are on the eve of settling the quarrel satisfactorily, by an appeal to blows* (*Boz* – 'Seven Dials').

Maryon, Captain: Captain of the sloop *Christopher*

107

Columbus. Brother of Marion Maryon. *Brave and bold (Christmas Stories – 'English Prisoners').*

Maryon, Marion: Captain Maryon's sister, living on Silver-Store Island. Gill Davies loves and protects her, but she marries Captain Carton. *Marion Maryon. Many a time have I run off those two names in my thoughts, like a bit of verse. Oh many, and many a time! (Christmas Stories – 'English Prisoners').*

Mask, The: Masked cavalier who meets Will Marks near Putney and orders him to take a corpse to London, in Mr. Pickwick's tale. *A man pretty far advanced in life, but of a firm and stately carriage. His dress was of a rich and costly kind, but so soiled and disordered that it was scarcely to be recognised for one of those gorgeous suits which the expensive taste and fashion of the time prescribed for men of any rank or station (Humphrey).*

Matinter, the two **Misses:** Ladies at the ball at Bath Assembly Rooms. *Being single and singular, paid great court to the Master of the Ceremonies, in the hope of getting a stray partner now and then (Pickwick).*

Matron: The superintendent of Watts's Charity, where the Six Poor Travellers lodge. *A decent body, of a wholesome matronly appearance (Christmas Stories – 'Seven Poor Travellers').*

Maunders: An old showman, subject of a reminiscence by Vuffin. *'I remember the time when old Maunders had in his cottage in Spa Fields in the winter time, when the season was over, eight male and female dwarfs setting down to dinner every day, who was waited on by eight old giants in green coats, red smalls, blue cotton stockings, and high-lows' (Curiosity Shop).*

Mawls, Master: Fellow pupil of the narrator at Our School. *Generally speaking, we may observe that whenever we see a child intently occupied with its nose, to the exclusion of all other subjects of interest, our mind reverts, in a flash, to Master Mawls (Reprinted – 'Our School').*

Maxby: Fellow pupil of the narrator at Our School, rumoured to be favoured because the usher was 'sweet upon' one of his sisters *(Reprinted – 'Our School').*

Maxey, Caroline: One of Mrs. Lirriper's succession of servants. *A good-looking black-eyed girl was Caroline and a comely-made girl to your cost when she did break out and laid about her (Christmas Stories – 'Mrs. Lirriper's Lodgings').*

Mayday: Friend of the Uncommercial Traveller who gives daunting birthday parties. *The guests have no knowledge of one another except on that one day in the year, and are annually terrified for a week by the prospect of meeting one another again (Uncommercial – 'Birthday Celebrations').*

Maylie, Mrs.: Mother of Harry, adoptive aunt of Rose. She befriends Oliver Twist after he has been shot helping Bill Sikes to burgle her house at Chertsey. *Well advanced in years; but the high-backed oaken chair in which she sat, was not more upright than she.*

Dressed with the utmost nicety and precision, in a quaint mixture of by-gone costume, and some slight concessions to the prevailing taste, which rather served to point the old style pleasantly than to impair its effect, she sat, in a stately manner, with her hands folded on the table before her (Twist).

Maylie, Harry: Mrs. Maylie's clergyman son. Marries Rose Maylie. *He seemed about five-and-twenty years of age, and was of the middle height; his countenance was frank and handsome; and his demeanour easy and prepossessing (Twist).*

Maylie, Rose: Adopted niece of Mrs. Maylie, she is really Rose Fleming, sister of Oliver Twist's deceased mother and a victim of the machinations of Monks. She marries Harry Maylie. *In the lovely bloom and springtime of womanhood; at that age, when, if ever angels be for God's good purposes enthroned in mortal forms, they may be, without impiety, supposed to abide in such as hers. She was not past seventeen. Cast in so slight and exquisite a mould; so mild and gentle; so pure and beautiful; that earth seemed not her element, nor its rough creatures her fit companions. The very intelligence that shone in her deep blue eye, and was stamped upon her noble head, seemed scarcely of her age, or of the world; and yet the changing expression of sweetness and good humour, the thousand lights that played about the face, and left no shadow there; above all, the smile, the cheerful, happy smile, were made for Home, and fireside peace and happiness (Twist).*

Meagles: Minnie's father, a retired banker who helps Clennam and Doyce. He and his wife adopt Harriet Beadle ('Tattycoram') from the Foundling Hospital. *With a whimsical good humour on him all the time (Dorrit).*

Meagles, Mrs.: Meagles's wife, mother of Minnie. *Comely and healthy, with a pleasant English face which had been looking at homely things for five-and-fifty years or more, and shone with a bright reflection of them (Dorrit).*

Meagles, Minnie ('Pet'): The Meagleses' daughter who marries Henry Gowan. *Pet was about twenty. A fair girl with rich brown hair hanging free in natural ringlets. A lovely girl, with a frank face, and wonderful eyes; so large, so soft, so bright, set to such perfection in her kind good head. She was round and fresh and dimpled and spoilt, and there was in Pet an air of timidity and dependence which was the best weakness in the world, and gave her the only crowning charm a girl so pretty and pleasant could have been without (Dorrit).*

'Mealy Potatoes': Boy employee with David Copperfield at Murdstone and Grinby's. *This youth had not been christened by that name, but ... it had been bestowed upon him in the workhouse, on account of his complexion, which was pale or mealy (Copperfield).*

Meek, Augustus George: The Meeks' baby. *When I saw the announcement in the Times, I dropped the paper. I had put it in, myself, and paid for it, but it* *looked so noble that it overpowered me. (Reprinted –* 'Births. Mrs. Meek, of a Son').

Meek, George: The proud father of Augustus George. *I hope and believe I am a quiet man. I will go farther. I know I am a quiet man. My constitution is tremulous, my voice was never loud, and, in point of stature, I have been from infancy, small (Reprinted –* 'Births. Mrs. Meek, of a Son').

Meek, Mrs. George (Maria Jane): Meek's wife. Mother of Augustus George and daughter of Mrs. Bigby. *Far from strong, and is subject to headaches, and nervous indigestion (Reprinted –* 'Births. Mrs. Meek, of a Son').

Melchisedech: Solicitor in Clifford's Inn to whom Tulkinghorn refers Trooper George *(Bleak House).*

'Melia: Servant at Dr. Blimber's. *The young woman seemed surprised at his appearance, and asked him where his mother was. When Paul told her she was dead, she took her gloves off, and gave him a kiss (Dombey).*

Mell, Mrs.: Mell's mother, residing in an almshouse at Blackheath *(Copperfield).*

Mell, Charles: Teacher at Salem House, dismissed because his mother lived in an almshouse. Later Dr. Mell of Colonial Salem-House Grammar School, Port Middlebay, Australia. *A gaunt, sallow young man, with hollow cheeks. . . . He was dressed in a suit of black clothes which were rather rusty and dry too, and rather short in the sleeves and legs; and he had a white neckerchief on, that was not over-clean (Copperfield).*

Mellows, J.: Landlord of the Dolphin's Head, the subject of the essay. *I found J. Mellows, looking at nothing, and apparently experiencing that it failed to raise his spirits (Uncommercial –* 'Old Stage-coaching House').

Melluka, Miss: Polly Tresham's doll, bought for her by Jackson. *Of Circassian descent, possessing as much boldness of beauty as was reconcilable with extreme feebleness of mouth, and combining a sky-blue silk pelisse with rose-coloured satin trousers, and a black velvet hat: which this fair stranger to our northern shores would seem to have founded on the portraits of the late Duchess of Kent (Christmas Stories –* 'Mugby Junction').

Meltham: Actuary of the Inestimable Life Assurance Company who devotes himself to the destruction of Julius Slinkton, whose niece, with whom Meltham had been in love, has been murdered by her uncle for her insurance money. Meltham assumes the identities of Alfred Beckwith and Major Banks in pursuing his vendetta, and helps to save Margaret Niner, another niece of Slinkton's, from being murdered also. His purpose achieved, he dies. *'He was at once the most profound, the most original, and the most energetic man I have ever known connected with Life Assurance'* ('Hunted Down').

Melvilleson, Miss M.: Singer at the Harmonic Meetings at the Sol's Arms, Chancery Lane. *She has been married a year and a half, though announced as Miss M. Melvilleson, the noted siren, and . . . her baby is clandestinely conveyed to the Sol's Arms every night to receive its natural nourishment during the entertainments (Bleak House).*

'Memory': Stryver's nickname for Sydney Carton *(Two Cities).*

'Mercury': The Dedlocks' footman. *Mercury, with his hands in the pockets of his bright peach-blossom small-clothes, stretches his symmetrical silk legs with the air of a man of gallantry (Bleak House).*

Mercy: The Uncommercial Traveller's childhood nurse and teller of gruesome tales. *This female bard – may she have been repaid my debt of obligation to her in the matter of nightmares and perspirations! – reappears in my memory as the daughter of a shipwright. Her name was Mercy, though she had none on me (Uncommercial –* 'Nurse's Stories').

Merdle, M.P.: Financier, banker, forger and thief. Speculation in his enterprises ruins Clennam, the Dorrits, and others, and he commits suicide. *Immensely rich; a man of prodigious enterprise; a Midas without the ears, who turned all he touched to gold. He was in everything good, from banking to building. . . . His desire was to the utmost to satisfy Society (whatever that was), and take up all its drafts upon him for tribute. He did not shine in company; he had not very much to say for himself; he was a reserved man, with a broad, overhanging, watchful head, that particular kind of dull red colour in his cheeks which is rather stale than fresh, and a somewhat uneasy expression about his coat-cuffs, as if they were in his confidence, and had reasons for being anxious to hide his hands (Dorrit).*

Merdle, Mrs.: Merdle's wife, mother of Edmund Sparkler by her first marriage. *The lady was not young and fresh from the hand of Nature, but was young and fresh from the hand of her maid. She had large unfeeling handsome eyes, and dark unfeeling handsome hair, and a broad unfeeling handsome bosom, and was made the most of in every particular. Either because she had a cold, or because it suited her face, she wore a rich white fillet tied over her head and under her chin. And if ever there were an unfeeling handsome chin that looked as if, for certain, it had never been, in familiar parlance, 'chucked' by the hand of man, it was the chin curbed up so tight and close by that laced bridle (Dorrit).*

Merrylegs: Signor Jupe's performing dog, which he takes with him when he decamps from Sleary's Circus. The dog eventually returns alone and dies *(Hard Times).*

Merrywinkle, Mr. and Mrs.: A couple who coddle themselves. *Mr. Merrywinkle is a rather lean and long-necked gentleman, middle-aged and middle-sized, and usually troubled with a cold in the head. Mrs. Merrywinkle is a delicate-looking lady, with very light hair, and is exceedingly subject to the same unpleasant disorder (Young Couples –* 'Couple Who Coddle Themselves').

Mesheck, Aaron: Jewish confidence trickster tracked down by Sergeant Dornton to the Tombs prison, New York (*Reprinted* – 'Detective Police').

'Mesrour': Nickname given to Tabby in the Seraglio fantasy (*Christmas Stories* – 'Haunted House').

Micawber, Master and **Miss:** Brother and sister, aged about four and three respectively, to Wilkins junior, Emma, and the twins (*Copperfield*).

Micawber, Emma: The Micawbers' second child, sister to Wilkins junior, Master and Miss Micawber, and the twins. She becomes Mrs. Ridger Begs, of Port Middlebay, Australia. *In whom, as Mr. Micawber told us, 'her mother renewed her youth, like the phoenix'* (*Copperfield*).

Micawber, Wilkins, jun.: The Micawbers' eldest child, brother of Emma, Master and Miss Micawber, and the twins. A talented singer. *'It was my hope when I came here,' said Mr. Micawber, 'to have got Wilkins into the Church: or perhaps I shall express my meaning more strictly, if I say the Choir. But there was no vacancy for a tenor in the venerable Pile for which this city is so justly eminent; and he has – in short, he has contracted a habit of singing in public-houses, rather than in sacred edifices'* (*Copperfield*).

Micawber, Wilkins, sen.: Agent of Murdstone and Grinby, and David Copperfield's landlord while he is employed there. Moving optimistically from employment to employment – interrupted by a spell in the Marshalsea for debt – he remains David's staunch friend, unmasks Uriah Heep for a villain, and is rewarded by Betsey Trotwood and others who pay his debts and send him and his family to Australia, where he becomes a prominent resident of Middlebay. *A stoutish, middle-aged person, in a brown surtout and black tights and shoes, with no more hair upon his head (which was a large one, and very shining) than there is upon an egg, and with a very extensive face, which he turned full upon me. His clothes were shabby, but he had an imposing shirt-collar on. He carried a jaunty sort of a stick, with a large pair of rusty tassels to it; and a quizzing-glass hung outside his coat, – for ornament* (*Copperfield*).

Micawber, Mrs. Wilkins, Sen. (Emma): Micawber's wife and champion in all adversity. Mother of Wilkins junior, Emma, Master and Miss Micawber, and twin babies. *A thin and faded lady, not at all young, who was sitting in the parlour (the first floor was altogether unfurnished, and the blinds were kept down to delude the neighbours), with a baby at her breast. . . . I have known her to be thrown into fainting fits by the king's taxes at three o'clock, and to eat lamb-chops breaded, and drink warm ale (paid for with two teaspoons that had gone to the pawnbroker's) at four* (*Copperfield*).

Micawber twins: The Micawbers' fifth and sixth children. *I may remark here that I hardly ever, in all my experience of the family, saw both the twins detached from Mrs. Micawber at the same time. One of them was always taking refreshment* (*Copperfield*).

Michael: The Poor Relation. He represents himself to be Christiana's husband, John Spatter's partner and Little Frank's friend, but it is all his day-dream. *Sometimes, one of my relations or acquaintances is so obliging as to ask me to dinner. Those are holiday occasions, and then I generally walk in the Park. I am a solitary man, and seldom walk with anybody. Not that I am avoided because I am shabby; for I am not at all shabby, having always a very good suit of black on (or rather Oxford mixture, which has the appearance of black and wears much better); but I have got into a habit of speaking low, and being rather silent, and my spirits are not high, and I am sensible that I am not an attractive companion* (*Christmas Stories* – 'Poor Relation').

'Middlesex Dumpling': Prizefighter whose contest with the Suffolk Bantam was stopped by Nupkins. *'Bless my soul, ma'am, are you aware of the activity of our local magistracy? Do you happen to have heard, ma'am, that I rushed into a prize-ring on the fourth of May last, attended by only sixty special constables; and, at the hazard of falling a sacrifice to the angry passions of an infuriated multitude, prohibited a pugilistic contest between the Middlesex Dumpling and the Suffolk Bantam?'* (*Pickwick*).

Miff, Mrs. Pew-opener at the church where Dombey marries Edith Granger and, later, Walter Gay marries Florence. *A vinegary face has Mrs. Miff, and a mortified bonnet, and eke a thirsty soul for sixpences and shillings. Beckoning to stray people to come into pews, has given Mrs. Miff an air of mystery; and there is reservation in the eye of Mrs. Miff, as always knowing of a softer seat, but having her suspicions of the fee* (*Dombey*).

Miggot: Parkle's laundress in Gray's Inn. *He had an idea which he could never explain, that Mrs. Miggot was in some way connected with the Church. When he was in particularly good spirits, he used to believe that a deceased uncle of hers had been a Dean* (*Uncommercial* – 'Chambers').

Miggs, Miss: The Vardens' disloyal servant and rival of Dolly Varden for Sim Tappertit, whom she follows to the Gordon Riots. Later a turnkey at Bridewell. *This Miggs was a tall young lady, very much addicted to pattens in private life; slender and shrewish, of a rather uncomfortable figure, and though not absolutely ill-looking, of a sharp and acid visage. As a general principle and abstract proposition, Miggs held the male sex to be utterly contemptible and unworthy of notice; to be fickle, false, base, sottish, inclined to perjury, and wholly undeserving. When particularly exasperated against them (which, scandal said, was when Sim Tappertit slighted her most) she was accustomed to wish with great emphasis that the whole race of women could but die off, in order that the men might be brought to know the real value of the blessings by which they set so little store; nay, her feeling for her order ran so high, that she sometimes declared, if she could only have good security for a fair, round number – say ten thousand – of young virgins following her example, she would, to spite mankind, hang, drown, stab, or poison herself, with a joy past all expression* (*Rudge*).

Mike: Client of Jaggers, rebuked for producing an invented witness (*Expectations*).

Miles, Bob: A villain encountered by Inspector Field's party in Saint Giles's (*Reprinted* – 'On Duty with Inspector Field').

Miles, Owen: One of Master Humphrey's circle and inseparable companion of Jack Redburn. *A most worthy gentleman . . . once a very rich merchant; but receiving a severe shock in the death of his wife, he retired from business, and devoted himself to a quiet, unostentatious life. He is an excellent man, of thoroughly sterling character: not of quick apprehension, and not without some amusing prejudices* (*Humphrey*).

Milkwash, John: A poetical young gentleman. *The favourite attitude of the poetical young gentleman is lounging on a sofa with his eyes fixed upon the ceiling, or sitting bolt-upright in a high-backed chair, staring with very round eyes at the opposite wall. When he is in one of these positions, his mother, who is a worthy affectionate old soul, will give you a nudge to bespeak your attention without disturbing the abstracted one, and whisper with a shake of the head, that John's imagination is at some extraordinary work or other, you may take her word for it. Hereupon John looks more fiercely intent upon vacancy than before, and suddenly snatching a pencil from his pocket, puts down three words, and a cross on the back of a card, sighs deeply, paces once or twice across the room, inflicts a most unmerciful slap upon his head, and walks moodily up to his dormitory* (*Young Gentlemen* – 'Poetical Young Gentleman').

Miller: A guest at Dingley Dell. *A little hard-headed, Ripstone-pippin-faced man* (*Pickwick*).

Miller, Jane Ann: Lime Tree Lodge, Groombridge Wells. Mrs. Wilding's married sister, who adopted Walter Wilding from the Foundling Hospital on her behalf (*Christmas Stories* – 'No Thoroughfare'; not in dramatised version).

Millers: One of Mrs. Matthew Pockets' nursemaids (*Expectations*).

Mills: Julia Mills's father. *Mr. Mills was not at home. I did not expect he would be. Nobody wanted him. Miss Mills was at home. Miss Mills would do* (*Copperfield*).

Mills, Julia: Dora Spenlow's pessimistic bosom friend. She goes to India and returns the disagreeable wife of a disagreeable rich man. *Comparatively stricken in years – almost twenty, I should say. . . . Miss Mills had had her trials in the course of a chequered existence . . . having been unhappy in a misplaced affection, and being understood to have retired from the world on her awful stock of experience, but still to take a calm interest in the unblighted hopes and loves of youth* (*Copperfield*).

Mills, Julia: Avid reader of romances contained in the library at our English watering-place. *She has left marginal notes on the pages, as 'Is not this truly touching? J.M.' 'How thrilling! J.M.' 'Entranced here by the Magician's potent spell. J.M.' She has also italicised her favourite traits in the description of the hero, as 'his hair, which was dark and wavy, clustered in rich profusion around a marble brow, whose lofty paleness bespoke the intellect within.' It reminds her of another hero. She adds, 'How like B.L. Can this be mere coincidence? J.M.'* (*Reprinted* – 'Our English Watering-Place').

Milvey, The Revd. Frank: Husband of Margaretta. Curate who introduces the Boffins to Betty Higden and marries Eugene Wrayburn to Lizzie Hexam. *He was quite a young man, expensively educated and wretchedly paid, with quite a young wife and half a dozen quite young children. He was under the necessity of teaching and translating from the classics, to eke out his scanty means, yet was generally expected to have more time to spare than the idlest person in the parish, and more money than the richest. He accepted the needless inequalities and inconsistencies of his life, with a kind of conventional submission that was almost slavish; and any daring layman who would have adjusted such burdens as his, more decently and graciously, would have had small help from him* (*Mutual Friend*).

Milvey, Mrs. Frank (Margaretta): The Revd. Frank's wife. *A pretty, bright little woman, something worn by anxiety, who had repressed many pretty tastes and bright fancies, and substituted in their stead, schools, soup, flannel, coals, and all the week-day cares and Sunday coughs of a large population, young and old* (*Mutual Friend*).

Mim: A showman, exhibitor of the giant Pickleson, and stepfather of Sophy, whom he sells to Dr. Marigold for six pairs of braces. *A wery hoarse man . . . a most ferocious swearer* (*Christmas Stories* – 'Doctor Marigold').

Mincin: A very friendly young gentleman; a medical man. *A gentleman who had been previously showing his teeth by the fireplace* (*Young Gentlemen* – 'Very Friendly Young Gentleman').

Minns, Augustus: Government clerk, at Somerset House, of private means. Cousin to Octavius Budden and proxy godfather to Alexander Augustus Budden. *A bachelor, of about forty as he said – of about eight-and-forty as his friends said. He was always exceedingly clean, precise, and tidy; perhaps somewhat priggish, and the most retiring man in the world. . . . There were two classes of created objects which he held in the deepest and most unmingled horror; these were dogs, and children. He was not unamiable, but he could, at any time, have viewed the execution of a dog, or the assassination of an infant, with the liveliest satisfaction. Their habits were at variance with his love of order; and his love of order was as powerful as his love of life* (*Boz* – 'Mr. Minns and his Cousin').

'Missis, Our': Formidable head of the Mugby Junction refreshment room. *You should hear Our Missis give the word, 'Here comes the Beast to be Fed!' and then you should hear 'em indignantly skipping across the Line, from the Up to the Down, or Wicer Warsaw, and begin to pitch the stale pastry into the plates, and chuck the sawdust sangwiches under the glass covers,*

111

and get out the – ha, ha, ha! – the sherry, – O my eye, my eye! – for your Refreshment (Christmas Stories – 'Mugby Junction').

Misty, X. X.: Speaker at the zoology and botany session of the second meeting of the Mudfog Association. *Communicated some remarks on the disappearance of dancing-bears from the streets of London, with observations on the exhibition of monkeys as connected with barrel-organs (Mudfog).*

Mith, Sergeant: One of the Detective Force officers of Scotland Yard. *A smooth-faced man with a fresh bright complexion, and a strange air of simplicity, is a dab at housebreakers (Reprinted – 'Detective Police').*

Mithers, Lady: Client of Miss Mowcher. 'There's *a woman! How* she wears! *– and Mithers himself came into the room where I was waiting for her –* there's a man! How he *wears! and his wig too, for he's had it these ten years' (Copperfield).*

Mitts, Mrs.: A Titbull's pensioner. *She had a way of passing her hands over and under one another as she spoke, that was not only tidy but propitiatory (Uncommercial – 'Titbull's Alms-Houses').*

Mivins ('The Zephyr'): A fellow prisoner of Pickwick in the Fleet. *A man in a broad-skirted green coat, with corduroy knee smalls and grey cotton stockings, was performing the most popular steps of a hornpipe, with a slang and burlesque caricature of grace and lightness, which, combined with the very appropriate character of his costume, was inexpressibly absurd (Pickwick).*

Mizzler, Marquis of and **Lord Bobby:** Subjects of an anecdote by which Chuckster seeks to impress the Garlands. *He was in a condition to relate the exact circumstances of the difference between the Marquis of Mizzler and Lord Bobby, which it appeared originated in a disputed bottle of champagne, and not in a pigeon-pie, as erroneously reported in the newspapers (Curiosity Shop).*

Mobbs: Pupil at Dotheboys Hall. *'Mobbs's mother-in-law,' said Squeers, 'took to her bed on hearing that he wouldn't eat fat, and has been very ill ever since. She wishes to know, by an early post, where he expects to go to, if he quarrels with his vittles; and with what feelings he could turn up his nose at the cow's liver broth, after his good master had asked a blessing on it' (Nickleby).*

Moddle, Augustus: The 'youngest gentleman' boarder at Todgers's. Falls hopelessly in love with Mercy Pecksniff, but she marries Jonas Chuzzlewit and Moddle transfers his affection to her sister Charity, whom he jilts in the nick of time and goes to America. *The youngest gentleman blew his melancholy into a flute. He didn't blow much out of it, but that was all the better. If the two Miss Pecksniffs and Mrs. Todgers had perished by spontaneous combustion, and the serenade had been in honour of their ashes, it would have been impossible to surpass the unutterable despair expressed in that one chorus, 'Go where glory waits thee!' It was a requiem, a dirge, a moan, a howl, a wail, a*

lament, an abstract of everything that is sorrowful and hideous in sound (Chuzzlewit).

Model, The: A gloomy artists' model encountered by the narrator on a Thames steamboat. *'I sets to the profession for a bob a-hour. . . . When I don't set for a head, I mostly sets for a throat and a pair of legs' (Reprinted – 'Ghost of Art').*

Molly: Mother of Estella by Magwitch, she had been tried for murder but successfully defended by Jaggers, who has since employed her as housekeeper. *She was a woman of about forty, I supposed – but I may have thought her younger than she was. Rather tall, of a lithe nimble figure, extremely pale, with large faded eyes, and a quantity of streaming hair. I cannot say whether any diseased affection of the heart caused her lips to be parted as if she were panting, and her face to bear a curious expression of sadness and flutter; but I know that I had been to see Macbeth at the theatre, a night or two before, and that her face looked to me as if it were all disturbed by fiery air, like the faces I had seen rise out of the Witches' cauldron (Expectations).*

Monflathers, Miss: Proprietress of a select school for young ladies whose pupils visit Jarley's waxwork show. *Was of rather uncertain temper, and lost no opportunity of impressing moral truths upon the tender minds of the young ladies (Curiosity Shop).*

Monks: See **Leeford, Edward** (*Twist*).

Montague, Julia: Singer who shares the bill with Amelia Martin at White Conduit. *Solo, Miss Montague (positively on this occasion only) – 'I am a Friar' – (enthusiasm) (Boz – 'Mistaken Milliner').*

Montague, Tigg: See **Tigg, Montague** (*Chuzzlewit*).

Moon: One of many doctors consulted by Our Bore. *Moon, whom half the town was then mad about (Reprinted – 'Our Bore').*

Mooney: Beadle officiating at the Coroner's Inquest on Hawdon. *Hopes to read in print what 'Mooney, the active and intelligent beadle of the district,' said and did; and even aspires to see the name of Mooney as familiarly and patronisingly mentioned as the name of the Hangman is (Bleak House).*

Mooney: Stargazer's partner. An astronomer and philosopher who has to be jerked out of his absent-minded ruminations by shocks from a strong battery. Stargazer wants him to marry Emma, but he declines (*Lamplighter* and 'Lamplighter's Story').

Mopes: The hermit on whom the story centres. *By suffering everything about him to go to ruin, and by dressing himself in a blanket and skewer, and by steeping himself in soot and grease and other nastiness, had acquired great renown in all that country-side. . . . He had even blanketed and skewered and sooted and greased himself, into the London papers (Christmas Stories – 'Tom Tiddler's Ground').*

Mordlin, Brother: Member of the Brick Lane Branch of the United Grand Junction Ebenezer Temperance Association who has adapted Dibdin's 'Who hasn't heard of a Jolly Young Waterman?' to the tune of the Old Hundredth, which Anthony Humm invites the meeting to sing. *He might take that opportunity of expressing his firm persuasion that the late Mr. Dibdin, seeing the errors of his former life, had written that song to show the advantages of abstinence. It was a temperance song (whirlwind of cheers). The neatness of the young man's attire, the dexterity of his feathering, the enviable state of mind which enabled him, in the beautiful words of the poet, to*

'Row along, thinking of nothing at all,'

all combined to prove that he must have been a water-drinker (cheers) (Pickwick).

Morfin: Under-manager at Dombey and Son. Staunch friend of John Carker and later husband to Harriet Carker. *A cheerful-looking, hazel-eyed elderly bachelor: gravely attired, as to his upper man, in black; and as to his legs, in pepper and salt colour. His dark hair was just touched here and there with specks of grey, as though the tread of Time had splashed it; and his whiskers were already white. . . . He was a great musical amateur in his way – after business; and had a paternal affection for the violoncello, which was once in every week transported from Islington, his place of abode, to a certain club-room hard by the Bank, where quartettes of the most tormenting and excruciating nature were executed every Wednesday evening by a private party (Dombey).*

Morgan: See **Jenkins** *(Young Couples – 'Contradictory Couple').*

Morgan, Becky: Deceased old woman about whose age David and the sexton argue in front of Little Nell *(Curiosity Shop).*

Morgan ap Kerrig: Woodcourt ancestor, lines about whose lineage Mrs. Woodcourt is fond of reciting from the Crumlinwallinwer and the Mewlinwillinwodd *(Bleak House).*

Mormon Agent: Organiser of the emigrants aboard the *Amazon. A compactly-made handsome man in black, rather short, with rich-brown hair and beard, and clear bright eyes. From his speech, I should set him down as American. Probably, a man who had 'knocked about the world' pretty much. A man with a frank open manner, and unshrinking look; withal a man of great quickness (Uncommercial – 'Bound for the Great Salt Lake').*

Mortair: A vice-president of the anatomy and medicine session at the second meeting of the Mudfog Association *(Mudfog).*

Mortimer: Name under which Micawber finds it expedient to live in Camden Town. *'The truth is,' said Traddles, in a whisper, 'he has changed his name to Mortimer, in consequence of his temporary embarrassments; and he don't come out till after dark – and then in spectacles' (Copperfield).*

Mortimer, Mrs.: A subject for one of Charles and Louisa's recriminations. *'You know as well as I do that I am particularly engaged to Mrs. Mortimer, and that it would be an act of the grossest rudeness and ill-breeding, after accepting a seat in her box and*

preventing her from inviting anybody else, not to go' (Young Couples – 'Cool Couple').

Mould: The undertaker who buries Anthony Chuzzlewit. Professionally in league with Mrs. Gamp. *A little elderly gentleman, bald, and in a suit of black; with a note-book in his hand, a massive gold watch-chain dangling from his fob, and a face in which a queer attempt at melancholy was at odds with a smirk of satisfaction; so that he looked as a man might, who, in the very act of smacking his lips over a choice old wine, tried to make believe it was physic (Chuzzlewit).*

Mould, Mrs. and the **Misses:** Mould's wife and daughters. *Plump as any partridge was each Miss Mould, and Mrs. M. was plumper than the two together. So round and chubby were their fair proportions, that they might have been the bodies once belonging to the angels' faces in the shop below, grown up, with other heads attached to make them mortal. Even their peachy cheeks were puffed out and distended, as though they ought of right to be performing on celestial trumpets (Chuzzlewit).*

Mowcher, Miss: A dwarf and visiting beauty specialist who attends Steerforth. She is instrumental in Littimer's arrest. *There came waddling round a sofa which stood between me and it, a pursy dwarf, of about forty or forty-five, with a very large head and face, a pair of roguish grey eyes, and such extremely little arms, that, to enable herself to lay a finger archly against her snub-nose as she ogled Steerforth, she was obliged to meet the finger half-way and lay her nose against it. Her chin, which was what is called a double-chin, was so fat that it entirely swallowed up the strings of her bonnet, bow and all. Throat she had none; waist she had none; legs she had none, worth mentioning; for though she was more than full-sized down to where her waist would have been, if she had had any, and though she terminated, as human beings generally do, in a pair of feet, she was so short that she stood at a common-sized chair as at a table, resting a bag she carried on the seat (Copperfield).*

Mr. F's Aunt: A strange old lady left to Flora Finching's care by her deceased husband. *An amazing little old woman, with a face like a staring wooden doll too cheap for expression, and a stiff yellow wig perched unevenly on the top of her head, as if the child who owned the doll had driven a tack through it anywhere, so that it only got fastened on. Another remarkable thing in this little old woman was, that the same child seemed to have damaged her face in two or three places with some blunt instrument in the nature of a spoon; her countenance, and particularly the tip of her nose, presenting the phenomena of several dints, generally answering to the bowl of that article. A further remarkable thing in this little old woman was, that she had no name but Mr. F's Aunt. . . . The major characteristics discoverable by the stranger in Mr. F's Aunt, were extreme severity and grim taciturnity; sometimes interrupted by a propensity to offer remarks in a deep warning voice, which, being totally uncalled for by anything said by anybody, and traceable to no association of ideas, confounded and terrified the mind (Dorrit).*

113

Mudberry, Mrs.: Neighbour quoted by Mrs. Sanders as having told her that Pickwick was engaged to Mrs. Bardell. *Mrs. Mudberry which kept a mangle (Pickwick).*

Muddlebrains: A vice-president at the zoology and botany session of the second meeting of the Mudfog Association *(Mudfog).*

Mudge, Jonas: Secretary of the Brick Lane Branch of the United Grand Junction Ebenezer Temperance Association. *Chandler's shop-keeper, an enthusiastic and disinterested vessel, who sold tea to the members (Pickwick).*

Muff and **Nogo, Professors:** Vice-presidents of the anatomy and medicine session of the first meeting of the Mudfog Association. They dissect Augustus (q.v.), a lady's pet dog, in their hotel room. *We are all very much delighted with the urbanity of their manners and the ease with which they adapt themselves to the forms and ceremonies of ordinary life. Immediately on their arrival they sent for the head waiter, and privately requested him to purchase a live dog, – as cheap a one as he could meet with, – and to send him up after dinner, with a pie-board, a knife and fork, and a clean plate. It is conjectured that some experiments will be tried upon the dog to-night (Mudfog).*

Mull, Professor: Member of the Mudfog Association *(Mudfog).*

Mullins, Jack: Regular drinker at the Six Jolly Fellowship Porters *(Mutual Friend).*

Mullion, John: Member of the *Golden Mary's* crew. *The man who had kept on burning the blue-lights (and who had lighted every new one at every old one before it went out, as quietly as if he had been at an illumination) (Christmas Stories – 'Golden Mary').*

Mullit, Professor: An American 'professor of education' whom Martin Chuzzlewit meets at Pawkins's Boarding-House, New York. *'He is a man of fine moral elements, sir, and not commonly endowed,' said the war correspondent. 'He felt it necessary, at the last election for President, to repudiate and denounce his father, who voted on the wrong interest. He has since written some powerful pamphlets, under the signature of "Suturb," or Brutus reversed' (Chuzzlewit).*

Muntle: Real name of Alfred Mantalini *(Nickleby).*

Murderer, Captain: Subject of one of the gruesome tales told by the Uncommercial Traveller's childhood nurse. *His warning name would seem to have awakened no general prejudice against him, for he was admitted into the best society and possessed immense wealth. Captain Murderer's mission was matrimony, and the gratification of a cannibal appetite with tender brides (Uncommercial – 'Nurse's Stories').*

Murdstone, Edward: Partner in Murdstone and Grinby, wine merchants. Brother of Jane, second husband to Clara Copperfield, and stepfather to David, whose spirit he tries to break by sending him to Salem House school and then into his own warehouse. He and his sister break Clara's heart, and Murdstone eventually re-marries, with similar results. *He had*

that kind of shallow black eye – I want a better word to express an eye that has no depth in it to be looked into – which, when it is abstracted, seems, from some peculiarity of light, to be disfigured, for a moment at a time, by a cast. Several times when I glanced at him, I observed that appearance with a sort of awe, and wondered what he was thinking about so closely. His hair and whiskers were blacker and thicker, looked at so near, than even I had given them credit for being. A squareness about the lower part of his face, and the dotted indication of the strong black beard he shaved close every day, reminded me of the wax-work that had travelled into our neighbourhood some half a year before. This, his regular eyebrows, and the rich white, and black, and brown, of his complexion – confound his complexion, and his memory! – made me think him, in spite of my misgivings, a very handsome man. I have no doubt that my poor dear mother thought him so too (Copperfield).

Murdstone, Mrs. Edward the First: See **Copperfield, Mrs. Clara** *(Copperfield).*

Murdstone, Mrs. Edward the Second: Murdstone's second wife, after Clara. *'A charming woman indeed, sir,' said Mr. Chillip; 'as amiable, I am sure, as it was possible to be! Mrs. Chillip's opinion is, that her spirit has been entirely broken since her marriage, and that she is all but melancholy mad' (Copperfield).*

Murdstone, Jane: Edward's sister. She is as hard as her brother and Clara Copperfield's death is much attributable to her. *A gloomy-looking lady she was, dark, like her brother, whom she greatly resembled in face and voice; and with very heavy eyebrows, nearly meeting over her large nose, as if, being disabled by the wrongs of her sex from wearing whiskers, she had carried them to that account. She brought with her two uncompromising hard black boxes, with her initials on the lids in hard brass nails. When she paid the coachman she took her money out of a hard steel purse, and she kept the purse in a very jail of a bag which hung upon her arm by a heavy chain, and shut up like a bite. I had never, at that time, seen such a metallic lady altogether as Miss Murdstone was (Copperfield).*

Murdstone and Grinby: Firm of wine merchants in which Edward Murdstone is partner, and in whose warehouse he employs and humiliates David Copperfield *(Copperfield).*

Murgatroyd: An undertaker, one of the admiring audience of the gentleman connected with the press at the Green Dragon, Westminster Bridge *(Mudfog – 'Mr. Robert Bolton').*

Mutanhed, Lord: A foppish young nobleman at the ball at Bath Assembly Rooms. *'The one with the long hair, and the particularly small forehead?' inquired Mr. Pickwick (Pickwick).*

Mutuel, Monsieur: Friend of Madame Bouclet. *A spectacled, snuffy, stooping old gentleman in carpet shoes and a cloth cap with a peaked shade, a loose blue frock-coat reaching to his heels, a large limp white shirt-frill, and cravat to correspond, – that is to say, white was the natural colour of his linen on Sundays,* but it toned down with the week (*Christmas Stories –* 'Somebody's Luggage').

Muzzle: Nupkins's footman and Job Trotter's rival for the cook. *An undersized footman, with a long body and short legs (Pickwick).*

Nadgett: Inquiry agent employed by the Anglo-Bengalee Disinterested Loan and Life Assurance Company to investigate Jonas Chuzzlewit, whose guilt he ultimately proves. *He was born to be a secret. He was a short, dried-up, withered, old man, who seemed to have secreted his very blood; for nobody would have given him credit for the possession of six ounces of it in his whole body. How he lived was a secret; where he lived was a secret; and even what he was, was a secret. In his musty old pocket-book he carried contradictory cards, in some of which he called himself a coal-merchant, in others a collector, in others an accountant: as if he really didn't know the secret himself (Chuzzlewit).*

Namby: Sheriff's officer who arrests Pickwick in execution of the judgment in Bardell and Pickwick. *A man of about forty, with black hair, and carefully combed whiskers. He was dressed in a particularly gorgeous manner, with plenty of articles of jewellery about him – all about three sizes larger than those which are usually worn by gentlemen – and a rough great-coat to crown the whole (Pickwick).*

Nancy: Member of Fagin's gang and mistress of Bill Sikes. She befriends Oliver Twist and helps him through Rose Maylie and Brownlow, but is overheard by Noah Claypole at a meeting with them, denounced to Fagin for treachery, and savagely murdered by Sikes. *The girl's life had been squandered in the streets, and among the most noisome of the stews and dens of London, but there was something of the woman's original nature left in her still (Twist).*

Nandy, John Edward: Mrs. Plornish's father. *A poor little reedy piping old gentleman, like a worn-out bird; who had been in what he called the music-binding business, and met with great misfortunes, and who had seldom been able to make his way, or to see it or to pay it, or to do anything at all with it but find it no thoroughfare, – had retired of his own accord to the Workhouse. . . . But no poverty in him and no coat on him that never was the mode, and no Old Men's Ward for his dwelling-place, could quench his daughter's admiration. Mrs. Plornish was as proud of her father's talents as she possibly could have been if they had made him Lord Chancellor. She had as firm a belief in the sweetness and propriety of his manners as she could possibly have had if he had been Lord Chamberlain. The poor little old man knew some pale and vapid little songs, long out of date, about Chloe, and Phyllis, and Strephon being wounded by the son of Venus; and for Mrs. Plornish there was no such music at the Opera, as the small internal flutterings and chirpings wherein he would discharge himself of these ditties, like a weak, little, broken barrel-organ, ground by a baby (Dorrit).*

Native, The: Major Bagstock's servant. *A dark servant of the major's, whom Miss Tox was quite content*

to classify as a 'native', without connecting him with any geographical idea whatever (Dombey).

Neckett: Sheriff's officer employed to arrest Skimpole. After his death Jarndyce provides for his three children, Charlotte, Tom, and Emma. *In a white greatcoat, with smooth hair upon his head and not much of it, which he was wiping smoother, and making less of, with a pocket-handkerchief (Bleak House).*

Neckett, Charlotte (Charley): Neckett's elder daughter, sister of Emma and Tom. She becomes Esther Summerson's maid. *A very little girl, childish in figure but shrewd and older-looking in the face – pretty-faced too – wearing a womanly sort of bonnet much too large for her, and drying her bare arms on a womanly sort of apron. Her fingers were white and wrinkled with washing, and the soap-suds were yet smoking which she wiped off her arms. But for this, she might have been a child playing at washing, and imitating a poor working-woman with a quick observation of the truth (Bleak House).*

Neckett, Emma: Neckett's infant daughter, sister of Charlotte and Tom. *A heavy child of eighteen months (Bleak House).*

Neckett, Tom: Neckett's infant son, brother of Charlotte and Emma. *A mite of a boy, some five or six years old (Bleak House).*

Ned: Chimney-sweep who kept his son small, for hiring out on burglary jobs to Bill Sikes and others. *'But the father gets lagged; and then the Juvenile Delinquent Society comes, and takes the boy away from a trade where he was earning money, teaches him to read and write, and in time makes a 'prentice of him. And so they go on,' said Mr. Sikes, his wrath rising with the recollection of his wrongs, 'so they go on; and, if they'd got money enough (which it's a Providence they haven't) we shouldn't have half a dozen boys left in the whole trade, in a year or two' (Twist).*

Neddy: One of Roker's fellow turnkeys in the Fleet Prison. *Of a taciturn and thoughtful cast (Pickwick).*

Neeshawts, Dr.: Member of the Mudfog Association (*Mudfog*).

Nell, Little: See **Trent, Nell** (*Curiosity Shop*).

'Nemo': See **Hawdon, Captain** (*Bleak House*).

Nettingall, the **Misses:** Principals of a Canterbury school for young ladies attended by Miss Shepherd (*Copperfield*).

Newcome, Clemency: Dr. Jeddler's maidservant, later married to his manservant, Benjamin Britain. *She was about thirty years old, and had a sufficiently plump and cheerful face, though it was twisted up into an odd expression of tightness that made it comical. But, the extraordinary homeliness of her gait and manner, would have superseded any face in the world. To say that she had two left legs, and somebody else's arms, and that all four limbs seemed to be out of joint, and to start from perfectly wrong places when they were set in motion, is to offer the mildest outline of the reality. To say that she was perfectly content and* satisfied with these arrangements, and regarded them as being no business of hers, and that she took her arms and legs as they came, and allowed them to dispose of themselves just as it happened, is to render faint justice to her equanimity (*Christmas Books* – 'Battle of Life').

Nicholas: Butler at Bellamy's restaurant in the Houses of Parliament. *A queer old fellow is Nicholas, and as completely a part of the building as the house itself ... looking as he always does, as if he had been in a bandbox ever since the last session. There he is, at his old post every night, just as we have described him: and, as characters are scarce, and faithful servants scarcer, long may he be there, say we!* (*Boz* – 'Parliamentary Sketch').

Nickleby, Godfrey: Deceased father of Ralph and Nicholas senior (*Nickleby*).

Nickleby, Kate: Sister of Nicholas junior. She marries Frank Cheeryble. *A slight, but very beautiful girl of about seventeen* (*Nickleby*).

Nickleby, Nicholas, jun.: Son of Mrs. Nickleby and the late Nicholas senior. Brother to Kate and nephew of Ralph. The central figure of the novel, he marries Madeline Bray, whose father he has helped rescue from the financial clutches of Ralph Nickleby and Arthur Gride. *His figure was somewhat slight, but manly and well-formed; and, apart from all the grace of youth and comeliness, there was an emanation from the warm young heart in his look* (*Nickleby*).

Nickleby, Nicholas, sen.: Deceased son of Godfrey, brother of Ralph, father of Nicholas and Kate (*Nickleby*).

Nickleby, Mrs. Nicholas, sen.: Widow of Nicholas senior and mother of Nicholas junior and Kate. Feckless and absent-minded, she fancies herself wooed by the Gentleman in Small-clothes, but nothing comes of it. *Mrs. Nickleby had begun to display unusual care in the adornment of her person, gradually superadding to those staid and matronly habiliments which had, up to that time, formed her ordinary attire, a variety of embellishments and decorations, slight perhaps in themselves, but, taken together, and considered with reference to the subject of her disclosure, of no mean importance. Even her black dress assumed something of a deadly-lively air from the jaunty style in which it was worn; and, eked out as its lingering attractions were, by a prudent disposal, here and there, of certain juvenile ornaments of little or no value, which had, for that reason alone, escaped the general wreck and been permitted to slumber peacefully in odd corners of old drawers and boxes where daylight seldom shone, her mourning garments assumed quite a new character. From being the outward tokens of respect and sorrow for the dead, they became converted into signals of very slaughterous and killing designs upon the living* (*Nickleby*).

Nickleby, Ralph: Son of Godfrey, brother of the late Nicholas senior, uncle to Nicholas and Kate. A rich and miserly moneylender who grudgingly helps his late brother's family but tries to humiliate Nicholas. He eventually hangs himself. *He wore a sprinkling of powder upon his head, as if to make himself look benevolent, but if that were his purpose, he would perhaps have done better to powder his countenance also, for there was something in its very wrinkles, and in his cold restless eye, which seemed to tell of cunning that would announce itself in spite of him* (*Nickleby*).

Nightingale, Christopher: Rosina's uncle and guardian. A hypochondriac who has been paying a regular allowance to Slap, believing the money to be going to his estranged wife, Maria, Slap's sister, who had actually died twelve years ago. He is saved from Slap's ultimate coup by Gabblewig (*Nightingale's Diary*).

Nightingale, Christopher, jun.: An imposture by Tip in aid of Slap's ultimate attempt at extortion from Mr. Nightingale (*Nightingale's Diary*).

Nightingale, Rosina: Nightingale's niece. She wishes to marry Gabblewig, of whom her uncle disapproves, so helps him redeem his character by unmasking Slap, in the course of which she assumes the disguises of Mrs. Poulter and Mrs. Trusty (*Nightingale's Diary*).

Niner, Margaret: Slinkton's surviving niece, whose murder for her insurance money is narrowly averted by Meltham and Sampson. *She was dressed in mourning, and I looked at her with great interest. She had the appearance of being extremely delicate, and her face was remarkably pale and melancholy; but she was very pretty* ('Hunted Down').

Nipper, Susan: Florence Dombey's maid and support. She marries Toots. *A short, brown, womanly girl of fourteen, with a little snub nose, and black eyes like jet beads* (*Dombey*).

Nixon, Mrs.: Felix's doting mother. *If you ask Felix how he finds himself to-day, he prefaces his reply with a long and minute bulletin of his mother's state of health; and the good lady in her turn, edifies her acquaintance with a circumstantial and alarming account, how she sneezed four times and coughed once after being out in the rain the other night* (*Young Gentlemen* – 'Domestic Young Gentleman').

Nixon, Felix: A domestic young gentleman. *Lives at home with his mother, just within the twopenny-post office circle of three miles from St. Martin le Grand. He wears India-rubber goloshes when the weather is at all damp, and always has a silk handkerchief neatly folded up in the right-hand pocket of his great-coat, to tie over his mouth when he comes home at night; moreover, being rather near-sighted, he carries spectacles for particular occasions, and has a weakish tremulous voice, of which he makes great use, for he talks as much as any old lady breathing. The two chief subjects of Felix's discourse, are himself and his mother, both of whom would appear to be very wonderful and interesting persons* (*Young Gentlemen* – 'Domestic Young Gentleman').

Noakes: A vice-president of the statistics session at the second meeting of the Mudfog Association (*Mudfog*).

Noakes, Mrs.: See **Williamson, Mrs.** (*Strange Gentleman*).

Noakes, Percy: A pleasure-loving law student, of Gray's Inn Square; prime organiser of the steam excursion. *He had a large circle of acquaintance, and seldom dined at his own expense. He used to talk politics to papas, flatter the vanity of mammas, do the amiable to their daughters, make pleasure engagements with their sons, and romp with the younger branches.... His sitting-room presented a strange chaos of dress-gloves, boxing-gloves, caricatures, albums, invitation-cards, foils, cricket-bats, cardboard drawings, paste, gum, and fifty other miscellaneous articles, heaped together in the strangest confusion. He was always making something for somebody, or planning some party of pleasure, which was his great forte. He invariably spoke with astonishing rapidity; was smart, spoffish, and eight-and-twenty* (Boz – 'Steam Excursion').

Nobody: Hero of the story. *It matters little what his name was. Let us call him Legion.... The story of Nobody is the story of the rank and file of the earth. They bear their share of the battle; they have their part in the victory; they fall; they leave no name but in the mass* (*Christmas Stories* – 'Nobody's Story').

Nockemorf: Bob Sawyer's predecessor in the medical practice at Bristol (*Pickwick*).

'Noddy': See **Boffin, Nicodemus** (*Mutual Friend*).

Noddy: Friend of Bob Sawyer, present at his supper party. *The scorbutic youth* (*Pickwick*).

Noggs, Newman: Ralph Nickleby's clerk, a former gentleman. He befriends and serves Nicholas, and is instrumental in Ralph's exposure and ruin. *A tall man of middle age, with two goggle eyes whereof one was a fixture, a rubicund nose, a cadaverous face, and a suit of clothes (if the term be allowable when they suited him not at all) much the worse for wear, very much too small, and placed upon such a short allowance of buttons that it was marvellous how he contrived to keep them on* (*Nickleby*).

Nogo, Professor: See **Muff** and **Nogo** (*Mudfog*).

Norah: Seven-year-old cousin to eight-year-old Harry Walmers, with whom she elopes to Gretna Green, hoping to marry. In adult life she marries a captain and dies in India. *The lady had got a parasol, a smelling-bottle, a round and a half of cold buttered toast, eight peppermint drops, and a hair-brush, – seemingly a doll's* (*Christmas Stories* – 'Holly-Tree').

Normandy: A gaming-booth attendant invited by Chops to join him in entering society. He is the instrument of Chops's ruin. *Had a wery genteel appearance* (*Christmas Stories* – 'Going into Society').

Norris Family: A wealthy New York family to whom Martin Chuzzlewit is introduced by Bevan on first arriving there. They drop him hastily when they learn that he had travelled steerage. *There were two young ladies – one eighteen; the other twenty – both very slender, but very pretty; their mother, who looked, as Martin thought, much older than she ought to have looked; and their grandmother, a little sharp-eyed,*

E

quick old woman, who seemed to have got past that stage, and to have come all right again. Besides these, there were the young ladies' father, and the young ladies' brother; the first engaged in mercantile affairs; the second, a student at college (*Chuzzlewit*).

Norton, Squire: Would-be seducer of Lucy Benson (*Village Coquettes*).

Nubbles, Mrs.: Widowed mother of Kit, Jacob, and a baby. A poor laundress. *Late as the Dutch clock showed it to be, the poor woman was still hard at work at an ironing-table* (*Curiosity Shop*).

Nubbles, Jacob: Kit's small brother. *A sturdy boy of two or three years old, very wide awake, with a very tight night-cap on his head, and a night-gown very much too small for him on his body, was sitting bolt upright in a clothes-basket, staring over the rim with his great round eyes, and looking as if he had thoroughly made up his mind never to go to sleep any more* (*Curiosity Shop*).

Nubbles, Kit: Little Nell's devoted friend and her grandfather's shop-boy at the Old Curiosity Shop. When the couple disappear he goes to work for Garland. Quilp gets him falsely accused of theft, but he is cleared and marries Barbara, the Garlands' maid. *A shock-headed shambling awkward lad with an uncommonly wide mouth, very red cheeks, a turned-up nose, and certainly the most comical expression of face I ever saw. He stopped short at the door on seeing a stranger, twirled in his hand a perfectly round old hat without any vestige of a brim, and, resting himself now on one leg, and now on the other, and changing them constantly, stood in the doorway, looking into the parlour with the most extraordinary leer I ever beheld* (*Curiosity Shop*).

Nupkins, George: Mayor of Ipswich, before whom the Pickwickians are taken on Miss Witherfield's complaint. *As grand a personage as the fastest walker would find out, between sunrise and sunset, on the twenty-first of June, which being, according to the almanacs, the longest day in the whole year, would naturally afford him the longest period for his search* (*Pickwick*).

Nupkins, Mrs. George: Nupkins's wife and mother of Henrietta. *A majestic female in a pink gauze turban and a light brown wig* (*Pickwick*).

Nupkins, Henrietta: The Nupkinses' daughter. *Possessed all her mamma's haughtiness without the turban, and all her ill-nature without the wig* (*Pickwick*).

Oakum-Head: One of the female delinquents in the workhouse visited by the Uncommercial Traveller (*Uncommercial* – 'Wapping Workhouse').

Obenreizer, Jules: London agent of Defresnier et Cie., Swiss wine merchants, and uncle of Marguerite. Fearing that Vendale is about to discover his frauds, Obenreizer tries to murder him in an Alpine pass. He is eventually killed in an avalanche. *A black-haired young man of a dark complexion, through whose swarthy skin no red glow ever shone. When colour* would have come into another cheek, a hardly discernible beat would come into his, as if the machinery for bringing up the ardent blood were there, but the machinery were dry.... But the great Obenreizer peculiarity was, that a certain nameless film would come over his eyes – apparently by the action of his own will – which would impenetrably veil, not only from those tellers of tales, but from his face at large, every expression save one of attention.... It was a comprehensive watchfulness of everything he had in his own mind, and everything that he knew to be, or suspected to be, in the minds of other men (Christmas Stories – 'No Thoroughfare' and in dramatised version).

Obenreizer, Marguerite: Obenreizer's niece, living with him in London. Courted by Vendale, she saves him after her uncle's murderous attack and eventually marries him. The young lady wore an unusual quantity of fair bright hair, very prettily braided about a rather rounder white forehead than the average English type, and so her face might have been a shade – or say a light – rounder than the average English face, and her figure slightly rounder than the figure of the average English girl at nineteen. A remarkable indication of freedom and grace of limb, in her quiet attitude, and a wonderful purity and freshness of colour in her dimpled face and bright gray eyes, seemed fraught with mountain air (Christmas Stories – 'No Thoroughfare' and in dramatised version).

O'Bleary, Frederick: Boarder at Mrs. Tibbs's, with ideas of marrying Mrs. Bloss. An Irishman, recently imported; he was in a perfectly wild state; and had come over to England to be an apothecary, a clerk in a government office, an actor, a reporter, or anything else that turned up – he was not particular.... He felt convinced that his intrinsic merits must procure him a high destiny. He wore shepherd's-plaid inexpressibles, and used to look under all the ladies' bonnets as he walked along the streets (Boz – 'Boarding-House').

O'Brien: See **Brown** and **O'Brien** (Boz – 'The River').

Odd Girl, The: One of the maids taken with them by the party investigating the haunted house. I have reason to record of the attendant last enumerated, who was one of the St. Lawrence's Union Female Orphans, that she was a fatal mistake and a disastrous engagement (Christmas Stories – 'Haunted House').

'Old Soldier, The': See **Markleham, Mrs.** (Copperfield).

Omer: Yarmouth draper and undertaker, father of Minnie. Employer, and later partner and father-in-law, of Joram. Employer of Little Em'ly before her elopement. A fat, short-winded, merry-looking, little old man in black, with rusty little bunches of ribbons at the knees of his breeches, black stockings, and a broad-brimmed hat (Copperfield).

Omer, Minnie: Omer's daughter, marries Joram. A pretty good-natured girl (Copperfield).

One Old Man: The Phantom of a hanged man who attends Goodchild in the Lancaster inn and tells his story. A chilled, slow, earthy, fixed old man. A cadaverous old man of measured speech. An old man who seemed as unable to wink, as if his eyelids had been nailed to his forehead.... His cravat appeared to trouble him. He put his hand to his throat, and moved his neck from side to side. He was an old man of a swollen character of face, and his nose was immoveably hitched up on one side, as if by a little hook inserted in that nostril (Two Apprentices).

Onowenever, Miss and **Mrs.:** An object of the Uncommercial Traveller's youthful admiration, and her mother. She was older than I, and had pervaded every chink and crevice of my mind for three or four years. I had held volumes of Imaginary Conversations with her mother on the subject of our union, and I had written letters more in number than Horace Walpole's, to that discreet woman, soliciting her daughter's hand in marriage. I had never had the remotest intention of sending any of those letters; but to write them, and after a few days tear them up, had been a sublime occupation (Uncommercial – 'Birthday Celebrations').

Orange, James: Mrs. Orange's 'husband' in Nettie Ashford's romantic tale ('Holiday Romance').

Orange, Mrs. James: A 'truly sweet young creature' in Nettie Ashford's romantic tale who had the misfortune to be sadly plagued by her numerous family of parents and other adults ('Holiday Romance').

'Orfling, The': See **Clickett** (Copperfield).

Orlick, Dolge: Joe Gargery's journeyman and implacable enemy to Pip, whom he nearly murders at Compeyson's instigation. He is Mrs. Joe Gargery's brutal attacker. He pretended that his Christian name was Dolge – a clear impossibility – but he was a fellow of that obstinate disposition that I believe him to have been the prey of no delusion in this particular, but wilfully to have imposed that name upon the village as an affront to its understanding. He was a broad-shouldered loose-limbed swarthy fellow of great strength, never in a hurry, and always slouching. He never even seemed to come to his work on purpose, but would slouch in as if by mere accident.... He always slouched, locomotively, with his eyes on the ground; and when accosted or otherwise required to raise them, he looked up in a half resentful, half puzzled way, as though the only thought he ever had, was, that it was rather an odd and injurious fact that he should never be thinking (Expectations).

Overton, Joseph: Solicitor and mayor of Great Winglebury, instructed by Julia Manners to arrange her elopement with Lord Peter. A sleek man ... in drab shorts and continuations, black coat, neckcloth, and gloves (Boz – 'Great Winglebury Duel'). He is renamed Owen Overton in the dramatic version, The Strange Gentleman.

Overton, Owen: Mayor of a small town on the road to Gretna (Strange Gentleman). This is the Joseph Overton (q.v.) of Boz – 'Great Winglebury Duel'.

Owen, John: A pupil at Marton's village school. 'A lad of good parts, sir, and frank, honest temper; but *too thoughtless, too playful, too light-headed by far. That boy, my good sir, would break his neck with pleasure, and deprive his parents of their chief comfort'* (Curiosity Shop).

Packer, Tom: Fellow Royal Marine private of Gill Davis in the sloop *Christopher Columbus. A wild, unsteady young fellow, but the son of a respectable shipwright in Portsmouth Yard, and a good scholar who had been well brought up* (Christmas Stories – 'English Prisoners').

Packlemerton, Jasper: One of Mrs. Jarley's wax-work figures. *'Of atrocious memory, who courted and married fourteen wives, and destroyed them all, by tickling the soles of their feet when they were sleeping in the consciousness of innocence and virtue'* (Curiosity Shop).

Palmer: Amateur actor. *Mister Palmer is to play* The Unknown Bandit (Boz – 'Private Theatres').

Pancks: Agent and rent collector for Casby, whom he eventually exposes. *He was dressed in black and rusty iron grey; had jet black beads of eyes; a scrubby little black chin; wiry black hair striking out from his head in prongs, like forks or hair-pins; and a complexion that was very dingy by nature, or very dirty by art, or a compound of nature and art. He had dirty hands and dirty broken nails, and looked as if he had been in the coals; he was in a perspiration, and snorted and sniffed and puffed and blew, like a little labouring steam-engine* (Dorrit).

Pangloss: A friend, in an official position, of the Uncommercial Traveller, with whom he visits wounded soldiers from India. *Lineally descended from a learned doctor of that name, who was once tutor to Candide, an ingenious young gentleman of some celebrity. In his personal character, he is as humane and worthy a gentleman as any I know; in his official capacity, he unfortunately preaches the doctrines of his renowned ancestor, by demonstrating on all occasions that we live in the best of all possible official worlds* (Uncommercial – 'Great Tasmania's Cargo').

Pankey, Miss: A fellow-boarder of the Dombey children at Mrs. Pipchin's. *A mild little blue-eyed morsel of a child, who was shampoo'd every morning, and seemed in danger of being rubbed away, altogether* (Dombey).

Paragon, Mary Anne: David and Dora Copperfield's first servant. *Her name was Paragon. Her nature was represented to us, when we engaged her, as being feebly expressed in her name. She had a written character, as large as a proclamation; and, according to this document, could do everything of a domestic nature that ever I heard of, and a great many things that I never did hear of. She was a woman in the prime of life; of a severe countenance; and subject (particularly in the arms) to a sort of perpetual measles or fiery rash. . . . Our treasure was warranted sober and honest. I am therefore willing to believe that she was in a fit when we found her under the boiler; and that the deficient tea-spoons were attributable to the dustman* (Copperfield).

Pardiggle, Egbert, Oswald, Francis, Felix, and **Alfred:** Sons, in order of seniority, of Mrs. Pardiggle. *'Egbert, my eldest (twelve), is the boy who sent out his pocket-money, to the amount of five-and-threepence, to the Tockahoopo Indians. Oswald, my second (ten-and-a-half), is the child who contributed two-and-ninepence to the Great National Smithers Testimonial. Francis, my third (nine), one-and-sixpence-halfpenny; Felix, my fourth (seven), eightpence to the Superannuated Widows; Alfred, my youngest (five), has voluntarily enrolled himself in the Infants Bonds of Joy, and is pledged never, through life, to use tobacco in any form'* (Bleak House).

Pardiggle, O. A.: Philanthropic neighbour of John Jarndyce. Father of Egbert, Oswald, Francis, Felix, and Alfred. *An obstinate-looking man with a large waistcoat and stubbly hair, who was always talking in a loud bass voice about his mite, or Mrs. Pardiggle's mite, or their five boys' mites* (Bleak House).

Pardiggle, Mrs. O. A.: Pardiggle's wife, a fervent philanthropist and committee woman. *A formidable style of lady, with spectacles, a prominent nose, and a loud voice, who had the effect of wanting a great deal of room. And she really did, for she knocked down little chairs with her skirts that were quite a great way off. As only Ada and I were at home, we received her timidly; for she seemed to come in like cold weather, and to make the little Pardiggles blue as they followed* (Bleak House).

Parker: Police constable who accompanies the narrator and Inspector Field to the Old Mint, Borough. *Parker, strapped and great-coated, and waiting in dim Borough doorway by appointment* (Reprinted – 'On Duty with Inspector Field').

Parker, Mrs. Johnson: Rival, with her seven spinster daughters, of the three Miss Browns in charitable endeavours. *A ladies' bible and prayer-book distribution society was instantly formed: president, Mrs. Johnson Parker; treasurers, auditors, and secretary, the Misses Johnson Parker* (Boz – 'Ladies' Societies').

Parkes, Phil: A ranger at Chigwell and *habitué* of the Maypole *(Rudge).*

Parkins: Friend of Our Bore with something about his wife's sister on his mind *(Reprinted – 'Our Bore').*

Parkins, Mrs.: The narrator's laundress, the porter's widow. *Had particular instructions to place a bedroom candle and a match under the staircase lamp on my landing, in order that I might light my candle there, whenever I came home. Mrs. Parkins invariably disregarding all instructions, they were never there* (Reprinted – 'Ghost of Art').

Parkle: A friend of the Uncommercial Traveller living in chambers in Gray's Inn Square. *They were so dirty that I could take off the distinctest impression of my figure on any article of furniture by merely lounging upon it for a few moments; and it used to be a private amusement of mine to print myself off – if I may use the expression – all over the rooms. It was the first large circulation I had. At other times I have actually shaken a window curtain while in animated conversa-*

119

tion with Parkle, and struggling insects which were certainly red, and were certainly not ladybirds, have dropped on the back of my hand. Yet Parkle lived in that top set years, bound body and soul to the superstition that they were clean (Uncommercial – 'Chambers').

Parksop, Brother: George Silverman's deceased grandfather, a brother of the same Nonconformist congregation as Hawkyard ('Silverman').

Parlour Orator, The: See **Rogers** and also **Snobee** (Boz – 'Parlour Orator').

Parsons, Mrs.: Subject of one of the Contradictory Couple's arguments. *Master James, growing talkative upon such prospects, asks his mamma how tall Mrs. Parsons is, and whether she is not six feet high; to which his mamma replies, 'Yes, she should think she was, for Mrs. Parsons is a very tall lady indeed; quite a giantess.' 'For Heaven's sake, Charlotte,' cries her husband, 'do not tell the child such preposterous nonsense. Six feet high!'* (Young Couples – 'Contradictory Couple').

Parsons, Gabriel: Tottle's old friend who pays Tottle's debts on condition that he will marry Miss Lillerton and pay him back handsomely from her estate. *A short elderly gentleman with a gruffish voice.... He was a rich sugar-baker, who mistook rudeness for honesty, and abrupt bluntness for an open and candid manner* (Boz – 'Watkins Tottle').

Parsons, Mrs. Gabriel (Fanny): Gabriel's wife, whom he had married against her parents' wishes. *'Our love was raised to such a pitch, and as my salary had been raised too, shortly before, we determined on a secret marriage.... Two girls – friends of Fanny's – acting as bridesmaids; and a man, who was hired for five shillings and a pint of porter, officiating as father'* (Boz – 'Watkins Tottle').

Parsons, Lætitia: Pianoforte soloist at the Misses Crumpton's ball. *Whose performance of 'The Recollections of Ireland' was universally declared to be almost equal to that of Moscheles himself* (Boz – 'Sentiment').

Parvis, Arson: Resident of Lanrean questioned by Captain Jorgan (Christmas Stories – 'Message from the Sea').

Passnidge: A friend with Murdstone at Lowestoft (Copperfield).

Patty: John's maiden sister, who moves into the haunted house with him. *I venture to call her eight-and-thirty, she is so very handsome, sensible, and engaging* (Christmas Stories – 'Haunted House').

Pawkins, Major: A Pennsylvania-born New Yorker and fraudulent speculator. *Distinguished by a very large skull, and a great mass of yellow forehead; in deference to which commodities, it was currently held in bar-rooms and other such places of resort, that the major was a man of huge sagacity. He was further to be known by a heavy eye and a dull slow manner; and for being a man of that kind who, mentally speaking, requires a good deal of room to turn himself in. But,* *in trading on his stock of wisdom, he invariably proceeded on the principle of putting all the goods he had (and more) into his window; and that went a great way with his constituency of admirers* (Chuzzlewit).

Pawkins, Mrs.: The Major's wife, proprietress of Pawkins's Boarding-House where Martin Chuzzlewit and Mark Tapley stay on arrival in New York. *Very straight, bony, and silent* (Chuzzlewit).

Payne, Dr.: Surgeon to the 43rd Regiment at Rochester. *A portly personage in a braided surtout* (Pickwick).

Pea or Peacoat: Officer conducting the narrator on a night inspection of the Thames Police (Reprinted – 'Down with the Tide').

Peak: Sir John Chester's manservant. *Was to the full as cool and negligent in his way as his master* (Rudge).

Peartree: Member of the Royal College of Surgeons and of the Eight Club (q.v.) at Cloisterham. *Mr. Peartree is not accountable to me for his opinions, and I say no more of them here than that he attends the poor gratis whenever they want him, and is not the parish doctor. Mr. Peartree may justify it to the grasp of his mind thus to do his republican utmost to bring an appointed officer into contempt. Suffice it that Mr. Peartree can never justify it to the grasp of mine.* (Drood fragment).

Pebbleson Nephew: City of London wine merchants to whom Walter Wilding was apprenticed by Mrs. Wilding. When he came of age she transferred her shareholding to him and later bought out the owners, enabling Wilding and Company to come into existence (Christmas Stories – 'No Thoroughfare'; not in dramatised version).

Pecksniff, Charity (Cherry): Pecksniff's shrewish elder daughter. She pursues Jonas Chuzzlewit and Moddle, but is evaded by both. *It was morning; and the beautiful Aurora, of whom so much hath been written, said, and sung, did, with her rosy fingers, nip and tweak Miss Pecksniff's nose ... or in more prosaic phrase, the tip of that feature in the sweet girl's countenance, was always very red at breakfast-time. For the most part, indeed, it wore, at the season of the day, a scraped and frosty look, as if it had been rasped; while a similar phenomenon developed itself in her humour, which was then observed to be of a sharp and acid quality, as though an extra lemon (figuratively speaking) had been squeezed into the nectar of her disposition, and had rather damaged its flavour* (Chuzzlewit).

Pecksniff, Mercy (Merry): Pecksniff's vain younger daughter. Marries Jonas Chuzzlewit. *She was the most arch and at the same time the most artless creature, was the youngest Miss Pecksniff, that you can possibly imagine. It was her great charm. She was too fresh and guileless, and too full of childlike vivacity, was the youngest Miss Pecksniff, to wear combs in her hair, or to turn it up, or to frizzle it, or braid it. She wore it in a crop, a loosely flowing crop, which had so many rows of curls in it, that the top row was only one curl. Moderately buxom was her shape,* *and quite womanly too; but sometimes – yes, sometimes – she even wore a pinafore; and how charming that was! (Chuzzlewit).*

Pecksniff, Seth: Architect and widower, of Salisbury, and hypocritical schemer after old Martin Chuzzlewit's money. Father of Charity and Mercy. *He was a most exemplary man: fuller of virtuous precept than a copybook. Some people likened him to a direction-post, which is always telling the way to a place, and never goes there: but these were his enemies; the shadows cast by his brightness; that was all. His very throat was moral. . . . It seemed to say, on the part of Mr. Pecksniff, 'There is no deception, ladies and gentlemen, all is peace, a holy calm pervades me.' So did his hair, just grizzled with an iron-grey, which was all brushed off his forehead, and stood bolt upright, or slightly drooped in kindred action with his heavy eyelids. So did his person, which was sleek though free from corpulency. So did his manner, which was soft and oily. In a word, even his plain black suit, and state of widower, and dangling double eye-glass, all tended to the same purpose, and cried aloud, 'Behold the moral Pecksniff!' (Chuzzlewit).*

Pedro: One of Jerry's performing dogs. *One of them had a cap upon his head, tied very carefully under his chin, which had fallen down upon his nose and completely obscured one eye (Curiosity Shop).*

Peecher, Emma: A teacher under Bradley Headstone, whom she loves. *Small, shining, neat, methodical, and buxom was Miss Peecher; cherry-cheeked and tuneful of voice. A little pincushion, a little housewife, a little book, a little workbox, a little set of tables and weights and measures, and a little woman, all in one. She could write a little essay on any subject, exactly a slate long, beginning at the left-hand top of one side and ending at the right-hand bottom of the other, and the essay should be strictly according to rule. If Mr. Bradley Headstone had addressed a written proposal of marriage to her, she would probably have replied in a complete little essay on the theme exactly a slate long, but would certainly have replied yes (Mutual Friend).*

Peepy, The Hon. Miss: A famous figure in the past of our English watering-place. *The Beauty of her day and the cruel occasion of innumerable duels (Reprinted – 'Our English Watering-place').*

Peerybingle, John: The carrier on whose hearth the Cricket sings. Husband of Mary. *A sturdy figure of a man . . . this lumbering, slow, honest John; this John so heavy, but so light of spirit; so rough upon the surface, but so gentle at the core; so dull without, so quick within; so stolid, but so good! (Christmas Books – 'Cricket').*

Peerybingle, Mrs. John (Mary, 'Dot'): John's wife, called Dot for her tiny size. *Fair she was, and young: though something of what is called the dumpling shape (Christmas Books – 'Cricket').*

Peffer and Snagsby: The law-stationer's business that is now Snagsby's alone. The deceased Peffer had been Mrs. Snagsby's uncle. *Peffer is never seen in Cook's Court now. His is not expected there, for he has been recumbent this quarter of a century in the churchyard of St. Andrew's, Holborn, with the waggons and hackney-coaches roaring past him, all the day and half the night, like one great dragon (Bleak House).*

Pegg (alias **Waterhouse**): A Liverpool crimp. *'This man's a regular bad one' (Uncommercial – 'Poor Mercantile Jack').*

Peggotty, Clara: Sister to Daniel. David Copperfield's nurse and lifelong friend. She serves his mother at Murdstone's and after Clara Copperfield's death marries Barkis. Eventually widowed, she spends the rest of her days with Miss Trotwood. *'Peggotty!' repeated Miss Betsey, with some indignation. 'Do you mean to say, child, that any human being has gone into a Christian church, and got herself named Peggotty?' . . . Peggotty, with no shape at all, and eyes so dark that they seemed to darken their whole neighbourhood in her face, and cheeks and arms so hard and red that I wondered the birds didn't peck her in preference to apples (Copperfield).*

Peggotty, Daniel: Yarmouth fisherman, bachelor brother to Clara. His household in a converted boat on Yarmouth beach includes his nephew Ham, niece Little Em'ly, and his partner's widow Mrs. Gummidge. He devotes months to searching for Little Em'ly after her elopement and then takes them all to Australia. *A hairy man with a very good-natured face. . . . He was but a poor man himself, said Peggotty, but as good as gold, and as true as steel – those were her similes. The only subject, she informed me, on which he ever showed a violent temper or swore an oath, was this generosity of his; and if it were ever referred to, by any one of them, he struck the table a heavy blow with his right hand (had split it on one such occasion), and swore a dreadful oath that he would be 'Gormed' if he didn't cut and run for good, if it was ever mentioned again (Copperfield).*

Peggotty, Ham: Son of the late Joe, nephew and adopted son of Daniel. Fiancé of Little Em'ly. Fisherman and boatbuilder. He is drowned trying to rescue his betrayer, Steerforth. *A huge, strong fellow of six feet high, broad in proportion, and round-shouldered; but with a simpering boy's face and curly light hair that gave him quite a sheepish look. He was dressed in a canvas jacket, and a pair of such very stiff trousers that they would have stood quite as well alone, without any legs in them. And you couldn't so properly have said he wore a hat, as that he was covered in atop, like an old building, with something pitchy (Copperfield).*

Peggotty, Joe: Daniel's deceased brother. Father of Ham *(Copperfield).*

Peggy: A housemaid *(Christmas Stories – 'Going into Society').*

Peggy: Lord Chamberlain to King Watkins the First in Alice Rainbird's romantic tale ('Holiday Romance').

Pegler, Mrs.: An old countrywoman who haunts Coketown and is finally revealed as Bounderby's mother. *It was an old woman, tall and shapely still,* *though withered by time, on whom his eyes fell when he stopped and turned. She was very cleanly and plainly dressed, had country mud upon her shoes, and was newly come from a journey. The flutter of her manner, in the unwonted noise of the streets; the spare shawl, carried unfolded on her arm; the heavy umbrella, and little basket; the loose long-fingered gloves, to which her hands were unused; all bespoke an old woman from the country, in her plain holiday clothes, come into Coketown on an expedition of rare occurrence (Hard Times).*

Pell, Solomon: A seedy attorney at the Insolvent Court who assists the Wellers. *A fat flabby pale man, in a surtout which looked green one minute and brown the next: with a velvet collar of the same cameleon tints. His forehead was narrow, his face wide, his head large, and his nose all on one side, as if Nature, indignant with the propensities she observed in him in his birth, had given it an angry tweak which it had never recovered. Being short-necked and asthmatic, however, he respired principally through this feature; so, perhaps, what it wanted in ornament it made up in usefulness (Pickwick).*

Peltirogus, Horatio: A supposed suitor of Kate Nickleby, whose name is evoked by Mrs. Nickleby in order to intrigue Frank Cheeryble. *She even went so far as to hint, obscurely, at an attachment entertained for her daughter by the son of an old neighbour of theirs, one Horatio Peltirogus (a young gentleman who might have been, at that time, four years old, or thereabouts), and to represent it, indeed, as almost a settled thing between the families – only waiting for her daughter's final decision, to come off with the sanction of the church, and to the unspeakable happiness and content of all parties (Nickleby).*

Penrewen: Resident of Lanrean questioned by Captain Jorgan (*Christmas Stories* – 'Message from the Sea').

Peplow, Mrs. and **Master:** See **Macklin, Walker,** and **Peplow** (*Boz* – 'The Streets – Night')

Pepper ('The Avenger'): Pip's boy servant. *I had got on so fast of late, that I had even started a boy in boots – top boots – in bondage and slavery to whom I might be said to pass my days. For, after I had made this monster (out of the refuse of my washerwoman's family) and had clothed him with a blue coat, canary waistcoat, white cravat, creamy breeches, and the boots already mentioned, I had to find him a little to do and a great deal to eat; and with both of these horrible requirements he haunted my existence (Expectations).*

Peps, Dr. Parker: Eminent physician who supervises the birth of Little Paul Dombey and is later present at his death. *One of the Court Physicians, and a man of immense reputation for assisting at the increase of great families, was walking up and down the drawing-room with his hands behind him, to the unspeakable admiration of the family surgeon (Dombey).*

Perch: Messenger to Dombey and Son. *When Perch the messenger, whose place was on a little bracket, like a time-piece, saw Mr. Dombey come in – or rather when he felt that he was coming, for he had usually an instinctive sense of his approach – he hurried into Mr. Dombey's room, stirred the fire, quarried fresh coals from the bowels of the coal-box, hung the newspaper to air upon the fender, put the chair ready, and the screen in its place, and was round upon his heel on the instant of Mr. Dombey's entrance, to take his great-coat and hat, and hang them up (Dombey).*

Perch, Mrs.: Perch's over-fertile wife. *Perch . . . jogging his elbow, begged his pardon, but wished to say in his ear, Did he think he could arrange to send home to England a jar of preserved ginger, cheap, for Mrs. Perch's own eating, in the course of her recovery from her next confinement (Dombey).*

Perker: A Gray's Inn solicitor who acts as election agent for Slumkey at Eatanswill and represents Pickwick in the case of Bardell and Pickwick. *A little high-dried man, with a dark squeezed-up face, and small restless black eyes, that kept winking and twinkling on each side of his little inquisitive nose, as if they were playing a perpetual game of peep-bo with that feature. He was dressed all in black, with boots as shiny as his eyes, a low white neckcloth, and a clean shirt with a frill to it. A gold watch-chain and seals, depended from his fob. He carried his black kid gloves in his hands, not on them; and as he spoke, thrust his wrists beneath his coat-tails, with the air of a man who was in the habit of propounding some regular posers (Pickwick).*

Perkins, Mrs.: See **Piper, Mrs. Anastasia** (*Bleak House*).

Perkinsop, Mary Anne: One of Mrs. Lirriper's succession of servants, enticed away for more wages by Miss Wozenham. *Was worth her weight in gold as overawing lodgers without driving them away, for lodgers would be far more sparing of their bells with Mary Anne than I ever knew them to be with Maid or Mistress, which is a great triumph especially when accompanied with a cast in the eye and a bag of bones, but it was the steadiness of her way with them through her father's having failed in Pork (Christmas Stories – 'Mrs. Lirriper's Lodgings').*

Pessell: A vice-president of the anatomy and medicine session at the second meeting of the Mudfog Association (*Mudfog*).

'Pet': See **Meagles, Minnie** (*Dorrit*).

Peter, Lord: Noble suitor of Julia Manners, for her money, who is unintentionally cut out by Alexander Trott. He is killed riding. *Lord Peter, who had been detained beyond his time by drinking champagne and riding a steeple-chase, went back to the Honourable Augustus Flair's, and drank more champagne, and rode another steeple-chase, and was thrown and killed (Boz – 'Great Winglebury Duel').*

Petowker, Henrietta: Actress at the Theatre Royal, Drury Lane, and friend of the Kenwigs family. She marries Lillyvick, but deserts him for a half-pay captain. *The great lion of the party, being the daughter of a theatrical fireman, who 'went on' in the* *pantomime, and had the greatest turn for the stage that was ever known, being able to sing and recite in a manner that brought the tears into Mrs. Kenwigs's eyes (Nickleby).*

Pettifer, Tom: Captain Jorgan's steward, whose hat contains the answer to the mystery. *A man of a certain plump neatness, with a curly whisker, and elaborately nautical in a jacket, and shoes, and all things correspondent. (Christmas Stories – 'Message from the Sea').*

Phib: See **Phoebe** *(Nickleby).*

Phibbs: Haberdasher neighbour of Trinkle who assists Inspector Wield's inquiries in the case of Eliza Grimwood's murder *(Reprinted – 'Three "Detective" Anecdotes').*

Phil: Serving man at Our School. *Our retrospective glance presents Phil as a shipwrecked carpenter, cast away upon the desert island of a school, and carrying into practice an ingenious inkling of many trades. He mended whatever was broken, and made whatever was wanted. . . . We particularly remember that Phil had a sovereign contempt for learning: which engenders in us a respect for his sagacity (Reprinted – 'Our School').*

Phoebe: Crippled daughter of 'Lamps', and exemplar to Jackson. *The room upstairs was a very clean white room with a low roof. Its only inmate lay on a couch that brought her face to a level with the window. The couch was white too; and her simple dress or wrapper being light blue, like the band around her hair, she had an ethereal look, and a fanciful appearance of lying among clouds. . . . He guessed her to be thirty. The charm of her transparent face and large bright brown eyes was, not that they were passively resigned, but that they were actively and thoroughly cheerful. Even her busy hands, which of their own thinness alone might have besought compassion, plied their task with a gay courage that made mere compassion an unjustifiable assumption of superiority, and an impertinence (Christmas Stories – 'Mugby Junction').*

Phoebe (Phib): The Squeerses' maid. *The hungry servant attended Miss Squeers in her own room according to custom, to curl her hair, perform the other little offices of her toilet, and administer as much flattery as she could get up (Nickleby).*

Phunky: Serjeant Snubbin's junior counsel for Pickwick in Bardell and Pickwick. *Although an infant barrister, he was a full-grown man. He had a very nervous manner, and a painful hesitation in his speech; it did not appear to be a natural defect, but seemed rather the result of timidity, arising from the consciousness of being 'kept down' by want of means, or interest, or connexion, or impudence, as the case might be (Pickwick).*

Pickles: The fishmonger from whose shop the magic fishbone comes in Alice Rainbird's romantic tale ('Holiday Romance').

Pickleson ('Rinaldo di Velasco'): A giant, exhibited by Mim who leases him from his mother. *This giant*

when on view figured as a Roman. He was a languid young man, which I attribute to the distance betwixt his extremities. He had a little head and less in it, he had weak eyes and weak knees, and altogether you couldn't look at him without feeling that there was greatly too much of him both for his joints and his mind. But he was an amiable though timid young man (his mother let him out and spent the money) (Christmas Stories – 'Doctor Marigold').

Pickwick, Samuel: General Chairman – Member Pickwick Club and leader of a group of Pickwickians – Snodgrass, Tupman, and Winkle – in a series of travels and adventures. *A casual observer, adds the secretary, to whose notes we are indebted for the following account – a casual observer might possibly have remarked nothing extraordinary in the bald head, and circular spectacles, which were intently turned towards his (the secretary's) face, during the reading of the above resolutions: to those who knew that the gigantic brain of Pickwick was working beneath that forehead, and that the beaming eyes of Pickwick were twinkling behind those glasses, the sight was indeed an interesting one. There sat the man who had traced to their source the mighty ponds of Hampstead, and agitated the scientific world with his Theory of Tittlebats, as calm and unmoved as the deep waters of the one on a frosty day, or as a solitary specimen of the other in the inmost recesses of an earthen jar. And how much more interesting did the spectacle become when, starting into full life and animation, as a simultaneous call for 'Pickwick' burst from his followers, that illustrious man slowly mounted into the Windsor chair, on which he had been previously seated, and addressed the club himself had founded. What a study for an artist did that exciting scene present! The eloquent Pickwick, with one hand gracefully concealed behind his coat tails, and the other waving in air, to assist his glowing declamation; his elevated position revealing those tights and gaiters, which, had they clothed an ordinary man, might have passed without observation, but which, when Pickwick clothed them – if we may use the expression – inspired voluntary awe and respect (Pickwick).*

Pidger: Deceased acquaintance of Lavinia Spenlow, believed by her to have been in love with her *(Copperfield).*

Piff, Miss: One of the attendants at Mugby Junction refreshment room *(Christmas Stories – 'Mugby Junction').*

Pigeon, Thomas: See **Thompson, Tally-Ho** *(Reprinted – 'Detective Police').*

Pilkins: The Dombey family physician when Little Paul is born. *The family surgeon, who had regularly puffed the case for the last six weeks, among all his patients, friends, and acquaintances, as one to which he was in hourly expectation day and night of being summoned, in conjuction with Doctor Parker Peps (Dombey).*

Pinch, Ruth: Tom's sister, governess to a Camberwell family. Marries John Westlock. *She had a good face; a very mild and prepossessing face; and a pretty little* *figure – slight and short, but remarkable for its neatness. There was something of her brother, much of him indeed, in a certain gentleness of manner, and in her look of timid trustfulness (Chuzzlewit).*

Pinch, Tom: Pecksniff's ingenuous assistant. *An ungainly, awkward-looking man, extremely short-sighted ... but notwithstanding his attire, and his clumsy figure, which a great stoop in his shoulders, and a ludicrous habit he had of thrusting his head forward, by no means redeemed, one would not have been disposed (unless Mr. Pecksniff said so) to consider him a bad fellow by any means. He was perhaps about thirty, but he might have been almost any age between sixteen and sixty: being one of those strange creatures who never decline into an ancient appearance, but look their oldest when they are very young, and get it over at once (Chuzzlewit).*

Pip: Friend of Montague Tigg. *'Mr. Pip – theatrical man – capital man to know – oh, capital man!' (Chuzzlewit).*

Pip (Philip Pirrip, jun.): Narrator and central figure of the novel about the rise and fall of his great expectations from a mysterious benefactor. *My father's family name being Pirrip, and my christian name Philip, my infant tongue could make of both names nothing longer or more explicit than Pip. So, I called myself Pip, and came to be called Pip (Expectations).*

Pipchin, Mrs.: Proprietor of the children's boarding-house at Brighton where the Dombey children stay. *A marvellous ill-favoured, ill-conditioned old lady, of a stooping figure, with a mottled face, like bad marble, a hook nose, and a hard grey eye, that looked as if it might have been hammered at on an anvil without sustaining any injury. Forty years at least had elapsed since the Peruvian mines had been the death of Mr. Pipchin; but his relict still wore black bombazeen, of such a lustreless, deep, dead, sombre shade, that gas itself couldn't light her up after dark, and her presence was a quencher to any number of candles. She was generally spoken of as 'a great manager' of children; and the secret of her management was, to give them everything that they didn't like, and nothing that they did – which was found to sweeten their dispositions very much. She was such a bitter old lady, that one was tempted to believe there had been some mistake in the application of the Peruvian machinery, and that all her waters of gladness and milk of human kindness, had been pumped out dry, instead of the mines (Dombey).*

Piper, Professor: A boarder at the National Hotel, in America, where Martin Chuzzlewit stays before embarking for Eden *(Chuzzlewit).*

Piper, Mrs. Anastasia and **Perkins, Mrs.:** Neighbours of Krook's and interested onlookers at the events at his house. *The potboy of the Sol's Arms appearing with her supper-pint well frothed, Mrs. Piper accepts that tankard and retires in-doors, first giving a fair good-night to Mrs. Perkins, who has had her own pint in her hand ever since it was fetched from the same hostelry by young Perkins before he was sent to bed (Bleak House).*

Pipkin, Mr., M.R.C.S.: Speaker at the anatomy and medicine session of the second meeting of the Mudfog Association. *Read a short but most interesting communication in which he sought to prove the complete belief of Sir William Courtenay, otherwise Thom, recently shot at Canterbury, in the Homœopathic system (Mudfog).*

Pipkin, Nathaniel: The parish clerk, in the tale of that title, who unsuccessfully loves Maria Lobbs. *A harmless, inoffensive, good-natured being, with a turned-up nose, and rather turned-in legs: a cast in his eye, and halt in his gait (Pickwick).*

Pipson, Miss: Fellow pupil of Master B. at Miss Griffin's school. *Having curly light hair and blue eyes (which was my idea of anything mortal and feminine that was called Fair) (Christmas Stories – 'Haunted House').*

Pirrip, Philip, jun.: See **Pip** *(Expectations).*

Pirrip, Philip, sen., Georgiana, Alexander, Bartholomew, Abraham, Tobias, and **Roger:** Pip's deceased father, mother, and infant brothers. *My first fancies regarding what they were like, were unreasonably derived from their tombstones. The shape of the letters on my father's, gave me an odd idea that he was a square, stout, dark man, with curly black hair. From the character and turn of the inscription, 'Also Georgiana Wife of the Above,' I drew a childish conclusion that my mother was freckled and sickly. To five little stone lozenges, each about a foot and a half long, which were arranged in a neat row beside their grave, and were sacred to the memory of five little brothers of mine ... I am indebted for a belief I religiously entertained that they had all been born on their backs with their hands in their trousers-pockets, and had never taken them out in this state of existence (Expectations).*

Pitcher: Pupil at Dotheboys Hall who contracts a fever. *'Never was such a boy, I do believe,' said Mrs. Squeers; 'whatever he has is always catching too. I say it's obstinacy' (Nickleby).*

Pitt, Jane: A matron at the school, where she is Old Cheeseman's only friend. They marry. *She was not quite pretty; but she had a very frank, honest, bright face, and all our fellows were fond of her. She was uncommonly neat and cheerful, and uncommonly comfortable and kind. And if anything was the matter with a fellow's mother, he always went and showed the letter to Jane (Christmas Stories – 'Schoolboy's Story').*

Plornish, Thomas: A plasterer, tenant of Casby in Bleeding Heart Yard. He and his wife befriend the Dorrits and Clennam, who lodge Cavalletto with them. *He was one of those many wayfarers on the road of life, who seem to be afflicted with supernatural corns, rendering it impossible for them to keep up even with their lame competitors. A willing, working, soft-hearted, not hard-headed fellow, Plornish took his fortune as smoothly as could be expected; but it was a rough one. It so rarely happened that anybody seemed to want him, it was such an exceptional case when his powers were in any request, that his misty mind could* *not make out how it happened. He took it as it came, therefore; he tumbled into all kinds of difficulties, and tumbled out of them; and, by tumbling through life, got himself considerably bruised. . . . A smooth-cheeked, fresh-coloured, sandy-whiskered man of thirty. Long in the legs, yielding at the knees, foolish in the face, flannel-jacketed, lime-whitened (Dorrit).*

Plornish, Mrs. Thomas (Sally): Plornish's wife. *A young woman, made somewhat slatternly in herself and her belongings by poverty; and so dragged at by poverty and the children together, that their united forces had already dragged her face into wrinkles (Dorrit).*

Pluck: One of Hawk's followers. *A gentleman with a flushed face and a flash air (Nickleby).*

Plummer, Bertha: Caleb's blind daughter, Edward's sister. To make her happy, Caleb pretends that their surroundings are not poor, and that Tackleton is not the hard master he is. Bertha comes to love her conception of Tackleton and her father has to reveal his deception. *The Blind Girl never knew that ceilings were discoloured, walls blotched and bare of plaster here and there, high crevices unstopped, and widening every day, beams mouldering and tending downward. The Blind Girl never knew that iron was rusting, wood rotting, paper peeling off; the size, and shape, and true proportion of the dwelling, withering away. The Blind Girl never knew that . . . sorrow and faint-heartedness were in the house; that Caleb's scanty hairs were turning greyer and more grey, before her sightless face. The Blind Girl never knew they had a master, cold, exacting, and uninterested – never knew that Tackleton was Tackleton in short (Christmas Books – 'Cricket').*

Plummer, Caleb: Father of Edward and Bertha, a poor toymaker employed by Gruff and Tackleton. *A little, meagre, thoughtful, dingy-faced man, who seemed to have made himself a great-coat from the sack-cloth covering of some old box; for, when he turned to shut the door, and keep the weather out, he disclosed upon the back of that garment, the inscription G & T in large black capitals. Also the word GLASS in bold characters (Christmas Books – 'Cricket').*

Plummer, Edward: Caleb's son, Bertha's brother. Returning after long absence abroad, he finds his sweetheart, May Fielding, about to marry Tackleton. He disguises himself as an old man to test the strength of her affections, and takes her for his own on her intended wedding morning. *Had long white hair, good features, singularly bold and well defined for an old man, and dark, bright, penetrating eyes (Christmas Books – 'Cricket').*

Plunder: One of Miss Flite's birds *(Bleak House).*

Pocket, Alick, Fanny, Jane, and **Joe:** Four of Matthew and Belinda's children, younger brothers and sisters to Herbert *(Expectations).*

Pocket, Herbert: Matthew's son, elder brother of Alick, Fanny, Jane, and Joe. Pip's close friend. They share lodgings and conspire to hide Magwitch and get

him out of England. Through Pip, Herbert gets a partnership in Clarriker and Co. and is enabled to marry Clara Barley. *I had never seen any one then, and I have never seen any one since, who more strongly expressed to me, in every look and tone, a natural incapacity to do anything secret and mean. There was something wonderfully hopeful about his general air, and something that at the same time whispered to me he would never be very successful or rich. . . . He was still a pale young gentleman, and had a certain conquered languor about him in the midst of his spirits and briskness, that did not seem indicative of natural strength. He had not a handsome face, but it was better than handsome: being extremely amiable and cheerful (Expectations).*

Pocket, Matthew: Father of Herbert, Alick, Fanny, Jane, and Joe. Cousin to Miss Havisham. *A gentleman with a rather perplexed expression of face, and with his very grey hair disordered on his head, as if he didn't quite see his way to putting anything straight. . . . By degrees I learnt, and chiefly from Herbert, that Mr. Pocket had been educated at Harrow and at Cambridge, where he had distinguished himself; but that when he had had the happiness of marrying Mrs. Pocket very early in life, he had impaired his prospects and taken up the calling of a Grinder (Expectations).*

Pocket, Mrs. Matthew (Belinda): Matthew's wife, mother of Herbert, Alick, Jane, Joe, and Fanny. *The only daughter of a certain accidental deceased Knight, who had invented for himself a conviction that his deceased father would have been made a Baronet but for somebody's determined opposition arising out of entirely personal motives. . . . He had directed Mrs. Pocket to be brought up from her cradle as one who in the nature of things must carry a title, and who was to be guarded from the acquisition of plebeian domestic knowledge. So successful a watch and ward had been established over the young lady by this judicious parent, that she had grown up highly ornamental, but perfectly helpless and useless (Expectations).*

Pocket, Sarah: Toadying cousin of Miss Havisham, who leaves her a derisory legacy in her will. *A little dry brown corrugated old woman, with a small face that might have been made of walnut shells, and a large mouth like a cat's without the whiskers (Expectations).*

Podder: A renowned member of the All-Muggleton Cricket Club. *The hitherto unconquered Podder (Pickwick).*

'Poddles': Pet name of one of Betty Higden's charges *(Mutual Friend).*

Podgers, John: Well-to-do widower of Windsor in the time of James I in Mr. Pickwick's tale. *Broad, sturdy, Dutch-built, short, and a very hard eater, as men of his figure often are. . . . He had several times been seen to look after fat oxen on market days, and had even been heard, by persons of good credit and reputation, to chuckle at the sight, and say to himself with great glee, 'Live beef, live beef!' (Humphrey).*

Podsnap, Georgiana: The Podsnaps' only daughter, whom Lammle attempts to manœuvre into marrying

Fledgeby. *This young rocking-horse was being trained in her mother's art of prancing in a stately manner without ever getting on. But the high parental action was not yet imparted to her, and in truth she was but an under-sized damsel, with high shoulders, low spirits, chilled elbows, and a rasped surface of nose, who seemed to take occasional frosty peeps out of childhood into womanhood, and to shrink back again, overcome by her mother's head-dress and her father from head to foot – crushed by the mere dead-weight of Podsnappery* (Mutual Friend).

Podsnap, John: Father of Georgiana. A complacent businessman. *Two little light-coloured wiry wings, one on either side of his else bald head, looking as like his hair-brushes as his hair, dissolving view of red beads on his forehead, large allowance of crumpled shirt-collar up behind. || Mr. Podsnap was well to do, and stood very high in Mr. Podsnap's opinion. Beginning with a good inheritance, he had married a good inheritance, and had thriven exceedingly in the Marine Insurance way, and was quite satisfied. He never could make out why everybody was not quite satisfied, and he felt conscious that he set a brilliant social example in being particularly well satisfied with most things, and, above all other things, with himself* (Mutual Friend).

Podsnap, Mrs. John: Podsnap's wife, Georgiana's mother. *Quantity of bone, neck and nostrils like a rocking-horse, hard features, majestic head-dress in which Podsnap has hung golden offerings* (Mutual Friend).

Pogram, The Hon. Elijah: A rabidly nationalistic American Congressman encountered by Martin Chuzzlewit in his travels. *'One of the master minds of our country.' || He had straight black hair, parted up the middle of his head, and hanging down upon his coat; a little fringe of hair upon his chin; wore no neck-cloth; a white hat; a suit of black, long in the sleeves, and short in the legs; soiled brown stockings, and laced shoes. His complexion, naturally muddy, was rendered muddier by too strict an economy of soap and water; and the same observation will apply to the washable part of his attire, which he might have changed with comfort to himself, and gratification to his friends. He was about five-and-thirty; was crushed and jammed up in a heap, under the shade of a large green cotton umbrella; and ruminated over his tobacco-plug like a cow* (Chuzzlewit).

Polly: Waitress upon Guppy and Jobling at the Slap-Bang dining-house. *The waitress returns, bearing what is apparently a model of the tower of Babel, but what is really a pile of plates, and flat tin dish-covers* (Bleak House).

Polreath, David: Resident of Lanrean questioned by Captain Jorgan (Christmas Stories – 'Message from the Sea').

Ponto: Jingle's sagacious dog of former days. *'Surprising instinct – out shooting one day – entering enclosure – whistled – dog stopped – whistled again – Ponto – no go; stock still – called him – Ponto, Ponto – wouldn't move – dog transfixed – staring at a board – looked up, saw an inscription – "Gamekeeper has orders to shoot all dogs found in this enclosure" – wouldn't pass it – wonderful dog – valuable dog that – very'* (Pickwick).

Poodles: A comical mongrel dog found starving at the door of the East London Children's Hospital and adopted there. *Trotting about among the beds, on familiar terms with all the patients. . . . An admirer of his mental endowments has presented him with a collar bearing the legend, 'Judge not Poodles by external appearances'* (Uncommercial – 'Small Star in the East' and 'On an Amateur Beat').

Poor Relation, The: See **Michael** (Christmas Stories – 'Poor Relation').

Pordage, Mr. Commissioner and **Mrs.:** Self-styled 'Government' of Silver-Store Island and his wife. In later years he is officially appointed Governor and a K.C.B., and dies of jaundice. *He was a stiff-jointed, high-nosed old gentleman, without an ounce of fat on him, of a very angry temper and a very yellow complexion. Mrs. Commissioner Pordage, making allowance for difference of sex, was much the same* (Christmas Stories – 'English Prisoners').

Porkenham (Sidney, Mrs. Sidney, and the Misses), Griggs, and **Slummintowken Families:** Social rivals of the Nupkins family, to whom the latter have boasted of their intimacy with Captain Fitz-Marshall, later unmasked as Jingle (Pickwick).

Porter, Emma: Mrs. Porter's daughter, contemptuous of the Gattleton girls for showing off in private theatricals. *Miss P., by the bye, had only the week before made 'an exhibition' of herself for four days, behind a counter at a fancy fair, to all and every of her Majesty's liege subjects who were disposed to pay a shilling each for the privilege of seeing some four dozen girls flirting with strangers, and playing at shop* (Boz – 'Mrs. Joseph Porter').

Porter, Mrs. Joseph: Mother of Emma. A notorious scandal-monger and great rival of the Gattletons, whose private theatricals she contrives to sabotage. *The good folks of Clapham and its vicinity stood very much in awe of scandal and sarcasm; and thus Mrs. Joseph Porter was courted, and flattered, and caressed, and invited, for much the same reason that induces a poor author, without a farthing in his pocket, to behave with extraordinary civility to a twopenny postman* (Boz – 'Mrs. Joseph Porter').

Porters, Mr.: See under **Twinkleton, Miss** (Drood).

Potkins, William: Waiter at the Blue Boar, Rochester (Expectations).

Pott: Editor of the *Eatanswill Gazette,* of whom Winkle falls foul over a newspaper item linking him with Mrs. Pott. *A tall, thin man, with a sandy-coloured head inclined to baldness, and a face in which solemn importance was blended with a look of unfathomable profundity* (Pickwick).

Pott, Mrs.: Pott's wife. *All men whom mighty genius has raised to a proud eminence in the world, have usually some little weakness which appears the more* conspicuous from the contrast it presents to their general character. If Mr. Pott had a weakness, it was, perhaps, that he was rather too submissive to the somewhat contemptuous control and sway of his wife (Pickwick).

Potter, Thomas and **Robert Smithers:** Two City clerks who spend their quarter's pay celebrating the receipt of it and paying the resultant fines. Their incomes were limited, but their friendship was unbounded. They lived in the same street, walked into town every morning at the same hour, dined at the same slap-bang every day, and revelled in each other's company every night. They were knit together by the closest ties of intimacy and friendship, or, as Mr. Thomas Potter touchingly observed, they were 'thick-and-thin pals, and nothing but it'. There was a spice of romance in Mr. Smithers's disposition, a ray of poetry, a gleam of misery, a sort of consciousness of he didn't exactly know what, coming across him he didn't precisely know why – which stood out in fine relief against the off-hand, dashing, amateur-pickpocket-sort-of-manner, which distinguished Mr. Potter in an eminent degree (Boz –'Making a Night of it').

Potterson, Abbey: Sister of Job and landlady of the Six Jolly Fellowship Porters. Miss Potterson, sole proprietor and manager of the Fellowship-Porters, reigned supreme on her throne, the Bar, and a man must have drunk himself mad drunk indeed if he thought he could contest a point with her. Being known on her own authority as Miss Abbey Potterson, some water-side heads, which (like the water) were none of the clearest, harboured muddled notions that, because of her dignity and firmness, she was named after, or in some sort related to, the Abbey at Westminster. But Abbey was only short for Abigail, by which name Miss Potterson had been christened at Limehouse Church, some sixty and odd years before.... She was a tall, upright, well-favoured woman, though severe of countenance, and had more of the air of a school-mistress than mistress of the Six Jolly Fellowship-Porters (Mutual Friend).

Potterson, Job: Abbey's brother, a steward in the ship in which John Harmon travels from Cape Colony to England. 'Lord bless my soul and body,' cried Mr. Inspector. 'Talk of trades, Miss Abbey, and the way they set their marks on men' (a subject which nobody had approached); 'who wouldn't know your brother to be a Steward! There's a bright and ready twinkle in his eye, there's a neatness in his action, there's a smartness in his figure, there's an air of reliability about him in case you wanted a basin, which points out the steward!' (Mutual Friend).

Pouch, Mrs. Joe: A widow whom Trooper George might have married. 'It was a chance for me, certainly,' returns the trooper, half-laughingly, half-seriously, 'but I shall never settle down into a respectable man now. Joe Pouch's widow might have done me good – there was something in her – and something of her – but I couldn't make up my mind to it' (Bleak House).

Poulter, Mr. and **Mrs.:** A reformed couple, charac-

ters assumed by Gabblewig and Rosina in order to unmask Slap (Nightingale's Diary).

Powler Family: An ancient line with which Mrs. Sparsit claims connection through her deceased husband. Could trace themselves so exceedingly far back that it was not surprising if they sometimes lost themselves – which they had rather frequently done, as respected horse-flesh, blind-hookey, Hebrew monetary transactions, and the Insolvent Debtors Court (Hard Times).

Pratchett, Mrs.: Head chambermaid of the hotel where Christopher works. Now Mrs. Pratchett was not a waitress, but a chambermaid. Now a chambermaid may be married; if Head, generally is married, – or says so. It comes to the same thing as expressing what is customary. (N.B. Mr. Pratchett is in Australia, and his address there is 'the Bush') (Christmas Stories – 'Somebody's Luggage').

Precedent: One of Miss Flite's birds (Bleak House).

Prentice Knights, later **United Bull-Dogs:** A brotherhood of London apprentices, led by Sim Tappertit, which allied itself with the Protestant cause and joined in the Gordon Riots (Rudge).

Price: A prisoner for debt, encountered by Pickwick at Namby's. A coarse vulgar young man of about thirty, with a sallow face and harsh voice: evidently possessed of that knowledge of the world, and captivating freedom of manner, which is to be acquired in public-house parlours, and at low billiard-tables (Pickwick).

Price, Matilda ('Tilda): Friend of Fanny Squeers. She marries Browdie. A miller's daughter of only eighteen (Nickleby).

Prig, Betsey: A nurse at St. Bartholomew's Hospital who shares engagements, including the nursing of Lewsome, with Mrs. Gamp until their famous quarrel. Mrs. Prig was of the Gamp build, but not so fat; and her voice was deeper and more like a man's. She had also a beard (Chuzzlewit).

Priscilla: The Jellybys' maid. 'Priscilla drinks – she's always drinking. It's a great shame and a great story of you, if you say you didn't smell her to-day. It was as bad as a public-house, waiting at dinner' (Bleak House).

Prodgit, Mrs.: Augustus George Meek's nurse. Stood in the corner behind the door, consuming Sherry Wine. From the nutty smell of that beverage pervading the apartment, I have no doubt she was consuming a second glassful. She wore a black bonnet of large dimensions, and was copious in figure. The expression of her countenance was severe and discontented (Reprinted – 'Births. Mrs. Meek, of a Son').

Prosee: Member of the Mudfog Association (Mudfog).

Pross, Miss: Companion of Lucie Manette, in trying to protect whom she struggles with Madame Defarge and the latter is killed. A wild-looking woman, whom even in his agitation, Mr. Lorry observed to be all of a red colour, and to have red hair, and to be dressed in some extraordinary tight-fitting fashion, and to have on her head a most wonderful bonnet like a Grenadier wooden measure, and good measure too, or a great Stilton cheese. . . . ('I really think this must be a man!' was Mr. Lorry's breathless reflection) (Two Cities).

Pross, Solomon (alias **John Barsad**): Miss Pross's corrupt brother who fleeces her of her possessions and abandons her. An informer in England and later spy and turnkey in France. *Of what profession? Gentleman. Ever been kicked? Might have been. Frequently? No. Ever kicked downstairs? Decidedly not; once received a kick on the top of a staircase, and fell downstairs of his own accord (Two Cities).*

Provis: See **Magwitch, Abel** (Expectations).

Pruffle: Manservant to the scientific gentleman Pickwick meets at Clifton. *The ingenious Mr. Pruffle (Pickwick).*

Pubsey and Co.: Moneylending business in the City of London run by Riah for Fledgeby (Mutual Friend).

Puffer, Princess: Keeper of the East End London opium den frequented by Jasper. *'Ah, my poor nerves! I got Heavens-hard drunk for sixteen year afore I took to this; but this don't hurt me, not to speak of. And it takes away the hunger as well as wittles, deary'* (Drood).

Pugstyles: A constituent of Gregsbury, M.P., and leader of the deputation demanding his resignation. *A plump old gentleman in a violent heat (Nickleby).*

Pumblechook, Uncle: Joe Gargery's uncle, a well-to-do corn-chandler. A notable hypocrite, he hints that he is Pip's secret benefactor. *A large hard-breathing middle-aged slow man, with a mouth like a fish, dull staring eyes, and sandy hair standing upright on his head, so that he looked as if he had just been all but choked, and had that moment come to. // Besides being possessed by my sister's idea that a mortifying and penitential character ought to be imparted to my diet . . . his conversation consisted of nothing but arithmetic. On my politely bidding him Good-morning, he said, pompously, 'Seven times nine, boy?' (Expectations).*

Pumpkinskull, Professor: Speaker at the zoology and botany session of the second meeting of the Mudfog Association. *No gentleman attending that section could fail to be aware of the fact that the youth of the present age evinced, by their behaviour in the streets, and at all places of public resort, a considerable lack of that gallantry and gentlemanly feeling which, in more ignorant times, had been thought becoming. He wished to know whether it were possible that a constant outward application of bears'-grease by the young gentlemen about town had imperceptibly infused into those unhappy persons something of the nature and quality of the bear (Mudfog).*

Pupford, Miss Euphemia: Principal of an academy for six young ladies of tender years. *One of the most amiable of her sex; it necessarily follows that she possesses a sweet temper, and would own to the possession of a great deal of sentiment if she considered it quite reconcilable with her duty to parents.*

// **Miss Pupford's Assistant** *has a little more bone than Miss Pupford, but is of the same trim orderly, diminutive cast, and, from long contemplation, admiration, and imitation of Miss Pupford, has grown like her (Christmas Stories – 'Tom Tiddler's Ground').*

Pupker, Sir Matthew, M.P.: Chairman of the United Metropolitan Improved Hot Muffin and Crumpet Baking and Punctual Delivery Company. *Had a little round head with a flaxen wig on the top of it (Nickleby).*

Purblind: Member of the Mudfog Association (Mudfog).

Purday, Captain: Ardent supporter of Bung for beadle of 'Our Parish'. *A determined opponent of the constituted authorities, whoever they may chance to be (Boz – 'Election for Beadle').* Purday is the unnamed 'Half-pay Captain' in the Boz sketch of that title.

Pyegrave, Charley: Son of a duke. Client of Miss Mowcher. *'What a man he is! There's a whisker! As to Charley's legs, if they were only a pair (which they ain't), they'd defy competition'* (Copperfield).

Pyke: One of Sir Mulberry Hawk's followers. *A sharp-faced gentleman (Nickleby).*

Quale: A philanthropic friend of the Jellybys, wishing to marry Caddy. *A loquacious young man . . . with large shining knobs for temples, and his hair all brushed to the back of his head . . . having a great deal to say for himself about Africa, and a project of his for teaching the coffee colonists to teach the natives to turn piano-forte legs and establish an export trade (Bleak House).*

Queerspeck, Professor: Speaker at the mechanical science session of the first meeting of the Mudfog Association. *Exhibited an elegant model of a portable railway, neatly mounted in a green case, for the waistcoat pocket. By attaching this beautiful instrument to his boots, any Bank or public-office clerk could transport himself from his place of residence to his place of business, at the easy rate of sixty-five miles an hour, which, to gentlemen of sedentary pursuits, would be an incalculable advantage (Mudfog).*

Quickear: One of the policemen visiting sailors' haunts with the Uncommercial Traveller (Uncommercial – 'Poor Mercantile Jack').

Quilp, Daniel: The villain of the story: a money-lender who cheats and ruins people on every hand and ill-treats his wife. Eventually pursued by the police, he drowns in the Thames. *An elderly man of remarkably hard features and forbidding aspect, and so low in stature as to be quite a dwarf, though his head and face were large enough for the body of a giant. His black eyes were restless, sly, and cunning; his mouth and chin, bristly with the stubble of a coarse hard beard; and his complexion was one of that kind which never looks clean or wholesome. But what added most to the grotesque appearance of his face, was a ghastly smile, which, appearing to be the mere result of habit* and to have no connection with any mirthful or complacent feeling, constantly revealed the few discoloured fangs that were yet scattered in his mouth, and gave him the aspect of a panting dog. His dress consisted of a large high-crowned hat, a worn dark suit, a pair of capacious shoes, and a dirty white neckerchief sufficiently limp and crumpled to disclose the greater part of his wiry throat. Such hair as he had, was of a grizzled black, cut short and straight upon his temples, and hanging in a frowsy fringe about his ears. His hands, which were of a rough coarse grain, were very dirty; his finger-nails were crooked, long, and yellow (Curiosity Shop).

Quilp, Mrs. Daniel (Betsey): Quilp's wife and Mrs. Jiniwin's daughter. She re-marries happily after Quilp's death. A pretty little, mild-spoken, blue-eyed woman, who having allied herself in wedlock to the dwarf in one of those strange infatuations of which examples are by no means scarce, performed a sound practical penance for her folly, every day of her life (Curiosity Shop).

Quinch, Mrs.: The oldest pensioner at Titbull's. 'Mrs. Quinch being the oldest and have totally lost her head' (Uncommercial – 'Titbull's Alms-Houses').

Quinion: Murdstone and Grinby's manager who introduces David Copperfield to Micawber (Copperfield).

Rachael: The Coketown factory hand for love of whom Stephen Blackpool wishes to divorce his drunken wife. He saw another of the shawled figures in advance of him, at which he looked so keenly that perhaps its mere shadow indistinctly reflected on the wet pavement – if he could have seen it without the figure itself moving along from lamp to lamp, brightening and fading as it went – would have been enough to tell him who was there. . . . She turned, being then in the brightness of a lamp; and raising her hood a little, showed a quiet oval face, dark and rather delicate, irradiated by a pair of very gentle eyes, and further set off by the perfect order of her shining black hair. It was not a face in its first bloom; she was a woman five-and-thirty years of age (Hard Times).

Rachael, Mrs.: See **Chadband, Mrs.** (Bleak House).

Raddle: Mrs. Raddle's husband. 'Oh! If ever a woman was troubled with a ruffi'nly creetur, that takes a pride and a pleasure in disgracing his wife on every possible occasion afore strangers, I am that woman!' (Pickwick).

Raddle, Mrs. (Mary Ann): Raddle's wife. Mrs. Cluppins's sister and Bob Sawyer's landlady at Lant Street, Borough. A little fierce woman bounced into the room, all in a tremble with passion, and pale with rage (Pickwick).

Radfoot, George: The seaman whose body is mistaken for Harmon's. Third mate on the ship in which Harmon had been returning to England, he had arranged to exchange with Harmon the clothes in which his body is clothed when found in the Thames by Hexam (Mutual Friend).

Rags: One of Miss Flite's birds (Bleak House).

Rainbird, Alice: 'Bride' of Robin Redforth and author of the romantic tale of Princess Alicia ('Holiday Romance').

Rairyganoo, Sally: One of Mrs. Lirriper's succession of maids. Which I still suspect of Irish extraction though family represented Cambridge, else why abscond with a bricklayer of the Limerick persuasion and be married in pattens not waiting till his black eye was decently got round with all the company fourteen in number and one horse fighting outside on the roof of the vehicle (Christmas Stories – 'Mrs. Lirriper's Legacy').

Ram Chowdar Doss Azuph Al Bowlar: Subject of an unlikely anecdote by Captain Helves, interrupted by dinner. 'A devilish pleasant fellow. As we were enjoying our hookahs one evening, in the cool verandah in front of his villa, we were rather surprised by the sudden appearance of thirty-four of his Kit-magars (for he had rather a large establishment there), accompanied by an equal number of Con-su-mars, approaching the house with a threatening aspect, and beating a tom-tom' (Boz – 'Steam Excursion'.

Rames, William: Second mate of the Golden Mary (Christmas Stories – 'Golden Mary').

Ramsey: Defendant in Bullman and Ramsey, the case discussed at length by Dodson and Fogg's clerks while Pickwick awaits attention (Pickwick).

Rarx: Passenger in the Golden Mary. He loses his reason in the long-boat after the wreck. An old gentleman, a good deal like a hawk if his eyes had been better and not so red, who was always talking, morning, noon, and night, about the gold discovery. But, whether he was making the voyage, thinking his old arms could dig for gold, or whether his speculation was to buy it, or to barter for it, or to cheat for it, or to snatch it anyhow from other people, was his secret (Christmas Stories – 'Golden Mary').

Ravender, William George: Captain of the Golden Mary. He dies in the long-boat after the wreck. I was apprenticed to the Sea when I was twelve years old, and I have encountered a great deal of rough weather, both literal and metaphorical. . . . I will add no more of the sort than that my name is William George Ravender, that I was born at Penrith half a year after my own father was drowned, and that I am on the second day of this present blessed Christmas week of one thousand eight hundred and fifty-six, fifty-six years of age (Christmas Stories – 'Golden Mary').

Raybrock, Mrs.: Draper and postmistress of Steepways village, Devon. Mother of Hugh and Alfred. A comely, elderly woman, short of stature, plump of form, sparkling and dark of eye, who, perfectly clean and neat herself, stood in the midst of her perfectly clean and neat arrangements. (Christmas Stories – 'Message from the Sea').

Raybrock, Alfred: A fisherman, younger brother to Hugh. Sweetheart and later husband of Kitty Tregarthen. A young fisherman of two or three and twenty, in the rough sea-dress of his craft, with a brown face, dark curling hair, and bright, modest eyes *under his Sou'wester hat, and with a frank, but simple and retiring manner (Christmas Stories – 'Message from the Sea').*

Raybrock, Hugh: Alfred's elder brother, a sailor presumed lost whose message and reappearance clear Tregarthen's name and enable Kitty and Alfred to marry. *A glance at this stranger assured the captain that he could be no other than the Seafaring Man (Christmas Stories – 'Message from the Sea').*

Raybrock, Mrs. Hugh (Margaret): Hugh's presumed widow. *A young widow, sitting at a neighbouring window across a little garden, engaged in needlework, with a young child sleeping on her bosom (Christmas Stories – 'Message from the Sea').*

Raybrock, Jorgan: Son of Alfred and Kitty, named after Captain Jorgan, who made their marriage possible (*Christmas Stories – 'Message from the Sea'*).

Raymond: Camilla's husband. Toadying relative of Miss Havisham. *'Cousin Raymond,' observed another lady, 'we are to love our neighbour.' 'Sarah Pocket,' returned Cousin Raymond, 'if a man is not his own neighbour, who is?' (Expectations).*

Red Whisker: Object of David Copperfield's jealousy at Dora Spenlow's birthday picnic. *Red Whisker pretended he could make a salad (which I don't believe), and obtruded himself on public notice. Some of the young ladies washed the lettuces for him, and sliced them under his directions. Dora was among these. I felt that fate had pitted me against this man, and one of us must fall (Copperfield).*

Redburn, Jack: One of Master Humphrey's closest friends and his librarian, steward, and household director. *He is something of a musician, something of an author, something of an actor, something of a painter, very much of a carpenter, and an extraordinary gardener, having had all his life a wonderful aptitude for learning everything that was of no use to him (Humphrey).*

Redforth, Lt.-Col. Robin: Alice Rainbird's 'bridegroom' in the romantic tale by his cousin William Tinkling, and himself author of the tale of Captain Boldheart ('Holiday Romance').

Redlaw: Chemist and lecturer who is visited by a phantom on Christmas Eve and endowed with the ability to forget past unhappiness, on condition that he passes the gift on to others. He does, with unhappy results, but Milly Swidger's goodness restores him. *Who could have seen his hollow cheek, his sunken brilliant eye; his black attired figure, indefinably grim, although well-knit and well-proportioned; his grizzled hair hanging, like tangled sea-weed, about his face, – as if he had been, through his whole life, a lonely mark for the chafing and beating of the great deep of humanity, – but might have said he looked like a haunted man? (Christmas Books – 'Haunted Man').*

Refractories: Female delinquents in the workhouse visited by the Uncommercial Traveller. *The oldest Refractory was, say twenty; youngest Refractory, say sixteen. I have never yet ascertained in the course of*

my uncommercial travels, why a Refractory habit should affect the tonsils and uvula; but, I have always observed that Refractories of both sexes and every grade, between a Ragged School and the Old Bailey, have one voice, in which the tonsils and the uvula gain a diseased ascendancy (Uncommercial – 'Wapping Workhouse').

Rest: One of Miss Flite's birds (*Bleak House*).

Reynolds, Miss: Inattentive fellow pupil of Rosa Bud at Miss Twinkleton's. *The impropriety of Miss Reynolds's appearing to stab herself in the band with a pin, is far too obvious, and too glaringly unlady-like, to be pointed out (Drood).*

Riah ('Aaron'): The Jew who runs Fledgeby's business for him and bears the odium meant for his master. He helps Lizzie Hexam and finally goes to share a home with Jenny Wren. *An old Jewish man in an ancient coat, long of skirt, and wide of pocket. A venerable man, bald and shining at the top of his head, and with long grey hair flowing down at its sides and mingling with his beard (Mutual Friend).*

Richard: Meg Veck's blacksmith fiancé. *A face as glowing as the iron on which his stout sledge-hammer daily rung. A handsome, well-made, powerful youngster he was; with eyes that sparkled like the red-hot droppings from a furnace fire; black hair that curled about his swarthy temples rarely; and a smile (Christmas Books – 'Chimes').*

Richard: Waiter at the Saracen's Head, Snow Hill (*Nickleby*).

Richards: The name by which Polly Toodle is required to be known while in service with the Dombeys. *Mrs. Toodle . . . dropped a curtsey and replied 'that perhaps if she was to be called out of her name, it would be considered in the wages' (Dombey).*

Rickits, Miss: Fellow pupil of Rosa Bud at Miss Twinkleton's. *A junior of weakly constitution (Drood).*

Riderhood, Roger ('Rogue'): Former partner of Jesse Hexam, whom he implicates in the supposed murder of Harmon. He blackmails Headstone after his attack on Wrayburn, but dies with him, of drowning, in a fight. *A waterside-man with a squinting leer (Mutual Friend).*

Riderhood, Pleasant: Roger's daughter, an unlicensed pawnbroker. She marries Venus. *In her four-and-twentieth year of life, Pleasant was already in her fifth year of this way of trade. . . . Why christened Pleasant, the late Mrs. Riderhood might possibly have been able at some time to explain, and possibly not. Her daughter had no information on that point. Pleasant she found herself, and she couldn't help it. She had not been consulted on the question, any more than on the question of her coming into these terrestrial parts, to want a name. Similarly, she found herself possessed of what is colloquially termed a swivel eye (derived from her father), which she might perhaps have declined if her sentiments on the subject had been taken. She was not otherwise positively ill-looking, though anxious, meagre, of a muddy com-*

plexion, and looking as old again as she really was (*Mutual Friend*).

Rigaud (alias **Blandois**, alias **Lagnier**): A Frenchman, imprisoned for murdering his wife (see **Barroneau, Madame Henri**). He escapes to England, tries to blackmail Mrs. Clennam for suppressing her husband's uncle's will, but is killed when the house in which he is awaiting her collapses. *His eyes, too close together, were not so nobly set in his head as those of the king of beasts are in his, and they were sharp rather than bright – pointed weapons with little surface to betray them. They had no depth or change; they glittered, and they opened and shut. . . . He had a hook nose, handsome after its kind, but too high between the eyes, by probably just as much as his eyes were too near to one another. For the rest, he was large and tall in frame, had thin lips, where his thick moustache showed them at all, and a quantity of dry hair, of no definable colour, in its shaggy state, but shot with red (Dorrit).*

'Rinaldo di Velasco': See **Pickleson** (*Christmas Stories* – 'Doctor Marigold').

'Rob the Grinder': See **Toodle, Robin** (*Dombey*).

Robert: Servant to John ('At Dusk').

Robert, Uncle and **Aunt Jane:** Husband and wife, guests at Christmas dinner (*Boz* – 'Christmas Dinner').

Robinson: Mrs. Tibbs's maid. *By way of making her presence known to her mistress, had been giving sundry hems and sniffs outside the door during the preceding five minutes (Boz – 'Boarding-House').*

Robinson: Husband of the youngest Miss Willis, who has to court her three sisters as well. *A gentleman in a public office, with a good salary and a little property of his own, beside (Boz – 'Four Sisters').*

Robinson: Clerk in Dombey's counting-house (*Dombey*).

Robinson, Mrs.: Robinson's wife, formerly the youngest of the four Misses Willis. *As the four sisters and Mr. Robinson continued to occupy the same house after this memorable occasion, and as the married sister, whoever she was, never appeared in public without the other three, we are not quite clear that the neighbours ever would have discovered the real Mrs. Robinson, but for a circumstance of the most gratifying description, which will happen occasionally in the best-regulated families (Boz – 'Four Sisters').*

Rodolph, Mr. and **Mrs. Jennings:** Amateur singers who encourage Amelia Martin's belief in her talents. *To hear them sing separately was divine, but when they went through the tragic duet of 'Red Ruffian, retire!' it was, as Miss Martin afterwards remarked, 'thrilling.' And why (as Mr. Jennings Rodolph observed) why were they not engaged at one of the patent theatres? If he was to be told that their voices were not powerful enough to fill the House, his only reply was, that he would back himself for any amount to fill Russell Square (Boz –'Mistaken Milliner').*

Rogers: The parlour orator. *A stoutish man of about forty, whose short, stiff, black hair curled closely round a broad high forehead, and a face to which something besides water and exercise had communicated a rather inflamed appearance. He was smoking a cigar, with his eyes fixed on the ceiling, and had that confident oracular air which marked him as the leading politician, general authority, and universal anecdote-relater, of the place. He had evidently just delivered himself of something very weighty; for the remainder of the company were puffing at their respective pipes and cigars in a kind of solemn abstraction, as if quite overwhelmed with the magnitude of the subject recently under discussion (Boz – 'Parlour Orator').*

Rogers: Police constable who accompanies Inspector Field and the narrator to Rats' Castle, Saint Giles's. *Rogers is ready, strapped and great-coated, with a flaming eye in the middle of his waist, like a deformed Cyclops (Reprinted – 'On Duty with Inspector Field').*

Rogers, Miss: Subject of one of Mrs. Nickleby's attempted recollections. *'A lady in our neighbourhood when we lived near Dawlish, I think her name was Rogers; indeed I am sure it was, if it wasn't Murphy' (Nickleby).*

Rogers, Mrs.: Mrs. Bardell's genteel lodger. *She was more gracious than intimate, in right of her position (Pickwick).*

Roker, Tom: Turnkey at the Fleet Prison (*Pickwick*).

Rokesmith, John: See **Harmon, John** (*Mutual Friend*).

Rokesmith, Mrs. John (Bella): see **Wilfer, Bella** (*Mutual Friend*).

Rolland: Junior partner in Defresnier et Cie who corresponds with Vendale about the discovery of fraud (*Christmas Stories* – 'No Thoroughfare').

Rosa: Lady Dedlock's maid who supplants Hortense. Marries Watt Rouncewell. *A dark-eyed, dark-haired, shy, village beauty comes in – so fresh in her rosy and yet delicate bloom, that the drops of rain, which have beaten on her hair, look like the dew upon a flower fresh gathered (Bleak House).*

Rose: The struggling young doctor's sweetheart. *How happy it would make Rose if he could only tell her that he had found a patient at last, and hoped to have more, and to come down again, in a few months' time, and marry her, and take her home to gladden his lonely fireside, and stimulate him to fresh exertions (Boz – 'Black Veil').*

Rose: Lucy Benson's cousin, sweetheart of John Maddox and the object of Flam's evil designs (*Village Coquettes*).

Ross, Frank: Bachelor friend of Gabriel Parsons (*Boz* – 'Watkins Tottle').

Rouncewell: Mrs. Rouncewell's son, brother of George, and father of Watt. An ironmaster. *Would have been provided for at Chesney Wold, and would have been made steward in due season; but he took,* when he was a schoolboy, to constructing steam-engines out of saucepans, and setting birds to draw their own water, with the least possible amount of labour; so assisting them with artful contrivance of hydraulic pressure, that a thirsty canary had only, in a literal sense, to put his shoulder to the wheel, and the job was done. This propensity gave Mrs. Rouncewell great uneasiness. She felt it with a mother's anguish, to be a move in the Wat Tyler direction (Bleak House).

Rouncewell, Mrs.: The Dedlocks' housekeeper at Chesney Wold. Mother of Rouncewell the ironmaster, and George, and grandmother of Watt. *She is rather deaf, which nothing will induce her to believe. She is a fine old lady, handsome, stately, wonderfully neat, and has such a back and such a stomacher, that if her stays should turn out when she dies to have been a broad old-fashioned family fire-grate, nobody who knows her would have cause to be surprised (Bleak House).*

Rouncewell, George (Mr. George or Trooper George): Mrs. Rouncewell's erratic son who, after serving in the army, runs a shooting-gallery in London until, restored to his mother by the Bagnets, he becomes Sir Leicester Dedlock's attendant. *A swarthy brown man of fifty; well-made, and good looking; with crisp dark hair, bright eyes, and a broad chest. His sinewy and powerful hands, as sunburnt as his face, have evidently been used to a pretty rough life. What is curious about him is, that he sits forward on his chair as if he were, from long habit, allowing space for some dress or accoutrements that he has altogether laid aside. His step too is measured and heavy, and would go well with a weighty clash and jingle of spurs. He is close-shaved now, but his mouth is set as if his upper lip had been for years familiar with a great moustache; and his manner of occasionally laying the open palm of his broad brown hand upon it, is to the same effect. Altogether, one might guess Mr. George to have been a trooper once upon a time (Bleak House).*

Rouncewell, Watt: Son of Rouncewell the ironmaster. Marries Rosa. *Perfectly good-humoured and polite; but, within such limits, evidently adapts his tone to his reception (Bleak House).*

Rudge: Barnaby's father. Supposed murdered by the slayer (actually himself) of his master, Reuben Haredale, he lives as a fugitive. Found out by Geoffrey Haredale, he is eventually executed. *The stranger took off his hat, and disclosed the hard features of a man of sixty or thereabouts, much weather-beaten and worn by time, and the naturally harsh expression of which was not improved by a dark handkerchief which was bound tightly round his head, and while it served the purpose of a wig, shaded his forehead, and almost hid his eyebrows. If it were intended to conceal or divert attention from a deep gash, now healed into an ugly seam, which when it was first inflicted must have laid bare his cheek-bone, the object was but indifferently attained, for it could scarcely fail to be noted at a glance. His complexion was of a cadaverous hue, and he had a grizzly jagged beard of some three weeks' date (Rudge)*

Rudge, Mrs. (Mary): Rudge's wife, supposed widow, and Barnaby's mother. *She was about forty – perhaps two or three years older – with a cheerful aspect, and a face that had once been pretty. . . . One thing about this face was very strange and startling. You could not look upon it in its most cheerful mood without feeling that it had some extraordinary capacity of expressing terror. It was not on the surface. It was in no one feature that it lingered. You could not take the eyes or mouth, or lines upon the cheek, and say, if this or that were otherwise, it would not be so. Yet there it always lurked (Rudge).*

Rudge, Barnaby: A simple-minded youth who wanders the roads between Chigwell and London with his raven, Grip. He ingenuously joins the Gordon Rioters, is arrested and sentenced to death, but reprieved through Gabriel Varden's efforts. *He was about three-and-twenty years old, and though rather spare, of a fair height and strong make. His hair, of which he had a great profusion, was red, and hanging in disorder about his face and shoulders, gave to his restless looks an expression quite unearthly – enhanced by the paleness of his complexion, and the glassy lustre of his large protruding eyes. Startling as his aspect was, his features were good, and there was something even plaintive in his wan and haggard aspect. . . . His dress was of green, clumsily trimmed here and there – apparently by his own hands – with gaudy lace; brightest where the cloth was most worn and soiled, and poorest where it was at the best. A pair of tawdry ruffles dangled at his wrists, while his throat was nearly bare. He had ornamented his hat with a cluster of peacock's feathers, but they were limp and broken, and now trailed negligently down his back. Girt to his side was the steel hilt of an old sword without blade or scabbard; and some parti-coloured ends of ribands and poor glass toys completed the ornamental portion of his attire. The fluttered and confused disposition of all the motley scraps that formed his dress, bespoke, in a scarcely less degree than his eager and unsettled manner, the disorder of his mind, and by a grotesque contrast set off and heightened the more impressive wildness of his face (Rudge).*

Rugg: A debt collector and agent, and Pancks's landlord. Father of Anastasia. *Mr. Rugg, who had a round white visage, as if all his blushes had been drawn out of him long ago, and who had a ragged yellow head like a worn-out hearth broom (Dorrit).*

Rugg, Anastasia: Rugg's daughter. *Miss Rugg, who had little nankeen spots, like shirt buttons, all over her face, and whose own yellow tresses were rather scrubby than luxuriant (Dorrit).*

Ruin: One of Miss Flite's birds (Bleak House).

Rummun, Professor: Member of the Mudfog Association (Mudfog).

'Rumty': see **Wilfer, Reginald** (Mutual Friend).

Saggers, Mrs.: Oldest but one pensioner at Titbull's and the centre of dissension there. *Has Mrs. Saggers any right to stand her pail outside her dwelling? (Uncommercial – 'Titbull's Alms-Houses').*

St. Evrémonde, Marquis: Elder of twin brothers. Father of Charles Darnay (*Two Cities*).

St. Evrémonde, Marquis: Younger of twin brothers. Uncle of Charles Darnay. Murdered by Gaspard whose child his carriage had killed. *A man of about sixty, handsomely dressed, haughty in manner, and with a face like a fine mask. A face of a transparent paleness; every feature in it clearly defined; one set expression on it. The nose, beautifully formed otherwise, was very slightly pinched at the top of each nostril. In those two compressions, or dints, the only little change that the face ever showed resided. They persisted in changing sometimes, and they would be occasionally dilated and contracted by something like a faint pulsation; then, they gave a look of treachery, and cruelty, to the whole countenance (Two Cities).*

St. Evrémonde, Charles: See **Darnay, Charles** (*Two Cities*).

St. Julien, Horatio: See **Larkins, Jem** (*Boz* – 'Private Theatres').

Salcy, the Family P.: Theatrical family appearing in a French-Flemish town visited by the Uncommercial Traveller. *The members of the Family P. Salcy were so fat and so like one another – fathers, mothers, sisters, brothers, uncles, and aunts – that I think the local audience were much confused about the plot of the piece under representation, and to the last expected that everybody must turn out to be the long-lost relative of everybody else (Uncommercial – 'In the French-Flemish Country').*

Sally: See under **Bill, Uncle** (*Boz* – 'London Recreations.).

Sally: See **Goldstraw, Mrs. Sarah** (*Christmas Stories* – 'No Thoroughfare').

Sally: Pauper attendant at Oliver Twist's birth. *A pauper old woman, who was rendered rather misty by an unwonted allowance of beer (Twist).*

Sam: Pecksniff's groom (*Chuzzlewit*).

Sam: The cab driver who suspects Pickwick to be an informant. *The cabman dashed his hat upon the ground, with a reckless disregard of his own private property, and knocked Mr. Pickwick's spectacles off, and followed up the attack with a blow on Mr. Pickwick's nose, and another on Mr. Pickwick's chest, and a third in Mr. Snodgrass's eye, and a fourth, by way of variety, in Mr. Tupman's waistcoat, and then danced into the road, and then back again to the pavement, and finally dashed the whole temporary supply of breath out of Mr. Winkle's body; and all in half a dozen seconds (Pickwick).*

Samba, Quanko: See under **Blazo, Colonel Sir Thomas** (*Pickwick*).

Sampson: Chief manager of a Life Assurance Office, who narrates the story. He helps Meltham save Margaret Niner from murder by Slinkton. *I think I have within the last thirty years seen more romances than the generality of men, however unpromising the opportunity may, at first sight, seem. As I have retired, and live at my ease, I possess the means that I used to*

want, of considering what I have seen, at leisure. My experiences have a more remarkable aspect, so reviewed, than they had when they were in progress. I have come home from the Play now, and can recall the scenes of the Drama upon which the curtain has fallen, free from the glare, bewilderment, and bustle of the Theatre ('Hunted Down').

Sampson, George: Friend of the Wilfers, admirer first of Bella, then of Lavinia. *The friend of the family was in that stage of the tender passion which bound him to regard everybody else as the foe of the family. He put the round head of his cane in his mouth, like a stopper, when he sat down. As if he felt himself full to the throat with affronting sentiments (Mutual Friend).*

Sanders, Mrs. Susannah: A crony of Mrs. Bardell. *A big, fat, heavy-faced personage (Pickwick).*

Sapsea, Thomas: Auctioneer and Mayor of Cloisterham. *Accepting the Jackass as the type of self-sufficient stupidity and conceit – a custom, perhaps, like some few other customs, more conventional than fair – then the purest Jackass in Cloisterham is Mr. Thomas Sapsea, Auctioneer.... Mr. Sapsea has many admirers; indeed, the proposition is carried by a large local majority, even including non-believers in his wisdom, that he is a credit to Cloisterham. He possesses the great qualities of being portentous and dull, and of having a roll in his speech, and another roll in his gait; not to mention a certain gravely flowing action with his hands, as if he were presently going to Confirm the individual with whom he holds discourse. Much nearer sixty years of age than fifty, with a flowing outline of stomach, and horizontal creases in his waistcoat; reputed to be rich; voting at elections in the strictly respectable interest; morally satisfied that nothing but he himself has grown since he was a baby; how can dunder-headed Mr. Sapsea be otherwise than a credit to Cloisterham, and society? (Drood).*

Sapsea, the late Mrs. Thomas (Ethelinda, née Brobity): Sapsea's late wife. *'Miss Brobity's Being, young man, was deeply imbued with homage to Mind. She revered Mind, when launched, or, as I say, precipitated, on an extensive knowledge of the world. When I made my proposal, she did me the honour to be so overshadowed with a species of Awe, as to be able to articulate only the two words, "O Thou!" meaning myself. Her limpid blue eyes were fixed upon me, her semi-transparent hands were clasped together, pallor overspread her aquiline features, and, though encouraged to proceed, she never did proceed a word further' (Drood).*

Sarah: See **Mary** and **Sarah** (*Boz* – 'Seven Dials').

Saunders: The Whifflers' bachelor friend who bears the brunt of their preoccupation with their children. *Whatever the attention of Mr. Saunders is called to, Mr. Saunders admires of course; though he is rather confused about the sex of the youngest branches and looks at the wrong children, turning to a girl when Mr. Whiffler directs his attention to a boy, and falling into raptures with a boy when he ought to be enchanted with a girl (Young Couples – 'Couple Who Dote Upon Their Children').*

Sawyer: A baker who beats his wife and then boils his son in the wash-house copper in a tale the gentleman connected with the press tells his admirers at the Green Dragon, Westminster Bridge (*Mudfog* – 'Mr. Robert Bolton').

Sawyer, Bob: Medical student, lodging at Mrs. Raddle's, Lant Street, Borough. It is intended that he marry Arabella, sister of his fellow student and drinking companion Ben Allen, but Winkle cuts him out. Sawyer and Allen eventually go to begin a new life in Bengal. *Mr. Bob Sawyer, who was habited in a coarse blue coat, which, without being either a great-coat or a surtout, partook of the nature and qualities of both, had about him that sort of slovenly smartness, and swaggering gait, which is peculiar to young gentlemen who smoke in the streets by day, shout and scream in the same by night, call waiters by their Christian names, and do various other acts and deeds of an equally facetious description. He wore a pair of plaid trousers, and a large rough double-breasted waistcoat; out of doors, he carried a thick stick with a big top. He eschewed gloves, and looked, upon the whole, something like a dissipated Robinson Crusoe* (*Pickwick*).

Sawyer, late Nockemorf: Medical practice owned by Bob Sawyer in Bristol. *'So snug, that at the end of a few years you might put all the profits in a wine glass, and cover 'em over with a gooseberry leaf'* (*Pickwick*).

Saxby, Long: One of Feenix's many acquaintances. *'Man of six foot ten'* (*Dombey*).

Scadder, Zephania: Agent of the Eden Land Corporation in America who persuades Martin Chuzzlewit to invest in the worthless scheme. *A gaunt man in a huge straw hat, and a coat of green stuff. The weather being hot, he had no cravat, and wore his shirt-collar wide open; so that every time he spoke something was seen to twitch and jerk up in his throat, like the little hammers in a harpsichord when the notes are struck. Perhaps it was the Truth feebly endeavouring to leap to his lips. If so, it never reached them* (*Chuzzlewit*).

Scadgers, Lady: Mrs. Sparsit's great-aunt. *An immensely fat old woman, with an inordinate appetite for butcher's meat, and a mysterious leg which had now refused to get out of bed for fourteen years* (*Hard Times*).

Scaley: Co-bailiff with Tix in possession at Madame Mantalini's. *Kate . . . started to hear a strange man's voice in the room, and started again, to observe, on looking round, that a white hat, and a red neckerchief, and a broad round face, and a large head, and part of a green coat were in the room too* (*Nickleby*).

Scarton, Charley: Amateur actor. *Charley Scarton is to take the part of an English sailor, and fight a broadsword combat with six unknown bandits, at one and the same time (one theatrical sailor is always equal to half a dozen men at least)* (*Boz* – 'Private Theatres').

Scientific Gentleman: An elderly gentleman 'of scientific attainments' who mistakes the flashes of Pickwick's lantern at Clifton for an undiscovered phenomenon of nature. *Full of this idea, the scientific gentleman seized his pen again, and committed to paper sundry notes of these unparalleled appearances, with the date, day, hour, minute, and precise second at which they were visible: all of which were to form the data of a voluminous treatise of great research and deep learning, which should astonish all the atmospherical sages that ever drew breath in any part of the civilised globe* (*Pickwick*).

Scott, Tom: Quilp's boy. Addicted to standing on his head, he becomes a successful professional acrobat after Quilp's death. *The first object that presented itself to his view was a pair of very imperfectly shod feet elevated in the air with the soles upwards, which remarkable appearance was referable to the boy, who being of an eccentric spirit and having a natural taste for tumbling was now standing on his head and contemplating the aspect of the river under these uncommon circumstances* (*Curiosity Shop*).

Screwzer, Tommy: One of Feenix's many acquaintances. *'Man of an extremely bilious habit'* (*Dombey*).

Scroo: A vice-president of the display of models and mechanical science session at the second meeting of the Mudfog Association (*Mudfog*).

Scrooge, Ebenezer: Central figure of the story. Surviving partner of the firm of Scrooge and Marley, and a grasping misanthrope, he is visited on Christmas Eve by the ghost of Marley and three Christmas spectres who show him the error of his ways and reform him. *Oh! But he was a tight-fisted hand at the grindstone, Scrooge! a squeezing, wrenching, grasping, scraping, clutching, covetous, old sinner! Hard and sharp as flint, from which no steel had ever struck out generous fire; secret, and self-contained, and solitary as an oyster. The cold within him froze his old features, nipped his pointed nose, shrivelled his cheek, stiffened his gait; made his eyes red, his thin lips blue; and spoke out shrewdly in his grating voice. A frosty rime was on his head, and on his eyebrows, and his wiry chin; he iced his office in the dog-days; and didn't thaw it one degree at Christmas* (*Christmas Books* – 'Christmas Carol').

Scrooge's Niece: Wife of his nephew Fred. *She was very pretty: exceedingly pretty. With a dimpled, surprised-looking, capital face; a ripe little mouth, that seemed made to be kissed – as no doubt it was; all kinds of good little dots about her chin, that melted into one another when she laughed; and the sunniest pair of eyes you ever saw in any little creature's head. Altogether she was what you would have called provoking, you know; but satisfactory, too. Oh, perfectly satisfactory* (*Christmas Books* – 'Christmas Carol').

Scuttlewig, Duke of: One of the aristocratic acquaintances claimed by the egotistical couple (*Young Couples* – 'Egotistical Couple').

Seamstress: Sydney Carton's fellow passenger in the tumbril on the way to the guillotine. *A young woman, with a slight girlish form, a sweet spare face in which there was no vestige of colour, and large widely opened patient eyes* (*Two Cities*).

Seraphina: Heroine of Jemmy Lirriper's tale: a schoolmaster's daughter. *The most beautiful creature that ever was seen, and she had brown eyes, and she had brown hair all curling beautifully, and she had a delicious voice, and she was delicious altogether* (*Christmas Stories* – 'Mrs. Lirriper's Lodgings').

Seven Poor Travellers: So styled by the narrator of that story, to comprise himself and the Six Poor Travellers lodging at Watts's Charity, Rochester. *I found the party to be thus composed. Firstly, myself. Secondly, a very decent man indeed, with his right arm in a sling, who had a certain clean, agreeable smell of wood about him, from which I judged him to have something to do with shipbuilding. Thirdly, a little sailor-boy, a mere child, with a profusion of rich dark brown hair, and deep womanly-looking eyes. Fourthly, a shabby-genteel personage in a threadbare black suit, and apparently in very bad circumstances, with a dry, suspicious look; the absent buttons on his waistcoat eked out with red tape; and a bundle of extraordinarily tattered papers sticking out of an inner breast-pocket. Fifthly, a foreigner by birth, but an Englishman in speech, who carried his pipe in the band of his hat, and lost no time in telling me, in an easy, simple, engaging way, that he was a watchmaker from Geneva, and travelled all about the Continent, mostly on foot, working as a journeyman, and seeing new countries, – possibly (I thought) also smuggling a watch or so, now and then. Sixthly, a little widow, who had been very pretty and was still very young, but whose beauty had been wrecked in some great misfortune, and whose manner was remarkably timid, scared, and solitary. Seventhly and lastly, a Traveller of a kind familiar to my boyhood, but now almost obsolete, – a Book-Pedler, who had a quantity of Pamphlets and Numbers with him, and who presently boasted that he could repeat more verses in an evening than he could sell in a twelvemonth* (*Christmas Stories* – 'Seven Poor Travellers').

Sexton, The: The old sexton at the village where Little Nell and her grandfather die. *Who peradventure, on a pinch, might have walked a mile with great difficulty in half a dozen hours* (*Curiosity Shop*).

Sexton, The: A deaf old man, one of the characters assumed by Gabblewig in order to unmask Slap (*Nightingale's Diary*).

Sharp: First master at Salem House. *A limp, delicate-looking gentleman, I thought, with a good deal of nose, and a way of carrying his head on one side, as if it were a little too heavy for him. His hair was very smooth and wavy; but I was informed by the very first boy who came back that it was a wig (a secondhand one he said), and that Mr. Sharp went out every Saturday afternoon to get it curled* (*Copperfield*).

Sharpeye: One of the policemen visiting sailors' haunts with the Uncommercial Traveller. *Had a skilful and quite professional way of opening doors – touched latches delicately, as if they were keys of musical instruments – opened every door he touched, as if he were perfectly confident that there was stolen property behind it – instantly insinuated himself, to*

prevent its being shut (*Uncommercial* – 'Poor Mercantile Jack').

Sheen and Gloss: Fashionable London mercers. *'To make this article go down, gentlemen,' says Sheen and Gloss the mercers, to their friends the manufacturers, 'you must come to us, because we know where to have the fashionable people, and we can make it fashionable'* (*Bleak House*).

Sheepskin: One of Miss Flite's birds (*Bleak House*).

Shepherd, Miss: A boarder at the Misses Nettingall's establishment. One of David Copperfield's first loves. *A little girl, in a spencer, with a round face and curly flaxen hair.... I touch Miss Shepherd's glove, and feel a thrill go up the right arm of my jacket, and come out at my hair. I say nothing tender to Miss Shepherd, but we understand each other. Miss Shepherd and myself live but to be united* (*Copperfield*).

Shepherd, The: One of Mrs. Tony Weller's spiritual comforters, observed by her husband. *'In comes a fat chap in black, vith a great white face, a smilin' avay like clockwork. Such goin' on, Sammy! "The kiss of peace," says the shepherd; and then he kissed the women all round.... I was just a thinkin' whether I hadn't better begin too – 'specially as there was a wery nice lady a sittin' next to me – ven in comes the tea, and your mother-in-law, as had been makin' the kettle bile downstairs. At it they went, tooth and nail.... I wish you could ha' seen the shepherd walkin' into the ham and muffins. I never see such a chap to eat and drink; never'* (*Pickwick*).

Shepherdson: Thief taken by Sergeant Mith who gains his confidence in the guise of a young butcher (*Reprinted* – 'Detective Police').

Shiny Villiam: Under-ostler at the Bull, Rochester. *So called, probably from his sleek hair and oily countenance* (*Pickwick*).

'Short' or 'Short Trotters': See **Harris** (*Curiosity Shop*).

Signal-man, The: The victim in the ghost story titled 'No. 1 Branch Line: The Signal-man' which forms ch. 4. *A dark, sallow man, with a dark beard and rather heavy eyebrows. His post was in as solitary and dismal a place as ever I saw* (*Christmas Stories* – 'Mugby Junction').

Sikes, Bill: Brutal thief associated with Fagin, lover and murderer of Nancy. He accidentally hangs himself trying to escape a mob hunting him down for the murder. *A stoutly-built fellow of about five-and-thirty, in a black velveteen coat, very soiled drab breeches, lace-up half boots, and grey cotton stockings, which inclosed a bulky pair of legs, with large swelling calves; – the kind of legs, which in such costume, always look in an unfinished and incomplete state without a set of fetters to garnish them. He had a brown hat on his head, and a dirty belcher handkerchief round his neck; with the long frayed ends of which he smeared the beer from his face as he spoke. He disclosed, when he had done so, a broad heavy countenance with a beard of three days' growth, and two scowling eyes; one of which displayed various*

135

parti-coloured symptoms of having been recently damaged by a blow (Twist).

Silverman, The Revd. George: Narrator of the story ('Silverman').

Silverstone, The Revd. and **Mrs.:** An egotistical couple. *Mrs. Silverstone, who launches into new praises of Mr. Silverstone's worth and excellence, to which he listens in the same meek silence, save when he puts in a word of self-denial relative to some question of fact, as – 'Not seventy-two christenings that week, my dear. Only seventy-one, only seventy-one.' At length his wife has quite concluded, and then he says, Why should he repine, why should he give way, why should he suffer his heart to sink within him? Is it he alone who toils and suffers? What has she gone through, he should like to know? What does she go through every day for him and society? With such an exordium Mr. Silverstone launches out into glowing praises of the conduct of Mrs. Silverstone in the production of eight young children, and the subsequent rearing and fostering of the same; and thus the husband magnifies the wife, and the wife the husband (Young Couples – 'Egotistical Couple').*

Simmery, Frank: Fellow stockbroker and betting friend of Wilkins Flasher. *A very smart young gentleman who wore his hat on his right whisker, and was lounging over the desk, killing flies with a ruler (Pickwick).*

Simmonds, Miss: Employee of Madame Mantalini *(Nickleby).*

Simmons: Parish beadle. *The parish beadle is one of the most, perhaps the most, important member of the local administration. He is not so well off as the churchwardens, certainly, nor is he so learned as the vestry-clerk, nor does he order things quite so much his own way as either of them. But his power is very great, notwithstanding; and the dignity of his office is never impaired by the absence of efforts on his part to maintain it. The beadle of our parish is a splendid fellow. It is quite delightful to hear him, as he explains the state of the existing poor laws to the deaf old women in the board-room passage on business nights (Boz – 'Beadle').* Simmons's death occurs in *Boz – 'Election for Beadle'.*

Simmons, Mrs. Henrietta: A neighbour and sympathiser of Mrs. Quilp's *(Curiosity Shop).*

Simmons, William: Van driver who gives Martin Chuzzlewit a ride from Salisbury to London after his dismissal by Pecksniff. *A red-faced burly young fellow; smart in his way, and with a good-humoured countenance (Chuzzlewit).*

Simpson: Boarder at Mrs. Tibbs's. He marries, but is deserted by, Julia Maplesone. *One of those young men, who are in society what walking gentlemen are on the stage, only infinitely worse skilled in his vocation than the most indifferent artist. He was as empty-headed as the great bell of St. Paul's; always dressed according to the caricatures published in the monthly fashions; and spelt Character with a K (Boz – 'Boarding-House').*

Simpson: Fellow prisoner of Pickwick in the Fleet. *Leaning out of window as far as he could without overbalancing himself, endeavouring, with great perseverance, to spit upon the crown of the hat of a personal friend on the parade below (Pickwick).*

Single Gentleman, The: The brother to Trent, Little Nell's grandfather, who narrates the story. He lodges with the Brass family and it emerges ultimately that he is Master Humphrey (q.v.) *(Curiosity Shop).*

Six Poor Travellers: See **Seven Poor Travellers** *(Christmas Stories –* 'Seven Poor Travellers').

Skettles, Lady: Wife of Sir Barnet Skettles, mother of Barnet junior *(Dombey).*

Skettles, Sir Barnet, M.P.: Father of Barnet junior, a pupil at Dr. Blimber's, and host for a time to Florence Dombey at Fulham. *Sir Barnet Skettles expressed his personal consequence chiefly through an antique gold snuff-box, and a ponderous silk pocket-handkerchief, which he had an imposing manner of drawing out of his pocket like a banner, and using with both hands at once. Sir Barnet's object in life was constantly to extend the range of his acquaintance. Like a heavy body dropped into water – not to disparage so worthy a gentleman by the comparison – it was in the nature of things that Sir Barnet must spread an ever-widening circle about him, until there was no room left. Or, like a sound in air, the vibration of which, according to the speculation of an ingenious modern philosopher, may go on travelling for ever through the interminable fields of space, nothing but coming to the end of his moral tether could stop Sir Barnet Skettles in his voyage of discovery through the social system (Dombey).*

Skettles, Barnet, jun.: Son of Sir Barnet and Lady Skettles. A fellow-pupil of the Dombey children at Doctor Blimber's *(Dombey).*

Skewton, The Hon. Mrs. ('Cleopatra'): Edith Dombey's elderly but coquettish mother. Aunt to Lord Feenix. *The discrepancy between Mrs. Skewton's fresh enthusiasm of words, and forlornly faded manner, was hardly less observable than that between her age, which was about seventy, and her dress, which would have been youthful for twenty-seven. Her attitude in the wheeled chair (which she never varied) was one in which she had been taken in a barouche, some fifty years before, by a then fashionable artist who had appended to his published sketch the name of Cleopatra: in consequence of a discovery made by the critics of the time, that it bore an exact resemblance to that princess as she reclined on board her galley. Mrs. Skewton was a beauty then, and bucks threw wine-glasses over their heads by dozens in her honour. The beauty and the barouche had both passed away, but she still preserved the attitude, and for this reason expressly, maintained the wheeled chair and the butting page: there being nothing whatever, except the attitude, to prevent her from walking (Dombey).*

Skewton, Edith: See **Dombey, Mrs. Paul the Second** *(Dombey).*

Skiffins, Miss: Marries Wemmick. *Miss Skiffins was of a wooden appearance.... She might have been some two or three years younger than Wemmick, and I judged her to stand possessed of portable property. The cut of her dress from the waist upward, both before and behind, made her figure very like a boy's kite; and I might have pronounced her gown a little too decidedly orange, and her gloves a little too intensely green. But she seemed to be a good sort of fellow (Expectations).*

Skimpin: Serjeant Buzfuz's junior counsel for Mrs. Bardell in Bardell and Pickwick. *Mr. Skimpin proceeded to 'open the case'; and the case appeared to have very little inside it when he had opened it, for he kept such particulars as he knew, completely to himself, and sat down, after a lapse of three minutes, leaving the jury in precisely the same advanced stage of wisdom as they were in before (Pickwick).*

Skimpole, Arethusa, Laura, and **Kitty:** The Skimpoles' daughters. *'This,' said Mr. Skimpole, 'is my Beauty daughter, Arethusa – plays and sings odds and ends like her father. This is my Sentiment daughter, Laura – plays a little but don't sing. This is my Comedy daughter, Kitty – sings a little but don't play' (Bleak House).*

Skimpole, Harold: Father of Arethusa, Laura, and Kitty. Protegé of John Jarndyce, whom he later estranges by vilifying him for selfishness. *He was a little bright creature, with a rather large head; but a delicate face, and a sweet voice, and there was a perfect charm in him. All he said was so free from effort and spontaneous, and was said with such a captivating gaiety, that it was fascinating to hear him talk.... He had more the appearance, in all respects, of a damaged young man, than a well-preserved elderly one. There was an easy negligence in his manner, and even in his dress (his hair carelessly disposed, and his neck-kerchief loose and flowing, as I have seen artists paint their own portraits), which I could not separate from the idea of a romantic youth who had undergone some unique process of depreciation. It struck me as being not at all like the manner or appearance of a man who had advanced in life, by the usual road of years, cares, and experiences (Bleak House).*

Skimpole, Mrs. Harold: Skimpole's wife, mother of Arethusa, Laura, and Kitty. *Had once been a beauty, but was now a delicate high-nosed invalid, suffering under a complication of disorders (Bleak House).*

Slackbridge: Militant trades-unionist whose oration drives Stephen Blackpool from his work and ultimately to his death. *Judging him by Nature's evidence, he was above the mass in very little but the stage on which he stood. In many great respects he was essentially below them. He was not so honest, he was not so manly, he was not so good-humoured; he substituted cunning for their simplicity, and passion for their safe solid sense. An ill-made, high-shouldered man, with lowering brows, and his features crushed into an habitually sour expression, he contrasted most unfavourably, even in his mongrel dress, with the great body of his hearers in their plain working clothes (Hard Times).*

Sladdery: Fashionable London lending librarian. *'If you want to get this print upon the tables of my high connexion, sir ... you must leave it, if you please, to me; for I have been accustomed to study the leaders of my high connexion, sir; and I may tell you, without vanity, that I can turn them round my finger' (Bleak House).*

Slammer, Dr.: Surgeon of the 97th Regiment at Rochester. Offended by Jingle, wearing Winkle's coat, he challenges Winkle to a duel. *One of the most popular personages, in his own circle, present was a little fat man, with a ring of upright black hair round his head, and an extensive bald plain on the top of it – Doctor Slammer, surgeon to the 97th. The Doctor took snuff with everybody, chatted with everybody, laughed, danced, made jokes, played whist, did everything, and was everywhere (Pickwick).*

Slammons: A name by which Mrs. Nickleby persists for a time in addressing Smike. *Which circumstance she attributed to the remarkable similarity of the two names in point of sound, both beginning with an S, and moreover being spelt with an M (Nickleby).*

Slang, Lord: One of the aristocratic acquaintances claimed by the egotistical couple (*Young Couples – 'Egotistical Couple'*).

Slap: A failed actor (stage name, Formiville) living by writing begging letters and extorting money from gullible people, principally Christopher Nightingale, estranged for many years from his wife, Slap's sister, but still paying a regular allowance, believing her to be alive. Posing as a friend of Mrs. Nightingale, Slap produces a 'Master Nightingale' in an attempt to make a final killing, but is foiled by Gabblewig (*Nightingale's Diary*).

Slasher: Eminent surgeon whose skill is described to Pickwick by Jack Hopkins. *'Took a boy's leg out of the socket last week – boy ate five apples and a gingerbread cake – exactly two minutes after it was all over, boy said he wouldn't lie there to be made game of, and he'd tell his mother if they didn't begin' (Pickwick).*

Slaughter, Lieutenant: Accomplice of the Waters. *Two iron-shod boots and one gruff voice (Boz – 'Tuggses at Ramsgate').*

Sleary: Circus proprietor and father of Josephine. He cares for Sissy Jupe after her father, his clown, has decamped, and helps Tom Gradgrind escape arrest. *A stout man ... with one fixed eye, and one loose eye, a voice (if it can be called so) like the efforts of a broken old pair of bellows, a flabby surface, and a muddled head which was never sober and never drunk (Hard Times).*

Sleary, Josephine: Sleary's daughter. Marries Childers. *A pretty fair-haired girl of eighteen, who had been tied on a horse at two years old, and had made a will at twelve, which she always carried about with her, expressive of her dying desire to be drawn to the grave by the two piebald ponies (Hard Times).*

Sliderskew, Peg: Arthur Gride's housekeeper. By stealing his papers she helps bring about his downfall, and is subsequently sentenced to transportation. *A short, thin, weasen, blear-eyed old woman, palsy-stricken and hideously ugly (Nickleby).*

Slingo: Horse-dealer. One of Tip Dorrit's many employers *(Dorrit).*

Slinkton, Julius: Murderer of one niece and intending murderer of another, Margaret Niner, for their insurance money, he is hunted down by Meltham, who had been in love with the former lady. Believing Meltham to be Beckwith, a drunkard near to death, Slinkton insures and tries to poison him, but is unmasked and kills himself with poison. *About forty or so, dark, exceedingly well dressed in black, – being in mourning, – and the hand he extended with a polite air, had a particularly well-fitting black-kid glove upon it. His hair, which was elaborately brushed and oiled, was parted straight up the middle; and he presented this parting to the clerk, exactly (to my thinking) as if he had said, in so many words: 'You must take me, if you please, my friend, just as I show myself. Come straight up here, follow the gravel path, keep off the grass, I allow no trespassing'* ('Hunted Down').

Slithers: Master Humphrey's barber. Captures Miss Benton from Tony Weller and marries her. *At all times a very brisk, bustling, active little man, – for he is, as it were, chubby all over, without being stout or unwieldy (Humphrey).*

Sloppy: An orphan brought up by Betty Higden, whom he helps with her laundry work. Boffin has him trained as a cabinet-maker. *A very long boy, with a very little head, and an open mouth of disproportionate capacity that seemed to assist his eyes in staring at the visitors (Mutual Friend).*

Slout: Master of the workhouse of which Mrs. Corney is matron. His death enables Bumble to become his successor and Mrs. Corney's husband. *'Oh, Mrs. Corney, what a prospect this opens! What a opportunity for a jining of hearts and housekeepings!'* (Twist).

Slowboy, Tilly: The Peerybingles' servant and nurse to their baby. *She was of a spare and straight shape, this young lady, insomuch that her garments appeared to be in constant danger of sliding off those sharp pegs, her shoulders, on which they were loosely hung. Her costume was remarkable for the partial development, on all possible occasions, of some flannel vestment of a singular structure; also for affording glimpses, in the region of the back, of a corset, or pair of stays, in colour a dead-green. Being always in a state of gaping admiration at everything, and absorbed, besides, in the perpetual contemplation of her mistress's perfections and the baby's, Miss Slowboy, in her little errors of judgment, may be said to have done equal honour to her head and to her heart; and though these did less honour to the baby's head, which they were the occasional means of bringing into contact with deal doors, dressers, stair-rails, bedposts, and other foreign substances, still they were the honest results of Tilly Slowboy's constant astonishment at finding herself so kindly treated (Christmas Books – 'Cricket').*

Sludberry, Thomas: Defendant in the brawling case of Bumple against Sludberry. *A little, red-faced, sly-looking, ginger-beer seller (Boz – 'Doctors' Commons').*

Sluffen: Speaker at the master sweeps' anniversary dinner at White Conduit House. *Expressed himself in a manner following: 'That now he'd cotcht the cheerman's hi, he vished he might be jolly vell blessed, if he worn't a goin' to have his innings, vich he vould say these here obserwashuns – that how some mischeevus coves as know'd nuffin about the consarn, had tried to sit people agin the mas'r swips, and take the shine out o' their bis'nes, and the bread out o' the traps o' their preshus kids, by a makin' o' this here remark, as chimblies could be as vell svept by 'sheenery as by boys; and that the makin' use o' boys for that there purpos vos barbareous; vereas, he 'ad been a chummy – he begged the cheerman's parding for usin' such a wulgar hexpression – more nor thirty year – he might say he'd been born in a chimbley – and he know'd uncommon vell as 'sheenery vor vus nor o' no use: and as to kerhewelty to the boys, everybody in the chimbley line know'd as vell as he did, that they liked the climbin' better nor nuffin as vos' (Boz – 'First of May').*

Slug: Speaker at the statistics session of the first meeting of the Mudfog Association. *He found that the total number of small carts and barrows engaged in dispensing provison to the cats and dogs of the metropolis was one thousand seven hundred and forty-three. The average number of skewers delivered daily with the provender, by each dogs'-meat cart or barrow, was thirty-six. . . . Allowing that . . . the odd two thousand seven hundred and forty-eight were accidentally devoured with the meat, by the most voracious of the animals supplied, it followed that sixty thousand skewers per day, or the enormous number of twenty-one millions nine hundred thousand skewers annually were wasted in the kennels and dustholes of London; which, if collected and warehoused, would in ten years' time afford a mass of timber more than sufficient for the construction of a first-rate vessel of war for the use of her Majesty's navy, to be called 'The Royal Skewer' (Mudfog).*

Slum: A writer of rhyming advertisements and friend of Mrs. Jarley. *A tallish gentleman with a hook nose and black hair, dressed in a military surtout very short and tight in the sleeves, and which had once been frogged and braided all over, but was now sadly shorn of its garniture and quite threadbare – dressed too in ancient grey pantaloons fitting tight to the leg, and a pair of pumps in the winter of their existence (Curiosity Shop).*

Slumkey, The Hon. Samuel: Successful parliamentary candidate against Fizkin at Eatanswill. *The Honourable Samuel Slumkey himself, in top-boots, and a blue neckerchief (Pickwick).*

Slummery and **Fithers:** Artist friends of the Bobtail

Widgers. *Mr. Slummery, say they, is unquestionably a clever painter, and would no doubt be very popular, and sell his pictures at a very high price, if that cruel Mr. Fithers had not forestalled him in his department of art, and made it thoroughly and completely his own; – Fithers, it is to be observed, being present and within hearing, and Slummery elsewhere* (Young Couples – 'Plausible Couple').

Slummintowken: See **Porkenham, Griggs,** and **Slummintowken Families** *(Pickwick).*

Slurk: Editor of the *Eatanswill Independent*, rival of Pott's *Gazette*. *A shortish gentleman, with very stiff black hair cut in the porcupine or blacking-brush style, and standing stiff and straight all over his head; his aspect was pompous and threatening; his manner was peremptory; his eyes were sharp and restless; and his whole bearing bespoke a feeling of great confidence in himself, and a consciousness of immeasurable superiority over all other people (Pickwick).*

Slyme, Chevy: Disreputable nephew of old Martin Chuzzlewit, closely associated with Montague Tigg. Later, as a police officer, he is concerned in Jonas Chuzzlewit's arrest. *Wrapped in an old blue camlet cloak with a lining of faded scarlet. His sharp features being much pinched and nipped by long waiting in the cold, and his straggling red whiskers and frowzy hair being more than usually dishevelled from the same cause, he certainly looked rather unwholesome and uncomfortable than Shakespearian or Miltonic (Chuzzlewit).*

Smalder Girls: See under **Johnson, Tom** *(Dombey).*

Smallweed, Bartholomew (Bart, 'Small', 'Chick Weed'): The Joshua Smallweeds' grandson, twin brother of Judith, and friend of Guppy. *He is a weird changeling, to whom years are nothing. He stands precociously possessed of centuries of owlish wisdom. If he ever lay in a cradle, it seems as if he must have lain there in a tail-coat. He has an old, old eye, has Smallweed: and he drinks and smokes, in a monkeyish way; and his neck is stiff in his collar; and he is never to be taken in; and he knows all about it, whatever it is. In short, in his bringing up, he has been so nursed by Law and Equity that he has become a kind of fossil Imp (Bleak House).*

Smallweed, Joshua (Grandfather Smallweed): Grandfather of Bartholomew and Judith. He obtains possession of the letters compromising Lady Dedlock and tries to blackmail Sir Leicester, but is foiled by Bucket. *He is in a helpless condition as to his lower, and nearly so as to his upper limbs; but his mind is unimpaired. It holds, as well as it ever held, the first four rules of arithmetic, and a certain small collection of the hardest facts. In respect of ideality, reverence, wonder, and other such phrenological attributes, it is no worse off than it used to be. Everything that Mr. Smallweed's grandfather ever put away in his mind was a grub at first, and is a grub at last. In all his life he has never bred a single butterfly (Bleak House).*

Smallweed, Mrs. Joshua (Grandmother Smallweed): Grandfather Smallweed's wife, grandmother of Bartholomew and Judith. *There has been only one child in the Smallweed family for several generations. Little old men and women there have been, but no child, until Mr. Smallweed's grandmother, now living, became weak in her intellect, and fell (for the first time) into a childish state. With such infantine graces as a total want of observation, memory, understanding and interest, and an eternal disposition to fall asleep over the fire and into it, Mr. Smallweed's grandmother has undoubtedly brightened the family (Bleak House).*

Smallweed, Judith (Judy): Bartholomew's twin sister and housekeeper for their grandparents. *Judy never owned a doll, never heard of Cinderella, never played at any game. She once or twice fell into children's company when she was about ten years old, but the children couldn't get on with Judy, and Judy couldn't get on with them. She seemed like an animal of another species, and there was instinctive repugnance on both sides. It is very doubtful whether Judy knows how to laugh. She has so rarely seen the thing done, that the probabilities are strong the other way. Of anything like a youthful laugh, she certainly can have no conception. If she were to try one, she would find her teeth in her way; modelling that action of her face, as she has unconsciously modelled all its other expressions, on her pattern of sordid age (Bleak House).*

Smangle: Fellow prisoner of Pickwick in the Fleet. *A tall fellow, with an olive complexion, long dark hair, and very thick bushy whiskers meeting under his chin. . . . There was a rakish, vagabond smartness, and a kind of boastful rascality, about the whole man, that was worth a mine of gold (Pickwick).*

Smart, Tom: Traveller for Bilson and Slum. Central character of 'The Bagman's Story'. *'Tom Smart, gentlemen, had always been very much attached to the public line. It had long been his ambition to stand in a bar of his own, in a green coat, knee-cords, and tops. He had a great notion of taking the chair at convivial dinners, and he had often thought how well he could preside in a room of his own in the talking way, and what a capital example he could set to his customers in the drinking department' (Pickwick).*

Smauker, John: Angelo Cyrus Bantam's footman who invites Sam Weller to the Bath footmen's soirée. *A powdered-headed footman in gorgeous livery, and of symmetrical stature (Pickwick).*

Smif, Putnam ('America Junior'): American shop assistant who writes to Martin Chuzzlewit seeking his patronage. *'I am young, and ardent. For there is a poetry in wildness, and every alligator basking in the slime is in himself an Epic, self-contained. I aspirate for fame. It is my yearning and my thirst' (Chuzzlewit).*

Smiggers, Joseph: *Perpetual Vice-President – Member Pickwick Club (Pickwick).*

Smike: Ralph Nickleby's son, abandoned at Dotheboys Hall, befriended and rescued by Nicholas Nickleby, with whom he acts for a time in Crummles's company under the name of Digby. He recovers some of his lost wits, but dies. *Although he could not have been less than eighteen or nineteen years old, and was tall for that age, he wore a skeleton suit, such as is usually put upon very little boys, and which, though most absurdly short in the arms and legs, was quite wide enough for his attenuated frame. In order that the lower part of his legs might be in perfect keeping with this singular dress, he had a very large pair of boots, originally made for tops, which might have been once worn by some stout farmer, but were now too patched and tattered for a beggar. Heaven knows how long he had been there, but he still wore the same linen which he had first taken down; for, round his neck, was a tattered child's frill, only half concealed by a coarse, man's neckerchief. He was lame; and as he feigned to be busy in arranging the table, glanced at the letters with a look so keen, and yet so dispirited and hopeless, that Nicholas could hardly bear to watch him (Nickleby).*

Smith: A London clerk. *He was a tall, thin, pale person, in a black coat, scanty grey trousers, little pinched-up gaiters, and brown beaver gloves. . . . We thought we almost saw the dingy little back-office into which he walks every morning, hanging his hat on the same peg, and placing his legs beneath the same desk: first, taking off that black coat which lasts the year through, and putting on the one which did duty last year, and which he keeps in his desk to save the other. There he sits till five o'clock, working on, all day, as regularly as did the dial over the mantelpiece, whose loud ticking is as monotonous as his whole existence (Boz – 'Thoughts About People').*

Smith: Member of the Mudfog Association *(Mudfog).*

Smith, M.P.: An eager new member. *Seizes both the hands of his gratified constituent, and, after greeting him with the most enthusiastic warmth, darts into the lobby with an extraordinary display of ardour in the public cause, leaving an immense impression in his favour (Boz – 'Parliamentary Sketch').*

Smith, Samuel: Real name of Horatio Sparkins (q.v.) *(Boz – 'Horatio Sparkins').*

Smithers, Miss: A boarder at Westgate House school, Bury St. Edmunds, on the night of Pickwick's escapade there. *Miss Smithers proceeded to go into hysterics of four young lady power (Pickwick).*

Smithers, Emily: Pupil of the Misses Crumpton. *The belle of the house (Boz – 'Sentiment').*

Smithers, Robert: See **Potter, Thomas** *(Boz – 'Making a Night of it').*

Smithick and Watersby: Liverpool owners of the *Golden Mary. I saw him bearing down upon me, head on. . . . It is, personally, neither Smithick, nor Watersby, that I here mention, nor was I ever acquainted with any man of either of those names, nor do I think that there has been any one of either of those names in that Liverpool House for years back. But, it is in reality the House itself that I refer to; and a wiser merchant or a truer gentleman never stepped (Christmas Stories – 'Golden Mary').*

Smithie, Mr., Mrs., and the **Misses:** A Chatham Dockyard official and his family, present at the charity ball at the Bull, Rochester *(Pickwick).*

Smorltork, Count: A guest at Mrs. Leo Hunter's fancy-dress breakfast at Eatanswill. *'The famous foreigner – gathering materials for his great work on England' (Pickwick).*

Smouch: Assistant to Namby at the arrest of Pickwick at the George and Vulture. *A shabby-looking man in a brown great-coat shorn of divers buttons (Pickwick).*

Smuggins: Professional entertainer at a harmonic meeting. *That little round-faced man, with the brown small surtout, white stockings and shoes, is in the comic line; the mixed air of self-denial, and mental consciousness of his own powers, with which he acknowledges the call of the chair, is particularly gratifying. . . . Smuggins, after a considerable quantity of coughing by way of symphony, and a most facetious sniff or two, which afford general delight, sings a comic song, with a fal-de-ral – tol-de-rol chorus at the end of every verse, much longer than the verse itself (Boz – 'The Streets – Night').*

Snagsby: Law stationer in Cook's Court, Cursitor Street, who employs Hawdon as a law writer. *A mild, bald, timid man, with a shining head, and a scrubby clump of black hair sticking out at the back. He tends to meekness and obesity. As he stands at his door in Cook's Court, in his grey shop-coat and black calico sleeves, looking up at the clouds; or stands behind a desk in his dark shop, with a heavy flat ruler, snipping and slicing at sheepskin, in company with his two 'prentices; he is emphatically a retiring and unassuming man (Bleak House).*

Snagsby, Mrs.: Snagsby's wife, niece of his deceased partner, Peffer. *Something too violently compressed about the waist, and with a sharp nose like a sharp autumn evening, inclining to be frosty towards the end. The Cook's-Courtiers had a rumour flying among them, that the mother of this niece did, in her daughter's childhood, moved by too jealous a solicitude that her figure should approach perfection, lace her up every morning with her maternal foot against the bed-post for a stronger hold and purchase; and further, that she exhibited internally pints of vinegar and lemon-juice: which acids, they held, had mounted to the nose and temper of the patient (Bleak House).*

Snap, Betsy: Uncle Chill's servant. *A withered, hard-favoured, yellow old woman – our only domestic – always employed, at this time of the morning, in rubbing my uncle's legs (Christmas Stories – 'Poor Relation').*

Snawley: Stepfather of two boys at Dotheboys Hall. Ralph Nickleby engages him to pose as Smike's father, but he is found out and exposes Nickleby. *The sleek and sanctified gentleman (Nickleby).*

Snawley, Mrs.: Snawley's wife *(Nickleby).*

Snevellici: Member of Crummles's theatrical company and father of Miss Snevellici. *Who had been in the profession ever since he had first played the* *ten-year-old imps in the Christmas pantomimes; who could sing a little, dance a little, fence a little, act a little, and do everything a little, but not much; who had been sometimes in the ballet, and sometimes in the chorus, at every theatre in London; who was always selected in virtue of his figure to play the military visitors and the speechless noblemen; who always wore a smart dress, and came on arm-in-arm with a smart lady in short petticoats, – and always did it too with such an air that people in the pit had been several times known to cry out 'Bravo!' under the impression that he was somebody (Nickleby).*

Snevellici, Miss: Snevellici's daughter. Member of Crummles's theatrical company. *Could do anything, from a medley dance to Lady Macbeth, and also always played some part in blue silk knee-smalls at her benefit (Nickleby).*

Snevellici, Mrs.: Snevellici's wife and Miss Snevellici's mother. Also a member of Crummles's theatrical company. *Still a dancer, with a neat little figure and some remains of good looks (Nickleby).*

Snewkes: A friend of the Kenwigses *(Nickleby).*

Sniff: Employed at Mugby Junction refreshment room, where his wife is chief assistant. *A regular insignificant cove. He looks arter the sawdust department in a back room, and is sometimes, when we are very hard put to it, let behind the counter with a corkscrew; but never when it can be helped, his demeanour towards the public being disgusting servile (Christmas Stories – 'Mugby Junction').*

Sniff, Mrs.: Sniff's wife, chief assistant at Mugby Junction refreshment room. *She's the one! She's the one as you'll notice to be always looking another way from you, when you look at her. She's the one with the small waist buckled in tight in front, and with the lace cuffs at her wrists, which she puts on the edge of the counter before her, and stands a-smoothing while the public foams. This smoothing the cuffs and looking another way while the public foams is the last accomplishment taught to the young ladies as come to Mugby to be finished by Our Missis; and it's always taught by Mrs. Sniff (Christmas Stories – 'Mugby Junction').*

Sniggs: Tulrumble's deceased predecessor as Mayor of Mudfog. *Despite the health-preserving air of Mudfog, the Mayor died. It was a most extraordinary circumstance; he had lived in Mudfog for eighty-five years. The corporation didn't understand it at all; indeed it was with great difficulty that one old gentleman, who was a great stickler for forms, was dissuaded from proposing a vote of censure on such unaccountable conduct. Strange as it was, however, die he did, without taking the slightest notice of the corporation (Mudfog).*

Snigsworth, Lord: First cousin to Twemlow, who dines out upon the relationship *(Mutual Friend).*

Snipe, The Hon. Wilmot: Ensign in the 97th Regiment at Rochester. *'Who's that little boy with the light hair and pink eyes, in fancy dress?' inquired Mr. Tupman. 'Hush, pray – pink eyes – fancy dress –*

little boy – nonsense – Ensign 97th – Honourable Wilmot Snipe – great family – Snipes – very' (Pickwick).

Snitchey, Jonathan: Partner in Snitchey and Craggs, Dr. Jeddler's lawyers. *Like a magpie or raven (only not so sleek) (Christmas Books – 'Battle of Life').*

Snitchey, Mrs. Jonathan: Wife of Mr. Snitchey, and friend of his partner's wife, Mrs. Craggs *(Christmas Books – 'Battle of Life').*

Snivey, Sir Hookham: Member of the Mudfog Association *(Mudfog).*

Snobb, The Hon. Mr.: A guest at Ralph Nickleby's dinner party *(Nickleby).*

Snobee: Parliamentary candidate suggested to the Old Street Suburban Representative Discovery Society by a Mr. Wilson, implacably opposed by Rogers, the Parlour Orator. *' "The abolitionist of the national debt, the unflinching opponent of pensions, the uncompromising advocate of the negro, the reducer of sinecures and the duration of Parliaments; the extender of nothing but the suffrages of the people," says Mr. Wilson. "Prove it," says I. "His acts prove it," says he. "Prove them," says I' (Boz – 'Parlour Orator').*

Snodgrass, Augustus: A member of the Pickwick Club and one of Pickwick's companions in his travels. He marries Emily Wardle. *The poetic Snodgrass ... poetically enveloped in a mysterious blue cloak with a canine-skin collar (Pickwick).*

Snore, Professor: President of the zoology and botany session at the first meeting of the Mudfog Association. *Wished to be informed how the ingenious gentleman proposed to open a communication with fleas generally, in the first instance, so that they might be thoroughly imbued with a sense of the advantages they must necessarily derive from changing their mode of life, and applying themselves to honest labour (Mudfog).*

Snorflerer, Dowager Lady: One of the aristocratic acquaintances claimed by the egotistical couple *(Young Couples – 'Egotistical Couple').*

Snow, Tom: Captain Ravender's negro steward in the *Golden Mary (Christmas Stories – 'Golden Mary').*

Snubbin, Serjeant: Pickwick's leading counsel in Bardell and Pickwick. *A lantern-faced, sallow-complexioned man, of about five-and-forty, or – as the novels say – he might be fifty. He had that dull-looking boiled eye which is often to be seen in the heads of people who have applied themselves during many years to a weary and laborious course of study; and which would have been sufficient, without the additional eye-glass which dangled from a broad black riband round his neck, to warn a stranger that he was very near-sighted. His hair was thin and weak, which was partly attributable to his having never devoted much time to its arrangement, and partly to his having worn for five-and-twenty years the forensic wig which hung on a block beside him (Pickwick).*

Snuffim, Sir Tumley: Mrs. Wititterly's doctor. *'Mrs. Wititterly,' said her husband, 'is Sir Tumley Snuffim's favourite patient. I believe I may venture to say, that Mrs. Wititterly is the first person who took the new medicine which is supposed to have destroyed a family at Kensington Gravel Pits'* (Nickleby).

Snuffletoffle, Q. J.: Speaker at the umbugology and ditchwaterisics session of the second meeting of the Mudfog Association. *Had heard of a pony winking his eye, and likewise of a pony whisking his tail, but whether they were two ponies or the same pony he could not undertake positively to say. At all events, he was acquainted with no authenticated instance of a simultaneous winking and whisking* (Mudfog).

Snugglewood: One of many doctors consulted by Our Bore (*Reprinted* – 'Our Bore').

Snuphanuph, The Dowager Lady: A whist partner introduced to Pickwick by Bantam at Bath Assembly Rooms. *'Hush, my dear sir – nobody's fat or old in Ba-ath. That's the Dowager Lady Snuphanuph'* (Pickwick)

Soemup, Dr.: President of the anatomy and medicine session at the second meeting of the Mudfog Association (Mudfog).

Sophia: Eldest of the Camberwell children to whom Ruth Pinch is governess. *A premature little woman of thirteen years old, who had already arrived at such a pitch of whalebone and education that she had nothing girlish about her* (Chuzzlewit).

Sophia: The Matthew Pockets' housemaid (Expectations).

Sophy: The deaf and dumb girl bought by Dr. Marigold from Mim for six pairs of braces. She marries a deaf and dumb man, goes to China with him, and returns with a perfectly normal little daughter. *The way she learnt to understand any look of mine was truly surprising. When I sold of a night, she would sit in the cart unseen by them outside, and would give a eager look into my eyes when I looked in, and would hand me straight the precise article or articles I wanted. And then she would clap her hands, and laugh for joy. And as for me, seeing her so bright, and remembering what she was when I first lighted on her, starved and beaten and ragged, leaning asleep against the muddy cart-wheel, it gave me such heart that I gained a greater heighth of reputation than ever* (Christmas Stories – 'Doctor Marigold').

Sophy: One of Mrs. Lirriper's succession of servants. *The willingest girl that ever came into a house half-starved poor thing, a girl so willing that I called her Willing Sophy down upon her knees scrubbing early and late and ever cheerful but always smiling with a black face* (Christmas Stories – 'Mrs. Lirriper's Lodgings').

Southcote, Mr. and **Mrs.:** A begging-letter writer, unsuccessfully prosecuted by the narrator, and his wife. *The Magistrate was wonderfully struck by his educational acquirements, deeply impressed by the excellence of his letters, exceedingly sorry to see a man of his attainments there, complimented him highly on his powers of composition, and was quite charmed to have the agreeable duty of discharging him. A collection was made for the 'poor fellow,' as he was called in the reports, and I left the court with a comfortable sense of being universally regarded as a sort of monster* (Reprinted – 'Begging-letter Writer').

Sowerberry: Undertaker to whom Oliver Twist is apprenticed briefly before running away after being thrashed for fighting with the other apprentice, Noah Claypole. *A tall, gaunt, large-jointed man, attired in a suit of threadbare black, with darned cotton stockings of the same colour, and shoes to answer. His features were not naturally intended to wear a smiling aspect, but he was in general rather given to professional jocosity* (Twist).

Sowerberry, Mrs.: Sowerberry's wife. *A short, thin, squeezed-up woman, with a vixenish countenance* (Twist).

Sownds: Beadle on duty at Little Paul Dombey's christening. *He gave Mr. Dombey a bow and a half-smile of recognition, importing that he (the beadle) remembered to have had the pleasure of attending on him when he buried his wife, and hoped he had enjoyed himself since* (Dombey).

Sowster: Beadle of Oldcastle where the second meeting of the Mudfog Association takes place. *A fat man, with a more enlarged development of that peculiar conformation of countenance which is vulgarly termed a double chin than I remember to have ever seen before. He has also a very red nose, which he attributes to a habit of early rising – so red, indeed, that but for this explanation I should have supposed it to proceed from occasional inebriety* (Mudfog).

Sparkins, Horatio: The name assumed by Samuel Smith, junior partner in the cut-price drapery business of Jones, Spruggins, and Smith, Tottenham-court Road, to take him into wealthy society, such as that of the Maldertons (q.v.), which he captivates by his superior manners and enigmatic air. *Who could he be? He was evidently reserved, and apparently melancholy. Was he a clergyman? – He danced too well. A barrister? – he said he was not called. He used very fine words, and talked a great deal. Could he be a distinguished foreigner, come to England for the purpose of describing the country, its manners and customs; and frequenting public balls and public dinners, with the view of becoming acquainted with high life, polished etiquette, and English refinement? – No, he had not a foreign accent. Was he a surgeon, a contributor to the magazines, a writer of fashionable novels, or an artist? – No; to each and all of these surmises, there existed some valid objection. – 'Then,' said everybody, 'he must be somebody'* (Boz – 'Horatio Sparkins').

Sparkler, Edmund: Mrs. Merdle's son by her first marriage. He marries Fanny Dorrit and rises high in the Circumlocution Office. *Of a chuckle-headed, high-shouldered make, with a general appearance of being, not so much a young man as a swelled boy. He had given so few signs of reason, that a by-word went* among his companions that his brain had been frozen up in a mighty frost which prevailed at St. John's, New Brunswick, at the period of his birth there, and had never thawed from that hour. Another by-word represented him as having in his infancy, through the negligence of a nurse, fallen out of a high window on his head, which had been heard by responsible witnesses to crack. It is probable that both these representations were of ex post facto origin; the young gentleman . . . being monomaniacal in offering marriage to all manner of undesirable young ladies, and in remarking of every successive young lady to whom he tendered a matrimonial proposal that she was 'a doosed fine gal – well educated too – with no biggodd nonsense about her' (Dorrit).

Sparkler, Mrs. Edmund: See **Dorrit, Fanny** (Dorrit).

Sparks, Tom: The one-eyed Boots at the St. James's Arms (Strange Gentleman).

Sparsit: Mrs. Sparsit's late husband. He inherited a fair fortune from his uncle, but owed it all before he came into it, and spent it twice over immediately afterwards. Thus, when he died, at twenty-four (the scene of his decease, Calais, and the cause, brandy), he did not leave his widow, from whom he had been separated soon after the honeymoon, in affluent circumstances (Hard Times).

Sparsit, Mrs.: Sparsit's widow and Bounderby's genteel housekeeper. Here she was now, in her elderly days, with the Coriolanian style of nose and the dense black eyebrows which had captivated Sparsit, making Mr. Bounderby's tea as he took his breakfast (Hard Times).

Spatter, John: Former schoolfriend, and imagined clerk, partner, and relative by marriage of Michael, the Poor Relation (Christmas Stories – 'Poor Relation').

Specks, Joe: Former schoolmate of the Uncommercial Traveller, who, revisiting his home town of Dullborough, finds Specks still there, a respected medical practitioner. Into a room, half surgery, half study, I was shown to await his coming, and I found it, by a series of elaborate accidents, bestrewn with testimonies to Joe. Portrait of Mr. Specks, bust of Mr. Specks, silver cup from grateful patient to Mr. Specks, presentation sermon from local clergyman, dedication poem from local poet, dinner-card from local nobleman, tract on balance of power from local refugee, inscribed Hommage de l'auteur à Specks (Uncommercial – 'Dullborough Town').

Specks, Mrs. Joe: Joe Specks's wife, whom the Uncommercial Traveller discovers to be the former friend of his youth, Lucy Green. She was fat, and if all the hay in the world had been heaped upon her, it could scarcely have altered her face more than Time had altered it from my remembrance of the face that had once looked down upon me (Uncommercial – 'Dullborough Town').

Speddie, Dr.: The doctor who treats Idle's sprained ankle in a Cumberland village and tells Goodchild the story of the corpse in the hotel bed. A tall, thin, large-boned, old gentleman, with an appearance at first sight of being hard-featured; but, at second glance, the mild expression of his face and some particular touches of sweetness and patience about his mouth, corrected this impression and assigned his long professional rides, by day and night, in the bleak hill-weather, as the true cause of that appearance (Two Apprentices).

Spenlow, Clarissa: Elder of Francis Spenlow's two maiden sisters, with whom Dora lives after her father's death. They were dressed alike, but this sister wore her dress with a more youthful air than the other, and perhaps had a trifle more frill, or tucker, or brooch, or bracelet, or some little thing of that kind, which made her look more lively (Copperfield).

Spenlow, Dora: Francis Spenlow's daughter. After his death she lives with her aunts Lavinia and Clarissa, is courted by David Copperfield, and becomes his first wife. Hopelessly immature and impractical, she soon dies. I don't remember who was there, except Dora. I have not the least idea what we had for dinner, besides Dora. My impression is, that I dined off Dora entirely, and sent away half a dozen plates untouched. I sat next to her. I talked to her. She had the most delightful little voice, the gayest little laugh, the pleasantest and most fascinating little ways, that ever led a lost youth into hopeless slavery. She was rather diminutive altogether. So much the more precious, I thought (Copperfield).

Spenlow, Francis: Dora's father. A partner in the law firm to which David Copperfield is apprenticed. He dies suddenly. He was a little light-haired gentleman, with undeniable boots, and the stiffest of white cravats and shirt-collars. He was buttoned up mighty trim and tight, and must have taken a great deal of pains with his whiskers, which were accurately curled. His gold watch-chain was so massive, that a fancy came across me, that he ought to have a sinewy golden arm, to draw it out with, like those which are put up over the gold-beater's shops. He was got up with such care, and was so stiff, that he could hardly bend himself; being obliged, when he glanced at some papers on his desk, after sitting down in his chair, to move his whole body, from the bottom of his spine, like Punch (Copperfield).

Spenlow, Lavinia: Younger of Francis Spenlow's two maiden sisters. Miss Lavinia was an authority in affairs of the heart, by reason of there having anciently existed a certain Mr. Pidger, who played short whist, and was supposed to have been enamoured of her. My private opinion is, that this was an entirely gratuitous assumption, and that Pidger was altogether innocent of any such sentiments – to which he had never given any sort of expression that I could ever hear of. Both Miss Lavinia and Miss Clarissa had a superstition, however, that he would have declared his passion, if he had not been cut short in his youth (at about sixty) by over-drinking his constitution, and over-doing an attempt to set it right again by swilling Bath water (Copperfield).

Spenlow and Jorkins: Law practice of Doctors' Commons of which Francis Spenlow is a proctor, and to which David Copperfield is articled. Spenlow uses Jorkins's reputed hardness as excuse for his refusal to release him *(Copperfield)*.

Sphynx, Sophronia: See **'Marchioness, The'** *(Curiosity Shop)*.

'Spider, The': See **Drummle, Bentley** *(Expectations)*.

Spiker, Henry: Solicitor, fellow dinner-guest with David Copperfield at the Waterbrooks'. *So cold a man, that his head, instead of being grey, seemed to be sprinkled with hoar-frost (Copperfield)*.

Spiker, Mrs. Henry ('Hamlet's Aunt'): Spiker's wife. *A very awful lady in a black velvet dress, and a great black velvet hat, whom I remember as looking like a near relation of Hamlet's – say his aunt (Copperfield)*.

Spinach: One of Miss Flite's birds *(Bleak House)*.

Spottletoe: Relative of the Chuzzlewits with designs on old Martin's money. *Was so bald and had such big whiskers, that he seemed to have stopped his hair, by the sudden application of some powerful remedy, in the very act of falling off his head, and to have fastened it irrevocably on his face (Chuzzlewit)*.

Spottletoe, Mrs.: Spottletoe's wife. *Much too slim for her years, and of a poetical constitution (Chuzzlewit)*.

Sprodgkin, Mrs. Sally: A pestiferous parishioner of the Revd. Frank Milvey. *A portentous old parishioner of the female gender, who was one of the plagues of their lives, and with whom they bore with most exemplary sweetness and good-humour notwithstanding her having an infection of absurdity about her, that communicated itself to everything with which, and everybody with whom, she came in contact. She was a member of the Reverend Frank's congregation and made a point of distinguishing herself in that body, by conspicuously weeping at everything, however cheering, said by the Reverend Frank in his public ministration; also by applying to herself the various lamentations of David, and complaining in a personally injured manner (much in arrear of the clerk and the rest of the respondents) that her enemies were digging pitfalls about her, and breaking her with rods of iron.... But this was not her most inconvenient characteristic, for that took the form of an impression, usually recurring in inclement weather and at about daybreak, that she had something on her mind and stood in immediate need of the Reverend Frank to come and take if off (Mutual Friend)*.

Spruggins, Thomas: Deafeated by Bung in election for beadle of 'Our Parish'. *'Spruggins for Beadle. Ten small children (two of them twins), and a wife!!!' ... Spruggins was a little thin man, in rusty black, with a long pale face, and a countenance expressive of care and fatigue, which might either be attributed to the extent of his family or the anxiety of his feelings (Boz – 'Election for Beadle')*.

Spruggins, Mrs. Thomas: Spruggins's wife. *Spruggins was the favourite at once, and the appearance of his lady, as she went about to solicit votes (which encouraged confident hopes of a still further addition to the house of Spruggins at no remote period), increased the general prepossession in his favour (Boz – 'Election for Beadle')*.

Spyers, Jem: Police officer who arrested Conkey Chickweed in Blathers's anecdote *(Twist)*.

Squeers, Fanny: The Squeerses' daughter, sister of Wackford junior, whom Nicholas Nickleby enrages by his indifference. *Miss Fanny Squeers was in her three-and-twentieth year. If there be any one grace of loveliness inseparable from that particular period of life, Miss Squeers may be presumed to have been possessed of it, as there is no reason to suppose that she was a solitary exception to a universal rule. She was not tall like her mother, but short like her father; from the former she inherited a voice of harsh quality; from the latter a remarkable expression of the right eye, something akin to having none at all (Nickleby)*.

Squeers, Wackford, jun.: The Squeerses' small son, brother of Fanny. *A striking likeness of his father (Nickleby)*.

Squeers, Wackford, sen.: Father of Fanny and Wackford junior. The brutal proprietor of Dotheboys Hall school in Yorkshire where Nicholas Nickleby finds work as a master. He is subsequently transported for possessing a will stolen from Gride. *He had but one eye, and the popular prejudice runs in favour of two. The eye he had, was unquestionably useful, but decidedly not ornamental; being of a greenish grey, and in shape resembling the fan-light of a street door. The blank side of his face was much wrinkled and puckered up, which gave him a very sinister appearance, especially when he smiled, at which times his expression bordered closely on the villainous. His hair was very flat and shiny, save at the ends, where it was brushed stiffly up from a low protruding forehead, which assorted well with his harsh voice and coarse manner. He was about two or three and fifty, and a trifle below the middle size; he wore a white neckerchief with long ends, and a suit of scholastic black; but his coat sleeves being a great deal too long, and his trousers a great deal too short, he appeared ill at ease in his clothes, and as if he were in a perpetual state of astonishment at finding himself so respectable (Nickleby)*.

Squeers, Mrs. Wackford, sen.: Squeers's wife. Mother of Fanny and Wackford junior. *The lady, who was of a large raw-boned figure, was about half a head taller than Mr. Squeers, and was dressed in a dimity night-jacket; with her hair in papers; she had also a dirty nightcap on, relieved by a yellow cotton handkerchief which tied it under the chin (Nickleby)*.

Squires, Olympia: A sweetheart of the Uncommercial Traveller's youth. *Olympia was most beautiful (of course), and I loved her to that degree, that I used to be obliged to get out of my little bed in the night, expressly to exclaim to Solitude, 'O, Olympia Squires!' (Uncommercial – 'Birthday Celebrations')*.

Squod, Phil: George's assistant at the shooting-gallery. *The little man is dressed something like a gunsmith, in a green baize apron and cap; and his face and hands are dirty with gunpowder, and begrimed with the loading of guns (Bleak House).*

Stables, The Hon. Bob: Cousin to Dedlock. *A better man than the Honourable Bob Stables to meet the Hunt at dinner, there could not possibly be (Bleak House).*

Stagg: Blind keeper of the drinking cellars in London where the Prentice Knights meet. He helps Rudge extort money from his wife and is shot dead as the Gordon Riots ringleaders are being rounded up. *The proprietor of this charming retreat ... wore an old tie-wig as bare and frouzy as a stunted hearth-broom.... His eyes were closed; but had they been wide open, it would have been easy to tell, from the attentive expression of the face he turned towards them – pale and unwholesome as might be expected in one of his underground existence – and from a certain anxious raising and quivering of the lids, that he was blind (Rudge).*

Stakes: See **Chops** (*Christmas Stories* – 'Going into Society').

Stalker, Inspector: One of the Detective Force officers of Scotland Yard. *A shrewd, hard-headed Scotchman – in appearance not at all unlike a very acute, thoroughly-trained schoolmaster, from the Normal Establishment at Glasgow (Reprinted – 'Detective Police').*

Stalker, Mrs.: Troublesome denizen of the Saint Giles district visited by the narrator and Inspector Field. *'Mrs. Stalker, I am something'd that need not be written here, if you won't get yourself into trouble, in about half a minute, if I see that face of yours again!' (Reprinted – 'On Duty with Inspector Field').*

Staple: Dingley Dell cricketer who speaks at the dinner after the match with All-Muggleton. *A little man with a puffy Say-nothing-to-me,-or-I'll-contradict-you sort of countenance, who remained very quiet; occasionally looking round him when the conversation slackened, as if he contemplated putting in something very weighty; and now and then bursting into a short cough of inexpressible grandeur (Pickwick).*

Stareleigh, Mr. Justice: The Judge in Bardell and Pickwick. *A most particularly short man, and so fat, that he seemed all face and waistcoat. He rolled in, upon two little turned legs, and having bobbed gravely to the bar, who bobbed gravely to him, put his little legs underneath his table, and his little three-cornered hat upon it; and when Mr. Justice Stareleigh had done this, all you could see of him was two queer little eyes, one broad pink face, and somewhere about half of a big and very comical-looking wig (Pickwick).*

Stargazer: Father of Emma and Galileo Isaac Newton Flamstead, and uncle to Fanny Brown. He wishes to marry off his daughter to his partner, Mooney, and predicts by the stars that Fanny is destined to marry Tom Grig (*Lamplighter*). Referred to as Mr. Stargazer in the dramatic version but given no specific name in 'The Lamplighter's Story'.

Stargazer, Emma: Stargazer's daughter, sister of Galileo Isaac Newton Flamstead. Her father wants her to marry his partner, Mooney, but the latter is not interested (*Lamplighter*). She has no surname in the subsequent prose version of this farce, entitled 'The Lamplighter's Story'.

Stargazer, Galileo Isaac Newton Flamstead: Son of Stargazer and brother of Emma. Although he is almost of age, his father regards him still as a child (*Lamplighter*). He has no surname in the subsequent prose version of this farce, entitled 'The Lamplighter's Story'.

Starling, Mrs.: Friend of the Leavers. *A widow lady who lost her husband when she was young, and lost herself about the same time – for by her own count she has never since grown five years older (Young Couples – 'Loving Couple').*

Starling, Alfred: Friend of John, the narrator, who makes one of the party visiting the haunted house. *An uncommonly agreeable young fellow of eight-and-twenty ... who pretends to be 'fast' (another word for loose, as I understand the term), but who is much too good and sensible for that nonsense, and who would have distinguished himself before now, if his father had not unfortunately left him a small independence of two hundred a year, on the strength of which his only occupation in life has been to spend six (Christmas Stories – 'Haunted House'),*

Startop: Fellow boarder with Pip at Matthew Pocket's who assists in the attempt to smuggle Magwitch out of the country. *Startop had been spoiled by a weak mother, and kept at home when he ought to have been at school, but he was devotedly attached to her, and admired her beyond measure. He had a woman's delicacy of feature, and was ... exactly like his mother (Expectations).*

Steadiman, John: Chief mate of the *Golden Mary*. He assumes command and takes up the narrative after Captain Ravender's death. *At this time of chartering the Golden Mary, he was aged thirty-two. A brisk, bright, blue-eyed fellow, a very neat figure and rather under the middle size, never out of the way and never in it, a face that pleased everybody and that all children took to, a habit of going about singing as cheerily as a blackbird, and a perfect sailor (Christmas Stories – 'Golden Mary').*

Steerforth, Mrs.: Steerforth's mother, an autocrat who, when he seduces Little Em'ly, blames her, and when he is killed cannot accept the fact of his death. *An elderly lady, though not very far advanced in years, with a proud carriage and a handsome face (Copperfield).*

Steerforth, James: Schoolfellow and later friend of David Copperfield, seducer of Little Em'ly, whom he later tries to pass on to his servant Littimer. He is drowned in a shipwreck off Yarmouth. *I was not considered as being formally received into the school, however, until J. Steerforth arrived. Before this boy, who was reputed to be a great scholar, and was very* good-looking, and at least half a dozen years my senior, I was carried as before a magistrate. // *What is natural in me, is natural in many other men, I infer, and so I am not afraid to write that I never had loved Steerforth better than when the ties that bound me to him were broken. In the keen distress of the discovery of his unworthiness, I thought more of all that was brilliant in him, I softened more towards all that was good in him, I did more justice to the qualities that might have made him a man of a noble nature and a great name, than ever I had done in the height of my devotion to him. Deeply as I felt my own unconscious part in his pollution of an honest home, I believed that if I had been brought face to face with him, I could not have uttered one reproach (Copperfield).*

Stetta, Violetta: See **Thigsberry, Duke of** *(Curiosity Shop).*

Stiggins, The Revd. Mr.: A drunken hypocrite and leading light at the Brick Lane Temperance meetings until exposed by Tony Weller, whose late wife had been one of Stiggins's gullible admirers and providers. *He was a prim-faced, red-nosed man, with a long, thin countenance, and a semi-rattlesnake sort of eye – rather sharp, but decidedly bad. He wore very short trousers, and black-cotton stockings, which, like the rest of his apparel, were particularly rusty. His looks were starched, but his white neckerchief was not, and its long limp ends straggled over his closely-buttoned waistcoat in a very uncouth and unpicturesque fashion (Pickwick).*

Stiltstalking, Lord Lancaster: A high-ranking oversea representative of the Circumlocution Office. *A grey old gentleman of dignified and sullen appearance.... This noble Refrigerator had iced several European courts in his time, and had done it with such complete success that the very name of Englishman yet struck cold to the stomachs of foreigners who had the distinguished honour of remembering him, at a distance of a quarter of a century (Dorrit).*

Stiltstalking, Tudor: See under **Barnacle, William** *(Dorrit).*

Stokes, Martin: A small farmer *(Village Coquettes).*

Strange Gentleman, The: See **Trott, Alexander** *(Strange Gentleman).*

Straudenheim: Shopkeeper-owner of a large house in Strasbourg, whose odd behaviour entertains the Uncommercial Traveller one wet Sunday evening. *He wore a black velvet skull-cap, and looked usurious and rich. A large-lipped, pear-nosed old man, with white hair, and keen eyes, though near-sighted (Uncommercial – 'Travelling Abroad').*

Straw, Sergeant: One of the Detective Force officers of Scotland Yard. *A little wiry Sergeant of meek demeanour and strong sense, would knock at a door and ask a series of questions in any mild character you choose to prescribe to him, from a charity-boy upwards, and seem as innocent as an infant (Reprinted – 'Detective Police').*

Streaker: Housemaid at the haunted house. *I am unable to say whether she was of an unusually*

lymphatic temperament, or what else was the matter with her, but this young woman became a mere Distillery for the production of the largest and most transparent tears I ever met with. Combined with these characteristics, was a peculiar tenacity of hold in those specimens, so that they didn't fall, but hung upon her face and nose (Christmas Stories – 'Haunted House').*

Strong, Dr.: David Copperfield's Canterbury schoolmaster, later his employer at Highgate. A temporary rift between him and his young wife, Annie, is healed by Mr. Dick. *Dr. Strong looked almost as rusty, to my thinking, as the tall iron rails and gates outside the house ... with his clothes not particularly well brushed, and his hair not particularly well combed; his knee-smalls unbraced; his long black gaiters unbuttoned; and his shoes yawning like two caverns on the hearthrug.... Outside his own domain, and unprotected, he was a very sheep for the shearers. He would have taken his gaiters off his legs, to give away. In fact, there was a story current among us ... that on a frosty day, one winter-time, he actually did bestow his gaiters on a beggar-woman, who occasioned some scandal in the neighbourhood by exhibiting a fine infant from door to door, wrapped in those garments, which were universally recognised, being as well known in the vicinity as the cathedral (Copperfield).*

Strong, Mrs. (Annie): Dr. Strong's wife. A misunderstanding about her relationship with Jack Maldon temporarily estranges them. *A very pretty young lady – whom he called Annie, and who was his daughter, I supposed (Copperfield).*

Struggles: Member of Dingley Dell Cricket Club. *The enthusiastic Struggles (Pickwick).*

Stryver: London barrister who defends Darnay at the Old Bailey. Much of his success is owed to Sydney Carton's 'devilling' for him. *A man of little more than thirty, but looking twenty years older than he was, stout, loud, red, bluff, and free from any drawback of delicacy, had a pushing way of shouldering himself (morally and physically) into companies and conversations, that argued well for his shouldering his way up in life (Two Cities).*

Stubbs: A pony placed at Esther Summerson's exclusive disposal by Lawrence Boythorn. *A chubby pony, with a short neck and a mane all over his eyes, who could canter – when he would – so easily and quietly, that he was a treasure (Bleak House).*

Stubbs, Mrs.: Percy Noakes's laundress. *A dirty old woman, with an inflamed countenance (Boz – 'Steam Excursion').*

Styles: A vice-president of the statistics session at the second meeting of the Mudfog Association *(Mudfog).*

'Suffolk Bantam': See **'Middlesex Dumpling'** *(Pickwick).*

Sulliwin, Mrs.: Resident of Seven Dials, the current bone of contention between Mary and Sarah. *'Here's poor dear Mrs. Sulliwin, as has five blessed children of her own, can't go out a charing for one arternoon, but what hussies must be a comin', and 'ticing away her* oun' 'usband, as she's been married to twelve year come next Easter Monday, for I see the certificate ven I vas drinkin' a cup o' tea vith her, only the werry last blessed Ven'sday as ever was sent' (Boz – 'Seven Dials').

Summerson, Esther ('Dame Durden'): Narrator of much of the story. An orphan, she is adopted by John Jarndyce and becomes companion to Ada Clare. Jarndyce subsequently wishes to marry her, but magnanimously gives her to Allan Woodcourt. She proves to be the illegitimate child of Lady Dedlock and Hawdon. *I am not clever. I always knew that. . . . I had always rather a noticing way – not a quick way, O no! – a silent way of noticing what passed before me, and thinking I should like to understand it better. I have not by any means a quick understanding. When I love a person very tenderly indeed, it seems to brighten. But even that may be my vanity (Bleak House).*

Superintendent: Liverpool police officer who conducts the Uncommercial Traveller on his tour of sailormen's haunts. *A tall well-looking well-set-up man of a soldierly bearing, with a cavalry air, a good chest, and a resolute but not by any means ungentle face. He carried in his hand a plain black walking-stick of hard wood; and whenever and wherever, at any after-time of the night, he struck it on the pavement with a ringing sound, it instantly produced a whistle out of the darkness, and a policeman (Uncommercial – 'Poor Mercantile Jack').*

Susan: Rosina Nightingale's maid *(Nightingale's Diary).*

Susan: Mrs. Mann's maid *(Twist).*

Sweedlepipe, Paul ('Poll'): Bird-fancier and barber. Mrs. Gamp's landlord in High Holborn and great friend of Bailey, whom he eventually takes into partnership. *A little elderly man, with a clammy cold right hand, from which even rabbits and birds could not remove the smell of shaving-soap. Poll had something of the bird in his nature; not of the hawk or eagle, but of the sparrow, that builds in chimney-stacks, and inclines to human company. He was not quarrelsome, though, like the sparrow; but peaceful, like the dove. In his walk he strutted; and, in this respect, he bore a faint resemblance to the pigeon, as well as in a certain prosiness of speech, which might, in its monotony, be likened to the cooing of that bird. He was very inquisitive; and when he stood at his shop-door in the evening-tide, watching the neighbours, with his head on one side, and his eye cocked knowingly, there was a dash of the raven in him. Yet, there was no more wickedness in Poll than in a robin (Chuzzlewit).*

Sweeney, Mrs.: The Uncommercial Traveller's servant when he is living in Gray's Inn. *In figure extremely like an old family-umbrella, whose dwelling confronts a dead wall in a court off Gray's Inn Lane, and who is usually fetched into the passage of that bower, when wanted, from some neighbouring home of industry, which has the curious property of imparting an inflammatory appearance to her visage. Mrs. Sweeney is one of the race of professed laundresses, and is the compiler of a remarkable manuscript volume entitled 'Mrs. Sweeney's Book,' from which much curious statistical information may be gathered respecting the high prices and small uses of soda, soap, sand, firewood, and other such articles (Uncommercial – 'Chambers').*

Swidger, George: Eldest son of Philip and brother of William. Repentant on his deathbed for his sins, he forgets them under Redlaw's influence and dies unregretful. *Redlaw paused at the bedside, and looked down on the figure that was stretched upon the mattress. It was that of a man, who should have been in the vigour of his life, but on whom it was not likely the sun would ever shine again. The vices of his forty or fifty years' career had so branded him, that, in comparison with their effects upon his face, the heavy hand of time upon the old man's face who watched him had been merciful and beautifying (Christmas Books – 'Haunted Man').*

Swidger, Philip: Father of George and William. He loses the happiness of his old age under Redlaw's influence, but it is restored through Milly Swidger. *'Superannuated keeper and custodian of this Institution, eighty-seven year old' (Christmas Books – 'Haunted Man').*

Swidger, William and **Mrs. William (Milly):** Redlaw's manservant, Philip Swidger's youngest son, brother of George; and his wife, Denham's ministering angel in his illness. *Mrs. William, like Mr. William, was a simple, innocent-looking person, in whose smooth cheeks the cheerful red of the husband's official waistcoat was very pleasantly repeated. But whereas Mr. William's light hair stood on end all over his head, and seemed to draw his eyes up with it in an excess of bustling readiness for anything, the dark brown hair of Mrs. William was carefully smoothed down, and waved away under a trim tidy cap, in the most exact and quiet manner imaginable. Whereas Mr. William's very trousers hitched themselves up at the ankles, as if it were not in their iron-grey nature to rest without looking about them, Mrs. William's neatly flowered skirts – red and white, like her own pretty face – were as composed and orderly, as if the very wind that blew so hard out of doors could not disturb one of their folds (Christmas Books – 'Haunted Man').*

Swillenhausen, Baron and **Baroness von:** Parents-in-law of Baron von Koëldwethout (q.v.) *(Nickleby).*

Swills, Little: Comic singer at the Harmonic Meetings at the Sol's Arms. *Sensation is created by the entrance of a chubby little man in a large shirt-collar, with a moist eye, and an inflamed nose, who modestly takes a position near the door as one of the general public, but seems familiar with the room too. A whisper circulates that this is Little Swills. It is considered not unlikely that he will get up an imitation of the Coroner, and make it the principal feature of the Harmonic Meeting in the evening (Bleak House).*

Swiveller, Dick: Friend of Fred Trent, who persuades him to give up Sophy Wackles and wait to marry Little Nell for her grandfather's money. Quilp manipulates him into becoming Brass's clerk, but he is repelled by what he discovers and helps to expose Brass and Quilp. He befriends, educates, and marries The Marchioness. *His wiry hair, dull eyes, and sallow face, would still have been strong witnesses against him. His attire was not, as he had himself hinted, remarkable for the nicest arrangement, but was in a state of disorder which strongly induced the idea that he had gone to bed in it. It consisted of a brown body-coat with a great many brass buttons up the front, and only one behind; a bright check neckerchief, a plaid waistcoat, soiled white trousers, and a very limp hat, worn with the wrong side foremost, to hide a hole in the brim. The breast of his coat was ornamented with an outside pocket from which there peeped forth the cleanest end of a very large and very ill-favoured handkerchief; his dirty wristbands were pulled down as far as possible and ostentatiously folded back over his cuffs; he displayed no gloves, and carried a yellow cane having at the top a bone hand with the semblance of a ring on its little finger and a black ball in its grasp (Curiosity Shop).*

Swoshle, Mrs. Henry George Alfred: See under **Tapkins, Mrs.** *(Mutual Friend).*

Swosser, Captain, R.N.: Deceased first husband of Mrs. Bayham Badger. *Mrs. Badger signified to us that she had never madly loved but once; and that the object of that wild affection, never to be recalled in its fresh enthusiasm, was Captain Swosser (Bleak House).*

Sylvia: Daughter of the farmhouse family at Hoghton Towers where George Silverman is placed by Hawkyard ('Silverman').

Tabblewick, Mrs.: Friend of the Bobtail Widgers. *She is no doubt beautiful, very beautiful; they once thought her the most beautiful woman ever seen; still if you press them for an honest answer, they are bound to say that this was before they had ever seen our lovely friend on the sofa, (the sofa is hard by, and our lovely friend can't help hearing the whispers in which this is said) (Young Couples – 'Plausible Couple').*

Tabby: Servant at Miss Griffin's school. *A grinning and good-natured soul called Tabby, who was the serving drudge of the house, and had no more figure than one of the beds, and upon whose face there was always more or less black-lead (Christmas Stories – 'Haunted House').*

Tacker: Mould the undertaker's chief mourner. *An obese person, with his waistcoat in closer connection with his legs than is quite reconcilable with the established ideas of grace; with that cast of feature which is figuratively called a bottle-nose; and with a face covered all over with pimples. He had been a tender plant once upon a time, but from constant blowing in the fat atmosphere of funerals, had run to seed (Chuzzlewit).*

Tackleton: Remaining partner of Gruff and Tackleton, by which name he is still known. He employs Caleb Plummer and is misguidedly adored by blind Bertha Plummer, and almost manages to marry May Fielding, being jilted on the wedding day. *Tackleton the Toy-merchant, was a man whose vocation had been quite misunderstood by his Parents and Guardians. If they had made him a Money Lender, or a sharp Attorney, or a Sheriff's Officer, or a Broker, he might have sown his discontented oats in his youth, and, after having had the full run of himself in ill-natured transactions, might have turned out amiable, at last, for the sake of a little freshness and novelty. But, cramped and chafing in the peaceable pursuit of toy-making, he was a domestic Ogre, who had been living on children all his life, and was their implacable enemy. He despised all toys; wouldn't have bought one for the world; delighted, in his malice, to insinuate grim expressions into the faces of brown-paper farmers who drove pigs to market, bell-men who advertised lost lawyers' consciences, moveable old ladies who darned stockings or carved pies; and other like samples of his stock-in-trade. In appalling masks; hideous, hairy, red-eyed Jacks in Boxes; Vampire Kites; demoniacal Tumblers who wouldn't lie down, and were perpetually flying forward, to stare infants out of countenance; his soul perfectly revelled. They were his only relief, and safety-valve (Christmas Books – 'Cricket').*

Tadger, Brother: Prominent official of the Brick Lane Branch of the United Grand Junction Ebenezer Temperance Association. *A little emphatic man, with a bald head, and drab shorts (Pickwick).*

Tamaroo: Successor to Bailey as Mrs. Todgers's servant. *An old woman whose name was reported to be Tamaroo – which seemed an · impossibility. Indeed it appeared in the fulness of time that the jocular boarders had appropriated the word from an English ballad, in which it is supposed to express the bold and fiery nature of a certain hackney-coachman; and that it was bestowed upon Mr. Bailey's successor by reason of her having nothing fiery about her, except an occasional attack of that fire which is called St. Anthony's.... She was chiefly remarkable for a total absence of all comprehension upon every subject whatever. She was a perfect Tomb for messages and small parcels; and when despatched to the Post-office with letters, had been seen frequently endeavouring to insinuate them into casual chinks in private doors, under the delusion that any door with a hole in it would answer the purpose (Chuzzlewit).*

Tangle: Counsel in the suit of Jarndyce and Jarndyce. *Knows more of Jarndyce and Jarndyce than anybody. He is famous for it – supposed never to have read anything else since he left school (Bleak House).*

Tape: Prince Bull's tyrannical old godmother, symbolising the Civil Service Establishment. *She was a Fairy, this Tape, and was a bright red all over. She was disgustingly prim and formal, and could never bend herself a hair's breadth this way or that way, out of her naturally crooked shape. But, she was very potent in her wicked art. She could stop the fastest thing in the world, change the strongest thing into the weakest, and the most useful into the most useless. To do this she had only to put her cold hand upon it, and repeat her own name, Tape. Then it withered away (Reprinted – 'Prince Bull').*

Tapkins, Mrs.: One of the first to leave her card on the newly-elevated Boffins. *All the world and his wife and daughter leave cards. Sometimes the world's wife has so many daughters, that her card reads rather like a Miscellaneous Lot at an Auction; comprising Mrs. Tapkins, Miss Tapkins, Miss Frederica Tapkins, Miss Antonina Tapkins, Miss Malvina Tapkins, and Miss Euphemia Tapkins; at the same time, the same lady leaves the card of Mrs. Henry George Alfred Swoshle, née Tapkins; also, a card, Mrs. Tapkins at Home, Wednesdays, Music, Portland Place (Mutual Friend).*

Tapkins, Felix: Bachelor friend of the Lovetowns, who flirts with Mrs. Lovetown *(Is She His Wife?).*

Tapley, Mark: Ostler at the Blue Dragon, Salisbury, renamed The Jolly Tapley after his marriage to its landlady, Mrs. Lupin. Later young Martin Chuzzlewit's servant, bosom friend and travelling companion. *Walked with a light quick step, and sang as he went: for certain in a very loud voice, but not unmusically. He was a young fellow, of some five or six-and-twenty perhaps, and was dressed in such a free and fly-away fashion, that the long ends of his loose red neckcloth were streaming out behind him quite as often as before. (Chuzzlewit).*

Taplin, Harry: Comedian who sings a comic duet with Amelia Martin at White Conduit. *'Go to work, Harry,' cried the comic gentleman's personal friends. 'Tap – tap – tap,' went the leader's bow on the music desk. The symphony began, and was soon afterwards followed by a faint kind of ventriloquial chirping, proceeding apparently from the deepest recesses of the interior of Miss Amelia Martin (Boz – 'Mistaken Milliner').*

Tappertit, Simon (Sim): Gabriel Varden's apprentice and Joe Willet's rival for Dolly. Leader of the Prentice Knights, later United Bull-Dogs (q.v.), he becomes a leader of the Gordon Riots but has his legs crushed. Discharged from prison, he is helped by Gabriel to set up as a shoe-black and marries a rag-and-bone man's widow. *An old-fashioned, thin-faced, sleek-haired, sharp-nosed, small-eyed little fellow, very little more than five feet high, and thoroughly convinced in his own mind that he was above the middle size; rather tall, in fact, than otherwise. Of his figure, which was well enough formed, though somewhat of the leanest, he entertained the highest admiration; and with his legs, which, in knee-breeches, were perfect curiosities of littleness, he was enraptured to a degree amounting to enthusiasm. He also had some majestic, shadowy ideas, which had never been quite fathomed by his intimate friends, concerning the power of his eye. . . . As certain liquors, confined in casks too cramped in their dimensions, will ferment, and fret, and chafe in their imprisonment, so the spiritual essence or soul of Mr. Tappertit would sometimes fume within that precious cask, his body, until, with great foam and froth and splutter, it would force a vent, and carry all before it (Rudge).*

Tappleton, Lieutenant: Dr. Slammer's second in the abortive duel at Rochester (Pickwick).

F

Tartar, Lieutenant, R.N.: Former schoolfellow of Canon Crisparkle. Neville Landless's neighbour at Staple Inn, he gives up his rooms to Rosa Bud after her flight from Cloisterham. *A handsome gentleman, with a young face, but with an older figure in its robustness and its breadth of shoulder; say a man of eight-and-twenty, or at the utmost thirty; so extremely sunburnt that the contrast between his brown visage and the white forehead shaded out of doors by his hat, and the glimpses of white throat below the neckerchief, would have been almost ludicrous but for his broad temples, bright blue eyes, clustering brown hair, and laughing teeth (Drood).*

Tarter, Bob: First Boy at the school, helped by Old Cheeseman, whom he has always persecuted. *His father was in the West Indies, and he owned, himself, that his father was worth Millions. He had great power among our fellows (Christmas Stories – 'Schoolboy's Story').*

Tatham, Mrs.: Pawnbroker's customer. *An old sallow-looking woman, who has been leaning with both arms on the counter with a small bundle before her, for half an hour previously (Boz – 'Pawnbroker's Shop').*

Tatt: Friend of Inspector Wield. His diamond pin is stolen at Epsom Station on Derby Day by the Swell Mob, but ingeniously recovered by Sergeant Witchem. *'A gentleman formerly in the public line, quite an amateur Detective in his way, and very much respected' (Reprinted – 'Three "Detective" Anecdotes').*

'Tattycoram': See **Beadle, Harriet** *(Dorrit).*

Taunton, Captain: Officer commanding Richard Doubledick's company. He is killed, as a Major, at Badajos. *A young gentleman not above five years his senior, whose eyes had an expression in them which affected Private Richard Doubledick in a very remarkable way. They were bright, handsome, dark eyes, – what are called laughing eyes generally, and, when serious, rather steady than severe, – but they were the only eyes now left in his narrowed world that Private Richard Doubledick could not stand. Unabashed by evil report and punishment, defiant of everything else and everybody else, he had but to know that those eyes looked at him for a moment, and he felt ashamed (Christmas Stories – 'Seven Poor Travellers').*

Taunton, Mrs.: Widowed mother of Emily and Sophia. They are the great rivals of Mrs. Briggs and her girls (q.v.). *A good-looking widow of fifty, with the form of a giantess and the mind of a child. The pursuit of pleasure, and some means of killing time, were the sole end of her existence. She doted on her daughters, who were as frivolous as herself (Boz – 'Steam Excursion').*

Taunton, Mrs.: Captain Taunton's mother. After his death she nurses and virtually adopts Richard Doubledick. *It gradually seemed to him as if in his maturity he had recovered a mother; it gradually seemed to her as if in her bereavement she had found a son (Christmas Stories – 'Seven Poor Travellers').*

Tellson's Bank: The London bank served by Jarvis Lorry as confidential clerk and messenger. *Tellson's Bank by Temple Bar was an old-fashioned place, even in the year one thousand seven hundred and eighty. It was very small, very dark, very ugly, very incommodious. It was an old-fashioned place, moreover, in the moral attribute that the partners in the House were proud of its smallness, proud of its darkness, proud of its ugliness, proud of its incommodiousness. They were even boastful of its eminence in those particulars, and were fired by an express conviction that, if it were less objectionable, it would be less respectable (Two Cities).*

Testator: Occupant of chambers in Lyon's Inn, who furnishes his rooms with items found in a cellar and is duly visited by their perhaps spectral owner (*Uncommercial* – 'Chambers').

Tetterby, Adolphus: Newsagent husband of Sophia and father of numerous children, including 'Dolphus, Johnny, and Sally. His customary good nature is temporarily lost under Redlaw's influence, but returns. *The small man who sat in the small parlour, making fruitless attempts to read his newspaper peaceably in the midst of this disturbance, was the father of the family, and the chief of the firm described in the inscription over the little shop front, by the name and title of A. TETTERBY AND CO., NEWSMEN. Indeed, strictly speaking, he was the only personage answering to that designation; as Co. was a mere poetical abstraction, altogether baseless and impersonal (Christmas Books* – 'Haunted Man').

Tetterby, Mrs. Adolphus (Sophia): Wife of Adolphus, who calls her his 'little woman'. Mother of 'Dolphus, Johnny, Sally and others. *The process of induction by which Mr. Tetterby had come to the conclusion that his wife was a little woman, was his own secret. She would have made two editions of himself, very easily. Considered as an individual, she was rather remarkable for being robust and portly; but considered with reference to her husband, her dimensions became magnificent (Christmas Books* – 'Haunted Man').

Tetterby, 'Dolphus: The Tetterbys' eldest son, brother of Johnny, Sally and others. *Was also in the newspaper line of life, being employed, by a more thriving firm than his father and Co., to vend newspapers at a railway station, where his chubby little person, like a shabbily disguised Cupid, and his shrill little voice (he was not much more than ten years old), were as well known as the hoarse panting of the locomotives, running in and out (Christmas Books* – 'Haunted Man').

Tetterby, Johnny: The Tetterbys' second son, brother of 'Dolphus, Sally and others. In constant charge of the baby, Sally. *Another little boy – the biggest there, but still little – was tottering to and fro, bent on one side, and considerably affected in the knees by the weight of a large baby, which he was supposed, by a fiction that obtains sometimes in sanguine families, to be hushing to sleep (Christmas Books* – 'Haunted Man').

Tetterby, Sally: The baby of the Tetterby family, sister of 'Dolphus, in the constant charge of her brother Johnny. *It was a very Moloch of a baby, on whose insatiate altar the whole existence of this particular young brother was offered up a daily sacrifice. Its personality may be said to have consisted in its never being quiet, in any one place, for five consecutive minutes, and never going to sleep when required. 'Tetterby's baby' was as well known in the neighbourhood as the postman or the pot-boy (Christmas Books* – 'Haunted Man').

Théophile, Corporal: A French soldier who cares for the orphan baby Bebelle until his death fighting a fire. *A smart figure of a man of thirty, perhaps a thought under the middle size, but very neatly made, – a sunburnt Corporal with a brown peaked beard.... Nothing was amiss or awry about the Corporal. A lithe and nimble Corporal, quite complete, from the sparkling dark eyes under his knowing uniform cap to his sparkling white gaiters. The very image and presentment of a Corporal of his country's army, in the line of his shoulders, the line of his waist, the broadest line of his Bloomer trousers, and their narrowest line at the calf of his leg (Christmas Stories* – 'Somebody's Luggage').

Thicknesse: A baker, one of the admiring audience of the gentleman connected with the press at the Green Dragon, Westminster Bridge. *A large stomach surmounted by a man's head, and placed on the top of two particularly short legs (Mudfog* – 'Mr. Robert Bolton').

Thigsberry, Duke of and **Stetta, Violetta:** Subjects of an anecdote by which Chuckster seeks to impress the Garlands. *Acquainted them with the precise amount of the income guaranteed by the Duke of Thigsberry to Violetta Stetta of the Italian Opera, which it appeared was payable quarterly, and not half-yearly, as the public had been given to understand, and which was exclusive, and not inclusive, (as had been monstrously stated), of jewellery, perfumery, hair-powder for five footmen, and two daily changes of kid-gloves for a page (Curiosity Shop).*

Thomas: Dedlock's groom (*Bleak House*).

Thomas: Waiter at the Winglebury Arms. *The waiter pulled down the window-blind, and then pulled it up again – for a regular waiter must do something before he leaves the room – adjusted the glasses on the sideboard, brushed a place that was not dusty, rubbed his hands very hard, walked stealthily to the door, and evaporated (Boz* – 'Great Winglebury Duel').

Thomas: Knag's boy. *Nearly half as tall as a shutter (Nickleby).*

Thomas: Waiter on the gentleman who killed himself in the cause of crumpet-eating (*Pickwick*).

Thompson, Mrs.: Friend of Fairfax who solicits his opinion of Mrs. Barker (*Young Gentlemen* – 'Censorious Young Gentleman').

Thompson, Bill: Popular performer at the Victoria Theatre. *The inimitable manner in which Bill*

Thompson can 'come the double monkey', or go through the mysterious involutions of a sailor's horn-pipe (Boz – 'The Streets – Night').

Thompson, Julia: A friend of Felix Nixon (*Young Gentlemen* – 'Domestic Young Gentleman').

Thompson, Tally-Ho (alias **Thomas Pigeon**): Notorious horse-stealer, couper, and magsman, taken by Sergeant Witchem (*Reprinted* – 'Detective Police').

Thomson, Sir John, M.P.: Eminent Parliamentarian (*Boz* – 'Parliamentary Sketch').

Tibbs, Mr. and Mrs.: Proprietress of a boarding house in Great Coram Street, London, and her hen-pecked husband. They eventually separate. *Mrs. Tibbs was somewhat short of stature, and Mr. Tibbs was by no means a large man. He had, moreover, very short legs, but, by way of indemnification, his face was peculiarly long. He was to his wife what the 0 is in 90 – he was of some importance with her – he was nothing without her. Mrs. Tibbs was always talking. Mr. Tibbs rarely spoke; but, if it were at any time possible to put in a word, when he should have said nothing at all, he had that talent. Mrs. Tibbs detested long stories, and Mr. Tibbs had one, the conclusion of which had never been heard by his most intimate friends. It always began, 'I recollect when I was in the volunteer corps, in eighteen hundred and six,' – but, as he spoke very slowly and softly, and his better-half very quickly and loudly, he rarely got beyond the introductory sentence (Boz – 'Boarding -House').*

Tickit, Mrs.: The Meagleses' cook and housekeeper. *Cook and Housekeeper when the family were at home, and Housekeeper only when the family were away.... When they went away, she always put on the silk-gown and the jet-black row of curls represented in that portrait (her hair was reddish-grey in the kitchen), established herself in the breakfast-room, put her spectacles between two particular leaves of Dr. Buchanan's Domestic Medicine, and sat looking over the blind all day until they came back again (Dorrit).*

Tickle: Exhibitor in the display of models and mechanical science at the second meeting of the Mudfog Association. *Displayed his newly-invented spectacles, which enabled the wearer to discern, in very bright colours, objects at a great distance, and rendered him wholly blind to those immediately before him (Mudfog).*

Tiddypot: Vestryman, of Gumption House (*Reprinted* – 'Our Vestry').

Tiffey: Senior clerk at Spenlow and Jorkins. *A little dry man, sitting by himself, who wore a stiff brown wig that looked as if it were made of ginger-bread (Copperfield).*

Tigg, Montague: A confidence-trickster associated with Chevy Slyme. Later, as Tigg Montague, he promotes the fraudulent Anglo-Bengalee Disinterested Loan and Life Assurance Company. Murdered by Jonas Chuzzlewit for knowing too much about his past. *Of that order of appearance, which is currently termed shabby-genteel.... His nether garments were*

of a bluish grey – violent in its colours once, but sobered now by age and dinginess – and were so stretched and strained in a tough conflict between his braces and his straps, that they appeared every moment in danger of flying asunder at the knees. His coat, in colour blue and of a military cut, was buttoned and frogged, up to his chin. His cravat was, in hue and pattern, like one of those mantles which hair-dressers are accustomed to wrap about their clients, during the progress of the professional mysteries. His hat had arrived at such a pass that it would have been hard to determine whether it was originally white or black. But he wore a moustache – a shaggy moustache too: nothing in the meek and merciful way, but quite in the fierce and scornful style: the regular Satanic sort of thing – and he wore, besides, a vast quantity of unbrushed hair. He was very dirty and very jaunty; very bold and very mean; very swaggering and very slinking; very much like a man who might have been something better, and unspeakably like a man who deserved to be something worse (Chuzzlewit).*

Tiggin and Welps: City house for which the Bagman's uncle travelled (*Pickwick*).

Tim, Tiny: see **Cratchit, Tim** (*Christmas Books* – 'Christmas Carol').

Timbered: A vice-president of the statistics session at the first meeting of the Mudfog Association (*Mudfog*).

Timberry, Snittle: Member of Crummles's theatrical company who chairs the farewell supper to the Crummles family. *It is observable that when people upon the stage are in any strait involving the very last extremity of weakness and exhaustion, they invariably perform feats of strength requiring great ingenuity and muscular power. Thus, a wounded prince or bandit-chief, who is bleeding to death and too faint to move, except to the softest music (and then only upon his hands and knees), shall be seen to approach a cottage door for aid, in such a series of writhings and twistings, and with such curlings up of the legs, and such rollings over and over, and such gettings up and tumblings down again, as could never be achieved save by a very strong man skilled in posture-making. And so natural did this sort of performance come to Mr. Snittle Timberry, that on their way out of the theatre and towards the tavern where the supper was to be holden, he testified the severity of his recent indisposition and its wasting effects upon the nervous system, by a series of gymnastic performances which were the admiration of all witnesses (Nickleby).*

Timkins: Candidate for election for beadle of 'Our Parish'. *'Timkins for Beadle. Nine small children!!!'* (*Boz* – 'Election for Beadle').

Timpson: Proprietor of coaches, including the Blue-Eyed Maid, whose business in Dullborough the Uncommercial Traveller finds taken over, and knocked down, by Pickford (*Uncommercial* – 'Dullborough Town').

Timson, The Revd. Charles: An unctuous friend of Gabriel Parsons, engaged to Miss Lillerton, whom he marries. *Mr. Timson, having conscientious scruples on the subject of card-playing, drank brandy-and-water* (Boz – 'Watkins Tottle').

Tinker, The: A laconic idler questioned by Mr. Traveller on his way to Mopes's. *A short-winded one, from whom no further breath of information was to be derived* (Christmas Stories – 'Tom Tiddler's Ground').

Tinker, The: A young ruffian who frightens David Copperfield on the Dover Road. *A tinker, I suppose, from his wallet and brazier* (Copperfield).

Tinkler: William Dorrit's valet. *Of a serious and composed countenance* (Dorrit).

Tinkles, Horatio: see **Hunter, Horace** (Strange Gentleman).

Tinkling, William: Eight-year-old author of the introductory romantic tale and editor of the others. 'Bridegroom' to Nettie Ashford ('Holiday Romance').

'Tip': see **Dorrit, Edward** (Dorrit).

Tip: Gabblewig's servant. He assists Slap in his final attempt to extort money from Nightingale by posing as Nightingale's son Christopher (Nightingale's Diary).

Tipkins against Bullock: A case conducted by Spenlow and David Copperfield. *It arose out of a scuffle between two church-wardens, one of whom was alleged to have pushed the other against a pump; the handle of which pump projecting into a school-house, which school-house was under a gable of the church-roof, made the push an ecclesiastical offence* (Copperfield).

Tipkisson: Leading supporter of our honourable friend's opponent for election to Parliament, discredited by religious aspersions. *Our honourable friend being come into the presence of his constituents, and having professed with great suavity that he was delighted to see his good friend Tipkisson there, in his working-dress – his good friend Tipkisson being an inveterate saddler, who always opposes him, and for whom he has a mortal hatred* (Reprinted – 'Our Honourable Friend').

Tipp: Carman at Murdstone and Grinby's warehouse. *Wore a red jacket, used to address me sometimes as 'David'* (Copperfield).

Tippin Family: A theatrical family appearing at Ramsgate. *A short female, in a blue velvet hat and feathers, was led into the orchestra, by a fat man in black tights and cloudy Berlins. . . . The talented Tippin having condescendingly acknowledged the clapping of hands, and shouts of 'bravo!' which greeted her appearance, proceeded to sing the popular cavatina of 'Bid me discourse,' accompanied on the piano by Mr. Tippin; after which, Mr. Tippin sang a comic song, accompanied on the piano by Mrs. Tippin: the applause consequent upon which, was only to be exceeded by the enthusiastic approbation bestowed upon an air with variations on the guitar, by Miss Tippin, accompanied on the chin by Master Tippin* (Boz – 'Tuggses at Ramsgate').

Tippins, Lady: Friend of Lightwood from his boyhood, and frequently at the Veneerings' gatherings. *With an immense obtuse drab oblong face, like a face in a tablespoon, and a dyed Long Walk up the top of her head, as a convenient public approach to the bunch of false hair behind. // She has a reputation for giving smart accounts of things, and she must be at these people's early, my dear, to lose nothing of the fun. Whereabout in the bonnet and drapery announced by her name, any fragment of the real woman may be concealed, is perhaps known to her maid; but you could easily buy all you see of her, in Bond Street: or you might scalp her, and peel her, and scrape her, and make two Lady Tippinses out of her, and yet not penetrate to the genuine article. She has a large gold eye-glass, has Lady Tippins, to survey the proceedings with. If she had one in each eye, it might keep that other drooping lid up, and look more uniform. But perennial youth is in her artificial flowers, and her list of lovers is full* (Mutual Friend).

Tisher, Mrs.: Miss Twinkleton's companion and assistant. *A deferential widow with a weak back, a chronic sigh, and a suppressed voice, who looks after the young ladies' wardrobes, and leads them to infer that she has seen better days* (Drood).

Titbull's: A group of east London alms-houses visited by the Uncommercial Traveller. *Of Titbull I know no more than that he deceased in 1723, that his Christian name was Sampson, and his social designation Esquire, and that he founded these Alms-Houses as Dwellings for Nine Poor Women and Six Poor Men by his Will and Testament. I should not know even this much, but for its being inscribed on a grim stone very difficult to read, let into the front of the centre house of Titbull's Alms-Houses, and which stone is ornamented a-top with a piece of sculptured drapery resembling the effigy of Titbull's bath-towel* (Uncommercial – 'Titbull's Alms-Houses').

Tix, Tom: Co-bailiff, with Scaley, in possession at Madame Mantalini's. *A little man in brown, very much the worse for wear, who brought with him a mingled fumigation of stale tobacco and fresh onions* (Nickleby).

Todd's Young Man: Baker's boy, a favourite with housemaids in the Covent Garden district. *Mr. Todd's young man, who being fond of mails, but more of females, takes a short look at the mails, and a long look at the girls* (Boz – 'The Streets – Morning').

'Toddles': Pet name of one of Betty Higden's charges (Mutual Friend).

Toddyhigh, Joe: Boyhood friend of the Lord Mayor Elect in the Deaf Gentleman's narrative, who overhears Gog and Magog talking in the Guildhall. *Not over and above well dressed, and was very far from being fat or rich-looking in any sense of the word, yet he spoke with a kind of modest confidence, and assumed an easy, gentlemanly sort of an air, to which nobody but a rich man can lawfully presume* (Humphrey).

Todgers, Mrs. M.: Proprietress of the boarding-house where the Pecksniffs lodge in London. *Rather a* *bony and hard-featured lady, with a row of curls in front of her head, shaped like little barrels of beer; and on the top of it something made of net – you couldn't call it a cap exactly – which looked like a black cobweb (Chuzzlewit).*

Tollimglower, Lady: Subject of obscure anecdotes told by old Mrs. Wardle. *The worthy old soul launched forth into a minute and particular account of her own wedding, with a dissertation on the fashion of wearing high-heeled shoes, and some particulars concerning the life and adventures of the beautiful Lady Tollimglower, deceased: at all of which the old lady herself laughed very heartily indeed, and so did the young ladies too, for they were wondering among themselves what on earth grandma was talking about (Pickwick).*

Tom: The struggling young doctor's servant. *A corpulent round-headed boy, who, in consideration of the sum of one shilling per week and his food, was let out by the parish to carry medicine and messages. As there was no demand for the medicine, however, and no necessity for the messages, he usually occupied his unemployed hours – averaging fourteen a day – in abstracting peppermint drops, taking animal nourishment, and going to sleep (Boz – 'Black Veil').*

Tom: Conductor of the 'Admiral Napier' omnibus. *Settled the contest in a most satisfactory manner, for all parties, by seizing Dumps round the waist, and thrusting him into the middle of his vehicle which had just come up and only wanted the sixteenth inside (Boz – 'Bloomsbury Christening').*

Tom: One of the officers who arrest William Warden (Boz – 'Drunkard's Death').

Tom: The Gattletons' servant, co-opted to appear as a fisherman in the private theatricals. *'When the revolt takes place, Tom must keep rushing in on one side and out on the other, with a pickaxe, as fast as he can. The effect will be electrical; it will look exactly as if there were an immense number of 'em' (Boz – 'Mrs. Joseph Porter').*

Tom: Gardener to Gabriel Parsons. *A gardener in a blue apron, who let himself out to do the ornamental for half-a-crown a day and his 'keep' (Boz – 'Watkins Tottle').*

Tom: The Revd. Charles Timson's servant (Boz – 'Watkins Tottle').

Tom: Driver of the train that kills the Signal-man (Christmas Stories – 'Mugby Junction').

Tom: The pavement-artist whose story forms part of this series. He is infatuated with Henrietta, but she leaves him for another pavement-artist. *If there's a blighted public character going, I am the party. And often as you have seen, do see, and will see, my Works, it's fifty thousand to one if you'll ever see me, unless, when the candles are burnt down and the Commercial character is gone, you should happen to notice a neglected young man perseveringly rubbing out the last traces of the pictures, so that nobody can renew the same. That's me (Christmas Stories – 'Somebody's Luggage').*

Tom: Captain Boldheart's cheeky cousin in Robin Redforth's romantic tale ('Holiday Romance').

Tom: Clerk at the employment agency where Nicholas Nickleby first sees Madeline Bray. *A lean youth with cunning eyes and a protruding chin (Nickleby).*

Tom: Wardle's coachman (Pickwick).

Tom: Waiter at the St. James's Arms (Strange Gentleman).

Tom: Driver of the Dover mailcoach (Two Cities).

Tom, Captain: Prisoner in Newgate visited by Pip and Wemmick (Expectations).

Tom, Honest: A Member of Parliament. *That smart-looking fellow in the black coat with velvet facings and cuffs, who wears his D'Orsay hat so rakishly is 'Honest Tom', a metropolitan representative (Boz – 'Parliamentary Sketch').*

Tomkins: Pupil at Dotheboys Hall. *A very little boy, habited still in his night-gear, and the perplexed expression of whose countenance as he was brought forward, seemed to intimate that he was as yet uncertain whether he was about to be punished or rewarded for the suggestion. He was not long in doubt (Nickleby).*

Tomkins, Miss: Principal of Westgate House boarding school for young ladies, Bury St. Edmunds (Pickwick).

Tomkins, Alfred: Boarder at Mrs. Tibbs's. *A clerk in a wine-house; he was a connoisseur in paintings, and had a wonderful eye for the picturesque (Boz – 'Boarding-House').*

Tomkins, Charles: Fiancé of Fanny Wilson, whom he has arranged to meet at the St. James's Arms in order to elope to Gretna Green. He is confused with the Strange Gentleman, and thought to be mad, but all comes clear eventually and the journey to Gretna proceeds (Strange Gentleman).

Tomlinson, Mrs.: Post-office keeper at Rochester, present at the charity ball at the Bull (Pickwick).

Tommy: Dissentient to Rogers's opinions. *A little greengrocer with a chubby face (Boz – 'Parlour Orator').*

Tommy: A waterman who obtains for Pickwick the cab whose driver, Sam, assaults the Pickwickians. *A strange specimen of the human race, in a sackcloth coat, and apron of the same, who with a brass label and number round his neck, looked as if he were catalogued in some collection of rarities (Pickwick).*

Toodle: Polly's husband, father of Robin and four other children. A stoker, later engine-driver. *A strong, loose, round-shouldered, shuffling, shaggy fellow, on whom his clothes sat negligently: with a good deal of hair and whisker, deepened in its natural tint, perhaps by smoke and coal-dust: hard knotty hands: and a square forehead, as coarse in grain as the bark of an oak (Dombey).*

Toodle, Mrs. (Polly, 'Richards'): Toodle's wife, and mother of Robin and four other children. Engaged by

Dombey as foster-mother to Florence and Little Paul, with the name 'Richards' imposed on her, but dismissed for paying a visit to her own home and children. *A plump rosy-cheeked wholesome apple-faced young woman (Dombey).*

Toodle, Robin ('Biler' and 'Rob the Grinder'): The Toodles' eldest son, used as a spy by James Carker and later servant to Miss Tox. *Known in the family by the name of Biler, in remembrance of the steam engine. // Poor Biler's life had been, since yesterday morning, rendered weary by the costume of the Charitable Grinders. The youth of the streets could not endure it. No young vagabond could be brought to bear its contemplation for a moment, without throwing himself upon the unoffending wearer, and doing him a mischief. . . . He had been stoned in the streets. He had been overthrown into gutters; bespattered with mud; violently flattened against posts. Entire strangers to his person had lifted his yellow cap off his head and cast it to the winds (Dombey).*

Toorell, Dr.: A vice-president of the anatomy and medicine session at the first meeting of the Mudfog Association *(Mudfog).*

Tootle, Tom: Regular drinker at the Six Jolly Fellowship Porters *(Mutual Friend).*

'Tootleum-Boots': Mrs. Lemon's baby in Nettie Ashford's romantic tale. *Mrs. Lemon's baby was leather and bran* ('Holiday Romance').

Toots, P.: Dr. Blimber's senior pupil. A friend to everyone, he woos Florence Dombey ardently, but accepts her rejection of him philosophically and eventually marries Susan Nipper. *Possessed of the gruffest of voices and the shrillest of minds; sticking ornamental pins into his shirt, and keeping a ring in his waistcoat pocket to put on his little finger by stealth, when the pupils went out walking; constantly falling in love by sight with nurserymaids, who had no idea of his existence; and looking at the gas-lighted world over the little iron bars in the left-hand corner window of the front three pairs of stairs, after bed-time, like a greatly overgown cherub who had sat up aloft much too long (Dombey).*

Toozellem, The Hon. Clementina: See under **Bilberry, Lady Jemima** *(Dorrit).*

Tope: Chief verger at Cloisterham Cathedral. Landlord of Jasper and, later, Datchery. *Mr. Tope, Chief Verger and Showman, and accustomed to be high with excursion parties (Drood).*

Tope, Mrs.: Tope's wife. *Mrs. Tope had indeed once upon a time let lodgings herself or offered to let them; but that as nobody had ever taken them, Mrs. Tope's window-bill, long a Cloisterham Institution, had disappeared (Drood).*

Topper: A guest at Fred's Christmas dinner. *Topper had clearly got his eye upon one of Scrooge's niece's sisters, for he answered that a bachelor was a wretched outcast (Christmas Books – 'Christmas Carol').*

Toppit, Miss: An American literary lady at Pogram's levee at the National Hotel. *One of the L.L.'s wore a brown wig of uncommon size (Chuzzlewit).*

Topsawyer: Mythical victim of ale-drinking at Yarmouth, invented by William, the waiter, in order to persuade young David Copperfield to let him dispose of his ale for him. *'He came in here,' said the waiter, looking at the light through the tumbler, 'ordered a glass of this ale* – would order it – *I told him not* – *drank it, and fell dead. It was too old for him. It oughtn't to be drawn; that's the fact. . . . But I'll drink it, if you like. I'm used to it, and use is everything. I don't think it'll hurt me, if I throw my head back, and take it off quick' (Copperfield).*

Tott, Mrs. Isabella (known as **'Belltott'**): A soldier's widow living on Silver-Store Island who fights gallantly against the pirates. *A little saucy woman, with a bright pair of eyes, rather a neat little foot and figure, and rather a neat little turned-up nose. The sort of young woman, I considered at the time, who appeared to invite you to give her a kiss, and who would have slapped your face if you accepted the invitation (Christmas Stories – 'English Prisoners').*

Tottle, Watkins: A bachelor, rescued from imprisonment for debt by his friend Gabriel Parsons, on condition that he marries Miss Lillerton and reimburses him handsomely from her estate. Miss Lillerton proves to be engaged to the Revd. Charles Timson, whom she marries, and Tottle drowns himself in the Regent's Canal. *A rather uncommon compound of strong uxorious inclinations, and an unparalleled degree of anti-connubial timidity. He was about fifty years of age; stood four feet six inches and three-quarters in his socks – for he never stood in stockings at all – plump, clean, and rosy. He looked something like a vignette to one of Richardson's novels, and had a clean-cravatish formality of manner, and kitchen-pokerness of carriage. . . . The idea of matrimony had never ceased to haunt him. Wrapt in profound reveries on this never-failing theme, fancy transformed his small parlour in Cecil Street, Strand, into a neat house in the suburbs; the half-hundredweight of coals under the kitchen-stairs suddenly sprang up into three tons of the best Wallsend; his small French bedstead was converted into a regular matrimonial four-poster; and in the empty chair on the opposite side of the fireplace, imagination seated a beautiful young lady, with a very little independence or will of her own, and a very large independence under a will of her father's (Boz – 'Watkins Tottle').*

'Toughey': See **Jo** *(Bleak House).*

Towlinson, Thomas: Dombey's footman. Marries Anne, the housemaid. *Adjourning in quest of the housemaid, and presently returning with that young lady on his arm, informs the kitchen that foreigners is only his fun, and that him and Anne have now resolved to take one another for better for worse, and to settle in Oxford Market in the general greengrocery and herb and leech line, where your kind favours is particularly requested (Dombey).*

Tox, Lucretia: Mrs. Chick's close spinster friend. She fails in her design to become the second Mrs. Dombey, but remains loyal throughout his misfortunes. She in turn is much admired by her neighbour, Major Bagstock. *A long lean figure, wearing such a faded air that she seemed not to have been made in what linen-drapers call 'fast colours' originally, and to have, by little and little, washed out. But for this she might have been described as the very pink of general propitiation and politeness. From a long habit of listening admirably to everything that was said in her presence, and looking at the speakers as if she were mentally engaged in taking off impressions of their images upon her soul, never to part with the same but with life, her head had quite settled on one side. Her hands had contracted a spasmodic habit of raising themselves of their own accord as in involuntary admiration. . . . She was accustomed to wear odd weedy little flowers in her bonnet and caps. Strange grasses were sometimes perceived in her hair; and it was observed, of all her collars, frills, tuckers, wrist-bands, and other gossamer articles – indeed of every-thing she wore which had two ends to it intended to unite – that the two ends were never on good terms, and wouldn't quite meet without a struggle* (Dombey).

Tozer: A room-mate of Paul Dombey at Dr. Blimber's. *A solemn young gentleman, whose shirt-collar curled up the lobes of his ears* (Dombey).

Tpschoffki, Major: See **Chops** (Christmas Stories – 'Going into Society').

Trabb: Obsequious master tailor who attends Pip. *A prosperous old bachelor, and his open window looked into a prosperous little garden and orchard, and there was a prosperous iron safe let into the wall at the side of his fireplace, and I did not doubt that heaps of his prosperity were put away in it in bags* (Expectations).

Trabb's Boy: The tailor's assistant. *The most auda-cious boy in all that countryside* (Expectations).

Traddles, Thomas: Pupil at Salem House; later a distinguished barrister. David Copperfield's great friend and best man. He marries Sophy Crewler. *Poor Traddles! In a tight sky-blue suit that made his arms and legs like German sausages, or roly-poly puddings, he was the merriest and most miserable of all the boys. He was always being caned – I think he was caned every day that half-year, except one holi-day Monday when he was only ruler'd on both hands – and was always going to write to his uncle about it, and never did. After laying his head on the desk for a little while, he would cheer up somehow, begin to laugh again, and draw skeletons all over his slate, before his eyes were dry. I used at first to wonder what comfort Traddles found in drawing skeletons; and for some time looked upon him as a sort of hermit, who reminded himself by those symbols of mortality that caning couldn't last for ever. But I believe he only did it because they were easy, and didn't want any features* (Copperfield).

Trampfoot: One of the policemen visiting sailors' haunts with the Uncommercial Traveller (Uncom-mercial – 'Poor Mercantile Jack').

Traveller, Mr.: Narrator of the story (Christmas Stories – 'Tom Tiddler's Ground').

Treasurer: Treasurer of the Foundling Hospital interviewed by Wilding (Christmas Stories – 'No Thoroughfare'; not in dramatised version).

Treasury: Whitehall magnate, guest at Merdle's (Dorrit).

Tredgear, John: Resident of Lanrean questioned by Captain Jorgan (Christmas Stories – 'Message from the Sea').

Tregarthen: Kitty's father, clerk to Dringworth Bros., cleared by the message from the sea of suspicion of theft. *A rather infirm man, but could scarcely be called old yet, with an agreeable face and a promising air of making the best of things* (Christmas Stories – 'Message from the Sea').

Tregarthen, Kitty: Tregarthen's daughter, sweet-heart and eventually wife of Alfred Raybrock. *A prettier sweetheart the sun could not have shone upon that shining day. As she stood before the captain, with her rosy lips just parted in surprise, her brown eyes a little wider open than was usual from the same cause, and her breathing a little quickened by the ascent . . . she looked so charming, that the captain felt himself under a moral obligation to slap both his legs again* (Christmas Stories – 'Message from the Sea').

Trent: Little Nell's grandfather. Proprietor of the Old Curiosity Shop. A compulsive gambler, he flees with Little Nell to escape his creditor, Quilp. Heartbroken by her death, he dies soon after. *A little old man with long grey hair, whose face and figure, as he held the light above his head and looked before him as he approached, I could plainly see. Though much altered by age, I fancied I could recognise in his spare and slender form something of that delicate mould which I had noticed in the child. Their bright blue eyes were certainly alike, but his face was so deeply furrowed, and so very full of care, that here all resemblance ended* (Curiosity Shop).

Trent, Frederick: Little Nell's dissolute brother, who tries to marry her off to his friend, Dick Swiveller. *A young man of one-and-twenty or thereabouts; well made, and certainly handsome, though the expression of his face was far from prepossessing, having in common with his manner and even his dress, a dis-sipated, insolent air which repelled one* (Curiosity Shop).

Trent, Nell (Little Nell): Central figure of the story: the child companion and support of her grandfather (see **Trent**). She wanders the roads with him and dies at a village. *Child she certainly was, although I thought it probable from what I could make out that her very small and delicate frame imparted a peculiar youthfulness to her appearance. Though more scantily attired than she might have been, she was dressed with perfect neatness, and betrayed no marks of poverty or neglect* (Curiosity Shop).

Tresham: Jackson's former colleague and friend, who had taken Beatrice from him and married her. Jackson's visit to Mugby is fortuitously in time to save them and their daughter Polly from the consequences of Tresham's illness and their poverty. *'My husband is* *very, very ill of a lingering disorder. He will never recover'* (*Christmas Stories* – 'Mugby Junction').

Tresham, Mrs. (Beatrice): A music teacher. Tresham's wife and Polly's mother. Jackson's lost love whom he helps in her poverty. *As you see what the rose was in its faded leaves; as you see what the summer growth of the woods was in their wintry branches; so Polly might be traced, one day, in a careworn woman like this, with her hair turned grey. Before him were the ashes of a dead fire that had once burned bright. This was the woman he had loved. This was the woman he had lost. Such had been the constancy of his imagination to her, so had Time spared her under its withholding, that now, seeing how roughly the inexorable hand had struck her, his soul was filled with pity and amazement* (*Christmas Stories* – 'Mugby Junction').

Tresham, Polly: Daughter of Tresham and Beatrice, who leads Jackson to his lost love. *A very little fair-haired girl.* // *'A most engaging little creature, but it's not that. A most winning little voice, but it's not that. That has much to do with it, but there is something more. How can it be that I seem to know this child? What was it she imperfectly recalled to me when I felt her touch in the street, and, looking down at her, saw her looking up at me?'* (*Christmas Stories* – 'Mugby Junction').

Trimmers: Friend of the Cheeryble brothers (*Nickleby*).

Trinkle: Son of a noted upholsterer in Cheapside. Inspector Wield's suspect for the murder of Eliza Grimwood, but proved not to be guilty (*Reprinted* – 'Three "Detective" Anecdotes').

Trott, Alexander: An umbrella-maker, rival to Horace Hunter for Emily Brown. Challenged to a duel by Hunter, he plans to save his skin by getting arrested, but is mistaken for Lord Peter, Julia Manners's suitor, and made to elope with her. The mistake revealed, they like one another enough to drive on to Gretna Green and marry. *Mr. Trott was a young man, had highly promising whiskers, an undeniable tailor, and an insinuating address – he wanted nothing but valour, and who wants that with three thousand a year?* (*Boz* – 'Great Winglebury Duel'). He appears as Walker Trott, the Strange Gentleman, in the dramatic version entitled *The Strange Gentleman*.

Trott, Walker: See **Trott, Alexander** (*Strange Gentleman*).

Trotter, Job: Jingle's servant and crony and Sam Weller's adversary. *A young fellow in mulberry-coloured livery . . . who had a large, sallow, ugly face, very sunken eyes, and a gigantic head, from which depended a quantity of lank black hair* (*Pickwick*).

'Trotters, Short': See **Harris** (*Curiosity Shop*).

Trottle: One of the listeners to the story (*Christmas Stories* – 'Going into Society').

Trotwood, Betsey: David Copperfield's great-aunt and later guardian, to whom he flies from Murdstone and Grinby's. She is actually married, but separated, and lives self-sufficiently, caring for Mr. Dick, David, and then David's successive wives, and combating such people as Jane Murdstone and Uriah Heep, as well as the donkeys which trample the grass in front of her house at Dover. Her husband appears at intervals to demand money, and eventually dies. *My aunt was a tall, hard-featured lady, but by no means ill-looking. There was an inflexibility in her face, in her voice, in her gait and carriage, amply sufficient to account for the effect she had made upon a gentle creature like my mother; but her features were rather handsome than otherwise, though unbending and austere. I particularly noticed that she had a very quick, bright eye* (*Copperfield*).

Truck: A vice-president of the mechanical science session at the first meeting of the Mudfog Association (*Mudfog*).

Trundle: The young man who marries Isabella Wardle (*Pickwick*).

Trusty, Mrs.: Captain Blower's nurse; one of the characters assumed by Rosina Nightingale to help Gabblewig unmask Slap (*Nightingale's Diary*).

Tuckle: A Bath footman, presiding at the footmen's soirée. *A stoutish gentleman in a bright crimson coat with long tails, vividly red breeches, and a cocked hat* (*Pickwick*).

Tugby: Sir Joseph Bowley's porter. He marries Mrs. Chickenstalker. *The great broad chin, with creases in it large enough to hide a finger in; the astonished eyes, that seemed to expostulate with themselves for sinking deeper and deeper into the yielding fat of the soft face; the nose afflicted with that disordered action of its functions which is generally termed The Snuffles; the short thick throat and labouring chest, with other beauties of the like description* (*Christmas Books* – 'Chimes').

Tuggs, Charlotte: The Tuggses' only daughter, and Simon's sister. When they come into money she calls herself Charlotta. *Fast ripening into that state of luxuriant plumpness which had enchanted the eyes, and captivated the heart, of Mr. Joseph Tuggs in his earlier days* (*Boz* – 'Tuggses at Ramsgate').

Tuggs, Joseph: Father of Charlotte and Simon. A London grocer who comes into a fortune, determines to live high at Ramsgate, and is duped by the Waterses. *A little dark-faced man, with shiny hair, twinkling eyes, short legs, and a body of very considerable thickness, measuring from the centre button of his waistcoat in front, to the ornamental buttons of his coat behind* (*Boz* – 'Tuggses at Ramsgate').

Tuggs, Mrs. Joseph: Tuggs's wife, and mother of Charlotte and Simon, in charge of the cheesemongery side of his business. *The figure of the amiable Mrs. Tuggs, if not perfectly symmetrical, was decidedly comfortable* (*Boz* – 'Tuggses at Ramsgate').

Tuggs, Simon: The Tuggses' only son, and Charlotte's brother. When they come into money he calls himself Cymon. Led on by Belinda Waters, he costs his father £1,500 of his fortune. *As differently formed in body, as he was differently constituted in mind, from the remainder of his family. There was that elongation in his thoughtful face, and that tendency to weakness in his interesting legs, which tell so forcibly of a great mind and romantic disposition. The slightest traits of character in such a being, possess no mean interest to speculative minds. He usually appeared in public, in capacious shoes with black cotton stockings; and was observed to be particularly attached to a black glazed stock, without tie or ornament of any description (Boz – 'Tuggses at Ramsgate').*

Tulkinghorn: The Dedlocks' family lawyer. He makes use of various people to discover Lady Dedlock's secret and is murdered by one of them, Hortense, for refusing to reward her sufficiently. *The old gentleman is rusty to look at, but is reputed to have made good thrift out of aristocratic marriage settlements and aristocratic wills, and to be very rich. He is surrounded by a mysterious halo of family confidences; of which he is known to be the silent depository. There are noble Mausoleums rooted for centuries in retired glades of parks, among the growing timber and the fern, which perhaps hold fewer noble secrets than walk abroad among men, shut up in the breast of Mr. Tulkinghorn. He is of what is called the old school – a phrase generally meaning any school that seems never to have been young – and wears knee breeches tied with ribbons, and gaiters or stockings. One peculiarity of his black clothes, and of his black stockings, be they silk or worsted, is, that they never shine. Mute, close, irresponsive to any glancing light, his dress is like himself. He never converses, when not professionally consulted. He is found sometimes, speechless but quite at home, at corners of dinner-tables in great country houses, and near doors of drawing-rooms, concerning which the fashionable intelligence is eloquent: where everybody knows him, and where half the Peerage stops to say 'How do you do, Mr. Tulkinghorn?' he receives these salutations with gravity, and buries them along with the rest of his knowledge (Bleak House).*

Tulrumble, Nicholas, jun.: The Tulrumbles' son. *Couldn't make up his mind to be anything but magnificent, so he went up to London and drew bills on his father; and when he had overdrawn, and got into debt, he grew penitent, and came home again (Mudfog).*

Tulrumble, Nicholas, sen.: Mayor of Mudfog in succession to Sniggs. Father of Nicholas junior. *Nicholas began life in a wooden tenement of four feet square, with a capital of two and ninepence, and a stock in trade of three bushels and a half of coals, exclusive of the large lump which hung, by way of a sign-board, outside. Then he enlarged the shed, and kept a truck; then he left the shed, and the truck too, and started a donkey and a Mrs. Tulrumble; then he moved again and set up a cart; the cart was soon afterwards exchanged for a waggon; and so he went on like his great predecessor Whittington – only without a cat for a partner – increasing in wealth and fame, until at last he gave up business altogether, and retired with Mrs. Tulrumble and family to Mudfog Hall,* which he had himself erected, on something which he attempted to delude himself into the belief was a hill, about a quarter of a mile distant from the town of Mudfog *(Mudfog).*

Tulrumble, Mrs. Nicholas, sen.: Tulrumble's wife, mother of Nicholas junior *(Mudfog).*

Tungay: Porter at Salem House school. *A stout man with a bull-neck, a wooden leg, over-hanging temples, and his hair cut close all round his head. . . . I heard that with the single exception of Mr. Creakle, Tungay considered the whole establishment, masters and boys, as his natural enemies, and that the only delight of his life was to be sour and malicious (Copperfield).*

Tupman, Tracy: A somewhat elderly member of the Pickwick Club and one of Pickwick's companions in his travels. He wins Rachael Wardle's heart, loses her through Jingle's scheming, and retires to bachelorhood at Richmond. *The too susceptible Tupman, who to the wisdom and experience of maturer years superadded the enthusiasm and ardour of a boy, in the most interesting and pardonable of human weaknesses – love. Time and feeding had expanded that once romantic form; the black silk waistcoat had become more and more developed; inch by inch had the gold watch-chain beneath it disappeared from within the range of Tupman's vision; and gradually had the capacious chin encroached upon the borders of the white cravat: but the soul of Tupman had known no change – admiration of the fair sex was still its ruling passion (Pickwick).*

Tupple: Guest at the Dobbles' New Year's Eve party. *A junior clerk in the same office; a tidy young man, with a tendency to cold and corns, who comes in a pair of boots with black cloth fronts, and brings his shoes in his coat-pocket (Boz – 'New Year').*

Turk: John the narrator's bloodhound. *I stationed him in his kennel outside, but unchained; and I seriously warned the village that any man who came in his way must not expect to leave him without a rip in his own throat (Christmas Stories – 'Haunted House').*

Turveydrop: Proprietor of a dancing academy in London and a celebrated arbiter of deportment. *A fat old gentleman with a false complexion, false teeth, false whiskers, and a wig. He had a fur collar, and he had a padded breast to his coat, which only wanted a star or a broad blue ribbon to be complete. He was pinched in, and swelled out, and got up, and strapped down, as much as he could possibly bear. He had such a neckcloth on (puffing his very eyes out of their natural shape) and his chin and even his ears so sunk into it, that it seemed as though he must inevitably double up, if it were cast loose. He had, under his arm, a hat of great size and weight, shelving downward from the crown to the brim; and in his hand a pair of white gloves, with which he flapped it, as he stood poised on one leg, in a high-shouldered, round-elbowed state of elegance not to be surpassed. He had a cane, he had an eye-glass, he had a snuffbox, he had rings, he had wristbands, he had everything but any touch of nature; he was not like youth, he was not like age, he* *was not like anything in the world but a model of Deportment (Bleak House).*

Turveydrop, Prince: Turveydrop's son and assistant, named after the Prince Regent. He marries Caddy Jellyby. *A little blue-eyed fair man of youthful appearance, with flaxen hair parted in the middle, and curling at the ends all round his head. He had a little fiddle, which we used to call at school a kit, under his left arm, and its little bow in the same ,hand. His little dancing shoes were particularly diminutive, and he had a little innocent, feminine manner, which not only appealed to me in an amiable way, but made this singular effect upon me: that I received the impression that he was like his mother, and that his mother had not been much considered or well used (Bleak House).*

Twemlow, Melvin: Frequent guest at the Veneerings' and elsewhere on the strength of his kinship (cousin) to Lord Snigsworth. *Grey, dry, polite, susceptible to east wind. First-Gentleman-in-Europe collar and cravat, cheeks drawn in as if he had made a great effort to retire into himself some years ago, and had got so far and had never got any farther. // At many houses might be said to represent the dining-table in its normal state. Mr. and Mrs. Veneering, for example, arranging a dinner, habitually started with Twemlow, and then put leaves in him, or added guests to him (Mutual Friend).*

Twigger, Edward ('Bottle-nosed Ned'): The town drunkard, who reduces Tulrumble's Mayor-making procession to chaos. *He was drunk upon the average once a day, and penitent upon an equally fair calculation once a month; and when he was penitent, he was invariably in the very last stage of maudlin intoxication. He was a ragged, roving, roaring kind of fellow, with a burly form, a sharp wit, and a ready head, and could turn his hand to anything when he chose to do it. . . . Notwithstanding his dissipation, Bottle-nosed Ned was a general favourite; and the authorities of Mudfog, remembering his numerous services to the population, allowed him in return to get drunk in his own way, without the fear of stocks, fine, or imprisonment. He had a general licence, and he showed his sense of the compliment by making the most of it (Mudfog).*

Twigger, Mrs. Edward: Edward's wife. *Ned no sooner caught a glimpse of her face and form, than from the mere force of habit he set off towards his home just as fast as his legs could carry him (Mudfog).*

Twinkleton, Miss: Principal of the Nuns' House Seminary for Young Ladies, Cloisterham, attended by Rosa Bud and Helena Landless. *Miss Twinkleton has two distinct and separate phases of being. Every night, the moment the young ladies have retired to rest, does Miss Twinkleton smarten up her curls a little, brighten up her eyes a little, and become a sprightlier Miss Twinkleton than the young ladies have ever seen. Every night, at the same hour, does Miss Twinkleton resume the topics of the previous night, comprehending the tenderer scandal of Cloisterham, of which she has no knowledge whatever by day, and references to*

a certain season at Tunbridge Wells . . . wherein a certain finished gentleman (compassionately called by Miss Twinkleton, in this stage of her existence, 'Foolish Mr. Porters') revealed a homage of the heart, whereof Miss Twinkleton, in her scholastic state of existence, is as ignorant as a granite pillar (Drood).

Twist, Oliver: Orphan natural son of Edwin Leeford and Agnes Fleming. Apprenticed to crime under Fagin and Bill Sikes, he is rescued and redeemed by Rose Maylie, Brownlow, and others, his identity is established, and Brownlow adopts him. *Oliver Twist's ninth birthday found him a pale thin child, somewhat diminutive in stature, and decidedly small in circumference. But nature or inheritance had implanted a good sturdy spirit in Oliver's breast. It had had plenty of room to expand, thanks to the spare diet of this establishment; and perhaps to this circumstance may be attributed his having any ninth birthday at all (Twist).*

Uncle, The Bagman's: See **Martin, Jack** (*Pickwick*).

Uncommercial Traveller: Narrator of the essays. *I am both a town traveller and a country traveller, and am always on the road. Figuratively speaking, I travel for the great house of Human Interest Brothers, and have rather a large connection in the fancy goods way. Literally speaking, I am always wandering here and there from my rooms in Covent Garden, London – now about the city streets: now, about the country by-roads – seeing many little things, and some great things, which, because they interest me, I think may interest others (Uncommercial – 'His General Line of Business').*

Undery: John the narrator's friend and solicitor who makes one of the party visiting the haunted house. *Plays whist better than the whole Law List, from the red cover at the beginning to the red cover at the end (Christmas Stories – 'Haunted House').*

United Bull-Dogs: See **Prentice Knights** (*Rudge*).

United Grand Junction Ebenezer Temperance Association: Sam and Tony Weller attend a meeting of the Brick Lane Branch in order to expose the Revd. Mr. Stiggins for a drunken hypocrite (*Pickwick*).

United Metropolitan Improved Hot Muffin and Crumpet Baking and Punctual Delivery Company: A company promoted by Bonney of which Ralph Nickleby is a director (*Nickleby*).

Upwitch, Richard: A greengrocer juryman in Bardell and Pickwick (*Pickwick*).

Valentine, Private: Capitaine de la Cour's batman. *Acting as sole housemaid, valet, cook, steward, and nurse . . . cleaning the floors, making the beds, doing the marketing, dressing the captain, dressing the dinners, dressing the salads, and dressing the baby, all with equal readiness (Christmas Stories – 'Somebody's Luggage').*

Varden, Dolly: Gabriel's daughter, loved by Joe Willet and Sim Tappertit. Seized by the mob, with Emma Haredale, during the Gordon Riots, she is rescued by Joe and subsequently marries him. *A roguish face met his; a face lighted up by the loveliest pair of sparkling eyes that ever locksmith looked upon; the face of a pretty, laughing, girl; dimpled and fresh, and healthful – the very impersonation of good-humour and blooming beauty (Rudge).*

Varden, Gabriel: Kindly, honest locksmith, husband of Martha and father of Dolly. *A round, red-faced, sturdy yeoman, with a double-chin, and a voice husky with good living, good sleeping, good humour, and good health. . . . Bluff, hale, hearty, and in a green old age: at peace with himself, and evidently disposed to be so with all the world. Although muffled up in divers coats and handkerchiefs – one of which, passed over his crown, and tied in a convenient crease of his double-chin, secured his three-cornered hat and bob-wig from blowing off his head – there was no disguising his plump and comfortable figure; neither did certain dirty finger-marks upon his face give it any other than an odd and comical expression, through which its natural good-humour shone with undiminished lustre (Rudge).*

Varden, Mrs. Gabriel (Martha): Gabriel's wife and Dolly's mother. *A lady of what is commonly called an uncertain temper – a phrase which being interpreted signifies a temper tolerably certain to make everybody more or less uncomfortable. Thus it generally happened, that when other people were merry, Mrs. Varden was dull; and that when other people were dull, Mrs. Varden was disposed to be amazingly cheerful. . . . It had been observed in this good lady (who did not want for personal attractions, being plump and buxom to look at, though like her fair daughter, somewhat short in stature) that this uncertainty of disposition strengthened and increased with her temporal prosperity; and divers wise men and matrons, on friendly terms with the locksmith and his family, even went so far as to assert, that a tumble down some half-dozen rounds in the world's ladder such as the breaking of the bank in which her husband kept his money, or some little fall of that kind – would be the making of her, and could hardly fail to render her one of the most agreeable companions in existence (Rudge).*

Veck, Margaret (Meg): Toby Veck's daughter, engaged to Richard. *Bright eyes they were. Eyes that would bear a world of looking in, before their depth was fathomed. Dark eyes, that reflected back the eyes which searched them; not flashingly, or at the owner's will, but with a clear, calm, honest, patient radiance, claiming kindred with that light which Heaven called into being. Eyes that were beautiful and true, and beaming with Hope. With Hope so young and fresh; with Hope so buoyant, vigorous, and bright, despite the twenty years of work and poverty on which they had looked (Christmas Books – 'Chimes').*

Veck, Toby ('Trotty'): A ticket-porter, or messenger, whose New Year's Eve dream of spirits inhabiting church bells forms the main theme of the story. *They called him Trotty from his pace, which meant speed if it didn't make it. He could have walked faster perhaps; most likely; but rob him of his trot, and Toby would*

have taken to his bed and died. It bespattered him with mud in dirty weather; it cost him a world of trouble; he could have walked with infinitely greater ease; but that was one reason for his clinging to it so tenaciously. A weak, small, spare old man, he was a very Hercules, this Toby, in his good intentions. He loved to earn his money. He delighted to believe – Toby was very poor, and couldn't well afford to part with a delight – that he was worth his salt. With a shilling or an eighteen-penny message or small parcel in his hand, his courage, always high, rose higher. As he trotted on, he would call out to fast Postmen ahead of him, to get out of the way; devoutly believing that in the natural course of things he must inevitably overtake and run them down; and he had perfect faith – not often tested – in his being able to carry anything that man could lift (Christmas Books – 'Chimes').*

Vendale, George: Partner in Wilding and Co. and head of it after Wilding's death. Courting Marguerite Obenreizer, he comes unwittingly close to discovering her uncle's frauds. Obenreizer tries to kill him in the Alps. He is saved by Marguerite, whom he marries. It transpires that he is the orphan who should have inherited Wilding and Co. in the first place. *A brown-cheeked handsome fellow . . . with a quick determined eye and an impulsive manner (Christmas Stories – 'No Thoroughfare' and the dramatised version).*

Veneering, Hamilton: A self-made rich man, sole remaining partner of Chicksey, Veneering and Stobbles, druggists, of which he had once been a lowly employee. Much given to Society life. He manages to buy a seat in Parliament through a rotten borough. *Forty, wavy-haired, dark, tending to corpulence, sly, mysterious, filmy – a kind of sufficiently well-looking veiled-prophet, not prophesying (Mutual Friend).*

Veneering, Mrs. Hamilton (Anastasia): Veneering's wife. *Fair, aquiline-nosed and fingered, not so much light hair as she might have, gorgeous in raiment and jewels, enthusiastic, propitiatory, conscious that a corner of her husband's veil is over herself (Mutual Friend).*

'Vengeance, The': Madame Defarge's chief associate among the women revolutionaries. *The short, rather plump wife of a starved grocer, and the mother of two children withal, this lieutenant had already earned the complimentary name of The Vengeance (Two Cities).*

Venning, Mrs.: A resident of Silver-Store Island and mother of Fanny Fisher. *One handsome elderly lady, with very dark eyes and gray hair (Christmas Stories – 'English Prisoners').*

Ventriloquist, Monsieur The: Performer at a Flemish country fair. *Thin and sallow, and of a weakly aspect (Uncommercial – 'In the French-Flemish Country').*

Venus: Taxidermist at Clerkenwell who purchased Silas Wegg's amputated leg and joins in his plot to blackmail Boffin, but repents and betrays Wegg. He marries Pleasant Riderhood, after her long hesitation out of objection to his business. *The face looking up is a sallow face with weak eyes, surmounted by a tangle* of reddish-dusty hair. *The owner of the face has no cravat on, and has opened his tumbled shirt-collar to work with the more ease. For the same reason he has no coat on: only a loose waistcoat over his yellow linen. His eyes are like the over-tried eyes of an engraver, but he is not that; his expression and stoop are like those of a shoemaker, but he is not that (Mutual Friend).*

Verisopht, Lord Frederick: A rich young man debauched by Hawk, who kills him in a duel after he has protested about Hawk's treatment of Kate Nickleby. *The gentleman addressed, turning round, exhibited a suit of clothes of the most superlative cut, a pair of whiskers of similar quality, a moustache, a head of hair, and a young face (Nickleby).*

Vholes: Richard Carstone's solicitor who turns him against Jarndyce. *A sallow man with pinched lips that looked as if they were cold, a red eruption here and there upon his face, tall and thin, about fifty years of age, high-shouldered, and stooping. Dressed in black, black-gloved, and buttoned to the chin, there was nothing so remarkable in him as a lifeless manner, and a slow fixed way he had of looking at Richard (Bleak House).*

Villam: Ostler of the Bull, Whitechapel *(Pickwick).*

Voigt, Maître: Chief notary at Neuchâtel who helps unmask Obenreizer. *A rosy, hearty, handsome old man. . . . Professionally and personally, the notary was a popular citizen. His innumerable kindnesses and his innumerable oddities had for years made him one of the recognised public characters of the pleasant Swiss town. His long brown frock-coat and his black skull-cap, were among the institutions of the place: and he carried a snuff-box which, in point of size, was popularly believed to be without a parallel in Europe (Christmas Stories – 'No Thoroughfare').* Maître Voigt's part in the story is given, in modified form, to Father Francis in the dramatised version.

Vuffin: A showman encountered by Little Nell and her grandfather. *The proprietor of a giant, and a little lady without legs or arms (Curiosity Shop).*

Wackles, Mrs.: Proprietress of a school for young ladies at Chelsea. *Corporal punishment, fasting, and other tortures and terrors, by Mrs. Wackles. . . . An excellent, but rather venomous old lady of three-score (Curiosity Shop).*

Wackles, the Misses Melissa, Sophy and **Jane:** Mrs. Wackles's daughters, in order of seniority; all teachers in her school for young ladies. Sophy is Dick Swiveller's intended, but he gives her up on hopes of Little Nell and she marries Cheggs. *English grammar, composition, geography, and the use of the dumb-bells, by Miss Melissa Wackles; writing, arithmetic, dancing, music, and general fascination, by Miss Sophy Wackles; the art of needle-work, marking, and samplery, by Miss Jane Wackles. . . . Miss Melissa might have been five-and-thirty summers or there-abouts, and verged on the autumnal; Miss Sophy was a fresh, good-humoured, buxom girl of twenty; and Miss Jane numbered scarcely sixteen years (Curiosity Shop).*

Wade, Miss: The Meagleses' moody friend who persuades Harriet Beadle to leave their service and live with her. *The shadow in which she sat, falling like a gloomy veil across her forehead, accorded very well with the character of her beauty. One could hardly see the face, so still and scornful, set off by the arched dark eyebrows, and the folds of dark hair, without wondering what its expression would be if a change came over it. That it could soften or relent, appeared next to impossible. . . . Although not an open face, there was no pretence in it. I am self-contained and self-reliant; your opinion is nothing to me; I have no interest in you, care nothing for you, and see and hear you with indifference – this it said plainly. It said so in the proud eyes, in the lifted nostril, in the handsome, but compressed and even cruel mouth. Cover either two of those channels of expression, and the third would have said so still. Mask them all, and the mere turn of the head would have shown an unsubduable nature (Dorrit).*

Waghorn: A vice-president of the mechanical science session at the first meeting of the Mudfog Association *(Mudfog).*

Wakefield, Mr. and **Mrs.:** Participants in the steam excursion, with their small daughter: *about six years old . . . dressed in a white frock with a pink sash and dog's-eared-looking little spencer: a straw bonnet and green veil, six inches by three and a half (Boz – 'Steam Excursion').*

Waldengarver: See **Wopsle** *(Expectations).*

Walker: A debtor in Solomon Jacobs's sponging-house. *A stout, hearty-looking man, of about forty, was eating some dinner which his wife – an equally comfortable-looking personage – had brought him in a basket (Boz – 'Watkins Tottle').*

Walker, Mrs.: See **Macklin, Walker,** and **Peplow** *(Boz – 'The Streets – Night').*

Walker, H.: Convert reported to the committee of the Brick Lane Branch of the United Grand Junction Ebenezer Temperance Association. *'Tailor, wife, and two children. When in better circumstances, owns to having been in the constant habit of drinking ale and beer; says he is not certain whether he did not twice a week, for twenty years, taste "dog's nose", which your committee find upon inquiry, to be compounded of warm porter, moist sugar, gin, and nutmeg' (a groan, and 'So it is!' from an elderly female) (Pickwick).*

Walker, Mick: Boy employee with David at Murdstone and Grinby's. *The oldest of the regular boys . . . he wore a ragged apron and a paper cap. He informed me that his father was a bargeman, and walked, in a black velvet head-dress, in the Lord Mayor's Show (Copperfield).*

Walmers: Father of Harry and employer of Cobbs. *He was a gentleman of spirit, and good-looking, and held his head up when he walked, and had what you may call Fire about him. He wrote poetry, and he rode, and he ran, and he cricketed, and he danced, and he acted, and he done it all equally beautiful (Christmas Stories – 'Holly-Tree').*

Walmers, Harry: Eight-year-old cousin of seven-year-old Norah, with whom he elopes to Gretna Green, hoping to marry, in the tale told by Cobbs to Charley. *The gentleman had got about half a dozen yards of string, a knife, three or four sheets of writing-paper folded up surprising small, a orange, and a Chaney mug with his name upon it* (*Christmas Stories* – 'Holly-Tree').

Walter, Edward M'Neville: See **Butler, Theodosius** (*Boz* – 'Sentiment').

Want: One of Miss Flite's birds (*Bleak House*).

Warden: A hopeless drunkard. His wife dies, one of his sons is killed and another hanged, and his daughter deserts him. He drowns himself in the Thames. *His dress was slovenly and disordered, his face inflamed, his eyes bloodshot and heavy. He had been summoned from some wild debauch to the bed of sorrow and death. . . . The time had been when many a friend would have crowded round him in his affliction, and many a heartfelt condolence would have met him in his grief. Where were they now? One by one, friends, relations, the commonest acquaintance even, had fallen off from and deserted the drunkard. His wife alone had clung to him in good and evil, in sickness and poverty, and how had he rewarded her? He had reeled from the tavern to her bedside in time to see her die* (*Boz* – 'Drunkard's Death').

Warden, Henry: Brother of John, William, and Mary. He is killed by a gamekeeper, who is murdered in turn by William (*Boz* – 'Drunkard's Death').

Warden, John: Brother of William, Henry, and Mary. He emigrates to America (*Boz* – 'Drunkard's Death').

Warden, Mary: Sister of John, Henry, and William. Like her dead mother she bears her father's excesses in order to care for him, but eventually deserts him. *A girl, whose miserable and emaciated appearance was only to be equalled by that of the candle which she shaded with her hand* (*Boz* – 'Drunkard's Death').

Warden, Michael: A dissolute client of Snitchey and Craggs. Marion Jeddler pretends to elope with him, and eventually marries him. *A man of thirty, or about that time of life, negligently dressed, and somewhat haggard in the face, but well-made, well-attired, and well-looking, who sat in the arm-chair of state, with one hand in his breast, and the other in his dishevelled hair, pondering moodily* (*Christmas Books* – 'Battle of Life').

Warden, William: Brother of John, Henry, and Mary. He murders a gamekeeper who has killed Henry, hides at his father's, but is unwittingly betrayed by his drunken parent, arrested, and hanged. *A young man of about two-and-twenty, miserably clad in an old coarse jacket and trousers* (*Boz* – 'Drunkard's Death').

Wardle: Owner of Manor Farm, Dingley Dell, where the Pickwickians enjoy Christmas sports and festivities. Father of Emily and Isabella and brother of Rachael. *A stout old gentleman, in a blue coat and bright buttons, corduroy breeches and top boots* (*Pickwick*).

Wardle, Mrs.: Wardle's mother. *A very old lady, in a lofty cap and faded silk gown – no less a personage than Mr. Wardle's mother – occupied the post of honour on the right-hand corner of the chimney-piece; and various certificates of her having been brought up in the way she should go when young, and of her not having departed from it when old, ornamented the walls, in the form of samplers of ancient date, worsted landscapes of equal antiquity, and crimson silk tea-kettle holders of a more modern period* (*Pickwick*).

Wardle, Emily: One of Wardle's daughters, sister to Isabella. She marries Snodgrass. *'Short girl – black eyes – niece Emily'* (*Pickwick*).

Wardle, Isabella: One of Wardle's daughters, sister to Emily. She marries Trundle. *A very amiable and lovely girl* (*Pickwick*).

Wardle, Rachael: Wardle's spinster sister. Tupman falls in love with her, but Jingle persuades her to elope with him and has to be bought off. *There was a dignity in the air, a touch-me-not-ishness in the walk, a majesty in the eye of the spinster aunt* (*Pickwick*).

'Warwick, The Earl of': One of the thieves living in Rats' Castle, Saint Giles's, visited by the narrator and Inspector Field. *'O there you are, my Lord. Come for'ard. There's a chest, sir, not to have a clean shirt on. An't it? Take your hat off, my Lord. Why, I should be ashamed if I was you – and an Earl, too – to show myself to a gentleman with my hat on!'* (*Reprinted* – 'On Duty with Inspector Field').

Waste: One of Miss Flite's birds (*Bleak House*).

Waterbrook: London solicitor, Wickfield's agent, with whom Agnes stays. *A middle-aged gentleman, with a short throat, and a good deal of shirt collar, who only wanted a black nose to be the portrait of a pug-dog* (*Copperfield*).

Waterbrook, Mrs.: Waterbrook's wife. *Mrs. Waterbrook, who was a large lady – or who wore a large dress: I don't exactly know which, for I don't know which was dress and which was lady* (*Copperfield*).

Waterhouse: See **Pegg** (*Uncommercial* – 'Poor Mercantile Jack').

'Waterloo': Toll-keeper on Waterloo Bridge who regales the narrator with tales of suicides there (*Reprinted* – 'Down with the Tide').

Waters, Captain Walter: A confidence trickster, husband of Belinda. *A stoutish, military-looking gentleman in a blue surtout buttoned up to his chin, and white trousers chained down to the soles of his boots* (*Boz* – 'Tuggses at Ramsgate').

Waters, Mrs. Walter (Belinda): Captain Waters's wife and accomplice. By arranging for Simon Tuggs to be found in compromising circumstances in her apartments she enables her husband to extort £1,500 of the Tuggs family's new fortune. *A young lady in a puce-coloured silk cloak, and boots of the same; with long black ringlets, large black eyes, brief petticoats,* *and unexceptionable ankles (Boz - 'Tuggses at Ramsgate').*

Watertoast Association of United Sympathisers: An American association in opposition to the British Lion, presided over by General Choke. *The Watertoast Association sympathised with a certain Public Man in Ireland, who held a contest upon certain points with England ... because they didn't love England at all – not by any means because they loved Ireland much (Chuzzlewit).*

Watkins: Kate Nickleby's godfather, recalled to her and Miss Knag by Mrs. Nickleby. *'He wasn't any relation, Miss Knag will understand, to the Watkins who kept the Old Boar in the village; by the bye, I don't remember whether it was the Old Boar or the George the Third, but it was one of the two, I know, and it's much the same – that Mr. Watkins said, when you were only two years and a half old, that you were one of the most astonishing children he ever saw. He did indeed, Miss Knag, and he wasn't at all fond of children, and couldn't have had the slightest motive for doing it. I know it was he who said so, because I recollect, as well as if it was only yesterday, his borrowing twenty pounds of her poor dear papa the very moment afterwards' (Nickleby).*

Watkins the First, King: Father of Princess Alicia in Alice Rainbird's romantic tale ('Holiday Romance').

Watson Family: Friends of Mincin (*Young Gentlemen* – 'Very Friendly Young Gentleman').

Watty: A bankrupt client of Perker. *A rustily-clad, miserable-looking man, in boots without toes and gloves without fingers (Pickwick).*

Wedgington Family: A husband-and-wife theatrical act and their infant son. *Mrs. B. Wedgington sang to a grand piano. Mr. B. Wedgington did the like, and also took off his coat, tucked up his trousers, and danced in clogs. Master B. Wedgington, aged ten months, was nursed by a shivering young person in the boxes, and the eye of Mrs. B. Wedgington wandered that way more than once (Reprinted – 'Out of the Season').*

Weedle, Anastasia: A Mormon emigrant aboard the *Amazon. A pretty girl, in a bright Garibaldi, this morning elected by universal suffrage the Beauty of the Ship (Uncommercial – 'Bound for the Great Salt Lake').*

'Weevle': See **Jobling, Tony** *(Bleak House).*

Wegg, Silas: A one-legged balladmonger and fruit-stall holder engaged by Boffin to improve his mind through literature. He finds Old Harmon's will and tries, with Venus, to blackmail Boffin, but is betrayed by his partner. *A knotty man, and a close-grained, with a face carved out of very hard material, that had just as much play of expression as a watchman's rattle. When he laughed, certain jerks occurred in it, and the rattle sprung. Sooth to say, he was so wooden a man that he seemed to have taken his wooden leg naturally, and rather suggested to the fanciful observer, that he might be expected – if his development received no untimely check – to be completely set up with a pair of wooden legs in about six months (Mutual Friend).*

Weller, Samuel: Son of Tony senior. Boots at the White Hart Inn, Borough. He becomes Pickwick's valet and faithful aide and eventually marries Mary, Nupkins's housemaid. *He was habited in a coarse-striped waistcoat, with black calico sleeves, and blue glass buttons; drab breeches and leggings. A bright red handkerchief was wound in a very loose and unstudied style round his neck, and an old white hat was carelessly thrown on one side of his head. // 'I wonder whether I'm meant to be a footman, or a groom, or a gamekeeper, or a seedsman. I looks like a sort of compo of every one on 'em. Never mind: there's a change of air, plenty to see, and little to do; and all this suits my complaint uncommon; so long life to the Pickvicks, say I!' (Pickwick).*

Weller, Tony, jun.: Sam Weller's infant son and Tony's grandson. *'There never wos any like that 'ere little Tony. He's alvays a playin' vith a quart pot, that boy is! To see him a settin' down on the doorstep pretending to drink out of it, and fetching a long breath artervards, and smoking a bit of fire-vood, and sayin', "Now I'm grandfather," – to see him a doin' that at two year old is better than any play as wos ever wrote' (Humphrey).*

Weller, Tony, sen.: Sam's father, a stage-coachman. *Among the number was one stout, red-faced, elderly man in particular, seated in an opposite box, who attracted Mr. Pickwick's attention. The stout man was smoking with great vehemence, but between every half-dozen puffs, he took his pipe from his mouth. . . . Then, he would bury in a quart pot as much of his countenance as the dimensions of the quart pot admitted of its receiving (Pickwick).*

Weller, Mrs. Tony, sen. (Susan): Second wife of Tony Weller senior and formerly the Widow Clarke. She is landlady of the Marquis of Granby, Dorking, where she drives Tony to despair by her infatuation with the hypocritical Revd. Mr. Stiggins, but restores him by dying and leaving him her property. *A rather stout lady of comfortable appearance. // 'Wy, I'll tell you what, Sammy,' said Mr. Weller, senior, with much solemnity in his manner; 'there never was a nicer woman as a widder, than that 'ere second wentur o' mine – a sweet creetur she was, Sammy; all I can say on her now, is, that as she was such an uncommon pleasant widder, it's a great pity she ever changed her condition' (Pickwick).*

Wemmick, sen.: See **'Aged, The'** *(Expectations).*

Wemmick, John: Jaggers's confidential clerk. He befriends Pip and Herbert Pocket and helps in the attempt to smuggle Magwitch out of the country. He marries Miss Skiffins. *A dry man, rather short in stature, with a square wooden face, whose expression seemed to have been imperfectly chiselled out with a dull-edged chisel. There were some marks in it that might have been dimples, if the material had been softer and the instrument finer, but which, as it was, were only dints. The chisel had made three or four of these attempts at embellishment over his nose, but had given them up without an effort to smooth them off. I judged him to be a bachelor from the frayed condition* *of his linen, and he appeared to have sustained a good many bereavements; for he wore at least four mourning rings, besides a brooch representing a lady and a weeping willow at a tomb with an urn on it. I noticed, too, that several rings and seals hung at his watch-chain, as if he were quite laden with remembrances of departed friends. He had glittering eyes – small, keen, and black – and thin wide mottled lips. He had had them, to the best of my belief, from forty to fifty years (Expectations).*

West, Dame: Grandmother of the child Harry (q.v.) *(Curiosity Shop).*

Westlock, John: Pupil of Pecksniff until he leaves in disgust, after failing to convince Tom Pinch of their master's malpractices. Eventually marries Ruth Pinch. *Not the old John of Pecksniff's, but a proper gentleman: looking another and grander person, with the consciousness of being his own master and having money in the bank: and yet in some respects the old John too, for he seized Tom Pinch by both his hands the instant he appeared, and fairly hugged him, in his cordial welcome (Chuzzlewit).*

Westwood: See **Adams, Captain** and **Westwood** *(Nickleby).*

Wharton, Granville: Pupil of George Silverman who self-sacrificially induces him to fall in love with Adelina Fareway, and marries them ('Silverman').

Wheezy, Professor: A vice-president of the zoology and botany session at the first meeting of the Mudfog Association *(Mudfog).*

'Whelp, The': See **Gradgrind, Tom** *(Hard Times).*

Whiff, Miss: One of the attendants at Mugby Junction refreshment room *(Christmas Stories – 'Mugby Junction').*

Whiffers: A Bath footman, present at the footmen's soirée, who announces his resignation from his employment because he has been required to eat cold meat. *He had a distinct recollection of having once consented to eat salt butter, and he had, moreover, on an occasion of sudden sickness in the house, so far forgotten himself as to carry a coal-scuttle up to the second floor. He trusted he had not lowered himself in the good opinion of his friends by this frank confession of his faults; and he hoped the promptness with which he had resented the last unmanly outrage on his feelings, to which he had referred, would reinstate him in their good opinion, if he had (Pickwick).*

Whiffin: Town crier of Eatanswill *(Pickwick).*

Whiffler: The doting father. *Mr. Whiffler must have to describe at his office such excruciating agonies constantly undergone by his eldest boy, as nobody else's eldest boy ever underwent; or he must be able to declare that there never was a child endowed with such amazing health, such an indomitable constitution, and such a cast-iron frame, as his child (Young Couples – 'Couple Who Dote Upon Their Children').*

Whiffler, Mrs.: Whiffler's wife, and doting mother of Georgiana, Ned, Dick, Tom, Bob, Mary Anne, Emily, Fanny, Carry and another on the way. *Mrs. Whiffler will never cease to recollect the last day of the old year as long as she lives, for it was on that day that the baby had the four red spots on its nose which they took for measles: nor Christmas-day, for twenty-one days after Christmas-day the twins were born; nor Good Friday, for it was on a Good Friday that she was frightened by the donkey-cart when she was in the family way with Georgiana (Young Couples – 'Couple Who Dote Upon Their Children').*

Whimple, Mrs.: The Barleys' landlady. *An elderly woman of a pleasant and thriving appearance (Expectations).*

Whisker: Garland's pony. *If the old gentleman remonstrated by shaking the reins, the pony replied by shaking his head. It was plain that the utmost the pony would consent to do, was to go in his own way up any street that the old gentleman particularly wished to traverse, but that it was an understanding between them that he must do this after his own fashion or not at all (Curiosity Shop).*

White: A pale, bald, grown-up child in Mrs. Lemon's school in Nettie Ashford's romantic tale ('Holiday Romance').

White: Police constable who accompanies the narrator and Inspector Field to the thieves' kitchen and seminary for the teaching of the art to children in Rotten Gray's Inn Lane *(Reprinted – 'On Duty with Inspector Field').*

White, Betsy: The species of girl preying on Liverpool sailors. *Betsy looks over the banisters . . . with a forcible expression in her protesting face, of an intention to compensate herself for the present trial by grinding Jack finer than usual when he does come (Uncommercial – 'Poor Mercantile Jack').*

White, Tom: The name given for Oliver Twist by a kindly jailor when, shocked and ill, Oliver is unable to give his name to the bullying magistrate, Fang *(Twist).*

Wickam, Mrs.: Paul Dombey's nurse after Polly Toodle's dismissal. *A waiter's wife – which would seem equivalent to being any other man's widow – whose application for an engagement in Mr. Dombey's service had been favourably considered, on account of the apparent impossibility of her having any followers, or any one to follow (Dombey).*

Wickfield: Betsey Trotwood's Canterbury lawyer; father of Agnes. Brought low by drink, he becomes the tool of Uriah Heep but is eventually rescued by Micawber. *His hair was quite white now, though his eyebrows were still black. He had a very agreeable face, and, I thought, was handsome. There was a certain richness in his complexion, which I had been long accustomed, under Peggotty's tuition, to connect with port wine; and I fancied it was in his voice, too, and referred his growing corpulency to the same cause (Copperfield).*

Wickfield, Agnes: David and Dora Copperfield's friend, and his second wife, by Dora's dying wish.

Although her face was quite bright and happy, there was a tranquillity about it, and about her – a quiet, good, calm spirit, – that I never have forgotten; that I never shall forget. . . . She had a little basket-trifle hanging at her side, with keys in it; and she looked as staid and as discreet a housekeeper as the old house could have. . . . I cannot call to mind where or when, in my childhood, I had seen a stained-glass window in a church. Nor do I recollect its subject. But I know that when I saw her turn round, in the grave light of the old staircase, and wait for us, above, I thought of that window; and I associated something of its tranquil brightness with Agnes Wickfield ever afterwards (Copperfield).

Wicks: A clerk at Dodson and Fogg's *(Pickwick).*

Widger, Bobtail and **Mrs. Bobtail (Lavinia):** A plausible couple. *No less plausible to each other than to third parties. They are always loving and harmonious. The plausible gentleman calls his wife 'darling,' and the plausible lady addresses him as 'dearest.' If it be Mr. and Mrs. Bobtail Widger, Mrs. Widger is 'Lavinia, darling,' and Mr. Widger is 'Bobtail, dearest.' Speaking of each other, they observe the same tender form. Mrs. Widger relates what 'Bobtail' said, and Mr. Widger recounts what 'darling' thought and did (Young Couples – 'Plausible Couple').*

Wield, Inspector Charles: One of the Detective Force officers of Scotland Yard. *A middle-aged man of a portly presence, with a large, moist, knowing eye, a husky voice, and a habit of emphasising his conversation by the aid of a corpulent fore-finger, which is constantly in juxta-position with his eyes or nose (Reprinted – 'Detective Police' and 'Three "Detective" Anecdotes').*

Wigs: One of Miss Flite's birds *(Bleak House).*

Wigsby: Speaker at the zoology and botany session of the first meeting of the Mudfog Association. *Produced a cauliflower somewhat larger than a chaise-umbrella, which had been raised by no other artificial means than the simple application of highly carbonated soda-water as manure. He explained that by scooping out the head, which would afford a new and delicious species of nourishment for the poor, a parachute . . . was at once obtained (Mudfog).*

Wigsby: A vestryman, of Chumbledon Square. *Mr. Wigsby replies (with his eye on next Sunday's paper) that in reference to the question which has been put to him by the honourable gentleman opposite, he must take leave to say, that if that honourable gentleman had had the courtesy of giving him notice of that question, he (Mr. Wigsby) would have consulted with his colleagues in reference to the advisability, in the present state of the discussions on the new paving-rate, of answering that question (Reprinted – 'Our Vestry').*

Wilding, Mrs.: The lady who adopts Walter Wilding from the Foundling Hospital and founds his fortunes as a wine merchant, believing him to be another child (*Christmas Stories* – 'No Thoroughfare'; not in dramatised version).

Wilding, Walter: Head of Wilding and Co., City of London wine merchants. Adopted from the Foundling Hospital in mistake for another baby, he had been left the business by Mrs. Wilding. Learning of the mistake from Mrs. Goldstraw, he determines to make restitution to the rightful heir, but dies while trying to trace him. *An innocent, open-speaking, unused-looking man, Mr. Walter Wilding, with a remarkably pink and white complexion, and a figure much too bulky for so young a man, though of a good stature. With crispy curling brown hair, and amiable bright blue eyes. An extremely communicative man: a man with whom loquacity was the irrestrainable outpouring of contentment and gratitude (Christmas Stories – 'No Thoroughfare' and in dramatised version).*

Wilfer, Bella: The Wilfer daughter intended under Harmon's will to marry his son. Bereaved before the event by his supposed murder, she marries him unknowingly as John Rokesmith and they have a baby. *A girl of about nineteen, with an exceedingly pretty figure and face, but with an impatient and petulant expression both in her face and in her shoulders (which in her sex and at her age are very expressive of discontent) (Mutual Friend).*

Wilfer, Lavinia ('The Irrepressible'): Bella's temperamental younger sister, loved by George Sampson. *'I'm not a child to be taken notice of by strangers' (Mutual Friend).*

Wilfer, Reginald ('The Cherub' and 'Rumty'): Father of Bella and Lavinia, a downtrodden clerk to Chicksey, Veneering and Stobbles. *So poor a clerk, through having a limited salary and an unlimited family, that he had never yet attained the modest object of his ambition: which was, to wear a complete new suit of clothes, hat and boots included, at one time. His black hat was brown before he could afford a coat, his pantaloons were white at the seams and knees before he could buy a pair of boots, his boots had worn out before he could treat himself to new pantaloons, and by the time he worked round to the hat again, that shining modern article roofed-in an ancient ruin of various periods. . . . His chubby, smooth, innocent appearance was a reason for his being always treated with condescension when he was not put down. A stranger entering his own poor house at about ten o'clock P.M. might have been surprised to find him sitting up to supper. So boyish was he in his curves and proportions, that his old schoolmaster meeting him in Cheapside, might have been unable to withstand the temptation of caning him on the spot (Mutual Friend).*

Wilfer, Mrs. Reginald: Wilfer's wife, mother of Bella and Lavinia. *A tall woman and an angular. Her lord being cherubic, she was necessarily majestic, according to the principle which matrimonially unites contrasts. She was much given to tying up her head in a pocket-handkerchief, knotted under the chin. This head-gear, in conjunction with a pair of gloves worn within doors, she seemed to consider as at once a kind of armour against misfortune (invariably assuming it when in low spirits or difficulties), and as a species of full dress (Mutual Friend).*

Wilhelm: German courier who narrates the story of James and John. *The stoutest courier* ('At Dusk').

Wilkins: Boldwig's gardener *(Pickwick)*.

Wilkins, Dick: A fellow apprentice of the young Scrooge *(Christmas Books – 'Christmas Carol')*.

Wilkins, Samuel: Journeyman carpenter courting Jemima Evans. *Of small dimensions, decidedly below the middle size – bordering, perhaps, upon the dwarfish. His face was round and shining, and his hair carefully twisted into the outer corner of each eye, till it formed a variety of that description of semi-curls, usually known as 'aggerawators'. His earnings were all-sufficient for his wants, varying from eighteen shillings to one pound five, weekly – his manner undeniable – his sabbath waistcoats dazzling. No wonder that, with these qualifications, Samuel Wilkins found favour in the eyes of the other sex* (Boz – 'Miss Evans and the Eagle').

Will: Waiter at the St. James's Arms *(Strange Gentleman)*.

Willet, Joe: Son of John, whose browbeating makes him run away. Rejected by Dolly Varden, he joins the army, loses an arm, and returns in time to save Dolly during the Gorden Riots, after which she marries him. *A broad-shouldered strapping young fellow of twenty, whom it pleased his father still to consider a little boy, and to treat accordingly (Rudge)*.

Willet, John: Landlord of the Maypole Inn, Chigwell, Essex. Father of Joe. *A burly, large-headed man with a fat face, which betokened profound obstinacy and slowness of apprehension, combined with a very strong reliance upon his own merits. It was John Willet's ordinary boast in his more placid moods that if he were slow he was sure; which assertion could, in one sense at least, be by no means gainsaid, seeing that he was in everything unquestionably the reverse of fast, and withal one of the most dogged and positive fellows in existence – always sure that what he thought or said or did was right, and holding it as a thing quite settled and ordained by the laws of nature and Providence, that anybody who said or did or thought otherwise must be inevitably and of necessity wrong (Rudge)*.

William: Young man who kills himself with hard work, copying and translating for publishers to keep himself and his widowed mother. *Night after night, two, three, four hours after midnight, could we hear the occasional raking up of the scanty fire, or the hollow and half-stifled cough, which indicated his being still at work; and day after day, could we see more plainly that nature had set that unearthly light in his plaintive face, which is the beacon of her worst disease* (Boz – 'Our Next-door Neighbour').

William: Yarmouth inn waiter who eats most of young David Copperfield's dinner for him. *It was quite delightful to me to find him so pleasant. He was a twinkling-eyed, pimple-faced man, with his hair standing upright all over his head. . . . 'What have we got here?' he said, putting a fork into my dish. 'Not chops?'* *(Copperfield)*.

William: Driver of the Canterbury coach taking David Copperfield to London. *'Is Suffolk your county, sir,' asked William. . . . 'I'm told the dumplings is uncommon fine down there'* *(Copperfield)*.

William: Waiter at the Saracen's Head inn, where Squeers stays in London *(Nickleby)*.

William: Sir Mulberry Hawk's coachman *(Nickleby)*.

William, Sweet: A travelling entertainer encountered by Little Nell and her grandfather. *A silent gentleman who earned his living by showing tricks upon the cards, and who had rather deranged the natural expression of his countenance by putting small leaden lozenges into his eyes and bringing them out at his mouth, which was one of his professional accomplishments (Curiosity Shop)*.

Williams: Police constable who accompanies the narrator and Inspector Field to sailors' haunts in Ratcliffe Highway *(Reprinted – 'On Duty with Inspector Field')*.

Williams, William: Regular drinker at the Six Jolly Fellowship Porters *(Mutual Friend)*.

Williamson, Mrs.: Landlady of the Winglebury Arms *(Boz – 'Great Winglebury Duel')*. In the dramatised version, *The Strange Gentleman*, she is renamed Mrs. Noakes.

Willis: A debtor in Solomon Jacobs's sponging-house. *A young fellow of vulgar manners dressed in the very extreme of the prevailing fashion, was pacing up and down the room, with a lighted cigar in his mouth and his hands in his pockets, ever and anon puffing forth volumes of smoke, and occasionally applying, with much apparent relish, to a pint pot, the contents of which were 'chilling' on the hob* (Boz – 'Watkins Tottle').

Willis, the four Misses: Four sisters who move into 'Our Parish', live completely interdependently, and eventually tantalise the neighbourhood with the question of which of them is to marry Robinson. *The eldest Miss Willis used to knit, the second to draw, the two others to play duets on the piano. They seemed to have no separate existence, but to have made up their minds just to winter through life together. . . . The eldest Miss Willis grew bilious – the four Miss Willises grew bilious immediately. The eldest Miss Willis grew ill-tempered and religious – the four Miss Willises were ill-tempered and religious directly. Whatever the eldest did, the others did, and whatever anybody else did, they all disapproved of* (Boz – 'Four Sisters').

Wilson: The Iago of the Gattletons' private presentation of *Othello*. *'Mr. Wilson, who was to have played Iago, is – that is, has been – or, in other words, Ladies and Gentlemen, the fact is, that I have just received a note, in which I am informed that Iago is unavoidably detained at the Post-office this evening'* (Boz – 'Mrs. Joseph Porter').

Wilson: Contender with Rogers, the Parlour Orator, at an Old Street Suburban Representative Discovery Society meeting over the Parliamentary candidature of Snobee (q.v.) *(Boz – 'Parlour Orator')*.

Wilson, Caroline: Pupil of the Misses Crumpton. *The ugliest girl in Hammersmith, or out of it (Boz – 'Sentiment').*

Wilson, Fanny: Sister of Mary and fiancée of Charles Tomkins *(Strange Gentleman).*

Wilson, Mary: Fanny's sister, on her way to Gretna Green with John Johnson *(Strange Gentleman).*

Wiltshire: A Wiltshire labourer aboard the emigrant ship *Amazon. A simple fresh-coloured farm-labourer, of eight-and-thirty (Uncommercial – 'Bound for the Great Salt Lake').*

Winking Charley: A character who frequently enters the narrator's night-thoughts as he drifts to sleep. *A sturdy vagrant, in one of her Majesty's jails (Reprinted – 'Lying Awake').* ·

Winkle, sen.: Nathaniel Winkle's father. A Birmingham wharfinger. *A little old gentleman in a snuff-coloured suit, with a head and face the precise counterpart of those belonging to Mr. Winkle, junior, excepting that he was rather bald (Pickwick).*

Winkle, Nathaniel: A member of the Pickwick Club and one of Pickwick's companions on his travels. An aspirant to fame as a sportsman, he makes his mark in a very different field by carrying off Arabella Allen as his wife. *The sporting Winkle ... communicating additional lustre to a new green shooting coat, plaid neckerchief, and close-fitted drabs (Pickwick).*

'Winks': Another name for Deputy (q.v.) *(Drood).*

Wisbottle: Boarder at Mrs. Tibbs's. *A high Tory. He was a clerk in the Woods and Forests Office, which he considered rather an aristocratic employment; he knew the peerage by heart, and could tell you, off-hand, where any illustrious personage lived. He had a good set of teeth, and a capital tailor. . . . It should be added, that, in addition to his partiality for whistling, Mr. Wisbottle had a great idea of his singing powers (Boz – 'Boarding-House').*

Wisk, Miss: Quale's fiancée, a like character and friend to Mrs. Jellyby. *Miss Wisk's mission, my guardian said, was to show the world that woman's mission was man's mission; and that the only genuine mission, of both man and woman, was to be always moving declaratory resolutions about things in general at public meetings (Bleak House).*

Witchem, Sergeant: One of the Detective Force officers of Scotland Yard. *Shorter and thicker-set, and marked with the small-pox, has something of a reserved and thoughtful air, as if he were engaged in deep arithmetical calculations. He is renowned for his acquaintance with the swell mob (Reprinted – 'Detective Police').*

Witherden: The notary to whom Abel Garland is articled. He is instrumental in unmasking Quilp and the Brasses. *Short, chubby, fresh-coloured, brisk and pompous (Curiosity Shop).*

Witherfield, Miss: Peter Magnus's fiancée, into whose bedroom Pickwick gets by mistake. *A middle-aged lady, in yellow curl-papers (Pickwick).*

Withers: Mrs. Skewton's page, who propels her invalid-carriage. *The chair having stopped, the motive power became visible in the shape of a flushed page pushing behind, who seemed to have in part outgrown and in part out-pushed his strength, for when he stood upright he was tall, and wan, and thin, and his plight appeared the more forlorn from his having injured the shape of his hat, by butting at the carriage with his head to urge it forward, as is sometimes done by elephants in Oriental countries (Dombey).*

Wititterly, Henry: Of Cadogan Place; Julia Wititterly's devoted husband. *An important gentleman of about eight-and-thirty, of rather plebeian countenance, and with a very light head of hair (Nickleby).*

Wititterly, Mrs. Henry (Julia): Henry's wife, whose companion Kate Nickleby is for a time. *The lady had an air of sweet insipidity, and a face of engaging paleness; there was a faded look about her, and about the furniture, and about the house. She was reclining on a sofa in such a very unstudied attitude, that she might have been taken for an actress all ready for the first scene in a ballet, and only waiting for the drop-curtain to go up (Nickleby).*

Wobbler: Clerk in the Circumlocution Office. *Spreading marmalade on bread with a paper-knife (Dorrit).*

Wolf: Friend of Montague Tigg. *'Mr. Wolf – literary character – you needn't mention it – remarkably clever weekly paper – oh, remarkably clever!' (Chuzzlewit).*

Wood Sawyer, The: A man who conversed with Lucie outside the prison of La Force whenever she went hoping to see her husband. *'See my saw! I call it my Little Guillotine. . . . I call myself the Samson of the firewood guillotine. See here again! Loo, loo, loo; Loo, loo, loo! And off her head comes! Now, a child. Tickle, tickle; Pickle, pickle! And off its head comes. All the family!' (Two Cities).*

Woodcourt: Mrs. Woodcourt's deceased husband and Allan's father. *'Poor Mr. Woodcourt, my dear,' she would say, and always with some emotion, for with her lofty pedigree she had a very affectionate heart, 'was descended from a great Highland family, the Mac Coorts of Mac Coort. He served his king and country as an officer in the Royal Highlanders, and he died on the field' (Bleak House).*

Woodcourt, Mrs.: Allan Woodcourt's widowed mother. *She was such a sharp little lady, and used to sit with her hands folded in each other, looking so very watchful while she talked to me, that perhaps I found that rather irksome. Or perhaps it was her being so upright and trim; though I don't think it was that, because I thought that quaintly pleasant. Nor can it have been the general expression of her face, which was very sparkling and pretty for an old lady. I don't know what it was (Bleak House).*

Woodcourt, Dr. Allan: The young medical man to whom Jarndyce relinquishes Esther Summerson's hand in marriage. *A gentleman of a dark complexion – a young surgeon. He was rather reserved, but I thought him very sensible and agreeable (Bleak House).*

Wooden Midshipman, The: Sol Gills's ship's instrument shop in the City of London, based by Dickens on Norie & Wilson's in Leadenhall Street, later Minories. Their original Midshipman sign is now in the Dickens House, London. *Little timber midshipmen in obsolete naval uniforms, eternally employed outside the shop-doors of nautical instrument-makers in taking observations of the hackney coaches.... One of these effigies ... thrust itself out above the pavement, right leg foremost, with a suavity the least endurable, and had the shoe buckles and flapped waistcoat the least reconcilable to human reason, and bore at its right eye the most offensively disproportionate piece of machinery* (Dombey).

Woodensconce: President of the statistics session at the first meeting of the Mudfog Association *(Mudfog).*

Woolford, Miss: Popular equestrienne at Astley's. *Another cut from the whip, a burst from the orchestra, a start from the horse, and round goes Miss Woolford again on her graceful performance, to the delight of every member of the audience, young or old* (Boz – 'Astley's').

Wopsle: Parish clerk and friend of the Gargerys. He becomes an actor under the name Waldengarver. *Mr. Wopsle, united to a Roman nose and a large shining bald forehead, had a deep voice which he was uncommonly proud of; indeed it was understood among his acquaintance that if you could only give him his head, he would read the clergyman into fits. ... He punished the Amens tremendously; and when he gave out the psalm – always giving the whole verse – he looked all round the congregation first, as much as to say, 'You have heard our friend overhead; oblige me with your opinion of this style!'* (Expectations).

Wopsle's Great-Aunt: *Kept an evening school in the village; that is to say, she was a ridiculous old woman of limited means and unlimited infirmity, who used to go to sleep from six to seven every evening, in the society of youth who paid twopence per week each, for the improving opportunity of seeing her do it* (Expectations).

Words: One of Miss Flite's birds *(Bleak House).*

Wosky, Dr.: Mrs. Bloss's physician. *A little man with a red face, – dressed of course in black, with a stiff white neckerchief. He had a very good practice, and plenty of money, which he had amassed by invariably humouring the worst fancies of all the females of all the families he had ever been introduced into* (Boz – 'Boarding-House').

Wozenham, Miss: Mrs. Lirriper's rival lodging-house keeper in Norfolk Street, Strand. *Some there are who do not think it lowering themselves to make their names that cheap, and even going the lengths of a portrait of the house not like it with a blot in every window and a coach and four at the door, but what will suit Wozenham's lower down on the other side of the way will not suit me* (Christmas Stories – 'Mrs. Lirriper's Lodgings' and 'Mrs. Lirriper's Legacy').

Wrayburn, Eugene: A reluctant barrister who spends his days in indolence and gloom until transformed by marriage with Lizzie Hexham, which he only achieves after nearly being murdered by the jealous Headstone. *'If there is a word in the dictionary under any letter from A to Z that I abominate, it is energy. It is such a conventional superstition, such parrot gabble! What the deuce! Am I to rush out into the street, collar the first man of a wealthy appearance that I meet, shake him, and say, "Go to law upon the spot, you dog, and retain me, or I'll be the death of you"? Yet that would be energy'* (Mutual Friend).

Wrayburn, Mrs. Eugene: See **Hexham, Lizzie** *(Mutual Friend).*

'Wren, Jenny': See **Cleaver, Fanny** *(Mutual Friend).*

Wrymug, Mrs.: Client of the General Agency Office. *'Pleasant Place, Finsbury. Wages, twelve guineas. No tea, no sugar. Serious family.... Three serious footmen. Cook, housemaid, and nursemaid; each female servant required to join the Little Bethel Congregation three times every Sunday – with a serious footman. If the cook is more serious than the footman, she will be expected to improve the footman; if the footman is more serious than the cook, he will be expected to improve the cook'* (Nickleby).

Wugsby, Mrs. Colonel: One of Pickwick's whist opponents at Bath Assembly Rooms *(Pickwick).*

Yawler: Former Salem House pupil who assists Traddles to enter the law. *'Yawler, with his nose on one side. Do you recollect him?'* No. He had not been there with me; all the noses were straight in my day (Copperfield).

York, The Five Sisters of: See **Five Sisters of York, The** *(Nickleby).*

Youth: One of Miss Flite's birds *(Bleak House).*

Zamiel: Nickname given to fellow-traveller in his railway compartment by the narrator. *Tall, grave, melancholy Frenchman, with black Vandyke beard, and hair close-cropped, with expansive chest to waistcoat, and compressive waist to coat: saturnine as to his pantaloons, calm as to his feminine boots, precious as to his jewellery, smooth and white as to his linen: dark-eyed, high-foreheaded, hawk-nosed – got up, one thinks, like Lucifer or Mephistopheles, or Zamiel, transformed into a highly genteel Parisian* (Reprinted – 'A Flight').

'Zephyr, The': See **Mivins** *(Pickwick).*

THE PLACES

A SELECTED TOPOGRAPHY OF DICKENS'S

WORKS AND LIFE

CONTENTS OF 'THE PLACES'

THE PLACES

PART ONE: THE WORLD, EXCEPT LONDON

Alderbury, Wiltshire: See **Salisbury.**

Amesbury, Wiltshire: See **Salisbury.**

Angel Inn: See **Bury St. Edmunds.**

Australia: Mentioned in several works, principally as a penal settlement for transported convicts (e.g. Magwitch, *Expectations*). Transportation to New South Wales ceased in 1840. Dickens was keenly interested in Australian colonisation as a remedy for bad living conditions in England. He sent the fictional Micawbers and Peggottys there (*Copperfield*), and also his own sons Alfred D'Orsay Tennyson Dickens and Edward Bulwer Lytton Dickens.

Barnard Castle, Durham: The King's Head Inn visited by Nicholas Nickleby on Newman Noggs's recommendation for its ale. Dickens and Hablôt K. Browne stayed at this inn in 1838 while investigating the notorious Yorkshire boarding schools. Opposite the inn were the premises of Mr. Humphrey, a clockmaker, which Dickens recalled when titling *Master Humphrey's Clock.*

Barnet, Hertfordshire: Scene of Oliver Twist's meeting with the Artful Dodger. Also mentioned in *Bleak House.* An important coaching stage on the Great North Road, close to London.

Barnstaple, Devon: Setting of 'A Message from the Sea' (*Christmas Stories*).

Bastille, The: Notorious Parisian prison, whose seizure by the revolutionaries on 14 July 1789 is a dramatic scene in *A Tale of Two Cities.*

Bath, Somerset: Setting for several episodes in *Pickwick*; for example, the footmen's 'swarry' attended by Sam Weller, and Winkle's escapade with Mrs. Dowler and the sedan chair. Dickens took Pickwick's name from Moses Pickwick, coach proprietor and owner of the White Hart Hotel.

Beckhampton, Wiltshire: The Wagon and Horses Inn on the Marlborough Downs is thought to be the original of the inn of Tom Smart's adventure with the old chair (*Pickwick*).

Birmingham, Warwickshire: Often visited by Dickens, who gave his first public readings there in 1853, and used by him in *Pickwick, Twist, Humphrey, Nickleby, Uncommercial, Reprinted, Dombey,* and *Rudge.*

Blackheath: See under Part Two.

Bleak House: Present-day name of Fort House, Dickens's holiday home at Broadstairs, which has no connection with the novel. The original of the fictional Bleak House is thought to have been either a house in Gombard's Road, St. Albans, or Great Nast Hyde, off the main St. Albans–Hatfield Road.

Blunderstone, Suffolk: David Copperfield's birthplace, based by Dickens on the village of Blundeston which he visited in 1848.

Bonchurch, Isle of Wight: Holiday home of Dickens and family in 1849. He hoped to make it an alternative to Broadstairs for family holidays, but found the climate unsuitable.

Borrioboola-Gha: Fictional African village, the object of Mrs. Jellyby's philanthropic activities (*Bleak House*).

Boulogne, France: Called 'Our French Watering-place' by Dickens, who frequently holidayed there. Mentioned in *Boz* – 'The Boarding-House', *Reprinted* – 'A Flight' and 'Our French Watering-place', and *Two Cities.*

Bowes, Yorkshire: See **Dotheboys Hall.**

Brentford, Middlesex: Featured in *Expectations, Mutual Friend,* and *Twist.*

Brieg, Switzerland: Township at the foot of the Simplon Pass. Starting-point of Vendale's and Obenreizer's mountain journey and scene of Vendale's marriage to Marguerite (*Christmas Stories* – 'No Thoroughfare').

Brighton, Sussex: Frequently visited by Dickens, who stayed at the Old Ship and Bedford hotels, and wrote there parts of *Twist, Rudge,* and *Bleak House.* Various claims have been made for the sites of Dr. Blimber's school and Mrs. Pipchin's 'Castle' (*Dombey*).

Bristol, Gloucestershire: Often visited by Dickens, who stayed there first in 1835 as a parliamentary reporter, and gave public readings at Clifton in 1866 and 1869. Bristol is featured in *Pickwick* as the site of Bob Sawyer's and Ben Allen's surgery, and of the Bush Inn (at which Dickens himself had stayed) to which Winkle fled from the wrath of Dowler. Arabella Allen lodged with her aunt in Clifton.

Broadstairs, Kent: Coastal resort, for many years the Dickens family's holiday place. They stayed at the Albion Hotel, Lawn House, and Fort House (now re-named Bleak House and open as a Dickens museum). Much of the work of his middle years was done at Broadstairs. It is 'Our English Watering-place'

(*Reprinted*), and the original of Betsey Trotwood is said to have lived in a house on the sea front (now 'Dickens House') which, in *Copperfield*, Dickens transfers to Dover.

Bury St. Edmunds, Suffolk: The Angel Inn is visited by Pickwick and Sam Weller in their pursuit of Jingle, and is the scene of Sam's encounter with Job Trotter and the starting point of Pickwick's adventure at the boarding school for young ladies. The town is also mentioned in *Copperfield, Boz* – 'Watkins Tottle', and *Uncommercial*. Dickens stayed there in 1835 while reporting a parliamentary election.

Cairo, Illinois: Probably the original of the barren estate, Eden, to which Martin Chuzzlewit goes in the hope of making his fortune.

Calais, France: Mentioned in *Two Cities, Dorrit, Mutual Friend, Uncommercial,* and *Hard Times*. Dickens went there many times when travelling to and from the Continent.

Cambridge, Cambridgeshire: Has associations with several stories, including *Two Cities,* 'Silverman' and *Expectations.* ·

Canongate, The: See **Edinburgh.**

Canterbury, Kent: David Copperfield attends school at Dr. Strong's (unidentified) and lodges with the Wickfields; the Micawbers lodge at the Sun Hotel, Sun Street, now a shop. Dickens was much attached to Canterbury and enjoyed personally showing his visitors over the Cathedral.

Chalk, Kent: Setting, with Higham, of the early part of *Great Expectations*. The original of Joe Gargery's forge and cottage may still be seen. Dickens spent his honeymoon in this village near Gravesend in 1836 and the neighbourhood was one of his favourites for walking in throughout his life.

Chatham, Kent: A busy naval base at the mouth of the River Medway, Kent. Mudfog of *Mudfog Sketches* and Dullborough of *The Uncommercial Traveller*. In *Pickwick*, the scene of Winkle's abortive duel with Dr. Slammer and of the Pickwickians' first meeting with Mr. Wardle and family. David Copperfield sells some of his clothing there during his walk to his aunt's. Also mentioned in 'Seven Poor Travellers' (*Christmas Stories*). Chatham was Dickens's childhood home, 1817–22, at Ordnance Terrace and St. Mary's Place. His father was a clerk in the Navy Pay Office in H.M. Dockyard. The Mitre Inn is associated with the childhood of Charley in 'Holly-Tree' (*Christmas Stories*) and with Dickens's own childhood: it was where he and his sister used to sing duets on the dining-room table. It is also probably the Crozier, where Datchery stays, in *Drood*.

Chertsey, Surrey: Scene of the attempted burglary of Mrs. Maylie's in which Oliver Twist is wounded and captured.

Chesney Wold, Lincolnshire: Home of Sir Leicester and Lady Dedlock (*Bleak House*). The original was Rockingham Castle, Northamptonshire (q.v.).

Chigwell, Essex: The King's Head Inn is the original of the Maypole in *Barnaby Rudge*. Chigwell was a favourite resort of Dickens.

Clifton: See **Bristol.**

Cloisterham: See **Rochester.**

Cobham, Kent: Village near Gad's Hill. The Leather Bottle, one of Dickens's favourite inns, is the setting of Pickwick's discovery of Tupman after his flight from Dingley Dell. The inn contains many items of Dickensian interest, including a reproduction of the stone bearing the mysterious cypher which intrigues Pickwick. The walk through Cobham Park, also mentioned in *Pickwick*, was a favourite of Dickens and the last he ever took. The Hall was the seat of Lord Darnley, a friend of Dickens, and is the scene of a ghost story in 'Holly-Tree' (*Christmas Stories*).

Coketown: See **Manchester** and **Preston.**

Conciergerie: Parisian prison where Sydney Carton substitutes himself for the condemned Charles Darnay (*Two Cities*). ·

Cooling, Kent: Pip's first encounter with Magwitch takes place in the churchyard (*Expectations*). The Comport graves are used by Dickens as those of Pip's brothers.

Deal, Kent: Richard Carstone is stationed at the Royal Marines barracks (*Bleak House*). Deal is still a Royal Marines centre, and in Dickens's time was also a thriving naval yard. It was familiar to him in walking between Broadstairs and Dover, and may be the watering place described in *Reprinted* – 'Out of the Season'.

Demerara: A colony in British Guiana where Jingle and Job Trotter are sent by Pickwick to give them a fresh chance in life (*Pickwick*).

Dijon, France: Rendezvous of Edith Dombey and James Carker in their elopement.

Dingley Dell: The home of Mr. Wardle and family where the Pickwickians spend Christmas and later attend Bella Wardle's wedding festivities. Cob Tree Hall, Sandling, near Maidstone, Kent, is much favoured as the original of Manor Farm.

Dorking, Surrey: Tony Weller and his second wife, Susan, keep the Marquis of Granby Inn, where Tony finally routs the persistent Revd. Mr. Stiggins (*Pickwick*).

Dotheboys Hall: A Yorkshire boarding school kept by Mr. and Mrs. Squeers where Nicholas Nickleby is employed as a master. Appalled by the conditions, he beats Squeers and escapes to London with the poor drudge, Smike. Dotheboys is the archetype of the notorious Yorkshire schools. The original was William Shaw's school at Bowes, visited by Dickens in 1838.

Dover, Kent: The setting for Betsey Trotwood's cottage, where David Copperfield finds refuge after tramping from London. Also featured in *Two Cities, Uncommercial, Pickwick,* and *Dorrit*. Often visited by Dickens travelling to and from the Continent.

Dullborough: The Uncommercial Traveller's home town. See **Chatham.**

Eatanswill: See **Sudbury.**

Eden: See **Cairo.**

Edinburgh: The Canongate is the setting for the story of the Bagman's Uncle (*Pickwick*). Dickens had visited the city in 1834 as a reporter. He gave readings there in 1858, 1861, and 1869.

Eel Pie Island, Twickenham: A small island in the Thames where the Kenwigs family picnic on 'bottled beer, shrub and shrimps' (*Nickleby*). Dickens often went there on pleasure outings.

Epping Forest, Essex: Part of the setting for *Rudge.* Chigwell (q.v.) stands on the edge of the forest.

Folkestone, Kent: Summer holiday home of the Dickens family in 1855. Dickens worked on *Dorrit* at 3 Albion Villas. Folkestone is Pavilionstone of *Reprinted* – 'Out of Town'.

Gad's Hill (also **Gadshill**): Between Gravesend and Rochester, Kent. Dickens first admired Gad's Hill Place as a child, and was told by his father that if he worked hard he might some day own it. In 1855 it became available to him by a coincidence; he bought it, used it as a holiday home until 1860, then made it his permanent home. It was there that he wrote *Two Cities, Expectations, Mutual Friend, Uncommercial,* and the unfinished *Drood.* He died there on 9 June 1870. The Swiss garden chalet in which he wrote is now in the grounds of Rochester Museum. Gad's Hill remained in the Dickens family until 1879 and is now a girls' school.

Glasgow: Dickens opened the Athenaeum in 1847. He gave many successful readings in Glasgow, the first in 1858.

Gravesend, Kent: Busy port on the Thames Estuary, well known to Dickens. He sets a number of scenes there, notably David Copperfield's and Peggotty's farewell to the emigrants for Australia, and the attempt to smuggle Magwitch out of England (*Expectations*).

Great Winglebury: See **Rochester.**

Greenwich, Kent (now Greater London): Bella Wilfer and her father take two notable meals at The Ship, the second after her wedding to John Rokesmith at Greenwich Church (*Mutual Friend*). Greenwich Fair is described in a *Boz* sketch of that name.

Greta Bridge, Yorkshire: Squeers and his party alight at the George and New Inn after their journey from London (*Nickleby*). Probably the original of the 'Holly-Tree' Inn (*Christmas Stories*). Dickens and H. K. Browne stayed here in 1838.

Gretna Green, Dumfriesshire: Traditional destination for eloping lovers, who could be married by the blacksmith. Featured in 'Holly-Tree' (*Christmas Stories*) and 'Great Winglebury Duel' (*Boz*).

Groombridge Wells: An amalgam of the neighbouring Groombridge, Sussex, and Tunbridge Wells,

Kent. Visited by Walter Wilding in his quest for his true identity (*Christmas Stories* – 'No Thoroughfare').

Ham House, near Twickenham, Middlesex: Historic mansion in whose neighbourhood Dickens sets the fatal duel between Sir Mulberry Hawk and Lord Frederick Verisopht (*Nickleby*).

Hampton, Middlesex: The quarrel between Hawk and Verisopht breaks out at the racecourse (*Nickleby*). Lightwood and Wrayburn occupy a bachelor cottage near Hampton (*Mutual Friend*). Sikes and Oliver Twist linger at a public house here on their way to the burglary at Chertsey.

Hatfield, Hertfordshire: Small town near London, site of the former royal palace of Hatfield. Bill Sikes pauses for refreshment at the Eight Bells Inn in his flight after murdering Nancy and helps fight a great fire at a mansion in the neighbourhood (*Twist*): Dickens was describing the fire at Hatfield House in 1835 when the Dowager Marchioness of Salisbury was burnt to death. Hatfield is also featured in 'Mrs. Lirriper's Legacy' (*Christmas Stories*).

Henley-on-Thames, Oxfordshire: The Red Lion Inn is probably the Anglers' Inn of *Mutual Friend* where Wrayburn is taken after Headstone's attempt to murder him. Marsh Mill was Paper Mill, where Lizzie Hexam worked. Plashwater Weir Mill Lock in the story is probably Hurley Lock, about six miles down the river.

Higham: See **Chalk.**

Hoghton Tower, Lancashire: Historic house between Preston and Blackburn where Dickens sends George Silverman ('Silverman').

Ipswich, Suffolk: Port and market town, scene of celebrated episodes in *Pickwick*: Pickwick's misadventure with the lady in curl-papers and the Pickwickians' appearance before the magistrate, Nupkins. Sam Weller meets Mary, the housemaid, here. The Great White Horse Inn is the centre of the action: Dickens had stayed there in 1836. Ipswich also features in 'Doctor Marigold' (*Christmas Stories*).

Kenilworth, Warwickshire: The historic castle ruins are visited by Dombey and Edith Granger on the day when he decides to propose to her. Dickens and H. K. Browne stayed there in 1838.

Kingston, Surrey: Thames-side town mentioned in *Expectations, Dombey, Mutual Friend,* and *Humphrey.*

Knebworth, Hertfordshire: Home of Sir Edward Bulwer-Lytton, Dickens's close friend. Dickens's theatrical company performed in the Banqueting Hall of Knebworth (now open to the public).

Lancaster, Lancashire: The former King's Arms Inn was the setting for the ghost story in *Two Apprentices.* Dickens and Wilkie Collins stayed there in 1857 while gathering material for the book. Lancaster is also mentioned in 'Doctor Marigold' (*Christmas Stories*).

Leamington, Warwickshire: Resort and spa, fashionable in Dickens's time. Dombey and Major Bagstock stay at Copp's Royal Hotel, and Bagstock introduces Dombey to Edith Granger.

Liverpool, Lancashire: Major seaport mentioned in several novels. The notorious sailors' haunts are described vividly in *Uncommercial*. Dickens went there in 1838, and again in 1842 when he embarked for America. He and his amateur theatrical company appeared there in 1847 and he read there several times, the last time in 1869.

London: See Part Two.

Lowestoft, Suffolk: Seaside town where Murdstone takes David Copperfield on an excursion.

Maidstone, Kent: County town of Kent. Probably the original of Muggleton *(Pickwick)*.

Manchester, Lancashire: A principal mercantile centre of the North of England, possibly Coketown of *Hard Times* (but see also **Preston**). Dickens went there often as a young man. His sister Fanny lived there: he modelled Tiny Tim ('Christmas Carol') and Paul Dombey on her crippled son. Two local Quaker brothers, William and Daniel Grant, were the originals of the Cheeryble brothers *(Nickleby)*.

Margate, Kent: Seaside resort familiar to Dickens and mentioned in several stories.

Marlborough Downs, Wiltshire: At an ancient inn on the Downs Tom Smart has his strange adventure with the chair *(Pickwick)*. There are several claimants to be the original of the inn.

Marseilles, France: Scene of the imprisonment of Rigaud and Cavalletto; also where Arthur Clennam and the Meagles family are kept in quarantine *(Dorrit)*.

Martigny, Switzerland: Scene of Mr. Dorrit's meeting with Mrs. Merdle and Mr. Sparkler.

Medway, River, Kent: The principal river of Kent, at whose mouth stand Chatham and Rochester, towns of much influence upon Dickens's early life and often represented in his works. He observed, 'If anybody present knows to a nicety where Rochester ends and Chatham begins, it is more than I do.' The Medway is referred to in *Pickwick* and the Medway Coal Trade in *Copperfield*.

Mudfog: Venue for the first meeting of the Mudfog Association. See **Chatham.**

Mugby Junction: Setting for 'Mugby Junction' *(Christmas Stories)*. A provincial railway junction with a characteristically bad refreshment room; held by some to have been Rugby.

Muggleton: Scene of the cricket match between All-Muggleton and Dingley Dell *(Pickwick)*. Of many Kentish claimants to be the original of this place, Maidstone is perhaps favourite.

Naples, Italy: Scene of Steerforth's desertion of Little Em'ly and of Peggotty's search for her *(Copperfield)*. Dickens, his wife, and Georgina Hogarth explored the city thoroughly in 1845, ascended Vesuvius, and visited Pompeii and Herculaneum.

New York: Dickens was first there in 1842. His uncomplimentary passages in the subsequent *American Notes* and *Chuzzlewit* earned him much American opprobrium, and copies of the latter were burnt; but by the time he returned to give readings in 1867 all had been forgiven.

'Our English Watering-place': See **Broadstairs.**

'Our French Watering-place': See **Boulogne.**

Paper Mill: See **Henley-on-Thames.**

Paris: Scene of much of *Two Cities*, during the Revolution, and subject of some of the *Reprinted Pieces*. Also featured in *Bleak House, Dorrit,* and *Dombey*. Dickens stayed there many times and was lionised by literary and theatrical society.

Pavilionstone: See **Folkestone.**

Pegwell Bay, Kent: A quiet shrimping bay near Ramsgate visited by the Tuggs family *(Boz* – 'Tuggses at Ramsgate'), and well known to Dickens.

Petersfield, Hampshire: The Coach and Horses is generally accepted to be the original of the unnamed inn where Nicholas Nickleby and Smike meet the Crummles family.

Plymouth, Devon: A major naval port, home of Micawber's in-laws *(Copperfield)*. Also mentioned in *Bleak House*.

Portsmouth, Hampshire: Dickens's birthplace, at 1 Mile End Terrace, Portsea: the house, now 393 Commercial Road, is a memorial museum to him. The subsequent family home at 16 Hawke Street no longer exists, but the font in which he was baptised in the now-demolished parish church of St. Mary, Kingston, is preserved in St. Stephen's Church, Portsea. The busy naval city is featured in *Nickleby*: Nicholas and Smike act with the Crummles company at the now-vanished theatre. Associated localities, such as their and the Crummleses' lodgings, are now unidentifiable, due to wartime destruction.

Preston, Lancashire: Industrial town near Manchester, the birthplace of George Silverman ('Silverman'). There are features of Coketown *(Hard Times)* in Preston that justify stronger identification than with the generally accepted original, Manchester.

Ramsgate, Kent: Seaside setting of *Boz* – 'Tuggses at Ramsgate'. Dickens paid visits there during his stays at the neighbouring Broadstairs.

Richmond, Surrey: A pleasant town on the Thames, much visited by river parties. Tupman retires there *(Pickwick)*, and Estella stays at Mrs. Brandley's, a 'staid old house' beside Richmond Green *(Expectations)*. The Star and Garter Hotel, where Dickens gave a party to celebrate *Copperfield*, was at the top of the Hill.

Rochester, Kent: Ancient city at the mouth of the River Medway and one of the most significant places in Dickens's life and work. It is bound up with his childhood and he was observed brooding there the day before his fatal seizure. The Royal Victoria and Bull is the Bull of *Pickwick*, the Blue Lion and Stomach

Warner of *Doz* 'Great Wingebury Duel', and the Blue Boar in *Expectations*. The Crispin and Crispianus, at the foot of Strood Hill, was one of Dickens's own favourite inns, mentioned in *Uncommercial*. Watts's Charity, of 'Seven Poor Travellers' (*Christmas Stories*), stands in the High Street. The original of the homes of Pumblechook (*Expectations*) and Sapsea (*Drood*) is in the High Street. Eastgate House, High Street, is the original of the Nuns' House, Cloisterham (*Drood*): it is the city's museum, and in its grounds stands the Swiss chalet from the grounds of Gad's Hill in which Dickens wrote up to the time of his death. The Cathedral, Minor Canon Row, and Jasper's Gatehouse, feature prominently in *Drood*. Restoration House, Maidstone Road, is Miss Havisham's Satis House (*Expectations*).

Rockingham Castle, Northamptonshire: Home of Dickens's friends, the Watsons. He used it as the original of Chesney Wold (*Bleak House*) and the local Sondes Arms is the original Dedlock Arms. The Castle is open to the public.

St. Albans, Hertfordshire: some scenes in *Bleak House* take place in this cathedral city. A house in Gombard's Road may have been the original of Bleak House itself.

St. Antoine, Paris: Setting for most of the Parisian scenes of *Two Cities*.

Salisbury, Wiltshire: Cathedral city. Home of Pecksniff and setting for many scenes of *Chuzzlewit*. The Blue Dragon Inn has been identified with the George, Amesbury, the Green Dragon, Alderbury, and the Lion's Head, Winterslow, all places nearby.

Sandling, Kent: A village near Maidstone, generally accepted as the original of Dingley Dell (*Pickwick*).

Satis House: Miss Havisham's home (*Expectations*). The original is Restoration House, Maidstone Road, Rochester.

Sens, France: Small cathedral town where Mrs. Lirriper and Jemmy visit the dying Edson (*Christmas Stories* – 'Mrs. Lirriper's Legacy').

Shanklin, Isle of Wight: Dickens visited the resort in 1849. He set the scene of the Lammles' mutual disillusionment on Shanklin sands (*Mutual Friend*).

Stevenage, Hertfordshire: Visited by Dickens in 1861 for the purpose of meeting a local eccentric known as Mad Lucas (used as Mopes in *Christmas Stories* –

'Tom Tiddler's Ground'). The White Hart Inn is the Peal of Bells in the same story.

Sudbury, Suffolk: Original of Eatanswill (*Pickwick*).

Tewkesbury, Gloucestershire: the Hop Pole Inn is the hostelry where Pickwick, Ben Allen, and Bob Sawyer dine on their way to Birmingham.

Tong, Shropshire: Village near Shifnal: scene of the deaths of Little Nell and her grandfather (*Curiosity Shop*).

Towcester, Northamptonshire: The Pomfret Arms is the inn (the Saracen's Head) where Pickwick and his party stay on their return from Birmingham and meet the rival editors, Pott and Slurk, who fight there.

Tunbridge Wells, Kent: An inland spa where one of Dickens's sons was educated. Scene of Miss Twinkleton's early romance with 'foolish Mr. Porters' (*Drood*), and of one of Mr. Finching's many proposals to Flora (*Dorrit*). Groombridge Wells (*Christmas Stories* – 'No Thoroughfare') is a combination of Tunbridge Wells and the nearby Groombridge, Sussex.

Twickenham, Middlesex: Dickens stayed there during the summer of 1838. He made it the setting of the fatal duel between Sir Mulberry Hawk and Lord Frederick Verisopht (*Nickleby*), and of the Meagleses' home (*Dorrit*).

Venice, Italy: The first place visited by the newly-rich Dorrits. Mr. Sparkler courts Fanny Dorrit there. It was one of Dickens's favourite continental cities.

Warwick, Warwickshire: Visited by Dickens and H. K. Browne in 1838. Its historic castle delights Mrs. Skewton on the outing arranged by Dombey. It is open to the public.

Windsor, Berkshire: Scene of John Podgers's adventures in Pickwick's story (*Humphrey*). Childhood home of Esther Summerson (*Bleak House*).

Winterslow, Wiltshire: See **Salisbury.**

Yarmouth, Norfolk: Seaside town visited by Dickens in 1848. Daniel Peggotty lives in an inverted boat on the beach, and Yarmouth is the setting for many other scenes in *Copperfield*.

York, Yorkshire: Dickens stayed at the Black Swan in 1838. This cathedral city is the setting for the story of 'The Five Sisters of York' (*Nickleby*). Visited by John Chivery in search of a clue to the Dorrit fortune.

PART TWO: LONDON

Adelphi: Residential terrace built by the Adam brothers just east of Charing Cross in 1768; now demolished. One of Dickens's favourite districts during his boyhood employment at the blacking warehouse. The vanished Adelphi Hotel, at the corner of John Adam Street, was Osborne's, Wardle's favourite London hostelry (*Pickwick*). 'Mrs. Edson' attempts

suicide from the Adelphi Terrace (*Christmas Stories* – 'Mrs. Lirriper's Lodgings'). David Copperfield lodges near the Adelphi, presumably at 15 Buckingham Street (demolished) where Dickens himself lodged briefly in youth. The Adelphi is the scene of Miss Wade's meeting with Blandois (*Dorrit*) and Martin Chuzzlewit lodges in a public house nearby.

Albany: Residential chambers near Burlington House in Piccadilly, where Fascination Fledgeby lives (*Mutual Friend*).

Aldersgate Street, City: Site of the warehouse of Chuzzlewit and Son. John Jasper stays in a lodging house here on his London visits (*Drood*).

Aldgate, City: Pickwick starts for Ipswich by coach from the Bull Inn. David Copperfield arrives at the Blue Boar, near the Bull, on his way to school at Salem House. Recognising that Florence Dombey's affections lie with Walter Gay, Toots consoles himself with a walk to Aldgate Pump, at the junction of Fenchurch and Leadenhall Streets.

'All the Year Round' Offices: The site is 26 Wellington Street, at the corner of Tavistock Street, Strand. Dickens occupied bachelor chambers above his editorial premises.

Angel, Islington: Famous tavern, now vanished, featured in *Twist*. The neighbourhood retains the name.

Arundel Street, Strand: No. 2 is the site of Chapman & Hall's former publishing premises (then 186 Strand) where Dickens bought the magazine containing his first story.

Astley's Royal Equestrian Amphitheatre stood on the site of 225–33 Westminster Bridge Road. The leading place of entertainment featuring equestrian acts, mentioned in *Curiosity Shop, Bleak House, Boz,* and elsewhere.

Athenaeum Club, Waterloo Place: Club founded in 1824, with a distinguished membership of learned men, to which Dickens was elected at the age of twenty-six. He and Thackeray ended their long estrangement there a few days before the latter's death.

Austin Friars, City: Old Martin Chuzzlewit's solicitor, Phipps, lives here.

Balls Pond, north London: Home of the Perches (*Dombey*) and the Butlers (*Boz* – 'Sentiment').

Bank of England: Established 1694 and located in Threadneedle Street since 1734. Mentioned in *Boz, Pickwick, Uncommercial, Chuzzlewit, Mutual Friend, Dombey,* and *Dorrit.*

Barbican, City: The inn where Sim Tappertit and the 'Prentice Knights hold their meetings (*Rudge*) is placed in the Barbican area, which has been virtually rebuilt since the Second World War. Also mentioned in *Twist, Chuzzlewit,* and *Dorrit.*

Barnard's Inn, Holborn: A now-vanished Inn of Chancery where Herbert Pocket and Pip share chambers (*Expectations*).

Barnet: See under Part One.

Bartholomew's Close, adjoining St. Bartholomew's Church, Little Britain: Pip sees Jaggers dealing with some of his importunate clients outside his office here (*Expectations*).

Battle Bridge: The old name for King's Cross. Nearby stood Boffin's Bower (*Mutual Friend*). Also mentioned in *Dombey, Twist,* and *Boz.*

Bayham Street, Camden Town: No. 16, now demolished, was the home of Dickens's parents and family in 1823. Probably the original of Bob Cratchit's (*Christmas Books* – 'Christmas Carol') and the lodging Traddles shares with the Micawbers (*Copperfield*).

Bedford Street, Strand: Warren's Blacking Warehouse was moved from Hungerford Stairs to the site of the present Civil Service Stores. This is where Dickens was humiliated by having to work in public view.

Bedlam: Actually Bethlehem Hospital, the lunatic asylum formerly in Moorfields, moved in Dickens's youth to Lambeth where the Imperial War Museum now stands. Referred to in *Uncommercial* – 'Night Walks'.

Bell Alley, Coleman Street (now Mason's Avenue): Pickwick is taken to the house of Namby, sheriff's officer, here before being put in the Fleet.

Bell Yard, Carter Lane: Dickens rented an office at No. 5 while reporting for one of the Proctors' offices in Doctors' Commons.

Bell Yard, Fleet Street: see **Cursitor Street.**

Belle Sauvage Inn, Ludgate Hill: Now-vanished headquarters of Tony Weller (*Pickwick*).

Bentinck Street, Portland Place: The home of John Dickens and family was here in 1833–34.

Berners Street, Oxford Street: Scene of Dickens's encounter with an eccentric woman in white, disappointed in marriage, who may have been the original of Miss Havisham in *Expectations.*

Bethnal Green: In Dickens's day a squalid East End region where Sikes and Nancy first kept house (*Twist*), and Eugene Wrayburn is spied on by Bradley Headstone (*Mutual Friend*).

Beulah Spa, Norwood: Opened in 1831 as a fashionable resort, but its popularity was short-lived (*Boz* – 'Watkins Tottle').

Bevis Marks, City: Sampson and Sally Brass live at No. 10; and Dick Swiveller enjoys 'exceedingly mild porter' at the Red Lion (*Curiosity Shop*).

Billingsgate: London's centuries-old fish market in the City features in *Dorrit, Expectations* and *Uncommercial.*

Bishopsgate: City terminus for eastern counties coaches where Brogley, the broker, keeps shop (*Dombey*).

Black Bull Inn: See **Holborn.**

Blackfriars Bridge: One of the Thames bridges: the bridge referred to by Dickens was demolished in 1863. As a child he had crossed it frequently, going from the blacking warehouse to the Marshalsea.

Blackfriars Road: Southern approach to the Blackfriars Bridge. In this road David Copperfield was robbed of his luggage and thus compelled to walk to Dover.

Blackheath: Residential district of south-east London where Dickens places Salem House School attended by David Copperfield (but see **Salem House School**). David shelters behind the school for a night on his walk to Dover. John and Bella Rokesmith have their first married home in Blackheath (*Mutual Friend*). The Dover Mail is ascending Shooter's Hill, Blackheath, as *A Tale of Two Cities* opens. Harry Walmers's father lives at the Elms, Shooter's Hill (*Christmas Stories* – 'Holly-Tree'). Tony Weller retires to a public house in the district at the end of *Pickwick*.

Bleeding Heart Yard, near Hatton Garden: The Plornish family lives here, and it contains the factory of Doyce and Clennam (*Dorrit*).

Bloomsbury: A residential part of Holborn. Dickens's last London home, **Tavistock House** (q.v.) was here. Mr. and Mrs. Kitterbell live at 14 Great Russell Street, and their 'Bloomsbury Christening' takes place at the church of St. George, Hart Street, now Bloomsbury Way (*Boz*). No. 29 Bloomsbury Square, burnt by the Gordon Rioters, was the home of Lord Mansfield, the Judge (*Rudge*).

Boffin's Bower: Name given by Mrs. Boffin to the house where she and Boffin lived before coming into their fortune (*Mutual Friend*). It was in Maiden Lane (now York Way), north London.

Bond Street: Fashionable West End shopping thoroughfare. The Uncommercial Traveller lodges here for a time in 'Arcadian London'.

Boot Tavern, Cromer Street, Bloomsbury: The present public house stands on the site of its former namesake, headquarters of the Gordon Rioters (*Rudge*).

Borough: District immediately south of London Bridge, incorporating Southwark. At the White Hart (now demolished, though its yard remains) Pickwick meets Sam Weller, and Pickwick and Wardle discover Jingle and Rachael after their elopement. Bob Sawyer lives in Lant Street (q.v.). The first half of *Dorrit* is set in and around the Marshalsea Prison, of which there are visible remains adjoining the churchyard of St. George's, the church where Little Dorrit is christened and married. The George, London's only surviving galleried inn, features in *Dorrit*. David Copperfield lodges in Lant Street. The King's Bench Prison (q.v.) stood at the corner of the Borough Road.

Bouverie Street: A street off Fleet Street where, in 1846, Dickens was editor of the *Daily News* for less than three weeks.

Bow: In Dickens's day a rural district of east London where the Cheeryble brothers let a cottage to Mrs. Nickleby and her family.

Bow Street Police Court, Covent Garden: The Artful Dodger appears before the Bow Street magistrate (*Twist*). Barnaby Rudge is questioned here after his arrest in the Gordon Riots. The page employed by David and Dora Copperfield is charged here with stealing Dora's watch. Bow Street Runners – London's first regular detective force, operating from Bow Street – appear in the characters of Blathers and Duff (*Twist*), and in *Expectations*, and Bow Street is the scene of *Boz* – 'Prisoners' Van'.

Brentford: See under Part One.

Brick Lane, Shoreditch: A mission hall here is the meeting place of the Brick Lane Branch of the United Grand Junction Ebenezer Temperance Association (*Pickwick*).

Bridewell: Workhouse and reformatory near Blackfriars, now demolished. Miss Miggs is appointed female turnkey (*Rudge*).

Brig Place, India Docks: Captain Cuttle lodges with Mrs. MacStinger at No. 9 (*Dombey*).

Britannia Theatre, Hoxton: Described in *Uncommercial* – 'Two Views of a Cheap Theatre'. Destroyed in 1940.

Brixton: In Dickens's time a prosperous suburb of south London where Pickwick carries out some of his researches.

Broad Court, off Bow Street, Covent Garden: Snevellici lives here (*Nickleby*).

Brook Street, Grosvenor Square: Mrs. Skewton borrows a house belonging to a Feenix relative for Edith's wedding to Dombey. Mr. Dorrit stays at a hotel here.

Buckingham Street, Strand: David Copperfield lodges with Mrs. Crupp at No. 15, now demolished, where Dickens lodged in his youth.

Burlington Arcade: A fashionable shopping arcade off Piccadilly (*Uncommercial* – 'Arcadian London').

Camberwell: In Dickens's time a rural south London suburb. Home of the Malderton family (*Boz* – 'Horatio Sparkins'). Pickwick pursues researches there. Wemmick and Miss Skiffins are married at St. Giles's Church (*Expectations*). Ruth Pinch is employed as governess in the house of a brass and copper founder (*Chuzzlewit*).

Camden Town: A rural area of north-west London, fast becoming urbanised in Dickens's time. His parents lodged at 16 Bayham Street (q.v.) and elsewhere. Dickens lodged with Mrs. Roylance, the original of Mrs. Pipchin, in Little College Street in 1824, when his father was committed to the Marshalsea. The Evans family live in Camden Town (*Boz* – 'Miss Evans and the Eagle'). The effect of the new railway on the district is described in *Miscellaneous Papers* – 'Unsettled Neighbourhood'. See also **Stagg's Gardens**.

Carnaby Street, behind Regent Street, near Oxford Circus: The Kenwigs family lives here (*Nickleby*).

Castle Street, Holborn (now Furnival Street): Traddles lodges here (*Copperfield*).

Cateaton Street, City (now Gresham Street): Tom Smart travels for Bilson and Slum's warehouse here *(Pickwick)*.

Cavendish Square, Marylebone: Madame Mantalini's showroom and workrooms are in this neighbourhood *(Nickleby)*. Silas Wegg has his pitch near the square *(Mutual Friend)*.

Cecil Street, Strand: The Dickens family lodged here in 1832. Watkins Tottle has a lodging here *(Boz – 'Watkins Tottle')*.

Chancery, Court of: Before the building of the Law Courts in the Strand, 1874, Chancery cases were heard at Lincoln's Inn Hall or Westminster Hall. Jarndyce and Jarndyce *(Bleak House)* was heard largely at the former but ended at the latter.

Chancery Lane, off Fleet Street: Much of the action of *Bleak House* is set here, old Tom Jarndyce having blown out his brains in a local coffee house. In Cook's Court (actually Took's Court) the Snagsbys live. Chichester Rents is the site of Krook's shop and the Sol's Arms. Watkins Tottle is imprisoned for debt in Cursitor Street *(Boz – 'Watkins Tottle')*. Pickwick is approached by a bail tout at Serjeant's Inn (now demolished).

Charing Cross: Regarded as the central point of London, it adjoins Trafalgar Square (laid out in 1829), formerly streets of houses, shops and, notably, the Golden Cross Hotel where Pickwick and his friends begin their travels. David Copperfield also stays there and takes Peggotty there after meeting him on the steps of St. Martin-in-the-Fields *(Copperfield)*.

Cheapside, City: Mould, the undertaker, lives here *(Chuzzlewit)*. Pickwick meets Tony Weller for the first time at an inn in Grocers Hall Court to which he is taken by Sam *(Pickwick)*.

Chelsea: Residential quarter of west London, on the river; semi-rural when Dickens married Catherine Hogarth in the Parish Church of St. Luke, 2 April 1836. Mr. and Mrs. Bayham Badger live here and Richard Carstone studies law under Mr. Badger's supervision *(Bleak House)*. Dick Swiveller visits Sophia Wackles here before she throws him over for Mr. Cheggs *(Curiosity Shop)*. Crummles shows Nicholas Nickleby a newspaper cutting: 'Crummles is NOT a Prussian, having been born in Chelsea'. The Royal East London Volunteers, in which Gabriel Varden is a sergeant, march to the Chelsea bun-house *(Rudge)*. Bucket's aunt lives next-door-but-two to the bun-house *(Bleak House)*.

Chichester Rents: See **Chancery Lane.**

Children's Hospital, Great Ormond Street, Bloomsbury: Probably the hospital to which Betty Higden's grandson Johnny is taken to die by Mrs. Boffin *(Mutual Friend)*. Dickens took a keen interest in this hospital and helped to raise funds for it.

Church Street, Smith Square, Westminster (now Dean Stanley Street): Jenny Wren lives here with her drunken father *(Mutual Friend)*.

City of London Theatre, Norton Folgate, Spitalfields, is featured in *Boz* – 'Making a Night of it'.

City Road, north London: The Micawbers lodge at Windsor Terrace *(Copperfield)*. See also **Eagle Inn.**

Clapham: Residential quarter of south London. Mr. Gattleton lives at Rose Villa, Clapham Rise, and presents the ill-fated amateur theatricals there *(Boz – 'Mrs. Joseph Porter')*. The Poor Relation lives in Clapham Road *(Christmas Stories – 'Poor Relation')*.

Clare Market, Holborn: The market no longer exists but a building survives as an antique shop, calling itself The Old Curiosity Shop and erroneously imagined by most visitors to be the original referred to in the novel. However, Dickens is said to have done business with a bookbinder there. This area may have been the site of the slum Tom-all-Alone's *(Bleak House)*. The local gin shops are referred to in *Boz* – 'Gin-shops'. The area also features in *Pickwick* and *Rudge*.

Clerkenwell: A north London borough. Gabriel Varden lives at his locksmith's premises, the Golden Key; prisoners are released from the New Gaol by the Gordon Rioters *(Rudge)*. Jarvis Lorry lives here *(Two Cities)*. Mr. Venus has his taxidermist's business here *(Mutual Friend)*, and Phil Squod plies his trade as a tinker *(Bleak House)*. Near Clerkenwell Green Mr. Brownlow has his pockets picked outside a bookshop by Charley Bates and the Artful Dodger, and Oliver Twist is arrested; and it is near here that he is later recaptured for Fagin by Nancy.

Clifford's Inn, Fleet Street: Oldest of the Chancery Inns, established 1345. It figures in one of Jack Bamber's stories of the Inns of Court *(Pickwick)*. Melchisedech, Old Smallweed's legal adviser, practises here *(Bleak House)*. Tip Dorrit works here for a year as a clerk. John Rokesmith takes Mr. Boffin to Clifford's Inn to discuss his secretaryship *(Mutual Friend)*.

Cock Lane, Snow Hill, Holborn: Scene in 1762 of the Cock Lane Ghost manifestations; referred to in *Nickleby* and *Two Cities*.

Coldbath Fields, Islington: Site of the present Mount Pleasant post office, where formerly stood one of the harshest London prisons, mentioned in *Boz* – 'Prisoners' Van'.

Commercial Road, Whitechapel: Where Captain Cuttle buys a 'ballad of considerable antiquity' about 'the courtship and nuptials of a promising coal-whipper with a certain "Lovely Peg"' *(Dombey)*. Also mentioned in *Uncommercial* – 'Wapping Workhouse'.

Cook's Court: See **Chancery Lane.**

Coram Street: See **Great Coram Street.**

Cornhill, City: Setting of several scenes in *Pickwick*. Freeman's Court, where Dodson and Fogg have their office, is now the Royal Exchange. The George and Vulture (q.v.) where Pickwick lodges is accessible from Cornhill. Bradley Headstone makes his appeal to

Lizzie Hexam in St. Peter's churchyard (*Mutual Friend*). Bob Cratchit here slides down the ice 'at the end of a lane of boys, twenty times' on Christmas Eve (*Christmas Books* – 'Christmas Carol').

Covent Garden: One of Dickens's favourite districts from childhood. The Uncommercial Traveller always begins his journeys from here, and Dickens's own offices were at 26 (originally 11) Wellington Street. Pip stays at Hummums Hotel, at the corner of Russell Street, when warned by Wemmick not to go home, and it was probably the meeting place of 'the Finches of the Grove' (*Expectations*). Tom Pinch strolls here with Ruth (*Chuzzlewit*). Sikes remarks that fifty boy-thieves could be obtained every night in Covent Garden (*Twist*). David Copperfield lodges temporarily in the area with Miss Trotwood, buys a bouquet for Dora in the Market, and attends the theatre. Job Trotter spends the night before Pickwick's release in a vegetable basket here. John Dounce sometimes attends Covent Garden Theatre for half price 'to see two acts of a five-act play' (*Boz* – 'Misplaced Attachment').

Craven Street, Strand: Brownlow and Rose Maylie meet in a lodging-house here before the rescue of Oliver (*Twist*).

Cross Keys Inn, Wood Street, Cheapside: A large coaching-office at which Dickens first arrived in London. Pip arrives here with Estella (*Expectations*), and Cavalletto is run over here (*Dorrit*). Also mentioned in *Uncommercial* and *Boz*.

Crown Inn, Golden Square: The favourite inn of Newman Noggs, now rebuilt and named the New Crown Inn (*Nickleby*).

Cursitor Street, Chancery Lane: John Dounce lives here with his three spinster daughters (*Boz* – 'Misplaced Attachment'). Watkins Tottle is detained in Solomon Jacobs's sponging-house (*Boz* – 'Watkins Tottle'). Skimpole takes Jarndyce, Ada, and Esther to 'Coavinses Castle', Bell Yard, the home of the late Neckett, to see Neckett's orphaned children (*Bleak House*). See also **Chancery Lane.**

Custom House, Lower Thames Street: Place of work of the late Mr. Bardell (*Pickwick*). Peepy Jellyby gets work here and prospers (*Bleak House*). Pip leaves his boat at a wharf nearby as part of the scheme to get Magwitch out of England (*Expectations*). Mrs. Clennam lives nearby (*Dorrit*). Florence Dombey reaches a wharf belonging to her father in Thames Street after her abduction by Good Mrs. Brown.

Cuttris's Hotel, James Street, Covent Garden, (now the Tavistock): This was Dickens's lodging when he came to London from Italy to give the first reading of 'The Chimes' to friends in 1844.

Deptford: A Thames dockside area where Toby Magsman recounts the story of Chops, the dwarf (*Christmas Stories* – 'Going into Society').

Devonshire Terrace, Marylebone Road: Dickens lived at No. 1 from 1839 to 1851. It was demolished in 1962, but the present office block incorporates a commemorative mural.

Doctors' Commons, City: The College of the Doctors of Law, founded 1768 and demolished 1867 to make way for the present Queen Victoria Street. Dickens rented an office in his reporting days at 5 Bell Yard, leading into the Commons. David Copperfield becomes an articled clerk here. Jingle applies for his licence to marry Rachael Wardle, and Tony Weller obtains his second wife's legacy here (*Pickwick*). It is featured in *Boz* – 'Doctors' Commons'.

Doughty Street, Bloomsbury: Dickens lived at No. 48 from 1837 to 1839. *Pickwick* and *Twist* were finished here, *Nickleby* written, and *Rudge* begun. It is now the headquarters of the Dickens Fellowship and a Dickens library and museum.

Dover Road: The road starting from Blackheath taken by David Copperfield on the walk to his aunt's house in Dover.

Drummond Street, Euston: Miss Martin lives at No. 47 (*Boz* – 'Mistaken Milliner'). Dickens and other boys from Wellington House Academy used to pretend to be beggars here.

Drury Lane: Dickens recalled ordering a small plate of beef during his blacking warehouse days at Johnson's alamode beef house, Clare Court, now vanished; and David Copperfield relates the same experience. Dick Swiveller lodges over a tobacconist's shop here (*Curiosity Shop*). Crown Court, Russell Street, leads into Drury Lane Garden, once a graveyard, where Hawdon is buried in *Bleak House*. Miss Petowker, of the Crummles company, is 'of the Theatre Royal, Drury Lane' (*Nickleby*), and John Dounce frequents the theatre at half-price in *Boz* – 'Misplaced Attachment'.

Duke Street, St. James's: Twemlow lodges over a livery stable (*Mutual Friend*).

Dulwich: An old residential district south of the Thames to which Pickwick retires at the end of his adventures.

Eagle Inn, City Road, north London: It stands on the site of the former Eagle Pleasure Gardens featured in *Boz* – 'Miss Evans and the Eagle'.

Ely Place, Charterhouse Street, City: Agnes Wickfield stays here with the Waterbrooks, and David Copperfield calls on her to apologise for his drunken behaviour at the theatre.

Essex Street, Strand: Pip finds a lodging here for Magwitch, under the name of Provis (*Expectations*).

Fenchurch Street, City: Bella Wilfer waits here in the Boffin coach for her father on her visit to his office (*Mutual Friend*).

Fetter Lane, Holborn: Augustus Cooper lives here (*Boz* – 'Dancing Academy').

Field Lane, Holborn: Slum area cleared for the building of Holborn Viaduct in 1867. Fagin's den is nearby (*Twist*).

Finchley: A north London suburb. After their escape from Newgate, Barnaby Rudge and his father spend a

179

night here in a shed in a field. Toots journeys to Finchley to get some chickweed for Florence Dombey's bird. Kit Nubbles is employed by Mr. and Mrs. Garland at Abel Cottage (*Curiosity Shop*). Dickens lodged at Cobley's Farm in 1843 while writing *Chuzzlewit* and got the idea for Mrs. Gamp there: the site is now occupied by No. 70 Queen's Avenue, which bears a commemorative tablet.

Fitzroy Street, Marylebone: Dickens lived with his parents at No. 15 (now 25) for part of 1832–3.

Fleet Prison. This stood in Farringdon Street, between Fleet Lane and the corner of Ludgate Hill. It was destroyed in the Gordon Riots (*Rudge*), rebuilt, and used until 1842, when debtors were removed to the Queen's Bench. Pickwick is imprisoned in the Fleet for refusing to pay Mrs. Bardell's damages and costs.

Fleet Street: It is prominent in Dickens's writings, and was a neighbourhood he knew intimately. Like David Copperfield he used to haunt it when he had no money, to look in food shops. David takes Peggotty to see Mrs. Salmon's waxworks here. When going to Doctors' Commons with his aunt he pauses to watch the giant figures outside the church of St. Dunstan's-in-the-West striking the hours on the bells. St. Dunstan's is the church of 'The Chimes' (*Christmas Books*). Jarvis Lorry works for Tellson's Bank by Temple Bar (actually Child's Bank) in *Two Cities*. Fleet Street in the early morning is described in *Christmas Stories* – 'Holly-Tree'.

Folly Ditch: See **Jacob's Island.**

Foster Lane, City: No. 5 is considered to be the original of the home of Anthony and Jonas Chuzzlewit.

Foundling Hospital, Bloomsbury: Now demolished, it stood north of Guilford Street, on a site now known as Coram's Fields. Walter Wilding's story largely revolves round it (*Christmas Stories* – 'No Thoroughfare'). On a Sunday morning, while listening to the foundlings singing, the Meagles family decide to adopt Tattycoram (*Dorrit*).

Fox under the Hill, near Charing Cross: This former riverside inn, where the Hotel Cecil now stands, was one of Dickens's haunts during his blacking warehouse days. He relates how he went there to watch the coal-heavers dancing.

Freeman's Court: See **Cornhill.**

Freemasons' Hall, Great Queen Street, Holborn: The scene of *Boz* – 'Public Dinners'. Dickens attended a farewell dinner here in 1867 before leaving for America.

Fresh Wharf, near London Bridge: Mrs. Gamp stands here, hoping to see Jonas and Mercy Chuzzlewit boarding the 'Ankwerks package'.

Fulham: Riverside district adjoining Chelsea. Florence Dombey stays here for a time at the home of Sir Barnet and Lady Skettles.

Furnival's Inn, Holborn: Former Inn of Court, demolished 1898. Dickens's chambers 1834–7, and

first married home, were here. He began *Pickwick* here. Wood's Hotel sends meals by 'flying waiter' to Grewgious, across at Staple Inn, and Rosa Bud stays at the hotel on the night after her flight from Jasper (*Drood*). John Westlock has chambers at the Inn (*Chuzzlewit*).

Garraway's, Change Alley, Cornhill: One of the oldest City coffee houses, it was demolished in 1874 but is commemorated by a plaque. Pickwick writes his famous 'chops and tomata sauce' letter to Mrs. Bardell from here. Nadgett keeps watch on Jonas Chuzzlewit from Garraway's. The Poor Relation sits here every day (*Christmas Stories* – 'Poor Relation'), and it is where Jeremiah Flintwinch transacts his business (*Dorrit*). The Uncommercial Traveller describes it on a Sunday, 'bolted and shuttered hard and fast'.

George Inn, Southwark: See **Borough.**

George and Vulture Inn, Lombard Street: Pickwick is 'at present suspended' at the George and Vulture when dealing with the legal business of Bardell and Pickwick. The Pickwickians are served with subpoenas here and Pickwick is arrested, to return after his eventual release from prison. Winkle and Arabella stay at the George and Vulture after their marriage and are visited by Winkle's father. The inn still exists, much as Dickens knew it.

Gerrard Street, Soho: Dickens's uncle, Thomas Barrow, lived at No. 10 over a bookseller's. Jaggers lives at a stately, if dingy, house probably based on Barrow's (*Expectations*).

Golden Cross: See Charing Cross.

Golden Square, Soho: It was going down in the world when Ralph Nickleby lived there, possibly at No. 7, now demolished. David Copperfield and Martha Endell find Little Em'ly at a house in a street off the square.

Goswell Road, City: Known in Dickens's time as Goswell Street, this is where Pickwick lodges in Mrs. Bardell's house and the misunderstanding occurs which leads to the breach of promise suit.

Gower Street, Bloomsbury: Dickens's parents lodged at No. 4 Gower Street North in 1823–4 and Mrs. Dickens unsuccessfully tried to conduct a young ladies' school.

Gray's Inn, Holborn: Dickens was a solicitor's clerk at 6 Raymond Buildings, 1828. Pickwick's legal adviser, Perker, has chambers in Gray's Inn Square, and Phunkey's chambers are in South Square, where Dickens's employers were previously located. David Copperfield stays in Gray's Inn after his return to England, in a room over the archway. Flora Finching makes a rendezvous with Arthur Clennam in Gray's Inn Gardens (*Dorrit*). The Inn is disparagingly described in *Uncommercial* – 'Chambers'.

Great Coram Street, Bloomsbury (now Coram Street): Mrs. Tibbs has her boarding-house in the neatest house in the street (*Boz* – 'Boarding-House').

Great Marlborough Street, Soho: The police court here is probably that to which Bucket takes Esther

Summerson before his search for Lady Dedlock *(Bleak House)*.

Great Queen Street, Holborn: Dick Swiveller buys a pair of boots on credit here, thus closing his last-but-one avenue to the Strand *(Curiosity Shop)*. The Freemasons' Hall (q.v.) stands here.

Great Russell Street, Bloomsbury: Charles Kitterbell *(Boz* – 'Bloomsbury Christening') lives at No. 14, now marked by a plaque.

Great Tower Street, City: Joe Willet enlists in the army through a recruiting sergeant at the Crooked Billet inn *(Rudge)*.

Green Dragon, Westminster: The public house near Westminster Bridge where Robert Bolton, the 'gentleman connected with the press', regales his regular audience with anecdotes *(Mudfog* – 'Mr. Robert Bolton').

Green Lanes, Marylebone: The name by which the area now covered by Cleveland Street and the northern end of Newman Street was known in the late eighteenth century. The Gordon Rioters are meeting here when Gashford arrives *(Rudge)*.

Greenwich: See under Part One.

Grocers Hall Court: See **Cheapside.**

Grosvenor Square, Mayfair: Tite Barnacle lives at 24 Mews Street *(Dorrit)*. Lord Rockingham's house was one of those defended against the Gordon Rioters *(Rudge)*.

Guildhall, City: The Court of Common Pleas (since rebuilt) is the scene of the Bardell and Pickwick trial. The giant figures of Gog and Magog figure prominently in *Master Humphrey's Clock*.

Guy's Hospital, Southwark: Bob Sawyer is a student at Guy's *(Pickwick)*, where Mrs. Gamp's late husband died *(Chuzzlewit)*.

Hammersmith: A south London riverside district. Matthew Pocket and his family live here; Pip is brought to study; Clara Barley completes her education at a school here and meets Herbert Pocket *(Expectations)*. The Misses Crumpton's finishing establishment, Minerva House, is the setting for *Boz* – 'Sentiment'.

Hampstead: A village on the northern heights of London. Dickens stayed in lodgings in North End in April or May 1832. After the death of his sister-in-law, Mary Hogarth, in 1837, Dickens and his wife spent most of the summer at Collins's Farm (now Wyldes Farm) on the Heath. Hampstead was a favourite place for Dickens, who rode out with friends to Jack Straw's Castle, an inn overlooking the Heath. David Copperfield likes to walk to Hampstead after bathing in the Roman bath in the Strand. Dick Swiveller and Sophronia live in a little cottage at Hampstead 'which had in the garden a smoking-box, the envy of the civilised world', where he is visited by Chuckster with news from London *(Curiosity Shop)*. One of Pickwick's papers for the Pickwick Club was 'Speculations on the Source of the Hampstead Ponds'; and Mrs. Bardell and
G

friends are enjoying tea at the Spaniards Inn beside the Heath when she is lured by Jackson into custody in the Fleet Prison. The Gordon Rioters march to Ken Wood House (then the seat of Lord Mansfield) intending to destroy it, but are foiled *(Rudge)*. Bill Sikes crosses the Heath on his flight after the murder of Nancy *(Twist)*. Mrs. Griffin's establishment, in 'Haunted House' *(Christmas Stories)*, is near Hampstead Ponds.

Hampstead Road (then New Road): In a terrace at the Mornington Crescent end stood Wellington House Academy, now demolished, attended by Dickens after his period at the blacking warehouse (see also **Pancras Road**). George Cruikshank's house, marked by a plaque, is at the end of the remaining part of the terrace.

Hampton: See under Part One.

Hanging Sword Alley, Whitefriars Street, Fleet Street: Jerry Cruncher and his family live here *(Two Cities)*. Mr. George sees possibly fatal symbolism in the alley's name as he passes on his way to the Bagnets' *(Bleak House)*.

Hanover Square, off Regent Street: At the Hanover Square Rooms, on the site of the present No. 4, several performances were given of Bulwer-Lytton's play *Not so Bad as we Seem* by Dickens's amateur company, and he later gave some of his readings here. Dickens's sister Fanny attended the Royal Academy of Music, then in Tenterden Street off the Square.

Harley Street, Marylebone: The Merdles live at the handsomest house in the Street *(Dorrit)*.

Hart Street: See **Bloomsbury.**

Hatton Garden, Holborn: The Metropolitan Police office presided over by Fang was the Hatton Garden police court, of which one of the magistrates was a Mr. Laing. Oliver Twist is taken there on suspicion of robbing Mr. Brownlow. The Garden forms part of Phil Squod's beat as a tinker, and the Jellybys take furnished lodgings here *(Bleak House)*.

Haymarket, off Pall Mall: Turveydrop is fond of dining at a French restaurant in the Opera Colonnade, now Royal Opera Arcade; Mr. George's shooting gallery is hereabouts *(Bleak House)*.

Highgate: A village on the northern heights of London. Dickens and his parents lodged here in 1832 at a house next to the old Red Lion Inn. The inn has disappeared but a house near the site bears a plaque. Dickens's parents and his daughter Dora are buried in Highgate Cemetery. Much of *David Copperfield* is set in the village: Mrs. Steerforth's house is said to be Church House, South Grove; Dr. Strong and Annie live in a cottage on the other side of the village, and David brings Dora here as his bride, while his aunt, Miss Trotwood, settles into the cottage next door. At the Archway toll Bucket first picks up the trail of Lady Dedlock on her last flight *(Bleak House)*. Pickwick undertakes some of his unwearied researches in the area. Noah Claypole and Charlotte enter London under the old Archway; Bill Sikes strides up Highgate Hill on his way north after the murder of Nancy

(*Twist*). In *Rudge*, Joe Willet, after his farewell to Dolly Varden, walks out to Highgate and meditates, 'but there were no voices in the bells to bid him turn' (a reference to Dick Whittington: Highgate is the place where he heard the bells of London summoning him back).

Hockley-in-the-Hole: A slum area now replaced by Clerkenwell Road and Rosebery Avenue. The Artful Dodger brings Oliver Twist through it on their way to Fagin's.

Holborn: A district deriving its name from a major thoroughfare running from Tottenham Court Road to the western boundary of the City of London. Mrs. Gamp lived in Kingsgate Street, High Holborn, above Poll Sweedlepipe's. At the now-vanished Black Bull, Holborn, she and Betsey Prig nurse Lewsome; Chicken Smivey lodges in Holborn (*Chuzzlewit*). Job Trotter runs up Holborn Hill to summon Perker when Pickwick decides to leave the Fleet Prison; and Oliver Twist walks the same way with Sikes en route for the crib at Chertsey. Langdale's warehouses on Holborn Hill are burnt by the Gordon Rioters (*Rudge*). Esther Summerson sees her first 'London particular' (fog) in Holborn when conducted by Guppy to Thavies Inn (*Bleak House*).

Holloway: Holloway Road was the old route into London from the North, approaching Islington. Some of it was still semi-rural in the 1860s, but the Wilfers lived between Holloway Road and the dustheaps at Battle Bridge (now King's Cross), 'a tract of suburban Sahara' (*Mutual Friend*).

Horn Coffee House: The Horn Tavern, 29 Knightrider Street, City, now occupies the site of the coffee house to which Pickwick sends out for 'a bottle or six' to celebrate Winkle's visit to the Fleet Prison.

Hornsey: A northern district of London where Pickwick conducts some of his unwearied researches. Betsey Trotwood's husband was born and buried here (*Copperfield*).

Horse Guards, Whitehall: After the loss of his legs Sim Tappertit is established by Gabriel Varden as a shoeblack under the archway near the Horse Guards (*Rudge*). Peggotty takes Mr. Dick to see the mounted guards (*Copperfield*).

Horsemonger Lane, Borough: Now Union Road. The notorious Horsemonger Lane gaol stood where there is now a recreation ground. In 1849 Dickens and 50,000 others witnessed the execution of the Mannings here, and he wrote a notable letter to *The Times* (13 November 1849) which helped to bring about the abolition of public hangings. He later based the character of Hortense on the French-born Mrs. Manning (*Bleak House*). Young John Chivery's mother keeps her 'snug tobacco business' at 5 Horsemonger Lane (*Dorrit*).

Hummums Hotel: See **Covent Garden.**

Hungerford Market: This stood on the site of Charing Cross station, was rebuilt in 1833, and demolished 1862. Hungerford Stairs, site of Warren's Blacking Warehouse, where the child Dickens worked, adjoined it. Mr. Dick lodges over a chandler's shop in the old market; the Micawbers leave from Hungerford Stairs to board their ship for Australia (*Copperfield*).

Hyde Park: The largest of London's parks. Dickens stayed briefly at several addresses in the neighbourhood: 16 Hyde Park Gate (1862), 16 Somers Place (1865), 6 Southwick Place (1866), and 5 Hyde Park Place (1870), his last London address.

Inns of Court: The old English meaning of inn was lodging, rather than tavern, and the Inns of Court take their names from their former owners whose London abodes they were – e.g. Lincoln's Inn, residence of the Earls of Lincoln. They became associated with the law as the premises of the four societies with the exclusive right to call persons to the Bar – Inner Temple, Middle Temple, Lincoln's Inn, and Gray's Inn. There were also nine Chancery Inns – Clifford's, Clement's, Lyon's, Strand, New, Furnival's, Thavies, Staple, and Barnard's. For story references see under individual Inn names.

Iron Bridge: Popular name for Southwark Bridge, built 1818, replaced 1921. Little Dorrit liked to walk here.

Islington: A northern district of London, once the site of numerous tea-gardens and places of entertainment, and the ancient Angel Inn (q.v.). Potter and Smithers live here (*Boz* – 'Making a Night of it'). Tom Pinch settles here with Ruth, possibly at a house in Terrett's Place, Upper Street (*Chuzzlewit*). Morfin lives here (*Dombey*). Mrs. Lirriper's first lodgings are here. Characters in several stories pass through Islington, e.g. Joe Willet and Barnaby Rudge, the Artful Dodger and Oliver Twist, Oliver Twist and Mr. Brownlow, John Browdie (*Nickleby*), Esther Summerson and Bucket (*Bleak House*), and Nicholas Nickleby's coach, *en route* to Yorkshire, stops at the Peacock Inn (now demolished).

Jack Straw's Castle: See **Hampstead.**

Jacob's Island, Bermondsey: Known as an island because it was cut off by Folly Ditch, since filled in, it was a slum district in Dickens's day. Escaping over the roof-tops from Toby Crackit's home here, Bill Sikes is accidentally hanged (*Twist*). A housing estate here is named after Dickens.

Jerusalem Chambers, Clerkenwell: Site of Tetterby's house and shop, possibly in the vicinity of the present Jerusalem Passage (*Christmas Books* – 'Haunted Man').

Johnson Street, Somers Town, north London (now Cranleigh Street): Dickens lived with his parents at No. 29 in 1825, while a pupil at Wellington House Academy. A modern building occupies the site of their home.

Johnson's Court: The *Monthly Magazine* had its offices at 166 Fleet Street. Into its letter-box in the side door in Johnson's Court Dickens 'stealthily, one evening at twilight, with fear and trembling,' put his first submitted story.

Ken Wood: See **Hampstead.**

Kensington: Fashionable district of west London, where Gabriel Parsons and his sweetheart meet secretly in the Gardens (*Boz* – 'Watkins Tottle').

Kent Street (now Tabard Street): The start of the London-Dover Road, referred to by the Uncommercial Traveller as one of the worst-kept parts of London.

Kentish Town: Populous district of north London, whose oldest inhabitant David Copperfield declares Mrs. Kidgerbury, his charwoman, to have been. Also mentioned in *Rudge*.

King's Bench Prison: Debtors' prison, at the junction of Newington Causeway and Borough Road, demolished 1869. Micawber is imprisoned there (*Copperfield*). Madeline Bray and her father live in the Rules of the King's Bench, an adjoining area where more favoured debtors lodged (*Nickleby*). The Uncommercial Traveller contemplates the prison in 'Night Walks'. The earlier building was destroyed by the Gordon Rioters (*Rudge*). (See also **Borough**.)

King's Bench Walk: An open space in the Temple (q.v.) where Sydney Carton strolls before commencing his work for Stryver (*Two Cities*).

Kingsgate Street: See **Holborn**.

Kingston: See under Part One.

Lambeth: Former slum district across the river from Westminster, where Peg Sliderskew hides after stealing Gride's papers, and is tracked down by Squeers (*Nickleby*).

Lant Street, Borough: Dickens lodged here as a boy while his father was imprisoned in the Marshalsea nearby, and later used his room as the model for Bob Sawyer's lodging with Mrs. Raddle (*Pickwick*). David Copperfield also lodges in Lant Street. There is a Charles Dickens school there today.

Leadenhall Market, City, near Cornhill and Gracechurch Street: The Green Dragon in Bull's Head Passage is believed to have been the original of the Blue Boar, where Sam Weller writes his Valentine to Mary (*Pickwick*). Sol Gills's shop, the Wooden Midshipman (*Dombey*), is said to have been 157 Leadenhall Street, since demolished, and the offices of Dombey and Son are also conjectured to have been in the street.

Leather Lane, Holborn: Barnaby and Hugh escape along it from the mob burning Langdale's Distillery (*Rudge*).

Leicester Square: Known as Leicester Fields at the time of the Gordon Riots, provoked by the Catholic Relief Bill of Sir George Saville, whose mansion was here (*Rudge*). Mr. George's shooting gallery was nearby (*Bleak House*), and the original Old Curiosity Shop may have been in Green Street (now Orange Street) connecting the Square with Castle Street, near Charing Cross Road. Dickens celebrated the completion of *Pickwick* by giving a dinner at the former Prince of Wales Hotel in Leicester Place, north of the Square.

Limehouse: Dockside quarter of east London. Dickens's godfather, Christopher Huffam, or Huffham, lived here. The Six Jolly Fellowship Porters Tavern was The Grapes, in Narrow Street, and Rogue Riderhood and the Hexams live nearby in Limehouse Hole (*Mutual Friend*). Near here Captain Cuttle encounters Jack Bunsby on his way to marry Mrs. MacStinger (*Dombey*). The Uncommercial Traveller describes the leadmills near Limehouse Church.

Lincoln's Inn: One of the oldest Inns of Court. *Bleak House* opens in the Court of Chancery, held here at the time, and this is the scene of the interminable Jarndyce and Jarndyce lawsuit; the offices of Kenge and Carboy are in Old Square; Krook's Rag and Bottle Warehouse is in Chichester Rents, near New Square (*Bleak House*). Pickwick and Perker visit Serjeant Snubbin in Old Square. Dickens was a clerk to a solicitor named Molloy in New Square. At No. 58 Lincoln's Inn Fields John Forster, Dickens's biographer and close friend, lived: his house, still standing, is Tulkinghorn's in *Bleak House*. Betsey Trotwood lodges at a private hotel in the Fields (*Copperfield*).

Little Britain: See **Bartholomew Close**.

Little College Street: See **Camden Town**.

Little Russell Street, Bloomsbury: The Albion Hotel is the scene of the bibulous celebrations of Potter and Smithers (*Boz* – 'Making a Night of it').

Lombard Street, City: Maria Beadnell, Dickens's first love, lived with her parents next door to the bank of Smith, Payne, and Smith, where her father was manager. The George and Vulture (q.v.) can be approached from Lombard Street. Barbox Brothers' office was in the vicinity (*Christmas Stories* – 'Mugby Junction').

London Bridge: In his days at Warren's Blacking Warehouse Dickens was fond of passing his spare time on London Bridge, an experience he relates through the young David Copperfield: 'I was wont to sit in one of the stone recesses, watching the people go by.' This was old London Bridge, the second being designed by Rennie and not opened for traffic until 1831; it has now been transported to America, and replaced by a new bridge. David Copperfield first sees the bridge when travelling to school at Blackheath, with Mr. Mell, whose old mother lived in an almshouse across the bridge. On the bridge, later, David meets 'the Orfling', a little servant who may have been based on the same original as 'the Marchioness' in *Curiosity Shop*, and tells her stories mostly proceeding from his own imagination about the riverside area. The Pickwickians, accompanied by Ben Allen, return across London Bridge after Bob Sawyer's memorable supper party in Lant Street. Pip crosses old London Bridge on his way from the interview in which he opens Miss Havisham's eyes to the wreck she has made of his life and Estella's (*Expectations*). Nancy has her fatal conversation with Rose Maylie on the steps of the new bridge, on the Surrey bank, near St. Saviour's Church (*Twist*). From the steps at the opposite end, on the Middlesex side, Jonas Chuzzlewit sinks the bundle of bloodstained clothes after murdering Tigg. Haredale, while in hiding, travels from Westminster to

London Bridge by water, to avoid possible encounters in the busy streets (*Rudge*). London Bridge Station, built in 1851 on the site of St. Thomas's Hospital, is mentioned in *Reprinted* – 'A Flight'.

London Coffee House: This was on the site of 42 Ludgate Hill. Here Arthur Clennam stays on the dreary Sunday evening after his return to England, listening to the monotonous sound of church bells *(Dorrit)*.

London Docks: Described in *Uncommercial* – 'Bound for the Great Salt Lake'. Mortimer Lightwood combs the docks for news of John Harmon (*Mutual Friend*).

London Hospital, Whitechapel: Founded 1741. Sally Brass buys her brother Sampson an office-stool in an open street market just opposite the Hospital *(Curiosity Shop)*.

London Tavern, Bishopsgate Street (now Bishopsgate): Now demolished. The first annual dinner of the General Theatrical Fund was held here in 1836, chaired by Dickens, who was also in the Chair at a similar dinner in 1841. The public meeting of the United Metropolitan Improved Hot Muffin and Crumpet Baking and Punctual Delivery Company is held here *(Nickleby)*.

London Wall, City: Clennam and Doyce share a house near London Wall *(Dorrit)*. Tom Pinch loses himself here when seeking Furnival's Inn, and finds himself at the Monument *(Chuzzlewit)*.

Long Acre, stretching between St. Martin's Lane and Great Queen Street: Dick Swiveller finds himself unable to pay for a meal he has eaten here, and is obliged to regard the street as being henceforth closed to him *(Curiosity Shop)*. Dickens gave his first series of paid public readings at the former St. Martin's Hall in 1858.

Long's Hotel, 15 New Bond Street: Cousin Feenix stays here *(Dombey)*.

Ludgate Hill: Until 1864, when it was widened, only the lower part was known as Ludgate Hill, the upper being Ludgate Street. David and his aunt are accosted here by her renegade husband *(Copperfield)*.

Lyon's Inn: One of the Inns of Chancery, in Newcastle Street, Holborn, it was demolished in 1863. Mentioned in *Uncommercial* – 'Chambers'.

Magpie and Stump: The meeting-place of Lowten and his friends *(Pickwick)* may have been the George IV (demolished in 1896 and later rebuilt) or the Old Black Jack, both in Portsmouth Street, Lincoln's Inn Fields. Another Magpie and Stump stands opposite the Old Bailey.

Maiden Lane, near Battle Bridge, now King's Cross: See **Boffin's Bower.**

Maiden Lane, Strand, between Bedford Place and Southampton Street: See **Strand.**

Manchester Buildings, Westminster: Gregsbury, M.P., lives in this block of chambers and Nicholas Nickleby applies to him here for a situation as secretary.

Mansion House, City: During the Gordon Riots the Lord Mayor is visited at the Mansion House by Haredale, who needs his help to get Rudge imprisoned; Langdale, the distiller, also arrives for aid, fearing the destruction of his premises *(Rudge)*. Kit Nubbles, arrested on a false charge, is taken to the Mansion House police court *(Curiosity Shop)*. Nicodemus Dumps leaves the Mansion House en route for the Kitterbells' in the Admiral Napier omnibus (*Boz* – 'Bloomsbury Christening').

Marshalsea Prison: See **Borough.**

Marylebone Church: Next door to the site of Dickens's home at No. 1 Devonshire Terrace stands St. Marylebone Parish Church, built in 1817. This is generally considered to be the church at which Paul was christened and Dombey married to Edith Granger *(Dombey)*.

Mile End, east London: The scene of Tony Weller's remarks to Pickwick on the life of tollpike keepers. Mrs. Jellyby has 'Borrioboolan business' at Mile End *(Bleak House)*.

Millbank: The riverside thoroughfare between Lambeth and Vauxhall Bridges. Lambeth Bridge is on the site of the horse-ferry, and the Penitentiary site is now occupied by the Tate Gallery. The ultimate destiny of the mutilated Sim Tappertit is to marry the widow of a rag-and-bone merchant of Millbank *(Rudge)*.

Mincing Lane, City: Herbalists and tea-merchants abounded here in Dickens's time. Rumty Wilfer works here in the firm of Chicksey, Veneering and Stobbles *(Mutual Friend)*.

Monmouth Street: Continuation of St. Martin's Lane. In Dickens's day the headquarters of second-hand clothing shops. Described in *Boz* – 'Meditations in Monmouth-street'.

Montague Place, Bloomsbury: The home of Perker *(Pickwick)*.

Montague Square, Marylebone: Jorkins, Spenlow's partner, lives in a dilapidated house here *(Copperfield)*.

Monument: Erected in 1667 as near as possible to the place where the Fire of London had broken out. Dickens (and David Copperfield) used to gaze at the golden flame on the top of it from London Bridge. Mrs. Todgers's boarding-house is almost in the shadow of the Monument, and Tom Pinch is disillusioned on hearing the comments of the guide *(Chuzzlewit)*. John Willet's idea of a pleasant day in London is to go to the top of the Monument and sit there *(Rudge)*. Dorrit's solicitors, Peddle and Pool, have their premises in Monument Yard.

Mount Pleasant, Islington: The way to Mr. Brownlow's house at Pentonville lay through Mount Pleasant *(Twist)*. The Smallweed family lived nearby, 'in a rather ill-favoured and ill-savoured neighbourhood' *(Bleak House)*.

Mutton Hill, often known as Mutton Lane, was the part of Vine Street between Hatton Garden and

Clerkenwell Green. The back door of the police court to which Oliver Twist was taken was beneath an archway leading out of Mutton Hill. The Field Lane Ragged School, one of Dickens's favourite charities, was here.

New River Head, Islington: Off the present Rosebery Avenue. Uriah Heep lodges in the district *(Copperfield)*.

Newgate, City: Newgate Market was the main meat market for London until the Central Meat Market was opened at Smithfield in 1855. Peepy Jellyby gets lost here *(Bleak House)*. The old Newgate prison was destroyed by fire in the Gordon Riots *(Rudge)*. Rebuilt in 1782, it provided the attraction of public executions. Lord George Gordon died there in 1793. Fagin has his last interview with Oliver Twist in the condemned cell, and is later executed here. Kit Nubbles is imprisoned here on a false charge *(Curiosity Shop)*. Wemmick takes Pip into the prison *(Expectations)*, which is described in detail in *Boz* – 'Visit to Newgate' and 'Criminal Courts'. In Newgate Street Sam Weller tells Pickwick the story of the sausage steam-engine inventor.

Newman Street, north of Oxford Street: Turveydrop lives at No. 26, and is joined there by Prince and Caddy after their marriage *(Bleak House)*.

Norfolk Street, off Fitzroy Square, Marylebone (now Cleveland Street): The Dickens family lodged at No. 10 (now 22) in 1829–31 and, more briefly, in Dickens's infancy.

Norfolk Street, Strand: Here are the boarding-houses of Mrs. Lirriper and Miss Wozenham *(Christmas Stories* – 'Mrs. Lirriper's Lodgings' and 'Mrs. Lirriper's Legacy').

Norwood: A residential district south of London, semi-rural in Dickens's youth. James Carker lives here in an unpretentious but tasteful house *(Dombey)*. Spenlow also lives here, and here David Copperfield first meets Dora. Gabriel Parsons has a pleasant villa at Norwood *(Boz* – 'Watkins Tottle').

Obelisk: A south London landmark which once stood at the centre of St. George's Circus, now in the grounds of the Imperial War Museum, Lambeth Road. Dickens had his clothes valued for debt repayment at a house near the Obelisk when the Dickens home was sold up and his father imprisoned. At the same point David Copperfield's luggage and money are stolen by a young man with a donkey-cart as he travels towards Dover. The Gordon Rioters gather at St. George's Fields *(Rudge)*. Solomon Pell lives in the area favoured by the attorneys to the Commissioners of the Insolvent Court, more or less within a radius of one mile from the Obelisk *(Pickwick)*.

Old Bailey: The street runs from Ludgate Hill to Newgate Street. At the Old Bailey Court (now the Central Criminal Court) Charles Darnay is tried *(Two Cities)*. Bailey Junior is said to have become thus nicknamed 'in contradistinction perhaps to the Old Bailey' *(Chuzzlewit)*.

Old Black Jack Inn: See **Magpie and Stump.**

Old Curiosity Shop: See **Leicester Square** and **Clare Market.**

Old Kent Road: David Copperfield's way to Dover lies through it. At Dolloby's shop he sells his waistcoat to buy food. In the New Kent Road, set in a public garden, is a modern reconstruction, placed there by the Dickens Fellowship, of the Triton statue at which David made his first halt. Dr. Marigold takes the child Sophy to the Asylum for the Deaf and Dumb for training *(Christmas Stories* – 'Doctor Marigold').

Old Square: See **Lincoln's Inn.**

Old Street: Formerly called Old Street Road. Between City Road and Shoreditch Church. Mrs. Guppy, mother of Esther Summerson's admirer, lives at 302 Old Street Road *(Bleak House)*.

Olympic Theatre: In Wych Street, Strand, it was opened in 1806 and burnt down in 1849. Madame Vestris, dancer and actress-manager, controlled it when Dickens wrote *Young Gentlemen* – 'Theatrical Young Gentleman'. The Olympic was known as the 'Pic', as the Victoria was the 'Vic'.

Opera Colonnade: See **Haymarket.**

Osnaburgh Terrace, Regent's Park: Dickens stayed at No. 9 in 1844.

Oxford Market: This was north of Oxford Street between Great Tichfield Street and Great Portland Street. Towlinson, Dombey's footman, aspires to lead 'an altered and blameless existence as a serious greengrocer' there *(Dombey)*.

Oxford Street: Known in Dickens's day as the Oxford Road, and largely residential for much of the nineteenth century. Esther, Ada, Richard, and John Jarndyce have a 'cheerful lodging' nearby *(Bleak House)*. Gabriel Parsons walks up and down the street for a week, in tight boots, hoping to meet his sweetheart *(Boz* – 'Watkins Tottle'). Micawber fancies a lodging at the west end, facing Hyde Park *(Copperfield)*. Clennam and Meagles search the streets nearby for Miss Wade *(Dorrit)*. Nicholas Nickleby first sees Madeline Bray at the General Agency Office, and meets Mr. Charles Cheeryble at the same spot. Mrs. Nickleby relates how Kate's grandmama once, turning into Oxford Street, collided with her hairdresser escaping from a bear: or it may have been the other way round.

Palace Yard, Westminster: Julius Handford (John Harmon) gives the Inspector the address of the Exchequer Coffee House, Old Palace Yard *(Mutual Friend)*.

Pall Mall: Nearby are the offices of the Anglo-Bengalee Disinterested Loan and Life Assurance Company, whose chairman, Tigg Montague, lives in Pall Mall *(Chuzzlewit)*. Twemlow spends a day in the window of his club here canvassing for Veneering *(Mutual Friend)*. Chops, the dwarf, lodged in Pall Mall and 'blazed away' his fortune *(Christmas Stories* – 'Going into Society').

Pancras Road: Running northward between St. Pancras and King's Cross Stations, neither of which existed in the first half of the nineteenth century. At old St. Pancras Church (still to be seen) Jerry Cruncher digs up what he imagines to be the coffin of Roger Cly (*Two Cities*). The churchyard contains the tombstone of Dickens's schoolmaster at Wellington House Academy (see **Hampstead Road**).

Paper Buildings: See **Temple**.

Park Lane, Mayfair: Clennam and Meagles lodge nearby while searching for Tattycoram and Miss Wade (*Dorrit*). Outside a hotel off Park Lane Nicholas Nickleby assaults Sir Mulberry Hawk for insulting language used about Kate.

Parliament, Houses of: The old Houses of Parliament were burnt down in 1834, with the exception of Westminster Hall. In 1855 Dickens, in his only political speech, attributed the fire to 'the burning up of the discarded notched sticks upon which exchequer accounts were kept ... worn-out, worm-eaten bits of wood.'

Parliament Street, Westminster: Dickens recalled how, during his blacking warehouse days, he went into the Red Lion public house in Parliament Street and ordered a glass of ale, which was served to him with kindness. David Copperfield does the same. The Red Lion still stands.

Peacock Inn, Islington: The narrator of 'Holly-Tree' (*Christmas Stories*) starts off from the Peacock (now demolished) on his journey to the North. Nicholas Nickleby leaves London with Squeers from the same point, a depot for the York coaches.

Peckham: South London district east of Camberwell. Feeder, in order to study 'the dark mysteries of London', proposes to stay with two maiden aunts in Peckham; Walter Gay is a weekly boarder at a Peckham school (*Dombey*).

Penton Place: Between Kennington Park Road and Newington Butts. Guppy lives at No. 87 (*Bleak House*).

Pentonville: A new and fashionable residential district of north London in the early nineteenth century. Brownlow lives here (*Twist*). Pancks lodges at Rugg's Agency (*Dorrit*). Nicodemus Dumps rents a first floor furnished which commends itself to him because it commands 'a dismal prospect of an adjacent churchyard' (*Boz* – 'Bloomsbury Christening'). Micawber's lodging is presumably in the part of Pentonville fronting the City Road (*Copperfield*).

Petersham: In Dickens's day a rural district, adjoining Richmond and Ham. Dickens spent the summer of 1839 at Elm Cottage, now Elm Lodge, and had lodged in Petersham in 1836 while writing *The Village Coquettes*. He gave his address there as 'Mrs. Denman's', which was perhaps the Dysart Arms, whose landlord was John Denman.

Piccadilly: Largely a fashionable residential area in Dickens's day. Piccadilly Circus was known as Regent's Circus. Fascination Fledgeby lives at Albany (q.v.) and the Lammles are married at St. James's Church (*Mutual Friend*). Micawber, in a burst of optimism, envisages himself and his family 'in the upper part of a house, over some respectable place of business – say in Piccadilly' (*Copperfield*). The White Horse Cellar, a coaching inn, stood at the corner of Dover Street. Esther Summerson meets Guppy at the inn (*Bleak House*). On the site of the present Piccadilly Hotel stood St. James's Hall, where Dickens gave his last reading in March 1870.

Polygon, Somers Town: A down-at-heel block of north London houses (now demolished) where John Dickens and his family lived in the late 1820s at No. 17. Harold Skimpole lives here (*Bleak House*).

Portland Place, Marylebone: The large family of Tapkinses live here and are 'At Home, Wednesdays, Music' (*Mutual Friend*).

Portman Square, Marylebone: The Podsnaps live 'in a shady angle' adjoining the Square (*Mutual Friend*).

Putney: South of Fulham, on the Surrey side of the Thames, a rural district in Dickens's time. Dora Spenlow's aunts, with whom she goes to live after her father's death, reside here, and Dora and David Copperfield may have been married in St. Mary's Church, on the riverside. Arthur Clennam strolls over Putney Heath en route for the Meagleses', to enjoy sunshine and exercise (*Dorrit*).

Quadrant, The: The curve of Regent Street between Vigo Street and Piccadilly Circus. Its arcades (demolished 1848) are mentioned in *Boz* – 'Misplaced Attachment'.

Queen Charlotte's Hospital: In Marylebone Road in Dickens's time, now removed to Goldhawk Road. It is applied to by Miss Tox for a suitable wet nurse for little Paul Dombey.

Queen Square, Bloomsbury, behind the present Southampton Row: John Jarndyce places Richard Carstone in a furnished lodging here (*Bleak House*).

Quilp's Wharf: Unidentified precisely by Dickens, it has been speculated that it may have been old Butler's Wharf, below Tower Bridge on the Surrey side (*Curiosity Shop*).

Ratcliff: East End riverside district, notable for crime in the early nineteenth century. Nancy lives there before moving to Field Lane (*Twist*). The *Cautious Clara* is lying hard by Ratcliff when Florence visits Captain Bunsby (*Dombey*).

Raymond Buildings: See **Gray's Inn**.

Red Lion, Highgate: See **Highgate**.

Red Lion, Parliament Street: See **Parliament Street**.

Red 'Us: The Red House, a popular pleasure resort of Londoners, it was a riverside tavern, on the Battersea shore (*Boz* – 'The River').

Regent Street: Completed in 1820, two years before Dickens came to London. Lord Frederick Verisopht lives here (*Nickleby*).

Regent's Canal, Regent's Park: Watkins Tottle may have drowned himself here after his disappointment in love (*Boz* – 'Watkins Tottle').

Regent's Park: Dickens lived for a time at 3 Hanover Terrace, writing part of *Great Expectations;* and 1 Devonshire Terrace (q.v.), his home for many years, was almost opposite the York Gate to the park.

Richmond: See under Part One.

Rolls Yard, Symond's Inn: Now demolished, this opened out of Chancery Lane, and was a spot where Snagsby 'loved to lounge about of a Sunday afternoon' *(Bleak House).*

Roman Bath, Strand Lane, Strand: More likely of seventeenth century origin, it was popular with gentlemen who had dined too well the night before, or who wanted a refreshing dip. Dickens often used it, as does David Copperfield.

Rookery of St. Giles's: There were many 'rookeries' in London, haunts of filth and vice, but that of St. Giles's was the most notorious. Removed when New Oxford Street was made in 1844–7, it is described in *Reprinted* – 'On Duty with Inspector Field'.

Royal Exchange: The old Exchange was burnt down in 1838 and rebuilt in 1844. Pip is surprised by the 'fluey' men sitting there, whom he takes to be great merchants; Herbert Pocket frequents 'Change *(Expectations).*

Sackville Street, off Piccadilly: Lammle's bachelor home and temporary married quarters *(Mutual Friend).*

Saffron Hill: A notorious criminal district, obliterated by the development of Holborn. The Three Cripples Inn, patronised by Fagin and his associates, stood here until about 1860 *(Twist).* Phil Squod has a tinker's round here *(Bleak House).*

St. Andrew's Church, Holborn: One of the old City churches still in existence, mentioned in *Twist, Copperfield,* and *Bleak House.*

St. Bartholomew's Hospital, Smithfield: The oldest London hospital. Jack Hopkins is a student here *(Pickwick).* Betsey Prig nurses here *(Chuzzlewit).* Cavalletto is taken to Bart's after being run over *(Dorrit).*

St. Clement Dane's Church, Strand: Scene of Mrs. Lirriper's wedding *(Christmas Stories – 'Mrs. Lirriper's Lodgings').*

St. Dunstan's-in-the-West: Church of 'The Chimes' *(Christmas Books).* See also **Fleet Street.**

St. George's Church, Southwark: See **Borough.**

St. George's Church, Hart Street, Bloomsbury: See **Bloomsbury.**

St. Giles's: Criminal slumland incorporating the Rookery (q.v.) and Seven Dials (q.v.)

St. James's Church, Piccadilly: Alfred Lammle marries Sophronia Akersham here *(Mutual Friend).*

St. James's Park: One of the Royal parks, adjoining Buckingham Palace. Ralph Nickleby is accosted by Brooker while sheltering here in a thunderstorm. Mark Tapley arranges a meeting here between young

Martin Chuzzlewit and Mary Graham. It was 'darkly whispered' that Sally Brass, enlisted as a private in the Guards, had been seen on sentry duty in the Park *(Curiosity Shop).*

St. James's Square, off Pall Mall: Twemlow frequently meditates here on his social status *(Mutual Friend).* The Gordon Rioters threw loot, including the keys of Newgate, into the pond then in the centre of the Square *(Rudge).*

St. James's Street, off St. James's Square: In chambers on the Piccadilly side lives the narrator of the Trial for Murder *(Christmas Stories* – 'Doctor Marigold').* In a hotel here Mrs. Sparsit tells Bounderby of Louisa's elopement *(Hard Times).*

St. James's Theatre: Now vanished from a corner of St. James's Square, it was the scene of the productions of Dickens's early plays, *The Strange Gentleman* and *The Village Coquettes* (1836) and *Is She His Wife?* (1837).

St. John's Church, Smith Square, Westminster: A fine and rare exercise in early Georgian baroque, Dickens thought it 'a very hideous church . . . generally resembling some petrified monster, frightful and gigantic, on its back with its legs in the air.' See also **Church Street.**

St. Luke's Church, Chelsea: See **Chelsea.**

St. Martin-in-the-Fields, Trafalgar Square: On the church steps, before Trafalgar Square was completed in 1841, David Copperfield encounters Peggotty returning from his search for Little Em'ly. Some of Dickens's childhood recollections of this neighbourhood, notably of a special pudding shop, are worked into the novel. The Uncommercial Traveller has a horrifying experience with a pauper on the church steps *(Uncommercial* – 'Night Walks').*

St. Mary Axe, City: Now a modern commercial area, it held the ancient office of Pubsey and Co., supervised by Riah. Lizzie Hexam and Jenny Wren often sit in the roof-garden to chat *(Mutual Friend).*

St. Mary-le-Strand Church: Dickens's parents were married here in 1809, when John Dickens was a clerk in Somerset House near the church.

St. Olave's Church, Hart Street: Referred to by the Uncommercial Traveller as St. Ghastly Grim; nevertheless, one of his favourite London churchyards *(Uncommercial* – 'The City of the Absent').*

St. Pancras Church: See **Pancras Road.**

St. Paul's Cathedral: It features in passing in several of the novels, including *Nickleby, Two Cities, Copperfield, Mutual Friend, Rudge, Expectations, Dombey,* etc. Doctors' Commons (q.v.) was joined to St. Paul's Churchyard by Paul's Chain.

St. Peter's Church, Cornhill: Bradley Headstone pleads with Lizzie Hexam in the churchyard to marry him *(Mutual Friend).*

Salem House School: It is sited near Blackheath *(Copperfield),* but was based on Wellington House Academy (q.v.).

Saracen's Head, Snow Hill: The inn where Squeers has his London headquarters, adjoining St. Sepulchre's Church (*Nickleby*). Demolished in 1868: the site is now occupied by a police station.

Scotland Yard, Westminster: Headquarters of the Metropolitan Police from 1829 until 1967. Its earlier appearance is described in *Boz* – 'Scotland-yard'.

Serjeant's Inn, Chancery Lane: Now demolished: Pickwick is taken there for commission to the Fleet prison after refusing to pay Mrs. Bardell's costs and damages.

Seven Dials: Once a notorious criminal slum district, where seven streets converge on St. Giles's Circus. Described in *Boz* – 'Seven Dials' and 'Meditations in Monmouth-street'. Mantalini is last discovered here by Nicholas and Kate Nickleby, turning a mangle.

Shadwell: Dockside district of low repute in Dickens's time. He visited an opium den here, and made it the setting for Princess Puffer's (*Drood*). The Mormon emigrant ship *Amazon* lies near Shadwell Church in *Uncommercial* – 'Bound for the Great Salt Lake'.

Shooter's Hill: See **Blackheath.**

Six Jolly Fellowship Porters: See **Limehouse.**

Smith Square, Westminster: See **Church Street** and **St. John's Church.**

Smithfield: London's wholesale meat market, near Holborn Viaduct. It is referred to in *Twist*, and it is in this neighbourhood that Barnaby helps his father to get rid of his fetters after his release from Newgate by the Gordon Rioters.

Snow Hill: Once a busy route from Holborn down into Farringdon Street. The Saracen's Head (q.v.) stood at the top. It is referred to principally in *Twist*, *Nickleby*, *Dorrit*, and *Rudge*.

Soho: A cosmopolitan district bounded by Regent Street, Oxford Street, Charing Cross Road, and Shaftesbury Avenue. Houses in Carlisle Street and Greek Street have been claimed as the original of Dr. Manette's (*Two Cities*). Obenreizer's house is on the north side of Soho Square (*Christmas Stories* – 'No Thoroughfare'). Caddy Jellyby and Esther Summerson have a rendezvous in the Square (*Bleak House*). At Carlisle House, near Carlisle Street, Emma Haredale encounters her uncle at a masquerade (*Rudge*).

Sol's Arms: The Old Ship, on the corner of Chancery Lane and Chichester Rents, was the original of this tavern where Little Swills entertains in *Bleak House*.

Somers Town: A cosmopolitan district north of Euston Station. See also **Polygon.**

Somerset House, Strand: Built in the eighteenth century for a ducal palace, it has long housed government record departments. Dickens's father and uncle, Thomas Culliford Barrow, were clerks there, as is Minns in *Boz* – 'Mr. Minns and his Cousin'.

Southampton Street, now Southampton Place, connecting High Holborn with Bloomsbury Square:

Grewgious finds lodgings for Miss Twinkleton and Rosa Bud at Billickins's, possibly at No. 20, next to the archway leading to Barter Street (*Drood*).

Southwark: See **Borough.**

Southwark Bridge: One of the Thames bridges, built of iron in 1815–19. John Chivery proposes to Little Dorrit on it. Southwark Bridge and London Bridge mark the limits of Gaffer Hexam's river beat in search of corpses (*Mutual Friend*).

Spa Fields: Once the name for an open area near the present Mount Pleasant post office, used as winter quarters by travelling showmen. Old Maunders keeps his eight dwarfs and eight giants in a cottage here (*Curiosity Shop*).

Spaniards, Hampstead: A historic inn, little changed from the day of Dickens, who used to walk there across the Heath. Its tea garden is where Jackson, of Dodson and Fogg, finds Mrs. Bardell and lures her away to the Fleet Prison (*Pickwick*).

Stagg's Gardens: A fictitious part of Camden Town (q.v.), typical of the district at the time, featured in *Dombey*.

Staple Inn, Holborn: This ancient Inn of Chancery was established in the fourteenth century. The Tudor shops which form its frontage – a unique one in central London – date from about 1545. Grewgious lives in chambers here, entertains Rosa Bud after her flight from Cloisterham, and conspires with Tartar and Crisparkle to outwit Jasper; while in another set of chambers, near Tartar's, Neville and Helena Landless lodge (*Drood*). Staple Inn received severe damage in the Second World War, but has been largely restored – the restorations including the inscription on the building lived in by Grewgious – 'P.J.T. 1747', standing for 'President James Taylor' (President of the Society of Antients of Staple Inn). Snagsby enjoys the countrified atmosphere of the Inn's courtyards in summertime (*Bleak House*).

Stock Exchange, City: Here Tony Weller receives from Wilkins Flasher a cheque for £530, the proceeds of his late wife's investments (*Pickwick*).

Strand: This thoroughfare appears very frequently in the stories. Warren's Blacking Warehouse was at Hungerford Stairs, at the western end of the Strand, and Dickens knew the whole area well when he worked there. Dickens worked as a reporter at the offices of the *Morning Chronicle*, and had a lodging in Buckingham Street (now demolished) which he described as Mrs. Crupp's house where David Copperfield has rooms. The editorial offices for *All the Year Round* were at No. 26 (formerly 11) Wellington Street, and those of *Household Words* opposite the Lyceum Theatre in the same street. Rule's Restaurant, in Maiden Lane, running parallel with the Strand off Bedford Street, was a favourite resort of Dickens, and still keeps a Dickens Corner. Miss La Creevy has her lodgings and studio in the Strand, conjecturally at No. 11 (*Nickleby*). Young Martin Chuzzlewit and Mark Tapley find lodgings in a court in the Strand, near Temple Bar.

Sun Court, Cornhill: Dickens places the George and Vulture here, when Dodson and Fogg's clerk goes to the inn to inquire for Pickwick.

Surrey Theatre: Now demolished, this stood at the end of the Blackfriars Road, near the original site of the Obelisk (q.v.). It was built in 1782 for Charles Dibdin, and was in Dickens's day the rival of Sadler's Wells for its presentations of legitimate drama. It is probably the theatre where Frederick Dorrit plays 'a clarinet as dirty as himself', and Fanny Dorrit is a dancer. Dickens and John Forster attended a performance of a dramatisation of *Oliver Twist* there in 1838, but Dickens was unable to watch it and 'laid himself down upon the floor in a corner of the box and never rose from it until the drop-scene fell.'

Symond's Inn: On the eastern side of Chancery Lane, backing on to Breams Buildings, it was mostly given over to private solicitors. Dickens probably worked there as a young clerk with a solicitor named Molloy. Vholes's offices 'in this dingy hatchment commemorative of Symond' *(Bleak House)* may be based on Molloy's.

Tavistock House, Tavistock Square, Bloomsbury: Dickens moved his household here from Devonshire Terrace in 1851, having bought the lease from Frank Stone, A.R.A. It stood in private gardens and he adapted its commodious schoolroom as a theatre for his amateur dramatic productions. Tavistock House was demolished about 1900. The offices of the British Medical Association on the site bear a commemorative plaque.

Tellson's Bank: See **Fleet Street.**

Temple: Extending from Fleet Street to the river in Dickens's day, before the building of the Embankment, this ancient area of Inns and chambers and quiet precincts figures frequently in the stories. Badly damaged in the Second World War, it has now been restored. Pip has chambers in Garden Court, where he is visited by Magwitch and learns the truth about his fortune. At Temple Stairs he keeps the boat used for the attempted escape of Magwitch *(Expectations)*. Sir John Chester *(Rudge)* has chambers in Paper Buildings, where Maypole Hugh calls on him. (These Paper Buildings were burnt down in 1838.) Tom Pinch is installed in chambers in Pump Court, to work as librarian for his mysterious benefactor, and in Fountain Court takes place the courtship of Ruth Pinch and John Westlock *(Chuzzlewit)*. Tartar keeps his boat at Temple Stairs (now vanished), at the end of King's Bench Walk, and rows Rosa up the river from there *(Drood)*. Mortimer Lightwood and Eugene Wrayburn have chambers on the site of Goldsmith's Buildings, near Temple Church *(Mutual Friend)*. Stryver has chambers in the Temple, in which Sydney Carton works for him *(Two Cities)*.

Temple Bar: This London landmark, dividing the Strand from Fleet Street, seems to have been unpopular with Dickens. In *Bleak House* he calls it 'that leaden-headed old obstruction' and remarks that in hot weather it is 'to the adjacent Strand and Fleet Street, what a heater is in an urn, and keeps them simmering all night.' Tom Pinch retires under it to laugh about Ruth's beefsteak pudding *(Chuzzlewit)*. The 'Prentice Knights swear not to damage Temple Bar during any rising they may instigate *(Rudge)*. Temple Bar was removed in 1878 to Sir Henry Bruce Meux's estate of Theobalds Park, near Waltham Cross.

Tenterden Street: See **Hanover Square.**

Thames Street: Running from Blackfriars to the Tower of London, it is probably the location of the dilapidated house owned by Ralph Nickleby, where he lodges his sister-in-law and Kate; and of the decaying home of Mrs. Clennam in *Dorrit*. See also **Custom House.**

Thavies Inn: One of the Inns of Chancery, near Holborn Circus, it was destroyed in the Second World War. In *Bleak House* the Jellybys live here.

Threadneedle Street, City: The offices of the brothers Cheeryble are in a courtyard off the street *(Nickleby)*. See also **Bank of England.**

Titbull's Almshouses: Described in *Uncommercial* – 'Titbull's Almshouses', they were probably the Vintners' Almshouses, in Mile End Road.

Took's Court: See **Chancery Lane.**

Tottenham Court Road: In Dickens's time it was noted for the number of its drapers' shops. Horatio Sparkins serves in one, Jones, Spruggins and Smith *(Boz* – 'Horatio Sparkins'). The table, flower-pot, and stand belonging to Traddles and Sophy, taken with Micawber's furniture when his Camden Town lodgings are seized by a broker, are found in a broker's shop at the top of Tottenham Court Road *(Copperfield)*. Miss Knag's brother, who keeps a stationer's shop and circulating library, lives in a by-street *(Nickleby)*. A wedding-party in Tottenham Court Road is described in *Boz* – 'Hackney-coach Stands'.

Tower of London: Lord George Gordon was imprisoned here. At the Crooked Billet in Tower Street (now demolished) Joe Willet enlists for the Army *(Rudge)*. Quilp lives on Tower Hill *(Curiosity Shop)*.

Turnham Green: District of west London where the Lord Mayor is held up and robbed by a highwayman *(Two Cities)*.

Turnstile, Holborn: Once a centre of the tailoring trade, it is a passage leading from Holborn to Lincoln's Inn. Snagsby recalls to his apprentices that he has heard of a crystal-clear brook once running down the middle of Holborn, when Turnstile was actually a stile leading into meadows *(Bleak House)*.

Twickenham: See under Part One.

Tyburn: Place of public execution sited near the present Marble Arch, used until 1783, after which executions took place outside Newgate Prison. Dickens recounts the tragic story of a young mother's death at Tyburn in the Preface to *Rudge*, and Dennis, hangman at Newgate, recalls when he held the same office at Tyburn.

Vauxhall Bridge: The bridge Dickens knew was replaced in 1906. It is referred to in *Boz, Mutual Friend,* and *Christmas Stories* – 'Somebody's Luggage'.

Vauxhall Gardens: Famous pleasure resort in the eighteenth and early nineteenth centuries, sited on the Surrey side of Vauxhall Bridge and closed in 1859. The gardens are described in *Boz* – 'Vauxhall-gardens by Day'.

Victoria Theatre, Waterloo Road: Referred to in *Boz* – 'The Streets – Night' and *Miscellaneous Papers* – 'Amusements of the People'. Built in 1817 as the Coburg Theatre, it is now the Old Vic.

Walcot Square, Kennington: Guppy offers his house in Walcot Square as an attraction when proposing to Esther *(Bleak House)*.

Walworth: Now a populous district south of the Borough, in Dickens's day it was a semi-rural area into which speculative builders were beginning to find their way. Wemmick lives with his aged father in 'Wemmick's Castle' *(Expectations)*. The Uncommercial Traveller records the high incidence of windy weather ('Refreshments for Travellers'). Walworth at the turn of the nineteenth century is described in *Boz* – 'Black Veil'.

Wapping: East London riverside district, described in *Uncommercial* – 'Wapping Workhouse'.

Waterloo Bridge: The bridge Dickens knew was opened in 1817 and demolished in 1939. Described in *Uncommercial* – 'Night Walks'. A suicide from the bridge steps is recounted in *Boz* – 'Drunkard's Death'. Sam Weller tells Pickwick how in his youth he had 'unfurnished lodgings for a fortnight' under 'the dry arches of Waterloo Bridge'.

Welbeck Street, Marylebone: Lord George Gordon lived at No. 64 (now rebuilt) *(Rudge)*.

Wellington House Academy: See **Hampstead Road** and **Salem House School.**

Wellington Street: See **Strand.**

West India Docks: Captain Cuttle's lodgings are 'on the brink of a little canal near the India Docks . . . a first floor and a top story, in Brig Place' *(Dombey)*. This was probably a reminiscence of Dickens's visits to his godfather, Christopher Huffam, at Church Street, Limehouse.

Westminster Abbey: Pip and Herbert Pocket go to a morning service at the Abbey *(Expectations)*. David and Daniel Peggotty follow Martha from Blackfriars, hoping she may lead them to Little Em'ly, and lose her at the Abbey *(Copperfield)*. Some of Miss Abbey Potterson's customers think that she is 'named after, or in some way related to, the Abbey at Westminster' *(Mutual Friend)*. Dickens was buried in Poets' Corner in the Abbey on 14 June 1870.

Westminster Bridge: The first stone bridge, built in 1739–50, was the one Dickens knew. It was demolished and replaced in 1862. Pickwick and his party cross it on their way to Kent by coach. Morleena Kenwigs is invited to a pleasure trip on Eel Pie Island (q.v., Part One) starting by steamer from Westminster Bridge *(Nickleby)*.

Westminster Hall: The only survivor of the fire which destroyed the old Houses of Parliament (q.v.). The old Law Courts, where the Jarndyce case was concluded, adjoined the Hall on the western side. Lord George Gordon was tried in the old Courts for high treason *(Rudge)*. John Harmon, under the name of Julius Handford, gives as his address the Exchequer Coffee House, Old Palace Yard.

White Conduit House: An inn with pleasure-grounds, it was a popular resort in Pentonville, on the fringes of Islington. It deteriorated and was demolished in 1849. The May Day procession of sweeps was exchanged for a formal anniversary dinner at White Conduit House *(Boz* – 'First of May').

White Hart Inn: See **Borough.**

White Horse Cellar: See **Piccadilly.**

Whitechapel: East End district, containing many coaching inns in Dickens's day. Joe Willet has meals on credit at the Black Lion, Whitechapel Road, begrudged by his father *(Rudge)*. Pickwick and Mr. Peter Magnus travel to Ipswich from the Bull. David Copperfield arrives in London for the first time at the Blue Boar. Sam Weller observes that poverty and oysters invariably go together, and points out to Pickwick that the Whitechapel streets are lined with oyster stalls *(Pickwick)*. After being recaptured by Sikes and Nancy, Oliver Twist is taken to a house in the Whitechapel district.

Whitefriars Street: See **Hanging Sword Alley.**

Whitehall: Jingle comments on the Banqueting Hall of Whitehall Palace as the coach containing himself and the Pickwickians sets out for Rochester. 'Fine place – little window – somebody else's head off there – eh, sir?'

Windsor Terrace, City Road: David Copperfield lodges with the Micawbers, and Mrs. Micawber advertises on a brass plate her Boarding Establishment for Young Ladies.

Wood Street, City: The Cross Keys inn (q.v.), a Rochester coaching house, is mentioned in *Expectations, Uncommercial, Dorrit,* and *Boz*. Mould, the undertaker, has premises near a small shady churchyard *(Chuzzlewit)*.

Wyldes Farm: See **Hampstead.**

CHARLES DICKENS: A TIME CHART

A TIME CHART

Year	Date	Life	Career	General Events
1812	February 7	Dickens born at 387 Mile End Road (also known as 1 Mile End Terrace), Landport, Portsmouth, son of John Dickens, employed in the Navy Pay Office, Portsmouth Dockyard, and Elizabeth Dickens, *née* Barrow; and brother of Frances Elizabeth, born 1810.		(George III on throne of England since 1760. Due to his illness the Prince of Wales had become Regent in 1811.) Assassination of Spencer Percival, Prime Minister; Lord Liverpool succeeds him. Viscount Castlereagh is Foreign Minister. Napoleon invades Russia; Battle of Borodino; French enter Moscow, then retreat. In the
	March	Dickens baptised Charles John Huffam (sometimes spelt Huffham) in Parish Church, Portsea.		Peninsular War Wellington advances to Madrid after the Battle of Salamanca, but is forced to retreat. War breaks out
	June 24	John Dickens family moves to Hawke Street, Kingston, Portsea.		between Britain and U.S.A. Early steamship *Comet* launched on the Clyde by Henry Bell. Gas Light and Coke Company developed by F. A. Winsor. Painless amputation developed by Napoleon's surgeon, Baron Larrey. Anti-machinery 'Luddite' riots break out in England. Beethoven's 7th and 8th symphonies first performed. Elgin Marbles brought to England. Discovery of Great Temple of Abu Simbel in Egypt.
				Publications: Grimms' *Fairy Tales*; first two cantos of Byron's *Childe Harold*.
1813		Alfred Dickens born. Died in infancy.		War of Liberation breaks out in Prussia. Prussia joins Russia against France; French retreat to the Elbe; Sweden joins Russia and Prussia; Napoleon defeats allied army but is defeated at Leipzig; Wellington's victory at Vittoria drives France out of

Year	Date	Life	Career	General Events
1813—contd				Spain. 'Puffing Billy' locomotive built in England by William Hedley. Last golden guineas issued in England. Publications: William Blake's *Day of Judgment*; Southey's *Life of Nelson*; Shelley's *Queen Mab*; Jane Austen's *Pride and Prejudice*; Scott's *Rokeby*.
1814	June 24	John Dickens transferred to a London post, probably at Somerset House. John Dickens family moves to Norfolk Street, St. Pancras, London.		Washington D.C. burnt by British; Treaty of Ghent ends Anglo-U.S. war. Allies invade France and capture Paris; Napoleon abdicates; Louis XVIII ascends French throne; first Treaty of Paris; Congress of Vienna. Tsar of Russia visits England. Construction of first efficient steam locomotive near Newcastle-upon-Tyne by George Stephenson. Development of steam cylinder-press printing. Term 'birth-control' first used. Publications: Jane Austen's *Mansfield Park*; Scott's *Waverley*; Wordsworth's *The Excursion*; Byron's *The Corsair and Lara*.
1815		Catherine Hogarth, later Mrs. Charles Dickens, born.		Napoleon escapes from Elba and regains Paris; Louis XVIII flees; Ney and Murat executed; Congress of Vienna dispersed; Napoleon's army defeated by Wellington at Waterloo; Napoleon abdicates; Louis XVIII returns; Napoleon banished to St. Helena and Congress of Vienna reassembles. Corn Law passed by British Parliament and income tax abolished. Schubert's 3rd symphony performed. Publications: Scott's novel *Guy Mannering* and poem *The Lord of the Isles*.
1816		Letitia Mary Dickens born.		Corn Law causes widespread hardship in England. U.S.A. introduces protection against British imports. Transatlantic packet service begins. First performance of Rossini's *The Barber of Seville*. Schubert's 4th and 5th symphonies performed.

Year		Dickens	World / Publications
			Publications: Coleridge's 'Kubla Khan' and 'Christabel'; Scott's *The Antiquary* and *Old Mortality*; Byron's *The Prisoner of Chillon*; Jane Austen's *Emma*.
1817		John Dickens reappointed to Chatham. John Dickens family moves to temporary lodgings in Chatham. John Dickens family moves to 2 Ordnance Terrace, Chatham.	Continued unrest in England: riots and marches. Death of Princess Charlotte, Prince Regent's daughter and heir, after him, to the English throne. Constable paints *Flatford Mill*. Rennie's Waterloo Bridge opened in London. Publications: Scott's *Rob Roy*; John Keats's *Poems*; Thomas Moore's *Lalla Rookh*; Byron's *Manfred*; Hazlitt's *Characters of Shakespear's Plays*; Coleridge's *Biographia Literaria*. *Blackwood's Magazine* founded.
1818			Count Bernadotte ascends Swedish throne as Charles XIV. Attempts to find the North-West Passage by Ross, Parry, and others. First iron passenger ship launched on the Clyde. Foundation of Bonn University. Publications: Keats's *Endymion*; Scott's *The Heart of Midlothian*; Mary Shelley's *Frankenstein*; Jane Austen's *Northanger Abbey* and *Persuasion*.
1819	August	Harriet Ellen Dickens born. Died in infancy.	Peterloo Massacre of Corn Law protesters in Manchester. First macadam roads laid in England. S.S. *Savannah* crosses Atlantic in 26 days. Factory Act protecting child workers in English cotton mills passed. Singapore founded by Raffles. Publications: Scott's *Ivanhoe*; Shelley's *The Cenci*; Byron's *Don Juan* and *Mazeppa*.
1820	July	Frederick William Dickens born.	Death of George III; Prince Regent succeeds him as George IV and brings unsuccessful divorce action against Queen Caroline. Constable paints *Dedham Mill*. Venus de Milo discovered on Greek Island of Melos. Publications: Shelley's *Prometheus Unbound*; Keats's *Hyperion* and 'Lamia'; Washington Irving's *Sketch-Book*.

Year	Date	Life	Career	General Events
1821		Dickens begins education at William Giles's school, Chatham. John Dickens in reduced circumstances due to improvidence. Family moves to 18 St. Mary's Place, Chatham.	Dickens writes a tragedy, *Mismar, the Sultan of India*.	Greek independence declared. Gold Coast becomes British Crown Colony. John Keats dies in Rome. Faraday demonstrates principle of electric motor. Wheatstone demonstrates sound reproduction. Weber's *Der Freischütz* performed. Constable paints *The Hay Wain*. Publications: De Quincey's *Confessions of an Opium-Eater*; Scott's *Kenilworth*; Shelley's 'Adonais' and *Defence of Poetry*.
1822	December (probably) December (late)	Alfred Lamert Dickens born. John Dickens transferred to London. John Dickens family moves to London: 16 Bayham Street, Camden Town, leaving Dickens in Chatham with William Giles. Dickens rejoins family.		English Foreign Secretary, Lord Castlereagh, commits suicide. Home Secretary, Lord Sidmouth, resigns; Lord Liverpool's Ministry re-formed. First railway locomotives used in Durham. Foundation of Royal Academy of Music, London. Shelley dies. Publications: Scott's *The Fortunes of Nigel*.
1823	October	John Dickens family moves to 4 Gower Street North. Mrs. Dickens opens school for young ladies, but no pupils arrive. Dickens living at home.		Home Secretary, Robert Peel, institutes penal reforms. First Ashanti war breaks out. World's first iron railway bridge built by Stephenson for Stockton and Darlington Railway. Foundation of Mechanics' Institutes in London and Glasgow. Present British Museum building erected. Schubert's *Rosamunde* performed. Publications: Scott's *Quentin Durward*; Lamb's *Essays of Elia*.
1824	February May 28	John Dickens arrested for debt. Imprisoned first in King's Bench, later transferred to Marshalsea. Mrs. Dickens and younger children join John Dickens in Marshalsea. Dickens lodging with Mrs. Roylance in Little College Street, Camden Town. Then moves to Lant Street, Borough, and employed through the agency of his cousin James Lamert at Warren's Blacking Warehouse. On release of John Dickens, family moves to lodgings in Camden Town, then to Seymour Street, Camden Town. Fanny		Poor Law Act of 1662 repealed. Byron dies at Missolonghi. Death of Louis XVIII of France; succeeded by Charles X. Beethoven's 9th symphony and *Missa Solemnis* performed. Blake paints *Beatrice Addressing Dante*. Athenaeum Club founded in London. Publications: Scott's *Redgauntlet*; Mary Russell Mitford's *Our Village*.

Date	The Life of Dickens	Historical and Cultural Events
June	Dickens resident at the Royal Academy of Music, Tenterden Street, off Hanover Square. Dickens removed from Warren's and sent to Wellington House Academy, Hampstead Road.	
1825	John Dickens family moves to 29 Johnson Street, Somers Town. John Dickens retired with small pension.	Suppression of Irish Catholic Association. Factory Act passed in Britain. Tsar Alexander I of Russia dies; succeeded by Nicholas I. Stephenson builds his first locomotive 'The Rocket' and opens his first passenger line, the Stockton and Darlington Railway. John Nash begins to re-build Buckingham Palace. Publications: Pepys's *Diary*; Scott's *The Talisman*.
1826	Dickens at Wellington House Academy. John Dickens writing for the *British Press* as city correspondent. The paper fails at the end of the year.	Telford's bridge over Menai Straits, Wales, opened. Berlioz's *Symphonie Fantastique* performed. Mendelssohn's *Midsummer Night's Dream* overture performed. Weber's *Oberon* performed. Schubert's String Quartet in D minor ('Death and the Maiden') performed. Constable paints *The Cornfield*. Publications: J. Fenimore Cooper's *The Last of the Mohicans*; Hölderlin's *Gedichte*.
March 1827	Augustus Dickens born. John Dickens family evicted for non-payment of rates. Dickens removed from Wellington House Academy, and Fanny from Royal Academy of Music. Dickens joins Ellis & Blackmore, 5 Holborn Court, Gray's Inn, as solicitor's clerk.	Lord Liverpool resigns British Premiership. George Canning succeeds him, but dies and is succeeded by Viscount Goderich. Turks capture the Acropolis at Athens. Turkish fleet destroyed by British, French, and Russians at Navarino. Publications: First parts of Audubon's *Birds of North America*; Heine's *Buch der Lieder*; John Clare's *The Shepherd's Calendar*; Manzoni's *I Promessi Sposi*; first Baedeker travel guide.
1828	Ellis & Blackmore move to 6 Raymond Buildings, Gray's Inn. Dickens employed for a time at this period by Charles Molloy, solicitor.	Duke of Wellington succeeds Goderich as Prime Minister. Daniel O'Connell debarred from standing for Parliament for County Clare because he is Catholic. Turks evacuate

Year	Date	Life	Career	General Events
1828— contd	November	John Dickens has learnt shorthand and is working as a reporter for the *Morning Herald*.		Greece; Greek independence declared. Schubert's 7th symphony performed. Constable paints *Salisbury Cathedral*. Publications: Webster's *Dictionary*; Casanova's *Mémoires*; Bulwer-Lytton's *Pelham*.
1829		John Dickens family moves to 10 Norfolk Street, Fitzroy Square.	Dickens has learnt shorthand and become a freelance reporter at Doctors' Commons, sharing Thomas Charlton's box to report legal proceedings.	Robert Peel establishes Metropolitan Police, London. Catholic Emancipation Act passed: O'Connell re-elected for County Clare. Colonisation of Western Australia begins. Horse-drawn omnibuses introduced in London. Louis Braille perfects his reading method for the blind. First boat race between Oxford and Cambridge Universities. Publications: Mérimée's *Mateo Falcone*; Balzac's *Les Chouans*, his first successful novel.
1830	February		Dickens admitted reader at British Museum.	George IV dies; succeeded by Duke of Clarence as William IV. Wellington resigns Premiership; succeeded by Earl Grey. Agricultural workers riot in Southern England ('Captain Swing' Riots). Plymouth Brethren founded. Charles X of France overthrown in 'July Revolution'; succeeded by Louis Philippe. Royal Geographic Society founded in London. Mendelssohn's *Reformation* symphony performed. Auber's *Fra Diavolo* performed. Corot paints *Houses at Honfleur*. Publications: Tennyson's *Poems, chiefly Lyrical*; Hugo's *Ernani*; Musset's *Poems*; Cobbett's *Rural Rides*.
	May	Dickens meets Maria Beadnell.		
1831		Forster sees Dickens for the first time.	Dickens working for John Henry Barrow, his uncle, reporting for the *Mirror of Parliament*.	Reform Bill passed by House of Commons but vetoed by Lords. Agricultural riots continue. Twelve-hour working day for persons under 18 in cotton mills becomes compulsory. Leopold of Saxe-Coburg becomes first King of Belgium. Charles Darwin sails as naturalist in H.M.S. *Beagle*.

1832		Dickens courting Maria Beadnell. John Dickens family living at 15 Fitzroy Street. Family lodges in Highgate for a fortnight in late summer.	Chloroform discovered by von Liebig. Faraday discovers electro-magnetic induction. British Association for the Advancement of Science founded. New London Bridge opens. Meyerbeer's *Robert le Diable* performed. Publications: Pushkin's *Boris Godunov*; Stendhal's *Le Rouge et le Noir*; Balzac's *La Peau de Chagrin*; Hugo's *Nôtre Dame de Paris*.
	? March	Dickens reporting for evening paper, the *True Sun*.	First Parliamentary Reform Act. Irish 'Tithe Strikes'. Anti-slavery movement begins in Boston, U.S.A. First U.S. railway built. Donizetti's *L'Elisir d'Amore* performed.
	April or May	Charles Dickens lodges briefly in Cecil Street, Strand.	Publications: George Sand's *Indiana*; Balzac's *Contes Drolatiques*; Hugo's *Le Roi s'amuse*.
1833	January	John Dickens family moves from Fitzroy Street to 18 Bentinck Street.	First session of reformed House of Commons. Tories adopt name Conservative. S.S. *Royal William* first vessel to cross Atlantic by steam alone. Mendelssohn's *Italian* symphony performed. Turner exhibits first Venetian paintings. Donizetti's *Lucrezia Borgia* performed.
	May	Dickens's romance with Maria Beadnell broken off.	Publications: Carlyle's *Sartor Resartus*; Balzac's *Le Médecin de Campagne*.
	December 1	Dickens's first story, 'A Dinner at Poplar Walk', published in the *Monthly Magazine*. It was later re-titled 'Mr. Minns and his Cousin'.	
1834	January–February 1835		Melbourne succeeds Grey as Prime Minister; is dismissed and succeeded by Peel. Poor Law Amendment Act passed. 'Tolpuddle Martyrs' transported for attempting to form a union. Establishment of Central Criminal Court in London. Slavery abolished in all British possessions. Faraday expounds laws of electrolysis. Hansom Cab patented by Joseph Hansom. Old Houses of Parliament destroyed by fire.
	August	8 more stories published in *Monthly Magazine*. Dickens becomes a reporter on the *Morning Chronicle*.	
	September–December	Dickens meets Catherine Hogarth.	'Street Sketches' 1–5 published in the *Morning Chronicle*.
	November	John Dickens arrested for debt and detained at sponging-house. Family home at 18 Bentinck Street broken up. On release John Dickens goes to lodgings in North End, Hampstead.	George Hogarth, Catherine's father, commissions 'Sketches of London' for his new paper, the *Evening Chronicle*. Publications: Bulwer-Lytton's *The Last Days of Pompeii*; Balzac's *Le Père Goriot*; Captain Marryat's *Peter Simple*.
	December	John Dickens family moves to 21 George Street, Adelphi. Dickens moves to 13 Furnival's Inn, Holborn.	

Year	Date	Life	Career	General Events
1835	January–August		'Sketches of London' 1-20 published in *Evening Chronicle*.	Peel resigns; replaced by Melbourne. Municipal Reform Act for England and Wales passed. Gas first used for cooking. Darwin studies Galapagos Islands, with important future results. Foundation of Melbourne, Australia. Schumann's *Carnaval* performed. Madame Tussaud's waxworks opens in London. Donizetti's *Lucia di Lammermoor* performed.
	? May	Dickens engaged to Catherine Hogarth. He takes lodgings at 11 Selwood Terrace, Queen's Elm, Brompton.		Publications: Gautier's *Mademoiselle de Maupin*; Browning's *Paracelsus*; John Clare's *The Rural Muse*.
	September–January 1836		'Scenes and Characters' 1-12 published in *Bell's Life in London*.	
1836	February 8		*Boz*, 1st series, published.	Boers make Great Trek from Cape Colony to found Republic of Orange Free State. Republic of Texas founded by Mexicans. Siege of El Alamo and Battle of San Jacinto. Births, Deaths, and Marriages Registration Act passed in Britain. Mendelssohn's *Saint Paul* performed. Meyerbeer's *Les Huguenots* performed. Glinka's *Life for the Czar* performed.
	February 10		First idea of *Pickwick* proposed to Dickens by Chapman & Hall.	Publications: Gogol's *The Inspector General*; Marryat's *Midshipman Easy*.
	February 17	Dickens moves to chambers at 15 Furnival's Inn, with brother Fred.	Dickens writing *Pickwick*.	
	March 31		*Pickwick* begins publication in 20 monthly parts (Chapman & Hall).	
	March–May		2 sketches published in the *Library of Fiction*.	
	April 2	Dickens marries Catherine Hogarth at St. Luke's Church, Chelsea. They go to Chalk, near Gravesend, for honeymoon, returning to live at Furnival's Inn, with Fred Dickens and Catherine's sister Mary Hogarth.		
	April 20		Robert Seymour, illustrator of *Pickwick*, commits suicide. Succeeded by Hablôt K. Browne ('Phiz').	
	June		'Sunday under Three Heads' published.	
	August 6		'Hospital Patient' published in the *Carlton Chronicle*.	
	August–September	Dickens and Catherine staying at Petersham.		
	September 29		*Strange Gentleman*, adapted from 'Great Winglebury Duel', begins run at St. James's Theatre of 60 nights.	
	November 4		Dickens agrees with Richard Bentley to edit *Bentley's Miscellany*.	
	November		Dickens leaves the *Morning Chronicle*.	

December 6		*Village Coquettes* produced at St. James's Theatre.
December 17		*Boz*, 2nd series, published.
December 22		*Village Coquettes* published.
? December 25	Dickens introduced to Forster by Harrison Ainsworth.	
? December (or January 1837)		*Strange Gentleman* published.
1837 January 1		First number of *Bentley's Miscellany* appears. The first of three pieces dealing with 'Mudfog' appears in it this month.	William IV dies. Victoria becomes Queen. Samuel B. Morse develops telegraph in U.S.A. Berlioz's *Requiem* performed. Isaac Pitman introduces his shorthand system. Joe Grimaldi dies, May 31.
January 6	Charles Culliford Boz (Charley) Dickens born.		Publications: Carlyle's *The French Revolution*.
January 21	Dickens elected member of Garrick Club.	
January 31		*Twist* begins publication in *Bentley's Miscellany*, February issue (24 monthly instalments).
February 4– ? March 6	Dickens and family at Chalk.	
March 6		*Is She His Wife?* produced at St. James's Theatre.
March	Dickens and family in lodgings at 30 Upper Norton Street.	
April (first week)	Dickens and family move to 48 Doughty Street.	
May 3		Dickens speaks in public for the first time at the Literary Fund Anniversary Dinner.
May 7	Mary Hogarth dies suddenly after a visit to the theatre. Dickens, Catherine, and Charley retire to Collins's Farm, Hampstead.	Writing of *Pickwick* and *Twist* suspended for a month.
June 16	Dickens introduced to William Charles Macready by Forster.	
July 2– ? 8	Dickens holidays in France and Belgium with Catherine and H. K. Browne.	
August 31– September ? 8/12	Dickens and family at 12 High Street, Broadstairs.	
September		First authoritative statement that 'Boz' is Dickens.
October 30		Last parts of *Pickwick* appear.

201

Year	Date	Life	Career	General Events
1837—contd	October 31–November 7	Dickens and Catherine at the Old Ship Hotel, Brighton.		
	November 17		Pickwick appears in book form.	
	November 18	Dinner to mark publication of Pickwick.		
1838	January 30–? February 6	Dickens on expedition to examine the Yorkshire schools with H. K. Browne.		Anti-Corn Law League founded in Manchester. First Afghan War breaks out. People's Charter (demanding universal suffrage, etc.) published at Glasgow, followed by several years of riots in its support. Daguerre perfects Daguerrotype system of photography. Regular Atlantic steamship service begins. Publications: Hugo's Ruy Blas.
	February 10		Young Gentlemen published.	
	February 26		Memoirs of Grimaldi published.	
	March 6	Mary (Mamie) Dickens born.		
	March 29	Dickens takes Catherine to the Star and Garter Hotel, Richmond, to convalesce and to celebrate their wedding anniversary.		
	March 31		Nickleby begins publication in 20 monthly instalments. (First issue dated April.)	
	June 21	Dickens elected member of the Athenaeum Club.		
	June–July	Dickens rents cottage at Twickenham.		
	September ? 3–12	Dickens and family in the Isle of Wight, staying at the Needles and Ventnor.		
	October 29–November 8	Dickens tours the Midlands and North Wales with H. K. Browne. Forster joins them at Liverpool on November 5.		
	November 9		Twist published in 3 vols.	
	November		Lamplighter, a play, written but not acted.	
1839	January		Dickens begins writing Rudge.	Queen Victoria becomes engaged to Albert of Saxe-Coburg. First Opium War between Britain and China breaks out. Fox Talbot introduces photographic paper. First Henley Regatta takes place. First Grand National run. Turner paints The Fighting Téméraire. Berlioz's Romeo et Juliette performed. Publications: Stendhal's La Chartreuse de Parme; Bradshaw's first railway timetable.
	January 12–17	Dickens visits Manchester with Harrison Ainsworth and Forster.		
	January 31		Dickens relinquishes editorship of Bentley's Miscellany.	
	March 4–11	Dickens visits Exeter to find a home for his parents. He stays at the New London Inn, and settles on Mile-End Cottage, Alphington.		
	March 13		Dickens elected to Literary Fund Committee.	
	March		Last part of Twist appears.	

Date	Biographical	Literary	Historical / Cultural
April 30–August 31	Dickens and family at Elm Cottage, Petersham.		
June		First complete edition of *Boz* published.	
September 3–? 1/2 October	Dickens and family at 40 Albion Street, Broadstairs.	Dickens completes *Nickleby*.	
October 1		Serialisation of *Nickleby* completed.	
October 23		*Nickleby* published in 1 vol.	
October 29	Kate Macready Dickens born.		
December 6	Dickens enrolled a student of Middle Temple, but does not 'eat dinners' there until many years later.		
December (early)	Dickens and family move to 1 Devonshire Terrace, Regent's Park.		
1840			Queen Victoria and Prince Albert marry. Princess Royal born (November). Act passed forbidding employment of boy chimney-sweeps in Britain, but proves ineffectual. Rowland Hill introduces penny post in England. First bicycle produced. Captain Hobson, first Governor of New Zealand, lands there and signs Treaty of Waitangi, acquiring land rights from Maoris. Barry builds new Houses of Parliament and Palace of Westminster in London. Nelson's column erected in Trafalgar Square. Donizetti's *La Fille du Régiment* performed. London Library opens. Publications: Browning's *Sordello*; W. Harrison Ainsworth's *The Tower of London*.
February 10		*Young Couples* published.	
February		Dickens writing *Humphrey*.	
February 29–March 4	Dickens at Bath with Forster, visiting Walter Savage Landor. They stay at York House Hotel.		
March		Dickens writing *Rudge* and *Curiosity Shop*.	
April 3–? 7	Dickens, Catherine, and Forster visit Birmingham, Stratford-upon-Avon, and Lichfield.		
April 4		First part of *Humphrey* appears.	
April 25		*Curiosity Shop* begins publication in the fourth number of *Humphrey* and runs for 40 instalments, sporadically up to June 20 and weekly thereafter.	
June 1–? 28	Dickens and family at 37 Albion Street, Broadstairs.		
June 29–30	Dickens, Forster, and Maclise visit Rochester and Cobham.		
July 27–August 4	Dickens visits his parents in Devon.		
August 30–October ? 10/11	Dickens at Lawn House, Broadstairs, with family.		
October 15		*Humphrey*, vol. I, published.	
1841			Melbourne resigns; Peel becomes Prime Minister. Albert Edward, Prince of Wales, born. New Zealand becomes separate
January		Dickens completes *Curiosity Shop*.	
February 6		End of serialisation of *Curiosity Shop*.	
February 8	Walter Landor Dickens born.		

Year	Date	Life	Career	General Events
1841—contd	February 13		*Rudge* begins publication in 42 weekly instalments in *Humphrey*.	British colony. Union of Upper and Lower Canada. Hong Kong founded as British settlement by British refugees from Canton. Schumann's 1st symphony performed. Thomas Cook's travel agency founded. German national anthem, *Deutschland, Deutschland Über Alles*, first heard.
	February 24–March 3	Dickens and Catherine at the Old Ship Hotel, Brighton.		
	April ? 12/15		*Humphrey*, vol. II, published.	Publications: Carlyle's *On Heroes and Hero-Worship*; Browning's *Pippa Passes*; *Punch* founded; *New York Tribune* founded.
	May 29	Dickens is invited to be Liberal parliamentary candidate for Reading. He declines.		
	June 19	Dickens and Catherine set off for Scotland.		
	June 22–July 4	They stay at the Royal Hotel, Edinburgh.	Dickens writing *Humphrey*.	
	June 25	Dinner at Waterloo Rooms, Edinburgh, in Dickens's honour.		
	June 29	Dickens is granted the Freedom of the City of Edinburgh.		
	July 4–16	Dickens and Catherine tour Scotland, with the sculptor Angus Fletcher.		
	July 18	Dickens and Catherine return to London.		
	August 1–October 2	Dickens and family at Lawn House, Broadstairs.		
	August 9		*The Pic Nic Papers* published, containing 'Lamplighter's Story'.	
	October 2–5	Dickens and Forster visit Rochester, Cobham and Gravesend.		
	October 8	Dickens undergoes an operation for fistula. He is convalescent during the following weeks.		
	October 24	Death of George Thomson Hogarth, Dickens's brother-in-law.		
	November 6–20	Dickens, still unwell, goes to Windsor to rest at the White Hart Hotel.	Dickens finishes *Rudge*.	
	November 27		End of serialisation of *Rudge*.	
	December 4		End of serialisation of *Humphrey*.	
	December 15		*Humphrey*, vol. III, published. *Curiosity Shop* and *Rudge* published in single-volume editions.	
1842	January 4	Dickens and Catherine sail on their first visit to America.		House of Commons rejects second Chartist petition; renewed rioting. South Australia

	Dickens (travels / personal)	Dickens (public life and works)	Contemporary events
January	Dickens and Catherine in Boston. Dickens meets Longfellow and R. H. Dana.	Dickens speaks on international copyright in Boston.	becomes a Crown Colony and wide-scale emigration commences. Women and children prevented from working in English collieries. Income tax reintroduced in Britain. Reformation of Corn Laws by Peel and beginning of Free Trade policies. American surgeon, Crawford Long, first to use anaesthetic for operation. Glinka's *Russlan and Ludmilla* performed. Wagner's *Rienzi* performed. Verdi's *Nabucco* performed. Publications: Tennyson's *Poems*; Macaulay's *Lays of Ancient Rome*; Samuel Lover's *Handy Andy*; Gogol's *Dead Souls*; *Illustrated London News* founded.
February	Dickens and Catherine in Worcester, Springfield, Hartford, and New Haven.	Dickens speaks on international copyright at Hartford.	
	Dickens and Catherine in New York. Dickens meets Washington Irving.	Dickens speaks on international copyright and investigates gaol conditions.	
March	Dickens and Catherine in Philadelphia, Washington, Richmond, Baltimore, York, and Harrisburgh.	Dickens investigates gaol conditions in Philadelphia, and criticises slavery in Richmond.	
April	Dickens and Catherine in Pittsburgh, Cincinnati, Louisville, St. Louis, Sandusky, and Buffalo.	Dickens inspects solitary confinement prison in Pittsburgh.	
May	Dickens and Catherine at Niagara, Toronto, Kingston, and Montreal, where Dickens performs in private theatricals with guards officers.		
July 1	Dickens and Catherine arrive back in England, stay briefly at 37 Albion Street, Broadstairs, then return to their London home, 1 Devonshire Terrace, where Georgina Hogarth joins the household.		
August	Dickens and family at Broadstairs.	Dickens writing *American Notes*.	
October 18		*American Notes* appears.	
October–November	Dickens, Forster, and Maclise make a 'bachelor' excursion to Cornwall.		
December (or January 1843)		Dickens begins writing *Chuzzlewit*.	
1843 January		First part of *Chuzzlewit* appears.	Princess Alice Maud Mary born to Queen Victoria. Establishment of Free Church of Scotland. Natal proclaimed a British possession. Irish government prohibit meeting in support of Daniel O'Connell's movement for repeal of Irish Act of Union. S.S. *Great Britain* is first screw-steamer to cross Atlantic. First public telegraph line established in England. Mendelssohn's music for *A Midsummer Night's Dream* performed. Donizetti's *Don Pasquale* performed. Wagner's *The Flying Dutchman* performed. First printed Christmas cards designed. Publications: George Borrow's *The Bible in Spain*; Thomas Hood's 'The Song of the
June	Dickens rents Cobley's Farm, Finchley, for a month's concentrated work on *Chuzzlewit*.		
August	Dickens and family at Albion Street, Broadstairs.		
October 4–6	Dickens presides at opening of Athenaeum Club, Manchester, with Richard Cobden and Benjamin Disraeli.		
October–November		Dickens writing 'Christmas Carol'.	
December		'Christmas Carol' appears.	

Year	Date	Life	Career	General Events
1843—contd				Shirt'; John Stuart Mill's *System of Logic*; *News of the World* newspaper founded; vol. I of Ruskin's *Modern Painters*.
1844	January		Dickens successfully takes proceedings in Chancery against pirates of his works.	Trial and sentence of O'Connell for sedition, later reversed by Lords. Tsar Nicholas I makes state visit to England. Retail Co-operative Movement founded by Rochdale Pioneers. Prince Alfred Ernest born to Queen Victoria. Polka introduced into Britain. Turner paints *Rain, Steam and Speed*. Verdi's *Ernani* performed.
	January 15	Francis Jeffrey (Frank) Dickens born.		Publications: Disraeli's *Coningsby*; Dumas's *Les Trois Mousquetaires* and *Monte Cristo*; Heine's *Neue Gedichte*; Kinglake's *Eothen*.
	February 26	Dickens takes the chair at the Mechanics' Institute, Liverpool.		
	February 28	Dickens takes the chair at the Polytechnic Institution, Birmingham.		
	May	Dickens family move to 9 Osnaburgh Terrace, having let 1 Devonshire Terrace for their forthcoming visit to Italy.		
	June		Dickens leaves Chapman & Hall for Bradbury & Evans. He completes *Chuzzlewit*.	
	July		*Chuzzlewit* completes serialisation and appears in book form.	
	July	Dickens family leave for Italy.		
	July 16	They arrive at Albaro, suburb of Genoa.		
	October	They rent rooms in the Palazzo Peschiere, Genoa.		
	October 10–November 3		Dickens writing 'Chimes'.	
	November 6	Dickens starts alone for England, visiting *en route* Parma, Modena, Bologna, Ferrava, Venice, Verona, Mantua, the Simplon Pass, Fribourg, Strasbourg, and Paris.		
	December 3	In London, Dickens reads 'Chimes' to a group of friends at Forster's house, Lincoln's Inn Fields. He leaves a few days later for Paris where he meets many literary celebrities.		
	December		'Chimes' published as Chapman & Hall's Christmas Book for 1844.	
	December 13	Dickens leaves Paris. Returns to Genoa by December 22.		

1845	January 20	Dickens and Catherine leave Genoa for Rome via Carrara, Pisa, and Siena.	Peel resigns over Corn Laws but is recalled. British agricultural holdings reformed by General Enclosure Act. Evangelical Alliance formed to oppose Roman Catholicism in Britain. First Sikh War breaks out. Faraday expounds electro-magnetic theory of light. Wagner's *Tannhäuser* performed. Mendelssohn's Violin Concerto performed.
	January 30	They arrive at Rome.	
	February–April	Dickens and Catherine visit Naples, where they are joined by Georgina Hogarth. From Naples, they return to Rome, then visit Florence in March, leaving on April 4 for Genoa.	
	April 9	They return to Genoa.	Publications: Disraeli's *Sybil*; Dumas's *La Tulipe Noire*; Engels's *The Condition of the Working Class in England*; Poe's *Tales of Mystery and Imagination*.
	June	Dickens, Catherine, and Georgina Hogarth leave Genoa for England via Switzerland. They are joined in Brussels by Maclise, Douglas Jerrold, and Forster, and arrive back at 1 Devonshire Terrace at the end of June.	Dickens conceives idea for 'Cricket'.
	July	Dickens engages Fanny Kelly's theatre, Dean Street, Soho, for amateur productions.	
	August	Dickens family at Broadstairs for three weeks.	
	September 21	Jonson's *Every Man in his Humour* produced at Fanny Kelly's theatre, Dickens playing Bobadil.	
	October		Dickens writing 'Cricket'.
	October 28	Alfred D'Orsay Tennyson Dickens born.	
	December	Performance of Beaumont and Fletcher's *The Elder Brother* at Fanny Kelly's theatre.	'Cricket' appears. Dickens begins writing *Pictures from Italy*.
1846	January 21		First issue of *Daily News* appears, with Dickens as editor. *Pictures from Italy* begins publication in it.	Peel, defeated after repeal of Corn Laws, is succeeded by Russell. Princess Helena Augusta Victoria born to Queen Victoria. American Richard March Hoe designs rotary printing press. Fleet Prison in London pulled down. Elizabeth Barrett marries Robert Browning. Mendelssohn's *Elijah* performed. Smithsonian Institute founded in Washington. Pneumatic tyre patented. First submarine cable laid across English Channel.
	February 9		Dickens resigns editorship of *Daily News*.	
	March 2		Serialisation of *Pictures from Italy* ends. It appears in volume form later in the month.	
	May 31	Dickens goes with his family to Switzerland, settling at the Villa Rosemont, Lausanne. Becomes interested in Swiss prison reform and Haldimand's work for the blind.	Dickens writing *Life of Our Lord* (it was not published until 1934).	Publications: Thackeray's *The Book of Snobs*; Edward Lear's *Book of Nonsense*; *Poems* by 'Currer, Ellis, and Acton Bell' (Charlotte, Emily and Anne Brontë).
	June 27		Dickens begins *Dombey*.	
	September		Dickens interrupts *Dombey* to write 'Battle of Life'.	

Year	Date	Life	Career	General Events
1846—contd	October		Dickens completes 'Battle of Life'. First monthly part of Dombey appears.	
	November 20	Dickens family arrive in Paris for a three month stay en route for England. They stay at the Hotel Brighton and then rent 48 rue de Courcelles, home of the Marquis de Castellane.		
	December		'Battle of Life' appears.	
	December 15–23	Dickens in London. He attends rehearsals of a dramatic version, by Albert Smith, of 'Battle of Life', then returns to Paris.		
1847	January–February	Dickens and family in Paris.	Dickens writing Dombey.	Mormons emigrate to Utah, establishing themselves at Salt Lake City. Britain undergoes financial crisis. Chloroform used successfully for first time in operation by James Y. Simpson. Verdi's Macbeth performed. Flotow's Martha performed. Berlioz's The Damnation of Faust performed. Publications: Disraeli's Tancred; Charlotte Brontë's Jane Eyre; Emily Brontë's Wuthering Heights; Marryat's The Children of the New Forest; Tennyson's The Princess.
	February	Dickens and family return to London prematurely because Charley, at King's College School, has scarlet fever. They stay at the Victoria Hotel, Euston Square. Their own house is still let, so they rent, furnished, 3 Chester Place, Regent's Park, for three months.		
	April 18	Sydney Smith Haldimand Dickens born.		
	May	Dickens and Catherine, Georgina Hogarth, and Charley holiday at Brighton, staying at 148 King's Road.		
	June–September	Dickens and family at the Albion Hotel, Broadstairs.	Dickens writing Dombey. Begins 'The Haunted Man', but lays it aside until winter 1848.	
	July	Dickens appears at Manchester and Liverpool in Every Man in his Humour with a cast of friends and relatives, for benefit of Leigh Hunt and John Poole. The play proper followed on alternate nights by farces: A Good Night's Rest, Turning the Tables and Comfortable Lodgings, or Paris in 1750.	Dickens writes an account of the Tour, 'a new Piljians Projiss', in the character of Mrs. Gamp, to be sold to augment the benefit fund. This never appeared because of the failure of the artists to provide illustrations.	
	September	Dickens and family return to Devonshire Terrace.		
	December 1	Dickens chairs a meeting of Leeds Mechanics' Society.		
	December 28	Dickens in Scotland, opening the Glasgow Athenaeum. Visits Edinburgh, where Catherine is taken ill, and they stay over the New Year period.		

Year	Date	Dickens's Works	Dickens's Life	World Events
1848	March	Last part of *Dombey* finished.		Revolution in Paris; Louis Philippe abdicates. Second Republic formed, and Louis Napoleon becomes Prince President. Revolutions break out in Berlin, Vienna, Venice, Rome, Milan, Naples, Prague, and Budapest. Francis Joseph becomes Emperor of Austria. Princess Louise Carolina Alberta born to Queen Victoria. Cholera epidemic breaks out in England. Successful steam-powered model aircraft flown by Stringfellow. First official settlers in California. First official settlers arrive at Dunedin, New Zealand. Spiritualist movement begins with experiences of the Fox Sisters in New York. Pre-Raphaelite Brotherhood founded in England. Publications: Mrs. Elizabeth Gaskell's *Mary Barton*; Thackeray's *Pendennis* begun (completed 1850); J. S. Mill's *Political Economy*; Anne Brontë's *The Tenant of Wildfell Hall* and *Agnes Grey*; first two vols. of Macaulay's *History of England*.
	April	Last part of *Dombey* appears and the work is published in book form.	Dickens and his company give eight performances in London in aid of the purchase and preservation of Shakespeare's birthplace, Stratford-upon-Avon: *The Merry Wives of Windsor*, Dickens playing Shallow, and a farce, *Love, Law and Physick*.	
	April–July		They tour with the plays, visiting Manchester, Liverpool, Birmingham, Edinburgh and Glasgow.	
	Summer		Dickens and family at Broadstairs on holiday.	
	August		Fanny Burnett, Dickens's sister, dies.	
	November	Dickens writing 'Haunted Man'.	Dickens at the Bedford Hotel, Brighton.	
	December	'Haunted Man' appears.		
	December 31		Dickens, John Leech, Mark Lemon, and Forster visit Norwich and Yarmouth for several days.	
1849	January 15		Henry Fielding Dickens born.	Britain annexes the Punjab. Dr. David Livingstone begins exploration of Central and South Africa, crossing the Kalahari Desert and reaching Lake Ngami. Discovery of reinforced concrete by J. Monier. 'Bloomers' introduced as women's wear by Amelia Jenks Bloomer. Publications: Charlotte Brontë's *Shirley*; Matthew Arnold's *The Strayed Reveller and other Poems*; first publication of *Who's Who*.
	February–June	Dickens writing *Copperfield*.	Dickens and family at Brighton, in lodgings and the Bedford Hotel.	
	May	First number of *Copperfield* appears.	Dickens and family at Fort House, Broadstairs.	
	July			
	July–October		Dickens, family, and friends at Bonchurch, Isle of Wight.	
	October 1		His original enthusiasm for the Isle of Wight having waned suddenly, Dickens takes his family back to Broadstairs, to the Albion Hotel.	
	October 7	In a letter to Forster, Dickens outlines the details of the proposed journal *Household Words*, an often-recurring idea which he has worked out at Bonchurch and Broadstairs.		
	November		Dickens and Catherine make first visit to Rockingham Castle, Northamptonshire.	
1850	March 30	First number of *Household Words* appears with Dickens as editor.		Death of Sir Robert Peel. Factory Act passed to define legal working hours.

Year	Date	Life	Career	General Events
1850—contd	April	Dickens and Catherine and Georgina Hogarth spend a week at Knebworth to discuss with Bulwer-Lytton his scheme for creating a Guild of Literature and Art to assist needy writers and artists.		Revival of trade unionism. Catholic hierarchy in Britain inaugurated. Prince Arthur William Patrick Albert born to Queen Victoria. Gold discovered in Australia. Meteorological Office established in England. Petrol refining first used. Pre-Raphaelite paintings include William Holman Hunt's *Claudio and Isabella* and John Everett Millais's *Christ in the House of His Parents*. Jean-François Millet paints *The Sower*. Schumann's 3rd symphony (The Rhenish) performed. Wagner's *Lohengrin* produced at Weimar. Sydney University, Australia, founded. Wordsworth dies.
	June	Dinner at Star and Garter, Richmond, in honour of *Copperfield*.		
	June	Dickens visits France with Maclise to see plays and pictures.		
	July	Dickens and family at Fort House, Broadstairs.		
	August 16	Dora Annie Dickens born in London. Dickens, who had joined his wife there for the event, then re-joins Georgina and his children at Fort House, Broadstairs.		
	October	Dickens back at Devonshire Terrace.	*Copperfield* finished.	Publications: Elizabeth Barrett Browning's *Sonnets from the Portuguese*; Nathaniel Hawthorne's *The Scarlet Letter*; Charles Kingsley's *Alton Locke*; Dante Gabriel Rossetti's *The Blessed Damozel*; Tennyson's *In Memoriam*; Ivan S. Turgenev's *A Month in the Country*; Wordsworth's *The Prelude*.
	November	Rehearsals at Knebworth for *Every Man in his Humour*, to be given in aid of the Guild of Literature and Art. Three private performances of *Every Man* given in the hall at Knebworth, followed by the farces *Animal Magnetism* and *Turning the Tables*, Dickens acting and directing.	Dickens writing *A Child's History of England*. Serialisation of *Copperfield* completed, and it appears in book form.	
1851	January	Performances of *Animal Magnetism* and *Used Up* at Rockingham Castle.	*A Child's History of England* begins in *Household Words*.	Palmerston dismissed from office as Foreign Secretary. Louis Napoleon gains control of all France. Crystal Palace built in Hyde Park, London, and Great Exhibition opens there. Isaac M. Singer markets first practical sewing-machine. Submarine cable links Dover and Calais. New York yacht *America* wins Royal Yacht Squadron cup, henceforward known as the America's Cup. Verdi's *Rigoletto* performed.
	February	Dickens visits Paris with Leech and the Hon. Spencer Lyttleton.		
	March	Catherine Dickens suffers a nervous collapse and goes to Malvern to recover. Dickens visits her, but is recalled to London to his father.		
	March 31	John Dickens dies in London.		
	April 14	Dickens takes the chair at the General Theatrical Fund meeting. Forster withholds the news until afterwards that Dickens's daughter Dora Annie has died at Devonshire Terrace.		Publications: Borrow's *Lavengro*; Herman Melville's *Moby Dick*; Harriet Beecher Stowe's *Uncle Tom's Cabin*; Henri Murger's *Scènes de la Vie de Bohème*; Ruskin's *Stones of Venice*.
	May 16	Dickens directs and plays in Bulwer-Lytton's *Not so Bad as we Seem* at Devonshire House, Piccadilly, home of the Duke of Devonshire.		

Date	Dickens's life	Dickens's work	Contemporary events
May 27	A second presentation at Devonshire House, at which Dickens plays in his own farce, *Nightingale's Diary*. The play is published privately this year, exact date unknown.		
May–June	Dickens decides to move his family to a larger house on the expiration of the Devonshire Terrace lease. He decides on Tavistock House, Bloomsbury, and supervises improvements during these months.		
May (late)	Dickens and family at Fort House, Broadstairs, for the last time, Dickens being driven out by the incessant noise of German bands and other street musicians.		
November	The Dickens family and Georgina Hogarth move into Tavistock House.	Dickens begins writing *Bleak House*.	
November	Catherine Dickens's only publication, a cookery book *What Shall We Have for Dinner?* appears under the pseudonym Lady Maria Clutterbuck.		
1852		First part of *Bleak House* appears.	Fall of Russell: coalition government. Duke of Wellington dies. New Zealand and Transvaal made self-governing. Wells Fargo & Co. founded in U.S.A. Holman Hunt paints *The Light of the World*. Millais paints *Ophelia*. Crystal Palace transferred to permanent site at Sydenham. Victoria and Albert Museum opened. Publications: Thackeray's *Henry Esmond*; Dumas *fils*'s *La Dame aux Camélias*; Matthew Arnold's *Empedocles on Etna and other Poems*.
March 13	Edward Bulwer Lytton Dickens born.		
July–October	Dickens's children staying at Camden Crescent, Dover, while he, accompanied by Catherine and Georgina Hogarth, tours in performances of Bulwer-Lytton's *Not so Bad as we Seem* at Derby, Sheffield, Nottingham, Sunderland, Newcastle, Manchester and Liverpool. Deaths of his friends, Count D'Orsay, in August, and Mrs. Macready, in September.	Dickens writing *Bleak House*.	
October	Dickens and Catherine and Georgina Hogarth in Boulogne, experimenting with it as a holiday place, after which they return to London for the rest of the year.	Dickens working on *Bleak House*; also on 'To be Read at Dusk' for *The Keepsake* at about this time.	
December		First bound volume of *A Child's History of England* appears. *Christmas Books* appears.	
1853			
January	Dickens receives ovation and presentations at Birmingham for his services to Mechanics' Institute. At Twelfth Night banquet Dickens makes offer to give two public readings at Christmas in aid of the new Midland Institute.	Dickens writing *Bleak House*, and *A Child's History of England*, and editing *Household Words*.	Gladstone's first Budget: Death Duty introduced. Napoleon III marries Eugénie. Russo-Turkish War breaks out. Queen Victoria allows use of chloroform during birth of Prince Leopold. Smallpox vaccination compulsory in England.

Year	Date	Life	Career	General Events
1853 — contd		Charley Dickens leaves Eton and goes to study at Leipzig.		Balmoral Castle rebuilt. Verdi's *Il Trovatore* and *La Traviata* performed.
	June 13	Dickens returns to Boulogne to escape nervous breakdown. Catherine and Georgina Hogarth accompany him and the family follow three weeks later. They have rented the Château des Moulineaux.		Publications: Charlotte Brontë's *Villette*; Mrs. Gaskell's *Cranford*; Nathaniel Hawthorne's *Tanglewood Tales*; Thackeray's *The Newcomes*; Matthew Arnold's *Sohrab and Rustum*.
	August		Dickens completes *Bleak House*.	
	September		Dickens completes *A Child's History of England*. Last monthly part of *Bleak House* appears, and it is published in volume form.	
	October–December	Dickens sends family home and goes on trip to Italy with Wilkie Collins and Augustus Egg. Revisits Haldimand's institution. Revisits Genoa, Naples, Rome, Florence, Venice.		
	Mid-December	Dickens returns to London.		
	December 10		*A Child's History of England* ends in *Household Words*. Second bound volume appears.	
	December 27		Dickens gives his first public reading, 'Christmas Carol', at Birmingham Town Hall, followed on December 29 by 'Cricket', and 'Christmas Carol' again on December 30. Henceforth, reading from his works in London and the provinces occupies much of his time and energy.	
1854	January 6	Twelfth Night celebrations at Tavistock House with *Tom Thumb* performed by the family.		Crimean War breaks out: Battles of Alma, Balaclava, Inkerman; siege of Sebastopol begins. Commodore Perry forces Japan to make trade treaty with U.S.A. W. P. Frith paints *Ramsgate Sands*, Millet paints *The Reapers*. Wagner begins composing *The Ring*.
	January	Dickens in Preston.	Dickens collecting material for *Hard Times*, which he begins.	
	April 1		First instalment of *Hard Times* in *Household Words*.	Publications: Tennyson's 'The Charge of the Light Brigade'; Thoreau's *Walden*.
	June–October	Dickens at Boulogne at the Villa Camp de Droite.	Dickens writing *Hard Times*.	
	August 12		Last instalment of *Hard Times* appears. It appears this month in volume form.	
	October	Dickens returns to Tavistock House.		

	December	Third and last bound volume of *A Child's History of England* appears.	
1855	January 6	Twelfth Night celebrations at Tavistock House: performance of *Fortunio and His Seven Gifted Servants*.	Crimean setbacks cause resignation of Aberdeen; succeeded by Palmerston. Queen Victoria and Prince Albert make state visit to France. Sebastopol falls; Britain and Turkey ally against Russia. Florence Nightingale becomes household name for her nursing work in the war. Death of Tsar Nicholas I; accession of Alexander II. Victoria Falls discovered by Livingstone. Liszt's *Faust* symphony performed. Ford Madox Brown paints *The Last England*.
	February	Dickens spends fortnight in Paris with Wilkie Collins.	
	May	Dickens begins writing *Dorrit*, first called *Nobody's Fault*. Dickens meets again Maria Winter, *née* Beadnell, and suffers disappointment in her.	
	June	Amateur theatricals at Tavistock House: *The Lighthouse, Nightingale's Diary,* and *Animal Magnetism*.	
	July	Dickens writing *Dorrit*. Dickens at 3 Albion Villas, Folkestone.	Publications: Kingsley's *Westward Ho!*; Longfellow's *Hiawatha*; Motley's *Rise of the Dutch Republic*; Browning's *Men and Women*; Trollope's *The Warden*; Tennyson's *Maud*; Whitman's *Leaves of Grass*; *Daily Chronicle* and *Daily Telegraph* newspapers first appear.
	November	Dickens and family winter in Paris at 49 Avenue des Champs-Elysées.	
	December	First monthly part of *Dorrit* appears. Dickens sits for Ary Scheffer for his portrait and meets the *élite* of Paris, including George Sand.	
1856	March 14	Dickens pays the purchase money for Gad's Hill Place. Returns to Paris until May. Dickens writing *Dorrit*.	Crimean War ends with Treaty of Paris. Second Anglo-Chinese war breaks out. Holman Hunt paints *The Scapegoat*. Millais paints *Autumn Leaves*. Victoria Cross instituted. Royal Opera House, Covent Garden, burns down.
	June–August	Dickens at Boulogne with family.	Publications: Flaubert's *Madame Bovary*; Kingsley's *The Heroes*; J. A. Froude's *The History of England*.
	September	Dickens returns to London.	
	November	Rehearsals at Tavistock House for Collins's melodrama *The Frozen Deep*.	
1857	January 6, 8, 12, 14	*The Frozen Deep* acted at Tavistock House, followed by farces *Animal Magnetism* and *Uncle John*.	Chinese fleet destroyed by British: British enter Canton. Indian Mutiny: Siege of Lucknow, Cawnpore Massacres, relief of Lucknow, capture of Delhi. Transportation for crime ends. Princess Beatrice born to Queen Victoria. Millet paints *The Gleaners*. Sir Charles Hallé founds Hallé concerts in Manchester.
	February	Dickens gets possession of Gad's Hill Place.	
	June	Last instalment of *Dorrit* appears, and it appears in volume form.	
	June 8	Douglas Jerrold, journalist and friend of Dickens, dies.	Publications: Charlotte Brontë's *The Professor*; Borrow's *The Romany Rye*; Elizabeth Barrett Browning's *Aurora Leigh*; Baudelaire's *Les Fleurs du Mal*; Thomas Hughes's *Tom Brown's Schooldays*; Herbert Spencer's *Essays*; Thackeray's *The*
	July 4	*The Frozen Deep* given as benefit performance for widow of Douglas Jerrold at Gallery of Illustration in Regent Street.	
	July 20	Walter Dickens leaves for India.	

H

Year	Date	Life	Career	General Events
1857— *contd*	July	Marital discord between Dickens and Catherine growing at this period.		*Virginians*; Trollope's *Barchester Towers*; Mrs. Craik's *John Halifax, Gentleman*.
	August	Dickens meets Ellen Ternan and she goes with his troupe to Manchester to play in the benefit performances of *The Frozen Deep* on August 21 and 22.		
	September	Dickens tours through the North of England with Wilkie Collins.	Dickens and Collins acquire material for *Two Apprentices*.	
	October 3–31		*Two Apprentices*, by Dickens and Wilkie Collins, appears in *Household Words*.	
1858	February	Dickens throws himself into work for Hospital for Sick Children.		Palmerston resigns; succeeded by Derby. Jews admitted to Parliament. Irish Republican Brotherhood, the Fenians, founded in U.S.A. Indian Mutiny suppressed, East India Company abolished and government transferred to British Crown. First recorded miracle at Lourdes. Lake Tanganyika, source of Nile, discovered. Suez Canal Company formed. Cathode rays discovered. First European oil well found. First Atlantic cable laid. Offenbach's *Orpheus in the Underworld* performed. Brahms's 1st piano concerto performed. Present Royal Opera House, Covent Garden, opened. Big Ben cast at White-chapel Bell Foundry. Frith paints *Derby Day*.
	April 15		Dickens gives reading in aid of Hospital.	
	April 29		First of the many public readings for Dickens's own benefit given at St. Martin's Hall, London.	
	[Date unknown]		*Reprinted Pieces* collected in 8th volume of Library Edition of Dickens's works (Chapman & Hall).	
	May	Dickens and Catherine separate.		
	June 12		Dickens makes unwise public statement in *Household Words* and quarrels with publishers Bradbury & Evans.	
	August 2– November 13		87 readings, beginning Clifton, ending Brighton, taking in Ireland and Scotland; 44 places altogether.	Publications: George Eliot's *Scenes from Clerical Life*; Frederic W. Farrar's *Eric, or Little by Little*; Oliver Wendell Holmes's *The Autocrat at the Breakfast-Table*; William Morris's *Defence of Guenevere and other Poems*; Longfellow's *The Courtship of Miles Standish*; Trollope's *Doctor Thorne*; Ibsen's *The Vikings in Heligoland*; Carlyle's *Frederick the Great*; first publication of *Crockford's Clerical Directory*.
1859	January 28		Dickens chooses title of *All the Year Round* for a new weekly journal.	Disraeli, Chancellor of the Exchequer, introduces Reform Bill, which is defeated. Derby's Government falls and Palmerston becomes Prime Minister for second term
	February		Takes offices at 11 Wellington Street, Strand.	

March	Dickens begins writing *Two Cities*.	of office. Growth of Fenian activity. First American oil wells drilled in Pennsylvania. T. B. Bishop composes *John Brown's Body* to commemorate raid at Harper's Ferry. Gounod's *Faust* performed. Millet paints *The Angelus*. Vauxhall Pleasure Gardens, London, closed.
April 30	First number of *All the Year Round* appears, containing opening instalment of *Two Cities*. As owner-editor, Dickens contributed to it throughout the remainder of his life, and willed his share in it to his son Charley. Chapman & Hall agree to publish the remainder of his books.	Publications: Charles Darwin's *The Origin of Species*; Edward FitzGerald's translation of *The Rubáiyát of Omar Khayyám*; George Eliot's *Adam Bede*; George Meredith's *The Ordeal of Richard Feverel*; Samuel Smiles's *Self-help*; J. S. Mill's *On Liberty*; Tennyson's *Idylls of the King*.
	Last number of *Household Words* appears.	
May 28		
Summer	Dickens at Gad's Hill with daughters, younger sons, and Georgina Hogarth as housekeeper. Moves to Broadstairs for a week at the end of the summer.	
	Dickens finishes *Two Cities*.	
August 20		
	First part of *Hunted Down* (in three parts) published in *New York Ledger*.	
November 26	Last instalment of *Two Cities* appears.	
December	*Two Cities* appears in volume form.	
1860		
January 28	*Uncommercial* begins in *All the Year Round*.	Free Trade Budget introduced by Gladstone. Cobden makes Free Trade Treaty with France. First Italian National Parliament formed at Turin. Capture of Sicily and Naples by Garibaldi.
July 17	Katey Dickens marries Charles Allston Collins.	Publications: Wilkie Collins's *The Woman in White*; George Eliot's *The Mill on the Floss*; Thackeray's *The Four Georges*.
July 27	Alfred Lamert Dickens dies in Manchester.	
July	Tavistock House given up.	
September	Dickens settles at Gad's Hill as his permanent residence.	
October	Dickens begins writing *Expectations*.	
November	Dickens and Wilkie Collins visit Devon and Cornwall.	
December 1	First instalment of *Expectations* appears in *All the Year Round*.	
December	First collection of *Uncommercial* pieces in book form appears.	
1861		
March	Dickens takes 3 Hanover Terrace, Regent's Park, as London base.	Death of Albert, Prince Consort. Abraham Lincoln elected President of U.S.A. American Civil War breaks out: Battles of Bull Run and Lexington. Italian unity (except for Roman Venice) achieved under Victor Emmanuel of Savoy. Serfdom abolished in Russia. London's first horse-drawn tramcars.
March	Sydney Dickens appointed to H.M.S. *Orlando*.	Dickens writing *Expectations*.
March–April	Second series of readings begins at St. James's Hall, ending April 18.	Publications: Mrs. Beeton's *Book of Household Management*; Palgrave's *Golden*
June	Dickens finishes writing *Expectations*.	
August 3	Dickens at Gad's Hill.	Last instalment of *Expectations* appears, and the work is published in 2 vols. this month.

Year	Date	Life	Career	General Events
1861—contd	October 28		A long series of provincial readings opens at Norwich, taking in Berwick-on-Tweed, Lancaster, Bury St. Edmunds, Cheltenham, Carlisle, Hastings, Plymouth, Birmingham, Canterbury, Torquay, Preston, Ipswich, Manchester, Brighton, Colchester, Dover, and Newcastle.	*Treasury*; Charles Reade's *The Cloister and the Hearth*; Turgenev's *Fathers and Sons*; Dostoievsky's *The House of the Dead*; George Eliot's *Silas Marner*.
	October	Dickens's tour manager, Arthur Smith, dies. Henry Austin, Dickens's brother-in-law, dies.		
	November	Charley Dickens marries Bessie Evans, daughter of Dickens's one-time publisher.		
1862	January		Provincial readings end at Chester.	American Civil War: Battles of Mill Springs and Williamsburg. Bismarck becomes Prime Minister of Prussia. Frith paints *The Railway Station*; Julia Ward Howe's 'Battle Hymn of the Republic' sung by Union forces in America; Berlioz's *Beatrice and Benedict* performed.
	February	Dickens takes 16 Hyde Park Gate for three months.		
	March	Georgina Hogarth seriously ill.		Publications: Hugo's *Les Misérables*; Mrs. Henry Wood's *The Channings*; Christina Rossetti's *Goblin Market and other Poems*; George Eliot's *Romola*; Flaubert's *Salammbo*; Herbert Spencer's *First Principles*; Ruskin's *Unto This Last*; Borrow's *Wild Wales*; Elizabeth Barrett Browning's *Last Poems*.
	March–June		Series of London readings at St. James's Hall, ending in mid-June.	
	October–December	Dickens takes Georgina Hogarth and Mamie Dickens to Paris, where they rent 24 rue du Faubourg St. Honoré.		
	December	Dickens home for Christmas.		
1863	January	Dickens returns to Paris with Georgina Hogarth and Mamie.	Dickens gives four readings at the British Embassy, Paris, for British Charitable Fund.	Edward, Prince of Wales, marries Princess Alexandra of Denmark. Abolition of slavery in U.S.A. American Civil War: Battles of Nashville, Winchester, Gettysburg, etc. Lincoln delivers Gettysburg Address. Work begins on London's underground railway, world's first. Bizet's *The Pearl Fishers* performed. Manet paints *Le Déjeuner sur l'Herbe*. Liszt's Symphony in A performed. Publications: Kingsley's *The Water Babies*.
	February	Dickens and his companions return to London.		
	June		Dickens gives 13 readings at the Hanover Square Rooms.	
	September 12	Death of Dickens's mother.		
	November	Dickens at Gad's Hill.	Dickens begins writing *Mutual Friend*.	
	December 24	Death of Thackeray.		
	December 31	Death of Walter Dickens in India.		
1864	January	Frank Dickens starts for India.		First Trade Union Conference. Chimney Sweeps Act forbidding employment of

February	Dickens moves London base to 57 Gloucester Place.	Dickens writing *Mutual Friend*.	children; proves ineffective. International Red Cross founded by Henry Dunant. Offenbach's *La Belle Hélène* performed. Bruckner's Symphony in D Minor performed. Publications: Le Fanu's *Uncle Silas*; Tennyson's *Enoch Arden*; Ségur's *Les Malheurs de Sophie*; Ibsen's *The Pretenders*; John Henry Newman's *Apologia pro Vita Sua*.
May 1		First part of *Mutual Friend* appears.	
June	Dickens leaves 57 Gloucester Place and returns to Gad's Hill for the remainder of year.		
October 29	Death of John Leech.		
December	Swiss chalet arrives at Gad's Hill, the gift of Fechter.		
1865 February	Dickens attacked by pain and lameness in left foot, probably early symptoms of thrombosis.		Death of Palmerston. Russell becomes Prime Minister. President Lincoln assassinated. First concrete roads laid in Britain. Queensberry Rules controlling boxing drawn up. Wagner's *Tristan and Isolde* performed. Whistler paints *Old Battersea Bridge*. Rimsky-Korsakov's Symphony in E Flat Minor performed. Publications: Lewis Carroll's *Alice in Wonderland*; Newman's *Dream of Gerontius*; Ouida's *Strathmore*; Ruskin's *Sesame and Lilies*; Swinburne's *Atalanta in Calydon*; Tolstoy's *War and Peace*.
March	Dickens takes furnished house at 16 Somers Place, Hyde Park, until June.		
June	Dickens takes short holiday in Paris, possibly accompanied by Ellen Ternan and her mother.	Dickens writing *Mutual Friend*.	
June 9	Dickens and companions in serious railway accident at Staplehurst, Kent. Dickens uninjured but permanently affected by shock.		
November		Last part of *Mutual Friend* appears, and the work is published in book form.	
December		Second collection of *Uncommercial* pieces appears in book form.	
1866 March	Dickens takes furnished house, 6 Southwick Place, Hyde Park. Suffers from heart trouble and general ill-health.	Dickens accepts offer from Chappells of Bond Street to undertake 30 readings.	Defeat of Gladstone's Reform Bill and resignation of Government. Derby becomes Prime Minister. Austria defeated by Prussia in Seven Weeks' War at Sadowa. Mary Baker Eddy formulates first ideas of Christian Science. Offenbach's *La Vie Parisienne* produced. Suppé's *Light Cavalry* produced. Publications: Paul Verlaine's *Poèmes saturniens*; Dostoievsky's *Crime and Punishment*; Kingsley's *Hereward the Wake*; Ruskin's *Crown of Wild Olive*; C. M. Yonge's *The Dove in the Eagle's Nest*; Emile Gaboriau's *L'Affaire Lerouge*; George Eliot's *Felix Holt*.
April		Reading tour begins at Liverpool.	
June		Tour ends.	
June	Dickens complains to various correspondents of exhaustion, and pain in left eye, hand, and foot. Returns to Gad's Hill for remainder of year.		
October 6	Augustus Dickens dies impoverished in Chicago.		
December		'Mugby Junction' published in *All the Year Round*.	

Year	Date	Life	Career	General Events
1867	January		Dickens begins new series of 50 provincial readings at Liverpool, taking in Scotland and Ireland.	Fenian rising in Ireland. Garibaldi invades Papal States. Emperor Maximilian executed by Mexican rebels. South African diamond fields discovered. Alfred B. Nobel produces dynamite. Lister demonstrates the use of carbolic antiseptic. Gounod's *Roméo et Juliette* produced. Johann Strauss's *The Blue Danube* performed. Sullivan provides music for Morton and Burnand's *Cox and Box*. Wagner's *Die Meistersinger von Nürnberg* performed. Bizet's *La Jolie Fille de Perth* performed.
	January 15	Dickens complains of exhaustion and faintness, and of nervousness produced by rail travel.		
	May	Death of Dickens's close friend Clarkson Stanfield.		
	May 14		Tour ends. After it, Dickens tells Forster of American offers, and that he is tempted to undertake an American tour.	
	August	Dickens suffers severely from pain and swelling in foot, and is unable to walk. Forster tries to dissuade him from undertaking the American project.	Dolby sails for America to reconnoitre.	Publications: Zola's *Thérèse Raquin*; first volume of Karl Marx's *Das Kapital*; Dostoievsky's *The Gambler*; Ibsen's *Peer Gynt*; Swinburne's *Song of Italy*.
	September		Dolby reports favourably on American conditions.	
	September 30		Dickens telegraphs acceptance to J. T. Fields in Boston.	
	? October–November		Dickens writes his last Christmas piece (with Wilkie Collins), 'No Thoroughfare', for *All the Year Round*. This and other Christmas pieces from *Household Words* and *All the Year Round* are now familiar as *Christmas Stories*.	
	November 9	Dickens sails for America.		
	November 19	Dickens arrives in Boston.		
	December 2	Dickens writes home of severe weather and trials of travelling, but enjoys warm hospitality in New England.	Dickens gives first reading in Boston. Is now making a clear profit of £1300 a week.	
	December 9		Gives first reading in New York.	
	December 26		First production of *No Thoroughfare*.	
	December 27	In New York, Dickens calls in doctor to treat persistent cold and catarrh.		
1868	January–February	Dickens continues ill. Comments on improvements in American conditions since his first visit.	Dickens reads in New York, Brooklyn (in Ward Beecher's chapel), Philadelphia, Baltimore, Washington (where he meets President Andrew Johnson).	Disraeli's first ministry, followed by Gladstone's first ministry. Ku Klux Klan founded in southern states of U.S.A. following the Civil War. Monet paints *Argenteuil-sur-Seine*; Renoir paints *Sisley*.
	February		'Silverman' published in *Household Words*.	
	January–March		'Silverman' published in *Atlantic Monthly*.	

January–May		'Holiday Romance' simultaneously begins publication in *Our Young Folks* (U.S.A.) and *All the Year Round*.	*and his Wife*; Moussorgsky's *Boris Godounov* performed; Rimsky-Korsakov's Symphony Number 2 performed. Maxim Gorky born. Publications: Browning's *The Ring and the Book*; Wilkie Collins's *The Moonstone*; Louisa May Alcott's *Little Women*; William Morris's *Earthly Paradise*; Queen Victoria's *Leaves from a Journal of Our Life in the Highlands*; Dostoievsky's *The Idiot*; first publication of *Whitaker's Almanac*.
March	Dickens revisits Niagara. Complains of being 'nearly used up'.	Dickens reads in Rochester, Syracuse, Buffalo, Springfield, Utica, Portland, New Bedford, etc. Returns to Boston.	
April	Public dinner given for Dickens at Delmonico's.	Dickens gives farewell readings in Boston and New York.	
April 22	Dickens sails for England.		
May 1	Dickens arrives in England. Appears in better health.		
Summer	Throughout summer Dickens entertains American and other friends at Gad's Hill.		
September	Dickens's youngest son, Edward Bulwer Lytton Dickens, sails for Australia.		
October 5		Dickens starts reading tour for Chappells.	
October 20	Dickens's only surviving brother Fred dies.		
November		Reading tour interrupted for anticipated general election. Dickens works up his 'Murder of Nancy' reading and first presents it privately at St. James's Hall, London, on November 14.	
1869 January		Readings resume; first public hearing of the 'Murder of Nancy' is on January 5.	Imprisonment for debt abolished. Irish Church Disestablishment Act. Suez Canal opened by Empress Eugénie. Union Pacific Railway completed. Blackfriars Bridge, London, built. *Cutty Sark*, tea-clipper, launched. Girton College for Women founded. Borodin's 1st Symphony performed; Manet painted *Portrait of Berthe Morisot*; Brahms completed *Ein Deutsches Requiem*. Publications: R. D. Blackmore's *Lorna Doone*; W. S. Gilbert's *Bab Ballads*; Mark Twain's *Innocents Abroad*; Flaubert's *L'Education Sentimentale*; Verlaine's *Fêtes Galantes*; Daudet's *Lettres de Mon Moulin*.
April 22		At Preston, Dickens is ordered by Dr. Beard and Sir Thomas Watson to discontinue readings, as paralysis threatens. The audience's money is returned and Dr. Beard escorts Dickens back to London. He continues unwell, but promises Chappells a series of London farewell readings.	
July	Dickens at Gad's Hill.		
October		Dickens conceives first ideas of *Drood*. Dickens begins writing *Drood*.	
1870 January	Dickens takes a furnished house, 5 Hyde Park Place, and visits Ellen Ternan regularly at Windsor Lodge, Peckham. Suffers much pain in left hand and failure in left eye.	Dickens writing *Drood*.	Irish Land Act passed. Outbreak of Franco-Prussian War; French defeated at Sedan; Siege of Paris. Second Empire ends, and Third Republic proclaimed. First Elementary Education Act results in the

Year	Date	Life	Career	General Events
1870— contd	January 11		Dickens begins 12 farewell readings at St. James's Hall.	establishment of Board Schools. First Caesarean operation performed. Millais paints *The Boyhood of Raleigh*. Delibes's music for *Coppélia* performed. Smetana's *The Bartered Bride* performed.
	March 9	Dickens received by Queen Victoria at Buckingham Palace.		Publications: Spencer's *Principles of Psychology*; D. G. Rossetti's *Poems*.
	March 15		Dickens gives final reading at St. James's Hall.	
	April 1		First number of *Drood* appears.	
	April 30	Daniel Maclise dies.	Dickens writing *Drood*.	
		Dickens attends Royal Academy Dinner and returns thanks for 'Literature', paying tribute to the recently-dead Maclise.		
	May	Dickens dines with Motley, American Minister, meets Disraeli at dinner at Lord Stanhope's, breakfasts with Gladstone. He is obliged to refuse invitation to attend Queen's ball with Mamie, because of illness. Dines with Lord Houghton, in company with Prince of Wales and King of the Belgians.		
	May 29	Dickens writes last letter to Forster.		
	June 7	Dickens drives from Gad's Hill to Cobham with Georgina Hogarth and walks in Cobham Park; expresses to her his desire to be buried at Rochester.		
	June 8	Dickens taken ill after a day of writing *Drood*.		
	June 9	Dickens dies of cerebral haemorrhage.	*Drood* is left unfinished.	
	June 14	(Buried in Poets' Corner, Westminster Abbey.)		
	August 12		First bound publication of *Drood*.	
	September		Sixth and last extant part of *Drood* appears.	

DICKENS AND HIS CIRCLE

THE FAMILY, FRIENDS AND ASSOCIATES

MOST INFLUENTIAL UPON DICKENS'S

WORKS AND LIFE

DICKENS AND HIS CIRCLE

Agassis, Jean Louis Rodolph (1807–73). Swiss American naturalist, geologist and teacher, the son of the Protestant pastor of Motier, Switzerland. At Erlangen he took the degree of Doctor of Philosophy and at Munich that of Doctor of Medicine. The study of fish-forms became his life-work, and he travelled widely to gather material for his important works *Recherches sur les Poissons Fossiles* and *Études Critiques sur les Mollusces,* and other volumes of scientific research. When Dickens visited America on his last reading tour Agassis was one of the notabilities introduced to him, and was present, with other American friends, when he left Boston for New York in December 1867.

Ainsworth, William Harrison (1805–82): Trained for the law, he became a publisher in 1826. His first novel, *Rookwood,* 1834, was an immediate success. He edited *Bentley's Miscellany,* 1840–2, and was the first professional writer to invite Dickens to his house as a fellow-author. His afternoon parties were a meeting-point for celebrities from the worlds of art and literature, and were often attended by Dickens. He wrote thirty-nine novels, mainly historical.

Andersen, Hans Christian (1805–75): After a varied career in Denmark as singer, dancer, and schoolmaster, he turned to literature and produced a successful novel in 1835. Later that year the first instalment of his *Fairy Tales* was published in Copenhagen and continued to appear until 1872, bringing him fame throughout Europe. In 1847 and 1857 he stayed with the Dickens family in England, and was one of Dickens's most ardent admirers.

Austin, Henry (d. 1861): Architect, and husband of Dickens's sister Letitia, he surveyed and gave advice on Dickens's purchases of Tavistock House and Gad's Hill. Skilled as an artist, he painted portraits of Maria Beadnell during Dickens's courtship of her.

Austin, Mrs. Henry (Letitia Mary, *née* **Dickens)** (1816–93): Younger sister of Dickens, she was a delicate child, subject to fits. In 1837 she married Henry Austin, architect and artist. Her husband's death left her in straitened circumstances, and Dickens obtained for her a pension of £60 a year as widow of the Secretary to the London Sanitary Commission. After Dickens's death his sister-in-law, Georgina Hogarth, continued to help Letitia.

Barham, Richard Harris (1788–1845): Author of *The Ingoldsby Legends* under the pen-name of Thomas Ingoldsby; minor canon of St. Paul's, 1821, divinity lecturer at St. Paul's and vicar of St. Faith's, London, 1842. Literary adviser to Bentley, 1839–43. The *Legends* were printed in *Bentley's Miscellany* and the *New Monthly Magazine*. Barham, born in Canterbury, was a friend of Dickens and Forster – 'the cordial Thomas Ingoldsby' – and shared Dickens's love for the supernatural, appreciating particularly 'The Chimes', of which, at his request, Dickens gave a second private reading in 1844.

Barrow, Charles (1759–1826): Father of Elizabeth Barrow and father-in-law of John Dickens. At the time of John Dickens's marriage to his daughter, Barrow was 'Chief Conductor of Monies in Town' at the Navy Pay Office, being responsible for the conveyance of money under armed guard to the ports of Plymouth, Portsmouth, Sheerness, and Chatham. Suspicion of dishonesty led to criminal proceedings being brought against him, and he admitted his guilt, pleading the heavy expenses of a family of ten children and his own ill-health. In 1810 he left England without repaying the sum he had embezzled.

Barrow, Edward (1798–1869): Son of Charles Barrow, younger brother of John Henry Barrow, and uncle of Charles Dickens. He married Janet Ross the miniaturist, who possibly provided some of the characteristics of Miss La Creevy in *Nicholas Nickleby*. She painted the earliest authentic portrait of Dickens.

Barrow, Elizabeth: See **Dickens, Mrs. John.**

Barrow, John Henry (1796–1858): Brother of Elizabeth Barrow (1789–1863). A Barrister-at-Law of Gray's Inn, he founded and edited the *Mirror of Parliament,* for which his brother Edward Barrow, his brother-in-law John Dickens and his nephew Charles became parliamentary reporters. He taught Dickens shorthand by the Gurney system. He was the author of *The Battle of Talavera,* an epic poem in the style of Scott, was a specialist in Indian affairs, and at the time of the trial of Queen Caroline was a Doctors' Commons reporter on the staff of *The Times*. When Charles Dickens became editor of the *Daily News* he appointed his uncle sub-editor.

Barrow, Thomas Culliford (?1793–1857): Uncle of Dickens. In 1805, aged 12, he became a clerk in the Navy Pay Office, and became friendly with a colleague, John Dickens, who later married Barrow's sister Elizabeth. He became head of the Prize Branch at a salary of £710 a year.

Beadnell, Anne: Second daughter of George

Beadnell, she married Dickens's friend Henry Kolle in 1833.

Beadnell, Maria (1810–86), later Mrs. Henry Winter: Youngest daughter of George Beadnell. Dickens was introduced to her family about 1830. He fell violently in love with Maria, but her parents disapproved of him as being young and irresponsible, and he was forbidden the house, while Maria was sent to a finishing school abroad. The courtship was later resumed, but ended by Maria. Dickens portrayed her as Dora in *David Copperfield* and, after meeting her again in 1855, when she had become middle-aged and matronly, as the ridiculous Flora Finching of *Little Dorrit*.

Beard, Dr. Francis Carr (1814–93): Thomas Beard's youngest brother; studied medicine at London University, M.R.C.S. in 1838, F.R.C.S. 1853. Dickens does not appear to have written to or consulted him much between the 1830s and 1859, after which date Beard became his regular medical attendant; he was at Dickens's death-bed.

Beard, Thomas (1807–91): Journalist, sometimes called Dickens's oldest friend; their friendship lasted until Dickens's death. Beard came of a family of brewers. A fellow shorthand-writer of Dickens when he entered the gallery of the House of Commons, he joined the *Morning Herald* about 1832 and in 1834 moved to the *Morning Chronicle*, where he was soon joined by Dickens. The two travelled the country widely as reporters, and Beard thought that 'there never *was* such a short-hand writer' as Dickens. He was best man at Dickens's wedding, godfather to Charley, Dickens's eldest son, and close friend of the family. To Dickens he was always 'Tom'.

Bentley, Richard (1794–1871): Publisher who went into partnership with Henry Colburn in 1829, but subsequently became his professional rival. He started *Bentley's Miscellany* with Dickens as editor in 1837. After some dissension over contractual matters Dickens agreed to edit a life of Grimaldi for Bentley. Despite other differences between them, the two men remained personally friendly, according to Forster, but it seems probable that Dickens never got over a certain dislike and distrust of Bentley, whom he had once called 'a nefarious rascal who expected to publish serials for his own benefit and authors to acquiesce in toiling to make him rich'. He founded the firm of Richard Bentley & Son.

Blackmore, Edward: Partner in the firm of Ellis & Blackmore, Gray's Inn, and Dickens's first employer. 'I was well acquainted with his parents,' Blackmore wrote, 'and being then in practice in Gray's Inn, they asked me if I could find employment for him. He was a bright, clever-looking youth, and I took him as a clerk.' Dickens worked for a salary of 13s. 6d., rising to 15s. a week. Blackmore noticed several incidents which had taken place in his offices making their appearance in *Pickwick* and *Nickleby*, and well re-called Dickens's passion for acting at minor theatres.

Blessington, Marguerite, Countess of (1789–1849): Born Margaret Power, she married in 1804 Captain Maurice St. Leger Farmer, separating from him after a few unhappy months. In 1818, after his death, she married Charles John Gardiner, first Earl of Blessington, and travelled with him on the Continent, returning, a widow once more, to London in 1831, after living in Paris for some time and making the acquaintance of Byron. She was accompanied by Alfred, Count D'Orsay, who had been married to and separated from Lady Harriet Gardiner, her step-daughter. Their *ménage* at Gore House, Kensington, gave rise to widespread scandal, and they were cold-shouldered by many leaders of London society, though artists, wits, dandies, politicians, scholars and men of letters flocked around them. Dickens was one of these, and met at her salon Walter Savage Landor, the young Disraeli, Bulwer-Lytton, Macready, and Harrison Ainsworth, among many others. He first met her about 1836, soon becoming a close friend of both her and D'Orsay. She edited the *Book of Beauty* and *The Keepsake* and wrote novels and memoirs. Ruined by extravagant entertaining, she was bankrupted in 1849 and fled to Paris with Count D'Orsay, dying there that summer. In July 1856 Dickens wrote to Landor, 'There in Paris ... I found Marguerite Power and little Nelly (Lady Blessington's nieces) living with their mother and a pretty sister, in a very small, neat apartment, and working (as Marguerite told me) very hard for a living. All that I saw of them filled me with respect, and revived the tenderest remembrances of Gore House.' Brilliant and beautiful, she was one of the most notable of London hostesses. Her portrait by Lawrence is in the Wallace Collection, Manchester Square, London.

Boyle, Mary (1810–90): Daughter of the Commissioner of Sheerness Dockyard, and niece of Lord Cork and of Mrs. Richard Watson of Rockingham Castle. A socialite and wit, her love of the theatre brought her into the Dickens circle of amateur players and she acted in many of his productions, often playing opposite him. To Dickens she was dearest 'Meery' for the twenty years of their close friendship.

'Boz': See **Dickens, Charles John Huffam.**

Bradbury & Evans: William Bradbury and Frederick Mullet Evans became partners in 1830 in the London publishing firm who replaced Chapman & Hall as Dickens's publishers in 1844. He broke with them in 1858 because of the refusal of *Punch*, of which they were the proprietors, to publish his 'separation document' denying the rumours of his attachment to Ellen Ternan. Bessie, Evans's daughter, married Charles Dickens junior.

Brown, Anne: Later Anne Cornelius. Maid in Dickens family from 1842 to sometime in the 1860s, she was held in great affection by Dickens. Before his separation from his wife she was personal maid to Catherine Dickens. After her marriage she asked Georgina Hogarth and Mamie Dickens for financial help during her husband's illness, and they raised a handsome subscription for her.

Browne, Hablôt Knight ('Phiz') (1815–82): Water-colour painter and book illustrator. His first illustration for Dickens was for 'Sunday under Three Heads' in 1836, followed by *Pickwick*. He continued to illustrate for Dickens for twenty-three years, ten of the novels being illustrated by him in etching or in wood-engraving. *A Tale of Two Cities* was the last book for which he drew, before being succeeded by Marcus Stone. His drawings are notable for grotesquerie and strong characterisation – caricatures rather than depictions of real life. His pseudonym 'Phiz' was chosen to match with the author's 'Boz'.

Bulwer, Edward: See Lytton.

Burdett-Coutts, Angela Georgina (1814–1906): Youngest daughter of Sir Francis Burdett, fifth Baronet, and his wife Sophia Coutts, in 1837 she assumed the additional surname of Coutts upon inheriting the great fortune of her maternal grandfather, the banker Thomas Coutts. Her father's social circle, as an eminent politician and reformer, included such famous men as Byron, Samuel Rogers, Moore, Wordsworth, and Dickens. The young heiress, who later became Baroness Burdett-Coutts, devoted her life to philanthropy, giving her time and wealth to such causes as education of the poor, the prevention of cruelty to children and animals, and the reclamation of prostitutes, in which cause she worked closely with Dickens. Their friendship lasted from about 1835 until his death, and their collaboration in good works until 1855, Dickens acting as unofficial almoner and secretary.

Burnett, Henry (1811–93): Singer, music teacher, and brother-in-law of Dickens. His character was influenced by his early life in the care of a deeply religious dissenter grandmother. Later he lived with his father in Brighton, and at the age of ten or thereabouts sang before George IV and his court at the Pavilion. Studied music with the organist of the Chapel Royal, entered the Royal Academy of Music in March 1832, met Fanny Dickens, with whom he sang in several concerts 1835–6, and married her in 1837. He took over from Braham the part of Squire Norton in *The Village Coquettes*, and in 1838 joined Macready's company at Covent Garden, but his inbred religious scruples soon made him doubt the propriety of the professional stage, and he left it in 1841, never afterwards entering a theatre.

Burnett, Mrs. Henry: See Dickens, Frances Elizabeth.

Carlyle, Mrs. Jane Baillie Welsh (1801–66): Born at Haddington, Scotland, she was a brilliant and beautiful young woman with a talent for versifying. She married Thomas Carlyle in 1826. Their home in Cheyne Row, Chelsea, became a centre for the literary ladies of her time and for literary society in general. Dickens admired her immensely and said of her 'none of the writing women come near her'.

Carlyle, Thomas (1795–1881): Essayist and historian. Scots-born, he came to London in 1831 with his wife Jane Welsh Carlyle. He first met Dickens in 1840 and a warm friendship began which lasted until Dickens's death, in spite of Carlyle's occasional criticisms. His *French Revolution,* published in 1837, made

his reputation, and his Collected Works appeared in 1857–8.

Cattermole, George (1800–68): Painter, exhibited at the Royal Academy 1819–27. A prolific book-illustrator, he was invited by Dickens to illustrate, together with 'Phiz', *Master Humphrey's Clock*. This was followed by *The Old Curiosity Shop* and *Barnaby Rudge,* the best-known of these drawings on wood being the church (Tong, Shropshire) which saw the end of Little Nell's travels, the scene of her deathbed, and the Maypole Inn in *Barnaby Rudge*. Cattermole was notable for his romanticism of style and the quaint elaboration of detail with which he fantasised ordinary buildings and scenes. From 1850 onwards he painted in oils, chiefly Biblical subjects.

Chapman, Edward (1804–80): With William Hall, of 186 Strand, bookseller and publisher from 1830. Chapman, son of a Richmond solicitor, was the more literary of the partners. It was he who commissioned Dickens to write the series of sketches which became *Pickwick Papers*. Also published *Nicholas Nickleby,* first complete edition of *Sketches by Boz, Master Humphrey's Clock,* incorporating *The Old Curiosity Shop* and *Barnaby Rudge, American Notes, Martin Chuzzlewit,* and 'The Chimes'. After this Dickens broke with the firm and became associated with the printers Bradbury & Evans. Chapman & Hall also published works for the Brownings, Lord Lytton, Trollope, and Meredith.

Chapman, Frederic (1823–95): Publisher, and cousin of Edward Chapman. He became a partner in the house of Chapman & Hall in 1847 and head of the firm in 1864.

Clarke, Mrs. Charles Cowden (Mary Victoria) (1809–98): Daughter of Vincent Novello, married Charles Cowden Clarke in 1828. Produced the *Complete Concordance to Shakespeare,* published in monthly parts 1844–5. Lived in Italy from 1856. She became a friend and admirer of Dickens through amateur theatricals and wrote of him in her *Recollections of Writers,* 1878.

Colburn, Henry (d. 1855): Publisher and magazine proprietor. He started a number of London magazines, 1814–29, kept a circulating library in 1816, and brought out a library of modern standard novelists, 1835–41. After an unsatisfactory partnership with Richard Bentley, he went into competition with him. Forster married Colburn's widow Eliza Ann in 1856, to Dickens's amused astonishment: 'I have the most prodigious, overwhelming, crushing, astounding, blinding, deafening, pulverising, scarifying secret, of which Forster is the hero ... after I knew it (from himself) this morning, I lay down flat as if an engine and tender had fallen on me.'

Collins, Charles Allston (1828–73): Son of William Collins, R.A., and brother of Wilkie Collins. Became a Pre-Raphaelite, exhibited at the Royal Academy, published essays and novels. Married Dickens's daughter Katey in 1860, and designed the famous green cover for *Edwin Drood* and some sample illustrations, but was prevented by ill-health from continuing the work.

Collins, Mrs. Charles Allston: See **Dickens, Kate Macready.**

Collins, William Wilkie (1824–89): Called to the bar in 1851, but turned to authorship. Contributed to *Household Words* from 1855. Collaborated with Dickens in *The Lazy Tour of Two Idle Apprentices* and 'A Message from the Sea'; contributed *The Woman in White* to *All the Year Round*. Wrote, with Dickens, 'No Thoroughfare', 1867, by which time he had become a close friend of, and a strong influence upon, Dickens. His later novels include *Armadale* and *The Moonstone*.

Cornelius, Mrs.: See **Brown, Anne.**

Cornwall, Barry: See **Procter, Bryan Waller.**

Cruikshank, George (1792–1878): Artist and caricaturist, son of Isaac Cruikshank, and brother of Robert, also artists. After an early career of caricaturing contemporary events and illustrating books, including the Grimms' *Popular Tales,* he was commissioned to illustrate *Sketches by Boz,* and later *Oliver Twist*. His drawings were essentially caricatures rather than portraits, comedy and drama being more conspicuous in them than beauty. Dickens, in an 1847 revival of the adventures of Mrs. Gamp, published in Forster's *Life,* made her speak of 'the great George'. Mrs. Gamp sees 'the wery man a-making pictures of me on his thumb nail, at the winder . . . a gentleman with a large shirt-collar and a hook nose, and an eye like one of Mr. Sweedlepipes's hawks, and long locks of hair, and wiskers that I wouldn't have no lady as I was engaged to meet suddenly a-turning round a corner.' In 1847 Cruikshank published *The Bottle,* and in 1848 *The Drunkard's Children,* a series of propagandist illustrations of the dangers of drink, against which he was now campaigning hotly. His *magnum opus* (1862) was *The Worship of Bacchus: or, the Drinking Customs of Society*. Dickens admired and remained friendly with him, in spite of Cruikshank's strange claims to have written *Oliver Twist* and originated *Pickwick*.

Dickens, Alfred D'Orsay Tennyson (1845–1912): Dickens's fourth son. 'A chopping boy' was his father's description of him at birth. Count D'Orsay and Tennyson stood godfathers to him. He was soon nicknamed 'Skittles'. Dickens attempted to press him into an army career, for which he was manifestly unsuited. After two years of work in a London China house he sailed for Australia at the age of 20, leaving a pile of unpaid bills behind him and confirming his father's fears that his sons were irresponsible and extravagant. In 1875 he married the 'Belle of Melbourne', Jessie Devlin, who was tragically killed in a carriage accident in 1879, leaving two daughters. Alfred did 'extremely well in the money way' with the London and Australian Agency Company Ltd., and after his father's death travelled in England and America lecturing on Dickens's life and works. He suffered from a weak heart and died suddenly in New York at the end of a lecture tour.

Dickens, Alfred Lamert (1822–60): Dickens's younger brother. Trained as a civil engineer, he became a sanitary inspector. His death left his widow Helen and her five children in straitened circumstances, for Alfred had been a bad manager of money. Dickens, despite other pressing commitments, undertook the support and housing of the family, and found a house for them on Haverstock Hill. Finding responsibility for Helen too much, he turned to his sister-in-law Georgina Hogarth for help with her and her affairs for, he said, 'I really can not bear the irritation she causes me.'

Dickens, Augustus (1827–66): Dickens's youngest brother. It was he whom Dickens, in honour of the Vicar of Wakefield, had nicknamed 'Moses', which facetiously pronounced through the nose became 'Boses', and ultimately 'Boz'. 'Boz was a very familiar household word to me, long before I was an author, and so I came to adopt it', Dickens told Forster. Augustus's life proved a disappointment to his brother: Thomas Chapman, of Chapman & Hall, found him 'City employment' about 1847, but he gave it up and deserted his blind wife to elope to America with another woman. From there he wrote to Dickens for funds, and died impoverished in Chicago, leaving his relict and several children penniless. 'Poor fellow! a sad business altogether,' said Dickens, and undertook the support not only of them but of Augustus's deserted wife. Until Dickens's death Augustus's eldest son, Bertram, received £50 a year.

Dickens, Charles Culliford Boz (1837–96): Dickens's eldest son and first child, known as Charley. For a time he worked in Baring's Bank. In 1860 he went to China to buy tea, and on his return in 1861 set himself up as an Eastern merchant. Dickens, hypercritical of his sons, thought Charley 'wanting in a sense of perseverance', and strongly disapproved of his marriage to Bessie Evans, daughter of one of the partners in the firm of Bradbury & Evans, with whom Dickens had quarrelled. In 1868 the papermill company which Charley had been running in association with Evans failed, and he was bankrupted. Dickens took him into the offices of *All the Year Round* as sub-editor. He attended Dickens during the final public readings when his health was rapidly failing. After his father's death Charley bought Gad's Hill, but was forced to give it up because of illness. He undertook reading tours in imitation of his father, whose works he edited, and died, as his father had done, of a stroke.

Dickens, Charles John Huffam ('Boz'): Born 1812 in Landport, Portsmouth; married Catherine Hogarth in 1836; died at Gad's Hill Place, Kent, in 1870. (See Time Chart.)

Dickens, Mrs. Charles John Huffam (Catherine) (1815–79): Eldest daughter of George and Georgina Hogarth, she was born in Scotland and came to England with her family in 1834. Through her father's journalistic connections she was introduced to Dickens, who was then writing sketches for the *Morning Chronicle,* of which her father was music critic. In April 1836 they were married. Dickens found Kate an incompatible partner, blamed her, somewhat unreasonably, for the birth of their ten children, and turned over the housekeeping to her sister Georgina. In 1858 their widely-publicised separation took place. From that time until Dickens's death they remained estranged, Catherine living with her eldest son, Charley, but she remained attached and loyal to her husband and to his memory until her own death from cancer.

Dickens, Dora Annie (1850-1): Dickens's youngest daughter. Born at Devonshire Terrace, she was named after David Copperfield's wife. Frail from birth, she died of convulsions aged only eight months, while her mother was recuperating from illness at Malvern. She is buried, with Dickens's parents, in Highgate cemetery.

Dickens, Edward Bulwer Lytton ('Plorn') (1852-1902): The tenth and last child of Dickens and Catherine, he was nicknamed 'the Plornishgenter' or 'Plornishmaroon tigunter', later shortened to 'Plorn'. Sensitive and shrinking by nature, he found Rochester High School too large and confusing, and was sent for private tuition at Tunbridge Wells. In 1868 he sailed for Australia to join his brother Alfred, but never prospered, having inherited his grandfather's spend-thrift and unworldly nature.

Dickens, Frances Elizabeth (Fanny) (1810-48): Dickens's elder sister. In 1823 she became a pupil at the Royal Academy of Music. Dickens, working at the blacking warehouse, was both proud and jealous at seeing her receive a prize there. She studied the piano under Moscheles and singing under Crivelli, winning the Academy's silver medal in June 1824. John Dickens found himself unable to pay her fees, and she was forced to leave the Academy in 1827, but later returned as pupil-teacher. About 1832 she met Henry Burnett, also studying there, and married him in 1837. On leaving the Academy in 1834 she was made Associate Honorary Member, a distinction kept for ex-students of exceptional ability. Performed at public concerts 1835-7. Her delicate, deformed son was the model for Tiny Tim and Paul Dombey, and she appears as Scrooge's sister in 'A Christmas Carol' and as herself in 'A Child's Dream of a Star'. She died of consumption aged only thirty-eight.

Dickens, Francis Jeffrey (Frank) (1844-86): Charles Dickens's third son. He aspired to become doctor, gentleman farmer and journalist, but none satisfied him and he joined the Bengal Mounted Police. Returning to England on leave in 1871, he overstayed, fell into debt, and after some drifting joined the Northwest Mounted Police. He resigned his commission in 1886 and died the same year.

Dickens, Frederick William (1820-68): Dickens's younger brother. Lived with Dickens before his marriage, and afterwards at Doughty Street. Dickens procured a clerkship for him in the Secretary's office of the Custom House. He joined the Dickens family on a Continental tour in 1844, and narrowly escaped drowning at Albaro. After Frederick's death Dickens commented, 'It was a wasted life, but God forbid that one should be hard upon it, or upon anything in this world that is not deliberately and coldly wrong.'

Dickens, Henry Fielding (1849-1933): Dickens's sixth son, known as Harry. Educated at Boulogne and Rochester, he edited with his brother 'Plorn' a small newspaper called *The Gad's Hill Gazette*, learning to operate a printing-press in the process. More robust and enterprising than his brothers, he became a notable sportsman. His early manifestations of a poetic gift were suppressed by his father. He became Head Censor at Wimbledon, organised the Higham Cricket Club, entered Trinity Hall, Cambridge, and to his father's delight won two scholarships and an essay prize. In 1873 he was called to the bar and started on a brilliant career. In 1876 he married Marie Thérèse Louise Roche. He undertook readings of his father's works for charity in 1904 with considerable success. The last years of Georgina Hogarth were cheered by Harry and his wife and two daughters.

Dickens, John (1785-1851): Charles Dickens's father. He married Elizabeth Barrow in 1809, when a clerk in the Navy Pay Office at Portsmouth Dockyard. Later he was transferred to London, and in 1817 to Chatham, transferring again to Somerset House in 1822. Described by a biographer as 'a jovial opportunist with no money sense', he was repeatedly in debt and in 1824 was arrested and imprisoned in the Marshalsea, to his son's humiliation. He returned to the Navy Pay Office, but in 1828 became a parliamentary reporter for the *Morning Herald*, and for the *Mirror of Parliament* of which his brother-in-law J. H. Barrow was editor. His recklessness in money matters continued to be a worry and annoyance to Charles, whose parents spent many years in shabby lodgings until in 1839 he found a cottage for them at Alphington, Devon. Dickens retained throughout his life warm affection and respect for his father, though deploring his unthrifty habits, and depicted him in the character of Wilkins Micawber in *David Copperfield*.

Dickens, Mrs. John (Elizabeth) (1789-1863): Daughter of Charles Barrow. She married John Dickens in 1809 and became the mother of Charles Dickens and seven other children. Although she appears to have devoted much time to cultivating her eldest son's mind and teaching him in early years, her attitude to his employment at Warren's Blacking Warehouse caused him to turn against her, and cool relations seem to have existed between them until her death. Dickens caricatured her as Mrs. Nickleby.

Dickens, Kate Macready (1839-1929): Dickens's second daughter; the actor Macready stood godfather to her. Pretty and spirited, she earned herself the nickname of 'Lucifer Box' because of her fiery temper. She had a talent for art and attended Bedford College for art lessons. The only one of his children to stand up to Dickens, she sided with her mother over the separation in 1858, and when she married Charles Allston Collins Dickens broke down and declared that 'but for me Katey would not have left home'. She appears to have entered upon the marriage more as a means to independence than because she loved Collins. She was the last person to talk at length with her father on the day before his death, and afterwards recorded something of the conversation. After Charles

Collins's death she married Carlo Perugini, a painter, as Collins had been. At the age of thirty-seven she gave birth to a son, who died aged seven months. She lived to a ripe and lively old age, and was the only member of Dickens's family to disclose any semi-intimate information about him to a biographer.

Dickens, Letitia Mary: See **Austin, Mrs. Henry.**

Dickens, Mary Angela (1838–96): Dickens's eldest daughter. Always known as 'Mamie', she was called after Mary Hogarth, who had died tragically the year before her birth. Dickens's nickname for her was 'Mild Glo'ster', a tribute to her gentleness, a strong contrast to her sister Katey's fire. She remained with Dickens until his death, taking second place to Georgina Hogarth as housekeeper and companion, and lived with Georgina afterwards. She left a book of memoirs, *My Father as I Recall Him,* and collaborated with Georgina in the editing and publication of Dickens's letters.

Dickens, Sydney Smith Haldimand (1847–72): Dickens's fifth son, nicknamed 'Ocean Spectre', later modified to 'Hoshen Peck', because of his curiously unchildlike way of gazing out to sea during his first holiday at Broadstairs. He may have contributed something to the character of Paul Dombey. Always a favourite with his father, he delighted Dickens by embarking on a naval career and returning from a successful examination 'all eyes and gold buttons', to be referred to thereafter as 'The Admiral'. In 1861 he gave Dickens further satisfaction by obtaining an excellent appointment in H.M.S. *Orlando,* but later showed ominous signs of the extravagance characteristic of his grandfather and brothers. While in America he appealed to his father for financial help, but Dickens, exasperated into sternness, refused and informed Sydney that he would not be received at Gad's Hill on his return to England. Aged only twenty-five, he died at sea aboard the *Malta* on his way home for sick leave. Georgina Hogarth wrote that 'poor Sydney's life was his Father's most bitter trial and grief for several years before his death'.

Dickens, Walter Landor (1841–63): Dickens's second son, and the first he was to name after a literary celebrity, though he was facetiously known as 'Young Skull' in childhood. Educated at Boulogne and Wimbledon, he was nominated at the age of sixteen, through the influence of Angela Burdett-Coutts, to a cadetship in the East India Company. Two years later he was promoted to the rank of lieutenant in the 42nd Highlanders, but got into debt, jeopardising his career. Soon after his family heard that he was being sent home on sick leave the news arrived that he was dead of an aortic aneurysm. Later in the year unpaid accounts were received from India, for the harassed Dickens to settle.

Dolby, George: Dickens's reading manager from 1866 to 1870. Devoted to Dickens, he was a large, amiable, highly competent man hampered in his business dealings by a speech impediment. He sustained the ailing Dickens through the English tours of 1866 and 1867, the arduous American tour of 1867–8, and

the 'Final Farewell' tour in the United Kingdom of 1868–70. After Dickens's retirement from his touring life Dolby was a frequent visitor to Gad's Hill, and left a detailed and rapturous account of his friendship with his beloved 'Chief', and of the tours, in the book *Charles Dickens as I Knew Him,* published in 1885.

D'Orsay, Alfred Guillaume Gabriel, Count (1801–52): Artist; served in the Bourbons' bodyguard in France, visited England for the coronation of George IV, 1821, became a leader of fashion in London, and gave rise to scandal because of his *ménage à trois* with Marguerite, Countess of Blessington, and her husband. After Blessington's death he presided at her fashionable soirées at Gore House, Kensington, becoming the friend of other dandies such as Bulwer and the young Disraeli. When Lady Blessington became bankrupt in 1849 she and D'Orsay fled to France. He was appointed director of the fine arts by Prince Louis Napoleon in 1852, shortly before his death. Dickens, in youth 'a highflyer at fashion', modelled himself on the elegantly flamboyant D'Orsay, to whom he had probably been introduced by Serjeant Talfourd in 1836.

Doyle, Richard (1824–83): Artist and caricaturist, son of John Doyle ('H.B.'), also famous for his political caricatures. He designed the cover of *Punch,* contributed cartoons and *Manners and Customs of ye Englyshe* to it, but resigned in consequence of its hostility to Roman Catholicism in 1850. With other artists he illustrated 'The Chimes' in a typically delicate and fantastic manner, and later illustrated Thackeray's *The Newcomes.* He was the uncle of Sir Arthur Conan Doyle.

Egg, Augustus Leopold (1816–63): Subject-painter, student at the Royal Academy, 1836, later an exhibitor. He acted in amateur theatricals with Dickens and designed some costumes for them. A comfortably-situated bachelor, he developed an attachment to Dickens's sister-in-law Georgina Hogarth, and Dickens did what he could to recommend Egg to Georgina. But Georgina declined to 'brighten up a good little man's house' as Dickens wished, and both died unmarried. Egg painted a charming portrait of Georgina sewing, commissioned by Dickens.

Ellis & Blackmore: See **Blackmore, Edward.**

Emerson, Ralph Waldo (1803–82): American poet and essayist, born in Boston of a family containing seven New England church ministers. After studying divinity at Cambridge, Mass., he was 'approbated to preach' by the Middlesex Association of Ministers; but doubts about the sacramental validity of the Lord's Supper caused him to abandon the formal ministry, though he continued to preach throughout his life. Thomas Carlyle introduced Emerson's essays into England, and Emerson published Carlyle's books in America. He turned to a lecturing career, and became leader of the transcendental school of philosophy – 'the Sage of Concord'. When Dickens visited America on his last reading tour Emerson was one of the famous men to become acquainted with him.

Evans, Bessie: See under **Dickens, Charles Culliford Boz.**

Evans, Frederick Mullet: See **Bradbury & Evans.**

Fagin, Bob: A boy who worked at Warren's Blacking Factory with Dickens in 1824. An orphan, he lived with his brother-in-law, a waterman. Dickens was at first deeply humiliated to find himself in the company of Bob and other boys of his kind, but grew to like him for his good nature. When Dickens had a bad attack of the pain in his side which often troubled him, 'Bob filled empty blacking-bottles with hot water, and applied relays of them to my side, half the day.' Bob then insisted of escorting Dickens home, but Dickens, too proud to let his friend know that his father was in the Marshalsea, 'shook hands with him on the steps of a house near Southwark Bridge on the Surrey side, making believe that I lived there. As a finishing piece of reality in case of his looking back, I knocked at the door . . . and asked, when the woman opened it, if that was Mr. Robert Fagin's house.'

Fechter, Charles (1822–79): Swiss actor-manager, first seen by Dickens in London when he was playing in *Hamlet* and *Ruy Blas*. In Paris Dickens was immensely impressed by the actor's performances in *Le Maître de Ravenswood* and *La Dame aux Camélias*. 'By Heavens!' he exclaimed, 'the man who can do that can do anything.' He was equally enthusiastic about Fechter's Othello, though his opinion was not that of many people, who considered him a mediocre player. Fechter became lessee of the Lyceum Theatre in London in 1863 with Dickens, by now his personal friend, as financial backer. In 1868 he played the leading role of Jules Obenreizer in Wilkie Collins's and Dickens's drama *No Thoroughfare*, adapted from the Christmas story written by them in collaboration. It was Fechter who presented Dickens with the Swiss chalet which became his writing-place in the garden at Gad's Hill (it is now preserved at Rochester Museum).

Field, Inspector Charles F.: Inspector in the R. Division (Greenwich) of the Metropolitan Constabulary in 1833, subsequently promoted to the Detective Force. Dickens portrays him as Detective Wield in *Reprinted Pieces*: 'The Detective Police', 'Three "Detective" Anecdotes', and 'On Duty with Inspector Field' (by this time his thin disguise had been abandoned). He took Dickens on conducted tours of London's underworld. Dickens drew a fairly close portrait of him as Inspector Bucket in *Bleak House*.

Fields, James T. (d. 1880): American publisher and editor, who appears to have met Dickens for the first time in 1859, when he attempted to persuade him to undertake reading tours in America, a project which was realised in 1867. Dickens stayed with Fields and his family in Boston and became friendly with his wife, Annie. After Dickens's return to England the Fields, with other American visitors, were lavishly entertained by Dickens in London and at Gad's Hill.

Fields, Mrs. James T. (Annie): Wife of Dickens's American publisher. When Dickens met Annie Fields at her Boston home she impressed him as 'a very nice woman, with a rare relish for humour and a most contagious laugh'. They became warm friends, Dickens being encouraged by Annie's sympathetic nature to confide in her to an unusual degree, his confidences apparently including his relationship with Ellen Ternan. When the Fields visited England Annie and Georgina Hogarth became equally friendly, and remained so for the rest of their lives. Annie wrote a biography of her husband after his death. Her unpublished diaries, containing accounts of Dickens's visits, are owned by the Massachusetts Historical Society at Boston.

Fildes, Sir Luke, R.A. (1844–1927): Subject-painter of great popularity in the last quarter of the nineteenth century, his most famous picture was *The Doctor*. When Charles Collins, through illness, was forced to abandon the illustrations for *Edwin Drood*, Fildes was called in and given by Dickens some guarded information about the solution of that mystery. Collins had set the story in the earlier years of Victoria's reign, but Fildes dressed his characters in contemporary (i.e. 1870) clothing.

Fitzgerald, Percy: One of 'Dickens's young men' and among his most ardent admirers and disciples, the Irish Fitzgerald was a frequent visitor to Gad's Hill in the 1860s and left glowing accounts of life there in his *Life of Charles Dickens*, published in 1905, and *Memoirs of an Author*, published in 1895. He was romantically interested in Mamie Dickens but, Dickens lamented, 'I am grievously disappointed that Mary can by no means be induced to think as highly of him as I do.' His Catholicism may have been a possible barrier to marriage with him in Mamie's eyes. After Dickens's death Fitzgerald drew upon himself the anger of the Dickens family by publishing a Dickens letter connecting John Dickens with Micawber, and an article speculating on the relationship between Dickens and his sister-in-law Mary Hogarth. In 1900 Fitzgerald founded the Boz Club, which met annually on Dickens's birthday, the celebration taking the form of a gala dinner.

Forster, John (1812–76): Historian and biographer, he was one of Dickens's closest friends. In 1843 he was a barrister of the Inner Temple, but had already embarked on a literary career, being dramatic critic to *The Examiner* and contributing *Lives of the Statesmen of the Commonwealth* to Lardner's *Cyclopaedia*. Editor of several journals, friend of Lamb, Leigh Hunt, and many of the Dickens circle, he constituted himself Boswell to Dickens's Johnson, and in 1872–4 produced *The Life of Charles Dickens*, dedicated to his god-daughters, Mamie and Katey Dickens. A detailed and valuable record of Dickens's life, providing essential material for later biographers, it slides over all remotely scandalous episodes, omitting much from the 'letters of unexampled candour and truthfulness' which he had received from his friend, thus presenting an idealised rather than an accurate portrait. In the later years of Dickens's life Forster maintained a somewhat jealous attitude to Wilkie Collins, by then an intimate of, and a strong influence upon, Dickens. Forster proof-read for Dickens, and claimed to know the truth of Dickens's solution to *The Mystery of*

Edwin Drood. A large, bluff, vociferous man, Forster was known to Dickens and other friends as 'Fuz'. He was probably the original of Podsnap in *Our Mutual Friend*.

Gaskell, Mrs. Elizabeth Cleghorn (1810–65): Brought up by her aunt at Knutsford, Cheshire, she later immortalised the town in her novel *Cranford*. She married William Gaskell, a Unitarian minister, in 1832, and wrote her first novel, *Mary Barton*, in 1848. Dickens thought her a very original writer, for whose powers he had a high admiration. She contributed to the first number of *Household Words* in 1850, and continued to be a contributor while writing her later novels and engaging in charitable works in the North of England.

Giles, The Revd. William, F.R.G.S. (1798–1856): Baptist minister and Dickens's first schoolmaster. Educated at St. Aldate's School, Oxford, he took over the 'classical, mathematical, and commercial school' at Chatham, attended by Dickens 1821–2. In 1831 he opened a boarding-school at Patricroft, near Manchester, and after 1837 opened schools in Manchester, Liverpool, and Chester. His scholars in Chatham were locally known as Giles's Cats. He was a liberal, intelligent man who recognised Dickens's quality, christened him 'The Inimitable', and remained friendly with him in later years. Dickens inscribed copies of *Sketches by Boz* and *Pickwick* to Giles, 'from his old and affectionate pupil'.

Grant, William and Daniel: The originals of the Cheeryble brothers in *Nicholas Nickleby*. Scots by birth, in youth the brothers had kept a shop in Bury St. Edmunds, but migrated to Manchester, where they became leading wool- and linen-drapers, famous for their philanthropy. Dickens met them in 1838 when he and Forster were the guests of Gilbert Winter of Stocks House, Manchester, but from Percy Fitzgerald's account it seems that John Dickens knew them much earlier and held them up as an example to his son.

Grip: Dickens admitted that the remarkable raven of *Barnaby Rudge* was based on 'two great originals, of whom I was at different times the proud possessor. The first was in the bloom of his youth when he was discovered in a modest retirement in London by a friend of mine, and given to me. He had from the first . . . "good gifts", which he improved by study and attention in a most exemplary manner.' Grip the First died of eating lead paint left about by workmen. Grip the Second, of Yorkshire origin, was a strong character who specialised in stable language, had no respect for anybody but the cook, and was once met by Dickens 'walking down the middle of a public street, attended by a pretty large crowd, and spontaneously exhibiting the whole of his accomplishments. His gravity under these trying circumstances I can never forget, nor the extraordinary gallantry with which, refusing to be brought home, he defended himself behind a pump, until overpowered by numbers.' After some years Grip the Second died: 'he kept his eyes to the last upon the meat as it roasted, and suddenly turned over on his back with a sepulchral cry of "Cuckoo!" ' Maclise sketched *The Apotheosis of Grip*

(the First) depicting him lying dead, a bird-soul emerging from his beak and ascending to a Heaven full of welcoming bird-angels. Both Grips lived at Devonshire Terrace.

Haldimand, William (1784–1862): Philanthropist, director of the Bank of England, M.P. for Ipswich 1820–6. He gave financial support to the cause of Greek independence, founded the Hortense Hospital at Aix-les-Bains and a blind asylum at Lausanne, where he met Dickens, who was deeply interested in the institution and visited it often.

Hall, William: See **Chapman, Edward.**

Harte, Francis Brett (1836–1902): American author who wrote under the name of Bret Harte. His early career was varied, and it was not until he was appointed secretary of the U.S. Mint in California in 1864 that he found time to devote himself to writing. In 1868 he became editor of the *Overland Monthly*, to which he contributed his famous western tale 'The Luck of Roaring Camp', the first of his vivid stories of pioneer life. It was just before this period that he was introduced to Dickens, then on his last American reading tour. After Dickens's death Harte paid him a poetical tribute in the verses 'Dickens in Camp'.

Hogarth, Catherine: See **Dickens, Mrs. Charles John Huffam.**

Hogarth, George (1783–1870): Father of Catherine, Mary, and Georgina Hogarth (and many other children), and father-in-law of Dickens. Educated for the law in Edinburgh, he was admitted to the practice in 1810. In 1814 he married Georgina Thomson, daughter of a musician friend of Burns. The couple moved in musical and literary circles, and when Sir Walter Scott was bankrupted by the failure of his publishing firm, Hogarth became his legal adviser. A violoncellist and composer, he served as joint secretary for the first Edinburgh Musical Festival in 1815, and was music critic for the Edinburgh *Courant*. In 1830 he abandoned the law for journalism, moved to Yorkshire and launched the *Halifax Guardian*, besides founding the Halifax Orchestral Society. In 1834 he moved his family to London and joined the staff of the *Morning Chronicle* as music critic. Here he met the young Dickens, who was writing a series of 'Street Sketches' for that paper, and when an offshoot, the *Evening Chronicle*, was launched, Hogarth asked Dickens for a contribution to the first issue: thus some of the earlier *Sketches by Boz* were commissioned by him. Hogarth also helped him to sell his libretto for *The Village Coquettes*. After a short courtship Dickens married the eldest of the Hogarth girls, Catherine, in 1836. George Hogarth died aged eighty-six, but still active in journalism.

Hogarth, Mrs. George (Georgina) (1793–1863): Wife of George Hogarth. In 1854, when Dickens's marriage was beginning to deteriorate, his relationship with his in-laws did likewise; he complained of Mrs. Hogarth's 'imbecility' and sluttishness, announced himself to be 'dead sick of the Scottish tongue' and found that the sight of his father-in-law at breakfast 'undermined his constitution'. He later became estranged from Mrs. Hogarth and her daughter Helen on the matter of his separation from Catherine.

Hogarth, Georgina (1827–1917): The youngest of the three elder Hogarth sisters introduced to Dickens by their father in 1834. From 1839, when Dickens, his wife and family removed to Devonshire Terrace, Marylebone, Georgina frequently visited them to play with the children. When Dickens and Catherine sailed for America in 1842 Georgina took such a part in the care of the young family they had left behind that Dickens invited her to become a member of the household. She remained with them as housekeeper, organiser, adviser and friend until her brother-in-law's death, and afterwards remained in close touch with his surviving relatives. She has been much blamed for the rift between Dickens and Catherine, and rumours were abroad at the time of the separation in 1858 that Georgina, as well as Ellen Ternan, was Dickens's mistress. Her relationship with Catherine seems to have been ambiguous, but it is supposed that any differences between them were made up before Catherine's death. With Mamie Dickens she edited Dickens's letters for publication, and the rest of her life was dedicated to the clearing of Dickens's reputation and the perpetuation of his memory. To the family she was always 'Aunt Georgy'.

Hogarth, Mary Scott (1819–37): Next in age to Catherine, and seven years older than Georgina, Mary was a pretty, lively girl, with whom Dickens may have been subconsciously in love, although he married her sister. She joined him and his bride when they set up house at Furnival's Inn in 1836, and moved with them to 48 Doughty Street in 1837. Her sudden death after a theatre outing in May of that year shattered Dickens's happiness. He grieved inordinately for her: 'the peace and life of our home – the admired of all for her beauty and excellence . . . she has been to us what we can never replace.' He took a ring from her dead finger and slipped it on his own, wearing it to the end of his life. She haunted his imagination, an ideal of youth and pure beauty, and his undying grief found expression in literary portraits of her as Rose Maylie, Little Nell, and other youthful victims. Her tombstone at Kensal Green bears Dickens's epitaph for her: 'Young, beautiful and good, God in his mercy numbered her with his angels at the early age of seventeen.'

Hood, Thomas (1799–1845): Poet and wit, he began his literary career with contributions to the *London Magazine*, which brought him the acquaintance of Lamb, Hazlitt, and De Quincey. He issued *Whims and Oddities* in 1826–7, became editor of the *Gem*, began the *Comic Annual*, 1830, lived at Coblenz and Ostend for a time, edited the *New Monthly Magazine*, and founded *Hood's Own* and *Hood's Magazine*. He was very friendly with Dickens, of whom he wrote in 1840, 'Boz is a very good fellow'. All his life he was dogged by ill-health and poverty. Dickens often wrote of him as 'poor Hood', and when he received Hood's book *Up the Rhine* for review he told Forster, 'It is rather poor, but I have not said so, because Hood is too, and ill besides.' Hood's most famous poem is 'The Song of the Shirt' and he wrote many punning ballads such as 'Faithless Nellie Gray'.

Huffam, Christopher: Godfather of Dickens. He lived at Limehouse Hole, and was an oar- and block-maker and rigger to His Majesty's Navy. He had come to the notice of the Prince Regent for fitting out a privateer against the French during the Napoleonic Wars, and was reputed to have been rewarded with an honour. He lived, said Forster, 'in a substantial handsome sort of way', and visits to him were among the young Dickens's greatest treats while he was living at Bayham Street in 1822–3. The atmosphere of Limehouse coloured the boy's imagination strongly, familiar as he was with shipping from his days at Chatham, and Huffam himself (sometimes spelt Huffham) probably contributed something to Captain Cuttle's character. Dickens's accomplishment of entertaining the company with comic songs, frequently nautical, was the admiration of one of his godfather's guests, who pronounced the child a 'progidy'.

Hunt, James Henry Leigh (1784–1859): Essayist and poet, friend of Keats, Byron, Moore, Shelley, and Lamb in his youth, and later of Dickens. He edited the *Examiner*, 1808, and the *Reflector*, 1810; was sentenced, with his brother John, to a fine and two years' imprisonment in 1813 for derogatory remarks about the Prince Regent, His literary career was versatile and distinguished and his personal charm considerable. The friendship with Dickens suffered when Hunt heard gossip to the effect that Dickens had based the character of Harold Skimpole in *Bleak House* upon him. Dickens wrote to him explaining that his intention was not to be offensive; he had certainly taken some of Hunt's characteristics and way of speaking in creating Skimpole, but had no intention of identifying him in any way with Skimpole's irresponsibility and dishonesty in money matters. After Hunt's death he published in *All the Year Round* a vindication of himself in the same connection, praising Hunt highly and denying any intention of hurting him.

Irving, Washington (1783–1859): American man of letters, born of an English mother and an Orcadian father. Trained for the law, he deserted it for literature, and when the family business in which he was a sleeping partner was bankrupted he turned to writing as a livelihood. Arriving in England, he became friendly with several prominent literary figures, and was introduced to the publishing firm of John Murray. His many works show a strong English influence, particularly in their style of humour. On his return to America, after extensive foreign travel, he found his name a household word. Dickens first met him on his American visit of 1842, when at the City Hotel, New York, Irving gave the toast of 'Charles Dickens, the Nation's guest, coupled with International Copyright', and observed, 'It is but fair that those who have laurels for their brows should be permitted to browse on their laurels.' (Irving realised, as did few American authors, the importance of the copyright question which so exercised Dickens.) Their correspondence had begun after the publication of *The Old Curiosity*

231

Shop, on which Irving wrote to congratulate Dickens. Many letters between them were destroyed when Dickens embarked upon the ritual burning of his private correspondence. Dickens's summing-up of Irving, after their first meeting, was 'Washington Irving is a *great* fellow. We have laughed most heartily together. He is just the man he ought to be.'

Jerrold, Douglas William (1803–57): Author and noted wit, he practised journalism while still a printer's assistant. He made his reputation as a playwright with *Black-eyed Susan* in 1829. By 1841 he was a constant contributor to *Punch,* and founded *Douglas Jerrold's Shilling Magazine* and *Douglas Jerrold's Weekly Newspaper* in 1845–6. He was on terms of the closest friendship with Dickens, who greatly admired his wit and charm, calling him 'one of the gentlest and most affectionate of men . . . in the company of children and young people he was particularly happy . . . he never was so gay, so sweettempered, and so pleased as then.' Many other tributes were paid to him by contemporaries, but against his charm was offset the bitter and biting quality of his satire. Dickens organised performances of *The Frozen Deep,* Wilkie Collins's play, for the benefit of Jerrold's widow.

Jones, William (1777–1836): Headmaster of Wellington House Academy, Mornington Crescent, London, which Dickens attended from 1824 to 1827. A Welshman, he appears to have been something of a tyrant: Dickens says that he 'was always ruling ciphering books with a bloated mahogany ruler, smiting the palms of offenders with the same diabolical instrument, or viciously drawing a pair of pantaloons tight with one of his large hands and caning the wearer with the other.' He was probably the model for Creakle in *David Copperfield.*

Kent, William Charles: Editor of the *Sun* newspaper and friend of Dickens. He was a particular admirer of Dickens's readings, and after the Final Farewell Reading on 15 March 1870, suggested to him that an accurate record should be made of all the readings given over the years. Dickens agreed, giving Kent *carte blanche* to compile such a record. (The resulting book, *Charles Dickens as a Reader,* published in 1872, was not entirely accurate, and it was left to Walter Dexter to provide a correct one. His 'Mr. Charles Dickens will Read' was published in *The Dickensian,* vols. 37–9, in 1941–3.) One of the last two letters written by Dickens was to Kent: dated 'Wednesday eighth June 1870', it is an apology for not calling on Kent, because of pressure of business, on the following day – the day on which, in fact, his fatal seizure occurred.

Kolle, Henry William (1808–81): Bank clerk. Son of a calico printer and manufacturer of household goods. He and Dickens met at the Beadnells' house about 1830. Kolle became engaged to Anne Beadnell, and Dickens strongly attracted to Maria, Kolle acting as go-between during the courtship. In 1833 he married Anne and by 1846 was a manufacturer of stoves, grates, and ranges in Jermyn Street, St. James's, painting in his spare time. Anne died in May 1836.

Lamert, James: Cousin of Dickens in a step-relationship. Dickens's mother's sister Mary married as her second husband Dr. Matthew Lamert, an army surgeon of Chatham, having joined the Dickens family there after her first husband's death. Lamert's son James, older than Dickens and with a passion for amateur theatricals, infected Dickens with his own enthusiasm and introduced him to the professional theatre at Chatham. In 1822 James was lodging with Dickens and his family at Bayham Street, Camden Town, and was responsible for Dickens's entry into Warren's Blacking Warehouse, which his cousin George Lamert had bought. A quarrel between Dickens's father and James Lamert resulted in Dickens being allowed to leave his hated employment. James's father Dr. Lamert was probably the model for Dr. Slammer in *Pickwick.*

Landon, Letitia Elizabeth ('L.E.L.') (1802–38): Poetess, she published under her initials and enjoyed a certain amount of popularity. In 1831 and 1834 she produced novels, and in 1836 a supposedly autobiographical novel, *Traits and Trials of Early Life.* A member of Lady Blessington's circle, she was frequently at Gore House at the time when Dickens visited there. At one time she was engaged to John Forster, but scandalous rumours about her ended this. In 1838 she married George Maclean, governor of Cape Coast Castle, West Africa, joined him there, and died mysteriously of poisoning.

Landor, Walter Savage (1775–1864): Poet and prolific author of belles-lettres, traveller, and godfather of Dickens's son Walter. In 1840 Dickens and Forster visited Landor at Bath, and Dickens there conceived the idea that was to develop into the character of Little Nell. Landor was immensely charmed by Nell, who became his favourite personage in fiction and, said Forster in his *Life of Landor,* in 'one of those whimsical bursts of comical extravagance out of which arose the fancy of Boythorn' (Dickens is supposed to have modelled Boythorn in *Bleak House* on Landor), he regretted that he had not purchased the house in Bath where the idea came to Dickens 'and then and there . . . burnt it to the ground, to the end that no meaner association should ever desecrate the birthplace of Nell. Then he would pause a little, become conscious of our sense of his absurdity, and break into a thundering peal of laughter.'

Landseer, Sir Edwin Henry (1802–73): Best known for his paintings of animals, he was a favourite of Queen Victoria and Prince Albert and frequently painted their portraits. He received a knighthood in 1850, and completed the lions for Nelson's monument in Trafalgar Square in 1866. A friend of Dickens's from Devonshire Terrace days, he grieved deeply over Dickens's death, somewhat to the surprise of Georgina Hogarth, who felt that 'Edwin was fonder of Charles than Charles of him'. Landseer drew the dog Boxer for 'The Cricket on the Hearth'.

La Rue, Mrs. Emile de: The English wife of a Swiss banker carrying on business in Genoa during the Dickens family's stay there in 1844. Dickens felt a 'magnetic attraction' towards this 'affectionate, excellent little woman', who confided to him that she suffered from alarming delusions. Dickens attempted to cure them by hypnotism, with Mr. de la Rue's co-operation but to the jealous anger of Catherine Dickens, who quarrelled with her husband about his visits to the lady's apartments. Mrs. de la Rue's phantom persecutors may have lent something to 'The Chimes: a Goblin Story', upon which Dickens was engaged at the time.

Layard, Sir Austen Henry (1817–94): Excavator of Nineveh, politician, world traveller, Lord Rector of Aberdeen University, 1855, and Liberal M.P. for Aylesbury, 1852–7; author of several books, mainly on art. A friend of Dickens, the correspondence between them was made available for publication in 1881, and printed in the third volume of the edition of Dickens's letters published by Chapman and Hall 1879–82. This was the first selection of Dickens's letters ever to appear.

Leech, John (1817–64): Humorous artist, made famous by his drawings for *Punch*, 1841–64. A schoolfellow at the Charterhouse was Thackeray, who became his life-long friend. After an interlude studying medicine Leech turned to art and offered himself, unsuccessfully, as illustrator of *Pickwick* after Seymour's death. In 1843 he married Annie Eaton, who was often his model. He became a personal friend of Dickens, contributed illustrations to all the *Christmas Books*, and was the sole illustrator of 'A Christmas Carol'. Leech was noted for his personal charm: George du Maurier said that he was 'the most charming companion conceivable', and Dean Hole of Rochester, meeting him in 1858, described his 'slim, elegant figure, over six feet in height, with a grand head, on which nature had written "gentleman" with a wonderful genius in his ample forehead; wonderful penetration, observation, humour, in his blue-gray Irish eyes, and wonderful sweetness, sympathy and mirth about his lips'.

Lemon, Mark (1809–70): Lifelong friend of Dickens; first editor of *Punch*, author of farces, melodramas, and operas, contributor to *Household Words* and *Illustrated London News* among other periodicals. In 1849 he adapted 'The Haunted Man' for the stage, in 1851 collaborated with Dickens in the farce *Mr. Nightingale's Diary*, and his children acted with the Dickens family in theatricals at Tavistock House. Dickens, in his continuation of Mrs. Gamp's adventures, published in Forster's *Life* makes her describe Lemon as 'a fat gentleman with curly black hair and a merry face, a-standing on the platform rubbing his two hands over one another, as if he was washing of 'em, and shaking his head and shoulders very much'. In the same year, inviting Lemon to Brighton after an illness, he sent his friend a poetical effusion, to be sung to the air of 'Lesbia hath a beaming eye', and beginning:

> *Lemon is a little hipped,*
> *And this is Lemon's true position –*
> *He is not pale, he's not white-lipped,*
> *Yet wants a little fresh condition.*
> *Sweeter 'tis to gaze upon*

> *Old Ocean's rising, falling billers,*
> *Than on the Houses every one*
> *That form the street called Saint Anne's Willers.*
> *Oh my Lemon, round and fat,*
> *Oh my bright, my right, my tight 'un,*
> *Think a little what you're at –*
> *Don't stay at home, but come to Brighton!*

Lewes, George Henry (1817–78): Author and contributor to quarterlies, he co-operated with Thornton Leigh Hunt in the *Leader*, 1850, wrote a play, two novels, and miscellaneous works. From 1854 to the end of his life he lived with Mary Ann Evans ('George Eliot') as her husband. Dickens had 'an old and great regard' for him, says Forster. A year after Dickens's death Lewes published a paper on 'Dickens in Relation to Criticism', which greatly annoyed Forster because of some implied depreciation of the man who had been his friend.

Linda: One of the St. Bernard dogs kept at Gad's Hill for protection against the vagrants who roamed the Dover Road. On Dickens's return from America in 1868 Linda, he said, 'was greatly excited; weeping profusely, and throwing herself on her back that she might caress my foot with her great forepaws'. Mamie Dickens recorded that she was soft-eyed, gentle, and good-tempered.

Linton, Mrs. Eliza Lynn (1822–98): Self-described 'a woman of letters', she wrote novels from 1845 onwards, was a member of the staff of the *Morning Chronicle*, contributed to *All the Year Round*, and married W. J. Linton in 1858 but soon separated from him. A protégée of Walter Savage Landor in her youth, she moved in Dickens's circle for many years. She was a somewhat formidable and plain-spoken lady, disliked Forster and reviewed his books with venom, but thought Dickens bright, gay, and charming, except when he blue-pencilled her contributions to *All the Year Round*. It was through her that Dickens gained possession of Gad's Hill Place, the house he had admired from boyhood: her father had left it to her and she could not afford to live in it.

Longfellow, Henry Wadsworth (1807–82): American poet, born in Portland, of an ancient New England family. Entering the world of literature against his father's wishes, he was offered in 1836 the Smith chair of modern languages at Harvard, which he accepted, and went abroad to study in England, Sweden, Denmark, and other countries. Dickens met him during the first American visit in 1842, and thought him a 'noble fellow'. On Dickens's return to England he invited Longfellow to become his guest at Devonshire Terrace. Longfellow accepted and Forster has left an amusing account of mild law-breaking at Rochester on the part of Dickens and Longfellow, and a tour of the haunts of tramps and thieves in London. The poet visited Dickens again in 1856 and 1868. Dickens, during his last American tour, was struck by the beauty of Longfellow's eldest daughter Alice, who with her sisters Edith and Allegra stayed at Gad's Hill during their father's 1868 visit. Of this Dickens wrote, 'Nothing can surpass the respect paid to Longfellow here, from the Queen downward. He is everywhere received and courted, and finds the working men at least as well acquainted with his books as the classes socially above them.'

Lowell, James Russell (1819–91): American author and diplomatist. His earliest work to be published was a collection of poems in 1843, followed by *Conversations on Some of the old Poets*. He became a regular contributor to the *National Anti-Slavery Standard* of New York, and was made editor of the *Atlantic Monthly* in 1857. In 1877 he was appointed minister resident at the court of Spain. Dickens met him when visiting Boston on his last American reading tour, 1867–8.

Lytton, Edward George Earle Lytton Bulwer-Lytton, first Baron (1803–73): Novelist, poet, playwright, writer for various periodicals, reformer in politics and supporter of authors' copyrights and the removal of taxes upon literature. His novels include *Falkland, Paul Clifford, Eugene Aram, The Last Days of Pompeii, Rienzi*, and *The Coming Race*, a remarkable prophecy of life in the twentieth century. Dickens, his friend and admirer, said of him, 'Some of you will connect him with prose, others will connect him with poetry. One will connect him with comedy, and another with the romantic passions of the stage, and his assertion of worthy ambition and earnest struggle against

> *Those twin gaolers of the human heart,*
> *Low birth and iron fortune.'*

With Dickens, he founded the Guild of Literature and Art, to improve the lot of impoverished writers. The scheme failed, but provided Dickens with the opportunity of producing and acting in a series of plays in London and at Knebworth, Lytton's home, with his amateur company. The repertoire included Lytton's comedy *Not so Bad as we Seem*. His marriage to Rosina Wheeler was a failure, and after their separation in 1836 she devoted herself to a series of verbal and literary attacks on him.

Maclise, Daniel (1806–70): Irish-born artist, close friend of Dickens from 1838, he painted the famous portrait of Dickens aged 27 which was exhibited at the Royal Academy in 1840, and several portraits of his family. Forster says, 'A greater enjoyment than the fellowship of Maclise at this period [1838] it would be difficult to imagine. Dickens hardly saw more than he did, while yet he seemed to be seeing nothing; and the small esteem in which this rare faculty was held by himself, a quaint oddity that in him gave to shrewdness itself an air of Irish simplicity . . . combined to render him attractive far beyond the common.' Dickens's last words to be spoken in public, at the Royal Academy Dinner of 1870, were a eulogy of the recently-dead Maclise: 'in wit a man, simplicity a child'.

Macready, William Charles (1793–1873): Distinguished actor. Made his first appearance as Romeo in 1810, and became famous for his Richard III. Manager of Drury Lane 1841–3. Forsook the stage in 1851, his last part being Macbeth at Drury Lane. Bulwer-Lytton gave him a farewell dinner, at which Dickens spoke; he and 'dear old gallant Macready' were friends for many years, and Macready's declining health was a constant anxiety to Dickens in the last year of his own life. Among his last words was an inquiry about Macready's son. A mutual friend recorded of Macready that 'When time and sorrow pressed him down, Dickens was his most frequent visitor; he cheered him with narratives of bygone days; he poured some of his own abundant warmth into his heart; he led him into new channels of thought . . . he conjured back his smile and his laugh.'

Macrone, John (1809–37): A Manx-born publisher, he met Dickens in 1836, introduced by Harrison Ainsworth, and persuaded him to sell the copyright of *Sketches by Boz* for £100. A dispute over the reissue of the *Sketches*, Macrone demanding £2,000 from Dickens and Chapman & Hall to relinquish the rights, ended the association. Dickens edited the *Pic Nic Papers*, 1841, which were published for the benefit of Macrone's family, left destitute by his sudden death.

Millais, Sir John Everett (1829–96): President of the Royal Academy, one of the founders of the Pre-Raphaelite movement, painter of such famous works as *Isabella, The Huguenot, The Boyhood of Raleigh, The Princes in the Tower* and *The Order of Release*. He was teacher of painting to Dickens's daughter Katey, and thought her talented. The day after Dickens's death he went to Gad's Hill to make a sketch of the dead face, which was later given to Katey. Millais had forgiven, if not forgotten, Dickens's slashing attack on the Pre-Raphaelites, and particularly Millais's *Christ in the House of his Parents*, in *Household Words*. He found Dickens personally amiable, and Katey sat to him for a figure in his painting *The Black Brunswicker*.

Milner-Gibson, Thomas (1806–84): Conservative M.P. for Ipswich, 1837–9, resigned on changing his views and became an active member and speaker of the Anti-Corn Law League; became Vice-President of the Board of Trade and Privy Councillor. His wife was a close friend of Mrs. Benjamin Disraeli, with whose husband Milner-Gibson had been at school. Early in 1870 Milner-Gibson briefly leased Dickens his Bayswater house, 5 Hyde Park Place.

Milnes, Richard Monckton, first Baron Houghton (1809–85): Politician and literary man, he was Conservative M.P. for Pontefract in 1837, and did much to secure the passing of the Copyright Act, to the pleasure of Dickens. He and his wife frequently entertained Dickens, and were entertained by him, from Tavistock House days onwards.

Mitton, Thomas (1812–78): He met Dickens in boyhood, possibly about 1827. Both were law-clerks in Lincoln's Inn, and he later became a solicitor. He remained friendly with Dickens throughout his life, and seems to have transacted the legal business of obtaining for Dickens the lease of 1 Devonshire Terrace.

Mrs. Bouncer (1859–74): A white Pomeranian dog belonging to Mamie Dickens at Gad's Hill. On her death Georgina Hogarth recalled how 'very, very kind and sweet to her' Dickens had been.

Nash, Mrs.: Landlady at the cottage at Chalk, Kent, where Dickens and Kate spent their honeymoon.

Ouvry, Frederic (1814–81): Dickens's friend and solicitor, who acted for him in the separation from his wife which occurred in 1858, and was still handling his affairs up to the drawing-up of the contract for *Edwin Drood* in 1870. He afterwards acted for Georgina Hogarth. In 1883, two years after his death, selections from Dickens's correspondence with Ouvry were published in America, unauthorised by Georgina, Dickens's executrix. But she refused to blame Ouvry, 'one of the most delicate, most discreet and judicious of men'.

Perugini, Carlo (c. 1839–1918): Artist, Italian by birth, a naturalised English citizen. He became Katey Dickens's second husband in 1874, after the death of Charles Collins. Georgina Hogarth described him as 'a most sensible, good, honourable and upright man, and devotedly attached to Katey'. In 1875 their only child was born, and christened Leonard Ralph Dickens Perugini, but died at the age of seven months. Perugini became a moderately well-known painter, exhibiting a series of genre pictures at the Royal Academy.

Perugini, Mrs. Carlo: See **Dickens, Kate Macready.**

'Phiz': See **Browne, Hablôt Knight.**

Procter, Bryan Waller (1787–1874): Poet and playwright, biographer of Charles Lamb, he started life as a solicitor and built up a large connection as conveyancer. In 1815 he began to contribute to the *Literary Gazette*. His tragedy *Mirandola* was produced at Covent Garden in 1821 under the pseudonym of Barry Cornwall. He was a close friend of both Dickens and Leigh Hunt, and was instrumental in reducing the likenesses between Hunt and the irresponsible Harold Skimpole of *Bleak House*.

Rogers, Samuel (1763–1855): Banker, poet, wit, and entertainer, his wealth enabled him to write poetry for pleasure. His 'breakfasts' were famous, gathering together luminaries of the arts and politics. Dickens was numbered among his friends, though he was not an 'out-and-out' admirer of the novelist's work, and brought his mordant wit to bear on 'A Christmas Carol'. Forster tells an amusing story of a dinner-party given by Dickens at which Rogers and another guest were taken ill, and Dickens was chaffingly accused of poisoning them.

Sala, George Augustus Henry (1828–96): Journalist. Once an artist and scene-painter, he wrote regularly for *Household Words*, and was sent to Russia by Dickens at the close of the Crimean War to write descriptive articles for it. When *All the Year Round* was founded he became a contributor. Dickens wrote of him to Forster in 1851, 'I find him a very conscientious fellow. When he gets money ahead, he is not like the imbecile youth who so often do the like in Wellington Street [the office of *Household Words*] and

walk off, but only works more industriously. I think he improves with everything he does.'

Seymour, Robert (1800–36): Artist and illustrator, he was famous for his sporting prints, usually of a slightly vulgar kind. He was engaged on a journal called the *Figaro in London*; practised art with a fellow-student at Canonbury Tower, Islington, and as a result produced an enormous picture representing scenes of German diablerie, rife with 'goblin incidents'. It was not a success, and he devoted himself to humorous sketches. In November 1835 Chapman & Hall published a small book called the *Squib Annual*, with plates by Seymour, and he expressed to them a wish to do a series of Cockney sporting prints of a superior kind. This was to deal with the adventures of the 'Nimrod Club', amateurs of shooting, fishing, and the like, who would get themselves into laughable difficulties. Chapman & Hall approached Dickens to write the text. He expressed no enthusiasm for it, regarding it as hackneyed and of no particular interest to himself, a non-sportsman. 'I would like to take my own way, with a freer range of English scenes and people,' he said; but such was the genesis of *The Pickwick Papers*. Dickens conceded the sporting Mr. Winkle as a sop to Seymour. Between the first and second numbers of *Pickwick* Seymour committed suicide, working to the last on his illustration for 'The Stroller's Tale', the original version of which Dickens had criticised slightly.

Shaw, William (?1783–1850): London-born schoolmaster, of Bowes, Yorkshire from 1822. Dickens had been much impressed in youth by reports of the trial of Shaw in 1823 for cruelty to his pupils, one of whom died. In 1838 he travelled up to Yorkshire to investigate the notorious Yorkshire boarding-schools or 'boy farms' to which unwanted boys were sent to be boarded, without holidays and under conditions of privation and brutality (Shaw's curriculum expressly stated 'No Vacations'). Shaw may have been no worse than the rest of his kind, and was apparently well regarded in Bowes, but Dickens made a scapegoat of him and caricatured him as Wackford Squeers, the one-eyed monster who rules Dotheboys Hall in *Nicholas Nickleby*. 'I have kept down the strong truth and thrown as much comicality over it as I could, rather than disgust and weary the reader with its fouler aspect,' said Dickens of the Dotheboys episodes in the book.

Smith, Arthur (1825–61): Manager of Dickens's first major reading-tour in 1858. He had been introduced to Dickens by his brother, Albert Smith, an entertainer, renowned for his one-man shows: travelogues interspersed with comic songs and sketches, and illustrated by dioramic views. Arthur Smith took over all the business details of the tour, and Dickens was impressed by his efficiency. 'He is all usefulness and service,' he told Wilkie Collins. 'I never could have done without him.' Smith died in 1861, to Dickens's great grief, plans for the readings on his mind to the last. Dickens composed an inscription for his gravestone.

Smith, Sydney (1771–1845): Canon of St. Paul's, he took orders in 1794 but became famous in a lay capacity as writer, campaigner, Whig reformer, and brilliant wit. Dickens probably met him at Gore House in the 'Blessington Set', and he became a friend and frequent guest. He accepted one of Dickens's invitations in these words: 'If I am invited by any man of greater genius than yourself or by one in whose works I have been more completely interested I will repudiate you and dine with the more splendid phenomenon of the two.'

Smith, Dr. Thomas Southwood (1788–1861): Studied medicine while a Unitarian minister in Edinburgh; helped to found the *Westminster Review,* 1824, the Useful Knowledge Society, the *Penny Cyclopaedia,* the Health of Towns Association; wrote valuable works on epidemics and sanitary improvements. Dickens first met him when Smith was Commissioner on the Employment of Young People early in the 1840s. The Commission's report on the conditions of children working in factories and mines aroused Dickens's indignation, though he seems to have held himself off from campaigning against these because he could not reconcile the necessary mighty change with the consequent reduction in income of poor families. However, Smith's influence led him to realise that good housing was essential if the terrible sanitary conditions of slum dwellings were to be banished; a conviction strengthened by the cholera outbreak of 1850, and an even worse one in 1854. Dickens's article 'To Working Men' published in *Household Words* called on the working classes to 'turn their intelligence, their energy, their numbers, their power of union . . . in this straight direction in earnest' in order that they might by Christmas find a worthy government in Downing Street.

Stanfield, Clarkson (1793–1867): Marine and landscape painter. He was pressed into the navy in 1812, but left the sea six years later. He became scene-painter at Drury Lane Theatre and painted the scenery for Dickens's productions of *The Lighthouse* and *The Frozen Deep,* the act-drops for which were used as hall-decorations at Gad's Hill. Stanfield contributed some illustrations to 'The Battle of Life'. Dickens had a warm affection for 'old Stanny', whom he called 'the soul of frankness, generosity, and simplicity, the most loving and most lovable of men'. The act-drop for *The Lighthouse* is preserved in the Dickens House, London.

Stone, Frank (1800–59): Painter, first exhibiting at the Royal Academy in 1837 and becoming A.R.A. in 1851. Dickens took Tavistock House from him in 1851 and they were close friends for many years, Stone painting several portraits of the Dickens children and taking part in Dickens's amateur theatricals. He made three of the drawings for 'The Haunted Man', and provided some extra illustrations for *Nicholas Nickleby* and *Martin Chuzzlewit.* He was the father of Marcus Stone, R.A., illustrator of *Our Mutual Friend.*

Stowe, Mrs. Harriet Elizabeth Beecher (1811–96): American writer and philanthropist, brought up in the intellectual society of New England, she devoted herself to the cause of anti-slavery and wrote her famous propagandist novel *Uncle Tom's Cabin,* published in 1852. Her travels brought her to England the year after, and she met Dickens at a banquet. 'Directly opposite me was Mr. Dickens, whom I now beheld for the first time, and was surprised to see looking so young. Mr. Justice Talfourd made allusion to the author of *Uncle Tom's Cabin* and Mr. Dickens, speaking of both as having employed fiction as a means of awakening the attention of the respective countries to the condition of the oppressed and suffering classes.'

Stroughill, George: Dickens's neighbour and playmate during Ordnance Terrace days. George, somewhat older than Dickens and of a bold and fearless nature, probably reappeared as the young Steerforth of *David Copperfield.*

Stroughill, Lucy: George's sister and Dickens's childhood sweetheart, the 'peach-faced creature in a blue sash' of 'Birthday Celebrations' and Golden Lucy of 'The Wreck of the Golden Mary'. Dickens uses the name Lucy five times in the novels.

Sultan: A St. Bernard-bloodhound cross given to Dickens by Percy Fitzgerald. Dickens remarked that he must be a Fenian, for no non-Fenian dog would have made such a point of rushing at and bearing down with fury anything in scarlet with the remotest resemblance to a soldier's uniform. Sultan had eventually to be shot for savagery.

Talfourd, Sir Thomas Noon (1795–1854): Judge and author, he published *Poems on various Subjects,* 1811, contributed articles and dramatic criticisms to numerous journals, and met the literary celebrities of the day. He was made Serjeant, 1833, and Justice of the Common Pleas, 1849; M.P. for Reading, 1835, 1837, and 1841; introduced the Custody of Infants Bill and the Copyright Bill, the latter particularly endearing him to Dickens and earning him the dedication of *The Pickwick Papers.* When he was made a judge Dickens was 'really quite enraptured at his success'. Forster observes that 'such small oddities or foibles as he had made him secretly only dearer to Dickens, who had no friend he was more attached to'. He was known among his friends as 'Ion', the title of a tragedy of his produced in 1836.

Tennyson, Alfred, first Baron Tennyson (1809––92): Author of *Maud, Idylls of the King, In Memoriam, The Princess,* 'The Charge of the Light Brigade', *Enoch Arden,* and many other poems, lyrical and heroic, who became Poet Laureate on the death of Wordsworth in 1850. He and Dickens had a reciprocal admiration. Forster says that in Dickens's brilliant middle years Tennyson gave him 'full allegiance and honoured welcome'. He appears as a young man in Frank Stone's painting *The Duet,* showing the Dickens family and guests at a musical evening in their Villa Rosemont, Lausanne. He was godfather to Dickens's son Alfred.

Ternan, Ellen Lawless (1839–1914): Presumed mistress of Dickens, she was a young actress whom he met in 1857, when she was appearing in Talfourd's play *Atalanta.* Dickens engaged her and her actress mother and sister, Frances Eleanor and Maria Ternan, for his next amateur production, *The Frozen*

Deep, followed by a farce, *Uncle John*. The meeting, and Dickens's subsequent infatuation, appear to have turned him finally against his long-suffering wife. In 1858 a separation was arranged, Catherine going to live with her eldest son Charley, while Dickens published an unwise and uncalled-for refutation of the supposed rumours and slanders that were flying about. Everyone, including Catherine, subscribed meekly to his will except Katey, who defied him and took her mother's part. It would seem (though the facts will never be known) that Ellen Ternan held out against him for some time after this date, but finally succumbed and entered with him into a furtive and somewhat unsatisfactory relationship, which added to the stresses of his last ten years. They apparently lived intermittently together at Peckham and Slough. Persistent legend says that a son was born to them, but no confirmation of this has ever been found. Ellen Ternan received £1,000 under Dickens's will, was present at his deathbed, and later remained on friendly terms with Georgina Hogarth and Mamie Dickens. In 1876 she married George W. Robinson, a clergyman who later became headmaster of a school in Margate.

Thackeray, William Makepeace (1811–63): Novelist. Born in India, he came to England in 1817; studied for the law, but abandoned it; failed in the management of a journal; studied drawing in Paris; and turned to miscellaneous literature and novel-writing, his most famous books being *Vanity Fair*, *Henry Esmond*, *The Newcomes*, and *The Virginians*. *Vanity Fair* completely established his reputation, which was enhanced by the later *Pendennis*. Dickens and he met in *Pickwick* days, when Dickens was in search of an illustrator, and Thackeray always remembered offering him some drawings 'which, strange to say, he did not find suitable'. In 1858 the two quarrelled over a critical comment on Thackeray by Edmund Yates, published in *Town Talk*. Thackeray tried to get Yates removed from membership of the Garrick Club; Dickens defended Yates, and the two literary giants remained estranged until a week before Thackeray's death. Dickens was deeply shocked by the death, and paid warm tribute to Thackeray's genius, learning, and humour.

Thompson, Mrs. T. J.: See **Weller, Christiana.**

Timber: A white spaniel who was a pet of Dickens's during Devonshire Terrace days. He travelled on the Continent with the family and was such an attraction to Italian fleas that he 'had to be clipped in lion style'. He survived into the 1850s. His original name was Mr. Snittle Timbery, later changed to Mr. Timber Doodle.

Turk: A mastiff owned by Dickens at Gad's Hill, and a great favourite; 'a noble animal', according to Forster, 'full of affection and intelligent'. By a strange coincidence he died as a result of a railway accident in 1865, shortly after his master had been involved in the Staplehurst disaster.

Victoria, Queen (1819–1901): When the Queen was married in 1840 to Prince Albert Dickens affected to be 'raving with love' for her, and wrote such lyrics on the subject as:

My heart is at Windsor,
My heart is not here,
My heart is at Windsor,
A following my dear.

He managed, however, to watch the wedding procession calmly enough. In 1857 when Dickens applied to the Queen for the Douglas Jerrold Memorial Fund, for which he was repeating his production of *The Frozen Deep*, she replied that she never patronised benefits for individuals, but would like to see the play, and invited Dickens to bring his troupe to the Palace. He replied that he preferred not to take the ladies of his company there 'in the quality of actresses', and the Queen accepted his invitation to a private presentation for herself and party at the Gallery of Illustration in Regent Street. They 'made a most excellent audience', reported Georgina Hogarth, '. . . cried and laughed and applauded'. In 1870 Dickens made his first appearance at Buckingham Palace, to receive Her Majesty's thanks for some American photographs he had sent at her request. He found her 'strangely shy . . . and like a girl in manner . . . but with a girlish sort of timidity which was very engaging'. He informed her that in his opinion the division of classes would gradually cease and, she commented in her journal, 'I earnestly hope it may.' On leaving he was presented with a copy of her book *Our Life in the Highlands*, given with the modest remark that she was really ashamed to offer such a book to such a writer. After Dickens's death the Queen telegraphed from Balmoral to Catherine, 'Deepest regret at the sad news.' A specially bound copy of his *Letters* was sent to her in 1879. There have been rumours that Dickens was offered a baronetcy, and accepted it, shortly before his death; but there seems to be no absolute proof of this. He certainly did not tell Forster about it, if it happened.

Warren, Jonathan: Original proprietor of the blacking warehouse in which Dickens worked in 1824, he sold out to the Lamerts his interest in the premises at 30 Hungerford Stairs, Strand, where he had set up a business in opposition to Robert Warren at 30, Strand. Both Jonathan and Robert claimed to hold the recipe for the blacking, and as no copyright law then existed, one firm exactly copied the pictorial advertisements of the other. Dickens's experience at Warren's is re-lived in David Copperfield's employment at Murdstone and Grinby's warehouse, and there are frequent glancing references to Warren in the novels.

Watson, The Hon. Richard (d. 1852): Owner of Rockingham Castle, Northamptonshire, and brother of Lord Sondes. Dickens first met Watson and his wife and family at the house of William Haldimand, former M.P. for Ipswich, who was living in Lausanne when the Dickenses lodged there in 1846. He formed a lasting friendship with them, cemented by Watson's strong Liberal views which chimed with Dickens's political sympathies. Invitations to Rockingham followed, and there, in 1849, Dickens met Mrs. Watson's niece, Mary Boyle, who became one of his closest friends. They acted together at Rockingham for the first time, in a farce called *Used Up*. Another production there was planned for 1852, but Watson died abroad before the plans could be implemented. Dickens wrote to Forster, 'I was so fond of him that I am sorry you didn't know him better. I believe he was as thoroughly good and true a man as ever lived; and I am sure I can have no greater affection for him than he felt for me. When I think of that bright house, and his fine simple honest heart, both so open to me, the blank and loss are like a dream.' As a tribute to Watson's memory he gave a reading of 'A Christmas Carol' in Peterborough. Chesney Wold, the home of the Dedlocks in *Bleak House*, is probably based on Rockingham Castle.

Weller, Christiana: On 26 February, 1844, Dickens took the chair at a soirée of the Mechanics' Institute in Liverpool. It included music, and as chairman Dickens announced, 'I am requested to introduce a young lady whom I have some difficulty and tenderness in announcing – Miss Weller – who will play a fantasia on the pianoforte.' The name Weller raised a great laugh, but Dickens's own amusement was tempered by his immediate infatuation with Christiana Weller, who possibly reminded him of Mary Hogarth. He wrote to his friend T. J. Thompson, 'I cannot joke about Miss Weller; for she is too good; and interest in her (spiritual young creature that she is, and destined to an early death, I fear) has become a sentiment with me.' Some days later Thompson confessed that he himself was in love with Miss Weller, to Dickens's shocked surprise, although he urged Thompson to win and marry her. Thompson did so, and far from being destined to an early death, Christiana became the mother of two daughters, one of whom became Lady Butler, the genre painter, and the other, Alice Meynell, the poet and essayist. Dickens visited them in Italy in 1853 and disapproved markedly of Christiana's Bohemian methods of running her household, and of the 'singularly untidy' state of her little girls.

Weller, Mary: Nurse to Dickens when the family lived at Ordnance Terrace, Chatham, she was an accomplished tale-spinner whose stories of ghosts, goblins, murders, and other ghoulish subjects stimulated the child's mind as well as frightening him a great deal; but it is not easy to reconcile the portrait in the essay 'Nurse's Stories' with the 'smart young girl' who looked after the Dickens family and remembered her young charge with such kindness in her old age. Dickens gave Mary's name to the immortal Sam. She married Thomas Gibson, a shipwright in Chatham Dockyard.

Williamina: Dickens's cat at Gad's Hill, the only one permitted there because of his fondness for bird-life. She had been presented to Georgina as a pretty white kitten, but became devoted to Dickens and was allowed, with her kittens, to live in his study. Her son, a completely deaf cat, was allowed to remain when homes were found for the others, and became known simply as The Master's Cat, following Dickens about like a dog and sitting beside him while he wrote. Mamie Dickens tells a charming anecdote about him in *My Father as I Recall Him*.

Wills, William Henry (1810–80): Appointed assistant editor of *Household Words* in 1850. It was Wills who in 1855 excitedly told Dickens, 'It is written that you were to have that house at Gad's Hill!' for the previous night he had learnt from Mrs. Lynn Linton that she wanted to sell the house Dickens had admired since boyhood. When Dickens's sons, Harry and 'Plorn', started their private newspaper *The Gad's Hill Gazette*, Wills presented the young journalists with a 'manifold writer' and a printing-press. In company with Forster and Georgina Hogarth he opposed Dickens's intention of embarking on the American tour of 1867–8, but Dickens pointed out the immense profits to be made from it, and made light of his growing ill-health. It appears from the correspondence of this date that Wills was privy to the liaison with Ellen Ternan: he received letters from Dickens written on Ellen's stationery, and among his instructions was a memorandum containing a code message for her by which she was to know whether or not to follow Dickens to America. After Dickens's death Wills sold out his one-eighth share in *All the Year Round* to Charley Dickens, with whom he quarrelled over money. Dickens had written to him in 1862, 'we doubt whether any two men can have gone on more happily, and smoothly, or with greater trust and confidence in each other', a passage which Wills was gratified to see in print when Dickens's *Letters* were published.

Winter, Mrs. Henry: See **Beadnell, Maria.**

Yates, Edmund (1831–94): Novelist and founder of the journal *The World*, he began his career as a post office worker. He was drama critic and reviewer of the *Daily News*, 1854–60, wrote several plays, and was editor of various periodicals as well as contributing to *All the Year Round*. Dickens took a great interest in him and in 1872 Yates followed Dickens's example by touring America, giving a series of literary lectures containing many reminiscences of his friendship with Dickens. Georgina Hogarth was disapproving of Yates's venture, fearing that some undesirable facts might come out during the lectures, for she thought Yates 'a harum-scarum creature', and it was he who had been the cause of the estrangement between Dickens and Thackeray.

QUOTATIONS

CONTENTS OF 'QUOTATIONS'

QUOTATIONS

SKETCHES BY BOZ

OUR PARISH

Our curate is a young gentleman of such prepossessing appearance, and fascinating manners, that within one month after his first appearance in the parish, half the young-lady inhabitants were melancholy with religion, and the other half, desponding with love. Never were so many young ladies seen in our parish-church on Sunday before; and never had the little round angels' faces on Mr. Tomkins's monument in the side aisle, beheld such devotion on earth as they all exhibited (*Chapter 2:* 'The Curate').

The curate began to cough, four fits of coughing one morning between the Litany and the Epistle, and five in the afternoon service. Here was a discovery – the curate was consumptive. How interestingly melancholy! If the young ladies were energetic before, their sympathy and solicitude now knew no bounds. Such a man as the curate – such a dear – such a perfect love – to be consumptive! It was too much. Anonymous presents of black-currant jam, and lozenges, elastic waistcoats, bosom friends, and warm stockings, poured in upon the curate until he was as completely fitted out with winter clothing, as if he were on the verge of an expedition to the North Pole: verbal bulletins of the state of his health were circulated throughout the parish half a dozen times a day; and the curate was in the very zenith of his popularity (*Chapter 2:* 'The Curate').

One of the old lady's next-door neighbours . . . is an old naval officer on half-pay, and his bluff and unceremonious behaviour disturbs the old lady's domestic economy, not a little. In the first place, he *will* smoke cigars in the front court, and when he wants something to drink with them – which is by no means an uncommon circumstance – he lifts up the old lady's knocker with his walking-stick, and demands to have a glass of table ale, handed over the rails. In addition to this cool proceeding, he is a bit of a Jack of all trades, or to use his own words 'a regular Robinson Crusoe'; and nothing delights him better than to experimentalise on the old lady's property. One morning he got up early, and planted three or four roots of full-grown marigolds in every bed of her front garden, to the inconceivable astonishment of the old lady, who actually thought when she got up and looked out of the window, that it was some strange eruption which had come out in the night. Another time he took to pieces the eight-day clock on the front landing, under pretence of cleaning the works, which he put together

again, by some undiscovered process, in so wonderful a manner, that the large hand has done nothing but trip up the little one ever since. Then he took to breeding silkworms, which he *would* bring in two or three times a day, in little paper boxes, to show the old lady, generally dropping a worm or two at every visit. The consequence was, that one morning a very stout silkworm was discovered in the act of walking upstairs – probably with a view of inquiring after his friends, for, on further inspection, it appeared that some of his companions had already found their way to every room in the house. The old lady went to the seaside in despair, and during her absence he completely effaced the name from her brass door-plate, in his attempts to polish it with aqua-fortis (*Chapter 2:* 'The Old Lady. The Half-pay Captain').

The life of this gentleman has been one of a very chequered description: he has undergone transitions – not from grave to gay, for he never was grave – not from lively to severe, for severity forms no part of his disposition; his fluctuations have been between poverty in the extreme, and poverty modified, or, to use his own emphatic language, 'between nothing to eat and just half enough.' He is not, as he forcibly remarks, 'one of those fortunate men who, if they were to dive under one side of a barge stark-naked, would come up on the other with a new suit of clothes on, and a ticket for soup in the waistcoat-pocket': neither is he one of those, whose spirit has been broken beyond redemption by misfortune and want. He is just one of the careless, good-for-nothing, happy fellows, who float, cork-like, on the surface, for the world to play at hockey with: knocked here and there, and everywhere: now to the right, then to the left, again up in the air, and anon to the bottom, but always reappearing and bounding with the stream buoyantly and merrily along (*Chapter 5:* 'The Broker's Man').

'If there is anything wrong in being the agent in such matters – not the principal, mind you – I'm sure the business, to a beginner like I was, at all events, carries its own punishment along with it. I wished again and again that the people would only blow me up, or pitch into me – that I wouldn't have minded, it's all in my way; but it's the being shut up by yourself in one room for five days, without so much as an old newspaper to look at, or anything to see out o' the winder but the roofs and chimneys at the back of the house, or anything to listen to, but the ticking, perhaps, of an old Dutch clock, the sobbing of the missis, now and then, the low talking of friends in the next room, who speak in whispers lest "the man" should overhear them, or perhaps the occasional opening of the door, as a child peeps in to look at you, and then runs half-frightened away – it's all this, that makes you feel sneaking somehow, and ashamed of yourself; and then, if it's winter time, they just give you fire enough to make you think you'd like more, and bring in your grub as if they wished it 'ud choke you – as I dare say they do, for the matter of that, most heartily. If they're very civil, they make you up a bed in the room at night, and if they don't, your master sends one in for you; but there you are, without being washed or shaved all the time, shunned by everybody, and spoken to by no one, unless some one comes in at dinner-time, and asks you whether you want any more, in a tone as much as to say, "I hope you don't," or, in the evening, to inquire whether you wouldn't rather have a candle, after you've been sitting in the dark half the night. When I was left in this way, I used to sit, think, think, thinking, till I felt as lonesome as a kitten in a wash-house copper with the lid on; but I believe the old brokers' men who are regularly trained to it, never think at all. I have heard some on 'em say, indeed, that they don't know how!' (*Chapter 5:* 'The Broker's Man' – Mr. Bung).

' "Who the devil are you, and how dare you walk into a gentleman's house without leave?" says the master, as fierce as a bull in fits' (*Chapter 5:* 'The Broker's Man' – Mr. Bung).

'A dirty striped curtain, on a very slack string, hung in the window, and a little triangular bit of broken looking-glass rested on the sill inside. I suppose it was meant for the people's use, but their appearance was so wretched, and so miserable, that I'm certain they never could have plucked up courage to look themselves in the face a second time, if they survived the fright of doing so once' (*Chapter 5:* 'The Broker's Man' – Mr. Bung).

We are very fond of speculating as we walk through a street, on the character and pursuits of the people who inhabit it; and nothing so materially assists us in these speculations as the appearance of the house-doors. The various expressions of the human countenance afford a beautiful and interesting study; but there is something in the physiognomy of street-door knockers, almost as characteristic, and nearly as infallible. Whenever we visit a man for the first time, we contemplate the features of his knocker with the greatest curiosity, for we well know, that between the man and his knocker, there will inevitably be a greater or less degree of resemblance and sympathy (*Chapter 7:* 'Our Next-door Neighbour').

In a day or two the single gentleman came in, and shortly afterwards his real character came out.

First of all, he displayed a most extraordinary partiality for sitting up till three or four o'clock in the morning, drinking whiskey-and-water, and smoking cigars; then he invited friends home, who used to come at ten o'clock, and begin to get happy about the small hours, when they evinced their perfect contentment by singing songs with half a dozen verses of two lines each, and a chorus of ten, which chorus used to be shouted forth by the whole strength of the company, in the most enthusiastic and vociferous manner, to the great annoyance of the neighbours, and the special discomfort of another single gentleman overhead (*Chapter 7:* 'Our Next-door Neighbour').

When the company *did* go away, instead of walking quietly down the street, as anybody else's company would have done, they amused themselves by making alarming and frightful noises, and counterfeiting the shrieks of females in distress; and one night, a red-faced gentleman in a white hat knocked in the most urgent manner at the door of the powdered-headed old gentleman at No. 3, and when the powdered-headed old gentleman, who thought one of his married daughters must have been taken ill prematurely, had groped downstairs, and after a great deal of unbolting and key-turning, opened the street door, the red-faced man in the white hat said he hoped he'd excuse his giving him so much trouble, but he'd feel obliged if he'd favour him with a glass of cold spring-water, and the loan of a shilling for a cab to take him home, on which the old gentleman slammed the door and went upstairs, and threw the contents of his water-jug out of window – very straight, only it went over the wrong man; and the whole street was involved in confusion (*Chapter 7:* 'Our Next-door Neighbour').

SCENES

The streets in the vicinity of the Marsh Gate and Victoria Theatre present an appearance of dirt and discomfort on such a night, which the groups who lounge about them in no degree tend to diminish. Even the little block-tin temple sacred to baked potatoes, surmounted by a splendid design in variegated lamps, looks less gay than usual; and as to the kidney-pie stand, its glory has quite departed. The candle in the transparent lamp, manufactured of oil-paper, embellished with 'characters,' has been blown out fifty times, so the kidney-pie merchant, tired with running backwards and forwards to the next wine-vaults, to get a light, has given up the idea of illumination in despair, and the only signs of his 'whereabout,' are the bright sparks, of which a long irregular train is whirled down the street every time he opens his portable oven to hand a hot kidney-pie to a customer (*Chapter 2:* 'The Streets – Night').

That wretched woman with the infant in her arms, round whose meagre form the remnant of her own scanty shawl is carefully wrapped, has been attempting to sing some popular ballad, in the hope of wringing a few pence from the compassionate passer-by. A brutal laugh at her weak voice is all she has gained. The tears fall thick and fast down her own pale face; the child is cold and hungry, and its low half-stifled wailing adds to the misery of its wretched mother, as she moans aloud, and sinks despairingly down, on a cold damp door-step.

Singing! How few of those who pass such a miserable creature as this, think of the anguish of heart, the sinking of soul and spirit, which the very effort of singing produces. Bitter mockery! Disease, neglect, and starvation, faintly articulating the words of the joyous ditty, that has enlivened your hours of feasting and merriment, God knows how often! It is no subject of jeering. The weak tremulous voice tells a fearful tale of want and famishing; and the feeble singer of this roaring song may turn away, only to die of cold and hunger (*Chapter 2:* 'The Streets – Night').

The more musical portion of the play-going community betake themselves to some harmonic meeting. As a matter of curiosity let us follow them thither for a few moments.

In a lofty room of spacious dimensions, are seated some eighty or a hundred guests knocking little pewter measures on the tables, and hammering away, with the handles of their knives, as if they were so many trunk-makers. They are applauding a glee, which has just been executed by the three 'professional gentlemen' at the top of the centre table, one of whom is in the chair – the little pompous man with the bald head just emerging from the collar of his green coat. The others are seated on either side of him – the stout man with the small voice, and the thin-faced dark man in black. The little man in the chair is a most amusing personage, – *such* condescending grandeur, and *such* a voice!

'Bass!' as the young gentleman near us with the blue stock forcibly remarks to his companion, 'bass! I b'lieve you; he can go down lower than any man: so low sometimes that you can't hear him.' And so he does. To hear him growling away, gradually lower and lower down, till he can't get back again, is the most delightful thing in the world, and it is quite impossible to witness unmoved the impressive solemnity with which he pours forth his soul in 'My 'art's in the 'ighlands,' or 'The brave old Hoak.' The stout man is also addicted to sentimentality, and warbles, 'Fly, fly from the world, my Bessy, with me,' or some such song, with ladylike sweetness, and in the most seductive tones imaginable.

'Pray give your orders, gen'l'm'n – pray give your orders,' – says the pale-faced man with the red head; and demands for 'goes' of gin and 'goes' of brandy, and pints of stout, and cigars of peculiar mildness, are vociferously made from all parts of the room. The 'professional gentlemen' are in the very height of their glory, and bestow condescending nods, or even a word or two of recognition, on the better-known frequenters of the room, in the most bland and patronising manner possible (*Chapter 2:* 'The Streets – Night').

What inexhaustible food for speculation, do the streets of London afford! We never were able to agree with Sterne in pitying the man who could travel from Dan to Beersheba, and say that all was barren; we have not the slightest commiseration for the man who can take up his hat and stick, and walk from Covent Garden to St. Paul's Churchyard, and back into the bargain, without deriving some amusement – we had almost said instruction – from his perambulation (*Chapter 3:* 'Shops and their Tenants').

On one side, a little crowd has collected round a couple of ladies, who having imbibed the contents of various 'three-outs' of gin-and-bitters in the course of the morning, have at length differed on some point of domestic arrangement, and are on the eve of settling the quarrel satisfactorily, by an appeal to blows, greatly to the interest of other ladies who live in the same house, and tenements adjoining, and who are all partisans on one side or other.

'Vy don't you pitch into her, Sarah?' exclaims one half-dressed matron, by way of encouragement. 'Vy don't you? If *my* 'usband had treated her with a drain last night, unbeknown to me, I'd tear her precious eyes out – a wixen!'

'What's the matter, ma'am?' inquires another old woman, who has just bustled up to the spot.

'Matter!' replies the first speaker, talking *at* the obnoxious combatant, 'matter! Here's poor dear Mrs. Sulliwin, as has five blessed children of her own, can't go out a charing for one arternoon, but what hussies must be a comin', and 'ticing avay her own' 'usband, as she's been married to twelve year come next Easter Monday, for I see the certificate ven I vas drinkin' a cup o' tea vith her, only the werry last blessed Ven'sday as ever was sent. I 'appen'd to say promiscuously, "Mrs. Sulliwin," says I –'

'What do you mean by hussies?' interrupts a champion of the other party, who has evinced a strong inclination throughout to get up a branch fight on her own account ('Hooroar,' ejaculates a pot-boy in parenthesis, 'put the kye-bosk on her, Mary!'), 'What do you mean by hussies?' reiterates the champion.

'Niver mind,' replies the opposition expressively, 'niver mind; *you* go home, and, ven you're quite sober, mend your stockings' (*Chapter 5:* 'Seven Dials').

Now anybody who passed through the Dials on a hot summer's evening, and saw the different women of the house gossiping on the steps, would be apt to think that all was harmony among them, and that a more primitive set of people than the native Diallers could not be imagined. Alas! the man in the shop ill-treats his family; the carpet-beater extends his professional pursuits to his wife; the one-pair front has an undying feud with the two-pair front, in consequence of the two-pair front persisting in dancing over his (the one-pair front's) head, when he and his family have retired for the night; the two-pair back *will* interfere with the front kitchen's children; the Irishman comes home drunk every other night, and attacks everybody; and the one-pair back screams at everything. Animosities spring up between floor and floor; the very cellar asserts his equality. Mrs. A. 'smacks' Mrs. B.'s child, for 'making faces.' Mrs. B. forthwith throws cold water over Mrs. A.'s child for 'calling names.' The husbands are embroiled – the quarrel becomes general – an assault is the consequence, and a police-officer the result (*Chapter 5:* 'Seven Dials').

It is the times that have changed, not Monmouth Street. Through every alteration and every change, Monmouth Street has still remained the burial-place of the fashions; and such, to judge from all present appearances, it will remain until there are no more fashions to bury.

We love to walk among these extensive groves of the illustrious dead, and to indulge in the speculations to which they give rise; now fitting a deceased coat, then a dead pair of trousers, and anon the mortal remains of a gaudy waistcoat, upon some being of our own conjuring up, and endeavouring, from the shape and fashion of the garment itself, to bring its former owner before our mind's eye. We have gone on speculating in this way, until whole rows of coats have started from their pegs, and buttoned up, of their own accord, round the waists of imaginary wearers; lines of trousers have jumped down to meet them; waistcoats have almost burst with anxiety to put themselves on; and half an acre of shoes have suddenly found feet to fit them, and gone stumping down the street with a noise which has fairly awakened us from our pleasant reverie, and driven us slowly away, with a bewildered stare, an object of astonishment to the good people of Monmouth Street, and of no slight suspicion to the policeman at the opposite street-corner (*Chapter 6:* 'Meditations in Monmouth-street').

We take great interest in hackney-coaches, but we seldom drive, having a knack of turning ourselves over when we attempt to do so. We are as great friends to horses, hackney-coach and otherwise, as the renowned Mr. Martin, of costermonger notoriety, and yet we never ride. We keep no horse, but a clothes-horse; enjoy no saddle so much as a saddle of mutton; and, following our own inclinations, have never followed the hounds. Leaving these fleeter means of getting over the ground, or of depositing one's-self upon it, to those who like them, by hackney-coach stands we take our stand (*Chapter 7:* 'Hackney-coach Stands').

If the regular City man, who leaves Lloyd's at five o'clock, and drives home to Hackney, Clapton, Stamford Hill, or elsewhere, can be said to have any daily recreation beyond his dinner, it is his garden. He never does anything to it with his own hands; but he takes great pride in it notwithstanding; and if you are desirous of paying your addresses to the youngest daughter, be sure to be in raptures with every flower and shrub it contains. If your poverty of expression compel you to make any distinction between the two, we would certainly recommend your bestowing more admiration on his garden than his wine. He always takes a walk round it, before he starts for town in the morning, and is particularly anxious that the fish-pond should be kept specially neat. If you call on him on Sunday in summer-time, about an hour before dinner, you will find him sitting in an arm-chair, on the lawn behind the house, with a straw hat on, reading a Sunday paper (*Chapter 9:* 'London Recreations').

In spring time, there is no end to the sowing of seeds, and sticking little bits of wood over them, with labels, which look like epitaphs to their memory; and in the evening, when the sun has gone down, the perseverance with which he lugs a great watering-pot about is perfectly astonishing (*Chapter 9:* 'London Recreations').

We grant that the banks of the Thames are very beautiful at Richmond and Twickenham, and other distant havens, often sought though seldom reached; but from the 'Red-us' back to Blackfriars Bridge, the scene is wonderfully changed. The Penitentiary is a noble building, no doubt, and the sportive youths who 'go in' at that particular part of the river, on a summer's evening, may be all very well in perspective; but when you are obliged to keep in shore coming home, and the young ladies will colour up, and look perseveringly the other way, while the married dittoes cough slightly, and stare very hard at the water, you feel awkward – especially if you happen to have been attempting the most distant approach to senti-mentality, for an hour or two previously (*Chapter 10:* 'The River').

We should very much like to see some piece in which all the dramatis personæ were orphans. Fathers are invariably great nuisances on the stage, and always have to give the hero or heroine a long explanation of what was done before the curtain rose, usually commencing with 'It is now nineteen years, my dear child, since your blessed mother (here the old villain's voice falters) confided you to my charge. You were then an infant,' etc., etc. Or else they have to discover, all of a sudden, that somebody whom they have been in constant communication with, during three long acts, without the slightest suspicion, is their own child: in which case they exclaim, 'Ah! what do I see? This bracelet! That smile! These documents! Those eyes! Can I believe my senses? – It must be! – Yes – it is, it is my child!' – 'My father!' exclaims the child; and they fall into each other's arms, and look over each other's shoulders, and the audience give three rounds of applause (*Chapter 11:* 'Astley's').

The chief place of resort in the daytime, after the public-houses, is [Greenwich] park, in which the principal amusement is to drag young ladies up the steep hill which leads to the Observatory, and then drag them down again, at the very top of their speed, greatly to the derangement of their curls and bonnet-caps, and much to the edification of lookers-on from below. 'Kiss in the Ring,' and 'Threading my Grand-mother's Needle,' too, are sports which receive their full share of patronage. Love-sick swains, under the influence of gin-and-water, and the tender passion, become violently affectionate: and the fair objects of their regard enhance the value of stolen kisses, by a vast deal of struggling, and holding down of heads, and cries of 'Oh! Ha' done, then, George – Oh, do tickle him for me, Mary – Well, I never!' and similar Lucretian ejaculations. Little old men and women, with a small basket under one arm, and a wine-glass, without a foot, in the other hand, tender 'a drop o' the right sort' to the different groups; and young ladies, who are persuaded to indulge in a drop of the afore-said right sort, display a pleasing degree of reluctance to taste it, and cough afterwards with great propriety (*Chapter 12:* 'Greenwich Fair').

This immense booth, with the large stage in front, so brightly illuminated with variegated lamps, and pots of burning fat, is 'Richardson's', where you have a melodrama (with three murders and a ghost), a pantomime, a comic song, an overture, and some incidental music, all done in five-and-twenty minutes.

The company are now promenading outside in all the dignity of wigs, spangles, red-ochre, and whitening. See with what a ferocious air the gentleman who personates the Mexican chief, paces up and down, and with what an eye of calm dignity the principal tragedian gazes on the crowd below, or converses confidentially with the harlequin! The four clowns, who are engaged in a mock broadsword combat, may be all very well for the low-minded holiday-makers; but these are the people for the reflective portion of the community. They look so noble in those Roman dresses, with their yellow legs and arms, long black curly heads, bushy eyebrows, and scowl expressive of assassination, and vengeance, and everything else that is grand and solemn. Then, the ladies – were there ever such innocent and awful-looking beings; as they walk up and down the platform in twos and threes, with their arms round each other's waists, or leaning for support on one of those majestic men? Their spangled muslin dresses and blue satin shoes and sandals (a *leetle* the worse for wear) are the admiration of all beholders; and the playful manner in which they check the advances of the clown, is perfectly enchanting (*Chapter 12:* 'Greenwich Fair').

'Just a going to begin! Pray come for'erd, come for'erd,' exclaims the man in the countryman's dress, for the seventieth time: and people force their way up the steps in crowds. The band suddenly strikes up, the harlequin and columbine set the example, reels are formed in less than no time, the Roman heroes place their arms akimbo, and dance with considerable agility; and the leading tragic actress, and the gentleman who enacts the 'swell' in the pantomime, foot it to perfection. 'All in to begin,' shouts the manager, when no more people can be induced to 'come for'erd,' and away rush the leading members of the company to do the dreadful in the first piece (*Chapter 12:* 'Greenwich Fair').

'RICHARD THE THIRD. – DUKE OF GLO'STER, 2*l.*; EARL OF RICHMOND, 1*l.*; DUKE OF BUCKINGHAM, 15*s.*; CATESBY, 12*s.*; TRESSEL, 10*s.* 6*d.*; LORD STANLEY, 5*s.*; LORD MAYOR OF LONDON 2*s.* 6*d.*'

Such are the written placards wafered up in the gentlemen's dressing-room, in the green-room (where there is any), at a private theatre; and such are the sums extracted from the shop-till, or overcharged in the office expenditure, by the donkeys who are prevailed upon to pay for permission to exhibit their lamentable ignorance and boobyism on the stage of a private theatre. This they do, in proportion to the scope afforded by the character for the display of their imbecility. For instance, the Duke of Glo'ster is well worth two pounds, because he has it all to himself; he must wear a real sword, and what is better still, he must draw it, several times in the course of the piece. The soliloquies alone are well worth fifteen shillings; then there is the stabbing King Henry – decidedly cheap at three-and-sixpence, that's eighteen-and-sixpence; bullying the coffin-bearers – say eighteenpence, though it's worth much more – that's a pound. Then the love scene with Lady Anne, and the bustle of the fourth act can't be dear at ten shillings more – that's only one pound ten, including the 'off with his head!'

J

– which is sure to bring down the applause, and it is very easy to do – 'Orf with his ed' (very quick and loud; – then slow and sneeringly) – 'So much for Bu-u-u-uckingham!' Lay the emphasis on the 'uck'; get yourself gradually into a corner, and work with your right hand, while you're saying it, as if you were feeling your way, and it's sure to do (*Chapter 13:* 'Private Theatres').

How different people *do* look by daylight, and without punch, to be sure! (*Chapter 14:* 'Vauxhall-gardens by Day').

We walked about, and met with a disappointment at every turn, our favourite views were mere patches of paint; the fountain that had sparkled so showily by lamplight, presented very much the appearance of a water-pipe that had burst; all the ornaments were dingy, and all the walks gloomy. There was a spectral attempt at rope-dancing in the little open theatre. The sun shone upon the spangled dresses of the performers, and their evolutions were about as inspiriting and appropriate as a country-dance in a family vault (*Chapter 14:* 'Vauxhall-gardens by Day').

If we had been a powerful churchman in those good times when blood was shed as freely as water, and men were mowed down like grass, in the sacred cause of religion, we would have lain by very quietly till we got hold of some especially obstinate miscreant, who positively refused to be converted to our faith, and then we would have booked him for an inside place in a small coach, which travelled day and night: and securing the remainder of the places for stout men with a slight tendency to coughing and spitting, we would have started him forth on his last travels: leaving him mercilessly to all the tortures which the waiters, landlords, coachmen, guards, boots, chambermaids, and other familiars on his line of road, might think proper to inflict (*Chapter 15:* 'Early Coaches').

It is very generally allowed that public conveyances afford an extensive field for amusement and observation. Of all the public conveyances that have been constructed since the days of the Ark – we think that is the earliest on record – to the present time, commend us to an omnibus. A long stage is not to be despised, but there you have only six insides, and the chances are, that the same people go all the way with you – there is no change, no variety. Besides, after the first twelve hours or so, people get cross and sleepy, and when you have seen a man in his night-cap, you lose all respect for him; at least, that is the case with us. Then on smooth roads people frequently get prosy, and tell long stories, and even those who don't talk, may have very unpleasant predilections. We once travelled four hundred miles, inside a stage-coach, with a stout man, who had a glass of rum-and-water, warm, handed in at the window at every place where we changed horses. This was decidedly unpleasant. We have also travelled occasionally, with a small boy of a pale aspect, with light hair, and no perceptible neck, coming up to town from school under the protection of the guard, and directed to be left at the Cross Keys till called for. This is, perhaps, even worse than rum-and-water in a close atmosphere. Then there is the whole train of evils consequent on a change of the coachman; and the misery of the discovery – which the guard is sure to make the moment you begin to doze – that he wants a brown-paper parcel, which he distinctly remembers to have deposited under the seat on which you are reposing. A great deal of bustle and groping takes place, and when you are thoroughly awakened, and severely cramped, by holding your legs up by an almost supernatural exertion, while he is looking behind them, it suddenly occurs to him that he put it in the fore-boot. Bang goes the door; the parcel is immediately found; off starts the coach again; and the guard plays the key-bugle as loud as he can play it, as if in mockery of your wretchedness.

Now, you meet with none of these afflictions in an omnibus; sameness there can never be. The passengers change as often in the course of one journey as the figures in a kaleidoscope, and though not so glittering, are far more amusing. We believe there is no instance on record, of a man's having gone to sleep in one of these vehicles. As to long stories, would any man venture to tell a long story in an omnibus? and even if he did, where would be the harm? nobody could possibly hear what he was talking about. Again; children, though occasionally, are not often to be found in an omnibus; and even when they are, if the vehicle be full, as is generally the case, somebody sits upon them, and we are unconscious of their presence. Yes, after mature reflection, and considerable experience, we are decidedly of opinion, that of all known vehicles, from the glass-coach in which we were taken to be christened, to that sombre caravan in which we must one day make our last earthly journey, there is nothing like an omnibus (*Chapter 16:* 'Omnibuses').

Some people object to the exertion of getting into cabs, and others object to the difficulty of getting out of them; we think both these are objections which take their rise in perverse and ill-conditioned minds. The getting into a cab is a very pretty and graceful process, which, when well performed, is essentially melo-dramatic. First, there is the expressive pantomime of every one of the eighteen cabmen on the stand, the moment you raise your eyes from the ground. Then there is your own pantomime in reply – quite a little ballet. Four cabs immediately leave the stand, for your especial accommodation; and the evolutions of the animals who draw them, are beautiful in the extreme, as they grate the wheels of the cabs against the curb-stones, and sport playfully in the kennel. You single out a particular cab, and dart swiftly towards it. One bound, and you are on the first step; turn your body lightly round to the right, and you are on the second; bend gracefully beneath the reins, working round to the left at the same time, and you are in the cab. There is no difficulty in finding a seat: the apron knocks you comfortably into it at once, and off you go (*Chapter 17:* 'The Last Cab-driver').

Well; many years ago we began to be a steady and matter-of-fact sort of people, and dancing in spring being beneath our dignity, we gave it up, and in course of time it descended to the sweeps – a fall certainly, because, though sweeps are very good fellows in their way, and moreover very useful in a civilised com-munity, they are not exactly the sort of people to give the tone to the little elegances of society. The sweeps, however, got the dancing to themselves, and they kept it up, and handed it down. This was a severe blow to the romance of spring-time, but, it did not entirely destroy it, either; for a portion of it descended to the sweeps with the dancing, and rendered them objects of great interest. A mystery hung over the sweeps in those days. Legends were in existence of wealthy gentlemen who had lost children, and who, after many years of sorrow and suffering, had found them in the character of sweeps. Stories were related of a young boy who, having been stolen from his parents in his infancy, and devoted to the occupation of chimney-sweeping, was sent, in the course of his professional career, to sweep the chimney of his mother's bedroom; and how, being hot and tired when he came out of the chimney, he got into the bed he had so often slept in as an infant, and was discovered and recognised therein by his mother, who once every year of her life, thereafter, requested the pleasure of the company of every London sweep, at half-past one o'clock, to roast beef, plum-pudding, porter, and sixpence.

Such stories as these, and there were many such, threw an air of mystery round the sweeps, and pro-duced for them some of those good effects which animals derive from the doctrine of the transmigration of souls. No one (except the masters) thought of ill-treating a sweep, because no one knew who he might be, or what nobleman's or gentleman's son he might turn out. Chimney-sweeping was, by many believers in the marvellous, considered as a sort of probationary term, at an earlier or later period of which, divers young noblemen were to come into possession of their rank and titles: and the profession was held by them in great respect accordingly.

We remember, in our young days, a little sweep about our own age, with curly hair and white teeth, whom we devoutly and sincerely believed to be the lost son and heir of some illustrious personage – an impression which was resolved into an unchangeable conviction on our infant mind, by the subject of our speculations informing us, one day, in reply to our question, propounded a few moments before his ascent to the summit of the kitchen chimney, 'that he believed he'd been born in the vurkis, but he'd never know'd his father.' We felt certain, from that time forth, that he would one day be owned by a lord; and we never heard the church-bells ring, or saw a flag hoisted in the neighbourhood, without thinking that the happy event had at last occurred, and that his long-lost parent had arrived in a coach and six, to take him home to Grosvenor Square. He never came, however; and, at the present moment, the young gentleman in question is settled down as a master sweep in the neighbourhood of Battle Bridge, his distinguishing characteristics being a decided anti-pathy to washing himself, and the possession of a pair of legs very inadequate to the support of his unwieldy and corpulent body (*Chapter 20:* 'The First of May').

Neither of these classes of brokers' shops, forms the subject of this sketch. The shops to which we advert, are immeasurably inferior to those on whose outward appearance we have slightly touched. Our readers must often have observed in some by-street, in a poor neighbourhood, a small dirty shop, exposing for sale the most extraordinary and confused jumble of old, worn-out, wretched articles, that can well be imagined. Our wonder at their ever having been bought, is only to be equalled by our astonishment at the idea of their ever being sold again. On a board, at the side of the door, are placed about twenty books – all odd volumes; and as many wine-glasses – all different patterns; several locks, an old earthenware pan, full of rusty keys; two or three gaudy chimney-ornaments – cracked, of course; the remains of a lustre, without any drops; a round frame like a capital O, which has once held a mirror; a flute, complete with the exception of the middle joint; a pair of curling-irons; and a tinder-box. In front of the shop-window, are ranged some half-dozen high-backed chairs, with spinal complaints and wasted legs; a corner cupboard; two or three very dark mahogany tables with flaps like mathematical problems; some pickle-jars, some surgeons' ditto, with gilt labels and without stoppers; an unframed portrait of some lady who flourished about the beginning of the thirteenth century, by an artist who never flourished at all; an incalculable host of miscellanies of every description, including bottles and cabinets, rags and bones, fenders and street-door knockers, fire-irons, wearing apparel and bedding, a hall-lamp, and a room-door. Imagine, in addition to this incongruous mass, a black doll in a white frock, with two faces – one looking up the street, and the other looking down, swinging over the door; a board with the squeezed-up inscription 'Dealer in marine stores,' in lanky white letters, whose height is strangely out of proportion to their width; and you have before you precisely the kind of shop to which we wish to direct your attention.

Although the same heterogeneous mixture of things will be found at all these places, it is curious to observe how truly and accurately some of the minor articles which are exposed for sale – articles of wearing apparel, for instance – mark the character of the neighbourhood. Take Drury Lane and Covent Garden for example.

This is essentially a theatrical neighbourhood. There is not a pot-boy in the vicinity who is not, to a greater or less extent, a dramatic character. The errand boys and chandler's-shop-keepers' sons, are all stage-struck: they 'gets up' plays in back-kitchens hired for the purpose, and will stand before a shop-window for hours, contemplating a great staring portrait of Mr. Somebody or other, of the Royal Coburg Theatre, 'as he appeared in the character of Tongo the Denounced.' The consequence is, that there is not a marine-store shop in the neighbourhood, which does not exhibit for sale some faded articles of dramatic finery, such as three or four pairs of soiled buff boots with turn-over red tops, heretofore worn by a 'fourth robber,' or 'fifth mob'; a pair of rusty broadswords, a few gauntlets, and certain resplendent ornaments, which, if they were yellow instead of white, might be taken for insurance plates of the Sun Fire Office. There are several of these shops in the narrow streets and dirty courts, of which there are so many near the national theatres, and they all have tempting goods of this description, with the addition, perhaps, of a lady's pink dress covered with spangles; white wreaths, stage shoes, and a tiara like a tin lamp-reflector. They have been purchased of some wretched supernumeraries, or sixth-rate actors, and are now offered for the benefit of the rising generation, who, on condition of making certain weekly payments, amounting in the whole to about ten times their value, may avail themselves of such desirable bargains (*Chapter 21:* 'Brokers' and Marine-store Shops').

The extensive scale on which these places are established, and the ostentatious manner in which the business of even the smallest among them is divided into branches, is amusing. A handsome plate of ground glass in one door directs you 'To the Counting-house;' another to the 'Bottle Department'; a third to the 'Wholesale Department'; a fourth to 'The Wine Promenade'; and so forth, until we are in daily expectation of meeting with a 'Brandy Bell,' or a 'Whiskey Entrance.' Then, ingenuity is exhausted in devising attractive titles for the different descriptions of gin; and the dram-drinking portion of the community as they gaze upon the gigantic black and white announcements, which are only to be equalled in size by the figures beneath them, are left in a state of pleasing hesitation between 'The Cream of the Valley,' 'The Out and Out,' 'The No Mistake,' 'The Good for Mixing,' 'The real Knock-me-down,' 'The celebrated Butter Gin,' 'The regular Flare-up,' and a dozen other, equally inviting and wholesome *liqueurs*. Although places of this description are to be met with in every second street, they are invariably numerous and splendid in precise proportion to the dirt and poverty of the surrounding neighbourhood. The gin-shops in and near Drury Lane, Holborn, St. Giles's, Covent Garden, and Clare Market, are the handsomest in London. There is more of filth and squalid misery near those great thoroughfares than in any part of this mighty city (*Chapter 22:* 'Gin-shops').

There are strange chords in the human heart, which will lie dormant through years of depravity and wickedness, but which will vibrate at last to some slight circumstance apparently trivial in itself, but connected by some undefined and indistinct association, with past days that can never be recalled, and with bitter recollections from which the most degraded creature in existence cannot escape (*Chapter 23:* 'The Pawnbroker's Shop').

CHARACTERS

It is strange with how little notice, good, bad, or indifferent, a man may live and die in London. He awakens no sympathy in the breast of any single person; his existence is a matter of interest to no one save himself; he cannot be said to be forgotten when he dies, for no one remembered him when he was alive. There is a numerous class of people in this great metropolis who seem not to possess a single friend, and whom nobody appears to care for. Urged by imperative necessity in the first instance, they have resorted to London in search of employment, and the means of subsistence (*Chapter 1:* 'Thoughts about People').

Christmas time! That man must be a misanthrope indeed, in whose breast something like a jovial feeling is not roused – in whose mind some pleasant associations are not awakened – by the recurrence of Christmas. There are people who will tell you that Christmas is not to them what it used to be; that each succeeding Christmas has found some cherished hope, or happy prospect, of the year before, dimmed or passed away; that the present only serves to remind them of reduced circumstances and straitened incomes – of the feasts they once bestowed on hollow friends, and of the cold looks that meet them now, in adversity and misfortune. Never heed such dismal reminiscences. There are few men who have lived long enough in the world, who cannot call up such thoughts any day in the year. Then do not select the merriest of the three hundred and sixty-five, for your doleful recollections, but draw your chair nearer the blazing fire – fill the glass and send round the song – and if your room be smaller than it was a dozen years ago, or if your glass be filled with reeking punch, instead of sparkling wine, put a good face on the matter, and empty it off-hand, and fill another, and troll off the old ditty you used to sing, and thank God it's no worse (*Chapter 2:* 'A Christmas Dinner').

A Christmas family-party! We know nothing in nature more delightful! There seems a magic in the very name of Christmas. Petty jealousies and discords are forgotten; social feelings are awakened, in bosoms to which they have long been strangers; father and son, or brother and sister, who have met and passed with averted gaze, or a look of cold recognition, for months before, proffer and return the cordial embrace, and bury their past animosities in their present happiness (*Chapter 2:* 'A Christmas Dinner').

'I wos a thinking,' said Mr. Samuel Wilkins, during a pause in the conversation – 'I wos a thinking of taking J'mima to the Eagle to-night.' – 'O my!' exclaimed Mrs. Ivins. 'Lor! how nice!' said the youngest Miss Ivins. 'Well, I declare!' added the youngest Miss Ivins but one. 'Tell J'mima to put on her white muslin, Tilly,' screamed Mrs. Ivins, with motherly anxiety; and down came J'mima herself soon afterwards in a white muslin gown carefully hooked and eyed, a little red shawl, plentifully pinned, a white straw bonnet trimmed with red ribbons, a small necklace, a large pair of bracelets, Denmark satin shoes, and open-worked stockings; white cotton gloves on her fingers, and a cambric pocket-handkerchief, carefully folded up, in her hand – all quite genteel and ladylike. And away went Miss J'mima Ivins and Mr. Samuel Wilkins, and a dress cane, with a gilt knob at the top, to the admiration and envy of the street in general, and to the high gratification of Mrs. Ivins, and the two youngest Miss Ivinses in particular. They had no sooner turned into the Pancras Road, than who should Miss J'mima Ivins stumble upon, by the most fortunate accident in the world, but a young lady as she knew, with *her* young man! – And it is so strange how things do turn out sometimes – they were

actually going to the Eagle too. So Mr. Samuel Wilkins was introduced to Miss J'mima Ivins's friend's young man, and they all walked on together, talking, and laughing, and joking away like anything; and when they got as far as Pentonville, Miss Ivins's friend's young man *would* have the ladies go into the Crown, to taste some shrub, which, after a great blushing and giggling, and hiding of faces in elaborate pocket-handkerchiefs, they consented to do. Having tasted it once, they were easily prevailed upon to taste it again; and they sat out in the garden tasting shrub, and looking at the busses alternately, till it was just the proper time to go to the Eagle; and then they resumed their journey, and walked very fast, for fear they should lose the beginning of the concert in the Rotunda.

'How ev'nly!' said Miss J'mima Ivins, and Miss J'mima Ivins's friend, both at once, when they had passed the gate and were fairly inside the gardens. There were the walks, beautifully gravelled and planted – and the refreshment-boxes, painted and ornamented like so many snuff-boxes – and the variegated lamps shedding their rich light upon the company's heads – and the place for dancing ready chalked for the company's feet – and a Moorish band playing at one end of the gardens – and an opposition military band playing away at the other. Then, the waiters were rushing to and fro with glasses of negus, and glasses of brandy-and-water, and bottles of ale, and bottles of stout; and ginger-beer was going off in one place, and practical jokes were going on in another; and people were crowding to the door of the Rotunda; and in short the whole scene was, as Miss J'mima Ivins, inspired by the novelty, or the shrub, or both, observed – 'one of dazzling excitement.' As to the concert-room, never was anything half so splendid. There was an orchestra for the singers, all paint, gilding, and plate-glass; and such an organ! Miss J'mima Ivins's friend's young man whispered it had cost 'four hundred pound,' which Mr. Samuel Wilkins said 'was not dear neither'; an opinion in which the ladies perfectly coincided (*Chapter 4:* 'Miss Evans and the Eagle').

TALES

'I shall be a good deal of trouble to you,' said Mrs. Bloss; 'but for that trouble I am willing to pay. I am going through a course of treatment which renders attention necessary. I have one mutton-chop in bed at half-past eight, and another at ten, every morning' (*Chapter 1:* 'The Boarding-House').

'It's rather singular,' continued Mrs. Tibbs, with what was meant for a most bewitching smile, 'that we have a gentleman now with us, who is in a very delicate state of health – a Mr. Gobler. His apartment is the back drawing-room.'
'The next room?' inquired Mrs. Bloss.
'The next room,' repeated the hostess.
'How very promiscuous!' ejaculated the widow.
'He hardly ever gets up,' said Mrs. Tibbs in a whisper.
'Lor!' cried Mrs. Bloss, in an equally low tone.

'And when he is up,' said Mrs. Tibbs, 'we never can persuade him to go to bed again.'

'Dear me!' said the astonished Mrs. Bloss, drawing her chair nearer Mrs. Tibbs. 'What is his complaint?'

'Why, the fact is,' replied Mrs. Tibbs, with a most communicative air, 'he has no stomach whatever.'

'No what?' inquired Mrs. Bloss, with a look of the most indescribable alarm.

'No stomach,' repeated Mrs. Tibbs, with a shake of the head.

'Lord bless us! what an extraordinary case!' gasped Mrs. Bloss, as if she understood the communication in its literal sense, and was astonished at a gentleman without a stomach finding it necessary to board anywhere (*Chapter 1:* 'The Boarding-House').

'God bless me!' exclaimed Tomkins, who had been looking out at the window. 'Here – Wisbottle – pray come here – make haste.'

Mr. Wisbottle started from the table, and every one looked up.

'Do you see,' said the connoisseur, placing Wisbottle in the right position – 'a little more this way: there – do you see how splendidly the light falls upon the left side of that broken chimney-pot at No. 48?'

'Dear me! I see,' replied Wisbottle, in a tone of admiration.

'I never saw an object stand out so beautifully against the clear sky in my life,' ejaculated Alfred. Everybody (except John Evenson) echoed the sentiment; for Mr. Tomkins had a great character for finding out beauties which no one else could discover – he certainly deserved it.

'I have frequently observed a chimney-pot in College Green, Dublin, which has a much better effect,' said the patriotic O'Bleary, who never allowed Ireland to be outdone on any point.

The assertion was received with obvious incredulity, for Mr. Tomkins declared that no other chimney-pot in the United Kingdom, broken or unbroken, could be so beautiful as the one at No. 48 (*Chapter 1:* 'The Boarding-House').

'We have some splendid steam-vessels in Ireland,' said O'Bleary.

'Certainly,' said Mrs. Bloss, delighted to find a subject broached in which she could take part.

'The accommodations are extraordinary,' said O'Bleary.

'Extraordinary indeed,' returned Mrs. Bloss. 'When Mr. Bloss was alive, he was promiscuously obliged to go to Ireland on business. I went with him, and raly the manner in which the ladies and gentlemen were accommodated with berths, is not creditable' (*Chapter 1:* 'The Boarding-House').

'By the bye,' said Mrs. Bloss, 'I have not seen Mr. What's-his-name yet.'

'Mr. Gobler?' suggested Mrs. Tibbs.

'Yes.'

'Oh!' said Mrs. Tibbs, 'he is a most mysterious person. He has his meals regularly sent upstairs, and sometimes don't leave his room for weeks together.'

'I haven't seen or heard nothing of him,' repeated Mrs. Bloss.

'I dare say you'll hear him to-night,' replied Mrs. Tibbs; 'he generally groans a good deal on Sunday evenings' (*Chapter 1:* 'The Boarding-House').

'How many beds have you got?' screamed Mrs. Tuggs out of the fly, to the woman who opened the door of the first house which displayed a bill intimating that apartments were to be let within.

'How many did you want, ma'am?' was, of course, the reply.

'Three.'

'Will you step in, ma'am?' Down got Mrs. Tuggs. The family were delighted. Splendid view of the sea from the front windows – charming! A short pause. Back came Mrs. Tuggs again. – One parlour and a mattress.

'Why the devil didn't they say so at first?' inquired Mr. Joseph Tuggs, rather pettishly.

'Don't know,' said Mrs. Tuggs.

'Wretches!' exclaimed the nervous Cymon. Another bill – another stoppage. Same question – same answer – similar result.

'What do they mean by this?' inquired Mr. Joseph Tuggs, thoroughly out of temper.

'Don't know,' said the placid Mrs. Tuggs.

'Orvis the vay here, sir,' said the driver, by way of accounting for the circumstance in a satisfactory manner; and off they went again, to make fresh inquiries, and encounter fresh disappointments (*Chapter 4:* 'The Tuggses at Ramsgate').

'How shall we go?' inquired the captain; 'it's too warm to walk.'

'A shay?' suggested Mr. Joseph Tuggs.

'Chaise,' whispered Mr. Cymon.

'I should think one would be enough,' said Mr. Joseph Tuggs aloud, quite unconscious of the meaning of the correction. 'However, two shays if you like' (*Chapter 4:* 'The Tuggses at Ramsgate').

Horatio's countenance brightened up, like an old hat in a shower of rain (*Chapter 5:* 'Horatio Sparkins').

Tom looked as happy as a cock on a drizzly morning (*Chapter 5:* 'Horatio Sparkins').

'How delightful!' said the interesting Horatio to his partner, as they promenaded the room at the conclusion of the set – 'how delightful, how refreshing it is, to retire from the cloudy storms, the vicissitudes, and the troubles, of life, even if it be but for a few short fleeting moments: and to spend those moments, fading and evanescent though they be, in the delightful, the blessed society of one individual – whose frowns would be death, whose coldness would be madness, whose falsehood would be ruin, whose constancy would be bliss; the possession of whose affection would be the brightest and best reward that Heaven could bestow on man?'

'What feeling! what sentiment!' thought Miss Teresa, as she leaned more heavily on her companion's arm (*Chapter 5:* 'Horatio Sparkins').

'And after all, sir, what is man?' said the metaphysical Sparkins. 'I say, what is man?'

'Ah! very true,' said Mr. Malderton; 'very true.'

'We know that we live and breathe,' continued Horatio; 'that we have wants and wishes, desires and appetites – '

'Certainly,' said Mr. Frederick Malderton, looking profound.

'I say, we know that we exist,' repeated Horatio, raising his voice, 'but there we stop; there, is an end to our knowledge; there, is the summit of our attainments; there, is the termination of our ends. What more do we know?'

'Nothing,' replied Mr. Frederick – than whom no one was more capable of answering for himself in that particular (*Chapter 5:* 'Horatio Sparkins').

'Pray, what is your opinion of woman, Mr. Sparkins?' inquired Mrs. Malderton. The young ladies simpered.

'Man,' replied Horatio, 'man, whether he ranged the bright, gay, flowery plains of a second Eden, or the more sterile, barren, and I may say, commonplace regions, to which we are compelled to accustom ourselves, in times such as these, man, under any circumstances, or in any place – whether he were bending beneath the withering blasts of the frigid zone, or scorching under the rays of a vertical sun – man, without woman, would be – alone' (*Chapter 5:* 'Horatio Sparkins').

He dressed himself, took a hasty apology for a breakfast, and sallied forth. The streets looked as lonely and deserted as if they had been crowded, overnight, for the last time. Here and there, an early apprentice, with quenched-looking, sleepy eyes, was taking down the shutters of a shop; and a policeman or milkwoman might occasionally be seen pacing slowly along; but the servants had not yet begun to clean the doors, or light the kitchen fires, and London looked the picture of desolation. At the corner of a by-street, near Temple Bar, was stationed a 'street-breakfast.' The coffee was boiling over a charcoal fire, and large slices of bread-and-butter were piled one upon the other, like deals in a timber-yard. The company were seated on a form, which, with a view both to security and comfort, was placed against a neighbouring wall. Two young men, whose uproarious mirth and disordered dress bespoke the conviviality of the preceding evening, were treating three 'ladies' and an Irish labourer. A little sweep was standing at a short distance, casting a longing eye at the tempting delicacies; and a policeman was watching the group from the opposite side of the street. The wan looks, and gaudy finery of the thinly-clad women contrasted as strangely with the gay sunlight, as did their forced merriment with the boisterous hilarity of the two young men, who, now and then, varied their amusements by 'bonneting' the proprietor of this itinerant coffee-house (*Chapter 7:* 'The Steam Excursion').

'How d'ye do, dear?' said the Misses Briggs to the Misses Taunton. (The word 'dear' among girls is frequently synonymous with 'wretch.') (*Chapter 7:* 'The Steam Excursion').

'Shall I accompany you, dear?' inquired one of the Miss Briggses, with the bland intention of spoiling the effect.

'Very much obliged to you, Miss Briggs,' sharply retorted Mrs. Taunton, who saw through the manœuvre; 'my daughters always sing without accompaniments.'

'And without voices,' tittered Mrs. Briggs, in a low tone.

'Perhaps,' said Mrs. Taunton, reddening, for she guessed the tenor of the observation, though she had not heard it clearly – 'Perhaps it would be as well for some people, if their voices were not quite so audible as they are to other people.'

'And, perhaps, if gentlemen who are kidnapped to pay attention to some person's daughters, had not sufficient discernment to pay attention to other persons' daughters,' returned Mrs. Briggs, 'some persons would not be so ready to display that ill-temper which, thank God, distinguishes them from other persons.'

'Persons!' ejaculated Mrs. Taunton.

'Persons,' replied Mrs. Briggs.

'Insolence!'

'Creature!'

'Hush! hush!' interrupted Mr. Percy Noakes, who was one of the very few by whom this dialogue had been overheard. 'Hush! – pray, silence for the duet' (*Chapter 7:* 'The Steam Excursion').

Impudence and the marvellous are pretty sure passports to any society (*Chapter 7:* 'The Steam Excursion').

Sea-sickness . . . is like a belief in ghosts – every one entertains some misgivings on the subject, but few will acknowledge any (*Chapter 7:* 'The Steam Excursion').

The throbbing motion of the engine was but too perceptible. There was a large, substantial, cold boiled leg of mutton, at the bottom of the table, shaking like blancmange; a previously hearty sirloin of beef looked as if it had been suddenly seized with the palsy; and some tongues, which were placed on dishes rather too large for them, went through the most surprising evolutions; darting from side to side, and from end to end, like a fly in an inverted wine-glass. Then, the sweets shook and trembled, till it was quite impossible to help them, and people gave up the attempt in despair; and the pigeon-pies looked as if the birds, whose legs were stuck outside, were trying to get them in. The table vibrated and started like a feverish pulse, and the very legs were convulsed – everything was shaking and jarring. The beams in the roof of the cabin seemed as if they were put there for the sole purpose of giving people headaches, and several elderly gentlemen became ill-tempered in consequence. As fast as the steward put the fire-irons up, they *would* fall down again; and the more the ladies and gentlemen tried to sit comfortably on their seats, the more the seats seemed to slide away from the ladies and gentlemen. Several ominous demands were made for small glasses of brandy; the countenances of the company gradually underwent most extraordinary changes; one gentleman was observed suddenly to rush from table without the slightest ostensible reason, and dart up the steps with incredible swiftness: thereby greatly damaging both himself, and the steward, who happened to be coming down at the same moment (*Chapter 7:* 'The Steam Excursion').

'I beg your pardon, sir,' said the steward, running up to Mr. Percy Noakes, 'I beg your pardon, sir, but the gentleman as just went on deck – him with the green spectacles – is uncommon bad, to be sure; and the young man as played the wiolin says, that unless he has some brandy he can't answer for the consequences. He says he has a wife and two children, whose werry subsistence depends on his breaking a wessel, and he expects to do so every moment. The flageolet's been werry ill, but he's better, only he's in a dreadful prusperation' (*Chapter 7:* 'The Steam Excursion').

Mr. Hardy was observed, some hours afterwards, in an attitude which induced his friends to suppose that he was busily engaged in contemplating the beauties of the deep; they only regretted that his taste for the picturesque should lead him to remain so long in a position, very injurious at all times, but especially so, to an individual labouring under a tendency of blood to the head (*Chapter 7:* 'The Steam Excursion').

'You are the upper-boots, I think?' inquired Mr. Trott.

'Yes, I am the upper-boots,' replied a voice from inside a velveteen case, with mother-of-pearl buttons – 'that is, I'm the boots as b'longs to the house; the other man's my man, as goes errands and does odd jobs. Top-boots and half-boots, I calls us.'

'You're from London?' inquired Mr. Trott.

'Driv a cab once,' was the laconic reply.

'Why don't you drive it now?' asked Mr. Trott.

'Over-driv the cab, and driv over a 'ooman,' replied the top-boots, with brevity (*Chapter 8:* 'The Great Winglebury Duel').

Matrimony is proverbially a serious undertaking. Like an overweening predilection for brandy-and-water, it is a misfortune into which a man easily falls, and from which he finds it remarkably difficult to extricate himself. It is of no use telling a man who is timorous on these points, that it is but one plunge, and all is over. They say the same thing at the Old Bailey, and the unfortunate victims derive as much comfort from the assurance in the one case as in the other (*Chapter 10:* 'A Passage in the Life of Mr. Watkins Tottle').

'Ladies and gentlemen,' resumed Dumps. . . . 'In accordance with what is, I believe, the established usage on these occasions, I, as one of the godfathers of Master Frederick Charles William Kitterbell – (here the speaker's voice faltered, for he remembered the mug) – venture to rise to propose a toast. I need hardly say that it is the health and prosperity of that young gentleman, the particular event of whose early life we are here met to celebrate – (applause). Ladies and gentlemen, it is impossible to suppose that our friends here, whose sincere well-wishers we all are, can pass through life without some trials, considerable suffering, severe affliction, and heavy losses!' – Here the arch-traitor paused, and slowly drew forth a long, white pocket-handkerchief – his example was followed by several ladies. 'That these trials may be long spared them is my most earnest prayer, my most fervent wish (a distinct sob from the grandmother). I hope and trust, ladies and gentlemen, that the infant whose christening we have this evening met to celebrate, may not be removed from the arms of his parents by premature decay (several cambrics were in requisition): that his young and now *apparently* healthy form, may not be wasted by lingering disease. (Here Dumps cast a sardonic glance around, for a great sensation was manifest among the married ladies.) You, I am sure, will concur with me in wishing that he may live to be a comfort and a blessing to his parents. ('Hear, hear!' and an audible sob from Mr. Kitterbell.) But should he not be what we could wish – should he forget in after-times the duty which he owes to them – should they unhappily experience that distracting truth, "how sharper than a serpent's tooth it is to have a thankless child" ' – Here Mrs. Kitterbell, with her handkerchief to her eyes, and accompanied by several ladies, rushed from the room, and went into violent hysterics in the passage, leaving her better-half in almost as bad a condition, and a general impression in Dumps's favour; for people like sentiment, after all (*Chapter 11:* 'The Bloomsbury Christening').

THE PICKWICK PAPERS

'May 12, 1827. Joseph Smiggers, Esq., P V P M P C.,[1] presiding. The following resolutions unanimously agreed to: –

'That this Association has heard read, with feelings of unmingled satisfaction, and unqualified approval, the paper communicated by Samuel Pickwick, Esq., G.C.M.P.C.,[2] entitled "Speculations on the Source of the Hampstead Ponds, with some Observations on the Theory of Tittlebats;" and that this Association does hereby return its warmest thanks to the said Samuel Pickwick, Esq., G.C.M.P.C., for the same' (*Chapter 1*).

'He (Mr. Pickwick) would not deny that he was influenced by human passions, and human feelings (cheers) – possibly by human weaknesses – (loud cries of "No"); but this he would say, that if ever the fire of self-importance broke out in his bosom, the desire to benefit the human race in preference effectually quenched it. The praise of mankind was his Swing; philanthropy was his insurance office. (Vehement cheering.) He had felt some pride – he acknowledged it freely, and let his enemies make the most of it – he had felt some pride when he presented his Tittlebatian Theory to the world; it might be celebrated or it might not. (A cry of "It is," and great cheering.)' (*Chapter 1*).

That punctual servant of all work, the sun, had just risen, and begun to strike a light on the morning of the thirteenth of May, one thousand eight hundred and twenty-seven, when Mr. Samuel Pickwick burst like another sun from his slumbers, threw open his chamber window, and looked out upon the world

1 Perpetual Vice-President – Member Pickwick Club
2 General Chairman – Member Pickwick Club.

beneath. Goswell Street was at his feet, Goswell Street was on his right hand – as far as the eye could reach, Goswell Street extended on his left; and the opposite side of Goswell Street was over the way. 'Such,' thought Mr. Pickwick, 'are the narrow views of those philosophers who, content with examining the things that lie before them, look not to the truths which are hidden beyond. As well might I be content to gaze on Goswell Street for ever, without one effort to penetrate to the hidden countries which on every side surround it.' And having given vent to this beautiful reflection, Mr. Pickwick proceeded to put himself into his clothes, and his clothes into his portmanteau (*Chapter 2*).

'How old is that horse, my friend?' inquired Mr. Pickwick, rubbing his nose with the shilling he had reserved for the fare.

'Forty-two,' replied the driver, eyeing him askant.

'What!' ejaculated Mr. Pickwick, laying his hand upon his note-book. The driver reiterated his former statement. Mr. Pickwick looked very hard at the man's face, but his features were immovable, so he noted down the fact forthwith.

'And how long do you keep him out at a time?' inquired Mr. Pickwick, searching for further information.

'Two or three weeks,' replied the man.

'Weeks!' said Mr. Pickwick, in astonishment – and out came the note-book again.

'He lives at Pentonwil when he's at home,' observed the driver, coolly, 'but we seldom takes him home on account of his weakness.'

'On account of his weakness!' reiterated the perplexed Mr. Pickwick.

'He always falls down when he's took out o' the cab,' continued the driver, 'but when he's in it, we bears him up werry tight, and takes him in werry short, so as he can't werry well fall down; and we've got a pair o' precious large wheels on, so ven he *does* move, they run after him, and he must go on – he can't help it.'

Mr. Pickwick entered every word of this statement in his note-book, with the view of communicating it to the club, as a singular instance of the tenacity of life in horses, under trying circumstances (*Chapter 2*).

'Here, waiter!' shouted the stranger, ringing the bell with tremendous violence, 'glasses round, – brandy-and-water, hot and strong, and sweet, and plenty, – eye damaged, sir? Waiter! raw beef-steak for the gentleman's eye, – nothing like raw beef-steak for a bruise, sir; cold lamp-post very good, but lamp-post inconvenient – damned odd standing in the open street half an hour, with your eye against a lamp-post – eh, – very good – ha! ha!' And the stranger, without stopping to take breath, swallowed at a draught full half a pint of the reeking brandy-and-water, and flung himself into a chair with as much ease as if nothing uncommon had occurred (*Chapter 2*: Jingle).

'Any luggage, sir?' inquired the coachman.

'Who – I? Brown paper parcel here, that's all, – other luggage gone by water, – packing cases, nailed up – big as houses – heavy, heavy, damned heavy,' replied the stranger, as he forced into his pocket as much as he could of the brown paper parcel, which presented most suspicious indications of containing one shirt and a handkerchief.

'Heads, heads – take care of your heads!' cried the loquacious stranger, as they came out under the low archway, which in those days formed the entrance to the coach-yard. 'Terrible place – dangerous work – other day – five children – mother – tall lady, eating sandwiches – forgot the arch – crash – knock – children look round – mother's head off – sandwich in her hand – no mouth to put it in – head of a family off – shocking, shocking! Looking at Whitehall, sir? – fine place – little window – somebody else's head off there, eh, sir? – he didn't keep a sharp look-out enough either – eh, sir, eh?' (*Chapter 2*: Jingle).

'My friend Mr. Snodgrass has a strong poetic turn,' said Mr. Pickwick.

'So have I,' said the stranger. 'Epic poem, – ten thousand lines – revolution of July – composed it on the spot – Mars by day, Apollo by night, – bang the fieldpiece, twang the lyre' (*Chapter 2*: Pickwick and Jingle).

'Sportsman, sir?' ...

'A little, sir,' replied that gentleman.

'Fine pursuit, sir, – fine pursuit. – Dogs, sir?'

'Not just now,' said Mr. Winkle.

'Ah! you should keep dogs – fine animals – sagacious creatures – dog of my own once – Pointer – surprising instinct – out shooting one day – entering enclosure – whistled – dog stopped – whistled again – Ponto – no go; stock still – called him – Ponto, Ponto – wouldn't move – dog transfixed – staring at a board – looked up, saw an inscription – "Gamekeeper has orders to shoot all dogs found in this enclosure" – wouldn't pass it – wonderful dog – valuable dog that – very' (*Chapter 2*: Jingle and Winkle).

'Magnificent ruin!' said Mr. Augustus Snodgrass, with all the poetic fervour that distinguished him, when they came in sight of the fine old castle.

'What a study for an antiquarian!' were the very words which fell from Mr. Pickwick's mouth, as he applied his telescope to his eye.

'Ah! fine place,' said the stranger, 'glorious pile – frowning walls – tottering arches – dark nooks – crumbling staircases – Old cathedral too – earthy smell – pilgrims' feet worn away the old steps – little Saxon doors – confessionals like money-takers' boxes at theatres – queer customers those monks – Popes, and Lord Treasurers, and all sorts of old fellows, with great red faces, and broken noses, turning up every day – buff jerkins too – match-locks – Sarcophagus – fine place – old legends too – strange stories: capital.' The stranger continued to soliloquise until they reached the Bull Inn, in the High Street, where the coach stopped.

'Do you remain here, sir?' inquired Mr. Nathaniel Winkle.

'Here – not I – but you'd better – good house – nice beds – Wright's next house, dear – very dear –

half-a-crown in the bill if you look at the waiter – charge you more if you dine at a friend's than they would if you dined in the coffee-room – rum fellows – very' (*Chapter 2:* Jingle).

We do not find, from a careful perusal of Mr. Pickwick's notes on the four towns, Stroud, Rochester, Chatham, and Brompton, that his impressions of their appearance differ in any material point from those of other travellers who have gone over the same ground. His general description is easily abridged.

'The principal productions of these towns,' says Mr. Pickwick, 'appear to be soldiers, sailors, Jews, chalk, shrimps, officers, and dockyard men. The commodities chiefly exposed for sale in the public streets are marine stores, hard-bake, apples, flat-fish, and oysters. The streets present a lively and animated appearance, occasioned chiefly by the conviviality of the military. It is truly delightful to a philanthropic mind, to see these gallant men staggering along under the influence of an overflow, both of animal and ardent spirits; more especially when we remember that the following them about, and jesting with them, affords a cheap and innocent amusement for the boy population. Nothing (adds Mr. Pickwick) can exceed their good humour. It was but the day before my arrival that one of them had been most grossly insulted in the house of a publican. The bar-maid had positively refused to draw him any more liquor; in return for which he had (merely in playfulness) drawn his bayonet, and wounded the girl in the shoulder. And yet this fine fellow was the very first to go down to the house next morning, and express his readiness to overlook the matter, and forget what had occurred.

'The consumption of tobacco in these towns (continues Mr. Pickwick) must be very great: and the smell which pervades the streets must be exceedingly delicious to those who are extremely fond of smoking. A superficial traveller might object to the dirt which is their leading characteristic; but to those who view it as an indication of traffic and commercial prosperity, it is truly gratifying' (*Chapter 2*).

'Many fine women in this town, do you know, sir?' inquired Mr. Tupman, with great interest.

'Splendid – capital. Kent, sir – everybody knows Kent – apples, cherries, hops, and women. Glass of wine, sir?' (*Chapter 2:* Jingle).

The wine, which had exerted its somniferous influence over Mr. Snodgrass and Mr. Winkle, had stolen upon the senses of Mr. Pickwick. That gentleman had gradually passed through the various stages which precede the lethargy produced by dinner, and its consequences. He had undergone the ordinary transitions from the height of conviviality to the depth of misery, and from the depth of misery to the height of conviviality. Like a gas lamp in the street, with the wind in the pipe, he had exhibited for a moment an unnatural brilliancy: then sunk so low as to be scarcely discernible: after a short interval he had burst out again, to enlighten for a moment, then flickered with an uncertain, staggering sort of light, and then gone out altogether. His head was sunk upon his bosom; and perpetual snoring, with a partial choke occasion-ally, were the only audible indications of the great man's presence (*Chapter 2*).

'Sir!' said the Doctor, in an awful voice, producing a card, and retiring into an angle of the passage, 'my name is Slammer, Doctor Slammer, sir – 97th Regiment' – Chatham Barracks – my card, sir, my card.' He would have added more, but his indignation choked him.

'Ah!' replied the stranger, coolly, 'Slammer – much obliged – polite attention – not ill now, Slammer – but when I am – knock you up.'

'You – you're a shuffler! sir,' gasped the furious Doctor, 'a poltroon – a coward – a liar – a – a – will nothing induce you to give me your card, sir!'

'Oh! I see,' said the stranger, half aside, 'negus too strong here – liberal landlord – very foolish – very – lemonade much better – hot rooms – elderly gentlemen – suffer for it in the morning – cruel – cruel' (*Chapter 2:* Jingle).

'I shall find you out, sir; I shall find you out.'

'Rather you found me out than found me at home,' replied the unmoved stranger (*Chapter 2:* Slammer and Jingle).

The evening grew more dull every moment, and a melancholy wind sounded through the deserted fields, like a distant giant whistling for his house-dog (*Chapter 2*).

Many authors entertain, not only a foolish, but a really dishonest objection to acknowledge the sources from whence they derive much valuable information. We have no such feeling. We are merely endeavouring to discharge, in an upright manner, the responsible duties of our editorial functions; and whatever ambition we might have felt under other circumstances to lay claim to the authorship of these adventures, a regard for truth forbids us to do more than claim the merit of their judicious arrangement and impartial narration. The Pickwick papers are our New River Head; and we may be compared to the New River Company. The labours of others have raised for us an immense reservoir of important facts. We merely lay them on, and communicate them, in a clear and gentle stream, through the medium of these numbers, to a world thirsting for Pickwickian knowledge (*Chapter 4*).

'It is indeed a noble and a brilliant sight,' said Mr. Snodgrass, in whose bosom a blaze of poetry was rapidly bursting forth, 'to see the gallant defenders of their country drawn up in brilliant array before its peaceful citizens; their faces beaming – not with warlike ferocity, but with civilised gentleness; their eyes flashing – not with the rude fire of rapine or revenge, but with the soft light of humanity and intelligence.'

Mr. Pickwick fully entered into the spirit of this eulogium, but he could not exactly re-echo its terms; for the soft light of intelligence burnt rather feebly in the eyes of the warriors, inasmuch as the command 'eyes front' had been given, and all the spectator saw before him was several thousand pairs of optics, staring straight forward, wholly divested of any expression whatever (*Chapter 4*).

There are very few moments in a man's existence when he experiences so much ludicrous distress, or meets with so little charitable commiseration, as when he is in pursuit of his own hat. A vast deal of coolness, and a peculiar degree of judgment, are requisite in catching a hat. A man must not be precipitate, or he runs over it; he must not rush into the opposite extreme, or he loses it altogether. The best way is, to keep gently up with the object of pursuit, to be wary and cautious, to watch your opportunity well, get gradually before it, then make a rapid dive, seize it by the crown, and stick it firmly on your head: smiling pleasantly all the time, as if you thought it as good a joke as anybody else (*Chapter 4*).

'Now, we must sit close,' said the stout gentleman. After a great many jokes about squeezing the ladies' sleeves, and a vast quantity of blushing at sundry jocose proposals, that the ladies should sit in the gentlemen's laps, the whole party were stowed down in the barouche; and the stout gentleman proceeded to hand the things from the fat boy (who had mounted up behind for the purpose) into the carriage.

'Now, Joe, knives and forks.' The knives and forks were handed in, and the ladies and gentlemen inside, and Mr. Winkle on the box, were each furnished with those useful instruments.

'Plates, Joe, plates.' A similar process employed in the distribution of the crockery.

'Now, Joe, the fowls. Damn that boy; he's gone to sleep again. Joe! Joe!' (Sundry taps on the head with a stick, and the fat boy, with some difficulty, roused from his lethargy.) 'Come, hand in the eatables.'

There was something in the sound of the last word which roused the unctuous boy. He jumped up: and the leaden eyes, which twinkled behind his mountainous cheeks, leered horribly upon the food as he unpacked it from the basket (*Chapter 4*: Wardle).

'Do you think my dear nieces pretty?' whispered their affectionate aunt to Mr. Tupman.

'I should, if their aunt wasn't here,' replied the ready Pickwickian, with a passionate glance.

'Oh, you naughty man - but really, if their complexions were a *little* better, don't you think they would be nice-looking girls - by candle-light?'

'Yes; I think they would,' said Mr. Tupman, with an air of indifference.

'Oh, you quiz - I know what you were going to say.'

'What?' inquired Mr. Tupman, who had not precisely made up his mind to say anything at all.

'You were going to say, that Isabel stoops - I know you were - you men are such observers. Well, so she does; it can't be denied; and, certainly, if there is one thing more than another that makes a girl look ugly, it is stooping. I often tell her, that when she gets a little older, she'll be quite frightful. Well, you *are* a quiz!' (*Chapter 4*).

'You have seen much trouble, sir,' said Mr. Pickwick, compassionately.

'I have,' said the dismal man, hurriedly; 'I have. More than those who see me now would believe possible.' He paused for an instant, and then said, abruptly -

'Did it ever strike you on such a morning as this, that drowning would be happiness and peace?'

'God bless me, no!' replied Mr. Pickwick, edging a little from the balustrade, as the possibility of the dismal man's tipping him over, by way of experiment, occurred to him rather forcibly (*Chapter 5*).

It was a curious little green box on four wheels, with a low place like a wine-bin for two behind, and an elevated perch for one in front, drawn by an immense brown horse, displaying great symmetry of bone. An hostler stood near, holding by the bridle another immense horse - apparently a near relative of the animal in the chaise - ready saddled for Mr. Winkle.

'Bless my soul!' said Mr. Pickwick, as they stood upon the pavement while the coats were being put in. 'Bless my soul! who's to drive? I never thought of that.'

'Oh! you, of course,' said Mr. Tupman.

'Of course,' said Mr. Snodgrass.

'I!' exclaimed Mr. Pickwick.

'Not the slightest fear, sir,' interposed the hostler. 'Warrant him quiet, sir; a hinfant in arms might drive him.'

'He don't shy, does he?' inquired Mr. Pickwick.

'Shy, sir? - He wouldn't shy if he was to meet a vaggin-load of monkeys with their tails burnt off' (*Chapter 5*).

Another game, with a similar result, was followed by a revoke from the unlucky Miller; on which the fat gentleman burst into a state of high personal excitement which lasted until the conclusion of the game, when he retired into a corner, and remained perfectly mute for one hour and twenty-seven minutes; at the end of which time he emerged from his retirement, and offered Mr. Pickwick a pinch of snuff with the air of a man who had made up his mind to a Christian forgiveness of injuries sustained. The old lady's hearing decidedly improved, and the unlucky Miller felt as much out of his element as a dolphin in a sentry-box (*Chapter 6*).

Mr. Pickwick was no sluggard; and he sprang like an ardent warrior from his tent-bedstead.

'Pleasant, pleasant country,' sighed the enthusiastic gentleman, as he opened his lattice window. 'Who could live to gaze from day to day on bricks and slates, who had once felt the influence of a scene like this? Who could continue to exist, where there are no cows but the cows on the chimney-pots; nothing redolent of Pan but pan-tiles; no crop but stone crop? Who could bear to drag out a life in such a spot? Who I ask could endure it?' and, having cross-examined solitude after the most approved precedents, at considerable length, Mr. Pickwick thrust his head out of the lattice, and looked around him (*Chapter 7*).

'Don't be frightened,' said the host.

'What's the matter?' screamed the ladies.

'Mr. Tupman has met with a little accident; that's all.'

The spinster aunt uttered a piercing scream, burst into an hysteric laugh, and fell backwards in the arms of her nieces.

'Throw some cold water over her,' said the old gentleman.

'No, no,' murmured the spinster aunt; 'I am better now. Bella, Emily – a surgeon! Is he wounded? – Is he dead? – Is he – ha, ha, ha!' Here the spinster aunt burst into fit number two, of hysteric laughter interspersed with screams.

'Calm yourself,' said Mr. Tupman, affected almost to tears by this expression of sympathy with his sufferings. 'Dear, dear, madam, calm yourself.'

'It is his voice!' exclaimed the spinster aunt; and strong symptoms of fit number three developed themselves forthwith.

'Do not agitate yourself, I entreat you, dearest madam,' said Mr. Tupman soothingly. 'I am very little hurt, I assure you.'

'Then you are not dead!' ejaculated the hysterical lady. 'Oh, say you are not dead!'

'Don't be a fool, Rachael,' interposed Mr. Wardle, rather more roughly than was quite consistent with the poetic nature of the scene. 'What the devil's the use of his *saying* he isn't dead?'

'No no, I am not,' said Mr. Tupman (*Chapter 7*).

Muggleton is an ancient and loyal borough, mingling a zealous advocacy of Christian principles with a devoted attachment to commercial rights; in demonstration whereof, the mayor, corporation, and other inhabitants, have presented at divers times, no fewer than one thousand four hundred and twenty petitions against the continuance of negro slavery abroad, and an equal number against any interference with the factory system at home; sixty-eight in favour of the sale of livings in the Church, and eighty-six for abolishing Sunday trading in the street (*Chapter 7*).

'Capital game – well played – some strokes admirable,' said the stranger, as both sides crowded into the tent, at the conclusion of the game.

'You have played it, sir?' inquired Mr. Wardle, who had been much amused by his loquacity.

'Played it! Think I have – thousands of times – not here – West Indies – exciting thing – hot work – very.'

'It must be rather a warm pursuit in such a climate,' observed Mr. Pickwick.

'Warm! – red hot – scorching – glowing. Played a match once – single wicket – friend the Colonel – Sir Thomas Blazo – who should get the greatest number of runs. – Won the toss – first innings – seven o'clock A.M. – six natives to look out – went in; kept in – heat intense – natives all fainted – taken away – fresh half-dozen ordered – fainted also – Blazo bowling – supported by two natives – couldn't bowl me out – fainted too – cleared away the Colonel – wouldn't give in – faithful attendant – Quanko Samba – last man left – sun so hot, bat in blisters – ball scorched brown – five hundred and seventy runs – rather exhausted – Quanko mustered up last remaining strength – bowled me out – had a bath, and went out to dinner.'

'And what became of what's-his-name, sir?' inquired an old gentleman.

'Blazo?'

'No – the other gentleman.'

'Quanko Samba?'

'Yes, sir.'

'Poor Quanko – never recovered it – bowled on, on my account – bowled off, on his own – died, sir.' Here the stranger buried his countenance in a brown jug, but whether to hide his emotion or imbibe its contents, we cannot distinctly affirm (*Chapter 7:* Jingle and Wardle).

'Is anything the matter?' inquired the three ladies.

'Nothing the matter,' replied Mr. Pickwick. 'We – we're all right. – I say, Wardle, we're all right, an't we?'

'I should think so,' replied the jolly host. – 'My dears, here's my friend, Mr. Jingle – Mr. Pickwick's friend, Mr. Jingle, come 'pon – little visit.'

'Is anything the matter with Mr. Snodgrass, sir?' inquired Emily, with great anxiety.

'Nothing the matter, ma'am,' replied the stranger. 'Cricket dinner – glorious party – capital songs – old port – claret – good – very good – wine, ma'am – wine.'

'It wasn't the wine,' murmured Mr. Snodgrass, in a broken voice. 'It was the salmon.' (Somehow or other, it never *is* the wine, in these cases.)

'Hadn't they better go to bed, ma'am?' inquired Emma. 'Two of the boys will carry the gentleman upstairs.'

'I won't go to bed,' said Mr. Winkle, firmly.

'No living boy shall carry me,' said Mr. Pickwick, stoutly, – and he went on smiling as before.

'Hurrah!' gasped Mr. Winkle, faintly.

'Hurrah!' echoed Mr. Pickwick, taking off his hat and dashing it on the floor, and insanely casting his spectacles into the middle of the kitchen (*Chapter 8*).

'Missus!' shouted the fat boy.

'Well, Joe,' said the trembling old lady. 'I'm sure I have been a good mistress to you, Joe. You have invariably been treated very kindly. You have never had too much to do; and you have always had enough to eat.'

This last was an appeal to the fat boy's most sensitive feelings. He seemed touched, as he replied, emphatically –

'I know I has.'

'Then what can you want to do now?' said the old lady, gaining courage.

'I wants to make your flesh creep,' replied the boy (*Chapter 8*).

There are in London several old inns, once the headquarters of celebrated coaches in the days when coaches performed their journeys in a graver and more solemn manner than they do in these times; but which have now degenerated into little more than the abiding and booking places of country waggons. The reader would look in vain for any of these ancient hostelries, among the Golden Crosses and Bull and Mouths, which rear their stately fronts in the improved streets of London. If he would light upon any of these old places, he must direct his steps to the obscurer quarters of the town; and there in some secluded nooks he will find several, still standing with a kind of gloomy sturdiness, amidst the modern innovations which surround them.

In the Borough especially, there still remain some half-dozen old inns, which have preserved their external features unchanged, and which have escaped alike the rage for public improvement, and the encroachments of private speculation. Great, rambling, queer, old places they are, with galleries, and passages, and staircases, wide enough and antiquated enough to furnish materials for a hundred ghost stories, supposing we should ever be reduced to the lamentable necessity of inventing any, and that the world should exist long enough to exhaust the innumerable veracious legends connected with old London Bridge, and its adjacent neighbourhood on the Surrey side (*Chapter 10*).

'Sam!'
'Hallo,' replied the man with the white hat.
'Number twenty-two wants his boots.'
'Ask number twenty-two, whether he'll have 'em now, or wait till he gets 'em,' was the reply.
'Come, don't be a fool, Sam,' said the girl, coaxingly, 'the gentleman wants his boots directly.'
'Well, you *are* a nice young 'ooman for a musical party, you are,' said the boot-cleaner. 'Look at these here boots – eleven pair o' boots; and one shoe as b'longs to number six, with the wooden leg. The eleven boots is to be called at half-past eight and the shoe at nine. Who's number twenty-two, that's to put all the others out? No, no; reg'lar rotation, as Jack Ketch said, wen he tied the men up. Sorry to keep you a waitin', sir, but I'll attend to you directly' (*Chapter 10:* Sam Weller).

'Touts for licences,' replied Sam. 'Two coves in white aprons – touches their hats wen you walk in – "Licence, sir, licence?" Queer sort, them, and their mas'rs too, sir – Old Bailey Proctors – and no mistake.'
'What do they do?' inquired the gentleman.
'Do! *You*, sir! That an't the wost on it, neither. They puts things into old gen'l'm'n's heads as they never dreamed of. My father, sir, wos a coachman. A widower he wos, and fat enough for anything – uncommon fat, to be sure. His missus dies, and leaves him four hundred pound. Down he goes to the Commons, to see the lawyer and draw the blunt – wery smart – top boots on – nosegay in his button-hole – broad-brimmed tile – green shawl – quite the gen'l'-m'n. Goes through the archvay, thinking how he should inwest the money – up comes the touter, touches his hat – "Licence, sir, licence?" – "What's that?" says my father. – "Licence, sir," says he. – "What licence?" says my father. – "Marriage licence," says the touter. – "Dash my veskit," says my father, "I never thought o' that." – "I think you wants one, sir," says the touter. My father pulls up and thinks a bit – "No," says he, "damme, I'm too old, b'sides I'm a many sizes too large," says he. – "Not a bit on it, sir," says the touter. – "Think not?" says my father. – "I'm sure not," says he; "we married a gen'l'm'n twice your size, last Monday." – "Did you, though?" said my father. – "To be sure, we did," says the touter, "you're a babby to him – this way, sir – this way!" ' (*Chapter 10:* Jingle and Sam Weller).

' "What's your name, sir?" says the lawyer. – "Tony Weller," says my father. – "Parish?" says the lawyer. – "Bell Savage," says my father; for he stopped there wen he drove up, and he know'd nothing about parishes, *he* didn't. – "And what's the lady's name?" says the lawyer. My father was struck all of a heap. "Blessed if I know," says he. – "Not know!" says the lawyer. – "No more nor you do," says my father, "can't I put that in arterwards?" – "Impossible!" says the lawyer. – "Wery well," says my father, after he'd though a moment, "put down Mrs. Clarke." – "What Clarke?" says the lawyer, dipping his pen in the ink. – "Susan Clarke, Markis o' Granby, Dorking," says my father; "she'll have me, if I ask, I des-say – I never said nothing to her, but she'll have me, I know." The licence was made out, and she *did* have him, and what's more she's got him now; and *I* never had any of the four hundred pounds, worse luck' (*Chapter 10:* Sam Weller).

'Wery well, I'm agreeable: I can't say no fairer than that, can I, sir? (Mr. Pickwick smiled). Then the next question is, what the devil do you want with me, as the man said wen he see the ghost?' (*Chapter 10:* Sam Weller).

'That's the pint, sir,' interposed Sam; 'out with it, as the father said to the child, wen he swallowed a farden' (*Chapter 12:* Sam Weller).

'Pray sit down. So you have carried your intention into effect. You have come down here to see an election – eh?'
Mr. Pickwick replied in the affirmative.
'Spirited contest, my dear sir,' said the little man.
'I am delighted to hear it,' said Mr. Pickwick, rubbing his hands. 'I like to see sturdy patriotism, on whatever side it is called forth; – and so it's a spirited contest?'
'Oh yes,' said the little man, 'very much so indeed. We have opened all the public-houses in the place, and left our adversary nothing but the beer-shops – masterly stroke of policy that, my dear sir, eh?' – the little man smiled complacently, and took a large pinch of snuff (*Chapter 13:* Perker).

'We are pretty confident, though,' said Mr. Perker, sinking his voice almost to a whisper. 'We had a little tea-party here, last night – five-and-forty women, my dear sir – and gave every one of 'em a green parasol when she went away.'
'A parasol!' said Mr. Pickwick.
'Fact, my dear sir, fact. Five-and-forty green parasols, at seven-and-sixpence a-piece. All women like finery, – extraordinary the effect of those parasols. Secured all their husbands, and half their brothers – beats stockings, and flannel, and all that sort of thing hollow. My idea, my dear sir, entirely. Hail, rain, or sunshine, you can't walk half a dozen yards up the street, without encountering half a dozen green parasols' (*Chapter 13*).

There was a moment of awful suspense as the procession waited for the Honourable Samuel Slumkey to step into his carriage. Suddenly the crowd set up a great cheering.

'He has come out,' said little Mr. Perker, greatly excited; the more so as their position did not enable them to see what was going forward.

Another cheer, much louder.

'He has shaken hands with the men,' cried the little agent.

Another cheer, far more vehement.

'He has patted the babies on the head,' said Mr. Perker, trembling with anxiety.

A roar of applause that rent the air.

'He has kissed one of 'em!' exclaimed the delighted little man.

A second roar.

'He has kissed another,' gasped the excited manager.

A third roar.

'He's kissing 'em all!' screamed the enthusiastic little gentleman. And hailed by the deafening shouts of the multitude, the procession moved on (*Chapter 13*).

'Gentlemen,' said the Mayor, at as loud a pitch as he could possibly force his voice to, 'Gentlemen. Brother electors of the Borough of Eatanswill. We are met here to-day for the purpose of choosing a representative in the room of our late – '

Here the Mayor was interrupted by a voice in the crowd.

'Suc-cess to the Mayor!' cried the voice, 'and may he never desert the nail and sarspan business, as he got his money by' (*Chapter 13*).

'Rum creeters is women,' said the dirty-faced man, after a pause.

'Ah! no mistake about that,' said a very red-faced man, behind a cigar.

After this little bit of philosophy there was another pause.

'There's rummer things than women in this world though, mind you,' said the man with the black eye, slowly filling a large Dutch pipe, with a most capacious bowl.

'Are you married?' inquired the dirty-faced man.

'Can't say I am.'

'I thought not.' Here the dirty-faced man fell into fits of mirth at his own retort, in which he was joined by a man of bland voice and placid countenance, who always made it a point to agree with everybody (*Chapter 14:* Bagman).

'Person's a waitin',' said Sam, epigrammatically.

'Does the person want me, Sam?' inquired Mr. Pickwick.

'He wants you particklar; and no one else'll do, as the Devil's private secretary said ven he fetched avay Doctor Faustus,' replied Mr. Weller (*Chapter 15*).

'Mrs. Pott's going,' were the first words with which he saluted his leader.

'Is she?' said Mr. Pickwick.

'As Apollo,' replied Mr. Winkle. 'Only Pott objects to the tunic.'

'He is right. He is quite right,' said Mr. Pickwick, emphatically.

Yes; – so she's going to wear a white satin gown with gold spangles.'

'They'll hardly know what she's meant for; will they?' inquired Mr. Snodgrass.

'Of course they will,' replied Mr. Winkle indignantly. 'They'll see her lyre, won't they?'

'True; I forgot that,' said Mr. Snodgrass (*Chapter 15*).

'Count Smorltork, Mr. Pickwick.'

Mr. Pickwick saluted the Count with all the reverence due to so great a man, and the Count drew forth a set of tablets.

'What you say, Mrs. Hunt?' inquired the Count, smiling graciously on the gratified Mrs. Leo Hunter, 'Pig Vig or Big Vig – what you call – lawyer – eh? I see – that is it. Big Vig' – and the Count was proceeding to enter Mr. Pickwick in his tablets, as a gentleman of the long robe, who derived his name from the profession to which he belonged, when Mrs. Leo Hunter interposed.

'No, no, Count,' said the lady, 'Pick-wick.'

'Ah, ah, I see,' replied the Count. 'Peak – Christian name; Weeks – surname; good, ver good. Peek Weeks. How do you do, Weeks?'

'Quite well, I thank you,' replied Mr. Pickwick, with all his usual affability (*Chapter 15*).

'The word politics, sir,' said Mr. Pickwick, 'comprises, in itself, a difficult study of no inconsiderable magnitude.'

'Ah!' said the Count, drawing out the tablets again, 'ver good – fine words to begin a chapter. Chapter forty-seven. Poltics. The word poltic surprises by himself – ' And down went Mr. Pickwick's remark, in Count Smorltork's tablets, with such variations and additions as the Count's exuberant fancy suggested, or his imperfect knowledge of the language, occasioned (*Chapter 15*).

As the enthusiasm in Count Smorltork's favour ran very high, his praises might have been sung until the end of the festivities, if the four something-ean singers had not ranged themselves in front of a small apple-tree, to look picturesque, and commenced singing their national songs, which appeared by no means difficult of execution, inasmuch as the grand secret seemed to be, that three of the something-ean singers should grunt, while the fourth howled (*Chapter 15*).

'Where's my servant?'

'Here you are, sir,' said Mr. Weller, emerging from a sequestered spot, where he had been engaged in discussing a bottle of Madeira, which he had abstracted from the breakfast-table, an hour or two before. 'Here's your servant, sir. Proud o' the title, as the Living Skellinton said, ven they show'd him' (*Chapter 15:* Pickwick and Sam Weller).

As the coach rolls swiftly past the fields and orchards which skirt the road, groups of women and children, piling the fruit in sieves, or gathering the scattered ears of corn, pause for an instant from their labour, and shading the sun-burnt face with a still browner hand, gaze upon the passengers with curious eyes, while some stout urchin, too small to work, but too mischievous to be left at home, scrambles over the side of the basket in which he has been deposited for security, and kicks and screams with delight. The reaper stops in his work, and stands with folded arms, looking at the vehicle as it whirls past; and the rough cart horses bestow a sleepy glance upon the smart coach team, which says, as plainly as a horse's glance can, 'It's all very fine to look at, but slow going, over a heavy field, is better than warm work like that, upon a dusty road, after all.' You cast a look behind you, as you turn a corner of the road. The women and children have resumed their labour: the reaper once more stoops to his work: the cart-horses have moved on: and all are again in motion *(Chapter 16)*.

'There's nothin' so refreshin' as sleep, sir, as the servant-girl said afore she drank the egg-cupful o' laudanum' *(Chapter 16: Sam Weller)*.

'You seem one of the jolly sort – looks as conwivial as a live trout in a lime basket,' added Mr. Weller, in an undertone *(Chapter 16)*.

'Come, come,' interposed Sam, who had witnessed Mr. Trotter's tears with considerable impatience, 'blow this here water-cart bis'ness. It won't do no good, this won't.'
'Sam,' said Mr. Pickwick, reproachfully, 'I am sorry to find that you have so little respect for this young man's feelings.'
'His feelin's is all wery well, sir,' replied Mr. Weller; 'and as they're so wery fine, and it's a pity he should lose 'em, I think he'd better keep 'em in his own buzzum, than let 'em ewaporate in hot water, 'specially as they do no good. Tears never yet wound up a clock, or worked a steam ingen'. The next time you go out to a smoking party, young fellow, fill your pipe with that 'ere reflection; and for the present just put that bit of pink gingham into your pocket. 'Tan't so handsome that you need keep waving it about, as if you was a tight-rope dancer' *(Chapter 16)*.

'Serpent!'
'Sir!' exclaimed Mr. Winkle, starting from his chair.
'Serpent, sir,' repeated Mr. Pott, raising his voice, and then suddenly depressing it; 'I said, Serpent, sir – make the most of it.'
When you have parted with a man, at two o'clock in the morning, on terms of the utmost good fellowship, and he meets you again, at half-past nine, and greets you as a serpent, it is not unreasonable to conclude that something of an unpleasant nature has occurred meanwhile *(Chapter 18)*.

'Pleasantry, sir! – but no, I will be calm; I will be calm, sir;' in proof of his calmness, Mr. Pott flung himself into a chair, and foamed at the mouth *(Chapter 18)*.

' ''LINES TO A BRASS POT

' ''Oh Pott! if you'd known
How false she'd have grown,
When you heard the marriage bells tinkle;
You'd have done then, I vow,
What you cannot help now,
And handed her over to W******'' '

'What,' said Mr. Pott, solemnly: 'what rhymes to "tinkle," villain?'

'What rhymes to tinkle?' said Mrs. Pott, whose entrance at the moment forestalled the reply. 'What rhymes to tinkle? Why, Winkle, I should conceive': saying this, Mrs. Pott smiled sweetly on the disturbed Pickwickian, and extended her hand towards him *(Chapter 18)*.

'Weal pie,' said Mr. Weller, soliloquising, as he arranged the eatables on the grass. 'Wery good thing is weal pie, when you know the lady as made it, and is quite sure it an't kittens; and arter all, though, where's the odds, when they're so like weal that the wery piemen themselves don't know the difference?' *(Chapter 19)*.

'I lodged in the same house with a pieman once, sir, and a wery nice man he was – reg'lar clever chap, too – make pies out o' anything, he could. "What a number o' cats you keep, Mr. Brooks," says I, when I'd got intimate with him. "Ah," says he, "I do – a good many," says he. "You must be wery fond o' cats," says I. "Other people is," says he, a winkin' at me; "they an't in season till the winter, though," says he. "Not in season!" says I. "No," says he, "fruits is in, cats is out." "Why, what do you mean?" says I. "Mean?" says he. "That I'll never be a party to the combination o' the butchers, to keep up the prices o' meat," says he. "Mr. Weller," says he, a squeezing my hand wery hard, and vispering in my ear – "don't mention this here agin – but it's the seasonin' as does it. They're all made o' them noble animals," says he, a pointin' to a wery nice little tabby kitten, "and I seasons 'em for beef-steak, weal, or kidney, 'cordin' to the demand. And more than that," says he, "I can make a weal a beef-steak, or a beef-steak a kidney, or any one on 'em a mutton, at a minute's notice, just as the market changes, and appetites wary!" '
'He must have been a very ingenious young man, that, Sam,' said Mr. Pickwick, with a slight shudder.
'Just was, sir,' replied Mr. Weller, continuing his occupation of emptying the basket, 'and the pies was beautiful' *(Chapter 19)*.

'You just come avay,' said Mr. Weller. 'Battledore and shuttlecock's a wery good game, vhen you an't the shuttlecock and two lawyers the battledores, in which case it gets too excitin' to be pleasant' *(Chapter 20)*.

'I should like a glass of brandy-and-water warm, Sam. Where can I have it, Sam?'
Mr. Weller's knowledge of London was extensive and peculiar. He replied without the slightest consideration –
'Second court on the right-hand side – last house but vun on the same side the vay – take the box as stands in the first fire-place, 'cos there an't no leg in the middle o' the table, which all the others has, and it's wery inconwenient' *(Chapter 20)*.

'Well done, father,' said Sam, 'take care, old fellow, or you'll have a touch of your old complaint, the gout.'
'I've found a sov'rin cure for that, Sammy,' said Mr. Weller, setting down the glass.
'A sovereign cure for the gout,' said Mr. Pickwick, hastily producing his note-book – 'what is it?'

'The gout, sir,' replied Mr. Weller, 'the gout is a complaint as arises from too much ease and comfort. If ever you're attacked with the gout, sir, jist you marry a widder as has got a good loud woice, with a decent notion of usin' it, and you'll never have the gout agin. It's a capital prescription, sir. I takes it reg'lar, and I can warrant it to drive away any illness as is caused by too much jollity' (*Chapter 20*).

'Well, what do you think of what your father says, Sam?' inquired Mr. Pickwick, with a smile.

'Think, sir!' replied Mr. Weller; 'why, I think he's the wictim o' connubiality, as Blue Beard's domestic chaplain said, with a tear of pity, ven he buried him' (*Chapter 20*).

'How many vain pleaders for mercy, do you think have turned away heart-sick from the lawyer's office, to find a resting-place in the Thames, or a refuge in the gaol? They are no ordinary houses, those. There is not a panel in the old wainscoting, but what, if it were endowed with the powers of speech and memory, could start from the wall, and tell its tale of horror – the romance of life, sir, the romance of life! Commonplace as they may seem now, I tell you they are strange old places, and I would rather hear many a legend with a terrific sounding name, than the true history of one old set of chambers' (*Chapter 21: Jack Bamber*).

'I know another case,' said the little old man. . . . 'It occurred in Clifford's Inn. Tenant of a top set – bad character – shut himself up in his bed-room closet, and took a dose of arsenic. The steward thought he had run away; opened the door, and put a bill up. Another man came, took the chambers, furnished them, and went to live there. Somehow or other he couldn't sleep – always restless and uncomfortable. "Odd," says he. "I'll make the other room my bed-chamber, and this my sitting-room." He made the change, and slept very well at night, but suddenly found that, somehow, he couldn't read in the evening: he got nervous and uncomfortable, and used to be always snuffing his candles and staring about him. "I can't make this out," said he, when he came home from the play one night, and was drinking a glass of cold grog, with his back to the wall, in order that he mightn't be able to fancy there was any one behind him – "I can't make it out," said he; and just then his eyes rested on the little closet that had been always locked up, and a shudder ran through his whole frame from top to toe. "I have felt this strange feeling before," said he, "I cannot help thinking there's something wrong about that closet." He made a strong effort, plucked up his courage, shivered the lock with a blow or two of the poker, opened the door, and there, sure enough, standing bolt upright in the corner, was the last tenant, with a little bottle clasped firmly in his hand, and his face – well!' As the little old man concluded, he looked round on the attentive faces of his wondering auditory with a smile of grim delight (*Chapter 21: Jack Bamber*).

A silent look of affection and regard when all other eyes are turned coldly away – the consciousness that we possess the sympathy and affection of one being when all others have deserted us – is a hold, a

comfort, in the deepest affliction, which no wealth could purchase or power bestow (*Chapter 21*).

'How's mother-in-law this mornin'?'

'Queer, Sammy, queer,' replied the elder Mr. Weller, with impressive gravity. 'She's been gettin' rayther in the Methodistical order lately, Sammy; and she is uncommon pious, to be sure. She's too good a creetur for me, Sammy. I feel I don't deserve her.'

'Ah,' said Mr. Samuel, 'that's wery self-denyin' o' you.'

'Wery,' replied his parent, with a sigh. 'She's got hold o' some inwention for grown-up people being born again, Sammy; the new birth, I thinks they calls it. I should wery much like to see that system in haction, Sammy. I should wery much like to see your mother-in-law born again. Wouldn't I put her out to nurse!' (*Chapter 22*).

'Company, you see – company is – is – it's a very different thing from solitude – ain't it?'

'There's no denying that 'ere,' said Mr. Weller, joining in the conversation, with an affable smile. 'That's what I call a self-evident proposition, as the dog's-meat man said, when the housemaid told him he warn't a gentleman' (*Chapter 22*).

'A very good name, indeed,' said Mr. Pickwick, wholly unable to repress a smile.

'Yes, I think it is,' replied Mr. Magnus. 'There's a good name before it, too, you will observe. Permit me, sir – if you hold the card a little slanting, this way, you catch the light upon the up-stroke. There – Peter Magnus – sounds well, I think, sir.'

'Very,' said Mr. Pickwick.

'Curious circumstance about those initials, sir,' said Mr. Magnus. 'You will observe – P.M. – post meridian. In hasty notes to intimate acquaintance, I sometimes sign myself "Afternoon." It amuses my friends very much, Mr. Pickwick.'

'It is calculated to afford them the highest gratification, I should conceive,' said Mr. Pickwick, rather envying the ease with which Mr. Magnus's friends were entertained (*Chapter 22*).

'Widders, Sammy,' replied Mr. Weller, slightly changing colour. 'Widders are 'ceptions to ev'ry rule. I *have* heerd how many ord'nary women, one widder's equal to, in pint o' comin' over you. I think it's five-and-twenty, but I don't rightly know vether it an't more.'

Well; that's pretty well,' said Sam.

'Besides,' continued Mr. Weller, not noticing the interruption, 'that's a wery different thing. You know what the counsel said, Sammy, as defended the gen'le-m'n as beat his wife with the poker, venever he got jolly. "And arter all, my Lord," says he, "it's a amiable weakness." So I says respectin' widders, Sammy, and so you'll say, ven you gets as old as me' (*Chapter 23*).

'Well, it's no use talking about it now,' said Sam. 'It's over, and can't be helped, and that's one consolation, as they always says in Turkey, ven they cuts the wrong man's head off' (*Chapter 23*).

'The family name depends wery much upon you, Samivel, and I hope you'll do wot's right by it. Upon all little pints o' breedin', I know I may trust you as vell as if it was my own self. So I've only this here one little bit of adwice to give you. If ever you gets to up'ards o' fifty, and feels disposed to go a marryin' anybody – no matter who – jist you shut yourself up in your own room, if you've got one, and pison yourself off hand. Hangin's wulgar, so don't you have nothin' to say to that. Pison yourself, Samivel, my boy, pison yourself, and you'll be glad on it arterwards.' With these affecting words, Mr. Weller looked steadfastly on his son, and turning slowly upon his heel, disappeared from his sight (*Chapter 23*).

There must be something very comprehensive in this phrase of 'Never mind,' for we do not recollect to have ever witnessed a quarrel in the street, at a theatre, public room, or elsewhere, in which it has not been the standard reply to all belligerent inquiries. 'Do you call yourself a gentleman, sir?' – 'Never mind, sir.' 'Did I offer to say anything to the young woman, sir?' – 'Never mind, sir.' 'Do you want your head knocked up against that wall, sir?' – 'Never mind, sir.' It is observable, too, that there would appear to be some hidden taunt in this universal 'Never mind,' which rouses more indignation in the bosom of the individual addressed, than the most lavish abuse could possibly awaken (*Chapter 24*).

'Business first, pleasure arterwards, as King Richard the Third said when he stabbed the t'other king in the Tower, afore he smothered the babbies' (*Chapter 25: Sam Weller*).

'Pickvick and principle!' exclaimed Mr. Weller, in a very audible voice.
'Sam, be quiet,' said Mr. Pickwick.
'Dum as a drum vith a hole in it, sir,' replied Sam (*Chapter 25*).

'Wery sorry to 'casion any personal inconwenience, ma'am, as the housebreaker said to the old lady when he put her on the fire' (*Chapter 26: Sam Weller*).

'Ven is it expected to come on?' inquired Sam.
Either in February or March,' replied Mrs. Bardell.
'What a number of witnesses there'll be, won't there?' said Mrs. Cluppins.
'Ah, won't there!' replied Mrs. Sanders.
'And won't Mr. Dodson and Fogg be wild if the plaintiff shouldn't get it?' added Mrs. Cluppins, 'when they do it all on speculation!'
'Ah! won't they!' said Mrs. Sanders.
'But the plaintiff must get it,' resumed Mrs. Cluppins.
'I hope so,' said Mrs. Bardell.
'Oh, there can't be any doubt about it,' rejoined Mrs. Sanders.
'Vell,' said Sam, rising and setting down his glass, 'all I can say is, that I wish you *may* get it.'
'Thank'ee, Mr. Weller,' said Mrs. Bardell, fervently.
'And of them Dodson and Foggs, as does these sort o' things on spec,' continued Mr. Weller, 'as well as for the other kind and gen'rous people o' the same purfession, as sets people by the ears, free gratis for

nothin', and sets their clerks to work to find out little disputes among their neighbours and acquaintances as vants settlin' by means o' law-suits – all I can say o' them is, that I vish they had the revard I'd give 'em.'
'Ah, I wish they had the reward that every kind and generous heart would be inclined to bestow upon them!' said the gratified Mrs. Bardell.
'Amen to that,' replied Sam, 'and a fat and happy livin' they'd get out of it! Wish you good night, ladies' (*Chapter 26*).

Mr. Stiggins groaned.
'What's the matter with that 'ere gen'l'm'n?' inquired Sam.
'He's shocked at the way your father goes on in,' replied Mrs. Weller.
'Oh, he is, is he?' said Sam.
'And with too good reason,' added Mrs. Weller, gravely. Mr. Stiggins took up a fresh piece of toast, and groaned heavily.
'He is a dreadful reprobate,' said Mrs. Weller.
'A man of wrath!' exclaimed Mr. Stiggins. He took a large semi-circular bite out of the toast, and groaned again (*Chapter 27*).

'Ugh, you wretch!' said Mrs. Weller.
'Thank 'ee, my love,' said Mr. Weller.
'Come, come, father,' said Sam, 'none o' these little lovin's afore strangers' (*Chapter 27*).

'I vish you could muffle that 'ere Stiggins, and take him with you,' said Mr. Weller.
'I am ashamed on you!' said Sam, reproachfully; 'what do you let him show his red nose in the Markis o' Granby at all, for?'
Mr. Weller the elder fixed on his son an earnest look, and replied, ' 'Cause I'm a married man, Samivel, 'cause I'm a married man. When you're a married man, Samivel, you'll understand a good many things as you don't understand now; but vether it's worth while goin' through so much, to learn so little, as the charity-boy said ven he got to the end of the alphabet, is a matter o' taste. *I* rayther think it isn't' (*Chapter 27*).

'I've only got to say this here,' said Sam, stopping short, 'that if *I* was the properiator o' the Markis o' Granby, and that 'ere Stiggins came and made toast in *my* bar, I'd – '
'What?' interposed Mr. Weller, with great anxiety. 'What?'
' – Pison his rum-and-water,' said Sam.
'No!' said Mr. Weller, shaking his son eagerly by the hand, 'would you raly, Sammy; would you, though?'
'I would,' said Sam. 'I wouldn't be too hard upon him at first. I'd drop him in the water-butt, and put the lid on; and if I found he was insensible to kindness, I'd try the other persvasion' (*Chapter 27*).

How many old recollections, and how many dormant sympathies, does Christmas time awaken!
We write these words now, many miles distant from the spot at which, year after year, we met on that day, a merry and joyous circle. Many of the hearts that throbbed so gaily then, have ceased to beat; many of the looks that shone so brightly then, have ceased to

glow; the hands we grasped, have grown cold; the eyes we sought, have hid their lustre in the grave; and yet the old house, the room, the merry voices and smiling faces, the jest, the laugh, the most minute and trivial circumstances connected with those happy meetings, crowd upon our mind at each recurrence of the season, as if the last assemblage had been but yesterday! Happy, happy Christmas, that can win us back to the delusions of our childish days; that can recall to the old man the pleasures of his youth; that can transport the sailor and the traveller, thousands of miles away, back to his own fireside and his quiet home! *(Chapter 28).*

A wedding is a licensed subject to joke upon, but there really is no great joke in the matter after all; we speak merely of the ceremony, and beg it to be distinctly understood that we indulge in no hidden sarcasm upon a married life. Mixed up with the pleasure and joy of the occasion, are the many regrets at quitting home, the tears of parting between parent and child, the consciousness of leaving the dearest and kindest friends of the happiest portion of human life, to encounter its cares and troubles with others still untried and little known: natural feelings which we would not render this chapter mournful by describing, and which we should be still more unwilling to be supposed to ridicule *(Chapter 28).*

'Vere does the mince pies go, young opium eater?' said Mr. Weller to the fat boy, as he assisted in laying out such articles of consumption as had not been duly arranged on the previous night.

The fat boy pointed to the destination of the pies.

'Wery good,' said Sam, 'stick a bit o' Christmas in 'em. T'other dish opposite. There; now we look compact and comfortable, as the father said ven he cut his little boy's head off, to cure him o' squintin'.' *(Chapter 28).*

'Well, Sam,' said Mr. Pickwick, as that favoured servitor entered his bed-chamber with his warm water, on the morning of Christmas Day, 'still frosty?'

'Water in the wash-hand basin's a mask o' ice, sir,' responded Sam.

'Severe weather, Sam,' observed Mr. Pickwick.

'Fine time for them as is well wrapped up, as the Polar Bear said to himself, ven he was practising his skating,' replied Mr. Weller *(Chapter 30).*

'Nothing like dissecting, to give one an appetite,' said Mr. Bob Sawyer, looking round the table.

Mr. Pickwick slightly shuddered.

'By the bye, Bob,' said Mr. Allen, 'have you finished that leg yet?'

'Nearly,' replied Sawyer, helping himself to half a fowl as he spoke. 'It's a very muscular one for a child's.'

'Is it?' inquired Mr. Allen, carelessly.

'Very,' said Bob Sawyer, with his mouth full.

'I've put my name down for an arm, at our place,' said Mr. Allen. 'We're clubbing for a subject, and the list is nearly full, only we can't get hold of any fellow that wants a head. I wish you'd take it.'

'No,' replied Bob Sawyer; 'can't afford expensive luxuries.'

'Nonsense!' said Allen.

'Can't indeed,' rejoined Bob Sawyer. 'I wouldn't mind a brain, but couldn't stand a whole head.'

'Hush, hush, gentlemen, pray,' said Mr. Pickwick, 'I hear the ladies' *(Chapter 30).*

The jovial party broke up next morning. Breakings-up are capital things in our school days, but in after life they are painful enough. Death, self-interest, and fortune's changes, are every day breaking up many a happy group, and scattering them far and wide; and the boys and girls never come back again *(Chapter 30).*

Mr. Benjamin Allen drew Mr. Pickwick aside with an air of some mystery; and Mr. Bob Sawyer thrusting his forefinger between two of Mr. Pickwick's ribs, and thereby displaying his native drollery, and his knowledge of the anatomy of the human frame, at one and the same time, inquired –

'I say, old boy, where do you hang out?'

Mr. Pickwick replied that he was at present suspended at the George and Vulture *(Chapter 30).*

The Serjeant's clerk laughed again; not a noisy boisterous laugh, but a silent, internal chuckle, which Mr. Pickwick disliked to hear. When a man bleeds inwardly, it is a dangerous thing for himself; but when he laughs inwardly, it bodes no good to other people. *(Chapter 31).*

'Now,' said Jack Hopkins, 'just to set us going again, Bob, I don't mind singing a song.' And Hopkins, incited thereto, by tumultuous applause, plunged himself at once into 'The King, God bless him,' which he sang as loud as he could, to a novel air, compounded of 'The Bay of Biscay,' and 'A Frog he would.' The chorus was the essence of the song; and, as each gentleman sang it to the tune he knew best, the effect was very striking indeed *(Chapter 32).*

'Ugh, you coward!' replied Mrs. Raddle, with supreme contempt. '*Do* you mean to turn them wretches out, or not, Mr. Sawyer?'

'They're going, Mrs. Raddle, they're going,' said the miserable Bob. 'I am afraid you'd better go,' said Mr. Bob Sawyer to his friends. 'I *thought* you were making too much noise.'

'It's a very unfortunate thing,' said the prim man. 'Just as we were getting so comfortable too!' The prim man was just beginning to have a dawning recollection of the story he had forgotten.

'It's hardly to be borne,' said the prim man, looking round. 'Hardly to be borne, is it?'

'Not to be endured,' replied Jack Hopkins; 'let's have the other verse, Bob. Come, here goes!'

'No, no, Jack, don't,' interposed Bob Sawyer; 'it's a capital song, but I am afraid we had better not have the other verse. They are very violent people, the people of the house.'

'Shall I step upstairs, and pitch into the landlord?' inquired Hopkins, 'or keep on ringing the bell, or go and groan on the staircase?' *(Chapter 32).*

The particular picture on which Sam Weller's eyes were fixed . . . was a highly coloured representation of a couple of human hearts skewered together with an arrow, cooking before a cheerful fire, while a male and female cannibal in modern attire: the gentleman being clad in a blue coat and white trousers, and the lady in a deep red pelisse with a parasol of the same: were approaching the meal with hungry eyes, up a serpentine gravel path leading thereunto. A decidedly indelicate young gentleman, in a pair of wings and nothing else, was depicted as superintending the cooking; a representation of the spire of the church in Langham Place, London, appeared in the distance; and the whole formed a 'valentine,' of which, as a written inscription in the window testified, there was a large assortment within, which the shopkeeper pledged himself to dispose of, to his countrymen generally, at the reduced rate of one and sixpence each *(Chapter 33)*.

'Wot's the matter now?' said Sam.

'Nev'r mind, Sammy,' replied Mr. Weller, 'It'll be a wery agonizin' trial to me at my time of life, but I'm pretty tough, that's vun consolation, as the wery old turkey remarked wen the farmer said he wos afeerd he should be obliged to kill him for the London market' *(Chapter 33)*.

'Go on, Sammy.'

' "Lovely creetur," ' repeated Sam.

'Tain't in poetry, is it?' interposed his father.

'No, no,' replied Sam.

'Wery glad to hear it,' said Mr. Weller. 'Poetry's unnat'ral; no man ever talked poetry 'cept a beadle on Boxin' Day, or Warren's blackin', or Rowlands' oil, or some o' them low fellows; never you let yourself down to talk poetry, my boy. Begin agin, Sammy' *(Chapter 33)*.

'That's a wery pretty sentiment,' said the elder Mr. Weller, removing his pipe to make way for the remark.

'Yes, I think it is rayther good,' observed Sam, highly flattered.

'Wot I like in that 'ere style of writin',' said the elder Mr. Weller, 'is, that there ain't no callin' names in it, – no Wenuses, nor nothin' o' that kind. Wot's the good o' callin' a young 'ooman a Wenus or a angel, Sammy?'

'Ah! what, indeed?' replied Sam.

'You might jist as well call her a griffin, or a unicorn, or a king's arms at once, which is wery well known to be a col-lection o' fabulous animals,' added Mr. Weller.

'Just as well,' replied Sam *(Chapter 33)*.

Sam resumed.

' "So I take the privilidge of the day, Mary, my dear – as the gen'l'm'n in difficulties did, ven he valked out of a Sunday, – to tell you that the first and only time I see you, your likeness was took on my hart in much quicker time and brighter colours than ever a likeness was took by the profeel macheen (wich p'raps you may have heerd on Mary my dear) altho it *does* finish a portrait and put the frame and glass on complete, with a hook at the end to hang it up by, and all in two minutes and a quarter." '

'I am afeerd that werges on the poetical, Sammy,' said Mr. Weller, dubiously.

'No it don't,' replied Sam, reading on very quickly, to avoid contesting the point –

' "Except of me Mary my dear as your walentine and think over what I've said. – My dear Mary I will now conclude." That's all,' said Sam.

'That's rather a sudden pull up, ain't it, Sammy?' inquired Mr. Weller.

'Not a bit on it,' said Sam; 'she'll vish there wos more, and that's the great art o' letter writin'.' *(Chapter 33)*.

The first matter relates to your governor, Sammy,' said Mr. Weller. 'He's a goin' to be tried to-morrow, ain't he?'

'The trial's a comin' on,' replied Sam.

'Vell,' said Mr. Weller, 'now I s'pose he'll want to call some witnesses to speak to his character, or p'raps to prove a alleybi. I've been a turnin' the bis'ness over in my mind, and he may make his-self easy, Sammy. I've got some friends as'll do either for him, but my adwice 'ud be this here – never mind the character, and stick to the alleybi. Nothing like a alleybi, Sammy, nothing' *(Chapter 33)*.

'Sammy,' whispered Mr. Weller, 'if some o' these people don't want tappin' to-morrow mornin', I ain't your father, and that's wot it is. Why, this here old lady next me is a drowndin' herself in tea.'

Be quiet, can't you?' murmured Sam.

'Sam,' whispered Mr. Weller, a moment afterwards, in a tone of deep agitation, 'mark my vords, my boy. If that 'ere secretary fellow keeps on for only five minutes more, he'll blow his-self up with toast and water.'

'Well, let him, if he likes,' replied Sam; 'it ain't no bis'ness o' your'n.'

'If this here lasts much longer, Sammy,' said Mr. Weller, in the same low voice, 'I shall feel it my duty, as a human bein', to rise and address the cheer. There's a young 'ooman on the next form but two, as has drunk nine breakfast cups and a half; and she's a swellin' wisibly before my wery eyes' *(Chapter 33)*.

The soft sex to a man – he begged pardon, to a female – rallied round the young waterman, and turned with disgust from the drinker of spirits (cheers). The Brick Lane Branch brothers were watermen (cheers and laughter). That room was their boat; that audience were the maidens; and he (Mr. Anthony Humm), however unworthily, was 'first oars' (unbounded applause).

'Wot does he mean by the soft sex, Sammy?' inquired Mr. Weller, in a whisper.

'The womin,' said Sam, in the same tone.

'He ain't far out there, Sammy,' replied Mr. Weller; 'they *must* be a soft sex, – a wery soft sex, indeed – if they let themselves be gammoned by such fellers as him' *(Chapter 33)*.

'The plaintiff, gentlemen,' continued Serjeant Buzfuz, in a soft and melancholy voice, 'the plaintiff is a widow; yes, gentlemen, a widow. The late Mr. Bardell, after enjoying, for many years, the esteem and confidence of his sovereign, as one of the guardians of his royal revenues, glided almost imperceptibly from the world, to seek elsewhere for that repose and peace which a custom-house can never afford.'

At this pathetic description of the decease of Mr.

Bardell, who had been knocked on the head with a quart-pot in a public-house cellar, the learned Serjeant's voice faltered, and he proceeded with emotion *(Chapter 34)*.

'These letters, too, bespeak the character of the man. They are not open, fervent, eloquent epistles, breathing nothing but the language of affectionate attachment. They are covert, sly, underhanded communications, but, fortunately, far more conclusive than if couched in the most glowing language and the most poetic imagery – letters that must be viewed with a cautious and suspicious eye – letters that were evidently intended at the time, by Pickwick, to mislead and delude any third parties into whose hands they might fall. Let me read the first:– "Garraway's, twelve o'clock. Dear Mrs. B. – Chops and Tomata sauce. Yours, PICKWICK." Gentlemen, what does this mean? Chops and Tomata sauce. Yours, Pickwick! Chops! Gracious heavens! and Tomata sauce! Gentlemen, is the happiness of a sensitive and confiding female to be trifled away by such shallow artifices as these? The next has no date whatever, which is in itself suspicious. "Dear Mrs. B., I shall not be at home till to-morrow. Slow coach." And then follows this very remarkable expression. "Don't trouble yourself about the warming-pan." The warming-pan! Why, gentlemen, who *does* trouble himself about a warming-pan? When was the peace of mind of man or woman broken or disturbed by a warming-pan, which is in itself a harmless, a useful, and I will add, gentlemen, a comforting article of domestic furniture? Why is Mrs. Bardell so earnestly entreated not to agitate herself about this warming-pan, unless (as is no doubt the case) it is a mere cover for hidden fire – a mere substitute for some endearing word or promise, agreeably to a preconcerted system of correspondence, artfully contrived by Pickwick with a view to his contemplated desertion, and which I am not in a condition to explain? And what does this allusion to the slow coach mean? For aught I know, it may be a reference to Pickwick himself, who has most unquestionably been a criminally slow coach during the whole of this transaction, but whose speed will now be very unexpectedly accelerated, and whose wheels, gentlemen, as he will find to his cost, will very soon be greased by you!' *(Chapter 34: Serjeant Buzfuz)*.

'What's your name, sir?' inquired the judge.

'Sam Weller, my Lord,' replied that gentleman.

'Do you spell it with a "V" or a "W"?' inquired the judge.

'That depends upon the taste and fancy of the speller, my Lord,' replied Sam; 'I never had occasion to spell it more than once or twice in my life, but I spells it with a "V." '

Here a voice in the gallery exclaimed aloud, 'Quite right too, Samivel, quite right. Put it down a we, my Lord, put it down a we' *(Chapter 34)*.

'Now, Mr. Weller,' said Serjeant Buzfuz.

'Now, sir,' replied Sam.

'I believe you are in the service of Mr. Pickwick, the defendant in this case. Speak up, if you please, Mr. Weller.'

'I mean to speak up, sir,' replied Sam; 'I am in the service o' that 'ere gen'l'm'n, and a wery good service it is.'

'Little to do, and plenty to get, I suppose?' said Serjeant Buzfuz with jocularity.

'Oh, quite enough to get, sir, as the soldier said ven they ordered him three hundred and fifty lashes,' replied Sam.

'You must not tell us what the soldier, or any other man, said, sir,' interposed the judge; 'it's not evidence.'

'Wery good, my Lord,' replied Sam *(Chapter 34)*.

'Now, attend, Mr. Weller,' said Serjeant Buzfuz, dipping a large pen into the inkstand before him, for the purpose of frightening Sam with a show of taking down his answer. 'You were in the passage, and yet saw nothing of what was going forward. Have you a pair of eyes, Mr. Weller?'

'Yes, I have a pair of eyes,' replied Sam, 'and that's just it. If they wos a pair o' patent double million magnifyin' gas microscopes of hextra power, p'raps I might be able to see through a flight o' stairs and a deal door; but bein' only eyes, you see, my wision's limited' *(Chapter 34)*.

Sam had put up the steps, and was preparing to jump upon the box, when he felt himself gently touched on the shoulder; and looking round, his father stood before him. The old gentleman's countenance wore a mournful expression, as he shook his head gravely, and said, in warning accents –

'I know'd what 'ud come o' this here mode o' doin' bis'ness. Oh Sammy, Sammy, vy worn't there a alleybi!' *(Chapter 34)*.

'But surely, my dear sir,' said little Perker, as he stood in Mr. Pickwick's apartment on the morning after the trial: 'surely you don't really mean – really and seriously now, and irritation apart – that you won't pay these costs and damages?'

'Not one halfpenny,' said Mr. Pickwick, firmly; 'not one halfpenny.'

'Hooroar for the principle, as the money-lender said ven he vouldn't renew the bill,' observed Mr. Weller *(Chapter 35)*.

The individual for whom the second place was taken, was a personage no less illustrious than Mrs. Dowler his lady wife.

'She's a fine woman,' said Mr. Dowler. 'I am proud of her. I have reason.'

'I hope I shall have the pleasure of judging,' said Mr. Pickwick, with a smile.

'You shall,' replied Dowler. 'She shall know you. She shall esteem you. I courted her under singular circumstances. I won her through a rash vow. Thus, I saw her; I loved her; I proposed; she refused me. – "You love another?" – "Spare my blushes." – "I know him." – "You do." – "Very good; if he remains here, I'll skin him." '

'Lord bless me!' exclaimed Mr. Pickwick, involuntarily.

'Did you skin the gentleman, sir?' inquired Mr. Winkle, with a very pale face.

'I wrote him a note. I said it was a painful thing. and so it was.'

'Certainly,' interposed Mr. Winkle.

'I said I had pledged my word as a gentleman to skin him. My character was at stake. I had no alternative. As an officer in his Majesty's service, I was bound to skin him. I regretted the necessity, but it must be done. He was open to conviction. He saw that the rules of the service were imperative. He fled. I married her. Here's the coach. That's her head' *(Chapter 35)*.

'I'm wery much afeerd, sir, that the properiator o' this here coach is playin' some imperence vith us.'

'How is that, Sam?' said Mr. Pickwick; 'aren't the names down on the way-bill?'

'The names is not only down on the vay-bill, sir,' replied Sam, 'but they've painted vun on 'em up,' on the door o' the coach.' As Sam spoke, he pointed to that part of the coach door on which the proprietor's name usually appears; and there, sure enough, gilt in letters of a good size, was the magic name of PICKWICK!

'Dear me,' exclaimed Mr. Pickwick, quite staggered by the coincidence; 'what a very extraordinary thing!'

'Yes, but that ain't all,' said Sam, again directing his master's attention to the coach door; 'not content vith writin' up Pickwick, they puts "Moses" afore it, vich I call addin' insult to injury, as the parrot said ven they not only took him from his native land, but made him talk the English langwidge arterwards' *(Chapter 35)*.

There are few things more worrying than sitting up for somebody, especially if that somebody be at a party. You cannot help thinking how quickly the time passes with them, which drags so heavily with you; and the more you think of this, the more your hopes of their speedy arrival decline. Clocks tick so loud, too, when you are sitting up alone, and you seem as if you had an undergarment of cobwebs on. First, something tickles your right knee, and then the same sensation irritates your left. You have no sooner changed your position, than it comes again in the arms; when you have fidgeted your limbs into all sorts of odd shapes, you have a sudden relapse in the nose, which you rub as if to rub it off – as there is no doubt you would, if you could. Eyes, too, are mere personal inconveniences; and the wick of one candle gets an inch and a half long, while you are snuffing the other. These, and various other little nervous annoyances, render sitting up for a length of time after everybody else has gone to bed, anything but a cheerful amusement *(Chapter 36)*.

Just as the clock struck three, there was blown into the Crescent a sedan-chair with Mrs. Dowler inside, borne by one short fat chairman, and one long thin one, who had had much ado to keep their bodies perpendicular: to say nothing of the chair. But on that high ground, and in the Crescent, which the wind swept round and round as if it were going to tear the paving stones up, its fury was tremendous. They were very glad to set the chair down, and give a good round loud double knock at the street-door.

They waited some time, but nobody came.

'Servants is in the arms o' Porpus, I think,' said the short chairman, warming his hands at the attendant link-boy's torch.

'I wish he'd give 'em a squeeze and wake 'em,' observed the long one *(Chapter 36)*.

Nobody came. It was all as silent and dark as ever.

'Dear me!' said Mrs. Dowler. 'You must knock again, if you please.'

'There ain't a bell, is there, ma'am?' said the short chairman.

'Yes, there is,' interposed the link-boy, 'I've been ringing at it ever so long.'

'It's only a handle,' said Mrs. Dowler, 'the wire's broken.'

'I wish the servants' heads wos,' growled the long man *(Chapter 36)*.

'How do you do, sir?'

'Why, reasonably conwalessent,' replied Sam. 'How do *you* find yourself, my dear feller?'

'Only so so,' said Mr. John Smauker.

'Ah, you've been a workin' too hard,' observed Sam. 'I was fearful you would; it won't do, you know; you must not give way to that 'ere uncompromisin' spirit o' your'n.'

'It's not so much that, Mr. Weller,' replied Mr. John Smauker, 'as bad wine; I'm afraid I've been dissipating.'

'Oh! that's it, is it?' said Sam; 'that's a wery bad complaint, that.'

'And yet the temptation, you see, Mr. Weller,' observed Mr. John Smauker.

'Ah, to be sure,' said Sam.

'Plunged into the very vortex of society, you know, Mr. Weller,' said Mr. John Smauker with a sigh.

'Dreadful indeed!' rejoined Sam.

'But it's always the way,' said Mr. John Smauker; 'if your destiny leads you into public life, and public station, you must expect to be subjected to temptations which other people is free from, Mr. Weller.'

'Precisely what my uncle said, ven *he* vent into the public line,' remarked Sam, 'and wery right the old gen'l'm'n wos, for he drank his-self to death in somethin' less than a quarter' *(Chapter 37)*.

'Have you drank the waters, Mr. Weller?' inquired his companion, as they walked towards High Street.

'Once,' replied Sam.

'What did you think of 'em, sir?'

'I thought they wos particklery unpleasant,' replied Sam.

'Ah,' said Mr. John Smauker, 'you disliked the killibeate taste, perhaps?'

'I don't know much about that 'ere,' said Sam. 'I thought they'd a wery strong flavour o' warm flat irons.'

'That *is* the killibeate, Mr. Weller,' observed Mr. John Smauker, contemptuously *(Chapter 37)*.

'I'm afraid you're a cunning fellow, Mr. Weller,' said that individual.

'No, no,' said Sam. 'I leave all that 'ere to you. It's a great deal more in your way than mine, as the gen'l'm'n on the right side o' the garden vall said to the man on the wrong 'un, ven the mad bull vos a comin' up the lane' *(Chapter 37)*.

'You ain't a goin', Blazes?'

'Yes, I am,' said the man with the cocked hat.

'Wot, and leave three-quarters of a bowl of punch behind you!' said Sam; 'nonsense, set down agin.'

Mr. Tuckle was not proof against this invitation. He laid aside the cocked hat and stick which he had just taken up, and said he would have one glass, for good fellowship's sake.

As the gentleman in blue went home the same way as Mr. Tuckle, he was prevailed upon to stop too. When the punch was about half gone, Sam ordered in some oysters from the greengrocer's shop; and the effect of both was so extremely exhilarating, that Mr. Tuckle, dressed out with the cocked hat and stick, danced the frog hornpipe among the shells on the table: while the gentleman in blue played an accompaniment upon an ingenious musical instrument formed of a hair-comb and a curl-paper. At last, when the punch was all gone, and the night nearly so, they sallied forth to see each other home. Mr. Tuckle no sooner got into the open air, than he was seized with a sudden desire to lie on the curb-stone; Sam thought it would be a pity to contradict him, and so let him have his own way. As the cocked hat would have been spoilt if left there, Sam very considerately flattened it down on the head of the gentleman in blue, and putting the big stick in his hand, propped him up against his own street-door, rang the bell, and walked quietly home *(Chapter 37)*.

'Lord, if I had known who you were, I should have rushed out, and caught you in my arms,' said Bob Sawyer; 'but upon my life, I thought you were the King's-taxes.'

'No!' said Mr. Winkle.

'I did, indeed,' responded Bob Sawyer, 'and I was just going to say that I wasn't at home, but if you'd leave a message I'd be sure to give it to myself; for he don't know me; no more does the Lighting and Paving. I think the Church-rates guesses who I am, and I know the Water-works does, because I drew a tooth of his when I first came down here. But come in, come in!' *(Chapter 38)*.

'You've been stopping to over all the posts in Bristol, you idle young scamp!' said Mr. Bob Sawyer.

'No, sir, I haven't,' replied the boy.

'You had better not!' said Mr. Bob Sawyer, with a threatening aspect. 'Who do you suppose will ever employ a professional man, when they see his boy playing at marbles in the gutter, or flying the garter in the horse-road? Have you no feeling for your profession, you groveller? Did you leave all the medicine?'

'Yes, sir.'

'The powders for the child, at the large house with the new family, and the pills to be taken four times a day at the ill-tempered old gentleman's with the gouty leg?'

'Yes, sir.'

'Then shut the door, and mind the shop' *(Chapter 38)*.

Mr. Bob Sawyer peeped into the shop to see that no stranger was within hearing, and leaning forward to Mr. Winkle, said, in a low tone –

'He leaves it all at the wrong houses.'

Mr. Winkle looked perplexed, and Bob Sawyer and his friend laughed.

'Don't you see?' said Bob. 'He goes up to a house, rings the area bell, pokes a packet of medicine without a direction into the servant's hand, and walks off. Servant takes it into the dining-parlour; master opens it and reads the label: "Draught to be taken at bed-time – pills as before – lotion as usual – *the* powder. From Sawyer's, late Nockemorf's. Physicians' prescriptions carefully prepared," and all the rest of it. Shows it to his wife – *she* reads the label; it goes down to the servants – *they* read the label. Next day, boy calls: "Very sorry – his mistake – immense business – great many parcels to deliver – Mr. Sawyer's compliments – late Nockemorf." The name gets known, and that's the thing, my boy, in the medical way. Bless your heart, old fellow, it's better than all the advertising in the world. We have got one four-ounce bottle that's been to half the houses in Bristol, and hasn't done yet' *(Chapter 38)*.

'Oh, Ben and I have hit upon a dozen such,' replied Bob Sawyer, with great glee. 'The lamplighter has eighteenpence a week to pull the night bell for ten minutes every time he comes round; and my boy always rushes into church, just before the psalms, when the people have got nothing to do but look about 'em, and calls me out, with horror and dismay depicted on his countenance. "Bless my soul," everybody says, "somebody taken suddenly ill! Sawyer, late Nockemorf, sent for. What a business that young man has!" ' *(Chapter 38)*.

'What do you mean by this conduct, Sam?' inquired Mr. Winkle, indignantly. 'Get out, sir, this instant. What do you mean, sir?'

'What do *I* mean,' retorted Sam; 'come, sir, this is rayther too rich, as the young lady said, wen she remonstrated with the pastry-cook, arter he'd sold her a pork-pie as had got nothin' but fat inside' *(Chapter 38)*.

'Vell,' said Sam at length, 'if this don't beat cock-fightin', nothin' never vill, as the Lord Mayor said, ven the chief secretary o' state proposed his missis's health arter dinner' *(Chapter 39)*.

The man in the spectacles was hard at work, swearing the clerks: the oath being invariably administered, without any effort at punctuation, and usually in the following terms:–

'Take the book in your right hand this is your name and handwriting you swear that the contents of this your affidavit are true so help you God a shilling you must get change I haven't got it.'

'Well, Sam,' said Mr. Pickwick, 'I suppose they are getting the habeas corpus ready.'

'Yes,' said Sam, 'and I vish they'd bring out the have-his-carcase. It's wery unpleasant keepin' us vaitin' here. I'd ha' got half a dozen have-his-carcases ready, pack'd up and all, by this time' *(Chapter 40)*.

'It strikes me, Sam,' said Mr. Pickwick, leaning over the iron rail at the stairhead, 'it strikes me, Sam, that imprisonment for debt is scarcely any punishment at all.'

'Think not, sir?' inquired Mr. Weller.

'You see how these fellows drink, and smoke, and roar,' replied Mr. Pickwick. 'It's quite impossible that they can mind it much.'

'Ah, that's just the wery thing, sir,' rejoined Sam, '*they* don't mind it; it's a regular holiday to them – all porter and skittles. It's the t'other vuns as gets done over, vith this sort o' thing: them down-hearted fellers as can't svig away at the beer, nor play at skittles neither; them as vould pay if they could, and gets low by being boxed up. I'll tell you wot it is, sir; them as is alvays a idlin' in public-houses it don't damage at all, and them as is alvays a workin' wen they can, it damages too much. "It's unekal," as my father used to say wen his grog worn't made half-and-half: "It's unekal, and that's the fault on it".' *(Chapter 41).*

'Mr. Pickwick!' exclaimed Job aloud.

'Eh?' said Jingle, starting from his seat. 'Mr. – ! So it is – queer place – strange things – serves me right – very.' Mr. Jingle thrust his hands into the place where his trousers pockets used to be, and, dropping his chin upon his breast, sank back into his chair.

Mr. Pickwick was affected; the two men looked so very miserable. The sharp involuntary glance Jingle had cast at a small piece of raw loin of mutton, which Job had brought in with him, said more of their reduced state than two hours' explanation could have done. Mr. Pickwick looked mildly at Jingle, and said –

'I should like to speak to you in private. Will you step out for an instant?'

'Certainly,' said Jingle, rising hastily. 'Can't step far – no danger of over-walking yourself here – Spike Park – grounds pretty – romantic, but not extensive – open for public inspection – family always in town – housekeeper desperately careful – very' *(Chapter 42).*

'Eh?' said Jingle. 'Spout – dear relation – uncle Tom – couldn't help it – must eat, you know. Wants of nature – and all that.'

'What do you mean?'

'Gone, my dear sir – last coat – can't help it. Lived on a pair of boots – whole fortnight. Silk umbrella – ivory handle – week – fact – honour – ask Job – knows it.'

'Lived for three weeks upon a pair of boots, and a silk umbrella with an ivory handle!' exclaimed Mr. Pickwick, who had only heard of such things in shipwrecks, or read of them in Constable's Miscellany.

'True,' said Jingle, nodding his head. 'Pawnbroker's shop – duplicates here – small sums – mere nothing – all rascals.'

'Oh,' said Mr. Pickwick, much relieved by this explanation; 'I understand you. You have pawned your wardrobe.'

'Everything – Job's too – all shirts gone – never mind – saves washing. Nothing soon – lie in bed – starve – die – Inquest – little bone-house – poor prisoner – common necessaries – hush it up – gentlemen of the jury – warden's tradesmen – keep it snug – natural death – coroner's order – workhouse funeral – serve him right – all over – drop the curtain' *(Chapter 42).*

266

'The have-his-carcase, next to the perpetual motion, is vun of the blessedest things as wos ever made. I've read that 'ere in the newspapers, wery of 'en' *(Chapter 43:* Sam Weller).

'Gentlemen,' said the coach-horser, 'rather than disturb the harmony of this delightful occasion, perhaps Mr. Samuel Weller will oblige the company.'

'Raly, gentlemen,' said Sam, 'I'm not wery much in the habit o' singin' without the instrument; but anythin' for a quiet life, as the man said wen he took the sitivation at the lighthouse' *(Chapter 43).*

ROMANCE

I.

Bold Turpin vunce, on Hounslow Heath,
His bold mare Bess bestrode-er;
Ven there he see'd the Bishop's coach
A coming along the road-er.
So he gallops close to the 'orse's legs,
And he claps his head vithin;
And the Bishop says, 'Sure as eggs is eggs,
This here's the bold Turpin!'

CHORUS

And the Bishop says, 'Sure as eggs is eggs,
This here's the bold Turpin!'

II.

Says Turpin, 'You shall eat your words,
With a sarse of leaden bul-let;'
So he puts a pistol to his mouth,
And he fires it down his gul-let.
The coachman he not likin' the job,
Set off at a full gal-lop,
But Dick put a couple of balls in his nob,
And perwailed on him to stop.

CHORUS *(sarcastically)*

But Dick put a couple of balls in his nob,
And perwailed on him to stop.

(Chapter 43: Sam Weller)

'It ain't o' no use, sir,' said Sam, again and again. 'He's a malicious, bad-disposed, vorldly-minded, spiteful, windictive creetur, with a hard heart as there ain't no soft'nin'. As the wirtuous clergyman remarked of the old gen'l'm'n with the dropsy, ven he said, that upon the whole he thought he'd rayther leave his property to his vife than build a chapel vith it' *(Chapter 44).*

'Wot's the matter?' says the doctor. "Wery ill," says the patient. "Wot have you been a eatin' on?" says the doctor. "Roast weal," says the patient. "Wot's the last thing you dewoured?" says the doctor. "Crumpets," says the patient. "That's it!" says the doctor. "I'll send you a box of pills directly, and don't you never take no more of 'em," he says. "no more o' wot?" says the patient – "Pills?" "No; crumpets," says the doctor. "Wy?" says the patient, starting up in bed; "I've eat four crumpets, ev'ry night for fifteen year, on principle." "Well, then, you'd better leave 'em off, on principle," says the doctor. "Crumpets is wholesome, sir," says the patient. "Crumpets is *not* wholesome, sir," says the doctor, wery fierce. "But they're so cheap," says the patient, comin' down a little, "and so wery fillin' at the price." "They'd be dear to you, at any price; dear if you wos paid to eat 'em," says the doctor. "Four crumpets a night," he says, "vill do your business in six months!" The patient looks him full in the face, and turns it over in his mind for a long time, and at last he says, "Are you sure o' that 'ere, sir?" "I'll stake my professional reputation on it," says the doctor. "How many crumpets, at a sittin', do you think 'ud kill me off at once?" says the patient. "I don't know," says the doctor. "Do you think half-a-crown's wurth 'ud do it?" says the patient. "I think it might," says the doctor. "Three shillin's' wurth 'ud be sure to do it, I s'pose?" says the patient. "Certainly," says the doctor. "Wery good," says the patient; "good night." Next mornin' he gets up, has a fire lit, orders in three shillin's' wurth o' crumpets, toasts 'em all, eats 'em all, and blows his brains out' (*Chapter 44: Sam Weller*).

'Mornin', gen'l'm'n,' said Sam, entering at the moment with the shoes and gaiters. 'Avay vith melincholly, as the little boy said ven his school-missis died' (*Chapter 44*).

'Yes, gen'l'm'n,' said Sam, 'I'm a – stand steady, sir, if you please – I'm a pris'ner, gen'l'm'n. Confined, as the lady said' (*Chapter 44*).

'Mother-in-law,' said Sam, politely saluting the lady, 'wery much obliged to you for this here wisit. Shepherd, how air you?'

'Oh, Samuel!' said Mrs. Weller. 'This is dreadful.'

'Not a bit on it, mum,' replied Sam. 'Is it, shepherd?'

Mr. Stiggins raised his hands, and turned up his eyes, till the whites – or rather the yellows – were alone visible; but made no reply in words.

'Is this here gen'l'm'n troubled with any painful complaint?' said Sam, looking to his mother-in-law for explanation.

'The good man is grieved to see you here, Samuel,' replied Mrs. Weller.

'Oh, that's it, is it?' said Sam. 'I was afeerd, from his manner, that he might ha' forgotten to take pepper vith that 'ere last cowcumber he eat. Set down, sir; ve make no extra charge for the settin' down, as the king remarked wen he blowed up his ministers' (*Chapter 45*).

Mr. Stiggins groaned.

'Hallo! Here's this unfort'nate gen'l'm'n took ill agin,' said Sam looking round. 'Where do you feel it now, sir?'

'In the same place, young man,' rejoined Mr. Stiggins: 'in the same place.'

'Where may that be, sir?' inquired Sam, with great outward simplicity.

'In the buzzim, young man,' replied Mr. Stiggins, placing his umbrella on his waistcoat.

At this affecting reply, Mrs. Weller, being wholly unable to suppress her feelings, sobbed aloud, and stated her conviction that the red-nosed man was a saint; whereupon Mr. Weller, senior, ventured to suggest, in an undertone, that he must be the representative of the united parishes of Saint Simon Without, and St. Walker Within (*Chapter 45*).

'Wot's your usual tap, sir?' replied Sam.

'Oh, my dear young friend,' replied Mr. Stiggins, 'all taps is vanities!'

'Too true, too true, indeed,' said Mrs. Weller, murmuring a groan, and shaking her head assentingly.

'Well,' said Sam, 'I des-say they may be, sir; but which is your partickler wanity? Vich wanity do you like the flavour on best, sir?'

'Oh, my dear young friend,' replied Mr. Stiggins, 'I despise them all. If,' said Mr. Stiggins, 'if there is any one of them less odious than another, it is the liquor called rum. Warm, my dear young friend, with three lumps of sugar to the tumbler.'

'Wery sorry to say, sir,' said Sam, 'that they don't allow that particular wanity to be sold in this here establishment.'

'Oh, the hardness of heart of these inveterate men!' ejaculated Mr. Stiggins. 'Oh, the accursed cruelty of these inhuman persecutors!' (*Chapter 45*).

'I'll tell you wot it is, Samivel, my boy,' whispered the old gentleman into his son's ear, after a long and steadfast contemplation of his lady and Mr. Stiggins; I think there must be somethin' wrong in your mother-in-law's inside, as vell as in that o' the red-nosed man.'

'Wot do you mean?' said Sam.

'I mean this here, Sammy,' replied the old gentleman, 'that wot they drink, don't seem no nourishment to 'em; it all turns to warm water, and comes a pourin' out o' their eyes. 'Pend upon it, Sammy, it's a constitootional infirmity' (*Chapter 45*).

'Sammy,' whispered Mr. Weller, looking cautiously round: 'my duty to your gov'ner, and tell him if he thinks better o' this here bis'ness, to commoonicate vith me. Me and a cab'net-maker has dewised a plan for gettin' him out. A pianner, Samivel, a pianner!' said Mr. Weller, striking his son on the chest with the back of his hand, and falling back a step or two.

'Wot do you mean?' said Sam.

'A pianner forty, Samivel,' rejoined Mr. Weller, in a still more mysterious manner, 'as he can have on hire; vun as von't play, Sammy.'

'And wot 'ud be the good o' that?' said Sam.

'Let him send to my friend, the cab'net-maker, to fetch it back, Sammy,' replied Mr. Weller. 'Are you avake, now?'

'No,' rejoined Sam.

'There ain't no vurks in it,' whispered his father. 'It 'ull hold him easy, vith his hat and shoes on, and breathe through the legs, vich his holler. Have a passage ready taken for 'Merriker. The 'Merrikin gov'ment will never give him up, ven they find as he's got money to spend, Sammy. Let the gov'ner stop there, till Mrs. Bardell's dead, or Mr. Dodson and Fogg's hung (wich last ewent I think is the most likely to happen first, Sammy), and then let him come back and write a book about the 'Merrikins as'll pay all his expenses and more, if he blows 'em up enough' (*Chapter 45*).

'Things has altered with me, sir,' said Job.

'I should think they had,' exclaimed Mr. Weller, surveying his companion's rags with undisguised wonder. 'This is rayther a change for the worse, Mr. Trotter, as the gen'l'm'n said, wen he got two doubtful shillin's and sixpenn'orth o' pocket pieces for a good half-crown' *(Chapter 45)*.

'How sweet the country is, to be sure!' sighed Mrs. Rogers; 'I almost wish I lived in it always.'

'Oh, you wouldn't like that, ma'am,' replied Mrs. Bardell, rather hastily; for it was not at all advisable, with reference to the lodgings, to encourage such notions; 'you wouldn't like it, ma'am.'

'Oh! I should think you was a deal too lively and sought after, to be content with the country, ma'am,' said little Mrs. Cluppins.

'Perhaps I am, ma'am. Perhaps I am,' sighed the first-floor lodger.

'For lone people as have got nobody to care for them, or take care of them, or as have been hurt in their mind, or that kind of thing,' observed Mr. Raddle, plucking up a little cheerfulness, and looking round, 'the country is all very well. The country for a wounded spirit, they say.'

Now, of all things in the world that the unfortunate man could have said, any would have been preferable to this. Of course Mrs. Bardell burst into tears, and requested to be led from the table instantly; upon which the affectionate child began to cry too, most dismally.

'Would anybody believe, ma'am,' exclaimed Mrs. Raddle, turning fiercely to the first-floor lodger, 'that a woman could be married to such a unmanly creetur, which can tamper with a woman's feelings as he does, every hour in the day, ma'am?'

'My dear,' remonstrated Mr. Raddle, 'I didn't mean anything, my dear.'

'You didn't mean!' repeated Mrs. Raddle, with great scorn and contempt. 'Go away. I can't bear the sight of you, you brute' *(Chapter 46)*.

The door swung heavily after them, and they descended a small flight of steps.

'Here we are, at last. All right and tight, Mrs. Bardell!' said Jackson, looking exultingly round.

'What do you mean?' said Mrs. Bardell, with a palpitating heart.

'Just this,' replied Jackson, drawing her a little on one side; 'don't be frightened, Mrs. Bardell. There never was a more delicate man than Dodson, ma'am, or a more humane man than Fogg. It was their duty, in the way of business, to take you in execution for them costs; but they were anxious to spare your feelings as much as they could. What a comfort it must be, to you, to think how it's been done! This is the Fleet, ma'am. Wish you good night, Mrs. Bardell' *(Chapter 46)*.

'Beg your pardon, sir,' rejoined Mr. Weller. 'But there's a lady here, sir, as says she's somethin' wery partickler to disclose.'

'I can't see any lady,' replied Mr. Pickwick, whose mind was filled with visions of Mrs. Bardell.

'I vouldn't make too sure o' that, sir,' urged Mr. Weller, shaking his head. 'If you know'd who was near, sir, I rayther think you'd change your note. As the hawk remarked to himself with a cheerful laugh, ven he heerd the robin redbreast a singin' round the corner' *(Chapter 47)*.

'I can never be grateful enough to you, Sam, I am sure,' said Arabella, with the sweetest smile imaginable. 'I shall not forget your exertions in the garden at Clifton.'

'Don't say nothin' wotever about it, ma'am,' replied Sam. 'I only assisted natur', ma'am; as the doctor said to the boy's mother, arter he'd bled him to death' *(Chapter 47: Arabella Allen and Sam Weller)*.

'Sir,' called out Mr. Weller to his master.

'Well, Sam,' replied Mr. Pickwick, thrusting his head out of the window.

'I wish them horses had been three months and better in the Fleet, sir.'

'Why, Sam?' inquired Mr. Pickwick.

'Wy, sir,' exclaimed Mr. Weller, rubbing his hands, 'how they would go if they had been!' *(Chapter 47)*.

'You shall do it, before you are twenty-four hours older,' retorted Ben, with desperate calmness. 'She *shall* have you, or I'll know the reason why. I'll exert my authority.'

'Well,' said Mr. Bob Sawyer, 'we shall see.'

'We *shall* see, my friend,' replied Mr. Ben Allen, fiercely. He paused for a few seconds, and added in a voice broken by emotion, 'You have loved her from a child, my friend. You loved her when we were boys at school together, and, even then, she was wayward, and slighted your young feelings. Do you recollect, with all the eagerness of a child's love, one day pressing upon her acceptance, two small caraway-seed biscuits and one sweet apple, neatly folded into a circular parcel with the leaf of a copybook?'

'I do,' replied Bob Sawyer.

'She slighted that, I think?' said Ben Allen.

'She did,' rejoined Bob. 'She said I had kept the parcel so long in the pockets of my corduroys, that the apple was unpleasantly warm.'

'I remember,' said Mr. Allen, gloomily. 'Upon which we ate it ourselves, in alternate bites' *(Chapter 48)*.

'I wonder what these ghosts of mail-coaches carry in their bags,' said the landlord, who had listened to the whole story with profound attention.

'The dead letters, of course,' said the Bagman.

'Oh, ah! To be sure,' rejoined the landlord. 'I never thought of that' *(Chapter 49)*.

'Wos you ever called in,' inquired Sam, glancing at the driver, after a short silence, and lowering his voice to a mysterious whisper: 'wos you ever called in, ven you wos 'prentice to a sawbones, to wisit a postboy?'

'I don't remember that I ever was,' replied Bob Sawyer.

'You never see a postboy in that 'ere hospital as you *walked* (as they says o' the ghosts), did you?' demanded Sam.

'No,' replied Bob Sawyer. 'I don't think I ever did.'

'Never know'd a churchyard where there wos a postboy's tombstone, or see a dead postboy, did you?' inquired Sam, pursuing his catechism.

'No,' rejoined Bob, 'I never did.'

'No!' rejoined Sam, triumphantly. 'Nor never vill, and there's another thing that no man never see, and that's a dead donkey. No man never see a dead donkey, 'cept the gen'l'm'n in the black silk smalls as know'd the young 'ooman as kep' a goat; and that wos a French donkey, so wery likely he warn't wun o' the reg'lar breed.'

'Well, what has that got to do with the postboys?' asked Bob Sawyer.

'This here,' replied Sam. 'Without goin' so far as to as-sert, as some wery sensible people do, that postboys and donkeys is both immortal, wot I say is this; that wenever they feels theirselves gettin' stiff and past their work, they just rides off together, wun postboy to a pair in the usual way; wot becomes on 'em nobody knows, but it's wery probable as they starts away to take their pleasure in some other vorld, for there ain't a man alive as ever see, either a donkey or a postboy, a takin' his pleasure in this!' *(Chapter 51).*

'In short, Sammy, I feel that I ain't safe anyveres but on the box.'

'How are you safer there than anyveres else?' interrupted Sam.

' 'Cos a coachman's a privileged indiwidual,' replied Mr. Weller, looking fixedly at his son. ' 'Cos a coach-man may do vithout suspicion wot other men may not; 'cos a coachman may be on the wery amicablest terms with eighty mile o' females, and yet nobody think that he ever means to marry any vun among 'em. And wot other man can say the same, Sammy?'

'Vell, there's somethin' in that,' said Sam *(Chapter 52).*

'Oh, my young friend,' said Mr. Stiggins, breaking the silence in a very low voice, 'here's a sorrowful affliction!'

Sam nodded very slightly.

'For the man of wrath, too!' added Mr. Stiggins; 'it makes a vessel's heart bleed!'

Mr. Weller was overheard by his son to murmur something relative to making a vessel's nose bleed; but Mr. Stiggins heard him not.

'Do you know, young man,' whispered Mr. Stiggins, drawing his chair closer to Sam, 'whether she has left Emanuel anything?'

'Who's he?' inquired Sam.

'The chapel,' replied Mr. Stiggins; 'our chapel; our fold, Mr. Samuel.'

'She hasn't left the fold nothin', nor the shepherd nothin', nor the animals nothin',' said Sam, decisively; 'nor the dogs neither' *(Chapter 52).*

'Don't go yet,' urged the fat boy.

'I must,' replied Mary. 'Good-bye, for the present.'

The fat boy, with elephantine playfulness, stretched out his arms to ravish a kiss; but as it required no great agility to elude him, his fair enslaver had vanished before he closed them again; upon which the apathetic youth ate a pound or so of steak with a sentimental countenance, and fell fast asleep *(Chapter 54).*

The ladies ran to Emily's bedroom to dress, and the lover taking up his hat, walked out of the room. He had scarcely got outside the door, when he heard Wardle's voice talking loudly, and looking over the banisters, beheld him, followed by some other gentlemen, coming straight upstairs. Knowing nothing of the house, Mr. Snodgrass in his confusion stepped hastily back into the room he had just quitted, and passing from thence into an inner apartment (Mr. Wardle's bed-chamber), closed the door softly, just as the persons he had caught a glimpse of, entered the sitting-room. These were Mr. Wardle, Mr. Pickwick, Mr. Nathaniel Winkle, and Mr. Benjamin Allen, whom he had no difficulty in recognising by their voices.

'Very lucky I had the presence of mind to avoid them,' thought Mr. Snodgrass with a smile, and walking on tip-toe to another door near the bedside; 'this opens into the same passage, and I can walk, quietly and comfortably, away.'

There was only one obstacle to his walking quietly and comfortably away, which was that the door was locked and the key gone *(Chapter 54).*

'Samivel,' said Mr. Weller, accosting his son on the morning after the funeral, 'I've found it, Sammy. I thought it wos there.'

'Thought wot wos where?' inquired Sam.

'Your mother-in-law's vill, Sammy,' replied Mr. Weller. 'In wirtue o' vich, them arrangements is to be made as I told you on, last night, respectin' the funs.'

'Wot, didn't she tell you where it was?' inquired Sam.

'Not a bit on it, Sammy,' replied Mr. Weller. 'We wos a adjestin' our little differences, and wos a cheerin' her spirits and bearin' her up, so that I forgot to ask anythin' about it. I don't know as I should ha' done it indeed, if I had remembered it,' added Mr. Weller, 'for it's a rum sort o' thing, Sammy, to go a hankerin' arter anybody's property, ven you're assistin' 'em in illness. It's like helping an outside passenger up, ven he's been pitched off a coach, and puttin' your hand in his pocket, vile you ask him vith a sigh how he finds his-self, Sammy' *(Chapter 55).*

Let us leave our old friend in one of those moments of unmixed happiness, of which, if we seek them, there are ever some, to cheer our transitory existence here. There are dark shadows on the earth, but its lights are stronger in the contrast. Some men, like bats or owls, have better eyes for the darkness than for the light. We, who have no such optical powers, are better pleased to take our last parting look at the visionary companions of many solitary hours, when the brief sunshine of the world is blazing full upon them.

It is the fate of most men who mingle with the world, and attain even the prime of life, to make many real friends, and lose them in the course of nature. It is the fate of all authors or chroniclers to create imaginary friends, and lose them in the course of art. Nor is this the full extent of their misfortunes; for they are required to furnish an account of them besides *(Chapter 57).*

OLIVER TWIST

What an excellent example of the power of dress, young Oliver Twist was! Wrapped in the blanket which had hitherto formed his only covering, he might have been the child of a nobleman or a beggar; it would have been hard for the haughtiest stranger to have assigned him his proper station in society. But now that he was enveloped in the old calico robes which had grown yellow in the same service, he was badged and ticketed, and fell into his place at once – a parish child – the orphan of a workhouse – the humble, half-starved drudge – to be cuffed and buffeted through the world – despised by all, and pitied by none.

Oliver cried lustily. If he could have known that he was an orphan, left to the tender mercies of churchwardens and overseers, perhaps he would have cried the louder *(Chapter 1)*.

Everybody knows the story of another experimental philosopher who had a great theory about a horse being able to live without eating, and who demonstrated it so well, that he had got his own horse down to a straw a day, and would unquestionably have rendered him a very spirited and rampacious animal on nothing at all, if he had not died, four-and-twenty hours before he was to have had his first comfortable bait of air *(Chapter 2)*.

'Now don't you be offended at what I'm a going to say,' observed Mrs. Mann, with captivating sweetness. 'You've had a long walk, you know, or I wouldn't mention it. Now, will you take a little drop of something, Mr. Bumble?'

'Not a drop. Not a drop,' said Mr. Bumble, waving his right hand in a dignified, but placid manner.

'I think you will,' said Mrs. Mann, who had noticed the tone of the refusal, and the gesture that had accompanied it. 'Just a leetle drop, with a little cold water, and a lump of sugar.'

Mr. Bumble coughed.

'Now, just a leetle drop, said Mrs. Mann persuasively.

'What is it?' inquired the beadle.

'Why, it's what I'm obliged to keep a little of in the house, to put into the blessed infants' Daffy, when they ain't well, Mr. Bumble,' replied Mrs. Mann as she opened a corner cupboard, and took down a bottle and glass. 'It's gin. I'll not deceive you, Mr. B. It's gin.'

'Do you give the children Daffy, Mrs. Mann?' inquired Bumble, following with his eyes the interesting process of mixing.

'Ah, bless 'em, that I do, dear as it is,' replied the nurse. 'I couldn't see 'em suffer before my very eyes, you know, sir' *(Chapter 2)*.

'Bow to the board,' said Bumble. Oliver brushed away two or three tears that were lingering in his eyes; and seeing no board but the table, fortunately bowed to that *(Chapter 2)*.

The members of this board were very sage, deep, philosophical men; and when they came to turn their attention to the workhouse, they found out at once, what ordinary folks would never have discovered – the poor people liked it! It was a regular place of public entertainment for the poorer classes; a tavern where there was nothing to pay; a public breakfast, dinner, tea and supper all the year round; a brick and mortar elysium, where it was all play and no work. 'Oho!' said the board, looking very knowing; 'we are the fellows to set this to rights; we'll stop it all, in no time.' So, they established the rule, that all poor people should have the alternative (for they would compel nobody, not they), of being starved by a gradual process in the house, or by a quick one out of it. With this view, they contracted with the water-works to lay on an unlimited supply of water; and with a corn-factor to supply periodically small quantities of oatmeal; and issued three meals of thin gruel a day, with an onion twice a week, and half a roll on Sundays. They made a great many other wise and humane regulations, having reference to the ladies, which it is not necessary to repeat; kindly undertook to divorce poor married people, in consequence of the great expense of a suit in Doctors' Commons; and, instead of compelling a man to support his family, as they had theretofore done, took his family away from him, and made him a bachelor! There is no saying how many applicants for relief, under these last two heads, might have started up in all classes of society, if it had not been coupled with the workhouse; but the board were long-headed men, and had provided for this difficulty. The relief was inseparable from the workhouse and the gruel; and that frightened people *(Chapter 2)*.

Boys have generally excellent appetites. Oliver Twist and his companions suffered the tortures of slow starvation for three months: at last they got so voracious and wild with hunger, that one boy, who was tall for his age, and hadn't been used to that sort of thing (for his father had kept a small cook-shop), hinted darkly to his companions, that unless he had another basin of gruel *per diem*, he was afraid he might some night happen to eat the boy who slept next him, who happened to be a weakly youth of tender age. He had a wild, hungry eye; and they implicitly believed him. A council was held; lots were cast who should walk up to the master after supper that evening, and ask for more; and it fell to Oliver Twist.

The evening arrived; the boys took their places. The master, in his cook's uniform, stationed himself at the copper; his pauper assistants ranged themselves behind him; the gruel was served out; and a long grace was said over the short commons. The gruel disappeared; the boys whispered each other, and winked at Oliver; while his next neighbours nudged him. Child as he was, he was desperate with hunger, and reckless with misery. He rose from the table; and advancing to the master, basin and spoon in hand, said: somewhat alarmed at his own temerity:

'Please, sir, I want some more.'

The master was a fat, healthy man; but he turned very pale. He gazed in stupefied astonishment on the small rebel for some seconds, and then clung for support to the copper. The assistants were paralysed with wonder; the boys with fear.

'What!' said the master at length, in a faint voice.

'Please, sir,' replied Oliver, 'I want some more.'

The master aimed a blow at Oliver's head with the ladle; pinioned him in his arms; and shrieked aloud for the beadle.

The board were sitting in solemn conclave, when Mr. Bumble rushed into the room in great excitement, and addressing the gentleman in the high chair, said,

'Mr. Limbkins, I beg your pardon, sir! Oliver Twist has asked for more!'

There was a general start. Horror was depicted on every countenance.

'For *more*!' said Mr. Limbkins. 'Compose yourself, Bumble, and answer me distinctly. Do I understand that he asked for more, after he had eaten the supper alloted by the dietary?'

'He did, sir,' replied Bumble.

'That boy will be hung,' said the gentleman in the white waistcoat. 'I know that boy will be hung' *(Chapter 2)*.

'If the parish vould like him to learn a right pleasant trade, in a good 'spectable chimbley-sweepin' bisness,' said Mr. Gamfield, 'I wants a 'prentis, and I am ready to take him.'

'Walk in,' said the gentleman in the white waistcoat. Mr. Gamfield having lingered behind, to give the donkey another blow on the head, and another wrench of the jaw, as a caution not to run away in his absence, followed the gentleman with the white waistcoat into the room where Oliver had first seen him.

'It's a nasty trade,' said Mr. Limbkins, when Gamfield had again stated his wish.

'Young boys have been smothered in chimneys before now,' said another gentleman.

'That's acause they damped the straw afore they lit it in the chimbley to make 'em come down agin,' said Gamfield; 'that's all smoke, and no blaze; vereas smoke ain't o' no use at all in making a boy come down, for it only sinds him to sleep, and that's wot he likes. Boys is wery obstinit, and wery lazy, gen'l'men, and there's nothink like a good hot blaze to make 'em come down vith a run. It's humane too, gen'l'men, acause, even if they've stuck in the chimbley, roasting their feet makes 'em struggle to hextricate theirselves' *(Chapter 3)*.

'I say you'll make your fortune, Mr. Sowerberry,' repeated Mr. Bumble, tapping the undertaker on the shoulder, in a friendly manner, with his cane.

'Think so?' said the undertaker in a tone which half admitted and half disputed the probability of the event. 'The prices allowed by the board are very small, Mr. Bumble.'

'So are the coffins,' replied the beadle: with precisely as near an approach to a laugh as a great official ought to indulge in.

Mr. Sowerberry was much tickled at this: as of course he ought to be; and laughed a long time without cessation. 'Well, well, Mr. Bumble,' he said at length, 'there's no denying that, since the new system of feeding has come in, the coffins are something narrower and more shallow than they used to be; but we must have some profit, Mr. Bumble. Well-seasoned timber is an expensive article, sir; and all the iron handles come, by canal, from Birmingham.'

'Well, well,' said Mr. Bumble, 'every trade has its drawbacks. A fair profit is, of course, allowable.'

'Of course, of course,' replied the undertaker; 'and if I don't get a profit upon this or that particular article, why, I make it up in the long-run, you see – he! he! he!'

'Just so,' said Mr. Bumble.

'Thought I must say,' continued the undertaker, resuming the current of observations which the beadle had interrupted: 'though I must say, Mr. Bumble, that I have to contend against one very great disadvantage; which is, that all the stout people go off the quickest. The people who have been better off, and have paid rates for many years, are the first to sink when they come into the house; and let me tell you, Mr. Bumble, that three or four inches over one's calculation makes a great hole in one's profits; especially when one has a family to provide for, sir' *(Chapter 4)*.

'Why, he *is* rather small,' replied Mr. Bumble: looking at Oliver as if it were his fault that he was no bigger; 'he *is* small. There's no denying it. But he'll grow, Mrs. Sowerberry – he'll grow.'

'Ah! I dare say he will,' replied the lady pettishly, 'on our victuals and our drink. I see no saving in parish children, not I; for they always cost more to keep, than they're worth. However, men always think they know best. There! Get downstairs, little bag o' bones.' With this, the undertaker's wife opened a side door, and pushed Oliver down a steep flight of stairs into a stone cell, damp and dark: forming the ante-room to the coal-cellar, and denominated 'kitchen': wherein sat a slatternly girl, in shoes down at heel, and blue worsted stockings very much out of repair.

'Here, Charlotte,' said Mrs. Sowerberry, who had followed Oliver down, 'give this boy some of the cold bits that were put by for Trip. He hasn't come home since the morning, so he may go without 'em. I dare say the boy isn't too dainty to eat 'em – are you, boy?'

Oliver, whose eyes had glistened at the mention of meat, and who was trembling with eagerness to devour it, replied in the negative; and a plateful of coarse broken victuals was set before him.

I wish some well-fed philosopher, whose meat and drink turn to gall within him; whose blood is ice, whose heart is iron; could have seen Oliver Twist clutching at the dainty viands that the dog had neglected. I wish he could have witnessed the horrible avidity with which Oliver tore the bits asunder with all the ferocity of famine. There is only one thing I should like better; and that would be to see the Philosopher making the same sort of meal himself, with the same relish *(Chapter 4)*.

'We only heard of the family the night before last,' said the beadle; 'and we shouldn't have known anything about them, then, only a woman who lodges in the same house made an application to the porochial committee for them to send the porochial surgeon to see a woman as was very bad. He had gone out to dinner; but his 'prentice (which is a very clever lad) sent 'em some medicine in a blacking-bottle, off-hand.'

'Ah, there's promptness,' said the undertaker.

'Promptness, indeed!' replied the beadle. 'But what's the consequence; what's the ungrateful behaviour of these rebels, sir? Why, the husband sends back word that the medicine won't suit his wife's complaint, and so she shan't take it – says she shan't take it, sir! Good, strong, wholesome medicine, as was given with great success to two Irish labourers and a coal-heaver, only a week before – sent 'em for nothing, with a blackin'-bottle in, – and he sends back word that she shan't take it, sir!'

As the atrocity presented itself to Mr. Bumble's mind in full force, he struck the counter sharply with his cane, and became flushed with indignation.

'Well,' said the undertaker, 'I ne-ver-did – '

'Never did, sir!' ejaculated the beadle. 'No, nor nobody never did; but, now she's dead, we've got to bury her; and that's the direction; and the sooner it's done, the better' (*Chapter 5:* Bumble and Sowerberry).

As Oliver accompanied his master in most of his adult expeditions, too, in order that he might acquire that equanimity of demeanour and full command of nerve which are essential to a finished undertaker, he had many opportunities of observing the beautiful resignation and fortitude with which some strong-minded people bear their trials and losses.

For instance; when Sowerberry had an order for the burial of some rich old lady or gentleman, who was surrounded by a great number of nephews and nieces, who had been perfectly inconsolable during the previous illness, and whose grief had been wholly irrepressible even on the most public occasions, they would be as happy among themselves as need be – quite cheerful and contented – conversing together with as much freedom and gaiety, as if nothing whatever had happened to disturb them. Husbands, too, bore the loss of their wives with the most heroic calmness. Wives, again, put on weeds for their husbands, as if, so far from grieving in the garb of sorrow, they had made up their minds to render it as becoming and attractive as possible. It was observable, too, that ladies and gentlemen who were in passions of anguish during the ceremony of interment, recovered almost as soon as they reached home, and became quite composed before the tea-drinking was over. All this was very pleasant and improving to see; and Oliver beheld it with great admiration (*Chapter 6*).

'Oliver!'

'Come; you let me out!' replied Oliver, from the inside.

'Do you know this here voice, Oliver?' said Mr. Bumble.

'Yes,' replied Oliver.

'Ain't you afraid of it, sir? Ain't you a-trembling while I speak, sir?' said Mr. Bumble.

'No!' replied Oliver, boldly.

An answer so different from the one he had expected to elicit, and was in the habit of receiving, staggered Mr. Bumble not a little. He stepped back from the keyhole; drew himself up to his full height; and looked from one to another of the three bystanders, in mute astonishment.

'Oh, you know, Mr. Bumble, he must be mad,' said Mrs. Sowerberry. 'No boy in half his senses could venture to speak so to you.'

'It's not Madness, ma'am,' replied Mr. Bumble, after a few moments of deep meditation. 'It's Meat.'

'What?' exclaimed Mrs. Sowerberry.

'Meat, ma'am, meat,' replied Bumble, with stern emphasis. 'You've over-fed him, ma'am. You've raised a artificial soul and spirit in him, ma'am, unbecoming a person of his condition: as the board, Mrs. Sowerberry, who are practical philosophers, will tell you. What have paupers to do with soul or spirit? It's quite enough that we let 'em have live bodies. If you had kept the boy on gruel, ma'am, this would never have happened'(*Chapter 7*).

'Hullo, my covey! What's the row?' said this strange young gentleman to Oliver.

'I am very hungry and tired,' replied Oliver: the tears standing in his eyes as he spoke. 'I have walked a long way. I have been walking these seven days.'

'Walking for sivin days!' said the young gentleman. 'Oh, I see. Beak's order, eh? But,' he added, noticing Oliver's look of surprise, 'I suppose you don't know what a beak is, my flash com-pan-i-on.'

Oliver mildly replied, that he had always heard a bird's mouth described by the term in question.

'My eyes, how green!' exclaimed the young gentleman. 'Why, a beak's a madgst'rate; and when you walk by a beak's order, it's not straight forerd, but always agoing up, and nivir a coming down agin. Was you never on the mill?'

'What mill?' inquired Oliver.

'What mill! Why, *the* mill – the mill as takes up so little room that it'll work inside a Stone Jug; and always goes better when the wind's low with people, than when it's high; acos then they can't get workmen. But come,' said the young gentleman; 'you want grub, and you shall have it. I'm at low-water mark myself – only one bob and a magpie; but *as* far *as* it goes, I'll fork out and stump. Up with you on your pins. There! Now then! Morrice!' (*Chapter 8:* Jack Dawkins and Oliver Twist).

When the breakfast was cleared away, the merry old gentleman and the two boys played at a very curious and uncommon game, which was performed in this way. The merry old gentleman, placing a snuff-box in one pocket of his trousers, a note-case in the other, and a watch in his waistcoat pocket, with a guard-chain round his neck, and sticking a mock diamond pin in his shirt: buttoned his coat tight round him, and putting his spectacle-case and handkerchief in his pockets, trotted up and down the room with a stick, in imitation of the manner in which old gentlemen walk about the streets any hour in the day. Sometimes he stopped at the fire-place, and sometimes at the door, making believe that he was staring with all his might into shop-windows. At such times, he would look constantly round him, for fear of thieves, and would keep slapping all his pockets in turn, to see that he hadn't lost anything, in such a very funny and natural manner, that Oliver laughed till the tears ran down his face. All this time, the two boys followed him closely about: getting out of his sight, so nimbly, every time he turned round, that it was impossible to follow their motions. At last, the Dodger trod upon his toes, or ran upon his boot accidentally, while Charley Bates stumbled up against him behind; and in that one moment they took from him, with the most extraordinary rapidity, snuff-box, note-case, watch-guard, chain, shirt-pin, pocket-handkerchief, even the spectacle-case. If the old gentleman felt a hand in any one of his pockets, he cried out where it was; and then the game began all over again *(Chapter 9)*.

Although Oliver had been brought up by philosophers, he was not theoretically acquainted with the beautiful axiom that self-preservation is the first law of nature. If he had been, perhaps he would have been prepared for this. Not being prepared, however, it alarmed him the more; so away he went like the wind, with the old gentleman and the two boys roaring and shouting behind him.

'Stop thief! Stop thief!' There is a magic in the sound. The tradesman leaves his counter, and the carman his waggon; the butcher throws down his tray; the baker his basket; the milkman his pail; the errand-boy his parcels; the school-boy his marbles; the paviour his pickaxe; the child his battledore. Away they run, pell-mell, helter-skelter, slap-dash: tearing, yelling, screaming, knocking down the passengers as they turn the corners, rousing up the dogs, and astonishing the fowls: and streets, squares, and courts, re-echo with the sound.

'Stop thief! Stop thief!' The cry is taken up by a hundred voices, and the crowd accumulate at every turning. Away they fly, splashing through the mud, and rattling along the pavements: up go the windows, out run the people, onward bear the mob, a whole audience desert Punch in the very thickest of the plot, and, joining the rushing throng, swell the shout, and lend fresh vigour to the cry, 'Stop thief! Stop thief!'

'Stop thief! Stop thief!' There is a passion *for hunting something* deeply implanted in the human breast. One wretched breathless child, panting with exhaustion; terror in his looks; agony in his eyes; large drops of perspiration streaming down his face; strains every nerve to make head upon his pursuers; and as they follow on his track, and gain upon him every instant, they hail his decreasing strength with still louder shouts, and whoop and scream with joy. 'Stop thief!' Ay, stop him for God's sake, were it only in mercy! *(Chapter 10)*.

'What are you up to? Ill-treating the boys, you covetous, avaricious, in-sa-ti-a-ble old fence?' said the man, seating himself deliberately. 'I wonder they don't murder you! *I* would if I was them. If I'd been your 'prentice, I'd have done it long ago, and – no, I couldn't have sold you afterwards, for you're fit for nothing but keeping as a curiosity of ugliness in a glass bottle, and I suppose they don't blow glass bottles large enough.'

'Hush! hush! Mr. Sikes,' said the Jew, trembling; 'don't speak so loud.'

'None of your mistering,' replied the ruffian; 'you always mean mischief when you come that. You know my name: out with it! I shan't disgrace it when the time comes.'

'Well, well, then – Bill Sikes,' said the Jew, with abject humility. 'You seem out of humour, Bill' *(Chapter 13: Sikes and Fagin)*.

'There are a good many books, are there not, my boy?' said Mr. Brownlow, observing the curiosity with which Oliver surveyed the shelves that reached from the floor to the ceiling.

'A great number, sir,' replied Oliver. 'I never saw so many.'

'You shall read them, if you behave well,' said the old gentleman kindly; 'and you will like that, better than looking at the outsides, – that is, in some cases; because there *are* books of which the backs and covers are by far the best parts.'

'I suppose they are those heavy ones, sir,' said Oliver, pointing to some large quartos, with a good deal of gilding about the binding.

'Not always those,' said the old gentleman, patting Oliver on the head, and smiling as he did so, 'there are other equally heavy ones, though of a much smaller size. How should you like to grow up a clever man, and write books, eh?'

'I think I would rather read them, sir,' replied Oliver.

'What! wouldn't you like to be a book-writer?' said the old gentleman.

Oliver considered a little while; and at last said, he should think it would be a much better thing to be a book-seller; upon which the old gentleman laughed heartily, and declared he had said a very good thing. Which Oliver felt glad to have done, though he by no means knew what it was.

'Well, well,' said the old gentleman, composing his features. 'Don't be afraid! We won't make an author of you, while there's an honest trade to be learnt, or brick-making to turn to' *(Chapter 14)*.

'Look here! do you see this! Isn't it a most wonderful and extraordinary thing that I can't call at a man's house but I find a piece of this poor surgeon's friend on the staircase? I've been lamed with orange-peel once, and I know orange-peel will be my death at last. It will, sir: orange-peel will be my death, or I'll be content to eat my own head, sir!'

This was the handsome offer with which Mr. Grimwig backed and confirmed nearly every assertion he made; and it was the more singular in his case, because, even admitting for the sake of argument, the possibility of scientific improvements being ever brought to that pass which will enable a gentleman to eat his own head in the event of his being so disposed, Mr. Grimwig's head was such a particularly large one, that the most sanguine man alive could hardly entertain a hope of being able to get through it at a sitting – to put entirely out of the question, a very thick coating of powder *(Chapter 14)*.

'I feel strongly on this subject, sir,' said the irritable old gentleman, drawing off his gloves. 'There's always more or less orange-peel on the pavement in our street; and I *know* it's put there by the surgeon's boy at the corner. A young woman stumbled over a bit last night, and fell against my garden-railings; directly she got up I saw her look towards his infernal red lamp with the pantomime-light. "Don't go to him," I called out of the window, "he's an assassin! A man-trap!" So he is. If he is not – ' Here the irascible old gentleman gave a great knock on the ground with his stick; which was always understood, by his friends, to imply the customary offer, whenever it was not expressed in words. Then, still keeping his stick in his hand, he sat down; and, opening a double eye-glass, which he wore attached to a broad black riband, took a view of Oliver: who, seeing that he was the object of inspection, coloured, and bowed again.

'That's the boy, is it?' said Mr. Grimwig, at length.

'That's the boy,' replied Mr. Brownlow.

'How are you, boy?' said Mr. Grimwig.

'A great deal better, thank you, sir,' replied Oliver.

Mr. Brownlow, seeming to apprehend that his singular friend was about to say something disagreeable, asked Oliver to step downstairs and tell Mrs. Bedwin they were ready for tea; which, as he did not half like the visitor's manner, he was very happy to do.

'He is a nice-looking boy, is he not?' inquired Mr. Brownlow.

'I don't know,' replied Mr. Grimwig, pettishly.

'Don't know?'

'No. I don't know. I never see any difference in boys. I only know two sorts of boys. Mealy boys, and beef-faced boys.'

'And which is Oliver?'

'Mealy. I know a friend who has a beef-faced boy; a fine boy, they call him; with a round head, and red cheeks, and glaring eyes; a horrid boy; with a body and limbs that appear to be swelling out of the seams of his blue clothes; with the voice of a pilot, and the appetite of a wolf. I know him! The wretch!' (Chapter 14).

'What the devil do you come in between me and my dog for?' said Sikes, with a fierce gesture.

'I didn't know, my dear, I didn't know,' replied Fagin, humbly; for the Jew was the new-comer.

'Didn't know, you white-livered thief!' growled Sikes. 'Couldn't you hear the noise?'

'Not a sound of it, as I'm a living man, Bill,' replied the Jew.

'Oh no! you hear nothing, you don't,' retorted Sikes with a fierce sneer. 'Sneaking in and out, so as nobody hears how you come or go! I wish you had been the dog, Fagin, half a minute ago.'

'Why?' inquired the Jew with a forced smile.

' 'Cause the government, as cares for the lives of such men as you, as haven't half the pluck of curs, lets a man kill a dog how he likes,' replied Sikes, shutting up the knife with a very expressive look; 'that's why' (Chapter 15).

The Jew inflicted a smart blow on Oliver's shoulders with the club; and was raising it for a second, when the girl, rushing forward, wrested it from his hand. She flung it into the fire, with a force that brought some of the glowing coals whirling out into the room.

'I won't stand by and see it done, Fagin,' cried the girl. 'You've got the boy, and what more would you have? – Let him be – let him be – or I shall put that mark on some of you, that will bring me to the gallows before my time.'

The girl stamped her foot violently on the floor as she vented this threat; and with her lips compressed, and her hands clenched, looked alternately at the Jew and the other robber: her face quite colourless from the passion of rage into which she had gradually worked herself.

'Why, Nancy!' said the Jew, in a soothing tone; after a pause, during which he and Mr. Sikes had stared at one another in a disconcerted manner; 'you – you're more clever than ever to-night. Ha! ha! my dear, you are acting beautifully.'

'Am I!' said the girl. 'Take care I don't overdo it. You will be the worse for it, Fagin, if I do; and so I tell you in good time to keep clear of me.'

There is something about a roused woman: especially if she add to all her other strong passions, the fierce impulses of recklessness and despair: which few men like to provoke. The Jew saw that it would be hopeless to affect any further mistake regarding the reality of Miss Nancy's rage; and, shrinking involuntarily back a few paces, cast a glance, half imploring and half cowardly, at Sikes: as if to hint that he was the fittest person to pursue the dialogue (Chapter 16).

It is the custom on the stage, in all good murderous melodramas, to present the tragic and the comic scenes, in as regular alternation, as the layers of red and white in a side of streaky bacon. The hero sinks upon his straw bed, weighed down by fetters and misfortunes; in the next scene, his faithful but unconscious squire regales the audience with a comic song. We behold, with throbbing bosoms, the heroine in the grasp of a proud and ruthless baron: her virtue and her life alike in danger, drawing forth her dagger to preserve the one at the cost of the other; and just as our expectations are wrought up to the highest pitch, a whistle is heard, and we are straightway transported to the great hall of the castle: where a grey-headed seneschal sings a funny chorus with a funnier body of vassals, who are free of all sorts of places, from church vaults to palaces, and roam about in company, carolling perpetually.

Such changes appear absurd; but they are not so unnatural as they would seem at first sight. The transitions in real life from well-spread boards to death-beds, and from mourning-weeds to holiday garments, are not a whit less startling; only, there, we are busy actors, instead of passive lookers-on, which makes a vast difference. The actors in the mimic life of the theatre, are blind to violent transitions and abrupt impulses of passion or feeling, which, presented before the eyes of mere spectators, are at once condemned as outrageous and preposterous (Chapter 17).

'Well, and good morning to you, sir,' replied Mrs. Mann, with many smiles; 'and hoping you find yourself well, sir!'

'So-so, Mrs. Mann,' replied the beadle. 'A porochial life is not a bed of roses, Mrs. Mann.'

'Ah, that it isn't indeed, Mr. Bumble,' rejoined the lady. And all the infant paupers might have chorused the rejoinder with great propriety, if they had heard it.

'A porochial life, ma'am,' continued Mr. Bumble, striking the table with his cane, 'is a life of worrit, and vexation, and hardihood; but all public characters, as I may say, must suffer prosecution' (Chapter 17).

'I suppose you don't even know what a prig is?' said the Dodger mournfully.

'I think I know that,' replied Oliver, looking up.

'It's a th – ; you're one, are you not?' inquired Oliver, checking himself.

'I am,' replied the Dodger. 'I'd scorn to be anything else.' Mr. Dawkins gave his hat a ferocious cock, after delivering this sentiment, and looked at Master Bates, as if to denote that he would feel obliged by his saying anything to the contrary.

'I am,' repeated the Dodger. 'So's Charley. So's Fagin. So's Sikes. So's Nancy. So's Bet. So we all are, down to the dog. And he's the downiest one of the lot!'

'And the least given to peaching,' added Charley Bates.

'He wouldn't so much as bark in a witness-box, for fear of committing himself; no, not if you tied him up in one, and left him there without wittles for a fortnight,' said the Dodger.

'Not a bit of it,' observed Charley.

'He's a rum dog. Don't he look fierce at any strange cove that laughs or sings when he's in company!' pursued the Dodger. 'Won't he growl at all, when he hears a fiddle playing! And don't he hate other dogs as ain't of his breed! Oh, no!'

'He's an out-and-out Christian,' said Charley *(Chapter 18)*.

'And always put this in your pipe, Nolly,' said the Dodger, as the Jew was heard unlocking the door above, 'if you don't take fogles and tickers – '

'What's the good of talking in that way?' interposed Master Bates: 'he don't know what you mean.'

'If you don't take pocket-handkechers and watches,' said the Dodger, reducing his conversation to the level of Oliver's capacity, 'some other cove will; so that the coves that lose 'em will be all the worse, and you'll be all the worse too, and and nobody half a ha'p'orth the better, except the chaps wot gets them – and you've just as good a right to them as they have.'

'To be sure, to be sure!' said the Jew, who had entered unseen by Oliver. 'It all lies in a nutshell, my dear; in a nutshell, take the Dodger's word for it. Ha! ha! ha! He understands the catechism of his trade' *(Chapter 18)*.

'Do you mean to tell me, Bill,' said the Jew: softening as the other grew heated: 'that neither of the two men in the house can be got over?'

'Yes, I do mean to tell you so,' replied Sikes. 'The old lady has had 'em these twenty year; and if you were to give 'em five hundred pound, they wouldn't be in it.'

'But do you mean to say, my dear,' remonstrated the Jew, 'that the women can't be got over?'

'Not a bit of it,' replied Sikes.

'Not by flash Toby Crackit?' said the Jew incredulously. 'Think what women are, Bill.'

'No; not even by flash Toby Crackit,' replied Sikes. 'He says he's worn sham whiskers, and a canary waistcoat, the whole blessed time he's been loitering down there, and it's all of no use.'

'He should have tried mustachios and a pair of military trousers, my dear,' said the Jew.

'So he did,' rejoined Sikes, 'and they warn't of no more use than the other plant' *(Chapter 19)*.

'Could you give my boy and me a lift as far as there?' demanded Sikes, pushing the ale towards his new friend.

'If you're going directly, I can,' replied the man, looking out of the pot. 'Are you going to Halliford?'

'Going on to Shepperton,' replied Sikes.

'I'm your man, as far as I go,' replied the other. 'Is all paid, Becky?'

'Yes, the other gentleman's paid,' replied the girl.

'I say!' said the man, with tipsy gravity; 'that won't do, you know.'

'Why not?' rejoined Sikes. 'You're a-going to accommodate us, and wot's to prevent my standing treat for a pint or so, in return?'

The stranger reflected upon this argument, with a very profound face; having done so, he seized Sikes by the hand: and declared he was a real good fellow. To which Mr. Sikes replied, he was joking; as, if he had been sober, there would have been strong reason to suppose he was *(Chapter 21)*.

Mrs. Corney was about to solace herself with a cup of tea. As she glanced from the table to the fireplace, where the smallest of all possible kettles was singing a small song in a small voice, her inward satisfaction evidently increased, – so much so, indeed, that Mrs. Corney smiled.

'Well!' said the matron, leaning her elbow on the table, and looking reflectively at the fire; 'I'm sure we have all on us a great deal to be grateful for! A great deal, if we did but know it. Ah!'

Mrs. Corney shook her head mournfully, as if deploring the mental blindness of those paupers who did not know it; and thrusting a silver spoon (private property) into the inmost recesses of a two-ounce tin tea-caddy, proceeded to make the tea.

How slight a thing will disturb the equanimity of our frail minds! The black teapot, being very small and easily filled, ran over while Mrs. Corney was moralising; and the water slightly scalded Mrs. Corney's hand.

'Drat the pot!' said the worthy matron, setting it down very hastily on the hob; 'a little stupid thing, that only holds a couple of cups! What use is it of, to anybody! Except,' said Mrs. Corney, pausing, 'except to a poor desolate creature like me. Oh dear!'

With these words, the matron dropped into her chair, and, once more resting her elbow on the table, thought of her solitary fate. The small teapot, and the single cup, had awakened in her mind sad recollections of Mr. Corney (who had not been dead more than five-and-twenty years); and she was overpowered.

'I shall never get another!' said Mrs. Corney, pettishly; 'I shall never get another – like him.'

Whether this remark bore reference to the husband, or the teapot, is uncertain. It might have been the latter; for Mrs. Corney looked at it as she spoke; and took it up afterwards *(Chapter 23)*.

'Hard weather, Mr. Bumble,' said the matron.

'Hard, indeed, ma'am,' replied the beadle. 'Anti-porochial weather this, ma'am. We've given away, Mrs. Corney, we've given away a matter of twenty quartern loaves and a cheese and a half, this very blessed afternoon; and yet them paupers are not contented.'

'Of course not. When would they be, Mr. Bumble?' said the matron, sipping her tea.

'When, indeed, ma'am!' rejoined Mr. Bumble. 'Why here's one man that, in consideration of his wife and large family, has a quartern loaf and a good pound of cheese, full weight. Is he grateful, ma'am? Is he grateful? Not a copper farthing's worth of it! What does he do, ma'am, but ask for a few coals; if it's only a pocket handkerchief full, he says! Coals! What would he do with coals? Toast his cheese with 'em, and then come back for more. That's the way with these people, ma'am; give 'em a apron full of coals to-day, and they'll come back for another, the day after to-morrow, as brazen as alabaster' *(Chapter 23)*.

'I never,' said Mr. Bumble, 'see anything like the pitch it's got to. The day afore yesterday, a man – you have been a married woman, ma'am, and I may mention it to you – a man, with hardly a rag upon his back (here Mrs. Corney looked at the floor), goes to our overseer's door when he has got company coming to dinner; and says, he must be relieved, Mrs. Corney. As he wouldn't go away, and shocked the company very much, our overseer sent him out a pound of potatoes and half a pint of oatmeal. "My heart!" says the ungrateful villain, "what's the use of *this* to me? You might as well give me a pair of iron spectacles!" "Very good," says our overseer, taking 'em away again, "you won't get anything else here." "Then I'll die in the streets!" says the vagrant. "Oh no, you won't," says our overseer.'

'Ha! ha! That was very good! So like Mr. Grannett, wasn't it?' interposed the matron. 'Well, Mr. Bumble?'

'Well, ma'am,' rejoined the beadle, 'he went away; and he *did* die in the streets. There's a obstinate pauper for you!' *(Chapter 23)*.

It was no unfit messenger of death, who had disturbed the quiet of the matron's room. Her body was bent by age; her limbs trembled with palsy; her face, distorted into a mumbling leer, resembled more the grotesque shaping of some wild pencil, than the work of nature's hand.

Alas! How few of nature's faces are left alone to gladden us with their beauty! The cares, and sorrows, and hungerings, of the world, change them as they change hearts; and it is only when those passions sleep, and have lost their hold for ever, that the troubled clouds pass off, and leave heaven's surface clear. It is a common thing for the countenances of the dead, even in that fixed and rigid state, to subside into the long-forgotten expression of sleeping infancy, and settle into the very look of early life; so calm, so peaceful, do they grow again, that those who knew them in their happy childhood, kneel by the coffin's side in awe, and see the Angel even upon earth *(Chapter 24)*.

'Mrs. Corney,' said Mr. Bumble, stooping over the matron, 'what is this, ma'am? Has anything happened, ma'am? Pray answer me: I'm on – on – ' Mr. Bumble, in his alarm, could not immediately think of the word 'tenterhooks,' so he said 'broken bottles.'

'Oh, Mr. Bumble!' cried the lady, 'I have been so dreadfully put out!'

'Put out, ma'am!' exclaimed Mr. Bumble; 'who has dared to – ? I know!' said Mr. Bumble, checking himself, with native majesty, 'this is them wicious paupers!'

'It's dreadful to think of!' said the lady, shuddering.

'Then *don't* think of it, ma'am,' rejoined Mr. Bumble.

'I can't help it,' whimpered the lady.

'Then take something, ma'am,' said Mr. Bumble soothingly. 'A little of the wine?'

'Not for the world!' replied Mrs. Corney. 'I couldn't, – oh! The top shelf in the right-hand corner – oh!' Uttering these words, the good lady pointed distractedly, to the cupboard, and underwent a convulsion from internal spasms. Mr. Bumble rushed to the closet; and, snatching a pint green-glass bottle from the shelf thus incoherently indicated, filled a tea-cup with its contents, and held it to the lady's lips.

'I'm better now,' said Mrs. Corney, falling back, after drinking half of it *(Chapter 27)*.

'The board allow you coals, don't they, Mrs. Corney?' inquired the beadle, affectionately pressing her hand.

'And candles,' replied Mrs. Corney, slightly returning the pressure.

'Coals, candles, and house-rent free,' said Mr. Bumble. 'Oh, Mrs. Corney, what a Angel you are!'

The lady was not proof against this burst of feeling. She sank into Mr. Bumble's arms; and that gentleman in his agitation, imprinted a passionate kiss upon her chaste nose.

'Such porochial perfection!' exclaimed Mr. Bumble, rapturously. 'You know that Mr. Slout is worse tonight, my fascinator?'

'Yes,' replied Mrs. Corney, bashfully.

'He can't live a week, the doctor says,' pursued Mr. Bumble. 'He is the master of this establishment; his death will cause a wacancy; that wacancy must be filled up. Oh, Mrs. Corney, what a prospect this opens! What a opportunity for a jining of hearts and housekeepings!'

Mrs. Corney sobbed.

'The little word?' said Mr. Bumble, bending over the bashful beauty. 'The one little, little, little word, my blessed Corney?'

'Ye-ye-yes!' sighed out the matron.

'One more,' pursued the beadle; 'compose your darling feelings for only one more. When is it to come off?'

Mrs. Corney twice essayed to speak: and twice failed. At length summoning up courage, she threw her arms round Mr. Bumble's neck, and said, it might be as soon as ever he pleased, and that he was 'a irresistible duck' *(Chapter 27)*.

The cloth was laid for supper; the table was covered with bread and butter, plates and glasses; a porter-pot and a wine-bottle. At the upper end of the table, Mr. Noah Claypole lolled negligently in an easy-chair, with his legs thrown over one of the arms: an open clasp-knife in one hand, and a mass of buttered bread in the other. Close beside him stood Charlotte, opening oysters from a barrel: which Mr. Claypole condescended to swallow, with remarkable avidity. A more than ordinary redness in the region of the young gentleman's nose, and a kind of fixed wink in his right eye, denoted that he was in a slight degree intoxicated; these symptoms were confirmed by the intense relish with which he took his oysters, for which nothing but a strong appreciation of their cooling properties, in cases of internal fever, could have sufficiently accounted.

'Here's a delicious fat one, Noah, dear!' said Charlotte; 'try him, do; only this one.'

'What a delicious thing is a oyster!' remarked Mr. Claypole, after he had swallowed it. 'What a pity it is, a number of 'em should ever make you feel uncomfortable; isn't it, Charlotte?'

'It's quite a cruelty,' said Charlotte.

'So it is,' acquiesced Mr. Claypole. 'An't yer fond of oysters?'

'Not overmuch,' replied Charlotte. 'I like to see you eat 'em, Noah dear, better than eating 'em myself.'

'Lor!' said Noah, reflectively; 'how queer!'

'Have another,' said Charlotte. 'Here's one with such a beautiful delicate beard!'

'I can't manage any more,' said Noah. 'I'm very sorry. Come here, Charlotte, and I'll kiss yer.'

'What!' said Mr. Bumble, bursting into the room. 'Say that again, sir.'

Charlotte uttered a scream, and hid her face in her apron. Mr. Claypole, without making any further change in his position than suffering his legs to reach the ground, gazed at the beadle in drunken terror.

'Say it again, you wile, owdacious fellow!' said Mr. Bumble. 'How dare you mention such a thing, sir? And how dare you encourage him, you insolent minx? Kiss her!' exclaimed Mr. Bumble, in strong indignation. 'Faugh!'

'I didn't mean to do it!' said Noah, blubbering. 'She's always a-kissing of me, whether I like it, or not.'

'Oh, Noah,' cried Charlotte, reproachfully.

'Yer are; yer know yer are!' retorted Noah. 'She's always a-doin' of it, Mr. Bumble, sir; she chucks me under the chin, please, sir; and makes all manner of love!'

'Silence!' cried Mr. Bumble, sternly. 'Take yourself downstairs, ma'am. Noah, you shut up the shop; say another word till your master comes home, at your peril; and, when he does come home, tell him that Mr. Bumble said he was to send a old woman's shell after breakfast to-morrow morning. Do you hear, sir? Kissing!' cried Mr. Bumble, holding up his hands. 'The sin and wickendness of the lower orders in this porochial district is frightful! If parliament don't take their abominable courses under consideration, this country's ruined, and the character of the peasantry gone for ever!' (*Chapter 27*: Noah Claypole and Charlotte).

'It was about half-past two,' said Mr. Giles, 'or I wouldn't swear that it mightn't have been a little nearer three, when I woke up, and, turning round in my bed, as it might be so, (here Mr. Giles turned round in his chair and pulled the corner of the table-cloth over him to imitate bed-clothes,) I fancied I heerd a noise.'

At this point of the narrative the cook turned pale, and asked the housemaid to shut the door: who asked Brittles, who asked the tinker, who pretended not to hear.

' – Heerd a noise,' continued Mr. Giles. 'I says, at first, "This is illusion;" and was composing myself off to sleep, when I heerd the noise again, distinct.'

'What sort of a noise?' asked the cook.

'A kind of a busting noise,' replied Mr. Giles, looking round him.

'More like the noise of powdering a iron bar on a nutmeg-grater,' suggested Brittles.

'It was, when *you* heerd it, sir,' rejoined Mr. Giles; 'but at this time, it had a busting sound. I turned down the clothes;' continued Giles, rolling back the table-cloth, 'sat up in bed; and listened.'

The cook and housemaid simultaneously ejaculated 'Lor!' and drew their chairs closer together.

'I heerd it now, quite apparent,' resumed Mr. Giles. ' "Somebody," I says, "is forcing of a door, or window; what's to be done? I'll call up that poor lad, Brittles, and save him from being murdered in his bed; or his throat," I says, "may be cut from his right ear to his left, without his ever knowing it." '

Here, all eyes were turned upon Brittles, who fixed his upon the speaker, and stared at him, with his mouth wide open, and his face expressive of the most unmitigated horror.

'I tossed off the clothes,' said Giles, throwing away the table-cloth, and looking very hard at the cook and housemaid, 'got softly out of bed; drew on a pair of – '

'Ladies present, Mr. Giles,' murmured the tinker.

' – Of *shoes*, sir,' said Giles, turning upon him, and laying great emphasis on the word; 'seized the loaded pistol that always goes upstairs with the plate-basket; and walked on tiptoes to his room. "Brittles," I says, when I had woke him, "don't be frightened!" '

'So you did,' observed Brittles, in a low voice.

' "We're dead men, I think, Brittles," I says,' continued Giles; ' "but don't be frightened." '

'*Was* he frightened?' asked the cook.

'Not a bit of it,' replied Mr. Giles. 'He was as firm – ah! pretty near as firm as I was' (*Chapter 28*).

Oliver told them all his simple history, and was often compelled to stop, by pain and want of strength. It was a solemn thing, to hear, in the darkened room, the feeble voice of the sick child recounting a weary catalogue of evils and calamities which hard men had brought upon him. Oh! if when we oppress and grind our fellow-creatures, we bestowed but one thought on the dark evidences of human error, which, like dense and heavy clouds, are rising, slowly it is true, but not less surely, to Heaven, to pour their after-vengeance on our heads; if we heard but one instant, in imagination, the deep testimony of dead men's voices, which no power can stifle, and no pride shut out; where would be the injury and injustice, the suffering, misery, cruelty, and wrong, that each day's life brings with it! (*Chapter 30*).

'Don't you see all this?'

'I see it, of course,' replied Rose, smiling at the doctor's impetuosity; 'but still I do not see anything in it, to criminate the poor child.'

'No,' replied the doctor; 'of course not! Bless the

bright eyes of your sex! They never see, whether for good or bad, more than one side of any question; and that is, always, the one which first presents itself to them' *(Chapter 31:* The Doctor and Rose Maylie).

Sending the plate, which had so excited Fagin's cupidity, to the banker's; and leaving Giles and another servant in care of the house, they departed to a cottage at some distance in the country, and took Oliver with them.

Who can describe the pleasure and delight, the peace of mind and soft tranquillity, the sickly boy felt in the balmy air, and among the green hills and rich woods, of an inland village! Who can tell how scenes of peace and quietude sink into the minds of pain-worn dwellers in close and noisy places, and carry their own freshness, deep into their jaded hearts! Men who have lived in crowded, pent-up streets, through lives of toil, and who have never wished for change; men, to whom custom has indeed been second nature, and who have come almost to love each brick and stone that formed the narrow boundaries of their daily walks; even they, with the hand of death upon them, have been known to yearn at last for one short glimpse of Nature's face; and, carried far from the scenes of their old pains and pleasures, have seemed to pass at once into a new state of being. Crawling forth, from day to day, to some green sunny spot, they have had such memories wakened up within them by the sight of sky, and hill and plain, and glistening water, that a foretaste of heaven itself has soothed their quick decline, and they have sunk into their tombs, as peacefully as the sun whose setting they watched from their lonely chamber window but a few hours before, faded from their dim and feeble sight! The memories which peaceful country scenes call up, are not of this world, nor of its thoughts and hopes. Their gentle influence may teach us how to weave fresh garlands for the graves of those we loved: may purify our thoughts, and bear down before it old enmity and hatred; but beneath all this, there lingers, in the least reflective mind, a vague and half-formed consciousness of having held such feelings long before, in some remote and distant time, which calls up solemn thoughts of distant times to come, and bends down pride and worldliness beneath it *(Chapter 32)*.

Oliver hurried up the inn-yard, with a somewhat lighter heart. He was turning out of the gateway when he accidentally stumbled against a tall man wrapped in a cloak, who was at that moment coming out of the inn door.

'Hah!' cried the man, fixing his eyes on Oliver, and suddenly recoiling. 'What the devil's this?'

'I beg your pardon, sir,' said Oliver; 'I was in a great hurry to get home, and didn't see you were coming.'

'Death!' muttered the man to himself, glaring at the boy with his large dark eyes. 'Who would have thought it! Grind him to ashes! He'd start up from a stone coffin, to come in my way!'

'I am sorry,' stammered Oliver, confused by the strange man's wild look. 'I hope I have not hurt you!'

'Rot you!' murmured the man, in a horrible passion; between his clenched teeth; 'if I had only had the courage to say the word, I might have been free of you in a night. Curses on your head, and black death on your heart, you imp!' *(Chapter 33:* Monks).

Oh! the suspense, the fearful, acute suspense, of standing idly by while the life of one we dearly love, is trembling in the balance! Oh! the racking thoughts that crowd upon the mind, and make the heart beat violently, and the breath come thick, by the force of the images they conjure up before it; the desperate anxiety *to be doing something* to relieve the pain, or lessen the danger, which we have no power to alleviate; the sinking of soul and spirit, which the sad remembrance of our helplessness produces; what tortures can equal these; what reflections or endeavours can, in the full tide and fever of the time, allay them! *(Chapter 33)*.

We need be careful how we deal with those about us, when every death carries to some small circle of survivors, thoughts of so much omitted, and so little done – of so many things forgotten, and so many more which might have been repaired! There is no remorse so deep as that which is unavailing; if we would be spared its tortures, let us remember this, in time *(Chapter 33)*.

There is a kind of sleep that steals upon us sometimes, which, while it holds the body prisoner, does not free the mind from a sense of things about it, and enable it to ramble at its pleasure. So far as an overpowering heaviness, a prostration of strength, and an utter inability to control our thoughts or power of motion, can be called sleep, this is it; and yet, we have a consciousness of all that is going on about us, and if we dream at such a time, words which are really spoken, or sounds which really exist at the moment, accommodate themselves with surprising readiness to our visions, until reality and imagination become so strangely blended that it is afterwards almost matter of impossibility to separate the two. Nor is this, the most striking phenomenon incidental to such a state. It is an undoubted fact, that although our senses of touch and sight be for the time dead, yet our sleeping thoughts, and the visionary scenes that pass before us, will be influenced, and materially influenced, by the *mere silent presence* of some external object; which may not have been near us when we closed our eyes: and of whose vicinity we have had no waking consciousness *(Chapter 34)*.

Mr. Bumble sat in the workhouse parlour, with his eyes moodily fixed on the cheerless grate, whence, as it was summer time, no brighter gleam proceeded, than the reflection of certain sickly rays of the sun, which were sent back from its cold and shining surface. A paper fly-cage dangled from the ceiling, to which he occasionally raised his eyes in gloomy thought; and, as the heedless insects hovered round the gaudy network, Mr. Bumble would heave a deep sigh, while a more gloomy shadow overspread his countenance. Mr. Bumble was meditating; it might be that the insects brought to mind, some painful passage in his own past life.

Nor was Mr. Bumble's gloom the only thing calculated to awaken a pleasing melancholy in the bosom of a spectator. There were not wanting other appearances, and those closely connected with his own person, which announced that a great change had taken place in the position of his affairs. The laced coat, and the cocked hat; where were they? He still wore knee-breeches, and dark cotton stockings on his nether limbs; but they were not *the* breeches. The coat was wide-skirted; and in that respect like *the* coat, but, oh, how different! The mighty cocked hat was replaced by a modest round one. Mr. Bumble was no longer a beadle.

There are some promotions in life, which, independent of the more substantial rewards they offer, acquire peculiar value and dignity from the coats and waistcoats connected with them. A field-marshal has his uniform; a bishop his silk apron; a counsellor his silk gown; a beadle his cocked hat. Strip the bishop of his apron, or the beadle of his hat and lace; what are they? Men. Mere men. Dignity, and even holiness too, sometimes, are more questions of coat and waistcoat than some people imagine *(Chapter 37)*.

'And to-morrow two months it was done!' said Mr. Bumble, with a sigh. 'It seems a age.'

Mr. Bumble might have meant that he had concentrated a whole existence of happiness into the short space of eight weeks; but the sigh – there was a vast deal of meaning in the sigh.

'I sold myself,' said Mr. Bumble, pursuing the same train of reflection, 'for six teaspoons, a pair of sugar-tongs, and a milk-pot; with a small quantity of second-hand furniture, and twenty pound in money. I went very reasonable. Cheap, dirt cheap!' *(Chapter 37)*.

Mrs. Bumble . . . dropped into a chair, and with a loud scream that Mr. Bumble was a hard-hearted brute, fell into a paroxysm of tears.

But tears were not the things to find their way to Mr. Bumble's soul; his heart was waterproof. Like washable beaver hats that improve with rain, his nerves were rendered stouter and more vigorous, by showers of tears, which, being tokens of weakness, and so far tacit admissions of his own power, pleased and exalted him. He eyed his good lady with looks of great satisfaction, and begged, in an encouraging manner, that she should cry her hardest: the exercise being looked upon, by the faculty, as strongly conducive to health.

'It opens the lungs, washes the countenance, exercises the eyes, and softens down the temper,' said Mr. Bumble. 'So cry away' *(Chapter 37)*.

'This is the woman, is it?' demanded Monks.

'Hem! That is the woman,' replied Mr. Bumble, mindful of his wife's caution.

'You think women never can keep secrets, I suppose?' said the matron, interposing, and returning, as she spoke, the searching look of Monks.

'I know they will always keep *one* till it's found out,' said Monks.

'And what may that be?' asked the matron.

'The loss of their own good name,' replied Monks. 'So, by the same rule, if a woman's a party to a secret that might hang or transport her, I'm not afraid of her telling it to anybody; not I!' *(Chapter 38)*.

'Why, what evil wind has blowed you here?' he asked Fagin.

'No evil wind at all, my dear, for evil winds blow nobody any good; and I've brought something good with me, that you'll be glad to see. Dodger, my dear, open the bundle; and give Bill the little trifles that we spent all our money on, this morning.'

In compliance with Mr. Fagin's request, the Artful untied this bundle, which was of large size, and formed of an old table-cloth; and handed the articles it contained, one by one, to Charley Bates: who placed them on the table, with various encomiums on their rarity and excellence.

'Sitch a rabbit pie, Bill,' exclaimed that young gentleman, disclosing to view a huge pasty; 'sitch delicate creeturs, with sitch tender limbs, Bill, that the wery bones melt in your mouth, and there's no occasion to pick 'em; half a pound of seven and sixpenny green, so precious strong that if you mix it with biling water, it'll go nigh to blow the lid of the tea-pot off; a pound and a half of moist sugar that the niggers didn't work at all at, afore they got it up to sitch a pitch of goodness, – oh no! Two half-quartern brans; pound of best fresh; piece of double Glo'ster; and, to wind up all, some of the richest sort you ever lushed!' *(Chapter 39)*.

'What do you mean by leaving a man in this state, three weeks and more, you false-hearted wagabond?'

'Only hear him, boys!' said Fagin, shrugging his shoulders. 'And us come to bring him all these beauti-ful things.'

'The things is well enough in their way,' observed Mr. Sikes: a little soothed as he glanced over the table; 'but what have you got to say for yourself, why you should leave me here, down in the mouth, health, blunt, and everything else; and take no more notice of me, all this mortal time, than if I was that 'ere dog. – Drive him down, Charley!'

'I never see such a jolly dog as that,' cried master Bates, doing as he was desired. 'Smelling the grub like a old lady a going to market! He'd make his fortun on the stage that dog would, and rewive the drayma besides' *(Chapter 39)*.

'A bad one! I'll eat my head if he is not a bad one,' growled Mr. Grimwig, speaking by some ventriloquial power, without moving a muscle of his face.

'He is a child of a noble nature and a warm heart,' said Rose, colouring; 'and that power which has thought fit to try him beyond his years, has planted in his breast affections and feelings which would do honour to many who have numbered his days six times over.'

'I'm only sixty-one,' said Mr. Grimwig, with the same rigid face. 'And, as the devil's in it if this Oliver is not twelve years old at least, I don't see the application of that remark.'

'Do not heed my friend, Miss Maylie,' said Mr. Brownlow; 'he does not mean what he says.'

'Yes, he does,' growled Mr. Grimwig.

'No, he does not,' said Mr. Brownlow, obviously rising in wrath as he spoke.

'He'll eat his head, if he doesn't,' growled Mr. Grimwig.

'He would deserve to have it knocked off, if he does,' said Mr. Brownlow.

'And he'd uncommonly like to see any man offer to do it,' responded Mr. Grimwig, knocking his stick upon the floor.

Having gone thus far, the two old gentlemen severally took snuff, and afterwards shook hands, according to their invariable custom *(Chapter 41)*.

'But, yer see,' observed Noah, 'as she will be able to do a good deal, I should like to take something very light.'

'A little fancy work?' suggested Fagin.

'Ah! something of that sort,' replied Noah. 'What do you think would suit me now? Something not too trying for the strength, and not very dangerous, you know. That's the sort of thing!'

'I heard you talk of something in the spy way upon the others, my dear,' said Fagin. 'My friend wants somebody who would do that well, very much.'

'Why, I did mention that, and I shouldn't mind turning my hand to it sometimes,' rejoined Mr. Claypole slowly; 'but it wouldn't pay by itself, you know.'

'That's true!' observed the Jew, ruminating or pretending to ruminate. 'No, it might not.'

'What do you think, then?' asked Noah, anxiously regarding him. 'Something in the sneaking way, where it was pretty sure work, and not much more risk than being at home.'

'What do you think of the old ladies?' asked Fagin. 'There's a good deal of money made in snatching their bags and parcels, and running round the corner.'

'Don't they holler out a good deal, and scratch sometimes?' asked Noah, shaking his head. 'I don't think that would answer my purpose. Ain't there any other line open?'

'Stop!' said Fagin, laying his hand on Noah's knee. 'The kinchin lay.'

'What's that?' demanded Mr. Claypole.

The kinchins, my dear,' said Fagin, 'is the young children that's sent on errands by their mothers, with sixpences and shillings; and the lay is just to take their money away – they've always got it ready in their hands, – then knock 'em into the kennel, and walk off very slow, as if there were nothing else the matter but a child fallen down and hurt itself. Ha! ha! ha!'

'Ha! ha!' roared Mr. Claypole, kicking up his legs in an ecstasy. 'Lord, that's the very thing!' *(Chapter 42)*.

'Some people are nobody's enemies but their own, yer know.'

'Don't believe that,' said Fagin. 'When a man's his own enemy, it's only because he's too much his own friend; not because he's careful for everybody but himself. Pooh! pooh! There ain't such a thing in nature.'

'There oughtn't to be, if there is,' replied Mr. Bolter.

'That stands to reason. Some conjurers say that number three is the magic number, and some say number seven. It's neither, my friend, neither. It's number one.'

'Ha! ha!' cried Mr. Bolter. 'Number one for ever' *(Chapter 43)*.

It was indeed Mr. Dawkins, who, shuffling into the office with the big coat sleeves tucked up as usual, his left hand in his pocket, and his hat in his right hand, preceded the jailer, with a rolling gait altogether indescribable, and, taking his place in the dock, requested in an audible voice to know what he was placed in that 'ere disgraceful sitivation for.

'Hold your tongue, will you?' said the jailer.

'I'm an Englishman, ain't I?' rejoined the Dodger. 'Where are my priwileges?'

'You'll get your privileges soon enough,' retorted the jailer, 'and pepper with 'em.'

'We'll see wot the Secretary of State for the Home Affairs has got to say to the beaks, if I don't,' replied Mr. Dawkins. 'Now then! Wot is this here business? I shall thank the madg'strates to dispose of this here little affair, and not to keep me while they read the paper, for I've got an appointment with a genelman in the City, and as I am a man of my word and wery punctual in business matters, he'll go away if I ain't there to my time, and then pr'aps there won't be an action for damage against them as kep me away. Oh no, certainly not!' *(Chapter 43)*.

'What is this?' inquired one of the magistrates.

'A pick-pocketing case, your worship.'

'Has the boy ever been here before?'

'He ought to have been, a many times,' replied the jailer. 'He has been pretty well everywhere else. *I* know him well, your worship.'

'Oh! you know me, do you?' cried the Artful, making a note of the statement. 'Wery good. That's a case of deformation of character, any way.'

Here there was another laugh, and another cry of silence *(Chapter 43)*.

'Have you anything to say at all?'

'Do you hear his worship ask if you've anything to say?' inquired the jailer, nudging the silent Dodger with his elbow.

'I beg your pardon,' said the Dodger, looking up with an air of abstraction. 'Did you redress yourself to me, my man?'

'I never see such an out-and-out young wagabond, your worship,' observed the officer with a grin. 'Do you mean to say anything, you young shaver?'

'No,' replied the Dodger, 'not here, for this ain't the shop for justice; besides which, my attorney is a-breakfasting this morning with the Wice President of the House of Commons; but I shall have something to say elsewhere, and so will he, and so will a wery numerous and 'spectable circle of acquaintance as'll make them beaks wish they'd never been born, or that they'd got their footmen to hang 'em up to their own hat-pegs, afore they let 'em come out this morning to try it on upon me. I'll – '

'There! He's fully committed!' interposed the clerk. 'Take him away.'

'Come on,' said the jailer.

'Oh ah! I'll come on,' replied the Dodger brushing his hat with the palm of his hand. 'Ah! (to the Bench) it's no use your looking frightened; I won't show you no mercy, not a ha'porth of it. *You'll* pay for this, my fine fellers. I wouldn't be you for something! I wouldn't go free, now, if you was to fall down on your knees and ask me. Here, carry me off to prison! Take me away!' *(Chapter 43)*.

'You did well yesterday, my dear,' said Fagin. 'Beautiful! Six shillings and ninepence halfpenny on the very first day! The kinchin lay will be a fortune to you.'

'Don't you forget to add three pint-pots and a milk-can,' said Mr. Bolter.

'No, no, my dear. The pint-pots were great strokes of genius: but the milk-can was a perfect masterpiece.'

'Pretty well, I think for a beginner,' remarked Mr. Bolter complacently. 'The pots I took off airy railings, and the milk-can was standing by itself outside a public-house. I thought it might get rusty with the rain, or catch cold, yer know. Eh? Ha! ha! ha!' (*Chapter 45*).

Speak to her kindly,' said the young lady to her companion. 'Poor creature! She seems to need it.'

'Your haughty religious people would have held their hands up to see me as I am to-night, and preached of flames and vengeance,' cried the girl. 'Oh, dear lady, why arn't those who claim to be God's own folks as gentle and as kind to us poor wretches as you, who, having youth, and beauty, and all that they have lost, might be a little proud instead of so much humbler?'

'Ah!' said the gentleman. 'A Turk turns his face, after washing it well, to the East, when he says his prayers; these good people, after giving their faces such a rub against the World as to take the smiles off, turn with no less regularity, to the darkest side of Heaven. Between the Mussulman and the Pharisee, commend me to the first!' (*Chapter 46:* Brownlow, Rose Maylie, and Nancy).

'Get up!' said the man.

'It *is* you, Bill!' said the girl, with an expression of pleasure at his return.

'It is,' was the reply. 'Get up.'

There was a candle burning, but the man hastily drew it from the candlestick, and hurled it under the grate. Seeing the faint light of early day without, the girl rose to undraw the curtain.

'Let it be,' said Sikes, thrusting his hand before her. 'There's light enough for wot I've got to do.'

'Bill,' said the girl, in the low voice of alarm, 'why do you look like that at me!'

The robber sat regarding her, for a few seconds, with dilated nostrils and heaving breast; and then, grasping her by the head and throat, dragged her into the middle of the room, and looking once towards the door, placed his heavy hand upon her mouth.

'Bill, Bill!' gasped the girl, wrestling with the strength of mortal fear, – 'I – I won't scream or cry – not once – hear me – speak to me – tell me what I have done!'

'You know, you she devil!' returned the robber, suppressing his breath. 'You were watched to-night; every word you said was heard.'

'Then spare my life for the love of Heaven, as I spared yours,' rejoined the girl, clinging to him. 'Bill, dear Bill, you cannot have the heart to kill me. Oh! think of all I have given up, only this one night, for you. You *shall* have time to think, and save yourself this crime; I will not loose my hold, you cannot throw me off. Bill, Bill, for dear God's sake, for your own, for mine, stop before you spill my blood! I have been true to you, upon my guilty soul I have!'

The man struggled violently, to release his arms; but those of the girl were clasped round his, and tear her as he would, he could not tear them away.

'Bill,' cried the girl, striving to lay her head upon his breast, 'the gentleman and that dear lady, told me to-night of a home in some foreign country where I could end my days in solitude and peace. Let me see them again, and beg them, on my knees, to show the same mercy and goodness to you; and let us both leave this dreadful place, and far apart lead better lives, and forget how we have lived, except in prayers, and never see each other more. It is never too late to repent. They told me so – I feel it now – but we must have time – a little, little time!'

The housebreaker freed one arm, and grasped his pistol. The certainty of immediate detection if he fired, flashed across his mind even in the midst of his fury; and he beat it twice with all the force he could summon, upon the upturned face that almost touched his own.

She staggered and fell: nearly blinded with the blood that rained down from a deep gash in her forehead; but raising herself, with difficulty, on her knees, drew from her bosom a white handkerchief – Rose Maylie's own – and holding it up, in her folded hands, as high towards Heaven as her feeble strength would allow, breathed one prayer for mercy to her Maker.

It was a ghastly figure to look upon. The murderer staggering backward to the wall, and shutting out the sight with his hand, seized a heavy club and struck her down (*Chapter 47:* Sikes and Nancy).

He wandered over miles and miles of ground, and still came back to the old place. Morning and noon had passed, and the day was on the wane, and still he rambled to and fro, and up and down, and round and round, and still lingered about the same spot. At last he got away, and shaped his course for Hatfield.

It was nine o'clock at night, when the man, quite tired out, and the dog, limping and lame from the unaccustomed exercise, turned down the hill by the church of the quiet village, and plodding along the little street, crept into a small public-house, whose scanty light had guided them to the spot. There was a fire in the taproom, and some country-labourers were drinking before it. They made room for the stranger, but he sat down in the furthest corner, and ate and drank alone, or rather with his dog: to whom he cast a morsel of food from time to time. . . .

The robber, after paying his reckoning, sat silent and unnoticed in his corner, and had almost dropped asleep, when he was half wakened by the noisy entrance of a new comer.

This was an antic fellow, half pedlar and half mountebank, who travelled about the country on foot to vend hones, strops, razors, washballs, harness-paste, medicine for dogs and horses, cheap perfumery, cosmetics, and such-like wares, which he carried in a case slung to his back. His entrance was the signal for various homely jokes with the countrymen, which slackened not until he had made his supper, and opened his box of treasures, when he ingeniously contrived to unite business with amusement.

'And what be that stoof? Good to eat, Harry?' asked a grinning countryman, pointing to some composition-cakes in one corner.

'This,' said the fellow, producing one, 'this is the infallible and invaluable composition for removing all sorts of stain, rust, dirt, mildew, spick, speck, spot, or spatter, from silk, satin, linen, cambric, cloth, crape, stuff, carpet, merino, muslin, bombazeen, or woollen stuff. Wine-stains, fruit-stains, beer-stains, water-stains, paint-stains, pitch-stains, any stains, all come out at one rub with the infallible and invaluable composition. If a lady stains her honour, she has only need to swallow one cake and she's cured at once – for it's poison. If a gentleman wants to prove this, he has only need to bolt one little square, and he has put it beyond question – for it's quite as satisfactory as a pistol-bullet, and a great deal nastier in the flavour, consequently the more credit in taking it. One penny a square. With all these virtues, one penny a square!'

There were two buyers directly, and more of the listeners plainly hesitated. The vendor observing this, increased in loquacity.

'It's all bought up as fast as it can be made,' said the fellow. 'There are fourteen water-mills, six steam-engines, and a galvanic battery, always a-working upon it, and they can't make it fast enough, though the men work so hard that they die off, and the widows is pensioned directly, with twenty pound a-year for each of the children, and a premium of fifty for twins. One penny a square! Two halfpence is all the same, and four farthings is received with joy. One penny a square! Wine-stains, fruit-stains, beer-stains, water-stains, paint-stains, pitch-stains, mud-stains, blood-stains! Here is a stain upon the hat of a gentleman in company, that I'll take clean out, before he can order me a pint of ale.'

'Hah!' cried Sikes starting up. 'Give that back.'

'I'll take it clean out, sir,' replied the man, winking to the company, 'before you can come across the room to get it. Gentlemen all, observe the dark stain upon this gentleman's hat, no wider than a shilling, but thicker than a half-crown. Whether it is a wine-stain, fruit-stain, beer-stain, water-stain, paint-stain, pitch-stain, mud-stain, or blood-stain –'

The man got no further, for Sikes with a hideous imprecation overthrew the table, and tearing the hat from him, burst out of the house *(Chapter 48)*.

'Anything new up in town, Ben?' asked the game-keeper, drawing back to the window-shutters, the better to admire the horses.

'No, nothing that I knows on,' replied the man, pulling on his gloves. 'Corn's up a little. I heerd talk of a murder, too, down Spitalfields way, but I don't reckon much upon it.'

'Oh, that's quite true,' said a gentleman inside, who was looking out of the window. 'And a dreadful murder it was.'

'Was it, sir?' rejoined the guard, touching his hat. 'Man or woman, pray, sir?'

'A woman,' replied the gentleman. 'It is supposed –'

'Now, Ben,' replied the coachman impatiently.

'Damn that 'ere bag,' said the guard; 'are you gone to sleep in there?'

'Coming!' cried the office keeper, running out.

'Coming,' growled the guard. 'Ah, and so's the young 'ooman of property that's going to take a fancy to me, but I don't know when. Here, give hold. All ri-ight!'

The horn sounded a few cheerful notes, and the coach was gone *(Chapter 48)*.

'They have him now,' cried a man on the nearest bridge. 'Hurrah!'

The crowd grew light with uncovered heads; and again the shout uprose.

'I will give fifty pounds,' cried an old gentleman from the same quarter, 'to the man who takes him alive. I will remain here, till he comes to ask me for it.' . . .

The man had shrunk down, thoroughly quelled by the ferocity of the crowd, and the impossibility of escape; but seeing this sudden change with no less rapidity than it had occurred, he sprang upon his feet, determined to make one last effort for his life by dropping into the ditch, and, at the risk of being stifled, endeavouring to creep away in the darkness and confusion.

Roused into new strength and energy, and stimulated by the noise within the house which announced that an entrance had really been effected, he set his foot against the stack of chimneys, fastened one end of the rope tightly and firmly round it, and with the other made a strong running noose by the aid of his hands and teeth almost in a second. He could let himself down by the cord to within a less distance of the ground than his own height, and had his knife ready in his hand to cut it then and drop.

At the very instant when he brought the loop over his head previous to slipping it beneath his arm-pits, and when the old gentleman before-mentioned (who had clung so tight to the railing of the bridge as to resist the force of the crowd, and retain his position) earnestly warned those about him that the man was about to lower himself down – at that very instant the murderer, looking behind him on the roof, threw his arms above his head, and uttered a yell of terror.

'The eyes again!' he cried in an unearthly screech.

Staggering as if struck by lightning, he lost his balance and tumbled over the parapet. The noose was on his neck. It ran up with his weight, tight as a bow-string, and swift as the arrow it speeds. He fell for five-and-thirty feet. There was a sudden jerk, a terrific convulsion of the limbs; and there he hung, with the open knife clenched in his stiffening hand.

The old chimney quivered with the shock, but stood it bravely. The murderer swung lifeless against the wall; and the boy, thrusting aside the dangling body which obscured his view, called to the people to come and take him out, for God's sake.

A dog, which had lain concealed till now, ran backwards and forwards on the parapet with a dismal howl, and collecting himself for a spring, jumped for the dead man's shoulders. Missing his aim, he fell into the ditch, turning completely over as he went; and striking his head against a stone, dashed out his brains *(Chapter 50)*.

'Do my hi's deceive me!' cried Mr. Bumble, with ill-feigned enthusiasm, 'or is that little Oliver? Oh O-li-ver, if you know'd how I've been a-grieving for you – '

'Hold your tongue, fool,' murmured Mrs. Bumble.

'Isn't natur, natur, Mrs. Bumble?' remonstrated the workhouse master. 'Can't I be supposed to feel – *I* as brought him up porochially – when I see him a-setting here among ladies and gentlemen of the very affablest description! I always loved that boy as if he'd been my – my – my own grandfather,' said Mr. Bumble, halting for an appropriate comparison. 'Master Oliver, my dear, you remember the blessed gentleman in the white waistcoat? Ah! he went to heaven last week, in a oak coffin with plated handles, Oliver' *(Chapter 51)*.

'It was all Mrs. Bumble. She *would* do it,' urged Mr. Bumble; first looking round to ascertain that his partner had left the room.

'That is no excuse,' replied Mr. Brownlow. 'You were present on the occasion of the destruction of these trinkets, and indeed are the more guilty of the two, in the eye of the law; for the law supposes that your wife acts under your direction.'

'If the law supposes that,' said Mr. Bumble, squeezing his hat emphatically in both hands, 'the law is a ass – a idiot. If that's the eye of the law, the law is a bachelor; and the worst I wish the law is, that his eye may be opened by experience – by experience' *(Chapter 51)*.

'It's a trying thing waiting supper for lovers,' said Mr. Grimwig, waking up, and pulling his pocket-handkerchief from over his head.

Truth to tell, the supper had been waiting a most unreasonable time. Neither Mrs. Maylie, nor Harry, nor Rose (who all came in together), could offer a word in extenuation.

'I had serious thoughts of eating my head to-night,' said Mr. Grimwig, 'for I began to think I should get nothing else. I'll take the liberty, if you'll allow me, of saluting the bride that is to be' *(Chapter 51)*.

The condemned criminal was seated on his bed, rocking himself from side to side, with a countenance more like that of a snared beast than the face of a man. His mind was evidently wandering to his old life, for he continued to mutter, without appearing conscious of their presence otherwise than as a part of his vision.

'Good boy, Charley – well done – ' he mumbled. 'Oliver, too, ha! ha! ha! Oliver too – quite the gentleman now – quite the – take that boy away to bed!'

The jailer took the disengaged hand of Oliver; and, whispering him not to be alarmed, looked on without speaking.

'Take him away to bed!' cried Fagin. 'Do you hear me, some of you? He has been the – the – somehow the cause of all this. It's worth the money to bring him up to it – Bolter's throat, Bill; never mind the girl – Bolter's throat as deep as you can cut. Saw his head off!'

'Fagin,' said the jailer.

'That's me!' cried the Jew, falling, instantly, into the attitude of listening he had assumed upon his trial. 'An old man, my Lord; a very old, old man!'

'Here,' said the turnkey, laying his hand upon his breast to keep him down. 'Here's somebody wants to see you, to ask you some questions, I suppose. Fagin, Fagin! Are you a man?'

'I shan't be one long,' he replied, looking up with a face retaining no human expression but rage and terror. 'Strike them all dead! What right have they to butcher me?' *(Chapter 52)*.

SKETCHES OF YOUNG GENTLEMEN

The theatrical young gentleman is a great advocate for violence of emotion and redundancy of action. If a father has to curse a child upon the stage, he likes to see it done in the thorough-going style, with no mistake about it: to which end it is essential that the child should follow the father on her knees, and be knocked violently over on her face by the old gentleman as he goes into a small cottage, and shuts the door behind him. He likes to see a blessing invoked upon the young lady, when the old gentleman repents, with equal earnestness, and accompanied by the usual conventional forms, which consist of the old gentleman looking anxiously up into the clouds, as if to see whether it rains, and then spreading an imaginary tablecloth in the air over the young lady's head – soft music playing all the while ('The Theatrical Young Gentleman').

In his milder and softer moments he occasionally lays down his neckcloth, and pens stanzas, which sometimes find their way into a Lady's Magazine, or the 'Poets' Corner' of some country newspaper; or which, in default of either vent for his genius, adorn the rainbow leaves of a lady's album. These are generally written upon some such occasions as contemplating the Bank of England by midnight, or beholding Saint Paul's in a snow-storm; and when these gloomy objects fail to afford him inspiration, he pours forth his soul in a touching address to a violet, or a plaintive lament that he is no longer a child, but has gradually grown up.

The poetical young gentleman is fond of quoting passages from his favourite authors, who are all of the gloomy and desponding school. He has a great deal to say too about the world, and is much given to opining, especially if he has taken anything strong to drink, that there is nothing in it worth living for. He gives you to understand, however, that for the sake of society, he means to bear his part in the tiresome play, manfully resisting the gratification of his own strong desire to make a premature exit; and consoles himself with the reflection, that immortality has some chosen nook for himself and the other great spirits whom earth has chafed and wearied ('The Poetical Young Gentleman').

NICHOLAS NICKLEBY

Some ill-conditioned persons who sneer at the life-matrimonial, may perhaps suggest, in this place, that the good couple would be better likened to two principals in a sparring match, who, when fortune is low and backers scarce, will chivalrously set to, for the mere pleasure of the buffeting; and in one respect indeed this comparison would hold good: for, as the adventurous pair of the Fives' Court will afterwards send round a hat, and trust to the bounty of the lookers-on for the means of regaling themselves, so Mr. Godfrey Nickleby and *his* partner, the honeymoon being over, looked wistfully out into the world, relying in no inconsiderable degree upon chance for the improvement of their means (*Chapter 1*).

Gold conjures up a mist about a man, more destructive of all his old senses and lulling to his feelings than the fumes of charcoal (*Chapter 1*).

Speculation is a round game; the players see little or nothing of their cards at first starting; gains *may* be great – and so may losses (*Chapter 1*).

'You didn't mention in your letter what my brother's complaint was, ma'am.'
'The doctors could attribute it to no particular disease,' said Mrs. Nickleby, shedding tears. 'We have too much reason to fear that he died of a broken heart.'
'Pooh!' said Ralph, 'there's no such thing. I can understand a man's dying of a broken neck, or suffering from a broken arm, or a broken head, or a broken leg, or a broken nose; but a broken heart! – nonsense, it's the cant of the day. If a man can't pay his debts, he dies of a broken heart, and his widow's a martyr' (*Chapter 3: Mrs. Nickleby and Ralph Nickleby*).

'EDUCATION. – At Mr. Wackford Squeers's Academy, Dotheboys Hall, at the delightful village of Dotheboys, near Greta Bridge in Yorkshire, Youth are boarded, clothed, booked, furnished with pocket-money, provided with all necessaries, instructed in all languages living and dead, mathematics, orthography, geometry, astronomy, trigonometry, the use of the globes, algebra, single stick (if required), writing, arithmetic, fortification, and every other branch of classical literature. Terms, twenty guineas per annum. No extras, no vacations, and diet unparalleled. Mr. Squeers is in town, and attends daily, from one till four, at the Saracen's Head, Snow Hill. N.B. An able assistant wanted. Annual salary £5. A Master of Arts would be preferred' (*Chapter 3*).

Snow Hill! What kind of place can the quiet towns-people who see the words emblazoned, in all the legibility of gilt letters and dark shading, on the north-country coaches, take Snow Hill to be? All people have some undefined and shadowy notion of a place whose name is frequently before their eyes, or often in their ears. What a vast number of random ideas there must be perpetually floating about, regarding this same Snow Hill. The name is such a good one. Snow Hill – Snow Hill too, coupled with a Saracen's Head: picturing to us by a double association of ideas, something stern and rugged! A bleak desolate tract of country, open to piercing blasts and fierce wintry storms – a dark, cold, gloomy heath, lonely by day, and scarcely to be thought of by honest folks at night

– a place which solitary wayfarers shun, and where desperate robbers congregate; – this, or something like this, should be the prevalent notion of Snow Hill, in those remote and rustic parts, through which the Saracen's Head, like some grim apparition, rushes each day and night with mysterious and ghost-like punctuality; holding its swift and headlong course in all weathers, and seeming to bid defiance to the very elements themselves (*Chapter 4*).

'You needn't hurry yourself,' said Squeers; 'there's plenty of time. Conquer your passions, boys, and don't be eager after vittles.' As he uttered this moral precept, Mr. Squeers took a large bite out of the cold beef (*Chapter 5*).

'When I say number one,' pursued Mr. Squeers, putting the mug before the children, 'the boy on the left hand nearest the window may take a drink; and when I say number two, the boy next him will go in, and so till we come to number five, which is the last boy. Are you ready?'
'Yes, sir,' cried all the little boys with great eagerness.
'That's right,' said Squeers, calmly getting on with his breakfast; 'keep ready till I tell you to begin. Subdue your appetites, my dears, and you've conquered human natur' (*Chapter 5*).

'This is the first class in English spelling and philosophy, Nickleby,' said Squeers, beckoning Nicholas to stand beside him. 'We'll get up a Latin one, and hand that over to you. Now, then, where's the first boy?'
'Please, sir, he's cleaning the back parlour window,' said the temporary head of the philosophical class.
'So he is, to be sure,' rejoined Squeers. 'We go upon the practical mode of teaching, Nickleby; the regular education system. C-l-e-a-n, clean, verb active, to make bright, to scour. W-i-n, win, d-e-r, der, winder, a casement. When the boy knows this out of book, he goes and does it. It's just the same principle as the use of the globes. Where's the second boy?'
'Please, sir, he's weeding the garden,' replied a small voice.
'To be sure,' said Squeers, by no means disconcerted. 'So he is. B-o-t, bot, t-i-n, tin, bottin, n-e-y, bottinney, noun substantive, a knowledge of plants. When he has learned that bottinney means a knowledge of plants, he goes and knows 'em. That's our system, Nickleby; what do you think of it?' (*Chapter 8*).

'Oh! that Knuckleboy,' said Mrs. Squeers impatiently. 'I hate him.'
'What do you hate him for, my dear?' asked Squeers.
'What's that to you?' retorted Mrs. Squeers. 'If I hate him, that's enough, ain't it?'
'Quite enough for him, my dear, and a great deal too much, I dare say, if he knew it,' replied Squeers in a pacific tone. 'I only asked from curiosity, my dear.'
'Well, then, if you want to know,' rejoined Mrs. Squeers, 'I'll tell you. Because he's a proud, haughty, consequential, turned-up-nosed peacock' (*Chapter 9*).

'Am I to take care of the school when I grow up a man, father?' said Wackford junior, suspending, in the excess of his delight, a vicious kick which he was administering to his sister.

'You are, my son,' replied Mr. Squeers, in a sentimental voice.

'Oh my eye, won't I give it to the boys!' exclaimed the interesting child, grasping his father's cane. 'Oh, father, won't I make 'em squeak again!'

It was a proud moment in Mr. Squeers's life, when he witnessed that burst of enthusiasm in his young child's mind, and saw in it a foreshadowing of his future eminence. He pressed a penny into his hand, and gave vent to his feelings (as did his exemplary wife also), in a shout of approving laughter. The infantine appeal to their common sympathies, at once restored cheerfulness to the conversation, and harmony to the company *(Chapter 9)*.

'What your uncle says, is very true, Kate, my dear,' said Mrs. Nickleby. 'I recollect when your poor papa and I came to town after we were married, that a young lady brought me home a chip cottage-bonnet, with white and green trimming, and green persian lining, in her own carriage, which drove up to the door full gallop; – at least, I am not quite certain whether it was her own carriage or a hackney chariot, but I remember very well that the horse dropped down dead as he was turning round, and that your poor papa said he hadn't had any corn for a fortnight' *(Chapter 10)*.

'My life,' said Mr. Mantalini, 'what a demd devil of a time you have been!'

'I didn't even know Mr. Nickleby was here, my love,' said Madame Mantalini.

'Then what a doubly demd infernal rascal that footman must be, my soul,' remonstrated Mr. Mantalini.

'My dear,' said Madame, 'that is entirely your fault.'

'My fault, my heart's joy?'

'Certainly,' returned the lady; 'what can you expect, dearest, if you will not correct the man?'

'Correct the man, my soul's delight!'

'Yes; I am sure he wants speaking to, badly enough,' said Madame, pouting.

'Then do not vex itself,' said Mr. Mantalini; 'he shall be horse-whipped till he cries out demnebly.' With this promise Mr. Mantalini kissed Madame Mantalini, and, after that performance, Madame Mantalini pulled Mr. Mantalini playfully by the ear: which done, they descended to business *(Chapter 10)*.

'We keep twenty young women constantly employed in the establishment,' said Madame.

'Indeed, ma'am!' replied Kate, timidly.

'Yes; and some of 'em demd handsome, too,' said the master.

'Mantalini!' exclaimed his wife, in an awful voice.

'My senses' idol!' said Mantalini.

'Do you wish to break my heart?'

'Not for twenty thousand hemispheres populated with – with – with little ballet-dancers,' replied Mantalini in a poetical strain *(Chapter 10)*.

'This day eight year,' said Mr. Kenwigs after a pause. 'Dear me – ah!'

This reflection was echoed by all present, who said 'Ah!' first, and 'dear me,' afterwards.

'I was younger then,' tittered Mrs. Kenwigs.

'No,' said the collector.

'Certainly not,' added everybody.

'I remember my niece,' said Mr. Lillyvick, surveying his audience with a grave air; 'I remember her, on that very afternoon, when she first acknowledged to her mother a partiality for Kenwigs. "Mother," she says, "I love him." '

' "Adore him," I said, uncle,' interposed Mrs. Kenwigs.

' "Love him," I think, my dear,' said the collector, firmly.

'Perhaps you are right, uncle,' replied Mrs. Kenwigs, submissively. 'I thought it was "adore." '

' "Love," my dear,' retorted Mr. Lillyvick. ' "Mother," she says, "I love him!" "What do I hear?" cries her mother; and instantly falls into strong convulsions' *(Chapter 14)*.

'Dotheboys Hall,
'Thursday Morning.

'Sir,

'My pa requests me to write to you, the doctors considering it doubtful whether he will ever recuvver the use of his legs which prevents his holding a pen.

'We are in a state of mind beyond everything, and my pa is one mask of brooses both blue and green likewise two forms are steepled in his Goar. We were kimpelled to have him carried down into the kitchen where he now lays. You will judge from this that he has been brought very low.

'When your nevew that you recommended for a teacher had done this to my pa and jumped upon his body with his feet and also langwedge which I will not pollewt my pen with describing, he assaulted my ma with dreadful violence, dashed her to the earth, and drove her back comb several inches into her head. A very little more and it must have entered her skull. We have a medical certifiket that if it had, the tortershell would have affected the brain.

'Me and my brother were then the victims of his feury since which we have suffered very much which leads us to the arrowing belief that we have received some injury in our insides, especially as no marks of violence are visible externally. I am screaming out loud all the time I write and so is my brother which takes off my attention rather and I hope will excuse mistakes.

'The monster having sasiated his thirst for blood ran away, taking with him a boy of desperate caracter that he had excited to rebellyon, and a garnet ring belonging to my ma, and not having been apprehended by the constables is supposed to have been took up by some stage-coach. My pa begs that if he comes to you the ring may be returned, and that you will let the thief and assassin go, as if we prosecuted him he would only be transported, and if he is let go he is sure to be hung before long which will save us trouble and be much more satisfactory. Hoping to hear from you when convenient.

'I remain
'Yours and cetrer
'Fanny Squeers.

'P.S. I pity his ignorance and despise him' *(Chapter 15)*.

'He has a very nice face and style, really,' said Mrs. Kenwigs.

'He certainly has,' added Miss Petowker. 'There's something in his appearance quite – dear, dear, what's that word again?'

'What word?' inquired Mr. Lillyvick.

'Why – dear me, how stupid I am,' replied Miss Petowker, hesitating. 'What do you call it, when Lords break off door-knockers and beat policemen, and play at coaches with other people's money, and all that sort of thing?'

'Aristocratic?' suggested the collector.

'Ah! aristocratic,' replied Miss Petowker; 'something very aristocratic about him, isn't there?' *(Chapter 15)*.

'My conduct, Pugstyles,' said Mr. Gregsbury, looking round upon the deputation with gracious magnanimity – 'My conduct has been, and ever will be, regulated by a sincere regard for the true and real interests of this great and happy country. Whether I look at home, or abroad; whether I behold the peaceful industrious communities of our island home: her rivers covered with steamboats, her roads with locomotives, her streets with cabs, her skies with balloons of a power and magnitude hitherto unknown in the history of aeronautics in this or any other nation – I say, whether I look merely at home, or, stretching my eyes farther, contemplate the boundless prospect of conquest and possession – achieved by British perseverance and British valour – which is outspread before me, I clasp my hands, and turning my eyes to the broad expanse above my head, exclaim, "Thank Heaven, I am a Briton!" ' *(Chapter 16)*.

The general impression seemed to be, that as an explanation of Mr. Gregsbury's political conduct, it did not enter quite enough into detail; and one gentleman in the rear did not scruple to remark aloud, that, for his purpose, it savoured rather too much of a 'gammon' tendency.

'The meaning of that term – gammon,' said Mr. Gregsbury, 'is unknown to me. If it means that I grow a little too fervid, or perhaps even hyperbolical, in extolling my native land, I admit the full justice of the remark. I *am* proud of this free and happy country. My form dilates, my eye glistens, my breast heaves, my heart swells, my bosom burns, when I call to mind her greatness and her glory' *(Chapter 16)*.

'I should wish my secretary to get together a few little flourishing speeches, of a patriotic cast. For instance, if any preposterous bill were brought forward, for giving poor grubbing devils of authors a right to their own property, I should like to say, that I for one would never consent to opposing an insurmountable bar to the diffusion of literature among *the people,* – you understand? – that the creations of the pocket, being man's, might belong to one man, or one family; but that the creations of the brain, being God's ought as a matter of course to belong to the people at large – and if I was pleasantly disposed, I should like to make a joke about posterity, and say that those who wrote for posterity should be content to be rewarded by the approbation *of* posterity; it might take with the

house, and could never do me any harm, because posterity can't be expected to know anything about me or my jokes either – do you see?'

'I see that, sir,' replied Nicholas.

'You must always bear in mind, in such cases as this, where our interests are not affected,' said Mr. Gregsbury, 'to put it very strong about the people, because it comes out very well at election-time; and you could be as funny as you liked about the authors; because I believe the greater part of them live in lodgings, and are not voters' *(Chapter 16)*.

'If you will be odiously, demnebly outr*i*geously jealous, my soul,' said Mr. Mantalini, 'you will be very miserable – horrid miserable – demnition miserable.' And then, there was a sound as though Mr. Mantalini were sipping his coffee.

'I *am* miserable,' returned Madame Mantalini, evidently pouting.

'Then you are an ungrateful, unworthy, demd unthankful little fairy,' said Mr. Mantalini.

'I am not,' returned Madame, with a sob.

'Do not put itself out of humour,' said Mr. Mantalini, breaking an egg. 'It is a pretty, bewitching little demd countenance, and it should not be out of humour, for it spoils its loveliness, and makes it cross and gloomy like a frightful, naughty, demd hobgoblin.'

'I am not to be brought round in that way, always,' rejoined Madame, sulkily.

'It shall be brought round in any way it likes best, and not brought round at all if it likes that better,' retorted Mr. Mantalini, with his egg-spoon in his mouth.

'It's very easy to talk,' said Mrs. Mantalini.

'Not so easy when one is eating a demnition egg,' replied Mr. Mantalini; 'for the yolk runs down the waistcoat, and yolk of egg does not match any waistcoat but a yellow waistcoat, demmit' *(Chapter 17)*.

'You can't want any more just now,' said Madame coaxingly.

'My life and soul,' returned her husband, 'there is a horse for sale at Scrubbs's, which it would be a sin and a crime to lose – going, my senses' joy, for nothing.'

'For nothing,' cried Madame, 'I am glad of that.'

'For actually nothing,' replied Mantalini. 'A hundred guineas down will buy him; mane, and crest, and legs, and tail, all of the demdest beauty. I will ride him in the park before the very chariots of the rejected countesses. The demd old dowager will faint with grief and rage; the other two will say, "He is married, he has made away with himself, it is a demd thing, it is all up!" They will hate each other demnebly, and wish you dead and buried. Ha! ha! Demmit' *(Chapter 17)*.

'Reduced – I should say poor people,' answered Kate, correcting herself hastily, for she was afraid of appearing proud, 'must live where they can.'

'Ah! very true, so they must; very proper indeed!' rejoined Miss Knag with that sort of half-sigh, which, accompanied by two or three slight nods of the head, is pity's small change in general society; 'and that's what I very often tell my brother, when our servants go away ill, one after another, and he thinks the back-kitchen's rather too damp for 'em to sleep in. These sort of people, I tell him, are glad to sleep anywhere! Heaven suits the back to the burden. What a nice thing it is to think that it should be so, isn't it?' (*Chapter 18: Kate Nickleby and Miss Knag*).

'She always was clever,' said poor Mrs. Nickleby, brightening up, 'always, from a baby. I recollect when she was only two years and a half old, that a gentleman who used to visit very much at our house – Mr. Watkins, you know, Kate, my dear, that your poor papa went bail for, who afterwards ran away to the United States, and sent us a pair of snow-shoes, with such an affectionate letter that it made your poor dear father cry for a week. You remember the letter? In which he said that he was very sorry he couldn't repay the fifty pounds just then, because his capital was all out at interest, and he was very busy making his fortune, but that he didn't forget you were his god-daughter, and he should take it very unkind if we didn't buy you a silver coral and put it down to his old account? Dear me, yes, my dear, how stupid you are! and spoke so affectionately of the old port wine that he used to drink a bottle and a half of every time he came. You must remember, Kate?' (*Chapter 18*).

'Have I lived to this day to be called a fright!' cried Miss Knag, suddenly becoming convulsive, and making an effort to tear her front off.

'Oh no, no,' replied the chorus, 'pray don't say so; don't now!'

'Have I deserved to be called an elderly person?' screamed Miss Knag, wrestling with the supernumeraries.

'Don't think of such things, dear,' answered the chorus.

'I hate her,' cried Miss Knag; 'I detest and hate her. Never let her speak to me again; never let anybody who is a friend of mine speak to her; a slut, a hussy, an impudent artful hussy!' Having denounced the object of her wrath, in these terms, Miss Knag screamed once, hiccupped thrice, gurgled in her throat several times, slumbered, shivered, woke, came to, composed her headdress, and declared herself quite well again (*Chapter 18*).

Mr. Mantalini put the tips of his whiskers, and, by degrees, his head, through the half-opened door, and cried in a soft voice –

'Is my life and soul there?'

'No,' replied his wife.

'How can it say so, when it is blooming in the front room like a little rose in a demnition flower-pot?' urged Mantalini. 'May its poppet come in and talk?'

'Certainly not,' replied Madame; 'you know I never allow you here. Go along!'

The poppet, however, encouraged perhaps by the relenting tone of this reply, ventured to rebel, and, stealing into the room, made towards Madame Mantalini on tiptoe, blowing her a kiss as he came along.

'Why will it vex itself, and twist its little face into bewitching nutcrackers?' said Mantalini, putting his left arm round the waist of his life and soul, and drawing her towards him with his right (*Chapter 21*).

'What's the demd total?' was the first question he asked.

'Fifteen hundred and twenty-seven pound, four and ninepence ha'penny,' replied Mr. Scaley, without moving a limb.

'The halfpenny be demd,' said Mr. Mantalini, impatiently.

'By all means if you vish it,' retorted Mr. Scaley; 'and the ninepence.'

'It don't matter to us if the fifteen hundred and twenty-seven pound went along with it, that I know on,' observed Mr. Tix.

'Not a button,' said Scaley (*Chapter 21*).

'My cup of happiness's sweetener,' said Mantalini, approaching his wife with a penitent air; 'will you listen to me for two minutes?'

'Oh! don't speak to me,' replied his wife, sobbing. 'You have ruined me, and that's enough.'

Mr. Mantalini, who had doubtless well considered his part, no sooner heard these words pronounced in a tone of grief and severity, than he recoiled several paces, assumed an expression of consuming mental agony, rushed headlong from the room, and was, soon afterwards, heard to slam the door of an upstairs dressing-room with great violence.

'Miss Nickleby,' cried Madame Mantalini, when this sound met her ear, 'make haste for Heaven's sake, he will destroy himself! I spoke unkindly to him, and he cannot bear it from me. Alfred, my darling Alfred.'

With such exclamations, she hurried upstairs, followed by Kate, who, although she did not quite participate in the fond wife's apprehensions, was a little flurried, nevertheless. The dressing-room door being hastily flung open, Mr. Mantalini was disclosed to view, with his shirt-collar symmetrically thrown back: putting a fine edge to a breakfast knife by means of his razor strop.

'Ah!' cried Mr. Mantalini. 'Interrupted!' and whisk went the breakfast knife into Mr. Mantalini's dressing-gown pocket, while Mr. Mantalini's eyes rolled wildly, and his hair floating in wild disorder, mingled with his whiskers.

'Alfred,' cried his wife, flinging her arms about him, 'I didn't mean to say it, I didn't mean to say it?'

'Ruined!' cried Mr. Mantalini. 'Have I brought ruin upon the best and purest creature that ever blessed a demnition vagabond! Demmit, let me go.' At this crisis of his ravings Mr. Mantalini made a pluck at the breakfast knife, and being restrained by his wife's grasp, attempted to dash his head against the wall – taking very good care to be at least six feet from it.

'Compose yourself, my own angel,' said Madame. 'It was nobody's fault; it was mine as much yours, we shall do very well yet. Come, Alfred, come' (*Chapter 21*).

'Excuse my saying so,' said the manager, leaning over to Nicholas, and sinking his voice, 'but what a capital countenance your friend has got!'

'Poor fellow!' said Nicholas, with a half-smile, 'I wish it were a little more plump, and less haggard.'

287

'Plump!' exclaimed the manager, quite horrified, 'you'd spoil it for ever.'

'Do you think so?'

'Think so, sir! Why, as he is now,' said the manager, striking his knee emphatically; 'without a pad upon his body, and hardly a touch of paint upon his face, he'd make such an actor for the starved business as was never seen in this country. Only let him be tolerably well up in the Apothecary in Romeo and Juliet with the slightest possible dab of red on the tip of his nose, and he'd be certain of three rounds the moment he put his head out of the practicable door in the front grooves O.P.' (*Chapter 22: Vincent Crummles*).

'Does no other profession occur to you, which a young man of your figure and address could take up easily, and see the world to advantage in?' asked the manager.

'No,' said Nicholas, shaking his head.

'Why, then, I'll tell you one,' said Mr. Crummles, throwing his pipe into the fire, and raising his voice. 'The stage.'

'The stage!' cried Nicholas, in a voice almost as loud.

'The theatrical profession,' said Mr. Vincent Crummles. 'I am in the theatrical profession myself, my wife is in the theatrical profession, my children are in the theatrical profession. I had a dog that lived and died in it from a puppy; and my chaise-pony goes on, in Timour the Tartar. I'll bring you out, and your friend too. Say the word. I want a novelty.'

'I don't know anything about it,' rejoined Nicholas, whose breath had been almost taken away, by this sudden proposal. 'I never acted a part in my life, except at school.'

'There's a genteel comedy in your walk and manner, juvenile tragedy in your eye, and touch-and-go farce in your laugh,' said Mr. Vincent Crummles. 'You'll do as well as if you had thought of nothing else but the lamps, from your birth downwards' (*Chapter 22*).

'We'll have a new show-piece out directly,' said the manager. 'Let me see – peculiar resources of this establishment – new and splendid scenery – you must manage to introduce a real pump and two washing-tubs.'

'Into the piece?' said Nicholas.

'Yes,' replied the manager. 'I bought 'em cheap, at a sale the other day, and they'll come in admirably. That's the London plan. They look up some dresses, and properties, and have a piece written to fit 'em. Most of the theatres keep an author on purpose.'

'Indeed!' cried Nicholas.

'Oh yes,' said the manager; 'a common thing. It'll look very well in the bills in separate lines – Real pump! – Splendid tubs! – Great attraction! You don't happen to be anything of an artist, do you?'

'That is not one of my accomplishments,' rejoined Nicholas.

'Ah! Then it can't be helped,' said the manager. 'If you had been, we might have had a large woodcut of the last scene for the posters, showing the whole depth of the stage, with the pump and tubs in the middle; but however, if you're not, it can't be helped' (*Chapter 22: Vincent Crummles and Nicholas Nickleby*).

The pony took his time upon the road, and – possibly in consequence of his theatrical education – evinced, every now and then, a strong inclination to lie down. However, Mr. Vincent Crummles kept him up pretty well, by jerking the rein, and plying the whip; and when these means failed, and the animal came to a stand, the elder Master Crummles got out and kicked him. By dint of these encouragements, he was persuaded to move from time to time, and they jogged on (as Mr. Crummles truly observed) very comfortably for all parties.

'He's a good pony at bottom,' said Mr. Crummles, turning to Nicholas.

He might has been at bottom, but he certainly was not at top, seeing that his coat was of the roughest and most ill-favoured kind. So, Nicholas merely observed that he shouldn't wonder if he was.

'Many and many is the circuit this pony has gone,' said Mr. Crummles, flicking him skilfully on the eyelid for old acquaintance' sake. 'He is quite one of us. His mother was on the stage.'

'Was she?' rejoined Nicholas.

'She ate apple-pie at a circus for upwards of fourteen years,' said the manager; 'fired pistols, and went to bed in a night-cap; and, in short, took the low comedy entirely. His father was a dancer.'

'Was he at all distinguished?'

'Not very,' said the manager. 'He was rather a low sort of pony. The fact is, he had been originally jobbed out by the day, and he never quite got over his old habits. He was clever in melodrama too, but too broad – too broad. When the mother died, he took the port-wine business.'

'The port-wine business!' cried Nicholas.

'Drinking port-wine with the clown,' said the manager; 'but he was greedy, and one night bit off the bowl of the glass, and choked himself, so his vulgarity was the death of him at last' (*Chapter 23*).

As Mrs. Vincent Crummles recrossed back to the table there bounded on to the stage from some mysterious inlet, a little girl in a dirty white frock with tucks up to the knees, short trousers, sandaled shoes, white spencer, pink gauze bonnet, green veil and curl-papers; who turned a pirouette, cut twice in the air, turned another pirouette, then, looking off at the opposite wing, shrieked, bounded forward to within six inches of the footlights, and fell into a beautiful attitude of terror, as a shabby gentleman in an old pair of buff slippers came in at one powerful slide, and chattering his teeth, fiercely brandished a walking-stick.

'They are going through the Indian Savage and the Maiden,' said Mrs. Crummles.

'Oh!' said the manager, 'the little ballet interlude. Very good, go on. A little this way, if you please, Mr. Johnson. That'll do. Now!'

The manager clapped his hands as a signal to proceed, and the savage, becoming ferocious, made a slide towards the maiden; but the maiden avoided him in six twirls, and came down, at the end of the last one, upon the very points of her toes. This seemed to make some impression upon the savage; for, after a little more ferocity and chasing of the maiden into corners, he began to relent, and stroked his face several times with his right thumb and four fingers, thereby intimating that he was struck with admiration of the maiden's beauty. Acting upon the impulse of this passion, he (the savage) began to hit himself severe thumps in the chest, and to exhibit other indications of being desperately in love, which being rather a prosy proceeding, was very likely the cause of the maiden's falling asleep; whether it was or no, asleep she did fall, sound as a church, on a sloping bank, and the savage perceiving it, leant his left ear on his left hand, and nodded sideways, to intimate to all whom it might concern that she *was* asleep, and no shamming. Being left to himself, the savage had a dance, all alone. Just as he left off, the maiden woke up, rubbed her eyes, got off the bank, and had a dance all alone too – such a dance that the savage looked on in ecstasy all the while, and when it was done, plucked from a neighbouring tree some botanical curiosity, resembling a small pickled cabbage, and offered it to the maiden, who at first wouldn't have it, but on the savage shedding tears relented. Then the savage jumped for joy; then the maiden jumped for rapture at the sweet smell of the pickled cabbage. Then the savage and the maiden danced violently together, and, finally, the savage dropped down on one knee, and the maiden stood on one leg upon his other knee; thus concluding the ballet, and leaving the spectators in a state of pleasing uncertainty, whether she would ultimately marry the savage, or return to her friends *(Chapter 23)*.

'You are welcome,' said Mrs. Crummles, turning round to Nicholas when they reached the bow-windowed front room on the first floor.

Nicholas bowed his acknowledgments, and was unfeignedly glad to see the cloth laid.

'We have but a shoulder of mutton with onion sauce,' said Mrs. Crummles, in the same charnel-house voice; 'but such as our dinner is, we beg you to partake of it.'

'You are very good,' replied Nicholas, 'I shall do it ample justice.'

'Vincent,' said Mrs. Crummles, 'what is the hour?'

'Five minutes past dinner-time,' said Mr. Crummles.

Mrs. Crummles rang the bell. 'Let the mutton and onion sauce appear' *(Chapter 23)*.

'Do you give lessons, ma'am?' inquired Nicholas.

'I do,' said Mrs. Crummles.

'There is no teaching here, I suppose!'

'There has been,' said Mrs. Crummles. 'I have received pupils here. I imparted tuition to the daughter of a dealer in ships' provision; but it afterwards appeared that she was insane when she first came to me. It was very extraordinary that she should come, under such circumstances' *(Chapter 23)*.

'I must have a dance of some kind, you know,' said Mr. Folair. 'You'll have to introduce one for the phenomenon, so you'd better make a *pas de deux,* and save time.'

'There's nothing easier than that,' said Mr. Lenville, observing the disturbed look of the young dramatist.

'Upon my word I don't see how it's to be done,' rejoined Nicholas.

'Why, isn't it obvious?' reasoned Mr. Lenville. 'Gadzooks, who can help seeing the way to do it? – you astonish me! You get the distressed lady, and the little child, and the attached servant, into the poor lodgings, don't you? – Well, look here. The distressed lady sinks into a chair, and buries her face in her pocket-handkerchief – "What makes you weep, mamma?" says the child. "Don't weep, mamma, or you'll make me weep too!" – "And me!" says the faithful servant, rubbing his eyes with his arm. "What can we do to raise your spirits, dear mamma?" says the little child. "Aye, what *can* we do?" says the faithful servant. "Oh, Pierre!" says the distressed lady; "would that I could shake off these painful thoughts." – "Try, ma'am, try," says the faithful servant; "rouse yourself, ma'am; be amused." – "I will," says the lady, "I will learn to suffer with fortitude. Do you remember that dance, my honest friend, which, in happier days, you practised with this sweet angel? It never failed to calm my spirits then. Oh! let me see it once again before I die!" – There it is – cue for the band, *before I die,* – and off they go. That's the regular thing; isn't it, Tommy?'

'That's it,' replied Mr. Folair. 'The distressed lady, overpowered by old recollections, faints at the end of the dance, and you close in with a picture' *(Chapter 24)*.

Hanging over the back of a chair was a half-finished muslin apron with little pockets ornamented with red ribbons, such as waiting-women wear on the stage, and (by consequence) are never seen with anywhere else. In one corner stood the diminutive pair of top-boots in which Miss Snevellicci was accustomed to enact the little jockey, and folded on a chair hard by, was a small parcel, which bore a very suspicious resemblance to the companion smalls.

But the most interesting object of all, was, perhaps, the open scrap-book, displayed in the midst of some theatrical duodecimos that were strewn upon the table; and pasted into which scrap-book were various critical notices of Miss Snevellicci's acting, extracted from different provincial journals, together with one poetic address in her honour, commencing –

> Sing, God of Love, and tell me in what dearth
> Thrice-gifted SNEVELLICCI came on earth,
> To thrill us with her smile, her tear, her eye,
> Sing, God of Love, and tell me quickly why.
>
> *(Chapter 24)*

Mr. Crummles unfolded a red poster, and a blue poster, and a yellow poster, at the top of each of which public notification was inscribed in enormous characters 'First appearance of the unrivalled Miss Petowker of the Theatre Royal, Drury Lane!'

'Dear me!' said Nicholas, 'I know that lady.'

'Then you are acquainted with as much talent as was ever compressed into one young person's body,' retorted Mr. Crummles, rolling up the bills again,' 'that is, talent of a certain sort – of a certain sort.

"The Blood Drinker," ' added Mr. Crummles with a prophetic sigh, ' "The Blood Drinker" will die with that girl; and she's the only sylph *I* ever saw, who could stand upon one leg, and play the tambourine on her other knee, *like* a sylph' *(Chapter 25)*.

'You don't quite know what Mrs. Crummles is, yet.'

Nicholas ventured to insinuate that he thought he did.

'No, no, you don't,' said Mr. Crummles; 'you don't, indeed. *I* don't, and that's fact. I don't think her country will, till she is dead. Some new proof of talent bursts from that astonishing woman every year of her life. Look at her, mother of six children, three of 'em alive, and all upon the stage!'

'Extraordinary!' cried Nicholas.

'Ah! extraordinary indeed,' rejoined Mr. Crummles, taking a complacent pinch of snuff, and shaking his head gravely. 'I pledge you my professional word I didn't even know she could dance till her last benefit, and then she played Juliet, and Helen Macgregor, and did the skipping-rope hornpipe between the pieces. The very first time I saw that admirable woman, Johnson,' said Mr. Crummles, drawing a little nearer, and speaking in the tone of confidential friendship, 'she stood upon her head on the butt-end of a spear, surrounded with blazing fireworks.'

'You astonish me!' said Nicholas.

'*She* astonished *me*!' returned Mr. Crummles, with a very serious countenance. 'Such grace, coupled with such dignity! I adored her from that moment!' *(Chapter 25)*.

'A – and how is Miss Nickleby?' said Lord Frederick. 'Well, I hope?'

'She is quite well, I'm obliged to you, my Lord,' returned Mrs. Nickleby, recovering. 'Quite well. She wasn't well for some days after that day she dined here, and I can't help thinking, that she caught cold in that hackney-coach coming home. Hackney-coaches, my lord, are such nasty things, that it's almost better to walk at any time, for although I believe a hackney-coachman can be transported for life, if he has a broken window, still they are so reckless, that they nearly all have broken windows. I once had a swelled face for six weeks, my lord, from riding in a hackney-coach – I think it was a hackney-coach,' said Mrs. Nickleby reflecting, 'though I'm not quite certain, whether it wasn't a chariot; at all events I know it was a dark green, with a very long number, beginning with a nought and ending with a nine – no, beginning with a nine, and ending with a nought, that was it, and of course the stamp-office people would know at once whether it was a coach or a chariot if any inquiries were made there – however that was, there it was with a broken window, and there was I for six weeks with a swelled face – I think that was the very same hackney-coach, that we found out afterwards, had the top open all the time, and we should never even have known it, if they hadn't charged us a shilling an hour extra for having it open, which it seems is the law, or was then, and a most shameful law it appears to be – I don't understand the subject, but I should say the Corn Laws could be nothing to *that* act of Parliament' *(Chapter 26)*.

'I had a cold once,' said Mrs. Nickleby, 'I think it was in the year eighteen hundred and seventeen; let me see, four and five are nine, and – yes, eighteen hundred and seventeen, that I thought I never should get rid of; actually and seriously, that I thought I never should get rid of. I was only cured at last by a remedy that I don't know whether you ever happened to hear of, Mr. Pluck. You have a gallon of water as hot as you can possibly bear it, with a pound of salt and sixpenn'orth of the finest bran, and sit with your head in it for twenty minutes every night just before going to bed; at least, I don't mean your head – your feet. It's a most extraordinary cure – a most extraordinary cure. I used it for the first time, I recollect, the day after Christmas Day, and by the middle of April following the cold was gone. It seems quite a miracle when you come to think of it, for I had it ever since the beginning of September' *(Chapter 27)*.

'Mrs. Wititterly is delighted,' said Mr. Wititterly, rubbing his hands; 'delighted, my lord, I am sure, with this opportunity of contracting an acquaintance which, I trust, my lord, we shall improve. Julia, my dear, you must not allow yourself to be too much excited, you must not. Indeed you must not. Mrs. Wititterly is of a most excitable nature, Sir Mulberry. The snuff of a candle, the wick of a lamp, the bloom on a peach, the down on a butterfly. You might blow her away, my lord; you might blow her away' *(Chapter 27)*.

'I take an interest, my lord,' said Mrs. Wititterly, with a faint smile, 'such an interest in the drama.'

'Ye-es. It's very interesting,' replied Lord Frederick.

'I'm always ill after Shakespeare,' said Mrs. Wititterly. 'I scarcely exist the next day; I find the reaction so very great after a tragedy, my lord, and Shakespeare is such a delicious creature.'

'Ye-es!' replied Lord Frederick. 'He was a clayver man.'

'Do you know, my lord,' said Mrs. Wititterly, after a long silence, 'I find I take so much more interest in his plays, after having been to that dear little dull house he was born in! Were you ever there, my lord?'

'No, nayver,' replied my lord.

'Then really you ought to go, my lord,' returned Mrs. Wititterly, in very languid and drawling accents. 'I don't know how it is, but after you've seen the place and written your name in the little book, somehow or other you seem to be inspired; it kindles up quite a fire within one' *(Chapter 27)*.

'I think there must be something in the place,' said Mrs. Nickleby, who had been listening in silence; 'for, soon after I was married, I went to Stratford with my poor dear Mr. Nickleby, in a post-chaise from Birmingham – was it a post-chaise though?' said Mrs. Nickleby, considering; 'yes, it must have been a post-chaise, because I recollect remarking at the time that the driver had a green shade over his left eye; – in a post-chaise from Birmingham, and after we had seen Shakespeare's tomb and birthplace, we went back to the inn there, where we slept that night, and I recollect that all night long I dreamt of nothing but a black gentleman, at full length, in plaster-of-Paris, with a lay-down collar tied with two tassels, leaning against a post and thinking; and when I woke in the morning and described him to Mr. Nickleby, he said it was Shakespeare just as he had been when he was alive, which was very curious indeed. Stratford – Stratford,' continued Mrs. Nickleby, considering. 'Yes, I am positive about that, because I recollect I was in the family way with my son Nicholas at the time, and I had been very much frightened by an Italian image boy that very morning. In fact, it was quite a mercy, ma'am,' added Mrs. Nickleby, in a whisper to Mrs. Wititterly, 'that my son didn't turn out to be a Shakespeare, and what a dreadful thing that would have been!' *(Chapter 27)*.

It was four in the afternoon – that is, the vulgar afternoon of the sun and the clock – and Mrs. Wititterly reclined, according to custom, on the drawing-room sofa, while Kate read aloud a new novel in three volumes, entitled 'The Lady Flabella,' which Alphonse the doubtful had procured from the library that very morning. And it was a production admirably suited to a lady labouring under Mrs. Wititterly's complaint, seeing that there was not a line in it, from beginning to end, which could, by the most remote contingency, awaken the smallest excitement in any person breathing.

Kate read on.

' "Cherizette," said the Lady Flabella, inserting her mouse-like feet in the blue satin slippers, which had unwittingly occasioned the half-playful, half-angry altercation between herself and the youthful Colonel Befillaire, in the Duke of Mincefenille's *salon de danse* on the previous night. *"Cherizette, ma chère, donnez-moi de l'eau de Cologne, s'il vous plaît, mon enfant."*

' *"Merci* – thank you," said the Lady Flabella, as the lively but devoted Cherizette, plentifully besprinkled with the fragrant compound the Lady Flabella's *mouchoir* of the finest cambric, edged with richest lace, and emblazoned at the four corners with the Flabella crest, and gorgeous heraldic bearing of that noble family; *"Merci* – that will do."

'At this instant, while the Lady Flabella yet inhaled that delicious fragrance by holding the *mouchoir* to her exquisite, but thoughtfully-chiselled nose, the door of the *boudoir* (artfully concealed by rich hangings of silken damask, the hue of Italy's firmament) was thrown open, and with noiseless tread two valets de chambre, clad in sumptuous liveries of peach-blossom and gold, advanced into the room followed by a page in *bas de soie* – silk stockings – who, while they remained at some distance making the most graceful obeisances, advanced to the feet of his lovely mistress, and dropping on one knee presented, on a golden salver gorgeously chased, a scented *billet*.

'The Lady Flabella, with an agitation she could not repress, hastily tore off the *envelope* and broke the scented seal. It *was* from Befillaire – the young, the slim, the low-voiced – *her own* Befillaire.'

'Oh, charming!' interrupted Kate's patroness, who was sometimes taken literally. 'Poetic, really. Read that description again, Miss Nickleby.'

Kate complied.

'Sweet, indeed!' said Mrs. Wititterly, with a sigh. 'So voluptuous, is it not? So soft?'

'Yes, I think it is,' replied Kate, gently; 'very soft' *(Chapter 28)*.

'Mrs. Wititterly,' said her husband, 'is Sir Tumley Snuffim's favourite patient. I believe I may venture to say, that Mrs. Wititterly is the first person who took the new medicine which is supposed to have destroyed a family at Kensington Gravel Pits. I believe she was. If I am wrong, Julia, my dear, you will correct me.'

'I believe I was,' said Mrs. Wititterly, in a faint voice.

As there appeared to be some doubt in the mind of his patron how he could best join in this conversation, the indefatigable Mr. Pyke threw himself into the breach, and, by way of saying something to the point, inquired – with reference to the aforesaid medicine – whether it was nice?

'No, sir, it was not. It had not even that recommendation,' said Mr. W.

'Mrs. Wititterly is quite a martyr,' observed Pyke, with a complimentary bow.

'I *think* I am,' said Mrs. Wititterly, smiling *(Chapter 28)*.

'Object of my scorn and hatred!' said Mr. Lenville, 'I hold ye in contempt.'

Nicholas laughed in very unexpected enjoyment of this performance; and the ladies, by way of encouragement, laughed louder than before; whereat Mr. Lenville assumed his bitterest smile, and expressed his opinion that they were 'minions.'

'But they shall not protect ye!' said the tragedian, taking an upward look at Nicholas, beginning at his boots and ending at the crown of his head, and then a downward one, beginning at the crown of his head, and ending at his boots – which two looks, as everybody knows, express defiance on the stage. 'They shall not protect ye – boy!'

Thus speaking, Mr. Lenville folded his arms, and treated Nicholas to that expression of face with which, in melodramatic performances, he was in the habit of regarding the tyrannical kings when they said, 'Away with him to the deepest dungeon beneath the castle moat;' and which, accompanied with a little jingling of fetters, had been known to produce great effects in its time *(Chapter 29)*.

'Then I am to make three last appearances, am I?' inquired Nicholas, smiling.

'Yes,' rejoined the manager, scratching his head with an air of some vexation; 'three is not enough, and it's very bungling and irregular not to have more, but if we can't help it we can't, so there's no use in talking. A novelty would be very desirable. You couldn't sing a comic song on the pony's back, could you?'

'No,' replied Nicholas, 'I couldn't indeed.'

'It has drawn money before now,' said Mr. Crummles, with a look of disappointment. 'What do you think of a brilliant display of fireworks?'

'That it would be rather expensive,' replied Nicholas, drily.

'Eighteenpence would do it,' said Mr. Crummles. 'You on the top of a pair of steps with the phenomenon in an attitude; "Farewell" on a transparency behind; and nine people at the wings with a squib in each hand – all the dozen and a half going off at once – it would be very grand – awful from the front, quite awful' (*Chapter 30*).

'So these are some of the stories they invent about us, and bandy from mouth to mouth!' thought Nicholas. 'If a man would commit an inexpiable offence against any society, large or small, let him be successful. They will forgive him any crime but that' (*Chapter 30*).

As they dashed by the quickly-changing and ever-varying objects, it was curious to observe in what a strange procession they passed before the eye. Emporiums of splendid dresses, the materials brought from every quarter of the world; tempting stores of everything to stimulate and pamper the sated appetite and give new relish to the oft-repeated feast; vessels of burnished gold and silver, wrought into every exquisite form of vase and dish, and goblet; guns, swords, pistols, and patent engines of destruction; screws and irons for the crooked, clothes for the newly-born, drugs for the sick, coffins for the dead, churchyards for the buried – all these jumbled each with the other and flocking side by side, seemed to flit by in motley dance like the fantastic groups of the old Dutch painter, and with the same stern moral for the unheeding restless crowd.

Nor were there wanting objects in the crowd itself to give new point and purpose to the shifting scene. The rags of the squalid ballad-singer fluttered in the rich light that showed the goldsmith's treasures; pale and pinched-up faces hovered about the windows where was tempting food; hungry eyes wandered over the profusion guarded by one thin sheet of brittle glass – an iron wall to them; half-naked shivering figures stopped to gaze at Chinese shawls and golden stuffs of India. There was a christening party at the largest coffin-maker's, and a funeral hatchment had stopped some great improvements in the bravest mansion. Life and death went hand in hand; wealth and poverty stood side by side; repletion and starvation laid them down together.

But it was London; and the old country lady inside, who had put her head out of the coach-window a mile or two on this side of Kensington, and had cried out to the driver that she was sure he must have passed it and forgotten to set her down, was satisfied at last (*Chapter 32*).

'What a demnition long time you have kept me ringing at this confounded old cracked tea-kettle of a bell, every tinkle of which is enough to throw a strong man into blue convulsions, upon my life and soul, oh demmit,' said Mr. Mantalini to Newman Noggs, scraping his boots as he spoke, on Ralph Nickleby's scraper.

'I didn't hear the bell more than once,' replied Newman.

'Then you are most immensely and outrigeously deaf,' said Mr. Mantalini, 'as deaf as a demnition post' (*Chapter 34*).

'Oh, you *are* here,' said Madame Mantalini, tossing her head.

'Yes, my life and soul, I am,' replied her husband, dropping on his knees, and pouncing with kitten-like playfulness upon a stray sovereign. 'I am here, my soul's delight, upon Tom Tiddler's ground, picking up the demnition gold and silver.'

'I am ashamed of you,' said Madame Mantalini, with much indignation.

'Ashamed? Of *me*, my joy? It knows it is talking demd charming sweetness, but naughty fibs,' returned Mr. Mantalini. 'It knows it is not ashamed of its own popolorum tibby.'

Whatever were the circumstances which had led to such a result, it certainly appeared as though the popolorum tibby had rather miscalculated, for the nonce, the extent of his lady's affection. Madame Mantalini only looked scornful in reply, and, turning to Ralph, begged him to excuse her intrusion.

'Which is entirely attributable,' said Madame, 'to the gross misconduct and most improper behaviour of Mr. Mantalini.'

'Of me, my essential juice of pine-apple!'

'Of you,' returned his wife. 'But I will not allow it. I will not submit to be ruined by the extravagance and profligacy of any man. I call Mr. Nickleby to witness the course I intend to pursue with you.'

'Pray don't call me to witness anything, ma'am,' said Ralph. 'Settle it between yourselves, settle it between yourselves.'

'No, but I must beg you as a favour,' said Madame Mantalini, 'to hear me give him notice of what is my fixed intention to do – my fixed intention, sir,' repeated Madame Mantalini, darting an angry look at her husband.

'Will she call me, "Sir"!' cried Mantalini. 'Me who dote upon her with the demdest ardour! She, who coils her fascinations round me like a pure and angelic rattlesnake! It will be all up with my feelings; she will throw me into a demd state' (*Chapter 34*).

'Demmit!' exclaimed Mr. Mantalini, opening his eyes at the sound of Ralph's voice, 'it is a horrid reality. She is sitting there before me. There is the graceful outline of her form; it cannot be mistaken – there is nothing like it. The two countesses had no outlines at all, and the dowager's was a demd outline. Why is she so excruciatingly beautiful that I cannot be angry with her, even now?'

'You have brought it upon yourself, Alfred,' returned Madame Mantalini – still reproachfully, but in a softened tone.

'I am a demd villain!' cried Mr. Mantalini, smiting himself on the head. 'I will fill my pockets with change for a sovereign in halfpence and drown myself in the Thames; but I will not be angry with her, even then, for I will put a note in the twopenny-post as I go along, to tell her where the body is. She will be a lovely widow. I shall be a body. Some handsome women will cry; she will laugh demnebly.'

'Alfred, you cruel, cruel creature,' said Madame Mantalini, sobbing at the dreadful picture.

'She calls me cruel – me – me – who for her sake will become a demd, damp, moist, unpleasant body!' exclaimed Mr. Mantalini (*Chapter 34*).

'You are the demdest, knowing hand,' replied Mr. Mantalini, in an admiring tone, 'the cunningest, rummest, superlativest old fox – oh dem! – to pretend now not to know that it was the little bright-eyed niece – the softest, sweetest, prettiest –'

'Alfred!' interposed Madame Mantalini.

'She is always right,' rejoined Mr. Mantalini soothingly, 'and when she says it is time to go, it is time, and go she shall; and when she walks along the streets with her own tulip, the women shall say with envy, she has got a demd fine husband; and the men shall say with rapture, he has got a demd fine wife; and they shall both be right and neither wrong, upon my life and soul – oh demmit!' *(Chapter 34)*.

'Why, this *is* a surprise!' said Ralph, bending his gaze upon the visitor, and half smiling as he scrutinised him attentively; 'I should know your face, Mr. Squeers.'

'Ah!' replied that worthy, 'and you'd have know'd it better sir, if it hadn't been for all that I've been a going through. Just lift that little boy off the tall stool in the back office, and tell him to come in here, will you, my man?' said Squeers, addressing himself to Newman. 'Oh, he's lifted his-self off! My son, sir, little Wackford. What do you think of him, sir, for a specimen of the Dotheboys Hall feeding? Ain't he fit to bust out of his clothes, and start the seams, and make the very buttons fly off with his fatness! Here's flesh!' cried Squeers, turning the boy about, and indenting the plumpest parts of his figure with divers pokes and punches, to the great discomposure of his son and heir. 'Here's firmness, here's solidness! Why, you can hardly get up enough of him between your finger and thumb to pinch him anywheres' *(Chapter 34:* Squeers and Ralph Nickleby).

'Have you quite recovered that scoundrel's attack?' asked Ralph.

'I've only just done it, if I've done it now,' replied Squeers. 'I was one blessed bruise, sir,' said Squeers, touching first the roots of his hair, and then the toes of his boots, 'from *here* to *there*. Vinegar and brown paper, vinegar and brown paper, from morning to night. I suppose there was a matter of half a ream of brown paper stuck upon me, from first to last. As I laid all of a heap in our kitchen, plastered all over, you might have thought I was a large brown-paper parcel, chock-full of nothing but groans. Did I groan loud, Wackford, or did I groan soft?' asked Mr. Squeers, appealing to his son.

Loud,' replied Wackford.

'Was the boys sorry to see me in such a dreadful condition, Wackford, or was they glad?' asked Mr. Squeers, in a sentimental manner.

'Gl –'

'Eh?' cried Squeers, turning sharp round.

'Sorry,' rejoined his son.

'Oh!' said Squeers, catching him a smart box on the ear. 'Then take your hands out of your pockets, and don't stammer when you're asked a question *(Chapter 34:* Ralph Nickleby and Squeers).

'Some bothering law business,' replied Squeers, scratching his head, 'connected with an action, for what they call neglect of a boy. I don't know what they would have. He had as good grazing, that boy had, as there is about us.'

Ralph looked as if he did not quite understand the observation.

'Grazing,' said Squeers, raising his voice, under the impression that as Ralph failed to comprehend him, he must be deaf. 'When a boy gets weak and ill and don't relish his meals, we give him a change of diet – turn him out, for an hour or so every day, into a neighbour's turnip-field, or sometimes, if it's a delicate case, a turnip-field and a piece of carrots alternately, and let him eat as many as he likes. There an't better land in the country than this perwerse lad grazed on, and yet he goes and catches cold and indigestion and what not, and then his friends brings a lawsuit against *me*! Now, you'd hardly suppose,' added Squeers, moving in his chair with the impatience of an ill-used man, 'that people's ingratitude would carry them quite as far as that; would you?' *(Chapter 34:* Squeers and Ralph Nickleby).

'You haven't got such a thing as twopence, Mr. Nickleby, have you?' said Squeers, rattling a bunch of keys in his coat pocket, and muttering something about its being all silver.

'I – think I have,' said Ralph, very slowly, and producing, after much rummaging in an old drawer, a penny, a halfpenny, and two farthings.

'Thankee,' said Squeers, bestowing it upon his son. 'Here! You go and buy a tart – Mr. Nickleby's man will show you where – and mind you buy a rich one. Pastry,' added Squeers, closing the door on Master Wackford, 'makes his flesh shine a good deal, and parents think that a healthy sign' *(Chapter 34)*.

After exhibiting every symptom of slow suffocation, in all its stages, and drinking about a tea-spoonful of water from a full tumbler, and spilling the remainder, Mrs. Nickleby *was* better, and remarked, with a feeble smile, that she was very foolish, she knew.

'It's a weakness in our family,' said Mrs. Nickleby, 'so, of course, I can't be blamed for it. Your gradmama, Kate, was exactly the same – precisely. The least excitement, the slightest surprise – she fainted away directly. I have heard her say, often and often, that when she was a young lady, and before she was married, she was turning a corner into Oxford Street one day, when she ran against her own hair-dresser who, it seems, was escaping from a bear; – the mere suddenness of the encounter made her faint away, directly. Wait, though,' added Mrs. Nickleby, pausing to consider, 'let me be sure I'm right. Was it her hair-dresser who had escaped from a bear, or was it a bear who had escaped from her hair-dresser's? I declare I can't remember just now, but the hair-dresser was a very handsome man, I know, and quite a gentleman in his manners; so that it has nothing to do with the point of the story' *(Chapter 35)*.

'I'm not coming an hour later in the morning, you know,' said Tim, breaking out all at once, and looking very resolute. 'I'm not going to sleep in the fresh air; no, nor I'm not going into the country either. A pretty thing at this time of day, certainly. Pho!'

293

'Damn your obstinacy, Tim Linkinwater,' said brother Charles, looking at him without the faintest spark of anger, and with a countenance radiant with attachment to the old clerk. 'Damn your obstinacy, Tim Linkinwater, what do you mean, sir?'

'It's forty-four year,' said Tim, making a calculation in the air with his pen, and drawing an imaginary line before he cast it up, 'forty-four year, next May, since I first kept the books of Cheeryble, Brothers. I've opened the safe every morning all that time (Sundays excepted) as the clock struck nine, and gone over the house every night at half-past ten (except on Foreign Post nights, and then twenty minutes before twelve) to see the doors fastened, and the fires out. I've never slept out of the back attic one single night. There's the same mignon-ette-box in the middle of the window, and the same four flower-pots, two on each side, that I brought with me when I first came. There an't – I've said it again and again, and I'll maintain it – there an't such a square as this in the world. I *know* there an't,' said Tim, with sudden energy, and looking sternly about him. 'Not one. For business or pleasure, in summer time or winter – I don't care which – there's nothing like it. There's not such a spring in England as the pump under the archway. There's not such a view in England as the view out of my window. I've seen it every morning before I shaved, and I ought to know something about it. I have slept in that room,' added Tim, sinking his voice a little, 'for four-and-forty year; and if it wasn't inconvenient, and didn't interfere with business, I should request leave to die there.'

'Damn you, Tim Linkinwater, how dare you talk about dying?' roared the twins by one impulse, and blowing their old noses violently (*Chapter 35:* Tim Linkinwater and the brothers Cheeryble).

'That girl grows more like her mother every day,' said Mr. Lumbey, suddenly stricken with an enthusiastic admiration of Morleena.

'There!' rejoined the married lady. 'What I always say; what I always did say! She's the very picter of her.' Having thus directed the general attention to the young lady in question, the married lady embraced the opportunity of taking another sip of brandy-and-water – and a pretty long sip too.

'Yes! there is a likeness,' said Mr. Kenwigs, after some reflection. 'But such a woman as Mrs. Kenwigs was, afore she was married! Good gracious, such a woman!'

Mr. Lumbey shook his head with great solemnity, as though to imply that he supposed she must have been rather a dazzler.

'Talk of fairies!' cried Mr. Kenwigs. '*I* never see anybody so light to be alive, never. Such manners too; so playful, and yet so sewerely proper! As for her figure! It isn't generally known,' said Mr. Kenwigs, dropping his voice; 'but her figure was such, at that time, that the sign of the Britannia over in the Holloway Road, was painted from it!' (*Chapter 36*).

'He desired me to give his kindest love,' said Nicholas.

'Very much obliged to him, I'm sure. Your great-uncle, Lillyvick, my dears,' interposed Mr. Kenwigs, condescendingly explaining it to the children.

'His kindest love,' resumed Nicholas; 'and to say that he had no time to write, but that he was married to Miss Petowker.'

Mr. Kenwigs started from his seat with a petrified stare, caught his second daughter by her flaxen tail, and covered his face with his pocket-handkerchief. Morleena fell, all stiff and rigid, into the baby's chair, as she had seen her mother fall when she fainted away, and the two remaining little Kenwigses shrieked in affright.

'My children, my defrauded, swindled infants!' cried Mr. Kenwigs, pulling so hard, in his vehemence, at the flaxen tail of his second daughter that he lifted her up on tiptoe, and kept her, for some seconds, in that attitude. 'Villain, ass, traitor!'

'Drat the man!' cried the nurse, looking angrily round. 'What does he mean by making that noise here?'

'Silence, woman!' said Mr. Kenwigs, fiercely.

'I won't be silent,' returned the nurse. 'Be silent yourself, you wretch. Have you no regard for your baby?'

'No!' returned Mr. Kenwigs.

'More shame for you,' retorted the nurse. 'Ugh! you unnatural monster.'

'Let him die,' cried Mr. Kenwigs, in the torrent of his wrath. 'Let him die! He has no expectations, no property to come into. We want no babies here,' said Mr. Kenwigs recklessly. 'Take 'em away, take 'em away to the Fondling!' (*Chapter 36*).

'The attentions,' said Mr. Kenwigs, looking around with a plaintive air, 'the attentions that I've shown to that man! The hyseters he has eat, and the pints of ale he has drank, in this house – !'

'It's very trying, and very hard to bear, we know,' said one of the married ladies; 'but think of your dear darling wife.'

'Oh yes, and what she's been a undergoing of, only this day,' cried a great many voices. 'There's a good man, do.'

'The presents that have been made to him,' said Mr. Kenwigs, reverting to his calamity, 'the pipes, the snuff-boxes – a pair of india-rubber goloshes, that cost six and six – '

'Ah! it won't bear thinking of, indeed,' cried the matrons generally; 'but it'll all come to him, never fear' (*Chapter 36*).

'Tim Linkinwater, sir,' said brother Charles; 'give me your hand, sir. This is your birthday. How dare you talk about anything else till you have been wished many happy returns of the day, Tim Linkinwater? God bless you, Tim! God bless you!'

'My dear brother,' said the other, seizing Tim's disengaged fist, 'Tim Linkinwater looks ten years younger than he did on his last birthday.'

'Brother Ned, my dear boy,' returned the other old fellow, 'I believe that Tim Linkinwater was born a hundred-and-fifty years old, and is gradually coming down to five-and-twenty; for he's younger every birthday than he was the year before.'

'So he is, brother Charles, so he is,' replied brother Ned. 'There's not a doubt about it.'

'Remember, Tim,' said brother Charles, 'that we

dine at half-past five to-day instead of two o'clock; we always depart from our usual custom on this anniversary, as you very well know, Tim Linkinwater. Mr. Nickleby, my dear sir, you will make one. Tim Linkinwater, give me your snuff-box as a remembrance to brother Charles and myself of an attached and faithful rascal, and take that, in exchange, as a feeble mark of our respect and esteem, and don't open it until you go to bed, and never say another word upon the subject, or I'll kill the blackbird. A dog! He should have had a golden cage half a dozen years ago, if it would have made him or his master a bit the happier. Now, brother Ned, my dear fellow, I'm ready. At half-past five, remember, Mr. Nickleby! Tim Linkinwater, sir, take care of Mr. Nickleby at half-past five. Now, brother Ned' (*Chapter 37:* The Cheeryble Brothers).

'People may say what they like,' observed Mrs. Nickleby, 'but there's a great deal of comfort in a night-cap, as I'm sure you would confess, Nicholas, my dear, if you would only have strings to yours, and wear it like a Christian, instead of sticking it upon the very top of your head like a blue-coat boy. You needn't think it an unmanly or quizzical thing to be particular about your night-cap, for I have often heard your poor dear papa, and the Reverend Mr. what's-his-name, who used to read prayers in that old church with the curious little steeple that the weathercock was blown off the night week before you were born, – I have often heard them say, that the young men at college are uncommonly particular about their night-caps, and that the Oxford night-caps are quite celebrated for their strength and goodness; so much so, indeed, that the young men never dream of going to bed without 'em, and I believe it's admitted on all hands that *they* know what's good, and don't coddle themselves' (*Chapter 37*).

'There can be no doubt,' said Mrs. Nickleby, 'that he *is* a gentleman, and has the manners of a gentleman, and the appearance of a gentleman, although he does wear smalls and grey worsted stockings. That may be eccentricity, or he may be proud of his legs. I don't see why he shouldn't be. The Prince Regent was proud of his legs, and so was Daniel Lambert, who was also a fat man; *he* was proud of his legs. So was Miss Biffin: she was – no,' added Mrs. Nickleby, correcting herself, 'I think she had only toes, but the principle is the same' (*Chapter 37*).

'My goodness me!' exclaimed Mrs. Nickleby, with a half-simper, 'suppose he was to go doing anything rash to himself. Could I ever be happy again, Nicholas?'

Despite his vexation and concern, Nicholas could scarcely help smiling, as he rejoined, 'Now, do you think, mother, that such a result would be likely to ensue from the most cruel repulse?'

'Upon my word, my dear, I don't know,' returned Mrs. Nickleby; 'really, I don't know. I am sure there was a case in the day before yesterday's paper, extracted from one of the French newspapers, about a journeyman shoe-maker who was jealous of a young girl in an adjoining village, because she wouldn't shut herself up in an air-tight three-pair of stairs, and charcoal herself to death with him; and who went and

hid himself in a Wood with a sharp-pointed knife, and rushed out, as she was passing by with a few friends, and killed himself first and then all the friends, and then her – no, killed all the friends first, and then herself, and them *him*self – which it is quite frightful to think of. Somehow or other,' added Mrs. Nickleby, after a momentary pause, 'they always *are* journeymen shoe-makers who do these things in France, according to the papers. I don't know how it is – something in the leather, I suppose' (*Chapter 37*).

Mr. Squeers related how, and in what manner, and when and where, he had picked up the runaway.

'It's clear that there has been a Providence in it, sir,' said Mr. Snawley, casting down his eyes with an air of humility, and elevating his fork, with a bit of lobster on the top of it, towards the ceiling.

'Providence is again him, no doubt,' replied Mr. Squeers, scratching his nose. 'Of course; that was to be expected. Anybody might have known that.'

'Hard-heartedness and evil-doing will never prosper, sir,' said Mr. Snawley.

'Never was such a thing known,' rejoined Squeers, taking a little roll of notes from his pocket-book, to see that they were all safe.

'I have been, Mrs. Snawley,' said Mr. Squeers, when he had satisfied himself upon this point, 'I have been that chap's benefactor, feeder, teacher, and clother. I have been that chap's classical, commercial, mathematical, philosophical, and trigonomical friend. My son – my only son, Wackford – has been his brother. Mrs. Squeers has been his mother, grandmother, aunt, – Ah! and I may say uncle too, all in one. She never cottoned to anybody, except them two engaging and delightful boys of yours, as she cottoned to this chap. What's my return? What's come of my milk of human kindness? It turns into curds and whey when I look at him' (*Chapter 38*).

Mystery and disappointment are not absolutely indispensable to the growth of love, but they are, very often, its powerful auxiliaries. 'Out of sight, out of mind,' is well enough as a proverb applicable to cases of friendship, though absence is not always necessary to hollowness of heart, even between friends, and truth and honesty, like precious stones, are perhaps most easily imitated at a distance, when the counterfeits often pass for real. Love, however, is very materially assisted by a warm and active imagination, which has a long memory, and will thrive for a considerable time on very slight and sparing food. Thus it is, that it often attains its most luxuriant growth in separation and under circumstances of the utmost difficulty (*Chapter 40*).

'Kate, my dear,' said Mrs. Nickleby; 'I don't know how it is, but a fine warm summer day like this, with the birds singing in every direction, always puts me in mind of roast pig, with sage and onion sauce, and made gravy.'

'That's a curious association of ideas, is it not, mamma?'

'Upon my word, my dear, I don't know,' replied Mrs. Nickleby. 'Roast pig; let me see. On the day five weeks after you were christened, we had a roast – no, that couldn't have been a pig, either, because I recollect there were a pair of them to carve, and your poor papa and I could never have thought of sitting down to two pigs – they must have been partridges. Roast pig! I hardly think we ever could have had one, now I come to remember, for your papa could never bear the sight of them in the shops, and used to say that they always put him in mind of very little babies, only the pigs had much fairer complexions; and he had a horror of little babies, too, because he couldn't very well afford any increase to his family, and had a natural dislike to the subject. It's very odd now, what can have put that in my head! I recollect dining once at Mrs. Bevan's, in that broad street round the corner by the coachmaker's, where the tipsy man fell through the cellar-flap of an empty house nearly a week before the quarter-day, and wasn't found till the new tenant went in – and we had roast pig there. It must be that, I think, that reminds me of it, especially as there was a little bird in the room that would keep on singing all the time of dinner – at least, not a little bird, for it was a parrot, and he didn't sing exactly, for he talked and swore dreadfully; but I think it must be that. Indeed I am sure it must. Shouldn't you say so, my dear?' *(Chapter 41)*.

'Suitors, my dear!' cried Mrs. Nickleby, with a smile of wonderful complacency. 'First and last, Kate, I must have had a dozen at least.'

'Mamma!' returned Kate, in a tone of remonstrance.

'I had indeed, my dear,' said Mrs. Nickleby; 'not including your poor papa, or a young gentleman who used to go, at that time, to the same dancing-school, and who *would* send gold watches and bracelets to our house in gilt-edged paper (which were always returned), and who afterwards unfortunately went out to Botany Bay in a cadet ship – a convict ship I mean – and escaped into a bush and killed sheep (I don't know how they got there), and was going to be hung, only he accidentally choked himself, and the government pardoned him. Then there was young Lukin,' said Mrs. Nickleby, beginning with her left thumb and checking off the names on her fingers – 'Mogley – Tipslark – Cabbery – Smifser – ' *(Chapter 41)*.

'Mamma!' cried Kate, really terrified for the moment, 'why do you stop, why do you lose an instant? Mamma, pray come in!'

'Kate, my dear,' returned her mother, still holding back, 'how can you be so foolish? I'm ashamed of you. How do you suppose you are ever to get through life if you're such a coward as this! What do you want, sir?' said Mrs. Nickleby, addressing the intruder with a sort of simpering displeasure. 'How dare you look into this garden?'

'Queen of my soul,' replied the stranger, folding his hands together, 'this goblet sip!'

'Nonsense, sir,' said Mrs. Nickleby. 'Kate, my love, pray be quiet.'

'Won't you sip the goblet?' urged the stranger, with his head imploringly on one side, and his right hand on his breast. 'Oh, do sip the goblet!'

'I shall not consent to do anything of the kind, sir,' said Mrs. Nickleby. 'Pray begone.'

'Why is it,' said the old gentleman, coming up a step higher, and leaning his elbows on the wall, with as much complacency as if he were looking out of a window, 'why is it that beauty is always obdurate, even when admiration is as honourable and respectful as mine?' Here he smiled, kissed his hand, and made several low bows. 'Is it owing to the bees, who, when the honey season is over, and they are supposed to have been killed with brimstone, in reality fly to Barbary and lull the captive Moors to sleep with their drowsy songs? Or is it,' he added, dropping his voice almost to a whisper, 'in consequence of the statue at Charing Cross having been lately seen, on the Stock Exchange at midnight, walking arm-in-arm with the Pump from Aldgate, in a riding-habit?' *(Chapter 41: Gentleman in Small-Clothes)*.

'Quite away?' said the gentleman, with a languishing look. 'Oh! quite away?'

'Yes,' returned Mrs. Nickleby, 'certainly. You have no business here. This is private property, sir; you ought to know that.'

'I do know,' said the old gentleman, laying his finger on his nose, with an air of familiarity, most reprehensible, 'that this is a sacred and enchanted spot, where the most divine charms' – here he kissed his hand and bowed again – 'waft mellifluousness over the neighbours' gardens, and force the fruit and vegetables into premature existence. That fact I am acquainted with. But will you permit me, fairest creature, to ask you one question, in the absence of the planet Venus, who has gone on business to the Horse Guards, and would otherwise – jealous of your superior charms – interpose between us?' *(Chapter 41: Gentleman in Small-Clothes)*.

'Are you a princess?'

'You are mocking me, sir,' replied Mrs. Nickleby, making a feint of retreating towards the house.

'No, but are you?' said the old gentleman.

'You know I am not, sir,' replied Mrs. Nickleby.

'Then are you any relation to the Archbishop of Canterbury?' inquired the old gentleman with great anxiety. 'Or to the Pope of Rome? Or the Speaker of the House of Commons? Forgive me, if I am wrong, but I was told you were niece to the Commissioners of Paving, and daughter-in-law to the Lord Mayor and Court of Common Council, which would account for your relationship to all three.'

'Whoever has spread such reports, sir,' returned Mrs. Nickleby, with some warmth, 'has taken great liberties with my name, and one which I am sure my son Nicholas, if he was aware of it, would not allow for an instant. The idea!' said Mrs. Nickleby, drawing herself up. 'Niece to the Commissioners of Paving!'

'Pray, mamma, come away!' whispered Kate.

' "Pray, mamma!" Nonsense, Kate,' said Mrs. Nickleby, angrily, 'but that's just the way. If they had said I was a niece to a piping bullfinch, what would you care! But I have no sympathy,' whimpered Mrs. Nickleby, 'I don't expect it, that's one thing.'

'Tears!' cried the old gentleman, with such an energetic jump, that he fell down two or three steps and grated his chin against the wall. 'Catch the crystal globules – catch 'em – bottle 'em up – cork 'em tight

– put sealing-wax on the top – seal 'em with a cupid – label 'em "Best quality" – and stow 'em away in the fourteen bin, with a bar of iron on the top to keep the thunder off!' *(Chapter 41:* Gentleman in Small-Clothes).

'I have estates, ma'am,' said the old gentleman, flourishing his right hand negligently, as if he made very light of such matters, and speaking very fast; 'jewels, light-houses, fish-ponds, a whalery of my own in the North Sea, and several oyster-beds of great profit in the Pacific Ocean. If you will have the kindness to step down to the Royal Exchange and to take the cocked hat off the stoutest beadle's head, you will find my card in the lining of the crown, wrapped up in a piece of blue paper. My walking-stick is also to be seen on application to the chaplain of the House of Commons, who is strictly forbidden to take any money for showing it. I have enemies about me, ma'am,' he looked towards his house and spoke very low, 'who attack me on all occasions, and wish to secure my property. If you bless me with your hand and heart, you can apply to the Lord Chancellor or call out the military if necessary – sending my toothpick to the commander-in-chief will be sufficient – and so clear the house of them before the ceremony is performed. After that, love bliss and rapture; rapture love and bliss. Be mine, be mine!' *(Chapter 41:* Gentleman in Small-Clothes).

'Be mine, be mine,' cried the old gentleman, 'Gog and Magog, Gog and Magog. Be mine, be mine!' *(Chapter 41:* Gentleman in Small-Clothes).

Mrs. Nickleby had scarcely finished speaking, when, to the great terror both of that lady and her daughter, he suddenly flung off his coat, and springing on the top of the wall, threw himself into an attitude which displayed his small clothes and grey worsteds to the fullest advantage, and concluded by standing on one leg, and repeating his favourite bellow with increased vehemence.

While he was still dwelling on the last note, and embellishing it with a prolonged flourish, a dirty hand was observed to glide stealthily and swiftly along the top of the wall, as if in pursuit of a fly, and then to clasp with the utmost dexterity one of the old gentleman's ankles. This done, the companion hand appeared, and clasped the other ankle.

Thus encumbered, the old gentleman lifted his legs awkwardly once or twice, as if they were very clumsy and imperfect pieces of machinery, and then looking down on his own side of the wall, burst into a loud laugh.

'It's you, is it?' said the old gentleman.

'Yes, it's me,' replied a gruff voice.

'How's the Emperor of Tartary?' said the old gentleman.

'Oh! he's much the same as usual,' was the reply. 'No better and no worse.'

'The young Prince of China,' said the old gentleman, with much interest. 'Is he reconciled to his father-in-law, the great potato salesman?'

'No,' answered the gruff voice; 'and he says he never will be, that's more.'

'If that's the case,' observed the old gentleman,

'perhaps I'd better come down' *(Chapter 41:* Gentleman in Small-Clothes).

'Do you know, Mr. Nickleby,' said Mrs. Browdie, with her archest smile, 'that I really think Fanny Squeers was very fond of you?'

'I am very much obliged to her,' said Nicholas; 'but, upon my word, I never aspired to making any impression upon her virgin heart.'

'How you talk!' tittered Mrs. Browdie. 'No, but do you know that really – seriously now and without any joking – I was given to understand by Fanny herself, that you had made an offer to her, and that you two were going to be engaged quite solemn and regular?'

'Was you, ma'am – was you?' cried a shrill female voice, 'was you given to understand that I – I – was going to be engaged to an assassinating thief that shed the gore of my pa? Do you – do you think, ma'am – that I was very fond of such dirt beneath my feet, as I couldn't condescend to touch with kitchen tongs, without blacking and crocking myself by the contract? Do you ma'am? Do you? Oh, base and degrading 'Tilda!' *(Chapter 42)*.

'This is the hend, is it?' continued Miss Squeers, who, being excited, aspirated her h's strongly; 'this is the hend, is it, of all my forbearance and friendship for that double-faced thing – that viper, that – that – mermaid?' (Miss Squeers hesitated a long time for this last epithet, and brought it out triumphantly at last, as if it quite clinched the business.) 'This is the hend, is it, of all my bearing with her deceitfulness, her lowness, her falseness, her laying herself out to catch the admiration of vulgar minds, in a way which made me blush for my – for my – '

'Gender,' suggested Mr. Squeers, regarding the spectators with a malevolent eye; literally *a* malevolent eye.

'Yes,' said Miss Squeers; 'but I thank my stars that my ma is of the same.'

'Hear, hear!' remarked Mr. Squeers; 'and I wish she was here to have a scratch at this company.'

'This is the hend, is it,' said Miss Squeers, tossing her head, and looking contemptuously at the floor, 'of my taking notice of that rubbishing creature, and demeaning myself to patronise her?' *(Chapter 42)*.

Is selfishness a necessary ingredient in the composition of that passion called love, or does it deserve all the fine things which poets, in the exercise of their undoubted vocation, have said of it? There are, no doubt, authenticated instances of gentlemen having given up ladies and ladies having given up gentlemen to meritorious rivals, under circumstances of great high-mindedness; but is it quite established that the majority of such ladies and gentlemen have not made a virtue of necessity, and nobly resigned what was beyond their reach; as a private soldier might register a vow never to accept the order of the Garter, or a poor curate of great piety and learning, but of no family – save a very large family of children – might renounce a bishopric? *(Chapter 43)*.

'Why, I don't believe now,' added Tim, taking off his spectacles, and smiling as with gentle pride, 'that there's such a place in all the world for coincidences as London is!'

'I don't know about that,' said Mr. Frank; 'but – '

'Don't know about it, Mr. Francis!' interrupted Tim, with an obstinate air. 'Well, but let us know. If there is any better place for such things, where is it? Is it in Europe? No, that it isn't. Is it in Asia? Why, of course it's not. Is it in Africa? Not a bit of it. Is it in America? *You* know better than that, at all events. Well, then,' said Tim, folding his arms resolutely, 'where is it?' (*Chapter 43:* Tim Linkinwater and Frank Cheeryble).

It is an exquisite and beautiful thing in our nature, that when the heart is touched and softened by some tranquil happiness or affectionate feeling, the memory of the dead comes over it most powerfully and irresistibly. It would almost seem as though our better thoughts and sympathies were charms, in virtue of which the soul is enabled to hold some vague and mysterious intercourse with the spirits of those whom we dearly loved in life. Alas! how often and how long may those patient angels hover above us, watching for the spell which is so seldom uttered, and so soon forgotten! (*Chapter 43*).

Pride is one of the seven deadly sins; but it cannot be the pride of a mother in her children, for that is a compound of two cardinal virtues – faith and hope (*Chapter 43*).

There are some men who, living with the one object of enriching themselves, no matter by what means, and being perfectly conscious of the baseness and rascality of the means which they will use every day towards this end, affect nevertheless – even to themselves – a high tone of moral rectitude, and shake their heads and sigh over the depravity of the world. Some of the craftiest scoundrels that ever walked this earth, or rather – for walking implies, at least, an erect position and the bearing of a man – that ever crawled and crept through life by its dirtiest and narrowest ways, will gravely jot down in diaries the events of every day, and keep a regular debtor and creditor account with Heaven, which shall always show a floating balance in their own favour. Whether this is a gratuitous (the only gratuitous) part of the falsehood and trickery of such men's lives, or whether they really hope to cheat Heaven itself, and lay up treasure in the next world by the same process which has enabled them to lay up treasure in this – not to question how it is, so it is. And, doubtless, such book-keeping (like certain autobiographies which have enlightened the world) cannot fail to prove serviceable, in the one respect of sparing the recording Angel some time and labour (*Chapter 44*).

'Nickleby,' said Mr. Mantalini in tears, 'you have been made a witness to this demnition cruelty, on the part of the demdest enslaver and captivator that never was, oh dem! I forgive that woman.'

'Forgive!' repeated Madame Mantalini, angrily.

'I do forgive her, Nickleby,' said Mr. Mantalini. 'You will blame me, the world will blame me, the women will blame me; everybody will laugh, and scoff, and smile, and grin most demnebly. They will say,

"She had a blessing. She did not know it. He was too weak; he was too good; he was a dem'd fine fellow, but he loved too strong; he could not bear her to be cross, and call him wicked names. It was a dem'd case, there never was a demder." But I forgive her' (*Chapter 44*).

'Be composed, sir,' said Ralph, with a gruff expression of sympathy; 'you have got him now.'

'Got him! Oh, haven't I got him! Have I got him, though?' cried Mr. Snawley, scarcely able to believe it. 'Yes, here he is, flesh and blood, flesh and blood.'

'Vary little flesh,' said John Browdie.

Mr. Snawley was too much occupied by his parental feelings to notice this remark; and, to assure himself more completely of the restoration of his child, tucked his head under his arm again, and kept it there.

'What was it,' said Snawley, 'that made me take such a strong interest in him, when that worthy instructor of youth brought him to my house? What was it that made me burn all over with a wish to chastise him severely for cutting away from his best friends, his pastors and masters?'

'It was parental instinct, sir,' observed Squeers.

'That's what it was, sir,' rejoined Snawley; 'the elevated feeling, the feeling of the ancient Romans and Grecians, and of the beasts of the field and birds of the air, with the exception of rabbits and tom-cats, which sometimes devour their offspring. My heart yearned towards him. I could have – I don't know what I couldn't have done to him in the anger of a father.'

'It only shows what Natur' is, sir,' said Mr. Squeers. 'She's a rum 'un, is Natur'.'

'She is a holy thing, sir,' remarked Snawley.

'I believe you,' added Mr. Squeers, with a moral sigh. 'I should like to know how we should ever get on without her. Natur',' said Mr. Squeers, solemnly, 'is more easier conceived than described. Oh what a blessed thing, sir, to be in a state of natur'!' (*Chapter 45*).

'My dear sir,' replied brother Charles, 'you fall into the very common mistake, of charging upon Nature, matters with which she has not the smallest connection, and for which she is in no way responsible. Men talk of nature as an abstract thing, and lose sight of what is natural while they do so. Here is a poor lad who has never felt a parent's care, who has scarcely known anything all his life but suffering and sorrow, presented to a man who he is told is his father, and whose first act is to signify his intention of putting an end to his short term of happiness, of consigning him to his old fate, and taking him from the only friend he has ever had – which is yourself. If Nature, in such a case, put into that lad's breast but one secret prompting which urged him towards his father and away from you, she would be a liar and an idiot. . . .

'The same mistake presents itself to me, in one shape or other, at every turn. Parents who never showed their love, complain of want of natural affection in their children; children who never showed their duty, complain of want of natural feeling in their parents; law-makers who find both so miserable that their affections have never had enough of life's sun to develop them, are loud in their moralisings over parents and children too, and cry that the very ties of nature are disregarded. Natural affections and instincts, my dear sir, are the most beautiful of the Almighty's works, but like other beautiful works of His, they must be reared and fostered, or it is as natural that they should be wholly obscured, and that new feelings should usurp their place, as it is that the sweetest productions of the earth, left untended, should be choked with weeds and briars. I wish we could be brought to consider this, and, remembering natural obligations a little more at the right time, talk about them a little less at the wrong one' (*Chapter 46: Charles Cheeryble*)

There is a dread disease which so prepares its victim, as it were, for death; which so refines it of its grosser aspect, and throws around familiar looks, unearthly indications of the coming change; a dread disease, in which the struggle between soul and body is so gradual, quiet, and solemn, and the result so sure, that day by day, and grain by grain, the mortal part wastes and withers away, so that the spirit grows light and sanguine with its lightening load, and, feeling immortality at hand, deems it but a new term of mortal life; a disease in which death and life are so strangely blended, that death takes the glow and hue of life, and life the gaunt and grisly form of death; a disease which medicine never cured, wealth never warded off, or poverty could boast exemption from; which sometimes moves in giant strides, and sometimes at a tardy sluggish pace, but, slow or quick, is ever sure and certain (*Chapter 49*).

'I hope,' said that lady, 'that this unaccountable conduct may not be the beginning of his taking to his bed and living there all his life, like the Thirsty Woman of Tutbury, or the Cock-lane Ghost, or some of those extraordinary creatures. One of them had some connection with our family. I forget, without looking back to some old letters I have upstairs, whether it was my great-grandfather who went to school with the Cock-lane Ghost, or the Thirsty Woman of Tutbury who went to school with my grandmother. Miss La Creevy, you know, of course. Which was it that didn't mind what the clergyman said? The Cock-lane Ghost, or the Thirsty Woman of Tutbury?'

'The Cock-lane Ghost, I believe.'

'Then I have no doubt,' said Mrs. Nickleby, 'that it was with him my great-grandfather went to school; for I know the master of his school was a Dissenter, and that would, in a great measure, account for the Cock-lane Ghost's behaving in such an improper manner to the clergyman when he grew up. Ah! Train up a Ghost – child, I mean – ' (*Chapter 49*).

Mrs. Nickleby, clasping her hands, uttered a sharp sound, something between a scream and an exclamation, and demanded to know whether the mysterious limbs were not clad in small-clothes and grey worsted stocking, or whether her eyes had deceived her?

'Yes,' cried Frank, looking a little closer. 'Small-clothes certainly, and – and – rough grey stockings, too. Do you know him, ma'am?'

'Kate, my dear,' said Mrs. Nickleby, deliberately sitting herself down in a chair with that sort of desperate resignation which seemed to imply that now matters had come to a crisis, and all disguise was useless, 'you will have the goodness, my love, to explain precisely how this matter stands. I have given him no encouragement – none whatever – not the least in the world. You know that, my dear, perfectly well. He was very respectful, exceedingly respectful, when he declared, as you were a witness to; still at the same time, if I am to be persecuted in this way, if vegetable what's-his-names and all kinds of garden-stuff are to strew my path out of doors, and gentlemen are to come choking up our chimneys at home, I really don't know – upon my word I do *not* know – what is to become of me. It's a very hard case – harder than anything I was ever exposed to, before I married your poor dear papa, though I suffered a good deal of annoyance then – but that, of course, I expected, and made up my mind for. When I was not nearly so old as you, my dear, there was a young gentleman who sat next us at church, who used, almost every Sunday, to cut my name in large letters in the front of his pew while the sermon was going on. It was gratifying, of course, naturally so, but still it was an annoyance, because the pew was in a very conspicuous place, and he was several times publicly taken out by the beadle for doing it. But that was nothing to this. This is a great deal worse, and a great deal more embarrassing. I would rather, Kate, my dear,' said Mrs. Nickleby, with great solemnity, and an effusion of tears: 'I would rather, I declare, have been a pig-faced lady, than exposed to such a life as this!' (*Chapter 49*).

'I am obliged to him, very much obliged to him, but I cannot listen to his addresses for a moment. It's quite impossible.'

While this address was in course of delivery, the old gentleman, with his nose and cheeks embellished with large patches of soot, sat upon the ground with his arms folded, eyeing the spectators in profound silence, and with a very majestic demeanour. He did not appear to take the smallest notice of what Mrs. Nickleby said, but when she ceased to speak he honoured her with a long stare, and inquired if she had quite finished?

'I have nothing more to say,' replied that lady modestly. 'I really cannot say anything more.'

'Very good,' said the old gentleman, raising his voice, 'then bring in the bottled lightning, a clean tumbler, and a corkscrew.'

Nobody executing this order, the old gentleman, after a short pause, raised his voice again and demanded a thunder sandwich. This article not being forthcoming either, he requested to be served with a fricassee of boot-tops and goldfish sauce, and then laughing heartily, gratified his hearers with a very long, very loud, and most melodious bellow (*Chapter 49: Gentleman in Small-Clothes*).

It happened that Miss La Creevy, finding her patient in no very threatening condition, and being strongly impelled by curiosity to see what was going forward, bustled into the room while the old gentleman was in the very act of bellowing. It happened, too, that the instant the old gentleman saw her, he stopped short, skipped suddenly on his feet, and fell to kissing his hand violently: a change of demeanour which almost terrified the little portrait-painter out of her senses, and caused her to retreat behind Tim Linkinwater with the utmost expedition.

'Aha!' cried the old gentleman, folding his hands, and squeezing them with great force against each other. 'I see her now, I see her now! My love, my life, my bride, my peerless beauty. She is come at last – at last – and all is gas and gaiters!'

Mrs. Nickleby looked rather disconcerted for a moment, but immediately recovering, nodded to Miss La Creevy and the other spectators several times, and frowned, and smiled gravely; giving them to understand that she saw where the mistake was, and would set it all to rights in a minute or two.

'She is come!' said the old gentleman, laying his hand upon his heart. 'Cormoran and Blunderbore! She is come! All the wealth I have is hers if she will take me for her slave. Where are grace, beauty, and blandishments, like those? In the Empress of Madagascar? No. In the Queen of Diamonds? No. In Mrs. Rowland, who every morning bathes in Kalydor for nothing? No. Melt all these down into one, with the three Graces, the nine Muses, and fourteen biscuit-bakers' daughters from Oxford Street, and make a woman half as lovely. Pho! I defy you' *(Chapter 49)*.

The two shots were fired, as nearly as possible, at the same instant. In that instant, the young lord turned his head sharply round, fixed upon his adversary a ghastly stare, and, without a groan or stagger, fell down dead.

'He's gone!' cried Westwood, who, with the other second, had run up to the body, and fallen on one knee beside it.

'His blood on his own head,' said Sir Mulberry. 'He brought this upon himself, and forced it upon me.'

'Captain Adams,' cried Westwood, hastily, 'I call you to witness that this was fairly done. Hawk, we have not a moment to lose. We must leave this place immediately, push for Brighton, and cross to France with all speed. This has been a bad business, and may be worse, if we delay a moment. Adams, consult your own safety, and don't remain here; the living before the dead. Good-bye!'

With these words, he seized Sir Mulberry by the arm, and hurried him away. Captain Adams – only pausing to convince himself, beyond all question, of the fatal result – sped off in the same direction, to concert measures with his servant for removing the body, and securing his own safety likewise.

So died Lord Frederick Verisopht, by the hand which he had loaded with gifts, and clasped a thousand times; by the act of him, but for whom, and others like him, he might have lived a happy man, and died with children's faces round his bed.

The sun came proudly up in all his majesty, the noble river ran its winding course, the leaves quivered and rustled in the air, the birds poured their cheerful songs from every tree, the short-lived butterfly fluttered its little wings; all the light and life of day came on; and, amidst it all, and pressing down the grass whose every blade bore twenty tiny lives, lay the dead man, with his stark and rigid face turned upward to the sky *(Chapter 50)*.

'Is anything the matter?' said Newman Noggs.

'Matter, sir!' cried Mr. Lillyvick. 'The plug of life is dry, sir, and but the mud is left.'

This speech – the style of which Newman attributed to Mr. Lillyvick's recent association with theatrical characters – not being quite explanatory, Newman looked as if he were about to ask another question, when Mr. Lillyvick prevented him by shaking his hand mournfully, and then waving his own.

'Let me be shaved!' said Mr. Lillyvick. 'It shall be done before Morleena; it *is* Morleena, isn't it?'

'Yes,' said Newman.

'Kenwigses have got a boy, haven't they?' inquired the collector.

Again Newman said 'Yes.'

'Is it a nice boy?' demanded the collector.

'It an't a very nasty one,' returned Newman, rather embarrassed by the question.

'Susan Kenwigs used to say,' observed the collector, 'that if ever she had another boy, she hoped it might be like me. Is this one like me, Mr. Noggs?'

This was a puzzling inquiry; but Newman evaded it, by replying to Mr. Lillyvick, that he thought the baby might possibly come like him in time.

'I should be glad to have somebody like me, somehow,' said Mr. Lillyvick, 'before I die.' *(Chapter 52)*.

Mr. Lillyvick said in a faltering voice –

'I never shall ask anybody here to receive my – I needn't mention the word; you know what I mean. Kenwigs and Susan, yesterday was a week she eloped with a half-pay captain!'

Mr. and Mrs. Kenwigs started together.

'Eloped with a half-pay captain,' repeated Mr. Lillyvick. 'Basely and falsely eloped with a half-pay captain. With a bottle-nosed captain, that any man might have considered himself safe from. It was in this room,' said Mr. Lillyvick, looking sternly round, 'that I first see Henrietta Petowker. It is in this room that I turn her off, for ever' *(Chapter 52)*.

'I know you have had great experience, dear mamma,' said Kate; 'I mean that perhaps you don't quite understand all the circumstances in this instance. We have stated them awkwardly, I dare say.'

'That I dare say you have,' retorted her mother, briskly. 'That's very likely. I am not to be held accountable for that; though, at the same time, as the circumstances speak for themselves, I shall take the liberty, my love, of saying that I do understand them, and perfectly well too; whatever you and Nicholas may choose to think to the contrary. Why is such a great fuss made because this Miss Magdalen is going to marry somebody who is older than herself? Your poor papa was older than I was, four years and a half older. Jane Dibabs – the Dibabses lived in the beautiful little thatched white house one story high, covered all over with ivy and creeping plants, with an exquisite little porch with twining honeysuckles and all sorts of things: where the earwigs used to fall into one's tea on a summer evening, and always fell upon their backs and kicked dreadfully, and where the frogs used to get into the rushlight shades when one stopped all night, and sit up and look through the little holes like Christians – Jane Dibabs, *she* married a man who was a great deal older than herself, and *would* marry him, notwithstanding all that could be said to the contrary, and she was so fond of him that nothing was ever equal to it' (*Chapter 55*: Mrs. Nickleby).

Nicholas snuffed the candles, put his hands in his pockets, and, leaning back in his chair, assumed a look of patient suffering and melancholy resignation.

'I think it my duty, Nicholas, my dear,' resumed his mother, 'to tell you what I know; not only because you have a right to know it too, and to know everything that happens in this family, but because you have it in your power to promote and assist the thing very much; and there is no doubt that the sooner one can come to a clear understanding on such subjects, it is always better, every way. There are a great many things you might do; such as taking a walk in the garden sometimes, or sitting upstairs in your own room for a little while, or making believe to fall asleep occasionally, or pretending that you recollected some business, and going out for an hour or so, and taking Mr. Smike with you. These seem very slight things, and I dare say you will be amused at my making them of so much importance, at the same time, my dear, I can assure you (and you'll find this out, Nicholas, for yourself one of these days, if you ever fall in love with anybody: as I trust and hope you will, provided she is respectable and well-conducted, and of course you'd never dream of falling in love with anybody who was not), I say, I can assure you that a great deal more depends upon these little things, than you would suppose possible. If your poor papa was alive, he would tell you how much depended on the parties being left alone. Of course, you are not to go out of the room as if you meant it and did it on purpose, but as if it was quite an accident, and to come back again in the same way. If you cough in the passage before you open the door, or whistle carelessly, or hum a tune, or something of that sort to let them know you're coming, it's always better; because, of course, though it's not only natural but perfectly correct and proper under the circumstances, still it is very confusing if you interrupt young people when they are – when they are sitting on the sofa, and – and all that sort of thing; which is very nonsensical perhaps, but still they will do it' (*Chapter 55*: Mrs. Nickleby).

A letter lay on his table. He let it lie there, for some time, as if he had not the courage to open it, but at length did so and turned deadly pale.

'The worst has happened,' he said, 'the house has failed. I see. The rumour was abroad in the City last night, and reached the ears of those merchants. Well, well!'

He strode violently up and down the room and stopped again.

'Ten thousand pounds! And only lying there for a day – for one day! How many anxious years, how many pinching days and sleepless nights, before I scraped together that ten thousand pounds! – Ten thousand pounds! How many proud painted dames would have fawned and smiled, and how many spend-thrift blockheads done me lip-service to my face and cursed me in their hearts, while I turned that ten thousand pounds into twenty! While I ground, and pinched, and used these needy borrowers for my pleasure and profit, what smooth-tongued speeches, and courteous looks, and civil letters, they would have given me! The cant of the lying world is, that men like me compass our riches by dissimulation and treachery: by fawning, cringing, and stooping. Why, how many lies, what mean evasions, what humbled behaviour from upstarts who, but for my money, would spurn me aside as they do their betters every day, would that ten thousand pounds have brought me in! Grant that I had doubled it – made cent. per cent. – for every sovereign told another – there would not be one piece of money in all the heap which wouldn't represent ten thousand mean and paltry lies, told, not by the money-lender, oh no! but by the money-borrowers, your liberal thoughtless generous dashing folks, who wouldn't be so mean as save a sixpence for the world!' (*Chapter 56*: Ralph Nickleby).

Making a halt in his reflections at this place, Mr. Squeers again put his glass to his lips, and drawing a dirty letter from his pocket, proceeded to con over its contents with the air of a man who had read it very often, and who now refreshed his memory rather in the absence of better amusement than for any specific information.

'The pigs is well,' said Mr. Squeers, 'the cows is well, and the boys is bobbish. Young Sprouter has been a winking, has he? I'll wink him when I get back. "Cobbey would persist in sniffing while he was a eating his dinner, and said that the beef was so strong it made him." – Very good, Cobbey, we'll see if we can't make you sniff a little without beef. "Pitcher was took with another fever," – of course he was – "and being fetched by his friends, died the day after he got home," – of course he did, and out of aggravation; it's part of a deep-laid system. There an't another chap in the school but that boy as would have died exactly at the end of the quarter: taking it out of me to the very last, and then carrying his spite to the utmost extremity. "The juniorest Palmer said he wished he was in Heaven." I really don't know, I do *not* know what's to be done with that young fellow; he's always a wishing something horrid. He said, once, he wished he was a donkey, because then he wouldn't have a father as didn't love him! Pretty wicious that for a child of six!' (*Chapter 57*).

Mr. Squeers drew a stool to the fire, and placing himself over against her, and the bottle and glass on the floor between them, roared out again very loud –

'Well, my Slider!'

I hear you,' said Peg, receiving him graciously.

'I've come according to promise,' roared Squeers.

'So they used to say in that part of the country I come from,' observed Peg, complacently, 'but I think oil's better.'

'Better than what?' roared Squeers, adding some rather strong language in an undertone.

'No,' said Peg, 'of course not.'

'I never saw such a monster as you are!' muttered Squeers, looking as amiable as he possibly could, the while; for Peg's eye was upon him, and she was chuckling fearfully, as though in delight at having made a choice repartee (*Chapter 57:* Peg Sliderskew).

'What's the reason,' said Mr. Squeers, deriving fresh facetiousness from the bottle; 'what's the reason of rheumatics? What do they mean? What do people have 'em for – eh?'

Mrs. Sliderskew didn't know, but suggested that it was possibly because they couldn't help it.

'Measles, rheumatics, hooping-cough, fevers, agers, and lumbagers,' said Mr. Squeers, 'is all philosophy together; that's what it is. The heavenly bodies is philosophy, and the earthly bodies is philosophy. If there's a screw loose in a heavenly body, that's philosophy; and if there's a screw loose in a earthly body, that's philosophy too; or it may be that sometimes there's a little metaphysics in it, but that's not often. Philosophy's the chap for me. If a parent asks a question in the classical, commercial, or mathematical line, says I, gravely, "Why, sir, in the first place, are you a philosopher?" – "No, Mr. Squeers," he says, "I an't." "Then, sir," says I, "I am sorry for you, for I shan't be able to explain it." Naturally, the parent goes away and wishes he was a philosopher, and, equally naturally, thinks I'm one' (*Chapter 57*).

'This,' said Squeers, 'is a bundle of overdue acceptances and renewed bills of six or eight young gentlemen; but they're all M.P.'s, so it's of no use to anybody. Throw it in the fire!'

Peg did as she was bidden, and waited for the next.

'This,' said Squeers, 'seems to be some deed of sale of the right of presentation to the rectory of Purechurch, in the valley of Cashup. Take care of that, Slider, literally for God's sake. It'll fetch its price at the Auction Mart.'

'What's the next?' inquired Peg.

'Why, this,' said Squeers, 'seems, from the two letters that's with it, to be a bond from a curate down in the country, to pay half a year's wages of forty pound for borrowing twenty. Take care of that; for if he don't pay it, his bishop will very soon be down upon him. We know what the camel and the needle's eye means; no man as can't live upon his income, whatever it is, must expect to go to heaven at any price' (*Chapter 57*).

'I say, young fellow, you've been and done it now; you have!'

'What's the matter with your head?' asked Ralph.

'Why, your man, your informing kidnapping man, has been and broke it,' rejoined Squeers sulkily; 'that's what's the matter with it. You've come at last, have you?'

'Why have you not sent to me?' said Ralph. 'How could I come till I knew what had befallen you?'

'My family!' hiccupped Mr. Squeers, raising his eye to the ceiling; 'my daughter, as is at that age when all the sensibilities is a coming out strong in blow – my son as is the young Norval of private life, and the pride and ornament of a doting willage – here's a shock for my family! The coat of arms of the Squeerses is tore, and their sun is gone down into the ocean wave!' (*Chapter 60*).

'Ah!' sighed Squeers, who, between the brandy-and-water and his broken head, wandered strangely, 'at the delightful village of Dotheboys near Greta Bridge in Yorkshire, youth are boarded, clothed, booked, washed, furnished with pocket-money, provided with all necessaries, instructed in all languages living and dead, mathematics, orthography, geometry, astronomy, trigonometry – this is a altered state of trigonomics, this is! A double 1 – all, everything – a cobbler's weapon. U-p-up, adjective, not down. S-q-u-double e-r-s-Squeers, noun substantive, a educator of youth. Total, all up with Squeers!' (*Chapter 60*).

'My moral influence with them lads,' added Mr. Squeers, with deeper gravity, 'is a tottering to its basis. The images of Mrs. Squeers, my daughter, and my son Wackford, all short of vittles, is perpetually before me; every other consideration melts away and vanishes, in front of these; the only number in all arithmetic that I know of, as a husband and a father, is number one, under this here most fatal go!' (*Chapter 60*).

'I am sure,' said Mrs. Nickleby, wiping her eyes, and sobbing bitterly, 'I have lost the best, the most zealous, and most attentive creature, that has ever been a companion to me in my life – putting you, my dear Nicholas, and Kate, and your poor papa, and that well-behaved nurse who ran away with the linen and the twelve small forks, out of the question, of course' (*Chapter 61*).

Ralph Nickleby left the City behind him and took the road to his own home.

The night was dark, and a cold wind blew, driving the clouds furiously and fast before it. There was one black gloomy mass that seemed to follow him: not hurrying in the wild chase with the others, but lingering sullenly behind, and gliding darkly and stealthily on. He often looked back at this, and, more than once, stopped to let it pass over; but, somehow, when he went forward again, it was still behind him, coming mournfully and slowly up, like a shadowy funeral train.

He had to pass a poor, mean burial-ground – a dismal place, raised a few feet above the level of the street, and parted from it by a low parapet-wall and an iron railing; a rank, unwholesome, rotten spot, where the very grass and weeds seemed, in their frowsy growth, to tell that they had sprung from paupers' bodies, and had struck their roots in the graves of men, sodden, while alive, in steaming courts and drunken hungry dens. And here, in truth, they lay, parted from the living by a little earth and a board or two – lay thick and close – corrupting in body as they had in mind – a dense and squalid crowd. Here they lay, cheek by jowl with life: no deeper down than the feet of the throng that passed there, every day, and piled high as their throats. Here they lay, a grisly family all these dear departed brothers and sisters of the ruddy clergyman who did his task so speedily when they were hidden in the ground! (*Chapter 62*).

The dead boy's love for Nicholas, and the attachment of Nicholas to him, was insupportable agony. The picture of his death-bed, with Nicholas at his side, tending and supporting him, and he breathing out his thanks and expiring in his arms, when he would have had them mortal enemies and hating each other to the last, drove him frantic. He gnashed his teeth, and smote the air, and looking wildly round, with eyes which gleamed through the darkness, cried aloud –

'I am trampled down and ruined. The wretch told me true. The night has come! Is there no way to rob them of further triumph, and spurn their mercy and compassion? Is there no Devil to help me?'

Swiftly, there glided again into his brain the figure he had raised that night. It seemed to lie before him. The head was covered now. So it was when he first saw it. The rigid upturned marble feet too, he remembered well. Then came before him, the pale and trembling relatives who had told their tale upon the inquest – the shrieks of women – the silent dread of men – the consternation and disquiet – the victory achieved by that heap of clay, which, with one motion of its hand, had let out the life and made this stir among them –

He spoke no more; but, after a pause, softly groped his way out of the room, and up the echoing stairs – up to the top – to the front garret – where he closed the door behind him, and remained.

It was a mere lumber-room now, but it yet contained an old dismantled bedstead; the one on which his son had slept; for no other had ever been there. He avoided it hastily, and sat down as far from it as he could.

The weakened glare of the lights in the street below, shining through the window which had no blind or curtain to intercept it, was enough to show the character of the room, though not sufficient fully to reveal the various articles of lumber, old corded trunks and broken furniture, which were scattered about. It had a shelving roof; high in one part, and at another descending almost to the floor. It was towards the highest part, that Ralph directed his eyes; and upon it he kept them fixed steadily for some minutes. Then he rose, and dragging thither an old chest upon which he had been seated, mounted on it, and felt along the wall above his head with both hands. At length, they touched a large iron hook, firmly driven into one of the beams (*Chapter 62:* Ralph Nickleby).

He listened to the man's retreating footsteps until the sound had passed, and then, gazing up into the sky, saw, or thought he saw, the same black cloud that had seemed to follow him home, and which now appeared to hover directly above the house.

'I know its meaning now,' he muttered, 'and the restless nights, the dreams, and why I have quailed of late. All pointed to this. Oh! if men by selling their own souls could ride rampant for a term, for how short a term would I barter mine to-night!'

The sound of a deep bell came along the wind. One.

'Lie on!' cried the usurer, 'with your iron tongue! Ring merrily for births that make expectants writhe, and for marriages that are made in hell, and toll ruefully for the dead whose shoes are worn already! Call men to prayers who are godly because not found out, and ring chimes for the coming in of every year that brings this cursed world nearer to its end. No bell or book for me! Throw me on a dunghill, and let me rot there, to infect the air!'

With a wild look around, in which frenzy, hatred, and despair, were horribly mingled, he shook his clenched hand at the sky above him, which was still dark and threatening, and closed the window.

The rain and hail pattered against the glass; the chimneys quaked and rocked; the crazy casement rattled with the wind, as though an impatient hand inside were striving to burst it open. But no hand was there, and it opened no more (*Chapter 62:* Ralph Nickleby).

'You nasty, idle, vicious, good-for-nothing brute,' cried the woman, stamping on the ground, 'why don't you turn the mangle?'

'So I am, my life and soul!' replied a man's voice. 'I am always turning. I am perpetually turning, like a demd old horse in a demnition mill. My life is one demd horrid grind!'

'Then why don't you go and list for a soldier?' retorted the woman, 'you're welcome to.'

'For a soldier!' cried the man. 'For a soldier! Would his joy and gladness see him in a coarse red coat with a little tail? Would she hear of his being slapped and beat by drummers demnebly? Would she have him fire off real guns, and have his hair cut, and his whiskers shaved, and his eyes turned right and left, and his trousers pipeclayed?' (*Chapter 64:* Laundry Woman and Mantalini).

'You're never to be trusted,' screamed the woman, 'you were out all day yesterday, and gallivanting somewhere I know. You know you were! Isn't it enough that I paid two pound fourteen for you, and took you out of prison and let you live here like a gentleman, but must you go on like this: breaking my heart besides?'

'I will never break its heart, I will be a good boy, and never do so any more; I will never be naughty again; I beg its little pardon,' said Mr. Mantalini, dropping the handle of the mangle, and folding his palms together, 'it is all up with its handsome friend! He has gone to the demnition bow-wows. It will have pity? It will not scratch and claw, but pet and comfort? Oh demmit' (*Chapter 64:* Laundry Woman and Mantalini).

SKETCHES OF YOUNG COUPLES

It not only appeared that the egotistical couple knew everybody, but that scarcely any event of importance or notoriety had occurred for many years with which they had not been in some way or other connected. Thus we learned that when the well-known attempt upon the life of George the Third was made by Hatfield in Drury lane theatre, the egotistical gentleman's grandfather sat upon his right hand and was the first man who collared him; and that the egotistical lady's aunt, sitting within a few boxes of the royal party, was the only person in the audience who heard his Majesty exclaim, 'Charlotte, Charlotte, don't be frightened, don't be frightened; they're letting off squibs, they're letting off squibs.' When the fire broke out, which ended in the destruction of the two Houses of Parliament, the egotistical couple, being at the time at a drawing-room window on Blackheath, then and there simultaneously exclaimed, to the astonishment of a whole party – 'It's the House of Lords!' ('The Egotistical Couple').

To those young ladies and gentlemen who are yet revolving singly round the church, awaiting the advent of that time when the mysterious laws of attraction shall draw them towards it in couples, we are desirous of addressing a few last words.

Before marriage and afterwards, let them learn to centre all their hopes of real and lasting happiness in their own fireside; let them cherish the faith that in home, and all the English virtues which the love of home engenders, lies the only true source of domestic felicity; let them believe that round the household gods, contentment and tranquillity cluster in their gentlest and most graceful forms; and that many weary hunters of happiness through the noisy world, have learnt this truth too late, and found a cheerful spirit and a quiet mind only at home at last ('Conclusion').

MASTER HUMPHREY'S CLOCK

I live in a venerable suburb of London, in an old house which in bygone days was a famous resort for merry roysterers and peerless ladies, long since departed. It is a silent, shady place, with a paved courtyard so full of echoes, that sometimes I am tempted to believe that faint responses to the noises of old times linger there yet, and that these ghosts of sound haunt my footsteps as I pace it up and down. I am the more confirmed in this belief, because, of late years, the echoes that attend my walks have been less loud and marked than they were wont to be; and it is pleasanter to imagine in them the rustling of silk brocade, and the light step of some lovely girl, than to recognise in their altered note the failing tread of an old man (*Chapter 1:* Master Humphrey).

Well, well, – all these sorrows are past. My glancing at them may not be without its use, for it may help in some measure to explain why I have all my life been attached to the inanimate objects that people my chamber, and how I have come to look upon them rather in the light of old and constant friends, than as mere chairs and tables which a little money could replace at will.

Chief and first among all these is my Clock, – my old, cheerful, companionable Clock. How can I ever convey to others an idea of the comfort and consolation that this old Clock has been for years to me!

It is associated with my earliest recollections. It stood upon the staircase at home (I call it home still mechanically), nigh sixty years ago. I like it for that; but it is not on that account, nor because it is a quaint old thing in a huge oaken case curiously and richly carved, that I prize it as I do. I incline to it as if it were alive, and could understand and give me back the love I bear it.

And what other thing that has not life could cheer me as it does? what other thing that has not life (I will not say how few things that have) could have proved the same patient, true, untiring friend? How often

have I sat in the long winter evenings feeling such society in its cricket-voice, that raising my eyes from my book and looking gratefully towards it, the face reddened by the glow of the shining fire has seemed to relax from its staid expression and to regard me kindly! how often in the summer twilight, when my thoughts have wandered back to a melancholy past, have its regular whisperings recalled them to the calm and peaceful present! how often in the dead tranquillity of night has its bell broken the oppressive silence, and seemed to give me assurance that the old clock was still a faithful watcher at my chamber-door! My easy-chair, my desk, my ancient furniture, my very books, I can scarcely bring myself to love even these last like my old clock (*Chapter 1:* Master Humphrey).

I have said that retirement has become a habit with me. When I add, that the deaf gentleman and I have two friends, I communicate nothing which is inconsistent with that declaration. I spend many hours of every day in solitude and study, have no friends or change of friends but these, only see them at stated periods, and am supposed to be of a retired spirit by the very nature and object of our association.

We are men of secluded habits, with something of a cloud upon our early fortunes, whose enthusiasm, nevertheless, has not cooled with age, whose spirit of romance is not yet quenched, who are content to ramble through the world in a pleasant dream, rather than ever waken again to its harsh realities. We are alchemists who would extract the essence of perpetual youth from dust and ashes, tempt coy Truth in many light and airy forms from the bottom of her well, and discover one crumb of comfort or one grain of good in the commonest and least-regarded matter that passes through our crucible. Spirits of past times, creatures of imagination, and people of to-day are alike the objects of our seeking, and, unlike the objects of search with most philosophers, we can insure their coming at our command (*Chapter 1:* Master Humphrey).

The popular faith in ghosts has a remarkable affinity with the whole current of our thoughts at such an hour as this, and seems to be their necessary and natural consequence. For who can wonder that man should feel a vague belief in tales of disembodied spirits wandering through those places which they once dearly affected, when he himself, scarcely less separated from his old world than they, is for ever lingering upon past emotions and bygone times, and hovering, the ghost of his former self, about the places and people that warmed his heart of old? It is thus that at this quiet hour I haunt the house where I was born, the rooms I used to tread, the scenes of my infancy, my boyhood, and my youth; it is thus that I prowl around my buried treasure (though not of gold or silver), and mourn my loss; it is thus that I revisit the ashes of extinguished fires, and take my silent stand at old bedsides. If my spirit should ever glide back to this chamber when my body is mingled with the dust, it will but follow the course it often took in the old man's lifetime, and add but one more change to the subjects of its contemplation (*Chapter 2:* Master Humphrey).

'I am very glad to see you in such good health, Mr. Weller,' said I.

'Why, thankee, sir,' returned Mr. Weller, 'the axle an't broke yet. We keeps up a steady pace, – not too sewere, but vith a moderate degree o' friction, – and the consekens is that ve're still a runnin' and comes in to the time reg'lar. – My son Samivel, sir, as you may have read on in history,' added Mr. Weller, introducing his first-born.

I received Sam very graciously, but before he could say a word his father struck in again.

'Samivel Veller, sir,' said the old gentleman, 'has conferred upon me the ancient title o' grandfather vich had long laid dormouse, and wos s'posed to be nearly hex-tinct in our family. Sammy, relate a anecdote o' vun o' them boys, – that 'ere little anecdote about young Tony sayin' as he *vould* smoke a pipe unbeknown to his mother.'

'Be quiet, can't you?' said Sam; 'I never see such a old magpie – never!' (*Chapter 3:* Tony Weller Senior and Sam Weller).

'It wos on the rail,' said Mr. Weller, with strong emphasis; 'I wos a goin' down to Birmingham by the rail, and I wos locked up in a close carriage vith a living widder. Alone we wos; the widder and me was alone; and I believe it wos only because we *wos* alone and there wos no clergyman in the conwayance, that that 'ere widder didn't marry me afore ve reached the half-way station. Ven I think how she began a screaming as we wos a goin' under them tunnels in the dark, – how she kept on a faintin' and ketchin' hold o' me, – and how I tried to bust open the door as was tight-locked and perwented all escape – Ah! It was a awful thing, most awful!' (*Chapter 3:* Tony Weller Senior).

'Here's the story,' said Sam. 'Vunce upon a time there wos a young hairdresser as opened a wery smart little shop vith four wax dummies in the winder, two gen'lmen and two ladies – the gen'lmen vith blue dots for their beards, wery large viskers, oudacious heads of hair, uncommon clear eyes, and nostrils of amazin' pinkness; the ladies with their heads o' one side, their right forefingers on their lips, and their forms deweloped beautiful, in vich last respect they had the adwantage over the gen'lmen, as wasn't allowed but wery little shoulder, and terminated rayther abrupt in fancy drapery. He had also a many hair-brushes and tooth-brushes bottled up in the winder, neat glasscases on the counter, a floor-clothed cuttin'-room upstairs, and a weighin'-macheen in the shop, right opposite the door. But the great attraction and ornament wos the dummies, which this here young hairdresser wos constantly a runnin' out in the road to look at, and constantly a runnin' in again to touch up and polish; in short, he wos so proud on 'em, that ven Sunday come, he wos always wretched and mis'rable to think they wos behind the shutters, and looked anxiously for Monday on that account. Vun o' these dummies wos a fav'rite vith him beyond the others; and ven any of his acquaintance asked him vy he didn't get married – as the young ladies he know'd, in partickler, often did – he used to say, "Never! I never vill enter into the bonds of vedlock," he says, "until I meet with a young 'ooman as realises my idea o' that 'ere fairest dummy vith the light hair. Then, and not till then," he says, "I vill approach the altar." All the young ladies he know'd as had got dark hair told him this wos wery sinful, and that he wos wurshippin' a idle; but them as wos at all near the same shade as the dummy coloured up wery much, and wos observed to think him a wery nice young man.'

'Samivel,' said Mr. Weller, gravely, 'a member o' this associashun bein' one o' that 'ere tender sex which is now immedetly referred to, I have to rekvest that you vill make no reflections.'

'I ain't a makin' any, am I?' inquired Sam.

'Order, sir!' rejoined Mr. Weller, with severe dignity. Then, sinking the chairman in the father, he added, in his usual tone of voice: 'Samivel, drive on!'

Sam interchanged a smile with the housekeeper, and proceeded:

'The young hairdresser hadn't been in the habit o' makin' this avowal above six months, ven he encountered a young lady as wos the wery picter o' the fairest dummy. "Now," he says, "it's all up. I am a slave!" The young lady wos not only the picter o' the fairest dummy, but she was wery romantic, as the young hairdresser was, too, and he says, "O!" he says, "here's a community o' feelin', here's a flow o' soul!" he says, "here's a interchange o' sentiment!" The young lady didn't say much, o' course, but she expressed herself agreeable, and shortly artervards vent to see him vith a mutual friend. The hairdresser rushes out to meet her, but d'rectly she sees the dummies she changes colour and falls a tremblin' wiolently. "Look up, my love," says the hairdresser, "behold your imige in my vinder, but not correcter than in my art!" "My imige!" she says. "Yourn!" replies the hairdresser. "But whose imige is *that*?" she says, a pinting at vun o' the gen'lmen. "No vun's, my love," he says, "it is but a idea." "A idea!" she cries, "it is a portrait, I feel it is a portrait, and that 'ere noble face must be in the millingtary!" "Wot do I hear!" says he, a crumplin' his curls. "Villiam Gibbs," she says, quite firm, "never renoo the subject. I respect you as a friend," she says, "but my affections is set upon that manly brow." "This," says the hairdresser, "is a reg'lar blight, and in it I perceive the hand of Fate. Farewell!" Vith these vords he rushes into the shop, breaks the dummy's nose with a blow of his curlin'-irons, melts him down at the parlour fire, and never smiles artervards.'

'The young lady, Mr. Weller?' said the housekeeper.

'Why, ma'am,' said Sam, 'finding that Fate had a spite agin her, and everybody she come into contact vith, she never smiled neither, but read a deal o' poetry and pined avay, – by rayther slow degrees, for she ain't dead yet. It took a deal o' poetry to kill the hairdresser, and some people say arter all that it was more the gin and water as caused him to be run over; p'r'aps it was a little o' both, and came o' mixing the two' (*Chapter 5*).

'It's in wain to deny it, mum,' said Mr. Weller, 'this here is a boy arter his grandfather's own heart, and beats out all the boys as ever wos or will be. Though at the same time, mum,' added Mr. Weller, trying to look gravely down upon his favourite, 'it was wery wrong

305

on him to want to – over all the posts as we come along, and wery cruel on him to force poor grandfather to lift him cross-legged over every vun of 'em. He wouldn't pass vun single blessed post, mum, and at the top o' the lane there's seven-and-forty on 'em all in a row, and wery close together.'

Here Mr. Weller, whose feelings were in a perpetual conflict between pride in his grandson's achievements and a sense of his own responsibility, and the importance of impressing him with moral truths, burst into a fit of laughter, and suddenly checking himself, remarked in a severe tone that little boys as made their grandfathers put 'em over posts never went to heaven at any price.

By this time the housekeeper had made tea, and little Tony, placed on a chair beside her, with his eyes nearly on a level with the top of the table, was provided with various delicacies which yielded him extreme contentment. The housekeeper (who seemed rather afraid of the child, notwithstanding her caresses) then patted him on the head, and declared that he was the finest boy she had ever seen.

'Wy, mum,' said Mr. Weller, 'I don't think you'll see a many sich, and that's the truth. But if my son Samivel vould give me my vay, mum, and only dispense with his – *might* I wenter to say the vurd?'

'What word, Mr. Weller?' said the housekeeper, blushing slightly.

'Petticuts, mum,' returned that gentleman, laying his hand upon the garments of his grandson. 'If my son Samivel, mum, vould only dis-pense with these here, you'd see such a alteration in his appearance, as the imagination can't depicter.'

'But what would you have the child wear instead, Mr. Weller?' said the housekeeper.

'I've offered my son Samivel, mum, agen and agen,' returned the old gentleman, 'to purwide him at my own cost vith a suit o' clothes as 'ud be the makin' on him, and form his mind in infancy for those pursuits as I hope the family o' the Vellers vill alvays dewote themselves to. Tony, my boy, tell the lady wot them clothes are, as grandfather says, father ought to let you vear.'

'A little white hat and a little sprig weskut and little knee cords and little top-boots and a little green coat with little bright buttons and a little welwet collar,' replied Tony, with great readiness and no stops.

'That's the cos-toom, mum,' said Mr. Weller, looking proudly at the housekeeper. 'Once make sich a model on him as that, and you'd say he *wos* a angel!' (*Chapter 6:* Tony Weller).

'It's wery wrong in little boys to make game o' their grandfathers, an't it, mum?' said Mr. Weller, shaking his head waggishly, until Tony looked at him, when he counterfeited the deepest dejection and sorrow.

'O very sad!' assented the housekeeper. 'But I hope no little boys do that?'

'There is vun young Turk, mum,' said Mr. Weller, 'as havin' seen his grandfather a little overcome vith drink on the occasion of a friend's birthday, goes a reelin' and staggerin' about the house, and makin' believe that he's the old gen'lm'n.'

'O, quite shocking!' cried the housekeeper.

'Yes, mum,' said Mr. Weller; 'and previously to so doin', this here young traitor that I'm a speakin' of, pinches his little nose to make it red, and then he gives a hiccup and says, "I'm all right," he says; "give us another song!" Ha, ha! "Give us another song," he says. Ha, ha, ha!'

In his excessive delight, Mr. Weller was quite unmindful of his moral responsibility, until little Tony kicked up his legs, and laughing immoderately, cried, 'That was me, that was;' whereupon the grandfather, by a great effort, became extremely solemn.

'No, Tony, not you,' said Mr. Weller. 'I hope it warn't you, Tony. It must ha' been that 'ere naughty little chap as comes sometimes out o' the empty watch-box round the corner, – that same little chap as wos found standing on the table afore the looking-glass, pretending to shave himself vith a oyster-knife.'

'He didn't hurt himself, I hope?' observed the housekeeper.

'Not he, mum,' said Mr. Weller proudly; 'bless your heart, you might trust that 'ere boy vith a steam-engine a'most, he's such a knowin' young' – but suddenly recollecting himself and observing that Tony perfectly understood and appreciated the compliment, the old gentleman groaned and observed that 'it wos all wery shockin' – wery.'

'O, he's a bad 'un,' said Mr. Weller, 'is that 'ere watch-box boy, makin' such a noise and litter in the back yard, he does, waterin' wooden horses and feedin' of 'em vith grass, and perpetivally spillin' his little brother out of a veelbarrow and frightenin' his mother out of her vits, at the wery moment wen she's expectin' to increase her stock of happiness vith another play-feller, – O, he's a bad one! He's even gone so far as to put on a pair of paper spectacles as he got his father to make for him, and walk up and down the garden vith his hands behind him in imitation of Mr. Pickwick, – but Tony don't do sich things, O no!'

'O no!' echoed Tony.

'He knows better, he does,' said Mr. Weller. 'He knows that if he wos to come sich games as these nobody wouldn't love him, and that his grandfather in partickler couldn't abear the sight on him; for vich reasons Tony's always good' (*Chapter 6:* Tony Weller Senior and grandson).

It is night. Calm and unmoved amidst the scenes that darkness favours, the great heart of London throbs in its Giant breast. Wealth and beggary, vice and virtue, guilt and innocence, repletion and the direst hunger, all treading on each other and crowding together, are gathered round it. Draw but a little circle above the clustering housetops, and you shall have within its space everything with its opposite extreme and contradiction, close beside. Where yonder feeble light is shining, a man is but this moment dead. The taper at a few yards' distance is seen by eyes that have this instant opened on the world. There are two houses separated by but an inch or two of wall. In one, there are quiet minds at rest; in the other, a waking conscience that one might think would trouble the very air. In that close corner where the roofs shrink down and cower together as if to hide their secrets from the handsome street hard by, there are such dark crimes, such miseries and horrors, as could be hardly told in whispers. In the handsome street, there are folks asleep who have dwelt there all their lives, and have no more knowledge of these things than if they had never been, or were transacted at the remotest limits of the world, – who, if they were hinted at, would shake their heads, look wise, and frown, and say they were impossible, and out of Nature, – as if all great towns were not. Does not this Heart of London, that nothing moves, nor stops, nor quickens, – that goes on the same let what will be done, – does it not express the City's character well?

The day begins to break, and soon there is the hum and noise of life. Those who have spent the night on doorsteps and cold stones crawl off to beg; they who have slept in beds come forth to their occupation, too, and business is astir. The fog of sleep rolls slowly off, and London shines awake. The streets are filled with carriages, and people gaily clad. The jails are full, too, to the throat, nor have the workhouses or hospitals much room to spare. The courts of law are crowded. Taverns have their regular frequenters by this time, and every mart of traffic has its throng. Each of these places is a world, and has its own inhabitants; each is distinct from, and almost unconscious of the existence of any other. There are some few people well to do, who remember to have heard it said, that numbers of men and women – thousands, they think it was – get up in London every day, unknowing where to lay their heads at night; and that there are quarters of the town where misery and famine always are. They don't believe it quite, – there may be some truth in it, but it is exaggerated, of course. So, each of these thousand worlds goes on, intent upon itself, until night comes again, – first with its lights and pleasures, and its cheerful streets; then with its guilt and darkness.

Heart of London, there is a moral in thy every stroke! as I look on at thy indomitable working, which neither death, nor press of life, nor grief, nor gladness out of doors will influence one jot, I seem to hear a voice within thee which sinks into my heart, bidding me, as I elbow my way among the crowd, have some thought for the meanest wretch that passes, and, being a man, to turn away with scorn and pride from none that bear the human shape (*Chapter 6:* Master Humphrey).

THE OLD CURIOSITY SHOP

'It always grieves me,' I observed. . .' to contemplate the initiation of children into the ways of life, when they are scarcely more than infants. It checks their confidence and simplicity – two of the best qualities that Heaven gives them – and demands that they share our sorrows before they are capable of entering into our enjoyments.'

'It will never check hers,' said the old man looking steadily at me, 'the springs are too deep. Besides, the children of the poor know but few pleasures. Even the cheap delights of childhood must be bought and paid for' (*Chapter 1:* Narrator and Grandfather).

All that night, waking or in my sleep, the same thoughts recurred, and the same images retained possession of my brain. I had, ever before me, the old dark murky rooms – the gaunt suits of mail with their ghostly silent air – the faces all awry, grinning from wood and stone – the dust, and rust, and worm that lives in wood – and alone in the midst of all this lumber and decay and ugly age, the beautiful child in her gentle slumber, smiling through her light and sunny dreams (*Chapter 1:* Narrator).

'There. It's Dick Swiveller,' said the young fellow, pushing him in. 'Sit down, Swiveller.'

'But is the old min agreeable?' said Mr. Swiveller in an under tone.

'Sit down,' repeated his companion.

Mr. Swiveller complied, and looking about him with a propitiatory smile, observed that last week was a fine week for the ducks, and this week was a fine week for the dust; he also observed that whilst standing by the post at the street-corner, he had observed a pig with a straw in his mouth issuing out of the tobacco-shop, from which appearance he argued that another fine week for the ducks was approaching, and that rain would certainly ensue. He furthermore took occasion to apologise for any negligence that might be perceptible in his dress, on the ground that last night he had had 'the sun very strong in his eyes'; by which expression he was understood to convey to his hearers in the most delicate manner possible, the information that he had been extremely drunk.

'But what,' said Mr. Swiveller with a sigh, 'what is the odds so long as the fire of soul is kindled at the taper of conwiviality, and the wing of friendship never moults a feather? What is the odds so long as the spirit is expanded by means of rosy wine, and the present moment is the least happiest of our existence?' (*Chapter 2:* Fred Trent and Dick Swiveller).

'It's a devil of a thing, gentlemen,' said Mr. Swiveller, 'when relations fall out and disagree. If the wing of friendship should never moult a feather, the wing of relationship should never be clipped, but be always expanded and serene. Why should a grandson and grandfather peg away at each other with mutual wiolence when all might be bliss and concord? Why not jine hands and forget it?' (*Chapter 2*).

Dick looked rather pale and foolish when he glanced at the direction, and still more so when he came to look at the inside; observing that this was one of the inconveniences of being a lady's man, and that it was very easy to talk as they had been talking, but he had quite forgotten her.

'*Her.* Who?' demanded Trent.

'Sophy Wackles,' said Dick.

'Who's she?'

'She's all my fancy painted her, sir, that's what she is,' said Mr. Swiveller, taking a long pull at 'the rosy' and looking gravely at his friend. 'She is lovely, she's divine. You know her.'

'I remember,' said his companion carelessly. 'What of her?'

'Why, sir,' returned Dick, 'between Miss Sophia Wackles and the humble individual who has now the honour to address you, warm and tender sentiments have been engendered – sentiments of the most honourable and inspiring kind. The Goddess Diana, sir, that calls aloud for the chase, is not more particular in her behaviour than Sophia Wackles; I can tell you that' *(Chapter 7).*

'May the present moment,' said Dick, sticking his fork into a large carbuncular potato, 'be the worst of our lives! I like this plan of sending 'em with the peel on; there's a charm in drawing a potato from its native element (if I may so express it) to which the rich and powerful are strangers. Ah! "Man wants but little here below, nor wants that little long!" How true that is! – after dinner' *(Chapter 8:* Dick Swiveller).

Richard Swiveller took a greasy memorandum-book from his pocket and made an entry therein.
'Is that a reminder, in case you should forget to call?' said Trent with a sneer.
'Not exactly, Fred,' replied the imperturbable Richard, continuing to write with a business-like air, 'I enter in this little book the names of the streets that I can't go down while the shops are open. This dinner to-day closes Long Acre. I bought a pair of boots in Great Queen Street last week, and made that no thoroughfare too. There's only one avenue to the Strand left open now, and I shall have to stop up that to-night with a pair of gloves. The roads are closing so fast in every direction, that in about a month's time, unless my aunt sends me a remittance, I shall have to go three or four miles out of town to get over the way' *(Chapter 8).*

'It's rather sudden,' said Dick shaking his head with a look of infinite wisdom, and running on (as he was accustomed to do) with scraps of verse as if they were only prose in a hurry; 'when the heart of a man is depressed with fears, the mist is dispelled when Miss Wackles appears: she's a very nice girl. She's like the red red rose that's newly sprung in June – there's no denying that – she's also like a melody that's sweetly played in tune. It's really very sudden. Not that there's any need, on account of Fred's little sister, to turn cool directly, but it's better not to go too far. If I begin to cool at all I must begin at once, I see that. There's the chance of an action for breach, that's one reason. There's the chance of Sophy's getting another husband, that's another. There's the chance of – no, there's no chance of that, but it's as well to be on the safe side' *(Chapter 8:* Dick Swiveller).

'Am I going?' echoed Dick bitterly. 'Yes, I am. What then?'
'Nothing, except that it's very early,' said Miss Sophy; 'but you are your own master of course.'
'I would that I had been my own mistress too,' said Dick, 'before I had ever entertained a thought of you. Miss Wackles, I believed you true, and I was blest in so believing, but now I mourn that e'er I knew, a girl so fair yet so deceiving' *(Chapter 8:* Dick Swiveller).

'I am sure I don't know what you mean, Mr. Swiveller,' said Miss Sophy with downcast eyes. 'I'm very sorry if – '
'Sorry, ma'am!' said Dick, 'sorry in the possession

of a Cheggs! But I wish you a very good-night; concluding with this slight remark, that there is a young lady growing up at this present moment for me, who has not only great personal attractions but great wealth, and who has requested her next of kin to propose for my hand, which, having a regard for some members of her family, I have consented to promise. It's a gratifying circumstance which you'll be glad to hear, that a young and lovely girl is growing into a woman expressly on my account, and is now saving up for me. I thought I'd mention it. I have now merely to apologise for trespassing so long upon your attention. Good-night!' *(Chapter 8:* Dick Swiveller).

We call this a state of childishness, but it is the same poor hollow mockery of it, that death is of sleep. Where, in the dull eyes of doting men, are the laughing light and life of childhood, the gaiety that has known no check, the frankness that has felt no chill, the hope that has never withered, the joys that fade in blossoming? Where, in the sharp lineaments of rigid and unsightly death, is the calm beauty of slumber, telling of rest for the waking hours that are past, and gentle hopes and loves for those which are to come? Lay death and sleep down, side by side, and say who shall find the two akin. Send forth the child and childish man together, and blush for the pride that libels our own old happy state, and gives its title to an ugly and distorted image *(Chapter 12).*

'You'll mention that I called, perhaps?' said Dick.
Mr. Quilp nodded, and said he certainly would, the very first time he saw them.
'And say,' added Mr. Swiveller, 'say, sir, that I was wafted here upon the pinions of concord; that I came to remove, with the rake of friendship, the seeds of mutual violence and heart-burning, and to sow in their place, the germs of social harmony. Will you have the goodness to charge yourself with that commission, sir?' *(Chapter 13).*

Why is it that we can better bear to part in spirit than in body, and while we have the fortitude to act farewell have not the nerve to say it? On the eve of long voyages or an absence of many years, friends who are tenderly attached will separate with the usual look, the usual pressure of the hand, planning one final interview for the morrow, while each well knows that it is but a poor feint to save the pain of uttering that one word, and that the meeting will never be. Should possibilities be worse to bear than certainties? We do not shun our dying friends; the not having distinctly taken leave of one among them, whom we left in all kindness and affection, will often embitter the whole remainder of a life *(Chapter 15).*

She was looking at a humble stone which told of a young man who had died at twenty-three years old, fifty-five years ago, when she heard a faltering step approaching, and looking round saw a feeble woman bent with the weight of years, who tottered to the foot of that same grave and asked her to read the writing on the stone. The old woman thanked her when she had done, saying that she had had the words by heart for many a long, long year, but could not see them now.

'Were you his mother?' said the child.

'I was his wife, my dear.'

She the wife of a young man of three-and-twenty! Ah, true! It was fifty-five years ago.

'You wonder to hear me say that,' remarked the old woman, shaking her head. 'You're not the first. Older folk than you have wondered at the same thing before now. Yes, I was his wife. Death doesn't change us more than life, my dear.'

'Do you come here often?' asked the child.

'I sit here very often in the summer time,' she answered, 'I used to come here once to cry and mourn, but that was a weary while ago, bless God!'

'I pluck the daisies as they grow, and take them home,' said the old woman after a short silence. 'I like no flowers so well as these, and haven't for five-and-fifty years. It's a long time, and I'm getting very old!' (*Chapter 17:* Nell and Old Woman).

Mr. Codlin sat smiling in the chimney-corner, eyeing the landlord as with a roguish look he held the cover in his hand, and, feigning that his doing so was needful to the welfare of the cookery, suffered the delightful steam to tickle the nostrils of his guest. The glow of the fire was upon the landlord's bald head, and upon his twinkling eye, and upon his watering mouth, and upon his pimpled face, and upon his round fat figure. Mr. Codlin drew his sleeve across his lips, and said in a murmuring voice, 'What is it?'

'It's a stew of tripe,' said the landlord smacking his lips, 'and cow-heel,' smacking them again, 'and bacon,' smacking them once more, 'and steak,' smacking them for the fourth time, 'and peas, cauliflowers, new potatoes, and sparrow-grass, all working up together in one delicious gravy.' Having come to the climax, he smacked his lips a great many times, and taking a long hearty sniff of the fragrance that was hovering about, put on the cover again with the air of one whose toils on earth were over (*Chapter 18*).

'Why didn't you tell me your little history – that about you and the poor old gentleman? I'm the best adviser that ever was, and *so* interested in you – so much more interested than Short. I think they're breaking up downstairs; you needn't tell Short, you know, that we've had this little talk together. God bless you. Recollect the friend. Codlin's the friend, not Short. Short's very well as far as he goes, but the real friend is Codlin – not Short' (*Chapter 19:* Codlin).

'Now, sir, will you have the goodness to go on; this is *not* the place,' said the old gentleman.

The pony looked with great attention into a fire-plug which was near him, and appeared to be quite absorbed in contemplating it.

'Oh dear, such a naughty Whisker!' cried the old lady. 'After being so good too, and coming along so well! I am quite ashamed of him. I don't know what we are to do with him, I really don't.'

The pony having thoroughly satisfied himself as to the nature and properties of the fire-plug, looked into the air after his old enemies the flies, and as there happened to be one off them tickling his ear at that moment he shook his head and whisked his tail, after which he appeared full of thought but quite com-

L

fortable and collected. The old gentleman having exhausted his powers of persuasion, alighted to lead him; whereupon the pony, perhaps because he held this to be a sufficient concession, perhaps because he happened to catch sight of the other brass plate, or perhaps because he was in a spiteful humour, darted off with the old lady and stopped at the right house, leaving the old gentleman to come panting on behind (*Chapter 20:* Mr. and Mrs. Garland).

'You know you must keep up your spirits, mother, and not be lonesome because I'm not at home. I shall very often be able to look in when I come into town I dare say, and I shall send you a letter sometimes, and when the quarter comes round, I can get a holiday of course; and then see if we don't take little Jacob to the play, and let him know what oysters means.'

'I hope plays mayn't be sinful, Kit, but I'm a'most afraid,' said Mrs. Nubbles.

'I know who has been putting that in your head,' rejoined her son disconsolately; 'that's Little Bethel again. Now I say, mother, pray don't take to going there regularly, for if I was to see your good-humoured face that has always made home cheerful, turned into a grievous one, and the baby trained to look grievous too, and to call itself a young sinner (bless its heart) and a child of the devil (which is calling its dead father names); if I was to see this, and see little Jacob looking grievous likewise, I should so take it to heart that I'm sure I should go and 'list for a soldier, and run my head on purpose against the first cannon-ball I saw coming my way.'

'Oh, Kit, don't talk like that.'

'I would, indeed, mother, and unless you want to make me feel very wretched and uncomfortable, you'll keep that bow on your bonnet which you'd more than half a mind to pull off last week. Can you suppose there's any harm in looking as cheerful and being as cheerful as our poor circumstances will permit? Do I see anything in the way I'm made, which calls upon me to be a snivelling, solemn, whispering chap, sneaking about as if I couldn't help it, and expressing myself in a most unpleasant snuffle? on the contrary, don't I see every reason why I shouldn't? Just hear this! Ha ha ha! An't that as nat'ral as walking, and as good for the health? Ha ha ha! An't that as nat'ral as a sheep's bleating, or a pig's grunting, or a horse's neighing, or a bird's singing? Ha ha ha! Isn't it, mother?' (*Chapter 22*).

Nell walked down it, and read aloud, in enormous black letters, the inscription, 'JARLEY'S WAX-WORK.'

'Read it again,' said the lady, complacently.

'Jarley's Wax-Work,' repeated Nell.

'That's me,' said the lady. 'I am Mrs. Jarley.'

Giving the child an encouraging look, intended to reassure her and let her know, that, although she stood in the presence of the original Jarley, she must not allow herself to be utterly overwhelmed and borne down, the lady of the caravan unfolded another scroll, whereon was the inscription, 'One hundred figures the full size of life,' and then another scroll, on which was written, 'The only stupendous collection of real wax-work in the world,' and then several smaller scrolls with such inscriptions as 'Now exhibiting within' –

'The genuine and only Jarley' – 'Jarley's unrivalled collection' – 'Jarley is the delight of the nobility and Gentry' – 'The Royal Family are the patrons of Jarley.' When she had exhibited these leviathans of public announcement to the astonished child, she brought forth specimens of the lesser fry in the shape of handbills, some of which were couched in the form of parodies on popular melodies, as 'Believe me if all Jarley's wax-work so rare' – 'I saw thy show in youthful prime' – 'Over the water to Jarley'; while, to consult all tastes, others were composed with a view to the lighter and more facetious spirits, as a parody on the favourite air of 'If I had a donkey,' beginning

> 'If I know'd a donkey wot wouldn't go
> To see Mrs. JARLEY's wax-work show,
> Do you think I'd acknowledge him?
> Oh no no!
> Then run to Jarley's

– besides several compositions in prose, purporting to be dialogues between the Emperor of China and an oyster, or the Archbishop of Canterbury and a dissenter on the subject of church-rates, but all having the same moral, namely, that the reader must make haste to Jarley's, and that children and servants were admitted at half-price. When she had brought all these testimonials of her important position in society to bear upon her young companion, Mrs. Jarley rolled them up, and having put them carefully away, sat down again, and looked at the child in triumph. 'Never go into the company of a filthy Punch any more,' said Mrs. Jarley, 'after this' *(Chapter 27)*.

'It isn't funny at all,' repeated Mrs. Jarley. 'It's calm and – what's that word again – critical? – no – classical, that's it – it's calm and classical. No low beatings and knockings about, no jokings and squeakings like your precious Punches, but always the same, with a constantly unchanging air of coldness and gentility; and so like life, that if wax-work only spoke and walked about, you'd hardly know the difference. I won't go so far as to say, that, as it is, I've seen wax-work quite like life, but I've certainly seen some life that was exactly like wax-work' *(Chapter 27)*.

When the festoons were all put up as tastily as they might be, the stupendous collection was uncovered, and there were displayed, on a raised platform some two feet from the floor, running round the room and parted from the rude public by a crimson rope breast-high, divers sprightly effigies of celebrated characters, singly and in groups, clad in glittering dresses of various climes and times, and standing more or less unsteadily upon their legs, with their eyes very wide open, and their nostrils very much inflated, and the muscles of their legs and arms very strongly developed, and all their countenances expressing great surprise. All the gentlemen were very pigeon-breasted and very blue about the beards; and all the ladies were miraculous figures; and all the ladies and all the gentlemen were looking intensely nowhere, and staring with extraordinary earnestness at nothing *(Chapter 28)*.

That,' said Mrs. Jarley in her exhibition tone, as Nell touched a figure at the beginning of the platform,

'is an unfortunate maid of honour in the Time of Queen Elizabeth, who died from pricking her finger in consequence of working upon a Sunday. Observe the blood which is trickling from her finger; also the gold-eyed needle of the period, with which she is at work' *(Chapter 28)*.

'That, ladies and gentlemen,' said Mrs. Jarley, 'is Jasper Packlemerton of atrocious memory, who courted and married fourteen wives, and destroyed them all, by tickling the soles of their feet when they were sleeping in the consciousness of innocence and virtue. On being brought to the scaffold and asked if he was sorry for what he had done, he replied yes, he was sorry for having let 'em off so easy, and hoped all Christian husbands would pardon him the offence. Let this be a warning to all young ladies to be particular in the character of the gentlemen of their choice. Observe that his fingers are curled as if in the act of tickling, and that his face is represented with a wink, as he appeared when committing his barbarous murders' *(Chapter 28)*.

'Don't you feel how naughty it is of you,' resumed Miss Monflathers, 'to be a wax-work child, when you might have the proud consciousness of assisting, to the extent of your infant powers, the manufactures of your country; of improving your mind by the constant contemplation of the steam-engine; and of earning a comfortable and independent subsistence of from two-and-ninepence to three shillings per week? Don't you know that the harder you are at work, the happier you are?' *(Chapter 31)*.

'The little busy bee,' said Miss Monflathers, drawing herself up, 'is applicable only to genteel children.

' "In books, or work, or healthful play"

is quite right as far as they are concerned; and the work means painting on velvet, fancy needlework, or embroidery. In such cases as these,' pointing to Nell, with her parasol, 'and in the case of all poor people's children, we should read it thus –

> ' "In work, work, work. In work alway
> Let my first years be past,
> That I may give for ev'ry day
> Some good account at last." '

(Chapter 31)

'Hallo!' he [Quilp] said, standing on tip-toe on the window-sill, and looking down into the room. 'Is there anybody at home? Is there any of the Devil's ware here? Is Brass at a premium, eh?'

'Ha, ha, ha!' laughed the lawyer in an affected ecstasy. 'Oh, very good, sir! Oh, very good indeed! Quite eccentric! Dear me, what humour he has!'

'Is that my Sally?' croaked the dwarf, ogling the fair Miss Brass. 'Is it Justice with the bandage off her eyes, and without the sword and scales? Is it the Strong Arm of the Law? Is it the Virgin of Bevis?'

'What an amazing flow of spirits!' cried Brass. 'Upon my word, it's quite extraordinary!' *(Chapter 33)*.

'Miss Sally will teach him law, the delightful study of the law,' said Quilp; 'she'll be his guide, his friend, his companion, his Blackstone, his Coke upon Littleton, his Young Lawyer's Best Companion.'

'He is exceedingly eloquent,' said Brass, like a man abstracted, and looking at the roofs of the opposite houses, with his hands in his pockets; 'he has an extraordinary flow of language. Beautiful, really.'

'With Miss Sally,' Quilp went on, 'and the beautiful fictions of the law, his days will pass like minutes. Those charming creations of the poet, John Doe and Richard Roe, when they first dawn upon him, will open a new world for the enlargement of his mind and the improvement of his heart.'

'Oh, beautiful, beautiful! Beau-ti-ful indeed!' cried Brass. 'It's a treat to hear him!' *(Chapter 33).*

He [Dick Swiveller] found favour in the eyes of Miss Sally Brass. Let not the light scorners of female fascination erect their ears to listen to a new tale of love which shall serve them for a jest, for Miss Brass, however accurately formed to be beloved, was not of the loving kind. That amiable virgin, having clung to the skirts of the Law from her earliest youth; having sustained herself by their aid, as it were, in her first running alone, and maintained a firm grasp upon them ever since; had passed her life in a kind of legal childhood. She had been remarkable, when a tender prattler, for an uncommon talent in counterfeiting the walk and manner of a bailiff: in which character she had learned to tap her little playfellows on the shoulder, and to carry them off to imaginary sponging-houses, with a correctness of imitation which was the surprise and delight of all who witnessed her performances, and which was only to be exceeded by her exquisite manner of putting an execution into her doll's house, and taking an exact inventory of the chairs and tables. These artless sports had naturally soothed and cheered the decline of her widowed father: a most exemplary gentleman, (called 'old Foxey' by his friends from his extreme sagacity,) who encouraged them to the utmost, and whose chief regret, on finding that he drew near to Houndsditch churchyard, was, that his daughter could not take out an attorney's certificate and hold a place upon the roll. Filled with this affectionate and touching sorrow, he had solemnly confided her to his son Sampson as an invaluable auxiliary; and from the old gentleman's decease to the period of which we treat, Miss Sally Brass had been the prop and pillar of his business *(Chapter 36).*

Oh! if those who rule the destinies of nations would but remember this – if they would but think how hard it is for the very poor to have engendered in their hearts, that love of home from which all domestic virtues spring, when they live in dense and squalid masses where social decency is lost, or rather never found, – if they would but turn aside from the wide thoroughfares and great houses, and strive to improve the wretched dwellings in by-ways where only poverty may walk, – many low roofs would point more truly to the sky, than the loftiest steeple that now rears proudly up from the midst of guilt, and crime, and horrible disease, to mock them by its contrast. In hollow voices from Workhouse, Hospital, and Jail, this truth is preached from day to day, and has been proclaimed for years. It is no light matter – no outcry from the working vulgar – no mere question of the people's health and comforts that may be whistled down on Wednesday nights. In love of home, the love of country has its rise; and who are the truer patriots or the better in time of need – those who venerate the land, owning its wood and stream, and earth, and all that they produce? or those who love their country, boasting not a foot of ground in all its wide domain? *(Chapter 38).*

Dear, dear, what a place it looked, that Astley's; with all the paint, gilding, and looking-glass; the vague smell of horses suggestive of coming wonders; the curtain that hid such gorgeous mysteries; the clean white sawdust down in the circus; the company coming in and taking their places; the fiddlers looking carelessly up at them while they tuned their instruments, as if they didn't want the play to begin, and knew it all beforehand! What a glow was that, which burst upon them all, when that long, clear, brilliant row of lights came slowly up; and what the feverish excitement when the little bell rang and the music began in good earnest, with strong parts for the drums, and sweet effects for the triangles! Well might Barbara's mother say to Kit's mother that the gallery was the place to see from, and wonder it wasn't much dearer than the boxes; well might Barbara feel doubtful whether to laugh or cry, in her flutter of delight.

Then the play itself! the horses which little Jacob believed from the first to be alive, and the ladies and gentlemen of whose reality he could be by no means persuaded, having never seen or heard anything at all like them – the firing, which made Barbara wink – the forlorn lady, who made her cry – the tyrant, who made her tremble – the man who sang the song with the lady's maid and danced the chorus, who made her laugh – the pony who reared up on his hind-legs when he saw the murderer, and wouldn't hear of walking on all fours again until he was taken into custody – the clown who ventured on such familiarities with the military man in boots – the lady who jumped over the nine-and-twenty ribbons and came down safe upon the horse's back – everything was delightful, splendid, and surprising! Little Jacob applauded till his hands were sore; Kit cried 'an-kor' at the end of everything, the three-act piece included; and Barbara's mother beat her umbrella on the floor, in her ecstasies, until it was nearly worn down to the gingham *(Chapter 39).*

Oh these holidays! why will they leave us some regret? why cannot we push them back, only a week or two in our memories, so as to put them at once at that convenient distance whence they may be regarded either with a calm indifference or a pleasant effort of recollection? why will they hang about us, like the flavour of yesterday's wine, suggestive of headaches and lassitude, and those good intentions for the future, which, under the earth, form the everlasting pavement of a large estate, and, upon it, usually endure until dinner-time or thereabouts? *(Chapter 40).*

Advancing more and more into the shadow of this mournful place, its dark depressing influence stole upon their spirits, and filled them with a dismal gloom. On every side, and far as the eye could see into the heavy distance, tall chimneys, crowding on each other, and presenting that endless repetition of the same dull, ugly form, which is the horror of oppressive dreams, poured out their plague of smoke, obscured the light, and made foul the melancholy air. On mounds of ashes by the wayside, sheltered only by a few rough boards, or rotten pent-house roofs, strange engines spun and writhed like tortured creatures; clanking their iron chains, shrieking in their rapid whirl from time to time as though in torment unendurable, and making the ground tremble with their agonies. Dismantled houses here and there appeared, tottering to the earth, propped up by fragments of others that had fallen down, unroofed, windowless, blackened, desolate, but yet inhabited. Men, women, children, wan in their looks and ragged in attire, tended the engines, fed their tributary fire, begged upon the road, or scowled half-naked from the doorless houses. Then, came more of the wrathful monsters, whose like they almost seemed to be in their wildness and their untamed air, screeching and turning round and round again; and still, before, behind, and to the right and left, was the same interminable perspective of brick towers, never ceasing in their black vomit, blasting all things living or inanimate, shutting out the face of day, and closing in on all these horrors with a dense dark cloud.

But, night-time in this dreadful spot! – night, when the smoke was changed to fire; when every chimney spirted up its flame; and places, that had been dark vaults all day, now shone red-hot, with figures moving to and fro within their blazing jaws, and calling to one another with hoarse cries – night, when the noise of every strange machine was aggravated by the darkness; when the people near them looked wilder and more savage; when bands of unemployed labourers paraded the roads, or clustered by torch-light round their leaders, who told them, in stern language, of their wrongs, and urged them on to frightful cries and threats; when maddened men, armed with sword and fire-brand, spurning the tears and prayers of women who would restrain them, rushed forth on errands of terror and destructon, to work no ruin half so surely as their own – night, when carts came rumbling by, filled with rude coffins (for contagious disease and death had been busy with the living crops); when orphans cried, and distracted women shrieked and followed in their wake – night, when some called for bread, and some for drink to drown their cares, and some with tears, and some with staggering feet, and some with bloodshot eyes, went brooding home – night, which, unlike the night that Heaven sends on earth, brought with it no peace, nor quiet, nor signs of blessed sleep – who shall tell the terrors of the night to the young wandering child! *(Chapter 45).*

They arranged to proceed upon their journey next evening, as a stage-waggon, which travelled for some distance on the same road as they must take, would stop at the inn to change horses, and the driver for a small gratuity would give Nell a place inside. A bargain was soon struck when the waggon came; and in due time it rolled away; with the child comfortably bestowed among the softer packages, her grandfather and the schoolmaster walking on beside the driver, and the landlady and all the good folks of the inn screaming out their good wishes and farewells.

What a soothing, luxurious, drowsy way of travelling, to lie inside that slowly-moving mountain, listening to the tinkling of the horses' bells, the occasional smacking of the carter's whip, the smooth rolling of the great broad wheels, the rattle of the harness, the cheery good-nights of passing travellers jogging past on little short-stepped horses – all made pleasantly indistinct by the thick awning, which seemed made for lazy listening under, till one fell asleep! The very going to sleep, still with an indistinct idea, as the head jogged to and fro upon the pillow, of moving onward with no trouble or fatigue, and hearing all these sounds like dreamy music, lulling to the senses – and the slow waking up, and finding one's-self staring out through the breezy curtain half-opened in the front, far up into the cold bright sky with its countless stars, and downward at the driver's lantern dancing on like its namesake Jack of the swamps and marshes, and sideways at the dark grim trees, and forward at the long bare road rising up, up, up, until it stopped abruptly at a sharp high ridge as if there were no more road, and all beyond was sky – and the stopping at the inn to bait, and being helped out, and going into a room with fire and candles, and winking very much, and being agreeably reminded that the night was cold, and anxious for very comfort's sake to think it colder than it was! – What a delicious journey was that journey in the waggon *(Chapter 46).*

'Ah!' said Mr. Brass, breaking the silence, and raising his eyes to the ceiling with a sigh, 'who knows but he may be looking down upon us now? Who knows but he may be surveying of us from – from somewheres or another, and contemplating us with a watchful eye? Oh Lor!'

Here Mr. Brass stopped to drink half his punch, and then resumed; looking at the other half, as he spoke, with a dejected smile.

'I can almost fancy,' said the lawyer shaking his head, 'that I see his eye glistening down at the very bottom of my liquor. When shall we look upon his like again? Never, never! One minute we are here' – holding his tumbler before his eyes – 'the next we are there' – gulping down its contents, and striking himself emphatically a little below the chest – 'in the silent tomb. To think that I should be drinking his very rum! It seems like a dream' *(Chapter 49).*

With regard to the descriptive advertisement,' said Sampson Brass, taking up his pen. 'It is a melancholy pleasure to recall his traits. Respecting his legs now – ?'

'Crooked, certainly,' said Mrs. Jiniwin.

'Do you think they *were* crooked?' said Brass, in an insinuating tone. 'I think I see them now coming up the street very wide apart, in nankeen pantaloons a little shrunk and without straps. Ah! what a vale of tears we live in. Do we say crooked?'

'I think they were a little so,' observed Mrs. Quilp with a sob.

'Legs crooked,' said Brass, writing as he spoke. 'Large head, short body, legs crooked – '

'Very crooked,' suggested Mrs. Jiniwin.

'We'll not say very crooked, ma'am,' said Brass piously. 'Let us not bear hard upon the weaknesses of the deceased. He is gone, ma'am, to where his legs will never come in question. – We will content ourselves with crooked, Mrs. Jiniwin' *(Chapter 49)*.

You're out of spirits,' said Quilp, drawing up a chair. 'What's the matter?'
'The law don't agree with me,' returned Dick. 'It isn't moist enough, and there's too much confinement. I have been thinking of running away.'
'Bah!' said the dwarf. 'Where would you run to, Dick?'
'I don't know,' returned Mr. Swiveller. 'Towards Highgate, I suppose. Perhaps the bells might strike up "Turn again, Swiveller, Lord Mayor of London." Whittington's name was Dick. I wish cats were scarcer' *(Chapter 50)*.

'What should you say this was?' demanded Mr. Swiveller.
'It looks like bride cake,' replied the dwarf, grinning.
'And whose should you say it was?' inquired Mr. Swiveller, rubbing the pastry against his nose with a dreadful calmness. 'Whose?'
'Not – '
'Yes,' said Dick, 'the same. You needn't mention her name. There's no such name now. Her name is Cheggs now, Sophy Cheggs. Yet loved I as man never loved that hadn't wooden legs, and my heart, my heart is breaking for the love of Sophy Cheggs' *(Chapter 50)*.

There are chords in the human heart – strange, varying strings – which are only struck by accident; which will remain mute and senseless to appeals the most passionate and earnest, and respond at last to the slightest casual touch. In the most insensible or childish minds, there is some truth of reflection which art can seldom lead, or skill assist, but which will reveal itself, as great truths have done, by chance, and when the discoverer has the plainest end in view *(Chapter 55)*.

'It has always been the same with me,' said Mr. Swiveller, 'always. 'Twas ever thus, from childhood's hour I've seen my fondest hopes decay, I never loved a tree or flower but 'twas the first to fade away; I never nursed a dear Gazelle, to glad me with its soft black eye, but when it came to know me well, and love me, it was sure to marry a market-gardener' *(Chapter 56)*.

'And this,' said Mr. Swiveller, with a kind of bantering composure, 'is life, I believe. Oh, certainly. Why not? I'm quite satisfied. I shall wear,' added Richard, taking off his hat again and looking hard at it, as if he were only deterred by pecuniary considerations from spurning it with his foot, 'I shall wear this emblem of woman's perfidy, in remembrance of her with whom I shall never again thread the windings of the mazy; whom I shall never more pledge in the rosy; who, during the short remainder of my existence, will murder the balmy. Ha, ha, ha!' *(Chapter 56)*.

'I respect *you*, Kit,' said Brass with emotion. 'I saw enough of your conduct, at that time, to respect you, though your station is humble, and your fortune lowly. It isn't the waistcoat that I look at. It is the heart. The checks in the waistcoat are but the wires of the cage. But the heart is the bird. Ah! How many sich birds are perpetually moulting, and putting their beaks through the wires to peck at all mankind!' *(Chapter 56: Brass and Kit Nubbles)*.

'Ah!' rejoins Mr. Brass, brimful of moral precepts and love of virtue. 'A charming subject of reflection for you, very charming. A subject of proper pride and congratulation, Christopher. Honesty is the best policy. – I always find it so myself. I lost forty-seven pound ten by being honest this morning. But it's all gain, it's gain!'
Mr. Brass slyly tickles his nose with his pen, and looks at Kit with the water standing in his eyes. Kit thinks that if ever there was a good man who belied his appearance, that man is Sampson Brass.
'A man,' says Sampson, 'who loses forty-seven pound ten in one morning by his honesty, is a man to be envied. If it had been eighty pounds, the luxuriousness of feeling would have been increased. Every pound lost, would have been a hundredweight of happiness gained. The still small voice, Christopher,' cries Brass, smiling, and tapping himself on the bosom, 'is a singing comic songs within me, and all is happiness and joy!' *(Chapter 57: Brass and Kit Nubbles)*.

Mr. Swiveller and his partner played several rubbers with varying success, until the loss of three sixpences, the gradual sinking of the purl, and the striking of ten o'clock, combined to render that gentleman mindful of the flight of Time, and the expediency of withdrawing before Mr. Sampson and Miss Sally Brass returned.
'With which object in view, Marchioness,' said Mr. Swiveller gravely, 'I shall ask your ladyship's permission to put the board in my pocket, and to retire from the presence when I have finished this tankard; merely observing, Marchioness, that since life like a river is flowing, I care not how fast it rolls on, ma'am, on, while such purl on the bank still is growing, and such eyes light the waves as they run. Marchioness, your health. You will excuse my wearing my hat, but the palace is damp, and the marble floor is – if I may be allowed the expression – sloppy' *(Chapter 58)*.

'I say,' quoth Miss Brass, abruptly breaking silence, 'you haven't seen a silver pencil-case this morning, have you?'
'I didn't meet many in the street,' rejoined Mr. Swiveller. 'I saw one – a stout pencil-case of respectable appearance – but as he was in company with an elderly penknife, and a young toothpick with whom he was in earnest conversation, I felt a delicacy in speaking to him' *(Chapter 58)*.

The world, being in constant commission of vast quantities of injustice, is a little too apt to comfort itself with the idea that if the victim of its falsehood and malice have a clear conscience, he cannot fail to be sustained under his trials, and somehow or other to come right at last– 'in which case,' say they who have hunted him down, '– though we certainly don't expect it – nobody will be better pleased than we.' Whereas, the world would do well to reflect, that injustice is in itself, to every generous and properly constituted mind, an injury, of all others the most insufferable, the most torturing, and the most hard to bear; and that many clear consciences have gone to their account elsewhere, and many sound hearts have broken, because of this very reason; the knowledge of their own deserts only aggravating their suffering, and rendering them the less endurable *(Chapter 61)*.

Quilp was out in an instant; not with his legs first, or his head first, or his arms first, but bodily – altogether.

'To be sure,' he said, taking up a lantern, which was now the only light in the place. 'Be careful how you go, my dear friend. Be sure to pick your way among the timber, for all the rusty nails are upwards. There's a dog in the lane. He bit a man last night, and a woman the night before, and last Tuesday he killed a child – but that was in play. Don't go too near him.'

'Which side of the road is he, sir?' asked Brass, in great dismay.

'He lives on the right-hand,' said Quilp, 'but sometimes he hides on the left, ready for a spring. He's uncertain in that respect. Mind you take care of yourself. I'll never forgive you if you don't. There's the light out – never mind – you know the way – straight on!' *(Chapter 62)*.

'Gentlemen, if I could express the pleasure it gives me to see three such men in a happy unity of feeling and concord of sentiment, I think you would hardly believe me. But though I am unfortunate – nay, gentlemen, criminal, if we are to use harsh expressions in a company like this – still, I have my feelings like other men. I have heard of a poet, who remarked that feelings were the common lot of all. If he could have been a pig, gentlemen, and have uttered that sentiment, he would still have been immortal' *(Chapter 66 Brass)*.

'If I had him here. If I only had him here – '

'Oh Quilp!' said his wife, 'what's the matter? Who are you angry with?'

'– I should drown him,' said the dwarf, not heeding her. 'Too easy a death, too short, too quick – but the river runs close at hand. Oh! if I had him here! Just to take him to the brink coaxingly and pleasantly, – holding him by the button-hole – joking with him, – and, with a sudden push, to send him splashing down! Drowning men come to the surface three times they say. Ah! To see him those three times, and mock him as his face came bobbing up, – oh, what a rich treat that would be!'

'Quilp!' stammered his wife, venturing at the same time to touch him on the shoulder: 'what has gone wrong?'

She was so terrified by the relish with which he pictured this pleasure to himself, that she could scarcely make herself intelligible.

'Such a bloodless cur!' said Quilp, rubbing his hands very slowly, and pressing them tight together. 'I thought his cowardice and servility were the best guarantee for his keeping silence. Oh Brass, Brass – my dear, good, affectionate, faithful, complimentary,

charming friend – if I only had you here!' *(Chapter 67)*.

For she was dead. There, upon her little bed, she lay at rest. The solemn stillness was no marvel now.

She was dead. No sleep so beautiful and calm, so free from trace of pain, so fair to look upon. She seemed a creature fresh from the hand of God, and waiting for the breath of life; not one who had lived and suffered death.

Her couch was dressed with here and there some winter berries and green leaves, gathered in a spot she had been used to favour. 'When I die, put near me something that has loved the light, and had the sky above it always.' Those were her words.

She was dead. Dear, gentle, patient, noble Nell was dead. Her little bird – a poor slight thing the pressure of a finger would have crushed – was stirring nimbly in its cage; and the strong heart of its child mistress was mute and motionless for ever.

Where were the traces of her early cares, her suffering, and fatigues? All gone. Sorrow was dead indeed in her, but peace and perfect happiness were born; imaged in her tranquil beauty and profound repose.

And still her former self lay there, unaltered in this change. Yes. The old fireside had smiled upon that same sweet face; it had passed, like a dream, through haunts of misery and care; at the door of the poor schoolmaster on the summer evening, before the furnace fire upon the cold wet night, at the still bedside of the dying boy, there had been the same mild lovely look. So shall we know the angels in their majesty, after death *(Chapter 71)*.

And now the bell – the bell she had so often heard, by night and day, and listened to with solemn pleasure almost as a living voice – rung its remorseless toll, for her, so young, so beautiful, so good. Decrepit age, and vigorous life, and blooming youth, and helpless infancy, poured forth – on crutches, in the pride of strength and health, in the full blush of promise, in the mere dawn of life – to gather round her tomb. Old men were there, whose eyes were dim and senses failing – grandmothers, who might have died ten years ago, and still been old – the deaf, the blind, the lame, the palsied, the living dead in many shapes and forms, to see the closing of that early grave. What was the death it would shut in, to that which still could crawl and creep above it?

Along the crowded path they bore her now; pure as the newly-fallen snow that covered it; whose day on earth had been as fleeting. Under the porch, where she had sat when Heaven in its mercy brought her to that peaceful spot, she passed again; and the old church received her in its quiet shade.

They carried her to one old nook, where she had many and many a time sat musing, and laid their burden softly on the pavement. The light streamed on it through the coloured window – a window, where the boughs of trees were ever rustling in the summer, and where the birds sang sweetly all day long. With every breath of air that stirred among those branches in the sunshine, some trembling, changing light would fall upon her grave.

Earth to earth, ashes to ashes, dust to dust! (*Chapter 72*).

Oh! it is hard to take to heart the lesson that such deaths will teach, but let no man reject it, for it is one that all must learn, and is a mighty universal Truth. When Death strikes down the innocent and young, for every fragile form from which he lets the panting spirit free, a hundred virtues rise, in shapes of mercy, charity, and love, to walk the world, and bless it. Of every tear that sorrowing mortals shed on such green graves, some good is born, some gentler nature comes. In the Destroyer's steps there spring up bright creations that defy his power, and his dark path becomes a way of light to Heaven (*Chapter 72*).

BARNABY RUDGE

'If, sir, Natur has fixed upon me the gift of argeyment, why should I not own to it, and rather glory in the same? Yes, sir, I *am* a tough customer that way. You are right, sir. My toughness has been proved, sir, in this room many and many a time, as I think you know; and if you don't know,' added John, putting his pipe in his mouth again, 'so much the better, for I an't proud and am not going to tell you' (*Chapter 1:* John Willet).

'Did you ever hear tell of mermaids, sir?' said Mr. Willet.
'Certainly I have,' replied the clerk.
'Very good,' said Mr. Willet. 'According to the constitution of mermaids, so much of a mermaid as is not a woman must be a fish. According to the constitution of young princes, so much of a young prince (if anything) as is not actually an angel, must be godly and righteous. Therefore if it's becoming and godly and righteous in the young princes (as it is at their ages) that they should be boys, they are and must be boys, and cannot by possibility be anything else' (*Chapter 1*).

'Something will come of this!' said Mr. Tappertit, pausing as if in triumph, and wiping his heated face upon his sleeve. 'Something will come of this. I hope it mayn't be human gore!' (*Chapter 4*).

'Oho!' cried Barnaby, glancing over his shoulder. 'He's a merry fellow, that shadow, and keeps close to me, though I *am* silly. We have such pranks, such walks, such runs, such gambols on the grass! Sometimes he'll be half as tall as a church-steeple, and sometimes no bigger than a dwarf. Now, he goes on before, and now behind, and anon he'll be stealing on, on this side, or on that, stopping whenever I stop, and thinking I can't see him, though I have my eye on him sharp enough. Oh! he's a merry fellow. Tell me – is he silly too? I think he is' (*Chapter 6*).

The raven, with his head very much on one side, and his bright eye shining like a diamond, preserved a thoughtful silence for a few seconds, and then replied in a voice so hoarse and distant, that it seemed to come through his thick feathers rather than out of his mouth.

'Halloa, halloa, halloa! What's the matter here? Keep up your spirits. Never say die. Bow wow wow. I'm a devil, I'm a devil, I'm a devil. Hurrah!' – And then, as if exulting in his infernal character, he began to whistle (*Chapter 6*).

'Good-night, noble captain,' whispered the blind man as he held it open for his passage out; 'Farewell, brave general. Bye, bye, illustrious commander. Good luck go with you for a – conceited, bragging, empty-headed, duck-legged idiot' (*Chapter 8:* Stagg).

'Why I wish I may only have a walking funeral, and never be buried decent with a mourning-coach and feathers, if the boy hasn't been and made a key for his own self!' cried Miggs. 'Oh the little villain!' (*Chapter 9*).

'Tell me one thing,' said Miggs. 'Is it thieves?'
'No – no – no!' cried Mr. Tappertit.
'Then,' said Miggs, more faintly than before, 'it's fire. Where is it, sir? It's near this room, I know. I've a good conscience, sir, and would much rather die than go down a ladder. All I wish is, respecting my love to my married sister, Golden Lion Court, number twenty-sivin, second bell-handle on the right-hand door-post' (*Chapter 9*).

Although the best room of the inn, it had the melancholy aspect of grandeur in decay, and was much too vast for comfort. Rich rustling hangings, waving on the walls; and, better far, the rustling of youth and beauty's dress; the light of women's eyes, outshining the tapers and their own rich jewels; the sound of gentle tongues, and music, and the tread of maiden feet, had once been there, and filled it with delight. But they were gone, and with them all its gladness. It was no longer a home; children were never born and bred there; the fireside had become mercenary – a something to be bought and sold – a very courtesan: let who would die, or sit beside, or leave it, it was still the same – it missed nobody, cared for nobody, had equal warmth and smiles for all. God help the man whose heart ever changes with the world, as an old mansion when it becomes an inn! (*Chapter 10*).

Every man smoked his pipe with a face of grave and serious delight, and looked at his neighbour with a sort of quiet congratulation. Nay, it was felt to be such a holiday and special night, that, on the motion of little Solomon Daisy, every man (including John himself) put down his sixpence for a can of flip, which grateful beverage was brewed with all despatch, and set down in the midst of them on the brick floor; both that it might simmer and stew before the fire, and that its fragrant steam, rising up among them, and mixing with the wreaths of vapour from their pipes, might shroud them in a delicious atmosphere of their own, and shut out all the world. The very furniture of the room seemed to mellow and deepen in its tone; the ceiling and walls looked blacker and more highly polished, the curtains of a ruddier red; the fire burnt clear and high, and the crickets in the hearthstone chirped with a more than wonted satisfaction (*Chapter 11*).

There are, still, worse places than the Temple, on a sultry day, for basking in the sun, or resting idly in the shade. There is yet a drowsiness in its courts, and a dreamy dulness in its trees and gardens; those who pace its lanes and squares may yet hear the echoes of their footsteps on the sounding stones, and read upon its gates, in passing from the tumult of the Strand or Fleet Street, 'Who enters here leaves noise behind.' There is still the plash of falling water in fair Fountain Court, and there are yet nooks and corners where dun-haunted students may look down from their dusty garrets, on a vagrant ray of sunlight patching the shade of the tall houses, and seldom troubled to reflect a passing stranger's form *(Chapter 15)*.

'As to our mode of life, every man has a right to live in the best way he can; and to make himself as comfortable as he can, or he is an unnatural scoundrel' *(Chapter 15: Chester)*.

'The very idea of marrying a girl whose father was killed, like meat! Good God, Ned, how disagreeable!' *(Chapter 15: Chester)*.

'Oh, Doll, Doll,' said her good-natured father. 'If you ever have a husband of your own – '
Dolly glanced at the glass.
' – Well, *when* you have,' said the locksmith, 'never faint, my darling. More domestic unhappiness has come of easy fainting, Doll, than from all the greater passions put together. Remember that, my dear, if you would be really happy, which you never can be, if your husband isn't' *(Chapter 19: Gabriel Varden)*.

'To make one's sweetheart miserable is well enough and quite right, but to be made miserable one's-self is a little too much!' *(Chapter 20: Dolly Varden)*.

'There are strings,' said Mr. Tappertit, flourishing his bread-and-cheese knife in the air, 'in the human heart that had better not be wibrated. That's what's the matter' *(Chapter 22)*.

'In every page of this enlightened writer, I find some captivating hypocrisy which has never occurred to me before, or some superlative piece of selfishness to which I was utterly a stranger. I should quite blush for myself before this stupendous creature, if, remembering his precepts, one might blush at anything. An amazing man! a nobleman indeed! any King or Queen may make a Lord, but only the devil himself – and the Graces – can make a Chesterfield' *(Chapter 23: Chester)*.

'You were drinking before you came here.'
'I always am when I can get it,' cried Hugh boisterously, waving the empty glass above his head, and throwing himself into a rude dancing attitude. 'I always am. Why not? Ha ha ha! What's so good to me as this? What ever has been? What else has kept away the cold on bitter nights, and driven hunger off in starving times? What else has given me the strength and courage of a man, when men would have left me to die, a puny child? I should never have had a man's heart but for this. I should have died in a ditch. Where's he who when I was a weak and sickly wretch, with trembling legs and fading sight, bade me cheer up, as this did? I never knew him; not I. I drink to the drink, master. Ha ha ha!' *(Chapter 23)*.

'We all change, but that's with Time; Time does his work honestly, and I don't mind him. A fig for Time, sir. Use him well, and he's a hearty fellow, and scorns to have you at a disadvantage. But care and suffering (and those have changed her) are devils, sir – secret, stealthy, undermining devils – who tread down the brightest flowers in Eden, and do more havoc in a month than Time does in a year' *(Chapter 26: Gabriel Varden)*.

Mr. Chester waved his hand, and smiled a courteous welcome.
'The door will be opened immediately,' he said. 'There is nobody but a very dilapidated female to perform such offices. You will excuse her infirmities? If she were in a more elevated station of society, she would be gouty. Being but a hewer of wood and drawer of water, she is rheumatic. My dear Haredale, these are natural class distinctions, depend upon it' *(Chapter 26)*.

'Master has no intentions, sir,' murmured Miggs . . . 'but to be as grateful as his natur will let him, for everythink he owns which it is in his powers to appreciate. But we never, sir' – said Miggs, looking sideways at Mrs. Varden, and interlarding her discourse with a sigh – 'we never know the full value of *some* wines and fig-trees till we love 'em. So much the worse, sir, for them as has the slighting of 'em on their consciences when they're gone to be in full blow elsewhere.' And Miss Miggs cast up her eyes to signify where that might be *(Chapter 27)*.

'Oh, mim,' said Miggs, returning with the candle. 'Oh gracious me, mim, there's a gentleman! Was there ever such an angel to talk as he is – and such a sweet-looking man! So upright and noble, that he seems to despise the very ground he walks on! and yet so mild and condescending, that he seems to say "but I will take notice on it too." And to think of his taking you for Miss Dolly, and Miss Dolly for your sister – Oh, my goodness me, if I was master wouldn't I be jealous of him!' *(Chapter 27)*.

The thoughts of worldly men are for ever regulated by a moral law of gravitation, which, like the physical one, holds them down to earth. The bright glory of day, and the silent wonders of a starlit night, appeal to their minds in vain. There are no signs in the sun, or in the moon, or in the stars, for their reading. They are like some wise men, who, learning to know each planet by its Latin name, have quite forgotten such small heavenly constellations as Charity, Forbearance, Universal Love, and Mercy, although they shine by night and day so brightly that the blind may see them; and who, looking upward at the spangled sky, see nothing there but the reflection of their own great wisdom and book-learning.
It is curious to imagine these people of the world, busy in thought, turning their eyes towards the countless spheres that shine above us, and making them reflect the only images their minds contain. The man who lives but in the breath of princes, has nothing in

his sight but stars for courtiers' breasts. The envious man beholds his neighbour's honours even in the sky; to the money-hoarder, and the mass of worldly folk, the whole great universe above glitters with sterling coin – fresh from the mint – stamped with the sovereign's head coming always between them and heaven, turn where they may. So do the shadows of our own desires stand between us and our better angels, and thus their brightness is eclipsed *(Chapter 29)*.

'Ah!' retorted Joe, 'but you don't care for glory.'
'For what?' said the Lion.
'Glory.'
'No,' returned the Lion, with supreme indifference. 'I don't. You're right in that, Mr. Willet. When Glory comes here, and calls for anything to drink and changes a guinea to pay for it, I'll give it him for nothing. It's my belief, sir, that the Glory's arms wouldn't do a very strong business' *(Chapter 31)*.

He [Joe Willet] went out by Islington and so on to Highgate, and sat on many stones and gates, but there were no voices in the bells to bid him turn. Since the time of noble Whittington, fair flower of merchants, bells have come to have less sympathy with human-kind. They only ring for money and on state occasions. Wanderers have increased in number; ships leave the Thames for distant regions, carrying from stem to stern no other cargo; the bells are silent; they ring out no entreaties or regrets; they are used to it and and have grown worldly *(Chapter 31)*.

The form of Mr. Tappertit stood confessed, with a brown-paper cap stuck negligently on one side of its head, and its arms very much a-kimbo.
'Have my ears deceived me,' said the 'prentice, 'or do I dream! am I to thank thee, Fortun', or to cus thee – which?'
He gravely descended from his elevation, took down his piece of looking-glass, planted it against the wall upon the usual bench, twisted his head round, and looked closely at his legs.
'If they're a dream,' said Sim, 'let sculptures have such wisions, and chisel 'em out when they wake. This is reality. Sleep has no such limbs as them. Tremble, Willet, and despair. She's mine! She's mine' *(Chapter 31)*.

Misfortunes, saith the adage, never come singly. There is little doubt that troubles are exceedingly gregarious in their nature, and flying in flocks, are apt to perch capriciously; crowding on the heads of some poor wights until there is not an inch of room left on their unlucky crowns, and taking no more notice of others who offer as good resting-places for the soles of their feet, than if they had no existence *(Chapter 32)*.

'You do wrong not to fill your glass,' said Mr. Chester, holding up his own before the light. 'Wine in moderation – not in excess, for that makes men ugly – has a thousand pleasant influences. It brightens the eye, improves the voice, imparts a new vivacity to one's thoughts and conversation: you should try it, Ned' *(Chapter 32)*.

'The hearts of animals – of bullocks, sheep, and so forth – are cooked and devoured, as I am told, by the lower classes, with a vast deal of relish. Men are sometimes stabbed to the heart, shot to the heart; but as to speaking from the heart, or to the heart, or being warm-hearted, or cold-hearted, or broken-hearted, or being all heart, or having no heart – pah! these things are nonsense, Ned' *(Chapter 32:* Chester).

'Edward, my father had a son, who being a fool like you, and, like you, entertaining low and disobedient sentiments, he disinherited and cursed one morning after breakfast. The circumstance occurs to me with a singular clearness of recollection this evening. I remember eating muffins at the time, with marmalade *(Chapter 32:* Chester).

The profusion too, the rich and lavish bounty, of that goodly tavern! It was not enough that one fire roared and sparkled on its spacious hearth; in the tiles which paved and compassed it, five hundred flickering fires burnt brightly also. It was not enough that one red curtain shut the wild night out, and shed its cheerful influence on the room. In every saucepan lid, and candlestick, and vessel of copper, brass, or tin that hung upon the walls, were countless ruddy hangings, flashing and gleaming with every motion of the blaze, and offering, let the eye wander where it might, interminable vistas of the same rich colour. The old oak wainscoting, the beams, the chairs, the seats, reflected it in a deep dull glimmer. There were fires and red curtains in the very eyes of the drinkers, in their buttons, in their liquor, in the pipes they smoked *(Chapter 33)*.

'When I left here to-night,' said Solomon Daisy, 'I little thought what day of the month it was. I have never gone alone into the church after dark on this day, for seven-and-twenty years. I have heard it said that as we keep our birthdays when we are alive, so the ghosts of dead people, who are not easy in their graves, keep the day they died upon. How the wind roars!' *(Chapter 33)*.

'You surprise me, Grueby,' said the gentleman. 'At a crisis like the present, when Queen Elizabeth, that maiden monarch, weeps within her tomb, and Bloody Mary, with a brow of gloom and shadow, stalks triumphant – '
'Oh, sir,' cried the man, gruffly, 'where's the use of talking of Bloody Mary, under such circumstances as the present, when my lord's wet through, and tired with hard riding?' Let's either go on to London, sir, or put up at once; or that unfort'nate Bloody Mary will have more to answer for – and she's done a deal more harm in her grave than she ever did in her lifetime, I believe' *(Chapter 35:* Gashford and Grueby).

'It is odd enough, but certain people seem to have as great a pleasure in pronouncing titles as their owners have in wearing them' *(Chapter 35:* John Willet).

It is the unhappy lot of thoroughly weak men, that their very sympathies, affections, confidences – all the qualities which in better constituted minds are virtues – dwindle into foibles, or turn into downright vices *(Chapter 36)*.

To surround anything, however monstrous or ridiculous, with an air of mystery, is to invest it with a secret charm, and power of attraction which to the crowd is irresistible. False priests, false prophets, false doctors, false patriots, false prodigies of every kind, veiling their proceedings in mystery, have always addressed themselves at an immense advantage to the popular credulity, and have been, perhaps, more indebted to that resource in gaining and keeping for a time the upper hand of Truth and Common Sense, than to any half-dozen items in the whole catalogue of imposture *(Chapter 37)*.

'These smalls,' said Dennis, rubbing his legs; 'these very smalls – they belonged to a friend of mine that's left off sich incumbrances for ever: this coat too – I've often walked behind this coat, in the street, and wondered whether it would ever come to me; this pair of shoes have danced a hornpipe for another man, afore my eyes, full half a dozen times at least: and as to my hat,' he said, taking it off, and whirling it round upon his fist – 'Lord! I've seen this hat go up Holborn on the box of a hackney-coach – ah, many and many a day!' *(Chapter 39)*.

'In an altered state of society – which must ensue if we break out and are victorious – when the locksmith's child is mine, Miggs must be got rid of somehow, or she'll poison the tea-kettle one evening when I'm out. He might marry Miggs, if he was drunk enough. It shall be done. I'll make a note of it' *(Chapter 39:* Simon Tappertit).

'Here she is at last!' cried Gabriel. 'And how well you look, Doll, and how late you are, my darling!'

How well she looked? Well? Why, if he had exhausted every laudatory adjective in the dictionary, it wouldn't have been praise enough. When and where was there ever such a plump, roguish, comely, bright-eyed, enticing, bewitching, captivating, maddening little puss in all this world, as Dolly! What was the Dolly of five years ago, to the Dolly of that day! How many coachmakers, saddlers, cabinet-makers, and professors of other useful arts, had deserted their fathers, mothers, sisters, brothers, and, most of all, their cousins, for the love of her! How many unknown gentlemen – supposed to be of mighty fortunes, if not titles – had waited round the corner after dark, and tempted Miggs the incorruptible, with golden guineas, to deliver offers of marriage folded up in love-letters! How many disconsolate fathers and substantial tradesmen had waited on the locksmith for the same purpose, with dismal tales of how their sons had lost their appetites, and taken to shut themselves up in dark bedrooms, and wandering in desolate suburbs with pale faces, and all because of Dolly Varden's loveliness and cruelty! How many young men, in all previous times of unprecedented steadiness, had turned suddenly wild and wicked for the same reason, and, in an ecstasy of unrequited love, taken to wrench off door-knockers, and invert the boxes of rheumatic watchmen! How had she recruited the king's service, both by sea and land, through rendering desperate his loving subjects between the ages of eighteen and twenty-five! How many young ladies had publicly professed, with tears in their eyes, that for their tastes she was much too short, too tall, too bold, too cold, too

stout, too thin, too fair, too dark – too everything but handsome! How many old ladies, taking counsel together, had thanked Heaven their daughters were not like her, and had hoped she might come to no harm, and had thought she would come to no good, and had wondered what people saw in her, and had arrived at the conclusion that she was 'going off' in her looks, or had never come on in them, and that she was a thorough imposition and a popular mistake! *(Chapter 41)*.

Mrs. Varden held that, in such stirring and tremendous times as those in which they lived, it would be much more to the purpose if Dolly became a regular subscriber to the Thunderer, where she would have an opportunity of reading Lord George Gordon's speeches word for word, which would be a greater comfort and solace to her, than a hundred and fifty Blue Beards ever could impart. She appealed in support of this proposition to Miss Miggs, then in waiting, who said that indeed the peace of mind she had derived from the perusal of that paper generally, but especially of one article of the very last week as ever was, entitled 'Great Britain drenched in gore,' exceeded all belief; the same composition, she added, had also wrought such a comforting effect on the mind of a married sister of hers, then resident at Golden Lion Court, number twenty-sivin, second bell-handle on the right-hand door-post, that, being in a delicate state of health, and in fact expecting an addition to her family, she had been seized with fits directly after its perusal, and had raved of the Inquisition ever since; to the great improvement of her husband and friends *(Chapter 41)*.

'Don't let there be words on my account, mim,' sobbed Miggs. 'It's much the best that we should part. I wouldn't stay – oh gracious me! – and make dissensions, not for a annual gold mine, and found in tea and sugar' *(Chapter 41)*.

'There are various degrees and kinds of blindness, widow. There is the connubial blindness, ma'am, which perhaps you may have observed in the course of your own experience, and which is a kind of wilful and self-bandaging blindness. There is the blindness of party, ma'am, and public men, which is the blindness of a mad bull in the midst of a regiment of soldiers clothed in red. There is the blind confidence of youth, which is the blindness of young kittens, whose eyes have not yet opened on the world; and there is that physical blindness, ma'am, of which I am, contrary to my own desire, a most illustrious example. Added to these, ma'am, is that blindness of the intellect, of which we have a specimen in your interesting son, and which, having sometimes glimmerings and dawnings of the light, is scarcely to be trusted as a total darkness *(Chapter 45:* Stagg).

In the exhaustless catalogue of Heaven's mercies to mankind, the power we have of finding some germs of comfort in the hardest trials must ever occupy the foremost place; not only because it supports and upholds us when we most require to be sustained, but because in this source of consolation there is something, we have reason to believe, of the divine spirit;

something of that goodness which detects amidst our own evil doings, a redeeming quality; something which, even in our fallen nature, we possess in common with the angels; which had its being in the old time when they trod the earth, and lingers on it yet, in pity *(Chapter 47)*.

'Grip, Grip, Grip – Grip the clever, Grip the wicked, Grip the knowing – Grip, Grip, Grip,' cried the raven, whom Barnaby had shut up on the approach of this stern personage. 'I'm a devil I'm a devil I'm a devil, Never say die Hurrah Bow wow wow, Polly put the kettle on we'll all have tea' *(Chapter 47)*.

They had torches among them, and the chief faces were distinctly visible. That they had been engaged in the destruction of some building was sufficiently apparent, and that it was a Catholic place of worship was evident from the spoils they bore as trophies, which were easily recognisable for the vestments of priests, and rich fragments of altar furniture. Covered with soot, and dirt, and dust, and lime; their garments torn to rags; their hair hanging wildly about them; their hands and faces jagged and bleeding with the wounds of rusty nails; Barnaby, Hugh, and Dennis hurried on before them all, like hideous madmen. After them, the dense throng came fighting on: some singing; some shouting in triumph; some quarelling among themselves; some menacing the spectators as they passed; some with great wooden fragments, on which they spent their rage as if they had been alive, rending them limb from limb, and hurling the scattered morsels high into the air; some in a drunken state, unconscious of the hurts they had received from falling bricks, and stones, and beams; one borne upon a shutter, in the very midst, covered with a dingy cloth, a senseless, ghastly heap. Thus a vision of coarse faces, with here and there a blot of flaring, smoky light; a dream of demon heads and savage eyes, and sticks and iron bars uplifted in the air, and whirled about; a bewildering horror, in which so much was seen, and yet so little, which seemed so long, and yet so short, in which there were so many phantoms, not to be forgotten all through life, and yet so many things that could not be observed in one distracting glimpse – it flitted onward, and was gone *(Chapter 50)*.

Miss Miggs, who, having arrived at that restless state and sensitive condition of the nervous system which are the result of long watching, did, by a constant rubbing and tweaking of her nose, a perpetual change of position (arising from the sudden growth of imaginary knots and knobs in her chair), a frequent friction of her eyebrows, the incessant recurrence of a small cough, a small groan, a gasp, a sigh, a sniff, a spasmodic start, and by other demonstrations of that nature, so file down and rasp, as it were, the patience of the locksmith, that after looking at her in silence for some time, he at last broke out into this apostrophe:–

'Miggs, my good girl, go to bed – do go to bed. You're really worse than the dripping of a hundred water-butts outside the window, or the scratching of as many mice behind the wainscot. I can't bear it. Do go to bed, Miggs. To oblige me – do.'

'You haven't got nothing to untie, sir,' returned Miss Miggs, 'and therefore your requests does not surprise me. But missis has – and while you sit up, mim' – she added, turning to the locksmith's wife, 'I couldn't, no, not if twenty times the quantity of cold water was aperiently running down my back at this moment, go to bed with a quiet spirit' *(Chapter 51)*.

At length, after the clock had struck two, there was a sound at the street door, as if somebody had fallen against the knocker by accident. Miss Miggs immediately jumping up and clapping her hands, cried with a drowsy mingling of the sacred and profane, 'Ally Looyer, mim! there's Simmuns's knock!' *(Chapter 51)*.

'Martha,' said the locksmith, turning to his wife, and shaking his head sorrowfully, while a smile at the absurd figure before him still played upon his open face, 'I trust it may turn out that this poor lad is not the victim of the knaves and fools we have so often had words about, and who have done so much harm to-day. If he has been at Warwick Street or Duke Street to-night – '

'He has been at neither, sir,' cried Mr. Tappertit in a loud voice, which he suddenly dropped into a whisper as he repeated, with eyes fixed upon the locksmith, 'he has been at neither.' . . .

'He was not at Duke Street, or at Warwick Street, G. Varden,' said Simon, sternly; 'but he *was* at Westminster. Perhaps, sir, he kicked a county member, perhaps, sir, he tapped a lord – you may stare, sir, I repeat it – blood flowed from noses, and perhaps he tapped a lord. Who knows? This,' he added, putting his hand into his waistcoat-pocket, and taking out a large tooth, at the sight of which both Miggs and Mrs. Varden screamed, 'this was a bishop's. Beware, G. Varden!' *(Chapter 51)*.

'Recollect from this time that all good things perverted to evil purposes, are worse than those which are naturally bad. A thoroughly wicked woman, is wicked indeed. When religion goes wrong, she is very wrong, for the same reason. Let us say no more about it, my dear' *(Chapter 51: Gabriel Varden)*.

A mob is usually a creature of very mysterious existence, particularly in a large city. Where it comes from or whither it goes, few men can tell. Assembling and dispersing with equal suddenness, it is as difficult to follow to its various sources as the sea itself; nor does the parallel stop here, for the ocean is not more fickle and uncertain, more terrible when roused, more unreasonable, or more cruel *(Chapter 51)*.

Yes. Here was the bar – the bar that the boldest never entered without special invitation – the sanctuary, the mystery, the hallowed ground: here it was, crammed with men, clubs, sticks, torches, pistols; filled with a deafening noise, oaths, shouts, screams, hootings; changed all at once into a bear-garden, a madhouse, an infernal temple: men darting in and out, by door and window, smashing the glass, turning the taps, drinking liquor out of China punchbowls, sitting astride of casks, smoking private and personal pipes, cutting down the sacred grove of lemons, hacking and hewing at the celebrated cheese, breaking open inviolable drawers, putting things in their pockets which didn't belong to them, dividing his own money before his own eyes, wantonly wasting, breaking, pulling down and tearing up: nothing quiet, nothing private: men everywhere – above, below, overhead, in the bedrooms, in the kitchen, in the yard, in the stables – clambering in at windows when there were doors wide open; dropping out of windows when the stairs were handy; leaping over the bannisters into chasms of passages: new faces and figures presenting themselves every instant – some yelling, some singing, some fighting, some breaking glass and crockery, some laying the dust with the liquor they couldn't drink, some ringing the bells till they pulled them down, others beating them with pokers till they beat them into fragments: more men still – more, more, more – swarming on like insects: noise, smoke, light, darkness, frolic, anger, laughter, groans, plunder, fear, and ruin! *(Chapter 54).*

The man was hurrying to the door, when suddenly there came towards them on the wind, the loud and rapid tolling of an alarm-bell, and then a bright and vivid glare streamed up, which illumined, not only the whole chamber, but all the country.

It was not the sudden change from darkness to this dreadful light, it was not the sound of distant shrieks and shouts of triumph, it was not this dread invasion of the serenity and peace of night, that drove the man back as though a thunderbolt had struck him. It was the Bell. If the ghastliest shape the human mind has ever pictured in its wildest dreams had risen up before him, he could not have staggered backward from its touch, as he did from the first sound of that loud iron voice. With eyes that started from his head, his limbs convulsed, his face most horrible to see, he raised one arm high up into the air, and holding something visionary back and down, with his other hand, drove at it as though he held a knife and stabbed it to the heart. He clutched his hair, and stopped his ears, and travelled madly round and round; then gave a frightful cry, and with it rushed away: still, still, the Bell tolled on and seemed to follow him – louder and louder, hotter and hotter yet. The glare grew brighter, the roar of voices deeper; the crash of heavy bodies falling, shook the air; bright streams of sparks rose up into the sky; but louder than them all – rising faster far, to Heaven – a million times more fierce and furious – pouring forth dreadful secrets after its long silence – speaking the language of the dead – the Bell – the Bell! *(Chapter 55).*

It ceased; but not in his ears. The knell was at his heart. No work of man had ever voice like that which sounded there, and warned him that it cried unceasingly to heaven. Who could hear that bell, and not know what it said! There was murder in its every note – cruel, relentless, savage murder – the murder of a confiding man, by one who held his every trust. Its ringing summoned phantoms from their graves. What face was that, in which a friendly smile changed to a look of half incredulous horror, which stiffened for a moment into one of pain, then changed again into an imploring glance at Heaven, and so fell idly down with

upturned eyes, like the dead stags' he had often peeped at when a little child: shrinking and shuddering – there was a dreadful thing to think of now! – and clinging to an apron as he looked! He sank upon the ground, and grovelling down as if he would dig himself a place to hide in, covered his face and ears: but no, no, no, – a hundred walls and roofs of brass would not shut out that bell, for in it spoke the wrathful voice of God, and from that voice, the whole wide universe could not afford a refuge! *(Chapter 55).*

If Bedlam gates had been flung open wide, there would not have issued forth such maniacs as the frenzy of that night had made. There were men there, who danced and trampled on the beds of flowers as though they trod down human enemies, and wrenched them from the stalks, like savages who twisted human necks. There were men who cast their lighted torches in the air, and suffered them to fall upon their heads and faces, blistering the skin with deep unseemly burns. There were men who rushed up to the fire, and paddled in it with their hands as if in water; and others who were restrained by force from plunging in, to gratify their deadly longing. On the skull of one drunken lad – not twenty, by his looks – who lay upon the ground with a bottle to his mouth, the lead from the roof came streaming down in a shower of liquid fire, white hot; melting his head like wax. When the scattered parties were collected, men – living yet, but singed as with hot irons – were plucked out of the cellars, and carried off upon the shoulders of others, who strove to wake them as they went along, with ribald jokes, and left them, dead, in the passages of hospitals. But of all the howling throng not one learnt mercy from, nor sickened at, these sights; nor was the fierce, besotted, senseless rage of one man glutted.

Slowly, and in small clusters, with hoarse hurrahs and repetitions of their usual cry, the assembly dropped away. The last few red-eyed stragglers reeled after those who had gone before; the distant noise of men calling to each other, and whistling for others whom they missed, grew fainter and fainter; at length even these sounds died away, and silence reigned alone *(Chapter 55).*

He sat down on the ground before the door, and putting his staff across his knees in case of alarm or surprise, summoned Grip to dinner.

This call, the bird obeyed with great alacrity; crying, as he sidled up to his master, 'I'm a devil, I'm a Polly, I'm a kettle, I'm a Protestant, No Popery!' Having learnt this latter sentiment from the gentry among whom he had lived of late, he delivered it with uncommon emphasis.

'Well said, Grip!' cried his master, as he fed him with the daintiest bits. 'Well said, old boy!'

'Never say die, bow wow wow, keep up your spirits, Grip Grip Grip, Holloa! We'll all have tea, I'm a Protestant kettle, No Popery!' cried the raven.

'Gordon for ever, Grip!' cried Barnaby *(Chapter 57).*

'I suppose the pigs will join 'em next,' said the serjeant, with an imprecation on the rioters, 'now that the birds have set 'em the example.'

'The birds!' repeated Tom Green.

'Ah – the birds,' said the serjeant testily; 'that's English, an't it?'

'I don't know what you mean.'

'Go to the guard-house, and see. You'll find a bird there, that's got their cry as pat as any of 'em, and bawls "No Popery," like a man – or like a devil, as he says he is. I shouldn't wonder. The devil's loose in London somewhere. Damme if I wouldn't twist his neck round, on the chance, if I had *my* way.'

The young man had taken two or three steps away, as if to go and see this creature, when he was arrested by the voice of Barnaby.

'It's mine,' he called out, half laughing and half weeping – 'my pet, my friend Grip. Ha ha ha! Don't hurt him, he has done no harm. I taught him; it's my fault. Let me have him, if you please. He's the only friend I have left now. He'll not dance, or talk, or whistle for you, I know; but he will for me, because he knows me and loves me – though you wouldn't think it – very well. You wouldn't hurt a bird, I'm sure. You're a brave soldier, sir, and wouldn't harm a woman or a child – no, no, nor a poor bird, I'm certain' *(Chapter 58)*.

'Miss Haredale,' said Sim, after a very awkward silence, 'I hope you're as comfortable as circumstances will permit of. Dolly Varden, my darling – my own, my lovely one – I hope *you're* pretty comfortable likewise.'

Poor little Dolly! She saw how it was; hid her face in her hands; and sobbed more bitterly than ever.

'You meet in me, Miss V.,' said Simon, laying his hand upon his breast, 'not a 'prentice, not a workman, not a slave, not the victim of your father's tyrannical behaviour, but the leader of a great people, the captain of a noble band, in which these gentlemen are, as I may say, corporals and serjeants. You behold in me, not a private individual, but a public character, not a mender of locks, but a healer of the wounds of his unhappy country. Dolly V., sweet Dolly V., for how many years have I looked forward to this present meeting! For how many years has it been my intention to exalt and ennoble you! I redeem it. Behold in me your husband. Yes beautiful Dolly – charmer – enslaver – S. Tappertit is all your own!' *(Chapter 59)*.

The prisoner [Rudge], left to himself, sat down upon his bedstead: and resting his elbows on his knees, and his chin upon his hands, remained in that attitude for hours. It would be hard to say, of what nature his reflections were. They had no distinctness, and, saving for some flashes now and then, no reference to his condition or the train of circumstances by which it had been brought about. The cracks in the pavement of his cell, the chinks in the wall where stone was joined to stone, the bars in the window, the iron ring upon the floor, – such things as these, subsiding strangely into one another, and awakening an indescribable kind of interest and amusement, engrossed his whole mind; and although at the bottom of his every thought there was an uneasy sense of guilt, and dread of death, he felt no more than that vague consciousness of it, which a sleeper has of pain. It pursues him through his dreams, gnaws at the heart of all his fancied pleasures,

robs the banquet of its taste, music of its sweetness, makes happiness itself unhappy, and yet is no bodily sensation, but a phantom without shape, or form, or visible presence; pervading everything, but having no existence; recognisable everywhere, but nowhere seen, or touched, or met with face to face, until the sleep is past, and waking agony returns *(Chapter 62)*.

There was another shriek, and another, and then a shrill voice cried, 'Is Simmun below!' At the same moment a lean neck was stretched over the parapet, and Miss Miggs, indistinctly seen in the gathering gloom of evening, screeched in a frenzied manner, 'Oh! dear gentlemen, let me hear Simmuns's answer from his own lips. Speak to me, Simmun. Speak to me!'

Mr. Tappertit, who was not at all flattered by this compliment, looked up, and bidding her hold her peace, ordered her to come down and open the door, for they wanted her master, and would take no denial.

'Oh good gentlemen!' cried Miss Miggs. 'Oh my own precious, precious Simmun – '

'Hold your nonsense, will you!' retorted Mr. Tappertit; 'and come down and open the door. – G. Varden, drop that gun, or it will be worse for you.'

'Don't mind his gun,' screamed Miggs. 'Simmun and gentlemen, I poured a mug of table-beer right down the barrel.'

The crowd gave a loud shout, which was followed by a roar of laughter.

'It wouldn't go off, not if you was to load it up to the muzzle,' screamed Miggs. 'Simmun and gentlemen, I'm locked up in the front attic, through the little door on the right hand when you think you've got to the very top of the stairs – and up the flight of corner steps, being careful not to knock your heads against the rafters, and not to tread on one side in case you should fall into the two-pair bedroom through the lath and plaster, which do not bear, but the contrairy, Simmun and gentlemen, I've been locked up here for safety, but my endeavours has always been, and always will be, to be on the right side – the blessed side – and to prenounce the Pope of Babylon, and all her inward and her outward workings, which is Pagin. My sentiments is of little consequences, I know,' cried Miggs, with additional shrillness, 'for my positions is but a servant, and as sich, of humilities, still I gives expressions to my feelings, and places my reliances on them which entertains my own opinions!' *(Chapter 63)*.

The man ... went back again to the rescue, and presently returned with Miss Miggs, limp and doubled up, and very damp from much weeping.

As the young lady had given no tokens of consciousness on their way downstairs, the bearer reported her either dead or dying; and being at some loss what to do with her, was looking round for a convenient bench or heap of ashes on which to place her senseless form, when she suddenly came upon her feet by some mysterious means, thrust back her hair, stared wildly at Mr. Tappertit, cried 'My Simmuns's life is not a wictim!' and dropped into his arms with such promptitude that he staggered and reeled some paces back, beneath his lovely burden.

'Oh bother!' said Mr. Tappertit. 'Here. Catch hold of her, somebody. Lock her up again; she never ought to have been let out.'

'My Simmun!' cried Miss Miggs, in tears, and faintly. 'My for ever, ever blessed Simmun!'

'Hold up, will you,' said Mr. Tappertit, in a very unresponsive tone, 'I'll let you fall if you don't. What are you sliding your feet off the ground for?'

'My angel Simmuns!' murmured Miggs – 'he promised – '

'Promised! Well, and I'll keep my promise,' answered Simon, testily. 'I mean to provide for you, don't I? Stand up!'

'Where am I to go? What is to become of me after my actions of this night!' cried Miggs. 'What resting-places now remains but in the silent tombses!'

'I wish you was in the silent tombses, I do,' cried Mr. Tappertit, 'and boxed up tight, in a good strong one. Here,' he cried to one of the bystanders, in whose ear he whispered for a moment: 'Take her off, will you. You understand where?' *(Chapter 63)*.

At the bidding of the mob, the houses were all illuminated that night – lighted up from top to bottom as at a time of public gaiety and joy. Many years afterwards, old people who lived in their youth near this part of the city, remembered being in a great glare of light, within doors and without, and as they looked, timid and frightened children, from the windows, seeing *a face* go by. Though the whole great crowd and all its other terrors had faded from their recollection, this one object remained; alone, distinct, and well remembered. Even in the unpractised mind of infants, one of these doomed men darting past, and but an instant seen, was an image of force enough to dim the whole concourse; to find itself an all-absorbing place, and hold it ever after *(Chapter 65)*.

There being now a great many parties in the streets, each went to work according to its humour, and a dozen houses were quickly blazing, including those of Sir John Fielding and two other justices, and four in Holborn – one of the greatest thoroughfares in London – which were all burning at the same time, and burned until they went out of themselves, for the people cut the engine hose, and would not suffer the firemen to play upon the flames. At one house near Moorfields, they found in one of the rooms some canary birds in cages, and these they cast into the fire alive. The poor little creatures screamed, it was said, like infants, when they were flung upon the blaze; and one man was so touched that he tried in vain to save them, which roused the indignation of the crowd, and nearly cost him his liffe.

At this same house, one of the fellows who went through the rooms, breaking the furniture and helping to destroy the building, found a child's doll – a poor toy – which he exhibited at the window to the mob below, as the image of some unholy saint which the late occupants had worshipped. While he was doing this, another man with an equally tender conscience (they had both been foremost in throwing down the canary birds for roasting alive), took his seat on the parapet of the house, and harangued the crowd from a pamphlet circulated by the Association, relative to the

true principles of Christianity! Meanwhile the Lord Mayor, with his hands in his pockets, looked on as an idle man might look at any other show, and seem mightily satisfied to have got a good place *(Chapter 66)*.

'Miss, miss,' whispered Dennis, beckoning to her with his forefinger, 'come here – I won't hurt you. Come here, my lamb, will you?'

On hearing this tender epithet, Miss Miggs, who had left off screaming when he opened his lips, and had listened to him attentively, began again; crying 'Oh I'm his lamb! He says I'm his lamb! Oh gracious, why wasn't I born old and ugly! Why was I ever made to be the youngest of six, and all of 'em dead and in their blessed graves, excepting one married sister, which is settled in Golden Lion Court, number twenty-sivin, second bell-handle on the – !' *(Chapter 70)*.

'I wouldn't,' cried Miggs, folding her hands and looking upwards with a kind of devout blankness, 'I wouldn't lay myself out as she does; I wouldn't be as bold as her; I wouldn't seem to say to all male creeturs "Come and kiss me" ' – and here a shudder quite convulsed her frame – 'for any earthly crowns as might be offered. Worlds,' Miggs added solemnly, 'should not reduce me. No. Not if I was Wenis.'

'Well, but you *are* Wenus you know,' said Mr. Dennis, confidentially.

'No, I am not, good gentleman,' answered Miggs, shaking her head with an air of self-denial which seemed to imply that she might be if she chose, but she hoped she knew better. 'No I am not, good gentleman. Don't charge me with it' *(Chapter 70)*.

Light hearts, light hearts, that float so gaily on a smooth stream, that are so sparkling and buoyant in the sunshine – down upon fruit, bloom upon flowers, blush in summer air, life of the winged insect, whose whole existence is a day – how soon ye sink in troubled water! *(Chapter 71)*.

'Ho, gracious me!' cried Miggs, with hysterical derision. 'Ho, gracious me! Yes, to be sure I will. Ho yes! I am an abject slave, and a toiling, moiling, constant-working, always-being-found-fault-with, never-giving-satisfactions, nor-having-no-time-to-clean-one-self, potter's wessel – an't I miss! Ho yes! My situations is lowly, and my capacities is limited, and my duties is to humble myself afore the base degenerating daughters of their blessed mothers as is fit to keep companies with holy saints but is born to persecutions from wicked relations – and to demean myself before them as is no better than Infidels – an't it, miss! Ho yes! My only becoming occupations is to help young flaunting pagins to brush and comb and titiwate theirselves into whitening and suppulchres, and leave the young men to think that there an't a bit of padding in it nor no pinching ins nor fillings out nor pompatums nor deceits nor earthly wanities – an't it, miss! Yes, to be sure it is – ho yes!' *(Chapter 71)*.

'It's been took off'

'By George!' said the Black Lion, striking the table with his hand, 'he's got it!'

'Yes, sir,' said Mr. Willet, with the look of a man

who felt that he had earned a compliment, and deserved it. 'That's where it is. It's been took off.'

'Tell him where it was done,' said the Black Lion to Joe.

'At the defence of the Savannah, father.'

'At the defence of the Salwanners,' repeated Mr. Willet, softly; again looking round the table.

'In America, where the war is,' said Joe.

'In America, where the war is,' repeated Mr. Willet. 'It was took off in the defence of the Salwanners in America where the war is.' Continuing to repeat these words to himself in a low tone of voice (the same information had been conveyed to him in the same terms, at least fifty times before), Mr. Willet arose from table, walked round to Joe, felt his empty sleeve all the way up, from the cuff to where the stump of his arm remained; shook his hand; lighted his pipe at the fire, took a long whiff, walked to the door, turned round once when he had reached it, wiped his left eye with the back of his forefinger, and said, in a faltering voice: 'My son's arm – was took off – at the defence of the – Salwanners – in America – where the war is' – with which words he withdrew, and returned no more that night (Chapter 72).

'Mother,' he said, after a long silence: 'how long, – how many days and nights, – shall I be kept here?'

'Not many, dear. I hope not many.'

'You hope! Ay, but your hoping will not undo these chains. I hope, but they don't mind that. Grip hopes, but who cares for Grip?'

The raven gave a short, dull, melancholy croak. It said 'Nobody,' as plainly as a croak could speak.

'Who cares for Grip, except you and me?' said Barnaby, smoothing the bird's rumpled feathers with his hand. 'He never speaks in this place; he never says a word in jail; he sits and mopes all day in his dark corner, dozing sometimes and sometimes looking at the light that creeps in through the bars, and shines in his bright eye as if a spark from those great fires had fallen into the room and was burning yet. But who cares for Grip?'

The raven croaked again – Nobody.

'And by the way,' said Barnaby, withdrawing his hand from the bird, and laying it upon his mother's arm, as he looked eagerly in her face; 'if they kill me – they may: I heard it said they would – what will become of Grip when I am dead?'

The sound of the word, or the current of his own thoughts, suggested to Grip his old phrase 'Never say die!' But he stopped short in the middle of it, drew a dismal cork, and subsided into a faint croak, as if he lacked the heart to get through the shortest sentence (Chapter 73).

Indeed this gentleman's stoicism was of that not uncommon kind, which enables a man to bear with exemplary fortitude the afflictions of his friends, but renders him, by way of counterpoise, rather selfish and sensitive in respect of any that happen to befall himself (Chapter 74).

'Ho master, ho mim!' cried Miggs, 'can I constrain my feelings in this here once agin united moments! Ho Mr. Warden, here's blessedness among relations, sir!

Here's forgivenesses of injuries, here's amicablenesses!' (Chapter 80).

The ashes of the commonest fire are melancholy things, for in them there is an image of death and ruin, – of something that has been bright, and is but dull, cold, dreary dust, – with which our nature forces us to sympathise. How much more sad the crumbled embers of a home: the casting down of that great altar, where the worst among us sometimes perform the worship of the heart; and where the best have offered up such sacrifices, and done such deeds of heroism, as, chronicled, would put the proudest temples of old Time, with all their vaunting annals, to the blush! (Chapter 81).

MARTIN CHUZZLEWIT

It has been rumoured, and it is needless to say the rumour originated in the same base quarters, that a certain male Chuzzlewit, whose birth must be admitted to be involved in some obscurity, was of very mean and low descent. How stands the proof? When the son of that individual, to whom the secret of his father's birth was supposed to have been communicated by his father in his lifetime, lay upon his death-bed, this question was put to him in a distinct, solemn, and formal way: 'Toby Chuzzlewit, who was your grandfather?' To which he, with his last breath, no less distinctly, solemnly, and formally replied: and his words were taken down at the time, and signed by six witnesses, each with his name and address in full: 'The Lord No Zoo' (Chapter 1).

It has been remarked that Mr. Pecksniff was a moral man. So he was. Perhaps there never was a more moral man than Mr. Pecksniff: especially in his conversation and correspondence. It was once said of him by a homely admirer, that he had a Fortunatus's purse of good sentiments in his inside. In this particular he was like the girl in the fairy tale, except that if they were not actual diamonds which fell from his lips, they were the very brightest paste, and shone prodigiously (Chapter 2).

'Even the worldly goods of which we have just disposed,' said Mr. Pecksniff, glancing round the table when he had finished, 'even cream, sugar, tea, toast, ham – '

'And eggs,' suggested Charity in a low voice.

'And eggs,' said Mr. Pecksniff, 'even they have their moral. See how they come and go! Every pleasure is transitory. We can't even eat, long. If we indulge in harmless fluids, we get the dropsy; if in exciting liquids, we get drunk. What a soothing reflection is that!'

'Don't say we get drunk, pa,' urged the eldest Miss Pecksniff.

'When I say, we my dear,' returned her father, 'I mean mankind in general; the human race, considered as a body, and not as individuals. There is nothing personal in morality, my love. Even such a thing as this,' said Mr. Pecksniff, laying the forefinger of his left hand upon the brown-paper patch on the top of his head, 'slight casual baldness though it be, reminds us that we are but' – he was going to say 'worms,' but recollecting that worms were not remarkable for heads of hair, he substituted 'flesh and blood' *(Chapter 2)*.

Mention has been already made more than once, of a certain Dragon who swung and creaked complainingly before the village ale-house door. A faded, and an ancient dragon he was; and many a wintry storm of rain, snow, sleet, and hail, had changed his colour from a gaudy blue to a faint lack-lustre shade of grey. But there he hung; rearing, in a state of monstrous imbecility, on his hind-legs; waxing, with every month that passed, so much more dim and shapeless, that as you gazed at him on one side of the sign-board it seemed as if he must be gradually melting through it, and coming out upon the other.

He was a courteous and considerate dragon too; or had been in his distincter days; for in the midst of his rampant feebleness, he kept one of his fore-paws near his nose, as though he would say, 'Don't mind me – it's only my fun'; while he held out the other, in polite and hospitable entreaty *(Chapter 3)*.

It was none of your frivolous and preposterously bright bedrooms, where nobody can close an eye with any kind of propriety or decent regard to the association of ideas; but it was a good, dull, leaden, drowsy place, where every article of furniture reminded you that you came there to sleep, and that you were expected to go to sleep. There was no wakeful reflection of the fire there, as in your modern chambers, which upon the darkest nights have a watchful consciousness of French polish; the old Spanish mahogany winked at it now and then, as a dozing cat or dog might, nothing more. The very size and shape, and hopeless immoveability, of the bedstead, and wardrobe, and in a minor degree of even the chairs and tables provoked sleep; they were plainly apoplectic and disposed to snore. There were no staring portraits to remonstrate with you for being lazy; no round-eyed birds upon the curtains, disgustingly wide awake, and insufferably prying. The thick neutral hangings, and the dark blinds, and the heavy heap of bed-clothes, were all designed to hold in sleep, and act as non-conductors to the day and getting up. Even the old stuffed fox upon the top of the wardrobe was devoid of any spark of vigilance, for his glass eye had fallen out, and he slumbered as he stood *(Chapter 3)*.

It would be no description of Mr. Pecksniff's gentleness of manner to adopt the common parlance, and say, that he looked at this moment as if butter wouldn't melt in his mouth. He rather looked as if any quantity of butter might have been made out of him, by churning the milk of human kindness, as it spouted upwards from his heart *(Chapter 3)*.

Mr. Pecksniff cast him off, as Saint George might have repudiated the Dragon in that animal's last moments *(Chapter 4)*.

'Sir, if there is a man on earth whom a gentleman would feel proud and honoured to be mistaken for, that man is my friend Slyme. For he is, without an exception, the highest-minded, the most independent-spirited, most original, spiritual, classical, talented, the most thoroughly Shakespearian, if not Miltonic, and at the same time the most disgustingly-unappreciated dog I know' *(Chapter 4:* Tigg).

'Every man of true genius has his peculiarity. Sir, the peculiarity of my friend Slyme is, that he is always waiting round the corner. He is perpetually round the corner, sir. He is round the corner at this instant. Now,' said the gentleman, shaking his fore-finger before his nose, and planting his legs wider apart as he looked attentively in Mr. Pecksniff's face, 'that is a remarkably curious and interesting trait in Mr. Slyme's character; and whenever Slyme's life comes to be written, that trait must be thoroughly worked out by his biographer, or society will not be satisfied!'
Mr. Pecksniff coughed.
'Slyme's biographer, sir, whoever he may be,' resumed the gentleman, 'must apply to me; or, if I am gone to that what's-his-name from which no thingumbob comes back, he must apply to my executors for leave to search among my papers' *(Chapter 4:* Tigg).

'Well, never mind! Moralise as we will, the world goes on. As Hamlet says, Hercules may lay about him with his club in every possible direction, but he can't prevent the cats from making a most intolerable row on the roofs of the houses, or the dogs from being shot in the hot weather if they run about the streets unmuzzled' *(Chapter 4:* Tigg).

If ever Mr. Pecksniff wore an apostolic look, he wore it on this memorable day. If ever his unruffled smile proclaimed the words, 'I am a messenger of peace!' that was its mission now. If ever man combined within himself all the mild qualities of the lamb with a considerable touch of the dove, and not a dash of the crocodile, or the least possible suggestion of the very mildest seasoning of the serpent, that man was he *(Chapter 4)*.

'Pecksniff,' said Anthony, who had been watching the whole party with peculiar keenness from the first: 'don't you be a hypocrite.'
'A what, my good sir?' demanded Mr. Pecksniff.
'A hypocrite.'
'Charity, my dear,' said Mr. Pecksniff, 'when I take my chamber candlestick to-night, remind me to be more than usually particular in praying for Mr. Anthony Chuzzlewit; who has done me an injustice' *(Chapter 4)*.

'Why, the truth is, my dear,' said Mr. Pecksniff, smiling upon his assembled kindred, 'that I am at a loss for a word. The name of those fabulous animals (pagan, I regret to say) who used to sing in the water, has quite escaped me.'
Mr. George Chuzzlewit suggested 'Swans.'
'No,' said Mr. Pecksniff. 'Not swans. Very like swans, too. Thank you.'
The nephew with the outline of a countenance, speaking for the first and last time on that occasion, propounded 'Oysters.'
'No,' said Mr. Pecksniff, with his own peculiar urbanity, 'nor oysters. But by no means unlike oysters;

a very excellent idea; thank you, my dear sir, very much. Wait! Sirens. Dear me! sirens, of course' *(Chapter 4)*.

The best of architects and land surveyors kept a horse, in whom the enemies already mentioned more than once in these pages, pretended to detect a fanciful resemblance to his master. Not in his outward person, for he was a raw-boned, haggard horse, always on a much shorter allowance of corn than Mr. Pecksniff; but in his moral character, wherein, said they, he was full of promise, but of no performance. He was always, in a manner, going to go, and never going. When at his slowest rate of travelling, he would sometimes lift up his legs so high, and display such mighty action, that it was difficult to believe he was doing less than fourteen miles an hour; and he was for ever so perfectly satisfied with his own speed, and so little disconcerted by opportunities of comparing himself with the fastest trotters, that the illusion was the more difficult of resistance. He was a kind of animal who infused into the breasts of strangers a lively sense of hope, and possessed all those who knew him better with a grim despair *(Chapter 5)*.

'I more than half believed, just now, seeing you so very smart,' said Pinch, 'that you must be going to be married, Mark.'
'Well, sir, I've thought of that, too,' he replied. 'There might be some credit in being jolly with a wife, 'specially if the children had the measles and that, and was very fractious indeed. But I'm a'most afraid to try it. I don't see my way clear' *(Chapter 5:* Pinch and Tapley).

'I was thinking ... of something in the grave-digging way.'
'Good gracious, Mark!' cried Mr. Pinch.
'It's a good damp, wormy sort of business, sir,' said Mark, shaking his head, argumentatively, 'and there might be some credit in being jolly, with one's mind in that pursuit, unless grave-diggers is usually given that way; which would be a drawback. You don't happen to know how that is, in general, do you, sir?'
'No,' said Mr. Pinch. 'I don't indeed. I never thought upon the subject.'
'In case of that not turning out as well as one could wish, you know,' said Mark, musing again, 'there's other businesses. Undertaking now. That's gloomy. There might be credit to be gained there. A broker's man in a poor neighbourhood wouldn't be bad perhaps. A jailer sees a deal of misery. A doctor's man is in the very midst of murder. A bailiff's an't a lively office nat'rally. Even a tax-gatherer must find his feelings rather worked upon, at times. There's lots of trades, in which I should have an opportunity, I think' *(Chapter 5)*.

'My daughters' room. A poor first-floor to us, but a bower to them. Very neat. Very airy. Plants you observe; hyacinths; books again; birds.' These birds, by the bye, comprised, in all, one staggering old sparrow without a tail, which had been borrowed expressly from the kitchen. 'Such trifles as girls love are here. Nothing more. Those who seek heartless

splendour, would seek here in vain' *(Chapter 5:* Pecksniff).

Mr. Pecksniff did honour to his own toast.
'This,' he said, in allusion to the party, not the wine, 'is a mingling that repays one for much disappointment and vexation. Let us be merry.' Here he took a captain's biscuit. 'It is a poor heart that never rejoices; and our hearts are not poor. No!' *(Chapter 5)*.

'I have a summons here to repair to London; on professional business, my dear Martin; strictly on professional business; and I promised my girls, long ago, that whenever that happened again, they should accompany me. We shall go forth to-night by the heavy coach – like the dove of old, my dear Martin – and it will be a week before we again deposit our olive-branches in the passage. When I say olive-branches,' observed Mr. Pecksniff, in explanation, 'I mean, our unpretending luggage' *(Chapter 6)*.

'Ardent child!' said Mr. Pecksniff, gazing on her in a dreamy way. 'And yet there is a melancholy sweetness in these youthful hopes! It is pleasant to know that they never can be realised. I remember thinking once myself, in the days of my childhood, that pickled onions grew on trees, and that every elephant was born with an impregnable castle on his back. I have not found the fact to be so; far from it; and yet those visions have comforted me under circumstances of trial' *(Chapter 6)*.

'Do you know, now,' said Mr. Pecksniff, folding his hands, and looking at his young relation with an air of pensive interest, 'that I should very much like to see your notion of a cow-house?'
But Martin by no means appeared to relish this suggestion.
'A pump,' said Mr. Pecksniff, 'is very chaste practice. I have found that a lamp-post is calculated to refine the mind and give it a classical tendency. An ornamental turnpike has a remarkable effect upon the imagination. What do you say to beginning with an ornamental turnpike?' *(Chapter 6)*.

'You remind me of Whittington, afterwards thrice Lord Mayor of London. I give you my unsullied word of honour, that you very strongly remind me of that historical character. You are a pair of Whittingtons, gents, without the cat; which is a most agreeable and blessed exception to me, for I am not attached to the feline species. My name is Tigg; how do you do?' *(Chapter 7)*.

'I swear,' cried Mr. Slyme, giving the table an imbecile blow with his fist, and then freely leaning his head upon his hand, while some drunken drops oozed from his eyes, 'that I am the wretchedest creature on record. Society is in a conspiracy against me. I'm the most literary man alive. I'm full of scholarship; I'm full of genius; I'm full of information; I'm full of novel views on every subject; yet look at my condition! I'm at this moment obliged to two strangers for a tavern bill!' *(Chapter 7)*.

'Was there ever such a Roman as our friend Chiv? Was there ever a man of such a purely classical turn of thought, and of such a toga-like simplicity of nature? Was there ever a man with such a flow of eloquence? Might he not, gents both, I ask, have sat upon a tripod in the ancient times, and prophesied to a perfectly unlimited extent, if previously supplied with gin-and-water at the public cost?' (*Chapter 7:* Tigg).

'What are we?' said Mr. Pecksniff, 'but coaches? Some of us are slow coaches' –
'Goodness, pa!' cried Charity.
'Some of us, I say,' resumed her parent with increased emphasis, 'are slow coaches; some of us are fast coaches. Our passions are the horses; and rampant animals too!' –
'Really, pa!' cried both the daughters at once. 'How very unpleasant.'
'And rampant animals too!' repeated Mr. Pecksniff, with so much determination, that he may be said to have exhibited, at the moment, a sort of moral rampancy himself: 'and Virtue is the drag. We start from The Mother's Arms, and we run to The Dust Shovel' (*Chapter 8*).

'The process of digestion, as I have been informed by anatomical friends, is one of the most wonderful works of nature. I do not know how it may be with others, but it is a great satisfaction to me to know, when regaling on my humble fare, that I am putting in motion the most beautiful machinery with which we have any acquaintance. I really feel at such times as if I was doing a public service. When I have wound myself up, if I may employ such a term,' said Mr. Pecksniff with exquisite tenderness, 'and know that I am Going, I feel that in the lesson afforded by the works within me, I am a Benefactor to my Kind!' (*Chapter 8*).

'Presiding over an establishment like this, makes sad havoc with the features, my dear Miss Pecksniffs,' said Mrs. Todgers. 'The gravy alone, is enough to add twenty years to one's age, I do assure you' (*Chapter 9*).

'There is no such passion in human nature, as the passion for gravy among commercial gentlemen' (*Chapter 9:* Mrs. Todgers).

'You, my dears, having to deal with your pa's pupils who can't help themselves, are able to take your own way,' said Mrs. Todgers, 'but in a commercial establishment, where any gentleman may say, any Saturday evening, "Mrs. Todgers, this day week we part, in consequence of the cheese," it is not so easy to preserve a pleasant understanding' (*Chapter 9*).

Mrs. Todgers vowed that anything one quarter so angelic she had never seen. 'She wanted but a pair of wings, a dear,' said that good woman, 'to be a young syrup': meaning, possibly, young sylph, or seraph (*Chapter 9*).

'My sweet child,' to the pupil, 'farewell! That fairy creature,' said Mr. Pecksniff, looking in his pensive mood hard at the footman, as if he meant him, 'has shed a vision on my path, refulgent in its nature, and not easily to be obliterated. My dears, are you ready?' (*Chapter 9*).

When he had completed his preparations, he grinned at the sisters, and expressed his belief that the approaching collation would be of 'rather a spicy sort.'
'Will it be long before it's ready, Bailey?' asked Mercy.
'No,' said Bailey, 'it *is* cooked. When I come up, she was dodging among the tender pieces with a fork, and eating of 'em' (*Chapter 9*).

'My feelings, Mrs. Todgers, will not consent to be entirely smothered, like the young children in the Tower. They are grown up, and the more I press the bolster on them, the more they look round the corner of it' (*Chapter 9:* Pecksniff).

'Has a voice from the grave no influence?' said Mr. Pecksniff, with dismal tenderness. 'This is irreligious! My dear creature.'
'Hush!' urged Mrs. Todgers. 'Really you mustn't.'
'It's not me,' said Mr. Pecksniff. 'Don't suppose it's me: it's the voice; it's her voice.'
Mrs. Pecksniff deceased, must have had an unusually thick and husky voice for a lady, and rather a stuttering voice, and to say the truth somewhat of a drunken voice, if it had ever borne much resemblance to that in which Mr. Pecksniff spoke just then. But perhaps this was delusion on his part (*Chapter 9*).

'Bless my life, Miss Pecksniffs!' cried Mrs. Todgers, aloud, 'your dear pa's took very poorly!'
Mr. Pecksniff straightened himself by a surprising effort, as every one turned hastily towards him; and standing on his feet, regarded the assembly with a look of ineffable wisdom. Gradually it gave place to a smile; a feeble, helpless, melancholy smile; bland, almost to sickliness. 'Do not repine, my friends,' said Mr. Pecksniff, tenderly. 'Do not weep for me. It is chronic.' And with these words, after making a futile attempt to pull off his shoes, he fell into the fireplace (*Chapter 9*).

'My friends,' cried Mr. Pecksniff, looking over the banisters, 'let us improve our minds by mutual inquiry and discussion. Let us be moral. Let us contemplate existence. Where is Jinkins?'
'Here,' cried that gentleman. 'Go to bed again!'
'To bed!' said Mr. Pecksniff. 'Bed! 'Tis the voice of the sluggard, I hear him complain, you have woke me too soon, I must slumber again. If any young orphan will repeat the remainder of that simple piece from Doctor Watts's collection an eligible opportunity now offers.'
Nobody volunteered.
'This is very soothing,' said Mr. Pecksniff, after a pause. 'Extremely so. Cool and refreshing; particularly to the legs! The legs of the human subject, my friends, are a beautiful production. Compare them with wooden legs, and observe the difference between the anatomy of nature and the anatomy of art. Do you know,' said Mr. Pecksniff, leaning over the banisters, with an odd recollection of his familiar manner among new pupils at home, 'that I should very much like to see Mrs. Todger's notion of a wooden leg, if perfectly agreeable to herself!' (*Chapter 9*).

The old man looked attentively from one to the other, and then at Mr. Pecksniff, several times.

'What,' he asked of Mr. Pecksniff, happening to catch his eye in its descent: for until now it had been piously upraised, with something of that expression which the poetry of ages has attributed to a domestic bird, when breathing its last amid the ravages of an electric storm: 'What are their names?' (*Chapter 10: Martin Chuzzlewit*).

'All hail to the vessel of Pecksniff the sire!
 And favouring breezes to fan;
While Tritons flock round it, and proudly admire
 The architect, artist, and man!'

(Chapter 11)

Mr. Bailey reserved his vocal offering until the morning, when he put his head into the room as the young ladies were kneeling before their trunks, packing up, and treated them to an imitation of the voice of a young dog, in trying circumstances: when that animal is supposed by persons of a lively fancy, to relieve his feelings by calling for pen and ink *(Chapter 11)*.

'Well?' said Martin.
'Well! as he landed there without a penny to bless himself with, of course they wos very glad to see him in the U-nited States.'
'What do you mean?' asked Martin, with some scorn.
'What do I mean?' said Bill. 'Why, *that*. All men are alike in the U-nited States, an't they? It makes no odds whether a man has a thousand pound, or nothing, there. Particular in New York, I'm told, where Ned landed.'
'New York, was it?' asked Martin, thoughtfully.
'Yes,' said Bill. 'New York. I know that, because he sent word home that it brought Old York to his mind, quite vivid, in consequence of being so exactly unlike it in every respect. I don't understand wot particular business Ned turned his mind to, when he got there; but he wrote home that him and his friends was always a singing, Ale Columbia, and blowing up the President, so I suppose it was something in the public line, or free-and-easy way again. Anyhow, he made his fortune' (*Chapter 13: Martin Chuzzlewit and Bill Simmons*).

'You're always full of your chaff,' said the shopman, rolling up the article (which looked like a shirt) quite as a matter of course, and nibbing his pen upon the counter.
'I shall never be full of my wheat,' said Mr. Tigg, 'as long as I come here. Ha, ha! Not bad! Make it two-and-six, my dear friend, positively for this occasion only. Half-a-crown is a delightful coin. Two-and-six! Going at two-and-six! For the last time at two-and-six!'
'It'll never be the last time till it's quite worn out,' rejoined the shopman. 'It's grown yellow in the service as it is.'
'Its master has grown yellow in the service, if you mean that, my friend,' said Mr. Tigg; 'in the patriotic service of an ungrateful country. You are making it two-and-six, I think?'
'I'm making it,' returned the shopman, 'what it always has been – two shillings. Same name as usual, I suppose?'

'Still the same name,' said Mr. Tigg; 'my claim to the dormant peerage not being yet established by the House of Lords.'
'The old address?'
'Not at all,' said Mr. Tigg; 'I have removed my town establishment from thirty-eight Mayfair, to number fifteen-hundred-and-forty-two, Park Lane.'
'Come, I'm not going to put down that, you know,' said the shopman with a grin.
'You may put down what you please, my friend,' quoth Mr. Tigg. 'The fact is still the same. The apartments for the under-butler and the fifth footman being of a most confounded low and vulgar kind at thirty-eight Mayfair, I have been compelled, in my regard for the feelings which do them so much honour, to take on lease, for seven, fourteen, or twenty-one years, renewable at the option of the tenant, the elegant and commodious family mansion, number fifteen-hundred-and-forty-two, Park Lane. Make it two-and-six, and come and see me!' (*Chapter 13*).

Oh, moralists, who treat of happiness and self-respect, innate in every sphere of life, and shedding light on every grain of dust in God's highway, so smooth below your carriage-wheels, so rough beneath the tread of naked feet, bethink yourselves in looking on the swift descent of men who *have* lived in their own esteem, that there are scores of thousands breathing now, and breathing thick with painful toil, who in that high respect have never lived at all, nor had a chance of life! Go ye, who rest so placidly upon the sacred Bard who had been young, and when he strung his harp was old, and had never seen the righteous forsaken, or his seed begging their bread; go, Teachers of content and honest pride, into the mine, the mill, the forge, the squalid depths of deepest ignorance, and uttermost abyss of man's neglect, and say can any hopeful plant spring up in air so foul that it extinguishes the soul's bright torch as fast as it is kindled! And, oh! ye Pharisees of the nineteen hundredth year of Christian Knowledge, who soundingly appeal to human nature, see first that it be human. Take heed it has not been transformed, during your slumber and the sleep of generations, into the nature of the Beasts (*Chapter 13*).

'Jolly sort of lodgings,' said Mark, rubbing his nose with the knob at the end of the fire-shovel, and looking round the poor chamber: 'that's a comfort. The rain's come through the roof too. That an't bad. A lively old bedstead, I'll be bound; popilated by lots of wampires, no doubt. Come! my spirits is a getting up again. An uncommon ragged night-cap this. A very good sign. We shall do yet!' (*Chapter 13: Tapley*).

'Hope is said by the poet, sir,' observed the gentleman, 'to be the nurse of Young Desire.'
Martin signified that he had heard of the cardinal virtue in question serving occasionally in that domestic capacity (*Chapter 16: Colonel Diver*).

It was a numerous company, eighteen or twenty perhaps. Of these some five or six were ladies, who sat wedged together in a little phalanx by themselves. All the knives and forks were working away at a rate that was quite alarming; very few words were spoken; and everybody seemed to eat his utmost in self-defence, as if a famine were expected to set in before breakfast-time to-morrow morning, and it had become high time to assert the first law of nature. The poultry, which may perhaps be considered to have formed the staple of the entertainment – for there was a turkey at the top, a pair of ducks at the bottom, and two fowls in the middle – disappeared as rapidly as if every bird had had the use of its wings, and had flown in desperation down a human throat. The oysters, stewed and pickled, leaped from their capacious reservoirs, and slid by scores into the mouths of the assembly. The sharpest pickles vanished, whole cucumbers at once, like sugar-plums, and no man winked his eye. Great heaps of indigestible matter melted away as ice before the sun. It was a solemn and an awful thing to see. Dyspeptic individuals bolted their food in wedges; feeding, not themselves, but broods of nightmares, who were continually standing at livery within them. Spare men, with lank and rigid cheeks, came out unsatisfied from the destruction of heavy dishes, and glared with watchful eyes upon the pastry. What Mrs. Pawkins felt each day at dinner-time is hidden from all human knowledge. But she had one comfort. It was very soon over *(Chapter 16)*.

'What course of lectures are you attending now, ma'am?' said Martin's friend, turning again to Mrs. Brick.
'The Philosophy of the Soul, on Wednesdays.'
'On Mondays?'
'The Philosophy of Crime.'
'On Fridays?'
'The Philosophy of Vegetables.'
'You have forgotten Thursdays; the Philosophy of Government, my dear,' observed the third lady.
'No,' said Mrs. Brick. 'That's Tuesdays.'
'So it is!' cried the lady. 'The Philosophy of Matter on Thursdays, of course.'
'You see Mr. Chuzzlewit, our ladies are fully employed,' said Bevan *(Chapter 17)*.

Change begets change. Nothing propagates so fast. If a man habituated to a narrow circle of cares and pleasures, out of which he seldom travels, step beyond it, though for never so brief a space, his departure from the monotonous scene on which he has been an actor of importance, would seem to be the signal for instant confusion. As if, in the gap he had left, the wedge of change were driven to the head, rending what was a solid mass to fragments, things cemented and held together by the usages of years, burst asunder in as many weeks. The mine which Time has slowly dug beneath familiar objects, is sprung in an instant; and what was rock before, becomes but sand and dust *(Chapter 18)*.

'How are they all at home? How's Charity?'
'Blooming, Mr. Jonas, blooming.'
'And the other one; how's she?'
'Volatile trifler!' said Mr. Pecksniff, fondly musing. 'She is well, she is well. Roving from parlour to bedroom, Mr. Jonas, like the bee; skimming from post to pillar, like the butterfly; dipping her young beak into our currant wine, like the humming-bird!' *(Chapter 18:* Jonas Chuzzlewit and Pecksniff*)*.

'Ah dear! When Gamp was summoned to his long home, and I see him a lying in Guy's Hospital with a penny-piece on each eye, and his wooden leg under his left arm, I thought I should have fainted away. But I bore up.'
If certain whispers current in the Kingsgate Street circles had any truth in them, she had indeed borne up surprisingly; and had exerted such uncommon fortitude, as to dispose of Mr. Gamp's remains for the benefit of science *(Chapter 19:* Mrs. Gamp*)*.

'If it wasn't for the nerve a little sip of liquor gives me (I never was able to do more than taste it), I never could go through with what I sometimes has to do. "Mrs. Harris," I says, at the very last case as ever I acted in, which it was but a young person, "Mrs. Harris," I says, "leave the bottle on the chimley-piece, and don't ask me to take none, but let me put my lips to it when I am so dispoged, and then I will do what I'm engaged to do, according to the best of my ability." ' *(Chapter 19:* Mrs. Gamp*)*.

'I have seen a deal of trouble my own self,' said Mrs. Gamp, laying greater and greater stress upon her words, 'and I can feel for them as has their feelings tried, but I am not a Rooshan or a Prooshan, and consequently cannot suffer spies to be set over me' *(Chapter 19)*.

'Ah! what a wale of grief!' cried Mrs. Gamp, possessing herself of the bottle and glass *(Chapter 19)*.

'Ay, Mrs. Gamp, you are right,' rejoined the undertaker. 'We should be an honoured calling. We do good by stealth, and blush to have it mentioned in our little bills. How much consolation may I, even I,' cried Mr. Mould, 'have diffused among my fellow-creatures by means of my four long-tailed prancers, never harnessed under ten pund ten!' *(Chapter 19)*.

' "If you should ever happen to go to bed there – you *may*, you know," he says, "in course of time as civilisation progresses – don't forget to take a axe with you." I look at him tolerable hard. "Fleas?" says I. "And more," says he. "Wampires?" says I. "And more," says he. "Musquitoes, perhaps?" says I. "And more," says he. "What more?" says I. "Snakes more," says he; "rattlesnakes. You're right to a certain extent, stranger. There air some catawampous chawers in the small way too, as graze upon a human pretty strong; but don't mind *them*, they're company. It's snakes," he says, "as you'll object to: and whenever you wake and see one in a upright poster on your bed," he says, "like a corkscrew with the handle off a sittin' on its bottom ring, cut him down, for he means wenom" ' *(Chapter 21:* Tapley*)*.

'I says to Mrs. Harris,' Mrs. Gamp continued, 'only t'other day; the last Monday evening fortnight as ever dawned upon this Piljian's Projiss of a mortal wale; I says to Mrs. Harris when she says to me, "Years and our trials, Mrs. Gamp, sets marks upon us all." – "Say not the words, Mrs. Harris, if you and me is to be continual friends, for such is not the case" ' *(Chapter 25)*.

Young ladies with such faces thinks of something else besides berryins, don't they, sir?'

'I am sure I don't know, Mrs. Gamp,' said Mould, with a chuckle. – 'Not bad in Mrs. Gamp, my dear?'

'Oh yes, you do know, sir!' said Mrs. Gamp, 'and so does Mrs. Mould, your ansome pardner too, sir; and so do I, although the blessing of a daughter was denigED me; which if we had had one, Gamp would certainly have drunk its little shoes right off its feet, as with our precious boy he did, and arterwards send the child a errand to sell his wooden leg for any money it would fetch as matches in the rough, and bring it home in liquor: which was truly done beyond his years, for ev'ry individgle penny that child lost at toss or buy for kidney ones; and come home arterwards quite bold, to break the news, and offering to drown himself if that would be a satisfaction to his parents' *(Chapter 25)*.

'Whether I sicks or monthlies, ma'am, I hope I does my duty, but I am but a poor woman, and I earns my living hard; therefore I *do* require it, which I makes confession, to be brought reg'lar and draw'd mild' *(Chapter 25: Mrs. Gamp)*.

'The pickled salmon,' Mrs. Prig replied, 'is quite delicious. I can partick'ler recommend it. Don't have nothink to say to the cold meat, for it tastes of the stable' *(Chapter 25)*.

'I think, young woman,' said Mrs. Gamp to the assistant-chambermaid, in a tone expressive of weakness, 'that I could pick a little bit of pickled salmon, with a nice little sprig of fennel, and a sprinkling of white pepper. I takes new bread, my dear, with jest a little pat of fresh butter, and a mossel of cheese. In case there should be such a thing as a cowcumber in the 'ouse, will you be so kind as bring it, for I'm rather partial to 'em, and they does a world of good in a sick room. If they draws the Brighton Old Tipper here, I takes *that* ale at night, my love; it bein' considered wakeful by the doctors. And whatever you do, young woman, don't bring more than a shillin's-worth of gin-and-water warm when I rings the bell a second time: for that is always my allowance, and I never takes a drop beyond!' *(Chapter 25)*.

'Ah!' sighed Mrs. Gamp, as she meditated over the warm shilling's-worth, 'what a blessed thing it is – living in a wale – to be contented! What a blessed thing it is to make sick people happy in their beds, and never mind one's-self as long as one can do a service! I don't believe a finer cowcumber was ever grow'd. I'm sure I never see one!' *(Chapter 25)*.

Mrs. Gamp, invoking a blessing upon the house, leered, winked, coughed, nodded, smiled, and curtsied herself out of the room.

'But I will say, and I would if I was led a Martha to the Stakes for it,' Mrs. Gamp remarked below-stairs, in a whisper, 'that she don't look much like a merry one at this present moment of time' *(Chapter 26)*.

'Talk of constitooshun!' Mrs. Gamp observed. 'A person's constitooshun need be made of bricks to stand it. Mrs. Harris jestly says to me, but t'other day. "Oh! Sairey Gamp," she says, "How is it done?" "Mrs. Harris, ma'am," I says to her, "we gives no trust ourselves, and puts a deal o' trust elsevere; these is our religious feelings, and we finds 'em answer." "Sairey,"

says Mrs. Harris, "sech is life. Vich likeways is the hend of all things!" ' *(Chapter 29)*.

'The families I've had,' said Mrs. Gamp, 'if all was know'd, and credit done where credit's doo, would take a week to chris'en at Saint Polge's fontin!' *(Chapter 29)*.

'I speak as I find, Mr. Sweedlepipes,' said Mrs. Gamp. 'Forbid it should be otherways! But we never knows wot's hidden in each other's hearts; and if we had glass winders there, we'd need keep the shetters up, some on us, I do assure you!'

'But you don't mean to say,' Poll Sweedlepipe began.

'No,' said Mrs. Gamp, cutting him very short, 'I don't. Don't think I do. The torters of the Imposition shouldn't make me own I did' *(Chapter 29)*.

'My eyes and ears are witnesses. I wouldn't have believed it otherwise. I wouldn't have believed it, Mr. Chuzzlewit, if a Fiery Serpent had proclaimed it from the top of Salisbury Cathedral' *(Chapter 31: Pecksniff)*.

'I ain't superstitious about toads,' said Mark, looking round the room, 'but if you could prevail upon the two or three I see in company, to step out at the same time, my young friends, I think they'd find the open air refreshing. Not that I at all object to 'em. A very handsome animal is a toad,' said Mr. Tapley, sitting down upon a stool: 'very spotted; very like a partickler style of old gentleman about the throat; very bright-eyed, very cool, and very slippy. But one sees 'em to the best advantage out of doors perhaps' *(Chapter 33)*.

"Mind and matter,' said the lady in the wig, 'glide swift into the vortex of immensity. Howls the sublime, and softly sleeps the calm Ideal, in the whispering chambers of Imagination. To hear it, sweet it is. But then, outlaughs the stern philosopher, and saith to the Grotesque, "What ho! arrest for me that Agency. Go, bring it here!" And so the vision fadeth' *(Chapter 34: Miss Toppitt)*.

'I was a thinking, sir,' returned Mark, 'that if I was a painter and was called upon to paint the American Eagle, how should I do it?'

'Paint it as like an Eagle as you could, I suppose.'

'No,' said Mark. 'That wouldn't do for me, sir. I should want to draw it like a Bat, for its short-sightedness; like a Bantam, for its bragging; like a Magpie, for its honesty; like a Peacock, for its vanity; like a Ostrich, for its putting its head in the mud, and thinking nobody sees it – '

'And like a Phoenix, for its power of springing from the ashes of its faults and vices, and soaring up anew into the sky!' said Martin. 'Well, Mark. Let us hope so' *(Chapter 34: Tapley and Martin Chuzzlewit)*.

'And which of all them smoking monsters is the Ankworks boat, I wonder? Goodness me!' cried Mrs. Gamp.

'What boat did you want?' asked Ruth.

'The Ankworks package,' Mrs. Gamp replied. 'I will not deceive you, my sweet. Why should I?'

'That is the Antwerp packet in the middle,' said Ruth.

'And I wish it was in Jonadge's belly, I do,' cried Mrs. Gamp; appearing to confound the prophet with the whale in this miraculous aspiration *(Chapter 40)*.

'Which shows,' said Mrs. Gamp, casting up her eyes, 'what a little way you've travelled into this wale of life, my dear young creetur! As a good friend of mine has frequent made remark to me, which her name, my love, is Harris, Mrs. Harris through the square and up the steps a turnin' round by the tobacker shop, "Oh Sairey, Sairey, little do we know wot lays afore us!" "Mrs. Harris, ma'am," I says, "not much, it's true, but more than you suppose. Our calcilations, ma'am," I says, "respectin' wot the number of a family will be, comes most times within one, and oftener than you would suppoge, exact." "Sairey," says Mrs. Harris, in a awful way, "Tell me wot is my indiwidgle number." "No, Mrs. Harris," I says to her, "ex-cuge me, if you please. My own," I says, "has fallen out of three-pair backs, and had damp doorsteps settled on their lungs, and one was turned up smilin' in a bedstead, unbeknown. Therefore, ma'am," I say, "seek not to proticipate, but take 'em as they come and as they go." Mine,' said Mrs. Gamp, 'mine is all gone, my dear young chick. And as to husbands, there's a wooden leg gone likeways home to its account, which in its constancy of walkin' into wine vaults, and never comin' out again till fetched by force, was quite as weak as flesh, if not weaker' *(Chapter 40)*.

'Oh drat you!' said Mrs. Gamp, shaking her umbrella at it, 'you're a nice spluttering nisy monster for a delicate young creeter to go and be a passinger by; ain't you? *You* never do no harm in that way, do you? With your hammering, and roaring, and hissing, and lamp-iling, you brute! Them Confugion steamers,' said Mrs. Gamp, shaking her umbrella again, 'has done more to throw us out of our reg'lar work and bring ewents on at times when nobody counted on 'em (especially them screeching railroad ones), than all the other frights that ever was took. I have heerd of one young man, a guard upon a railway, only three years opened – well does Mrs. Harris know him, which indeed he is her own relation by her sister's marriage with a master sawyer – as is godfather at this present time to six-and-twenty blessed little strangers, equally unexpected, and all on 'um named after the Ingeins as was the cause. Ugh!' said Mrs. Gamp, resuming her apostrophe, 'one might easy know you was a man's invention, from your dis-regardlessness of the weakness of our naturs, so one might, you brute!' *(Chapter 40)*.

'There she identically goes! Poor sweet young creetur, there she goes, like a lamb to the sacrifige! If there's any illness when that wessel gets to sea,' said Mrs. Gamp, prophetically, 'it's murder, and I'm the witness for the persecution' *(Chapter 40)*.

'I hope, sir,' returned Mrs. Gamp, dropping an indignant curtsey, 'as no bones is broke by me and Mrs. Harris a walkin' down upon a public wharf. Which was the very words she says to me (although

they was the last I ever had to speak) was these: "Sairey," she says, "is it a public wharf?" "Mrs. Harris," I makes answer, "can you doubt it? You have know'd me now, ma'am, eight and thirty year; and did you ever know me go, or wish to go, where I was not made welcome, say the words." "No, Sairey," Mrs. Harris says, "contrairy quite." And well she knows it too. I am but a poor woman, but I've been sought after, sir, though you may not think it. I've been knocked up at all hours of the night, and warned out by a many landlords, in consequence of being mistook for Fire. I goes out working for my bread, 'tis true, but I maintains my indepency, with your kind leave, and which I will till death. I has my feelings as a woman, sir, and I have been a mother likeways; but touch a pipkin as belongs to me, or make the least remarks on what I eats or drinks, and though you was the favouritest young for'ard hussy of a servant-gal as ever come into a house, either you leaves the place, or me. My earnings is not great, sir, but I will not be impoged upon. Bless the babe, and save the mother, is my mortar, sir; but I makes so free as add to that, Don't try no impogician with the Nuss, for she will not abear it!' *(Chapter 40)*.

'Your bosom's lord sits lightly on its throne, Mr. Chuzzlewit, as what's-his-name says in the play. I wish he said it in a play which did anything like common justice to our profession, by the bye. There is an apothecary in that drama, sir, which is a low thing; vulgar, sir; out of nature altogether' *(Chapter 41: Jobling)*.

'Behold the wonders of the firmament, Mrs. Lupin! How glorious is the scene! When I look up at those shining orbs, I think that each of them is winking to the other to take notice of the vanity of men's pursuits. My fellow-men!' cried Mr. Pecksniff, shaking his head in pity; 'you are much mistaken; my wormy relatives, you are much deceived! The stars are perfectly contented (I suppose so) in their several spheres. Why are not you? Oh! do not strive and struggle to enrich yourselves, or to get the better of each other, my deluded friends, but look up there, with me!' *(Chapter 44)*.

Mrs. Gamp was a lady of that happy temperament which can be ecstatic without any other stimulating cause than a general desire to establish a large and profitable connection *(Chapter 46)*.

'I knows a lady, which her name, I'll not deceive you, Mrs. Chuzzlewit, is Harris, her husband's brother bein' six foot three, and marked with a mad bull in Wellington boots upon his left arm, on account of his precious mother havin' been worrited by one into a shoemaker's shop, when in a sitiwation which blessed is the man as has his quiver full of sech, as many times I've said to Gamp when words has roge betwixt us on account of the expense – and often have I said to Mrs. Harris, "Oh, Mrs. Harris, ma'am! your countenance is quite a angel's!" Which, but for Pimples, it would be. "No, Sairey Gamp," says she, "you best of hard-working and industrious creeturs as ever was underpaid at any price, which underpaid you are, quite diff'rent. Harris had it done afore marriage at ten and six," she says, "and wore it faithful next his heart till the colour run, when the money was declined to be give back, and no arrangement could be come to. But he never said it was a angel's, Sairey, wotever he might have thought." If Mrs. Harris's husband was here now,' said Mrs. Gamp, looking round, and chuckling as she dropped a general curtsey, 'he'd speak out plain, he would, and his dear wife would be the last to blame him! For if ever a woman lived as know'd not wot it was to form a wish to pizon them as had good looks, and had no reagion give her by the best of husbands, Mrs. Harris is that ev'nly dispogician!' *(Chapter 46)*.

'If you should turn at all faint, we can soon revive you, sir, I promige you. Bite a person's thumbs, or turn their fingers the wrong way,' said Mrs. Gamp, smiling with the consciousness of at once imparting pleasure and instruction to her auditors, 'and they comes to, wonderful, Lord bless you!' *(Chapter 46)*.

'You wasn't here, sir, when he was took so strange. I never see a poor dear creatur took so strange in all my life, except a patient much about the same age, as I once nussed, which his calling was the custom-'us, and his name was Mrs. Harris's own father, as pleasant a singer, Mr. Chuzzlewit, as ever you heard, with a voice like a Jew's-harp in the bass notes, that it took six men to hold at sech times, foaming frightful' *(Chapter 46: Mrs. Gamp)*.

'There! Now drat you, Betsey, don't be long!' said Mrs. Gamp, apostrophising her absent friend. 'For I can't abear to wait, I do assure you. To wotever place I goes, I sticks to this one mortar, "I'm easy pleased; it is but little as I wants; but I must have that little of the best, and to the minute when the clock strikes, else we do not part as I could wish, but bearin' malice in our arts" ' *(Chapter 49)*.

'And don't go a dropping none of your snuff in it,' said Mrs. Prig. 'In gruel, barley-water, apple-tea, mutton-broth, and that, it don't signify. It stimulates a patient. But I don't relish it myself.'
'Why, Betsey Prig!' cried Mrs. Gamp, 'how *can* you talk so?'
'Why, ain't your patients, wotever their diseases is, always a sneezin' their wery heads off, along of your snuff?' said Mrs. Prig.
'And wot if they are?' said Mrs. Gamp.
'Nothing if they are,' said Mrs. Prig. 'But don't deny it, Sairah.'
'Who deniges of it?' Mrs. Gamp inquired.
Mrs. Prig returned no answer.
'WHO deniges of it, Betsey?' Mrs. Gamp inquired again. Then Mrs. Gamp, by reversing the question, imparted a deeper and more awful character of solemnity to the same. 'Betsey, who deniges of it?' *(Chapter 49)*.

'Betsey,' said Mrs. Gamp, filling her own glass, and passing the tea-pot, 'I will now propoge a toast. My frequent pardner, Betsey Prig!'
'Which, altering the name to Sairah Gamp; I drink,' Said Mrs. Prig, 'with love and tenderness.'
From this moment symptoms of inflammation

began to lurk in the nose of each lady; and perhaps, notwithstanding all appearances to the contrary, in the temper also *(Chapter 49)*.

'If you have anythink to say contrairy to the character of Mrs. Harris, which well I knows behind her back, afore her face, or anywhere, is not to be impeaged, out with it, Betsey. I have know'd that sweetest and best of women,' said Mrs. Gamp, shaking her head, and shedding tears, 'ever since afore her First, which Mr. Harris who was dreadful timid went and stopped his ears in a empty dog-kennel, and never took his hands away or come out once till he was showed the baby, wen bein' took with fits, the doctor collared him and laid him on his back upon the airy stones, and she was told to ease her mind, his owls was organs. And I have know'd her, Betsey Prig, when he was hurt her feelin' art by sayin' of his Ninth that it was one too many, if not two, while that dear innocent was cooin' in his face, which thrive it did though bandy, but I have never know'd as you had occagion to be glad, Betsey, on accounts of Mrs. Harris not requiring you. Required she never will, depend upon it, for her constant words in sickness is, and will be, "Send for Sairey!" ' *(Chapter 49)*.

Mrs. Gamp resumed:
'Mrs. Harris, Betsey – '
'Bother Mrs. Harris!' said Betsey Prig.
Mrs. Gamp looked at her with amazement, incredulity, and indignation; when Mrs. Prig, shutting her eye still closer, and folding her arms still tighter, uttered these memorable and tremendous words:
'I don't believe there's no sich a person!'
After the utterance of which expressions, she leaned forward, and snapped her fingers once, twice, thrice; each time nearer to the face of Mrs. Gamp, and then rose to put on her bonnet, as one who felt that there was now a gulf between them, which nothing could ever bridge across *(Chapter 49)*.

'I'm a goin', ma'am, ain't I?' said Mrs. Prig, stopping as she said it.
'You had better, ma'am,' said Mrs. Gamp.
'Do you know who you're talking to, ma'am?' inquired her visitor.
'Aperiently,' said Mrs. Gamp, surveying her with scorn from head to foot, 'to Betsey Prig. Aperiently so. *I* know her. No one better. Go along with you!' *(Chapter 49)*.

'If she had abuged me, bein' in liquor, which I thought I smelt her wen she come, but could not so believe, not bein' used myself' – Mrs. Gamp, by the way was pretty far gone, and the fragrance of the tea-pot was strong in the room – 'I could have bore it with a thankful art. But the words she spoke of Mrs. Harris, lambs could not forgive. No, Betsey!' said Mrs. Gamp, in a violent burst of feeling, 'nor worms forget!' *(Chapter 49)*.

'Never mind,' said John. 'You know it is not true.'
'Isn't true!' cried Mrs. Gamp. 'True! Don't I know as that dear woman is expecting me at this minnit, Mr. Westlock, and is a lookin' out of window down the street, with little Tommy Harris in her arms, as calls

me his own Gammy, and truly calls, for bless the mottled little legs of that there precious child (like Canterbury Brawn his own dear father says, which so they are) his own I have been, ever since I found him, Mr. Westlock, with his small red worsted shoe a gurglin' in his throat, where he had put it in his play, a chick, wile they was leavin' of him on the floor a looking for it through the ouse and him a choakin' sweetly in the parlour! Oh, Betsey Prig, what wickedness you've showed this night, but never shall you darken Sairey's doors agen, you twining serpiant!' (*Chapter 49*).

'A pleasant evenin',' said the voice of Mrs. Gamp, 'though warm, which, bless you, Mr. Chuzzlewit, we must expect when cowcumbers is three for twopence' (*Chapter 51*).

Mrs. Gamp replied in the affirmative, and softly discharged herself of her familiar phrase, 'Turn and turn about; one off, one on.' But she spoke so tremulously that she felt called upon to add, 'which fiddle-strings is weakness to expredge my nerves this night!' (*Chapter 51*).

'There's a surprisin' number of men, sir, who as long as they've only got their own shoes and stockings to depend upon, will walk down-hill, along the gutters quiet enough, and by themselves, and not do much harm. But set any on 'em up with a coach and horses, sir; and it's wonderful what a knowledge of drivin' he'll show, and how he'll fill his vehicle with passengers, and start off in the middle of the road, neck or nothing, to the Devil!' (*Chapter 52*: Tapley).

'And if you ever contemplate the silent tomb, sir, which you will excuse me for entertaining some doubt of your doing, after the conduct into which you have allowed yourself to be betrayed this day; if you ever contemplate the silent tomb, sir, think of me. If you find yourself approaching to the silent tomb, sir, think of me. If you should wish to have anything inscribed upon your silent tomb, sir, let it be, that I – ah, my remorseful sir! that I – the humble individual who has now the honour of reproaching you, forgave you' (*Chapter 52*: Pecksniff).

'Excuge the weakness of the man,' said Mrs. Gamp, eyeing Mr. Sweedlepipe with great indignation; 'and well I might expect it, as I should have know'd, and wishin' he was drownded in the Thames afore I had brought him here, which not a blessed hour ago he nearly shaved the noge off from the father of as lovely a family as ever, Mr. Chuzzlewit, was born three sets of twins, and would have done it, only he see it a goin' in the glass, and dodged the rager' (*Chapter 52*).

'Which, Mr. Chuzzlewit,' she said, 'is well beknown to Mrs. Harris as has one sweet infant (though she *do* not wish it known) in her own family by the mother's side, kep in spirits in a bottle; and that sweet babe she see at Greenwich Fair a travelling in company with the pink-eyed lady, Prooshan dwarf, and livin' skelinton, which judge her feelins wen the barrel organ played, and she was showed her own dear sister's child, the same not bein' expected from the outside picter, where it was painted quite contrairy in a livin'

state, a many sizes larger, and performing beautiful upon the Arp, which never did that dear child know or do: since breathe it never did, to speak on, in this wale!' (*Chapter 52*: Mrs. Gamp).

They went away, but not through London's streets! Through some enchanted city, where the pavements were of air; where all the rough sounds of a stirring town were softened into gentle music; where everything was happy; where there was no distance, and no time. There were two good-tempered, burly draymen letting down big butts of beer into a cellar, somewhere; and when John helped her – almost lifted her – the lightest, easiest, neatest thing you ever saw – across the rope, they said he owed them a good turn for giving him the chance. Celestial draymen! *(Chapter 53)*.

CHRISTMAS BOOKS

A CHRISTMAS CAROL

Marley was dead, to begin with. There is no doubt whatever about that. The register of his burial was signed by the clergyman, the clerk, the undertaker, and the chief mourner. Scrooge signed it. And Scrooge's name was good upon 'Change, for anything he chose to put his hand to.

Old Marley was as dead as a door-nail.

Mind! I don't mean to say that I know, of my own knowledge, what there is particularly dead about a door-nail. I might have been inclined, myself, to regard a coffin-nail as the deadest piece of ironmongery in the trade. But the wisdom of our ancestors is in the simile; and my unhallowed hands shall not disturb it, or the Country's done for. You will therefore permit me to repeat, emphatically, that Marley was as dead as a door-nail *(Stave 1)*.

'Don't be cross, uncle!' said the nephew.

'What else can I be,' returned the uncle, 'when I live in such a world of fools as this? Merry Christmas! Out upon merry Christmas! What's Christmas time to you but a time for paying bills without money; a time for finding yourself a year older, but not an hour richer; a time for balancing your books and having every item in 'em through a round dozen of months presented dead against you? If I could work my will,' said Scrooge indignantly, 'every idiot who goes about with "Merry Christmas" on his lips, should be boiled with his own pudding, and buried with a stake of holly through his heart. He should!'

'Uncle!' pleaded the nephew.

'Nephew!' returned the uncle, sternly, 'keep Christmas in your own way, and let me keep it in mine.'

'Keep it!' repeated Scrooge's nephew. 'But you don't keep it.'

'Let me leave it alone, then,' said Scrooge. 'Much good may it do you! Much good it has ever done you!'

'There are many things from which I might have derived good, by which I have not profited, I dare say,' returned the nephew. 'Christmas among the rest. But I am sure I have always thought of Christmas time, when it has come round – apart from the veneration due to its sacred name and origin, if anything belonging to it can be apart from that – as a good time; a kind, forgiving, charitable, pleasant time:.the only time I know of, in the long calendar of the year, when men and women seem by one consent to open their shut-up hearts freely, and to think of people below them as if they really were fellow-passengers to the grave, and not another race of creatures bound on other journeys. And therefore, uncle, though it has never put a scrap of gold or silver in my pocket, I believe that it *has* done me good, and *will* do me good; and I say, God bless it!' *(Stave 1:* Scrooge and Fred).

'At this festive season of the year, Mr. Scrooge,' said the gentleman, taking up a pen, 'it is more than usually desirable that we should make some slight provision for the Poor and destitute, who suffer greatly at the present time. Many thousands are in want of common necessaries; hundreds of thousands are in want of common comforts, sir.'

'Are there no prisons?' asked Scrooge.

'Plenty of prisons,' said the gentleman, laying down the pen again.

'And the Union workhouses?' demanded Scrooge. 'Are they still in operation?'

'They are. Still,' returned the gentleman, 'I wish I could say they were not.'

'The Treadmill and the Poor Law are in full vigour, then?' said Scrooge.

'Both very busy, sir.'

'Oh! I was afraid, from what you said at first, that something had occurred to stop them in their useful course,' said Scrooge. 'I'm very glad to hear it' *(Stave 1)*.

'What shall I put you down for?'

'Nothing!' Scrooge replied.

'You wish to be anonymous?'

'I wish to be left alone,' said Scrooge. 'Since you ask me what I wish, gentlemen, that is my answer. I don't make merry myself at Christmas and I can't afford to make idle people merry. I help to support the establishments I have mentioned – they cost enough; and those who are badly off must go there.'

'Many can't go there; and many would rather die.'

'If they would rather die,' said Scrooge, 'they had better do it, and decrease the surplus population. Besides – excuse me – I don't know that.'

'But you might know it,' observed the gentleman.

'It's not my business,' Scrooge returned. 'It's enough for a man to understand his own business, and not to interfere with other people's. Mine occupies me constantly. Good afternoon, gentlemen!' *(Stave 1)*.

Scrooge took his melancholy dinner in his usual melancholy tavern; and having read all the newspapers, and beguiled the rest of the evening with his banker's-book, went home to bed. He lived in chambers which had once belonged to his deceased partner. They were a gloomy suite of rooms, in a lowering pile of building up a yard, where it had so little business to be, that one could scarcely help fancying it must have run there when it was a young house, playing at hide-and-seek with other houses, and forgotten the way out again. *(Stave 1)*.

Now, it is a fact, that there was nothing at all particular about the knocker on the door, except that it was very large. It is also a fact, that Scrooge had seen it, night and morning, during his whole residence in that place; also that Scrooge had as little of what is called fancy about him as any man in the city of London, even including – which is a bold word – the corporation, aldermen, and livery. Let it also be borne in mind that Scrooge had not bestowed one thought on Marley, since his last mention of his seven-years' dead partner that afternoon. And then let any man explain to me, if he can, how it happened that Scrooge, having his key in the lock of the door, saw in the knocker, without its undergoing any intermediate process of change – not a knocker, but Marley's face.

Marley's face. It was not in impenetrable shadow as the other objects in the yard were, but had a dismal light about it, like a bad lobster in a dark cellar. It was not angry or ferocious, but looked at Scrooge as Marley used to look: with ghostly spectacles turned up on its ghostly forehead. The hair was curiously stirred, as if by breath or hot air; and, though the eyes were wide open, they were perfectly motionless. That, and its livid colour, made it horrible; but its horror seemed to be in spite of the face and beyond its control, rather than a part of its own expression.

As Scrooge looked fixedly at this phenomenon, it was a knocker again *(Stave 1)*.

'You don't believe in me,' observed the Ghost.

'I don't,' said Scrooge.

'What evidence would you have of my reality beyond that of your senses?'

I don't know,' said Scrooge.

'Why do you doubt your senses?'

'Because,' said Scrooge, 'a little thing affects them. A slight disorder of the stomach makes them cheats. You may be an undigested bit of beef, a blot of mustard, a crumb of cheese, a fragment of an underdone potato. There's more of gravy than of grave about you, whatever you are!' *(Stave 1:* Marley's Ghost and Scrooge).

'Man of the worldly mind!' replied the Ghost, 'do you believe in me or not?'

'I do,' said Scrooge. 'I must. But why do spirits walk the earth, and why do they come to me?'

'It is required of every man,' the Ghost returned, 'that the spirit within him should walk abroad among his fellow-men, and travel far and wide; and if that spirit goes not forth in life, it is condemned to do so after death. It is doomed to wander through the world – oh, woe is me! – and witness what it cannot share, but might have shared on earth, and turned to happiness!'

Again the spectre raised a cry, and shook its chain and wrung its shadowy hands *(Stave 1:* Marley's Ghost and Scrooge).

The moment Scrooge's hand was on the lock, a strange voice called him by his name, and bade him enter. He obeyed.

It was his own room. There was no doubt about that. But it had undergone a surprising transformation. The walls and ceiling were so hung with living green, that it looked a perfect grove; from every part of which, bright gleaming berries glistened. The crisp leaves of holly, mistletoe, and ivy reflected back the light, as if so many little mirrors had been scattered there; and such a mighty blaze went roaring up the chimney, as that dull petrifaction of a hearth had never known in Scrooge's time, or Marley's, or for many and many a winter season gone. Heaped up on the floor, to form a kind of throne, were turkeys, geese, game, poultry, brawn, great joints of meat, sucking-pigs, long wreaths of sausages, mince-pies, plum puddings, barrels of oysters, red-hot chestnuts, cherry-cheeked apples, juicy oranges, luscious pears, immense twelfth-cakes, and seething bowls of punch, that made the chamber dim with their delicious steam. In easy state upon this couch, there sat a jolly Giant, glorious to see; who bore a glowing torch, in shape not unlike Plenty's horn, and held it up, high up, to shed its light on Scrooge, as he came peeping round the door (*Stave 3:* Ghost of Christmas Present).

There never was such a goose. Bob said he didn't believe there ever was such a goose cooked. Its tenderness and flavour, size and cheapness, were the themes of universal admiration. Eked out by apple sauce and mashed potatoes, it was a sufficient dinner for the whole family: indeed, as Mrs. Cratchit said with great delight (surveying one small atom of a bone upon the dish), they hadn't ate it all at last! Yet every one had had enough, and the youngest Cratchits in particular, were steeped in sage and onion to the eyebrows! But now, the plates being changed by Miss Belinda, Mrs. Cratchit left the room alone – too nervous to bear witnesses – to take the pudding up and bring it in.

Suppose it should not be done enough! Suppose it should break in turning out! Suppose somebody should have got over the wall of the back-yard, and stolen it, while they were merry with the goose – a supposition at which the two young Cratchits became livid! All sorts of horrors were supposed.

Hallo! A great deal of steam! The pudding was out of the copper. A smell like a washing-day! That was the cloth. A smell like an eating-house and a pastrycook's next door to each other, with a laundress's next door to that! That was the pudding! In half a minute Mrs. Cratchit entered – flushed, but smiling proudly – with the pudding, like a speckled cannon-ball, so hard and firm, blazing in half of half-a-quartern of ignited brandy, and bedight with Christmas holly stuck into the top.

Oh, a wonderful pudding! Bob Cratchit said, and calmly too, that he regarded it as the greatest success achieved by Mrs. Cratchit since their marriage. Mrs. Cratchit said that now the weight was off her mind, she would confess she had had her doubts about the quantity of flour. Everybody had something to say about it, but nobody said or thought it was at all a small pudding for a large family. It would have been flat heresy to do so. Any Cratchit would have blushed to hint at such a thing (*Stave 3*).

'Spirit!' he cried, tight clutching at its robe, 'hear me! I am not the man I was. I will not be the man I must have been but for this intercourse. Why show me this, if I am past all hope!'

For the first time the hand appeared to shake.

'Good Spirit,' he pursued, as down upon the ground he fell before it: 'Your nature intercedes for me, and pities me. Assure me that I yet may change these shadows you have shown me, by an altered life!'

The kind hand trembled.

'I will honour Christmas in my heart, and try to keep it all the year. I will live in the Past, the Present, and the Future. The Spirits of all Three shall strive within me. I will not shut out the lessons that they teach. Oh, tell me I may sponge away the writing on this stone!' (*Stave 4:* Scrooge).

'Hallo!' growled Scrooge, in his accustomed voice, as near as he could feign it. 'What do you mean by coming here at this time of day?'

'I am very sorry, sir,' said Bob. 'I *am* behind my time.'

'You are?' repeated Scrooge. 'Yes. I think you are. Step this way, sir, if you please.'

'It's only once a year, sir,' pleaded Bob, appearing from the Tank. 'It shall not be repeated. I was making rather merry yesterday, sir.'

'Now, I'll tell you what, my friend,' said Scrooge, 'I am not going to stand this sort of thing any longer. And therefore,' he continued, leaping from his stool, and giving Bob such a dig in the waistcoat that he staggered back into the Tank again: 'and therefore I am about to raise your salary!' (*Stave 5*).

He had no further intercourse with Spirits, but lived upon the Total Abstinence Principle, ever afterwards; and it was always said of him, that he knew how to keep Christmas well, if any man alive possessed the knowledge. May that be truly said of us, and all of us! And so, as Tiny Tim observed, God bless Us, Every One! (*Stave 5*).

THE CHIMES

They were old Chimes, trust me. Centuries ago, these Bells had been baptized by bishops: so many centuries ago, that the register of their baptism was lost long, long before the memory of man, and no one knew their names. They had had their Godfathers and Godmothers, these Bells (for my own part, by the way, I would rather incur the responsibility of being God-father to a Bell than a Boy), and had their silver mugs no doubt, besides. But Time had mowed down their sponsors, and Henry the Eighth had melted down their mugs; and they now hung, nameless and mugless, in the church-tower (*First Quarter*).

'Dinner-time, eh!' repeated Toby, using his right-hand muffler like an infantile boxing-glove, and punishing his chest for being cold. 'Ah-h-h-h!'

He took a silent trot, after that, for a minute or two.

'There's nothing,' said Toby, breaking forth afresh – but here he stopped short in his trot, and with a face of great interest and some alarm, felt his nose carefully all the way up. It was but a little way (not being much of a nose) and he had soon finished.

'I thought it was gone,' said Toby, trotting off again. 'It's all right, however. I am sure I couldn't blame it if it was to go. It has a precious hard service of it in the bitter weather, and precious little to look forward to; for I don't take snuff myself. It's a good deal tried, poor creetur, at the best of times; for when it *does* get hold of a pleasant whiff or so (which an't too often), it's generally from somebody else's dinner, a-coming home from the baker's.' *(First Quarter:* Toby Veck).

'There's nothing,' said Toby, 'more regular in its coming round than dinner-time, and nothing less regular in its coming round than dinner. That's the great difference between 'em. It's took me a long time to find it out. I wonder whether it would be worth any gentleman's while, now, to buy that observation for the Papers; or the Parliament!' *(First Quarter:* Toby Veck).

'But who eats tripe?' said Mr. Filer, looking round. 'Tripe is without an exception the least economical, and the most wasteful article of consumption that the markets of this country can by possibility produce. The loss upon a pound of tripe has been found to be, in the boiling, seven-eighths of a fifth more than the loss upon a pound of any other animal substance whatever. Tripe is more expensive, properly understood, than the hothouse pine-apple. Taking into account the number of animals slaughtered yearly within the bills of mortality alone; and forming a low estimate of the quantity of tripe which the carcasses of those animals, reasonably well butchered, would yield; I find that the waste on that amount of tripe, if boiled, would victual a garrison of five hundred men for five months of thirty-one days each, and a February over. The Waste, the Waste!' *(First Quarter).*

Famous man for the common people, Alderman Cute! Never out of temper with them! Easy, affable, joking, knowing gentleman!

'You see, my friend,' pursued the Alderman, 'there's a great deal of nonsense talked about Want – "hard up," you know; that's the phrase, isn't it? ha! ha! ha! – and I intend to Put it Down. There's a certain amount of cant in vogue about Starvation, and I mean to Put it Down. That's all! Lord bless you,' said the Alderman, turning to his friends again, 'you may Put Down anything among this sort of people, if you only know the way to set about it' *(First Quarter).*

The Year was Old, that day. The patient Year had lived through the reproaches and misuses of its slanderers, and faithfully performed its work. Spring, summer, autumn, winter. It had laboured through the destined round, and now laid down its weary head to die. Shut out from hope, high impulse, active happiness, itself, but active messenger of many joys to others, it made appeal in its decline to have its toiling days and patient hours remembered, and to die in peace. Trotty might have read a poor man's allegory in the fading year; but he was past that, now.

And only he? Or has the like appeal been ever made, by seventy years at once upon an English labourer's head, and made in vain! *(Second Quarter).*

'I don't agree with Cute here, for instance,' said Sir Joseph. . . . 'I don't agree with the Filer party. I don't agree with any party. My friend the Poor Man, has no business with anything of that sort, and nothing of that sort has any business with him. My friend the Poor Man, in my district, is my business. No man or body of men has any right to interfere between my friend and me. That is the ground I take. I assume a – a paternal character towards my friend. I say, "My good fellow, I will treat you paternally." '

Toby listened with great gravity, and began to feel more comfortable.

'Your only business, my good fellow,' pursued Sir Joseph, looking abstractedly at Toby; 'your only business in life is with me. You needn't trouble yourself to think about anything. I will think for you; I know what is good for you; I am your perpetual parent. Such is the dispensation of an all-wise Providence! Now, the design of your creation is – not that you should swill, and guzzle, and associate your enjoyments, brutally, with food'; Toby thought remorsefully of the tripe; 'but that you should feel the Dignity of Labour. Go forth erect into the cheerful morning air, and – and stop there. Live hard and temperately, be respectful, exercise your self-denial, bring up your family on next to nothing, pay your rent as regularly as the clock strikes, be punctual in your dealings (I set you a good example; you will find Mr. Fish, my confidential secretary, with a cash-box before him at all times); and you may trust to me to be your Friend and Father' *(Second Quarter:* Sir Joseph Bowley).

'Unnatural and cruel!' Toby cried. 'Unnatural and cruel! None but people who were bad at heart, born bad, who had no business on the earth, could do such deeds. It's too true, all I've heard to-day; too just, too full of proof. We're Bad!'

The Chimes took up the words so suddenly – burst out so loud, and clear, and sonorous – that the Bells seemed to strike him in his chair.

And what was that they said?

'Toby Veck, Toby Veck, waiting for you Toby! Toby Veck, Toby Veck, waiting for you Toby! Come and see us, come and see us, Drag him to us, drag him to us, Haunt and hunt him, haunt and hunt him, Break his slumbers, break his slumbers! Toby Veck, Toby Veck, door open wide Toby, Toby Veck, Toby Veck, door open wide Toby – ' then fiercely back to their impetuous strain again, and ringing in the very bricks and plaster on the walls.

Toby listened. Fancy, fancy! His remorse, for having run away from them that afternoon! No, no. Nothing of the kind. Again, again, and yet a dozen times again. 'Haunt and hunt him, haunt and hunt him, Drag him to us, drag him to us!' Deafening the whole town! *(Second Quarter).*

Black are the brooding clouds, and troubled the deep waters, when the sea of Thought, first heaving from a calm, gives up its Dead. Monsters uncouth and wild, arise in premature imperfect resurrection; the several parts and shapes of different things are joined and mixed by chance; and when, and how, and by what wonderful degrees, each separates from each, and every sense and object of the mind resumes its usual form and lives again, no man – though every man is every day the casket of this type of the Great Mystery – can tell.

So, when and how the darkness of the night-black steeple changed to shining light; when and how the solitary tower was peopled with a myriad figures; when and how the whispered 'Haunt and hunt him,' breathing monotonously through his sleep or swoon, became a voice exclaiming in the waking ears of Trotty, 'Break his slumbers;' when and how he ceased to have a sluggish and confused idea that such things were, companioning a host of others that were not; there are no dates or means to tell. But, awake and standing on his feet upon the boards where he had lately lain, he saw this Goblin Sight *(Third Quarter)*.

'The voice of Time,' said the Phantom, 'cries to man, Advance! Time is for his advancement and improvement; for his greater worth, his greater happiness, his better life; his progress onward to that goal within its knowledge and its view, and set there, in the period when Time and He began. Ages of darkness, wickedness, and violence, have come and gone – millions uncountable, have suffered, lived, and died – to point the way before him. Who seeks to turn him back, or stay him on his course, arrests a mighty engine which will strike the meddler dead; and be the fiercer and the wilder, ever, for its momentary check!'

'I never did so to my knowledge, sir,' said Trotty. 'It was quite by accident if I did. I wouldn't go to do it, I'm sure.'

'Who puts into the mouth of Time, or of its servants,' said the Goblin of the Bell, 'a cry of lamentation for days which have had their trial and their failure, and have left deep traces of it which the blind may see – a cry that only serves the present time, by showing men how much it needs their help when any ears can listen to regrets for such a past – who does this, does a wrong. And you have done that wrong, to us, the Chimes' *(Third Quarter: Goblin of the Bell and Toby Veck)*.

'I have learnt it!' cried the old man. 'From the creature dearest to my heart! O, save her, save her!'

He could wind his fingers in her dress; could hold it! As the words escaped his lips, he felt his sense of touch return, and knew that he detained her.

The figures looked down steadfastly upon him.

'I have learnt it!' cried the old man. 'O, have mercy on me in this hour, if, in my love for her, so young and good, I slandered Nature in the breasts of mothers rendered desperate! Pity my presumption, wickedness, and ignorance, and save her.'

He felt his hold relaxing. They were silent still.

'Have mercy on her!' he exclaimed, 'as one in whom this dreadful crime has sprung from Love perverted; from the strongest, deepest Love we fallen creatures know! Think what her misery must have been, when such seed bears such fruit! Heaven meant her to be good. There is no loving mother on the earth who might not come to this, if such a life had gone before. O, have mercy on my child, who, even at this pass, means mercy to her own, and dies herself, and perils her immortal soul, to save it!'

She was in his arms. He held her now. His strength was like a giant's.

'I see the Spirit of the Chimes among you!' cried the old man, singling out the child, and speaking in some inspiration, which their looks conveyed to him. 'I know that our inheritance is held in store for us by Time. I know there is a sea of Time to rise one day, before which all who wrong us or oppress us will be swept away like leaves. I see it, on the flow! I know that we must trust and hope, and neither doubt ourselves, nor doubt the good in one another. I have learnt it from the creature dearest to my heart. I clasp her in my arms again. O Spirits, merciful and good, I take your lesson to my breast along with her! O Spirits, merciful and good, I am grateful!' *(Fourth Quarter)*.

THE CRICKET ON THE HEARTH

The kettle began it! Don't tell me what Mrs. Peerybingle said. I know better. Mrs. Peerybingle may leave it on record to the end of time that she couldn't say which of them began it; but, I say the kettle did. I ought to know, I hope! The kettle began it, full five minutes by the little waxy-faced Dutch clock in the corner, before the Cricket uttered a chirp.

As if the clock hadn't finished striking, and the convulsive little Haymaker at the top of it, jerking away right and left with a scythe in front of a Moorish Palace, hadn't mowed down half an acre of imaginary grass before the Cricket joined in at all! *(Chirp the First)*.

Besides, the kettle was aggravating and obstinate. It wouldn't allow itself to be adjusted on the top bar; it wouldn't hear of accommodating itself kindly to the knobs of coal; it *would* lean forward with a drunken air, and dribble, a very Idiot of a kettle, on the hearth. It was quarrelsome, and hissed and spluttered morosely at the fire. To sum up all, the lid, resisting Mrs. Peerybingle's fingers, first of all turned topsy-turvy, and then, with an ingenious pertinacity deserving of a better cause, dived sideways in – down to the very bottom of the kettle. And the hull of the Royal George has never made half the monstrous resistance to coming out of the water, which the lid of that kettle employed against Mrs. Peerybingle, before she got it up again.

It looked sullen and pig-headed enough, even then; carrying its handle with an air of defiance, and cocking its spout pertly and mockingly at Mrs. Peerybingle, as if it said, 'I won't boil. Nothing shall induce me!' *(Chirp the First)*.

This song of the kettle's was a song of invitation and welcome to somebody out of doors: to somebody at that moment coming on, towards the snug small home and the crisp fire: there is no doubt whatever. Mrs. Peerybingle knew it, perfectly, as she sat musing before the hearth. It's a dark night, sang the kettle, and the rotten leaves are lying by the way; and, above, all is mist and darkness, and, below, all is mire and clay; and there's only one relief in all the sad and murky air; and I don't know that it is one, for it's nothing but a glare; of deep and angry crimson, where the sun and wind together; set a brand upon the clouds for being guilty of such weather; and the wildest open country is a long dull streak of black; and there's hoar-frost on the finger-post, and thaw upon the track, and the ice it isn't water, and the water isn't free; and you couldn't say that anything is what it ought to be; but he's coming, coming, coming! –

And here, if you like, the Cricket DID chime in! with a Chirrup, Chirrup, Chirrup of such magnitude, by way of chorus; with a voice so astoundingly disproportionate to its size, as compared with the kettle; (size! you couldn't see it!) that if it had then and there burst itself like an overcharged gun, if it had fallen a victim on the spot, and chirruped its little body into fifty pieces, it would have seemed a natural and inevitable consequence, for which it had expressly laboured. *(Chirp the First)*.

'Why what's this round box? Heart alive, John, it's a wedding-cake!'

'Leave a woman alone to find out that,' said John, admiringly. 'Now a man would never have thought of it. Whereas, it's my belief that if you was to pack a wedding-cake up in a tea-chest, or a turn-up bedstead, or a pickled salmon keg, or any unlikely thing, a woman would be sure to find it out directly. Yes; I called for it at the pastry-cook's' *(Chirp the First: Dot and John Peerybingle)*.

The Stranger [Edward Plummer] raised his head; and glancing from the latter to the former, said,

'Your daughter, my good friend?'

'Wife,' returned John.

'Niece?' said the Stranger.

'Wife,' roared John.

'Indeed?' observed the Stranger. 'Surely? Very young!'

He quietly turned over, and resumed his reading. But, before he could have read two lines, he again interrupted himself to say:

'Baby, yours?'

John gave him a gigantic nod; equivalent to an answer in the affirmative, delivered through a speaking trumpet.

'Girl?'

'Bo-o-oy!' roared John.

'Also very young, eh?'

Mrs. Peerybingle instantly struck in. 'Two months and three da-ays! Vaccinated just six weeks ago-o! Took very fine-ly! Considered, by the doctor, a remarkably beautiful chi-ild! Equal to the general run of children at five months o-old! Takes notice, in a way quite won-der-ful! May seem impossible to you, but feels his legs al-ready!' *(Chirp the First)*.

'Humph! Caleb, come here! Who's that with the grey hair?'

'I don't know, sir,' returned Caleb in a whisper. 'Never see him before, in all my life. A beautiful figure for a nut-cracker; quite a new model. With a screw-jaw opening down into his waistcoat, he'd be lovely.'

'Not ugly enough,' said Tackleton.

'Or for a firebox, either,' observed Caleb, in deep contemplation, 'what a model! Unscrew his head to put the matches in; turn him heels up'ards for the light; and what a firebox for a gentleman's mantel-shelf, just as he stands!'

'Not half ugly enough,' said Tackleton. 'Nothing in him at all!' *(Chirp the First: Tackleton and Caleb Plummer)*.

'I beg your pardon, friend,' said the old gentleman, advancing to him; 'the more so, as I fear your wife has not been well; but the Attendant whom my infirmity,' he touched his ears and shook his head, 'renders almost indispensable, not having arrived, I fear there must be some mistake. The bad night which made the shelter of your comfortable cart (may I never have a worse!) so acceptable, is still as bad as ever. Would you, in your kindness, suffer me to rent a bed here?'

'Yes, yes,' cried Dot. 'Yes! Certainly!'

'Oh!' said the Carrier, surprised by the rapidity of this consent. 'Well! I don't object; but still I'm not quite sure that – '

'Hush!' she interrupted. 'Dear John!'

'Why, he's stone deaf,' urged John.

'I know he is, but – Yes, sir, certainly. Yes! certainly! I'll make him up a bed, directly, John.'

As she hurried off to do it, the flutter of her spirits, and the agitation of her manner, were so strange, that the Carrier stood looking after her, quite confounded.

'Did its mothers make it up a Bed then!' cried Miss Slowboy to the Baby; 'and did its hair grow brown and curly, when its caps was lifted off, and frighten it, a precious Pets, a-sitting by the fires!' *(Chirp the First)*.

Gruff and Tackleton was also there, doing the agreeable, with the evident sensation of being as perfectly at home, and as unquestionably in his own element, as a fresh young salmon on the top of the Great Pyramid *(Chirp the Second)*.

Tilly was hushing the Baby, and she crossed and re-crossed Tackleton, a dozen times, repeating drowsily:

'Did the knowledge that it was to be its wifes, then, wring its hearts almost to breaking; and did its fathers deceive it from its cradles but to break its hearts at last!' *(Chirp the Second: Tilly Slowboy)*.

His little wife, being left alone, sobbed piteously; but often dried her eyes and checked herself, to say how good he was, how excellent he was! and once or twice she laughed; so heartily, triumphantly, and incoherently (still crying all the time), that Tilly was quite horrified.

'Ow if you please don't!' said Tilly. 'It's enough to dead and bury the Baby, so it is if you please.'

'Will you bring him sometimes, to see his father, Tilly,' inquired her mistress, drying her eyes; 'when I can't live here, and have gone to my old home?'

'Ow if you please don't!' cried Tilly, throwing back her head, and bursting out into a howl – she looked at the moment uncommonly like Boxer; 'Ow if you please don't! Ow, what has everybody gone and been and done with everybody, making everybody else so wretched! Ow-w-w-w!' *(Chirp the Third)*.

Everybody tumbled over Tilly Slowboy and the Baby, everywhere. Tilly never came out in such force before. Her ubiquity was the theme of general admiration. She was a stumbling-block in the passage at five-and-twenty minutes past two; a man-trap in the kitchen at half-past two precisely; and a pitfall in the garret at five-and-twenty minutes to three. The Baby's head was, as it were, a test and touchstone for every description of matter – animal, vegetable, and mineral. Nothing was in use that day that didn't come, at some time or other, into close acquaintance with it (*Chirp the Third*).

THE BATTLE OF LIFE

'The French wit,' said Mr. Snitchley, peeping sharply into his blue bag, 'was wrong, Doctor Jeddler, and your philosophy is altogether wrong, depend upon it, as I have often told you. Nothing serious in life! What do you call law?'

'A joke,' replied the Doctor.

'Did you ever go to law?' asked Mr. Snitchey, looking out of the blue bag.

'Never,' returned the Doctor.

'If you ever do,' said Mr. Snitchey, 'perhaps you'll alter that opinion' (*Part the First*).

'Granted, if you please, that war is foolish,' said Snitchey. 'There we agree. For example. Here's a smiling country,' pointing it out with his fork, 'once overrun by soldiers – trespassers every man of 'em – and laid waste by fire and sword. He, he, he! The idea of any man exposing himself, voluntarily, to fire and sword! Stupid, wasteful, positively ridiculous; you laugh at your fellow-creatures, you know, when you think of it! But take this smiling country as it stands. Think of the laws appertaining to real property; to the bequest and devise of real property; to the mortgage and redemption of real property; to leasehold, freehold, and copyhold estate; think,' said Mr. Snitchey, with such great emotion that he actually smacked his lips, 'of the complicated laws relating to title and proof of title, with all the contradictory precedents and numerous acts of parliament connected with them; think of the infinite number of ingenious and interminable chancery suits, to which this pleasant prospect may give rise; and acknowledge, Dr. Jeddler, that there is a green spot in the scheme about us! I believe,' said Mr. Snitchey, looking at his partner, 'that I speak for Self and Craggs?' (*Part the First*).

'Mr. Craggs, sir,' observed Snitchey, 'didn't find life, I regret to say, as easy to have and to hold as his theory made it out, or he would have been among us now. It's a great loss to me. He was my right arm, my right leg, my right ear, my right eye, was Mr. Craggs. I am paralytic without him. He bequeathed his share of the business to Mrs. Craggs, her executors, administrators, and assigns. His name remains in the Firm to this hour. I try, in a childish sort of way, to make believe, sometimes, he's alive. You may observe that I speak for Self and Craggs – deceased, sir – deceased,' said the tender-hearted attorney, waving his pocket-handkerchief. (*Part the Third*).

THE HAUNTED MAN

You should have seen him in his dwelling about twilight, in the dead winter time.

When the wind was blowing, shrill and shrewd, with the going down of the blurred sun. When it was just so dark, as that the forms of things were indistinct and big – but not wholly lost. When sitters by the fire began to see wild faces and figures, mountains and abysses, ambuscades, and armies, in the coals. When people in the streets bent down their heads and ran before the weather. When those who were obliged to meet it, were stopped at angry corners, stung by wandering snow-flakes alighting on the lashes of their eyes, – which fell too sparingly, and were blown away too quickly, to leave a trace upon the frozen ground. When windows of private houses closed up tight and warm. When lighted gas began to burst forth in the busy and the quiet streets fast blackening otherwise. When stray pedestrians, shivering along the latter, looked down at the glowing fires in kitchens, and sharpened their appetites by sniffing up the fragrance of whole miles of dinners.

When travellers by land were bitter cold, and looked wearily on gloomy landscapes, rustling and shuddering in the blast. When mariners at sea, outlying upon icy yards, were tossed and swung above the howling ocean dreadfully. When lighthouses, on rocks and headlands, showed solitary and watchful; and benighted sea-birds breasted on against their ponderous lanterns, and fell dead. When little readers of story-books, by the firelight, trembled to think of Cassim Baba cut into quarters, hanging in the Robbers' Cave, or had some small misgivings that the fierce little old woman, with the crutch, who used to start out of the box in the merchant Abudah's bedroom, might one of these nights, be found upon the stairs, in the long, cold, dusky journey up to bed.

When, in rustic places, the last glimmering of daylight died away from the ends of avenues; and the trees, arching overhead, were sullen and black. When, in parks and woods, the high wet fern and sodden moss and beds of fallen leaves, and trunks of trees, were lost to view, in masses of impenetrable shade. When mists arose from dyke, and fen, and river. When lights in old halls and cottage windows, were a cheerful sight. When the mill stopped, the wheelwright and the blacksmith shut their workshops, the turnpike-gate closed, the plough and harrow were left lonely in the fields, the labourer and team went home, and the striking of the church clock had a deeper sound than at noon, and the churchyard wicket would be swung no more that night.

When twilight everywhere released the shadows, prisoned up all day, that now closed in and gathered like mustering swarms of ghosts. When they stood lowering, in corners of rooms, and frowned out from behind half-opened doors. When they had full possession of unoccupied apartments. When they danced upon the floors, and walls, and ceilings of inhabited chambers, while the fire was low, and withdrew like ebbing waters when it sprung into a blaze. When they fantastically mocked the shapes of household objects, making the nurse an ogress, the rocking-horse a monster, the wondering child half-scared and half-amused, a stranger to itself, – the very tongs upon the hearth, a straddling giant with his arms a-kimbo, evidently smelling the blood of Englishmen, and wanting to grind people's bones to make his bread (*Chapter 1*).

'Mrs. William is of course subject at any time, sir, to be taken off her balance by the elements. She is not formed superior to *that*.'

'No,' returned Mr. Redlaw good-naturedly, though abruptly.

'No, sir. Mrs. William may be taken off her balance by Earth; as, for example, last Sunday week, when sloppy and greasy, and she going out to tea with her newest sister-in-law, and having a pride in herself, and wishing to appear perfectly spotless though pedestrian. Mrs. William may be taken off her balance by Air; as being once over-persuaded by a friend to try a swing at Peckham Fair, which acted on her constitution instantly like a steam-boat. Mrs. William may be taken off her balance by Fire; as on a false alarm of engines at her mother's, when she went two miles in her nightcap. Mrs. William may be taken off her balance by Water; as at Battersea, when rowed into the piers by her young nephew, Charley Swidger junior, aged twelve, which had no idea of boats whatever. But these are elements. Mrs. William must be taken out of elements for the strength of *her* character to come into play' (*Chapter 1:* William Swidger).

'I thank'ee, sir, I thank'ee!' said the old man, 'for Mouse, and for my son William, and for myself. Where's my son William? William, you take the lantern and go on first, through them long dark passages, as you did last year and the year afore. Ha, ha! *I* remember – though I'm eighty-seven! "Lord keep my memory green!" It's a very good prayer, Mr. Redlaw, that of the learned gentleman in the peaked beard, with a ruff round his neck – hangs up, second on the right above the panelling, in what used to be, afore our ten poor gentlemen commuted, our great Dinner Hall. "Lord keep my memory green!" It's very good and pious, sir. Amen! Amen!' (*Chapter 1:* Philip Swidger).

'If I could forget my sorrow and wrong, I would,' the Ghost repeated. 'If I could forget my sorrow and wrong, I would!'

'Evil spirit of myself,' returned the haunted man, in a low, trembling tone, 'my life is darkened by that incessant whisper.'

'It is an echo,' said the Phantom.

'If it be an echo of my thoughts – as now, indeed, I know it is,' rejoined the haunted man, 'why should I, therefore, be tormented? It is not a selfish thought. I suffer it to range beyond myself. All men and women have their sorrows, – most of them their wrongs; ingratitude, and sordid jealousy, and interest, besetting all degrees of life. Who would not forget their sorrows and their wrongs?'

'Who would not, truly, and be the happier and better for it?' said the Phantom.

'These revolutions of years, which we commemorate,' proceeded Redlaw, 'what do *they* recall! Are there any minds in which they do not re-awaken some sorrow, or some trouble? What is the remembrance of the old man who was here to-night? A tissue of sorrow and trouble' (*Chapter 1*).

Tetterby himself, however, in his little parlour, as already mentioned, having the presence of a young family impressed upon his mind in a manner too clamorous to be disregarded, or to comport with the quiet perusal of a newspaper, laid down his paper, wheeled, in his distraction, a few times round the parlour, like an undecided carrier-pigeon, made an ineffectual rush at one or two flying little figures in bed-gowns that skimmed past him, and then, bearing suddenly down upon the only unoffending member of the family, boxed the ears of little Moloch's nurse.

'You bad boy!' said Mr. Tetterby, 'haven't you any feeling for your poor father after the fatigues and anxieties of a hard winter's day, since five o'clock in the morning, but must you wither his rest, and corrode his latest intelligence, with *your* wicious tricks? Isn't it enough, sir, that your brother 'Dolphus is toiling and moiling in the fog and cold, and you rolling in the lap of luxury with a – with a baby, and everything you can wish for,' said Mr. Tetterby, heaping this up as a great climax of blessings, 'but must you make a wilderness of home, and maniacs of your parents? Must you, Johnny? Hey?' At each interrogation, Mr. Tetterby made a feint of boxing his ears again, but thought better of it, and held his hand.

'Oh father!' whimpered Johnny, 'when I wasn't doing anything, I'm sure, but taking such care of Sally, and getting her to sleep. Oh, father!' (*Chapter 2*).

'I wish my little woman would come home!' said Mr. Tetterby, relenting and repenting, 'I only wish my little woman would come home! I an't fit to deal with 'em. They make my head go round, and get the better of me. Oh, Johnny! Isnt' it enough that your dear mother has provided you with that sweet sister?' indicating Moloch; 'isn't it enough that you were seven boys before, without a ray of gal, and that your dear mother went through what she *did* go through, on purpose that you might all of you have a little sister, but must you so behave yourself as to make my head swim?'

Softening more and more, as his own tender feelings and those of his injured son were worked on, Mr. Tetterby concluded by embracing him, and immediately breaking away to catch one of the real delinquents. A reasonably good start occurring, he succeeded, after a short but smart run, and some rather severe cross-country work under and over the bedsteads, and in and out among the intricacies of the chairs, in capturing his infant, whom he condignly punished, and bore to bed. This example had a powerful, and apparently mesmeric influence on him of the boots, who instantly fell into a deep sleep, though he had been, but a moment before, broad awake, and in the highest possible feather. Nor was it lost upon the two young architects, who retired to bed, in an adjoining closet, with great privacy and speed. The comrade of the Intercepted One also shrinking into his nest with similar discretion, Mr. Tetterby, when he paused for breath, found himself unexpectedly in a scene of peace.

'My little woman herself,' said Mr. Tetterby, wiping his flushed face, 'could hardly have done it better! I only wish my little woman had had it to do, I do indeed!'

Mr. Tetterby sought upon his screen for a passage appropriate to be impressed upon his children's minds on the occasion, and read the following.

' "It is an undoubted fact that all remarkable men have had remarkable mothers, and have respected them in after life as their best friends." Think of your own remarkable mother, my boys,' said Mr. Tetterby, 'and know her value while she is still among you!'

He sat down in his chair by the fire, and composed himself, cross-legged, over his newspaper.

'Let anybody, I don't care who it is, get out of bed again,' said Tetterby, as a general proclamation, delivered in a very soft-hearted manner, 'and astonishment will be the portion of that respected contemporary!' – which expression Mr. Tetterby selected from his screen. 'Johnny, my child, take care of your only sister, Sally; for she's the brightest gem that ever sparkled on your early brow' *(Chapter 2)*.

'I am sure, 'Dolphus,' sobbed Mrs. Tetterby, 'coming home, I had no more idea than a child unborn – '

Mr. Tetterby seemed to dislike this figure of speech, and observed, 'Say than the baby, my dear.'

' – Had no more idea than the baby,' said Mrs. Tetterby. – 'Johnny, don't look at me, but look at her, or she'll fall out of your lap and be killed, and then you'll die in agonies of a broken heart, and serve you right. – No more idea I hadn't than that darling, of being cross when I came home; but somehow, 'Dolphus – ' Mrs. Tetterby paused, and again turned her wedding-ring round and round upon her finger.

'I see!' said Mr. Tetterby. 'I understand! My little woman was put out. Hard times, and hard weather, and hard work, make it trying now and then. I see, bless your soul! No wonder! 'Dolf, my man,' continued Mr. Tetterby, exploring the basin with a fork, 'here's your mother been and bought, at the cook's shop, besides pease pudding, a whole knuckle of a lovely roast leg of pork, with lots of crackling left upon it, and with seasoning gravy and mustard quite unlimited. Hand in your plate, my boy, and begin while it's simmering' *(Chapter 2)*.

'My little woman,' said her husband, dubiously, 'are you quite sure you're better? Or are you, Sophia, about to break out in a fresh direction?'

'No, 'Dolphus, no,' replied his wife. 'I'm quite myself.' With that, settling her hair, and pressing the palms of her hands upon her eyes, she laughed again.

'What a wicked fool I was, to think so for a moment!' said Mrs. Tetterby. 'Come nearer, 'Dolphus, and let me ease my mind, and tell you what I mean. Let me tell you all about it.'

Mr. Tetterby bringing his chair closer, Mrs. Tetterby laughed again, gave him a hug, and wiped her eyes.

'You know, 'Dolphus, my dear,' said Mrs. Tetterby, 'that when I was single, I might have given myself away in several directions. At one time, four after me at once; two of them were sons of Mars.'

'We're all sons of Ma's, my dear,' said Mr. Tetterby, 'jointly with Pa's' *(Chapter 2)*.

'You had better read your paper than do nothing at all,' said Mrs. Tetterby.

'What's there to read in a paper?' returned Mr. Tetterby, with excessive discontent.

'What?' said Mrs. Tetterby. 'Police.'

'It's nothing to me,' said Tetterby. 'What do I care what people do, or are done to?'

'Suicides,' suggested Mrs. Tetterby.

'No business of mine,' replied her husband.

'Births, deaths, and marriages, are those nothing to you?' said Mrs. Tetterby.

'If the births were all over for good, and all to-day; and the deaths were all to begin to come off to-morrow; I don't see why it should interest me, till I thought it was a-coming to my turn,' grumbled Tetterby. 'As to marriages, I've done it myself. I know quite enough about *them*' *(Chapter 3)*.

'One Christmas morning,' pursued the old man, 'that you come here with her – and it began to snow, and my wife invited the young lady to walk in, and sit by the fire that is always a-burning on Christmas Day in what used to be, before our ten poor gentlemen commuted, our great Dinner Hall. I was there; and I recollect, as I was stirring up the blaze for the young lady to warm her pretty feet by, she read the scroll out loud, that is underneath that picter. "Lord, keep my memory green!" She and my poor wife fell a-talking about it; and it's a strange thing to think of, now, that they both said (both being so unlike to die) that it was a good prayer, and that it was one they would put up very earnestly, if they were called away young, with reference to those who were dearest to them. "My brother," says the young lady – "My husband," says my poor wife. – "Lord, keep his memory of me, green, and do not let me be forgotten!" ' *(Chapter 3: Philip Swidger)*.

DOMBEY AND SON

Dombey was about eight-and-forty years of age. Son about eight and forty minutes. Dombey was rather bald, rather red, and though a handsome well-made man, too stern and pompous in appearance to be prepossessing. Son was very bald, and very red, and though (of course) an undeniably fine infant, somewhat crushed and spotty in his general effect, as yet. On the brow of Dombey, Time and his brother Care had set some marks, as on a tree that was to come down in good time – remorseless twins they are for striding through their human forests, notching as they go – while the countenance of Son was crossed and recrossed with a thousand little creases, which the same deceitful Time would take delight in smoothing out and wearing away with the flat part of his scythe, as a preparation of the surface for his deeper operations *(Chapter 1)*.

'He will be christened Paul, my – Mrs. Dombey – of course.'

She feebly echoed, 'Of course,' or rather expressed it by the motion of her lips, and closed her eyes again.

'His father's name, Mrs. Dombey, and his grandfather's! I wish his grandfather were alive this day!' And again he said 'Dom-bey and Son,' in exactly the same tone as before.

Those three words conveyed the one idea of Mr. Dombey's life. The earth was made for Dombey and Son to trade in, and the sun and moon were made to give them light. Rivers and seas were formed to float their ships; rainbows gave them promise of fair weather; winds blew for or against their enterprises; stars and planets circled in their orbits, to preserve inviolate a system of which they were the centre. Common abbreviations took new meanings in his eyes, and had sole reference to them: A. D. had no concern with anno Domini, but stood for anno Dombei – and Son (*Chapter 1: Dombey and Mrs. Dombey*).

'I shall never cease to congratulate myself,' said Mrs. Chick, 'on having said, when I little thought what was in store for us, – really as if I was inspired by something, – that I forgave poor dear Fanny everything. Whatever happens, that must always be a comfort to me!'

Mrs. Chick made this impressive observation in the drawing-room after having descended thither from the inspection of the mantua-makers upstairs, who were busy on the family mourning. She delivered it for the behoof of Mr. Chick, who was a stout bald gentleman, with a very large face, and his hands continually in his pockets, and who had a tendency in his nature to whistle and hum tunes, which, sensible of the indecorum of such sounds in a house of grief, he was at some pains to repress at present.

'Don't you over-exert yourself, Loo,' said Mr. Chick, 'or you'll be laid up with spasms, I see. Right tol loor rul! Bless my soul, I forgot! We're here one day and gone the next!'

Mrs. Chick contented herself with a glance of reproof, and then proceeded with the thread of her discourse.

'I am sure,' she said, 'I hope this heart-rending occurrence will be a warning to all of us, to accustom ourselves to rouse ourselves, and to make efforts in time where they're required of us. There's a moral in everything, if we would only avail ourselves of it. It will be our own faults if we lose sight of this one.'

Mr. Chick invaded the grave silence which ensued on this remark with the singularly inappropriate air of 'A cobbler there was'; and checking himself, in some confusion, observed that it was undoubtedly our own faults if we didn't improve such melancholy occasions as the present.

'Which might be better improved, I should think, Mr. C.,' retorted his helpmate, after a short pause, 'than by the introduction, either of the College Hornpipe, or the equally unmeaning and unfeeling remark of rump-te-iddity, bow-wow-wow!' – which Mr. Chick had indeed indulged in, under his breath, and which Mrs. Chick repeated in a tone of withering scorn (*Chapter 2*).

M

'It would have occurred to most men,' said Mrs. Chick, 'that poor dear Fanny being no more, it becomes necessary to provide a nurse.'

'Oh! Ah!' said Mr. Chick. 'Toor-rul – such is life, I mean. I hope you are suited, my dear.'

'Indeed I am not,' said Mrs. Chick; 'nor likely to be, so far as I can see. Meanwhile, of course, the child is –'

'Going to the very deuce,' said Mr. Chick, thoughtfully, 'to be sure.'

Admonished, however, that he had committed himself, by the indignation expressed in Mrs. Chick's countenance at the idea of a Dombey going there; and thinking to atone for his misconduct by a bright suggestion, he added – 'Couldn't something temporary be done with a teapot?' (*Chapter 2*).

Mr. Dombey's house was a large one, on the shady side of a tall, dark, dreadfully genteel street in the region between Portland Place and Bryanstone Square. It was a corner house, with great wide areas containing cellars frowned upon by barred windows, and leered at by crooked-eyed doors leading to dustbins. It was a house of dismal state, with a circular back to it, containing a whole suit of drawing-rooms looking upon a gravelled yard, where two gaunt trees, with blackened trunks and branches, rattled rather than rustled, their leaves were so smoke-dried. The summer sun was never on the street, but in the morning about breakfast-time, when it came with the water-carts and the old clothes-men, and the people with geraniums, and the umbrella-mender, and the man who trilled the little bell of the Dutch clock as he went along. It was soon gone again to return no more that day; and the bands of music and the straggling Punch's shows going after it, left it a prey to the most dismal of organs, and white mice; with now and then a porcupine, to vary the entertainments; until the butlers whose families were dining out, began to stand at the house-doors in the twilight, and the lamp-lighter made his nightly failure in attempting to brighten up the street with gas (*Chapter 3*).

'My darling,' said Richards, 'you wear that pretty black frock in remembrance of your Mamma.'

'I can remember my Mamma,' returned the child, with tears springing to her eyes, 'in any frock.'

'But people put on black, to remember people when they're gone.'

'Where gone?' asked the child.

'Come and sit down by me.' said Richards, 'and I'll tell you a story.'

With a quick perception that it was intended to relate to what she had asked, little Florence laid aside the bonnet she had held in her hand until now, and sat down on a stool at the nurse's feet, looking up into her face.

'One upon a time,' said Richards, 'there was a lady – a very good lady, and her little daughter dearly loved her.'

'A very good lady and her little daughter dearly loved her,' repeated the child.

'Who, when God thought it right that it should be so, was taken ill and died.'

The child shuddered.

341

'Died, never to be seen again by any one on earth, and was buried in the ground where the trees grow.'

'The cold ground?' said the child, shuddering again.

'No! The warm ground,' returned Polly, seizing her advantage, 'where the ugly little seeds turn into beautiful flowers, and into grass, and corn, and I don't know what all besides. Where good people turn into bright angels, and fly away to heaven!'

The child, who had drooped her head, raised it again, and sat looking at her intently.

'So; let me see,' said Polly, not a little flurried between this earnest scrutiny, her desire to comfort the child, her sudden success, and her very slight confidence in her own powers. 'So, when this lady died, wherever they took her, or wherever they put her, she went to GOD! and she prayed to Him, this lady did,' said Polly, affecting herself beyond measure; being heartily in earnest, 'to teach her little daughter to be sure of that in her heart: and to know that she was happy there and loved her still: and to hope and try – Oh, all her life – to meet her there one day, never, never, never to part any more.'

'It was my Mamma!' exclaimed the child, springing up, and clasping her round the neck (*Chapter 3: Polly Richards and Florence Dombey*).

'Oh well, Miss Floy! And won't your Pa be angry neither!' cried a quick voice at the door, proceeding from a short brown, womanly girl of fourteen, with a little snub nose, and black eyes like jet beads. 'When it was 'tickerleyly given out that you wasn't to go and worrit the wet nurse.'

'She don't worry me,' was the surprised rejoinder of Polly. 'I am very fond of children.'

'Oh! but begging your pardon, Mrs. Richards, that don't matter, you know,' returned the black-eyed girl, who was so desperately sharp and biting that she seemed to make one's eyes water. 'I may be very fond of pennywinkles, Mrs. Richards, but it don't follow that I'm to have 'em for tea' (*Chapter 3: Susan Nipper and Polly Richards*).

'Lork, Mrs. Richards!' cried Miss Nipper, taking up her words with a jerk. 'Don't. See her dear Papa indeed! I should like to see her do it!'

'Won't she then?' asked Polly.

'Lork, Mrs. Richards, no, her Pa's a deal too wrapped up in somebody else, and before there was a somebody else to be wrapped up in she never was a favourite, girls are thrown away in this house, Mrs. Richards, *I* assure you.'

The child looked quickly from one nurse to the other, as if she understood and felt what was said.

'You surprise me!' cried Polly. 'Hasn't Mr. Dombey seen her since – '

'No,' interrupted Susan Nipper. 'Not once since, and he hadn't hardly set his eyes upon her before that for months and months, and I don't think he'd have known her for his own child if he had met her in the streets, or would know her for his own child if he was to meet her in the streets to-morrow, Mrs. Richards, as to *me*,' said Spitfire, with a giggle, 'I doubt if he's aweer of my existence.'

'Pretty dear!' said Richards; meaning, not Miss Nipper, but the little Florence.

'Oh! there's a Tartar within a hundred miles of where we're now in conversation, I can tell you, Mrs. Richards, present company always excepted too,' said Susan Nipper; 'wish you good morning, Mrs. Richards, now Miss Floy, you come along with me, and don't go hanging back like a naughty wicked child that judgments is no example to, don't' (*Chapter 3*).

'It ain't right of you to ask it, Miss Floy, for you know I can't refuse you, but Mrs. Richards and me will see what can be done, if Mrs. Richards likes, I may wish, you see, to take a voyage to Chaney, Mrs. Richards, but I mayn't know how to leave the London Docks.'

Richards assented to the proposition.

'This house ain't so exactly ringing with merry-making,' said Miss Nipper, 'that one need be lonelier than one must be. Your Toxes and your Chickses may draw out my two front double teeth, Mrs. Richards, but that's no reason why I need offer 'em the whole set' (*Chapter 3*).

Though the offices of Dombey and Son were within the liberties of the City of London, and within hearing of Bow Bells, when their clashing voices were not drowned by the uproar in the streets, yet were there hints of adventurous and romantic story to be observed in some of the adjacent objects. Gog and Magog held their state within ten minutes' walk; the Royal Exchange was close at hand; the Bank of England, with its vaults of gold and silver 'down among the dead men' underground, was their magnificent neighbour. Just round the corner stood the rich East India House, teeming with suggestions of precious stuffs and stones, tigers, elephants, howdahs, hookahs, umbrellas, palm trees, palanquins, and gorgeous princes of a brown complexion sitting on carpets, with their slippers very much turned up at the toes. Anywhere in the immediate vicinity there might be seen pictures of ships speeding away full sail to all parts of the world; outfitting warehouses ready to pack off anybody anywhere, fully equipped in half an hour; and little timber midshipmen in obsolete naval uniforms, eternally employed outside the shopdoors of nautical instrument-makers in taking observations of the hackney coaches (*Chapter 4*).

Solomon Gills rubbed his hands with an air of stealthy enjoyment, as he talked of the sea, though, and looked on the seafaring objects about him with inexpressible complacency.

'Think of this wine for instance,' said old Sol, 'which has been to the East Indies and back, I'm not able to say how often, and has been once round the world. Think of the pitch-dark nights, the roaring winds, and rolling seas!'

'The thunder, lightning, rain, hail, storm of all kinds,' said the boy.

'To be sure,' said Solomon, – 'that this wine has passed through. Think what a straining and creaking of timbers and masts: what a whistling and howling of the gale through ropes and rigging!'

'What a clambering aloft of men, vying with each other who shall lie out first upon the yards to furl the icy sails, while the ship rolls and pitches, like mad!' cried his nephew.

'Exactly so,' said Solomon: 'has gone on, over the old cask that held this wine. Why, when the Charming Sally went down in the – '

'In the Baltic Sea, in the dead of the night; five-and-twenty minutes past twelve when the captain's watch stopped in his pocket; he lying dead against the main-mast – on the fourteenth of February, seventeen forty-nine!' cried Walter, with great animation.

'Ay, to be sure!' cried old Sol, 'quite right! Then there were five hundred casks of such wine aboard; and all hands (except the first mate, first lieutenant, two seamen, and a lady, in a leaky boat) going to work to stave the casks, got drunk and died drunk, singing, "Rule Britannia," when she settled and went down, and ending with one awful scream in chorus' (*Chapter 4:* Solomon Gills and Walter Gay).

'Wal'r!' he said arranging his hair (which was thin) with his hook, and then pointing it at the instrument-maker, 'look at him! Love! Honour! And Obey! Overhaul your catechism till you find that passage, and when found turn the leaf down. Success, my boy!' (*Chapter 4:* Captain Cuttle).

'I suppose he could make a clock if he tried?'

'I shouldn't wonder, Captain Cuttle,' returned the boy.

'And it would go!' said Captain Cuttle, making a species of serpent in the air with his hook. 'Lord, how that clock would go!'

For a moment or two he seemed quite lost in contemplating the pace of this ideal timepiece, and sat looking at the boy as if his face were the dial.

'But he's chock-full of science,' he observed, waving his hook towards the stock-in-trade. 'Look ye here! Here's a collection of 'em. Earth, air, or water. It's all one. Only say where you'll have it. Up in a balloon? There you are. Down in a bell? There you are. D'ye want to put the North Star in a pair of scales and weigh it? He'll do it for you' *Chapter 4).*

'Florence will never, never, never, be a Dombey,' said Mrs. Chick, 'not if she lives to be a thousand years old.'

Miss Tox elevated her eyebrows and was again full of commiseration.

'I quite fret and worry myself about her,' said Mrs. Chick, with a sigh of modest merit. 'I really don't see what is to become of her when she grows older, or what position she is to take. She don't gain on her Papa, in the least. How can one expect she should, when she is so very unlike a Dombey?'

Miss Tox looked as if she saw no way out of such a cogent argument as that, at all.

'And the child, you see,' said Mrs. Chick, in deep confidence, 'has poor Fanny's nature. She'll never make an effort in after-life, I'll venture to say. Never! She'll never wind and twine herself about her papa's heart like – '

'Like the ivy?' suggested Miss Tox.

'Like the ivy,' Mrs. Chick assented. 'Never! she'll never glide and nestle into the bosom of her papa's affections like – the – '

'Startled fawn?' suggested Miss Tox.

'Like the startled fawn,' said Mrs. Chick. 'Never! Poor Fanny! yet, how I loved her!' *(Chapter 5).*

'Oh! bless your heart, Mrs. Richards,' cried Susan, 'temporaries always orders permanencies here, didn't you know that, why wherever was you born, Mrs. Richards? But wherever you was born, Mrs. Richards,' pursued Spitfire, shaking her head resolutely, 'and whenever, and however (which is best known to yourself), you may bear in mind, please, that it's one thing to give orders, and quite another thing to take 'em. A person may tell a person to dive off a bridge head foremost into five-and-forty feet of water, Mrs. Richards, but a person may be very far from diving.'

'There now,' said Polly, 'you're angry because you're a good little thing, and fond of Miss Florence; and yet you turn round on me, because there's nobody else.'

'It's very easy for some to keep their tempers, and be soft-spoken, Mrs. Richards,' returned Susan, slightly mollified, 'when their child's made as much of as a prince, and is petted and patted till it wishes its friends further, but when a sweet young pretty innocent, that never ought to have a cross word spoken to or of it, is run down, the case is very different indeed. My goodness gracious me, Miss Floy, you naughty, sinful child, if you don't shut your eyes this minute, I'll call in them hobgoblins that lives in the cock-loft to come and eat you up alive!'

Here Miss Nipper made a horrible lowing, supposed to issue from a conscientious goblin of the bull species, impatient to discharge the severe duty of his position. Having further composed her young charge by covering her head with the bed-clothes, and making three or four angry dabs at the pillow, she folded her arms, and screwed up her mouth, and sat looking at the fire for the rest of the evening *(Chapter 5).*

'Please to bring the child in quick out of the air there,' whispered the beadle, holding open the inner door of the church.

Little Paul might have asked with Hamlet 'into my grave?' so chill and earthy was the place. The tall shrouded pulpit and reading-desk; the dreary perspective of empty pews stretching away under the galleries, and empty benches mounting to the roof and lost in the shadow of the great grim organ; the dusty matting and cold stone slabs; the grisly free seats in the aisles; and the damp corner by the bell-rope, where the black tressels used for funerals were stowed away, along with some shovels and baskets, and a coil or two of deadly-looking rope; the strange, unusual, uncomfortable smell, and the cadaverous light; were all in unison. It was a cold and dismal scene. . . .

Over the fireplace was a ground-plan of the vaults underneath the church; and Mr. Chick, skimming the literary portion of it aloud, by way of enlivening the company, read the reference to Mrs. Dombey's tomb in full, before he could stop himself.

After another cold interval, a wheezy little pew-opener, afflicted with an asthma, appropriate to the churchyard, if not to the church, summoned them to the font. Here they waited some little time while the marriage party enrolled themselves; and meanwhile the wheezy little pew-opener – partly in consequence of her infirmity, and partly that the marriage party might not forget her – went about the building coughing like a grampus.

Presently the clerk (the only cheerful-looking object there, and *he* was an undertaker) came up with a jug of warm water, and said something, as he poured it into the font, about taking the chill off; which millions of gallons boiling hot could not have done for the occasion. Then the clergyman, an amiable and mild-looking young curate but obviously afraid of the baby, appeared like the principal character in a ghost-story, 'a tall figure all in white'; at sight of whom Paul rent the air with his cries, and never left off again till he was taken out black in the face *(Chapter 5)*.

Mr. Chick was twice heard to hum a tune at the bottom of the table, but on both occasions it was a fragment of the Dead March in Saul. The party seemed to get colder and colder, and to be gradually resolving itself into a congealed and solid state, like the collation round which it was assembled. At length Mrs. Chick looked at Miss Tox, and Miss Tox returned the look, and they both rose and said it was really time to go. Mr. Dombey receiving this announcement with perfect equanimity, they took leave of that gentleman, and presently departed under the protection of Mr. Chick; who, when they had turned their backs upon the house and left its master in his usual solitary state, put his hands in his pockets, threw himself back in the carriage, and whistled 'With a hey ho chevy!' all through; conveying into his face as he did so, an expression of such gloomy and terrible defiance, that Mrs. Chick dared not protest, or in any way molest him *(Chapter 5)*.

The first shock of a great earthquake had, just at that period, rent the whole neighbourhood to its centre. Traces of its course were visible on every side. Houses were knocked down; streets broken through and stopped; deep pits and trenches dug in the ground; enormous heaps of earth and clay thrown up; buildings that were undermined and shaking, propped by great beams of wood. Here, a chaos of carts, overthrown and jumbled together, lay topsy-turvy at the bottom of a steep unnatural hill; there, confused treasures of iron soaked and rusted in something that had accidentally become a pond. Everywhere were bridges that led nowhere; thoroughfares that were wholly impassable; Babel towers of chimneys, wanting half their height; temporary wooden houses and enclosures, in the most unlikely situations; carcasses of ragged tenements, and fragments of unfinished walls and arches, and piles of scaffolding, and wildernesses of bricks, and giant forms of cranes, and tripods straddling above nothing. There were a hundred thousand shapes and substances of incompleteness, wildly mingled out of their places, upside down, burrowing in the earth, aspiring in the air, mouldering in the water, and unintelligible as any dream. Hot springs and fiery eruptions, the usual attendants upon earthquakes, lent their contributions of confusion to the scene. Boiling water hissed and heaved within dilapidated walls; whence, also, the glare and roar of flames came issuing forth; and mounds of ashes blocked up rights of way, and wholly changed the law and custom of the neighbourhood.

In short, the yet unfinished and unopened railroad was in progress; and, from the very core of all this dire disorder, trailed smoothly away, upon its mighty course of civilisation and improvement *(Chapter 6)*.

Some philosophers tell us that selfishness is at the root of our best loves and affections. Mr. Dombey's young child was, from the beginning, so distinctly important to him as a part of his own greatness, or (which is the same thing) of the greatness of Dombey and Son, that there is no doubt his parental affection might have been easily traced, like many a goodly superstructure of fair fame, to a very low foundation *(Chapter 8)*.

'Floy,' he said one day, 'where's India, where that boy's friends live?'

'Oh, it's a long, long distance off,' said Florence, raising her eyes from her work.

'Weeks off?' asked Paul.

'Yes, dear. Many weeks' journey, night and day.'

'If you were in India, Floy,' said Paul, after being silent for a minute, 'I should – what is that Mamma did? I forget.'

'Loved me!' answered Florence.

'No, no. Don't I love you now, Floy? What is it? – Died. If you were in India, I should die, Floy.'

She hurriedly put her work aside, and laid her head down on his pillow, caressing him. And so would she, she said, if he were there. He would be better soon.

'Oh! I am a great deal better now!' he answered. 'I don't mean that. I mean that I should die of being so sorry and so lonely, Floy!'

Another time, in the same place, he fell asleep, and slept quietly for a long time. Awaking suddenly, he listened, started up, and sat listening.

Florence asked him what he thought he heard.

'I want to know what it says,' he answered, looking steadily in her face. 'The sea, Floy, what is it that it keeps on saying?'

She told him that it was only the noise of the rolling waves.

'Yes, yes,' he said. 'But I know that they are always saying something. Always the same thing. What place is over there?' He rose up, looking eagerly at the horizon.

She told him that there was another country opposite, but he said he didn't mean that; he meant farther away – farther away!

Very often afterwards, in the midst of their talk, he would break off, to try to understand what it was that the waves were always saying; and would rise up in his couch to look towards that invisible region, far away *(Chapter 8: Paul and Florence Dombey)*.

'I have the honour of addressing Mr. Dombey, I believe?'

'I am the present unworthy representative of that name, Major,' returned Mr. Dombey.

'By G – , Sir,' said the Major, 'it's a great name. It's a name, Sir,' said the Major firmly, as if he defied Mr. Dombey to contradict him, and would feel it his painful duty to bully him if he did, 'that is known and honoured in the British possessions abroad. It is a name, Sir, that a man is proud to recognise. There is nothing adulatory in Joseph Bagstock, Sir. His Royal Highness the Duke of York observed on more than one occasion, "there is no adulation in Joey. He is a plain old soldier is Joe. He is tough to a fault is Joseph;" but it's a great name, Sir. By the Lord, it's a great name!' said the Major, solemnly *(Chapter 10:* Major Bagstock).

Captain Cuttle advanced to the table; and clearing a space among the breakfast-cups at Mr. Dombey's elbow, produced the silver watch, the ready money, the tea-spoons, and the sugar-tongs; and piling them up into a heap that they might look as precious as possible, delivered himself of these words:

'Half a loaf's better than no bread, and the same remark holds good with crumbs. There's a few. Annuity of one hundred pound prannum, also ready to be made over. If there is a man chock-full of science in the world, it's old Sol Gills. If there is a lad of promise – one flowing,' added the Captain, in one of his happy quotations, 'with milk and honey – it's his nevy!' *(Chapter 10)*.

It is when our budding hopes are nipped beyond recovery by some rough wind, that we are the most disposed to picture to ourselves what flowers they might have borne, if they had flourished *(Chapter 10)*.

'Berry's very fond of you, ain't she?' Paul once asked Mrs. Pipchin when they were sitting by the fire with the cat.

'Yes,' said Mrs. Pipchin.

'Why?' asked Paul.

'Why!' returned the disconcerted old lady. 'How can you ask such things, Sir! Why are you fond of your sister Florence?'

'Because she's very good,' said Paul. 'There's nobody like Florence.'

'Well!' retorted Mrs. Pipchin, shortly, 'and there's nobody like me, I suppose.'

'Ain't there really though?' asked Paul, leaning forward in his chair, and looking at her very hard.

'No,' said the old lady.

'I am glad of that,' observed Paul, rubbing his hands thoughtfully. 'That's a very good thing' *(Chapter 11:* Paul Dombey and Mrs. Pipchin).

Whenever a young gentleman was taken in hand by Doctor Blimber, he might consider himself sure of a pretty tight squeeze. The Doctor only undertook the charge of ten young gentlemen, but he had, always ready, a supply of learning for a hundred, on the lowest estimate; and it was at once the business and delight of his life to gorge the unhappy ten with it.

In fact, Doctor Blimber's establishment was a great hothouse, in which there was a forcing apparatus incessantly at work. All the boys blew before their time. Mental green-peas were produced at Christmas, and intellectual asparagus all the year round. Mathematical gooseberries (very sour ones too) were common at untimely seasons, and from mere sprouts of bushes, under Doctor Blimber's cultivation. Every description of Greek and Latin vegetable was got off the driest twigs of boys, under the frostiest circum-stances. Nature was of no consequence at all. No matter what a young gentleman was intended to bear, Doctor Blimber made him bear to pattern, somehow or other *(Chapter 11)*.

'Mr. Dombey, my love,' pursued the Doctor turning to his wife, 'is so confiding as to – do you see our little friend?'

Mrs. Blimber, in an excess of politeness, of which Mr. Dombey was the object, apparently did not, for she was backing against the little friend, and very much endangering his position on the table. But, on this hint, she turned to admire his classical and intellectual lineaments, and turning again to Mr. Dombey, said, with a sigh, that she envied his dear son.

'Like a bee, Sir,' said Mrs. Blimber, with uplifted eyes, 'about to plunge into a garden of the choicest flowers, and sip the sweets for the first time. Virgil, Horace, Ovid, Terence, Plautus, Cicero. What a world of honey have we here. It may appear remarkable, Mr. Dombey, in one who is a wife – the wife of such a husband – '

'Hush, hush,' said Doctor Blimber. 'Fie for shame.'

'Mr. Dombey will forgive the partiality of a wife,' said Mrs. Blimber, with an engaging smile.

Mr. Dombey answered 'Not at all': applying those words, it is to be presumed, to the partiality, and not to the forgiveness.

' – And it may seem remarkable in one who is a mother also,' resumed Mrs. Blimber.

'And such a mother,' observed Mr. Dombey, bow-ing with some confused idea of being complimentary to Cornelia.

'But really,' pursued Mrs. Blimber, 'I think if I could have known Cicero, and been his friend, and talked with him in his retirement at Tusculum (beauti-ful Tusculum!), I could have died contented' *(Chapter 11)*.

Despite his entreaty that they would not think of stirring, Doctor Blimber, Mrs. Blimber, and Miss Blimber all pressed forward to attend him to the hall; and thus Mrs. Pipchin got into a state of entanglement with Miss Blimber and the Doctor, and was crowded out of the study before she could clutch Florence. To which happy accident Paul stood afterwards indebted for the dear remembrance, that Florence ran back to throw her arms round his neck, and that hers was the last face in the doorway: turned towards him with a smile of encouragement, the brighter for the tears through which it beamed.

It made his childish bosom heave and swell when it was gone; and sent the globes, the books, blind Homer and Minerva, swimming round the room. But they stopped, all of a sudden; and then he heard the loud clock in the hall still gravely inquiring 'how, is, my, lit, tle, friend?' how, is, my, lit, tle, friend?' as it had done before.

He sat, with folded hands, upon his pedestal, silently listening. But he might have answered 'weary, weary! very lonely, very sad!' And there, with an aching void in his young heart, and all outside so cold, and bare, and strange, Paul sat as if he had taken life unfurnished, and the upholsterer were never coming *(Chapter 11)*.

'Now, Dombey,' said Miss Blimber. 'How have you got on with those books?'

They comprised a little English, and a deal of Latin – names of things, declensions of articles and substantives, exercises thereon, and preliminary rules – a trifle of orthography, a glance at ancient history, a wink or two at modern ditto, a few tables, two or three weights and measures, and a little general information. When poor Paul had spelt out number two, he found he had no idea of number one; fragments whereof afterwards obtruded themselves into number three, which slided into number four, which grafted itself on to number two. So that whether twenty Romuluses made a Remus, or hic haec hoc was troy weight, or a verb always agreed with an ancient Briton, or three times four was Taurus a bull, were open questions with him.

'Oh, Dombey, Dombey!' said Miss Blimber, 'this is very shocking.'

'If you please,' said Paul, 'I think if I might sometimes talk a little to old Glubb, I should be able to do better' *(Chapter 12).*

He grew more thoughtful and reserved, every day; and had no such curiosity in any living member of the Doctor's household, as he had in Mrs. Pipchin. He loved to be alone; and in those short intervals when he was not occupied with his books, liked nothing so well as wandering about the house by himself, or sitting on the stairs, listening to the great clock in the hall. He was intimate with all the paperhanging in the house; saw things that no one else saw in the patterns; found out miniature tigers and lions running up the bedroom walls, and squinting faces leering in the squares and diamonds of the floor-cloth.

The solitary child lived on, surrounded by this arabesque work of his musing fancy, and no one understood him. Mrs. Blimber thought him 'odd,' and sometimes the servants said among themselves that little Dombey 'moped'; but that was all.

Unless young Toots had some idea on the subject, to the expression of which he was wholly unequal. Ideas, like ghosts (according to the common notion of ghosts), must be spoken to a little before they will explain themselves; and Toots had long left off asking any questions of his own mind. Some mist there may have been, issuing from that leaden casket, his cranium, which, if it could have taken shape and form, would have become a genie; but it could not; and it only so far followed the example of the smoke in the Arabian story, as to roll out in a thick cloud, and there hang and hover. But it left a little figure visible upon a lonely shore, and Toots was always staring at it *(Chapter 12).*

Mr. Feeder, after imbibing several custard-cups of negus, began to enjoy himself. The dancing in general was ceremonious, and the music rather solemn – a little like church music in fact – but after the custard-cups Mr. Feeder told Mr. Toots that he was going to throw a little spirit into the thing. After that, Mr. Feeder not only began to dance as if he meant dancing and nothing else, but secretly to stimulate the music to perform wild tunes. Further, he became particular in his attentions to the ladies; and dancing with Miss Blimber, whispered to her – whispered to her! – though not so softly but that Paul heard him say this remarkable poetry,

'Had I a heart for falsehood framed,
I ne'er could injure You!'

This, Paul heard him repeat to four young ladies in succession. Well might Mr. Feeder say to Mr. Toots, that he was afraid he should be worse for it to-morrow! *(Chapter 14).*

He could not even remember whether he had often said to Florence, 'Oh Floy, take me home, and never leave me!' but he thought he had. He fancied sometimes he had heard himself repeating, 'Take me home, Floy! take me home!'

But he could remember, when he got home, and was carried up the well-remembered stairs, that there had been the rumbling of a coach for many hours together, while he lay upon the seat, with Florence still beside him, and old Mrs. Pipchin sitting opposite. He remembered his old bed too, when they laid him down in it: his aunt, Miss Tox, and Susan: but there was something else, and recent too, that still perplexed him.

'I want to speak to Florence, if you please,' he said. 'To Florence by herself, for a moment!'

She bent down over him, and the others stood away.

'Floy, my pet, wasn't that Papa in the hall, when they brought me from the coach?'

'Yes, dear.'

'He didn't cry, and go into his room, Floy, did he, when he saw me coming in?'

Florence shook her head, and pressed her lips against his cheek.

'I'm very glad he didn't cry,' said little Paul. 'I thought he did. Don't tell them that I asked' *(Chapter 14: Paul and Florence Dombey).*

'Wal'r, my boy,' replied the Captain, 'in the Proverbs of Solomon you will find the following words, "May we never want a friend in need, nor a bottle to give him!" When found, make a note of' *(Chapter 15: Captain Cuttle).*

'There's a friend of mine,' murmured the Captain, in an absent manner, 'but he's at present coasting round to Whitby, that would deliver such an opinion on this subject, or any other that could be named, as would give Parliament six and beat 'em. Been knocked overboard, that man,' said the Captain, 'twice, and none the worse for it. Was beat in his apprenticeship, for three weeks (off and on), about the head with a ringbolt. And yet a clearer-minded man don't walk.'

In spite of his respect for Captain Cuttle, Walter could not help inwardly rejoicing at the absence of this sage, and devoutly hoping that his limpid intellect might not be brought to bear on his difficulties until they were quite settled *(Chapter 15).*

'Do you want to go to Staggs's Gardens, Susan?' inquired Walter.

'Ah! *She* wants to go there! WHERE IS IT?' growled the coachman.

'I don't know where it is!' exclaimed Susan, wildly, 'Mr. Walter, I was there once myself, along with Miss

Floy and our poor darling Master Paul, on the very day when you found Miss Floy in the City, for we lost her coming home, Mrs. Richards and me, and a mad bull, and Mrs. Richards's eldest, and though I went there afterwards, I can't remember where it is, I think it's sunk into the ground. Oh, Mr. Walter, don't desert me, Staggs's Gardens, if you please! Miss Floy's darling – all our darlings – little, meek, meek Master Paul! Oh Mr. Walter!"

'Good God!' cried Walter. 'Is he very ill?'

'The pretty flower!' cried Susan, wringing her hands, 'has took the fancy that he'd like to see his old nurse, and I've come to bring her to his bedside, Mrs. Staggs, of Polly Toodle's Gardens, some one pray!'

Greatly moved by what he heard, and catching Susan's earnestness immediately, Walter, now that he understood the nature of her errand, dashed into it with such ardour that the coachman had enough to do to follow closely as he ran before, inquiring here and there and everywhere, the way to Staggs's Gardens.

There was no such place as Staggs's Gardens. It had vanished from the earth. Where the old rotten summer-houses once had stood, palaces now reared their heads, and granite columns of gigantic girth opened a vista to the railway world beyond. The miserable waste ground, where the refuse-matter had been heaped of yore, was swallowed up and gone; and in its frowsy stead were tiers of warehouses, crammed with rich goods and costly merchandise. The old by-streets now swarmed with passengers and vehicles of every kind: the new streets that had stopped dis-heartened in the mud and waggon-ruts, formed towns within themselves, originating wholesome comforts and conveniences belonging to themselves, and never tried nor thought of until they sprung into existence. Bridges that had led to nothing, led to villas, gardens, churches, healthy public walks. The carcasses of houses, and beginnings of new thoroughfares, had started off upon the line at steam's own speed, and shot away into the country in a monster train.

As to the neighbourhood which had hesitated to acknowledge the railroad in its straggling days, that had grown wise and penitent, as any Christian might in such a case, and now boasted of its powerful and prosperous relation. There were railway patterns in its drapers' shops, and railway journals in the windows of its newsmen. There were railway hotels, coffee-houses, lodging-houses, boarding-houses; railway plans, maps, views, wrappers, bottles, sandwich-boxes, and time-tables; railway hackney-coach and cabstands; railway omnibuses, railway streets and buildings, railway hangers-on and parasites, and flatterers out of all calculation. There was even railway time observed in clocks, as if the sun itself had given in. Among the vanquished was the master chimney-sweeper, whilom incredulous at Staggs's Gardens, who now lived in a stuccoed house three stories high, and gave himself out, with golden flourishes upon a varnished board, as contractor for the cleansing of railway chimneys by machinery.

To and from the heart of this great change, all day and night, throbbing currents rushed and returned incessantly like its life's blood. Crowds of people and mountains of goods, departing and arriving scores upon scores of times in every four-and-twenty hours, produced a fermentation in the place that was always in action. The very houses seemed disposed to pack up and take trips. Wonderful Members of Parliament, who, little more then twenty years before, had made themselves merry with the wild railroad theories of engineers, and given them the liveliest rubs in cross-examination, went down into the north with their watches in their hands, and sent on messages before by the electric telegraph, to say that they were coming. Night and day the conquering engines rumbled at their distant work, or, advancing smoothly to their journey's end, and gliding like tame dragons into the allotted corners grooved out to the inch for their reception, stood bubbling and trembling there, making the walls quake, as if they were dilating with the secret knowledge of great powers yet unsuspected in them, and strong purposes not yet achieved.

But Staggs's Gardens had been cut up root and branch. Oh woe the day when 'not a rood of English ground' – laid out in Staggs's Gardens – is secure! *(Chapter 15).*

'Has the little boy been long ill, Susan?' inquired Walter, as they hurried on.

'Ailing for a deal of time, but no one knew how much,' said Susan; adding, with excessive sharpness, 'Oh, them Blimbers!'

Blimbers?' echoed Walter.

'I couldn't forgive myself at such a time as this, Mr. Walter,' said Susan, 'and when there's so much serious distress to think about, if I rested hard on any one, especially on them that little darling Paul speaks well of, but I *may* wish that the family was set to work in a stony soil to make new roads, and that Miss Blimber went in front, and had the pickaxe!' *(Chapter 15: Susan Nipper and Walter Gay).*

'Now lay me down,' he said, 'and Floy, come close to me, and let me see you!'

Sister and brother wound their arms around each other, and the golden light came streaming in, and fell upon them, locked together.

'How fast the river runs, between its green banks and the rushes, Floy! But it's very near the sea. I hear the waves! They always said so!'

Presently he told her that the motion of the boat upon the stream was lulling him to rest. How green the banks were now, how bright the flowers growing on them, and how tall the rushes! Now the boat was out at sea, but gliding smoothly on. And now there was a shore before him. Who stood on the bank!

He put his hands together, as he had been used to do at his prayers. He did not remove his arms to do it; but they saw him fold them so, behind her neck.

'Mamma is like you, Floy. I know her by the face! But tell them that the print upon the stairs at school is not divine enough. The light about the head is shining on me as I go!'

The golden ripple on the wall came back again, and nothing else stirred in the room. The old, old fashion! The fashion that came in with our first garments, and will last unchanged until our race has run its course, and the wide firmament is rolled up like a scroll. The old, old fashion – Death!

Oh thank GOD, all who see it, for that older fashion yet, of Immortality! And look upon us, angels of young children, with regards not quite estranged, when the swift river bears us to the ocean! (*Chapter 16: Paul and Florence Dombey*).

Now the rosy children living opposite to Mr. Dombey's house, peep from their nursery windows down into the street; for there are four black horses at his door, with feathers on their heads; and feathers tremble on the carriage that they draw; and these and an array of men with scarves and staves, attract a crowd. The juggler who was going to twirl the basin, puts his loose coat on again over his fine dress; and his trudging wife, one-sided with her heavy baby in her arms, loiters to see the company come out. But closer to her dingy breast she presses her baby, when the burden that is so easily carried is borne forth; and the youngest of the rosy children at the high window opposite, needs no restraining hand to check her in her glee, when, pointing with dimpled finger, she looks into her nurse's face, and asks, 'What's that?'

And now, among the knot of servants dressed in mourning, and the weeping women, Mr. Dombey passes through the hall to the other carriage that is waiting to receive him. He is not 'brought down,' these observers think, by sorrow and distress of mind. His walk is as erect, his bearing is as stiff as ever it has been. He hides his face behind no handkerchief, and looks before him. But that his face is something sunk and rigid, and is pale, it bears the same expression as of old. He takes his place within the carriage, and three other gentlemen follow. Then the grand funeral moves slowly down the street. The feathers are yet nodding in the distance, when the juggler has the basin spinning on a cane, and has the same crowd to admire it. But the juggler's wife is less alert than usual with the money-box, for a child's burial has set her thinking that perhaps the baby underneath her shabby shawl may not grow up to be a man, and wear a sky-blue fillet round his head, and salmon-coloured worsted drawers, and tumble in the mud.

The feathers wind their gloomy way along the streets, and come within the sound of a church bell. In this same church, the pretty boy received all that will soon be left of him on earth – a name. All of him that is dead, they lay there, near the perishable substance of his mother. It is well. Their ashes lie where Florence in her walks – oh lonely, lonely walks! – may pass them any day (*Chapter 18*).

There is sounder sleep and deeper rest in Mr. Dombey's house to-night, than there has been for many nights. The morning sun awakens the old household, settled down once more in their old ways. The rosy children opposite run past with hoops. There is a splendid wedding in the church. The juggler's wife is active with the money-box in another quarter of the town. The mason sings and whistles as he chips out P-A-U-L in the marble slab before him (*Chapter 18*).

'How d'ye do, Miss Dombey?' said Mr. Toots. 'I'm very well, I thank you; how are you?'
Mr. Toots – than whom there were few better fellows in the world, though there may have been one or two brighter spirits – had laboriously invented this long burst of discourse with the view of relieving the feelings both of Florence and himself. But finding that he had run through his property, as it were, in an injudicious manner, by squandering the whole before taking a chair, or before Florence had uttered a word, or before he had well got in at the door, he deemed it advisable to begin again.
'How d'ye do, Miss Dombey?' said Mr. Toots. 'I'm very well, I thank you; how are you?'
Florence gave him her hand, and said she was very well.
'I'm very well indeed,' said Mr. Toots, taking a chair. 'Very well indeed, I am. I don't remember,' said Mr. Toots, after reflecting a little, 'that I was ever better, thank you' (*Chapter 18*).

'Papa! Papa! Speak to me, dear Papa!'
He started at her voice, and leaped up from his seat. She was close before him, with extended arms, but he fell back.
'What is the matter?' he said, sternly. 'Why do you come here? What has frightened you?'
If anything had frightened her, it was the face he turned upon her. The glowing love within the breast of his young daughter froze before it, and she stood and looked at him as if stricken into stone.
There was not one touch of tenderness or pity in it. There was not one gleam of interest, parental recognition, or relenting in it. There was a change in it, but not of that kind. The old indifference and cold constraint had given place to something: what, she never thought and did not dare to think, and yet she felt it in its force, and knew it well without a name: that as it looked upon her, seemed to cast a shadow on her head.
Did he see before him the successful rival of son, in health and life? Did he look upon his own successful rival in that son's affection? Did a mad jealousy and withered pride, poison sweet remembrances that should have endeared and made her precious to him? Could it be possible that it was gall to him to look upon her in her beauty and her promise: thinking of his infant boy?
Florence had no such thoughts. But love is quick to know when it is spurned and hopeless: and hope died out of hers, as she stood looking in her father's face (*Chapter 18: Florence Dombey and Dombey*).

Walter's heart felt heavy as he looked round his old bedroom, up among the parapets and chimney-pots, and thought that one more night already darkening would close his acquaintance with it, perhaps for ever. Dismantled of his little stock of books and pictures, it looked coldly and reproachfully on him for his desertion, and had already a foreshadowing upon it of its coming strangeness. 'A few hours more,' thought Walter, 'and no dream I ever had here when I was a school-boy will be so little mine as this old room. The dream may come back in my sleep, and I may return waking to this place, it may be: but the dream at least will serve no other master, and the room may have a score, and every one of them may change, neglect, misuse it' (*Chapter 19*).

'Going away, Walter!' said Florence.

'Yes, Miss Dombey,' he replied, but not so hopefully as he endeavoured: 'I have a voyage before me.'

'And your uncle,' said Florence, looking back at Solomon. 'He is sorry you are going, I am sure. Ah! I see he is! Dear Walter, I am very sorry too.'

'Goodness knows,' exclaimed Miss Nipper, 'there's a many we could spare instead, if numbers is a object, Mrs. Pipchin as a overseer would come cheap at her weight in gold, and if a knowledge of black slavery should be required, them Blimbers is the very people for the sitiwation' *(Chapter 19)*.

'Hear him!' cried the Captain. 'Good morality! Wal'r, my lad. Train up a fig-tree in the way it should go, and when you are old sit under the shade on it. Overhaul the – Well,' said the Captain on second thoughts, 'I an't quite certain where that's to be found, but when found, make a note of. Sol Gills, heave ahead again!' *(Chapter 19: Captain Cuttle).*

The power that forced itself upon its iron way – its own – defiant of all paths and roads, piercing through the heart of every obstacle, and dragging living creatures of all classes, ages, and degrees behind it, was a type of the triumphant monster, Death.

Away, with a shriek, and a roar, and a rattle, from the town, burrowing among the dwellings of men and making the streets hum, flashing out into the meadows for a moment, mining in through the damp earth, booming on in darkness and heavy air, bursting out again into the sunny day so bright and wide; away, with a shriek, and a roar, and a rattle, through the fields, through the woods, through the corn, through the hay, through the chalk, through the mould, through the clay, through the rock, among objects close at hand and almost in the grasp, ever flying from the traveller, and a deceitful distance ever moving slowly within him: like as in the track of the remorseless monster, Death!

Through the hollow, on the height, by the heath, by the orchard, by the park, by the garden, over the canal, across the river, where the sheep are feeding, where the mill is going, where the barge is floating, where the dead are lying, where the factory is smoking, where the stream is running, where the village clusters, where the great cathedral rises, where the bleak moor lies, and the wild breeze smooths or ruffles it at its inconstant will; away, with a shriek, and a roar, and a rattle, and no trace to leave behind but dust and vapour: like as in the track of the remorseless monster, Death!

Breasting the wind and light, the shower and sunshine, away, and still away, it rolls and roars, fierce and rapid, smooth and certain, and great works and massive bridges crossing up above, fall like a beam of shadow an inch broad, upon the eye, and then are lost. Away, and still away, onward and onward ever: glimpses of cottage-homes, of houses, mansions, rich estates, of husbandry and handicraft, of people, of old roads and paths that look deserted, small, and insignificant as they are left behind: and so they do, and what else is there but such glimpses, in the track of the indomitable monster, Death!

Away, with a shriek, and a roar, and a rattle,
plunging down into the earth again, and working on in such a storm of energy and perseverance, that amidst the darkness and whirlwind the motion seems reversed, and to tend furiously backward, until a ray of light upon the wet wall shows its surface flying past like a fierce stream. Away once more into the day, and through the day, with a shrill yell of exultation, roaring, rattling, tearing on, spurning everything with its dark breath, sometimes pausing for a minute where a crowd of faces are, that in a minute more are not: sometimes lapping water greedily, and before the spout at which it drinks has ceased to drip upon the ground, shrieking, roaring, rattling through the purple distance!

Louder and louder yet, it shrieks and cries as it comes tearing on resistless to the goal: and now its way, still like the way of Death, is strewn with ashes thickly. Everything around is blackened. There are dark pools of water, muddy lanes, and miserable habitations far below. There are jagged walls and falling houses close at hand, and through the battered roofs and broken windows, wretched rooms are seen, where want and fever hide themselves in many wretched shapes, while smoke and crowded gables, and distorted chimneys, and deformity of brick and mortar penning up deformity of mind and body, choke the murky distance. As Mr. Dombey looks out of his carriage window, it is never in his thoughts that the monster who has brought him there has let the light of day in on these things: not made or caused them. It was the journey's fitting end, and might have been the end of everything; it was so ruinous and dreary *(Chapter 20)*.

'There is only one change, Mr. Dombey,' observed Mrs. Skewton, with a mincing sigh, 'for which I really care, and that I fear I shall never be permitted to enjoy. People cannot spare one. But seclusion and contemplation are my what's-his-name – '

'If you mean Paradise, Mamma, you had better say so, to render yourself intelligible,' said the younger lady.

'My dearest Edith,' returned Mrs. Skewton, 'you know that I am wholly dependent upon you for those odious names. I assure you, Mr. Dombey, nature intended me for an Arcadian. I am thrown away in society. Cows are my passion. What I have ever sighed for, has been to retreat to a Swiss farm, and live entirely surrounded by cows – and china.'

This curious association of objects, suggesting a remembrance of the celebrated bull who got by mistake into a crockery shop, was received with perfect gravity by Mr. Dombey, who intimated his opinion that nature was, no doubt, a very respectable institution *(Chapter 21)*.

'Do you know, Mr. Dombey,' said her languishing mother, playing with a hand-screen, 'that occasionally my dearest Edith and myself actually almost differ – '

'Not quite, sometimes, Mamma?' said Edith.

'Oh, never quite, my darling! Fie, fie, it would break my heart,' returned her mother, making a faint attempt to pat her with the screen, which Edith made no movement to meet, ' – about these cold conventionalities of manner that are observed in little things?

349

Why are we not more natural! Dear me! With all those yearnings, and gushings, and impulsive throbbings that we have implanted in our souls, and which are so very charming, why are we not more natural?' (*Chapter 21: Mrs. Skewton and Edith*).

'Cleopatra commands,' returned the Major, kissing his hand, 'and Antony Bagstock obeys.'

'The man has no sensitiveness,' said Mrs. Skewton, cruelly holding up the hand-screen so as to shut the Major out. 'No sympathy. And what do we live for *but* sympathy! What else is so extremely charming! Without that gleam of sunshine on our cold cold earth,' said Mrs. Skewton, arranging her lace tucker, and complacently observing the effect of her bare lean arm, looking upward from the wrist, 'how could we possibly bear it? In short, obdurate man!' glancing at the Major round the screen, 'I would have my world all heart; and Faith is so excessively charming, that I won't allow you to disturb it, do you hear?' (*Chapter 21*).

'If I hadn't,' said Susan Nipper, evidently struggling with some latent anxiety and alarm, and looking full at her young mistress, while endeavouring to work herself into a state of resentment with the unoffending Mr. Perch's image, 'if I hadn't more manliness than that insipidest of his sex, I'd never take pride in my hair again, but turn it up behind my ears, and wear coarse caps, without a bit of border, until death released me from my insignificance. I may not be a Amazon, Miss Floy, and wouldn't so demean myself by such disfigurement, but anyways I'm not a giver up, I hope' (*Chapter 23*).

'Hush, Susan! If you please!' said Florence. 'Perhaps you can have the goodness to tell us where Captain Cuttle lives, ma'am, as he don't live her.'

'Who says he don't live here?' retorted the implacable MacStinger. 'I said it wasn't Cap'en Cuttle's house – and it ain't his house – and forbid it, that it ever should be his house – for Cap'en Cuttle don't know how to keep a house – and don't deserve to have a house – it's *my* house – and when I let the upper floor to Cap'en Cuttle, oh I do a thankless thing, and cast pearls before swine!' (*Chapter 23*).

'When my friend Dombey, Sir,' added the Major, 'talks to you of Major Bagstock, I must crave leave to set him and you right. He means plain Joe, Sir – Joey B. – Josh. Bagstock – Joseph – rough and tough Old J., Sir. At your service' (*Chapter 26*).

'Oh it's you, is it? On second thoughts, you may enter,' observed Cleopatra.

The Major entered accordingly, and advancing to the sofa pressed her charming hand to his lips.

'Sit down,' said Cleopatra, listlessly waving her fan, 'a long way off. Don't come too near me, for I am frightfully faint and sensitive this morning, and you smell of the sun. You are absolutely tropical.'

'By George, Ma'am,' said the Major, 'the time has been when Joseph Bagstock has been grilled and blistered by the sun; the time was, when he was forced, Ma'am, into such full blow, by high hothouse heat in the West Indies, that he was known as the Flower. A man never heard of Bagstock, Ma'am, in those days; he heard of the Flower - the Flower of Ours. The Flower may have faded, more or less, Ma'am,' observed the Major, dropping into a much nearer chair than had been indicated by his cruel Divinity, 'but it is a tough plant yet, and constant as the evergreen' (*Chapter 26: Mrs. Skewton and Bagstock*).

'Really,' cried Mrs. Skewton, who had taken this opportunity of inspecting Mr. Carker through her glass, and satisfying herself (as she lisped audibly to the Major) that he was all heart; 'really now, this is one of the most enchanting coincidences that I ever heard of. The idea! My dearest Edith, there is such an obvious destiny in it, that really one might almost be induced to cross one's arms upon one's frock, and say, like those wicked Turks, there is no What's-his-name but Thingummy, and What-you-may-call-it is his prophet!' (*Chapter 27*).

'Oh!' cried Mrs. Skewton, with a faded little scream of rapture, 'the Castle is charming! – associations of the Middle Ages – and all that – which is so truly exquisite. Don't you dote upon the Middle Ages, Mr. Carker?'

'Very much, indeed,' said Mr. Carker.

'Such charming times!' cried Cleopatra. 'So full of faith! So vigorous and forcible! So picturesque! So perfectly removed from commonplace! Oh dear! If they would only leave us a little more of the poetry of existence in these terrible days!' (*Chapter 27*).

'Those darling bygone times, Mr. Carker,' said Cleopatra, 'with their delicious fortresses, and their dear old dungeons, and their delightful places of torture, and their romantic vengeances, and their picturesque assaults and sieges, and everything that makes life truly charming! How dreadfully we have degenerated!'

'Yes, we have fallen off deplorably,' said Mr. Carker (*Chapter 27*).

'We have no faith left, positively,' said Mrs. Skewton, advancing her shrivelled ear; for Mr. Dombey was saying something to Edith. 'We have no faith in the dear old barons, who were the most delightful creatures – or in the dear old priests, who were the most warlike of men – or even in the days of that inestimable Queen Bess, upon the wall there, which were so extremely golden. Dear creature! She was all heart! And that charming father of hers! I hope you dote on Harry the Eighth!'

'I admire him very much,' said Carker.

'So bluff!' cried Mrs. Skewton, 'wasn't he? So burly. So truly English. Such a picture, too, he makes, with his dear little peepy eyes, and his benevolent chin!' (*Chapter 27*).

'Oh, how de do, Miss Dombey?' said the stricken Toots, always dreadfully disconcerted when the desire of his heart was gained, and he was speaking to her; 'thank you, I'm very well indeed, I hope you're the same, so was Diogenes yesterday.'

'You are very kind,' said Florence.

'Thank you, it's of no consequence,' retorted Mr. Toots. 'I thought perhaps you wouldn't mind, in this fine weather, coming home by water, Miss Dombey. There's plenty of room in the boat for your maid.'

'I am very much obliged to you,' said Florence, hesitating. 'I really am – but I would rather not.'

'Oh, it's of no consequence,' retorted Mr. Toots. 'Good morning!'

'Won't you wait and see Lady Skettles?' asked Florence, kindly.

'Oh no, thank you,' returned Mr. Toots, 'it's of no consequence at all.'

So shy was Mr. Toots on such occasions, and so flurried! *(Chapter 28).*

Dawn, with its passionless blank face , steals shivering to the church beneath which lies the dust of little Paul and his mother, and looks in at the windows. It is cold and dark. Night crouches yet, upon the pavement, and broods, sombre and heavy, in nooks and corners of the building. The steeple-clock, perched up above the houses, emerging from beneath another of the countless ripples in the tide of time that regularly roll and break on the eternal shore, is greyly visible, like a stone beacon, recording how the sea flows on; but within doors, dawn, at first, can only peep at night, and see that it is there.

Hovering feebly round the church, and looking in, dawn moans and weeps for its short reign, and its tears trickle on the window-glass, and the trees against the church-wall bow their heads, and wring their many hands in sympathy. Night, growing pale before it, gradually fades out of the church, but lingers in the vaults below, and sits upon the coffins. And now comes bright day, burnishing the steeple-clock, and reddening the spire, and drying up the tears of dawn, and stifling its complaining; and the scared dawn, following the night, and chasing it from its last refuge, shrinks into the vaults itself and hides, refreshed, to drive it out.

And now, the mice, who have been busier with the prayer-books than their proper owners, and with the hassocks, more worn by their little teeth than by human knees, hide their bright eyes in their holes, and gather close together in affright at the resounding clashing of the church-door *(Chapter 31).*

'Dombey,' says the Major, with appropriate action, 'that is the hand of Joseph Bagstock: of plain old Joey B., Sir, if you like that better! That is the hand of which His Royal Highness the late Duke of York did me the honour to observe, Sir, to His Royal Highness the late Duke of Kent, that it was the hand of Josh.: a rough and tough, and possibly an up-to-snuff, old vagabond. Dombey, may the present moment be the least unhappy of our lives. God bless you!' *(Chapter 31).*

'Do you think Miss Dombey will be very much affected, Captain Gills – I mean Mr. Cuttle?'

'Why, Lord love you,' returned the Captain, with something of compassion for Mr. Toot's innocence. 'When she warn't no higher than that, they were as fond of one another as two young doves.'

'Were they though?' said Mr. Toots, with a considerably lengthened face.

'They were made for one another,' said the Captain, mournfully; 'but what signifies that now?'

'Upon my word and honour,' cried Mr. Toots, blurting out his words through a singular combination of awkward chuckles and emotion, 'I'm even more sorry than I was before. You know, Captain Gills, I – I positively adore Miss Dombey; – I – I am perfectly sore with loving her'; the burst with which this confession forced itself out of the unhappy Mr. Toots, bespoke the vehemence of his feelings; 'but what would be the good of my regarding her in this manner, if I wasn't truly sorry for her feeling pain, whatever was the cause of it? Mine an't a selfish affection, you know,' said Mr. Toots, in the confidence engendered by his having been a witness of the Captain's tenderness. 'It's the sort of thing with me, Captain Gills, that if I could be run over – or – or trampled upon – or – or thrown off a very high place – or anything of that sort – for Miss Dombey's sake, it would be the most delightful thing that could happen to me' *(Chapter 32).*

'Although I am very well off,' said Mr. Toots, with energy, 'you can't think what a miserable beast I am. The hollow crowd, you know, when they see me with the Chicken, and characters of distinction like that, suppose me to be happy; but I'm wretched. I suffer for Miss Dombey, Captain Gills. I can't get through my meals; I have no pleasure in my tailor; I often cry when I'm alone *(Chapter 32).*

'But what makes you say this along of Rob, father?' asked his wife, anxiously.

'Polly, old 'ooman,' said Mr. Toodle, 'I don't know as I said it partickler along o' Rob, I'm sure. I starts light with Rob only; I comes to a branch; I takes on what I finds there; and a whole train of ideas gets coupled on to him, afore I knows where I am, or where they comes from. What a junction a man's thoughts is,' said Mr. Toodle, 'to-be-sure!' *(Chapter 38).*

'Now look'ee here: you've made some observations to me, which gives me to understand as you admire a certain sweet creetur. Hey?'

'Captain Gills,' said Mr. Toots, gesticulating violently with the hand in which he held his hat, 'admiration is not the word. Upon my honour, you have no conception what my feelings are. If I could be dyed black, and made Miss Dombey's slave, I should consider it a compliment. If, at the sacrifice of all my property, I could get transmigrated into Miss Dombey's dog – I – I really think I should never leave off wagging my tail. I should be so perfectly happy, Captain Gills!' *(Chapter 39).*

'If you're in 'arnest, you see, my lad,' said the Captain, 'you're a object of clemency, and clemency is the brightest jewel in the crown of a Briton's head, for which you'll overhaul the constitution as laid down in Rule Britannia, and, when found, *that* is the charter as them garden angels was a singing of, so many times over. Stand by! *(Chapter 39:* Captain Cuttle).

The Captain therefore hemmed to clear his throat, and read the letter aloud.

' "My dear Ned Cuttle. When I left home for the West Indies – " '

Here the Captain stopped, and looked hard at Bunsby, who looked fixedly at the coast of Greenland.

– ' "in forlorn search of intelligence of my dear boy, I knew that if you were acquainted with design, you would thwart it, or accompany me; and therefore I kept it secret. If you ever read this letter, Ned, I am likely to be dead. You will easily forgive an old friend's folly then and will feel for the restlessness and uncertainty in which he wandered away on such a wild voyage. So no more of that. I have little hope that my poor boy will ever read these words, or gladden your eyes with the sight of his frank face any more." No, no; no more,' said Captain Cuttle, sorrowfully meditating; 'no more. There he lays, all his days – '

Mr. Bunsby, who had a musical ear, suddenly bellowed, 'In the Bays of Biscay, O!' which so affected the good Captain, as an appropriate tribute to departed worth, that he shook him by the hand in acknowledgment, and was fain to wipe his eyes.

'Well, well!' said the Captain with a sigh, as the Lament of Bunsby ceased to ring and vibrate in the skylight. 'Affliction sore, long time he bore, and let us overhaul the wollume, and there find it.'

'Physicians,' observed Bunsby, 'was in vain.'

'Aye, aye, to be sure,' said the Captain, 'what's the good o' *them* in two or three hundred fathoms o' water!' *(Chapter 39)*.

'Oh, I was a weak and trusting fool when I took you under *my* roof, Cap'en Cuttle, I was!' cried Mrs. MacStinger. 'To think of the benefits I've showered on that man, and the way in which I brought my children up to love and *honour* him as if he was a father to 'em, when there an't a 'ouse-keeper, no nor a lodger in our street, don't know that I lost money by that man, and by his guzzlings and his muzzlings' – Mrs. MacStinger used the last word for the joint sake of alliteration and aggravation, rather than for the expression of any idea – 'and when they cried out one and all, shame upon him for putting upon an industrious woman, up early and late for the good of her young family, and keeping her poor place so clean that a individual might have ate his dinner, yes, and his tea too, if he was so disposed, off any one of the floors or stairs, in spite of all his guzzlings *and* his muzzlings, such was the care and pains bestowed upon him!'

Mrs. MacStinger stopped to fetch her breath; and her face flushed with triumph in this second happy introduction of Captain Cuttle's muzzlings.

'And he runs awa-a-a-ay!' cried Mrs. MacStinger, with a lengthening out of the last syllable that made the unfortunate Captain regard himself as the meanest of men; 'and keeps away a twelvemonth! From a woman! Sitch is his conscience! He hasn't the courage to meet her hi-i-i-igh'; long syllable again; 'but steals away, like a felion. Why, if that baby of mine,' said Mrs. MacStinger, with sudden rapidity, 'was to offer to go and steal away, I'd do my duty as a mother by him, till he was covered with whales!' *(Chapter 39)*.

'Oh, it's very well to say "don't" Miss Floy,' returned the Nipper, much exasperated; 'but raly begging your pardon we're coming to such passes that it turns all the blood in a person's body into pins and needles, with their pints all ways. Don't mistake me,

Miss Floy, I don't mean nothing again your ma-in-law who has always treated me as a lady should though she is rather high I must say not that I have any right to object to that particular, but when we come to Mrs. Pipchinses and having them put over us and keeping guard at your pa's door like crocodiles (only make us thankful that they lay no eggs!) we are growing too outrageous!'

'Papa thinks well of Mrs. Pipchin, Susan,' returned Florence, 'and has a right to choose his housekeeper, you know. Pray don't!'

'Well Miss Floy,' returned the Nipper, 'when you say don't, I never do I hope but Mrs. Pipchin acts like early gooseberries upon me Miss, and nothing less' *(Chapter 43)*.

'I have been in your service, Sir,' said Susan Nipper, with her usual rapidity, 'now twelve year a waiting on Miss Floy my own young lady who couldn't speak plain when I first come here and I was old in this house when Mrs. Richards was new, I may not be Meethosalem, but I am not a child in arms.'

Mr. Dombey raised upon his arm and looking at her, offered no comment on this preparatory statement of facts.

'There never was a dearer or a blesseder young lady than is my young lady, Sir,' said Susan, 'and I ought to know a great deal better than some for I have seen her in her grief and I have seen her in her joy (there's not been much of it) and I have seen her with her brother and I have seen her in her loneliness and some have never seen her, and I say to some and all – I do!' and here the black-eyed shook her head, and slightly stamped her foot; 'that she's the blessedest and dearest angel is Miss Floy that ever drew the breath of life, the more that I was torn to pieces Sir the more I'd say it though I may not be a Fox's Martyr' *(Chapter 44)*.

Alas! are there so few things in the world, about us, most unnatural, and yet most natural in being so? Hear the magistrate or judge admonish the unnatural outcasts of society; unnatural in brutal habits, unnatural in want of decency, unnatural in losing and confounding all distinctions between good and evil; unnatural in ignorance, in vice, in recklessness, in contumacy, in mind, in looks, in everything. But follow the good clergyman or doctor, who, with his life imperilled at every breath he draws, goes down into their dens, lying within the echoes of our carriage-wheels and daily tread upon the pavement stones. Look round upon the world of odious sights – millions of immortal creatures have no other world on earth – at the lightest mention of which humanity revolts, and dainty delicacy living in the next street, stops her ears, and lisps, 'I don't believe it!' Breathe the polluted air, foul with every impurity that is poisonous to health and life; and have every sense, conferred upon our race for its delight and happiness, offended, sickened and disgusted, and made a channel by which misery and death alone can enter. Vainly attempt to think of any simple plant, or flower, or wholesome weed, that, set in this foetid bed, could have its natural growth, or put its little leaves off to the sun as GOD designed it. And then, calling up some ghastly child, with stunted form and wicked face, hold forth on its unnatural sinfulness, and lament its being, so early, far away from Heaven – but think a little of its having been conceived, and born and bred, in Hell! *(Chapter 47)*.

'And bear a hand and cheer up,' said the Captain, patting him on the back. 'What! There's more than one sweet creetur in the world!'

'Not to me, Captain Gills,' replied Mr. Toots gravely. 'Not to me, I assure you. The state of my feelings towards Miss Dombey is of that unspeakable description, that my heart is a desert island, and she lives in it alone. I'm getting more used up every day, and I'm proud to be so. If you could see my legs when I take my boots off, you'd form some idea of what unrequited affection is. I have been prescribed bark, but I don't take it, for I don't wish to have any tone whatever given to my constitution. I'd rather not. This, however, is forbidden ground. Captain Gills, good-bye!' *(Chapter 48)*.

'My lady lass,' said the Captain, 'cheer up, and try to eat a deal. Stand by, my deary! Liver wing it is. Sarse it is. Sassage it is. And potato!' all which the Captain ranged symmetrically on a plate, and pouring hot gravy on the whole with the useful spoon, set before his cherished guest.

'The whole row o' dead lights is up, for'ard, lady lass,' observed the Captain, encouragingly, 'and everythink is made snug. Try and pick a bit, my pretty' *(Chapter 49: Captain Cuttle)*.

'You never was at sea, my own?'

'No,' replied Florence.

'Aye,' said the Captain, reverentially; 'it's a almighty element. There's wonders in the deep, my pretty. Think on it when the winds is roaring and the waves is rowling. Think on it when the stormy nights is so pitch dark,' said the Captain, solemnly holding up his hook, 'as you can't see your hand afore you, excepting when the wiwid lightning reweals the same; and when you drive, drive, drive through the storm and dark, as if you was a driving, head on, to the world without end, evermore, amen, and when found making a note of. Them's the times, my beauty, when a man may say to his messmate (previously a overhauling of the wollume), "A stiff nor-wester's blowing, Bill; hark, don't you hear it roar now! Lord help 'em, how I pitys all unhappy folks ashore now!"' Which quotation, as particularly applicable to the terrors of the ocean, the Captain delivered in a most impressive manner, concluding with a sonorous 'Stand by!' *(Chapter 49: Captain Cuttle)*.

'Hope, you see, Wal'r,' said the Captain, sagely, 'Hope. It's that as animates you. Hope is a buoy, for which you overhaul your Little Warbler, sentimental diwision, but Lord, my lad, like any other buoy, it only floats; it can't be steered nowhere. Along with the figure-head of Hope,' said the Captain, 'there's a anchor; but what's the good of my having a anchor, if I can't find no bottom to let it go in' *(Chapter 50: Captain Cuttle)*.

He paid the money for his journey to the country-place he had thought of; and was walking to and fro, alone, looking along the lines of iron, across the valley in one direction, and towards a dark bridge near at hand in the other; when, turning in his walk, where it was bounded by one end of the wooden stage on which he paced up and down, he saw the man from whom he had fled, emerging from the door by which he himself had entered there. And their eyes met.

In the quick unsteadiness of the surprise, he staggered, and slipped on to the road below him. But recovering his feet immediately, he stepped back a pace or two upon that road, to interpose some wider space between them, and looked at his pursuer, breathing short and quick.

He heard a shout – another – saw the face change from its vindictive passion to a faint sickness and terror – felt the earth tremble – knew in a moment that the rush was come – uttered a shriek – looked round – saw the red eyes, bleared and dim, in the daylight, close upon him – was beaten down, caught up, and whirled away upon a jagged mill, that spun him round and round and struck him limb from limb, and licked his stream of life up with its fiery heat, and cast his mutilated fragments in the air.

When the traveller, who had been recognised, recovered from a swoon, he saw them bringing from a distance something covered, that lay heavy and still, upon a board, between four men, and saw that others drove some dogs away that sniffed upon the road, and soaked his blood up, with a train of ashes *(Chapter 56)*.

Mr. Toots and Captain Cuttle heaved a sigh in concert.

'What then?' said the Captain. 'She loves him true. He loves her true. Them as should have loved and tended of her, treated of her like the beasts as perish. When she, cast out of home, come here to me, and dropped upon them planks, her wounded heart was broke. I know it. I, Ed'ard Cuttle, see it. There's nowt but true, kind, steady love, as can ever piece it up again. If so be I didn't know that, and didn't know as Wal'r was her true love, brother, and she his, I'd have these here blue arms and legs chopped off, afore I'd let her go. But I *do* know it, and what then? Why, then, I say, Heaven go with 'em both, and so it will! Amen!'

'Captain Gills,' said Mr. Toots, 'let me have the pleasure of shaking hands. You've a way of saying things, that gives me an agreeable warmth, all up my back. *I* say Amen. You are aware, Captain Gills, that I, too, have adored Miss Dombey.'

'Cheer up!' said the Captain, laying his hand on Mr. Toots's shoulder. 'Stand by, boy!'

'It is my intention, Captain Gills,' returned the spirited Mr. Toots, '*to* cheer up. Also to stand by, as much as possible. When the silent tomb shall yawn, Captain Gills, I shall be ready for burial; not before' *(Chapter 56)*.

'Besides,' said Walter, 'long ago – before I went to sea – I had a little purse presented to me, dearest, which had money in it.'

'Ah!' returned Florence, laughing sorrowfully, 'very little! Very little, Walter! But, you must not think,' and here she laid her light hand on his shoulder, and looked into his face, 'that I regret to be this burden on you. No, dear love, I am glad of it. I am happy in it. I wouldn't have it otherwise for all the world!'

353

'Nor I, indeed, dear Florence.'

'Aye! but Walter, you can never feel it as I do. I am so proud of you! It makes my heart swell with such delight to know that those who speak of you must say you married a poor disowned girl, who had taken shelter here; who had no other home, no other friends; who had nothing – nothing! Oh, Walter, if I could have brought you millions, I never could have been so happy for your sake, as I am!'

'And you, dear Florence? are you nothing?' he returned.

'No, nothing, Walter. Nothing but your wife.' The light hand stole about his neck, and the voice came nearer – nearer. 'I am nothing any more, that is not you. I have no earthly hope any more, that is not you. I have nothing dear to me any more, that is not you!' (*Chapter 56:* Florence and Walter Gay).

'Chock full o' science,' said the radiant Captain, 'as ever he was! Sol Gills, Sol Gills, what have you been up to, for this many a long day, my ould boy?'

'I'm half blind, Ned,' said the old man, 'and almost deaf and dumb with joy.'

'His wery woice,' said the Captain, looking round with an exultation to which even his face could hardly render justice – 'his wery woice as chock full o' science as ever it was! Sol Gills, lay to, my lad, upon your own wines and fig-trees, like a taut ould patriark as you are, and overhaul them there adwentures o' yourn, in your own formilior woice. 'Tis *the* woice,' said the Captain, impressively, and announcing a quotation with his hook, 'of the sluggard, I heerd him complain, you have woke me too soon, I must slumber again. Scatter his ene-mies, and make 'em fall!' (*Chapter 56:* Captain Cuttle).

Mrs. Pipchin ... looms dark in her black bombazeen skirts, black bonnet and shawl; and has her personal property packed up; and has her chair (late a favourite chair of Mr. Dombey's and the dead bargain of the sale) ready near the street door; and is only waiting for a fly van, going to-night to Brighton on private service, which is to call for her, by private contract, and convey her home.

Presently it comes. Mrs. Pipchin's wardrobe being handed in and stowed away, Mrs. Pipchin's chair is next handed in, and placed in a convenient corner among certain trusses of hay; it being the intention of the amiable woman to occupy the chair during her journey. Mrs. Pipchin herself is next handed in, and grimly takes her seat. There is a snaky gleam in her hard grey eye, as of anticipated rounds of buttered toast, relays of hot chops, worryings and quellings of young children, sharp snappings at poor Berry, and all the other delights of her ogress's castle. Mrs. Pipchin almost laughs as the fly van drives off, and she composes her black bombazeen skirts, and settles herself among the cushions of her easy-chair (*Chapter 59*).

Mr. Toots felt it incumbent on him to make a speech; and in spite of a whole code of telegraphic dissuasions from Mrs. Toots, appeared on his legs for the first time in his life.

'I really,' said Mr. Toots, 'in this house, where whatever was done to me in the way of – of any mental confusion sometimes – which is of no consequence and I impute to nobody – I was always treated like one of Doctor Blimber's family, and had a desk to myself for a considerable period – can – not – allow – my friend Feeder to be – '

Mrs. Toots suggested 'married.'

It may not be inappropriate to the occasion, or altogether uninteresting,' said Mr. Toots with a delighted face, 'to observe that my wife is a most extraordinary woman, and would do this much better than myself – allow my friend Feeder to be married – especially to – '

Mrs. Toots suggested 'to Miss Blimber.'

'To Mrs. Feeder, my love!' said Mr. Toots, in a subdued tone of private discussion: ' "whom God hath joined," you know, "let no man" – don't you know? I cannot allow my friend, Feeder, to be married – especially to Mrs. Feeder – without proposing their – their toasts; and may,' said Mr. Toots, fixing his eyes on his wife, as if for inspiration in a high flight, 'may the torch of Hymen be the beacon of joy, and may the flowers we have this day strewed in their path, be the – the banishers of – of gloom!' (*Chapter 60*).

DAVID COPPERFIELD

The first objects that assume a distinct presence before me, as I look far back, into the blank of my infancy, are my mother with her pretty hair and youthful shape, and Peggotty, with no shape at all, and eyes so dark that they seemed to darken their whole neighbourhood in her face, and cheeks and arms so hard and red that I wondered the birds didn't peck her in preference to apples.

I believe I can remember these two at a little distance apart, dwarfed to my sight by stooping down or kneeling on the floor, and I going unsteadily from the one to the other. I have an impression on my mind which I cannot distinguish from actual remembrance, of the touch of Peggotty's forefinger as she used to hold it out to me, and of its being roughened by needlework, like a pocket nutmeg-grater.

This may be fancy, though I think the memory of most of us can go farther back into such times than many of us suppose; just as I believe the power of observation in numbers of very young children to be quite wonderful for its closeness and accuracy. Indeed, I think that most grown men who are remarkable in this respect, may with greater propriety be said not to have lost the faculty, than to have acquired it; the rather, as I generally observe such men to retain a certain freshness, and gentleness, and capacity of being pleased, which are also an inheritance they have preserved from their childhood (*Chapter 2:* David Copperfield).

Ham carrying me on his back and a small box of ours under his arm, and Peggotty carrying another small box of ours, we turned down lanes bestrewn with bits of chips and little hillocks of sand, and went past gas-works, rope-walks, boat-builders' yards, shipwrights' yards, ship-breakers' yards, caulkers' yards, riggers' lofts, smiths' forges, and a great litter of such places, until we came out upon the dull waste I had already seen at a distance; when Ham said –

'Yon's our house, Mas'r Davy!'

I looked in all directions, as far as I could stare over the wilderness, and away at the sea, and away at the river, but no house could *I* make out. There was a black barge, or some other kind of superannuated boat, not far off, high and dry on the ground, with an iron funnel sticking out of it for a chimney and smoking very cosily; but nothing else in the way of a habitation that was visible to *me*.

'That's not it?' said I. 'That ship-looking thing?'

'That's it, Mas'r Davy,' returned Ham.

If it had been Aladdin's palace, roc's egg and all, I suppose I could not have been more charmed with the romantic idea of living in it. There was a delightful door cut in the side, and it was roofed in, and there were little windows in it; but the wonderful charm of it was, that it was a real boat which had no doubt been upon the water hundreds of times, and which had never been intended to be lived in, on dry land. That was the captivation of it to me. If it had ever been meant to be lived in, I might have thought it small, or inconvenient, or lonely; but never having been designed for any such use, it became a perfect abode.

It was beautifully clean inside, and as tidy as possible. There was a table, and a Dutch clock, and a chest of drawers, and on the chest of drawers there was a tea-tray with a painting on it of a lady with a parasol, taking a walk with a military-looking child who was trundling a hoop. The tray was kept from tumbling down, by a bible; and the tray, if it had tumbled down, would have smashed a quantity of cups and saucers and a teapot that were grouped around the book. On the walls there were some common coloured pictures, framed and glazed, of scripture subjects; such as I have never seen since in the hands of pedlars, without seeing the whole interior of Peggotty's brother's house again, at one view. Abraham in red going to sacrifice Isaac in blue, and Daniel in yellow cast into a den of green lions, were the most prominent of these. Over the little mantel-shelf, was a picture of the *Sarah Jane* lugger, built at Sunderland, with a real little wooden stern stuck on to it; a work of art, combining composition with carpentry, which I considered to be one of the most enviable possessions that the world could afford. There were some hooks in the beams of the ceiling, the use of which I did not divine then; and some lockers and boxes and conveniences of that sort, which served for seats and eked out the chairs *(Chapter 3)*.

'Besides,' said Em'ly as she looked about for shells and pebbles, 'your father was a gentleman and your mother is a lady; and my father was a fisherman and my mother was a fisherman's daughter, and my uncle Dan is a fisherman.'

'Dan is Mr. Peggotty, is he?' said I.

'Uncle Dan – yonder,' answered Em'ly, nodding at the boat-house.

'Yes. I mean him. He must be very good, I should think?'

'Good?' said Em'ly. 'If I was ever to be a lady, I'd give him a sky-blue coat with diamond buttons, nankeen trousers, a red velvet waistcoat, a cocked hat, a large gold watch, a silver pipe, and a box of money' *(Chapter 3)*.

Mrs. Gummidge had been in a low state all day, and had burst into tears in the forenoon, when the fire smoked. 'I am a lone lorn creetur',' were Mrs. Gummidge's words, when that unpleasant occurrence took place, 'and everythink goes contrairy with me.'

'Oh, it'll soon leave off,' said Peggotty – I again mean our Peggotty – 'and besides, you know, it's not more disagreeable to you than to us.'

'I feel it more,' said Mrs. Gummidge.

It was a very cold day, with cutting blasts of wind. Mrs. Gummidge's peculiar corner of the fireside seemed to me to be the warmest and snuggest in the place, as her chair was certainly the easiest, but it didn't suit her that day at all. She was constantly complaining of the cold, and of its occasioning a visitation in her back which she called 'the creeps.' At last she shed tears on that subject, and said again that she was 'a lone lorn creetur' and everythink went contrairy with her.'

'It is certainly very cold,' said Peggotty. 'Everybody must feel it so.'

'I feel it more than other people,' said Mrs. Gummidge *(Chapter 3)*.

'What's amiss, dame?' said Mr. Peggotty.

'Nothing,' returned Mrs. Gummidge. 'You've come from The Willing Mind, Dan'l?'

'Why yes, I've took a short spell at The Willing Mind to-night,' said Mr. Peggotty.

'I'm sorry I should drive you there,' said Mrs. Gummidge.

'Drive! I don't want no driving,' returned Mr. Peggotty, with an honest laugh. 'I only go too ready.'

'Very ready,' said Mrs. Gummidge, shaking her head, and wiping her eyes. 'Yes, yes, very ready. I am sorry it should be along of me that you're so ready.'

'Along o' you! It an't along o' you!' said Mr. Peggotty. 'Don't ye believe a bit on it.'

'Yes, yes, it is,' cried Mrs. Gummidge. 'I know what I am. I know that I am a lone lorn creetur', and not only that everythink goes contrairy with me, but that I go contrairy with everybody. Yes, yes, I feel more than other people do, and I show it more. It's my misfortun' ' *(Chapter 3)*.

'Master Davy,' said Peggotty, untying her bonnet with a shaking hand, and speaking in a breathless sort of way. 'What do you think? You have got a pa!'

I trembled, and turned white. Something – I don't know what, or how – connected with the grave in the churchyard and the raising of the dead, seemed to strike me like an unwholesome wind.

'A new one,' said Peggotty.

'A new one?' I repeated.

Peggotty gave a gasp, as if she were swallowing something that was very hard, and, putting out her hand, said –

'Come and see him.'

'I don't want to see him.'

– 'And your mamma,' said Peggotty.

I ceased to draw back, and we went straight to the best parlour, where she left me. On one side of the fire, sat my mother; on the other, Mr. Murdstone. My mother dropped her work, and arose hurriedly, but timidly I thought.

'Now, Clara my dear,' said Mr. Murdstone. 'Recollect! control yourself, always control yourself! Davy boy, how do you do?'

I gave him my hand. After a moment of suspense, I went and kissed my mother: she kissed me, patted me gently on the shoulder, and sat down again to her work. I could not look at her, I could not look at him, I knew quite well that he was looking at us both; and I turned to the window and looked out there at some shrubs that were drooping their heads in the cold.

As soon as I could creep away, I crept upstairs. My old dear bedroom was changed, and I was to lie a long way off. I rambled downstairs to find anything that was like itself, so altered it all seemed; and roamed into the yard. I very soon started back from there, for the empty dog-kennel was filled up with a great dog – deep-mouthed and black-haired like Him – and he was very angry at the sight of me, and sprang out to get at me *(Chapter 3)*.

'Are you only going to Yarmouth, then?' I asked.

'That's about it,' said the carrier. 'And there I shall take you to the stage-cutch, and the stage-cutch that'll take you to – wherever it is.'

As this was a great deal for the carrier (whose name was Mr. Barkis) to say – he being, as I observed in a former chapter, of a phlegmatic temperament, and not at all conversational – I offered him a cake as a mark of attention, which he ate at one gulp, exactly like an elephant, and which made no more impression on his big face than it would have done on an elephant's.

'Did *she* make 'em, now?' said Mr. Barkis, always leaning forward, in his slouching way, on the foot-board of the cart with an arm on each knee.

'Peggotty, do you mean, sir?'

'Ah!' said Mr. Barkis. 'Her.'

'Yes. She makes all our pastry and does all our cooking.'

'Do she though?' said Mr. Barkis.

He made up his mouth as if to whistle, but he didn't whistle. He sat looking at the horse's ears, as if he saw something new there; and sat so for a considerable time. By-and-by, he said:

'No sweethearts, I b'lieve?'

'Sweetmeats did you say, Mr. Barkis?' For I thought he wanted something else to eat, and had pointedly alluded to that description of refreshment.

'Hearts,' said Mr. Barkis. 'Sweethearts; no person walks with her?'

'With Peggotty?'

'Ah!' he said. 'Her.'

'Oh, no. She never had a sweetheart.'

'Didn't she, though?' said Mr. Barkis.

Again he made up his mouth to whistle, and again he didn't whistle, but sat looking at the horse's ears.

'So she makes,' said Mr. Barkis, after a long interval of reflection, 'all the apple parsties, and does all the cooking, do she?'

I replied that such was the fact.

'Well. I'll tell you what,' said Mr. Barkis. 'P'raps you might be writin' to her?'

'I shall certainly write to her,' I rejoined.

'Ah!' he said, slowly turning his eyes towards me. 'Well! If you was writin' to her, p'raps you'd recollect to say that Barkis was willin'; would you?'

'That Barkis was willing,' I repeated, innocently. 'Is that all the message?'

'Ye-es,' he said, considering. 'Ye-es. Barkis is willin' ' *(Chapter 5)*.

'There's half a pint of ale for you. Will you have it now?'

I thanked him and said 'Yes.' Upon which he poured it out of a jug into a large tumbler, and held it up against the light, and made it look beautiful.

'My eye!' he said. 'It seems a great deal, don't it?'

'It does seem a good deal,' I answered with a smile. For it was quite delightful to me to find him so pleasant. He was a twinkling-eyed, pimple-faced man, with his hair standing upright all over his head; and as he stood with one arm akimbo, holding up the glass to the light with the other hand, he looked quite friendly.

'There was a gentleman here yesterday,' he said – 'a stout gentleman, by the name of Topsawyer – perhaps you know him?'

'No,' I said, 'I don't think – '

'In breeches and gaiters, broad-brimmed hat, grey coat, speckled choker,' said the waiter.

'No,' I said bashfully, 'I haven't the pleasure – '

'He came in here,' said the waiter, looking at the light through the tumbler, 'ordered a glass of this ale – *would* order it – I told him not – drank it, and fell dead. It was too old for him. It oughtn't to be drawn; that's the fact.'

I was very much shocked to hear of this melancholy accident, and said I thought I had better have some water.

'Why you see,' said the waiter, still looking at the light through the tumbler, with one of his eyes shut up, 'our people don't like things being ordered and left. It offends 'em. But *I'll* drink it if you like. I'm used to it, and use is everything. I don't think it'll hurt me, if I throw my head back, and take it off quick. Shall I?'

I replied that he would much oblige me by drinking it, if he thought he could do it safely, but by no means otherwise. When he did throw his head back, and take it off quick, I had a horrible fear, I confess, of seeing him meet the fate of the lamented Mr. Topsawyer, and fall lifeless on the carpet. But it didn't hurt him. On the contrary, I thought he seemed the fresher for it.

'What have we got here?' he said, putting a fork into my dish. 'Not chops?'

'Chops,' I said.

'Lord bless my soul!' he exclaimed, 'I didn't know they were chops. Why a chop's the very thing to take off the bad effects of that beer! Ain't it lucky?'

So he took a chop by the bone in one hand, and a potato in the other, and ate away with a very good appetite, to my extreme satisfaction. He afterwards took another chop, and another potato; and after that another chop and another potato. When he had done, he brought me a pudding, and having set it before me, seemed to ruminate, and to become absent in his mind for some moments.

'How's the pie?' he said, rousing himself.

'It's a pudding,' I made answer.

'Pudding!' he exclaimed. 'Why, bless me, so it is! What?' looking at it nearer. 'You don't mean to say it's a batter-pudding?'

'Yes, it is indeed.'

'Why, a batter-pudding,' he said, taking up a table-spoon, 'is my favourite pudding! Ain't that lucky? Come on, little 'un, and let's see who'll get most.'

The waiter certainly got most. He entreated me more than once to come in and win, but what with his table-spoon to my tea-spoon, his despatch to my despatch, and his appetite to my appetite, I was left far behind at the first mouthful, and had no chance with him. I never saw any one enjoy a pudding so much, I think; and he laughed, when it was all gone, as if his enjoyment of it lasted still.

Finding him so very friendly and companionable, it was then that I asked for the pen and ink and paper to write to Peggotty. He not only brought it immediately, but was good enough to look over me while I wrote the letter. When I had finished it, he asked me where I was going to school.

I said, 'Near London,' which was all I knew.

'Oh! my eye!' he said, looking very low-spirited, 'I am sorry for that.'

'Why?' I asked him.

'Oh, Lord!' he said, shaking his head, 'that's the school where they broke the boy's ribs – two ribs – a little boy he was. I should say he was – let me see – how old are you, about?'

I told him between eight and nine.

'That's just his age,' he said. 'He was eight years and six months old when they broke his first rib; eight years and eight months old when they broke his second and did for him.'

I could not disguise from myself, or from the waiter, that this was an uncomfortable coincidence, and inquired how it was done. His answer was not cheering to my spirits, for it consisted of two dismal words: 'With whopping.'

The blowing of the coach-horn in the yard was a seasonable diversion, which made me get up and hesitatingly inquire in the mingled pride and diffidence of having a purse (which I took out of my pocket), if there were anything to pay.

'There's a sheet of letter-paper,' he returned. 'Did you ever buy a sheet of letter-paper?'

I could not remember that I ever had.

'It's dear,' he said, 'on account of the duty. Three-pence. That's the way we're taxed in this country. There's nothing else, except the waiter. Never mind the ink. *I* lose by that.'

'What should you – what should I – how much ought I to – what would it be right to pay the waiter, if you please?' I stammered, blushing.

'If I hadn't a family, and that family had'nt the cowpock,' said the waiter, 'I wouldn't take a sixpence. If I didn't support a aged pairint, and a lovely sister,' – here the waiter was greatly agitated – 'I wouldn't take a farthing. If I had a good place, and was treated well here, I should beg acceptance of a trifle, instead of taking of it. But I live on broken wittles – and I sleep on the coals' – here the waiter burst into tears *(Chapter 5)*.

'I was sorry, David, I remarked,' said Murdstone, turning his head and eyes stiffly towards me, 'to observe that you are of a sullen disposition. This is not a character that I can suffer to develop itself beneath my eyes without an effort at improvement. You must endeavour, sir, to change it. We must endeavour to change it for you.'

'I beg your pardon, sir,' I faltered. 'I have never meant to be sullen since I came back.'

'Don't take refuge in a lie, sir!' he returned so fiercely, that I saw my mother involuntarily put out her trembling hand as if to interpose between us. 'You have withdrawn yourself in your sullenness to your own room. You have kept your own room when you ought to have been here. You know now, once for all, that I require you to be here, and not there. Further, that I require you to bring obedience here. You know me, David. I will have it done.'

Miss Murdstone gave a hoarse chuckle.

'I will have a respectful, prompt, and ready bearing towards myself,' he continued, 'and towards Jane Murdstone, and towards your mother. I will not have this room shunned as if it were infected, at the pleasure of a child. Sit down.'

He ordered me like a dog, and I obeyed like a dog *(Chapter 8)*.

I retreated to my own room no more; I took refuge with Peggotty no more; but sat wearily in the parlour day after day looking forward to night, and bed-time.

What irksome constraint I underwent, sitting in the same attitude hours upon hours, afraid to move an arm or a leg lest Miss Murdstone should complain (as she did on the least pretence) of my restlessness, and afraid to move an eye lest she should light on some look of dislike or scrutiny that would find new cause for complaint in mine! What intolerable dulness to sit listening to the ticking of the clock; and watching Miss Murdstone's little shiny steel beads as she strung them; and wondering whether she would ever be married, and if so, to what sort of unhappy man; and counting the divisions in the moulding on the chimney-piece; and wandering away with my eyes, to the ceiling, among the curls and corkscrews in the paper on the wall!

What walks I took alone, down muddy lanes, in the bad winter weather, carrying that parlour, and Mr. and Miss Murdstone in it, everywhere: a monstrous load that I was obliged to bear, a daymare that there was no possibility of breaking in, a weight that brooded on my wits, and blunted them!

What meals I had in silence and embarrassment, always feeling that there were a knife and fork too many, and those mine; an appetite too many, and that mine; a plate and chair too many, and those mine; a somebody too many, and that I!

What evenings, when the candles came, and I was expected to employ myself, but not daring to read an entertaining book, pored over some hard-headed harder-hearted treatise on arithmetic; when the tables of weights and measures set themselves to tunes, as Rule Britannia, or Away with Melancholy; when they wouldn't stand still to be learnt, but would go threading my grandmother's needle through my unfortunate head, in at one ear and out at the other!

What yawns and dozes I lapsed into, in spite of all my care; what starts I came out of concealed sleeps with; what answers I never got, to little observations that I rarely made; what a blank space I seemed, which everybody overlooked, and yet was in everybody's way; what a heavy relief it was to hear Miss Murdstone hail the first stroke of nine at night, and order me to bed!

Thus the holidays lagged away, until the morning came when Miss Murdstone said: 'Here's the last day off!' and gave me the closing cup of tea of the vacation *(Chapter 8)*.

Again Mr. Barkis appeared at the gate, and again Miss Murdstone in her warning voice said: 'Clara!' when my mother bent over me, to bid me farewell.

I kissed her, and my baby brother, and was very sorry then; but not sorry to go away, for the gulf between us was there, and the parting was there, every day. And it is not so much the embrace she gave me, that lives in my mind, though it was as fervent as could be, as what followed the embrace.

I was in the carrier's cart when I heard her calling to me. I looked out, and she stood at the garden-gate alone, holding her baby up in her arms for me to see. It was cold still weather; and not a hair of her head, nor a fold of her dress, was stirred, as she looked intently at me, holding up her child.

So I lost her. So I saw her afterwards, in my sleep at school – a silent presence near my bed – looking at me with the same intent face – holding up her baby in her arms *(Chapter 8)*.

Mr. Barkis's wooing, as I remember it, was altogether of a peculiar kind. He very seldom said anything; but would sit by the fire in much the same attitude as he sat in his cart, and stare heavily at Peggotty, who was opposite. One night, being, as I suppose, inspired by love, he made a dart at the bit of wax-candle she kept for her thread, and put it in his waistcoat-pocket and carried it off. After that, his great delight was to produce it when it was wanted, sticking to the lining of his pocket, in a partially melted state, and pocket it again when it was done with. He seemed to enjoy himself very much, and not to feel at all called upon to talk. Even when he took Peggotty out for a walk on the flats, he had no uneasiness on that head, I believe; contenting himself with now and then asking her if she was pretty comfortable; and I remember that sometimes, after he was gone, Peggotty would throw her apron over her face, and laugh for half an hour. Indeed, we were all more or less amused, except that miserable Mrs. Gummidge, whose courtship would appear to have been of an exactly parallel nature, she was so continually reminded by these transactions of the old one *(Chapter 10)*.

And now I fell into a state of neglect, which I cannot look back upon without compassion. I fell at once into a solitary condition, – apart from all

friendly notice, apart from the society of all other boys of my own age, apart from all companionship but my own spiritless thoughts, – which seems to cast its gloom upon this paper as I write.

What would I have given, to have been sent to the hardest school that ever was kept? – to have been taught something, anyhow, anywhere? No such hope dawned upon me. They disliked me; and they sullenly, sternly, steadily, overlooked me *(Chapter 10)*.

I know enough of the world now, to have almost lost the capacity of being much surprised by anything; but it is matter of some surprise to me, even now, that I can have been so easily thrown away at such an age. A child of excellent abilities, and with strong powers of observation, quick, eager, delicate, and soon hurt bodily or mentally, it seems wonderful to me that nobody should have made any sign in my behalf. But none was made; and I became, at ten years old, a little labouring hind in the service of Murdstone and Grinby *(Chapter 11)*.

'Master Copperfield,' said Mrs. Micawber, 'I make no stranger of you, and therefore do not hesitate to say that Mr. Micawber's difficulties are coming to a crisis.'

It made me very miserable to hear it, and I looked at Mrs. Micawber's red eyes with the utmost sympathy.

'With the exception of the heel of a Dutch cheese – which is not adapted to the wants of a young family' – said Mrs. Micawber, 'there is really not a scrap of anything in the larder. I was accustomed to speak of the larder when I lived with papa and mamma, and I use the word almost unconsciously. What I mean to express is, that there is nothing to eat in the house' *(Chapter 11)*.

At last Mr. Micawber's difficulties came to a crisis, and he was arrested early one morning, and carried over to the King's Bench Prison in the Borough. He told me, as he went out of the house, that the God of day had now gone down upon him – and I really thought his heart was broken and mine too. But I heard, afterwards, that he was seen to play a lively game at skittles, before noon *(Chapter 11)*.

Mr. Micawber was waiting for me within the gate, and we went up to his room (top story but one), and cried very much. He solemnly conjured me, I remember, to take warning by his fate; and to observe that if a man had twenty pounds a year for his income, and spent nineteen pounds nineteen shillings and sixpence, he would be happy, but that if he spent twenty pounds one he would be miserable. After which he borrowed a shilling of me for porter, gave me a written order on Mrs. Micawber for the amount, and put away his pocket-handkerchief, and cheered up *(Chapter 11)*.

I was sent up to 'Captain Hopkins' in the room overhead, with Mr. Micawber's compliments, and I was his young friend and would Captain Hopkins lend me a knife and fork.

Captain Hopkins lent me the knife and fork, with his compliments to Mr. Micawber. There was a very dirty lady in his little room, and two wan girls, his daughters, with shock heads of hair. I thought it was better to borrow Captain Hopkin's knife and fork, than Captain Hopkin's comb. The captain himself was in the last extremity of shabbiness, with large whiskers, and an old, old brown greatcoat with no other coat below it. I saw his bed rolled up in a corner; and what plates and dishes and pots he had, on a shelf; and I divined (God knows how) that though the two girls with the shock heads of hair were Captain Hopkin's children, the dirty lady was not married to Captain Hopkins. My timid station on his threshold was not occupied more than a couple of minutes at most; but I came down again with all this in my knowledge, as surely as the knife and fork were in my hand *(Chapter 11)*.

As I walked to and fro daily between Southwark and Blackfriars, and lounged about at meal-times in obscure streets, the stones of which may, for anything I know, be worn at this moment by my childish feet, I wonder how many of these people were wanting in the crowd that used to come filing before me in review again, to the echo of Captain Hopkin's voice! When my thoughts go back now, to that slow agony of my youth, I wonder how much of the histories I invented for such people hangs like a mist of fancy over well-remembered facts! When I tread the old ground, I do not wonder that I seem to see and pity, going on before me, an innocent romantic boy, making his imaginative world out of such strange experiences and sordid things *(Chapter 11)*.

'My family,' said Mrs. Micawber, who always said those two words with an air, though I never could discover who came under the denomination, 'my family are of opinion that Mr. Micawber should quit London, and exert his talents in the country. Mr. Micawber is a man of great talent, Master Copperfield.'

I said I was sure of that.

'Of great talent,' repeated Mrs. Micawber. 'My family are of opinion, that, with a little interest, something might be done for a man of his ability in the Custom House. The influence of my family being local, it is their wish that Mr. Micawber should go down to Plymouth. They think it indispensable that he should be upon the spot.'

'That he may be ready?' I suggested.

'Exactly,' returned Mrs. Micawber. 'That he may be ready in case of anything turning up.'

'And do you go too, ma'am?'

The events of the day, in combination with the twins, if not with the flip, had made Mrs. Micawber hysterical, and she shed tears as she replied:–

'I never will desert Mr. Micawber. Mr. Micawber may have concealed his difficulties from me in the first instance, but his sanguine temper may have led him to expect that he would overcome them. The pearl necklace and bracelets which I inherited from mamma, have been disposed of for less than half their value; and the set of coral, which was the wedding gift of my papa, has been actually thrown away for nothing. But I never will desert Mr. Micawber. No!' cried Mrs. Micawber, more affected than before, 'I never will do it! It's of no use asking me!' *(Chapter 12)*.

'My other piece of advice, Copperfield,' said Mr. Micawber, 'you know. Annual income twenty pounds, annual expenditure nineteen nineteen six, result happiness. Annual income twenty pounds, annual expenditure twenty pounds ought and six, result misery. The blossom is blighted, the leaf is withered, the God of day goes down upon the dreary scene, and – in short you are for ever floored. As I am!'

To make his example the more impressive, Mr. Micawber drank a glass of punch with an air of great enjoyment and satisfaction, and whistled the College Hornpipe *(Chapter 12)*.

I had had a hard day's work, and was pretty well jaded when I came climbing out, at last, upon the level of Blackheath. It cost me some trouble to find out Salem House; but I found it, and I found a haystack in the corner, and I lay down by it; having first walked round the wall, and looked up at the windows, and seen that all was dark and silent within. Never shall I forget the lonely sensation of first lying down, without a roof above my head!

Sleep came upon me as it came on many other outcasts, against whom house-doors were locked, and house-dogs barked, that night – and I dreamed of lying on my old school-bed, talking to the boys in my room; and found myself sitting upright, with Steerforth's name upon my lips, looking wildly at the stars that were glistening and glimmering above me. When I remembered where I was at that untimely hour, a feeling stole upon me that made me get up, afraid of I don't know what, and walk about. But the fainter glimmering of the stars, and the pale light in the sky where the day was coming, reassured me: and my eyes being very heavy, I lay down again, and slept – though with a knowledge in my sleep that it was cold – until the warm beams of the sun, and the ringing of the getting-up bell at Salem House, awoke me. If I could have hoped that Steerforth was there, I would have lurked about until he came out alone; but I knew he must have left long since. Traddles still remained, perhaps, but it was very doubtful; and I had not sufficient confidence in his discretion or good luck, however strong my reliance was on his good-nature, to wish to trust him with my situation. So I crept away from the wall as Mr. Creakle's boys were getting up, and struck into the long dusty track which I had first known to be the Dover Road when I was one of them, and when I little expected that any eyes would ever see me the wayfarer I was now, upon it.

What a different Sunday morning from the old Sunday morning at Yarmouth! In due time I heard the church-bells ringing, as I plodded on; and I met people who were going to church; and I passed a church or two where the congregation were inside, and the sound of singing came out into the sunshine, while the beadle sat and cooled himself in the shade of the porch, or stood beneath the yew-tree, with his hand to his forehead, glowering at me going by. But the peace and rest of the old Sunday morning were on everything except me. That was the difference. I felt quite wicked in my dirt and dust, with my tangled hair. But for the quiet picture I had conjured up, of my mother in her youth and beauty, weeping by the fire, and my aunt relenting to her, I hardly think I should have had courage to go on until next day. But it always went before me, and I followed *(Chapter 13)*.

This modesty of mine directed my attention to the marine-store shops, and such shops as Mr. Dolloby's, in preference to the regular dealers. At last I found one that I thought looked promising, at the corner of a dirty lane, ending in an inclosure full of stinging-nettles, against the palings of which some second-hand sailors' clothes, that seemed to have overflowed the shop, were fluttering among some cots, and rusty guns, and oilskin hats, and certain trays full of so many old rusty keys of so many sizes that they seemed various enough to open all the doors in the world.

Into this shop, which was low and small, and which was darkened rather than lighted by a little window, overhung with clothes, and was descended into by some steps, I went with a palpitating heart; which was not relieved when an ugly old man, with the lower part of his face all covered with a stubbly grey beard, rushed out of a dirty den behind it, and seized me by the hair of my head. He was a dreadful old man to look at, in a filthy flannel waistcoat, and smelling terribly of rum. His bedstead, covered with a tumbled and ragged piece of patchwork, was in the den he had come from, where another little window showed a prospect of more stinging-nettles and a lame donkey.

'Oh, what do you want?' grinned this old man, in a fierce, monotonous whine. 'Oh, my eyes and limbs, what do you want? Oh, my lungs and liver, what do you want? Oh, goroo, goroo!'

I was so much dismayed by these words, and particularly by the repetition of the last unknown one, which was a kind of rattle in his throat, that I could make no answer; hereupon the old man, still holding me by the hair, repeated:

'Oh, what do you want? Oh, my eyes and limbs, what do you want? Oh, my lungs and liver, what do you want? Oh, goroo!' – which he screwed out of himself, with an energy that made his eyes start in his head.

'I wanted to know,' I said, trembling, 'if you would buy a jacket.'

'Oh, let's see the jacket!' cried the old man. 'Oh, my heart on fire, show the jacket to us! Oh, my eyes and limbs, bring the jacket out!'

With that he took his trembling hands, which were like the claws of a great bird, out of my hair; and put on a pair of spectacles, not at all ornamental to his inflamed eyes.

'Oh, how much for the jacket?' cried the old man, after examining it. 'Oh – goroo! – how much for the jacket?'

'Half-a-crown,' I answered, recovering myself.

'Oh, my lungs and liver,' cried the old man, 'no! Oh, my eyes, no! Oh, my limbs, no! Eighteenpence. Goroo!'

Every time he uttered this ejaculation, his eyes seemed to be in danger of starting out; and every sentence he spoke, he delivered in a sort of tune, always exactly the same, and more like a gust of wind, which begins low, mounts up high, and falls again, than any other comparison I can find for it.

'Well,' said I, glad to have closed the bargain, 'I'll take eighteenpence.'

'Oh, my liver!' cried the old man, throwing the jacket on a shelf. 'Get out of the shop! Oh, my lungs, get out of the shop! Oh, my eyes and limbs – goroo! – don't ask for money; make it an exchange.'

I never was so frightened in my life, before or since; but I told him humbly that I wanted money, and that nothing else was of any use to me, but that I would wait for it, as he desired, outside, and had no wish to hurry him. So I went outside, and sat down in the shade in a corner. And I sat there so many hours, that the shade became sunlight, and the sunlight became shade again, and still I sat there waiting for the money.

There never was such another drunken madman in that line of business, I hope. That he was well known in the neighbourhood, and enjoyed the reputation of having sold himself to the devil, I soon understood from the visits he received from the boys, who continually came skirmishing about the shop, shouting that legend, and calling to him to bring out his gold. 'You ain't poor, you know, Charley, as you pretend. Bring out your gold. Bring out some of the gold you sold yourself to the devil for. Come! It's in the lining of the mattress, Charley. Rip it open and let's have some!' This, and many offers to lend him a knife for the purpose, exasperated him to such a degree, that the whole day was a succession of rushes on his part, and flights on the part of the boys. Sometimes in his rage he would take me for one of them, and come at me, mouthing as if he were going to tear me in pieces; then, remembering me, just in time, would dive into the shop, and lie upon his bed, as I thought from the sound of his voice, yelling in a frantic way, to his own windy tune, the Death of Nelson; with an Oh! before every line, and innumerable Goroos interspersed. As if this were not bad enough for me, the boys, connecting me with the establishment, on account of the patience and perseverance with which I sat outside, half-dressed, pelted me, and used me very ill all day.

He made many attempts to induce me to consent to an exchange; at one time coming out with a fishing-rod, at another with a fiddle, at another with a cocked hat, at another with a flute. But I resisted all these overtures, and sat there in desperation; each time asking him, with tears in my eyes, for my money or my jacket. At last he began to pay me in halfpence at a time; and was full two hours getting by easy stages to a shilling.

'Oh, my eyes and limbs!' he then cried, peeping hideously out of the shop, after a long pause, 'will you go for twopence more?'

'I can't,' I said; 'I shall be starved.'

'Oh, my lungs and liver, will you go for threepence?'

'I would go for nothing, if I could,' I said, 'but I want the money badly.'

'Oh, go-roo!' (it is really impossible to express how he twisted this ejaculation out of himself, as he peeped round the door-post at me, showing nothing but his crafty old head;) 'will you go for fourpence?'

I was so faint and weary that I closed with this offer; and taking the money out of his claw, not without trembling, went away more hungry and thirsty than I had ever been, a little before sunset *(Chapter 13).*

But under this difficulty, as under all the other difficulties of my journey, I seemed to be sustained and led on by my fanciful picture of my mother in her youth, before I came into the world. It always kept me company. It was there, among the hops, when I lay down to sleep; it was with me on my waking in the morning; it went before me all day. I have associated it, ever since, with the sunny street of Canterbury, dozing as it were in the hot light; and with the sight of its old houses and gateways, and the stately, grey Cathedral, with the rooks sailing round the towers.

When I came, at last, upon the bare, wide downs near Dover, it relieved the solitary aspect of the scene with hope; and not until I reached that first great aim of my journey, and actually set foot in the town itself, on the sixth day of my flight, did it desert me. But then, strange to say, when I stood with my ragged shoes, and my dusty, sunburnt, half-clothed figure, in the place so long desired, it seemed to vanish like a dream, and to leave me helpless and dispirited.

I inquired about my aunt among the boatmen first, and received various answers. One said she lived in the South Foreland Light, and had singed her whiskers by doing so; another, that she was made fast to the great buoy outside the harbour, and could only be visited at half-tide; a third, that she was locked up in Maidstone Jail for child-stealing; a fourth, that she was seen to mount a broom, in the last high wind, and make direct for Calais *(Chapter 13).*

I followed the young woman, and we soon came to a very neat little cottage with cheerful bow-windows: in front of it, a small square gravelled court or garden full of flowers, carefully tended, and smelling deliciously.

'This is Miss Trotwood's,' said the young woman. 'Now you know; and that's all I have got to say.' With which words she hurried into the house, as if to shake off the responsibility of my appearance; and left me standing at the garden-gate, looking disconsolately over the top of it towards the parlour-window, where a muslin curtain, partly undrawn in the middle, a large round green screen or fan fastened on to the window-sill, a small table, and a great chair, suggested to me that my aunt might be at that moment seated in awful state *(Chapter 13).*

The unbroken stillness of the parlour-window leading me to infer, after a while, that she was not there, I lifted up my eyes to the window above it, where I saw a florid, pleasant-looking gentleman, with a grey head, who shut up one eye in a grotesque manner, nodded his head at me several times, shook it at me as often, laughed, and went away.

I had been discomposed enough before; but I was so much the more discomposed by this unexpected be-haviour, that I was on the point of slinking off, to think how I had best proceed, when there came out of the house a lady with a handkerchief tied over her cap, and a pair of gardening gloves on her hands, wearing a gardening-pocket like a toll-man's apron, and carrying a great knife. I knew her immediately to be Miss

Betsey, for she came stalking out of the house exactly as my poor mother had so often described her stalking up our garden at Blunderstone Rookery.

'Go away!' said Miss Betsey, shaking her head, and making a distant chop in the air with her knife. 'Go along! No boys here!'

I watched her, with my heart at my lips, as she marched to a corner of her garden, and stooped to dig up some little root there. Then, without a scrap of courage, but with a great deal of desperation, I went softly in and stood beside her, touching her with my finger.

'If you please, ma'am,' I began.

She started and looked up.

'If you please, aunt.'

'EH?' exclaimed Miss Betsey, in a tone of amaze-ment I have never heard approached.

'If you please, aunt, I am your nephew.'

'Oh, Lord!' said my aunt. And sat flat down in the garden-path *(Chapter 13).*

Janet had gone away to get the bath ready, when my aunt, to my great alarm, became in one moment rigid with indignation, and had hardly voice to cry out, 'Janet! Donkeys!'

Upon which, Janet came running up the stairs as if the house were in flames, darted out on a little piece of green in front, and warned off two saddle-donkeys, lady-ridden, that had presumed to set hoof upon it; while my aunt, rushing out of the house, seized the bridle of a third animal laden with a bestriding child, turned him, led him forth from those sacred precincts, and boxed the ears of the unlucky urchin in attend-ance who had dared to profane that hallowed ground.

To this hour I don't know whether my aunt had any lawful right of way over that patch of green; but she had settled it in her own mind that she had, and it was all the same to her. The one great outrage of her life, demanding to be constantly avenged, was the passage of a donkey over that immaculate spot. In whatever occupation she was engaged, however interesting to her the conversation in which she was taking part, a donkey turned the current of her ideas in a moment, and she was upon him straight. Jugs of water, and watering pots, were kept in secret places ready to be discharged on the offending boys; sticks were laid in ambush behind the door; sallies were made at all hours; and incessant war prevailed. Perhaps the more sagacious of the donkeys, understanding how the case stood, delighted with constitutional obstinacy in coming that way. I only know that there were three alarms before the bath was ready; and that on the occasion of the last and most desperate of all, I saw my aunt engage, single-handed, with a sandy-headed lad of fifteen, and bump his sandy head against her own gate, before he seemed to comprehend what was the matter. These interruptions were the more ridiculous to me, because she was giving me broth out of a table-spoon at the time (having firmly persuaded her-self that I was actually starving, and must receive nourishment at first in very small quantities), and, while my mouth was yet open to receive the spoon, she would put it back into the basin, cry 'Janet! Donkeys!' and go out to the assault *(Chapter 13).*

'Now, Mr. Dick,' said my aunt, with her grave look, and her forefinger up as before, 'I am going to ask you another question. Look at this child.'

'David's son?' said Mr. Dick, with an attentive, puzzled face.

'Exactly so,' returned my aunt. 'What would you do with him, now?'

'Do with David's son?' said Mr. Dick.

'Ay,' replied my aunt, 'with David's son.'

'Oh!' said Mr. Dick. 'Yes. Do with – I should put him to bed.'

'Janet!' cried my aunt, with the same complacent triumph that I had remarked before. 'Mr. Dick sets us all right. If the bed is ready, we'll take him up to it' *(Chapter 13)*.

'You have been to school?'

'Yes, sir,' I answered; 'for a short time.'

'Do you recollect the date,' said Mr. Dick, looking earnestly at me, and taking up his pen to note it down, 'when King Charles the First had his head cut off?'

I said I believed it happened in the year sixteen hundred and forty-nine.

'Well,' returned Mr. Dick, scratching his ear with his pen, and looking dubiously at me. 'So the books say; but I don't see how that can be. Because, if it was so long ago, how could the people about him have made that mistake of putting some of the trouble out of *his* head, after it was taken off, into *mine?*'

I was very much surprised by the inquiry; but could give no information on this point.

'It's very strange,' said Mr. Dick, with a despondent look upon his papers, and with his hand among his hair again, 'that I never can get that quite right. I never can make that perfectly clear. But no matter, no matter!' he said cheerfully, and rousing himself, 'there's time enough! My compliments to Miss Trotwood, I am getting on very well indeed' *(Chapter 14)*.

'Trot,' said my aunt in conclusion, 'be a credit to yourself, to me, and Mr. Dick, and Heaven be with you!'

I was greatly overcome, and could only thank her, again and again, and send my love to Mr. Dick.

'Never,' said my aunt, 'be mean in anything; never be false; never be cruel. Avoid those three vices, Trot, and I can always be hopeful of you' *(Chapter 15:* Miss Trotwood and David Copperfield).

You are working late to-night, Uriah,' says I.

'Yes, Master Copperfield,' says Uriah.

As I was getting on the stool opposite, to talk to him more conveniently, I observed that he had not such a thing as a smile about him, and that he could only widen his mouth and make two hard creases down his cheeks, one on each side, to stand for one.

'I am not doing office-work, Master Copperfield,' said Uriah.

'What work, then?' I asked.

'I am improving my legal knowledge, Master Copperfield,' said Uriah. 'I am going through Tidd's Practice. Oh, what a writer Mr. Tidd is, Master Copperfield!'

My stool was such a tower of observation, that as I watched him reading on again, after this rapturous exclamation, and following up the lines with his fore-finger, I observed that his nostrils, which were thin and pointed, with sharp dints in them, had a singular and most uncomfortable way of expanding and contracting themselves; that they seemed to twinkle instead of his eyes, which hardly ever twinkled at all.

'I suppose you are quite a great lawyer?' I said, after looking at him for some time.

'Me, Master Copperfield?' said Uriah. 'Oh, no! I'm a very umble person.'

It was no fancy of mine about his hands, I observed; for he frequently ground the palms against each other as if to squeeze them dry and warm, besides often wiping them, in a stealthy way, on his pocket-handkerchief.

'I am well aware that I am the umblest person going,' said Uriah Heep, modestly; 'let the other be where he may. My mother is likewise a very umble person. We live in a numble abode, Master Copperfield, but have much to be thankful for. My father's former calling was umble. He was a sexton.'

'What is he now?' I asked.

'He is a partaker of glory at present, Master Copperfield,' said Uriah Heep. 'But we have much to be thankful for. How much have I to be thankful for in living with Mr. Wickfield!' *(Chapter 16)*.

'Shall we go and see Mrs. Micawber, sir?' I said, to get Mr. Micawber away.

'If you will do her that favour, Copperfield,' replied Mr. Micawber, rising. 'I have no scruple in saying, in the presence of our friends here, that I am a man who has, for some years, contended against the pressure of pecuniary difficulties.' I knew he was certain to say something of this kind; he always would be so boastful about his difficulties. 'Sometimes I have risen superior to my difficulties. Sometimes my difficulties have – in short, have floored me. There have been times when I have administered a succession of facers to them; there have been times when they have been too many for me, and I have given in, and said to Mrs. Micawber in the words of Cato, "Plato, thou reasonest well. It's all up now. I can show fight no more." But at no time of my life,' said Mr. Micawber, 'have I enjoyed a higher degree of satisfaction than in pouring my griefs (if I describe difficulties, chiefly arising out of warrants of attorney and promissory notes at two and four months, by that word) into the bosom of my friend Copperfield' *(Chapter 17)*.

'My Dear Young Friend,

'The die is cast – all is over. Hiding the ravages of care with a sickly mask of mirth, I have not informed you, this evening, that there is no hope of the remittance! Under these circumstances, alike humiliating to endure, humiliating to contemplate, and humiliating to relate, I have discharged the pecuniary liability contracted at this establishment, by giving a note of hand, made payable fourteen days after date, at my residence, Pentonville, London. When it becomes due, it will not be taken up. The result is destruction. The bolt is impending, and the tree must fall.

'Let the wretched man who now addresses you, my

dear Copperfield, be a beacon to you through life. He writes with that intention, and in that hope. If he could think himself of so much use, one gleam of day might, by possibility, penetrate into the cheerless dungeon of his remaining existence – though his longevity is, at present (to say the least of it), extremely problematical.

'This is the last communication, my dear Copperfield, you will ever receive

'From
'The
'Beggared Outcast,
'WILKINS MICAWBER.'

I was so shocked by the contents of this heartrending letter, that I ran off directly towards the little hotel with the intention of taking it on my way to Doctor Strong's, and trying to soothe Mr. Micawber with a word of comfort. But, half-way there, I met the London coach with Mr. and Mrs. Micawber up behind; Mr. Micawber, the very picture of tranquil enjoyment, smiling at Mrs. Micawber's conversation, eating walnuts out of a paper bag, with a bottle sticking out of his breast-pocket. As they did not see me, I thought it best, all things considered, not to see them. So, with a great weight taken off my mind, I turned into a by-street that was the nearest way to school, and felt, upon the whole, relieved that they were gone: though I still liked them very much, nevertheless *(Chapter 17)*.

Why do I secretly give Miss Shepherd twelve Brazil nuts for a present, I wonder? They are not expressive of affection, they are difficult to pack into a parcel of any regular shape, they are hard to crack, even in room-doors, and they are oily when cracked; yet I feel that they are appropriate to Miss Shepherd. Soft, seedy biscuits, also, I bestow upon Miss Shepherd; and oranges innumerable. Once, I kiss Miss Shepherd in the cloak-room. Ecstasy! What are my agony and indignation next day, when I hear a flying rumour that the Misses Nettingall have stood Miss Shepherd in the stocks for turning in her toes!

Miss Shepherd being the one pervading theme and vision of my life, how do I ever come to break with her? I can't conceive. And yet a coolness grows between Miss Shepherd and myself. Whispers reach me of Miss Shepherd having said she wished I wouldn't stare so, and having avowed a preference for Master Jones – for Jones! a boy of no merit whatever! The gulf between me and Miss Shepherd widens. At last, one day, I meet the Misses Nettingalls' establishment out walking. Miss Shepherd makes a face as she goes by, and laughs to her companion. All is over. The devotion of a life – it seems a life, it is all the same – is at an end; Miss Shepherd comes out of the morning service, and the Royal Family know her no more *(Chapter 18)*.

The shade of a young butcher rises, like the apparition of an armed head in Macbeth. Who is this young butcher? He is the terror of the youth of Canterbury. There is a vague belief abroad, that the beef suet with which he anoints his hair gives him unnatural strength, and that he is a match for a man. He is a broad-faced, bull-necked young butcher, with rough red cheeks, an ill-conditioned mind, and an injurious tongue. His main use of this tongue, is, to disparage Doctor Strong's young gentlemen. He says, publicly, that if they want anything he'll give it 'em. He names individuals among them (myself included), whom he could undertake to settle with one hand, and the other tied behind him. He waylays the smaller boys to punch their unprotected heads, and calls challenges after me in the open streets. For these sufficient reasons I resolve to fight the butcher.

It is a summer evening, down in a green hollow, at the corner of a wall. I meet the butcher by appointment. I am attended by a select body of our boys; the butcher, by two other butchers, a young publican, and a sweep. The preliminaries are adjusted, and the butcher and myself stand face to face. In a moment the butcher lights ten thousand candles out of my left eyebrow. In another moment, I don't know where the wall is, or where I am, or where anybody is. I hardly know which is myself and which the butcher, we are always in such a tangle and tussle, knocking about upon the trodden grass. Sometimes I see the butcher, bloody but confident; sometimes I see nothing, and sit gasping on my second's knee; sometimes I go in at the butcher madly, and cut my knuckles open against his face, without appearing to discompose him at all. At last I awake, very queer about the head, as from a giddy sleep, and see the butcher walking off, congratulated by the two other butchers and the sweep and publican, and putting on his coat as he goes; from which I augur, justly, that the victory is his *(Chapter 18)*.

What other changes have come upon me, besides the changes in my growth and looks, and in the knowledge I have garnered all this while? I wear a gold watch and chain, a ring upon my little finger, and a long-tailed coat; and I use a great deal of bear's grease – which, taken in conjunction with the ring, looks bad. Am I in love again? I am. I worship the eldest Miss Larkins.

The eldest Miss Larkins is not a little girl. She is a tall, dark, black-eyed, fine figure of a woman. The eldest Miss Larkins is not a chicken; for the youngest Miss Larkins is not that, and the eldest must be three or four years older. Perhaps the eldest Miss Larkins may be about thirty. My passion for her is beyond all bounds.

The eldest Miss Larkins knows officers. It is an awful thing to bear. I see them speaking to her in the street. I see them cross the way to meet her, when her bonnet (she has a bright taste in bonnets) is seen coming down the pavement, accompanied by her sister's bonnet. She laughs and talks, and seems to like it. I spend a good deal of my own spare time in walking up and down to meet her. If I can bow to her once in the day (I know her to bow to, knowing Mr. Larkins), I am happier. I deserve a bow now and then. The raging agonies I suffer on the night of the Race Ball, where I know the eldest Miss Larkins will be dancing with the military, ought to have some compensation, if there be even-handed justice in the world.

My passion takes away my appetite, and makes me

wear my newest silk neckerchief continually. I have no relief but in putting on my best clothes, and having my boots cleaned over and over again. I seem, then, to be worthier of the eldest Miss Larkins. Everything that belongs to her, or is connected with her, is precious to me. Mr. Larkins (a gruff old gentleman with a double chin, and one of his eyes immovable in his head) is fraught with interest to me. When I can't meet his daughter, I go where I am likely to meet him. To say, 'How do you do, Mr. Larkins? Are the young ladies and all the family quite well?' seems so pointed, that I blush *(Chapter 18)*.

'And the Punches,' said William. 'There's cattle! A Suffolk Punch, when he's a good 'un, is worth his weight in gold. Did you ever breed any Suffolk Punches yourself, sir?'

'N-no,' I said, 'not exactly.'

'Here's a gen'l'm'n behind me, I'll pound it,' said William, 'as has bred 'em by wholesale.'

The gentleman spoken of was a gentleman with a very unpromising squint, and a prominent chin, who had a tall white hat on with a narrow flat brim, and whose close-fitting drab trousers seemed to button all the way up outside his legs from his boots to his hips. His chin was cocked over the coachman's shoulder, so near to me, that his breath quite tickled the back of my head; and as I looked round at him, he leered at the leaders with the eye with which he didn't squint, in a very knowing manner.

'Ain't you?' asked William.

'Ain't I what?' said the gentleman behind.

'Bred them Suffolk Punches by wholesale?'

'I should think so,' said the gentleman. 'There ain't no sort of orse that I ain't bred, and no sort of dorg. Orses and dorgs is some men's fancy. They're wittles and drink to me – lodging, wife, and children – reading, writing, and 'rithmetic – snuff, tobacker, and sleep.'

'That ain't a sort of man to see sitting behind a coach-box, is it though?' said William in my ear, as he handled the reins.

I construed this remark into an indication of a wish that he should have my place, so I blushingly offered to resign it.

'Well, if you don't mind, sir,' said William, 'I think it *would* be more correct' *(Chapter 19)*.

'I believe my breath will get long next, my memory's getting so much so,' said Mr. Omer. 'Well, sir, we've got a young relation of hers here, under articles to us, that has as elegant a taste in the dressmaking business – I assure you I don't believe there's a duchess in England can touch her.'

'Not little Em'ly?' said I, involuntarily.

'Em'ly's her name,' said Mr. Omer, 'and she's little too. But if you'll believe me, she has such a face of her own that half the women in this town are mad against her.'

'Nonsense, father!' cried Minnie.

'My dear,' said Mr. Omer, 'I don't say it's the case with you,' winking at me, 'but I say that half the women in Yarmouth, ah! and in five mile round, are mad against that girl.'

'Then she should have kept to her own station in life, father,' said Minnie, 'and not have given them any hold to talk about her, and then they couldn't have done it.'

'Couldn't have done it, my dear!' retorted Mr. Omer. 'Couldn't have done it! Is that *your* knowledge of life? What is there that any woman couldn't do, that she shouldn't do – especially on the subject of another woman's good looks?' *(Chapter 21)*.

'What name was it as I wrote up in the cart, sir?' said Mr. Barkis, with a slow rheumatic smile.

'Ah! Mr. Barkis, we had some grave talks about that matter, hadn't we?'

'I was willin' a long time, sir?' said Mr. Barkis.

'A long time,' said I.

'And I don't regret it,' said Mr. Barkis. 'Do you remember what you told me once, about her making all the apple parsties and doing all the cooking?'

'Yes, very well,' I returned.

'It was as true,' said Mr. Barkis, 'as turnips is. It was as true,' said Mr. Barkis, nodding his night-cap, which was his only means of emphasis, 'as taxes is. And nothing's truer than them' *(Chapter 21)*.

'Mr. Copperfield,' said Steerforth; 'he wants to know you.'

'Well then, he shall! I thought he looked as if he did!' returned Miss Mowcher, waddling up to me, bag in hand, and laughing on me as she came. 'Face like a peach!' standing on tiptoe to pinch my cheek as I sat. 'Quite tempting! I'm very fond of peaches. Happy to make your acquaintance, Mr. Copperfield, I'm sure.'

I said that I congratulated myself on having the honour to make hers, and that the happiness was mutual.

'Oh, my goodness, how polite we are!' exclaimed Miss Mowcher, making a preposterous attempt to cover her large face with her morsel of a hand. 'What a world of gammon and spinnage it is, though, ain't it!'

This was addressed confidentially to both of us, as the morsel of a hand came away from the face, and buried itself, arm and all, in the bag again.

'What do you mean, Miss Mowcher?' said Steerforth.

'Ha! ha! ha! What a refreshing set of humbugs we are, to be sure, ain't we, my sweet child?' replied that morsel of a woman, feeling in the bag with her head on one side, and her eye in the air. 'Look here!' taking something out. 'Scraps of the Russian Prince's nails. Prince Alphabet turned topsy-turvy, *I* call him, for his name's got all the letters in it, higgledy-piggledy.'

'The Russian Prince is a client of yours, is he?' said Steerforth.

'I believe you, my pet,' replied Miss Mowcher. 'I keep his nails in order for him. Twice a week! Fingers *and* toes.'

'He pays well, I hope?' said Steerforth.

'Pays as he speaks, my dear child – through the nose,' replied Miss Mowcher. 'None of your close shavers the Prince ain't. You'd say so, if you saw his moustachios. Red by nature, black by art.'

'By your art, of course,' said Steerforth.

Miss Mowcher winked assent. 'Forced to send for

me. Couldn't help it. The climate affected *his* dye; it did very well in Russia, but it was no go here. You never saw such a rusty prince in all your born days as he was. Like old iron!' *(Chapter 22)*.

She then selected two or three of the little instruments, and a little bottle, and asked (to my surprise) if the table would bear. On Steerforth replying in the affirmative, she pushed a chair against it, and begging the assistance of my hand, mounted up, pretty nimbly, to the top, as if it were a stage.

'If either of you saw my ankles,' she said, when she was safely elevated, 'say so, and I'll go home and destroy myself.'

'*I* did not,' said Steerforth.

'*I* did not,' said I.

'Well then,' cried Miss Mowcher, 'I'll consent to live. Now, ducky, ducky, ducky, come to Mrs. Bond and be killed.'

This was an invocation to Steerforth to place himself under her hands; who, accordingly, sat himself down, with his back to the table, and his laughing face towards me, and submitted his head to her inspection, evidently for no other purpose than our entertainment. To see Miss Mowcher standing over him, looking at his rich profusion of brown hair through a large round magnifying glass, which she took out of her pocket, was a most amazing spectacle.

'*You're* a pretty fellow!' said Miss Mowcher, after a brief inspection. 'You'd be as bald as a friar on the top of your head in twelve months, but for me. Just half a minute, my young friend, and we'll give you a polishing that shall keep your curls on for the next ten years!' *(Chapter 22)*.

'Ah!' she said. 'Such things are not much in demand hereabouts. That sets me off again! I haven't seen a pretty woman since I've been here, Jemmy.'

'No?' said Steerforth.

'Not the ghost of one,' replied Miss Mowcher.

'We could show her the substance of one, I think?' said Steerforth, addressing his eyes to mine. 'Eh, Daisy?'

'Yes, indeed,' said I.

'Aha?' cried the little creature, glancing sharply at my face, and then peeping round at Steerforth's. 'Umph?'

The first exclamation sounded like a question put to both of us, and the second like a question put to Steerforth only. She seemed to have found no answer to either, but continued to rub, with her head on one side and her eye turned up, as if she were looking for an answer in the air, and were confident of its appearing presently.

'A sister of yours, Mr. Copperfield?' she cried, after a pause, and still keeping the same look-out. 'Aye, aye?'

'No,' said Steerforth, before I could reply. 'Nothing of the sort. On the contrary, Mr. Copperfield used – or I am much mistaken – to have a great admiration for her.'

'Why, hasn't he now?' returned Miss Mowcher. 'Is he fickle? oh, for shame! Did he sip every flower, and change every hour, until Polly his passion requited? Is her name Polly?'

The elfin suddenness with which she pounced upon me with this question, and a searching look, quite disconcerted me for a moment.

'No, Miss Mowcher,' I replied. 'Her name is Emily.'

'Aha?' she cried exactly as before. 'Umph? What a rattle I am! Mr. Copperfield, ain't I volatile?' *(Chapter 22)*.

'The fee,' said Steerforth, 'is – '

'Five bob,' replied Miss Mowcher, 'and dirt cheap, my chicken. Ain't I volatile, Mr. Copperfield?'

I replied politely: 'Not at all.' But I though she was rather so, when she tossed up his two half-crowns like a goblin pieman, caught them, dropped them in her pocket, and gave it a loud slap.

'That's the till!' observed Miss Mowcher, standing at the chair again, and replacing in the bag a miscellaneous collection of little objects she had emptied out of it. 'Have I got all my traps? It seems so. It won't do to be like long Ned Beadwood, when they took him to church "to marry him to somebody," as he says, and left the bride behind. Ha! ha! ha! A wicked rascal, Ned, but droll! Now, I know I'm going to break your hearts, but I am forced to leave you. You must call up all your fortitude, and try to bear it. Good-bye, Mr. Copperfield! Take care of yourself, Jockey of Norfolk! How I *have* been rattling on! It's all the fault of you two wretches. *I* forgive you! "Bob swore!" – as the Englishman said for "Good-night," when he first learnt French, and though it so like English. "Bob swore," my ducks!'

With the bag slung over her arm, and rattling as she waddled away, she waddled to the door; where she stopped to inquire if she should leave us a lock of her hair. 'Ain't I volatile?' she added, as a commentary on this offer, and, with her finger on her nose, departed *(Chapter 22)*.

'What *is* a proctor, Steerforth?' said I.

'Why, he is a sort of monkish attorney,' replied Steerforth. 'He is, to some faded courts held in Doctors' Commons – a lazy old nook near St. Paul's Churchyard – what solicitors are to the courts of law and equity. He is a functionary whose existence, in the natural course of things, would have terminated about two hundred years ago. I can tell you best what he is, by telling you what Doctors' Commons is. It's a little out-of-the-way place, where they administer what is called ecclesiastical law, and play all kinds of tricks with obsolete old monsters of Acts of Parliament, which three-fourths of the world know nothing about, and the other fourth supposes to have been dug up, in a fossil state, in the days of the Edwards. It's a place that has an ancient monopoly in suits about people's wills and people's marriages, and disputes among ships and boats.'

'Nonsense, Steerforth!' I exclaimed. 'You don't mean to say that there is any affinity between nautical matters and ecclesiastical matters?'

'I don't, indeed, my dear boy,' he returned; 'but I mean to say that they are managed and decided by the same set of people, down in that same Doctors' Commons. You shall go there one day, and find them blundering through half the nautical terms in Young's Dictionary, apropos of the "Nancy" having run down the "Sarah Jane," or Mr. Peggotty and the Yarmouth boatmen having put off in a gale of wind with an anchor and cable to the "Nelson" Indiaman in distress; and you shall go there another day, and find them deep in the evidence, pro and con., respecting a clergyman who has misbehaved himself; and you shall find the judge in the nautical case, the advocate in the clergyman's case, or contrariwise. They are like actors: now a man's a judge, and now he is not a judge; now he's one thing, now he's another; now he's something else, change and change about; but it's always a very pleasant profitable little affair of private theatricals, presented to an uncommonly select audience' *(Chapter 23).*

'So you have left Mr. Dick behind, aunt?' said I. 'I am sorry for that. Ah, Janet, how do you do?'

As Janet curtsied, hoping I was well, I observed my aunt's visage lengthen very much.

'I am sorry for it, too,' said my aunt, rubbing her nose. 'I have had no peace of mind, Trot, since I have been here.'

Before I could ask why, she told me.

'I am convinced,' said my aunt, laying her hand with melancholy firmness on the table, 'that Dick's character is not a character to keep the donkeys off. I am confident he wants strength of purpose. I ought to have left Janet at home instead, and then my mind might perhaps have been at ease. If ever there was a donkey trespassing on my green,' said my aunt, with emphasis, 'there was one this afternoon at four o'clock. A cold feeling came over me from head to foot, and I *know* it was a donkey!' *(Chapter 23:* Miss Trotwood).

Supper was comfortably served and hot, though my aunt's rooms were very high up – whether that she might have more stone stairs for her money, or might be nearer to the door in the roof, I don't know – and consisted of a roast fowl, a steak, and some vegetables, to all of which I did ample justice, and which were all excellent. But my aunt had her own ideas concerning London provision, and ate but little.

'I suppose this unfortunate fowl was born and brought up in a cellar,' said my aunt, 'and never took the air except on a hackney coach-stand. I *hope* the steak may be beef, but I don't believe it. Nothing's genuine in the place, in my opinion, but the dirt.'

'Don't you think the fowl may have come out of the country, aunt?' I hinted.

'Certainly not,' returned my aunt. 'It would be no pleasure to a London tradesman to sell anything which was what he pretended it was' *(Chapter 23).*

'And so, Mr. Copperfield, you think of entering into our profession? I casually mentioned to Miss Trotwood, when I had the pleasure of an interview with her the other day ... that there was a vacancy here. Miss Trotwood was good enough to mention that she had a nephew who was her peculiar care, and for whom she was seeking to provide genteelly in life. That nephew, I believe, I have now the pleasure of' ....

I bowed my acknowledgments, and said, my aunt had mentioned to me that there was that opening, and

that I believed I should like it very much. That I was strongly inclined to like it, and had taken immediately to the proposal. That I could not absolutely pledge myself to like it, until I knew something more about it. That although it was little else than a matter of form, I presumed I should have an opportunity of trying how I liked it, before I bound myself to it irrevocably.

'Oh surely! surely!' said Mr. Spenlow. 'We always, in this house, propose a month – an initiatory month. I should be happy, myself, to propose two months – three – an indefinite period, in fact – but I have a partner. Mr. Jorkins.'

'And the premium, sir,' I returned, 'is a thousand pounds.'

'And the premium, stamp included, is a thousand pounds,' said Mr. Spenlow. 'As I have mentioned to Miss Trotwood, I am actuated by no mercenary considerations; few men are less so, I believe; but Mr. Jorkins has his opinions. Mr. Jorkins thinks a thousand pounds too little, in short.'

'I suppose, sir,' said I, still desiring to spare my aunt, 'that it is not the custom here, if an articled clerk were particularly useful, and made himself a perfect master of his profession' – I could not help blushing, this looked so like praising myself – 'I suppose it is not the custom, in the later years of his time, to allow him any – '

Mr. Spenlow, by a great effort, just lifted his head far enough out of his cravat, to shake it, and answered, anticipating the word 'salary.'

'No. I will not say what consideration I might give to that point myself, Mr. Copperfield, if I were unfettered. Mr. Jorkins is immovable' *(Chapter 23).*

'Why, this is the very thing, aunt!' said I, flushed with the possible dignity of living in chambers.

'Then come,' replied my aunt, immediately resuming the bonnet she had a minute before laid aside. 'We'll go and look at 'em.'

Away we went. The advertisement directed us to apply to Mrs. Crupp on the premises, and we rung the area bell, which we supposed to communicate with Mrs. Crupp. It was not until we had rung three or four times that we could prevail on Mrs. Crupp to communicate with us, but at last she appeared, being a stout lady with a flounce of flannel petticoat below a nankeen gown.

'Let us see these chambers of yours, if you please, ma'am,' said my aunt.

'For this gentleman?' said Mrs. Crupp, feeling in her pocket for her keys.

'Yes, for my nephew,' said my aunt.

'And a sweet set they is for sich!' said Mrs. Crupp.

So we went upstairs.

They were on the top of the house – a great point with my aunt, being near the fire-escape – and consisted of a little half-blind entry where you could see hardly anything, a little stone-blind pantry where you could see nothing at all, a sitting-room, and a bedroom. The furniture was rather faded, but quite good enough for me; and, sure enough, the river was outside the windows.

As I was delighted with the place, my aunt and Mrs. Crupp withdrew into the pantry to discuss the terms, while I remained on the sitting-room sofa, hardly daring to think it possible that I could be destined to live in such a noble residence. After a single combat of some duration they returned, and I saw, to my joy, both in Mrs. Crupp's countenance and in my aunt's, that the deed was done.

'Is it the last occupant's furniture?' inquired my aunt.

'Yes, it is, ma'am,' said Mrs. Crupp.

'What's become of him?' asked my aunt.

Mrs. Crupp was taken with a troublesome cough, in the midst of which she articulated with much difficulty. 'He was took ill here, ma'am, and – ugh! ugh! ugh! dear me! – and he died!'

'Hey! What did he die of?' asked my aunt.

'Well, ma'am, he died of drink,' said Mrs. Crupp, in confidence. 'And smoke.'

'Smoke? You don't mean chimneys?' said my aunt.

'No, ma'am,' returned Mrs. Crupp. 'Cigars and pipes.'

'*That's* not catching, Trot, at any rate,' remarked my aunt, turning to me.

'No, indeed,' said I *(Chapter 23).*

It was a remarkable instance of want of forethought on the part of the ironmonger who had made Mrs. Crupp's kitchen fire-place, that it was capable of cooking nothing but chops and mashed potatoes. As to a fish-kittle, Mrs. Crupp said, well! would I only come and look at the range? She couldn't say fairer than that. Would I come and look at it? As I should not have been much the wiser if I *had* looked at it, I declined, and said, 'Never mind fish.' But Mrs. Crupp said, Don't say that; oysters was in, and why not them? So *that* was settled. Mrs. Crupp then said what she would recommend would be this. A pair of hot roast fowls – from the pastry-cook's; a dish of stewed beef, with vegetables – from the pastry-cook's; two little corner things, as a raised pie and a dish of kidneys – from the pastry-cook's; a tart, and (if I liked) a shape of jelly – from the pastry-cook's. This, Mrs. Crupp said, would leave her at full liberty to concentrate her mind on the potatoes, and to serve up the cheese and celery as she could wish to see it done.

I acted on Mrs. Crupp's opinion, and gave the order at the pastry-cook's myself. Walking along the Strand, afterwards, and observing a hard mottled substance in the window of a ham and beef shop, which resembled marble, but was labelled 'Mock Turtle,' I went in and bought a slab of it, which I have since seen reason to believe would have sufficed for fifteen people. This preparation, Mrs. Crupp, after some difficulty, consented to warm up; and it shrunk so much in a liquid state, that we found it what Steerforth called 'rather a tight fit' for four *(Chapter 24).*

I began by being singularly cheerful and light-hearted; all sorts of half-forgotten things to talk about, came rushing into my mind, and made me hold forth in a most unwonted manner. I laughed heartily at my own jokes, and everybody else's; called Steerforth to order for not passing the wine; made several engagements to go to Oxford; announced that I meant to have a dinner-party exactly like that, once a week until further notice; and madly took so much snuff out

of Grainger's box, that I was obliged to go into the pantry, and have a private fit of sneezing ten minutes long.

I went on, by passing the wine faster and faster yet, and continually starting up with a corkscrew to open more wine, long before any was needed. I proposed Steerforth's health. I said he was my dearest friend, the protector of my boyhood, and the companion of my prime. I said I was delighted to propose his health. I said I owed him more obligations than I could ever repay, and held him in a higher admiration than I could ever express. I finished by saying, 'I'll give you Steerforth! God bless him! Hurrah!' We gave him three times, and another, and a good one to finish with. I broke my glass in going round the table to shake hands with him, and I said (in two words) 'Steerforth, you'retheguidingstarofmyexistence.'

I went on, by finding suddenly that somebody was in the middle of a song. Markham was the singer, and he sang, 'When the heart of a man is depressed with care.' He said, when he had sung it, he would give us 'Woman!' I took objection to that, and I couldn't allow it. I said it was not a respectful way of proposing the toast, and I would never permit that toast to be drunk in my house otherwise than as 'The Ladies!' I was very high with him, mainly I think because I saw Steerforth and Grainger laughing at me – or at him – or at both of us. He said a man was not to be dictated to. I said a man *was*. He said a man was not to be insulted, then. I said he was right there – never under my roof, where the Lares were sacred, and the laws of hospitality paramount. He said it was no derogation from a man's dignity to confess that I was a devilish good fellow. I instantly proposed his health *(Chapter 24).*

I found Mr. Waterbrook to be a middle-aged gentleman, with a short throat, and a good deal of shirt collar, who only wanted a black nose to be the portrait of a pug-dog. He told me he was happy to have the honour of making my acquaintance; and when I had paid my homage to Mrs. Waterbrook, presented me, with much ceremony, to a very awful lady in a black velvet dress, and a great black velvet hat, whom I remember as looking like a near relation of Hamlet's – say his aunt.

Mrs. Henry Spiker was this lady's name; and her husband was there too: so cold a man, that his head, instead of being grey, seemed to be sprinkled with hoar-frost. Immense deference was shown to the Henry Spikers, male and female; which Agnes told me was on account of Mr. Henry Spiker being solicitor to something or to somebody, I forget what or which, remotely connected with the Treasury *(Chapter 25).*

Traddles and I were separated at table, being billeted in two remote corners: he in the glare of a red velvet lady: I, in the gloom of Hamlet's aunt. The dinner was very long, and the conversation was about the Aristocracy – and Blood. Mrs. Waterbrook repeatedly told us, that if she had a weakness, it was Blood.

It occurred to me several times that we should have got on better, if we had not been quite so genteel. We were so exceedingly genteel, that our scope was very limited. A Mr. and Mrs. Gulpidge were of the party, who had something to do at second-hand (at least, Mr. Gulpidge had), with the law business of the Bank; and what with the Bank, and what with the Treasury, we were as exclusive as the Court Circular. To mend the matter, Hamlet's aunt had the family failing of indulging in soliloquy, and held forth in a desultory manner, by herself, on every topic that was introduced. These were few enough, to be sure; but as we always fell back upon Blood, she had as wide a field for abstract speculation as her nephew himself.

We might have been a party of ogres, the conversation assumed such a sanguine complexion.

'I confess I am of Mrs. Waterbrook's opinion,' said Mr. Waterbrook, with his wine-glass at his eye. 'Other things are all very well in their way, but give me Blood!'

'Oh! There is nothing,' observed Hamlet's aunt, 'so satisfactory to one! There is nothing that is so much one's *beau-ideal* of – of all that sort of thing, speaking generally. There are some low minds (not many, I am happy to believe, but there are *some*) that would prefer to do what *I* should call bow down before idols. Positively idols! Before services, intellect, and so on. But these are intangible points. Blood is not so. We see Blood in a nose, and we know it. We meet with it in a chin, and we say, "There it is! That's Blood!" It is an actual matter of fact. We point it out. It admits of no doubt.'

The simpering fellow with the weak legs, who had taken Agnes down, stated the question more decisively yet, I thought.

'Oh, you know, deuce take it,' said this gentleman, looking round the board with an imbecile smile, 'we can't forego Blood, you know. Some young fellows, you know, may be a little behind their station, perhaps, in point of education and behaviour, and may go a little wrong, you know, and get themselves and other people into a variety of fixes – and all that – but deuce take it, it's delightful to reflect that they've got Blood in 'em! Myself, I'd rather at any time be knocked down by a man who had got Blood in him, than I'd be picked up by a man who hadn't!' *(Chapter 25).*

'Oh, really, Master Copperfield, – I mean Mister Copperfield,' said Uriah, 'to see you waiting upon me is what I never could have expected! But, one way and another, so many things happen to me which I never could have expected, I am sure, in my umble station, that it seems to rain blessings on my ed. You have heard something, I des-say, of a change in my expectations, Master Copperfield, – *I* should say, Mister Copperfield?'

As he sat on my sofa, with his long knees drawn up under his coffee-cup, his hat and gloves upon the ground close to him, his spoon going softly round and round, his shadowless red eyes, which looked as if they had scorched their lashes off, turned towards me without looking at me, the disagreeable dints I have formerly described in his nostrils coming and going with his breath, and a snaky undulation pervading his frame from his chin to his boots, I decided in my own mind that I disliked him intensely. It made me very uncomfortable to have him for a guest, for I was young then, and unused to disguise what I so strongly felt.

'You have heard something, I des-say, of a change in my expectations, Master Copperfield, – I should say, Mister Copperfield?' observed Uriah.

'Yes,' said I, 'something.'

'Ah! I thought Miss Agnes would know of it!' he quietly returned. 'I'm glad to find Miss Agnes knows of it. Oh, thank you, Master – Mister Copperfield!'

I could have thrown my bootjack at him (it lay ready on the rug), for having entrapped me into the disclosure of anything concerning Agnes, however immaterial. But I only drank my coffee.

'What a prophet you have shown yourself, Mister Copperfield!' pursued Uriah. 'Dear me, what a prophet you have proved yourself to be! Don't you remember saying to me once, that perhaps I should be a partner in Mr. Wickfield's business, and perhaps it might be Wickfield and Heep? *You* may not recollect it; but when a person is umble, Master Copperfield, a person treasures such things up!' *(Chapter 25).*

'So, Mr. Wickfield,' said I, at last, 'who is worth five hundred of you – or me'; for my life, I think, I could not have helped dividing that part of the sentence with an awkward jerk; 'has been imprudent, has he, Mr. Heep?'

'Oh, very imprudent indeed, Master Copperfield,' returned Uriah, sighing modestly. 'Oh, very much so! But I wish you'd call me Uriah, if you please. It's like old times.'

'Well! Uriah,' said I, bolting it out with some difficulty.

'Thank you!' he returned, with fervour. 'Thank you, Master Copperfield! It's like the blowing of old breezes or the ringing of old bellses to hear *you* say Uriah. I beg your pardon. Was I making any observation?'

'About Mr. Wickfield,' I suggested.

'Oh! Yes, truly,' said Uriah. 'Ah! Great imprudence, Master Copperfield. It's a topic that I wouldn't touch upon, to any soul but you. Even to you I can only touch upon it, and no more. If any one else had been in my place during the last few years, by this time he would have had Mr. Wickfield (oh, what a worthy man he is, Master Copperfield, too!) under his thumb. Un-der-his thumb,' said Uriah, very slowly, as he stretched out his cruel-looking hand above my table, and pressed his own thumb down upon it, until it shook, and shook the room *(Chapter 25).*

'Master Copperfield,' he began – 'but am I keeping you up?'

'You are not keeping me up. I generally go to bed late.'

'Thank you, Master Copperfield! I have risen from my umble station since first you used to address me, it is true; but I am umble still. I hope I never shall be otherwise than umble. You will not think the worse of my umbleness, if I make a little confidence to you, Master Copperfield? Will you?'

'Oh no,' said I, with an effort.

'Thank you!' He took out his pocket-handkerchief, and began wiping the palms of his hands. 'Miss Agnes, Master Copperfield – '

'Well, Uriah?'

'Oh, how pleasant to be called Uriah, spontaneously!' he cried; and gave himself a jerk, like a convulsive fish. 'You thought her looking very beautiful to-night, Master Copperfield?'

'I thought her looking as she always does: superior, in all respects, to every one around her,' I returned.

'Oh, thank you! It's so true!' he cried. 'Oh, thank you very much for that!'

'Not at all,' I said, loftily. 'There is no reason why you should thank me.'

'Why that, Master Copperfield,' said Uriah, 'is, in fact, the confidence that I am going to take the liberty of reposing. Umble as I am,' he wiped his hands harder, and looked at them and at the fire by turns, 'umble as my mother is, and lowly as our poor but honest roof has ever been, the image of Miss Agnes (I don't mind trusting you with my secret, Master Copperfield, for I have always overflowed towards you since the first moment I had the pleasure of beholding you in a pony-shay) has been in my breast for years. Oh, Master Copperfield, with what a pure affection do I love the ground my Agnes walks on!'

I believe I had a delirious idea of seizing the red-hot poker out of the fire, and running him through with it. It went from me with a shock, like a ball fired from a rifle: but the image of Agnes, outraged by so much as a thought of this red-headed animal's, remained in my mind (when I looked at him, sitting all awry as if his mean soul griped his body), and made me giddy. He seemed to swell and grow before my eyes; the room seemed full of the echoes of his voice; and the strange feeling (to which, perhaps, no one is quite a stranger) that all this had occurred before, at some indefinite time, and that I knew what he was going to say next, took possession of me *(Chapter 25)*.

There was a lovely garden to Mr. Spenlow's house; and though that was not the best time of the year for seeing a garden, it was so beautifully kept, that I was quite enchanted. There was a charming lawn, there were clusters of trees, and there were perspective walks that I could just distinguish in the dark, arched over with trellis-work, on which shrubs and flowers grew in the growing season. 'Here Miss Spenlow walks by herself,' I thought. 'Dear me!'

We went into the house, which was cheerfully lighted up, and into a hall where there were all sorts of hats, caps, great-coats, plaids, gloves, whips, and walking sticks. 'Where is Miss Dora?' said Mr. Spenlow to the servant. 'Dora!' I thought. 'What a beautiful name!'

We turned into a room near at hand (I think it was the identical breakfast-room, made memorable by the brown East Indian sherry), and I heard a voice say, 'Mr. Copperfield, my daughter Dora, and my daughter Dora's confidential friend!' It was, no doubt, Mr. Spenlow's voice, but I didn't know it, and I didn't care whose it was. All was over in a moment. I had fulfilled my destiny. I was a captive and a slave. I loved Dora Spenlow to distraction! *(Chapter 26)*.

I had not been walking long, when I turned a corner, and met her. I tingle again from head to foot as my recollection turns that corner, and my pen shakes in my hand.

'You – are – out early, Miss Spenlow,' said I.

'It's so stupid at home,' she replied, 'and Miss Murdstone is so absurd! She talks such nonsense about its being necessary for the day to be aired, before I come out. Aired!' (She laughed here, in the most melodious manner.) 'On a Sunday morning, when I don't practise, I must do something. So I told papa last night I *must* come out. Besides, it's the brightest time of the whole day. Don't you think so?'

I hazarded a bold flight, and said (not without stammering) that it was very bright to me then, though it had been very dark to me a minute before.

'Do you mean a compliment?' said Dora, 'or that the weather has really changed?'

I stammered worse than before, in replying that I meant no compliment, but the plain truth; though I was not aware of any change having taken place in the weather. It was in the state of my own feelings, I added bashfully: to clench the explanation.

I never saw such curls – how could I, for there never were such curls! – as those she shook out to hide her blushes. As to the straw hat and blue ribbons which was on the top of the curls, if I could only have hung it up in my room in Buckingham Street, what a priceless possession it would have been!

'You have just come home from Paris,' said I.

'Yes,' said she. 'Have you ever been there?'

'No.'

'Oh! I hope you'll go soon! You would like it so much!'

Traces of deep-seated anguish appeared in my countenance. That she should hope I would go, that she should think it possible I *could* go, was insupportable. I depreciated Paris; I depreciated France. I said I wouldn't leave England, under existing circumstances, for any earthly consideration. Nothing should induce me. In short, she was shaking the curls again, when the little dog came running along the walk to our relief.

He was mortally jealous of me, and persisted in barking at me. She took him up in her arms – oh my goodness! – and caressed him, but he persisted upon barking still. He wouldn't let me touch him, when I tried; and then she beat him. It increased my sufferings greatly to see the pats she gave him for punishment on the bridge of his blunt nose, while he winked his eyes, and licked her hand, and still growled within himself like a little double-bass. At length he was quiet – well he might be with her dimpled chin upon his head! – and we walked away to look at a greenhouse *(Chapter 26)*.

'It is very hard, because we have not a kind mamma, that we are to have, instead, a sulky, gloomy old thing like Miss Murdstone, always following us about – isn't it, Jip? Never mind, Jip. We won't be confidential, and we'll make ourselves as happy as we can in spite of her, and we'll teaze her, and not please her – won't we, Jip?'

If it had lasted any longer, I think I must have gone down on my knees on the gravel, with the probability before me of grazing them, and of being presently ejected from the premises besides. But, by good fortune the greenhouse was not far off, and these words brought us to it.

It contained quite a show of beautiful geraniums. We loitered along in front of them, and Dora often stopped to admire this one or that one, and I stopped to admire the same one, and Dora, laughing, held the dog up childishly, to smell the flowers; and if we were not all three in Fairy-land, certainly *I* was. The scent of a geranium leaf, at this day, strikes me with a half-comical, half-serious wonder as to what change has come over me in a moment; and then I see a straw hat and blue ribbons, and a quantity of curls, and a little black dog being held up, in two slender arms, against a bank of blossoms and bright leaves *(Chapter 26)*.

We departed early in the morning, for we had a salvage case coming on in the Admiralty Court, requiring a rather accurate knowledge of the whole science of navigation, in which (as we couldn't be expected to know much about those matters in the Commons) the judge had entreated two old Trinity Masters, for charity's sake, to come and help him out. Dora was at the breakfast-table to make the tea again, however; and I had the melancholy pleasure of taking off my hat to her in the phaeton, as she stood on the door-step with Jip in her arms.

What the Admiralty was to me that day; what nonsense I made of our case in my mind, as I listened to it; how I saw 'DORA' engraved upon the blade of the silver oar which they lay upon the table, as the emblem of that high jurisdiction; and how I felt when Mr. Spenlow went home without me (I had had an insane hope that he might take me back again), as if I were a mariner myself, and the ship to which I belonged had sailed away and left me on a desert island; I shall make no fruitless effort to describe. If that sleepy old Court could rouse itself, and present in any visible form the day-dreams I have had in it about Dora, it would reveal my truth.

I don't mean the dreams that I dreamed on that day alone, but day after day, from week to week, and term to term. I went there, not to attend to what was going on, but to think about Dora. If ever I bestowed a thought upon the cases, as they dragged their slow length before me, it was only to wonder, in the matrimonial cases (remembering Dora), how it was that married people could ever be otherwise than happy; and, in the Prerogative cases, to consider, if the money in question had been left to me, what were the foremost steps I should immediately have taken in regard to Dora. Within the first week of my passion, I bought four sumptuous waistcoats – not for myself; *I* had no pride in them; for Dora – and took to wearing straw-coloured kid gloves in the streets, and laid the foundations of all the corns I have ever had. If the boots I wore at that period could only be produced and compared with the natural size of my feet, they would show what the state of my heart was, in a most affecting manner.

And yet, wretched cripple as I made myself by this act of homage to Dora, I walked miles upon miles daily in the hope of seeing her. Not only was I soon as well known on the Norwood Road as the postmen on that beat, but I pervaded London likewise. I walked about the streets where the best shops for ladies were, I haunted the Bazaar like an unquiet spirit, I fagged through the Park again and again, long after I was quite knocked up. Sometimes, at long intervals and on rare occasions, I saw her. Perhaps I saw her glove waved in a carriage-window; perhaps I met her, walked with her and Miss Murdstone a little way, and spoke to her. In the latter case I was always very miserable afterwards, to think that I had said nothing to the purpose; or that she had no idea of the extent of my devotion, or that she cared nothing about me. I was always looking out, as may be supposed, for another invitation to Mr. Spenlow's house. I was always being disappointed, for I got none *(Chapter 26)*.

Mrs. Crupp must have been a woman of penetration, for even in that early stage, she found it out. She came up to me one evening, when I was very low, to ask (she being then afflicted with the disorder I have mentioned) if I could oblige her with a little tincture of cardamums mixed with rhubarb, and flavoured with seven drops of the essence of cloves, which was the best remedy for her complaint; – or, if I had not such a thing by me, with a little brandy, which was the next best. It was not, she remarked, so palatable to her, but it was the next best. As I had never even heard of the first remedy, and always had the second in the closet, I gave Mrs. Crupp a glass of the second, which (that I might have no suspicion of its being devoted to any improper use) she began to take in my presence.

'Cheer up, sir,' said Mrs. Crupp. 'I can't abear to see you so, sir: I'm a mother myself.'

I did not quite perceive the application of this fact to *my*self, but I smiled on Mrs. Crupp, as benignly as was in my power.

'Come, sir,' said Mrs. Crupp. 'Excuse me. I know what it is, sir. There's a lady in the case.'

'Mrs. Crupp?' I returned, reddening.

'Oh, bless you! Keep a good heart, sir!' said Mrs. Crupp, nodding encouragement. 'Never say die, sir! If She don't smile upon you, there's a many as will. You're a young gentleman to *be* smiled on, Mr. Copperfull, and you must learn your walue, sir.'

Mrs. Crupp always called me Mr. Copperfull: firstly, no doubt, because it was not my name; and secondly, I am inclined to think, in some indistinct association with a washing-day.

'What makes you suppose there is any young lady in the case, Mrs. Crupp?' said I.

'Mr. Copperfull,' said Mrs. Crupp, with a great deal of feeling. 'I'm a mother myself.'

For some time Mrs. Crupp could only lay her hand upon her nankeen bosom, and fortify herself against returning pain with sips of her medicine. At length she spoke again.

'When the present set were took for you by your dear aunt, Mr. Copperfull,' said Mrs. Crupp, 'my remark were, I had now found summun I could care for. "Thank Ev'in!" were the expression, "I have now found summun I can care for!" – You don't eat enough, sir, nor yet drink.'

'Is that what you found your supposition on, Mrs. Crupp?' said I.

'Sir,' said Mrs. Crupp, in a tone approaching to severity, 'I've laundressed other young gentlemen besides yourself. A young gentleman may be over-careful of himself, or he may be under-careful of himself. He may brush his hair too regular, or too unregular. He may wear his boots much too large for him, or much too small. That is according as the young gentleman has his original character formed. But let him go to which extreme he may, sir, there's a young lady in both of 'em.'

Mrs. Crupp shook her head in such a determined manner, that I had not an inch of 'vantage-ground left.

'It was but the gentleman which died here before yourself,' said Mrs. Crupp, 'that fell in love – with a barmaid – and had his waistcoats took in directly, though much swelled by drinking.'

'Mrs. Crupp,' said I, 'I must beg you not to connect the young lady in my case with a barmaid, or anything of that sort, if you please.'

'Mr. Copperfull,' returned Mrs. Crupp, 'I'm a mother myself, and not likely. I ask your pardon, sir, if I intrude. I should never wish to intrude where I were not welcome. But you are a young gentleman, Mr. Copperfull, and my advice to you is, to cheer up, sir, to keep a good heart, and to know your own walue. If you was to take to something, sir,' said Mrs. Crupp, 'If you was to take to skittles, now, which is healthy, you might find it divert your mind, and do you good.'

With these words, Mrs. Crupp, affecting to be very careful of the brandy – which was all gone – thanked me with a majestic curtsey, and retired. As her figure disappeared into the gloom of the entry, this counsel certainly presented itself to my mind in the light of a slight liberty on Mrs. Crupp's part; but, at the same time, I was content to receive it, in another point of view, as a word to the wise, and a warning in future to keep my secret better *(Chapter 26)*.

All this time, Mr. Micawber had not known me in the least, though he had stood face to face with me. But now, seeing me smile, he examined my features with more attention, fell back, cried, 'Is it possible? Have I the pleasure of again beholding Copperfield?' and shook me by both hands with the utmost fervour.

'Good Heaven, Mr. Traddles!' said Mr. Micawber, 'to think that I should find you acquainted with the friend of my youth, the companion of earlier days! My dear!' calling over the banisters to Mrs. Micawber, while Traddles looked (with reason) not a little amazed at this description of me. 'Here is a gentleman in Mr. Traddles's apartment, whom he wishes to have the pleasure of presenting to you, my love!'

Mr. Micawber immediately reappeared, and shook hands with me again.

'And how is our good friend the Doctor, Copperfield?' said Mr. Micawber, 'and all the circle at Canterbury?'

'I have none but good accounts of them,' said I.

'I am most delighted to hear it,' said Mr. Micawber. 'It was at Canterbury where we last met. Within the shadow, I may figuratively say, of that religious edifice, immortalised by Chaucer, which was anciently the resort of pilgrims from the remotest corners of – in short,' said Mr. Micawber, 'in the immediate neigh-bourhood of the cathedral.'

I replied that it was. Mr. Micawber continued talking as volubly as he could; but not, I thought, without showing, by some marks of concern in his countenance, that he was sensible of sounds in the next room, as of Mrs. Micawber washing her hands, and hurriedly opening and shutting drawers that were uneasy in their action.

'You find us, Copperfield,' said Mr. Micawber, with one eye on Traddles, 'at present established, on what may be designated as a small and unassuming scale; but, you are aware that I have, in the course of my career, surmounted difficulties, and conquered obstacles. You are no stranger to the fact, that there have been periods of my life, when it has been requisite that I should pause, until certain expected events should turn up; when it has been necessary that I should fall back, before making what I trust I shall not be accused of presumption in terming – a spring. The present is one of those momentous stages in the life of man. You find me, fallen back, *for* a spring; and I have every reason to believe that a vigorous leap will shortly be the result' *(Chapter 27)*.

'My dear Copperfield,' said Mr. Micawber, 'I need hardly tell you that to have beneath our roof, under existing circumstances, a mind like that which gleams – if I may be allowed the expression – which gleams – in your friend Traddles, is an unspeakable comfort. With a washerwoman, who exposes hard-bake for sale in her parlour-window, dwelling next door, and a Bow-street officer residing over the way, you may imagine that his society is a source of consolation to myself and to Mrs. Micawber. I am at present, my dear Copperfield, engaged in the sale of corn upon commission. It is not an avocation of a remunerative description – in other words, it does *not* pay – and some temporary embarrassments of a pecuniary nature have been the consequence. I am, however, delighted to add that I have now an immediate prospect of something turning up (I am not at liberty to say in what direction), which I trust will enable me to provide, permanently, both for myself and for your friend Traddles, in whom I have an unaffected inter-est. You may, perhaps, be prepared to hear that Mrs. Micawber is in a state of health which renders it not wholly improbable that an addition may be ultimately made to those pledges of affection which – in short, to the infantine group. Mrs. Micawber's family have been so good as to express their dissatisfaction at this state of things. I have merely to observe, that I am not aware it is any business of theirs, and that I repel that exhibition of feeling with scorn, and with defiance!'

Mr. Micawber then shook hands with me again, and left me *(Chapter 27)*.

Until the day arrived on which I was to entertain my newly-found old friends, I lived principally on Dora and coffee. In my love-lorn condition, my appetite languished; and I was glad of it, for I felt as though it would have been an act of perfidy towards Dora to have a natural relish for my dinner. The quantity of walking exercise I took, was not in this respect attended with its usual consequence, as the disappointment counteracted the fresh air. I have my doubts, too, founded on the acute experience acquired at this period of my life, whether a sound enjoyment of animal food can develop itself freely in any human subject who is always in torment from tight boots. I think the extremities require to be at peace before the stomach will conduct itself with vigour *(Chapter 28)*.

Having laid in the materials for a bowl of punch, to be compounded by Mr. Micawber; having provided a bottle of lavender-water, two wax candles, a paper of mixed pins, and a pincushion, to assist Mrs. Micawber in her toilette, at my dressing-table; having also caused the fire in my bed-room to be lighted for Mrs. Micawber's convenience; and having laid the cloth with my own hands, I awaited the result with composure.

At the appointed time, my three visitors arrived together. Mr. Micawber with more shirt-collar than usual, and a new ribbon to his eye-glass; Mrs. Micawber with her cap in a whity-brown paper parcel; Traddles carrying the parcel, and supporting Mrs. Micawber on his arm. They were all delighted with my residence. When I conducted Mrs. Micawber to my dressing-table, and she saw the scale on which it was prepared for her, she was in such raptures, that she called Mr. Micawber to come in and look.

'My dear Copperfield,' said Mr. Micawber, 'this is luxurious. This is a way of life which reminds me of the period when I was myself in a state of celibacy, and Mrs. Micawber had not yet been solicited to plight her faith at the Hymeneal altar.'

'He means, solicited by him, Mr. Copperfield,' said Mrs. Micawber, archly. 'He cannot answer for others.'

'My dear,' returned Mr. Micawber with sudden seriousness, 'I have no desire to answer for others. I am too well aware that when, in the inscrutable decrees of Fate, you were reserved for me, it is possible you may have been reserved for one, destined, after a protracted struggle, at length to fall a victim to pecuniary involvements of a complicated nature. I understand your allusion, my love. I regret it, but I can bear it.'

'Micawber!' exclaimed Mrs. Micawber, in tears. 'Have I deserved this? I, who never have deserted you; who never *will* desert you, Micawber!'

'My love,' said Mr. Micawber, much affected, 'you will forgive, and our old and tried friend Copperfield will, I am sure, forgive, the momentary laceration of a wounded spirit, made sensitive by a recent collision with the Minion of Power – in other words, with a ribald attached to the waterworks – and will pity, not condemn, its excesses' *(Chapter 28)*.

I suppose – I never ventured to inquire, but I suppose – that Mrs. Crupp, after frying the soles, was taken ill. Because we broke down at that point. The leg of mutton came up very red within, and very pale without: besides having a foreign substance of a gritty nature sprinkled over it, as if it had had a fall into the ashes of that remarkable kitchen fireplace. But we were not in a condition to judge of this fact from the appearance of the gravy, forasmuch as the 'young gal'

had dropped it all upon the stairs – where it remained, by-the-bye, in a long train, until it was worn out. The pigeon-pie was not bad, but it was a delusive pie: the crust being like a disappointing head, phrenologically speaking: full of lumps and bumps, with nothing particular underneath. In short, the banquet was such a failure that I should have been quite unhappy – about the failure, I mean, for I was always unhappy about Dora – if I had not been relieved by the great good-humour of my company, and by a bright suggestion from Mr. Micawber.

'My dear friend Copperfield,' said Mr. Micawber, 'accidents will occur in the best-regulated families; and in families not regulated by that pervading influence which sanctifies while it enhances the – a – I would say in short, by the influence of Woman, in the lofty character of Wife, they may be expected with confidence, and must be borne with philosophy. If you will allow me to take the liberty of remarking that there are few comestibles better, in their way, than a Devil, and that I believe, with a little divison of labour, we could accomplish a good one if the young person in attendance could produce a gridiron, I would put it to you, that this little misfortune may be easily repaired.'

There was a gridiron in the pantry, on which my morning rasher of bacon was cooked. We had it in, in a twinkling, and immediately applied ourselves to carrying Mr. Micawber's idea into effect. The division of labour to which he had referred was this: – Traddles cut the mutton into slices; Mr. Micawber (who could do anything of this sort to perfection) covered them with pepper, mustard, salt, and cayenne; I put them on the gridiron, turned them with a fork, and took them off, under Mr. Micawber's direction; and Mrs. Micawber heated, and continually stirred, some mushroom ketchup in a little saucepan. When we had slices enough done to begin upon, we fell-to with our sleeves still tucked up at the wrists, more slices sputtering and blazing on the fire, and our attention divided between the mutton on our plates, and the mutton then preparing.

What with the novelty of this cookery, the excellence of it, the bustle of it, the frequent starting up to look after it, the frequent sitting down to dispose of it as the crisp slices came off the gridiron hot and hot, the being so busy, so flushed with the fire, so amused, and in the midst of such a tempting noise and savour, we reduced the leg of mutton to the bone. My own appetite came back miraculously. I am ashamed to record it, but I really believe I forgot Dora for a little while. I am satisfied that Mr. and Mrs. Micawber could not have enjoyed the feast more, if they had sold a bed to provide it. Traddles laughed as heartily, almost the whole time, as he ate and worked. Indeed we all did, all at once; and I dare say there never was a greater success *(Chapter 28)*.

'But punch, my dear Copperfield,' said Mr. Micawber, tasting it, 'like time and tide, waits for no man. Ah! it is at the present moment in high flavour. My love, will you give me your opinion?'

Mrs. Micawber pronounced it excellent.

'Then I will drink,' said Mr. Micawber, 'if my

friend Copperfield will permit me to take that social liberty, to the days when my friend Copperfield and myself were younger, and fought our way in the world side by side. I may say, of myself and Copperfield, in words we have sung together before now, that

> "We twa' hae run about the braes
> And pu'd the gowans fine"

– in a figurative point of view – on several occasions. I am not exactly aware,' said Mr. Micawber, with the old roll in his voice, and the old indescribable air of saying something genteel, 'what gowans may be, but I have no doubt that Copperfield and myself would frequently have taken a pull at them, if it had been feasible.'

Mr. Micawber, at the then present moment, took a pull at his punch. So we all did: Traddles evidently lost in wondering at what distant time Mr. Micawber and I could have been comrades in the battle of the world.

'Ahem!' said Mr. Micawber, clearing his throat, and warming with the punch and with the fire. 'My dear, another glass?' *(Chapter 28)*.

'I will not conceal from you, my dear Mr. Copperfield,' said Mrs. Micawber, 'that *I* have long felt the brewing business to be particularly adapted to Mr. Micawber. Look at Barclay and Perkins! Look at Truman, Hanbury, and Buxton! It is on that extensive footing that Mr. Micawber, I know from my own knowledge of him, is calculated to shine; and the profits, I am told, are e-NOR-mous! But if Mr. Micawber cannot get into those firms, – which decline to answer his letters, when he offers his services even in an inferior capacity – what is the use of dwelling upon that idea? None. I may have a conviction that Mr. Micawber's manners – '

'Hem! Really, my dear,' interposed Mr. Micawber.

'My love, be silent,' said Mrs. Micawber, laying her brown glove on his hand. 'I may have a conviction, Mr. Copperfield, that Mr. Micawber's manners peculiarly qualify him for the banking business. I may argue within myself, that if *I* had a deposit at a banking-house, the manners of Mr. Micawber, as representing that banking-house, would inspire confidence, and must extend the connection. But if the various banking-houses refuse to avail themselves of Mr. Micawber's abilities, or receive the offer of them with contumely, what is the use of dwelling upon *that* idea? None. As to originating a banking business, I may know that there are members of my family who, if they chose to place their money in Mr. Micawber's hands, might found an establishment of that description. But if they do *not* choose to place their money in Mr. Micawber's hands – which they don't – what is the use of that? Again I contend that we are no farther advanced than we were before' *(Chapter 28)*.

'I will not,' said Mrs. Micawber, finishing her punch, and gathering her scarf about her shoulders, preparatory to her withdrawal to my bedroom: 'I will not protract these remarks on the subject of Mr. Micawber's pecuniary affairs. At your fireside, my dear Mr. Copperfield, and in the presence of Mr. Traddles, who, though not so old a friend, is quite

N

one of ourselves, I could not refrain from making you acquainted with the course I advise Mr. Micawber to take. I feel that the time is arrived when Mr. Micawber should exert himself and – I will add – assert himself, and it appears to me that these are the means. I am aware that I am merely a female, and that a masculine judgment is usually considered more competent to the discussion of such questions; still I must not forget that, when I lived at home with my papa and mamma, my papa was in the habit of saying, "Emma's form is fragile, but her grasp of a subject is inferior to none." That my papa was too partial, I well know; but that he was an observer of character in some degree, my duty and my reason equally forbid me to doubt.'

With these words, and resisting our entreaties that she would grace the remaining circulation of the punch with her presence, Mrs. Micawber retired to my bedroom. And really I felt that she was a noble woman – the sort of woman who might have been a Roman matron, and done all manner of heroic things, in times of public trouble *(Chapter 28)*.

'She is playing her harp,' said Steerforth, softly, at the drawing-room door, 'and nobody but my mother has heard her do that, I believe, these three years.' He said it with a curious smile, which was gone directly; and we went into the room and found her alone.

'Don't get up,' said Steerforth (which she had already done); 'my dear Rosa, don't! Be kind for once, and sing us an Irish song.'

'What do you care for an Irish song?' she returned.

'Much!' said Steerforth. 'Much more than for any other. Here is Daisy, too, loves music from his soul. Sing us an Irish song, Rosa! and let me sit and listen as I used to do.'

He did not touch her, or the chair from which she had risen, but sat himself near the harp. She stood beside it for some little while, in a curious way, going through the motion of playing it with her right hand, but not sounding it. At length she sat down, and drew it to her with one sudden action, and played and sang.

I don't know what it was, in her touch or voice, that made that song the most unearthly I have ever heard in my life, or can imagine. There was something fearful in the reality of it. It was as if it had never been written, or set to music, but sprung out of the passion within her; which found imperfect utterance in the low sounds of her voice, and crouched again when all was still. I was dumb when she leaned beside the harp again, playing it, but not sounding it, with her right hand.

A minute more, and this had roused me from my trance: – Steerforth had left his seat, and gone to her, and had put his arm laughingly about her, and had said, 'Come, Rosa, for the future we will love each other very much!' And she had struck him, and had thrown him off with the fury of a wild cat, and had burst out of the room *(Chapter 29: Rosa Dartle)*.

'Daisy, if anything should ever separate us, you must think of me at my best, old boy. Come! Let us make that bargain. Think of me at my best, if circumstances should ever part us!'

'You have no best to me, Steerforth,' said I, 'and no

worst. You are always equally loved, and cherished in my heart.'

So much compunction for having ever wronged him, even by a shapeless thought, did I feel within me, that the confession of having done so was rising to my lips. But for the reluctance I had, to betray the confidence of Agnes, but for my uncertainty how to approach the subject with no risk of doing so, it would have reached them before he said, 'God bless you, Daisy, and good-night!' In my doubt, it did *not* reach them; and we shook hands, and we parted.

I was up with the dull dawn, and, having dressed as quietly as I could, looked into his room. He was fast asleep; lying easily, with his head upon his arm, as I had often seen him lie at school.

The time came in its season, and that was very soon, when I almost wondered that nothing troubled his repose, as I looked at him. But he slept – let me think of him so again – as I had often seen him sleep at school; and thus, in this silent hour, I left him.

– Never more, oh, God forgive you, Steerforth! to touch that passive hand in love and friendship. Never, never more! (*Chapter 29*).

'Barkis, my dear!' said Peggotty, almost cheerfully: bending over him, while her brother and I stood at the bed's foot. 'Here's my dear boy – my dear boy, Master Davy, who brought us together, Barkis! That you sent messages by, you know! Won't you speak to Master Davy?'

He was as mute and senseless as the box, from which his form derived the only expression it had.

'He's a going out with the tide,' said Mr. Peggotty to me, behind his hand.

My eyes were dim, and so were Mr. Peggotty's; but I repeated in a whisper, 'With the tide?'

'People can't die, along the coast,' said Mr. Peggotty, 'except when the tide's pretty nigh out. They can't be born, unless it's pretty nigh in – not properly born, till flood. He's a going out with the tide. It's ebb at half-arter three, slack water half an hour. If he lives till it turns, he'll hold his own till past the flood, and go out with the next tide.'

We remained there, watching him, a long time – hours. What mysterious influence my presence had upon him in that state of his senses, I shall not pretend to say; but when he at last began to wander feebly, it is certain he was muttering about driving me to school.

'He's coming to himself,' said Peggotty.

Mr. Peggotty touched me, and whispered with much awe and reverence, 'They are both a going out fast.'

'Barkis, my dear!' said Peggotty.

'C. P. Barkis,' he cried faintly. 'No better woman anywhere!'

'Look! Here's Master Davy!' said Peggotty. For he now opened his eyes.

I was on the point of asking him if he knew me, when he tried to stretch out his arm, and said to me, distinctly, with a pleasant smile:

'Barkis is willin'!'

And, it being low water, he went out with the tide (*Chapter 30*).

Mr. Peggotty seemed very much shocked at himself for having made a speech capable of this unfeeling construction, but was prevented from replying, by Peggotty's pulling his sleeve, and shaking her head. After looking at Mrs. Gummidge for some moments, in sore distress of mind, he glanced at the Dutch clock, rose, snuffed the candle, and put it in the window.

'Theer!' said Mr. Peggotty, cheerily. 'Theer we are, Missis Gummidge!' Mrs. Gummidge slightly groaned. 'Lighted up, accordin' to custom! You're a wonderin' what that's fur, sir! Well, it's fur our little Em'ly. You see, the path ain't over light or cheerful arter dark; and when I'm here at the hour as she's a comin' home, I puts the light in the winder. That, you see,' said Mr. Peggotty, bending over me with great glee, 'meets two objects. She says, says Em'ly, "Theer's home!" she says. And likewise, says Em'ly, "My uncle's theer!" Fur if I an't theer, I never have no light showed.'

'You're a baby!' said Peggotty; very fond of him for it, if she thought so.

'Well,' returned Mr. Peggotty, standing with his legs pretty wide apart, and rubbing his hands up and down them in his comfortable satisfaction, as he looked alternately at us and at the fire, 'I doen't know but I am. Not, you see, to look at.'

'Not azackly,' observed Peggotty.

'No,' laughed Mr. Peggotty, 'not to look at, but to – to consider on, you know. *I* don't care, bless you! Now I tell you. When I go a looking and looking about that theer pritty house of our Em'ly's, I'm – I'm Gormed,' said Mr. Peggotty with sudden emphasis – 'theer! I can't say more – if I doen't feel as if the littlest things was her, a'most. I takes 'em up and I puts 'em down, and I touches of 'em as delicate as if they was our Em'ly. So 'tis with her little bonnets and that. I couldn't see one on 'em rough used a purpose – not fur the whole wureld. There's a babby for you, in the form of a great sea porkypine!' said Mr. Peggotty, relieving his earnestness with a roar of laughter (*Chapter 31*).

'A strange chay and hosses was outside town, this morning, on the Norwich road, a'most afore the day broke,' Ham went on. 'The servant went to it, and come from it, and went to it again. When he went to it again, Em'ly was nigh him. The t'other was inside. He's the man.'

'For the Lord's love,' said Mr. Peggotty, falling back, and putting out his hand, as if to keep off what he dreaded. 'Doen't tell me his name's Steerforth.'

'Mas'r Davy,' exclaimed Ham, in a broken voice, 'it ain't no fault of yourn – and I am far from laying of it to you – but his name is Steerforth, and he's a damned villain!'

Mr. Peggotty uttered no cry, and shed no tear, and moved no more, until he seemed to wake again, all at once, and pulled down his rough coat from its peg in a corner.

'Bear a hand with this! I'm struck of a heap, and can't do it,' he said, impatiently. 'Bear a hand and help me. Well!' when somebody had done so. 'Now give me that theer hat!'

Ham asked him whither he was going.

'I'm a going to seek my niece. I'm a going to seek

my Em'ly. I'm a going, first, to stave in that theer boat, and sink it where I would have drownded *him*, as I'm a livin' soul, if I had had one thought of what was in him! As he sat afore me,' he said, wildly, holding out his clenched right hand, 'as he sat afore me, face to face, strike me down dead, but I'd have drownded him, and thought it right! I'm a going to seek my niece.'

'Where?' cried Ham, interposing himself before the door.

'Anywhere! I'm a going to seek my niece through the wureld. I'm a going to find my poor niece in her shame, and bring her back. No one stop me! I tell you I'm a going to seek my niece!'

'No, no!' cried Mrs. Gummidge, coming between them in a fit of crying. 'No, no, Dan'l, not as you are now. Seek her in a little while, my lone lorn Dan'l, and that'll be but right! but not as you are now. Sit ye down, and give me your forgiveness for having ever been a worrit to you, Dan'l – what have *my* contrairies ever been to this! – and let us speak a word about them times when she was first an orphan, and when Ham was too, and when I was a poor widder woman, and you took me in. It'll soften your poor heart, Dan'l,' laying her head upon his shoulder, 'and you'll bear your sorrow better; for you know the promise, Dan'l, "As you have done it unto one of the least of these, you have done it unto Me"; and that can never fail under this roof, that's been our shelter for so many, many year!'

He was quite passive now; and when I heard him crying, the impulse that had been upon me to go down upon my knees, and ask their pardon for the desolation I had caused, and curse Steerforth, yielded to a better feeling. My over-charged heart found the same relief, and I cried too *(Chapter 31)*.

'Miss Dartle,' I returned, 'you are surely not so unjust as to condemn *me?*'

'Why do you bring division between these two mad creatures?' she returned. 'Don't you know that they are both mad with their own self-will and pride?'

'Is it my doing?' I returned.

'Is it your doing!' she retorted. 'Why do you bring this man here?'

'He is a deeply injured man, Miss Dartle,' I replied. 'You may not know it.'

'I know that James Steerforth,' she said, with her hand on her bosom, as if to prevent the storm that was raging there, from being loud, 'has a false, corrupt heart, and is a traitor. But what need I know or care about this fellow, and his common niece?'

'Miss Dartle,' I returned, 'you deepen the injury. It is sufficient already. I will only say, at parting, that you do him a great wrong.'

'I do him no wrong,' she returned. 'They are a depraved, worthless set. I would have her whipped!'

Mr. Peggotty passed on, without a word, and went out at the door.

'Oh, shame, Miss Dartle! shame!' I said indignantly. 'How can you bear to trample on his undeserved affliction?'

'I would trample on them all,' she answered. 'I would have his house pulled down. I would have her branded on the face, drest in rags, and cast out in the

streets to starve. If I had the power to sit in judgment on her, I would see it done. See it done? I would do it! I detest her. If I ever could reproach her with her infamous condition, I would go anywhere to do so. If I could hunt her to her grave, I would. If there was any word of comfort that would be a solace to her in her dying hour, and only I possessed it, I wouldn't part with it for life itself.'

The mere vehemence of her words can convey, I am sensible, but a weak impression of the passion by which she was possessed, and which made itself articulate in her whole figure, though her voice, instead of being raised, was lower than usual. No description I could give of her would do justice to my recollection of her, or to her entire deliverance of herself to her anger. I have seen passion in many forms, but I have never seen it in such a form as that *(Chapter 32)*.

If I may so express it, I was steeped in Dora. I was not merely over head and ears in love with her, but I was saturated through and through. Enough love might have been wrung out of me, metaphorically speaking, to drown anybody in; and yet there would have remained enough within me, and all over me, to pervade my entire existence.

The first thing I did, on my own account, when I came back, was to take a night-walk to Norwood, and, like the subject of a venerable riddle of my childhood, to go 'round and round the house, without ever touching the house,' thinking about Dora. I believe the theme of this incomprehensible conundrum was the moon. No matter what it was, I, the moon-struck slave of Dora, perambulated round and round the house and garden for two hours, looking through crevices in the palings, getting my chin by dint of violent exertion above the rusty nails on the top, blowing kisses at the lights in the windows, and romantically calling on the night, at intervals, to shield my Dora – I don't exactly know what from, I suppose from fire. Perhaps from mice, to which she had a great objection *(Chapter 33)*.

I have set all this down, in my present blissful chapter, because here it comes into its natural place. Mr. Spenlow and I falling into this conversation, prolonged it and our saunter to and fro, until we diverged into general topics. And so it came about, in the end, that Mr. Spenlow told me this day week was Dora's birthday, and he would be glad if I would come down and join a little picnic on the occasion. I went out of my senses immediately; became a mere driveller next day, on receipt of a little lace-edged sheet of note-paper, 'Favoured by papa. To remind;' and passed the intervening period in a state of dotage.

I think I committed every possible absurdity, in the way of preparation for this blessed event. I turn hot when I remember the cravat I bought. My boots might be placed in any collection of instruments of torture. I provided, and sent down by the Norwood coach the night before, a delicate little hamper, amounting in itself, I thought, almost to a declaration. There were crackers in it with the tenderest mottoes that could be got for money. At six in the morning, I was in Covent Garden Market, buying a bouquet for Dora. At ten I was on horseback (I hired a gallant grey, for the occasion), with the bouquet in my hat, to keep it fresh, trotting down to Norwood.

I suppose that when I saw Dora in the garden and pretended not to see her, and rode past the house pretending to be anxiously looking for it, I committed two small fooleries which other young gentlemen in my circumstances might have committed – because they came so very natural to me. But oh! when I *did* find the house, and *did* dismount at the garden gate, and drag those stony-hearted boots across the lawn to Dora sitting on a garden seat under a lilac-tree, what a spectacle she was, upon that beautiful morning, among the butterflies, in a white chip bonnet and a dress of celestial blue!

There was a young lady with her – comparatively stricken in years – almost twenty, I should say. Her name was Miss Mills, and Dora called her Julia. She was the bosom friend of Dora. Happy Miss Mills!

Jip was there, and Jip *would* bark at me again. When I presented my bouquet, he gnashed his teeth with jealousy. Well he might. If he had the least idea how I adored his mistress, well he might!

'Oh, thank you, Mr. Copperfield! What dear flowers!' said Dora.

I had had an intention of saying (and had been studying the best form of words for three miles) that I thought them beautiful before I saw them so near *her*. But I couldn't manage it. She was too bewildering. To see her lay the flowers against her little dimpled chin, was to lose all presence of mind and power of language in a feeble ecstasy. I wonder I didn't say, 'Kill me, if you have a heart, Miss Mills. Let me die here!'

Then Dora held my flowers to Jip to smell. Then Jip growled, and wouldn't smell them. Then Dora laughed, and held them a little closer to Jip, to make him. Then Jip laid hold of a bit of geranium with his teeth, and worried imaginary cats in it. Then Dora beat him, and pouted, and said, 'My poor beautiful flowers!' as compassionately, I thought, as if Jip had laid hold of me. I wished he had! *(Chapter 33).*

But now Mr. Spenlow came out of the house, and Dora went to him, saying, 'Look, papa, what beautiful flowers!' And Miss Mills smiled thoughtfully, as who should say, 'Ye May-flies enjoy your brief existence in the bright morning of life!' And we all walked from the lawn towards the carriage, which was getting ready.

I shall never have such a ride again. I have never had such another. There were only those three, their hamper, my hamper, and the guitar-case, in the phaeton; and, of course, the phaeton was open; and I rode behind it, and Dora sat with her back to the horses, looking towards me. She kept the bouquet close to her on the cushion, and wouldn't allow Jip to sit on that side of her at all, for fear he should crush it. She often carried it in her hand, often refreshed herself with its fragrance. Our eyes at those times often met; and my great astonishment is that I didn't go over the head of my gallant grey into the carriage.

There was dust, I believe. There was a good deal of dust, I believe. I have a faint impression that Mr. Spenlow remonstrated with me for riding in it; but I knew of none. I was sensible of a mist of love and beauty about Dora, but of nothing else. He stood up sometimes, and asked me what I thought of the prospect. I said it was delightful, and I dare say it was; but it was all Dora to me. The sun shone Dora, and the birds sang Dora. The south wind blew Dora, and the wild flowers in the hedges were all Doras, to a bud. My comfort is, Miss Mills understood me. Miss Mills alone could enter into my feelings thoroughly *(Chapter 33).*

I was debating whether I should pretend that I was not well and fly – I don't know where – upon my gallant grey, when Dora and Miss Mills met me.

'Mr. Copperfield,' said Miss Mills, 'you are dull.'

I begged her pardon. Not at all.

'And Dora,' said Miss Mills, '*you* are dull.'

Oh dear no! Not in the least.

'Mr. Copperfield and Dora,' said Miss Mills, with an almost venerable air. 'Enough of this. Do not allow a trivial misunderstanding to wither the blossoms of spring, which, once put forth and blighted, can not be renewed. I speak,' said Miss Mills, 'from experience of the past – the remote irrevocable past. The gushing fountains which sparkle in the sun, must not be stopped in mere caprice; the oasis in the desert of Sahara, must not be plucked up idly.'

I hardly knew what I did, I was burning all over to that extraordinary extent; but I took Dora's little hand and kissed it – and she let me! I kissed Miss Mills's hand; and we all seemed, to my thinking, to go straight up to the seventh heaven.

We did not come down again. We stayed up there all the evening. At first we strayed to and fro among the trees: I with Dora's shy arm drawn through mine: and Heaven knows, folly as it all was, it would have been a happy fate to have been struck immortal with those foolish feelings, and have strayed among the trees for ever!

But, much too soon, we heard the others laughing and talking, and calling 'where's Dora?' So we went back, and they wanted Dora to sing. Red Whisker would have got the guitar-case out of the carriage, but Dora told him nobody knew where it was but I. So Red Whisker was done for in a moment; and *I* got it, and *I* unlocked it, and *I* took the guitar out, and *I* sat by her, and *I* held her handkerchief and gloves, and *I* drank in every note of her dear voice, and she sang to *me* who loved her, and all the others might applaud as much as they liked, but they had nothing to do with it! *(Chapter 33).*

Miss Mills was very glad to see me, and very sorry her papa was not at home: though I thought we all bore that with fortitude. Miss Mills was conversational for a few minutes, and then, laying down her pen upon Affection's Dirge, got up, and left the room.

I began to think I would put it off till to-morrow.

'I hope your poor horse was not tired, when he got home at night,' said Dora, lifting up her beautiful eyes. 'It was a long way for him.'

I began to think I would do it to-day.

'It was a long way for *him*,' said I, 'for he had nothing to uphold him on the journey.'

'Wasn't he fed, poor thing?' asked Dora.

I began to think I would put it off till to-morrow.

'Ye-es,' I said, 'he was well taken care of. I mean he

had not the unutterable happiness that I had in being so near you.'

Dora bent her head over her drawing, and said, after a little while – I had sat, in the interval, in a burning fever, and with my legs in a very rigid state –

'You didn't seem to be sensible of that happiness yourself, at one time of the day.'

I saw now that I was in for it, and it must be done on the spot.

'You didn't care for that happiness in the least,' said Dora, slightly raising her eyebrows, and shaking her head, 'when you were sitting by Miss Kitt.'

Kitt, I should observe, was the name of the creature in pink, with the little eyes.

'Though certainly I don't know why you should,' said Dora, 'or why you should call it a happiness at all. But of course you don't mean what you say. And I am sure no one doubts your being at liberty to do whatever you like. Jip, you naughty boy, come here!'

I don't know how I did it. I did it in a moment. I intercepted Jip. I had Dora in my arms. I was full of eloquence. I never stopped for a word. I told her how I loved her. I told her I should die without her. I told her that I idolised and worshipped her. Jip barked madly all the time.

When Dora hung her head and cried, and trembled, my eloquence increased so much the more. If she would like me to die for her, she had but to say the word, and I was ready. Life without Dora's love was not a thing to have on any terms. I couldn't bear it, and I wouldn't. I had loved her every minute, day and night, since I first saw her. I loved her at that minute to distraction. I should always love her, every minute, to distraction. Lovers had loved before, and lovers would love again; but no lover had ever loved, might, could, would, or should ever love, as I loved Dora. The more I raved, the more Jip barked. Each of us, in his own way, got more mad every moment.

Well, well! Dora and I were sitting on the sofa by and by, quiet enough, and Jip was lying in her lap, winking peacefully at me. It was off my mind. I was in a state of perfect rapture. Dora and I were engaged *(Chapter 33)*.

What an idle time it was! What an unsubstantial, happy, foolish time it was!

When I measured Dora's finger for a ring that was to be made of Forget-me-nots, and when the jeweller, to whom I took the measure, found me out, and laughed over his order book, and charged me anything he liked for the pretty little toy, with its blue stones – so associated in my remembrance with Dora's hand, that yesterday, when I saw such another, by chance, on the finger of my own daughter, there was a momentary stirring in my heart, like pain!

When I walked about, exalted with my secret, and full of my own interest, and felt the dignity of loving Dora, and of being beloved, so much, that if I had walked the air, I could not have been more above the people not so situated, who were creeping on the earth!

When we had those meetings in the garden of the square, and sat within the dingy summer-house, so happy, that I love the London sparrows to this hour, for nothing else, and see the plumage of the tropics in their smoky feathers!

When we had our first great quarrel (within a week of our betrothal), and when Dora sent me back the ring, enclosed in a despairing cocked-hat note, wherein she used the terrible expression that 'our love had begun in folly, and ended in madness!' which dreadful words occasioned me to tear my hair, and cry that all was over!

When, under cover of the night, I flew to Miss Mills, whom I saw by stealth in a back-kitchen where there was a mangle, and implored Miss Mills to interpose between us and avert insanity. When Miss Mills undertook the office and returned with Dora, exhorting us, from the pulpit of her own bitter youth, to mutual concession, and the avoidance of the desert of Sahara!

When we cried, and made it up, and were so blest again, that the back-kitchen, mangle and all, changed to Love's own temple, where we arranged a plan of correspondence through Miss Mills, always to comprehend at least one letter on each side every day!

What an idle time! What an unsubstantial, happy, foolish time! Of all the times of mine that Time has in his grip, there is none that in one retrospect I can smile at half so much, and think of half so tenderly *(Chapter 33)*.

How miserable I was, when I lay down. How I thought and thought about my being poor, in Mr. Spenlow's eyes; about my not being what I thought I was, when I proposed to Dora; about the chivalrous necessity of telling Dora what my worldly condition was, and releasing her from her engagement if she thought fit; about how I should contrive to live, during the long term of my articles, when I was earning nothing; about doing something to assist my aunt, and seeing no way of doing anything; about coming down to have no money in my pocket, and to wear a shabby coat, and to be able to carry Dora no little presents, and to ride no gallant greys, and to show myself in no agreeable light! Sordid and selfish as I knew it was, and as I tortured myself by knowing that it was, to let my mind run on my own distress so much, I was so devoted to Dora that I could not help it. I knew that it was base in me not to think more of my aunt, and less of myself; but, so far, selfishness was inseparable from Dora, and I could not put Dora on one side for any mortal creature. How exceedingly miserable I was, that night.

As to sleep, I had dreams of poverty in all sorts of shapes, but I seemed to dream without the previous ceremony of going to sleep. Now I was ragged, wanting to sell Dora matches, six bundles for a halfpenny; now I was at the office in a night-gown and boots, remonstrated with by Mr. Spenlow on appearing before the clients in that airy attire; now I was hungrily picking up the crumbs that fell from old Tiffey's daily biscuit, regularly eaten when St. Paul's struck one; now I was hopelessly endeavouring to get a licence to marry Dora, having nothing but one of Uriah Heep's gloves to offer in exchange, which the whole Commons rejected; and still, more or less conscious of my own room, I was always tossing about like a distressed ship in a sea of bed-clothes *(Chapter 35)*.

'And how do you think we are looking, Master Copperfield, – I should say, Mister?' fawned Uriah. 'Don't you find Mr. Wickfield blooming, sir? Years don't tell much in our firm, Master Copperfield, except in raising up the umble, namely, mother and self – and in developing,' he added, as an after-thought, 'the beautiful, namely, Miss Agnes.'

He jerked himself about, after this compliment, in such an intolerable manner, that my aunt, who had sat looking straight at him, lost all patience.

'Deuce take the man!' said my aunt, sternly, 'what's he about? Don't be galvanic, sir!'

'I ask your pardon, Miss Trotwood,' returned Uriah; 'I'm aware you're nervous.'

'Go along with you, sir!' said my aunt, anything but appeased. 'Don't presume to say so! I am nothing of the sort. If you're an eel, sir, conduct yourself like one. If you're a man, control your limbs, sir! Good God!' said my aunt, with great indignation, 'I am not going to be serpentined and corkscrewed out of my senses!' *(Chapter 35)*.

'My dear Mr. Copperfield,' said Mrs. Micawber, 'of your friendly interest in all our affairs, I am well assured. My family may consider it banishment, if they please; but I am a wife and mother, and I never will desert Mr. Micawber.'

Traddles, appealed to, by Mrs. Micawber's eye, feelingly acquiesced.

'That,' said Mrs. Micawber, 'that, at least, is my view, my dear Mr. Copperfield and Mr. Traddles, of the obligation which I took upon myself when I repeated the irrevocable words, "I, Emma, take thee, Wilkins." I read the service over with a flat-candle on the previous night, and the conclusion I derived from it was, that I never could desert Mr. Micawber. And,' said Mrs. Micawber, 'though it is possible I may be mistaken in my view of the ceremony, I never will!' *(Chapter 36)*.

'My dear Copperfield,' said Mr. Micawber, rising with one of his thumbs in each of his waistcoat-pockets, 'the companion of my youth: if I may be allowed the expression – and my esteemed friend Traddles: if I may be permitted to call him so – will allow me, on the part of Mrs. Micawber, myself, and our offspring, to thank them in the warmest and most uncompromising terms for their good wishes. It may be expected that on the eve of a migration which will consign us to a perfectly new existence,' Mr. Micawber spoke as if they were going five hundred thousand miles, 'I should offer a few valedictory remarks to two such friends as I see before me. But all that I have to say in this way I have said. Whatever station in society I may attain, through the medium of the learned profession of which I am about to become an unworthy member, I shall endeavour not to disgrace, and Mrs. Micawber will be safe to adorn. Under the temporary pressure of pecuniary liabilities, contracted with a view to their immediate liquidation, but remaining unliquidated through a combination of circumstances, I have been under the necessity of assuming a garb from which my natural instincts recoil – I allude to spectacles – and possessing myself of a cognomen, to which I can establish no legitimate pretensions. All I have to say on that score is, that the cloud has passed from the dreary scene, and the God of Day is once more high upon the mountain tops. On Monday next, on the arrival of the four o'clock afternoon coach at Canterbury, my foot will be on my native heath – my name, Micawber!' *(Chapter 36)*.

'Dora, my own life, I am your ruined David!'

'I declare I'll make Jip bite you!' said Dora, shaking her curls, 'if you are so ridiculous.'

But I looked so serious, that Dora left off shaking her curls, and laid her trembling little hand upon my shoulder, and first looked scared and anxious, then began to cry. That was dreadful. I fell upon my knees before the sofa, caressing her, and imploring her not to rend my heart; but, for some time, poor little Dora did nothing but exclaim Oh dear! Oh dear! And oh, she was so frightened! And where was Julia Mills? And oh, take her to Julia Mills, and go away, please! until I was almost beside myself.

At last, after an agony of supplication and protestation, I got Dora to look at me, with a horrified expression of face, which I gradually soothed until it was only loving, and her soft, pretty cheek was lying against mine. Then I told her, with my arms clasped round her, how I loved her, so dearly, and so dearly; how I felt it right to offer to release her from her engagement, because now I was poor; how I never could bear it, or recover it, if I lost her; how I had no fears of poverty, if she had none, my arm being nerved and my heart inspired by her; how I was already working with a courage such as none but lovers knew; how I had begun to be practical, and look into the future; how a crust well earned was sweeter far than a feast inherited; and much more to the same purpose, which I delivered in a burst of passionate eloquence quite surprising to myself, though I had been thinking about it, day and night, ever since my aunt had astonished me.

'Is your heart mine still, dear Dora?' said I, rapturously, for I knew by her clinging to me that it was.

'Oh, yes!' cried Dora. 'Oh, yes, it's all yours. Oh, don't be dreadful!'

I dreadful! To Dora!

'Don't talk about being poor, and working hard!' said Dora, nestling closer to me. 'Oh, don't, don't!'

'My dearest love said I, 'the crust well earned – '

'Oh, yes; but I don't want to hear any more about crusts!' said Dora. 'And Jip must have a mutton-chop every day at twelve, or he'll die!' *(Chapter 37)*.

How I found time to haunt Putney, I am sure I don't know; but I contrived, by some means or other, to prowl about the neighbourhood pretty often. Miss Mills, for the more exact discharge of the duties of friendship, kept a journal; and she used to meet me sometimes, on the Common, and read it, or (if she had not time to do that) lend it to me. How I treasured up the entries, of which I subjoin a sample:

'Monday. My sweet D. still much depressed. Headache. Called attention to J. as being beautifully sleek. D. fondled J. Associations thus awakened, opened floodgates of sorrow. Rush of grief admitted. (Are tears the dewdrops of the heart? J.M.)

'Tuesday. D. weak and nervous. Beautiful in pallor. (Do we not remark this in moon likewise? J.M.) D., J. M., and J. took airing in carriage. J. looking out of window, and barking violently at dustman, occasioned smile to overspread features of D. (Of such slight links is chain of life composed! J.M.)

'Wednesday. D. comparatively cheerful. Sang to her, as congenial melody, Evening Bells. Effect not soothing, but reverse. D. inexpressibly affected. Found sobbing afterwards, in own room. Quoted verses respecting self and young Gazelle. Ineffectually. Also referred to Patience on Monument. (Qy. Why on monument? J.M.)

'Thursday. D. certainly improved. Better night. Slight tinge of damask revisiting cheek. Resolved to mention name of D.C. Introduced same, cautiously, in course of airing. D. immediately overcome. "Oh, dear, dear Julia! Oh, I have been a naughty and undutiful child!" Soothed and caressed. Drew ideal picture of D. C. on verge of tomb. D. again overcome. "Oh, what shall I do, what shall I do? Oh, take me somewhere!" Much alarmed. Fainting of D. and glass of water from public-house. (Poetical affinity. Chequered sign on doorpost: chequered human life. Alas! J.M.)

'Friday. Day of incident. Man appears in kitchen, with blue bag, "for lady's boots left out to heel." Cook replies, "No such orders." Man argues point. Cook withdraws to inquire, leaving man alone with J. On Cook's return, man still argues point, but ultimately goes. J. missing. D. distracted. Information sent to police. Man to be identified by broad nose, and legs like balustrades of bridge. Search made in every direction. No J. D. weeping bitterly, and inconsolable. Renewed reference to young Gazelle. Appropriate, but unavailing. Towards evening, strange boy calls. Brought into parlour. Broad nose, but no balustrades. Says he wants a pound, and knows a dog. Declines to explain further, though much pressed. Pound being produced by D., takes Cook to little house, where J. alone tied up to leg of table. Joy of D. who dances round J. while he eats his supper. Emboldened by this happy change, mention D.C. upstairs. D. weeps afresh, cries piteously, "Oh, don't, don't, don't! It is so wicked to think of anything but poor papa!" – embraces J. and sobs herself to sleep. (Must not D.C. confine himself to the broad pinions of Time? J.M.)' (Chapter 38).

'I am charmed, Copperfield,' said Mr. Micawber, 'let me assure you, with Miss Wickfield. She is a very superior young lady, of very remarkable attractions, graces, and virtues. Upon my honour,' said Mr. Micawber, indefinitely kissing his hand and bowing with his genteelest air, 'I do Homage to Miss Wickfield! Hem!'

'I am glad of that, at least,' said I.

'If you had not assured us, my dear Copperfield, on the occasion of that agreeable afternoon we had the happiness of passing with you, that D. was your favourite letter,' said Mr. Micawber, 'I should unquestionably have supposed that A. had been so.'

We have all some experience of a feeling, that comes over us occasionally, of what we are saying and doing having been said and done before, in a remote time – of our having been surrounded, dim ages ago, by the same faces, objects, and circumstances – of our knowing perfectly what will be said next, as if we suddenly remembered it! I never had this mysterious impression more strongly in my life, than before he uttered those words (Chapter 39).

'There now!' said Uriah, looking flabby and lead-coloured in the moonlight.... 'But how little you think of the rightful umbleness of a person in my station, Master Copperfield! Father and me was both brought up at a foundation school for boys; and mother, she was likewise brought up at a public, sort of charitable, establishment. They taught us all a deal of umbleness – not much else that I know of, from morning to night. We was to be umble to this person, and umble to that; and to pull off our caps here, and to make bows there; and always to know our place, and abase ourselves before our betters. And we had such a lot of betters! Father got the monitor-medal by being umble. So did I. Father got made a sexton by being umble. He had the character, among the gentle-folks, of being such a well-behaved man, that they were determined to bring him in. "Be umble, Uriah," says father to me, "and you'll get on. It was what was always being dinned into you and me at school; it's what goes down best. Be umble," says father, "and you'll do!" And really it ain't done bad!'

It was the first time it had ever occurred to me, that this detestable cant of false humility might have originated out of the Heep family. I had seen the harvest, but had never thought of the seed.

'When I was quite a young boy,' said Uriah, 'I got to know what umbleness did, and I took to it. I ate umble pie with an appetite. I stopped at the umble point of my learning, and says I, "Hold hard!" When you offered to teach me Latin, I knew better. "People like to be above you," says father, "keep yourself down." I am very umble to the present moment, Master Copperfield, but I've got a little power!' (Chapter 39).

'By-the-bye, my dear Traddles,' said I, 'your experience may suggest something to me. When you became engaged to the young lady whom you have just mentioned, did you make a regular proposal to her family? Was there anything like – what we are going through to-day, for instance?' I added, nervously.

'Why,' replied Traddles, on whose attentive face a thoughtful shade had stolen, 'it was rather a painful transaction, Copperfield, in my case. You see, Sophy being of so much use in the family, none of them could endure the thought of her ever being married. Indeed, they had quite settled among themselves that she never was to be married, and they called her the old maid. Accordingly, when I mentioned it, with the greatest precaution, to Mrs. Crewler – '

'The mamma?' said I.

'The mamma,' said Traddles – 'Reverend Horace Crewler – when I mentioned it with every possible precaution to Mrs. Crewler, the effect upon her was such that she gave a scream and became insensible. I couldn't approach the subject again, for months.'

'You did at last?' said I.

'Well, the Reverend Horace did,' said Traddles. 'He is an excellent man, most exemplary in every way; and he pointed out to her that she ought, as a Christian, to reconcile herself to the sacrifice (especially as it was so uncertain), and to bear no uncharitable feeling towards me. As to myself, Copperfield, I give you my word, I felt a perfect bird of prey towards the family.'

'The sisters took your part, I hope, Traddles?'

'Why, I can't say they did,' he returned. 'When we had comparatively reconciled Mrs. Crewler to it, we had to break it to Sarah. You recollect my mentioning Sarah, as the one that has something the matter with her spine?'

'Perfectly!'

'She clenched both her hands,' said Traddles, looking at me in dismay; 'shut her eyes; turned leadcolour; became perfectly stiff; and took nothing for two days but toast-and-water, administered with a teaspoon' *(Chapter 41)*.

'Sister Lavinia,' said Miss Clarissa, having now relieved her mind, 'you can go on, my dear.'

Miss Lavinia proceeded:

'Mr. Copperfield, my sister Clarissa and I have been very careful indeed in considering this letter; and we have not considered it without finally showing it to our niece, and discussing it with our niece. We have no doubt that you think you like her very much.'

'Think, ma'am,' I rapturously began, 'oh – '

But Miss Clarissa giving me a look (just like a sharp canary), as requesting that I would not interrupt the oracle, I begged pardon.

'Affection,' said Miss Lavinia, glancing at her sister for corroboration, which she gave in the form of a little nod to every clause, 'mature affection, homage, devotion, does not easily express itself. Its voice is low. It is modest and retiring, it lies in ambush, waits and waits. Such is the mature fruit. Sometimes a life glides away, and finds it still ripening in the shade.'

Of course I did not understand then that this was an allusion to her supposed experience of the stricken Pidger; but I saw, from the gravity with which Miss Clarissa nodded her head, that great weight was attached to these words *(Chapter 41)*.

I have been very fortunate in worldly matters; many men have worked much harder, and not succeeded half so well; but I never could have done what I have done, without the habits of punctuality, order, and diligence, without the determination to concentrate myself on one object at a time, no matter how quickly its successor should come upon its heels, which I then formed. Heaven knows I write this, in no spirit of self-laudation. The man who reviews his own life, as I do mine, in going on here, from page to page, had need to have been a good man indeed, if he would be spared the sharp consciousness of many talents neglected, many opportunities wasted, many erratic and perverted feelings constantly at war within his breast, and defeating him. I do not hold one natural gift, I dare say, that I have not abused. My meaning simply is, that whatever I have tried to do in life, I have tried with all my heart to do well; that whatever I have devoted myself to, I have devoted myself to completely; that in great aims and in small, I have always been thoroughly in earnest. I have never believed it possible that any natural or improved ability can claim immunity from the companionship of the steady, plain, hard-working qualities, and hope to gain its end. There is no such thing as such fulfilment on this earth. Some happy talent, and some fortunate opportunity, may form the two sides of the ladder on which some men mount, but the rounds of that ladder must be made of stuff to stand wear and tear; and there is no substitute for thorough-going, ardent, and sincere earnestness. Never to put one hand to anything, on which I could throw my whole self; and never to affect depreciation of my work, whatever it was; I find, now, to have been my golden rules *(Chapter 42)*.

I have come legally to man's estate. I have attained the dignity of twenty-one. But this is a sort of dignity that may be thrust upon one. Let me think what I have achieved.

I have tamed that savage stenographic mystery. I make a respectable income by it. I am in high repute for my accomplishment in all pertaining to the art, and am joined with eleven others in reporting the debates in Parliament for a Morning Newspaper. Night after night, I record predictions that never come to pass, professions that are never fulfilled, explanations that are only meant to mystify. I wallow in words. Britannia, that unfortunate female, is always before me, like a trussed fowl: skewered through and through with office-pens, and bound hand and foot with red tape. I am sufficiently behind the scenes to know the worth of political life. I am quite an infidel about it, and shall never be converted *(Chapter 43)*.

I have come out in another way. I have taken with fear and trembling to authorship. I wrote a little something, in secret, and sent it to a magazine, and it was published in the magazine. Since then, I have taken heart to write a good many trifling pieces. Now, I am regularly paid for them. Altogether, I am well off; when I tell my income on the fingers of my left hand, I pass the third finger and take in the fourth to the middle joint *(Chapter 43)*.

I doubt whether two young birds could have known less about keeping house, than I and my pretty Dora did. We had a servant, of course. She kept house for us. I have still a latent belief that she must have been Mrs. Crupp's daughter in disguise, we had such an awful time of it with Mary Anne.

Her name was Paragon. Her nature was represented to us, when we engaged her, as being feebly expressed in her name. She had a written character, as large as a proclamation; and, according to this document, could do everything of a domestic nature that ever I heard of, and a great many things that I never did hear of. She was a woman in the prime of life; of a severe countenance; and subject (particularly in the arms) to a sort of perpetual measles or fiery rash. She had a cousin in the Life Guards, with such long legs that he looked like the afternoon shadow of somebody else. His shell-jacket was as much too little for him as he was too big for the premises. He made the cottage smaller than it need have been, by being so very much out of proportion to it. Besides which, the walls were not thick, and whenever he passed the evening at our house, we always knew of it by hearing one continual growl in the kitchen.

Our treasure was warranted sober and honest. I am therefore willing to believe that she was in a fit when we found her under the boiler; and that the deficient tea-spoons were attributable to the dustman *(Chapter 44)*.

'Now, my own Dora,' said I, 'you are very childish, and are talking nonsense. You must remember, I am sure, that I was obliged to go out yesterday when dinner was half over; and that, the day before, I was made quite unwell by being obliged to eat underdone veal in a hurry; to-day, I don't dine at all – and I am afraid to say how long we waited for breakfast – and *then* the water didn't boil. I don't mean to reproach you, my dear, but this is not comfortable.'

'Oh, you cruel, cruel boy, to say I am a disagreeable wife!' cried Dora.

'Now, my dear Dora, you must know that I never said that!'

'You said I wasn't comfortable!' said Dora.

'I said the housekeeping was not comfortable.'

'It's exactly the same thing!' cried Dora. And she evidently thought so, for she wept most grievously.

I took another turn across the room, full of love for my pretty wife, and distracted by self-accusatory inclinations to knock my head against the door. I sat down again, and said:

'I am not blaming you, Dora. We have both a great deal to learn. I am only trying to show you, my dear, that you must – you really must' (I was resolved not to give this up) 'accustom yourself to look after Mary Anne. Likewise to act a little for yourself, and me.'

'I wonder, I do, at your making such ungrateful speeches,' sobbed Dora. 'When you know that the other day, when you said you would like a little bit of fish, I went out myself, miles and miles, and ordered it to surprise you.'

'And it was very kind of you, my own darling,' said I. 'I felt it so much that I wouldn't on any account have even mentioned that you bought a salmon – which was too much for two. Or that it cost one pound six – which was more than we can afford.'

'You enjoyed it very much,' sobbed Dora. 'And you said I was a mouse.'

'And I'll say so again,' I returned, 'a thousand times!'

But I had wounded Dora's soft little heart, and she was not to be comforted *(Chapter 44)*.

The next domestic trial we went through, was the Ordeal of Servants. Mary Anne's cousin deserted into our coal-hole, and was brought out, to our great amazement, by a piquet of his companions in arms, who took him away handcuffed in a procession that covered our front-garden with ignominy. This nerved me to get rid of Mary Anne, who went so mildly, on receipt of wages, that I was surprised, until I found out about the tea-spoons, and also about the little sums she had borrowed in my name of the tradespeople without

authority. After an interval of Mrs. Kidgerbury – the oldest inhabitant of Kentish Town, I believe, who went out charing, but was too feeble to execute her conceptions of that art – we found another treasure, who was one of the most amiable of women, but who generally made a point of falling either up or down the kitchen-stairs with the tray, and almost plunged into the parlour, as into a bath, with the tea-things. The ravages committed by this unfortunate rendering her dismissal necessary, she was succeeded (with intervals of Mrs. Kidgerbury) by a long line of Incapables; terminating in a young person of genteel appearance, who went to Greenwich Fair in Dora's bonnet. After whom I remember nothing but an average equality of failure *(Chapter 44)*.

As to the washerwoman pawning the clothes, and coming in a state of penitent intoxication to apologise, I suppose that might have happened several times to anybody. Also the chimney on fire, the parish engine, and perjury on the part of the beadle. But I apprehend that we were personally unfortunate in engaging a servant with a taste for cordials, who swelled our running account for porter at the public-house by such inexplicable items as 'quartern rum shrub (Mrs. C.);' 'Half-quartern gin and cloves (Mrs. C.);' 'Glass rum and peppermint (Mrs. C.)' – the parenthesis always referring to Dora, who was supposed, it appeared on explanation, to have imbibed the whole of these refreshments *(Chapter 44)*.

'Will you call me a name I want you to call me?' inquired Dora, without moving.

'What is it?' I asked with a smile.

'It's a stupid name,' she said, shaking her curls for a moment. 'Child-wife.'

I laughingly asked my child-wife, what her fancy was in desiring to be so called. She answered without moving, otherwise than as the arm I twined about her may have brought her blue eyes nearer to me –

'I don't mean, you silly fellow, that you should use the name instead of Dora. I only mean that you should think of me that way. When you are going to be angry with me, say to yourself, "it's only my child-wife!" When I am very disappointing, say, "I knew, a long time ago, that she would make but a child-wife!" When you miss what I should like to be, and I think can never be, say, "still my foolish child-wife loves me!" For indeed I do.'

I had not been serious with her; having no idea, until now, that she was serious herself. But her affectionate nature was so happy in what I now said to her with my whole heart, that her face became a laughing one before her glittering eyes were dry. She was soon my child-wife indeed; sitting down on the floor outside the Chinese house, ringing all the little bells one after another, to punish Jip for his recent bad behaviour; while Jip lay blinking in the doorway with his head out, even too lazy to be teased.

This appeal of Dora's made a strong impression on me. I look back on the time I write of; I invoke the innocent figure that I dearly loved, to come out from the mists and shadows of the past, and turn its gentle head towards me once again; and I can still declare that this one little speech was constantly in my memory. I may not have used it to the best account; I was young and inexperienced; but I never turned a deaf ear to its artless pleading *(Chapter 44)*.

I had a great deal of work to do, and had many anxieties, but the same considerations made me keep them to myself. I am far from sure, now, that it was right to do this, but I did it for my child-wife's sake. I search my breast, and I commit its secrets, if I know them, without any reservation to this paper. The old unhappy loss or want of something had, I am conscious, some place in my heart; but not to the embitterment of my life. When I walked alone in the fine weather, and thought of the summer days when all the air had been filled with my boyish enchantment, I did miss something of the realisation of my dreams; but I thought it was a softened glory of the past, which nothing could have thrown upon the present time. I did feel, sometimes, for a little while, that I could have wished my wife had been my counsellor; had had more character and purpose, to sustain me, and improve me by; had been endowed with power to fill up the void which somewhere seemed to be about me; but I felt as if this were an unearthly consummation of my happiness, that never had been meant to be, and never could have been *(Chapter 44)*.

'A specimen of the thanks one gets,' cried Mrs. Markleham, in tears, 'for taking care of one's family! I wish I was a Turk!'

('I wish you were, with all my heart – and in your native country!' said my aunt.)

'It was at that time that mamma was most solicitous about my cousin Maldon. I had liked him:' she spoke softly, but without any hesitation: 'very much. We had been little lovers once. If circumstances had not happened otherwise, I might have come to persuade myself that I really loved him, and might have married him, and been most wretched. There can be no disparity in marriage like unsuitability of mind and purpose.'

I pondered on those words, even while I was studiously attending to what followed, as if they had some particular interest, or some strange application that I could not divine. 'There can be no disparity in marriage like unsuitability of mind and purpose' – 'no disparity in marriage like unsuitability of mind and purpose' *(Chapter 45: Annie Strong, Miss Trotwood)*.

'That's a settler for our military friend, at any rate,' said my aunt, on the way home. 'I should sleep the better for that, if there was nothing else to be glad of!'

'She was quite overcome, I am afraid,' said Mr. Dick, with great commiseration.

'What? Did you ever see a crocodile overcome?' inquired my aunt.

'I don't think I ever saw a crocodile,' returned Mr. Dick, mildly.

'There never would have been anything the matter, if it hadn't been for that old Animal,' said my aunt, with strong emphasis. 'It's very much to be wished that some mothers would leave their daughters alone after marriage, and not be so violently affectionate. They seem to think the only return that can be made them for bringing an unfortunate young woman into the world – God bless my soul, as if she asked to be brought, or wanted to come! – is full liberty to worry her out of it again. What are you thinking of, Trot?'

I was thinking of all that had been said. My mind was still running on some of the expressions used. 'There can be no disparity, in marriage like unsuitability of mind and purpose.' 'The first mistaken impulse of an undisciplined heart.' 'My love was founded on a rock.' But we were at home; and the trodden leaves were lying underfoot, and the autumn wind was blowing *(Chapter 45)*.

'I'll put my hand in no man's hand,' said Mr. Micawber, gasping, puffing, and sobbing, to that degree that he was like a man fighting with cold water, 'until I have – blown to fragments – the – a – detestable – serpent – HEEP! I'll partake of no one's hospitality, until I have – a – moved Mount Vesuvius – to eruption – on a – the abandoned rascal – HEEP! Refreshment – a – underneath this roof – particularly punch – would – a – choke me – unless – I had – previously – choked the eyes – out of the head – a – of – interminable cheat, and liar – HEEP! I – a – I'll know nobody – and – a – say nothing – and – a – live nowhere – until I have crushed – to – a – undiscoverable atoms – the – transcendent and immortal hypocrite and perjurer – HEEP!' *(Chapter 49)*.

'No, Copperfield! – No communication – a until – Miss Wickfield – a – redress from wrongs inflicted by consummate scoundrel – HEEP!' (I am quite convinced he could not have uttered three words, but for the amazing energy with which this word inspired him when he felt it coming.) 'Inviolable secret – a – from the whole world – a – no exceptions – this day week – a – at breakfast time – a – everybody present – including aunt – a – and extremely friendly gentleman – to be at the hotel at Canterbury – a – where – Mrs. Micawber and myself – Auld Lang Syne in chorus – and – a – will expose intolerable ruffian – HEEP! No more to say – a – or listen to persuasion – go immediately – not capable – a – bear society – upon the track of devoted and doomed traitor – HEEP!' *(Chapter 49: Micawber)*.

'Dear me!' said Mr. Omer, 'when a man is drawing on to a time of life, where the two ends of life meet; when he finds himself, however hearty he is, being wheeled about for the second time, in a speeches of go-cart; he should be over-rejoiced to do a kindness if he can. He wants plenty. And I don't speak of myself, particular,' said Mr. Omer, 'because, sir, the way I look at it is, that we are all drawing on to the bottom of the hill, whatever age we are, on account of time never standing still for a single moment. So let us always do a kindness, and be over-rejoiced. To be sure!' *(Chapter 51)*.

'And that eldest young gentleman, now,' said my aunt, musing. 'What has *he* been brought up to?'

'It was my hope when I came here,' said Mr. Micawber, 'to have got Wilkins into the Church: or perhaps I shall express my meaning more strictly, if I say the Choir. But there was no vacancy for a tenor in the venerable Pile for which this city is so justly eminent; and he has – in short, he has contracted a habit of singing in public-houses, rather than in sacred edifices.'

'But he means well,' said Mrs. Micawber, tenderly *(Chapter 52)*.

I think now, how odd it was, but how wonderfully like Mr. Micawber, that, when he went from London to Canterbury, he should have talked as if he were going to the farthest limits of the earth; and, when he went from England to Australia, as if he were going for a little trip across the channel.

'On the voyage I shall endeavour,' said Mr. Micawber, 'occasionally to spin them a yarn; and the melody of my son Wilkins will, I trust, be acceptable at the galley-fire. When Mrs. Micawber has her sea-legs on – an expression in which I hope there is no conventional impropriety – she will give them, I dare say, Little Tafflin. Porpoises and dolphins, I believe, will be frequently observed athwart our Bows, and, either on the Starboard or the Larboard Quarter, objects of interest will be continually descried. In short,' said Mr. Micawber, with the old genteel air, 'the probability is, all will be found so exciting, alow and aloft, that when the look-out, stationed in the main-top, cries Land-oh! we shall be very considerably astonished!'

With that he flourished off the contents of his little tin pot, as if he had made the voyage, and had passed a first-class examination before the highest naval authorities *(Chapter 57)*.

The time was come. I embraced him, took my weeping nurse upon my arm, and hurried away. On deck, I took leave of poor Mrs. Micawber. She was looking distractedly about for her family, even then; and her last words to me were, that she never would desert Mr. Micawber.

We went over the side into our boat, and lay at a little distance to see the ship wafted on her course. It was then calm, radiant sunset. She lay between us, and the red light; and every taper line and spar was visible against the glow. A sight at once so beautiful, so mournful, and so hopeful, as the glorious ship, lying, still, on the flushed water, with all the life on board her crowded at the bulwarks, and there clustering, for a moment, bare-headed and silent, I never saw.

Silent, only for a moment. As the sails rose to the wind, and the ship began to move, there broke from all the boats three resounding cheers, which those on board took up, and echoed back, and which were echoed and re-echoed. My heart burst out when I heard the sound, and beheld the waving of the hats and handkerchiefs – and then I saw her!

Then I saw her, at her uncle's side, and trembling on his shoulder. He pointed to us with an eager hand; and she saw us, and waved her last good-bye to me. Aye, Emily, beautiful and drooping, cling to him with the utmost trust of thy bruised heart; for he has clung to thee, with all the might of his great love!

Surrounded by the rosy light, and standing high upon the deck, apart together, she clinging to him, and he holding her, they solemnly passed away. The night had fallen on the Kentish hills when we were rowed ashore – and fallen darkly upon me *(Chapter 57)*.

I was in Switzerland. I had come out of Italy, over one of the great passes of the Alps, and had since wandered with a guide among the by-ways of the mountains. If those awful solitudes had spoken to my heart, I did not know it. I had found sublimity and wonder in the dread heights and precipices, in the roaring torrents, and the wastes of ice and snow; but as yet, they had taught me nothing else.

I came, one evening before sunset, down into a valley, where I was to rest. In the course of my descent to it, by the winding track along the mountain-side, from which I saw it shining far below, I think some long-unwonted sense of beauty and tranquillity, some softening influence awakened by its peace, moved faintly in my breast. I remember pausing once, with a kind of sorrow that was not all oppressive, not quite despairing. I remember almost hoping that some better change was possible within me.

I came into the valley, as the evening sun was shining on the remote heights of snow, that closed it in, like eternal clouds. The bases of the mountains forming the gorge in which the little village lay, were richly green; and high above this gentler vegetation, grew forests of dark fir, cleaving the wintry snow-drift, wedge-like, and stemming the avalanche. Above these, were range upon range of craggy steeps, grey rock, bright ice, and smooth verdure-specks of pasture, all gradually blending with the crowning snow. Dotted here and there on the mountain's side, each tiny dot a home, were lonely wooden cottages, so dwarfed by the towering heights that they appeared too small for toys. So did even the clustered village in the valley, with its wooden bridge across the stream, where the stream tumbled over broken rocks, and roared away among the trees. In the quiet air, there was a sound of distant singing – shepherd voices; but, as one bright evening cloud floated midway along the mountain's side, I could almost have believed it came from there, and was not earthly music. All at once, in this serenity, great Nature spoke to me; and soothed me to lay down, my weary head upon the grass, and weep as I had not wept yet, since Dora died! *(Chapter 58)*.

'Now, Twenty Seven,' said Mr. Creakle, entering on a clear stage with *his* man, 'is there anything that any one can do for you? If so, mention it.'

'I would umbly ask, sir,' returned Uriah, with a jerk of his malevolent head, 'for leave to write again to mother.'

'It shall certainly be granted,' said Mr. Creakle.

'Thank you, sir! I am anxious about mother. I am afraid she ain't safe.'

Somebody incautiously asked, what from? But there was a scandalised whisper of 'Hush!'

'Immortally safe, sir,' returned Uriah, writhing in the direction of the voice. 'I should wish mother to be got into my state. I never should have been got into my present state if I hadn't come here. I wish my mother had come here. It would be better for everybody, if they got took up, and was brought here.'

This sentiment gave unbounded satisfaction – greater satisfaction, I think, than anything that had passed yet.

'Before I come here,' said Uriah, stealing a look at

us, as if he would have blighted the outer world to which we belonged, if he could, 'I was given to follies; but now I am sensible of my follies. There's a deal of sin outside. There's a deal of sin in mother. There's nothing but sin everywhere – except here.'

'You are quite changed?' said Mr. Creakle.

'Oh, dear, yes, sir!' cried this hopeful penitent.

'You wouldn't relapse, if you were going out?' asked somebody else.

'Oh de-ar no, sir!'

'Well,' said Mr. Creakle, 'this is very gratifying. You have addressed Mr. Copperfield, Twenty Seven. Do you wish to say anything further to him?'

'You knew me a long time before I came here and was changed, Mr. Copperfield,' said Uriah, looking at me; and a more villainous look I never saw, even on his visage. 'You knew me when, in spite of my follies, I was umble among them that was proud, and meek among them that was violent – you was violent to me yourself, Mr. Copperfield. Once, you struck me a blow in the face, you know.'

General commiseration. Several indignant glances directed at me.

'But I forgive you, Mr. Copperfield,' said Uriah, making his forgiving nature the subject of a most impious and awful parallel, which I shall not record. 'I forgive everybody. It would ill become me to bear malice. I freely forgive you, and I hope you'll curb your passions in future. I hope Mr. W. will repent, and Miss W., and all of that sinful lot. You've been visited with affliction, and I hope it may do you good; but you'd better have come here. Mr. W. had better have come here, and Miss W. too. The best wish I could give you, Mr. Copperfield, and give all of you gentlemen, is, that you could be took up and brought here. When I think of my past follies and my present state, I am sure it would be best for you. I pity all who ain't brought here!'

He sneaked back into his cell, amidst a chorus of approbation; and both Traddles and I experienced a great relief when he was locked in *(Chapter 61)*.

REPRINTED PIECES

In the Autumn-time of the year, when the great metropolis is so much hotter, so much noisier, so much more dusty or so much more water-carted, so much more crowded, so much more disturbing and distracting in all respects, than it usually is, a quiet sea-beach becomes indeed a blessed spot. Half awake and half asleep, this idle morning in our sunny window on the edge of a chalk-cliff in the old-fashioned watering-place to which we are a faithful resorter, we feel a lazy inclination to sketch its picture.

The place seems to respond. Sky, sea, beach, and village, lie as still before us as if they were sitting for the picture. It is dead low-water. A ripple plays among the ripening corn upon the cliff, as if it were faintly trying from recollection to imitate the sea; and the world of butterflies hovering over the crop of radish-seed are as restless in their little way as the gulls are in their larger manner when the wind blows. But the ocean lies winking in the sunlight like a drowsy lion –

its glassy waters scarcely curve upon the shore – the fishing-boats in the tiny harbour are all stranded in the mud – our two colliers (our watering-place has a maritime trade employing that amount of shipping) have not an inch of water within a quarter of a mile of them, and turn, exhausted, on their sides, like faint fish of an antediluvian species. Rusty cables and chains, ropes and rings, undermost parts of posts and piles and confused timber-defences against the waves, lie strewn about, in a brown litter of tangled sea-weed and fallen cliff which looks as if a family of giants had been making tea here for ages, and had observed an untidy custom of throwing their tea-leaves on the shore ('Our English Watering-Place').

Our French watering-place, when it is once got into, is a very enjoyable place. It has a varied and beautiful country around it, and many characteristic and agreeable things within it. To be sure, it might have fewer bad smells and less decaying refuse, and it might be better drained, and much cleaner in many parts, and therefore infinitely more healthy. Still, it is a bright, airy, pleasant, cheerful town; and if you were to walk down either of its three well-paved main streets, towards five o'clock in the afternoon, when delicate odours of cookery fill the air, and its hotel windows (it is full of hotels) give glimpses of long tables set out for dinner, and made to look sumptuous by the aid of napkins folded fan-wise, you would rightly judge it to be an uncommonly good town to eat and drink in.

We have an old walled town, rich in cool public wells of water, on the top of a hill within and above the present business-town; and if it were some hundreds of miles further from England, instead of being, on a clear day, within sight of the grass growing in the crevices of the chalk-cliffs of Dover, you would long ago have been bored to death about that town. It is more picturesque and quaint than half the innocent places which tourists, following their leader like sheep, have made impostors of. To say nothing of its houses with grave courtyards, its queer by-corners, and its many-windowed streets white and quiet in the sunlight, there is an ancient belfry in it that would have been in all the Annuals and Albums, going and gone, these hundred years, if it had but been more expensive to get at ('Our French Watering-Place').

The voice of Nature, however, cries aloud in behalf of Augustus George, my infant son. It is for him that I wish to utter a few plaintive household words. I am not at all angry; I am mild – but miserable.

I wish to know why, when my child, Augustus George, was expected in our circle, a provision of pins was made, as if the little stranger were a criminal who was to be put to the torture immediately on his arrival, instead of a holy babe? I wish to know why haste was made to stick those pins all over his innocent form, in every direction? I wish to be informed why light and air are excluded from Augustus George, like poisons? Why, I ask, is my unoffending infant so hedged into a basket-bedstead, with dimity and calico, with miniature sheets and blankets, that I can only hear him snuffle (and no wonder!) deep down under the pink hood of a little bathing-machine, and can never peruse even so much of his lineaments as his nose.

Was I expected to be the father of a French Roll, that the brushes of All Nations were laid in, to rasp Augustus George? Am I to be told that his sensitive skin was ever intended by Nature to have rashes brought out upon it by the premature and incessant use of those formidable little instruments?

Is my son a Nutmeg, that he is to be grated on the stiff edges of sharp frills? Am I the parent of a Muslin boy, that his yielding surface is to be crimped and small plaited? Or is my child composed of Paper or of Linen, that impressions of the finer getting-up art, practised by the laundress, are to be printed off, all over his soft arms and legs, as I constantly observe them? The starch enters his soul; who can wonder that he cries?

Was Augustus George intended to have limbs, or to be born a Torso? I presume that limbs were the intention, as they are the usual practice. Then, why are my poor child's limbs fettered and tied up? Am I to be told that there is any analogy between August George Meek and Jack Sheppard? ('Births. Mrs. Meek, of a Son' – Mr. Meek).

Sitting, on a bright September morning, among my books and papers at my open window on the cliff over-hanging the sea-beach, I have the sky and ocean framed before me like a beautiful picture. A beautiful picture, but with such movement in it, such changes of light upon the sails of ships and wake of steamboats, such dazzling gleams of silver far out at sea, such fresh touches on the crisp wave-tops as they break and roll towards me – a picture with such music in the billowy rush upon the shingle, the blowing of morning wind through the corn-sheaves where the farmers' waggons are busy, the singing of the larks, and the distant voices of children at play – such charms of sight and sound as all the Galleries on earth can but poorly suggest.

So dreamy is the murmur of the sea below my window, that I may have been here, for anything I know, one hundred years. Not that I have grown old, for, daily on the neighbouring downs and grassy hill-sides, I find that I can still in reason walk any distance, jump over anything, and climb up anywhere; but, that the sound of the ocean seems to have become so customary to my musings, and other realities seem to have gone aboard ship and floated away over the horizon, that, for aught I will undertake to the contrary, I am the enchanted son of the King my father, shut up in a tower on the sea-shore, for protection against the old she-goblin who insisted on being my godmother, and who foresaw at the font – wonderful creature! – that I should get into a scrape before I was twenty-one ('Out of Town').

Cooke's Circus (Mr. Cooke is my friend, and always leaves a good name behind him) gives us only a night in passing through. Nor does the travelling menagerie think us worth a longer visit. It gave us a look-in the other day, bringing with it the residentiary van with the stained glass windows, which Her Majesty kept ready-made at Windsor Castle, until she found a suitable opportunity of submitting it for the proprietor's acceptance. I brought away five wonderments from this exhibition. I have wondered ever since,

Whether the beasts ever do get used to those small places of confinement; Whether the monkeys have that very horrible flavour in their free state; Whether wild animals have a natural ear for time and tune, and therefore every four-footed creature began to howl in despair when the band began to play; What the giraffe does with his neck when his cart is shut up; and, Whether the elephant feels ashamed of himself when he is brought out of his den to stand on his head in the presence of the whole Collection ('Out of Town').

We went to look at it, only this last Midsummer, and found that the Railway had cut it up root and branch. A great trunk-line had swallowed the playground, sliced away the schoolroom, and pared off the corner of the house; which, thus curtailed of its proportions, presented itself, in a green stage of stucco, profilewise towards the road, like a forlorn flat-iron without a handle, standing on end ('Our School').

Our School was rather famous for mysterious pupils. There was another – a heavy young man, with a large double-cased silver watch, and a fat knife the handle of which was a perfect tool-box – who unaccountably appeared one day at a special desk of his own, erected close to that of the Chief, with whom he held familiar converse. He lived in the parlour, and went out for his walks, and never took the least notice of us – even of us, the first boy – unless to give us a deprecatory kick, or grimly to take our hat off and throw it away, when he encountered us out of doors, which unpleasant ceremony he always performed as he passed – not even condescending to stop for the purpose. Some of us believed that the classical attainments of this phenomenon were terrific, but that his penmanship and arithmetic were defective, and he had come there to mend them; others, that he was going to set up a school, and had paid the Chief 'twenty-five pound down,' for leave to see Our School at work. The gloomier spirits even said that he was going to buy us; against which contingency, conspiracies were set on foot for a general defection and running away. However, he never did that. After staying for a quarter, during which period, though closely observed, he was never seen to do anything but make pens out of quills, write small hand in a secret portfolio, and punch the point of the sharpest blade in his knife into his desk all over it, he too disappeared, and his place knew him no more.

There was another boy, a fair, meek boy, with a delicate complexion and rich curling hair, who, we found out, or thought we found out (we have no idea now, and probably had none then, on what grounds, but it was confidentially revealed from mouth to mouth), was the son of a Viscount who had deserted his lovely mother. It was understood that if he had his rights, he would be worth twenty thousand a year. And that if his mother ever met his father, she would shoot him with a silver pistol, which she carried, always loaded to the muzzle, for that purpose. He was a very suggestive topic. So was a young Mulatto, who was always believed (though very amiable) to have a dagger about him somewhere. But, we think they were both outshone, upon the whole, by another boy who claimed to have been born on the twenty-ninth of February, and to have only one birthday in five years. We suspect this to have been a fiction – but he lived upon it all the time he was at Our School ('Our School').

Our School was remarkable for white mice. Red-polls, linnets, and even canaries, were kept in desks, drawers, hat-boxes, and other strange refuges for birds; but white mice were the favourite stock. The boys trained the mice, much better than the masters trained the boys. We recall one white mouse, who lived in the cover of a Latin dictionary, who ran up ladders, drew Roman chariots, shouldered muskets, turned wheels, and even made a very creditable appearance on the stage as the Dog of Montargis. He might have achieved greater things, but for having the misfortune to mistake his way in a triumphal procession to the Capitol, when he fell into a deep inkstand, and was dyed black and drowned. The mice were the occasion of some most ingenious engineering, in the construction of their houses and instruments of performance. The famous one belonged to a company of proprietors, some of whom have since made Railroads, Engines, and Telegraphs; the chairman has erected mills and bridges in New Zealand ('Our School').

It is unnecessary to say we keep a bore. Everybody does. But, the bore whom we have the pleasure and honour of enumerating among our particular friends, is such a generic bore, and has so many traits (as it appears to us) in common with the great bore family, that we are tempted to make him the subject of the present notes. May he be generally accepted! ('Our Bore').

Our bore has travelled. He could not possibly be a complete bore without having travelled. He rarely speaks of his travels without introducing, sometimes on his own plan of construction, morsels of the language of the country – which he always translates. You cannot name to him any little remote town in France, Italy, Germany, or Switzerland but he knows it well; stayed there a fortnight under peculiar circumstances. And talking of that little place, perhaps you know a statue over an old fountain, up a little court, which is the second – no, the third – stay – yes, the third turning on the right, after you come out of the Post-house, going up the hill towards the market? You *don't* know that statue? Nor that fountain? You surprise him! They are not usually seen by travellers (most extraordinary, he has never yet met with a single traveller who knew them, except one German, the most intelligent man he ever met in his life!) but he thought that YOU would have been the man to find them out. And then he describes them, in a circumstantial lecture half an hour long, generally delivered behind a door which is constantly being opened from the other side; and implores you, if you ever revisit that place, now do go and look at that statue and fountain!

Our bore, in a similar manner, being in Italy, made a discovery of a dreadful picture, which has been the terror of a large portion of the civilised world ever since. We have seen the liveliest men paralysed by it, across a broad dining-table. He was lounging among the mountains, sir, basking in the mellow influences of the climate, when he came to *una piccola chiesa* – a little church – or perhaps it would be more correct to say *una piccolissima cappella* – the smallest chapel you can possibly imagine – and walked in. There was nobody inside but a *cieco* – a blind man – saying his prayers, and a *vecchio padre* – old friar – rattling a money-box. But, above the head of that friar, and immediately to the right of the altar as you enter – to the right of the altar? No. To the left of the altar as you enter – or say near the centre – there hung a painting (subject, Virgin and Child) so divine in its expression, so pure and yet so warm and rich in its tone, so fresh in its touch, at once so glowing in its colour and so statuesque in its repose, that our bore cried out in an ecstasy, 'That's the finest picture in Italy!' And so it is, sir. There is no doubt of it. It is astonishing that that picture is so little known. Even the painter is uncertain. He afterwards took Blumb, of the Royal Academy (it is to be observed that our bore takes none but eminent people to see sights, and that none but eminent people take our bore), and you never saw a man so affected in your life as Blumb was. He cried like a child! And then our bore begins his description in detail – for all this is introductory – and strangles his hearers with the folds of the purple drapery ('Our Bore').

Slaughter-houses, in the large towns of England, are always (with the exception of one or two enterprising towns) most numerous in the most densely crowded places, where there is the least circulation of air. They are often underground, in cellars; they are sometimes in close back yards; sometimes (as in Spitalfields) in the very shops where the meat is sold. Occasionally, under good private management, they are ventilated and clean. For the most part, they are unventilated and dirty; and, to the reeking walls, putrid fat and other offensive animal matter clings with a tenacious hold. The busiest slaughter-houses in London are in the neighbourhood of Smithfield, in Newgate Market, in Whitechapel, in Newport Market, in Leadenhall Market, in Clare Market. All these places are surrounded by houses of a poor description, swarming with inhabitants. Some of them are close to the worst burial-grounds in London. When the slaughter-house is below the ground, it is a common practice to throw the sheep down areas, neck and crop – which is exciting, but not at all cruel. When it is on the level surface, it is often extremely difficult of approach. Then, the beasts have to be worried, and goaded, and pronged, and tail-twisted, for a long time before they can be got in – which is entirely owing to their natural obstinacy. When it is not difficult of approach, but is in a foul condition, what they see and scent makes them still more reluctant to enter – which is their natural obstinacy again. When they do get in at last, after no trouble and suffering to speak of (for, there is nothing in the previous journey into the heart of London, the night's endurance in Smithfield, the struggle out again, among the crowded multitude, the coaches, carts, waggons, omnibuses, gigs, chaises, phaetons, cabs, trucks, dogs, boys, whoopings, roarings, and ten thousand other distractions), they are represented to be in a most unfit state to be killed, according to microscopic examinations made of their fevered blood by one of the most distinguished physiologists in the world, PROFESSOR OWEN – but that's humbug. When they *are* killed, at last, their reeking carcasses are hung in impure air, to become, as the same Professor will explain to you, less nutritious and more unwholesome – but he is only an *un*common counsellor, so don't mind *him*. In half a quarter of a mile's length of Whitechapel, at one time, there shall be six hundred newly slaughtered oxen hanging up, and seven hundred sheep – but, the more the merrier – proof of prosperity. Hard by Snow Hill and Warwick Lane, you shall see the little children, inured to sights of brutality from their birth, trotting along the alleys, mingled with troops of horribly busy pigs, up to their ankles in blood – but it makes the young rascals hardy. Into the imperfect sewers of this overgrown city, you shall have the immense mass of corruption, engendered by these practices, lazily thrown out of sight, to rise, in poisonous gases, into your house at night, when your sleeping children will most readily absorb them, and to find its languid way, at last, into the river that you drink – but, the French are a frog-eating people who wear wooden shoes, and it's O the roast beef of England, my boy, the jolly old English roast beef ('A Monument of French Folly').

CHRISTMAS STORIES

A CHRISTMAS TREE

I have been looking on, this evening, at a merry company of children assembled round that pretty German toy, a Christmas Tree. The tree was planted in the middle of a great round table, and towered high above their heads. It was brilliantly lighted by a multitude of little tapers; and everywhere sparkled and glittered with bright objects. There were rosy-cheeked dolls, hiding behind the green leaves; and there were real watches (with moveable hands, at least, and an endless capacity of being wound up) dangling from innumerable twigs; there were French-polished tables, chairs, bedsteads, wardrobes, eight-day clocks, and various other articles of domestic furniture (wonderfully made, in tin, at Wolverhampton), perched among the boughs, as if in preparation for some fairy housekeeping; there were jolly, broad-faced little men, much more agreeable in appearance than many real men – and no wonder, for their heads took off, and showed them to be full of sugar-plums; there were fiddles and drums; there were tambourines, books, work-boxes, paint-boxes, sweetmeat-boxes, peep-show boxes, and all kinds of boxes; there were trinkets for the elder girls, far brighter than any grown-up gold and jewels; there were baskets and pincushions in all devices; there were guns, swords, and banners; there were witches standing in enchanted rings of pasteboard, to tell fortunes; there were teetotums, humming-tops, needle-cases, pen-wipers, smelling-bottles, conversation-cards, bouquet-holders; real fruit, made artificially dazzling with gold leaf; imitation apples, pears, and walnuts, crammed with surprises; in short, as a pretty child before me, delightedly whispered to another pretty child, her bosom friend, 'There was

everything, and more.' This motley collection of odd objects, clustering on the tree like magic fruit, and flashing back the bright looks directed towards it from every side – some of the diamond-eyes admiring it were hardly on a level with the table, and a few were languishing in timid wonder on the bosoms of pretty mothers, aunts, and nurses – made a lively realisation of the fancies of childhood; and set me thinking how all the trees that grow and all the things that come into existence on the earth, have their wild adornments at that well-remembered time.

I begin to consider, what do we all remember best upon the branches of the Christmas Tree of our own young Christmas days, by which we climbed to real life.

Straight, in the middle of the room, cramped in the freedom of its growth by no encircling walls or soon-reached ceiling, a shadowy tree arises; and, looking up into the dreamy brightness of its top – for I observe in this tree the singular property that it appears to grow downwards towards the earth – I look into my youngest Christmas recollections!

All toys at first, I find. Up yonder, among the green holly and red berries, is the Tumbler with his hands in his pockets, who wouldn't lie down, but whenever he was put upon the floor, persisted in rolling his fat body about, until he rolled himself still, and brought those lobster eyes of his to bear upon me – when I affected to laugh very much, but in my heart of hearts was extremely doubtful of him. Close beside him is that infernal snuff-box, out of which there sprang a demoniacal Counsellor in a black gown, with an obnoxious head of hair, and a red cloth mouth, wide open, who was not to be endured on any terms, but could not be put away either; for he used suddenly, in a highly magnified state, to fly out of Mammoth Snuff-boxes in dreams, when least expected. Nor is the frog with cobbler's wax on his tail, far off; for there was no knowing where he wouldn't jump; and when he flew over the candle, and came upon one's hand with that spotted back – red on a green ground – he was horrible. The cardboard lady in a blue-silk skirt, who was stood up against the candlestick to dance, and whom I see on the same branch, was milder, and was beautiful; but I can't say as much for the larger cardboard man, who used to be hung against the wall and pulled by a string; there was a sinister expression in that nose of his; and when he got his legs round his neck (which he very often did), he was ghastly, and not a creature to be alone with.

When did that dreadful Mask first look at me? Who put it on, and why was I so frightened that the sight of it is an era in my life? It is not a hideous visage in itself; it is even meant to be droll; why then were its stolid features so intolerable? Surely not because it hid the wearer's face. An apron would have done as much; and though I should have preferred even the apron away, it would not have been absolutely insupportable, like the mask. Was it the immovability of the mask? The doll's face was immovable, but I was not afraid of *her*. Perhaps that fixed and set change coming over a real face, infused into my quickened heart some remote suggestion and dread of the universal change that is to come on every face, and make it still? Nothing reconciled me to it. No drummers, from whom proceeded a melancholy chirping on the turning of a handle; no regiment of soldiers, with a mute band, taken out of a box, and fitted, one by one, upon a stiff and lazy little set of lazy-tongs; no old woman, made of wires and a brown-paper composition, cutting up a pie for two small children; could give me a permanent comfort, for a long time. Nor was it any satisfaction to be shown the Mask, and see that it was made of paper, or to have it locked up and be assured that no one wore it. The mere recollection of that fixed face, the mere knowledge of its existence anywhere, was sufficient to awake me in the night all perspiration and horror, with, 'O I know it's coming! O the mask!'

Ah! The Doll's house! – of which I was not proprietor, but where I visited. I don't admire the Houses of Parliament half so much as that stone-fronted mansion with real glass windows, and door-steps, and a real balcony – greener than I ever see now, except at watering-places; and even they afford but a poor imitation. And though it *did* open all at once, the entire house-front (which was a blow, I admit, as cancelling the fiction of a staircase), it was but to shut it up again, and I could believe. Even open, there were three distinct rooms in it: a sitting-room and bed-room, elegantly furnished, and best of all, a kitchen, with uncommonly soft fire-irons, a plentiful assortment of diminutive utensils – oh, the warming-pan! – and a tin man-cook in profile, who was always going to fry two fish. What Barmecide justice have I done to the noble feasts wherein the set of wooden platters figures, each with its own peculiar delicacy, as a ham or turkey, glued tight on to it, and garnished with something green, which I recollect as moss! Could all the Temperance Societies of these latter days, united, give me such a tea-drinking as I have had through the means of yonder little set of blue crockery, which really would hold liquid (it ran out of the small wooden cask, I recollect, and tasted of matches), and which made tea, nectar. And if the two legs of the ineffectual little sugar-tongs did tumble over one another, and want purpose, like Punch's hands, what does it matter? And I did once shriek out, as a poisoned child, and strike the fashionable company with consternation, by reason of having drunk a little teaspoon, inadvertently dissolved in too hot tea, I was never the worse for it, except by a powder!

And now, I see a wonderful row of little lights rise smoothly out of the ground, before a vast green curtain. Now, a bell rings – a magic bell, which still sounds in my ears, unlike all other bells – and music plays, amidst a buzz of voices, and a fragrant smell of orange-peel and oil. Anon, the magic bell commands the music to cease, and the great green curtain rolls itself up majestically, and The Play begins! The devoted dog of Montargis avenges the death of his master, foully murdered in the Forest of Bondy; and a humorous Peasant with a red nose and a very little hat, whom I take from this hour forth to my bosom as a friend (I think he was a Waiter or an Hostler at a village Inn, but many years have passed since he and I

have met), remarks that the sassigassity of that dog is indeed surprising; and evermore this jocular conceit will live in my remembrance fresh and unfading, over-topping all possible jokes, unto the end of time. Or now, I learn with bitter tears how poor Jane Shore, dressed all in white, and with her brown hair hanging down, went starving through the streets; or how George Barnwell killed the worthiest uncle that ever man had, and was afterwards so sorry for it that he ought to have been let off. Comes swift to comfort me, the Pantomime - stupendous Phenomenon! - when clowns are shot from loaded mortars into the great chandelier, bright constellation that it is; when Harlequins, covered all over with scales of pure gold, twist and sparkle, like amazing fish; when Pantaloon (whom I deem it no irreverence to compare in my own mind to my grandfather) puts red-hot pokers in his pocket, and cries 'Here's somebody coming!' or taxes the Clown with petty larceny, by saying, 'Now, I sawed you do it!' when Everything is capable, with the greatest ease, of being changed into Anything; and 'Nothing is, but thinking makes it so.' Now, too, I perceive my first experience of the dreary sensation – often to return in after-life – of being unable, next day, to get back to the dull, settled world; of wanting to live for ever in the bright atmosphere I have quitted; of doting on the little Fairy, with the wand like a celestial Barber's Pole, and pining for a Fairy immortality along with her. Ah, she comes back, in many shapes, as my eye wanders down the branches of my Christmas Tree, and goes as often, and has never yet stayed by me!

But hark! The Waits are playing, and they break my childish sleep! What images do I associate with the Christmas music as I see them set forth on the Christmas Tree? Known before all the others, keeping far apart from all the others, they gather round my little bed. An angel, speaking to a group of shepherds in a field; some travellers, with eyes uplifted, following a star; a baby in a manger; a child in a spacious temple, talking with grave men; a solemn figure, with a mild and beautiful face, raising a dead girl by the hand; again, near a city gate, calling back the son of a widow, on his bier, to life; a crowd of people looking through the opened roof of a chamber where he sits, and letting down a sick person on a bed, with ropes; the same, in a tempest, walking on the water to a ship; again, on a sea-shore, teaching a great multitude; again, with a child upon his knee, and other children round; again, restoring sight to the blind, speech to the dumb, hearing to the deaf, health to the sick, strength to the lame, knowledge to the ignorant; again, dying upon a Cross, watched by armed soldiers, a thick darkness coming on, the earth beginning to shake, and only one voice heard, 'Forgive them, for they know not what they do.'

If I no more come home at Christmas-time, there will be boys and girls (thank Heaven!) while the World lasts; and they do! Yonder they dance and play upon the branches of my Tree, God bless them, merrily, and my heart dances and plays too!

And I *do* come home at Christmas. We all do, or we all should. We all come home, or ought to come home, for a short holiday – the longer, the better – from the great boarding-school, where we are for ever working at our arithmetical slates, to take, and give a rest. As to going a visiting, where can we not go, if we will; where have we not been, when we would; starting our fancy from our Christmas Tree!

There is probably a smell of roasted chestnuts and other good comfortable things all the time, for we are telling Winter Stories – Ghost stories, or more shame for us – round the Christmas fire; and we have never stirred, except to draw a little nearer to it. But, no matter for that. We came to the house, and it is an old house, full of great chimneys where wood is burnt on ancient dogs upon the hearth, and grim portraits (some of them with grim legends, too) lower distrustfully from the oaken panels of the walls. We are a middle-aged nobleman, and we make a generous supper with our host and hostess and their guests – it being Christmas-time, and the old house full of company – and then we go to bed. Our room is a very old room. It is hung with tapestry. We don't like the portrait of a cavalier in green, over the fireplace. There are great black beams in the ceiling, and there is a great black bedstead, supported at the foot by two great black figures, who seem to have come off a couple of tombs in the old baronial church in the park, for our particular accommodation. But, we are not a superstitious nobleman, and we don't mind. Well! we dismiss our servant, lock the door, and sit before the fire in our dressing-gown, musing about a great many things. At length we go to bed. Well! we can't sleep. We toss and tumble, and can't sleep. The embers on the hearth burn fitfully and make the room look ghostly. We can't help peeping out over the counterpane, at the two black figures and the cavalier – that wicked-looking cavalier – in green. In the flickering light they seem to advance and retire: which, though we are not by any means a superstitious nobleman, is not agreeable. Well! we get nervous – more and more nervous. We say 'This is very foolish, but we can't stand this; we'll pretend to be ill, and knock up somebody.' Well! we are just going to do it, when the locked door opens, and there comes in a young woman, deadly pale, and with long fair hair, who glides to the fire, and sits down in the chair we have left there, wringing her hands. Then, we notice that her clothes are wet. Our tongue cleaves to the roof of our mouth, and we can't speak; but, we observe her accurately. Her clothes are wet; her long hair is dabbled with moist mud; she is dressed in the fashion of two hundred years ago; and she has at her girdle a bunch of rusty keys. Well! there she sits, and we can't even faint, we are in such a state about it. Presently she gets up, and tries all the locks in the room with the rusty keys, which won't fit one of them; then, she fixes her eyes on the portrait of the cavalier in green, and says, in a low, terrible voice, 'The stags know it!' After that, she wrings her hands again, passes the bedside, and goes out at the door.

There is no end to the old houses, with resounding galleries, and dismal state-bedchambers, and haunted wings shut up for many years, through which we may ramble, with an agreeable creeping up our back, and

encounter any number of ghosts, but (it is worthy of remark perhaps) reducible to a very few general types and classes; for, ghosts have little originality, and 'walk' in a beaten track. Thus, it comes to pass, that a certain room in a certain old hall, where a certain bad lord, baronet, knight, or gentleman, shot himself, has certain planks in the floor from which the blood *will not* be taken out. You may scrape and scrape, as the present owner has done, or plane and plane, as his father did, or scrub and scrub, as his grandfather did, or burn and burn with strong acids, as his great-grandfather did, but there the blood will still be – no readder and no paler – no more and no less – always just the same. Thus, in such another house there is a haunted door, that never will keep open; or another door that never will keep shut; or a haunted sound of a spinning-wheel, or a hammer, or a footstep, or a cry, or a sigh, or a horse's tramp, or the rattling of a chain. Or else, there is a turret-clock, which, at the midnight hour, strikes thirteen when the head of the family is going to die; or a shadowy, immovable black carriage which at such a time is always seen by somebody, waiting near the great gates in the stable-yard.

Now, the tree is decorated with bright merriment, and song, and dance, and cheerfulness. And they are welcome. Innocent and welcome be they ever held, beneath the branches of the Christmas Tree, which cast no gloomy shadow! But, as it sinks into the ground, I hear a whisper going through the leaves. 'This, in commemoration of the law of love and kindness, mercy and compassion. This, in remembrance of Me!'

WHAT CHRISTMAS IS AS WE GROW OLDER

Welcome, everything! Welcome, alike what has been, and what never was, and what we hope may be, to your shelter underneath the holly, to your places round the Christmas fire, where what is sits open-hearted! In yonder shadow, do we see obtruding furtively upon the blaze, an enemy's face? By Christmas Day we do forgive him! If the injury he has done us may admit of such companionship, let him come here and take his place. If otherwise, unhappily, let him go hence, assured that we will never injure nor accuse him.

On this day we shut out Nothing!

'Pause,' says a low voice. 'Nothing? Think!'

'On Christmas Day, we will shut out from our fireside, Nothing.'

'Not the shadow of a vast City where the withered leaves are lying deep?' the voice replies. 'Not the shadow that darkens the whole globe? Not the shadow of the City of the Dead?'

Not even that. Of all days in the year, we will turn our faces towards that City upon Christmas Day, and from its silent hosts bring those we loved, among us. City of the Dead, in the blessed name wherein we are gathered together at this time, and in the Presence that is here among us according to the promise, we will receive, and not dismiss, thy people who are dear to us!

Yes. We can look upon these children angels that alight, so solemnly, so beautifully among the living children by the fire, and can bear to think how they departed from us. Entertaining angels unawares, as the Patriarchs did, the playful children are unconscious of their guests; but we can see them – can see a radiant arm around one favourite neck, as if there were a tempting of that child away.... There was a dear girl – almost a woman – never to be one – who made a mourning Christmas in a house of joy, and went her trackless way to the silent City. Do we recollect her, worn out, faintly whispering what could not be heard, and falling into that last sleep for weariness? O look upon her now! O look upon her beauty, her serenity, her changeless youth, her happiness! The daughter of Jairus was recalled to life, to die; but she, more blest, has heard the same voice, saying unto her, 'Arise for ever!'

THE HOLLY-TREE

It was still dark when we left the Peacock. For a little while, pale, uncertain ghosts of houses and trees appeared and vanished, and then it was hard, black, frozen day. People lighting their fires; smoke was mounting straight up high into the rarefied air; and we were rattling for Highgate Archway over the hardest ground I have ever heard the ring of iron shoes on. As we got into the country, everything seemed to have grown old and gray. The roads, the trees, thatched roofs of cottages and homesteads, the ricks in farmers' yards. Out-door work was abandoned, horse-troughs at roadside inns were frozen hard, no stragglers lounged about, doors were close shut, little turnpike houses had blazing fires inside, and children (even turnpike people have children, and seem to like them) rubbed the frost from the little panes of glass with their chubby arms, that their bright eyes might catch a glimpse of the solitary coach going by. I don't know when the snow began to set in; but I know that we were changing horses somewhere when I heard the guard remark, 'That the old lady up in the sky was picking her geese pretty hard to-day.' Then, indeed, I found the white down falling fast and thick ('First Branch').

My first impressions of an Inn dated from the Nursery; consequently I went back to the Nursery for a starting-point, and found myself at the knee of a sallow woman with a fishy eye, an aquiline nose, and a green gown, whose specialty was a dismal narrative of a landlord by the roadside, whose visitors unaccountably disappeared for many years, until it was discovered that the pursuit of his life had been to convert them into pies. For the better devotion of himself to this branch of industry, he had constructed a secret door behind the head of the bed; and when the visitor (oppressed with pie) had fallen asleep, this wicked landlord would look softly in with a lamp in one hand and a knife in the other, would cut his throat, and would make him into pies; for which purpose he had coppers, underneath a trap-door, always boiling; and rolled out his pastry in the dead of the night. Yet even he was not insensible to the stings of conscience, for he never went to sleep without being heard to mutter, 'Too much pepper!' which was eventually the cause of his being brought to justice ('First Branch').

This same narrator, who had a Ghoulish pleasure, I have long been persuaded, in terrifying me to the utmost confines of my reason, had another authentic anecdote within her own experience, founded, I now believe, upon *Raymond and Agnes, or the Bleeding Nun*. She said it happened to her brother-in-law, who was immensely rich, – which my father was not; and immensely tall, – which my father was not. It was always a point with this Ghoul to present my dearest relations and friends to my youthful mind under circumstances of disparaging contrast. The brother-in-law was riding once through a forest on a magnificent horse (we had no magnificent horse at our house), attended by a favourite and valuable Newfoundland dog (we had no dog), when he found himself benighted, and came to an Inn. A dark woman opened the door, and he asked her if he could have a bed there. She answered yes, and put his horse in the stable, and took him into a room where there were two dark men. While he was at supper, a parrot in the room began to talk, saying, 'Blood, blood! Wipe up the blood!' Upon which one of the dark men wrung the parrot's neck, and said he was fond of roasted parrots, and he meant to have this one for breakfast in the morning. After eating and drinking heartily, the immensely rich, tall brother-in-law went up to bed; but he was rather vexed, because they had shut his dog in the stable, saying that they never allowed dogs in the house. He sat very quiet for more than an hour, thinking and thinking, when just as his candle was burning out, he heard a scratch at the door. He opened the door, and there was the Newfoundland dog! The dog came softly in, smelt about him, went straight to some straw in the corner which the dark men had said covered apples, tore the straw away, and disclosed two sheets steeped in blood. Just at that moment the candle went out, and the brother-in-law, looking through a chink in the door, saw the two dark men stealing upstairs; one armed with a dagger that long (about five feet); the other carrying a chopper, a sack, and a spade. Having no remembrance of the close of this adventure, I suppose my faculties to have been always so frozen with terror at this stage of it, that the power of listening stagnated within me for some quarter of an hour ('First Branch').

More than a year before I made the journey in the course of which I put up at that Inn, I had lost a very near and dear friend by death. Every night since, at home or away from home, I had dreamed of that friend; sometimes as still living; sometimes as returning from the world of shadows to comfort me; always as being beautiful, placid, and happy, never in association with any approach to fear or distress. It was at a lonely Inn in a wide moorland place, that I halted to pass the night. When I had looked from my bedroom window over the waste of snow on which the moon was shining, I sat down by my fire to write a letter. I had always, until that hour, kept it within my own breast that I dreamed every night of the dear lost one. But in the letter that I wrote I recorded the circumstance, and added that I felt much interested in proving whether the subject of my dream would still be faithful to me, travel-tired, and in that remote place. No. I lost the beloved figure of my vision in parting with the secret. My sleep has never looked upon it since, in sixteen years, but once. I was in Italy, and awoke (or seemed to awake), the well-remembered voice distinctly in my ears, conversing with it. I entreated it, as it rose above my bed and soared up to the vaulted roof of the old room, to answer me a question I had asked touching the Future Life. My hands were still outstretched towards it as it vanished, when I heard a bell ringing by the garden wall, and a voice in the deep stillness of the night calling on all good Christians to pray for the souls of the dead; it being All Souls' Eve ('First Branch').

Once I passed a fortnight at an Inn in the North of England, where I was haunted by the ghost of a tremendous pie. It was a Yorkshire pie, like a fort, – an abandoned fort with nothing in it; but the waiter had a fixed idea that it was a point of ceremony at every meal to put the pie on the table. After some days I tried to hint, in several delicate ways, that I considered the pie done with; as, for example, by emptying fag-ends of glasses of wine into it; putting cheese-plates and spoons into it, as into a basket; putting wine-bottles into it, as into a cooler; but always in vain, the pie being invariably cleaned out again and brought up as before. At last, beginning to be doubtful whether I was not the victim of a spectral illusion, and whether my health and spirits might not sink under the horrors of an imaginary pie, I cut a triangle out of it, fully as large as the musical instrument of that name in a powerful orchestra. Human prevision could not have foreseen the result – but the waiter mended the pie. With some effectual species of cement, he adroitly fitted the triangle in again, and I paid my reckoning and fled ('First Branch').

A desperate idea came into my head. Under any other circumstances I should have rejected it; but, in the strait at which I was, I held it fast. Could I so far overcome the inherent bashfulness which withheld me from the landlord's table and the company I might find there, as to call up the Boots, and ask him to take a chair, – and something in a liquid form, – and talk to me? I could. I would. I did.

Where had he been in his time? he repeated, when I asked him the question. Lord, he had been everywhere! And what had he been? Bless you, he had been everything you could mention a'most!

Seen a good deal? Why, of course he had. I should say so, he could assure me, if I only knew about a twentieth part of what had come in his way. Why, it would be easier for him, he expected, to tell what he hadn't seen than what he had. Ah! A deal, it would.

What was the curiousest thing he had seen? Well! He didn't know. He couldn't momently name what was the curiousest thing he had seen, – unless it was a Unicorn, – and he see him once at a Fair. But supposing a young gentleman not eight year old was to run away with a fine young woman of seven, might I think that a queer start? Certainly. Then that was a start as he himself had had his blessed eyes on, and he had cleaned the shoes they run away in – and they was so little that he couldn't get his hand into 'em ('Second Branch').

Boots could assure me that it was better than a picter, and equal to a play, to see them babies, with their long, bright, curling hair, their sparkling eyes, and their beautiful light tread, a rambling about the garden, deep in love. Boots was of opinion that the birds believed they was birds, and kept up with 'em, singing to please 'em. Sometimes they would creep under the Tulip-tree, and would sit there with their arms round one another's necks, and their soft cheeks touching, a reading about the Prince and the Dragon, and the good and bad enchanters and the king's fair daughter. Sometimes he would hear them planning about having a house in a forest, keeping bees and a cow, and living entirely on milk and honey. Once he came upon them by the pond, and heard Master Harry say, 'Adorable Norah, kiss me, and say you love me to distraction, or I'll jump in head-foremost.' And Boots made no question he would have done it if she hadn't complied. On the whole, Boots said it had a tendency to make him feel as if he was in love himself – only he didn't exactly know who with ('Second Branch').

In the evening, Boots went into the room to see how the runaway couple was getting on. The gentleman was on the window-seat, supporting the lady in his arms. She had tears upon her face, and was lying, very tired and half asleep, with her head upon his shoulder.

'Mrs. Harry Walmers, Junior, fatigued, sir?' says Cobbs.

'Yes, she is tired, Cobbs; but she is not used to be away from home, and she has been in low spirits again. Cobbs, do you think you could bring a biffin, please?'

'I ask your pardon, sir,' says Cobbs. 'What was it you – ?'

'I think a Norfolk biffin would rouse her, Cobbs. She is very fond of them' ('Second Branch').

A biled fowl, and baked bread-and-butter pudding, brought Mrs. Walmers up a little; but Boots could have wished, he must privately own to me, to have seen her more sensible of the woice of love, and less abandoning of herself to currants ('Second Branch').

Finally, Boots says, that's all about it. Mr. Walmers drove away in the chaise, having hold of Master Harry's hand. The elderly lady and Mrs. Harry Walmers, Junior, that was never to be (she married a Captain long afterwards, and died in India), went off next day. In conclusion, Boots put it to me whether I hold with him in two opinions: firstly, that there are not many couples on their way to be married who are half as innocent of guile as those two children; secondly, that it would be a jolly good thing for a great many couples on their way to be married, if they could only be stopped in time, and brought back separately ('Second Branch').

GOING INTO SOCIETY

Some inquiries were making about that House, and would he object to say why he left it?

Not at all; why should he? He left it, along of a Dwarf.

Along of a Dwarf?

Mr. Magsman repeated, deliberately and emphatically, Along of a dwarf.

Might it be compatible with Mr. Magsman's inclination and convenience to enter, as a favour, into a few particulars?

Mr. Magsman entered into the following particulars.

It was a long time ago, to begin with; – afore lotteries and a deal more was done away with. Mr. Magsman was looking about for a good pitch, and he see that house, and he says to himself, 'I'll have you, if you're to be had. If money'll get you, I'll have you.'

The neighbours cut up rough, and made complaints; but Mr. Magsman don't know what they *would* have had. It was a lovely thing. First of all, there was the canvass, representin the picter of the Giant, in Spanish trunks and a ruff, who was himself half the heighth of the house, and was run up with a line and pulley to a pole on the roof, so that his Ed was coeval with the parapet. Then, there was the canvass, representin the picter of the Albina lady, showing her white air to the Army and Navy in correct uniform. Then, there was the canvass, representin the picter of the Wild Indian a scalpin a member of some foreign nation. Then, there was the canvass, representin the picter of a child of a British Planter, seized by two Boa Constrictors – not that *we* never had no child, nor no Constrictors neither. Similarly, there was the canvass, representin the picter of the Wild Ass of the Prairies – not that *we* never had no wild asses, nor wouldn't have had 'em at a gift. Last, there was the canvass, representin the picter of the Dwarf, and like him too (considerin), with George the Fourth in sych a state of astonishment at him as His Majesty couldn't with his utmost politeness and stoutness express. The front of the House was so covered with canvasses, that there wasn't a spark of daylight ever visible on that side. 'MAGSMAN'S AMUSEMENTS,' fifteen foot long by two foot high, ran over the front door and parlour winders. The passage was a Arbour of green baize and gardenstuff. A barrel-organ performed there unceasing. And as to respectability, – if threepence ain't respectable, what is?

But, the Dwarf is the principal article at present, and he was worth the money. He was wrote up as MAJOR TPSCHOFFKI, OF THE IMPERIAL BULGRADERIAN BRIGADE. Nobody couldn't pronounce the name, and it never was intended anybody should. The public always turned it, as a regular rule, into Chopski. In the line he was called Chops; partly on that account, and partly because his real name, if he ever had any real name (which was very dubious), was Stakes.

He was always in love, of course; every human nat'ral phenomenon is. And he was always in love with a large woman; *I* never knowed the Dwarf as could be got to love a small one. Which helps to keep 'em the Curiosities they are.

One sing'ler idea he had in that Ed of his, which must have meant something, or it wouldn't have been there. It was always his opinion that he was entitled to property. He never would put his name to anything. He had been taught to write, by the young man without arms, who got his living with his toes (quite a

writing master *he* was, and taught scores in the line), but Chops would have starved to death, afore he'd have gained a bit of bread by putting his hand to a paper. This is the more curious to bear in mind, because HE had no property, nor hopes of property, except his house and a sarser. When I say his house, I mean the box, painted and got up outside like a reg'lar six-roomer, that he used to creep into, with a diamond ring (or quite as good to look at) on his forefinger, and ring a little bell out of what the Public believed to be the Drawing-room winder. And when I say a sarser, I mean a Chaney sarser in which he made a collection for himself at the end of every Entertainment. His cue for that, he took from me; 'Ladies and gentlemen, the little man will now walk three times round the Cairawan, and retire behind the curtain.' When he said anything important, in private life, he mostly wound it up with this form of words, and they was generally the last thing he said to me at night afore he went to bed.

He had what I consider a fine mind – a poetic mind. His ideas respectin his property never come upon him so strong as when he sat upon a barrel-organ and had the handle turned. Arter the wibration had run through him a little time, he would screech out, 'Toby, I feel my property coming – grind away! I'm counting my guineas by thousands, Toby – grind away! Toby, I shall be a man of fortun! I feel the Mint a jingling in me, Toby, and I'm swelling out into the Bank of England!' Such is the influence of music on a poetic mind. Not that he was partial to any other music but a barrel-organ; on the contrary, hated it.

He had a kind of a everlasting grudge agin the Public: which is a thing you may notice in many phenomenons that get their living out of it. What riled him most in the nater of his occupation was, that it kep him out of Society. He was continiwally saying, 'Toby, my ambition is, to go into Society. The curse of my position towards the Public is, that it keeps me hout of Society. This don't signify to a low beast of a Indian; he an't formed for Society. This don't signify to a Spotted Baby; *he* an't formed for Society. – I am.'

When I set him on the door-mat in the hall, he kep me close to him by holding on to my coat-collar, and he whispers:

'I ain't 'appy, Magsman.'

'What's on your mind, Mr. Chops?'

'They don't use me well. They an't grateful to me. They puts me on the mantel-piece when I won't have in more Champagne-wine, and they locks me in the sideboard when I won't give up my property.'

'Get rid of 'em, Mr. Chops.'

'I can't. We're in Society together, and what would Society say?'

'Come out of Society!' says I.

'I can't. You don't know what you're talking about. When you have once gone into Society, you mustn't come out of it.'

'Then if you'll excuse the freedom, Mr. Chops,' were my remark, shaking my head grave, 'I think it's a pity you ever went in.'

Mr. Chops shook that deep Ed of his, to a surprisin extent, and slapped it half a dozen times with his hand, and with more Wice than I thought were in him. Then, he says, 'You're a good fellow, but you don't understand. Good night, go along. Magsman, the little man will now walk three times round the Cairawan, and retire behind the curtain.'

I perceived, you understand, that he was soured by his misfortuns, and I felt for Mr. Chops.

'As to Fat Ladies,' says he, giving his head a tremendous one agin the wall, 'ther's lots of *them* in Society, and worse than the original. *Hers* was a outrage upon Taste – simply a outrage upon Taste – awakenin contempt carryin its own punishment in the form of a Indian!' Here he giv himself another tremendous one. 'But *theirs*, Magsman, *theirs* is mercenary outrages. Lay in Cashmeer shawls, buy bracelets, strew 'em and a lot of 'andsome fans and things about your rooms, let it be known that you give away like water to all as come to admire, and the Fat Ladies that don't exhibit for so much down upon the drum, will come from all the pints of the compass to flock about you, whatever you are. They'll drill holes in your 'art, Magsman, like a Cullender. And when you've no more left to give, they'll laugh at you to your face, and leave you to have your bones picked dry by Wulturs, like the dead Wild Ass of the Prairies that you deserve to be!' Here he giv himself the most tremendous one of all, and dropped.

I thought he was gone. His Ed was so heavy, and he knocked it so hard, and he fell so stoney, and the sassagerial disturbance in him must have been so immense, that I thought he was gone. But, he soon come round with care, and he sat up on the floor, and he said to me, with wisdom comin out of his eyes, if ever it come:

'Magsman! The most material difference between the two states of existence through which your un-happy friend has passed;' he reached out his poor little hand, and his tears dropped down on the moustachio which it was a credit to him to have done his best to grow, but it is not in mortals to command success, – 'the difference is this. When I was out of Society, I was paid light for being seen. When I went into Society, I paid heavy for being seen. I prefer the former, even if I wasn't forced upon it. Give me out through the trumpet, in the hold way, to-morrow.'

Arter that, he slid into the line again as easy as if he had been iled all over. But the organ was kep from him, and no allusions was ever made, when a company was in, to his property. He got wiser every day; his views of Society and the Public was luminous, be-wilderin, awful; and his Ed got bigger and bigger as his wisdom expanded it.

He took well, and pulled 'em in most excellent for nine weeks. At the expiration of that period, when his Ed was a sight, he expressed one evenin, the last Company havin been turned out, and the door shut, a wish to have a little music.

'Mr. Chops,' I said (I never dropped the 'Mr.' with him; the world might do it, but not me); 'Mr. Chops, are you sure as you are in a state of mind and body to sit upon the organ?'

His answer was this: 'Toby, when next met with on the tramp, I forgive her and the Indian. And I am.'

It was with fear and trembling that I begun to turn the handle; but he sat like a lamb. It will be my belief to my dying day, that I see his Ed expand as he sat; you may therefore judge how great his thoughts was. He sat out all the changes, and then he come off.

'Toby,' he says, with a quiet smile, 'the little man will now walk three times round the Cairawan, and retire behind the curtain.'

When we called him in the morning, we found him gone into a much better Society than mine or Pall Mall's. I giv Mr. Chops as comfortable a funeral as lay in my power, followed myself as Chief, and had the George the Fourth canvass carried first, in the form of a banner. But, the House was so dismal arterwards, that I giv it up, and took to the Wan again.

THE HAUNTED HOUSE

'I have nothing to do with you, sir,' returned the gentleman; 'pray let me listen – O.'

He enunciated this vowel after a pause, and noted it down.

At first I was alarmed, for an Express lunatic and no communication with the guard, is a serious posi-tion. The thought came to my relief that the gentle-man might be what is popularly called a Rapper: one of a sect for (some of) whom I have the highest respect, but whom I don't believe in. I was going to ask him the question, when he took the bread out of my mouth.

'You will excuse me,' said the gentleman con-temptuously, 'if I am too much in advance of common humanity to trouble myself at all about it. I passed the night – as indeed I pass the whole of my time now – in spiritual intercourse.'

'O!' said I, something snappishly.

'The conferences of the night begin,' continued the gentleman, turning several leaves of his note-book, 'with this message: "Evil communications corrupt good manners." '

'Sound,' said I; 'but, absolutely new?'

'New from spirits,' returned the gentleman.

I could only repeat my rather snappish 'O!' and ask if I might be favoured with the last communication.

' "A bird in the hand," ' said the gentleman, read-ing his last entry with great solemnity, ' "is worth two in the Bosh." '

'Truly I am of the same opinion,' said I; 'but shouldn't it be Bush?'

'It came to me, Bosh,' returned the gentleman.

The gentleman then informed me that the spirit of Socrates had delivered this special revelation in the course of the night. 'My friend, I hope you are pretty well. There are two in this railway carriage. How do you do? There are seventeen thousand four hundred and seventy-nine spirits here, but you cannot see them. Pythagoras is here. He is not at liberty to mention it, but hopes you like travelling.' Galileo likewise had dropped in, with this scientific intelligence. 'I am glad to see you, *amico. Come sta?* Water will freeze when it is cold enough. *Addio!*' In the course of the night, also, the following phenomena had occurred. Bishop Butler had insisted on spelling his name, 'Blubler,' for which offence against orthography and good manners he had been dismissed as out of temper. John Milton (suspected of wilful mystification) had repudiated the authorship of Paradise Lost, and had introduced, as joint authors of that poem, two Unknown gentlemen, respectively named Grungers and Scadgingtone. And Prince Arthur, nephew of King John of England, had described himself as tolerably comfortable in the seventh circle, where he was learning to paint on velvet, under the direction of Mrs. Trimmer and Mary Queen of Scots.

If this should meet the eye of the gentleman who favoured me with these disclosures, I trust he will excuse my confessing that the sight of the rising sun, and the contemplation of the magnificent Order of the vast Universe, made me impatient of them. In a word, I was so impatient of them, that I was mightily glad to get out at the next station, and to exchange these clouds and vapours for the free air of Heaven ('The Mortals in the House').

No period within the four-and-twenty hours of day and night is so solemn to me, as the early morning. In the summer time, I often rise very early, and repair to my room to do a day's work before breakfast, and I am always on those occasions deeply impressed by the stillness and solitude around me. Besides that there is something awful in the being surrounded by familiar faces asleep – in the knowledge that those who are dearest to us and to whom we are dearest, are profoundly unconscious of us, in an impassive state, anticipative of that mysterious condition to which we are all tending – the stopped life, the broken threads of yesterday, the deserted seat, the closed book, the unfinished but abandoned occupation, all are images of Death. The tranquillity of the hour is the tranquillity of Death. The colour and the chill have the same association. Even a certain air that familiar household objects take upon them when they first emerge from the shadows of the night into the morning, of being newer, and as they used to be long ago, has its counterpart in the subsidence of the worn face of maturity or age, in death, into the old youthful look. Moreover, I once saw the apparition of my father, at this hour. He was alive and well, and nothing ever came of it, but I saw him in the daylight, sitting with his back towards me, on a seat that stood beside my bed. His head was resting on his hand, and whether he was slumbering or grieving, I could not discern. Amazed to see him there, I sat up, moved my position, leaned out of bed, and watched him. As he did not move, I spoke to him more than once. As he did not move then, I became alarmed and laid my hand upon his shoulder, as I thought – and there was no such thing ('The Mortals in the House').

'This gentleman wants to know,' said the landlord, 'if anything's seen at the Poplars.'

' 'Ooded woman with a howl,' said Ikey, in a state of great freshness.

'Do you mean a cry?'

'I mean a bird, sir.'

'A hooded woman with an owl. Dear me! Did you ever see her?'

'I seen the howl.'

'Never the woman?'

'Not so plain as the howl, but they always keeps together.'

'Has anybody ever seen the woman as plainly as the owl?'

'Lord bless you, sir! Lots.'

'Who?'

'Lord bless you, sir! Lots.'

'The general-dealer opposite, for instance, who is opening his shop?'

'Perkins? Bless you, Perkins wouldn't go a-nigh the place. No!' observed the young man, with considerable feeling; 'he an't over-wise, an't Perkins, but he an't such a fool as *that*.'

(Here, the landlord murmured his confidence in Perkins's knowing better.)

'Who is – or who was – the hooded woman with the owl? Do you know?'

'Well!' said Ikey, holding up his cap with one hand while he scratched his head with the other, 'they say, in general, that she was murdered, and the howl he 'ooted the while' ('The Mortals in the House').

Above stairs and below, waste tracts of passage intervened between patches of fertility represented by rooms; and there was a mouldy old well with a green growth upon it, hiding like a murderous trap, near the bottom of the back-stairs, under the double row of bells. One of these bells was labelled, on a black ground in faded white letters, MASTER B. This, they told me, was the bell that rang the most.

'Who was Master B.?' I asked. 'Is it known what he did while the owl hooted?'

'Rang the bell,' said Ikey ('The Mortals in the House').

The year was dying early, the leaves were falling fast, it was a raw cold day when we took possession, and the gloom of the house was most depressing. The cook (an amiable woman, but of a weak turn of intellect) burst into tears on beholding the kitchen, and requested that her silver watch might be delivered over to her sister (2 Tuppintock's Gardens, Liggs's Walk, Clapham Rise), in the event of anything happening to her from the damp. Streaker, the housemaid, feigned cheerfulness, but was the greater martyr. The Odd Girl, who had never been in the country, alone was pleased, and made arrangements for sowing an acorn in the garden outside the scullery window, and rearing an oak ('The Mortals in the House').

Let me do Ikey no injustice. He was afraid of the house, and believed in its being haunted; and yet he would play false on the haunting side, so surely as he got an opportunity. The Odd Girl's case was exactly similar. She went about the house in a state of real terror, and yet lied monstrously and wilfully, and invented many of the alarms she spread, and made many of the sounds we heard. I had had my eye on the two, and I know it. It is not necessary for me, here, to account for this preposterous state of mind; I content myself with remarking that it is familiarly known to every intelligent man who has had fair medical, legal, or other watchful experience; that it is as well established and as common a state of mind as any with which observers are acquainted; and that it is one of the first elements, above all others, rationally to be suspected in, and strictly looked for, and separated from, any question of this kind ('The Mortals in the House').

We went into a room by ourselves, and Miss Griffin called in to her assistance, Mesrour, chief of the dusky guards of the Hareem. Mesrour, on being whispered to, began to shed tears.

'Bless you, my precious!' said that officer, turning to me; 'your Pa's took bitter bad!'

I asked, with a fluttered heart, 'Is he very ill?'

'Lord temper the wind to you, my lamb!' said the good Mesrour, kneeling down, that I might have a comforting shoulder for my head to rest on, 'your Pa's dead!'

Haroun Alraschid took to flight at the words; the Seraglio vanished; from that moment, I never again saw one of the eight of the fairest of the daughters of men.

I was taken home, and there was Debt at home as well as Death, and we had a sale there. My own little bed was so superciliously looked upon by a Power unknown to me, hazily called 'The Trade,' that a brass coal-scuttle, a roasting-jack, and a birdcage, were obliged to be put into it to make a Lot of it, and then it went for a song. So I heard mentioned, and I wondered what song, and thought what a dismal song it must have been to sing!

Then, I was sent to a great, cold, bare, school of big boys; where everything to eat and wear was thick and clumpy, without being enough; where everybody, large and small, was cruel; where the boys knew all about the sale, before I got there, and asked me what I had fetched, and who had bought me, and hooted at me, 'Going, going, gone!' I never whispered in that wretched place that I had seen Haroun, or had had a Seraglio, for, I knew that if I mentioned my reverses, I should be so worried, that I should have to drown myself in the muddy pond near the playground, which looked like the beer.

Ah me, ah me! No other ghost has haunted the boy's room, my friends, since I have occupied it, than the ghost of my own childhood, the ghost of my own innocence, the ghost of my own airy belief. Many a time have I pursued the phantom: never with this man's stride of mine to come up with it, never with these man's hands of mine to touch it, never more to this man's heart of mine to hold it in its purity. And here you see me working out, as cheerfully and thankfully as I may, my doom of shaving in the glass a constant change of customers, and of lying down and rising up with the skeleton allotted to me for my mortal companion ('The Ghost in Master B.'s Room').

TOM TIDDLER'S GROUND

'Pray shake hands,' said Mr. Traveller.

'Take care, sir,' was the Tinker's caution, as he reached up his hand in surprise; 'the black comes off.'

'I am glad of it,' said Mr. Traveller. 'I have been for several hours among other black that does not come off.'

'You are speaking of Tom in there?'

'Yes.'

'Well now,' said the Tinker, blowing the dust off his job: which was finished. 'Ain't it enough to disgust a pig, if he could give his mind to it?'

'If he could give his mind to it,' returned the other, smiling, 'the probability is that he wouldn't be a pig' (Chapter 7).

SOMEBODY'S LUGGAGE

Then, what is the inference to be drawn respecting time Waitering? You must be bred to it. You must be born to it. Would you know how born to it, Fair Reader, – if of the adorable female sex? Then learn from the biographical experience of one that is a Waiter in the sixty-first year of his age.

You were conveyed, – ere yet your dawning powers were otherwise developed than to harbour vacancy in your inside, – you were conveyed, by surreptitious means, into a pantry adjoining the Admiral Nelson, Civil and General Dining-Rooms, there to receive by stealth that healthful sustenance which is the pride and boast of the British female constitution. Your mother was married to your father (himself a distant Waiter) in the profoundest secrecy; for a Waitress known to be married would ruin the best of businesses, – it is the same as on the stage. Hence your being smuggled into the pantry, and that – to add to the infliction – by an unwilling grandmother. Under the combined influence of the smells of roast and boiled, and soup, and gas, and malt liquors, you partook of your earliest nourishment; your unwilling grandmother sitting prepared to catch you when your mother was called and dropped you; your grandmother's shawl ever ready to stifle your natural complainings; your innocent mind surrounded by uncongenial cruets, dirty plates, dish-covers, and cold gravy, your mother calling down the pipe for veals and porks, instead of soothing you with nursery rhymes. Under these untoward circumstances you were early weaned (Chapter 1).

MRS. LIRRIPER'S LODGINGS

Whoever would begin to be worried with letting Lodgings that wasn't a lone woman with a living to get is a thing inconceivable to me, my dear; excuse the familiarity, but it comes natural to me in my own little room, when wishing to open my mind to those that I can trust, and I should be truly thankful if they were all mankind, but such is not so, for have but a Furnished bill in the window and your watch on the mantelpiece, and farewell to it if you turn your back for but a second, however gentlemanly the manners; nor is being of your own sex any safeguard, as I have reason, in the form of sugar-tongs to know, for that lady (and a fine woman she was) got me to run for a glass of water, on the plea of going to be confined, which certainly turned out true, but it was in the Station-house.

Number Eighty-one Norfolk Street, Strand – situated midway between the City and St. James's, and within five minutes' walk of the principal places of public amusement – is my address. I have rented this house many years, as the parish rate-books will testify; and I could wish my landlord was as alive to the fact as I am myself; but no, bless you, not a half a pound of paint to save his life, nor so much, my dear, as a tile upon the roof, though on your bended knees (*Chapter 1: Mrs. Lirriper*).

My poor Lirriper being behindhand with the world and being buried at Hatfield Church in Hertfordshire, not that it was his native place but that he had a liking for the Salisbury Arms where we went upon our wedding-day and passed as happy a fortnight as ever happy was, I went round to the creditors and I says 'Gentlemen I am acquainted with the fact that I am not answerable for my late husband's debts but I wish to pay them for I am his lawful wife and his good name is dear to me. I am going into the Lodgings gentlemen as a business and if I prosper every farthing that my late husband owed shall be paid for the sake of the love I bore him, by this right hand.' It took a long time to do but it was done, and the silver cream-jug which is between ourselves and the bed and the mattress in my room up-stairs (or it would have found legs so sure as ever the Furnished bill was up) being presented by the gentlemen engraved 'To Mrs. Lirriper a mark of grateful respect for her honourable conduct' gave me a turn which was too much for my feelings, till Mr. Betley which at that time had the parlours and loved his joke says 'Cheer up Mrs. Lirriper, you should feel as if it was only your christening and they were your godfathers and god-mothers which did promise for you.' And it brought me round, and I don't mind confessing to you my dear that I then put a sandwich and a drop of sherry in a little basket and went down to Hatfield churchyard outside the coach and kissed my hand and laid it with a kind of proud and swelling love on my husband's grave, though bless you it had taken me so long to clear his name that my wedding-ring was worn quite fine and smooth when I laid it on the green green waving grass (*Chapter 1*).

'Well, Madam,' says the Major rubbing his nose – as I did fear at the moment with the black sponge but it was only his knuckle, he being always neat and dexterous with his fingers – 'well, Madam, I suppose you would be glad of the money?'

I was delicate of saying 'Yes' too out, for a little extra colour rose into the Major's cheeks and there was irregularity which I will not particularly specify in a quarter which I will not name.

'I am of opinion, Madam,' says the Major 'that when money is ready for you – when it is ready for you, Mrs. Lirriper – you ought to take it. What is there against it, Madam, in this case up-stairs?'

'I really cannot say there is anything against it sir, still I thought I would consult you.'

'You said a newly-married couple, I think, Madam?' says the Major.

I says 'Ye-es. Evidently. And indeed the young lady mentioned to me in a casual way that she had not been married many months.'

The Major rubbed his nose again and stirred the varnish round and round in its little saucer with his piece of sponge and took to his whistling in a whisper for a few moments. Then he says 'You would call it a Good Let, Madam?'

'O certainly a Good Let sir.'

'Say they renew for the additional six months. Would it put you about very much Madam if – if the worst was to come to the worst?' said the Major.

'Well I hardly know,' I says to the Major. 'It depends upon circumstances. Would *you* object Sir for instance?'

'I?' says the Major. 'Object? Jemmy Jackman? Mrs. Lirriper close with the proposal' (*Chapter 1*).

His letter never came when it ought to have come and what she went through morning after morning when the postman brought none for her the very postman himself compassionated when she ran down to the door, and yet we cannot wonder at its being calculated to blunt the feelings to have all the trouble of other people's letters and none of the pleasure and doing it oftener in the mud and mizzle than not and at a rate of wages more resembling Little Britain than Great. But at last one morning when she was too poorly to come running downstairs he says to me with a pleased look in his face that made me next to love the man in his uniform coat though he was dripping wet 'I have taken you first in the street this morning Mrs. Lirriper, for here's the one for Mrs. Edson.' I went up to her bedroom with it as fast as ever I could go, and she sat up in bed when she saw it and kissed it and tore it open and then a blank stare came upon her. 'It's very short!' she says lifting her large eyes to my face. 'O Mrs. Lirriper it's very short?' I says 'My dear Mrs. Edson no doubt that's because your husband hadn't time to write more just at that time.' 'No doubt, no doubt,' says she, and puts her two hands on her face and turns round in her bed.

I shut her softly in and I crept downstairs and I tapped at the Major's door, and when the Major having his thin slices of bacon in his own Dutch oven saw me he came out of his chair and put me down on the sofa. 'Hush!' says he, 'I see something's the matter. Don't speak – take time.' I says 'O Major I'm afraid there's cruel work upstairs.' 'Yes, yes' says he 'I had begun to be afraid of it – take time.' And then in opposition to his own words he rages out frightfully, and says 'I shall never forgive myself Madam, that I, Jemmy Jackman, didn't see it all that morning – didn't go straight upstairs when my boot-sponge was in my hand – didn't force it down his throat – and choke him dead with it on the spot!' (*Chapter 1*).

Something merciful, something wiser and better far than my own self, had moved me while it was yet light to sit in my bonnet and shawl, and as the shadows fell and the tide rose I could sometimes – when I put out my head and looked at her window below – see that she leaned out a little looking down the street. It was just settling dark when I saw *her* in the street.

So fearful of losing sight of her that it almost stops my breath while I tell it, I went downstairs faster than I ever moved in all my life and only tapped with my hand at the Major's door in passing it and slipping out. She was gone already. I made the same speed down the street and when I came to the corner of

Howard Street I saw that she had turned it and was there plain before me going towards the west. O with what a thankful heart I saw her going along!

She was quite unacquainted with London and had very seldom been out for more than an airing in our own street where she knew two or three little children belonging to neighbours and had sometimes stood among them at the street looking at the water. She must be going at hazard I knew, still she kept the bye-streets quite correctly as long as they would serve her, and then turned up into the Strand. But at every corner I could see her head turned one way, and that way was always the river way.

It may have been only the darkness and quiet of the Adelphi that caused her to strike into it but she struck into it much as readily as if she had set out to go there, which perhaps was the case. She went straight down to the Terrace and along it and looked over the iron rail, and I often woke afterwards in my own bed with the horror of seeing her do it. The desertion of the wharf below and the flowing of the high water there seemed to settle her purpose. She looked about as if to make out the way down, and she struck out the right way or the wrong way – I don't know which, for I don't know the place before or since – and I followed her the way she went.

It was noticeable that all this time she never once looked back. But there was now a great change in the manner of her going, and instead of going at a steady quick walk with her arms folded before her, – among the dark dismal arches she went in a wild way with her arms open wide, as if they were wings and she was flying to her death.

We were on the wharf and she stopped. I stopped. I saw her hands at her bonnet-strings, and I rushed between her and the brink and took her round the waist with both my arms. She might have drowned me, I felt then, but she could never have got quit of me.

Down to that moment my mind had been all in a maze and not half an idea had I had in it what I should say to her, but the instant I touched her it came to me like magic and I had my natural voice and my senses and even almost my breath.

Mrs. Edson!' I says 'My dear! Take care. How ever did you lose your way and stumble on a dangerous place like this? Why you must have come here by the most perplexing streets in all London. No wonder you are lost, I'm sure. And this place too! Why I thought nobody ever got here, except me to order my coals and the Major in the parlours to smoke his cigar!' – for I saw that blessed man close by, pretending to it.

'Hah – Hah – Hum!' coughs the Major.

'And good gracious me,' I says, 'why here he is!'

'Halloa! who goes there?' says the Major in a military manner.

'Well!' I says, 'if this don't beat everything! Don't you know us Major Jackman?'

'Halloa!' says the Major. 'Who calls on Jemmy Jackman!' (and more out of breath he was, and did it less life like than I should have expected.)

'Why here's Mrs. Edson Major' I says, 'strolling out to cool her poor head which has been very bad, has missed her way and got lost, and Goodness knows

where she might have got to but for me coming here to drop an order into my coal merchant's letter-box and you coming here to smoke your cigar! – And you really are not well enough my dear' I says to her 'to be half so far from home without me. – And your arm will be very acceptable I am sure Major' I says to him 'and I know she may lean upon it as heavy as she likes.' And now we had both got her – thanks be Above! – one on each side.

She was all in a cold shiver and she so continued till I laid her on her own bed, and up to the early morning she held me by the hand and moaned and moaned 'O wicked, wicked, wicked!' But when at last I made believe to droop my head and be overpowered with a dead sleep, I heard that poor young creature give such touching and such humble thanks for being preserved from taking her own life in her madness that I thought I should have cried my eyes out on the counterpane and I knew she was safe *(Chapter 1)*.

The miles and miles that me and the Major have travelled with Jemmy in the dusk between the lights are not to be calculated, Jemmy driving on the coach-box which is the Major's brass-bound writing desk on the table, me inside in the easy-chair and the Major Guard up behind with a brown-paper horn doing it really wonderful. I do assure you my dear that sometimes when I have taken a few winks in my place inside the coach and have come half awake by the flashing light of the fire and have heard that precious pet driving and the Major blowing up behind to have the change of horses ready when we got to the Inn, I have half believed we were on the old North Road that my poor Lirriper knew so well. Then to see that child and the Major both wrapped up getting down to warm their feet and going stamping about and having glasses of ale out of the paper match-boxes on the chimney-piece is to see the Major enjoying it fully as much as the child I am very sure, and it's equal to any play when Coachee opens the coach-door to look in at me inside and say 'Wery 'past that 'tage. – 'Prightened old lady?' *(Chapter 1)*.

My dear the system upon which the Major commenced and as I may say perfected Jemmy's learning when he was so small that if the dear was on the other side of the table you had to look under it instead of over it to see him with his mother's own bright hair in beautiful curls, is a thing that ought to be known to the Throne and Lords and Commons and then might obtain some promotion for the Major which he well deserves and would be none the worse for (speaking between friends) L. S. D.-ically. When the Major first undertook his learning he says to me:

'I'm going Madam,' he says 'to make our child a Calculating Boy.'

'Major,' I says, 'you terrify me and may do the pet a permanent injury you would never forgive yourself.'

'Madam,' says the Major, 'next to my regret that when I had my boot-sponge in my hand, I didn't choke that scoundrel with it – on the spot – '

'There! For Gracious' sake,' I interrupts, 'let his conscience find him without sponges.'

' – I say next to that regret, Madam,' says the Major 'would be the regret with which my breast,'

397

which he tapped, 'would be surcharged if this fine mind was not early cultivated. But mark me Madam,' says the Major holding up his forefinger 'cultivated on a principle that will make it a delight.'

'Major,' I says 'I will be candid with you and tell you openly that if ever I find the dear child fall off in his appetite I shall know it is his calculations and shall put a stop to them at two minutes' notice. Or if I find them mounting to his head' I says, 'or striking anyways cold to his stomach or leading to anything approaching flabbiness in his legs, the result will be the same, but Major you are a clever man and have seen much and you love the child and are his own godfather, and if you feel a confidence in trying try.'

'Spoken Madam' says the Major 'like Emma Lirriper' (*Chapter 1*).

MRS. LIRRIPER'S LEGACY

If I hadn't passed my word and raised their hopes, I doubt if I could have gone through with the undertaking but it was too late to go back now. So on the second day after Midsummer Day we went off by the morning mail. And when we came to the sea which I had never seen but once in my life and that when my poor Lirriper was courting me, the freshness of it and the deepness and the airiness and to think that it had been rolling ever since and that it was always a rolling and so few of us minding, made me feel quite serious. But I felt happy too and so did Jemmy and the Major and not much motion on the whole, though me with a swimming in the head and a sinking but able to take notice that the foreign insides appear to be constructed hollower than the English, leading to much more tremenjous noises when bad sailors.

But my dear the blueness and the lightness and the coloured look of everything and the very sentry-boxes striped and the shining rattling drums and the little soldiers with their waists and tidy gaiters, when we got across to the Continent – it made me feel as if I don't know what – as if the atmosphere had been lifted off me. And as to lunch why bless you if I kept a man-cook and two kitchen-maids I couldn't get it done for twice the money, and no injured young woman a glaring at you and grudging you and acknowledging your patronage by wishing that your food might choke you, but so civil and so hot and attentive and every way comfortable except Jemmy pouring wine down his throat by tumblers-full and me expecting to see him drop under the table (*Chapter 1:* Mrs. Lirriper)

And of Paris I can tell you no more my dear than that it's town and country both in one, and carved stone and long streets of high houses and gardens and fountains and statues and trees and gold, and immensely big soldiers and immensely little soldiers and the pleasantest nurses with the whitest caps a playing at skipping-rope with the bunchiest babies in the flattest caps, and clean table-cloths spread everywhere for dinner and people sitting out of doors smoking and sipping all day long and little plays being acted in the open air for little people and every shop a complete and elegant room, and everybody seeming to play at everything in this world. And as to the sparkling lights my dear after dark, glittering high up and low down and on before and on behind and all round, and the crowd of theatres and the crowd of people and the crowd of all sorts, it's pure enchantment. And pretty well the only thing that grated on me was that whether you pay your fare at the railway or whether you change your money at a money-dealer's or whether you take your ticket at the theatre, the lady or gentleman is caged up (I suppose by government) behind the strongest iron bars having more of a Zoological appearance than a free country.

Well to be sure when I did after all get my precious bones to bed that night, and my Young Rogue came in to kiss me and asks 'What do you think of this lovely lovely Paris, Gran?' I says 'Jemmy I feel as if it was beautiful fireworks being let off in my head' (*Chapter 1:* Mrs. Lirriper).

Well my dear and so the evening readings of those jottings of the Major's brought us round at last to the evening when we were all packed and going away next day, and I do assure you that by that time though it was deliciously comfortable to look forward to the dear old house in Norfolk Street again, I had formed quite a high opinion of the French nation and had noticed them to be much more homely and domestic in their families and far more simple and amiable in their lives than I had ever been led to expect, and it did strike me between ourselves that in one particular they might be imitated to advantage by another nation which I will not mention, and that is in the courage with which they take their little enjoyments on little means and with little things and don't let solemn big-wigs stare them out of countenance or speechify them dull, of which said solemn big-wigs I have ever had the one opinion that I wish they were all made comfortable separately in coppers with the lids on and never let out any more (*Chapter 2:* Mrs. Lirriper).

DOCTOR MARIGOLD

Now I'll tell you what. I mean to go down into my grave declaring that of all the callings ill used in Great Britain, the Cheap Jack calling is the worst used. Why ain't we a profession? Why ain't we endowed with privileges? Why are we forced to take out a hawker's license, when no such thing is expected of the political hawkers? Where's the difference betwixt us? Except that we are Cheap Jacks, and they are Dear Jacks, I don't see any difference but what's in our favour.

For look here! Say it's election time. I am on the footboard of my cart in the market-place, on a Saturday night. I put up a general miscellaneous lot. I say: 'Now here, my free and independent voters, I'm a going to give you such a chance as you never had in all your born days, nor yet the days preceding. Now I'll show you what I am a going to do with you. Here's a pair of razors that'll shave you closer than the Board of Guardians; here's a flat-iron worth its weight in gold; here's a frying-pan artificially flavoured with essence of beefsteaks to that degree that you've only got for the rest of your lives to fry bread and dripping in it and there you are replete with animal food; here's a genuine chronometer watch in such a solid silver case that you may knock at the door with it when you come home late from a social meeting, and rouse your wife and family, and save up your knocker for the postman; and here's half a dozen dinner plates that you may play the cymbals with to charm the baby when it's fractious. Stop! I'll throw you in another article, and I'll give you that, and it's a rolling-pin, and if the baby can only get it well into its mouth when its teeth is coming and rub the gums once with it, they'll come through double, in a fit of laughter equal to being tickled. Stop again! I'll throw you in another article, because I don't like the looks of you, for you haven't the appearance of buyers unless I lose by you, and because I'd rather lose than not take money to-night, and that's a looking-glass in which you may see how ugly you look when you don't bid. What do you say now? Come! Do you say a pound? Not you, for you haven't got it. Do you say ten shillings? Not you, for you owe more to the tally-man. Well then, I'll tell you what I'll do with you. I'll heap 'em all on the footboard of the cart, – there they are! razors, flat-iron, frying-pan, chronometer watch, dinner plates, rolling-pin, and looking-glass, – take 'em all away for four shillings, and I'll give you sixpence for your trouble!' This is me, the Cheap Jack (*Chapter 1: Doctor Marigold*).

Next Saturday that come, I pitched the cart on the same pitch, and I was in very high feather indeed, keeping 'em laughing the whole of the time, and getting off the goods briskly. At last I took out of my waistcoat-pocket a small lot wrapped in soft paper, and I put it this way (looking up at the window where she was). 'Now here, my blooming English maidens, is an article, the last article of the present evening's sale, which I offer to only you, the lovely Suffolk Dumplings biling over with beauty, and I won't take a bid of a thousand pounds for from any man alive. Now what is it? Why, I'll tell you what it is. It's made of fine gold, and it's not broke, though there's a hole in the middle of it, and it's stronger than any fetter that ever was forged, though it's smaller than any finger in my set of ten. Why ten? Because, when my parents made over my property to me, I tell you true, there was twelve sheets, twelve towels, twelve table-cloths, twelve knives, twelve forks, twelve tablespoons, and twelve teaspoons, but my set of fingers was two short of a dozen, and could never since be matched. Now what else is it? Come, I'll tell you. It's a hoop of solid gold, wrapped in a silver curl-paper, that I myself took off the shining locks of the ever beautiful old lady in Threadneedle Street, London city; I wouldn't tell you so if I hadn't the paper to show, or you mightn't believe it even of me. Now what else is it? It's a man-trap and a handcuff, the parish stocks and a leg-lock, all in gold and all in one. Now what else is it? It's a wedding-ring. Now I'll tell you what I'm a going to do with it. I'm not a going to offer this lot for money; but I mean to give it to the next of you beauties that laughs, and I'll pay her a visit to-morrow morning at exactly half after nine o'clock as the chimes go, and I'll take her out for a walk to put up the banns.' *She* laughed, and got the ring handed up to her. When I called in the morning, she says, 'O

dear! It's never you, and you never mean it.' 'It's ever me,' says I, 'and I am ever yours, and I ever mean it'. So we got married, after being put up three times – which, by the bye, is quite the Cheap Jack way again, and shows once more how the Cheap Jack customs pervade society (*Chapter 1*).

She wasn't a bad wife, but she had a temper. If she could have parted with that one article at a sacrifice, I wouldn't have swopped her away in exchange for any other woman in England. Not that I ever did swop her away, for we lived together till she died, and that was thirteen year. Now, my lords and ladies and gentle-folks all, I'll let you into a secret, though you won't believe it. Thirteen year of temper in a Palace would try the worst of you, but thirteen year of temper in a Cart would try the best of you. You are kept so very close to it in a cart, you see. There's thousands of couples among you getting on like sweet ile upon a whetstone in houses five and six pairs of stairs high, that would go to the Divorce Court in a cart. Whether the jolting makes it worse, I don't undertake to decide; but in a cart it does come home to you, and stick to you. Wiolence in a cart is *so* wiolent, and aggrawation in a cart is *so* aggrawating.

We might have had such a pleasant life! A roomy cart, with the large goods hung outside, and the bed slung underneath it when on the road, an iron pot and a kettle, a fireplace for the cold weather, a chimney for the smoke, a hanging-shelf and a cupboard, a dog and a horse. What more do you want? You draw off upon a bit of turf in a green lane or by the roadside, you hobble your old horse and turn him grazing, you light your fire upon the ashes of the last visitors, you cook your stew, and you wouldn't call the Emperor of France you father. But have a temper in the cart, flinging language and the hardest goods in stock at you, and where are you then? Put a name to your feelings.

My dog knew as well when she was on the turn as I did. Before she broke out, he would give a howl, and bolt. How he knew it, was a mystery to me; but the sure and certain knowledge of it would wake him up out of his soundest sleep, and he would give a howl, and bolt. At such times I wished I was him (*Chapter 1*).

It was while the second ladies' lot was holding 'em enchained that I felt her lift herself a little on my shoulder, to look across the dark street. 'What troubles you, darling?' 'Nothing troubles me, father. I am not at all troubled. But don't I see a pretty churchyard over there?' 'Yes, my dear.' 'Kiss me twice, dear father, and lay me down to rest upon that churchyard grass so soft green.' I staggered back into the cart with her head dropped on my shoulder, and I says to her mother, 'Quick. Shut the door! Don't let those laughing people see!' 'What's the matter?' she cries. 'O woman, woman, 'I tells her, 'you'll never catch my little Sophy by her hair again, for she has flown away from you!'

Maybe those were harder words than I meant 'em; but from that time forth my wife took to brooding, and would sit in the cart or walk beside it, hours at a stretch, with her arms crossed, and her eyes looking on the ground. When her furies took her (which was rather seldomer than before) they took her in a new way, and she banged herself about to that extent that I was forced to hold her. She got none the better for a little drink now and then, and through some years I used to wonder, as I plodded along at the old horse's head, whether there was many carts upon the road that held so much dreariness as mine, for all my being looked up to as the King of the Cheap Jacks. So sad our lives went on till one summer evening, when, as we were coming into Exeter, out of the farther West of England, we saw a woman beating a child in a cruel manner, who screamed, 'Don't beat me! O mother, mother, mother!' Then my wife stopped her ears, and ran away like a wild thing, and next day she was found in the river *(Chapter 1)*.

I am a neat hand at cookery, and I'll tell you what I knocked up for my Christmas-eve dinner in the Library Cart. I knocked up a beefsteak-pudding for one, with two kidneys, a dozen oysters, and a couple of mushrooms thrown in. It's a pudding to put a man in good humour with everything, except the two bottom buttons of his waistcoat. Having relished that pudding and cleared away, I turned the lamp low, and sat down by the light of the fire, watching it as it shone upon the backs of Sophy's books.

Sophy's books so brought up Sophy's self, that I saw her touching face quite plainly, before I dropped off dozing by the fire. This may be a reason why Sophy, with her deaf-and-dumb child in her arms, seemed to stand silent by me all through my nap. I was on the road, off the road, in all sorts of places, North and South and West and East. Winds liked best and winds liked least. Here and there and gone astray, Over the hills and far away, and still she stood silent by me, with her silent child in her arms. Even when I woke with a start, she seemed to vanish, as if she had stood by me in that very place only a single instant before.

I had started at a real sound, and the sound was on the steps of the cart. It was the light hurried tread of a child, coming clambering up. That tread of a child had once been so familiar to me, that for half a moment I believed I was a-going to see a little ghost.

But the touch of a real child was laid upon the outer handle of the door, and the handle turned, and the door opened a little way, and a real child peeped in. A bright little comely girl with large dark eyes.

Looking full at me, the tiny creature took off her mite of a straw hat, and a quantity of dark curls fell all about her face. Then she opened her lips, and said in a pretty voice,

'Grandfather!'

'Ah, my God!' I cries out. 'She can Speak!'

'Yes, dear grandfather. And I am to ask you whether there was ever any one that I remind you of?'

In a moment Sophy was round my neck, as well as the child, and her husband was a-wringing my hand with his face hid, and we all had to shake ourselves together before we could get over it. And when we did begin to get over it, and I saw the pretty child a-talking, pleased and quick and eager and busy, to

her mother, in the signs that I had first taught her mother, the happy and yet pitying tears fell rolling down my face *(Chapter 3)*.

MUGBY JUNCTION

A place replete with shadowy shapes, this Mugby Junction in the black hours of the four-and-twenty. Mysterious goods trains, covered with palls and gliding on like vast weird funerals, conveying themselves guiltily away from the presence of the few lighted lamps, as if their freight had come to a secret and unlawful end. Half-miles of coal pursuing in a Detective manner, following when they lead, stopping when they stop, backing when they back. Red-hot embers showering out upon the ground, down this dark avenue, and down the other, as if torturing fires were being raked clear; concurrently, shrieks and groans and grinds invading the ear, as if the tortured were at the height of their suffering. Iron-barred cages full of cattle jangling by midway, the drooping beasts with horns entangled, eyes frozen with terror, and mouths too: at least they have long icicles (or what seem so) hanging from their lips. Unknown languages in the air, conspiring in red, green, and white characters. An earthquake, accompanied with thunder and lightning, going up express to London. Now, all quiet, all rusty, wind and rain in possession, lamps extinguished, Mugby Junction dead and indistinct, with its robe drawn over its head, like Caesar *(Chapter 1)*.

What a lark it is! We are the Model Establishment, we are, at Mugby. Other Refreshment Rooms send their imperfect young ladies up to be finished off by Our Missis. For some of the young ladies, when they're new to the business, come into it mild! Ah! Our Missis, she soon takes that out of 'em. Why, I originally come into the business meek myself. But Our Missis, she soon took that out of *me (Chapter 3: Ezekiel)*.

You should see our Bandolining Room at Mugby Junction. It's led to by the door behind the counter, which you'll notice usually stands ajar, and it's the room where Our Missis and our young ladies Bandolines their hair. You should see 'em at it, betwixt trains, Bandolining away, as if they was anointing themselves for the combat. When you're telegraphed, you should see their noses all a-going up with scorn, as if it was a part of the working of the same Cooke and Wheatstone electrical machinery. You should hear Our Missis give the word, 'Here comes the Beast to be Fed!' and then you should see 'em indignantly skipping across the Line, from the Up to the Down, or Wicer Warsaw, and begin to pitch the stale pastry into the plates, and chuck the sawdust sangwiches under the glass covers, and get out the – ha, ha, ha! – the sherry, – O my eye, my eye! – for your Refreshment.

It's only in the Isle of the Brave and Land of the Free (by which, of course, I mean to say Britannia) that Refreshmenting is so effective, so 'olesome, so constitutional a check upon the public. There was a Foreigner, which having politely, with his hat off, beseeched our young ladies and Our Missis for 'a leetel gloss hoff prarndee,' and having had the Line surveyed through him by all and no other acknowledgment, was a-proceeding at last to help himself, as seems to be the custom in his own country, when Our Missis, with her hair almost a-coming un-Bandolined with rage, and her eyes omitting sparks, flew at him, cotched the decanter out of his hand, and said, 'Put it down! I won't allow that!' The foreigner turned pale, stepped back with his arms stretched out in front of him, his hands clasped, and his shoulders riz, and exclaimed: 'Ah! Is it possible, this! That these disdaineous females and this ferocious old woman are placed here by the administration, not only to empoison the voyagers, but to affront them! Great Heaven! How arrives it? The English people. Or is he then a slave? Or idiot?' *(Chapter 3)*.

I think it was her standing up agin the Foreigner as giv' Our Missis the idea of going over to France, and droring a comparison betwixt Refreshmenting as followed among the frog-eaters, and Refreshmenting as triumphant in the Isle of the Brave and Land of the Free (by which, of course, I mean to say agin, Britannia). Our young ladies, Miss Whiff, Miss Piff, and Mrs. Sniff, was unanimous opposed to her going; for, as they says to Our Missis one and all, it is well beknown to the hends of the herth as no other nation except Britain has a idea of anythink, but above all of business. Why then should you tire yourself to prove what is already proved? Our Missis, however (being a teazer at all pints) stood out grim obstinate, and got a return pass by South-eastern Tidal, to go right through, if such should be her dispositions, to Marseilles *(Chapter 3)*.

When Our Missis went away upon her journey, Mrs. Sniff was left in charge. She did hold the public in check most beautiful! In all my time, I never see half so many cups of tea given without milk to people as wanted it with, nor half so many cups of tea with milk given to people as wanted it without. When foaming ensued, Mrs. Sniff would say: 'Then you'd better settle it among yourselves, and change with one another.' It was a most highly delicious lark. I enjoyed the Refreshmenting business more than ever, and was so glad I had took to it when young *(Chapter 3)*.

'I should not enter, ladies,' says Our Missis, 'on the revolting disclosures I am about to make, if it was not in the hope that they will cause you to be yet more implacable in the exercise of the power you wield in a constitutional country, and yet more devoted to the constitutional motto which I see before me,' – it was behind her, but the words sounded better so, – ' "May Albion never learn!" '

Here the pupils as had made the motto admired it, and cried, 'Hear! Hear! Hear!' Sniff, showing an inclination to join in chorus, got himself frowned down by every brow.

'The baseness of the French,' pursued Our Missis, 'as displayed in the fawning nature of their Refreshmenting, equals, if not surpasses, anythink as was ever heard of the baseness of the celebrated Bonaparte.'

Miss Whiff, Miss Piff, and me, we drored a heavy breath, equal to saying, 'We thought as much!' Miss Whiff and Miss Piff seeming to object to my droring mine along with theirs, I drored another to aggravate 'em.

'Shall I be believed,' says Our Missis, with flashing eyes, 'when I tell you that no sooner had I set my foot upon that treacherous shore – '

Here Sniff, either bursting out mad, or thinking aloud, says in a low voice: 'Feet. Plural, you know.'

The cowering that came upon him when he was spurned by all eyes, added to his being beneath contempt, was sufficient punishment for a cove so grovelling. In the midst of a silence rendered more impressive by the turned-up female noses with which it was pervaded, Our Missis went on:

'Shall I be believed when I tell you, that no sooner had I landed,' this word with a killing look at Sniff, 'on that treacherous shore, than I was ushered into a Refreshment Room where there were – I do not exaggerate – actually eatable things to eat?'

A groan burst from the ladies. I not only did myself the honour of jining, but also of lengthening it out.

'Where there were,' Our Missis added, 'not only eatable things to eat, but also drinkable things to drink?'

A murmur, swelling almost into a scream, ariz. Miss Piff, trembling with indignation, called out, 'Name?'

'I *will* name,' said Our Missis. 'There was roast fowls, hot and cold; there was smoking roast veal surrounded with browned potatoes; there was hot soup with (again I ask shall I be credited?) nothing bitter in it, and no flour to choke off the consumer; there was a variety of cold dishes set off with jelly; there was salad; there was – mark me! *fresh* pastry, and that of a light construction; there was a luscious show of fruit; there was bottles and decanters of sound small wine, of every size, and adapted to every pocket; the same odious statement will apply to brandy; and these were set out upon the counter so that all could help themselves.'

Our Missis's lips so quivered, that Mrs. Sniff, though scarcely less convulsed than she were, got up and held the tumbler to them.

'This,' proceeds Our Missis, 'was my first unconstitutional experience. Well would it have been if it had been my last and worst. But no. As I proceeded farther into that enslaved and ignorant land, its aspect became more hideous. I need not explain to this assembly the ingredients and formation of the British Refreshment sangwich?'

Universal laughter, – except from Sniff, who, as sangwich-cutter, shook his head in a state of the utmost dejection as he stood with it agin the wall.

'Well!' said Our Missis, with dilated nostrils. 'Take a fresh, crisp, long, crusty penny loaf made of the whitest and best flour. Cut it longwise through the middle. Insert a fair and nicely fitting slice of ham. Tie a smart piece of ribbon round the middle of the whole to bind it together. Add at one end a neat wrapper of clean white paper by which to hold it. And the universal French Refreshment sangwich busts on your disgusted vision' *(Chapter 3)*.

'Putting everything together,' said Our Missis, 'French Refreshmenting comes to this, and oh, it comes to a nice total! First: eatable things to eat, and drinkable things to drink.'

A groan from the young ladies, kep' up by me.

'Second: convenience, and even elegance.'

Another groan from the young ladies, kep' up by me.

'Third: moderate charges.'

This time a groan from me, kep' up by the young ladies.

'Fourth: – and here,' says Our Missis, 'I claim your angriest sympathy, – attention, common civility, nay, even politeness!'

Me and the young ladies regularly raging mad all together (Chapter 3).

I resumed my downward way, and stepping out upon the level of the railroad, and drawing nearer to him, saw that he was a dark, sallow man, with a dark beard and rather heavy eyebrows. His post was in as solitary and dismal a place as ever I saw. On either side, a dripping-wet wall of jagged stone, excluding all view but a strip of sky; the perspective one way only a crooked prolongation of this great dungeon; the shorter perspective in the other direction terminating in a gloomy red light, and the gloomier entrance to a black tunnel, in whose massive architecture there was a barbarous, depressing, and forbidding air. So little sunlight ever found its way to this spot, that it had an earthy, deadly smell; and so much cold wind rushed through it, that it struck chill to me, as if I had left the natural world.

Before he stirred, I was near enough to him to have touched him. Not even then removing his eyes from mine, he stepped back one step, and lifted his hand.

This was a lonesome post to occupy (I said), and it had riveted my attention when I looked down from up yonder. A visitor was a rarity. I should suppose; not an unwelcome rarity, I hoped? In me, he merely saw a man who had been shut up within narrow limits all his life, and who, being at last set free, had a newly-awakened interest in these great works. To such purpose I spoke to him; but I am far from sure of the terms I used; for, besides that I am not happy in opening any conversation, there was something in the man that daunted me.

He directed a most curious look towards the red light near the tunnel's mouth, and looked all about it, as if something were missing from it, and then looked at me.

That light was part of his charge? Was it not?

He answered in a low voice, – 'Don't you know it is?'

The monstrous thought came into my mind, as I perused the fixed eyes and the saturnine face, that this was a spirit, not a man. I have speculated since, whether there may have been infection in his mind (Chapter 4: Signalman).

'I have made up my mind, sir,' he began, bending forward as soon as we were seated, and speaking in a tone but a little above a whisper, 'that you shall not have to ask me twice what troubles me. I took you for some one else yesterday evening. That troubles me.'

'That mistake?'

'No. That some one else.'

'Who is it?'

'I don't know.'

'Like me?'

'I don't know. I never saw the face. The left arm is across the face, and the right arm is waved, – violently waved. This way.'

I followed his action with my eyes, and it was the action of an arm gesticulating, with the utmost passion and vehemence, 'For God's sake, clear the way!'

'One moonlight night,' said the man, 'I was sitting here, when I heard a voice cry, "Halloa! Below there!" I started up, looked from that door, and saw this Some one else standing by the red light near the tunnel, waving as I just now showed you. The voice seemed hoarse with shouting, and it cried, "Look out! Look out!" And then again, "Halloa! Below there! Look out!" I caught up my lamp, turned it on red, and ran towards the figure, calling, "What's wrong? What has happened? Where?" It stood just outside the blackness of the tunnel. I advanced so close upon it that I wondered at its keeping the sleeve across its eyes. I ran right up at it, and had my hand stretched out to pull the sleeve away, when it was gone.'

'Into the tunnel?' said I.

'No. I ran on into the tunnel, five hundred yards. I stopped, and held my lamp above my head, and saw the figures of the measured distance, and saw the wet stains stealing down the walls and trickling through the arch. I ran out again faster than I had run in (for I had a mortal abhorrence of the place upon me), and I looked all round the red light with my own red light, and I went up the iron ladder to the gallery atop of it, and I came down again, and ran back here. I telegraphed both ways, "An alarm has been given. Is anything wrong?" The answer came back, both ways, "All well." '

Resisting the slow touch of a frozen finger tracing out my spine, I showed him how that this figure must be a deception of his sense of sight; and how that figures, originating in disease of the delicate nerves that minister to the functions of the eye, were known to have often troubled patients, some of whom had become conscious of the nature of their affliction, and had even proved it by experiments upon themselves. 'As to an imaginary cry,' said I, 'do but listen for a moment to the wind in this unnatural valley while we speak so low, and to the wild harp it makes of the telegraph wires' (Chapter 4: Signalman).

With an irresistible sense that something was wrong, – with a flashing self-reproachful fear that fatal mischief had come of my leaving the man there, and causing no one to be sent to overlook or correct what he did, – I descended the notched path with all the speed I could make.

'What is the matter?' I asked the men.

'Signal-man killed this morning, sir.'

'Not the man belonging to that box?'

'Yes, sir.'

'Not the man I know?'

'You will recognize him, sir, if you knew him,' said the man who spoke for the others, solemnly uncovering his own head, and raising an end of the tarpaulin, 'for his face is quite composed.'

'O, how did this happen, how did this happen?' I asked, turning from one to another as the hut closed in again.

'He was cut down by an engine, sir. No man in England knew his work better. But somehow he was not clear of the outer rail. It was just at broad day. He had struck the light, and had the lamp in his hand. As the engine came out the tunnel, his back was towards her, and she cut him down. That man drove her, and was showing how it happened. Show the gentleman, Tom.'

The man, who wore a rough dark dress, stepped back to his former place at the mouth of the tunnel.

'Coming round the curve in the tunnel, sir,' he said, 'I saw him at the end, like as if I saw him down a perspective-glass. There was no time to check speed, and I knew him to be very careful. As he didn't seem to take heed of the whistle, I shut it off when we were running down upon him, and called to him as loud as I could call.'

'What did you say?'

'I said, "Below there! Look out! Look out! For God's sake, clear the way!" '

I started.

'Ah! it was a dreadful time, sir. I never left off calling to him. I put this arm before my eyes not to see, and I waved this arm to the last; but it was no use' *(Chapter 4).*

NO THOROUGHFARE

'Yes. I hope we shall all be a united family, Joey.'

'Ah!' said Joey. 'I hope they may be.'

'They? Rather say we, Joey.'

Joey Ladle shook his head. 'Don't look to me to make we on it, Young Master Wilding, not at my time of life and under the circumstances which has formed my disposition. I have said to Pebbleson Nephew many a time, when they have said to me, "Put a livelier face upon it, Joey" – I have said to them, "Gentlemen, it is all wery well for you that has been accustomed to take your wine into your systems by the conwivial channel of your throttles, to put a lively face upon it; but," I says, "I have been accustomed to take *my* wine in at the pores of the skin, and, took that way, it acts different. It acts depressing. It's one thing, gentlemen," I says to Pebbleson Nephew, "to charge your glasses in a dining-room with a Hip Hurrah and a Jolly Companions Every One, and it's another thing to be charged yourself, through the pores, in a low dark cellar and a mouldy atmosphere. It makes all the difference betwixt bubbles and wapours," I tells Pebbleson Nephew. And so it do. I've been a cellarman my life through, with my mind fully given to the business. What's the consequence? I'm as muddled a man as lives – you won't find a muddleder man than me – nor yet you won't find my equal in molloncolly. Sing of Filling the bumper fair, Every drop you sprinkle, O'er the brow of care, Smooths away a wrinkle? Yes. P'raps so. But try filling yourself through the pores, underground, when you don't want to it!' *(Act 1).*

BLEAK HOUSE

London. Michaelmas Term lately over, and the Lord Chancellor sitting in Lincoln's Inn Hall. Implacable November weather. As much mud in the streets, as if the waters had but newly retired from the face of the earth, and it would not be wonderful to meet a Megalosaurus, forty feet long or so, waddling like an elephantine lizard up Holborn Hill. Smoke lowering down from chimney-pots, making a soft black drizzle, with flakes of soot in it as big as full-grown snow-flakes – gone into mourning, one might imagine, for the death of the sun. Dogs, undistinguishable in mire. Horses, scarcely better; splashed to their very blinkers. Foot passengers, jostling one another's umbrellas, in a general infection of ill-temper, and losing their foothold at street corners, where tens of thousands of other foot passengers have been slipping and sliding since the day broke (if this day ever broke), adding new deposits to the crust upon crust of mud, sticking at those points tenaciously to the pavement, and accumulating at compound interest.

Fog everywhere. Fog up the river, where it flows among green aits and meadows; fog down the river, where it rolls defiled among the tiers of shipping, and the waterside pollutions of a great (and dirty) city. Fog on the Essex marshes, fog on the Kentish heights. Fog creeping into the cabooses of collier-brigs; fog lying out on the yards, and hovering in the rigging of great ships; fog dropping on the gunwales of barges and small boats. Fog in the eyes and throats of ancient Greenwich pensioners, wheezing by the firesides of their wards; fog in the stem and bowl of the afternoon pipe of the wrathful skipper, down in his close cabin; fog cruelly pinching the toes and fingers of his shivering little 'prentice boy on deck. Chance people on the bridges peeping over the parapets into a nether sky of fog, with fog all round them, as if they were up in a balloon, and hanging in the misty clouds.

Gas looming through the fog in divers places in the streets, much as the sun may, from the spongy fields, be seen to loom by husbandman and ploughboy. Most of the shops lighted two hours before their time – as the gas seems to know, for it has a haggard and unwilling look.

The raw afternoon is rawest, and the dense fog is densest, and the muddy streets are muddiest, near that leaden-headed old obstruction, appropriate ornament for the threshold of a leaden-headed old corporation: Temple Bar. And hard by Temple Bar, in Lincoln's Inn Hall, at the very heart of the fog, sits the Lord High Chancellor in his High Court of Chancery *(Chapter 1).*

On such an afternoon, if ever, the Lord High Chancellor ought to be sitting here – as here he is – with a foggy glory round his head, softly fenced in with crimson cloth and curtains, addressed by a large advocate with great whiskers, a little voice, and an interminable brief, and outwardly directing his contemplation to the lantern in the roof, where he can see nothing but fog. On such an afternoon, some score of members of the High Court of Chancery bar ought to be – as they are – mistily engaged in one of the ten thousand stages of an endless cause, tripping one another up on slippery precedents, groping knee-deep in technicalities, running their goat-hair and horse-hair warded heads against walls of words, and making a pretence of equity with serious faces, as players might. On such an afternoon, the various solicitors in the cause, some two or three of whom have inherited it from their fathers, who made a fortune by it, ought to be – as are they not? – ranged in a line, in a long matted well (but you might look in vain for Truth at the bottom of it), between the registrar's red table and the silk gowns, with bills, cross-bills, answers, rejoinders, injunctions, affidavits, issues, references to masters, masters' reports, mountains of costly nonsense, piled before them. Well may the court be dim, with wasting candles here and there; well may the fog hang heavy in it, as if it would never get out; well may the stained glass windows lose their colour, and admit no light of day into the place; well may the uninitiated from the streets, who peep in through the glass panes in the door, be deterred from entrance by its owlish aspect, and by the drawl languidly echoing to the roof from the padded daïs where the Lord High Chancellor looks into the lantern that has no light in it, and where the attendant wigs are all stuck in a fog-bank! This is the Court of Chancery; which has its decaying houses and its blighted lands in every shire; which has its worn-out lunatic in every mad-house, and its dead in every churchyard; which has its ruined suitor, with his slipshod heels and thread-bare dress, borrowing and begging through the round of every man's acquaintance; which gives to monied might, the means abundantly of wearying out the right; which so exhausts finances, patience, courage, hope; so overthrows the brain and breaks the heart; that there is not an honourable man among its practitioners who would not give – who does not often give – the warning, 'Suffer any wrong that can be done you, rather than come here!' (*Chapter 1*).

'Is it possible,' pursued Mr. Kenge, putting up his eye-glasses, 'that our young friend – I *beg* you won't distress yourself! – never heard of Jarndyce and Jarndyce!'

I shook my head, wondering even what it was.

'Not of Jarndyce and Jarndyce?' said Mr. Kenge, looking over his glasses at me, and softly turning the case about and about, as if he were petting something. 'Not of one of the greatest Chancery suits known? Not of Jarndyce and Jarndyce – the – a – in itself a monument of Chancery practice. In which (I would say) every difficulty, every contingency, every masterly fiction, every form of procedure known in that court, is represented over and over again? It is a cause that could not exist, out of this free and great country. I should say that the aggregate of costs in Jarndyce and Jarndyce, Mrs. Rachael'; I was afraid he addressed himself to her, because I appeared inattentive; 'amounts at the present hour to from SIX-ty to SEVEN-ty THOUSAND POUNDS!' said Mr. Kenge, leaning back in his chair (*Chapter 3:* Esther Summerson).

He was very obliging; and as he handed me into a fly, after superintending the removal of my boxes, I asked him whether there was a great fire anywhere? For the streets were so full of dense brown smoke that scarcely anything was to be seen.

'O dear no, miss,' he said. 'This is a London particular.'

I had never heard of such a thing.

'A fog, miss,' said the young gentleman.

'O indeed!' said I (*Chapter 3:* Esther and Guppy).

'You find me, my dears,' said Mrs. Jellyby, snuffing the two great office candles in tin candlesticks which made the room taste strongly of hot tallow (the fire had gone out, and there was nothing in the grate but ashes, a bundle of wood, and a poker), 'you find me, my dears, as usual, very busy; but that you will excuse. The African project at present employs my whole time. It involves me in correspondence with public bodies and with private individuals anxious for the welfare of their species all over the country. I am happy to say it is advancing. We hope by this time next year to have from a hundred and fifty to two hundred healthy families cultivating coffee and educating the natives of Borrioboola-Gha, on the left bank of the Niger' (*Chapter 4*).

'May I come in?' she shortly and unexpectedly asked me in the same sulky way.

'Certainly,' said I. 'Don't wake Miss Clare.'

She would not sit down, but stood by the fire, dipping her inky finger in the egg-cup, which contained vinegar, and smearing it over the ink stains on her face; frowning, the whole time, and looking very gloomy.

'I wish Africa was dead!' she said, on a sudden.

I was going to remonstrate.

'I do!' she said. 'Don't talk to me, Miss Summerson. I hate it and detest it. It's a beast!' (*Chapter 4:* Caddy Jellyby).

Mr. Krook shrunk into his former self as suddenly as he had leaped out of it.

'You see I have so many things here,' he resumed, holding up the lantern, 'of so many kinds, and all as the neighbours think (but *they* know nothing), wasting away and going to rack and ruin, that that's why they have given me and my place a christening. And I have so many old parchmentses and papers in my stock. And I have a liking for rust and must and cobwebs. And all's fish that comes to my net. And I can't abear to part with anything I once lay hold of (or so my neighbours think, but what do *they* know?) or to alter anything, or to have any sweeping, nor scouring, nor cleaning, nor repairing going on about me. That's the way I've got the ill name of Chancery. *I* don't mind. I go to see my noble and learned brother pretty well every day, when he sits in the Inn. He don't notice me, but I notice him. There's no great odds betwixt us. We both grub on in a muddle. Hi, Lady Jane!'

A large grey cat leaped from some neighbouring shelf on his shoulder, and startled us all (*Chapter 5*).

'The little Jellybys,' said Richard, coming to my relief, 'are really – I can't help expressing myself strongly, sir – in a devil of a state.'

'She means well,' said Mr. Jarndyce, hastily. 'The wind's in the east.'

'It was in the north, sir, as we came down,' observed Richard.

'My dear Rick,' said Mr. Jarndyce, poking the fire; 'I'll take an oath it's either in the east, or going to be. I am always conscious of an uncomfortable sensation now and then when the wind is blowing in the east' (*Chapter 6:* Richard Carstone and Jarndyce).

'Come, Rick, come! I must settle this before I sleep. How much are you out of pocket? You two made the money up, you know! Why did you? How could you? – O Lord, yes, it's due east – must be!

'Really, sir,' said Richard, 'I don't think it would be honourable in me to tell you. Mr. Skimpole relied upon us – '

'Lord bless you, my dear boy! He relies upon everybody!' said Mr. Jarndyce, giving his head a great rub, and stopping short.

'Indeed, sir?'

'Everybody! And he'll be in the same scrape again, next week!' said Mr. Jarndyce, walking again at a great pace, with a candle in his hand that had gone out. 'He's always in the same scrape. He was born in the same scrape. I verily believe that the announcement in the newspapers when his mother was confined, was "On Tuesday last, at her residence in Botheration Building, Mrs. Skimpole of a son in difficulties" '(*Chapter 6*).

There may be some motions of fancy among the lower animals at Chesney Wold. The horses in the stables – the long stables in a barren, red-brick courtyard, where there is a great bell in a turret, and a clock with a large face, which the pigeons who live near it, and who love to perch upon its shoulders, seem to be always consulting – *they* may contemplate some mental pictures of fine weather on occasions, and may be better artists at them than the grooms. The old roan, so famous for cross-country work, turning his large eyeball to the grated window near his rack, may remember the fresh leaves that glisten there at other times, and the scents that stream in, and may have a fine run with the hounds, while the human helper, clearing out the next stall, never stirs beyond his pitchfork and birch-broom. The grey, whose place is opposite the door, and who, with an impatient rattle of his halter, pricks his ears and turns his head so wistfully when it is opened, and to whom the opener says, 'Woa grey, then, steady! Noabody wants you to-day!' may know it quite as well as the man. The whole seemingly monotonous and uncompanionable half-dozen, stabled together, may pass the long wet hours, when the door is shut, in livelier communication than is held in the servants' hall, or at the Dedlock Arms; – or may even beguile the time by improving (perhaps corrupting) the pony in the loose-box in the corner.

So the mastiff, dozing in his kennel, in the court-yard, with his large head on his paws, may think of the hot sunshine, when the shadows of the stable-buildings tire his patience out by changing, and leave him, at one time of the day, no broader refuge than the shadow of his own house, where he sits on end,

panting and growling short, and very much wanting something to worry, besides himself and his chain. So, now, half-waking, and all-winking, he may recall the house full of company, the coach-houses full of vehicles, the stables full of horses, and the out-buildings full of attendants upon horses, until he is undecided about the present, and comes forth to see how it is. Then, with that impatient shake of himself, he may growl in the spirit, 'Rain, rain, rain! Nothing but rain – and no family here!' as he goes in again, and lies down with a gloomy yawn (*Chapter 7*).

I was passing through the passages on my return with my basket of keys on my arm, when Mr. Jarndyce called me into a small room next his bed-chamber, which I found to be in part a little library of books and papers, and in part quite a little museum of his boots and shoes, and hat-boxes.

'Sit down, my dear,' said Mr. Jarndyce. 'This, you must know, is the Growlery. When I am out of humour, I come and growl here.'

'You must be here very seldom, sir,' said I.

'O, you don't know me!' he returned. 'When I am deceived or disappointed in – the wind, and it's Easterly, I take refuge here. The Growlery is the best-used room in the house. You are not aware of half my humours yet. My dear, how you are trembling!' (*Chapter 8:* Jarndyce and Esther Summerson).

'He must have a profession; he must make some choice for himself. There will be a world more Wiglomeration about it, I suppose, but it must be done.'

'More what, Guardian?' said I.

'More Wiglomeration,' said he. 'It's the only name I know for the thing. He is a ward in Chancery, my dear. Kenge and Carboy will have something to say about it; Master Somebody – a sort of ridiculous Sexton, digging graves for the merits of causes in a back room at the end of Quality Court, Chancery Lane – will have something to say about it; Counsel will have something to say about it; the Chancellor will have something to say about it; the Satellites will have something to say about it; they will all have to be handsomely fee'd, all round, about it; the whole thing will be vastly ceremonious, wordy, unsatisfactory, and expensive, and I call it, in general Wiglomeration. How mankind ever came to be afflicted with Wiglomeration, or for those sins these young people ever fell into a pit of it, I don't know; so it is' (*Chapter 8:* Jarndyce).

'Not half a glass?' said Mr. Guppy; 'quarter? No! Then, to proceed. My present salary, Miss Summerson, at Kenge and Carboy's, is two pound a-week. When I first had the happiness of looking upon you, it was one-fifteen, and had stood at that figure for a lengthened period. A rise of five has since taken place, and a further rise of five is guaranteed at the expiration of a term not exceeding twelve months from the present date. My mother has a little property, which takes the form of a small life annuity: upon which she lives in an independent though unassuming manner, in the Old Street Road. She is eminently calculated for a mother-in-law. She never interferes, is all for peace,

O

and her disposition easy. She has her failings – as who has not? – but I never knew her do it when company was present; at which time you may freely trust her with wines, spirits, or malt liquors. My own abode is lodgings at Penton Place, Pentonville. It is lowly, but airy, open at the back, and considered one of the 'ealthiest outlets. Miss Summerson! In the mildest language, I adore you. Would you be so kind as to allow me (as I may say) to file a declaration – to make an offer!' *(Chapter 9)*.

Then the active and intelligent, who has got into the morning papers as such, comes with his pauper company to Mr. Krook's, and bears off the body of our dear brother here departed, to a hemmed-in church-yard, pestiferous and obscene, whence malignant diseases are communicated to the bodies of our dear brothers and sisters who have not departed; while our dear brothers and sisters who hang about official backstairs – would to Heaven they *had* departed! – are very complacent and agreeable. Into a beastly scrap of ground which a Turk would reject as a savage abomination, and a Caffre would shudder at, they bring our dear brother here departed, to receive Christian burial.

With houses looking on, on every side, save where a reeking little tunnel of a court gives access to the iron gate – with every villainy of life in action close on death, and every poisonous element of death in action close on life – here, they lower our dear brother down a foot or two: here, sow him in corruption, to be raised in corruption; an avenging ghost at many a sick-bedside: a shameful testimony to future ages, how civilisation and barbarism walked this boastful island together.

Come night, come darkness, for you cannot come too soon, or stay too long, by such a place as this! Come, straggling lights into the windows of the ugly houses; and you who do iniquity therein, do it at least with this dread scene shut out! Come, flame of gas, burning so sullenly above the iron gate, on which the poisoned air deposits its witch-ointment slimy to the touch! It is well that you should call to every passer-by, 'Look here!'

With the night, comes a slouching figure through the tunnel-court, to the outside of the iron gate. It holds the gate with its hands, and looks in between the bars; stands looking in, for a little while.

It then, with an old broom it carries, softly sweeps the step, and makes the archway clean. It does so, very busily and trimly; looks in again, a little while; and so departs.

Jo, is it thou? Well, well! Though a rejected witness, who 'can't exactly say' what will be done to him in greater hands than men's, thou art not quite in outer darkness. There is something like a distant ray of light in thy muttered reason for this:

'He wos wery good to me, he wos!' *(Chapter 11)*.

The brilliant and distinguished circle comprehends within it, no contracted amount of education, sense, courage, honour, beauty, and virtue. Yet there is something a little wrong about it, in despite of its immense advantages. What can it be?

Dandyism? There is no King George the Fourth now (more's the pity!) to set the dandy fashion; there are no clear-starched jack-towel neckcloths, no short-waisted coats, no false calves, no stays. There are no caricatures, now, of effeminate Exquisites so arrayed, swooning in opera boxes with excess of delight, and being revived by other dainty creatures, poking long-necked scent-bottles at their noses. There is no beau whom it takes four men at once to shake into his buck-skins, or who goes to see all the executions, or who is troubled with the self-reproach of having once consumed a pea. But is there Dandyism in the brilliant and distinguished circle notwithstanding, Dandyism of a more mischievous sort, that has got below the surface and is doing less harmless things than jack-towelling itself and stopping its own digestion, to which no rational person need particularly object?

Why, yes. It cannot be disguised. There *are*, at Chesney Wold this January week, some ladies and gentlemen of the newest fashion, who have set up a Dandyism – in Religion, for instance. Who, in mere lackadaisical want of an emotion, have agreed upon a little dandy talk about the Vulgar wanting faith in things in general; meaning, in the things that have been tried and found wanting, as though a low fellow should unaccountably lose faith in a bad shilling, after finding it out! Who would make the Vulgar very picturesque and faithful, by putting back the hands upon the Clock of Time, and cancelling a few hundred years of history *(Chapter 12)*.

'The dear old Crippler!' said Mrs. Badger, shaking her head. 'She was a noble vessel. Trim, ship-shape, all a taunto, as Captain Swosser used to say. You must excuse me if I occasionally introduce a nautical expression; I was quite a sailor once. Captain Swosser loved that craft for my sake. When she was no longer in commission, he frequently said that if he were rich enough to buy her old hulk, he would have an inscription let into the timbers of the quarter-deck where we stood as partners in the dance, to mark the spot where he fell – raked fore and aft (Captain Swosser used to say) by the fire from my tops. It was his naval way of mentioning my eyes' *(Chapter 13)*.

'Go on, Prince! Go on!' said Mr. Turveydrop, standing with his back to the fire, and waving his gloves condescendingly. 'Go on, my son!'

At this command, or by this gracious permission, the lesson went on. Prince Turveydrop sometimes played the kit, dancing; sometimes played the piano, standing; sometimes hummed the tune with what little breath he could spare, while he set a pupil right; always conscientiously moved with the least proficient through every step and every part of the figure; and never rested for an instant. His distinguished father did nothing whatever, but stand before the fire, a model of Deportment.

'And he never does anything else,' said the old lady of the censorious countenance. 'Yet would you believe that it's *his* name on the door-plate?'

'His son's name is the same, you know,' said I.

'He wouldn't let his son have any name, if he could take it from him,' returned the old lady. 'Look at the son's dress!' It certainly was plain – threadbare – almost shabby. 'Yet the father must be garnished and tricked out,' said the old lady, 'because of his Deportment. I'd deport him! Transport him would be better!' *(Chapter 14).*

'What, you're looking at my lodger's birds, Mr. Jarndyce?' The old man had come by little and little into the room, until he now touched my guardian with his elbow, and looked close up into his face with his spectacled eyes. 'It's one of her strange ways, that she'll never tell the names of these birds if she can help it, though she named 'em all.' This was in a whisper. 'Shall I run 'em over, Flite?' he asked aloud, winking at us and pointing at her as she turned away, affecting to sweep the grate.

'If you like,' she answered hurriedly.

The old man, looking up at the cages, after another look at us, went through the list.

'Hope, Joy, Youth, Peace, Rest, Life, Dust, Ashes, Waste, Want, Ruin, Despair, Madness, Death, Cunning, Folly, Words, Wigs, Rags, Sheepskin, Plunder, Precedent, Jargon, Gammon and Spinach. That's the whole collection,' said the old man, 'all cooped up together, by my noble and learned brother.'

'This is a bitter wind!' muttered my guardian.

'When my noble and learned brother gives his Judgment, they're to be let go free,' said Krook, winking at us again. 'And then,' he added, whispering and grinning, 'if that ever was to happen – which it won't – the birds that have never been caged would kill 'em' *(Chapter 14).*

Jo lives – that is to say, Jo has not yet died – in a ruinous place, known to the like of him by the name of Tom-all-Alone's. It is a black, dilapidated street, avoided by all decent people; where the crazy houses were seized upon, when their decay was far advanced, by some bold vagrants, who, after establishing their own possession, took to letting them out in lodgings. Now, these tumbling tenements contain, by night, a swarm of misery. As, on the ruined human wretch, vermin parasites appear, so, these ruined shelters have bred a crowd of foul existence that crawls in and out of gaps in walls and boards; and coils itself to sleep, in maggot numbers, where the rain drips in; and comes and goes, fetching and carrying fever, and sowing more evil in its every footprint than Lord Coodle, and Sir Thomas Doodle, and the Duke of Foodle, and all the fine gentlemen in office, down to Zoodle, shall set right in five hundred years – though born expressly to do it.

Twice, lately, there has been a crash and a cloud of dust, like the springing of a mine, in Tom-all-Alone's; and, each time, a house has fallen. These accidents have made a paragraph in the newspapers, and have filled a bed or two in the nearest hospital. The gaps remain, and there are not unpopular lodgings among the rubbish. As several more houses are nearly ready to go, the next crash in Tom-all-Alone's may be expected to be a good one *(Chapter 16).*

'He was put there,' says Jo, holding to the bars and looking in.

'Where? O, what a scene of horror!'

'There!' says Jo, pointing. 'Over yinder. Among them piles of bones and close to that there kitchin

winder! They put him wery nigh the top. They was obliged to stamp upon it to git it in. I could unkiver it for you with my broom, if the gate was open. That's why they locks it, I s'pose,' giving it a shake. 'It's always locked. Look at the rat!' cried Jo, excited. 'Hi! Look! There he goes! Ho! Into the ground!'

The servant shrinks into a corner – into a corner of that hideous archway, with its deadly stains contaminating her dress; and putting out her two hands, and passionately telling him to keep away from her, for he is loathsome to her, so remains for some moments. Jo stands staring, and is still staring when she recovers herself.

'Is this place of abomination, consecrated ground?'

'I don't know nothink of consequential ground,' says Jo, still staring.

'Is it blessed?'

'WHICH?'. says Jo, in the last degree amazed.

'Is it blessed?'

'I'm blest if I know,' says Jo, staring more than ever; 'but I shouldn't think it warn't. Blest?' repeats Jo, something troubled in his mind. 'It ain't done it much good if it is. Blest? I should think it was t'othered myself. But I don't know nothink!' *(Chapter 16).*

'Why, Mr. Carstone,' said Mrs. Badger, 'is very well, and is, I assure you, a great acquisition to our society. Captain Swosser used to say of me that I was always better than land a-head and a breeze a-starn to the midshipmen's mess when the purser's junk had become as tough as the fore-topsel weather earrings. It was his naval way of mentioning generally that I was an acquisition to any society' *(Chapter 17).*

'It was a maxim of Captain Swosser's,' said Mrs. Badger, 'speaking in his figurative naval manner, that when you make pitch hot, you cannot make it too hot; and that if you only have to swab a plank, you should swab it as if Davy Jones were after you. It appears to me that this maxim is applicable to the medical, as well as to the nautical profession' *(Chapter 17).*

'People objected to Professor Dingo, when we were staying in the North of Devon, after our marriage,' said Mrs. Badger, 'that he disfigured some of the houses and other buildings, by chipping off fragments of those edifices with his little geological hammer. But the Professor replied, that he knew of no building, save the Temple of Science. The principle is the same, I think?'

'Precisely the same,' said Mr. Badger. 'Finely expressed! The Professor made the same remark, Miss Summerson, in his last illness; when (his mind wandering) he insisted on keeping his little hammer under the pillow, and chipping at the countenances of the attendants. The ruling passion!' *(Chapter 17).*

He lived in a pretty house, formerly the Parsonage house, with a lawn in front, a bright flower-garden at the side, and a well-stocked orchard and kitchen-garden in the rear, enclosed with a venerable wall that had of itself a ripened ruddy look. But, indeed, everything about the place wore an aspect of maturity and abundance. The old lime-tree walk was like green cloisters, the very shadows of the cherry-trees and apple-trees were heavy with fruit, the gooseberry-bushes were so laden that their branches arched and rested on the earth, the strawberries and raspberries grew in like profusion, and the peaches basked by the hundred on the wall. Tumbled about among the spread nets and the glass frames sparkling and winking in the sun, there were such heaps of drooping pods, and marrows, and cucumbers, that every foot of ground appeared a vegetable treasury, while the smell of sweet herbs and all kinds of wholesome growth (to say nothing of the neighbouring meadows where the hay was carrying) made the whole air a great nosegay. Such stillness and composure reigned within the orderly precincts of the old red wall, that even the feathers hung in garlands to scare the birds hardly stirred; and the wall had such a ripening influence that where, here and there high up, a disused nail and scrap of list still clung to it, it was easy to fancy that they had mellowed with the changing seasons, and that they had rusted and decayed according to the common fate *(Chapter 18)*.

'But excellent Boythorn might say,' returned our host, swelling and growing very red, 'I'll be – '
'I understand,' said Mr. Skimpole. 'Very likely he would.'
' – if I *will* go to dinner!' cried Mr. Boythorn, in a violent burst, and stopping to strike his stick upon the ground. 'And he would probably add, "Is there such a thing as principle, Mr. Harold Skimpole?" '
'To which Harold Skimpole would reply, you know,' he returned in his gayest manner, and with his most ingenuous smile, ' "Upon my life I have not the least idea! I don't know what it is you call by that name, or where it is, or who possesses it. If you possess it, and find it comfortable, I am quite delighted, and congratulate you heartily. But I know nothing about it, I assure you; for I am a mere child, and I lay no claim to it, and I don't want it!" So, you see, excellent Boythorn and I would go to dinner after all!' *(Chapter 18)*.

It is the hottest long vacation known for many years. All the young clerks are madly in love, and, according to their various degrees, pine for bliss with the beloved object, at Margate, Ramsgate, or Gravesend. All the middle-aged clerks think their families too large. All the unowned dogs who stray into the Inns of Court, and pant about staircases and other dry places, seeking water, give short howls of aggravation. All the blind men's dogs in the streets draw their masters against pumps, or trip them over buckets. A shop with a sun-blind, and a watered pavement, and a bowl of gold and silver fish in the window, is a sanctuary. Temple Bar gets so hot, that it is, to the adjacent Strand and Fleet Street, what a heater is in an urn, and keeps them simmering all night *(Chapter 19)*.

From Mr. Chadband's being much given to describe himself, both verbally and in writing, as a vessel, he is occasionally mistaken by strangers for a gentleman connected with navigation; but, he is, as he expresses it, 'in the ministry.' Mr. Chadband is attached to no particular denomination; and is considered by his persecutors to have nothing so very

remarkable to say on the greatest of subjects as to render his volunteering, on his own account, at all incumbent on his conscience; but, he has his followers, and Mrs. Snagsby is of the number *(Chapter 19)*.

'My little woman,' says Mr. Snagsby to the sparrows in Staple, 'likes to have her religion rather sharp, you see!' *(Chapter 19)*.

'My friends,' says Mr. Chadband, 'Peace be on this house! On the master thereof, on the mistress thereof, on the young maidens, and on the young men! My friends, why do I wish for peace? What is peace? Is it war? No. Is it strife? No. Is it lovely, and gentle, and beautiful, and pleasant, and serene, and joyful? O yes! Therefore, my friends, I wish for peace, upon you and upon yours' *(Chapter 19)*.

'My friends,' says Chadband, 'eightpence is not much; it might justly have been one and fourpence; it might justly have been half-a-crown. O let us be joyful, joyful! O let us be joyful!'
With which remark, which appears from its sound to be an extract in verse, Mr. Chadband stalks to the table, and, before taking a chair, lifts up his admonitory hand.
'My friends,' says he, 'what is this which we now behold as being spread before us? Refreshment. Do we need refreshment then, my friends? We do. And why do we need refreshment, my friends? Because we are but mortal, because we are but sinful, because we are but of the earth, because we are not of the air. Can we fly, my friends? We cannot. Why can we not fly, my friends?'
Mr. Snagsby, presuming on the success of his last point, ventures to observe in a cheerful and rather knowing tone, 'No wings.' But, is immediately frowned down by Mrs. Snagsby *(Chapter 19)*.

'He's as obstinate a young gonoph as I know. He WON'T move on.'
'O my eye! Where can I move to!' cries the boy, clutching quite desperately at his hair, and beating his bare feet upon the floor of Mr. Snagsby's passage.
'Don't you come none of that, or I shall make blessed short work of you!' says the constable, giving him a passionless shake. 'My instructions are, that you are to move on. I have told you so five hundred times.'
'But where?' cries the boy.
'Well! Really, constable, you know,' says Mr. Snagsby wistfully, and coughing behind his hand his cough of great perplexity and doubt; 'really that does seem a question. Where, you know?'
'My instructions don't go to that,' replies the constable. 'My instructions are that this boy is to move on.'
Do you hear, Jo? It is nothing to you or to any one else, that the great lights of the parliamentary sky have failed for some few years, in this business, to set you the example of moving on. The one grand recipe remains for you – the profound philosophical prescription – the be-all and the end-all of your strange existence upon earth. Move on! You are by no means to move off, Jo, for the great lights can't at all agree about that. Move on! *(Chapter 19)*.

'My young friend, stand forth!'

Jo, thus apostrophised, gives a slouch backward, and another slouch forward, and another slouch to each side, and confronts the eloquent Chadband, with evident doubts of his intentions.

'My young friend,' says Chadband, 'you are to us a pearl, you are to us a diamond, you are to us a gem, you are to us a jewel. And why, my young friend?'

'*I* don't know,' replies Jo. 'I don't know nothink.'

'My young friend,' says Chadband, 'it is because you know nothing that you are to us a gem and jewel. For what are you, my young friend? Are you a beast of the field? No. A bird of the air? No. A fish of the sea or river? No. You are a human boy, my young friend. A human boy. O glorious to be a human boy! And why glorious, my young friend? Because you are capable of receiving the lessons of wisdom, because you are capable of profiting by this discourse which I now deliver for your good, because you are not a stick, or a staff, or a stock, or a stone, or a post, or a pillar.

O running stream of sparkling joy
To be a soaring human boy!

And do you cool yourself in that stream now, my young friend? No. Why do you not cool yourself in that stream now? Because you are in a state of darkness, because you are in a state of obscurity, because you are in a state of sinfulness, because you are in a state of bondage. My young friend, what *is* bondage? Let us, in a spirit of love, inquire.'

At this threatening stage of the discourse, Jo, who seems to have been gradually going out of his mind, smears his right arm over his face, and gives a terrible yawn. Mrs. Snagsby indignantly expresses her belief that he is a limb of the archfiend *(Chapter 19)*.

Jo moves on, through the long vacation, down to Blackfriars Bridge, where he finds a baking stony corner, wherein to settle to his repast.

And there he sits, munching and gnawing, and looking up at the great Cross on the summit of St. Paul's Cathedral, glittering above a red and violet-tinted cloud of smoke. From the boy's face one might suppose that sacred emblem to be, in his eyes, the crowning confusion of the great, confused city; so golden, so high up, so far out of his reach. There he sits, the sun going down, the river running fast, the crowd flowing by him in two streams – everything moving on to some purpose and to one end – until he is stirred up, and told to 'move on' too *(Chapter 19)*.

'Well, and how are you?' says Mr. Guppy, shaking hands with him.

'So, so. How are you?'

Mr. Guppy replying that he is not much to boast of, Mr. Jobling ventures on the question, 'How is *she?*' This Mr. Guppy resents as a liberty; retorting, 'Jobling, there *are* chords in the human mind – ' Jobling begs pardon.

'Any subject but that!' says Mr. Guppy, with a gloomy enjoyment of his injury. 'For there *are* chords, Jobling – '

Mr. Jobling begs pardon again *(Chapter 20)*.

'Then, what's a fellow to do? I have been keeping out of the way, and living cheap, down about the market-gardens; but what's the use of living cheap when you have got no money? You might as well live dear.'

'Better,' Mr. Smallweed thinks.

'Certainly. It's the fashionable way; and fashion and whiskers have been my weaknesses, and I don't care who knows it,' says Mr. Jobling. 'They are great weaknesses – Damme, sir, they are great. Well!' proceeds Mr. Jobling, after a defiant visit to his rum-and-water, 'what can a fellow do, I ask you, *but* enlist?' *(Chapter 20)*.

Some time elapses, in the present instance, before the old gentleman is sufficiently cool to resume his discourse; and even then he mixes it up with several edifying expletives addressed to the unconscious partner of his bosom, who holds communication with nothing on earth but the trivets. As thus:

'If your father, Bart, had lived longer, he might have been worth a deal of money – you brimstone chatterer! – but just as he was beginning to build up the house that he had been making the foundations for, through many a year – you jade of a magpie, jackdaw, and poll-parrot, what do you mean! – he took ill and died of a low fever, always being a sparing and a spare man, full of business care – I should like to throw a cat at you instead of a cushion, and I will too if you make such a confounded fool of yourself! – and your mother, who was a prudent woman as dry as a chip, just dwindled away like touchwood after you and Judy were born – You are an old pig. You are a brimstone pig. You're a head of swine!' *(Chapter 21: 'Mr. Smallweed')*.

'You're a brimstone idiot. You're a scorpion – a brimstone scorpion! You're a sweltering toad. You're a chattering clattering broomstick witch, that ought to be burnt!' gasps the old man, prostrate in his chair. 'My dear friend, will you shake me up a little?' *(Chapter 21: Smallweed)*.

Allegory looks pretty cool in Lincoln's Inn Fields, though the evening is hot; for, both Mr. Tulkinghorn's windows are wide open, and the room is lofty, gusty, and gloomy. These may not be desirable characteristics when November comes with fog and sleet, or January with ice and snow; but they have their merits in the sultry long vacation weather. They enable Allegory, though it has cheeks like peaches, and knees like bunches of blossoms, and rosy swellings for calves to its legs and muscles to its arms, to look tolerably cool to-night.

Plenty of dust comes in at Mr. Tulkinghorn's windows, and plenty more has generated among his furniture and papers. It lies thick everywhere. When a breeze from the country that has lost its way, takes fright, and makes a blind hurry to rush out again, it flings as much dust in the eyes of Allegory as the law – or Mr. Tulkinghorn, one of its trustiest representatives – may scatter, on occasion, in the eyes of the laity *(Chapter 22)*.

'My children,' said Mr. Turveydrop, paternally encircling Caddy with his left arm as she sat beside him, and putting his right hand gracefully on his hip. 'My son and daughter, your happiness shall be my care. I will watch over you. You shall always live with me'; meaning, of course, I will always live with you; 'this house is henceforth as much yours as mine; consider it your home. May you long live to share it with me!'

The power of his Deportment was such, that they really were as much overcome with thankfulness as if, instead of quartering himself upon them for the rest of his life, he were making some munificent sacrifice in their favour.

'For myself, my children,' said Mr. Turveydrop, 'I am falling into the sear and yellow leaf, and it is impossible to say how long the last feeble traces of gentlemanly Deportment may linger in this weaving and spinning age. But, so long, I will do my duty to society, and will show myself, as usual, about town. My wants are few and simple. My little apartment here, my few essentials for the toilet, my frugal morning meal, and my little dinner, will suffice. I charge your dutiful affection with the supply of these requirements, and I charge myself with all the rest.'

They were overpowered afresh by his uncommon generosity *(Chapter 23)*.

The Lord Chancellor leaned back in his very easy chair, with his elbow on the cushioned arm, and his forehead resting on his hand; some of those who were present, dozed; some read the newspapers; some walked about, or whispered in groups: all seemed perfectly at their ease, by no means in a hurry, very unconcerned and extremely comfortable.

To see everything going on so smoothly, and to think of the roughness of the suitors' lives and deaths; to see all that full dress and ceremony, and to think of the waste, and want, and beggared misery it represented; to consider that, while the sickness of hope deferred was raging in so many hearts, this polite show went calmly on from day to day, and year to year, in such good order and composure; to behold the Lord Chancellor, and the whole array of practitioners under him, looking at one another and at the spectators, as if nobody had ever heard that all over England the name in which they were assembled was a bitter jest: was held in universal horror, contempt, and indignation; was known for something so flagrant and bad, that little short of a miracle could bring any good out of it to any one: this was so curious and self-contradictory to me, who had no experience of it, that it was at first incredible, and I could not comprehend it *(Chapter 24)*.

'Of all my old associations, of all my old pursuits and hopes, of all the living and the dead world, this one poor soul alone comes natural to me, and I am fit for. There is a tie of many suffering years between us two, and it is the only tie I ever had on earth that Chancery has not broken!' *(Chapter 24*: Richard Carstone).

'Or, my juvenile friends,' says Chadband, descending to the level of their comprehension, with a very obtrusive demonstration, in his greasily meek smile, of coming a long way downstairs for the purpose, 'if the master of this house was to go forth into the city and there see an eel, and was to come back, and was to call

unto him the mistress of this house, and was to say, "Sarah, rejoice with me, for I have seen an elephant!" would *that* be Terewth?'

Mrs. Snagsby in tears.

'Or put it, my juvenile friends, that he saw an elephant, and returning said "Lo, the city is barren, I have seen but an eel," would *that* be Terewth?'

Mrs. Snagsby sobbing loudly *(Chapter 25)*.

'The old girl,' says Mr. Bagnet ... 'saves. Has a stocking somewhere. With money in it. I never saw it. But I know she's got it. Wait till the greens is off her mind. Then she'll set you up.'

'She is a treasure!' exclaims Mr. George.

'She's more. But I never own to it before her. Discipline must be maintained. It was the old girl that brought out my musical abilities. I should have been in the artillery now, but for the old girl. Six years I hammered at the fiddle. Ten at the flute. The old girl said it wouldn't do; intention good, but want of flexibility; try the bassoon. The old girl borrowed a bassoon from the bandmaster of the Rifle Regiment. I practised in the trenches. Got on, got another, get a living by it!'

George remarks that she looks as fresh as a rose, and as sound as an apple.

'The old girl,' says Mr. Bagnet in reply, 'is a thoroughly fine woman. Consequently, she is like a thoroughly fine day. Gets finer as she gets on. I never saw the old girl's equal. But I never own to it before her. Discipline must be maintained!' *(Chapter 27)*.

'My dear Caddy,' said Mr. Jellyby. 'Never have – '

'Not Prince Pa?' faltered Caddy. 'Not have Prince?'

'Yes, my dear,' said Mr. Jellyby. 'Have him, certainly. But, never have – '

I mentioned, in my account of our first visit in Thavies Inn, that Richard described Mr. Jellyby as frequently opening his mouth after dinner without saying anything. It was a habit of his. He opened his mouth now, a great many times, and shook his head in a melancholy manner.

'What do you wish me not to have? Don't have what, dear Pa?' asked Caddy, coaxing him, with her arms round his neck.

'Never have a Mission, my dear child' *(Chapter 30)*.

It is night in Lincoln's Inn – perplexed and troublous valley of the shadow of the law, where suitors generally find but little day – and fat candles are snuffed out in offices, and clerks have rattled down the crazy wooden stairs, and dispersed. The bell that rings at nine o'clock, has ceased its doleful clangour about nothing; the gates are shut; and the night-porter, a solemn warder with a mighty power of sleep, keeps guard in his lodge. From tiers of staircase windows, clogged lamps like the eyes of Equity, bleared Argus with a fathomless pocket for every eye and an eye upon it, dimly blink at the stars. In dirty upper casements, here and there, hazy little patches of candlelight reveal where some wise draughtsman and conveyancer yet toils for the entanglement of real estate in meshes of sheep-skin, in the average ratio of about a dozen of sheep to an acre of land. Over which bee-like industry, these benefactors of their species linger yet, though office-hours be past; that they may give, for every day, some good account at last (*Chapter 32*).

'I thought you had gone to Jericho at least, instead of coming here,' says Tony.

Why, I said about ten.'

'You said about ten,' Tony repeats. 'Yes, so you did say about ten. But, according to my count, it's ten times ten – it's a hundred o'clock. I never had such a night in my life!'

'What has been the matter?'

'That's it!' says Tony. 'Nothing has been the matter. But, here have I been stewing and fuming in this jolly old crib, till I have had the horrors falling on me as thick as hail. *There's* a blessed-looking candle!' says Tony, pointing to the heavily burning taper on his table with a great cabbage head and a long winding-sheet.

'That's easily improved,' Mr. Guppy observed, as he takes the snuffers in hand.

'*Is* it?' returns his friend. 'Not so easily as you think. It has been smouldering like that, ever since it was lighted' (*Chapter 32:* Weevle and Guppy).

'No! Dash it, Tony,' says that gentleman [Mr. Guppy], 'you really ought to be careful how you wound the feelings of a man, who has an unrequited image imprinted on his art, and who is *not* altogether happy in those chords which vibrate to the tenderest emotions. You, Tony, possess in yourself all that is calculated to charm the eye, and allure the taste. It is not – happily for you, perhaps, and I may wish that I could say the same – it is not your character to hover around the flower. The ole garden is open to you, and your airy pinions carry through it. Still, Tony, far be it from me, I am sure, to wound even your feelings without a cause!' (*Chapter 32*).

Mr. Guppy has been biting his thumb-nail during this dialogue, generally changing the thumb when he has changed the cross leg. As he is going to do so again, he happens to look at his coat-sleeve. It takes his attention. He stares at it, aghast.

'Why, Tony, what on earth is going on in this house to-night? Is there a chimney on fire?'

'Chimney on fire!'

'Ah!' returns Mr. Guppy. 'See how the soot's falling. See here, on my arm! See again, on the table here! Confound the stuff, it won't blow off – smears, like black fat!'

They look at one another, and Tony goes listening to the door, and a little way upstairs, and a little way downstairs. Comes back, and says it's all right, and all quiet; and quotes the remark he lately made to Mr. Snagsby, about their cooking chops at the Sol's Arms.

'And it was then,' resumes Mr. Guppy, still glancing with remarkable aversion at the coat-sleeve, as they pursue their conversation before the fire, leaning on opposite sides of the table, with their heads very neat together, 'that he told you of his having taken the bundle of letters from his lodger's portmanteau?'

'That was the time, sir,' answers Tony, faintly adjusting his whiskers. 'Whereupon I wrote a line to my dear boy, the Honourable William Guppy, informing him of the appointment for to-night, and advising him not to call before: Boguey being a Slyboots.'

The light vivacious tone of fashionable life which is usually assumed by Mr. Weevle, sits so ill upon him to-night, that he abandons that and his whiskers together; and, after looking over his shoulder, appears to yield himself up, a prey to the horrors again (*Chapter 32*).

'What's that?'

'It's eleven o'clock striking by the bell of Saint Paul's. Listen, and you'll hear all the bells in the city jangling.'

Both sit silent, listening to the metal voices, near and distant, resounding from towers of various heights, in tones more various than their situations. When these at length cease, all seems more mysterious and quiet than before. One disagreeable result of whispering is, that it seems to evoke an atmosphere of silence, haunted by the ghosts of sound – strange cracks and tickings, the rustling of garments that have no substance in them, and the tread of dreadful feet, that would leave no mark on the sea-sand or the winter snow. So sensitive the two friends happen to be, that the air is full of these phantoms; and the two look over their shoulders by one consent, to see that the door is shut (*Chapter 32:* Guppy and Weevle).

'Fah! Here's more of this hateful soot hanging about,' says he. 'Let us open the window a bit, and get a mouthful of air. It's too close.'

He raises the sash, and they both rest on the window-sill, half in and half out of the room (*Chapter 32:* Guppy).

Mr. Guppy sitting on the window-will . . . continues thoughtfully to tap it, and clasp it, and measure it with his hand, until he hastily draws his hand away.

'What, in the Devil's name,' he says, 'is this! Look at my fingers!'

A thick, yellow liquor defiles them, which is offensive to the touch and sight and more offensive to the smell. A stagnant, sickening oil, with some natural repulsion in it that makes them both shudder.

'What have you been doing here? What have you been pouring out of the window?'

'I pouring out of window! Nothing, I swear! Never, since I have been here!' cries the lodger.

And yet look here – and look here! When he brings the candle, here, from the corner of the window-sill, it slowly drips, and creeps away down the bricks; here, lies in a little thick nauseous pool.

'This is a horrible house,' says Mr. Guppy, shutting down the window. 'Give me some water, or I shall cut my hand off' (*Chapter 33:* Guppy).

In no more than a minute or two the stairs creak, and Tony comes swiftly back.

'Have you got them?'

'Got them! No. The old man's not there.'

He has been so horribly frightened in the short interval, that his terror seizes the other, who makes a rush at him, and asks loudly, 'What's the matter?'

411

'I couldn't make him hear, and I softly opened the door and looked in. And the burning smell is there – and the soot is there, and the oil is there – and he is not there!' – Tony ends this with a groan.

Mr. Guppy takes the light. They go down, more dead than alive, and holding one another, push open the door of the back shop. The cat has retreated close to it, and stands snarling – not at them; at something on the ground before the fire. There is a very little fire left in the grate, but there, is a smouldering, suffocating vapour in the room, and a dark greasy coating on the walls and ceiling. The chairs and table, and the bottle so rarely absent from the table, all stand as usual. On one chair-back, hang the old man's hairy cap and coat.

'Look!' whispers the lodger, pointing his friend's attention to these objects with a trembling finger. 'I told you so. When I saw him last, he took his cap off, took out the little bundle of old letters, hung his cap on the back of the chair – his coat was there already, for he had pulled that off, before he went to put the shutters up – and I left him turning the letters over in his hand, standing just where that crumbled black thing is upon the floor' (*Chapter 32:* Guppy and Weevle).

'What's the matter with the cat?' says Mr. Guppy. 'Look at her!'

'Mad, I think. And no wonder in this evil place.'

They advance slowly, looking at all these things. The cat remains where they found her, still snarling at the something on the ground, before the fire and between the two chairs. What is it? Hold up the light.

Here is a small burnt patch of flooring; here is the tinder from a little bundle of burnt paper, but not so light as usual, seeming to be steeped in something; and here is – is it the cinder of a small charred and broken log of wood sprinkled with white ashes, or is it coal? O Horror, he IS here! and this from which we run away, striking out the light and overturning one another into the street, is all that represents him.

Help, help, help! come into this house for Heaven's sake!

Plenty will come in, but none can help. The Lord Chancellor of that Court, true to his title in his last act, had died the death of all Lord Chancellors in all Courts, and of all authorities in all places under all names soever, where false pretences are made, and where injustice is done. Call the death by any name Your Highness will, attribute it to whom you will, or say it might have been prevented how you will, it is the same death eternally – inborn, inbred, engendered in the corrupted humours of the vicious body itself, and that only – Spontaneous Combustion, and none other of all the deaths than can be died (*Chapter 32*).

'O Lord!' gasps Mr. Smallweed, looking about him, breathless, from an arm-chair. 'O dear me! O my bones and back! O my aches and pains! Sit down, you dancing, prancing, shambling, scrambling poll-parrot! Sit down!'

This little apostrophe to Mrs. Smallweed is occasioned by a propensity on the part of that unlucky old lady, whenever she finds herself on her feet, to amble about and 'set' to inanimate objects, accompanying herself with a chattering noise, as in a witch dance. A nervous affection has probably as much to do with these demonstrations, as any imbecile intention in the poor old woman; but on the present occasion they are so particularly lively in connexion with the Windsor arm-chair, fellow to that in which Mr. Smallweed is seated, that she only quite desists when her grandchildren have held her down in it: her lord in the meanwhile bestowing upon her, with great volubility, the endearing epithet of 'a pig-headed Jackdaw,' repeated a surprising number of times (*Chapter 33*).

'George, you know the old girl – she's as sweet and mild as milk. But touch her on the children – or myself – and she's off like gunpowder.'

'It does her credit, Mat!'

'George,' says Mr. Bagnet, looking straight before him, 'the old girl – can't do anything – that don't do her credit. More or less. I never say so. Discipline must be maintained.'

'She's worth her weight in gold,' says the trooper.

'In gold?' says Mr. Bagnet. 'I'll tell you what. The old girl's weight – is twelve stone six. Would I take that weight – in any metal – *for* the old girl? No. Why not? Because the old girl's metal is far more precious – than the preciousest metal. And she's *all* metal!'

'You are right, Mat!'

'When she took me – and accepted the ring – she 'listed under me and the children – heart and head; for life. She's that earnest,' says Mr. Bagnet, 'and true to her colours – that, touch us with a finger – and she turns out – and stands to her arms. If the old girl fires wide – once in a way – at the call of duty – look over it, George. For she's loyal!' (*Chapter 34*).

'My dear,' said she as she carefully folded up her scarf and gloves, 'my brave physician ought to have a Title bestowed upon him. And no doubt he will. You are of that opinion?'

That he well deserved one, yes. That he would ever have one, no.

'Why not, Fitz-Jarndyce?' she asked, rather sharply.

I said it was not the custom in England to confer titles on men distinguished by peaceful services, however good and great; unless occasionally, when they consisted of the accumulation of some very large amount of money.

'Why, good gracious,' said Miss Flite, 'how can you say that? Surely you know, my dear, that all the greatest ornaments of England in knowledge, imagination, active humanity, and improvement of every sort, are added to its nobility! Look round you, my dear, and consider. *You* must be rambling a little now, I think, if you don't know that this is the great reason why titles will always last in the land!'

I am afraid she believed what she said; for there were moments when she was very mad indeed (*Chapter 35:* Miss Flite and Esther Summerson).

'It's a gentleman, miss, and his compliments, and will you please to come without saying anything about it.'

'Whose compliments, Charley?'

'His'n, miss,' returned Charley: whose grammatical education was advancing, but not very rapidly.

'And how do you come to be the messenger, Charley?'

'I am not the messenger, if you please, miss,' returned my little maid. 'It was W. Grubble, miss.'

'And who is W. Grubble, Charley?'

'Mister Grubble, miss,' returned Charley. 'Don't you know, miss? The Dedlock Arms, by W. Grubble,' which Charley delivered as if she were slowly spelling out the sign.

'Aye? The landlord, Charley?'

'Yes, miss. If you please, miss, his wife is a beautiful woman, but she broke her ankle, and it never joined. And her brother's the sawyer, that was put in the cage, miss, and they expect he'll drink himself to death entirely on beer,' said Charley *(Chapter 37).*

'My dear Miss Summerson, here is our friend Richard,' said Mr. Skimpole, 'full of the brightest visions of the future, which he evokes out of the darkness of Chancery. Now that's delightful, that's inspiriting, that's full of poetry! In old times, the woods and solitudes were made joyous to the shepherd by the imaginary piping and dancing of Pan and the Nymphs. This present shepherd, our pastoral Richard, brightens the dull Inns of Court by making Fortune and her train sport through them to the melodious notes of a judgment from the bench. That's very pleasant, you know! Some ill-conditioned growling fellow may say to me, "What's the use of these legal and equitable abuses? How do you defend them?" I reply, "My growling friend, I *don't* defend them, but they are very agreeable to me. There is a shepherd-youth, a friend of mine, who transmutes them into something highly fascinating to my simplicity. I don't say it is for this that they exist – for I am a child among your worldly grumblers, and not called upon to account to you or myself for anything – but it may be so' *(Chapter 37).*

Mr. Skimpole soon afterwards appeared, and made us merry for an hour. He particularly requested to see Little Coavinses (meaning Charley), and told her, with a patriarchal air, that he had given her late father all the business in his power; and that if one of her little brothers would make haste to get set-up in the same profession, he hoped he should still be able to put a good deal of employment in his way.

'For I am constantly being taken in these nets,' said Mr. Skimpole, looking beamingly at us over a glass of wine-and-water, 'and am constantly being bailed out – like a boat. Or paid off – like a ship's company. Somebody always does it for me. *I* can't do it, you know, for I never have any money. But Somebody does it. I get out by Somebody's means; I am not like the starling; I get out. If you were to ask me who Somebody is, upon my word I couldn't tell you. Let us drink to Somebody. God bless him!' *(Chapter 37).*

'See, my dear Miss Summerson,' he took a handful of loose silver and halfpence from his pocket, there's so much money. I have not an idea how much. I have not the power of counting. Call it four and ninepence – call it four pound nine. They tell me I owe more than that. I dare say I do. I dare say I owe as much as good-natured people will let me owe. If they don't

stop, why should I? There you have Harold Skimpole in little. If that's responsibility, I am responsible.'

The perfect ease of manner with which he put the money up again, and looked at me with a smile on his refined face, as if he had been mentioning a curious little fact about somebody else, almost made me feel as if he really had nothing to do with it.

'Now when you mention responsibility,' he resumed, 'I am disposed to say, that I never had the happiness of knowing any one whom I should consider so refreshingly responsible as yourself. You appear to me to be the very touchstone of responsibility. When I see you, my dear Miss Summerson, intent upon the perfect working of the whole little orderly system of which you are the centre, I feel inclined to say to myself – in fact I do say to myself, very often – *that's* responsibility!'

It was difficult, after this, to explain what I meant; but I persisted so far as to say, that we all hoped he would check and not confirm Richard in the sanguine views he entertained just then.

'Most willingly,' he retorted, 'if I could. But, my dear Miss Summerson, I have no art, no disguise. If he takes me by the hand, and leads me through Westminster Hall in an airy procession after Fortune, I must go. If he says, "Skimpole, join the dance!" I must join it. Common sense wouldn't, I know; but I have *no* common sense.'

'It was very unfortunate for Richard,' I said.

'Do you think so!' returned Mr. Skimpole. 'Don't say that, don't say that. Let us suppose him keeping company with Common Sense – an excellent man – a good deal wrinkled – dreadfully practical – change for a ten-pound note in every pocket – ruled account book in his hand – say, upon the whole, resembling a taxgatherer. Our dear Richard, sanguine, ardent, overleaping obstacles, bursting with poetry like a young bud, says to this highly respectable companion, "I see a golden prospect before me; it's very bright, it's very beautiful, it's very joyous; here I go, bounding over the landscape to come at it!" The respectable companion instantly knocks him down with the ruled account-book; tells him, in a literal prosaic way, that he sees no such thing; shows him it's nothing but fees, fraud, horsehair wigs, and black gowns. Now you know that's a painful change; – sensible in the last degree, I have no doubt, but disagreeable. *I* can't do it. I haven't got the ruled account-book, I have none of the tax-gathering elements in my composition, I am not at all respectable, and I don't want to be. Odd perhaps, but so it is!' *(Chapter 37).*

'Miss Summerson,' said Mr. Guppy, 'you will excuse the waywardness of a parent every mindful of a son's appiness. My mother, though highly exasperating to the feelings, is actuated by maternal dictates.'

I could hardly have believed that anybody could in a moment have turned so red, or changed so much, as Mr. Guppy did when I now put up my veil.

'I asked the favour of seeing you for a few moments here.' said I, 'in preference to calling at Mr. Kenge's, because, remembering what you said on an occasion when you spoke to me in confidence, I feared I might otherwise cause you some embarrasssment, Mr. Guppy.'

I caused him embarrassment enough as it was, I am sure. I never saw such faltering, such confusion, such amazement and apprehension.

'Miss Summerson,' stammered Mr. Guppy, 'I – I – beg your pardon, but in our profession – we – we – find it necessary to be explicit. You have referred to an occasion, miss, when I – when I did myself the honour of making a declaration which – '

Something seemed to rise in his throat that he could not possibly swallow. He put his hand there, coughed, made faces, tried again to swallow it, coughed again, made faces again, looked all round the room, and fluttered his papers.

'A kind of giddy sensation has come upon me, miss,' he explained, 'which rather knocks me over. I – er – a little subject to this sort of thing – er – By George!'

I gave him a little time to recover. He consumed it in putting his hand to his forehead and taking it away again, and in backing his chair into the corner behind him.

'My intention was to remark, miss,' said Mr. Guppy, ' – dear me – something bronchial, I think – hem! – to remark that you was so good on that occasion as to repel and repudiate that declaration. You – you wouldn't perhaps object to admit that? Though no witnesses are present, it might be a satisfaction to – to your mind – if you was to put in that admission.'

'There can be no doubt,' said I, 'that I declined your proposal without any reservation or qualification whatever, Mr. Guppy.'

'Thank you, miss,' he returned, measuring the table with his troubled hands. 'So far that's satisfactory, and it does you credit. Er – this is certainly bronchial! – must be in the tubes – er – you wouldn't perhaps be offended if I was to mention – not that it's necessary, for your own good sense or any person's sense must show 'em that – if I was to mention that such declaration on my part was final, and there terminated?'

'I quite understand that,' said I.

'Perhaps – er – it may not be worth the form, but it might be a satisfaction to your mind – perhaps you wouldn't object to admit that, miss?' said Mr. Guppy.

'I admit it most fully and freely,' said I.

'Thank you,' returned Mr. Guppy. 'Very honourable, I am sure. I regret that my arrangements in life, combined with circumstances over which I have no control, will put it out of my power ever to fall back upon that offer, or to renew it in any shape or form whatever; but it will ever be a retrospect entwined – er – with friendship's bowers.' Mr. Guppy's bronchitis came to his relief, and stopped his measurement of the table *(Chapter 38)*.

The one great principle of the English law is, to make business for itself. There is no other principle distinctly, certainly, and consistently maintained through all its narrow turnings. Viewed by this light it becomes a coherent scheme and not the monstrous maze the laity are apt to think it. Let them but once clearly perceive that its grand principle is to make business for itself at their expense, and surely they will cease to grumble *(Chapter 39)*.

England has been in a dreadful state for some weeks. Lord Coodle would go out, Sir Thomas Doodle wouldn't come in, and there being nobody in Great Britain (to speak of) except Coodle and Doodle, there has been no Government. It is a mercy that the hostile meeting between those two great men, which at one time seemed inevitable, did not come off; because if both pistols had taken effect, and Coodle and Doodle had killed each other, it is to be presumed that England must have waited to be governed until young Coodle and young Doodle, now in frocks and long stockings, were grown up. This stupendous national calamity, however, was averted by Lord Coodle's making the timely discovery, that if in the heat of debate he had said that he scorned and despised the whole ignoble career of Sir Thomas Doodle, he had merely meant to say that party differences should never induce him to withold from it the tribute of his warmest admiration; while it as opportunely turned out, on the other hand, that Sir Thomas Doodle had in his own bosom expressly booked Lord Coodle to go down to posterity as the mirror of virtue and honour. Still England has been some weeks in the dismal strait of having no pilot (as was well observed by Sir Leicester Dedlock) to weather the storm; and the marvellous part of the matter is, that England has not appeared to care very much about it, but has gone on eating and drinking and marrying and giving in marriage, as the old world did in the days before the flood. But Coodle knew the danger, and Doodle knew the danger, and all their followers and hangers-on had the clearest possible perception of the danger. At last Sir Thomas Doodle has not only condescended to come in, but has done it handsomely, bringing in with him all his nephews, all his male cousins, and all his brothers-in-law. So there is hope for the old ship yet *(Chapter 40)*.

Through some of the fiery windows, beautiful from without, and set, at this sunset hour, not in dull grey stone but in a glorious house of gold, the light excluded at other windows pours in, rich, lavish, overflowing like the summer plenty in the land. Then do the frozen Dedlocks thaw. Strange movements come upon their features, as the shadows of leaves play there. A dense Justice in a corner is beguiled into a wink. A staring Baronet, with a truncheon, gets a dimple in his chin. Down into the bosom of a stony shepherdess there steals a fleck of light and warmth, that would have done it good, a hundred years ago. One ancestress of Volumnia . . . casting the shadow of that virgin event before her full two centuries – shoots out into a halo and becomes a saint. A maid of honour of the court of Charles the Second, with large round eyes (and other charms to correspond), seems to bathe in glowing water, and it ripples as it glows.

But the fire of the sun is dying. Even now the floor is dusky, and shadow slowly mounts the walls, bringing the Dedlocks down like age and death. And now, upon my lady's picture over the great chimney-piece, a weird shade falls from some old tree, that turns it pale, and flutters it, and looks as if a great arm held a veil or hood, watching an opportunity to draw it over her. Higher and darker rises shadow on the wall – now a red gloom on the ceiling – now the fire is out *(Chapter 40)*.

'My experience teaches me,' says Mr. Tulkinghorn, who has by this time got his hands in his pockets, and is going on in his business consideration of the matter, like a machine. 'My experience teaches me, Lady Dedlock, that most of the people I know would do far better to leave marriage alone. It is at the bottom of three-fourths of their troubles' *(Chapter 41)*.

He [Harold Skimpole] was not in the least disconcerted by our appearance, but rose and received us in his usual airy manner.

'Here I am, you see!' he said, when we were seated; not without some little difficulty, the greater part of the chairs being broken. 'Here I am! This is my frugal breakfast. Some men want legs of beef and mutton for breakfast; I don't. Give me my peach, my cup of coffee, and my claret; I am content. I don't want them for themselves; but they remind me of the sun. There's nothing solar about legs of beef and mutton. Mere animal satisfaction!' *(Chapter 43)*.

'This is a day,' said Mr. Skimpole, gaily taking a little claret in a tumbler, 'that will ever be remembered here. We shall call it Saint Clare and Saint Summerson day. You must see my daughters. I have a blue-eyed daughter who is my Beauty daughter, I have a Sentiment daughter, and I have a Comedy daughter. You must see them all. They'll be enchanted' *(Chapter 43)*.

'It is pleasant,' said Mr. Skimpole, turning his sprightly eyes from one to the other of us, 'and it is whimsically interesting, to trace peculiarities in families. In this family we are all children, and I am the youngest.'

The daughters, who appeared to be very fond of him, were amused by this droll fact; particularly the Comedy daughter.

'My dears, it is true,' said Mr. Skimpole, 'is it not? So it is, and so it must be, because, like the dogs in the hymn, "it is our nature to." Now, here is Miss Summerson with a fine administrative capacity, and a knowledge of details perfectly surprising. It will sound very strange in Miss Summerson's ears, I dare say, that we known nothing about chops in this house. But we don't; not the least. We can't cook anything whatever. A needle and thread we don't know how to use. We admire the people who possess the practical wisdom we want; but we don't quarrel with them. Then why should they quarrel with us? Live, and let live, we say to them. Live upon your practical wisdom, and let us live upon you!' *(Chapter 43)*.

Darkness rests upon Tom-all-Alone's. Dilating and dilating since the sun went down last night, it has gradually swelled until it fills every void in the place. For a time there were some dungeon lights burning, as the lamp of Life burns in Tom-all-Alone's, heavily, heavily, in the nauseous air, and winking – as that lamp, too, winks in Tom-all-Alone's – at many horrible things. But they are blotted out. The moon has eyed Tom with a dull cold stare, as admitting some puny emulation of herself in his desert region unfit for life and blasted by volcanic fires; but she has passed on, and is gone. The blackest nightmare in the infernal stables grazes on Tom-all-Alone's, and Tom is fast asleep.

Much mighty speech-making there has been, both in and out of Parliament, concerning Tom, and much wrathful disputation how Tom shall be got right. Whether he shall be put into the main road by constables, or by beadles, or by bell-ringing, or by force of figures, or by correct principles of taste, or by high church, or by low church, or by no church; whether he shall be set to splitting trusses of polemical straws with the crooked knife of his mind, or whether he shall be put to stone-breaking instead. In the midst of which dust and noise, there is but one thing perfectly clear, to wit, that Tom only may and can, or shall and will, be reclaimed according to somebody's theory but nobody's practice. And in the hopeful meantime, Tom goes to perdition head foremost in his old determined spirit.

But he has his revenge. Even the winds are his messengers, and they serve him in these hours of darkness. There is not a drop of Tom's corrupted blood but propagates infection and contagion somewhere. It shall pollute, this very night, the choice stream (in which chemists on analysis would find the genuine nobility) of a Norman house, and his Grace shall not be able to say Nay to the infamous alliance. There is not an atom of Tom's slime, not a cubic inch of any pestilential gas in which he lives, not one obscenity or degradation about him, not an ignorance, not a wickedness, not a brutality of his committing, but shall work its retribution, through every order of society, up to the proudest of the proud, and to the highest of the high. Verily, what with tainting, plundering, and spoiling, Tom has his revenge *(Chapter 46)*.

Jo is brought in. He is not one of Mrs. Pardiggle's Tockahoopo Indians; he is not one of Mrs. Jellyby's lambs, being wholly unconnected with Borrioboola-Gha; he is not softened by distance and unfamiliarity; he is not a genuine foreign-grown savage; he is the ordinary home-made article. Dirty, ugly, disagreeable to all the senses, in body a common creature of the common streets, only in soul a heathen. Homely filth begrimes him, homely parasites devour him, homely sores are in him, homely rags are on him: native ignorance, the growth of English soil and climate, sinks his immortal nature lower than the beasts that perish. Stand forth, Jo, in uncompromising colour! From the sole of thy foot to the crown of thy head, there is nothing interesting about thee *(Chapter 47)*.

'I thought,' says Jo, who has started, and is looking round, 'I thought I was in Tom-all-Alone's agin. Ain't there nobody here but you, Mr. Woodcot?'

'Nobody.'

'And I ain't took back to Tom-all-Alone's. Am I, sir?'

'No.' Jo closes his eyes, muttering, 'I'm wery thankful.'

After watching him closely a little while, Allan puts his mouth very near his ear, and says to him in a low, distinct voice:

'Jo! Did you ever know a prayer?'

'Never knowd nothink, sir.'

'Not so much as one short prayer?'

'No, sir. Nothink at all. Mr. Chadbands he wos a-prayin wunst at Mr. Snagsby's and I heerd him, but he sounded as if he wos a-speakin' to hisself, and not to me. He prayed a lot, but *I* couldn't make out nothink on it. Different times, there was other genlmen come down Tom-all-Alone's a-prayin, but they all mostly sed as the t'other wuns prayed wrong, and all mostly sounded to be a-talkin to theirselves, or a-passing blame on the t'others, and not a-talkin to us. *We* never knowd nothink. *I* never knowd what it wos all about.'

It takes him a long time to say this; and few but an experienced and attentive listener could hear, or, hearing, understand him. After a short relapse into sleep or stupor, he makes, of a sudden, a strong effort to get out of bed.

'Stay, Jo! What now?'

'It's time for me to go to that there berryin ground, sir,' he returns with a wild look.

'Lie down, and tell me. What burying ground, Jo?'

'Where they laid him as wos wery good to me, wery good to me indeed, he wos. It's time fur me to go down to that there berryin ground, sir, and ask to put along with him. I wants to go there and be berried. He used fur to say to me, "I am as poor as you to-day, Jo," he ses. I wants to tell him that I am as poor as him now, and have come there to be laid along with him.'

'By and by, Jo. By and by.'

'Ah! P'raps they wouldn't do it if I wos to go myself. But will you promise to have me took there, sir, and laid along with him?'

'I will, indeed.'

'Thank'ee, sir. Thank'ee, sir. They'll have to get the key of the gate afore they can take me in, for it's allus locked. And there's a step there, as I used for to clean with my broom. – It's turned wery dark, sir. Is there any light a-comin?'

'It is coming fast, Jo.'

Fast. The cart is shaken all to pieces, and the rugged road is very near its end.

'Jo, my poor fellow!'

'I hear you, sir, in the dark, but I'm a-gropin – a-gropin – let me catch hold of your hand.'

'Jo, can you say what I say?'

'I'll say anythink as you say, sir, for I knows it's good.'

'OUR FATHER.'

'Our Father! – yes, that's wery good, sir.'

'WHICH ART IN HEAVEN.'

'Art in Heaven – is the light a-comin' sir?'

'It is close at hand. HALLOWED BE THY NAME!'

'Hallowed be – thy –'

The light is come upon the dark benighted way. Dead! Dead, your Majesty. Dead, my lords and gentlemen. Dead, Right Reverends and Wrong Reverends of every order. Dead, men and women, born with Heavenly compassion in your hearts. And dying thus around us every day *(Chapter 47)*.

There is a splendid clock upon the staircase, famous as splendid clocks not often are, for its accuracy. 'And what do *you* say?' Mr. Tulkinghorn inquires, referring to it. 'What do you say?'

If it said now, 'Don't go home!' What a famous clock, hereafter, if it said to-night of all the nights that it has counted off, to this old man of all the young and old men who have ever stood before it, 'Don't go home!' With its sharp clear bell, it strikes three-quarters after seven, and ticks on again. 'Why, you are worse than I thought you,' says Mr. Tulkinghorn, muttering reproof to his watch. 'Two minutes wrong? At this rate you won't last my time.' What a watch to return good for evil, if it ticked in answer, 'Don't go home!'

He passes out into the streets, and walks on, with his hands behind him, under the shadow of the lofty houses, many of whose mysteries, difficulties, mortgages, delicate affairs of all kinds, are treasured up within his old black satin waistcoat. He is in the confidence of the very bricks and mortar. The high chimney-stacks telegraph family secrets to him. Yet there is not a voice in a mile of them to whisper, 'Don't go home!'

Through the stir and motion of the commoner streets; through the roar and jar of many vehicles, many feet, many voices; with the blazing shop lights lighting him on, the west wind blowing him on, and the crowd pressing him on; he is pitilessly urged upon his way, and nothing meets him, murmuring, 'Don't go home!' Arrived at last in his dull room, to light his candles, and look round and up, and see the Roman pointing from the ceiling, there is no new significance in the Roman's hand to-night, or in the flutter of the attendant groups, to give him the late warning, 'Don't come here!' *(Chapter 48)*.

What's that? Who fired a gun or pistol? Where was it?

The few foot-passengers start, stop, and stare about them. Some windows and doors are opened, and people come out to look. It was a loud report, and echoed and rattled heavily. It shook one house, or so a man says who was passing. It has aroused all the dogs in the neighbourhood, who bark vehemently. Terrified cats scamper across the road. While the dogs are yet barking and howling – there is one dog howling like a demon – the church-clocks, as if they were startled too, begin to strike. The hum from the streets, like-wise, seems to swell into a shout. But it is soon over. Before the last clock begins to strike ten, there is a lull. When it has ceased, the fine night, the bright large moon, and multitudes of stars, are left at peace again.

Has Mr. Tulkinghorn been disturbed? His windows are dark and quiet, and his door is shut. It must be something unusual indeed, to bring him out of his shell. Nothing is heard of him, nothing is seen of him. What power of cannon might it take to shake that rusty old man out of his immovable composure?

For many years, the persistent Roman has been pointing, with no particular meaning, from that ceiling. It is not likely that he has any new meaning in him to-night. Once pointing, always pointing, – like any Roman, or even Briton, with a single idea. There he is, no doubt, in his impossible attitude, pointing, unavailingly, all night long. Moonlight, darkness, dawn, sunrise, day. There he is still, eagerly pointing, and no one minds him.

But, a little after the coming of the day, come people to clean the rooms. And either the Roman has some new meaning in him, not expressed before, or the foremost of them goes wild; for, looking up at his outstretched hand, and looking down at what is below it, that person shrieks and flies. The others, looking in as the first one looked, shriek and fly too, and there is an alarm in the street.

What does it mean? No light is admitted into the darkened chamber, and people unaccustomed to it, enter, and, treading softly, but heavily, carry a weight into the bedroom, and lay it down. There is whispering and wondering all day, strict search of every corner, careful tracing of steps, and careful noting of the disposition of every article of furniture. All eyes look up at the Roman, and all voices murmur, 'If he could only tell what he saw!'

He is pointing at a table, with a bottle (nearly full of wine) and a glass upon it, and two candles that were blown out suddenly, soon after being lighted. He is pointing at an empty chair, and at a stain upon the ground before it that might be almost covered with a hand. These objects lie directly within his range. An excited imagination might suppose that there was something in them so terrific, as to drive the rest of the composition, not only the attendant big-legged boys, but the clouds and flowers and pillars too – in short, the very body and soul of Allegory, and all the brains it has – stark mad. It happens surely, that every one who comes into the darkened room and looks at these things, looks up at the Roman, and that he is invested in all eyes with mystery and awe, as if he were a paralysed dumb witness.

So, it shall happen surely, through many years to come, that ghostly stories shall be told of the stain upon the floor, so easy to be covered, so hard to be got out; and that the Roman, pointing from the ceiling, shall point, so long as dust and damp and spiders spare him, with far greater significance than he ever had in Mr. Tulkinghorn's time, and with a deadly meaning. For, Mr. Tulkinghorn's time is over for evermore; and the Roman pointed at the murderous hand uplifted against his life, and pointed helplessly at him, from night to morning, lying face downward on the floor, shot through the heart (*Chapter 48*).

It is the old girl's birthday; and that is the greatest holiday and reddest-letter day in Mr. Bagnet's calendar. The auspicious event is always commemorated according to certain forms, settled and prescribed by Mr. Bagnet some years since. Mr. Bagnet being deeply convinced that to have a pair of fowls for dinner is to attain the highest pitch of imperial luxury, invariably goes forth himself very early in the morning of this day to buy a pair; he is, as invariably, taken in by the vendor, and installed in the possession of the oldest inhabitants of any coop in Europe. Returning with these triumphs of toughness tied up in a clean blue and white cotton handkerchief (essential to the arrangements), he in a casual manner invites Mrs. Bagnet to declare at breakfast what she would like for dinner. Mrs. Bagnet, by a coincidence never known to fail, replying Fowls, Mr. Bagnet instantly produces his bundle from a place of concealment, amidst general

amazement and rejoicing. He further requires that the old girl shall do nothing all day long, but sit in her very best gown, and be served by himself and the young people. As he is not illustrious for his cookery, this may be supposed to be a matter of state rather than enjoyment on the old girl's part; but she keeps her state with all imaginable cheerfulness (*Chapter 49*).

It is well for the old girl that she has but one birthday in a year, for two such indulgences in poultry might be injurious. Every kind of finer tendon and ligament that is in the nature of poultry to possess, is developed in these specimens in the singular form of guitar-strings. Their limbs appear to have struck roots into their breasts and bodies, as aged trees strike roots into the earth. Their legs are so hard, as to encourage the idea that they must have devoted the greater part of their long and arduous lives to pedestrian exercises, and the walking of matches. But Mr. Bagnet, unconscious of these little defects, sets his heart on Mrs. Bagnet eating a most severe quantity of the delicacies before her; and as that good old girl would not cause him a moment's disappointment on any day, least of all on such a day, for any consideration, she imperils her digestion fearfully. How young Woolwich cleans the drum-sticks without being of ostrich descent, his anxious mother is at a loss to understand (*Chapter 49*).

'Lord, he's wonderfully like you! But about what you may call the brow, you know, *there* his father comes out!' Mr. Bucket compares the faces with one eye shut up, while Mr. Bagnet smokes in stolid satisfaction.

This is an opportunity for Mrs. Bagnet to inform him, that the boy is George's godson.

'George's godson, is he?' rejoins Mr. Bucket, with extreme cordiality. 'I must shake hands over again with George's godson. Godfather and godson do credit to one another. And what do you intend to make of him, ma'am? Does he show any turn for any musical instrument?'

Mr. Bagnet suddenly interposes, 'Plays the Fife. Beautiful.'

'Would you believe it, governor,' says Mr. Bucket, struck by the coincidence, 'that when I was a boy I played the fife myself? Not in a scientific way, as I expect he does, but by ear. Lord bless you! British Grenadiers – there's a tune to warm an Englishman up! *Could* you give us British Grenadiers, my fine fellow?'

Nothing could be more acceptable to the little circle than this call upon young Woolwich, who immediately fetches his fife and performs the stirring melody; during which performance Mr. Bucket, much enlivened, beats time, and never fails to come in sharp with the burden, 'Brit Ish Gra-a-anadeers!' In short, he shows so much musical taste, that Mr. Bagnet actually takes his pipe from his lips to express his conviction that he is a singer. Mr. Bucket receives the harmonious impeachment so modestly; confessing how that he did once chaunt a little, for the expression of the feelings of his own bosom, and with no presumptuous idea of entertaining his friends: that he is asked to sing. Not to be behindhand in the sociality of the evening, he complies, and gives them 'Believe me if all those endearing young charms.' This ballad, he informs Mrs. Bagnet, he considers to have been his most powerful ally in moving the heart of Mrs. Bucket when a maiden, and inducing her to approach the altar – Mr. Bucket's own words are, to come up to the scratch (*Chapter 49*).

Then there was old Mr. Turveydrop, who was from morning to night and from night to morning the subject of innumerable precautions. If the baby cried, it was nearly stifled lest the noise should make him uncomfortable. If the fire wanted stirring in the night, it was surreptitiously done lest his rest should be broken. If Caddy required any little comfort that the house contained, she first carefully discussed whether he was likely to require it too. In return for this consideration, he would come into the room once a day, all but blessing it – showing a condescension, and a patronage, and a grace of manner, in dispensing the light of his high-shouldered presence, from which I might have supposed him (if I had not known better) to have been the benefactor of Caddy's life.

'My Caroline,' he would say, making the nearest approach that he could to bending over her. 'Tell me that you are better to-day.'

'O much better, thank you, Mr. Turveydrop,' Caddy would reply.

'Delighted! Enchanted! And our dear Miss Summerson. She is not quite prostrated by fatigue!' Here he would crease up his eyelids, and kiss his fingers to me; though I am happy to say he had ceased to be particular in his attentions, since I had been so altered.

'Not at all,' I would assure him.

'Charming! We must take care of our dear Caroline, Miss Summerson. We must spare nothing that will restore her. We must nourish her. My dear Caroline'; he would turn to his daughter-in-law with infinite generosity and protection; 'want for nothing, my love. Frame a wish and gratify it, my daughter. Everything this house contains, everything my room contains, is at your service, my dear. Do not,' he would sometimes add, in a burst of Deportment, 'even allow my simple requirements to be considered, if they should at any time interfere with your own, my Caroline. Your necessities are greater than mine.'

He had established such a long prescriptive right to this Deportment (his son's inheritance from his mother), that I several times knew both Caddy and her husband to be melted to tears by these affectionate self-sacrifices.

'Nay, my dears,' he would remonstrate; and when I saw Caddy's thin arm about his fat neck as he said it, I would be melted too, though not by the same process; 'Nay, nay! I have promised never to leave ye. Be dutiful and affectionate towards me, and I ask no other return. Now, bless ye! I am going to the Park' (*Chapter 50*).

Mrs. Bagnet made another application to her skirts, and brought forth a leathern purse in which she hastily counted over a few shillings, and which she then shut up with perfect satisfaction.

'Never you mind for me, miss. I'm a soldier's wife, and accustomed to travel my own way. Lignum, old boy,' kissing him, 'one for yourself; three for the children. Now, I'm away into Lincolnshire after George's mother.'

And she actually set off while we three stood looking at one another lost in amazement. She actually trudged away in her grey cloak at a sturdy pace, and turned the corner and was gone.

'Mr. Bagnet,' said my guardian. 'Do you mean to let her go in that way!'

'Can't help it,' he returned. 'Made her way home once. From another quarter of the world. With the same grey cloak. And same umbrella. Whatever the old girl says, do. Do it! Whenever the old girl says, *I'*ll do it. She does it.'

'Then she is as honest and genuine as she looks,' rejoined my guardian, 'and it is impossible to say more for her.'

'She's Colour-Serjeant of the Nonpareil battalion,' said Mr. Bagnet, looking at us over his shoulder, as he went his way also. 'And there's not such another. But I never own to it before her. Discipline must be maintained' (*Chapter 52*).

My Lady's out, ain't she?'

'Out to dinner.'

'Goes out pretty well every day, don't she?'

'Yes.'

'Not to be wondered at!' says Mr. Bucket. 'Such a fine woman as her, so handsome and so graceful and so elegant, is like a fresh lemon on a dinner-table, ornamental wherever she goes' (*Chapter 53: Mercury and Bucket*).

Railroads shall soon traverse all this country, and with a rattle and a glare the engine and train shall shoot like a meteor over the wide night-landscape, turning the moon paler; but, as yet, such things are non-existent in these parts, though not wholly unexpected. Preparations are afoot, measurements are made, ground is staked out. Bridges are begun, and their not yet united piers desolately look at one another over roads and streams, like brick and mortar couples with an obstacle to their union; fragments of embankments are thrown up, and left as precipices with torrents of rusty carts and barrows tumbling over them; tripods of tall poles appear on hilltops, where there are rumours of tunnels; everything looks chaotic, and abandoned in full hopelessness. Along the freezing roads, and through the night, the post-chaise makes its way without a railroad on its mind (*Chapter 55*).

'Ah!' said Mr. Bucket. 'Here we are, and a nice retired place it is. Puts a man in mind of the country house in the Woodpecker-tapping, that was known by the smoke which so gracefully curled. They're early with the kitchen fire, and that denotes good servants. But what you've always got to be careful of with servants, is, who comes to see 'em; you never know what they're up to, if you don't know that. And another thing, my dear. Whenever you find a young man behind the kitchen-door, you give that young man in charge on suspicion of being secreted in a dwelling-house with an unlawful purpose' (*Chapter 57*).

'Now, Miss Summerson, I'll give you a piece of advice that your husband will find useful when you are happily married and have got a family about you. Whenever a person says to you that they are as innocent as can be in all concerning money, look well after your own money, for they are dead certain to collar it, if they can. Whenever a person proclaims to you "In worldly matters I'm a child," you consider that that person is only a-crying off from being held accountable, and that you have got that person's number, and it's Number One. Now, I am not a poetical man myself, except in a vocal way when it goes round a company, but I'm a practical one, and that's my experience. So's this rule. Fast and loose in one thing, Fast and loose in everything. I never knew it fail. No more will you. Nor no one. With which caution to the unwary, my dear, I take the liberty of pulling this here bell, and so go back to our business' (*Chapter 57:* Bucket).

'Another secret, my dear. I have added to my collection of birds.'
'Really, Miss Flite?' said I, knowing how it pleased her to have her confidence received with an appearance of interest.
She nodded several times, and her face became overcast and gloomy. 'Two more. I call them the Wards in Jarndyce. They are caged up with all the others. With Hope, Joy, Youth, Peace, Rest, Life, Dust, Ashes, Waste, Want, Ruin, Despair, Madness, Death, Cunning, Folly, Words, Wigs, Rags, Sheepskin, Plunder, Precedent, Jargon, Gammon and Spinach!' (*Chapter 60*).

Mr. Skimpole, lying on the sofa in his room, playing the flute a little, was enchanted to see me. Now, who should receive me, he asked? Who would I prefer for mistress of the ceremonies? Would I have his Comedy daughter, his Beauty Daughter, or his Sentiment daughter? Or would I have all the daughters at once, in a perfect nosegay?
I replied, half defeated already, that I wished to speak to himself only, if he would give me leave.
'My dear Miss Summerson, most joyfully! Of course,' he said, bringing his chair nearer mine, and breaking into his fascinating smile, 'of course it's not business. Then it's pleasure!'
I said it certainly was not business that I came upon, but it was not quite a pleasant matter.
'Then, my dear Miss Summerson,' said he, with the frankest gaiety, 'don't allude to it. Why should you allude to anything that is *not* a pleasant matter? *I* never do. And you are a much pleasanter creature, in every point of view, than I. You are perfectly pleasant; I am imperfectly pleasant; then, if I never allude to an unpleasant matter, how much less should you! So that's disposed of, and we will talk of something else' (*Chapter 61*).

A most beautiful summer morning succeeded; and after breakfast we went out arm in arm, to see the house of which I was to give my mighty housekeeping opinion. We entered a flower-garden by a gate in a side wall, of which he had the key; and the first thing I saw, was, that the beds and flowers were all laid out according to the manner of my beds and flowers at home.
'You see, my dear,' observed my guardian, standing still, with a delighted face, to watch my looks; 'knowing there could be no better plan, I borrowed yours.'
We went on by a pretty little orchard, where the cherries were nestling among the green leaves, and the shadows of the apple-trees were sporting on the grass, to the house itself, – a cottage, quite a rustic cottage of doll's rooms; but such a lovely place, so tranquil and so beautiful, with such a rich and smiling country spread around it; with water sparkling away into the distance, here all overhung with summer-growth, there turning a humming mill; at its nearest point glancing through a meadow by the cheerful town, where cricket-players were assembling in bright groups, and a flag was flying from a white tent that rippled in the sweet west wind. And still, as we went through the pretty rooms, out at the little rustic verandah doors, and underneath the tiny wooden colonnades, garlanded with woodbine, jasmine, and honeysuckle, I saw, in the papering on the walls, in the colours of the furniture, in the arrangement of all the pretty objects, *my* little tastes and fancies, *my* little methods and inventions which they used to laugh at while they praised them, my odd ways everywhere.
I could not say enough in admiration of what was all so beautiful, but one secret doubt arose in my mind, when I saw this. I thought, O would he be the happier for it! Would it not have been better for his peace that I should not have been so brought before him? Because, although I was not what he thought me, still he loved me very dearly, and it might remind him mournfully of what he believed he had lost. I did not wish him to forget me, – perhaps he might not have done so, without these aids to his memory, – but my way was easier than his, and I could have reconciled myself even to that, so that he had been the happier for it.
'And now, little woman,' said my guardian, whom I had never seen so proud and joyful as in showing me these things, and watching my appreciation of them, 'now, last of all, for the name of this house.'
'What is it called, dear Guardian?'
'My child,' said he, 'come and see.'
He took me to the porch, which he had hitherto avoided, and said, pausing before we went out:
'My dear child, don't you guess the name?'
'No!' said I.
We went out of the porch; and he showed me written over it, BLEAK HOUSE (*Chapter 64:* Jarndyce and Esther Summerson).

'Ada, my darling!'
He sought to raise himself a little. Allan raised him so that she could hold him on her bosom: which was what he wanted.
'I have done you many wrongs, my own. I have fallen like a poor stray shadow on your way, I have married you to poverty and trouble, I have scattered your means to the winds. You will forgive me all this, my Ada, before I begin the world?'
A smile irradiated his face, as she bent to kiss him. He slowly laid his face down upon her bosom, drew his arms closer round her neck, and with one parting sob

began the world. Not this world, O not this! The world that sets this right.

When all was still, at a late hour, poor crazed Miss Flite came weeping to me, and told me she had given her birds their liberty (*Chapter 65:* Richard Carstone).

HARD TIMES

BOOK THE FIRST: SOWING

'Bitzer', said Thomas Gradgrind. 'Your definition of a horse.'

'Quadruped. Graminivorous. Forty teeth, namely twenty-four grinders, four eye-teeth, and twelve incisive. Sheds coat in the spring; in marshy countries, sheds hoofs, too. Hoofs hard, but requiring to be shod with iron. Age known by marks in mouth.' Thus (and much more) Bitzer.

'Now girl number twenty,' said Mr. Gradgrind. 'You know what a horse is' (*Chapter 1*).

'Very well,' said this gentleman, briskly smiling, and folding his arms. 'That's a horse. Now, let me ask you girls and boys. Would you paper a room with representations of horses?'

After a pause, one half of the children cried in chorus, 'Yes, sir!' Upon which the other half, seeing in the gentleman's face that Yes was wrong, cried out in chorus, 'No, sir!' – as the custom is, in these examinations.

'Of course, No. Why wouldn't you?' . . .

'I'll explain to you, then,' said the gentleman, after another and a dismal pause, 'Why you wouldn't paper a room with representations of horses. Do you ever see horses walking up and down the sides of rooms in reality – in fact? Do you?'

'Yes, sir!' from one half. 'No, sir!' from the other.

'Of course no,' said the gentleman, with an indignant look at the wrong half. 'Why, then, you are not to see anywhere, what you don't have in fact. What is called Taste, is only another name for Fact.'

Thomas Gradgrind nodded his approbation.

'This is a new principle, a discovery, a great discovery,' said the gentleman. 'Now, I'll try you again. Suppose you were going to carpet a room. Would you use a carpet having a representation of flowers upon it?'

There being a general conviction by this time that 'No, sir!' was always the right answer to this gentleman, the chorus of No was very strong. Only a few feeble stragglers said Yes; among them Sissy Jupe.

'Girl number twenty,' said the gentleman, smiling in the calm strength of knowledge.

Sissy blushed, and stood up.

'So you would carpet your room – or your husband's room, if you were a grown woman, and had a husband – with representations of flowers, would you?' said the gentleman. 'Why would you?'

'If you please, sir, I am very fond of flowers,' returned the girl.

'And is that why you would put tables and chairs upon them, and have people walking over them with heavy boots?'

'It wouldn't hurt them, sir. They wouldn't crush and wither, if you please, sir. They would be the pictures of what was very pretty and pleasant, and I would fancy –'

'Ay, ay, ay! But you mustn't fancy,' cried the gentleman, quite elated by coming so happily to his point. 'That's it! You are never to fancy' (*Chapter 2:* Government Officer).

There were five young Gradgrinds, and they were models every one. They had been lectured at, from their tenderest years; coursed, like little hares. Almost as soon as they could run alone, they had been made to run to the lecture-room. The first object with which they had an association, or of which they had a remembrance, was a large black board with a dry Ogre chalking ghastly white figures on it.

Not that they knew, by name or nature, anything about an Ogre. Fact forbid! I only use the word to express a monster in a lecturing castle, with Heaven knows how many heads manipulated into one, taking childhood captive, and dragging it into gloomy statistical dens by the hair.

No little Gradgrind had ever seen a face in the moon; it was up in the moon before it could speak distinctly. No little Gradgrind had ever learnt the silly jingle, Twinkle, twinkle little star; how I wonder what you are! No little Gradgrind had ever known wonder on the subject, each little Gradgrind having at five years old dissected the Great Bear like a Professor Owen, and driven Charles's Wain like a locomotive engine-driver. No little Gradgrind had ever associated a cow in a field with that famous cow with the crumpled horn who tossed the dog who worried the cat who killed the rat who ate the malt, or with that yet more famous cow who swallowed Tom Thumb; it had never heard of those celebrities, and had only been introduced to a cow as a graminivorous ruminating quadruped with several stomachs (*Chapter 3*).

In the formal drawing-room of Stone Lodge, standing on the hearthrug, warming himself before the fire, Mr. Bounderby delivered some observations to Mrs. Gradgrind on the circumstance of its being his birthday. He stood before the fire, partly because it was a cool spring afternoon, though the sun shone; partly because the shade of Stone Lodge was always haunted by the ghost of damp mortar; partly because he thus took up a commanding position, from which to subdue Mrs. Gradgrind.

'I hadn't a shoe to my foot. As to a stocking, I didn't know such a thing by name. I passed the day in a ditch, and the night in a pigsty. That's the way I spent my tenth birthday. Not that a ditch was new to me, for I was born in a ditch'. . . .

Mrs. Gradgrind hoped it was a dry ditch?

'No! As wet as a sop. A foot of water in it,' said Mr. Bounderby.

'Enough to give a baby cold,' Mrs. Gradgrind considered.

'Cold? I was born with inflammation of the lungs, and of everything else, I believe, that was capable of inflammation,' returned Mr. Bounderby. 'For years, ma'am, I was one of the most miserable little wretches ever seen. I was so sickly, that I was always moaning and groaning. I was so ragged and dirty, that you wouldn't have touched me with a pair of tongs.'

Mrs. Gradgrind faintly looked at the tongs, as the most appropriate thing her imbecility could think of doing.

'How I fought through it, *I* don't know,' said Bounderby. 'I was determined, I suppose. I have been a determined character in later life, and I suppose I was then. Here I am, Mrs. Gradgrind, anyhow, and nobody to thank for my being here, but myself.' . . .

Mrs. Gradgrind meekly and weakly hoped that his mother –

'*My* mother? Bolted, ma'am!' said Bounderby.

Mrs. Gradgrind, stunned as usual, collapsed and gave it up.

'My mother left me to my grandmother,' said Bounderby; 'and, according to the best of my remembrance, my grandmother was the wickedest and the worst old woman that ever lived. If I got a little pair of shoes by any chance, she would take 'em off and sell 'em for drink. Why, I have known that grandmother of mine lie in her bed and drink her four-teen glasses of liquor before breakfast!' . . .

'She kept a chandler's shop,' pursued Bounderby, 'and kept me in an egg-box. That was the cot of *my* infancy; an old egg-box. As soon as I was big enough to run away, of course I ran away. Then I became a young vagabond; and instead of one old woman knocking me about and starving me, everybody of all ages knocked me about and starved me. They were right; they had no business to do anything else. I was a nuisance, and incumbrance, and a pest. I know that very well' *(Chapter 4)*.

'You know, as well as I do, no young people have circus masters, or keep circuses in cabinets, or attend lectures about circuses. What can you possibly want to know of circuses then? I am sure you have enough to do, if that's what you want. With my head in its present state, I couldn't remember the mere names of half the facts you have got to attend to.'

'That's the reason!' pouted Louisa.

'Don't tell me that's the reason, because it can be nothing of the sort,' said Mrs. Gradgrind. 'Go and be somethingological directly,' Mrs. Gradgrind was not a scientific character, and usually dismissed her children to their studies with this general injunction to choose their pursuit *(Chapter 4)*.

Let us strike the key-note, Coketown, before pursuing our tune.

It was a town of red brick, or of brick that would have been red if the smoke and ashes had allowed it; but as matters stood it was a town of unnatural red and black like the painted face of a savage. It was a town of machinery and tall chimneys, out of which interminable serpents of smoke trailed themselves for ever and ever, and never got uncoiled. It had a black canal in it, and a river that ran purple with ill-smelling dye, and vast piles of building full of windows where there was a rattling and a trembling all day long, and where the piston of the steam-engine worked monton-ously up and down, like the head of an elephant in a state of melancholy madness. It contained several large streets all very like one another, and many small

streets still more like one another, inhabited by people equally like one another, who all went in and out at the same hours, with the same sound upon the same pavements, to do the same work, and to whom every day was the same as yesterday and to-morrow, and every year the counterpart of the last and the next *(Chapter 5)*.

The name of the public-house was the Pegasus's Arms. The Pegasus's legs might have been more to the purpose; but, underneath the winged horse upon the signboard, the Pegasus's Arms was inscribed in Roman letters. Beneath that inscription again, in a flowing scroll, the painter had touched off the lines:

> Good malt makes good beer,
> Walk in, and they'll draw it here;
> Good wine makes good brandy,
> Give us a call, and you'll find it handy.

Framed and glazed upon the wall behind the dingy little bar, was another Pegasus – a theatrical one – with real gauze let in for his wings, golden stars stuck on all over him, and his ethereal harness made of red silk *(Chapter 6)*.

'Very well,' said Bounderby. 'I was born in a ditch, and my mother ran away from me. Do I excuse her for it? No. Have I ever excused her for it? Not I. What do I call her for it? I call her probably the very worst woman that ever lived in the world, except my drunken grandmother. There's no family pride about me, there's no imaginative sentimental humbug about me. I call a spade a spade; and I call the mother of Josiah Bounderby of Coketown, without any fear or any favour, what I should call her if she had been the mother of Dick Jones of Wapping. So, with this man. He is a runaway rogue and a vagabond, that's what he is, in English' *(Chapter 6)*.

Mrs. Sparsit had not only seen different days, but was highly connected. She had a great aunt living in these very times called Lady Scadgers. Mr. Sparsit, deceased, of whom she was the relict, had been by the mother's side what Mrs. Sparsit called 'a Powler.' Strangers of limited information and dull apprehension were sometimes observed not to know what a Powler was, and even to appear uncertain whether it might be a business, or a political party, or a profession of faith. The better class of minds, however, did not need to be informed that the Powlers were an ancient stock, who could trace themselves so exceedingly far back that it was not surprising if they sometimes lost themselves – which they had rather frequently done, as respected horse-flesh, blind-hockey, Hebrew monetary transactions, and the Insolvent Debtors Court *(Chapter 7)*.

'You have been in the habit now of reading to your father, and those people I found you among, I dare say?' said Mr. Gradgrind, beckoning her nearer to him before he said so, and dropping his voice.

'Only to father and Merrylegs, sir. At least I mean to father when Merrylegs was always there.'

'Never mind Merrylegs, Jupe,' said Mr. Gradgrind, with a passing frown. 'I don't ask about him. I understand you to have been in the habit of reading to your father?'

'O yes, sir, thousands of times. They were the happiest – O, of all the happy times we had together, sir!'

It was only now when her sorrow broke out, that Louisa looked at her.

And what,' asked Mr. Gradgrind, in a still lower voice, 'did you read to your father, Jupe?'

'About the Fairies, sir, and the Dwarf, and the Hunchback, and the Genies,' she sobbed out; 'and about – '

'Hush!' said Mr. Gradgrind, 'that is enough. Never breathe a word of such destructive nonsense any more. Bounderby, this is a case for rigid training, and I shall observe it with interest' *(Chapter 7)*.

There was a library in Coketown, to which general access was easy. Mr. Gradgrind greatly tormented his mind about what the people read in this library: a point whereon little rivers of tabular statements periodically flowed into the howling ocean of tabular statements, which no diver ever got to any depth in and came up sane. It was a disheartening circumstance, but a melancholy fact, that even these readers persisted in wondering. They wondered about human nature, human passions, human hopes and fears, the struggles, triumphs and defeats, the cares and joys and sorrows, the lives and deaths of common men and women! They sometimes, after fifteen hours' work, sat down to read mere fables about men and women, more or less like themselves, and about children, more or less like their own. They took De Foe to their bosoms, instead of Euclid, and seemed to be on the whole more comforted by Goldsmith than by Cocker. Mr. Gradgrind was for ever working, in print and out of print, at this eccentric sum, and he never could make out how it yielded this unaccountable product *(Chapter 8)*.

'As to me,' said Tom, tumbling his hair all manner of ways with his sulky hands, 'I am a Donkey, that's what *I* am. I am as obstinate as one, I am more stupid than one, I get as much pleasure as one, and I should like to kick like one. ... And I am a Mule too, which you're not. If father was determined to make me either a Prig or a Mule, and I am not a Prig, why, it stands to reason, I must be a Mule. And so I am,' said Tom, desperately *(Chapter 8: Tom Gradgrind)*.

'Mr. M'Choakumchild said he would try me once more. And he said, Here are the stutterings – '

'Statistics,' said Louisa.

'Yes, Miss Louisa – they always remind me of stutterings, and that's another of my mistakes – of accidents upon the sea. And I find (Mr. M'Choakumchild said) that in a given time a hundred thousand persons went to sea on long voyages, and only five hundred of them were drowned or burnt to death. What is the percentage? And I said, Miss'; here Sissy fairly sobbed as confessing with extreme contrition to her greatest error; 'I said it was nothing.'

'Nothing, Sissy?'

'Nothing, Miss – to the relations and friends of the people who were killed. I shall never learn,' said Sissy. 'And the worst of all is, that although my poor father wished me so much to learn, and although I am so anxious to learn, because he wished me to, I am afraid I don't like it' *(Chapter 9:* Sissy Jupe and Louisa Gradgrind).

'And your father was always kind? To the last?' ...

'Always, always!' returned Sissy, clasping her hands. 'Kinder and kinder than I can tell. He was angry only one night, and that was not to me, but Merrylegs. Merrylegs'; she whispered the awful fact; 'is his performing dog.'

'Why was he angry with the dog?' Louisa demanded.

'Father, soon after they came home from performing, told Merrylegs to jump up on the back of the two chairs and stand across them – which is one of his tricks. He looked at father, and didn't do it once. Everything of father's had gone wrong that night, and he hadn't pleased the public at all. He cried out that the very dog knew he was failing, and had no compassion on him. Then he beat the dog, and I was frightened, and said, "Father, father! Pray don't hurt the creature who is so fond of you! O Heaven forgive you, father, stop!" And he stopped, and the dog was bloody, and father lay down crying on the floor with the dog in his arms, and the dog licked his face' *(Chapter 9:* Sissy Jupe).

I entertain a weak idea that the English people are as hard-worked as any people upon whom the sun shines. I acknowledge to this ridiculous idiosyncrasy, as a reason why I would give them a little more play *(Chapter 10)*.

The Fairy palaces burst into illumination, before pale morning showed the monstrous serpents of smoke trailing themselves over Coketown. A clattering of clogs upon the pavement; a rapid ringing of bells; and all the melancholy mad elephants, polished and oiled up for the day's monotony, were at their heavy exercise again. ...

So many hundred Hands in this Mill; so many hundred horse Steam Power. It is known, to the force of a single pound weight, what the engine will do; but, not all the calculators of the National Debt can tell me the capacity for good or evil, for love or hatred, for patriotism or discontent, for the decomposition of virtue into vice, or the reverse, at any single moment in the soul of one of these its quiet servants, with the composed faces and the regulated actions. There is no mystery in it; there is an unfathomable mystery in the meanest of them, for ever. – Supposing we were to reserve our arithmetic for material objects, and to govern these awful unknown quantities by other means! *(Chapter 11)*.

'I mun' be ridden o' her. I cannot bear 't nommore. I ha' lived under 't so long, for that I ha' had'n the pity and comforting words o' th' best lass living or dead. Haply, but for her, I should ha' gone hottering mad.'

'He wishes to be free, to marry the female of whom he speaks, I fear, sir,' observed Mrs. Sparsit in an undertone, and much dejected by the immorality of the people.

'I do. The lady says what's right. I do. I were a coming to 't. I ha' read i' th' papers that great fok (fair faw 'em a'! I wishes 'em no hurt!) are not bonded together for better for worst so fast, but that they can be set free fro' *their* misfortnet marriages, an' marry ower agen. When they dunnot agree, for that their tempers is ill-sorted, they has room o' one kind an' another in their houses, above a bit, and they can live asunders. We fok ha' only one room, and we can't. When that won't do, they ha' gows an' other cash, an' they can say "This for yo' an' that for me," an' they can go their separate ways. We can't. Spite o' all that, they can be set free for smaller wrongs than mine. So, I mun be ridden o' this woman, and I want t' know how?' *(Chapter 11:* Stephen Blackpool).

Stephen added to his other thoughts the stern reflection, that of all the casualties of this existence upon earth, not one was dealt out with so unequal a hand as Death. The inequality of Birth was nothing to it. For, say that the child of a King and the child of a Weaver were born to-night in the same moment, what was that disparity, to the death of any human creature who was serviceable to, or beloved by, another, while this abandoned woman lived on! *(Chapter 13)*.

She [Louisa Gradgrind] gave him an affectionate good-night, and went out with him to the door, whence the fires of Coketown could be seen, making the distance lurid. She stood there, looking steadfastly towards them, and listening to his departing steps. They retreated quickly, as glad to get away from Stone Lodge; and she stood there yet, when he was gone and all was quiet. It seemed as if, first in her own fire within the house, and then in the fiery haze without, she tried to discover what kind of woof Old Time, that greatest and longest-established Spinner of all, would weave from the threads he had already spun into a woman. But this factory is a secret place, his work is noiseless, and his Hands are mutes *(Chapter 14)*.

'Are you consulting the chimneys of the Coketown works, Louisa?'

'There seems to be nothing there but languid and monotonous smoke. Yet when the night comes, Fire bursts out, father!' she answered, turning quickly.

'Of course I know that, Louisa. I do not see the application of the remark.' To do him justice he did not, at all.

She passed it away with a slight motion of her hand, and concentrating her attention upon him again, said, 'Father, I have often thought that life is very short.' – This was so distinctly one of his subjects that he interposed.

'It is short, no doubt, my dear. Still, the average duration of human life is proved to have increased of late years. The calculations of various life assurance and annuity offices, among other figures which cannot go wrong, have established the fact' *(Chapter 15:* Gradgrind and Louisa).

'What do *I* know, father,' said Louisa in her quiet manner, 'of tastes and fancies; of aspirations and affections; of all that part of my nature in which such light things might have been nourished? What escape have I had from problems that could be demonstrated, and realities that could be grasped?' As she said it, she unconsciously closed her hand, as if upon a solid object, and slowly opened it as though she were releasing dust or ash.

'My dear,' assented her eminently practical parent, 'quite true, quite true.'

'Why, father,' she pursued, 'what a strange question to ask *me*! The baby-preference that even I have heard of as common among children, has never had its innocent resting-place in my breast. You have been so careful of me, that I never had a child's heart. You have trained me so well, that I never dreamed a child's dream. You have dealt so wisely with me, father, from my cradle to this hour, that I never had a child's belief or a child's fear' *(Chapter 15:* Louisa and Gradgrind).

'Oh!' said Mrs. Gradgrind, 'so you have settled it! Well, I'm sure I hope your health may be good, Louisa; for if your head begins to split as soon as you are married, which was the case with mine, I cannot consider that you are to be envied, though I have no doubt you think you are, as all girls do. However, I give you joy, my dear – and I hope you may now turn all your ological studies to good account, I am sure I do! I must give you a kiss of congratulation, Louisa; but don't touch my right shoulder, for there's something running down it all day long. And now you see,' whimpered Mrs. Gradgrind, adjusting her shawls after the affectionate ceremony, 'I shall be worrying myself, morning, noon, and night, to know what I am to call him!'

'Mrs. Gradgrind,' said her husband, solemnly, 'what do you mean?'

'Whatever I am to call him, Mr. Gradgrind, when he is married to Louisa! I must call him something. It's impossible,' said Mrs. Gradgrind, with a mingled sense of politeness and injury, 'to be constantly addressing him and never giving him a name. I cannot call him Josiah, for the name is insupportable to me. You yourself wouldn't hear of Joe, you very well know. Am I to call my own son-in-law, Mister! Not, I believe, unless the time has arrived when, as an invalid, I am to be trampled upon by my relations. Then, what am I to call him!' *(Chapter 15)*.

'As to the wedding, all I ask, Louisa, is, – and I ask it with a fluttering in my chest, which actually extends to the soles of my feet, – that it may take place soon. Otherwise, I know it is one of those subjects I shall never hear the last of' *(Chapter 15:* Mrs. Gradgrind).

On his [Bounderby's] way home, on the evening he set aside for this momentous purpose, he took the precaution of stepping into a chemist's shop and buying a bottle of the very strongest smelling-salts. 'By George!' said Mr. Bounderby, 'if she takes it in the fainting way, I'll have the skin off her nose, at all events!' But, in spite of being thus forearmed, he entered his own house with anything but a courageous air; and appeared before the object of his misgivings, like a dog who was conscious of coming direct from the pantry *(Chapter 16)*.

It was in vain for Bounderby to bluster or to assert himself in any of his explosive ways; Mrs. Sparsit was resolved to have compassion on him, as a Victim. She was polite, obliging, cheerful, hopeful; but, the more polite, the more obliging, the more cheerful, the more hopeful, the more exemplary altogether, she; the forlorner Sacrifice and Victim, he. She had that tenderness for his melancholy fate, that his great red countenance used to break out into cold perspirations when she looked at him (*Chapter 16*).

'Ladies and gentlemen, I am Josiah Bounderby of Coketown. Since you have done my wife and myself the honour of drinking our healths and happiness, I suppose I must acknowledge the same; though, as you all know me, and know what I am, and what my extraction was, you won't expect a speech from a man who, when he sees a Post, says "that's a Post," and when he sees a Pump, says "that's a Pump," and is not to be got to call a Post a Pump, or a Pump a Post, or either of them a Toothpick. If you want a speech this morning, my friend and father-in-law, Tom Gradgrind, is a Member of Parliament, and you know where to get it. I am not your man. However, if I feel a little independent when I look around this table to-day, and reflect how little I thought of marrying Tom Gradgrind's daughter when I was a ragged street-boy, who never washed his face unless it was at a pump, and that not oftener than once a fortnight, I hope I may be excused. So, I hope you like my feeling independent; if you don't, I can't help it. I *do* feel independent. Now I have mentioned, and you have mentioned, that I am this day married to Tom Gradgrind's daughter. I am very glad to be so. It has long been my wish to be so. I have watched her bringing-up, and I believe she is worthy of me. At the same time – not to deceive you – I believe I am worthy of her. So, I thank you, on both our parts, for the good-will you have shown towards us; and the best wish I can give the unmarried part of the present company, is this: I hope every bachelor may find as good a wife as I have found. And I hope every spinster may find as good a husband as my wife has found' (*Chapter 16*).

BOOK THE SECOND: REAPING

'What do you think of the gentleman, Bitzer? she asked the light porter, when he came to take away.

'Spends a deal of money on his dress, ma'am.'

'It must be admitted,' said Mrs. Sparsit, 'that it's very tasteful.'

'Yes, ma'am,' returned Bitzer, 'if that's worth the money.'

'Besides which, ma'am,' resumed Bitzer, while he was polishing the table, 'he looks to me as if he gamed.'

'It's immoral to game,' said Mrs. Sparsit.

'It's ridiculous, ma'am,' said Bitzer, 'because the chances are against the players' (*Chapter 1*).

'What, repeated Mr. Bounderby, folding his arms, 'do you people, in a general way, complain of?'

Stephen looked at him with some little irresolution for a moment, and then seemed to make up his mind.

'Sir, I were never good at showing o 't, though I ha' had'n my share in feeling o't. 'Deed we are in a muddle, sir. Look round town – so rich as 'tis – and see the numbers o' people as has been broughten into being' heer, fur to weave, an' to card, an' to piece out a livin,' aw the same one way, somehows, 'twixt their cradles and their graves. Look how we live, an' wheer we live, an' in what numbers, an' by what chances, and wi' what sameness; and look how the mills is awlus a goin', and how they never works us no nigher to ony dis'ant object – ceptin' awlus, Death. Look how you considers of us, and writes of us, and talks of us, and goes up wi' yor deputations to Secretaries o' State 'bout us, and how yo are awlus right, and how we are awlus wrong, and never had'n no reason in us sin ever we were born. Look how this ha' growen an' growen, sir, bigger an' bigger, broader an' broader, harder an' harder, fro year to year, fro generation unto generation. Who can look on 't, sir, and fairly tell a man 'tis not a muddle?' (*Chapter 5:* Stephen Blackpool).

It afforded Mr. Bounderby supreme satisfaction to instal himself in this snug little estate, and with demonstrative humility to grow cabbages in the flower-garden. He delighted to live, barrack-fashion, among the elegant furniture, and he bullied the very pictures with his origin. 'Why, sir,' he would say to a visitor, 'I am told that Nickits,' the later owner, 'gave seven hundred pound for that Seabeach. Now, to be plain with you, if I ever, in the whole course of my life, take seven looks at it, at a hundred pound a look, it will be as much as I shall do. No, by George! I don't forget that I am Josiah Bounderby of Coketown. For years upon years, the only pictures in my possession, or that I could have got into my possession, by any means, unless I stole 'em, were the engravings of a man shaving himself in a boot, on the blacking bottles that I was overjoyed to use in cleaning boots with, and that I sold when they were empty for a farthing a-piece, and glad to get it!' (*Chapter 7*).

When the Devil goeth about like a roaring lion, he goeth about in a shape by which few but savages and hunters are attracted. But, when he is trimmed, smoothed, and varnished, according to the mode: when he is aweary of vice, and aweary of virtue, used up as to brimstone, and used up as to bliss; then, whether he take to the serving out of red tape, or to the kindling of red fire, he is the very Devil (*Chapter 8*).

She [Mrs. Sparsit] was a most wonderful woman for prowling about the house. How she got from story to story was a mystery beyond solution. A lady so decorous in herself, and so highly connected, was not to be suspected of dropping over the banisters or sliding down them, yet her extraordinary facility of locomotion suggested the wild idea. Another noticeable circumstance in Mrs. Sparsit was, that she was never hurried. She would shoot with consummate velocity from the roof to the hall, yet would be in full possession of her breath and dignity on the moment of her arrival there. Neither was she ever seen by human vision to go at a great pace (*Chapter 9*).

The dreams of childhood – its airy fables; its graceful, beautiful, humane, impossible adornments of the world beyond: so good to be believed in once, so good to be remembered when outgrown, for then the least among them rises to the stature of a great Charity in the heart, suffering little children to come into the midst of it, and to keep with their pure hands a garden in the stony ways of this world, wherein it were better for all the children of Adam that they should oftener sun themselves, simple and trustful, and not worldly-wise – what had she to do with these? Remembrances of how she had journeyed to the little that she knew, by the enchanted roads of what she and millions of innocent creatures had hoped and imagined; of how, first coming upon Reason through the tender light of Fancy, she had seen it a beneficent god, deferring to gods as great as itself: not a grim Idol, cruel and cold, with its victims bound hand to foot, and its big dumb shape set up with a sightless stare, never to be moved by anything but so many calculated tons of leverage – what had she to do with these? Her remembrances of home and childhood were remembrances of the drying up of every spring and fountain in her young heart as it gushed out. The golden waters were not there. They were flowing for the fertilisation of the land where grapes are gathered from thorns, and figs from thistles (*Chapter 9:* Louisa Bounderby).

'Are you in pain, dear mother?'

'I think there's a pain somewhere in the room,' said Mrs. Gradgrind, 'but I couldn't positively say that I have got it' (*Chapter 9*).

'You learnt a great deal, Louisa, and so did your brother. Ologies of all kind from morning to night. If there is any Ology left, of any description, that has not been worn to rags in this house, all I can say is, I hope I shall never hear its name.'

'I can hear you, mother, when you have strength to go on.' This, to keep her from floating away.

'But there is something – not an Ology at all – that your father has missed, or forgotten, Louisa. I don't know what it is. I have often sat with Sissy near me, and thought about it. I shall never get its name now. But your father may. It makes me restless. I want to write to him, to find out for God's sake, what it is. Give me a pen, give me a pen.'

Even the power of restlessness was gone, except from the poor head, which could just turn from side to side.

She fancied, however, that her request had been complied with, and that the pen she could not have held was in her hand. It matters little what figures of wonderful no-meaning she began to trace upon her wrappers. The hand soon stopped in the midst of them; the light that had always been feeble and dim behind the weak transparency, went out; and even Mrs. Gradgrind, emerged from the shadow in which man walketh and disquieteth himself in vain, took upon her the dread solemnity of the sages and patri-archs (*Chapter 9*).

'This is a device to keep him out of the way,' said Mrs. Sparsit, starting from the dull office window whence she had watched him last. 'Harthouse is with his sister now!'

It was the conception of an inspired moment, and she shot off with her utmost swiftness to work it out. The station for the country house was at the opposite end of the town, the time was short, the road not easy; but she was so quick in pouncing on a disengaged coach, so quick in darting out of it, producing her money, seizing her ticket, and diving into the train, that she was borne along the arches spanning the land of coal-pits past and present, as if she had been caught up in a cloud and whirled away.

All the journey, immovable in the air though never left behind; plain to the dark eyes of her mind, as the electric wires which ruled a colossal strip of music-paper out of the evening sky, were plain to the dark eyes of her body; Mrs. Sparsit saw her staircase, with the figure coming down. Very near the bottom now. Upon the brink of the abyss.

An overcast September evening, just as nightfall, saw beneath its drooping eyelid Mrs. Sparsit glide out of her carriage, pass down the wooden steps of the little station into a stony road, cross it into a green lane, and become hidden in a summer-growth of leaves and branches. One or two late birds sleepily chirping in their nests, and a bat heavily crossing and recross-ing her, and the reek of her own tread in the thick dust that felt like velvet, were all Mrs. Sparsit heard or saw until she very softly closed a gate.

She went up to the house, keeping within the shrubbery, and went round it, peeping between the leaves at the lower windows. Most of them were open, as they usually were in such warm weather, but there were no lights yet, and all was silent. She tried the garden with no better effect. She thought of the wood, stole towards it, heedless of long grass and briers; of worms, snails, and slugs, and all the creeping things that be. With her dark eyes and her hook nose warily in advance of her, Mrs. Sparsit softly crushed her way through the thick undergrowth, so intent upon her object that she probably would have done no less, if the wood had been a wood of adders.

Hark!

The smaller birds might have tumbled out of their nests, fascinated by the glittering of Mrs. Sparsit's eyes in the gloom, as she stopped and listened (*Chapter 11*).

BOOK THE THIRD: GARNERING

'I doubt whether I have understood Louisa. I doubt whether I have been quite right in the manner of her education.'

'There you hit it,' returned Bounderby. 'There I agree with you. You have found it out at last, have you? Education! I'll tell you what education is – To be tumbled out of doors, neck and crop, and put upon the shortest allowance of everything except blows. That's what *I* call education' (*Chapter 3:* Gradgrind and Bounderby).

'Thou'rt in great pain, my own dear Stephen?'

'I ha' been, but not now. I ha' been – dreadful, and dree, and long, my dear – but 'tis ower now. Ah, Rachael, aw a muddle! Fro' first to last, a muddle!'

The spectre of his old look seemed to pass as he said the word.

'I ha' fell into th' pit, my dear, as have cost wi'in the knowledge o' old fok now livin', hundreds and hundreds o' men's lives – fathers, sons, brothers, dear to thousands an' thousands, an' keeping 'em fro' want and hunger. I ha' fell into a pit that ha' been wi' th'

Fire-damp crueller than battle. I ha' read on't in the public petition, as onny one may read, fro' the men that works in pits, in which they ha' pray'n and pray'n the lawmakers for Christ's sake not to let their work be murder to 'em, but to spare 'em for th' wives and children that they loves as well as gentlefok loves theirs. When it were in work, it killed wi'out need; when 'tis let alone, it kills wi'out need. See how we die an' no need, one way an' another – in a muddle – every day!' (*Chapter 6:* Stephen Blackpool).

'Thethilia,' said Mr. Sleary, who had brandy-and-water at hand, 'it doth me good to thee you. You wath alwayth a favourite with uth, and you've done uth credit thinth the old timeth I'm thure. You mutht thee our people, my dear, afore we thpeak of bithnith, or they'll break their hearth – ethpethially the women. Here'th Jothphine hath been and got married to E. W. B. Childerth, and thee hath got a boy, and though he'th only three yearth old, he thtickth on to any pony you can bring againtht him. He'th named The Little Wonder of Thcolathtic Equitation; and if you don't hear of that boy, at Athley'th, you'll hear of him at Parith. And you recollect Kidderminthter, that wath thought to be rather thweet upon yourthelf? Well. He'th married too. Married a widder. Old enough to be hith mother. Thee wath Tightrope, thee wath, and now thee'th nothing – on accounth of fat. They've got two children, tho we're throng in the Fairy bithnith and the Nurthery dodge. If you wath to thee our Children in the Wood, with their father and mother both a dyin' on a horthe – their uncle a retheiving of 'em ath hith wardth, upon a horthe – themthelvth both a goin' a blackberryin' on a horthe – and the Robinth a coming in to cover 'em with leavth, upon a horthe – you'd thay it wath the completetht thing ath ever you thet your eyeth on! And you remember Emma Gordon, my dear, ath wath a'motht a mother to you? Of courthe you do; I needn't athk. Well! Emma, thee lotht her huthband. He wath throw'd a heavy back-fall off a Elephant in a thort of a Pagoda thing ath the Thultan of the Indieth, and he never got the better of it; and thee married a thecond time – married a Cheethemonger ath fell in love with her from the front – and he'th a Overtheer and makin' a fortun' (*Chapter 7*).

'Thquire, you don't need to be told that dogth ith wonderful animalth.'

'Their instinct,' said Mr. Gradgrind, 'is surprising.'

'Whatever you call it – and I'm bletht if *I* know what to call it' – said Sleary, 'it ith athtonithing. The way in whith a dog'll find you – the dithtanthe he'll come!'

'His scent,' said Mr. Gradgrind, 'being so fine.'

'I'm bletht if I know what to call it,' repeated Sleary, shaking his head, 'but I have had dogth find me, Thquire, in a way that made me think whether that dog hadn't gone to another dog, and thed, "You don't happen to know a perthon of the name of Thleary, do you? Perthon of the name of Thleary, in the Horthe-Riding way – thtout man – game eye?" And whether that dog mightn't have thed, "Well, I can't thay I know him mythelf, but I know a dog that I think would be likely to be acquainted with him."

And whether that dog mightn't have thought it over, and thed, "Thleary, Thleary! O yeth, to be thure! A friend of mine menthioned him to me at one time. I can get you hith adreth directly." In conthequenth of my being afore the public, and going about tho muth, you thee, there mutht be a number of dogth acquainted with me, Thquire, that *I* don't know!' (*Chapter 8*).

'Any way,' said Sleary, after putting his lips to his brandy-and-water, 'ith fourteen month ago, Thquire, thinthe we wath at Chethter. We wath getting up our Children in the Wood one morning, when there cometh into our Ring, by the thtage door, a dog. He had travelled a long way, he wath in very bad condithon, he wath lame, and pretty well blind. He went round to our children, one after another, as if he wath a theeking for a child he know'd; and then he come to me, and throwd hithelf up behind, and thtood on hith two forelegth, weak ath he wath, and then he wagged hith tail and died. Thquire, that dog wath Merrylegth' (*Chapter 8*).

'It theemth to prethent two thingth to a perthon, don't it, Thquire?' said Mr. Sleary, musing as he looked down into the depths of his brandy-and-water: 'one, that there ith a love in the world, not all Thelf-interetht after all, but thomething very different; t'other, that it hath a way of ith own of calculating or not calculating, whith thomehow or another ith at leatht ath hard to give a name to, ath the wayth of the dogth ith!' (*Chapter 8*).

LITTLE DORRIT

BOOK THE FIRST: POVERTY

'Adieu, my birds!' said the keeper of the prison, taking his pretty child in his arms, and dictating the words with a kiss.

'Adieu, my birds!' the pretty child repeated.

Her innocent face looked back so brightly over his shoulder, as he walked away with her, singing her the song of the child's game:

> 'Who passes by this road so late?
> Compagnon de la Majolaine!
> Who passes by this road so late?
> Always gay!'

that John Baptist felt it a point of honour to reply at the grate, and in good time and tune, though a little hoarsely:

> 'Of all the king's knights 'tis the flower,
> Compagnon de la Majolaine!
> Of all the king's knights 'tis the flower,
> Always gay!'

Which accompanied them so far down the few steep stairs, that the prison-keeper had to stop at last for his little daughter to hear the song out, and repeat the Refrain while they were yet in sight. Then the child's head disappeared, and the prison-keeper's head disappeared, but the little voice prolonged the strain until the door clashed (*Chapter 1*).

Excited into a still greater resemblance to a caged wild animal by his anxiety to know more, the prisoner leaped nimbly down, ran round the chamber, leaped nimbly up again, clasped the grate and tried to shake it, leaped down and ran, leaped up and listened, and never rested until the noise, becoming more and more distant, had died away. How many better prisoners have worn their noble hearts out so; no man thinking of it; not even the beloved of their souls realising it; great kings and governors, who had made them captive, careering in the sunlight jauntily, and men cheering them on. Even the said great personages dying in bed, making exemplary ends and sounding speeches; and polite history, more servile than their instruments, embalming them! *(Chapter 1)*.

'I bear those monotonous walls no ill-will now,' said Mr. Meagles. 'One always begins to forgive a place as soon as it's left behind; I dare say a prisoner begins to relent towards his prison, after he is let out' *(Chapter 2)*.

'Good-bye!' said Mr. Meagles. 'This is the last good-bye upon the list, for Mother and I have just said it to Mr. Clennam here, and he only waits to say it to Pet. Good-bye! We may never meet again.'
'In our course through life we shall meet the people who are coming to meet *us*, from many strange places and by many strange roads,' was the composed reply; 'and what it is set to us to do to them, and what it is set to them to do to us, will all be done' *(Chapter 2)*.

It was a Sunday evening in London, gloomy, close and stale. Maddening church bells of all degrees of dissonance, sharp and flat, cracked and clear, fast and slow, made the brick-and-mortar echoes hideous. Melancholy streets in a penitential garb of soot, steeped the souls of the people who were condemned to look at them out of windows, in dire despondency. In every thoroughfare, up almost every alley, and down almost every turning, some doleful bell was throbbing, jerking, tolling, as if the Plague were in the city and the dead-carts were going round. Everything was bolted and barred that could by possibility furnish relief to an overworked people. No pictures, no unfamiliar animals, no rare plants or flowers, no natural or artificial wonders of the ancient world – all *taboo* with that enlightened strictness, that the ugly South Sea gods in the British Museum might have supposed themselves at home again. Nothing to see but streets, streets, streets. Nothing to breathe but streets, streets, streets. Nothing to change the brooding mind, or raise it up. Nothing for the spent toiler to do, but to compare the monotony of his seventh day with the monotony of his six days, think what a weary life he led, and make the best of it – or the worst, according to the probabilities *(Chapter 3)*.

Ten thousand responsible houses surrounded him [Arthur Clennam], frowning as heavily on the streets they composed, as if they were every one inhabited by the ten young men of the Calender's story, who blackened their faces and bemoaned their miseries every night. Fifty thousand lairs surrounded him where people lived so unwholesomely that fair water put into their crowded rooms on Saturday night, would be corrupt on Sunday morning; albeit my lord, their county member, was amazed that they failed to sleep in company with their butcher's meat. Miles of close wells and pits of houses, where the inhabitants gasped for air, stretched far away towards every point of the compass. Through the heart of the town a deadly sewer ebbed and flowed, in the place of a fine fresh river. What secular want could the million or so of human beings whose daily labour, six days in the week, lay among these Arcadian objects, from the sweet sameness of which they had no escape between the cradle and the grave – what secular want could they possibly have upon their seventh day? Clearly they could want nothing but a stringent policeman *(Chapter 3)*.

Her diminutive figure, small features, and slight spare dress, gave her the appearance of being much younger than she was. A woman, probably of not less than two-and-twenty, she might have been passed in the street for little more than half that age. Not that her face was very youthful, for in truth there was more consideration and care in it than naturally belonged to her utmost years; but she was so little and light, so noiseless and shy, and appeared so conscious of being out of place among the three hard elders, that she had all the manner and much of the appearance of a subdued child *(Chapter 5: Little Dorrit)*.

'Thank you,' said the doctor, 'thank you. Your good lady is quite composed. Doing charmingly.'
'I am very happy and very thankful to know it,' said the debtor, 'though I little thought once, that – '
'That a child would be born to you in a place like this?' said the doctor. 'Bah, bah, sir, what does it signify? A little more elbow-room is all we want here. We are quiet here; we don't get badgered here; there's no knocker here, sir, to be hammered at by creditors and bring a man's heart into his mouth. Nobody comes here to ask if a man's at home, and to say he'll stand on the door mat till he is. Nobody writes threatening letters about money to this place. It's freedom, sir it's freedom! I have had to-day's practice at home and abroad, on a march, and aboard ship, and I'll tell you this: I don't know that I have every pursued it under such quiet circumstances, as here this day. Elsewhere, people are restless, worried, hurried about, anxious respecting one thing, anxious respecting another. Nothing of the kind here, sir. We have done all that – we know the worst of it; we have got to the bottom, we can't fall, and what have we found? Peace. That's the word for it. Peace.' With this profession of faith, the doctor, who was an old jail-bird, and was more sodden than usual, and had the additional and unusual stimulus of money in his pocket, returned to his associate and chum in hoarseness, puffiness, red-facedness, all-fours, tobacco, dirt, and brandy *(Chapter 6)*.

'When Maggy was ten years old,' said Dorrit, watching her face while she spoke, 'she had a bad fever, sir, and she has never grown any older ever since.'
'Ten years old,' said Maggy, nodding her head. 'But what a nice hospital! So comfortable, wasn't it? Oh so nice it was. Such a Ev'nly place!'
'She had never been at peace before, sir,' said Dorrit, turning towards Arthur for an instant and speaking low, 'and she always runs off upon that.'

'Such beds there is there!' cried Maggy. 'Such lemonades! Such oranges! Such d'licious broth and wine! Such Chicking! Oh, AIN'T it a delightful place to go and stop at!' *(Chapter 9)*.

The Circumlocution Office was (as everybody knows without being told) the most important Department under Government. No public business of any kind could possibly be done at any time, without the acquiescence of the Circumlocution Office. Its finger was in the largest public pie, and in the smallest public tart. It was equally impossible to do the plainest right and to undo the plainest wrong, without the express authority of the Circumlocution Office. If another Gunpowder Plot had been discovered half an hour before the lighting of the match, nobody would have been justified in saving the parliament until there had been half a score of boards, half a bushel of minutes, several sacks of official memoranda, and a family-vault full of ungrammatical correspondence, on the part of the Circumlocution Office.

This glorious establishment had been early in the field, when the one sublime principle involving the difficult art of governing a country, was first distinctly revealed to statesmen. It had been foremost to study that bright revelation, and to carry its shining influence through the whole of the official proceedings. Whatever was required to be done, the Circumlocution Office was beforehand with all the public departments in the art of perceiving – HOW NOT TO DO IT.

Through this delicate perception, through the tact with which it invariably seized it, and through the genius with which it always acted on it, the Circumlocution Office had risen to over-top all the public departments; and the public condition had risen to be – what it was *(Chapter 10)*.

Numbers of people were lost in the Circumlocution Office. Unfortunates with wrongs, or with projects for the general welfare (and they had better have had wrongs at first, than have taken that bitter English recipe for certainly getting them), who in slow lapse of time and agony had passed safely through other public departments; who, according to rule, had been bullied in this, over-reached by that, and evaded by the other; got referred at last to the Circumlocution Office, and never reappeared in the light of day. Boards sat upon them, secretaries minuted upon them, commissioners gabbled about them, clerks registered, entered, checked, and ticked them off, and they melted away. In short, all the business of the country went through the Circumlocution Office, except the business that never came out of it; and *its* name was Legion *(Chapter 10)*.

Mews Street, Grosvenor Square, was not absolutely Grosvenor Square itself, but it was very near it. It was a hideous little street of dead wall, stables, and dunghills, with lofts over coach-houses inhabited by coachmen's families, who had a passion for drying clothes, and decorating their window-sills with miniature turnpike-gates. The principal chimney-sweep of that fashionable quarter lived at the blind end of Mews Street; and the same corner contained an establishment much frequented about early morning and twilight, for the purchase of wine-bottles and kitchen-stuff. Punch's shows used to lean against the dead wall in Mews Street, while their proprietors were dining elsewhere; and the dogs of the neighbourhood made appointments to meet in the same locality. Yet there were two or three small airless houses at the entrance end of Mews Street, which went at enormous rents on account of their being abject hangers-on to a fashionable situation; and whenever one of these fearful little coops was to be let (which seldom happened, for they were in great request), the house agent advertised it as a gentlemanly residence in the most aristocratic part of town, inhabited solely by the élite of the beau monde *(Chapter 10)*.

'Mr. Wobbler?' inquired the suitor.
Both gentleman glanced at him, and seemed surprised at his assurance.
'So he went,' said the gentleman with the gun-barrel, who was an extremely deliberate speaker, 'down to his cousin's place, and took the Dog with him by rail. Inestimable Dog. Flew at the porter fellow when he was put into the dog-box, and flew at the guard when he was taken out. He got half a dozen fellows into a Barn, and a good supply of Rats, and timed the Dog. Finding the Dog able to do it immensely, made the match, and heavily backed the Dog. When the match came off, some devil of a fellow was bought over, Sir, Dog was made drunk, Dog's master was cleaned out.'
'Mr. Wobbler?' inquired the suitor.
The gentleman who was spreading the marmalade returned, without looking up from that occupation, 'What did he call the Dog?'
'Called him Lovely,' said the other gentleman. 'Said the Dog was the perfect picture of the old aunt from whom he had expectations. Found him particularly like her when hocussed.'
'Mr. Wobbler?' said the suitor *(Chapter 10:* Clennam and Wobbler).

At this end of the Yard and over the gateway, was the factory of Daniel Doyce, often heavily beating like a bleeding heart of iron, with the clink of metal upon metal.
The opinion of the Yard was divided respecting the derivation of its name. The more practical of its inmates abided by the tradition of a murder; the gentler and more imaginative inhabitants, including the whole of the tender sex, were loyal to the legend of a young lady of former times closely imprisoned in her chamber by a cruel father for remaining true to her own true love, and refusing to marry the suitor he chose for her. The legend related how that the young lady used to be seen up at her window behind the bars, murmuring a love-lorn song of which the burden was, 'Bleeding Heart, Bleeding Heart, bleeding away,' until she died. It was objected by the murderous party that this Refrain was notoriously the invention of a tambour-worker, a spinster and romantic, still lodging in the Yard. But, forasmuch as all favourite legends must be associated with the affections, and as many more people fall in love than commit murder – which it may be hoped, howsoever bad we are, will continue until the end of the world to be the dispensation under which we shall live – the Bleeding Heart, Bleeding

Heart, bleeding away story, carried the day by a great majority. Neither party would listen to the antiquaries who delivered learned lectures in the neighbourhood, showing the Bleeding Heart to have been the heraldic cognizance of the old family to whom the property had once belonged. And, considering that the hour-glass they turned from year to year was filled with the earthiest and coarsest sand, the Bleeding Heart Yarders had reason enough for objecting to be despoiled of the one little golden grain of poetry that sparkled in it *(Chapter 12)*.

On the way, Arthur elicited from his new friend a confused summary of the interior life of Bleeding Heart Yard. They was all hard up there, Mr. Plornish said, uncommon hard up, to be sure. Well, he couldn't say how it was; he didn't know as anybody *could* say how it was; all he know'd was, that so it was. When a man felt, on his own back and in his own belly, that poor he was, that man (Mr. Plornish gave it as his decided belief) know'd well that he was poor somehow or another, and you couldn't talk it out of him, no more than you could talk Beef into him. Then you see, some people as was better off said, and a good many such people lived pretty close up to the mark themselves if not beyond it so he'd heerd, that they was 'improvident' (that was the favourite word) down the Yard. For instance, if they see a man with his wife and children going to Hampton Court in a Wan, perhaps once in a year, they says, 'Hallo! I thought you was poor, my improvident friend!' Why, Lord, how hard it was upon a man! What was a man to do? He couldn't go mollancholly mad, and even if he did, you wouldn't be the better for it. In Mr. Plornish's judgment you would be the worse for it. Yet you seemed to want to make a man mollancholly mad. You was always at it – if not with your right hand, with your left. What was they a doing in the Yard? Why, take a look at 'em and see. There was the girls and their mothers a working at their sewing, or their shoe-binding, or their trimming, or their waistcoat making, day and night and night and day, and not more than able to keep body and soul together after all – often not so much. There was people of pretty well all sorts of trades you could name, all wanting to work, and yet not able to get it. There was old people, after working all their lives, going and being shut up in the workhouse, much worse fed and lodged and treated altogether, than – Mr. Plornish said manufacturers, but appeared to mean malefactors. Why, a man didn't know where to turn himself for a crumb of comfort. As to who was to blame for it, Mr. Plornish didn't know who was to blame for it. He could tell you who suffered, but he couldn't tell you whose fault it was. It wasn't *his* place to find out, and who'd mind what he said, if he did find out? He only know'd that it wasn't put right by them what undertook that line of business, and that it didn't come right of itself. And in brief his illogical opinion was, that if you couldn't do nothing for him, you had better take nothing from him for doing of it; so far as he could make out, that was about what it come to *(Chapter 12)*.

Most men will be found sufficiently true to themselves to be true to an old idea. It is no proof of an inconstant mind, but exactly the opposite, when the idea will not bear close comparison with the reality, and the contrast is a fatal shock to it. Such was Clennam's case. In his youth he had ardently loved this woman, and had heaped upon her all the locked-up wealth of his affection and imagination. That wealth had been, in his desert home, like Robinson Crusoe's money; exchangeable with no one, lying idle in the dark to rust, until he poured it out for her. Ever since that memorable time, though he had, until the night of his arrival, as completely dismissed her from any association with his Present or Future as if she had been dead (which she might easily have been for anything he knew), he had kept the old fancy of the Past unchanged, in its old sacred place. And now, after all, the last of the Patriarchs coolly walked into the parlour, saying in effect, 'Be good enough to throw it down and dance upon it. This is Flora' *(Chapter 13)*.

'Indeed I have little doubt,' said Flora, running on with astonishing speed, and pointing her conversation with nothing but commas, and very few of them, 'that you are married to some Chinese lady, being in China so long and being in business and naturally desirous to settle and extend your connection nothing was more likely than that you should propose to a Chinese lady and nothing was more natural I am sure than that the Chinese lady should accept you and think herself very well off too, I only hope she's not a Pagodian dissenter.'
'I am not,' returned Arthur, smiling in spite of himself, 'married to any lady, Flora.'
'Oh good gracious me I hope you never kept yourself a bachelor so long on my account!' tittered Flora; 'but of course you never did why should you, pray don't answer, I don't know where I'm running to, oh do tell me something about the Chinese ladies whether their eyes are really so long and narrow always putting me in mind of mother-of-pearl fish at cards and do they really wear tails down their back and plaited too or is it only the men, and when they pull their hair so very tight off their foreheads don't they hurt themselves, and why do they stick little bells all over their bridges and temples and hats and things or don't they really do it!' Flora gave him another of her old glances *(Chapter 13:* Flora Finching and Arthur Clennam).

'One remark,' said Flora, giving their conversation, without the slightest notice and to the great terror of Clennam, the tone of a love-quarrel, 'I wish to make, one explanation I wish to offer, when your Mama came and made a scene of it with my Papa and when I was called down into the little breakfast-room where they were looking at one another with your Mama's parasol between them seated on two chairs like mad bulls what was I to do?'
'My dear Mrs. Finching,' urged Clennam – 'all so long ago and so long concluded, is it worth while seriously to – '
'I can't Arthur,' returned Flora, 'be denounced as heartless by the whole society of China without setting myself right when I have the opportunity of doing so, and you must be very well aware that there was Paul and Virginia which had to be returned and which was returned without note or comment, not that I mean to say you could have written to me watched as I was but

if it had only come back with a red wafer on the cover I should have known that meant Come to Pekin Nankeen and What's the third place barefoot.'

'My dear Mrs. Finching, you were not to blame, and I never blamed you. We were both too young, too dependent and helpless, to do anything but accept our separation. – Pray think how long ago,' gently remonstrated Arthur.

'One more remark,' proceeded Flora with unslackened volubility, 'I wish to make, one more explanation I wish to offer, for five days I had a cold in the head from crying which I passed entirely in the back drawing-room – there is the back drawing-room still on the first floor and still at the back of the house to confirm my words – when that dreary period had passed a lull succeeded years rolled on and Mr. F became acquainted with us at a mutual friend's, he was all attention he called next day he soon began to call three evenings a week and to send in little things for supper, it was not love on Mr. F's part it was adoration, Mr. F proposed with the full approval of Papa and what could I do?'

'Nothing whatever,' said Arthur, with the cheerfulest readiness, 'but what you did' (Chapter 13).

The major characteristics discoverable by the stranger in Mr. F's Aunt, were extreme severity and grim taciturnity; sometimes interrupted by a propensity to offer remarks in a deep warning voice, which, being totally uncalled for by anything said by anybody, and traceable to no association of ideas, confounded and terrified the mind. Mr. F's Aunt may have thrown in these observations on some system of her own, and it may have been ingenious, or even subtle; but the key to it was wanted (Chapter 13).

Mr. F's Aunt, after regarding the company for ten minutes with a malevolent gaze, delivered the following fearful remark.

'When we lived at Henley, Barnes's gander was stole by tinkers' (Chapter 13).

Flora had just said, 'Mr. Clennam, will you give me a glass of port for Mr. F's Aunt?'

'The Monument near London Bridge,' that lady instantly proclaimed, 'was put up arter the Great Fire of London; and the Great Fire of London was not the fire in which your uncle George's workshops was burned down.'

Mr. Pancks, with his former courage, said 'Indeed, ma'am? All right!' But appearing to be incensed by imaginary contradiction, or other ill-usage, Mr. F's Aunt, instead of relapsing into silence, made the following additional proclamation.

'I hate a fool!' (Chapter 13).

'There, Little Dorrit, there, there, there! We will suppose that you did know this person, and that you might do all this, and that it was all done. And now tell me, who am quite another person – who am nothing more than the friend who begged you to trust him – why you are out at midnight, and what it is that brings you so far through the streets at this late hour, my slight, delicate,' child was on his lips again, 'Little Dorrit!'

'Maggy and I have been to-night,' she answered, subduing herself with the quiet effort that had long

been natural to her, 'to the theatre where my sister is engaged.'

'And oh ain't it a Ev'nly place,' suddenly interrupted Maggy, who seemed to have the power of going to sleep and waking up whenever she chose. 'Almost as good as a hospital. Only there ain't no Chicking in it.'

Here she shook herself, and fell asleep again (Chapter 14: Arthur Clennam and Little Dorrit).

Strange, if the little sick-room fire were in effect a beacon fire, summoning some one, and that the most unlikely some one in the world, to the spot that must be come to. Strange, if the little sick-room light were in effect a watch-light, burning in that place every night until an appointed event should be watched out! Which of the vast multitude of travellers, under the sun and the stars, climbing the dusty hills and toiling along the weary plains, journeying by land and journeying by sea, coming and going so strangely, to meet and to act and re-act on one another, which of the host may, with no suspicion of the journey's end, be travelling surely hither?

Time shall show us. The post of honour and the post of shame, the general's station and the drummer's, a peer's statue in Westminster Abbey and a seaman's hammock in the bosom of the deep, the mitre and the workhouse, the woolsack and the gallows, the throne and the guillotine – the travellers to all are on the great high road; but it has wonderful divergences, and only Time shall show us whither each traveller is bound (Chapter 15).

As he knew the house well, he conducted Arthur to it by the way that showed it to the best advantage. It was a charming place (none the worse for being a little eccentric), on the road by the river, and just what the residence of the Meagles family ought to be. It stood in a garden, no doubt as fresh and beautiful in the May of the Year, as Pet now was in the May of her life; and it was defended by a goodly show of handsome trees and spreading evergreens, as Pet was by Mr. and Mrs. Meagles. It was made out of an old brick house, of which a part had been altogether pulled down, and another part had been changed into the present cottage; so there was a hale elderly portion, to represent Mr. and Mrs. Meagles, and a young picturesque, very pretty portion to represent Pet. There was even the later addition of a conservatory sheltering itself against it, uncertain of hue in its deep-stained glass, and in its more transparent portions flashing to the sun's rays, now like fire and now like harmless water drops; which might have stood for Tattycoram. Within view was the peaceful river and the ferry-boat, to moralise to all the inmates, saying: Young or old, passionate or tranquil, chafing or content, you, thus runs the current always. Let the heart swell into what discord it will, thus plays the rippling water on the prow of the ferry-boat ever the same tune. Year after year, so much allowance for the drifting of the boat, so many miles an hour the flowing of the stream, here the rushes, there the lilies, nothing uncertain or unquiet, upon this road that steadily runs away; while you, upon your flowing road of time, are so capricious and distracted (Chapter 16).

Tatty stood for a moment, immovable.

'Hey?' cried Mr. Meagles. 'Count another five-and-twenty, Tattycoram.'

She might have counted a dozen, when she bent and put her lips to the caressing hand. It patted her cheek, as it touched the owner's beautiful curls, and Tattycoram went away.

'Now, there,' said Mr. Meagles, softly, as he gave a turn to the dumb-waiter on his right hand, to twirl the sugar towards himself. 'There's a girl who might be lost and ruined, if she wasn't among practical people. Mother and I know, solely from being practical, that there are times when that girl's whole nature seems to roughen itself against seeing us so bound up in Pet. No father and mother were bound up in her, poor soul. I don't like to think of the way in which that unfortunate child, with all that passion and protest in her, feels when she hears the Fifth Commandment on a Sunday. I am always inclined to call out, Church, Count five-and-twenty, Tattycoram' *(Chapter 16)*.

Though too humble before the rule of his heart to be sanguine, Young John had considered the object of his attachment in all its lights and shades. Following it out to blissful results, he had descried, without self-commendation, a fitness in it. Say things prospered, and they were united. She, the child of the Marshalsea; he, the lock-keeper. There was a fitness in that. Say he became a resident turnkey. She would officially succeed to the chamber she had rented so long. There was a beautiful propriety in that. It looked over the wall, if you stood on tip-toe; and, with a trellis-work of scarlet beans and a canary or so, would become a very Arbour. There was a charming idea in that. Then, being all in all to one another, there was even an appropriate grace in the lock. With the world shut out (except that part of it which would be shut in); with its troubles and disturbances only known to them by hearsay, as they would be described by the pilgrims tarrying with them on their way to the Insolvent Shrine; with the Arbour above, and the Lodge below; they would glide down the stream of time, in pastoral domestic happiness. Young John drew tears from his eyes by finishing the picture with a tombstone in the adjoining churchyard, close against the prison wall, bearing the following touching inscription: 'Sacred to the Memory of JOHN CHIVERY, Sixty years Turnkey, and Fifty years Head Turnkey, of the neighbouring Marshalsea, Who departed this life, universally respected, on the thirty-first of December, One thousand eight hundred and eighty-six, Aged eighty-three years. Also of his truly beloved and truly loving wife, AMY, whose maiden name was DORRIT, Who survived his loss not quite forty-eight hours, And who breathed her last in the Marshalsea aforesaid. There she was born, There she lived, There she died *(Chapter 18)*.

The tobacco business round the corner of Horsemonger Lane was carried on in a rural establishment one storey high, which had the benefit of the air from the yards of Horsemonger Lane Jail, and the advantage of a retired walk under the wall of that pleasant establishment. The business was of too modest a character to support a life-size Highlander, but it maintained a little one on a bracket on the door-post, who looked like a fallen Cherub that had found it necessary to take to a kilt *(Chapter 18)*.

It was an affecting illustration of the fallacy of human projects, to behold her lover with the great hat pulled over his eyes, the velvet collar turned up as if it rained, the plum-coloured coat buttoned to conceal the silken waistcoat of golden sprigs, and the little direction-post pointing inexorably home, creeping along by the worst back streets, and composing, as he went, the following new inscription for a tombstone in St. George's Churchyard:

'Here lie the mortal remains of JOHN CHIVERY, Never anything worth mentioning, Who died about the end of the year one thousand eight hundred and twenty-six, Of a broken heart, Requesting with his last breath that the word AMY might be inscribed over his ashes, Which was accordingly directed to be done, By his afflicted Parents' *(Chapter 18)*.

Society,' said Mrs. Merdle, with another curve of her little finger, 'is so difficult to explain to young persons (indeed is so difficult to explain to most persons), that I am glad to hear that. I wish Society was not so arbitrary, I wish it was not so exacting – Bird, be quiet!'

The parrot had given a most piercing shriek, as if its name were Society and it asserted its right to its exactions.

'But,' resumed Mrs. Merdle, 'we must take it as we find it. We know it is hollow and conventional and wordly and very shocking, but unless we are Savages in the Tropical seas (I should have been charmed to be one myself – most delightful life and perfect climate I am told), we must consult it. It is the common lot. Mr. Merdle is a most extensive merchant, his transactions are on the vastest scale, his wealth and influence are very great, but even he – Bird, be quiet!' *(Chapter 20)*.

'You may see him now,' said she, 'if you'll condescend to take a peep.'

With these mysterious words, she preceded the visitor into a little parlour behind the shop, with a little window in it commanding a very little dull back-yard. In this yard a wash of sheets and table-cloths tried (in vain, for want of air) to get itself dried on a line or two; and among those flapping articles was sitting in a chair, like the last mariner left alive on the deck of a damp ship without the power of furling the sails, a little woe-begone young man.

'Our John,' said Mrs. Chivery.

Not to be deficient in interest, Clennam asked what he might be doing there?

'It's the only change he takes,' said Mrs. Chivery, shaking her head afresh. 'He won't go out, even in the back-yard, when there's no linen; but when there's linen to keep the neighbours' eyes off, he'll sit there, hours. Hours he will. Says he feels as if it was groves!' Mrs. Chivery shook her head again, put her apron in a motherly way to her eyes, and reconducted her visitor into the regions of the business *(Chapter 22)*.

The wheeled chair had its associated remembrances and reveries, one may suppose, as every place that is made the station of a human being has. Pictures of demolished streets and altered houses, as they formerly were when the occupant of the chair was familiar with them; images of people as they too used to be, with little or no allowance made for the lapse of time since they were seen; of these, there must have been many in the long routine of gloomy days. To stop the clock of busy existence, at the hour when we were personally sequestered from it; to suppose mankind stricken motionless, when we were brought to a stand-still; to be unable to measure the changes beyond our view, by any larger standard than the shrunken one of our own uniform and contracted existence; is the infirmity of many invalids, and the mental unhealthiness of almost all recluses *(Chapter 29)*.

Anybody may pass, any day, in the thronged thoroughfares of the metropolis, some meagre, wrinkled, yellow old man (who might be supposed to have dropped from the stars, if there were any star in the Heavens dull enough to be suspected of casting off so feeble a spark), creeping along with a scared air, as though bewildered and a little frightened by the noise and bustle. This old man is always a little old man. If he were ever a big old man, he has shrunk into a little old man; if he were always a little old man, he has dwindled into a less old man. His coat is of a colour, and cut, that never was the mode anywhere, at any period. Clearly, it was not made for him, or for any individual mortal. Some wholesale contractor measured Fate for five thousand coats of such quality, and Fate has lent this old coat to this old man, as one of a long unfinished line of many old men. It has always large dull metal buttons, similar to no other buttons. This old man wears a hat, a thumbed and napless and yet an obdurate hat, which has never adapted itself to the shape of his poor head. His coarse shirt and his coarse neckcloth have no more individuality than his coat and hat; they have the same character of not being his – of not being anybody's. Yet this old man wears these clothes with a certain unaccustomed air of being dressed and elaborated for the public ways; as though he passed the greater part of his time in the nightcap and gown. And so, like the country mouse in the second year of a famine, come to see the town mouse, and timidly threading his way to the town-mouse's lodging through a city of cats, this old man passes in the streets.

Sometimes, on holidays towards the evening, he will be seen to walk with a slightly increased infirmity, and his old eyes will glimmer with a moist and marshy light. Then the little old man is drunk. A very small measure will overset him; he may be bowled off his unsteady legs with a half-pint pot. Some pitying acquaintance – chance acquaintance very often – has warmed up his weakness with a treat of beer, and the consequence will be the lapse of a longer time than usual before he shall pass again. For, the little old man is going home to the Workhouse; and on his good behaviour they do not let him out often (though methinks they might, considering the few years he has before him to go out in, under the sun); and on his bad behaviour they shut him up closer than ever, in a grove of two score and nineteen more old men, every one of whom smells of all the others *(Chapter 31)*.

'Miss Dorrit,' said Mrs. Plornish, 'Here's Father! Ain't he looking nice? And such voice he's in!'

Little Dorrit gave him her hand, and smilingly said she had not seen him this long time.

'No, they're rather hard on poor Father,' said Mrs. Plornish with a lengthening face, 'and don't let him have half as much change and fresh air as would benefit him. But he'll soon be home for good, now. Won't you, Father?'

'Yes, my dear, I hope so. In good time, please God.'

Here Mr. Plornish delivered himself of an oration which he invariably made, word for word the same, on all such opportunities. It was couched in the following terms:

'John Edward Nandy. Sir. While there's a ounce of wittles or drink of any sort in this present roof, you're fully welcome to your share on it. While there's a handful of fire or a mouthful of bed in this present roof, you're fully welcome to your share on it. If so be as there should be nothing in this present roof, you should be as welcome to your share on it as if it was something much or little. And this is what I mean and so I don't deceive you, and consequently which is to stand out is to entreat of you, and therefore why not do it?' *(Chapter 31)*.

'Thank you, John. How is your mother, Young John?'

'Thank you, sir, she's not quite as well as we could wish – in fact, we none of us are, except father, – but she's pretty well, sir.'

'Say we sent our remembrances, will you? Say, kind remembrances, if you please, Young John.'

'Thank you, sir, I will.' And Mr. Chivery, junior, went his way, having spontaneously composed on the spot an entirely new epitaph for himself, to the effect that Here lay the body of John Chivery, Who, Having at such a date, Beheld the idol of his life, In grief and tears, And feeling unable to bear the harrowing spectacle, Immediately repaired to the abode of his inconsolable parents, And terminated his existence, by his own rash act *(Chapter 31: The Father of the Marshalsea and Young John Chivery)*.

Among the friends of Mrs. Gowan (who piqued herself at once on being Society, and on maintaining intimate and easy relations with that Power), Mrs. Merdle occupied a front row. True, the Hampton Court Bohemians, without exception, turned up their noses at Merdle as an upstart; but they turned them down again, by falling flat on their faces to worship his wealth. In which compensating adjustment of their noses, they were pretty much like Treasury, Bar, and Bishop, and all the rest of them *(Chapter 33)*.

Mrs. Merdle reviewed the bosom which Society was accustomed to review; and having ascertained that show-window of Mr. Merdle's and the London jewellers' to be in good order, replied:

'As to marriage on the part of a man, my dear, Society requires that he should retrieve his fortunes by marriage. Society requires that he should gain by marriage. Society requires that he should found a handsome establishment by marriage. Society does not see, otherwise, what he has to do with marriage. Bird, be quiet!'

For the parrot on his cage above them, presiding over the conference as if he were a Judge (and indeed he looked rather like one), had wound up the exposition with a shriek *(Chapter 33)*.

'But, young men,' resumed Mrs. Merdle, 'and by young men you know what I mean, my love – I mean people's sons who have the world before them – they must place themselves in a better position towards Society by marriage, or Society really will not have any patience with their making fools of themselves. Dreadfully worldly all this sounds,' said Mrs. Merdle, leaning back in her nest and putting up her glass again, 'does it not?'

'But it is true,' said Mrs. Gowan, with a highly moral air.

'My dear, it is not to be disputed for a moment,' returned Mrs. Merdle; 'because Society has made up its mind on the subject, and there is nothing more to be said. If we were in a more primitive state, if we lived under roofs of leaves, and kept cows and sheep and creatures, instead of banker's accounts (which would be delicious; my dear, I am pastoral to a degree, by nature), well and good. But we don't live under leaves, and keep cows and sheep and creatures. I perfectly exhaust myself sometimes, in pointing out the distinction to Edmund Sparkler' *(Chapter 33)*.

The conference was held at four or five o'clock in the afternoon, when all the region of Harley Street, Cavendish Square, was resonant of carriage-wheels and double-knocks. It had reached this point when Mr. Merdle came home, from his daily occupation of causing the British name to be more and more respected in all parts of the civilised globe, capable of the appreciation of world-wide commercial enterprise and gigantic combinations of skill and capital. For, though nobody knew with the least precision what Mr. Merdle's business was, except that it was to coin money, these were the terms in which everybody defined it on all ceremonious occasions, and which it was the last new polite reading of the parable of the camel and the needle's eye to accept without inquiry.

For a gentleman who had this splendid work cut out for him, Mr. Merdle looked a little common, and rather as if, in the course of his vast transactions, he had accidentally made an interchange of heads with some inferior spirit *(Chapter 33)*.

BOOK THE SECOND: RICHES

It was the vintage time in the valleys on the Swiss side of the Pass of the Great Saint Bernard, and along the banks of the Lake of Geneva. The air there was charged with the scent of gathered grapes. Baskets, troughs, and tubs of grapes, stood in the dim village doorways, stopped the steep and narrow village streets, and had been carrying all day along the roads and lanes. Grapes, split and crushed under foot, lay about everywhere. The child carried in a sling by the laden peasant woman toiling home, was quieted with picked-up grapes; the idiot sunning his big goître under the eaves of the wooden châlet by the way to the waterfall, sat munching grapes, the breath of the cows and goats was redolent of leaves and stalks of grapes; the company in every little cabaret were eating, drinking, talking grapes. A pity that no ripe touch of this generous abundance could be given to the thin, hard, stony wine, which after all was made from the grapes! *(Chapter 1)*.

Mrs. General was the daughter of a clerical dignitary in a cathedral town, where she had led the fashion until she was as near forty-five as a single lady can be. A stiff commissariat officer of sixty, famous as a martinet, had then become enamoured of the gravity with which she drove the proprieties four-in-hand through the cathedral town society, and had solicited to be taken beside her on the box of the cool coach of ceremony to which that team was harnessed. His proposal of marriage being accepted by the lady, the commissary took his seat behind the proprieties with great decorum, and Mrs. General drove until the commissary died. In the course of their united journey, they ran over several people who came in the way of the proprieties; but always in a high style, and with composure *(Chapter 2)*.

Mrs. General was not to be told of anything shocking. Accidents, miseries, and offences, were never to be mentioned before her. Passion was to go to sleep in the presence of Mrs. General, and blood was to change to milk and water. The little that was left in the world, when all these deductions were made, it was Mrs. General's province to varnish. In that formation process of hers, she dipped the smallest of brushes into the largest of pots, and varnished the surface of every object that came under consideration. The more cracked it was, the more Mrs. General varnished it.

There was varnish in Mrs. General's voice, varnish in Mrs. General's touch, an atmosphere of varnish round Mrs. General's figure. Mrs. General's dreams ought to have been varnished – if she had any – lying asleep in the arms of the good Saint Bernard, with the feathery snow falling on his house-top *(Chapter 2)*.

It being that period of the forenoon when the various members of the family had coffee in their own chambers, some couple of hours before assembling at breakfast in a faded hall which had once been sumptuous, but was now the prey of watery vapours and a settled melancholy, Mrs. General was accessible to the valet. That envoy found her on a little square of carpet, so extremely diminutive in reference to the size of her stone and marble floor, that she looked as if she might have had it spread for the trying on of a ready-made pair of shoes; or as if she had come into possession of the enchanted piece of carpet, bought for forty purses by one of the three princes in the Arabian Nights, and had that moment been transported on it, at wish, into a palatial saloon with which it had no connexion *(Chapter 5)*.

'I would not,' said Mrs. General, 'be understood to say, observe, that there is nothing to improve in Fanny. But there is material there – perhaps, indeed, a little too much.'

'Will you be kind enough, madam,' said Mr. Dorrit, 'to be – ha – more explicit? I do not quite understand my elder daughter's having – hum – too much material. What material?'

'Fanny,' returned Mrs. General, 'at present forms too many opinions. Perfect breeding forms none, and is never demonstrative' *(Chapter 5)*.

'I think, father, I required a little time.'
'Papa is a preferable mode of address,' observed Mrs. General. 'Father is rather vulgar, my dear. The word Papa, besides, gives a pretty form to the lips. Papa, potatoes, poultry, prunes, and prism, are all very good words for the lips: especially prunes and prism. You will find it serviceable, in the formation of a demeanour, if you sometimes say to yourself in company – on entering a room, for instance – Papa, potatoes, poultry, prunes and prism, prunes and prism' *(Chapter 5:* Little Dorrit and Mrs. General).

'My goodness Arthur!' cried Flora, rising to give him a cordial reception, 'Doyce and Clennam what a start and a surprise for though not far from the machinery and foundry business and surely might be taken sometimes if at no other time about mid-day when a glass of sherry and a humble sandwich of whatever cold meat in the larder might not come amiss nor taste the worse for being friendly for you know you buy it somewhere and wherever bought a profit must be made or they would never keep the place it stands to reason without a motive still never seen and learnt now not to be expected, for as Mr. F himself said if seeing is believing not seeing is believing too and when you don't see you may fully believe you're not remembered not that I expect you Arthur Doyce and Clennam to remember me why should I for the days are gone but bring another tea-cup here directly and tell her fresh toast and pray sit near the fire' *(Chapter 9:* Flora Finching).

'And now pray tell me something all you know,' said Flora, drawing her chair near to his, 'about the good dear quiet little thing and all the changes of her fortunes carriage people now no doubt and horses without number most romantic, a coat of arms of course and wild beasts on their hind legs showing it as if it was a copy they had done with mouths from ear to ear good gracious, and has she her health which is the first consideration after all for what is wealth without it Mr. F himself so often saying when his twinges came that sixpence a day and find yourself and no gout so much preferable, not that he could have lived on anything like it being the last man or that the precious little thing through far too familiar an expression now had any tendency of that sort much too slight and small but looked so fragile bless her?' *(Chapter 5:* Flora Finching).

"In Italy is she really?' said Flora, 'with the grapes and figs growing everywhere and lava necklaces and bracelets too that land of poetry with burning mountains picturesque beyond belief though if the organ-boys come away from the neighbourhood not to be scorched nobody can wonder being so young and bringing their white mice with them most humane, and is she really in that favoured land with nothing but blue about her and dying gladiators and Belvederas though Mr. F himself did not believe for his objection when in spirits was that the images could not be true there being no medium between expensive quantities of linen badly got up and all in creases and none whatever, which certainly does not seem probable though perhaps in consequence of the extremes of rich and poor which may account for it' *(Chapter 5:* Flora Finching).

'None of your eyes at me,' said Mr. F's Aunt, shivering with hostility. 'Take that.'
'That' was the crust of the piece of toast. Clennam accepted the boon with a look of gratitude, and held it in his hand under the pressure of a little embarrassment, which was not relieved when Mr. F's Aunt, elevating her voice into a cry of considerable power, exclaimed, 'He has a proud stomach, this chap! He's too proud a chap to eat it!' and, coming out of her chair, shook her venerable fist so very close to his nose as to tickle the surface. But for the timely return of Flora, to find him in this difficult situation, further consequences might have ensued. Flora, without the least discomposure or surprise, but congratulating the old lady in an approving manner on being 'very lively to-night,' handed her back to her chair.
'He has a proud stomach, this chap,' said Mr. F's relation, on being reseated. 'Give him a meal of chaff!'
'Oh! I don't think he would like that, aunt,' returned Flora.
'Give him a meal of chaff, I tell you,' said Mr. F's Aunt, glaring round Flora on her enemy. 'It's the only thing for a proud stomach. Let him eat up every morsel. Drat him, give him a meal of chaff!' *(Chapter 5)*.

Mrs. Plornish's shop-parlour had been decorated under her own eye, and presented, on the side towards the shop, a little fiction in which Mrs. Plornish unspeakably rejoiced. This poetical heightening of the parlour consisted in the wall being painted to represent the exterior of a thatched cottage; the artist having introduced (in as effective a manner as he found compatible with their highly disproportioned dimensions) the real door and window. The modest sunflower and hollyhock were depicted as flourishing with great luxuriance on this rustic dwelling, while a quantity of dense smoke issuing from the chimney indicated good cheer within, and also, perhaps, that it had not been lately swept. A faithful dog was represented as flying at the legs of the friendly visitor, from the threshold; and a circular pigeon-house, enveloped in a cloud of pigeons, arose from behind the garden-paling. On the door (when it was shut), appeared the semblance of a brass-plate presenting the inscription, Happy Cottage, T. and M. Plornish; the partnership expressing man and wife. No Poetry and no Art ever charmed the imagination more than the union of the two in this counterfeit cottage charmed Mrs. Plornish. It was nothing to her that Plornish had a habit of leaning against it as he smoked his pipe after work, when his hat blotted out the pigeon-house and all the pigeons, when his back swallowed up the dwelling, when his hands in his pockets uprooted the blooming garden and laid waste the adjacent country. To Mrs. Plornish, it was still a most beautiful cottage, a most wonderful deception; and it made no difference that Mr. Plornish's eye was some inches above the level of the gable bedroom in the thatch. To come out into the shop after it was shut, and hear her father sing a song inside this cottage, was a perfect Pastoral to Mrs. Plornish, the Golden Age revived. And truly if that famous period had been revived, or had ever been at all, it may be doubted whether it would have produced many more heartily admiring daughters than the poor woman *(Chapter 13)*.

Mr. Pancks listened with such interest that regardless of the charms of the Eastern pipe, he put it in the grate among the fire-irons, and occupied his hands during the whole recital in so erecting the loops and hooks of hair all over his head, that he looked, when it came to a conclusion, like a journeyman Hamlet in conversation with his father's spirit *(Chapter 13)*.

'I beg Mr. Dorrit to offer a thousand apologies and indeed they would be far too few for such an intrusion which I know must appear extremely bold in a lady and alone too, but I thought it best upon the whole however difficult and even apparently improper though Mr. F's Aunt would have willingly accompanied me and as a character of great force and spirit would probably have struck one possessed of such a knowledge of life as no doubt with so many changes must have been acquired, for Mr. F himself said frequently that although well educated in the neighbourhood of Blackheath at as high as eighty guineas which is a good deal for parents and the plate kept back too on going away but that is more a meanness than its value that he had learnt more in his first year as a commercial traveller with a large commission on the sale of an article that nobody would hear of much less buy which preceded the wine trade a long time than in the whole six years in that academy conducted by a college Bachelor, though why a Bachelor more clever than a married man I do not see and never did but pray excuse me that is not the point' *(Chapter 17: Flora Finching)*.

As ill at ease as on the first night of his lying down to sleep within those dreary walls, he wore the night out with such thoughts. What time Young John lay wrapt in peaceful slumber, after composing and arranging the following monumental inscription on his pillow:–

STRANGER!
RESPECT THE TOMB OF
JOHN CHIVERY, JUNIOR,
WHO DIED AT AN ADVANCED AGE
NOT NECESSARY TO MENTION.
HE ENCOUNTERED HIS RIVAL IN A DISTRESSED
STATE, AND FELT INCLINED
TO HAVE A ROUND WITH HIM;
BUT, FOR THE SAKE OF THE LOVED ONE,
CONQUERED THOSE FEELINGS OF BITTERNESS; AND
BECAME
MAGNANIMOUS.
(Chapter 27).

'I am, in general,' said Mr. Pancks, 'a dry, uncomfortable, dreary Plodder and Grubber. That's your humble servant. There's his full length portrait, painted by himself and presented to you, warranted a likeness! But what's a man to be, with such a man as this for his Proprietor? What can be expected of him?

Did anybody ever find boiled mutton and caper-sauce growing in a cocoa-nut?' *(Chapter 32)*.

'It is a mighty fine sign-post is The Casby's Head,' said Mr. Pancks, surveying it with anything rather than admiration; 'but the real name of the House is the Sham's Arms. Its motto is, Keep the Grubber always at it. Is any· gentleman present,' said Mr. Pancks, breaking off and looking round, 'acquainted with the English Grammar?'

Bleeding Heart Yard was shy of claiming that acquaintance.

'It's no matter,' said Mr. Pancks. 'I merely wish to remark that the task this Proprietor has set me, has been never to leave off conjugating the Imperative Mood Present Tense of the verb To keep always at it. Keep thou always at it. Let him keep always at it. Keep we or do we keep always at it. Keep ye or do ye or you keep always at it. Let them keep always at it. Here is your benevolent Patriarch of a Casby, and there is his golden rule' *(Chapter 32)*.

'The withered chaplet my dear,' said Flora, with great enjoyment, 'is then perished the column is crumbled and the pyramid is standing upside down upon its what's-his-name call it not giddiness call it not weakness call it not folly I must now retire into privacy and look upon the ashes of departed joys no more but taking the further liberty of paying for the pastry which has formed the humble pretext of our interview will for ever say Adieu!' *(Chapter 34: Flora Finching)*.

THE LAZY TOUR OF TWO IDLE APPRENTICES

The Innkeeper was not idle enough – was not idle at all, which was a great fault in him – but was a fine specimen of a north-country man, or any kind of man. He had a ruddy cheek, a bright eye, a well-knit frame, an immense hand, a cheery, outspeaking voice, and a straight, bright, broad look. He had a drawing-room, too, upstairs, which was worth a visit to the Cumberland Fells. (This was Mr. Francis Goodchild's opinion, in which Mr. Thomas Idle did not concur.)

The ceiling of this drawing-room was so crossed and re-crossed by beams of unequal lengths, radiating from a centre, in a corner, that it looked like a broken starfish. The room was comfortably and solidly furnished with good mahogany and horsehair. It had a snug fireside, and a couple of well-curtained windows, looking out upon the wild country behind the house. What it most developed was, an unexpected taste for little ornaments and nick-nacks, of which it contained a most surprising number. They were not very various, consisting in great part of waxen babies with their limbs more or less mutilated, appealing on one leg to the parental affections from under little cupping-glasses; but, Uncle Tom was there, in crockery, receiving theological instructions from Miss Eva, who grew out of his side like a wen, in an exceedingly rough state of profile propagandism. Engravings of Mr. Hunt's country boy, before and after his pie, were on the wall, divided by a highly-coloured nautical piece, the subject of which had all her colours (and more) flying, and was making great way through a sea of a regular pattern, like a lady's collar. A benevolent, elderly gentleman of the last century, with a powdered head, kept guard, in oil and varnish, over a most perplexing piece of furniture on a table; in appearance between a driving seat and an angular knife-box, but, when opened, a musical instrument of tinkling wires, exactly like David's harp packed for travelling. Everything became a nick-nack in this curious room. The copper tea-kettle, burnished up to the highest point of glory, took his station on a stand of his own at the greatest possible distance from the fireplace, and said: 'By your leave, not a kettle, but a bijou.' The Staffordshire-ware butter-dish with the cover on, got upon a little round occasional table in a window, with a worked top, and announced itself to the two chairs accidentally placed there, as an aid to polite conversation, a graceful trifle in china to be chatted over by callers, as they airily trifled away the visiting moments of a butterfly existence, in that rugged old village on the Cumberland Fells. The very footstool could not keep the floor, but got upon a sofa, and therefrom proclaimed itself, in high relief of white relief of white and liver-coloured wool, a favourite spaniel coiled up for repose. Though, truly, in spite of its bright glass eyes, the spaniel was the least successful assumption in the collection: being perfectly flat, and dismally suggestive of a recent mistake in sitting down on the part of some corpulent member of the family (*Chapter 1*).

By night, in its unconscious state, the Station was not so much as visible. Something in the air, like an enterprising chemist's established in business on one of the boughs of Jack's beanstalk, was all that could be discerned of it under the stars. In a moment it would break out, a constellation of gas. In another moment, twenty rival chemists, on twenty rival beanstalks, came into existence. Then, the Furies would be seen, waving their lurid torches up and down the confused perspectives of embankments and arches – would be heard, too, wailing and shrieking. Then, the Station would be full of palpitating trains, as in the day; with the heightening difference that they were not so clearly seen as in the day, whereas the Station walls, starting forward under the gas, like a hippopotamus's eyes, dazzled the human locomotives with the sauce-bottle, the cheap music, the bedstead, the distorted range of buildings where the patent safes are made, the gentleman in the rain with the registered umbrella, the lady returning from the ball with the registered respirator, and all their other embellishments. And now, the human locomotives, creased as to their countenances and purblind as to their eyes, would swarm forth in a heap, addressing themselves to the mysterious urns and the much-injured women; while the iron locomotives, dripping fire and water, shed their steam about plentifully, making the dull oxen in their cages, with heads depressed, and foam hanging from their mouths as their red looks glanced fearfully at the surrounding terrors, seem as though they had been drinking at half-frozen waters and were hung with icicles. Through the same steam would be caught glimpses of their fellow-travellers, the sheep, getting their white kid faces together, away from the bars, and

stuffing the interstices with trembling wool. Also, down among the wheels, of the man with the sledge-hammer, ringing the axles of the fast night-train; against whom the oxen have a misgiving that he is the man with the pole-axe who is to come by-and-by, and so the nearest of them try to get back, and get a purchase for a thrust at him through the bars. Suddenly, the bell would ring, the steam would stop with one hiss and a yell, the chemists on the beanstalks would be busy, the avenging Furies would bestir themselves, the fast night-train would melt from eye and ear, the other trains going their ways more slowly would be heard faintly rattling in the distance like old-fashioned watches running down, the sauce-bottle and cheap music retired from view, even the bedstead went to bed, and there was no such visible thing as the Station to vex the cool wind in its blowing, or perhaps the autumn lightning, as it found out the iron rails (*Chapter 3*).

'This place fills me with a dreadful sensation,' said Thomas, 'of having something to do. Remove me, Francis.'

'Where would you like to go next?' was the question of the ever-engaging Goodchild.

'I have heard there is a good old Inn at Lancaster, established in a fine old house: an Inn where they give you Bride-cake every day after dinner,' said Thomas Idle. 'Let us eat Bride-cake without the trouble of being married, or of knowing anybody in that ridiculous dilemma.'

Mr. Goodchild, with a lover's sigh, assented (*Chapter 3*).

Mr. Goodchild concedes Lancaster to be a pleasant place. A place dropped in the midst of a charming landscape, a place with a fine ancient fragment of castle, a place of lovely walks, a place possessing staid old houses richly fitted with old Honduras mahogany, which has grown so dark with time that it seems to have got something of a retrospective mirror-quality into itself, and to show the visitor, in the depth of its grain, through all its polish, the hue of the wretched slaves who groaned long ago under old Lancaster merchants. And Mr. Goodchild adds that the stones of Lancaster do sometimes whisper, even yet, of rich men passed away – upon whose great prosperity some of these old doorways frowned sullen in the brightest weather – that their slave-gain turned to curses, as the Arabian Wizard's money turned to leaves, and that no good ever came of it, even unto the third and fourth generations, until it was wasted and gone.

It was a gallant sight to behold, the Sunday procession of the Lancaster elders to Church – all in black, and looking fearfully like a funeral without the Body – under the escort of Three Beadles (*Chapter 3*).

The house was a genuine old house of a very quaint description, teeming with old carvings, and beams, and panels, and having an excellent old staircase, with a gallery or upper staircase, cut off from it by a curious fence-work of old oak, or of the old Honduras Mahogany wood. It was, and is, and will be, for many a long year to come, a remarkably picturesque house; and a certain grave mystery lurking in the depth of the old mahogany panels, as if they were so many deep pools of dark water – such, indeed, as they had been much among when they were trees – gave it a very mysterious character after nightfall.

When Mr. Goodchild and Mr. Idle had first alighted at the door, and stepped into the sombre, handsome old hall, they had been received by half a dozen noiseless old men in black, all dressed exactly alike, who glided up the stairs with the obliging landlord and waiter – but without appearing to get into their way, or to mind whether they did or no – and who had filed off to the right and left on the old staircase, as the guests entered their sitting-room. It was then broad, bright day. But, Mr. Goodchild had said, when their door was shut, 'Who on earth are those old men?' And afterwards both on going out and coming in, he had noticed that there were no old men to be seen (*Chapter 4*).

They had been discussing several idle subjects of speculation, not omitting the strange old men, and were still so occupied, when Mr. Goodchild abruptly changed his attitude to wind up his watch. They were just becoming drowsy enough to be stopped in their talk by any such slight check. Thomas Idle, who was speaking at the moment, paused and said, 'How goes it?'

'One,' said Goodchild.

As if he had ordered One old man, and the order were promptly executed (truly, all orders were so, in that excellent hotel), the door opened, and One old man stood there.

He did not come in, but stood with the door in his hand.

'One of the six, Tom, at last!' said Mr. Goodchild, in a surprised whisper. – 'Sir, your pleasure?'

'Sir, *your* pleasure?' said the One old man.

'I didn't ring.'

'The bell did,' said the One old man.

He said BELL, in a deep, strong way, that would have expressed the church Bell. . . .

'If you are an old inhabitant of this place,' Francis Goodchild resumed:

'Yes.'

'Perhaps you can decide a point my friend and I were in doubt upon, this morning. They hang condemned criminals at the Castle, I believe?'

'*I* believe so,' said the old man.

'Are their faces turned towards that noble prospect?'

'Your face is turned,' replied the old man, 'to the Castle wall. When you are tied up, you see its stones expanding and contracting violently, and a similar expansion and contraction seem to take place in your own head and breast. Then, there is a rush of fire and an earthquake, and the Castle springs into the air, and you tumble down a precipice.'

His cravat appeared to trouble him. He put his hand to his throat, and moved his neck from side to side. He was an old man of a swollen character of face, and his nose was immovably hitched up on one side, as if by a little hook inserted in that nostril. Mr. Goodchild felt exceedingly uncomfortable, and began to think the night was hot, and not cold.

'A strong description, sir,' he observed.

'A strong sensation,' the old man rejoined (*Chapter 4*).

'I must tell it to you,' said the old man, with a ghastly and a stony stare.

'What?' asked Francis Goodchild.

'You know where it took place. Yonder!'

Whether he pointed to the room above, or to the room below, or to any room in that old house, or to a room in some other old house in that old town, Mr. Goodchild was not, nor is, nor ever can be, sure. He was confused by the circumstance that the right forefinger of the One old man seemed to dip itself in one of the threads of fire, light itself, and make a fiery start in the air, as it pointed somewhere. Having pointed somewhere, it went out.

'You know she was a Bride,' said the old man.

'I know they still send up Bride-cake,' Mr. Goodchild faltered. 'This is a very oppressive air.'

'She was a Bride,' said the old man. 'She was a fair, flaxen-haired, large-eyed girl, who had no character, no purpose. A weak, credulous, incapable, helpless nothing. . . .

'She was twenty-one years and twenty-days old, when he brought her home to the gloomy house, his half-witted, frightened, and submissive Bride of three weeks. . . .

'She turned to him upon the threshold, as the rain was dripping from the porch, and said:

' "O sir, it is the Death-watch ticking for me!"

' "Well!" he answered. "And if it were?"

' "O sir!" she returned to him, "look kindly on me, and be merciful to me! I beg your pardon. I will do anything you wish, if you will only forgive me!"

'That had become the poor fool's constant song: "I beg your pardon," and "Forgive me!"

'She was not worth hating; he felt nothing but contempt for her. But, she had long been in the way, and he had long been weary, and the work was near its end, and had to be worked out.

' "You fool," he said. "Go up the stairs!"

'She obeyed very quickly, murmuring, "I will do anything you wish!" When he came into the Bride's Chamber, having been a little retarded by the heavy fastenings of the great door (for they were alone in the house, and he had arranged that the people who attended on them should come and go in the day), he found her withdrawn to the furthest corner, and there standing pressed against the panelling as if she would have shrunk through it: her flaxen hair all wild about her face, and her large eyes staring at him in vague terror.

' "What are you afraid of? Come and sit down by me."

' "I will do anything you wish. I beg your pardon, sir. Forgive me!" Her monotonous tune as usual.

' "Ellen, here is a writing that you must write out to-morrow, in your own hand. You may as well be seen by others, busily engaged upon it. When you have written it all fairly, and corrected all mistakes, call in any two people there may be about the house, and sign your name to it before them. Then, put it in your bosom to keep it safe, and when I sit here again to-morrow night, give it to me."

' "I will do it all, with the greatest care. I will do anything you wish."

' "Don't shake and tremble, then."

' "I will try my utmost not to do it – if you will only forgive me!" . . .

'He saw her follow the directions she had received, in all particulars; and at night, when they were alone again in the same Bride's Chamber, and he drew his chair to the hearth, she timidly approached him from her distant seat, took the paper from her bosom, and gave it into his hand.

'It secured all her possessions to him, in the event of her death. He put her before him, face to face, that he might look at her steadily; and he asked her, in so many plain words, neither fewer nor more, did she know that?

'There were spots of ink upon the bosom of her white dress, and they made her face look whiter and her eyes look larger as she nodded her head. There were spots of ink upon the hand with which she stood before him, nervously plaiting and folding her white skirts.

He took her by the arm, and looked her, yet more closely and steadily, in the face. "Now, die! I have done with you."

'She shrunk, and uttered a low, suppressed cry.

' "I am not going to kill you. I will not endanger my life for yours. Die!"

'He sat before her in the gloomy Bride's Chamber, day after day, night after night, looking the word at her when he did not utter it. As often as her large unmeaning eyes were raised from the hands in which she rocked her head, to the stern figure, sitting with crossed arms and knitted forehead, in the chair, they read in it, "Die!" When she dropped asleep in exhaustion, she was called back to shuddering consciousness, by the whisper, "Die!" When she fell upon her old entreaty to be pardoned, she was answered, "Die!" When she had out-watched and out-suffered the long night, and the rising sun flamed into the sombre room, she heard it hailed with, "Another day and not dead? – Die!" . . .

'It was done, upon a windy morning, before sunrise. He computed the time to be half-past four; but, his forgotten watch had run down, and he could not be sure. She had broken away from him in the night, with loud and sudden cries – the first of that kind to which she had given vent – and he had had to put his hands over her mouth. Since then, she had been quiet in the corner of the panelling where she had sunk down; and he had left her, and had gone back with his folded arms and his knitted forehead to his chair.

'Paler in the pale light, more colourless than ever in the leaden dawn, he saw her coming, trailing herself along the floor towards him – a white wreck of hair, and dress, and wild eyes, pushing itself on by an irresolute and bending hand.

' "O, forgive me! I will do anything. O, sir, pray tell me I may live!"

' "Die!"

' "Are you so resolved? Is there no hope for me?"

' "Die!"

'Her large eyes strained themselves with wonder and fear; wonder and fear changed to reproach;

reproach to blank nothing. It was done. He was not at first so sure it was done, but that the morning sun was hanging jewels in her hair – he saw the diamond, emerald, and ruby, glittering among it in little points, as he stood looking down at her – when he lifted her and laid her on her bed. . . .

'There was no doubt for which of the two murders he should be first tried; but, the real one was chosen, and he was found Guilty, and cast for Death. Bloodthirsty wretches! They would have made him Guilty of anything, so set they were upon having his life.

'His money could do nothing to save him, and he was hanged. *I* am He, and I was hanged at Lancaster Castle with my face to the wall, a hundred years ago!' *(Chapter 4)*.

A TALE OF TWO CITIES

BOOK THE FIRST: RECALLED TO LIFE

It was the best of times, it was the worst of times, it was the age of wisdom, it was the age of foolishness, it was the epoch of belief, it was the epoch of incredulity, it was the season of Light, it was the season of Darkness, it was the spring of hope, it was the winter of despair, we had everything before us, we had nothing before us, we were all going direct to Heaven, we were all going direct the other way – in short, the period was so far like the present period, that some of its noisiest authorities insisted on its being received, for good or for evil, in the superlative degree of comparison only.

There were a king with a large jaw and a queen with a plain face, on the throne of England; there were a king with a large jaw and a queen with a fair face, on the throne of France. In both countries it was clearer than crystal to the lords of the State preserves of loaves and fishes, that things in general were settled for ever.

It was the year of Our Lord one thousand seven hundred and seventy-five. Spiritual revelations were conceded to England at that favoured period, as at this. Mrs. Southcott had recently attained her five-and-twentieth blessed birthday, of whom a prophetic private in the Life Guards had heralded the sublime appearance by announcing that arrangements were made for the swallowing up of London and Westminster. Even the Cock Lane ghost had been laid only a round dozen of years, after rapping out its messages, as the spirits of this very year last past (supernaturally deficient in originality) rapped out theirs. Mere messages in the earthly order of events had lately come to the English Crown and People, from a congress of British subjects in America: which, strange to relate, have proved more important to the human race than any communications yet received through any of the chickens of the Cock Lane brood.

France, less favoured on the whole as to matters spiritual than her sister of the shield and trident, rolled with exceeding smoothness downhill, making paper money and spending it. Under the guidance of her Christian pastors, she entertained herself, besides, with such humane achievements as sentencing a youth to have his hands cut off, his tongue torn out with pincers, and his body burned alive, because he had not kneeled down in the rain to do honour to a dirty procession of monks which passed within his view, at a distance of some fifty or sixty yards. It is likely enough that, rooted in the woods of France and Norway, there were growing trees, when that sufferer was put to death, already marked by the Woodman, Fate, to come down and be sawn into boards, to make a certain movable framework with a sack and a knife in it, terrible in history. It is likely enough that in the rough outhouses of some tillers of the heavy lands adjacent to Paris, there were sheltered from the weather that very day, rude carts, bespattered with rustic mire, snuffed about by pigs, and roosted in by poultry, which the Farmer, Death, had already set apart to be his tumbrils of the Revolution. But that Woodman and that Farmer, though they work unceasingly, work silently, and no one heard them as they went about with muffled tread: the rather, forasmuch as to entertain any suspicion that they were awake, was to be atheistical and traitorous. . . .

All these things, and a thousand like them, came to pass in and close upon the dear old year one thousand seven hundred and seventy-five. Environed by them, while the Woodman and the Farmer worked unheeded, those two of the large jaws, and those other two of the plain and the fair faces, trod with stir enough, and carried their divine rights with a high hand. Thus did the year one thousand seven hundred and seventy-five conduct their Greatnesses, and myriads of small creatures – the creatures of this chronicle among the rest – along the roads that lay before them *(Chapter 1)*.

A wonderful fact to reflect upon, that every human creature is constituted to be that profound secret and mystery to every other. A solemn consideration, when I enter a great city by night, that every one of those darkly clustered houses encloses its own secret; that every room in every one of them encloses its own secret; that every beating heart in the hundreds of thousands of breasts there, is, in some of its imaginings, a secret to the heart nearest it! Something of the awfulness, even of Death itself, is referable to this. No more can I turn the leaves of this dear book that I loved, and vainly hope in time to read it all. No more can I look into the depths of this unfathomable water, wherein, as momentary lights glanced into it, I have had glimpses of buried treasure and other things submerged. It was appointed that the book should shut with a spring, for ever and for ever, when I had read but a page. It was appointed that the water should be locked in an eternal frost, when the light was playing on its surface, and I stood in ignorance on the shore. My friend is dead, my neighbour is dead, my love, the darling of my soul, is dead; it is the inexorable consolidation and perpetuation of the secret that was always in that individuality, and which I shall carry in mine to my life's end. In any of the burial places of this city through which I pass, is there a sleeper more inscrutable than its busy inhabitants are, in their innermost personality, to me, or than I am to them? *(Chapter 3)*.

Tellson's Bank had a run upon it in the mail. As the bank passenger – with an arm drawn through the

leathern strap, which did what lay in it to keep him from pounding against the next passenger, and driving him into his corner, whenever the coach got a special jolt – nodded in his place, with half-shut eyes, the little coach-windows, and the coach-lamp dimly gleaming through them, and the bulky bundle of opposite passenger, became the bank, and did a great stroke of business. The rattle of the harness was the chink of money, and more drafts were honoured in five minutes than even Tellson's, with all its foreign and home connection, ever paid in thrice the time. Then the strongrooms underground, at Tellson's, with such of their valuable stores and secrets as were known to the passenger (and it was not a little that he knew about them), opened before him, and he went in among them with the great keys and the feebly-burning candle, and found them safe, and strong, and sound, and still, just as he had last seen them.

But, though the bank was almost always with him, and though the coach (in a confused way, like the presence of pain under an opiate) was always with him, there was another current of impression that never ceased to run, all through the night. He was on his way to dig some one out of a grave.

Now, which of the multitude of faces that showed themselves before him was the true face of the buried person, the shadows of the night did not indicate; but they were all the faces of a man of five-and-forty years, and they differed principally in the passions they expressed, and in the ghastliness of their worn and wasted state. Pride, contempt, defiance, stubbornness, submission, lamentation, succeeded one another; so did varieties of sunken cheek, cadaverous colour, emaciated hands and figures. But the face was in the main one face, and every head was prematurely white. A hundred times the dozing passenger inquired of this spectre:

'Buried how long?'

The answer was always the same: 'Almost eighteen years.'

'You had abandoned all hope of being dug out?'

'Long ago.'

'You know that you are recalled to life?'

'They tell me so.'

'I hope you care to live?'

'I can't say.'

'Shall I show her to you? Will you come and see her?'

The answers to this question were various and contradictory. Sometimes the broken reply was, 'Wait! It would kill me if I saw her too soon.' Sometimes it was given in a tender rain of tears, and then it was, 'Take me to her.' Sometimes it was staring and bewildered, and then it was, 'I don't know her, I don't understand' *(Chapter 3)*.

The little narrow, crooked town of Dover hid itself away from the beach, and ran its head into the chalk cliffs, like a marine ostrich. The beach was a desert of heaps of sea and stones tumbling wildly about, and the sea did what it liked, and what it liked was destruction. It thundered at the town, and thundered at the cliffs, and brought the coast down, madly. The air among the houses was of so strong a piscatory flavour that one might have supposed sick fish went up to be dipped in it, as sick people went down to be dipped in the sea. A little fishing was done in the port, and a quantity of strolling about by night, and looking seaward: particularly at those times when the tide made, and was near flood. Small tradesmen, who did no business whatever, sometimes unaccountably realised large fortunes, and it was remarkable that nobody in the neighbourhood could endure a lamplighter *(Chapter 4)*.

A narrow winding street [in Paris], full of offence and stench, with other narrow winding streets diverging, all peopled by rags and nightcaps, and all smelling of rags and nightcaps, and all visible things with a brooding look upon them that looked ill. In the hunted air of the people there was yet some wild-beast thought of the possibility of turning at bay. Depressed and slinking though they were, eyes of fire were not wanting among them; nor compressed lips, white with what they suppressed; nor foreheads knitted into the likeness of the gallows-rope they mused about enduring, or inflicting. The trade signs (and they were almost as many as the shops) were, all, grim illustrations of Want. The butcher and the porkman painted up, only the leanest scrags of meat; the baker, the coarsest of meagre loaves. The people rudely pictured as drinking in the wine-shops, croaked over their scanty measures of thin wine and beer, and were gloweringly confidential together. Nothing was represented in a flourishing condition, save tools and weapons; but, the cutler's knives and axes were sharp and bright, the smith's hammers were heavy, and the gunmaker's stock was murderous. The crippling stones of the pavement, with their many little reservoirs of mud and water, had no footways, but broke off abruptly at the doors. The kennel, to make amends, ran down the middle of the street – when it ran at all: which was only after heavy rains, and then it ran, by many eccentric fits, into the houses. Across the streets, at wide intervals, one clumsy lamp was slung by a rope and pulley; at night, when the lamplighter had let these down, and lighted, and hoisted them again, a feeble grove of dim wicks swung in a sickly manner overhead, as if they were at sea. Indeed they were at sea, and the ship and crew were in peril of tempest.

For, the time was to come, when the gaunt scarecrows of that region should have watched the lamplighter, in their idleness and hunger, so long, as to conceive the idea of improving on his method, and hauling up men by those ropes and pulleys, to flare upon the darkness of their condition. But, the time was not come yet; and every wind that blew over France shook the rags of the scarecrows in vain, for the birds, fine of song and feather, took no warning *(Chapter 5)*.

'Hark!' he exclaimed. 'Whose voice was that?'

His hands released her as he uttered this cry, and went up to his white hair, which they tore in a frenzy. It died out, as everything but his shoemaking did die out of him, and he refolded his little packet and tried to secure it in his breast: but he still looked at her, and gloomily shook his head.

'No, no, no; you are too young, too blooming. It can't be. See what the prisoner is. These are not the hands she knew, this is not the face she knew, this is not a voice she ever heard. No, no. She was – and He

was – before the slow years of the North Tower – ages ago. What is your name, my gentle angel?'

Hailing his softened tone and manner, his daughter fell upon her knees before him, with her appealing hands upon his breast.

'O, sir, at another time you shall know my name, and who my mother was, and who my father, and how I never knew their hard, hard history. But I cannot tell you at this time, and I cannot tell you here. All that I may tell you, here and now, is, that I pray to you to touch me and to bless me. Kiss me, kiss me! O my dear, my dear!'

His cold white head mingled with her radiant hair, which warmed and lighted it as though it were the light of Freedom shining on him.

'If you hear in my voice – I don't know that it is so, but I hope it is – if you hear in my voice any resemblance to a voice that once was sweet music in your ears, weep for it, weep for it! If you touch, in touching my hair, anything that recalls a beloved head that lay on your breast when you were young and free, weep for it, weep for it! If, when I hint to you of a Home that is before us, where I will be true to you with all my duty and with all my faithful service, I bring back the remembrance of a Home long desolate, while your poor heart pined away, weep for it, weep for it!' *(Chapter 6:* Lucie Manette and her father).

Under the over-swinging lamps – swinging ever brighter in the better streets, and ever dimmer in the worse – and by the lighted shops, gay crowds, illuminated coffee-houses, and theatre-doors, to one of the city gates. Soldiers with lanterns, at the guard-house there. 'Your papers, travellers!' 'See here then, Monsieur the Officer,' said Defarge, getting down, and taking him gravely apart, 'these are the papers of monsieur inside, with the white head. They were consigned to me, with him, at the –' He dropped his voice, there was a flutter among the military lanterns, and one of them being handed into the coach by an arm in uniform, the eyes connected with the arm looked, not an every day or an every night look, at monsieur with the white head. 'It is well. Forward!' from the uniform. 'Adieu!' from Defarge. And so, under a short grove of feebler and feebler over-swinging lamps, out under the great grove of stars.

Beneath that arch of unmoved and eternal lights; some, so remote from this little earth that the learned tell us it is doubtful whether their rays have even yet discovered it, as a point in space where anything is suffered or done: the shadows of the night were broad and black. All through the cold and restless interval, until dawn, they once more whispered in the ears of Mr. Jarvis Lorry – sitting opposite the buried man who had been dug out, and wondering what subtle powers were for ever lost to him, and what were capable of restoration – the old inquiry:

'I hope you care to be recalled to life?'

And the old answer:

'I can't say' *(Chapter 6)*.

BOOK THE SECOND: THE GOLDEN THREAD

Mr. Cruncher reposed under a patchwork counterpane, like a Harlequin at home. At first, he slept heavily, but, by degrees, began to roll and surge in bed, until he rose above the surface, with his spiky hair looking as if it must tear the sheets to ribbons. At which juncture, he exclaimed, in a voice of dire exasperation:

'Bust me, if she ain't at it agin!'

A woman of orderly and industrious appearance rose from her knees in a corner, with sufficient haste and trepidation to show that she was the person referred to.

'What!' said Mr. Cruncher, looking out of bed for a boot. 'You're at it agin, are you?'

After hailing the morn with this second salutation, he threw a boot at the woman as a third. It was a very muddy boot, and may introduce the odd circumstance connected with Mr. Cruncher's domestic economy, that, whereas he often came home after banking hours with clean boots, he often got up next morning to find the same boots covered with clay.

'What,' said Mr. Cruncher, varying his apostrophe after missing his mark – 'what are you up to, Aggerawayter?'

'I was only saying my prayers.'

'Saying your prayers! You're a nice woman! What do you mean by flopping yourself down and praying agin me?'

'I was not praying against you; I was praying for you.'

'You weren't. And if you were, I won't be took the liberty with. Here! your mother's a nice woman, young Jerry, going a praying agin your father's prosperity. You've got a dutiful mother, you have, my son. You've got a religious mother, you have, my boy: going and flopping herself down, and praying that the bread-and-butter may be snatched out of the mouth of her only child' *(Chapter 1)*.

'And what do you suppose, you conceited female,' said Mr. Cruncher, with unconscious inconsistency, 'that the worth of *your* prayers may be? Name the price that you put *your* prayers at!'

'They only come from the heart, Jerry. They are worth no more than that.'

'Worth no more than that,' repeated Mr. Cruncher. 'They ain't worth much, then. Whether or no, I won't be prayed agin, I tell you. I can't afford it. I'm not a going to be made unlucky by *your* sneaking. If you must go flopping yourself down, flop in favour of your husband and child, and not in opposition to 'em. If I had had any but a unnat'ral wife, and this poor boy had had any but a unnat'ral mother, I might have made some money last week instead of being counter-prayed and countermined and religiously circum-wented into the worst of luck. B-u-u-ust me!' said Mr. Cruncher, who all this time had been putting on his clothes, 'if I ain't, what with piety and one blowed thing and another, been choused this last week into as bad luck as ever a poor devil of a honest tradesman met with! Young Jerry, dress yourself, my boy, and while I clean my boots keep a eye upon your mother now and then, and if you see any signs of more flopping, give me a call. For, I tell you,' here he addressed his wife once more, 'I won't be gone agin, in this manner. I am as rickety as a hackney-coach, I'm

as sleepy as laudanum, my lines is strained to that degree that I shouldn't know, if it wasn't for the pain in 'em, which was me and which somebody else, yet I'm none the better for it in pocket; and it's my suspicion that you've been at it from morning to night to prevent me from being the better for it in pocket, and I won't put up with it, Aggerawayter, and what do you say now!' *(Chapter 1)*.

'Well then! Pledge me to the pretty witness,' said Stryver, holding up his glass. 'Are you turned in a pleasant direction?'

Apparently not, for he became gloomy again.

'Pretty witness,' he muttered, looking down into his glass. 'I have had enough of witnesses to-day and to-night; who's your pretty witness?'

'The picturesque doctor's daughter, Miss Manette.'

'*She* pretty?'

'Is she not?'

'No.'

'Why, man alive, she was the admiration of the whole Court!'

'Rot the admiration of the whole Court! Who made the Old Bailey a judge of beauty? She was a golden-haired doll!'

'Do you know, Sydney,' said Mr. Stryver, looking at him with sharp eyes, and slowly drawing a hand across his florid face: 'do you know, I rather thought, at the time, that you sympathised with the golden-haired doll, and were quick to see what happened to the golden-haired doll?'

'Quick to see what happened! If a girl, doll or no doll, swoons within a yard or two of a man's nose, he can see it without a perspective-glass. I pledge you, but I deny the beauty. And now I'll have no more drink; I'll get to bed.'

When his host followed him out on the staircase with a candle, to light him down the stairs, the day was coldly looking in through its grimy windows. When he got out of the house, the air was cold and sad, the dull sky overcast, the river dark and dim, the whole scene like a lifeless desert. And wreaths of dust were spinning round and round before the morning blast, as if the desert-sand had risen far away, and the first spray of it in its advance had begun to overwhelm the city.

Waste forces within him, and a desert all around, this man stood still on his way across a silent terrace, and saw for a moment, lying in the wilderness before him, a mirage of honourable ambition, self-denial, and perseverance. In the fair city of this vision, there were airy galleries from which the loves and graces looked upon him, gardens in which the fruits of life hung ripening, waters of Hope that sparkled in his sight. A moment, and it was gone. Climbing to a high chamber in a well of houses, he threw himself down in his clothes on a neglected bed, and its pillow was wet with wasted tears.

Sadly, sadly, the sun rose; it rose upon no sadder sight than the man of good abilities and good emotions, incapable of their directed exercise, incapable of his own help and his own happiness, sensible of the blight on him, and resigning himself to let it eat him away *(Chapter 5:* Stryver and Sydney Carton).

Monseigneur, one of the great lords in power at the Court, held his fortnightly reception in his grand hotel in Paris. Monseigneur was in his inner room, his sanctuary of sanctuaries, the Holiest of Holiests to the crowd of worshippers in the suite of rooms without. Monseigneur was about to take his chocolate. Monseigneur could swallow a great many things with ease, and was by some few sullen minds supposed to be rather rapidly swallowing France; but, his morning's chocolate could not so much as get into the throat of Monseigneur, without the aid of four strong men besides the Cook.

Yes. It took four men, all four a-blaze with gorgeous decoration, and the Chief of them unable to exist with fewer than two gold watches in his pocket, emulative of the noble and chaste fashion set by Monseigneur, to conduct the happy chocolate to Monseigneur's lips. One lacquey carried the chocolate pot into the sacred presence; a second, milled and frothed the chocolate with the little instrument he bore for that function; a third, presented the favoured napkin; a fourth (he of the two gold watches), poured the chocolate out. It was impossible for Monseigneur to dispense with one of these attendants on the chocolate and hold his high place under the admiring Heavens. Deep would have been the blot upon his escutcheon if his chocolate had been ignobly waited on by only three men; he must have died of two *(Chapter 7)*.

Dress was the one unfailing talisman and charm used for keeping all things in their places. Everybody was dressed for a Fancy Ball that was never to leave off. From the Palace of the Tuileries, through Monseigneur and the whole Court, through the Chambers, the Tribunals of Justice, and all society (except the scarecrows), the Fancy Ball descended to the Common Executioner: who, in pursuance of the charm, was required to officiate 'frizzled, powdered, in a gold-laced coat, pumps, and white silk stockings.' At the gallows and the wheel – the axe was a rarity – Monsieur Paris, as it was the episcopal mode among his brother Professors of the provinces, Monsieur Orleans, and the rest, to call him, presided in this dainty dress. And who among the company at Monseigneur's reception in that seventeen hundred and eightieth year of our Lord, could possibly doubt, that a system rooted in frizzled hangman, powdered, gold-laced, pumped, and white-silk stockinged, would see the very stars out! *(Chapter 7)*.

With a wild rattle and clatter, and an inhuman abandonment of consideration not easy to be understood in these days, the carriage dashed through streets and swept round corners, with women screaming before it, and men clutching each other and clutching children out of its way. At last, swooping at a street corner by a fountain, one of its wheels came to a sickening little jolt, and there was a loud cry from a number of voices, and the horses reared and plunged.

But for the latter inconvenience, the carriage probably would not have stopped; carriages were often known to drive on, and leave their wounded behind, and why not? But the frightened valet had got down in a hurry, and there were twenty hands at the horses' bridles.

'What has gone wrong?' said Monsieur, calmly looking out.

A tall man in a nightcap had caught up a bundle from among the feet of the horses, and had laid it on the basement of the fountain, and was down in the mud and wet, howling over it like a wild animal.

'Pardon, Monsieur the Marquis!' said a ragged and submissive man, 'it is a child.'

'Why does he make that abominable noise? Is it his child?'

'Excuse me, Monsieur the Marquis – it is a pity – yes.'

The fountain was a little removed; for the street opened, where it was, into a space some ten or twelve yards square. As the tall man suddenly got up from the ground, and came running at the carriage, Monsieur the Marquis clapped his hand for an instant on his sword-hilt.

'Killed!' shrieked the man, in wild desperation, extending both arms at their length above his head, and staring at him. 'Dead!'

The people closed round, and looked at Monsieur the Marquis. There was nothing revealed by the many eyes that looked at him but watchfulness and eagerness; there was no visible menacing or anger. Neither did the people say anything; after the first cry, they had been silent, and they remained so. The voice of the submissive man who had spoken, was flat and tame in its extreme submission. Monsieur the Marquis ran his eyes over them all, as if they had been mere rats come out of their holes.

He took out his purse.

'It is extraordinary to me,' said he, 'that you people cannot take care of yourselves and your children. One or other of you is for ever in the way. How do I know what injury you have done my horses? See! Give him that' *(Chapter 7)*.

All the people of the village were at the fountain, standing about in their depressed manner, and whispering low, but showing no other emotions than grim curiosity and surprise. The led cows, hastily brought in and tethered to anything that would hold them, were looking stupidly on, or lying down chewing the cud of nothing particularly repaying their trouble, which they had picked up in their interrupted saunter. Some of the people of the château, and some of those of the posting-house, and all the taxing authorities, were armed more or less, and were crowded on the other side of the little street in a purposeless way, that was highly fraught with nothing. Already, the mender of roads had penetrated into the midst of a group of fifty particular friends, and was smiting himself in the breast with his blue cap. What did all this portend, and what portended the swift hoisting-up of Monsieur Gabelle behind a servant on horseback, and the conveying away of the said Gabelle (double-laden though the horse was), at a gallop, like a new version of the German ballad of Leonora?

It portended that there was one stone face too many, up at the château.

The Gorgon had surveyed the building again in the night, and had added the one stone face wanting; the stone face for which it had waited through about two hundred years.

It lay back on the pillow of Monsieur the Marquis. It was like a fine mask, suddenly startled, made angry, and petrified. Driven home into the heart of the stone figure attached to it, was a knife. Round its hilt was a frill of paper, on which was scrawled:

'*Drive him fast to his tomb. This from* JACQUES.' *(Chapter 9).*

'Pray forgive me, Miss Manette. I break down before the knowledge of what I want to say to you. Will you hear me?'

'If it will do you any good, Mr. Carton, if it would make you happier, it would make me very glad!'

'God bless you for your sweet compassion!'

He unshaded his face after a little while, and spoke steadily.

'Don't be afraid to hear me. Don't shrink from anything I say. I am like one who died young. All my life might have been.'

'No, Mr. Carton. I am sure that the best part of it might still be; I am sure that you might be much, much worthier of yourself.'

'Say of you, Miss Manette, and although I know better – although in the mystery of my own wretched heart I know better – I shall never forget it!'

She was pale and trembling. He came to her relief with a fixed despair of himself which made the interview unlike any other that could have been holden.

'If it had been possible, Miss Manette, that you could have returned the love of the man you see before you – self-flung away, wasted, drunken, poor creature of misuse as you know him to be – he would have been conscious this day and this hour, in spite of his happiness, that he would bring you to misery, bring you to sorrow and repentance, blight you, disgrace you, pull you down with him. I know very well that you can have no tenderness for me; I ask for none; I am even thankful that it cannot be. . . .

'If you will hear me through a very little more, all you can ever do for me is done. I wish you to know that you have been the last dream of my soul. In my degradation I have not been so degraded but that the sight of you with your father, and of this home made such a home by you, has stirred old shadows that I thought had died out of me. Since I knew you, I have been troubled by a remorse that I thought would never reproach me again, and have heard whispers from old voices impelling me upward, that I thought were silent for ever. I have had unformed ideas of striving afresh, beginning anew, shaking off sloth and sensuality, and fighting out the abandoned fight. A dream, all a dream, that ends in nothing, and leaves the sleeper where he lay down, but I wish you to know that you inspired it' *(Chapter 13).*

'You and your yes, Jerry,' said Mr. Cruncher, taking a bite out of his bread-and-butter, and seeming to help it down with a large invisible oyster out of his saucer. 'Ah! I think so. I believe you.'

'You are going out to-night?' asked his decent wife, when he took another bite.

'Yes, I am.'

'May I go with you, father?' asked his son, briskly.

'No, you mayn't. I'm a going – as your mother knows – a fishing. That's where I'm going to. Going a fishing.'

'Your fishing-rod gets rayther rusty; don't it, father?'

'Never you mind.'

'Shall you bring any fish home, father?'

'If I don't, you'll have short commons, to-morrow,' returned that gentleman, shaking his head; 'that's questions enough for you; I ain't a-going out, till you've been long abed.' . . .

Thus the evening wore away with the Cruncher family, until Young Jerry was ordered to bed, and his mother, laid under similar injunctions, obeyed them. Mr. Cruncher beguiled the earlier watches of the night with solitary pipes, and did not start upon his excursion until nearly one o'clock. Towards that small and ghostly hour, he rose up from his chair, took a key out of his pocket, opened a locked cupboard, and brought forth a sack, a crowbar of convenient size, a rope and chain, and other fishing tackle of that nature. Disposing these articles about him in skilful manner, he bestowed a parting defiance on Mrs. Cruncher, extinguished the light, and went out.

Young Jerry, who had only made a feint of undressing when he went to bed, was not long after his father. Under cover of the darkness he followed out of the room, followed down the stairs, followed down the court, followed out into the streets. He was in no uneasiness concerning his getting into the house again, for it was full of lodgers, and the door stood ajar all night.

Impelled by a laudable ambition to study the art and mystery of his father's honest calling, Young Jerry, keeping as close to house fronts, walls, and doorways, as his eyes were close to one another, held his honoured parent in view. The honoured parent steering Northward, had not gone far, when he was joined by another disciple of Izaak Walton, and the two trudged on together.

Within half an hour from the first starting, they were beyond the winking lamps, and the more than winking watchmen, and were out upon a lonely road. Another fisherman was picked up here – and that so silently, that if Young Jerry had been superstitious, he might have supposed the second follower of the gentle craft to have, all of a sudden, split himself into two.

The three went on, and Young Jerry went on, until the three stopped under a bank overhanging the road. Upon the top of the bank was a low brick wall, surmounted by an iron railing. In the shadow of bank and wall the three turned out of the road, and up a blind lane, of which the wall – there, risen to some eight or ten feet high – formed one side. Crouching down in a corner, peeping up the lane, the next object that Young Jerry saw, was the form of his honoured parent, pretty well defined against a watery and clouded moon, nimbly scaling an iron gate. He was soon over, and then the second fisherman got over, and then the third. They all dropped softly on the ground within the gate, and lay there a little – listening perhaps. Then, they moved away on their hands and knees.

It was now young Jerry's turn to approach the gate:

which he did, holding his breath. Crouching down again in a corner there, and looking in, he made out the three fishermen creeping through some rank grass, and all the gravestones in the churchyard – it was a large churchyard that they were in – looking on like ghosts in white, while the church tower itself looked on like the ghost of a monstrous giant. They did not creep far, before they stopped and stood upright. And then they began to fish.

They fished with a spade, at first. Presently the honoured parent appeared to be adjusting some instrument like a great corkscrew. Whatever tools they worked with, they worked hard, until the awful striking of the church clock so terrified Young Jerry, that he made off, with his hair as stiff as his father's.

But, his long-cherished desire to know more about these matters, not only stopped him in his running away, but lured him back again. They were still fishing perseveringly, when he peeped in at the gate for the second time; but now they seemed to have got a bite. There was a screwing and complaining sound down below, and their bent figures were strained, as if by a weight. By slow degrees the weight broke away the earth upon it, and came to the surface. Young Jerry very well knew what it would be; but, when he saw it, and saw his honoured parent about to wrench it open, he was so frightened, being new to the sight, that he made off again, and never stopped until he had run a mile or more *(Chapter 14)*.

From his oppressed slumber, Young Jerry in his closet was awakened after daybreak and before sunrise, by the presence of his father in the family room. Something had gone wrong with him; at least, so Young Jerry inferred, from the circumstance of his holding Mrs. Cruncher by the ears, and knocking the back of her head against the head-board of the bed *(Chapter 14)*.

'Father,' said Young Jerry, as they walked along: taking care to keep at arm's length and to have the stool well between them: 'what's a Resurrection-Man?'

Mr. Cruncher came to a stop on the pavement before he answered, 'How should I know?'

'I thought you knowed everything, father,' said the artless boy.

'Hem! Well,' returned Mr. Cruncher, going on again, and lifting off his hat to give his spikes free play, 'he's a tradesman.'

'What's his goods, father?' asked the brisk Young Jerry.

'His goods,' said Mr. Cruncher, after turning it over in his mind, 'is a branch of Scientific goods.'

'Persons' bodies, ain't it, father?' asked the lively boy.

'I believe it is something of that sort,' said Mr. Cruncher.

'Oh, father, I should so like to be a Resurrection-Man when I'm quite growed up?'

Mr. Cruncher was soothed, but shook his head in a dubious and moral way. 'It depends upon how you dewelop your talents. Be careful to dewelop your talents, and never to say no more than you can help to nobody, and there's no telling at the present time what you may not come to be fit for.' As Young Jerry, thus

encouraged, went on a few yards in advance, to plant the stool in the shadow of the Bar, Mr. Cruncher added to himself: 'Jerry, you honest tradesman, there's hopes wot that boy will yet be a blessing to you, and a recompense to you for his mother!' *(Chapter 14)*.

'How say you, Jacques?' demanded Number One. 'To be registered?'

'To be registered, as doomed to destruction,' returned Defarge.

'Magnificent!' croaked the man with the craving.

'The château and all the race?' inquired the first.

'The château and all the race,' returned Defarge. 'Extermination.'

The hungry man repeated, in a rapturous croak, 'Magnificent!' and began gnawing another finger.

'Are you sure,' asked Jacques Two, of Defarge, 'that no embarrassment can arise from our manner of keeping the register? Without doubt it is safe, for no one beyond ourselves can decipher it; but shall we always be able to decipher it – or, I ought to say, will she?'

'Jacques,' returned Defarge, drawing himself up, 'if madame my wife undertook to keep the register in her memory alone, she would not lose a word of it – not a syllable of it. Knitted, in her own stitches and her own symbols, it will always be as plain to her as the sun. Confide in Madame Defarge, it would be easier ' weakest poltroon that lives, to erase himself from existence, than to erase one letter of his name or crimes from the knitted register of Madame Defarge' *(Chapter 15)*.

Madame Defarge looked superciliously at the client. . . .

'As to you,' said she, 'You would shout and shed tears for anything, if it made a show and a noise. Say! Would you not?'

'Truly, madame, I think so. For the moment.'

'If you were shown a great heap of dolls, and were set upon them to pluck them to pieces and despoil them for your own advantage, you would pick out the richest and gayest. Say! Would you not?'

'Truly yes, madame.'

'Yes. And if you were shown a flock of birds, unable to fly, and were set upon them to strip them of their feathers for your own advantage, you would set upon the birds of the finest feathers: would you not?'

'It is true, madame.'

'You have seen both dolls and birds to-day,' said Madame Defarge, with a wave of her hand towards the place where they had last been apparent; 'now, go home!' *(Chapter 15)*.

In the evening, at which season of all others Saint Antoine turned himself inside out, and sat on doorsteps and window-ledges, and came to the corners of vile streets and courts, for a breath of air, Madame Defarge with her work in her hand was accustomed to pass from place to place and from group to group: a Missionary – there were many like her – such as the world will do well never to breed again. All the women knitted. They knitted worthless things; but, the mechanical work was a mechanical substitute for eating and drinking; the hands moved for the jaws and the digestive apparatus: if the bony fingers had been still, the stomachs would have been more famine-pinched.

But, as the fingers went, the eyes went, and the thoughts. And as Madame Defarge moved on from group to group, all three went quicker and fiercer among every little knot of women that she had spoken with, and left behind.

Her husband smoked at his door, looking after her with admiration. 'A great woman,' said he, 'a strong woman, a grand woman, a frightfully grand woman!'

Darkness closed around, and then came the ringing of church bells and the distant beating of the military drums in the Palace Court-Yard, as the women sat knitting, knitting. Darkness encompassed them. Another darkness was closing in as surely, when the church bells, then ringing pleasantly in many an airy steeple over France, should be melted into thundering cannon; when the military drums should be beating to drown a wretched voice, that night all-potent as the voice of Power and Plenty, Freedom and Life. So much was closing in about the women who sat knitting, knitting, that they their very selves were closing in around a structure yet unbuilt, where they were to sit knitting, knitting, counting dropping heads *(Chapter 16)*.

Headlong, mad, and dangerous footsteps to force their way into anybody's life, footsteps not easily made clean again if once stained red, the footsteps raging in Saint Antoine afar off, as the little circle sat in the dark London window.

Saint Antoine had been, that morning, a vast dusky mass of scarecrows heaving to and fro, with frequent gleams of light above the billowy heads, where steel blades and bayonets shone in the sun. A tremendous roar arose from the throat of Saint Antoine, and a forest of naked arms struggled in the air like shrivelled branches of trees in a winter wind: all the fingers convulsively clutching at every weapon or semblance of a weapon that was thrown up from the depths below, no matter how far off.

Who gave them out, whence they last came, where they began, through what agency they crookedly quivered and jerked, scores at a time, over the heads of the crowd, like a kind of lightning, no eye in the throng could have told; but, muskets were being distributed – so were cartridges, powder, and ball, bars of iron and wood, knives, axes, pikes, every weapon that distracted ingenuity could discover or devise. People who could lay hold of nothing else, set themselves with bleeding hands to force stones and bricks out of their places in walls. Every pulse and heart in Saint Antoine was on high-fever strain and at high-fever heat. Every living creature there held life as of no account, and was demented with a passionate readiness to sacrifice it.

As a whirlpool of boiling waters has a centre point, so, all this raging circled round Defarge's wine-shop, and every human drop in the caldron had a tendency to be sucked towards the vortex where Defarge himself, already begrimed with gunpowder and sweat, issued orders, issued arms, thrust this man back, dragged this man forward, disarmed one to arm another, laboured and strove in the thickest of the uproar.

'Keep near to me, Jacques Three,' cried Defarge; 'and do you, Jacques One and Two, separate and put yourselves at the head of as many of these patriots as you can. Where is my wife?'

'Eh, well! Here you see me!' said madame, composed as ever, but not knitting to-day. Madame's resolute right hand was occupied with an axe, in place of the usual softer implements, and in her girdle were a pistol and a cruel knife.

'Where do you go, my wife?'

'I go,' said madame, 'with you at present. You shall see me at the head of women, by and by.'

'Come, then!' cried Defarge, in a resounding voice. 'Patriots and friends, we are ready! The Bastille!' *(Chapter 21).*

'Say then, my husband. What is it?'

'News from the other world!'

'How then?' cried madame, contemptuously. 'The other world?'

'Does everybody here recall old Foulon, who told the famished people that they might eat grass, and who died, and went to Hell?'

'Everybody!' from all throats.

'The news is of him. He is among us!'

'Among us!' from the universal throat again. 'And dead?'

'Not dead! He feared us so much – and with reason – that he caused himself to be represented as dead, and had a grand mock-funeral. But they have found him alive, hiding in the country, and have brought him in. I have seen him but now, on his way to the Hotel de Ville, a prisoner. I have said he had reason to fear us. Say all! *Had* he reason?.

Wretched old sinner of more than threescore years and ten, if he had never known it yet, he would have known it in his heart of hearts if he could have heard the answering cry.

A moment of profound silence followed. Defarge and his wife looked steadfastly at one another. The Vengeance stooped, and the jar of a drum was heard as she moved it at her feet behind the counter.

'Patriots!' said Defarge, in a determined voice, 'are we ready?'

Instantly Madame Defarge's knife was in her girdle; the drum was beating in the streets, as if it and a drummer had flown together by magic; and The Vengeance, uttering terrific shrieks, and flinging her arms about her head like all the forty Furies at once, was tearing from house to house, rousing the women.

The men were terrible, in the bloody-minded anger with which they looked from windows, caught up what arms they had, and came pouring down into the streets; but, the women were a sight to chill the boldest. From such household occupations as their bare poverty yielded, from their children, from their aged and their sick crouching on the bare ground famished and naked, they ran out with streaming hair, urging one another, and themselves, to madness with the wildest cries and actions. Villain Foulon taken, my sister! Old Foulon taken, my mother! Miscreant Foulon taken, my daughter! Then, a score of others ran into the midst of these, beating their breasts, tearing their hair, and screaming, Foulon alive! Foulon who told my old father that he might eat grass, when I had no bread to give Him! Foulon who told my baby it might suck grass, when these breasts were dry with want! O mother of God, this Foulon! O Heaven, our suffering! Hear me, my dead baby and my withered father: I swear on my knees, on these stones, to avenge you on Foulon! Husbands, and brothers, and young men, Give us the blood of Foulon, Give us the head of Foulon, Give us the heart of Foulon, Give us the body and soul of Foulon, Rend Foulon to pieces, and dig him into the ground, that grass may grow from him! With these cries, numbers of the women, lashed into blind frenzy, whirled about, striking and tearing at their own friends until they dropped into a passionate swoon, and were only saved by the men belonging to them from being trampled under foot *(Chapter 22)*.

BOOK THE THIRD:
THE TRACK OF A STORM

'Come!' said the chief, at length taking up his keys, 'come with me, emigrant.'

Through the dismal prison twilight, his new charge accompanied him by corridor and staircase, many doors clanging and locking behind them, until they came into a large, low, vaulted chamber, crowded with prisoners of both sexes. The women were seated at a long table, reading and writing, knitting, sewing, and embroidering; the men were for the most part standing behind their chairs, or lingering up and down the room.

In the instinctive association of prisoners with shameful crime and disgrace, the new-comer recoiled from this company. But the crowning unreality of his long unreal ride, was, their all at once rising to receive him, with every refinement of manner known to the time, and with all the engaging graces and courtesies of life.

So strangely clouded were these refinements by the prison manners and gloom, so spectral did they become in the inappropriate squalor and misery through which they were seen, that Charles Darnay seemed to stand in a company of the dead. Ghosts all! The ghost of beauty, the ghost of stateliness, the ghost of elegance, the ghost of pride, the ghost of frivolity, the ghost of wit, the ghost of youth, the ghost of age, all waiting their dismissal from the desolate shore, all turning on him eyes that were changed by the death they had died in coming there.

It struck him motionless. The gaoler standing at his side, and the other gaolers moving about, who would have been well enough as to appearance in the ordinary exercise of their functions, looked so extravagantly coarse contrasted with sorrowing mothers and blooming daughters who were there – with the apparitions of the coquette, the young beauty, and the mature woman delicately bred – that the inversion of all experience and likelihood which the scene of shadows presented, was heightened to its utmost. Surely, ghosts all. Surely, the long unreal ride some progress of disease that had brought him to these gloomy shades! ·

'In the name of the assembled companions in misfortune,' said a gentleman of courtly appearance and address, coming forward, 'I have the honour of giving you welcome to La Force, and of condoling with you on the calamity that has brought you among us. May it soon terminate happily!' *(Chapter 1)*.

'There's all manner of things wanted,' said Miss Pross, 'and we shall have a precious time of it. We want wine, among the rest. Nice toasts these Redheads will be drinking, wherever we buy it.'

'It will be much the same to your knowledge, miss, I should think,' retorted Jerry, 'whether they drink your health or the Old Un's.'

'Who's he?' said Miss Pross.

Mr. Cruncher, with some diffidence, explained himself as meaning 'Old Nick's.'

'Ha!' said Miss Pross, 'it doesn't need an interpreter to explain the meaning of these creatures. They have but one, and it's Midnight Murder, and Mischief.'

'Hush, dear! Pray, pray, be cautious!' cried Lucie.

'Yes, yes, yes, I'll be cautious,' said Miss Pross; 'but I may say among ourselves, that I do hope there will be no oniony and tobaccoey smotherings in the form of embracings all round, going on in the streets. Now, Ladybird, never you stir from that fire till I come back! Take care of the dear husband you have recovered, and don't move your pretty head from his shoulder as you have it now, till you see me again! May I ask a question, Doctor Manette, before I go?'.

'I think you may take that liberty,' the Doctor answered, smiling.

'For gracious sake, don't talk about Liberty; we have quite enough of that,' said Miss Pross.

'Hush, dear! Again?' Lucie remonstrated.

'Well, my sweet,' said Miss Pross, nodding her head emphatically, 'the short and the long of it is, that I am a subject of His Most Gracious Majesty King George the Third'; Miss Pross curtseyed at the name; 'and as such, my maxim is, Confound their politics, Frustrate their knavish tricks, On him our hopes we fix, God save the King!' *(Chapter 7)*.

'See you then, Jacques,' said Madame Defarge, wrathfully; 'and see you, too, my little Vengeance; see you both! Listen! For other crimes as tyrants and oppressors, I have this race a long time on my register, doomed to destruction and extermination. Ask my husband, is that so.'

'It is so,' assented Defarge, without being asked.

'In the beginning of the great days, when the Bastille falls, he finds this paper of to-day, and he brings it home, and in the middle of the night when this place is clear and shut, we read it, here on this spot, by the light of this lamp. Ask him, is that so.'

'It is so,' assented Defarge.

'That night, I tell him, when the paper is read though, and the lamp is burnt out, and the day is gleaming in above those shutters and between those iron bars, that I have now a secret to communicate. Ask him, is that so.'

'It is so,' assented Defarge again.

'I communicate to him that secret. I smite his bosom with these two hands as I smite it now, and I tell him, "Defarge, I was brought up among the fishermen of the sea-shore, and that peasant family so injured by the two Evrémonde brothers, as that Bastille paper describes, is my family. Defarge, that sister of the mortally wounded boy upon the ground was my sister, that husband was my sister's husband, that unborn child was their child, that brother was my brother, that father was my father, those dead are my dead, and that summons to answer for those things descends to me!" Ask him, is that so.'

'It is so,' assented Defarge once more.

'Then tell Wind and Fire where to stop,' returned madame; but don't tell me' *(Chapter 12)*.

'Look back, look back, and see if we are pursued!'

'The road is clear, my dearest. So far, we are not pursued.'

Houses in twos and threes pass by us, solitary farms, ruinous buildings, dye-works, tanneries, and the like, open country, avenues of leafless trees. The hard uneven pavement is under us, the soft deep mud is on either side. Sometimes, we strike into the skirting mud, to avoid the stones that clatter us and shake us; sometimes, we stick in ruts and sloughs there. The agony of our impatience is then so great, that in our wild alarm and hurry we are for getting out and running – hiding – doing anything but stopping.

Out of the open country, in again among ruinous buildings, solitary farms, dye-works, tanneries, and the like, cottages in twos and threes, avenues of leafless trees. Have these men deceived us, and taken us back by another road? Is not this the same place twice over? Thank Heaven, no. A village. Look back, look back and see if we are pursued! Hush! the posting-house.

Leisurely, our four horses are taken out; leisurely, the coach stands in the little street, bereft of horses, and with no likelihood upon it of ever moving again; leisurely, the new horses come into visible existence, one by one; leisurely, the new postilions follow, sucking and plaiting the lashes of their whips; leisurely, the old postilions count their money, make wrong additions, and arrive at dissatisfied results. All the time, our over-fraught hearts are beating at a rate that would far outstrip the fastest gallop of the fastest horses ever foaled.

At length the new positilions are in their saddles, and the old are left behind. We are through the village, up the hill, and down the hill, and on the low watery grounds. Suddenly, the postilions exchange speech with animated gesticulation, and the horses are pulled up, almost on their haunches. We are pursued?

'Ho! within the carriage there. Speak then!'

'What is it?' asks Mr. Lorry, looking out at window.

'How many did they say?'

'I do not understand you.'

'– At the last post. How many to the Guillotine to-day?'

'Fifty-two.'

'I said so! A brave number! My fellow-citizen here would have it forty-two; ten more heads are worth having. The Guillotine goes handsomely. I love it. Hi forward. Whoop!'

The night comes on dark. He moves more; he is beginning to revive, and to speak intelligibly; he thinks they are still together; he asks him, by his name, what he has in his hand. O pity us, kind Heaven, and help us! Look out, look out, and see if we are pursued.

The wind is rushing after us, and the clouds are flying after us, and the moon is plunging after us, and the whole wild night is in pursuit of us; but, so far, we are pursued by nothing else *(Chapter 13:* Dr. Manette and Lucie, Darnay and Lorry).

'Now what do you think, Mr. Cruncher,' said Miss Pross, whose agitation was so great that she could hardly speak, or stand, or move, or live: 'what do you think of our not starting from this court-yard? Another carriage having already gone from here to-day, it might awaken suspicion.'

'My opinion, miss,' returned Mr. Cruncher, 'is as you're right. Likewise wot I'll stand by you, right or wrong.'

'I am so distracted with fear and hope for our precious creatures,' said Miss Pross, wildly crying, 'that I am incapable of forming any plan. Are *you* capable of forming any plan, my dear good Mr. Cruncher?'

'Respectin' a future spear o' life, miss,' returned Mr. Cruncher, 'I hope so. Respectin' any present use o' this here blessed old head o' mine, I think not. Would you do me the favour, miss, to take notice o' two promises and wows wot it is my wishes fur to record in this here crisis?'

'Oh, for gracious sake!' cried Miss Pross, still wildly crying, 'record them at once, and get them out the way, like an excellent man.'

'First,' said Mr. Cruncher, who was all in a tremble, and who spoke with an ashy and solemn visage, 'them poor things well out o' this, never no more will I do it, never no more!'

'I am quite sure, Mr. Cruncher,' returned Miss Pross, 'that you never will do it again, whatever it is, and I beg you not to think it necessary to mention more particularly what it is.'

'No, miss,' returned Jerry, 'it shall not be named to you. Second: them poor things well out o' this, and never no more will I interfere with Mrs. Cruncher's flopping, never no more!'

'Whatever housekeeping arrangement that may be,' said Miss Pross, striving to dry her eyes and compose herself, 'I have no doubt it is best that Mrs. Cruncher should have it entirely under her own superintendence. – O my poor darlings!'

'I go so far as to say, miss, moreover,' proceeded Mr. Cruncher, with a most alarming tendency to hold forth as from a pulpit – 'and let my words be took down and took to Mrs. Cruncher through yourself – that wot my opinions respectin' flopping has undergone a change, and that wot I only hope with all my heart as Mrs. Cruncher may be a flopping at the present time.'

'There, there, there! I hope she is, my dear man,' cried the distracted Miss Pross, 'and I hope she finds it answering her expectations.'

'Forbid it,' proceeded Mr. Cruncher, with additional solemnity, additional slowness, and additional tendency to hold forth and hold out, 'as anything wot I have ever said or done should be wisited on my earnest wishes for them poor creeturs now! Forbid it as we shouldn't all flop (if it was anyways conwenient) to get 'em out o' this here dismal risk! Forbid it, miss! Wot I say, for – BID it!' This was Mr. Cruncher's conclusion after a protracted but vain endeavour to find a better one *(Chapter 14)*.

Madame Defarge looked coldly at her, and said, 'The wife of Evrémonde; where is she?'

It flashed upon Miss Pross's mind that the doors were all standing open, and would suggest the flight. Her first act was to shut them. There were four in the room, and she shut them all. She then placed herself before the door of the chamber which Lucie had occupied.

Madame Defarge's dark eyes followed her through this rapid movement, and rested on her when it was finished. Miss Pross had nothing beautiful about her; years had not tamed the wildness, or softened the grimness, of her appearance; but, she too was a determined woman in her different way, and she measured Madame Defarge with her eyes, every inch.

'You might, from your appearance, be the wife of Lucifer,' said Miss Pross, in her breathing. 'Nevertheless, you shall not get the better of me. I am an Englishwoman.'

Madame Defarge looked at her scornfully, but still with something of Miss Pross's own perception that they two were at bay. She saw a tight, hard, wiry woman before her, as Mr. Lorry had seen in the same figure a woman with a strong hand, in the years gone by. She knew full well that Miss Pross was the family's devoted friend; Miss Pross knew full well that Madame Defarge was the family's malevolent enemy.

'On my way yonder,' said Madame Defarge with a slight movement of her hand towards the fatal spot, 'where they reserve my chair and my knitting for me, I am come to make my compliments to her in passing. I wish to see her.'

'I know that your intentions are evil,' said Miss Pross, 'and you may depend upon it, I'll hold my own against them.'

Each spoke in her own language; neither understood the other's words; both were very watchful, and intent to deduce from look and manner, what the unintelligible words meant.

'It will do her no good to keep herself concealed from me at this moment,' said Madame Defarge. 'Good patriots will know what that means. Let me see her. Go tell her that I wish to see her. Do you hear?.'

'If those eyes of yours were bed-winches,' returned Miss Pross, 'and I was an English four-poster, they shouldn't loose a splinter of me. No, you wicked foreign woman; I am your match.'

Madame Defarge was not likely to follow these idiomatic remarks in detail; but, she so far understood them as to perceive that she was set at naught.

'Woman imbecile and pig-like!' said Madame Defarge, frowning. 'I take no answer from you. I demand to see her. Either tell her that I demand to see her, or stand out of the way of the door and let me go to her!' This, with an angry explanatory wave of her right arm.

'I little thought,' said Miss Pross, 'that I should ever want to understand your nonsensical language; but I would give all I have, except the clothes I wear, to know whether you suspect the truth, or any part of it.'

Neither of them for a single moment released the other's eyes. Madame Defarge had not moved from the spot where she stood when Miss Pross first became aware of her; but, she now advanced one step.

'I am a Briton,' said Miss Pross, 'I am desperate. I don't care an English Twopence for myself. I know that the longer I keep you here, the greater hope there is for my Ladybird. I'll not leave a handful of that dark hair upon your head, if you lay a finger on me!' *(Chapter 14)*.

Madame Defarge made at the door. Miss Pross, on the instinct of the moment, seized her round the waist in both her arms, and held her tight. It was in vain for Madame Defarge to struggle and to strike; Miss Pross, with the vigorous tenacity of love, always so much stronger than hate, clasped her tight, and even lifted her from the floor in the struggle that they had. The two hands of Madame Defarge buffetted and tore her face; but, Miss Pross, with her head down, held her round the waist, and clung to her with more than the hold of a drowning woman.

Soon, Madame Defarge's hands ceased to strike, and felt at her encircled waist. 'It is under my arm,' said Miss Pross, in smothered tones, 'you shall not draw it. I am stronger than you, I bless Heaven for it. I'll hold you till one or other of us faints or dies!'

Madame Defarge's hands were at her bosom. Miss Pross looked up, saw what it was, struck at it, struck out a flash and a crash, and stood alone – blinded with smoke.

All this was in a second. As the smoke cleared, leaving an awful stillness, it passed out on the air, like the soul of the furious woman whose body lay lifeless on the ground *(Chapter 14)*.

'Is there any noise in the streets?' she asked him.

'The usual noises,' Mr. Cruncher replied; and looked surprised by the question and by her aspect.

'I don't hear you,' said Miss Pross. 'What do you say?'

It was in vain for Mr. Cruncher to repeat what he said; Miss Pross could not hear him. 'So I'll nod my head,' thought Mr. Cruncher, amazed, 'at all events she'll see that.' And she did.

'Is there any noise in the streets now?' asked Miss Pross again, presently.

Again Mr. Cruncher nodded his head.

'I don't hear it.'

'Gone deaf in a hour?' said Mr. Cruncher, ruminating, with his mind much disturbed; 'wot's come to her?'

'I feel,' said Miss Pross, 'as if there had been a flash and a crash, and that crash was the last thing I should ever hear in this life.'

'Blest if she ain't in a queer condition!' said Mr. Cruncher, more and more disturbed. 'Wot can she have been a takin', to keep her courage up? Hark! There's the roll of them dreadful carts! You can hear that, miss?'

'I can hear,' said Miss Pross, seeing that he spoke to her, 'nothing. O, my good man, there was first a great crash, and then a great stillness, and that stillness seems to be fixed and unchangeable, never to be broken any more as long as my life lasts.'

'If she don't hear the roll of those dreadful carts, now very nigh their journey's end,' said Mr. Cruncher, glancing over his shoulder, 'it's my opinion that indeed she never will hear anything else in this world.'

And indeed she never did. (*Chapter 14*).

He gently places her with her back to the crashing engine that constantly whirrs up and falls, and she looks into his face and thanks him.

'But for you, dear stranger, I should not be so composed, for I am naturally a poor little thing, faint of heart; nor should I have been able to raise my thoughts to Him who was put to death, that we might have hope and comfort here to-day. I think you were sent to me by Heaven.'

'Or you to me,' says Sydney Carton. 'Keep your eyes upon me, dear child, and mind no other object.'

'I mind nothing while I hold your hand. I shall mind nothing when I let it go, if they are rapid.'

'They will be rapid. Fear not!'

The two stand in the fast-thinning throng of victims, but they speak as if they were alone. Eye to eye, voice to voice, hand to hand, heart to heart, these two children of the Universal Mother, else so wide apart and differing, have come together on the dark highway, to repair home together, and to rest in her bosom.

'Brave and generous friend, will you let me ask you one last question? I am very ignorant, and it troubles me – just a little.'

'Tell me what it is.'

'I have a cousin, an only relative and an orphan, like myself, whom I love very dearly. She is five years younger than I, and she lives in a farmer's house in the south country. Poverty parted us, and she knows nothing of my fate – for I cannot write – and if I could, how should I tell her! It is better as it is.'

'Yes, yes: better as it is.'

'What I have been thinking as we came along, and what I am still thinking now, as I look into your kind strong face which gives me so much support, is this:- If the Republic really does good to the poor, and they come to be less hungry, and in all ways to suffer less, she may live a long time: she may even live to be old.'

'What then, my gentle sister?'

'Do you think:' the uncomplaining eyes in which there is so much endurance, fill with tears, and the lips part a little more and tremble: 'that it will seem long to me, while I wait for her in the better land where I trust both you and I will be mercifully sheltered?'

'It cannot be, my child; there is no Time there, and no trouble there.'

'You comfort me so much! I am so ignorant. Am I to kiss you now? Is the moment come?'

'Yes.'

She kisses his lips; he kisses hers; they solemnly bless each other. The spare hand does not tremble as he releases it; nothing worse than a sweet, bright constancy is in the patient face. She goes next before him – is gone; the knitting-women count Twenty-Two.

'I am the Resurrection and the Life, saith the Lord: he that believeth in me, though he were dead, yet shall he live: and whosoever liveth and believeth in me shall never die.'

The murmuring of many voices, the upturning of many faces, the pressing on of many footsteps in the outskirts of the crowd, so that it swells forward in a mass, like one great heave of water, all flashes away. Twenty-Three (*Chapter 15:* The Little Seamstress and Sydney Carton).

One of the most remarkable sufferers by the same axe – a woman – had asked at the foot of the same scaffold, not long before, to be allowed to write down the thoughts that were inspiring her. If he had given any utterance to his, and they were prophetic, they would have been these:

'I see Barsad, the Cly, Defarge, The Vengeance, the Juryman, the Judge, long ranks of the new oppressors who have risen on the destruction of the old, perishing by this retributive instrument, before it shall cease out of its present use. I see a beautful city and a brilliant people rising from this abyss, and, in their struggles to be truly free, in their triumphs and defeats, through long long years to come, I see the evil of this time and of the previous time of which this is the natural birth, gradually making expiation for itself and wearing out.

'I see the lives for which I lay down my life, peaceful, useful, prosperous and happy, in that England which I shall see no more. I see Her with a child upon her bosom, who bears my name. I see her father, aged and bent, but otherwise restored, and faithful to all men in his healing office, and at peace. I see the good old man, so long their friend, in ten years' time enriching them with all he has, and passing tranquilly to his reward.

'I see that I hold a sanctuary in their hearts, and in the hearts of their descendants, generations hence. I see her, an old woman, weeping for me on the anniversary of this day. I see her and her husband, their course done, lying side by side in their last earthly bed, and I know that each was not more honoured and held sacred in the other's soul, than I was in the souls of both.

'I see that child who lay upon her bosom and who bore my name, a man winning his way up in that path of life which once was mine. I see him winning it so well, that my name is made illustrious there by the light of his. I see the blots I threw upon it, faded away. I see him, foremost of just judges and honoured men, bringing a boy of my name, with a forehead that I know and golden hair, to this place – then fair to look upon, with not a trace of this day's disfigurement – and I hear him tell the child my story, with a tender and a faltering voice.

'It is a far, far better thing that I do, than I have ever done; it is a far, far better rest that I go to than I have ever known' (*Chapter 15:* Sydney Carton).

HUNTED DOWN

There is nothing truer than physiognomy, taken in connection with manner. The art of reading that book of which Eternal Wisdom obliges every human creature to present his or her own page with the individual character written on it, is a difficult one, perhaps, and is little studied. It may require some natural aptitude, and it must require (for everything does) some patience and some pains. That these are not usually given to it, – that numbers of people accept a few stock commonplace expressions of the face as the whole list of characteristics, and neither seek nor know the refinements that are truest, – that You, for instance, give a great deal of time and attention to the reading of music, Greek, Latin, French, Italian, Hebrew, if you please, and do not qualify yourself to read the face of the master or mistress looking over your shoulder teaching it to you, – I assume to be five hundred times more probable than improbable. Perhaps a little self-sufficiency may be at the bottom of this; facial expression requires no study from you, you think; it comes by nature to you to know enough about it, and you are not to be taken in.

I confess, for my part, that I *have* been taken in, over and over again. I have been taken in by acquaintances, and I have been taken in (of course) by friends; far oftener by friends than by any other class of persons. How came I to be so deceived? Had I quite misread their faces?

No. Believe me, my first impression of those people, founded on face and manner alone, was invariably true. My mistake was in suffering them to come nearer to me and explain themselves away (*Chapter 1:* Sampson).

As he [Julius Slinkton] talked and talked – but really not too much, for the rest of us seemed to force it upon him – I became quite angry with myself. I took his face to pieces in my mind, like a watch, and examined it in detail. I could not say much against any of his features separately; I could say even less against them when they were put together. 'Then is it not monstrous,' I asked myself, 'that because a man happens to part his hair straight up the middle of his head, I should permit myself to suspect, and even to detest him?'

(I may stop to remark that this was no proof of my sense. An observer of men who finds himself steadily repelled by some apparently trifling thing in a stranger is right to give it great weight. It may be the clue to the whole mystery. A hair or two will show where a lion is hidden. A very little key will open a very heavy door) (*Chapter 2:* Sampson).

'Apart from the general human disinclination to do anything that ought to be done, I dare say there is a specialty about assuring one's life. You find it like will-making. People are too superstitious, and take it for granted they will die soon afterwards' (*Chapter 3:* Julius Slinkton).

THE UNCOMMERCIAL TRAVELLER

You are going off by railway, from any Terminus. You have twenty minutes for dinner, before you go. You want your dinner, and like Dr. Johnson, Sir, you like to dine. You present to your mind, a picture of the refreshment-table at that terminus. The conventional

shabby evening-party supper – accepted as the model for all termini and all refreshment-stations, because it is the last repast known to this state of existence of which any human creature would partake, but in the direst extremity – sickens your contemplation, and your words are these: 'I cannot dine on stale sponge-cakes that turn to sand in the mouth. I cannot dine on shining brown patties, composed of unknown animals within, and offering to my view the device of an indigestible star-fish in leaden pie-crust without. I cannot dine on a sandwich that has long been pining under an exhausted receiver. I cannot dine on barley-sugar. I cannot dine on Toffee.' You repair to the nearest hotel, and arrive agitated, in the coffee-room.

It is a most astonishing fact that the waiter is very cold to you. Account for it how you may, smooth it over how you will, you cannot deny that he is cold to you. He is not glad to see you, he does not want you, he would much rather you hadn't come. He opposes to your flushed condition, an immovable composure. As if this were not enough, another waiter, born, as it would seem, expressly to look at you in this passage of your life, stands at a little distance, with his napkin under his arm and his hands folded, looking at you with all his might. You impress on your waiter that you have ten minutes for dinner, and he proposes that you shall begin with a bit of fish which will be ready in twenty. That proposal declined, he suggests – as a neat originality – 'a weal or mutton cutlet.' You close with either cutlet, any cutlet, anything. He goes, leisurely, behind a door and calls down some unseen shaft. A ventriloquial dialogue ensues, tending finally to the fact that weal only, is available on the spur of the moment. You anxiously call out 'Veal then!' Your waiter having settled that point, returns to array your tablecloth, with a napkin folded cocked-hat wise (slowly, for something out of window engages his eye), a white wine-glass, a green wine-glass, a blue finger-glass, a tumbler and a powerful field battery of fourteen casters with nothing in them; or at all events – which is enough for your purpose – with nothing in them that will come out. All this time, the other waiter looks at you – with an air of mental comparison and curiosity, now, as if it had occurred to him that you are rather like his brother. Half your time gone, and nothing come but the jug of ale and the bread, you implore your waiter to 'see after that cutlet, waiter; pray do!' He cannot go at once, for he is carrying in seventeen pounds of American cheese for you to finish with, and a small Landed Estate of celery and water-cresses. The other waiter changes his leg, and takes a new view of you, doubtfully, now, as if he had rejected the resemblance to his brother, and had begun to think you more like his aunt or his grandmother. Again you beseech your waiter with pathetic indignation, to 'see after that cutlet!' He steps out to see after it, and by and by, when you are going away without it, comes back with it. Even then, he will not take the sham silver cover off, without a pause for a flourish, and a look at the musty cutlet as if he were surprised to see it – which cannot possibly be the case, he must have seen it so often before. A sort of fur has been produced upon its surface by the cook's art, and in a sham silver vessel staggering on two feet instead of three, is a cutaneous kind of sauce, of brown pimples and pickled cucumber. You order the bill, but your waiter cannot bring your bill yet, because he is bringing, instead, three flinty-hearted potatoes and two grim head of broccoli, like the occasional ornaments on area railings, badly boiled. You know that you will never come to this pass, any more than to the cheese and celery, and you imperatively demand your bill; but it takes time to get, even when gone for, because your waiter has to communicate with a lady who lives behind a sash-window in a corner, and who appears to have to refer to several Ledgers before she can make it out – as if you had been staying there a year. You become distracted to get away, and the other waiter, once more changing his leg, still looks at you – but suspiciously, now, as if you had begun to remind him of the party who took the great-coats last winter. Your bill at last brought and paid, at the rate of sixpence a mouthful, your waiter reproachfully reminds you that 'attendance is not charged for a single meal,' and you have to search in all your pockets for sixpence more. He has a worse opinion of you than ever, when you have given it to him, and lets you out into the street with the air of one saying to himself, as you cannot doubt he is, 'I hope we never shall see *you* here again!'(6: 'Refreshments for Travellers').

So smooth was the old high road, and so fresh were the horses, and so fast went I, that it was midway between Gravesend and Rochester, and the widening river was bearing the ships, white-sailed or black-smoked, out to sea, when I noticed by the wayside a very queer small boy.

'Holloa!' said I, to the very queer small boy, 'where do you live?'

'At Chatham,' says he.

'What do you do there?' says I.

'I go to school,' says he.

I took him up in a moment and we went on. Presently, the very queer small boy says, 'This is Gads-hill we are coming to, where Falstaff went out to rob those travellers, and ran away.'

'You know something about Falstaff, eh?' said I.

'All about him,' says the very queer small boy. 'I am old (I am nine), and I read all sorts of books. But *do* let us stop at the top of the hill, and look at the house there, if you please!'

'You admire that house?' said I.

'Bless you, sir,' said the very queer small boy, 'when I was not more than half as old as nine, it used to be a treat for me to be brought to look at it. And now, I am nine, I come by myself to look at it. And ever since I can recollect, my father, seeing me so fond of it, has often said to me, "If you were to be very persevering and were to work hard, you might some day come to live in it." Though that's impossible!' said the very queer small boy, drawing a low breath, and now staring at the house out of window with all his might.

I was rather amazed to be told this by the very queer small boy; for that house happens to be *my* house, and I have reason to believe that what he said was true (7: 'Travelling Abroad').

Whenever I am at Paris, I am dragged by invisible force into the Morgue. I never want to go there, but am always pulled there. One Christmas Day, when I would rather have been anywhere else, I was attracted in, to see an old grey man lying all alone on his cold bed, with a tap of water turned on over his grey hair, and running, drip, drip, drip, down his wretched face until it got to the corner of his mouth, where it took a turn, and made him look sly. One New Year's Morning (by the same token, the sun was shining outside, and there was a mountebank balancing a feather on his nose within a yard of the gate), I was pulled in again to look at a flaxen-haired boy of eighteen, with a heart hanging on his breast – 'from his mother,' was engraven on it – who had come into the net across the river, with a bullet wound in his fair forehead and his hands cut with a knife, but whence or how was a blank mystery. This time, I was forced into the same dread place, to see a large dark man whose disfigurement by water was in a frightful manner comic, and whose expression was that of a prize-fighter who had closed his eyelids under a heavy blow, but was going immediately to open them, shake his head, and 'come up smiling.' Oh what this large dark man cost me in that bright city!

It was very hot weather, and he was none the better for that, and I was much the worse. Indeed, a very neat and pleasant little woman with the key of her lodging on her forefinger, who had been showing him to her little girl while she and the child ate sweetmeats, observed monsieur looking poorly as we came out together, and asked monsieur, with her wondering little eyebrows prettily raised, if there were anything the matter? Faintly replying in the negative, monsieur crossed the road to a wine-shop, got some brandy, and resolved to freshen himself with a dip in the great floating bath on the river.

The bath was crowded in the usual airy manner, by a male population in striped drawers of various gay colours, who walked up and down arm in arm, drank coffee, smoked cigars, sat at little tables, conversed politely with the damsels who dispensed the towels, and every now and then pitched themselves into the river head foremost, and came out again to repeat this social routine. I made haste to participate in the water part of the entertainments, and was in the full enjoyment of a delightful bath, when all in a moment I was seized with an unreasonable idea that the large dark body was floating straight at me.

I was out of the river, and dressing instantly. In the shock I had taken some water into my mouth, and it turned me sick, for I fancied that the contamination of the creature was in it. I had got back to my cool darkened room in the hotel, and was lying on a sofa there, before I began to reason with myself.

Of course, I knew perfectly well that the large dark creature was stone dead, and that I should no more come upon him out of the place where I had seen him dead, than I should come upon the cathedral of Notre-Dame in an entirely new situation. What troubled me was the picture of the creature; and that had so curiously and strongly painted itself upon my brain, that I could not get rid of it until it was worn out (7: 'Travelling Abroad').

Another Sunday.

After being again rung for by conflicting bells, like a

leg of mutton or a laced hat a hundred years ago, I make selection of a church oddly put away in a corner among a number of lanes – a smaller church than the last, and an ugly: of about the date of Queen Anne. As a congregation, we are fourteen strong: not counting an exhausted charity school in gallery, which has dwindled away to four boys, and two girls. In the porch, is a benefaction of loaves of bread, which there would seem to be nobody left in the exhausted congregation to claim, and which I saw an exhausted beadle, long faded out of uniform, eating with his eyes for self and family when I passed in. There is also an exhausted clerk in a brown wig, and two or three exhausted doors and windows have been bricked up, and the service books are musty, and the pulpit cushions are threadbare, and the whole of the church furniture is in a very advanced state of exhaustion. We are three old women (habitual), two young lovers (accidental), two tradesmen, one with a wife and one alone, an aunt and nephew, again two girls (these two girls dressed out for church with everything about them limp that should be stiff, and *vice versa*, are an invariable experience,) and three sniggering boys. The clergyman is, perhaps, the chaplain of a civic company; he has the moist and vinous look, and eke the bulbous boots, of one acquainted with 'Twenty port, and comet vintages . . .

The clergyman, who is of a prandial presence, and a muffled voice, may be scant of hearing as well as of breath, but he only glances up, as having an idea that somebody has said Amen in a wrong place, and continues his steady jog-trot, like a farmer's wife going to market. He does all he has to do, in the same easy way, and gives us a concise sermon, still like the jog-trot of the farmer's wife on a level road. Its drowsy cadence soon lulls the three old women asleep, and the unmarried tradesman sits looking out at window, and the married tradesman sits looking at his wife's bonnet, and the lovers sit looking at one another, so superlatively happy, that I mind when I, turned of eighteen, went with my Angelica to a City church on account of a shower (by this special coincidence that it was Huggin Lane), and when I said to my Angelica, 'Let the blessed event, Angelica, occur at no altar but this!' and when my Angelica consented that it should occur at no other – which it certainly never did, for it never occurred anywhere. And O, Angelica, what has become of you, this present Sunday morning when I can't attend to the sermon; and, more difficult question than that, what has become of Me as I was when I sat by your side? (9: 'City of London Churches').

We talk of men keeping dogs, but we might often talk more expressively of dogs keeping men. I know a bull-dog in a shy corner of Hammersmith who keeps a man. He keeps him up a yard, and makes him go to public-houses and lay wagers on him, and obliges him to lean against posts and look at him, and forces him to neglect work for him, and keeps him under rigid coercion. I once knew a fancy terrier who kept a gentleman – a gentleman who had been brought up at Oxford, too. The dog kept the gentleman entirely for his glorification, and the gentleman never talked about anything but the terrier (10: 'Shy Neighbourhoods').

As the dogs of shy neighbourhoods usually betray a slinking consciousness of being in poor circumstances – for the most part manifested in an aspect of anxiety, an awkwardness in their play, and a misgiving that somebody is going to harness them to something, to pick up a living – so the cats of shy neighbourhoods exhibit a strong tendency to relapse into barbarism. Not only are they made selfishly ferocious by ruminating on the surplus population around them, and on the densely crowded state of all the avenues to cat's meat; not only is there a moral and politico-economical haggardness in them, traceable to these reflections; but they evince a physical deterioration. Their linen is not clean, and is wretchedly got up; their black turns rusty, like old mourning; they wear very indifferent fur; and take to the shabbiest cotton velvet, instead of silk velvet. I am on terms of recognition with several small streets of cats, about the Obelisk in St. George's Fields, and also in the vicinity of Clerkenwell Green, and also in the back settlements of Drury Lane. In appearance they are very like the women among whom they live. They seem to turn out of their unwholesome beds into the street, without any preparation. They leave their young families to stagger about the gutters, unassisted, while they frouzily quarrel and swear and scratch and spit, at street corners. In particular, I remark that when they are about to increase their families (an event of frequent recurrence) the resemblance is strongly expressed in a certain dusty dowdiness, down-at-heel self-neglect, and general giving up of things. I cannot honestly report that I have ever seen a feline matron of this class washing her face when in an interesting condition (10: 'Shy Neighbourhoods').

I have my eye upon a piece of Kentish road, bordered on either side by a wood, and having on one hand, between the road-dust and the trees, a skirting patch of grass. Wild flowers grow in abundance on this spot, and it lies high and airy, with a distant river stealing away steadily to the ocean, like a man's life. To gain the milestone here, which the moss, primroses, violets, blue-bells, and wild roses, would soon render illegible but for peering travellers pushing them aside with their sticks, you must come up a steep hill, come which way you may. So, all the tramps with carts or caravans – the Gipsy-tramp, the Show-tramp, the Cheap-Jack – find it impossible to resist the temptations of the place, and all turn the horse loose when they come to it, and boil the pot. Bless the place, I love the ashes of the vagabond fires that have scorched its grass! What tramp children do I see here, attired in a handful of rags, making a gymnasium of the shafts of the cart, making a feather-bed of the flints and brambles, making a toy of the hobbled old horse who is not much more like a horse than any cheap toy would be! Here, do I encounter the cart of mats and brooms and baskets – with all thoughts of business given to the evening wind – with the stew made and being served out – with Cheap Jack and Dear Jill striking soft music out of the plates that are rattled like warlike cymbals when put up for auction at fairs and markets – their minds so influenced (no doubt) by the melody of the nightingales as they begin to sing in the woods behind them, that if I were to propose a deal, they would sell me anything at cost price. On this hallowed ground has it been my happy privilege (let me whisper it), to behold the White-haired Lady with the pink eyes, eating meat-pie with the Giant: while, by the hedge-side, on the box of blankets which I knew contained the snakes, were set forth the cups and saucers and the teapot. It was on an evening in August that I chanced upon this ravishing spectacle, and I noticed that, whereas the Giant reclined half concealed beneath the overhanging boughs and seemed indifferent to Nature, the white hair of the gracious Lady streamed free in the breath of evening, and her pink eyes found pleasure in the landscape. I heard only a single sentence of her uttering, yet it bespoke a talent for modest repartee. The ill-mannered Giant – accursed be his evil race! – had interrupted the Lady in some remark, and, as I passed that enchanted corner of the wood, she gently reproved him, with the words, 'Now, Cobby'; – Cobby! so short a name! – 'ain't one fool enough to talk at a time?' (11: 'Tramps').

I call my boyhood's home (and I feel like a Tenor in an English Opera when I mention it) Dullborough. Most of us come from Dullborough who come from a country town.

As I left Dullborough in the days when there were no railroads in the land, I left it in a stage-coach. Through all the years that have since passed, have I ever lost the smell of the damp straw in which I was packed – like game – and forwarded, carriage paid, to the Cross Keys, Wood Street, Cheapside, London? There was no other inside passenger, and I consumed my sandwiches in solitude and dreariness, and it rained hard all the way, and I thought life sloppier than I had expected to find it.

With this tender remembrance upon me, I was cavalierly shunted back into Dullborough the other day, by train. My ticket had been previously collected, like my taxes, and my shining new portmanteau had had a great plaster stuck upon it, and I had been defied by Act of Parliament to offer an objection to anything that was done to it, or me, under a penalty of not less than forty shillings or more than five pounds, compoundable for a term of imprisonment. When I had sent my disfigured property on to the hotel, I began to look about me; and the first discovery I made, was, that the Station had swallowed up the playing-field.

It was gone. The two beautiful hawthorn-trees, the hedge, the turf, and all those buttercups and daisies, had given place to the stoniest of jolting roads: while, beyond the Station, an ugly dark monster of a tunnel kept its jaws open, as if it had swallowed them and were ravenous for more destruction. The coach that had carried me away, was melodiously called Timpson's Blue-Eyed Maid, and belonged to Timpson, at the coach-office up-street; the locomotive engine that had brought me back, was called severely No. 97, and belonged to S.E.R., and was spitting ashes and hot water over the blighted ground (12: 'Dullborough Town').

It is a mercy I have not a red and green lamp and a night-bell at my door, for in my very young days I was taken to so many lyings-in that I wonder I escaped becoming a professional martyr to them in after-life. I suppose I had a very sympathetic nurse, with a large circle of married acquaintance. However that was, as I continued my walk through Dullborough, I found many houses to be solely associated in my mind with this particular interest. At one little greengrocer's shop, down certain steps from the street, I remember to have waited on a lady who had had four children (I am afraid to write five, though I fully believe it was five) at a birth. This meritorious woman held quite a reception in her room on the morning when I was introduced there, and the sight of the house brought vividly to my mind how the four (five) deceased young people lay, side by side, on a clean cloth on a chest of drawers; reminding me by a homely association, which I suspect their complexion to have assisted, of pigs' feet as they are usually displayed at a neat tripe-shop. Hot caudle was handed round on the occasion, and I further remembered as I stood contemplating the greengrocer's, that a subscription was entered into among the company, which becomes extremely alarming to my consciousness of having pocket-money on my person. This fact being known to my conductress, whoever she was, I was earnestly exhorted to contribute, but resolutely declined: therein disgusting the company, who gave me to understand that I must dismiss all expectations of going to Heaven (12: 'Dullborough Town').

A very curious disease the Dry Rot in men, and difficult to detect the beginning of. It had carried Horace Kinch inside the wall of the old King's Bench prison, and it had carried him out with his feet foremost. He was a likely man to look at, in the prime of life, well to do, as clever as he needed to be, and popular among many friends. He was suitably married, and had healthy and pretty children. But, like some fair-looking houses or fair-looking ships, he took the Dry Rot. The first strong external revelation of the Dry Rot in men, is a tendency to lurk and lounge; to be at street-corners without intelligible reason; to be going anywhere when met; to be about many places rather than at any; to do nothing tangible, but to have an intention of performing a variety of intangible duties to-morrow or the day after (13: 'Night Walks').

When a church clock strikes, on houseless ears in the dead of the night, it may be at first mistaken for company and hailed as such. But, as the spreading circles of vibration, which you may perceive at such a time with great clearness, go opening out, for ever and ever afterwards widening perhaps (as the philosopher has suggested) in external space, the mistake is rectified and the sense of loneliness is profounder. Once – it was after leaving the Abbey and turning my face north – I came to the great steps of St. Martin's church as the clock was striking Three. Suddenly a thing that in a moment more I should have trodden upon without seeing, rose up at my feet with a cry of loneliness and houselessness, struck out of it by the bell, the like of which I never heard. We then stood face to face looking at one another, frightened by one another. The creature was like a bettle-browed hair-lipped youth of twenty, and it had a loose bundle of rags on, which it held together with one of its hands. It shivered from head to foot, and its teeth chattered, and as it stared at me – persecutor, devil, ghost, whatever it thought me – it made with its whining mouth as if it were snapping at me, like a worried dog. Intending to give this ugly object money, I put out my hand to stay it – for it recoiled as it whined and snapped – and laid my hand upon its shoulder. Instantly, it twisted out of its garment, like the young man in the New Testament, and left me standing alone with its rags in my hands (13: 'Night Walks').

I look upon Gray's Inn generally as one of the most depressing institutions in brick and mortar, known to the children of men. Can anything be more dreary than its arid Square, Sahara Desert of the law, with the ugly old tiled-topped tenements, the dirty windows, the bills To Let, To Let, the door-posts inscribed like gravestones, the crazy gateway giving upon the filthy Lane, the scowling iron-barred prison-like passage into Verulam-buildings, the mouldy red-nosed ticket-porters with little coffin plates, and why with aprons, the dry, hard, atomy-like appearance of the whole dust-heap? When my uncommercial travels tend to this dismal spot, my comfort is its rickety state. Imagination gloats over the fulness of time when the staircases shall have quite tumbled down – they are daily wearing into an ill-savoured powder, but have not quite tumbled down yet – when the last old prolix bencher all of the olden time, shall have been got out of an upper window by means of a Fire Ladder, and carried off to the Holborn Union; when the last clerk shall have engrossed the last parchment behind the last splash on the last of the mud-stained windows, which, all through the miry year, are pilloried out of recognition in Gray's Inn Lane. Then, shall a squalid little trench, with rank grass and a pump in it, lying between the coffee-house and South Square, be wholly given up to cats and rats, and not, as now, have its empire divided between those animals and a few briefless bipeds – surely called to the Bar by voices of deceiving spirits, seeing that they are wanted there by no mortal – who glance down, with eyes better glazed than their casements, from their dreary and lack-lustre rooms. Then shall the way Nor' Westward, now lying under a short grim colonnade where in summer-time pounce flies from law-stationering windows into the eyes of laymen, be choked with rubbish and happily become impassable. Then shall the gardens where turf, trees, and gravel wear a legal livery of black, run rank, and pilgrims go to Gorhambury to see Bacon's effigy as he sat, and not come here (which in truth they seldom do) to see where he walked. Then, in a word, shall the old-established vendor of periodicals sit alone in his little crib of a shop behind the Holborn Gate, like that lumbering Marius among the ruins of Carthage, who has sat heavy on a thousand million of similes (14: 'Chambers').

On the same staircase with my friend Parkle, and on the same floor, there lived a man of law who pursued his business elsewhere, and used those chambers as his place of residence. For three or four years, Parkle rather knew of him than knew him, but after that – for Englishmen – short pause of consideration, they began to speak. Parkle exchanged words with him in his private character only, and knew nothing of his business ways, or means. He was a man a good deal about town, but always alone. We used to remark to one another, that although we often encountered him in theatres, concert-rooms, and similar public places, he was always alone. Yet he was not a gloomy man, and was of a decidedly conversational turn; insomuch that he would sometimes of an evening lounge with a cigar in his mouth, half in and half out of Parkle's rooms, and discuss the topics of the day by the hour. He used to hint on these occasions that he had four faults to find with life; firstly, that it obliged a man to be always winding up his watch; secondly, that London was too small; thirdly, that it therefore wanted variety; fourthly, that there was too much dust in it. There was so much dust in his own faded chambers, certainly, that they reminded me of a sepulchre, furnished in prophetic anticipation of the present time, which had newly been brought to light, after having remained buried a few thousand years. One dry hot autumn evening at twilight, this man, being then five years turned of fifty, looked in upon Parkle in his usual lounging way, with his cigar in his mouth as usual, and said, 'I am going out of town.' As he never went out of town, Parkle said, 'Oh, indeed! At last?' 'Yes,' says he, 'at last. For what is a man to do? London is so small! If you go West, you come to Hounslow. If you go East, you come to Bow. If you go South, there's Brixton or Norwood. If you go North, you can't get rid of Barnet. Then, the monotony of all the streets, streets, streets – and of all the roads, roads, roads – and the dust, dust, dust!' When he had said this, he wished Parkle a good evening, but came back again and said, with his watch in his hand, 'Oh, I really cannot go on winding up this watch over and over again; I wish you would take care of it.' So, Parkle laughed and consented, and the man went out of town. The man remained out of town so long, that his letter-box became choked, and no more letters could be got into it, and they began to be left at the lodge and to accumulate there. At last the head-porter decided, on conference with the steward, to use his master-key and look into the chambers, and give them the benefit of a whiff of air. Then, it was found that he had hanged himself to his bedstead, and had left this written memorandum: 'I should prefer to be cut down by my neighbour and friend (if he will allow me to call him so), H. Parkle, Esq.' This was an end of Parkle's occupancy of chambers. He went into lodgings immediately (14: 'Chambers').

The first diabolical character who intruded himself on my peaceful youth ... was a certain Captain Murderer. This wretch must have been an offshoot of the Blue Beard family, but I had no suspicion of the consanguinity in those times. His warning name would seem to have awakened no general prejudice against him, for he was admitted into the best society and possessed immense wealth. Captain Murderer's mission was matrimony, and the gratification of a cannibal appetite with tender brides. On his marriage morning, he always caused both sides of the way to church to be planted with curious flowers; and when his bride said, 'Dear Captain Murderer, I never saw flowers like these before: what are they called?' he answered, 'They are called Garnish for house-lamb,' and laughed at his ferocious practical joke in a horrid manner, disquieting the minds of the noble bridal company, with a very sharp show of teeth, then displayed for the first time. He made love in a coach and six, and married in a coach and twelve, and all his horses were milk-white horses with one red spot on the back which he caused to be hidden by the harness. For, the spot *would* come there, though every horse was milk-white when Captain Murderer bought him. And the spot was young bride's blood. (To this terrific point I am indebted for my personal experience of a shudder and cold beads on the forehead.) When Captain Murderer had made an end of feasting and revelry, and had dismissed the noble guests, and was alone with his wife on the day month of their marriage, it was his whimsical custom to produce a golden rolling-pin and a silver pie-board. Now, there was this special feature in the Captain's courtships, that he always asked if the young lady could make pie-crust; and if she couldn't by nature or education, she was taught. Well. When the bride saw Captain Murderer produce the golden rolling-pin and silver pie-board, she remembered this, and turned up her laced-silk sleeves to make a pie. The Captain brought out a silver pie-dish of immense capacity, and the Captain brought out flour and butter and eggs and all things needful, except the inside of the pie; of materials for the staple of the pie itself, the Captain brought out none. Then said the lovely bride, 'Dear Captain Murderer, what pie is this to be?' He replied, 'A meat pie.' Then said the lovely bride, 'Dear Captain Murderer, I see no meat.' The Captain humorously retorted, 'Look in the glass.' She looked in the glass, but still she saw no meat, and then the Captain roared with laughter, and suddenly frowning and drawing his sword, bade her roll out the crust. So she rolled out the crust, dropping large tears upon it all the time because he was so cross, and when she had lined the dish with crust and had cut the crust all ready to fit the top, the Captain called out, '*I* see the meat in the glass!' And the bride looked up at the glass just in time to see the Captain cutting her head off; and he chopped her in pieces, and peppered her, and salted her, and put her in the pie, and sent it to the baker's, and ate it all, and picked the bones.

Captain Murderer went on in this way, prospering exceedingly, until he came to choose a bride from two twin sisters, and at first didn't know which to choose. For, though one was fair and the other dark, they were both equally beautiful. But the fair twin loved him, and the dark twin hated him, so he chose the fair one. The dark twin would have prevented the marriage if she could, but she couldn't; however, on the night before it, much suspecting Captain Murderer, she stole out and climbed his garden wall, and looked in at his window through a chink in the shutter, and saw him having his teeth filed sharp. Next day she listened all day, and heard him make his joke about the house-lamb. And that day month, he had the paste rolled out, and cut the fair twin's head off, and chopped her in pieces, and peppered her, and salted her, and put her in the pie, and sent it to the baker's, and ate it all, and picked the bones.

Now, the dark twin had had her suspicions much increased by the filing of the Captain's teeth, and again by the house-lamb joke. Putting all things together when he gave out that her sister was dead, she divined the truth, and determined to be revenged. So, she went up to Captain Murderer's house, and knocked at the knocker and pulled at the bell, and when the Captain came to the door, said: 'Dear Captain Murderer, marry me next, for I always loved you and was jealous of my sister.' The Captain took it as a compliment, and made a polite answer, and the marriage was quickly arranged. On the night before it, the bride again climbed to his window, and again saw him having his teeth filed sharp. At this sight she laughed such a terrible laugh at the chink in the shutter, that the Captain's blood curdled, and he said: 'I hope nothing has disagreed with me!' At that, she laughed again, a still more terrible laugh, and the shutter was opened and search made, but she was nimbly gone, and there was no one. Next day they went to church in a coach and twelve, and were married. And that day month, she rolled the pie-crust out, and Captain Murderer cut her head off, and chopped her in pieces, and peppered her, and salted her, and put her in the pie, and sent it to the baker's, and ate it all, and picked the bones.

But before she began to roll out the paste she had taken a deadly poison of a most awful character, distilled from toads' eyes and spiders' knees; and Captain Murderer had hardly picked her last bone, when he began to swell, and to turn blue, and to be all spots, and to scream. And he went on swelling and turning bluer, and being more all over spots and screaming, until he reached from floor to ceiling and from wall to wall; and then, at one o'clock in the morning, he blew up with a loud explosion. At the sound of it, all the milk-white horses in the stables broke their halters and went mad, and then they galloped over everybody in Captain Murderer's house (beginning with the family blacksmith who had filed his teeth) until the whole were dead, and then they galloped away (15: 'Nurses' Stories').

The Dentist's servant. Is that man no mystery to us, no type of invisible power? The tremendous individual knows (who else does?) what is done with the extracted teeth; he knows what goes on in the little room where something is always being washed or filed; he knows what warm spicy infusion is put into the comfortable tumbler from which we rinse our wounded mouth, with a gap in it that feels a foot wide; he knows whether the thing we spit into is a fixture communicating with the Thames, or could be cleared away for a dance; he sees the horrible parlour when there are no patients in it, and he could reveal, if he would, what becomes of the Every-Day book then. The conviction of my coward conscience when I see that man in a professional light, is, that he knows all the statistics of my teeth and gums, my double teeth, my single teeth, my stopped teeth, and my sound (16: 'Arcadian London').

The wind blows stiffly from the Nor'-East, the sea runs high, we ship a deal of water, the night is dark and cold, and the shapeless passengers lie about in melancholy bundles, as if they were sorted out for the laundress; but for my own uncommercial part I cannot pretend that I am much inconvenienced by any of those things. A general howling whistling flopping gurgling and scooping, I am aware of, and a general knocking about of Nature; but the impressions I receive are very vague. In a sweet faint temper, something like the smell of damaged oranges, I think I should feel languidly benevolent if I had time. I have not time, because I am under a curious compulsion to occupy myself with the Irish melodies. 'Rich and rare were the gems she wore,' is the particular melody to which I find myself devoted. I sing it to myself in the most charming manner and with the greatest expression. Now and then, I raise my head (I am sitting on the hardest of wet seats, in the most uncomfortable of wet attitudes, but I don't mind it,) and notice that I am a whirling shuttlecock between a fiery battledore of a lighthouse on the French coast and a fiery battledore of a lighthouse on the English coast; but I don't notice it particularly, except to feel envenomed in my hatred of Calais. Then I go on again, 'Rich and rare were the ge-ems she-e-e-e wore, And a bright gold ring on her wa-and she bo-ore, But O her beauty was fa-a-a-a-r beyond' – I am particularly proud of my execution here, when I become aware of another awkward shock from the sea, and another protest from the funnel, and a fellow-creature at the paddle-box more audibly indisposed than I think he need be – 'Her sparkling gems or snow-white wand, But O her beauty was fa-a-a-a-r beyond' – another awkward one here, and the fellow-creature with the umbrella down and picked up – 'Her spa-a-rkling ge-ems, or her Port! port! steady! steady! snow-white fellow-creature at the paddle-box very selfishly audible, bump, roar, wash, white wand' (18: 'The Calais Night Mail').

One of my best beloved churchyards, I call the church-yard of Saint Ghastly Grim; touching what men in general call it, I have no information. It lies at the heart of the City, and the Blackwall Railway shrieks at it daily. It is a small small church-yard, with a ferocious strong spiked iron gate, like a jail. This gate is ornamented with skulls and cross-bones, larger than the life, wrought in stone; but it likewise came into the mind of Saint Ghastly Grim, that to stick iron spikes a-top of the stone skulls, as though they were impaled, would be a pleasant device. Therefore the skulls grin aloft horribly, thrust through and through with iron spears. Hence, there is attraction of repulsion for me in Saint Ghastly Grim, and, having often contemplated it in the daylight and the dark, I once felt drawn towards it in a thunderstorm at midnight. 'Why not?' I said, in self-excuse. 'I have been to see the Colosseum by the light of the moon; is it worse to go to see Saint Ghastly Grim by the light of the lightning?' I repaired to the Saint in a hackney cab, and found the skulls most effective, having the air of a public execution, and seeming, as the lightning

flashed, to wink and grin with the pain of the spikes. Having no other person to whom to impart my satisfaction, I communicated it to the driver. So far from being responsive, he surveyed me – he was naturally a bottle-nosed, red-faced man – with a blanched countenance. And as he drove me back, he ever and again glanced in over his shoulder through the little front window of his carriage, as mistrusting that I was a fare originally from a grave in the churchyard of Saint Ghastly Grim, who might have flitted home again without paying (23: 'The City of the Absent').

GREAT EXPECTATIONS

My father's family name being Pirrip, and my christian name Philip, my infant tongue could make of both names nothing longer or more explicit than Pip. So, I called myself Pip, and came to be called Pip.

I give Pirrip as my father's family name, on the authority of his tombstone and my sister – Mrs. Joe Gargery, who married the blacksmith. As I never saw my father or my mother, and never saw any likeness of either of them (for their days were long before the days of photographs), my first fancies regarding what they were like, were unreasonably derived from their tombstones. The shape of the letters on my father's, gave me an odd idea that he was a square, stout, dark man, with curly black hair. From the character and turn of the inscription, *'Also Georgiana Wife of the Above,'* I drew a childish conclusion that my mother was freckled and sickly. To five little stone lozenges, each about a foot and a half long, which were arranged in a neat row beside their grave, and were sacred to the memory of five little brothers of mine – who gave up trying to get a living exceedingly early in that universal struggle – I am indebted for a belief I religiously entertained that they had all been born on their backs with their hands in their trousers-pockets, and had never taken them out in this state of existence *(Chapter 1)*.

He gave me a most tremendous dip and roll, so that the church jumped over its own weather-cock. Then, he held me by the arms in an upright position on the top of the stone, and went on in these fearful terms:

'You bring me, to-morrow morning early, that file and them wittles. You bring the lot to me, at that old Battery over yonder. You do it, and you never dare to say a word or dare to make a sign concerning your having seen such a person as me, or any person sumever, and you shall be let to live. You fail, or you go from my words in any partickler, no matter how small it is, and your heart and your liver shall be tore out, roasted and ate. Now, I ain't alone, as you may think I am. There's a young man hid with me, in comparison with which young man I am a Angel. That young man hears the words I speak. That young man has a secret way pecooliar to himself, of getting at a boy, and at his heart, and at his liver. It is in wain for a boy to attempt to hide himself from that young man. A boy may lock his door, may be warm in bed, may tuck himself up, may draw the clothes over his head, may think himself comfortable and safe, but that young man will softly creep and creep his way to him and tear him open. I am keeping that young man from harming of you at the present moment, with great difficulty. I find it wery hard to hold that young man off of your inside. Now, what do you say?' (*Chapter 1: The Convict*).

'I have only been to the churchyard,' said I, from my stool, crying and rubbing myself.

'Churchyard!' repeated my sister. 'If it warn't for me you'd have been to the churchyard long ago, and stayed there. Who brought you up by hand?'

'You did,' said I.

'And why did I do it, I should like to know?' exclaimed my sister.

I whimpered, 'I don't know.'

'*I* don't!' said my sister. 'I'd never do it again! I know that. I may truly say I've never had this apron of mine off, since born you were. It's bad enough to be a blacksmith's wife (and him a Gargery), without being your mother' (*Chapter 2: Pip and Mrs. Gargery*).

I was never allowed a candle to light me to bed, and, as I went upstairs in the dark, with my head tingling – from Mrs. Joe's thimble having played the tambourine upon it, to accompany her last words – I felt fearfully sensible of the great convenience that the hulks were handy for me. I was clearly on my way there. I had begun by asking questions, and I was going to rob Mrs. Joe.

Since that time, which is far enough away now, I have often thought that few people know what secrecy there is in the young, under terror. No matter how unreasonable the terror, so that it be terror. I was in mortal terror of the young man who wanted my heart and liver; I was in mortal terror of my interlocutor with the iron leg; I was in mortal terror of myself, from whom an awful promise had been extracted; I had no hope of deliverance through my all-powerful sister, who repulsed me at every turn; I am afraid to think of what I might have done on requirement, in the secrecy of my terror (*Chapter 2: Pip*).

I was regaled with the scaly tips of the drumsticks of the fowls, and with those obscure corners of pork of which the pig, when living, had had the least reason to be vain (*Chapter 4: Pip*).

'Swine,' pursued Mr. Wopsle, in his deepest voice, and pointing his fork at my blushes, as if he were mentioning my christian name; 'Swine were the companions of the prodigal. The gluttony of Swine is put before us, as an example to the young.' (I thought this pretty well in him who had been praising up the pork for being so plump and juicy.) 'What is detestable in a pig, is more detestable in a boy.'

'Or girl,' suggested Mr. Hubble.

'Of course, or girl, Mr. Hubble,' assented Mr. Wopsle, rather irritably, 'but there is no girl present' (*Chapter 4*).

I think the Romans must have aggravated one another very much, with their noses. Perhaps, they became the restless people they were, in consequence. Anyhow, Mr. Wopsle's Roman nose so aggravated me, during the recital of my misdemeanours, that I should have liked to pull it until he howled (*Chapter 4:* Pip).

'Good stuff, eh, sergeant?' said Mr. Pumblechook.

'I'll tell you something,' returned the sergeant; 'I suspect that stuff's of *your* providing.'

Mr. Pumblechook, with a fat sort of laugh, said, 'Ay, ay? Why?'

'Because,' returned the sergeant, clapping him on the shoulder, 'you're a man that knows what's what.'

'D'ye think so?' said Mr. Pumblechook, with his former laugh. 'Have another glass!'

'With you. Hob and nob,' returned the sergeant. 'The top of mine to the foot of yours – the foot of yours to the top of mine – Ring once, ring twice – the best tune on the Musical Glasses! Your health. May you live a thousand years, and never be a worse judge of the right sort than you are at the present moment of your life!' (*Chapter 5*).

Mr. Wopsle's great-aunt kept an evening school in the village; that is to say, she was a ridiculous old woman of limited means and unlimited infirmity, who used to go to sleep from six to seven every evening, in the society of youth who paid twopence per week each, for the improving opportunity of seeing her do it. She rented a small cottage, and Mr. Wopsle had the room upstairs, where we students used to overhear him reading aloud in a most dignified and terrific manner, and occasionally bumping on the ceiling. There was a fiction that Mr. Wopsle 'examined' the scholars, once a quarter. What he did on those occasions was to turn up his cuffs, stick up his hair, and give us Mark Antony's oration over the body of Caesar. This was always followed by Collins's Ode on the Passions, wherein I particularly venerated Mr. Wopsle as Revenge, throwing his blood-stained sword in thunder down, and taking the War-denouncing trumpet with a withering look. It was not with me then, as it was in later life, when I fell into the society of the Passions, and compared them with Collins and Wopsle, rather to the disadvantage of both gentlemen (*Chapter 7*).

In an arm-chair, with an elbow resting on the table and her head leaning on that hand, sat the strangest lady I have ever seen, or shall ever see.

She was dressed in rich materials – satins, and lace, and silks – all of white. Her shoes were white. And she had a long white veil dependent from her hair, and she had bridal flowers in her hair, but her hair was white. Some bright jewels sparkled on her neck and on her hands, and some other jewels lay sparkling on the table. Dresses, less splendid than the dress she wore, and half-packed trunks, were scattered about. She had not quite finished dressing, for she had but one shoe on – the other was on the table near her hand – her veil was but half arranged, her watch and chain were not put on, and some lace for her bosom lay with those trinkets, and with her handkerchief, and gloves, and some flowers, and a Prayer-book, all confusedly heaped about the looking-glass.

It was not in the first few moments that I saw all these things, though I saw more of them in the first moments than might be supposed. But, I saw that everything within my view which ought to be white, had been white long ago, and had lost its lustre, and was faded and yellow. I saw that the bride within the bridal dress had withered like the dress, and like the flowers, and had no brightness left but the brightness of her sunken eyes. I saw that the dress had been put upon the rounded figure of a young woman, and that the figure upon which it now hung loose, had shrunk to skin and bone. Once, I had been taken to see some ghastly waxwork at the Fair, representing I know not what impossible personage lying in state. Once, I had been taken to one of our old marsh churches to see a skeleton in the ashes of a rich dress, that had been dug out of a vault under the church pavement. Now, waxwork and skeleton seemed to have dark eyes that moved and looked at me. I should have cried out, if I could (*Chapter 8:* Pip).

My sister's bringing up had made me sensitive. In the little world in which children have their existence, whosoever brings them up, there is nothing so finely perceived and so finely felt, as injustice. It may be only small injustice that the child can be exposed to; but the child is small, and its rocking-horse stands as many hands high, according to scale, as a big-boned Irish hunter (*Chapter 8:* Pip).

'Now, boy! What was she a doing of, when you went in to-day?' asked Mr. Pumblechook.

'She was sitting,' I answered, 'in a black velvet coach.'

Mr. Pumblechook and Mrs. Joe stared at one another – as they well might – and both repeated, 'In a black velvet coach?'

'Yes,' said I. 'And Miss Estella – that's her niece, I think – handed her in cake and wine at the coach-window, on a gold plate. And we all had cake and wine on gold plates. And I got up behind the coach to eat mine, because she told me to.'

'Was anybody else there?' asked Mr. Pumblechook.

'Four dogs,' said I.

'Large or small?'

'Immense,' said I. 'And they fought for veal cutlets out of a silver basket.'

Mr. Pumblechook and Mrs. Joe stared at one another again, in utter amazement. I was perfectly frantic – a reckless witness under the torture – and would have told them anything (*Chapter 9*).

'What did you play at, boy?'

'We played with flags,' I said. (I beg to observe that I think of myself with amazement, when I recall the lies I told on this occasion.)

Flags!' echoed my sister.

'Yes,' said I. 'Estella waved a blue flag, and I waved a red one, and Miss Havisham waved one sprinkled all over with little gold stars, out at the coach-window. And then we all waved our swords and hurrahed.'

'Swords!' repeated my sister. 'Where did you get swords from?'

'Out of a cupboard,' said I. 'And I saw pistols in it – and jam – and pills. And there was no daylight in the room, but it was all lighted up with candles' (*Chapter 9*).

That was a memorable day to me, for it made great changes in me. But it is the same with any life.

Imagine one selected day struck out of it, and think how different its course would have been. Pause you who read this, and think for a moment of the long chain of iron or gold, of thorns or flowers, that would never have bound you, but for the formation of the first link on one memorable day (*Chapter 9:* Pip).

'Poor soul!' Camilla presently went on . . .' he is so very strange! Would any one believe that when Tom's wife died, he actually could not be induced to see the importance of the children's having the deepest of trimmings to their mourning? "Good Lord!" says he, 'Camilla, what can it signify so long as the poor bereaved little things are in black?" So like Matthew! The idea!'

'Good points in him, good points in him,' said Cousin Raymond; 'Heaven forbid I should deny good points in him; but he never had, and he never will have, any sense of the proprieties.'

'You know I was obliged,' said Camilla, 'I was obliged to be firm. I said, "It WILL NOT DO, for the credit of the family." I told him that, without deep trimmings, the family was disgraced. I cried about it from breakfast till dinner. I injured my digestion. And at last he flung out in his violent way, and said, with a D, "Then do as you like." Thank Goodness it will always be a consolation to me to know that I instantly went out in a pouring rain and bought the things' (*Chapter 11*).

I crossed the staircase landing, and entered the room she indicated. From that room, too, the daylight was completely excluded, and it had an airless smell that was oppressive. A fire had been lately kindled in the damp old-fashioned grate, and it was more disposed to go out than to burn up, and the reluctant smoke which hung in the room seemed colder than the clearer air – like our own marsh mist. Certain wintry branches of candles on the high chimneypiece faintly lighted the chamber; or, it would be more expressive to say, faintly troubled its darkness. It was spacious, and I dare say had once been handsome, but every discernible thing in it was covered with dust and mould, and dropping to pieces. The most prominent object was a long table with a tablecloth spread on it, as if a feast had been in preparation when the house and the clocks all stopped together. An épergne or centre-piece of some kind was in the middle of this cloth; it was so heavily overhung with cobwebs that its form was quite undistinguishable; and, as I looked along the yellow expanse out of which I remember its seeming to grow, like a black fungus, I saw speckled-legged spiders with blotchy bodies running home to it, and running out from it, as if some circumstance of the greatest public importance had just transpired in the spider community.

I heard the mice too, rattling behind the panels, as if the same occurrence were important to their interests. But, the blackbeetles took no notice of the agitation, and groped about the hearth in a ponderous elderly way, as if they were short-sighted and hard of hearing, and not on terms with one another (*Chapter 11*).

'Why, what's the matter with you?' asked Miss Havisham, with exceeding sharpness.

'Nothing worth mentioning,' replied Camilla. 'I don't wish to make a display of my feelings, but I have habitually thought of you more in the night than I am quite equal to.'

'Then don't think of me,' retorted Miss Havisham.

'Very easily said!' remarked Camilla, amiably repressing a sob, while a hitch came into her upper lip, and her tears overflowed. 'Raymond is a witness what ginger and sal volatile I am obliged to take in the night. Raymond is a witness what nervous jerkings I have in my legs. Chokings and nervous jerkings, however, are nothing new to me when I think with anxiety of those I love. If I could be less affectionate and sensitive, I should have a better digestion and an iron set of nerves. I am sure I wish it could be so. But as to not thinking of you in the night – the idea!' (Chapter 11).

There was a song Joe used to hum fragments of at the forge, of which the burden was Old Clem. This was not a very ceremonious way of rendering homage to a patron saint; but I believe Old Clem stood in that relation towards smiths. It was a song that imitated the measure of beating upon iron, and was a mere lyrical excuse for the introduction of Old Clem's respected name. Thus, you were to hammer boys round – Old Clem! With a thump and a sound – Old Clem! Beat it out, beat it out – Old Clem! With a clink for the stout – Old Clem! Blow the fire, blow the fire – Old Clem! Roaring dryer, soaring higher – Old Clem! One day soon after the appearance of the chair, Miss Havisham suddenly saying to me, with the impatient movement of her fingers, 'There, there, there! Sing!' I was surprised into crooning this ditty as I pushed her over the floor (Chapter 12: Pip).

My only other remembrances of the great festival are, That they wouldn't let me go to sleep, but whenever they saw me dropping off, woke me up and told me to enjoy myself. That, rather late in the evening Mr. Wopsle gave us Collins's ode, and threw his blood-stain'd sword in thunder down, with such effect that a waiter came in and said, 'The Commercials underneath sent up their compliments, and it wasn't the Tumblers' Arms.' That, they were all in excellent spirits on the road home, and sang O Lady Fair! Mr. Wopsle taking the bass, and asserting with a tremendously strong voice (in reply to the inquisitive bore who leads that piece of music in a most impertinent manner, by wanting to know all about everybody's private affairs) that he was the man with his white locks flowing, and that he was upon the whole the weakest pilgrim going (Chapter 13).

A highly popular murder had been committed, and Mr. Wopsle was imbrued in blood to the eyebrows. He gloated over every abhorrent adjective in the description, and identified himself with every witness at the Inquest. He faintly moaned, 'I am done for,' as the victim, and he barbarously bellowed, 'I'll serve you out,' as the murderer. He gave the medical testimony, in pointed imitation of our local practitioner; and he piped and shook, as the aged turnpike-keeper who had heard blows, to an extent so very paralytic as to suggest a doubt regarding the mental competency of that witness. The coroner, in Mr. Wopsle's hands, became Timon of Athens; the beadle, Coriolanus. He enjoyed himself thoroughly, and we all enjoyed ourselves, and were delightfully comfortable. In this cozy state of mind we came to the verdict of Wilful Murder (Chapter 18).

Mr. Pumblechook helped me to the liver wing, and to the best slice of tongue (none of those out-of-the-way No Thoroughfares of Pork now), and took, comparatively speaking, no care of himself at all. 'Ah! poultry, poultry! You little thought,' said Mr. Pumblechook, apostrophising the fowl in the dish, 'when you was a young fledgling, what was in store for you. You little thought you was to be refreshment beneath this humble roof for one as – Call it a weakness, if you will,' said Mr. Pumblechook, getting up again, 'but may I? may I – ?'

It began to be unnecessary to repeat the form of saying he might, so he did it at once. How he ever did it so often without wounding himself with my knife, I don't know (Chapter 19).

I walked away at a good pace, thinking it was easier to go than I had supposed it would be, and reflecting that it would never have done to have an old shoe thrown after the coach, in sight of all the High Street. I whistled and made nothing of going. But the village was very peaceful and quiet, and the light mists were solemnly rising, as if to show me the world, and I had been so innocent and little there, and all beyond was so unknown and great, that in a moment with a strong heave and sob I broke into tears. It was by the finger-post at the end of the village, and I laid my hand upon it, and said, "Good-bye, O my dear, dear friend!'

Heaven knows we need never be ashamed of our tears, for they are rain upon the blinding dust of earth, overlying our hard hearts. I was better after I had cried, than before – more sorry, more aware of my own ingratitude, more gentle. If I had cried before, I should have had Joe with me then (Chapter 19: Pip).

There was a knot of three men and two women standing at a corner, and one of the women was crying on her dirty shawl, and the other comforted her by saying, as she pulled her own shawl over her shoulders, 'Jaggers is for him, 'Melia, and what more could you have?' There was a red-eyed little Jew who came into the Close while I was loitering there, in company with a second little Jew whom he sent upon an errand; and while the messenger was gone, I remarked this Jew, who was of a highly excitable temperament, performing a jig of anxiety under a lamp-post, and accompanying himself, in a kind of frenzy, with the words, 'Oh Jaggereth, Jaggereth, Jaggereth! all otherth ith Cag-Maggerth, give me Jaggerth!' (Chapter 20).

'Holy father, Mithter Jaggerth!' cried my excitable acquaintance, turning white, 'don't thay you're again Habraham Latharuth!'

'I am,' said Mr. Jaggers, 'and there's an end of it. Get out of the way.'

'Mithter Jaggerth! Half a moment! My hown cuthen'th gone to Mithter Wemmick at thith pre-

thenth minute to hoffer him hany termth. Mithter
Jaggerth! Half a quarter of a moment! If you'd have
the condethenthun to be bought off from the t'other
thide – at any thuperior prithe! – money no object! –
Mithter Jaggerth – Mithter – !'

My guardian threw his supplicant off with supreme
indifference, and left him dancing on the pavement as
if it were red-hot *(Chapter 20)*.

I informed him in exchange that my christian name
was Philip.

'I don't take to Philip,' said he, smiling, 'for it
sounds like a moral boy out of the spelling-book, who was
so lazy that he fell into a pond, or so fat that he couldn't
see out of his eyes, or so avaricious that he locked up his
cake till the mice ate it, or so determined to go a
bird's-nesting that he got himself eaten by bears who
lived handy in the neighbourhood. I tell you what I
should like. We are so harmonious, and you have been
a blacksmith – would you mind it?'

'I shouldn't mind anything that you propose,' I
answered, 'but I don't understand you.'

'Would you mind Handel for a familiar name?
There's a charming piece of music by Handel, called
the Harmonious Blacksmith' *(Chapter 22: Pip and
Herbert Pocket)*.

We had made some progress in the dinner, when I
reminded Herbert of his promise to tell me about Miss
Havisham.

'True,' he replied. 'I'll redeem it at once. Let me
introduce the topic, Handel, by mentioning that in
London it is not the custom to put the knife in the
mouth – for fear of accidents – and that while the
fork is reserved for that use, it is not put further in
than necessary. It is scarcely worth mentioning, only
it's as well to do as other people do. Also the spoon is
not generally used over-hand, but under. This has two
advantages. You get at your mouth better (which after
all is the object), and you save a good deal of the
attitude of opening oysters, on the part of the right
elbow' *(Chapter 22: Herbert Pocket)*.

'Take another glass of wine, and excuse my
mentioning that society as a body does not expect one
to be so strictly conscientious in emptying one's glass,
as to turn it bottom upwards with the rim on one's
nose.'

I had been doing this, in an excess of attention to
his recital. I thanked him and apologised. He said,
'Not at all,' and resumed *(Chapter 22: Herbert
Pocket)*.

To my unutterable amazement, I now, for the first
time, saw Mr. Pocket relieve his mind by going
through a performance that struck me as very extraordinary, but which made no impression on anybody
else, and with which I soon became as familiar as the
rest. He laid down the carving-knife and fork – being
engaged in carving at the moment – put his two hands
into his disturbed hair, and appeared to make an
extraordinary effort to lift himself up by it. When he
had done this, and had not lifted himself up at all, he
quietly went on with what he was about *(Chapter 23)*.

'This is a pretty thing, Belinda!' said Mr. Pocket,
returning with a countenance expressive of grief and
despair. 'Here's the cook lying insensibly drunk on the
kitchen floor, with a large bundle of fresh butter made
up in the cupboard ready to sell for grease!'

Mrs. Pocket instantly showed much amiable
emotion, and said, 'This is that odious Sophia's doing!'

'What do you mean, Belinda?' demanded Mr.
Pocket.

'Sophia has told you,' said Mrs. Pocket. 'Did I not
see her, with my own eyes, and hear her with my own
ears, come into the room just now and ask to speak to
you?'

'But has she not taken me downstairs, Belinda,'
returned Mr. Pocket, 'and shown me the woman, and
the bundle too?'

'And do you defend her, Matthew,' said Mrs.
Pocket, 'for making mischief?'

Mr. Pocket uttered a dismal groan.

'Am I, grandpapa's granddaughter, to be nothing in
the house?' said Mrs. Pocket. 'Besides, the cook has
always been a very nice respectful woman, and said in
the most natural manner when she came to look after
the situation, that she felt I was born to be a Duchess.'

There was a sofa where Mr. Pocket stood, and he
dropped upon it in the attitude of a Dying Gladiator.
Still in that attitude he said, with a hollow voice,
'Good-night, Mr. Pip,' when I deemed it advisable to
go to bed and leave him *(Chapter 23)*.

There came between me and them, the housekeeper,
with the first dish for the table.

She was a woman of about forty, I supposed – but I
may have thought her younger than she was. Rather
tall, of a lithe nimble figure, extremely pale, with large
faded eyes, and a quantity of streaming hair. I cannot
say whether any diseased affection of the heart caused
her lips to be parted as if she were panting, and her
face to bear a curious expression of suddenness and
flutter; but I know that I had been to see Macbeth at
the theatre, a night or two before, and that her face
looked to me as if it were all disturbed by fiery air, like
the faces I had seen rise out of the Witches' cauldron
(Chapter 22).

No other attendant than the housekeeper appeared.
She set on every dish; and I always saw in her face, a
face rising out of the caldron. Years afterwards, I
made a dreadful likeness of that woman, by causing a
face that had no other natural resemblance to it than
it derived from flowing hair, to pass behind a bowl of
flaming spirits in a dark room *(Chapter 26)*.

'And all friends is no backerder, if not no forarder.
'Ceptin' Wopsle: he's had a drop.'. . .

'Had a drop, Joe?'

'Why yes,' said Joe, lowering his voice, 'he's left the
Church and went into the playacting. Which the
playacting have likewise brought him to London along
with me. And his wish were,' said Joe, getting the
bird's-nest under his left arm for the moment, and
groping in it for an egg with his right; 'if no offence, as
I would 'and you that.'

I took what Joe gave me, and found it to be the
crumpled playbill of a small metropolitan theatre,
announcing the first appearance, in that very week, of
'the celebrated Provincial Amateur of Roscian

renown, whose unique performance in the highest tragic walk of our National Bard has lately occasioned so great a sensation in local dramatic circles.'

'Were you at his performance, Joe?' I inquired.

'I *were*,' said Joe, with emphasis and solemnity.

'Was there a great sensation?'

'Why,' said Joe, 'yes, there certainly were a peck of orange-peel. Partickler when he see the ghost. Though I put it to yourself, sir, whether it were calc'lated to keep a man up to his work with a good hart, to be continiwally cutting in betwixt him and the Ghost with "Amen!" A man may have had a misfortun' and been in the Church,' said Joe, lowering his voice to an argumentative and feeling tone, 'but that is no reason why you should put him out at such a time. Which I meantersay, if the ghost of a man's own father cannot be allowed to claim his attention, what can, Sir? Still more, when his mourning 'at is unfortunately made so small as that the weight of the black feathers brings it off, try to keep it on how you may' (*Chapter 27:* Joe Gargery).

'Have you seen anything of London, yet?'

'Why, yes, Sir,' said Joe, 'me and Wopsle went off straight to look at the Blacking Ware'us. But we didn't find that it come up to its likeness in the red bills at the shop doors: which I meantersay,' added Joe, in an explanatory manner, 'as it is there drawd too architectooralooral' (*Chapter 27:* Joe Gargery).

'Pip, dear old chap, life is made of ever so many partings welded together, as I may say, and one man's a blacksmith, and one's a whitesmith, and one's a goldsmith, and one's a coppersmith. Diwisions among such must come, and must be met as they come' (*Chapter 27:* Joe Gargery).

All other swindlers upon earth are nothing to the self-swindlers, and with such pretences did I cheat myself. Surely a curious thing. That I should innocently take a bad half-crown of somebody else's manufacture, is reasonable enough; but that I should knowingly reckon the spurious coin of my own make, as good money! An obliging stranger, under pretence of compactly folding up my banknotes for security's sake, abstracts the notes and gives me nutshells; but what is his sleight of hand to mine, when I fold up my own nutshells and pass them on myself as notes! (*Chapter 28*).

Estella being gone and we two left alone, she turned to me and said in a whisper:

'Is she beautiful, graceful, well-grown? Do you admire her?'

'Everybody must who sees her, Miss Havisham.'

She drew an arm round my neck, and drew my head close down to hers as she sat in the chair. 'Love her, love her, love her! How does she use you?'

Before I could answer (if I could have answered so difficult a question at all), she repeated, 'Love her, love her, love her! If she favours you, love her. If she wounds you, love her. If she tears your heart to pieces – and as it gets older and stronger it will tear deeper – love her, love her, love her!'

Never had I seen such passionate eagerness as was joined to her utterance of these words. I could feel the muscles of the thin arm round my neck, swell with the vehemence that possessed her.

'Hear me, Pip! I adopted her to be loved. I bred her and educated her, to be loved. I developed her into what she is, that she might be loved. Love her!' (*Chapter 29*).

Casting my eyes along the street at a certain point of my progress, I beheld Trabb's boy approaching, lashing himself with an empty blue bag. Deeming that a serene and unconscious contemplation of him would best beseem me, and would be most likely to quell his evil mind, I advanced with that expression of countenance, and was rather congratulating myself on my success, when suddenly the knee of Trabb's boy smote together, his hair uprose, his cap fell off, he trembled violently in every limb, staggered out into the road, and crying to the populace, 'Hold me! I'm so frightened!' feigned to be in a paroxysm of terror and contrition, occasioned by the dignity of my appearance. As I passed him, his teeth loudly chattered in his head, and with every mark of extreme humiliation, he prostrated himself in the dust (*Chapter 30*).

'May I ask you if you have ever had an opportunity of remarking, down in your part of the country, that the children of not exactly suitable marriages, are always most particularly anxious to be married?'

This was such a singular question, that I asked him, in return, 'Is it so?'

'I don't know,' said Herbert; 'that's what I want to know. Because it is decidedly the case with us. My poor sister Charlotte who was next me and died before she was fourteen, was a striking example. Little Jane is the same. In her desire to be matrimonially established, you might suppose her to have passed her short existence in the perpetual contemplation of domestic bliss. Little Alick in a frock has already made arrangements for his union with a suitable young person at Kew. And, indeed, I think we are all engaged, except the baby' (*Chapter 30:* Herbert Pocket).

A folded piece of paper . . . attracting my attention, I opened it and found it to be the playbill I had received from Joe, relative to the celebrated provincial amateur of Roscian renown. 'And bless my heart,' I involuntarily added aloud, 'it's to-night!'. . . .

On our arrival in Denmark, we found the king and queen of that country elevated in two arm-chairs on a kitchen-table, holding a Court. The whole of the Danish nobility were in attendance; consisting of a noble boy in the wash-leather boots of a gigantic ancestor, a venerable Peer with a dirty face, who seemed to have risen from the people late in life, and the Danish chivalry with a comb in its hair and a pair of white silk legs, and presenting on the whole a feminine appearance. My gifted townsman stood gloomily apart, with folded arms, and I could have wished that his curls and forehead had been more probable.

Several curious little circumstances transpired as the action proceeded. The late king of the country not only appeared to have been troubled with a cough at the time of his decease, but to have taken it with him to the tomb, and to have brought it back. The royal phantom also carried a ghostly manuscript round its truncheon, to which it had the appearance of occasionally referring, and that, too, with an air of anxiety and a tendency to lose the place of reference which were suggestive of a state of mortality. It was this, I conceive, which led to the Shade's being advised by the gallery to 'turn over!' – a recommendation which it took extremely ill. It was likewise to be noted of this majestic spirit that whereas it always appeared with an air of having been out a long time and walked an immense distance, it perceptibly came from a closely-contiguous wall. This occasioned its terrors to be received derisively. The Queen of Denmark, a very buxom lady, though no doubt historically brazen, was considered by the public to have too much brass about her; her chin being attached to her diadem by a broad band of that metal (as if she had a gorgeous tooth-ache), her waist being encircled by another, and each of her arms by another, so that she was openly mentioned as 'the kettle-drum.' The noble boy in the ancestral boots, was inconsistent; representing himself, as it were in one breath, as an able seaman, a strolling actor, a grave-digger, a clergyman, and a person of the utmost importance at a Court fencing-match, on the authority of whose practised eye and nice discrimination the finest strokes were judged. This gradually led to a want of toleration for him, and even – on his being detected in holy orders, and declining to perform the funeral service – to the general indignation taking the form of nuts. Lastly, Ophelia was a prey to such slow musical madness, that when, in course of time, she had taken off her white muslin scarf, folded it up, and buried it, a sulky man who had been long cooling his impatient nose against an iron bar in the front row of the gallery, growled, 'Now the baby's put to bed, let's have supper!' Which, to say the least of it, was out of keeping.

Upon my unfortunate townsman all these incidents accumulated with playful effect. Whenever that undecided Prince had to ask a question or state a doubt, the public helped him out with it. As for example; on the question whether 'twas nobler in the mind to suffer, some roared yes, and some no, and some inclining to both opinions said 'toss up for it'; and quite a Debating Society arose. When he asked what should such fellows as he do crawling between earth and heaven, he was encouraged with loud cries of 'Hear, hear!' When he appeared with his stocking disordered (its disorder expressed, according to usage, by one very neat fold in the top, which I suppose to be always got up with a flat iron), a conversation took place in the gallery respecting the paleness of his leg, and whether it was occasioned by the turn the ghost had given him. On his taking the recorders – very like a little black flute that had just been played in the orchestra and handed out at the door – he was called upon unanimously for Rule Britannia. When he recommended the player not to saw the air thus, the sulky man said, 'And don't *you* do it, neither; you're a deal worse than *him*!' And I grieve to add that peals of laughter greeted Mr. Wopsle on every one of these occasions.

But his greatest trials were in the churchyard: which had the appearance of a primeval forest, with a

kind of small ecclesiastical wash-house on one side, and a turnpike gate on the other. Mr. Wopsle, in a comprehensive black cloak, being descried entering at the turnpike, the gravedigger was admonished in a friendly way, 'Look out! Here's the undertaker a coming, to see how you're getting on with your work!' I believe it is well known in a constitutional country that Mr. Wopsle could not possibly have returned the skull, after moralising over it, without dusting his fingers on a white napkin taken from his breast; but even that innocent and indispensable action did not pass without the comment 'Wai-ter!' The arrival of the body for interment (in an empty black box with the lid tumbling open), was the signal for a general joy which was much enhanced by the discovery, among the bearers, of an individual obnoxious to identification. The joy attended Mr. Wopsle through his struggle with Laertes on the brink of the orchestra and the grave, and slackened no more until he had tumbled the king off the kitchen-table, and had died by inches from the ankles upwards *(Chapter 30–1)*.

I requested a waiter who had been staring at the coach like a man who had never seen such a thing in his life, to show us a private sitting-room. Upon that, he pulled out a napkin, as if it were a magic clue without which he couldn't find the way upstairs, and led us to the black hole of the establishment: fitted up with a diminishing mirror (quite a superfluous article considering the whole's proportions), an anchovy sauce-cruet, and somebody's pattens. On my objecting to this retreat, he took us into another room with a dinner-table for thirty, and in the grate a scorched leaf of a copy-book under a bushel of coal-dust. Having looked at this extinct conflagration and shaken his head, he took my order: which, proving to be merely 'Some tea for the lady,' sent him out of the room in a very low state of mind.

I was, and I am, sensible that the air of this chamber, in its strong combination of stable with soup-stock, might have led one to infer that the coaching department was not doing well, and that the enterprising proprietor was boiling down the horses for the refreshment department *(Chapter 33)*.

We came to Richmond all too soon, and our destination there, was a house by the Green: a staid old house, where hoops and powder and patches, embroidered coats, rolled stockings, ruffles, and swords, had had their court days many a time. Some ancient trees before the house were still cut into fashions as formal and unnatural as the hoops and wigs and stiff skirts; but their own allotted places in the great procession of the dead were not far off, and they would soon drop into them and go the silent way of the rest.

A bell with an old voice – which I dare say in its time had often said to the house, Here is the green farthingale, Here is the diamond-hilted sword, Here are the shoes with red heels and the blue solitaire, – sounded gravely in the moonlight, and two cherry-coloured maids came fluttering out to receive Estella *(Chapter 33)*.

At Startop's suggestion, we put ourselves down for election into a club called the Finches of the Grove:

the object of which institution I have never divined, if it were not that the members should dine expensively once a fortnight, to quarrel among themselves as much as possible after dinner, and to cause six waiters to get drunk on the stairs. I know that these gratifying social ends were so invariably accomplished, that Herbert and I understood nothing else to be referred to in the first standing toast of the society: which ran, 'Gentlemen, may the present promotion of good feeling ever reign predominant among the Finches of the Grove' (*Chapter 34*).

I came within sight of the house, and saw that Trabb and Co. had put in a funereal execution and taken possession. Two dismally absurd persons, each ostentatiously exhibiting a crutch done up in a black bandage – as if that instrument could possibly communicate any comfort to anybody – were posted at the front door; and in one of them I recognised a postboy discharged from the Boar for turning a young couple into a sawpit on their bridal morning in consequence of intoxication rendering it necessary for him to ride his horse clasped round the neck with both arms. All the children of the village, and most of the women, were admiring these sable warders and the closed windows of the house and forge; and as I came up, one of the two warders (the postboy) knocked at the door – implying that I was far too much exhausted by grief, to have strength remaining to knock for myself.

Another sable warder (a carpenter, who had once eaten two geese for a wager) opened the door, and showed me into the best parlour. Here, Mr. Trabb had taken unto himself the best table, and had got all the leaves up, and was holding a kind of black Bazaar, with the aid of a quantity of black pins. At the moment of my arrival, he had just finished putting somebody's hat into black long-clothes, like an African baby; so he held out his hand for mine. But I, misled by the action, and confused by the occasion, shook hands with him with every testimony of warm affection (*Chapter 35: Pip*).

'Pocket-handkerchiefs out, all!' cried Mr. Trabb at this point, in a depressed business-like voice – 'Pocket-handkerchiefs out! We are ready!'

So, we all put our pocket-handkerchiefs to our faces, as if our noses were bleeding, and filed out two and two; Joe and I; Biddy and Pumblechook; Mr. and Mrs. Hubble. The remains of my poor sister had been brought round by the kitchen door, and, it being a point of Undertaking ceremony that the six bearers must be stifled and blinded under a horrible black velvet housing with a white border, the whole looked like a blind monster with twelve human legs, shuffling and blundering along under the guidance of two keepers – the postboy and his comrade (*Chapter 35*).

'Mr. Pip,' said Wemmick, 'I should like just to run over with you on my fingers, if you please, the names of the various bridges up as high as Chelsea Reach. Let's see; there's London, one; Southwark, two; Blackfriars, three; Waterloo, four; Westminster, five; Vauxhall, six.' He had checked off each bridge in its turn, with the handle of his safe-key on the palm of his hand. 'There's as many as six, you see, to choose from.'

'I don't understand you,' said I.

'Choose your bridge, Mr. Pip,' returned Wemmick, 'and take a walk upon your bridge, and pitch your money into the Thames over the centre arch of your bridge, and you know the end of it. Serve a friend with it, and you may know the end of it too – but it's a less pleasant and profitable end.'

I could have posted a newspaper in his mouth, he made it so wide after saying this.

'This is very discouraging,' said I.

'Meant to be so,' said Wemmick.

'Then is it your opinion,' I inquired, with some little indignation, 'that a man should never – '

'– Invest portable property in a friend?' said Wemmick. 'Certainly he should not. Unless he wants to get rid of the friend – and then it becomes a question how much portable property it may be worth to get rid of him' (*Chapter 36*).

Miss Skiffins was of a wooden appearance, and was, like her escort, in the post-office branch of the service. She might have been some two or three years younger than Wemmick, and I judged her to stand possessed of portable property. The cut of her dress from the waist upward, both before and behind, made her figure very like a boy's kite; and I might have pronounced her gown a little too decidedly orange, and her gloves a little too intensely green. But she seemed to be a good sort of fellow, and showed a high regard for the Aged. I was not long in discovering that she was a frequent visitor at the Castle; for, on our going in, and my complimenting Wemmick on his ingenious contrivance for announcing himself to the Aged, he begged me to give my attention for a moment to the other side of the chimney, and disappeared. Presently another click came, and another little door tumbled open with 'Miss Skiffins' on it; then Miss Skiffins shut up and John tumbled open; then Miss Skiffins and John both tumbled open together, and finally shut up together. On Wemmick's return from working these mechanical appliances, I expressed the great admiration with which I regarded them, and he said, 'Well, you know, they're both pleasant and useful to the Aged. And by George, sir, it's a thing worth mentioning, that of all the people who come to this gate, the secret of those pulls is only known to the Aged, Miss Skiffins, and me!' (*Chapter 37*).

We returned into the Castle, where we found Miss Skiffins preparing tea. The responsible duty of making the toast was delegated to the Aged, and that excellent old gentleman was so intent upon it that he seemed to be in some danger of melting his eyes. It was no nominal meal that we were going to make, but a vigorous reality. The Aged prepared such a haystack of buttered toast, that I could scarcely see him over it as it simmered on an iron stand hooked on to the top-bar; while Miss Skiffins brewed such a jorum of tea, that the pig in the back premises became strongly excited, and repeatedly expressed his desire to participate in the entertainment (*Chapter 37*).

Wemmick explained to me while the Aged got his spectacles out, that this was according to custom, and that it gave the old gentleman infinite satisfaction to read the news aloud. 'I won't offer an apology,' said Wemmick, 'for he isn't capable of many pleasures – are you, Aged P.?'

'All right, John, all right,' returned the old man, seeing himself spoken to.

'Only tip him a nod every now and then when he looks off his paper,' said Wemmick, 'and he'll be as happy as a king. We are all attention, Aged One.'

'All right, John, all right!' returned the cheerful old man: so busy and so pleased, that it really was quite charming.

The Aged's reading reminded me of the classes at Mr. Wopsle's great-aunt's, with pleasanter peculiarity that it seemed to come through a keyhole. As he wanted the candles close to him, and as he was always on the verge of putting either his head or the newspaper into them, he required as much watching as a powder-mill. But Wemmick was equally untiring and gentle in his vigilance, and the Aged read on, quite unconscious of his many rescues. Whenever he looked at us, we all expressed the greatest interest and amazement, and nodded until he resumed again.

As Wemmick and Miss Skiffins sat side by side, and as I sat in a shadowy corner, I observed a slow and gradual elongation of Mr. Wemmick's mouth, powerfully suggestive of his slowly and gradually stealing his arm round Miss Skiffins's waist. In course of time I saw his hand appear on the other side of Miss Skiffins; but at that moment Miss Skiffins neatly stopped him with the green glove, unwound his arm again as if it were an article of dress, and with the greatest deliberation laid it on the table before her. Miss Skiffins's composure while she did this was one of the most remarkable sights I have ever seen, and if I could have thought the act consistent with abstraction of mind, I should have deemed that Miss Skiffins performed it mechanically.

By and by, I noticed Wemmick's arm beginning to disappear again, and gradually fading out of view. Shortly afterwards his mouth began to widen again. After an interval of suspense on my part that was quite enthralling and almost painful, I saw his hand appear on the other side of Miss Skiffins. Instantly, Miss Skiffins stopped it with the neatness of a placid boxer, took off that girdle or cestus as before, and laid it on the table. Taking the table to represent the path of virtue, I am justified in stating that during the whole time of the Aged's reading, Wemmick's arm was straying from the path of virtue and being recalled to it by Miss Skiffins *(Chapter 37)*.

In the Eastern story, the heavy slab that was to fall on the bed of state in the flush of conquest was slowly wrought out of the quarry, the tunnel for the rope to hold it in its place was slowly carried through the leagues of rock, the slab was slowly raised and fitted in the roof, the rope was rove to it and slowly taken through the miles of hollow to the great iron ring. All being made ready with much labour, and the hour come, the sultan was aroused in the dead of the night, and the sharpened axe that was to sever the rope from the great iron ring was put into his hand, and he struck with it, and the rope parted and rushed away,

and the ceiling fell. So, in my case; all the work, near and afar, that tended to the end, had been accomplished; and in an instant the blow was struck, and the roof of my stronghold dropped upon me *(Chapter 39)*.

He ate in a ravenous way that was very disagreeable, and all his actions were uncouth, noisy, and greedy. Some of his teeth had failed him since I saw him eat on the marshes, and as he turned his food in his mouth, and turned his head sideways to bring his strongest fangs to bear upon it, he looked terribly like a hungry old dog.

If I had begun with any appetite, he would have taken it away, and I should have sat much as I did – repelled from him by an insurmountable aversion, and gloomily looking at the cloth.

'I'm a heavy grubber, dear boy,' he said, as a polite kind of apology when he had made an end of his meal, 'but I always was. If it had been in my constitution to be a lighter grubber, I might ha' got into lighter trouble. Similarly, I must have my smoke. When I was first hired out as a shepherd t'other side the world, it's my belief I should ha' turned into a molloncolly-mad sheep myself, if I hadn't a had my smoke' *(Chapter 40: Magwitch)*.

As he was at present dressed in a seafaring slop suit, in which he looked as if he had some parrots and cigars to dispose of, I next discussed with him what dress he should wear. He cherished an extraordinary belief in the virtues of 'shorts' as a disguise, and had in his own mind sketched a dress for himself that would have made him something between a dean and a dentist *(Chapter 40)*.

'Not a particle of evidence, Pip,' said Mr. Jaggers, shaking his head and gathering up his skirts. 'Take nothing on its looks; take everything on evidence. There's no better rule' *(Chapter 40)*.

The influences of his solitary hut-life were upon him besides, and gave him a savage air that no dress could tame; added to these were the influences of his subsequent branded life among men, and, crowning all, his consciousness that he was dodging and hiding now. In all his ways of sitting and standing, and eating and drinking – of brooding about, in a high-shouldered reluctant style – of taking out his great horn-handled jack-knife and wiping it on his legs and cutting his food – of lifting light glasses and cups to his lips, as if they were clumsy pannikins – of chopping a wedge off his bread, and soaking up with it the last fragments of gravy round and round his plate, as if to make the most of an allowance, and then drying his fingers on it, and then swallowing it – in these ways and a thousand other small nameless instances arising every minute in the day, there was Prisoner, Felon, Bondsman, plain as plain could be *(Chapter 40)*.

'Arthur lived at the top of Compeyson's house (over nigh Brentford it was), and Compeyson kept a careful account agen him for board and lodging, in case he should ever get better to work it out. But Arthur soon settled the account. The second or third time as ever I see him, he come a tearing down into Compeyson's parlour late at night, in only a flannel gown, with his hair all in a sweat, and he says to Compeyson's wife, "Sally, she really is upstairs alonger me, now, and I can't get rid of her. She's all in white," he says, "wi' white flowers in her hair, and she's awful mad, and she's got a shroud hanging over her arm, and she says she'll put it on me at five in the morning."

Says Compeyson: "Why, you fool, don't you know she's got a living body? And how should she be up there, without coming through the door, or in at the window, and up the stairs?"

' "I don't know how she's there," says Arthur, shivering dreadful with the horrors, "but she's standing in the corner at the foot of the bed, awful mad. And over where her heart's broke – *you* broke it! – there's drops of blood."

'Compeyson spoke hardy, but he was always a coward. "Go up alonger this drivelling sick man," he says to his wife, "and, Magwitch, lend her a hand, will you?" But he never come nigh himself.

'Compeyson's wife and me took him up to bed agen, and he raved most dreadful. "Why look at her!" he cried out. "She's a shaking the shroud at me! Don't you see her? Look at her eyes! Ain't it awful to see her so mad?" Next, he cries, "She'll put it on me, and then I'm done for! Take it away from her, take it away!" And then he catched hold of us, and kep on a talking to her, and answering of her, till I half-believed I see her myself.

'Compeyson's wife, being used to him, gave him some liquor to get the horrors off, and by and by he quieted. "Oh, she's gone! Has her keeper been for her?" he says. "Yes," says Compeyson's wife. "Did you tell him to lock and bar her in?" "Yes." "And to take that ugly thing away from her?" "Yes, yes, all right." "You're a good creetur," he says, "don't leave me, whatever you do, and thank you!"

'He rested pretty quiet till it might want a few minutes of five, and then he starts up with a scream, and screams out, "Here she is! She's got the shroud again. She's unfolding it. She's coming out of the corner. She's coming to the bed. Hold me, both on you – one of each side – don't let her touch me with it. Hah! She missed me that time. Don't let her throw it over my shoulders. Don't let her lift me up to get it round me. She's lifting me up. Keep me down!" Then he lifted himself up hard, and was dead' (*Chapter 42:* Magwitch).

'Nonsense,' she returned, 'nonsense. This will pass in no time.'

'Never, Estella!'

'You will get me out of your thoughts in a week.'

'Out of my thoughts! You are part of my existence, part of myself. You have been in every line I have ever read, since I first came here, the rough common boy whose poor heart you wounded even then. You have been in every prospect I have ever seen since – on the river, on the sails of the ships, on the marshes, in the clouds, in the light, in the darkness, in the wind, in the woods, in the sea, in the streets. You have been the embodiment of every graceful fancy that my mind has ever become acquainted with. The stones of which the strongest London buildings are made, are not more real, or more impossible to be displaced by your hands,

than your presence and influence have been to me, there and everywhere, and will be. Estella, to the last hour of my life, you cannot choose but remain part of my character, part of the little good in me, part of the evil. But, in this separation I associate you only with the good, and I will faithfully hold you to that always, for you must have done me far more good than harm, let me feel now what sharp distress I may. O God bless you, God forgive you!' (*Chapter 44:* Pip).

Suddenly the growl swelled into a roar again, and a frightful bumping noise was heard above, as if a giant with a wooden leg were trying to bore it through the ceiling to come at us. Upon this Clara said to Herbert, 'Papa wants me, darling!' and ran away.

'There is an unconscionable old shark for you!' said Herbert. 'What do you suppose he wants now, Handel?'

'I don't know,' said I. 'Something to drink?'

'That's it!' cried Herbert, as if I had made a guess of extraordinary merit. 'He keeps his grog ready-mixed in a little tub on the table. Wait a moment, and you'll hear Clara lift him up to take some. – There he goes!' Another roar, with a prolonged shake at the end. 'Now,' said Herbert, as it was succeeded by silence, 'he's drinking. Now,' said Herbert, as the growl resounded in the beam once more, 'he's down again on his back!'

Clara returned soon afterwards, and Herbert accompanied me upstairs to see our charge. As we passed Mr. Barley's door, he was heard hoarsely muttering within, in a strain that rose and fell like wind, the following Refrain; in which I substitute good wishes for something quite the reverse.

'Ahoy! Bless your eyes, here's old Bill Barley. Here's old Bill Barley, bless your eyes. Here's old Bill Barley on the flat of his back, by the Lord. Lying on the flat of his back, like a drifting old dead flounder, here's your old Bill Barley, bless your eyes. Ahoy! Bless you' (*Chapter 46:* Clara Barley and Herbert Pocket).

I was aware that Mr. Wopsle had not succeeded in reviving the Drama, but, on the contrary, had rather partaken of its decline. He had been ominously heard of, through the playbills, as a faithful Black, in connection with a little girl of noble birth, and a monkey. And Herbert had seen him as a predatory Tartar, of comic propensities, with a face like a red brick, and an outrageous hat all over bells.

I dined at what Herbert and I used to call a Geographical chop-house – where there were maps of the world in porter-pot rims on every half-yard of the tablecloths, and charts of gravy on every one of the knives – to this day there is scarcely a single chop-house within the Lord Mayor's dominions which is not Geographical – and wore out the time in dozing over crumbs, staring at gas, and baking in a hot blast of dinners. By-and-by, I roused myself and went to the play.

There, I found a virtuous boatswain in his Majesty's service – a most excellent man, though I could have wished his trousers not quite so tight in some places and not quite so loose in others – who knocked all the little men's hats over their eyes, though he was very generous and brave, and who wouldn't hear of anybody's paying taxes, though he was very patriotic. He had a bag of money in his pocket, like a pudding in the cloth, and on that property married a young person in bed-furniture, with great rejoicings; the whole population of Portsmouth (nine in number at the last Census) turning out on the beach, to rub their own hands and shake everybody else's, and sing, 'Fill, fill!' A certain dark-complexioned Swab, however, who wouldn't fill, or do anything else that was proposed to him, and whose heart was openly stated (by the boatswain) to be as black as his figure-head, proposed to two other Swabs to get all mankind into difficulties; which was so effectually done (the Swab family having considerable political influence) that it took half the evening to set things right, and then it was only brought about through an honest little grocer with a white hat, black gaiters, and red nose, getting into a clock, with a gridiron, and listening, and coming out, and knocking everybody down from behind with the gridiron whom he couldn't confute with what he had overheard. This led to Mr. Wopsle's (who had never been heard of before) coming in with a star and garter on, as a plenipotentiary of great power direct from the Admiralty, to say that the Swabs were all to go to prison on the spot, and that he had brought the boatswain down the Union Jack, as a slight acknowledgment of his public services. The boatswain, unmanned for the first time, respectfully dried his eyes on the Jack, and then cheering up and addressing Mr. Wopsle as Your Honour, solicited permission to take him by the fin. Mr. Wopsle conceding his fin with a gracious dignity, was immediately shoved into a dusty corner while everybody danced a hornpipe (*Chapter 47*).

I looked into the room where I had left her, and I saw her seated in the ragged chair upon the hearth close to the fire, with her back towards me. In the moment when I was withdrawing my head to go quietly away, I saw a great flaming light spring up. In the same moment I saw her running at me, shrieking, with a whirl of fire blazing all about her, and soaring at least as many feet above her head as she was high.

I had a double-caped great-coat on, and over my arm another thick coat. That I got them off, closed with her, threw her down, and got them over her; that I dragged the great cloth from the table for the same purpose, and with it dragged down the heap of rottenness in the midst, and all the ugly things that sheltered there; that we were on the ground struggling like desperate enemies, and that the closer I covered her, the more wildly she shrieked and tried to free herself; that this occurred I knew through the result, but not through anything I felt, or thought, or knew I did. I knew nothing until I knew that we were on the floor by the great table, and that patches of tinder yet alight were floating in the smoky air, which a moment ago had been her faded bridal dress.

Then, I looked round and saw the disturbed beetles and spiders running away over the floor, and the servants coming in with breathless cries at the door. I still held her forcibly down with all my strength, like a prisoner who might escape; and I doubt if I even knew who she was, or why we had struggled, or that she had been in flames, or that the flames were out, until I saw the patches of tinder that had been her garments, no longer alight, but falling in a black shower around us (*Chapter 49:* Pip and Miss Havisham).

Punctual to my appointment, I rang at the Castle gate on the Monday morning, and was received by Wemmick himself: who struck me as looking tighter than usual, and having a sleeker hat on. Within, there were two glasses of rum-and-milk prepared, and two biscuits. The Aged must have been stirring with the lark, for, glancing into the perspective of his bedroom, I observed that his bed was empty.

When we had fortified ourselves with the rum-and-milk and biscuits, and were going out for the walk with that training preparation on us, I was considerably surprised to see Wemmick take up a fishing-rod, and put it over his shoulder. 'Why, we are not going fishing!' said I. 'No,' returned Wemmick, 'but I like to walk with one.'

I thought this odd: however, I said nothing, and we set off. We went towards Camberwell Green, and when we were thereabouts, Wemmick said suddenly:

'Halloa! Here's a church!'

There was nothing very surprising in that; but again, I was rather surprised, when he said, as if he were animated by a brilliant idea:

'Let's go in!'

We went in, Wemmick leaving his fishing-rod in the porch, and looked all round. In the mean time, Wemmick was diving into his coat-pockets, and getting something out of paper there.

'Halloa!' said he. 'Here's a couple of pair of gloves! Let's put 'em on!'

As the gloves were white kid gloves, and as the post-office was widened to its utmost extent, I now began to have my strong suspicions. They were strengthened into certainty when I beheld the Aged enter at a side door, escorting a lady.

'Halloa!' said Wemmick. 'Here's Miss Skiffins! Let's have a wedding.'

That discreet damsel was attired as usual, except that she was now engaged in substituting for her green kid gloves, a pair of white. The Aged was likewise occupied in preparing a similar sacrifice for the altar of Hymen. The old gentleman, however, experienced so much difficulty in getting his gloves on, that Wemmick found it necessary to put him with his back against a pillar, and then to get behind the pillar himself and pull away at them, while I for my part held the old gentleman round the waist, that he might present an equal and safe resistance. By dint of this ingenious scheme, his gloves were got on to perfection.

The clerk and clergyman then appearing, we were ranged in order at those fatal rails. True to his notion of seeming to do it all without preparation, I heard Wemmick say to himself as he took something out of his waistcoat-pocket before the service began, 'Halloa! Here's a ring!' (*Chapter 55*).

Not to make Joe uneasy by talking too much, even if I had been able to talk much, I deferred asking him about Miss Havisham until next day. He shook his head when I then asked him if she had recovered?

'Is she dead, Joe?'

'Why, you see, old chap,' said Joe, in a tone of remonstrance, and by way of getting at it by degrees, 'I wouldn't go so far as to say that, for that's a deal to say; but she ain't – '

'Living, Joe?'

'That's nigher where it is,' said Joe; 'she ain't living' (*Chapter 57:* Joe Gargery and Pip).

'Miss Sarah,' said Joe, 'she have twenty-five pound perannium fur to buy pills, on account of being bilious. Miss Georgiana, she have twenty pound down. Mrs. – what's the name of them wild beasts with humps, old chap?'

'Camels?' said I, wondering why he could possibly want to know.

Joe nodded. 'Mrs. Camels,' by which I presently understood he meant Camilla, 'she have five pound fur to buy rushlights to put her in spirits when she wake up in the night' (*Chapter 57:* Joe Gargery).

'Old Orlick he's been a bustin' open a dwelling-ouse.'

'Whose?' said I.

'Not, I grant you, but what his manners is given to blusterous,' said Joe, apologetically; 'still, a English-man's ouse is his Castle, and castles must not be busted 'cept when done in war time. And wotsume'er the failings on his part, he were a corn and seedsman in his hart.'

'Is it Pumblechook's house that has been broken into, then?'

'That's it, Pip,' said Joe; 'and they took his till, and they took his cash-box, and they drinked his wine, and they partook of his wittles, and they slapped his face, and they pulled his nose, and they tied him up to his bedpust, and they giv' him a dozen, and they stuffed his mouth full of flowering annuals to perwent his crying out. But he knowed Orlick, and Orlick's in the county jail' (*Chapter 57:* Joe Gargery).

'Lord! To think of your poor sister and her Ramp-ages! And don't you remember Tickler?'

'I do indeed, Joe.'

'Look 'ee here, old chap,' said Joe. 'I done what I could to keep you and Tickler in sunders, but my power were not always fully equal to my inclinations. For when your poor sister had a mind to drop into you, it were not so much,' said Joe, in his favourite argumentative way, 'that she dropped into me too, if I put myself in opposition to her, but that she dropped into you always heavier for it. I noticed that. It ain't a grab at a man's whisker, nor yet a shake or two of a man (to which your sister was quite welcome), that 'ud put a man off from getting a little child out of punishment. But when that little child is dropped into, heavier, for that grab of whisker or shaking, then that man naterally up and says to himself, "Where is the good as you are a doing? I grant you I see the 'arm," says the man, "but I don't see the good. I call upon you, sir, therefore, to pint out the good."'

'The man says?' I observed, as Joe waited for me to speak.

'The man says,' Joe assented. 'Is he right, that man?'

'Dear Joe, he is always right' (*Chapter 57:* Joe Gargery and Pip).

'Hah!' he went on, handing me the bread-and-butter. 'And air you a-going to Joseph?'

'In Heaven's name,' said I, firing in spite of myself, 'what does it matter to you where I am going? Leave that teapot alone.'

It was the worst course I could have taken, because it gave Pumblechook the opportunity he wanted.

'Yes, young man,' said he, releasing the handle of the article in question, retiring a step or two from my table, and speaking for the behoof of the landlord and waiter at the door, 'I *will* leave that teapot alone. You are right, young man. For once, you are right. I forgit myself when I take such an interest in your breakfast, as to wish your frame, exhausted by the debilitating effects of prodigygality, to be stimilated by the 'olesome nourishment of your forefathers. And yet,' said Pumblechook, turning to the landlord and waiter, and pointing me out at arm's length, 'this is him as I ever sported with in his days of happy infancy! Tell me not it cannot be; I tell you this is him!'

A low murmur from the two replied. The waiter appeared to be particularly affected.

'This is him,' said Pumblechook, 'as I have rode in my shay-cart. This is him as I have seen brought up by hand. This is him untoe the sister of which I was uncle by marriage, as her name was Georgiana M'ria from her own mother, let him deny it if he can!' (*Chapter 58:* Pumblechook and Pip).

'I little thought,' said Estella, 'that I should take leave of you in taking leave of this spot. I am very glad to do so.'

'Glad to part again, Estella? To me, parting is a painful thing. To me, the remembrance of our last parting has been ever mournful and painful.'

'But you said to me,' returned Estella, very earnestly, ' "God bless you, God forgive you!" And if you could say that to me then, you will not hesitate to say that to me now – now, when suffering has been stronger than all other teaching, and has taught me to understand what your heart used to be. I have been bent and broken, but – I hope – into a better shape. Be as considerate and good to me as you were, and tell me we are friends.'

'We are friends,' said I, rising and bending over her, as she rose from the bench.

'And will continue friends apart,' said Estella.

I took her hand in mine, and we went out of the ruined place; and, as the morning mists had risen long ago when I first left the forge, so, the evening mists were rising now, and in all the broad expanse of tranquil light they showed to me, I saw no shadow of another parting from her (*Chapter 59:* Estella and Pip).

OUR MUTUAL FRIEND

BOOK THE FIRST: THE CUP AND THE LIP

Mr. and Mrs. Veneering were bran-new people in a bran-new house in a bran-new quarter of London.

Everything about the Veneerings was spick and span new. All their furniture was new, all their friends were new, all their servants were new, their plate was new, their carriage was new, their harness was new, their horses were new, their pictures were new, they themselves were new, they were as newly married as was lawfully compatible with their having a bran-new baby, and if they had set up a great-grandfather, he would have come home in matting from the Pantechnicon, without a scratch upon him, French polished to the crown of his head *(Chapter 2)*.

'Dinner is on the table!'
Thus the melancholy retainer, as who should say, 'Come down and be poisoned, ye unhappy children of men!' *(Chapter 2)*.

The retainer goes round, like a gloomy Analytical Chemist; always seeming to say, after 'Chablis, sir?' – 'You wouldn't if you knew what it's made of' *(Chapter 2)*.

'Now, my dear Mrs. Veneering,' quoth Lady Tippins, 'I appeal to you whether this is not the basest conduct ever known in this world? I carry my lovers about, two or three at a time, on condition that they are very obedient and devoted; and here is my old lover-in-chief, the head of all my slaves, throwing off his allegiance before company! And here is another of my lovers, a rough Cymon at present, certainly, but of whom I had most hopeful expectations as to his turning out well in course of time, pretending that he can't remember his nursery rhymes! On purpose to annoy me, for he knows how I dote upon them!'
A grisly little fiction concerning her lovers is Lady Tippins's point. She is always attended by a lover or two, and she keeps a little list of her lovers, and she is always booking a new lover, or striking out an old lover, or putting a lover in her black list, or promoting a lover to her blue list, or adding up her lovers, or otherwise posting her book. Mrs. Veneering is charmed by the humour, and so is Veneering. Perhaps it is enhanced by a certain yellow play in Lady Tippins's throat, like the legs of scratching poultry *(Chapter 2)*.

It is always noticeable at the table of the Veneerings, that no man troubles himself much about the Veneerings themselves, and that any one who has anything to tell, generally tells it to anybody else in preference *(Chapter 2)*.

'He [Harmon Sen.] grew rich as a Dust Contractor, and lived in a hollow in a hilly country entirely composed of Dust. On his own small estate the growling old vagabond threw up his own mountain range, like an old volcano, and its geological formation was Dust. Coal-dust, vegetable-dust, bone-dust, crockery dust, rough dust, and sifted dust – all manner of Dust' *(Chapter 2: Mortimer)*.

The Analytical Chemist returning, everybody looks at him. Not because anybody wants to see him, but because of that subtle influence in nature which impels humanity to embrace the slightest opportunity of looking at anything, rather than the person who addresses it *(Chapter 2)*.

'I am one by myself, one,' said Mortimer, 'high up an awful staircase commanding a burial-ground, and I have a whole clerk to myself, and he has nothing to do but look at the burial-ground, and what he will turn out when arrived at maturity, I cannot conceive. Whether, in that shabby rook's nest, he is always plotting wisdom, or plotting murder; whether he will grow up, after so much solitary brooding, to enlighten his fellow-creatures, or to poison them; is the only speck of interest that presents itself to my professional view. Will you give me a light? Thank you' *(Chapter 3)*.

According to the success with which you put this and that together, you get a woman and fish apart, or a Mermaid in combination *(Chapter 3)*.

He [Wilfer] was shy, and unwilling to own to the name of Reginald, as being too aspiring and self-assertive a name. In his signature he used only the initial R., and imparted what it really stood for, to none but chosen friends, under the seal of confidence. Out of this, the facetious habit had arisen in the neighbourhood surrounding Mincing Lane of making Christian names for him of adjectives and participles beginning with R. Some of these were more or less appropriate: as Rusty, Retiring, Ruddy, Round, Ripe, Ridiculous, Ruminative; others derived their point from their want of application: as Raging, Rattling, Roaring, Raffish. But, his popular name was Rumty, which in a moment of inspiration had been bestowed upon him by a gentleman of convivial habits connected with the drug market, as the beginning of a social chorus, his leading part in the execution of which had led this gentleman to the Temple of Fame, and of which the whole expressive burden ran:

'Rumty iddity, row dow dow,
Sing toodlely, teedlely, bow wow wow.'

(Chapter 4).

'No, R. W. Lavinia has not known the trial that Bella has known. The trial that your daughter Bella has undergone, is, perhaps, without a parallel, and has been borne, I will say, Nobly. When you see your daughter Bella in her black dress, which she alone of all the family wears, and when you remember the circumstances which have led to her wearing it, and when you know how those circumstances have been sustained, then, R. W., lay your head upon your pillow and say, "Poor Lavinia!"'
Here, Miss Lavinia, from her kneeling situation under the table, put in that she didn't want to be 'poored by pa,' or anybody else *(Chapter 4: Mrs. Wilfer)*.

'This is another of the consequences of being poor! The idea of a girl with a really fine head of hair, having to do it by one flat candle and a few inches of looking-glass!' *(Chapter 4: Bella Wilfer)*.

' "A literary man – *with* a wooden leg – and all Print is open to him!" That's what I thought to myself, that morning,' pursued Mr. Boffin, leaning forward to describe, uncramped by the clothes-horse, as large an arc as his right arm could make; ' "all Print is open to him!" And it is, ain't it?'

'Why, truly, sir,' Mr. Wegg admitted with modesty; 'I believe you couldn't show me the piece of English print, that I wouldn't be equal to collaring and throwing.'

'On the spot?' said Mr. Boffin.

'On the spot.'

'I know'd it! Then consider this. Here am I, a man without a wooden leg, and yet all print is shut to me' *(Chapter 5)*.

'I see no difficulty if you wish it. You are provided with the needful implement – a book, sir?'

'Bought him at a sale,' said Mr. Boffin. 'Eight wollumes. Red and gold. Purple ribbon in every wollume, to keep the place where you leave off. Do you know him?'

'The book's name, sir?' inquired Silas.

'I thought you might have know'd him without it,' said Mr. Boffin, slightly disappointed. 'His name is Decline-and-Fall-Off-The-Rooshan-Empire' *(Chapter 5)*.

'Beside that cottage door, Mr. Boffin,
    A girl was on her knees;
She held aloft a snowy scarf, Sir,
    Which (my eldest brother noticed) fluttered in the breeze.
She breathed a prayer for him, Mr. Boffin;
    A prayer he coold not hear.
And my eldest brother lean'd upon his sword, Mr. Boffin,
    And wiped away a tear.'

                                   (Chapter 5: Wegg).

His gravity was unusual, portentous, and immeasurable, not because he admitted any doubt of himself, but because he perceived it necessary to forestall any doubt of himself in others. And herein he ranged with that very numerous class of impostors, who are quite as determined to keep up appearances to themselves, as to their neighbours *(Chapter 5)*.

'Do you like it, Wegg?' asked Mr. Boffin, in his pouncing manner.

'I admire it greatly, sir,' said Wegg. 'Peculiar comfort at this fireside, sir.'

'Do you understand it, Wegg?'

'Why, in a general way, sir,' Mr. Wegg was beginning slowly and knowingly, with his head stuck on one side, as evasive people do begin, when the other cut him short:

'You *don't* understand it, Wegg, and I'll explain it. These arrangements is made by mutual consent between Mrs. Boffin and me. Mrs. Boffin, as I've mentioned, is a highflyer at Fashion, at present I'm not. I don't go higher than comfort, and comfort of the sort that I'm equal to the enjoyment of. Well then. Where would be the good of Mrs. Boffin and me quarrelling over it? We never did quarrel, before we come into Boffin's Bower as a property; why quarrel when we *have* come into Boffin's Bower as a property? So Mrs. Boffin, she keeps up her part of the room, in her way; I keep up my part of the room in mine. In consequence of which we have at once, Sociability (I should go melancholy mad without Mrs. Boffin), Fashion, and Comfort. If I get by degrees to be a highflyer at Fashion, then Mrs. Boffin will by degrees come for'arder. If Mrs. Boffin should
Q

ever be less of a dab at Fashion than she is at the present time, then Mrs. Boffin's carpet would go back'arder. If we should both continny as we are, why then *here* we are, and give us a kiss, old lady' *(Chapter 5)*.

'This is a charming spot, is the Bower, but you must get to appreciate it by degrees. It's a spot to find out the merits of, little by little, and a new 'un every day. There's a serpentining walk up each of the mounds, that gives you the yard and neighbourhood changing every moment. When you get to the top, there's a view of the neighbouring premises, not to be surpassed. The premises of Mrs. Boffin's late father (Canine Provision Trade), you look down into, as if they was your own. And the top of the High Mound is crowned with a lattice-work Arbour, in which, if you don't read out loud many a book in the summer, ay, and as a friend, drop many a time into poetry too, it shan't be my fault' *(Chapter 5: Boffin)*.

'When you come in here of an evening, and look round you, and notice anything on a shelf that happens to catch your fancy, mention it.'

Wegg, who had been going to put on his spectacles, immediately laid them down, with the sprightly observation:

'You read my thoughts, sir. *Do* my eyes deceive me, or is that object up there a – a pie? It can't be a pie.'

'Yes, it's a pie, Wegg,' replied Mr. Boffin, with a glance of some little discomfiture at the Decline and Fall.

'*Have* I lost my smell for fruits, or is it a apple pie, sir?' asked Wegg.

'It's a veal and ham pie,' said Mr. Boffin.

'Is it, indeed, sir? And it would be hard, sir, to name the pie that is a better pie than a weal and hammer,' said Mr. Wegg, nodding his head emotionally.

'Have some, Wegg?'

'Thank you, Mr. Boffin, I think I will, at your invitation. I wouldn't at any other party's, at the present juncture; but at yours, sir! – And meaty jelly too, especially when a little salt, which is the case where there's ham, is mellering to the organ, is very mellering to the organ.' Mr. Wegg did not say what organ, but spoke with a cheerful generality *(Chapter 5)*.

'Commodious,' gasped Mr. Boffin, staring at the moon, after letting Wegg out of the gate and fastening it: 'Commodious fights in that wild-beast show, seven hundred and thirty-five times, in one character only! As if that wasn't stunning enough, a hundred lions is turned into the same wild-beast show all at once! As if that wasn't stunning enough, Commodious, in another character, kills 'em all off in a hundred goes! As if that wasn't stunning enough, Vittle-us (and well named too) eats six millions' worth, English money, in seven months! Wegg takes it easy, but upon-my-soul to a old bird like myself these are scarers. And even now that Commodious is strangled, I don't see a way to our bettering ourselves.' Mr. Boffin added as he turned his pensive steps towards the Bower and shook his head, 'I didn't think this morning there was half so many Scarers in Print. But I'm in for it now!' *(Chapter 5)*.

The wood forming the chimney-pieces, beams, partitions, floors, and doors, of the Six Jolly Fellowship-Porters, seemed in its old age fraught with confused memories of its youth. In many places it had become gnarled and riven, according to the manner of old trees; knots started out of it; and here and there it seemed to twist itself into some likeness of boughs. In this state of second childhood, it had an air of being in its own way garrulous about its early life. Not without reason was it often asserted by the regular frequenters of the Porters, that when the light shone full upon the grain of certain panels, and particularly upon an old corner cupboard of walnut-wood in the bar, you might trace little forests there, and tiny trees like the parent tree, in full umbrageous leaf *(Chapter 6)*.

'And you mean to say you are still obstinate?'
'Not obstinate, Miss, I hope.'
'Firm (I suppose you call it) then?'
'Yes, Miss. Fixed like.'
'Never was an obstinate person yet, who would own to the word!' remarked Miss Potterson, rubbing her vexed nose: 'I'm sure I would, if I was obstinate; but I am a pepperer, which is different' *(Chapter 6:* Lizzie Hexam and Abbey Potterson).

'My tea is drawing, and my muffin is on the hob, Mr. Wegg; will you partake?'
It being one of Mr. Wegg's guiding rules in life always to partake, he says he will. But, the little shop is so excessively dark, is stuck so full of black shelves and brackets and nooks and corners, that he sees Mr. Venus's cup and saucer only because it is close under the candle, and does not see from what mysterious recess Mr. Venus produces another for himself, until it is under his nose. Concurrently, Wegg perceives a pretty little dead bird lying on the counter, with its head drooping on one side against the rim of Mr. Venus's saucer, and a long stiff wire piercing its breast. As if it were Cock Robin, the hero of the ballad, and Mr. Venus were the sparrow with his bow and arrow, and Mr. Wegg were the fly with his little eye *(Chapter 7)*.

The greasy door is violently pushed inward, and a boy follows it, who says, after having let it slam:
'Come for the stuffed canary.'
'It's three and ninepence,' returns Venus; 'have you got the money?'
The boy produces four shillings. Mr. Venus, always in exceedingly low spirits, and making whimpering sounds, peers about for the stuffed canary. On his taking the candle to assist his search, Mr. Wegg observes that he has a convenient little shelf near his knees, exclusively appropriated to skeleton hands, which have very much the appearance of wanting to lay hold of him. From these Mr. Venus rescues the canary in a glass case, and shows it to the boy.
'There!' he whimpers. 'There's animation! On a twig, making up his mind to hop! Take care of him; he's a lovely specimen. – And three is four' *(Chapter 7)*.

'Oh dear me, dear me!' sighs Mr. Venus, heavily, snuffing the candle, 'the world that appeared so flowery has ceased to blow! You're casting your eye round the shop, Mr. Wegg. Let me show you a light. My working bench. My young man's bench. A Wice. Tools. Bones, warious. Skulls, warious. Preserved Indian baby. African ditto. Bottled preparations, warious. Everything within reach of your hand, in good preservation. The mouldy ones a-top. What's in those hampers over them again, I don't quite remember. Say, human warious. Cats. Articulated English baby. Dogs. Ducks. Glass eyes, warious. Mummied bird. Dried cuticle, warious. Oh dear me! That's the general panoramic view' *(Chapter 7)*.

'Mr. Wegg, if you was brought here loose in a bag to be articulated, I'd name your smallest bones blindfold equally with your largest, as fast as I could pick 'em out, and I'd sort 'em all, and sort your wertebrae, in a manner that would equally surprise and charm you' *(Chapter 7:* Venus).

' "Mr. Venus," '
'Yes. Go on.'
' "Preserver of Animals and Birds," '
'Yes. Go on.'
' "Articulator of human bones." '
'That's it,' with a groan. 'That's it! Mr. Wegg, I'm thirty-two, and a bachelor. Mr. Wegg, I love her. Mr. Wegg, she is worthy of being loved by a Potentate!' Here Silas is rather alarmed by Mr. Venus springing to his feet in the hurry of his spirits, and haggardly confronting him with his hand on his coat collar; but Mr. Venus, begging pardon, sits down again, saying, with the calmness of despair, 'She objects to the business.'
'Does she know the profits of it?'
'She knows the profits of it, but she don't appreciate the art of it, and she objects to it. "I do not wish," she writes in her own handwriting, "to regard myself, nor yet to be regarded, in that bony light" ' *(Chapter 7)*.

'Mrs. Boffin and me had no child of our own, and had sometimes wished that how we had one. But not now. "We might both of us die," says Mrs. Boffin, "and other eyes might see that lonely look in our child." So of a night, when it was very cold, or when the wind roared, or the rain dripped heavy, she would wake sobbing, and call out in a fluster, "Don't you see the poor child's face? O shelter the poor child!" – till in course of years it gently wore out, as many things do' *(Chapter 8)*.

'I object on principle,' said Eugene, 'as a biped – '
'As a what?' asked Mr. Boffin.
'As a two-footed creature, to being constantly referred to insects and four-footed creatures. I object to being required to model my proceedings according to the proceedings of the bee, or the dog, or the spider, or the camel. I fully admit that the camel, for instance, is an excessively temperate person; but he has several stomachs to entertain himself with, and I have only one. Besides, I am not fitted up with a convenient cool cellar to keep my drink in' *(Chapter 8:* Eugene Wrayburn).

'Conceding for a moment that there is any analogy between a bee and a man in a shirt and pantaloons (which I deny), and that it is settled that the man is to learn from the bee (which I also deny), the question still remains, what is he to learn? To imitate? Or to avoid? When your friends the bees worry themselves to that highly fluttered extent about their sovereign, and become perfectly distracted touching the slightest monarchical movement, are we men to learn the greatness of Tuft-hunting, or the littleness of the Court Circular? I am not clear, Mr. Boffin, but that the hive may be satirical' (*Chapter 8: Eugene Wrayburn*).

As is well known to the wise in their generation, traffic in Shares is the one thing to have to do with in this world. Have no antecedents, no established character, no cultivation, no ideas, no manners; have Shares. Have Shares enough to be on Boards of Direction in capital letters, oscillate on mysterious business between London and Paris, and be great. Where does he come from? Shares. Where is he going to? Shares. What are his tastes? Shares. Has he any principles? Shares. What squeezes him into parliament? Shares. Perhaps he never of himself achieved success in anything, never originated anything, never produced anything! Sufficient answer to all; Shares. O mighty Shares! To set those blaring images so high, and to cause us smaller vermin, as under the influence of henbane or opium, to cry out night and day, 'Relieve us of our money, scatter it for us, buy us and sell us, ruin us, only we beseech ye take rank among the powers of the earth, and fatten on us!' (*Chapter 10*).

Twemlow goes home to Duke Street, St. James's, to take a plate of mutton broth with a chop in it, and a look at the marriage service, in order that he may cut in at the right place to-morrow; and he is low, and feels it dull over the livery stable-yard, and is distinctly aware of a dint in his heart, made by the most adorable of the adorable bridesmaids. For, the poor little harmless gentleman once had his fancy, like the rest of us, and she didn't answer (as she often does not), and he thinks the adorable bridesmaid is like the fancy as she was then (which she is not at all), and that if the fancy had not married some one else for money, but had married him for love, he and she would have been happy (which they wouldn't have been), and that she has a tenderness for him still (whereas her toughness is a proverb). Brooding over the fire, with his dried little head in his dried little hands, and his dried little elbows on his dried little knees, Twemlow is melancholy. 'No Adorable to bear me company here!' thinks he. 'No Adorable at the club! A waste, a waste, a waste, my Twemlow!' And so drops asleep, and has galvanic starts all over him (*Chapter 10*).

More carriages at the gate, and lo, the rest of the characters. Whom Lady Tippins, standing on a cushion, surveying through the eye-glass, thus checks off: 'Bride; five-and-forty if a day, thirty shillings a yard, veil fifteen pounds, pocket-handkerchief a present. Bridesmaids; kept down for fear of outshining bride, consequently not girls, twelve and sixpence a yard, Veneering's flowers, snub-nosed one rather pretty but too conscious of her stockings, bonnets three pound ten. Twemlow; blessed release for the dear man if she really was his daughter, nervous even under the pretence that she is, well he may be. Mrs. Veneering; never saw such velvet, say two thousand pounds as she stands, absolute jeweller's window, father must have been a pawnbroker, or how could these people do it? Attendant unknowns; pokey' (*Chapter 10*).

Hideous solidity was the characteristic of the Podsnap plate. Everything was made to look as heavy as it could, and to take up as much room as possible. Everything said boastfully, 'Here you have as much of me in my ugliness as if I were only lead; but I am so many ounces of precious metal worth so much an ounce; – wouldn't you like to melt me down?' A corpulent straddling épergne, blotched all over as if it had broken out in an eruption rather than been ornamented, delivered this address from an unsightly silver platform in the centre of the table. Four silver wine-coolers, each furnished with four staring heads, each head obtrusively carrying a big silver ring in each of its ears, conveyed the sentiment up and down the table, and handed it on to the pot-bellied silver salt-cellars. All the big silver spoons and forks widened the mouths of the company expressly for the purpose of thrusting the sentiment down their throats with every morsel they ate (*Chapter 11*).

It was not summer yet, but spring; and it was not gentle spring ethereally mild, as in Thomson's Seasons, but nipping spring with an easterly wind, as in Johnson's, Jackson's, Dickson's, Smith's, and Jones's Seasons. The grating wind sawed rather than blew; and as it sawed, the sawdust whirled about the sawpit. Every street was a sawpit, and there were no top-sawyers; every passenger was an under-sawyer, with the sawdust blinding him and choking him.

That mysterious paper currency which circulates in London when the wind blows, gyrated here and there and everywhere. Whence can it come, whither can it go? It hangs on every bush, flutters in every tree, is caught flying by the electric wires, haunts every enclosure, drinks at every pump, cowers at every grating, shudders upon every plot of grass, seeks rest in vain behind the legions of iron rails. In Paris, where nothing is wasted, costly and luxurious city though it be, but where wonderful human ants creep out of holes and pick up every scrap, there is no such thing. There, it blows nothing but dust. There, sharp eyes and sharp stomachs reap even the east wind, and get something out of it (*Chapter 12*).

When the spring evenings are too long and light to shut out, and such weather is rife, the city which Mr. Podsnap so explanatorily called London, Londres, London, is at its worst. Such a black shrill city, combining the qualities of a smoky house and a scolding wife; such a gritty city; such a hopeless city, with no rent in the leaden canopy of its sky; such a beleaguered city, invested by the great Marsh Forces of Essex and Kent. So the two old schoolfellows felt it to be, as, their dinner done, they turned towards the fire to smoke. Young Blight was gone, the coffee-house waiter was gone, the plates and dishes were gone, the wine was going – but not in the same direction *(Chapter 12)*.

As they glided slowly on, keeping under the shore, and sneaking in and out among the shipping, by back-alleys of water, in a pilfering way that seemed to be their boatman's normal manner of progression, all the objects among which they crept were so huge in contrast with their wretched boat as to threaten to crush it. Not a ship's hull, with its rusty iron links of cable run out of hawse-holes long discoloured with the iron's rusty tears, but seemed to be there with a fell intention. Not a figure-head but had the menacing look of bursting forward to run them down. Not a sluice gate, or a painted scale upon a post or wall, showing the depth of water, but seemed to hint, like the dreadfully facetious Wolf in bed in Grand-mamma's cottage, 'That's to drown *you* in, my dears!' Not a lumbering black barge, with its cracked and blistered side impending over them, but seemed to suck at the river with a thirst for sucking them under. And everything so vaunted the spoiling influences of water – discoloured copper, rotten wood, honey-combed stone, green dank deposit – that the after-consequences of being crushed, sucked under, and drawn down, looked as ugly to the imagination as the main event *(Chapter 14)*.

' "I'll tell thee how the maiden wept, Mrs. Boffin,
'When her true love was slain, ma'am,
'And how her broken spirit slept, Mrs. Boffin,
'And never woke again, ma'am.
'I'll tell thee (if agreeable to Mr. Boffin) how the steed drew nigh,
'And left his lord afar;
'And if my tale (which I hope Mr. Boffin might excuse) should make you sigh,
'I'll strike the light guitar." '

(Chapter 15)'

A gloomy house the Bower, with sordid signs on it of having been, through its long existence as Harmony Jail, in miserly holding. Bare of paint, bare of paper on the walls, bare of furniture, bare of experience of human life. Whatever is built by man for man's occupation, must, like natural creations, fulfil the intention of its existence, or soon perish. This old house had wasted more from desuetude than it would have wasted from use, twenty years for one *(Chapter 15)*.

The man of low cunning had, of course, acquired a mastery over the man of high simplicity. The mean man had, of course, got the better of the generous man. How long such conquests last, is another matter; that they are achieved, is every-day experience, not even to be flourished away by Podsnappery itself *(Chapter 15)*.

'The Poor-house?' said the Secretary.

Mrs. Higden set that resolute old face of hers, and darkly nodded yes.

'You dislike the mention of it.'

'Dislike the mention of it?' answered the old woman. 'Kill me sooner than take me there. Throw this pretty child under cart-horses' feet and a loaded waggon, sooner than take him there. Come to us and find us all a-dying, and set a light to us all where we lie, and let us all blaze away with the house into a heap of cinders, sooner than move a corpse of us there!' *(Chapter 16)*.

BOOK THE SECOND: BIRDS OF A FEATHER

'What do I make with my straw?'

'Dinner-mats.'

'A schoolmaster, and says dinner-mats! I'll give you a clue to my trade in a game of forfeits. I love my love with a B because she's Beautiful; I hate my love with a B because she is Brazen; I took her to the sign of the Blue Boar, and I treated her with bonnets; her name's Bouncer, and she lives in Bedlam. – Now, what do I make with my straw?'

'Ladies' bonnets?'

'Fine ladies',' said the person of the house, nodding assent. 'Dolls'. I'm a Dolls' Dressmaker.'

'I hope it's a good business?'

The person of the house shrugged her shoulders and shook her head. 'No. Poorly paid. And I'm often so pressed for time! I had a doll married, last week, and was obliged to work all night. And it's not good for me, on account of my back being so bad and my legs so queer' *(Chapter 1: Fanny Cleaver and Charley Hexam)*.

'Am I so little to be relied upon?'

'You're more to be relied upon than silver and gold.' As she said it, Miss Wren suddenly broke off, screwed up her eyes and her chin, and looked prodigiously knowing. 'Aha!

'Who comes here?
'A Grenadier.
'What does he want?
'A pot of beer.

– And nothing else in the world, my dear!' *(Chapter 2)*.

'Talking of ideas, my Lizzie,' they were sitting side by side as they had sat at first, 'I wonder how it happens that when I am work, work, working here, all alone in the summer-time, I smell flowers.'

'As a common-place individual, I should say,' Eugene suggested languidly – for he was growing weary of the person of the house – 'that you smell flowers because you *do* smell flowers.'

'No, I don't,' said the little creature, resting one arm upon the elbow of her chair, resting her chin upon that hand, and looking vacantly before her; 'this is not a flowery neighbourhood. It's anything but that. And yet, as I sit at work, I smell miles of flowers. I smell roses till I think I see the rose-leaves lying in heaps, bushels, on the floor. I smell fallen leaves till I put down my hand – so – and expect to make them rustle. I smell the white and the pink May in the hedges, and all sorts of flowers that I never was among. For I have seen very few flowers indeed, in my life *(Chapter 2 – Miss Wren)*.

'I dare say my birds sing better than other birds, and my flowers smell better than other flowers. For when I was a little child,' in a tone as though it were ages ago, 'the children that I used to see early in the morning were very different from any others that I ever saw. They were not like me: they were not chilled, anxious, ragged, or beaten; they were never in pain. They were not like the children of the neighbours; they never made me tremble all over, by setting up shrill noises, and they never mocked me. Such numbers of them, too! All in white dresses, and with something shining on the borders, and on their head, that I have never been able to imitate with my work, though I know it so well. They used to come down in long bright slanting rows, and say altogether, "Who is this in pain! Who is this in pain!" When I told them who it was, they answered, "Come and play with us!" When I said, "I never play! I can't play!" they swept about me and took me up, and made me light. Then it was all delicious ease and rest till they laid me down, and said, all together, "Have patience, and we will come again." Whenever they came back, I used to know they were coming before I saw the long bright rows, by hearing them ask, all together a long way off, "Who is this in pain! Who is this in pain!" And I used to cry out, "O my blessed children, it's poor me. Have pity on me. Take me up and make me light!"' (*Chapter 2: Miss Wren*).

Veneering having instructed his driver to charge at the Public in the streets, like the life-guards at Waterloo, is driven furiously to Duke Street, St. James's. There, he finds Twemlow in his lodgings, fresh from the hands of a secret artist who has been doing something to his hair with yolks of eggs. The process requiring that Twemlow shall, for two hours after the application, allow his hair to stick upright and dry gradually, he is in an appropriate state for the receipt of startling intelligence; looking equally like the Monument on Fish Street Hill, and King Priam on a certain incendiary occasion not wholly unknown as a neat point from the classics (*Chapter 3*).

More is done, or considered to be done – which does as well – by taking cabs, and 'going about,' than the fair Tippins knew of. Many vast vague reputations have been made, solely by taking cabs and going about. This particularly obtains in all Parliamentary affairs. Whether the business in hand be to get a man in, or get a man out, or get a man over, or promote a railway, or jockey a railway, or what else, nothing is understood to be so effectual as scouring nowhere in a violent hurry – in short, as taking cabs and going about (*Chapter 3*).

'But *you* are not dead, you know,' said Jenny Wren. 'Get down to life!'
Mr. Fledgeby seemed to think it rather a good suggestion, and with a nod turned round. As Riah followed to attend him down the stairs, the little creature called out to the Jew in a silvery tone, 'Don't be long gone. Come back, and be dead!' And still as they went down they heard the little sweet voice, more and more faintly, half calling and half singing, 'Come back and be dead, Come back and be dead!' (*Chapter 5*).

'As one that was ever an ornament to human life,' says Mr. Wegg, again holding out Mr. Venus's palm as if he were going to tell his fortune by chiromancy, and holding his own up ready for smiting it when the time

should come; as one that the poet might have had his eye on, in writing the national naval words:

> Helm a-weather, now lay her close,
> Yard arm and yard arm she lies;
> Again, cried I, Mr. Venus, give her t'other dose,
> Man shrouds and grapple, sir, or she flies!

– that is to say, regarded in the light of true British Oak; for such you are – explain, Mr. Venus, the expression "papers"!' (*Chapter 7*).

'Now, Pa,' said Bella, hugging him close, 'take this lovely woman out to dinner.'
'Where shall we go, my dear?'
'Greenwich!' said Bella, valiantly. 'And be sure you treat this lovely woman with everything of the best' (*Chapter 8*).

'Your mother has, throughout life, been a companion that any man might – might look up to – and – and commit the sayings of, to memory – and – form himself upon – if he – '
'If he liked the model?' suggested Bella.
'We-ell, ye-es,' he returned, thinking about it, not quite satisfied with the phrase: 'or perhaps I might say, if it was in him. Supposing, for instance, that a man wanted to be always marching, he would find your mother an inestimable companion. But if he had any taste for walking, or should wish at any time to break into a trot, he might sometimes find it a little difficult to keep step with your mother. Or take it this way, Bella,' he added, after a moment's reflection: 'Supposing that a man had to go through life, we won't say with a companion, but we'll say to a tune. Very good. Supposing that the tune allotted to him was the Dead March in Saul. Well. It would be a very suitable tune for particular occasions – none better – but it would be difficult to keep time with in the ordinary run of domestic transactions. For instance, if he took his supper after a hard day, to the Dead March in Saul, his food might be likely to sit heavy on him. Or, if he was at any time inclined to relieve his mind by singing a comic song or dancing a hornpipe, and was obliged to do it to the Dead March in Saul, he might find himself put out in the execution of his lively intentions.'
'Poor Pa!' thought Bella, as she hung upon his arm (*Chapter 8: Reginald Wilfer*).

'Talk to me of love!' said Bella, contemptuously: though her face and figure certainly rendered the subject no incongruous one. 'Talk to me of fiery dragons! But talk to me of poverty and wealth, and there indeed we touch upon realities' (*Chapter 8*).

On the grateful impulse of the moment, Mr. Sloppy kissed Mrs. Boffin's hand, and then detaching himself from that good creature that he might have room enough for his feelings, threw back his head, opened his mouth wide, and uttered a dismal howl. It was creditable to his tenderness of heart, but suggested that he might on occasion give some offence to the neighbours: the rather, as the footman looked in, and begged pardon, finding he was not wanted, but excused himself, on the ground 'that he thought it was Cats' (*Chapter 10*).

Love at first sight is a trite expression quite sufficiently discussed; enough that in certain smouldering natures like this man's, that passion leaps into a blaze, and makes such head as fire does in a rage of wind, when other passions, but for its mastery, could be held in chains. As a multitude of weak, imitative natures are always lying by, ready to go mad upon the next wrong idea that may be broached – in these times, generally some form of tribute to Somebody for something that never was done, or, if ever done, that was done by Somebody Else – so these less ordinary natures may lie by for years, ready on the touch of an instant to burst into flame (*Chapter 11*).

'Humph! If he – I mean, of course, my dear, the party who is coming to court me when the time comes – should be *that* sort of man, he may spare himself the trouble. *He* wouldn't do to be trotted about and made useful. He'd take fire and blow up while he was about it.'
'And so you would be rid of him,' said Lizzie, humouring her.
'Not so easily,' returned Miss Wren. 'He wouldn't blow up alone. He'd carry me up with him. *I* know his tricks and his manners.'
'Would he want to hurt you, do you mean?' asked Lizzie.
'Mightn't exactly want to do it, my dear,' returned Miss Wren; 'but a lot of gunpowder among lighted lucifer-matches in the next room might almost as well be here' (*Chapter 11*).

Pleasant Riderhood had it in the blood, or had been trained, to regard seamen, within certain limits, as her prey. Show her a man in a blue jacket, and, figuratively speaking, she pinned him instantly. Yet, all things considered, she was not of an evil mind or an unkindly disposition. For, observe how many things were to be considered according to her own unfortunate experience. Show Pleasant Riderhood a Wedding in the street, and she only saw two people taking out a regular license to quarrel and fight. Show her a Christening, and she saw a little heathen personage having a quite superfluous name bestowed upon it, inasmuch as it would be commonly addressed by some abusive epithet; which little personage was not in the least wanted by anybody, and would be shoved and banged out of everybody's way, until it should grow big enough to shove and bang. Show her a Funeral, and she saw an unremunerative ceremony in the nature of a black masquerade, conferring a temporary gentility on the performers, at an immense expense, and representing the only formal party ever given by the deceased. Show her a live father, and she saw but a duplicate of her own father, who from her infancy had been taken with fits and starts of discharging his duty to her, which duty was always incorporated in the form of a fist or a leathern strap, and being discharged hurt her. All things considered, therefore, Pleasant Riderhood was not so very, very bad (*Chapter 12*).

At the great iron gate of the churchyard he stopped and looked in. He looked up at the high tower spectrally resisting the wind, and he looked round at the white tombstones, like enough to the dead in their winding-sheets, and he counted the nine tolls of the clock-bell.

'It is a sensation not experienced by many mortals,' said he, 'to be looking into a churchyard on a wild windy night, and to feel that I no more hold a place among the living than these dead do, and even to know that I lie buried somewhere else, as they lie buried here. Nothing uses me to it. A spirit that was once a man could hardly feel stranger or lonelier, going unrecognised among mankind, than I feel' (*Chapter 13: John Harmon*).

A grey dusty withered evening in London city has not a hopeful aspect. The closed warehouses and offices have an air of death about them, and the national dread of colour has an air of mourning. The towers and steeples of the many house-encompassed churches, dark and dingy as the sky that seems descending on them, are no relief to the general gloom; a sun-dial on a church-wall has the look, in its useless black shade, of having failed in its business enterprise and stopped payment for ever; melancholy waifs and strays of housekeepers and porters sweep melancholy waifs and strays of papers and pins into the kennels, and other more melancholy waifs and strays explore them, searching and stooping and poking for anything to sell. The set of humanity outward from the City is as a set of prisoners departing from gaol, and dismal Newgate seems quite as fit a stronghold for the mighty Lord Mayor as his own state-dwelling (*Chapter 15*).

'No man knows till the time comes, what depths are within him. To some men it never comes; let them rest and be thankful. To me, you brought it; on me, you forced it; and the bottom of this raging sea,' striking himself upon the breast, 'has been heaved up ever since' (*Chapter 15: Bradley Headstone*).

'You know what I am going to say. I love you. What other men may mean when they use that expression, I cannot tell; what *I* mean is, that I am under the influence of some tremendous attraction which I have resisted in vain, and which overmasters me. You could draw me to fire, you could draw me to water, you could draw me to the gallows, you could draw me to any death, you could draw me to anything I have most avoided, you could draw me to any exposure and disgrace. This and the confusion of my thoughts, so that I am fit for nothing, is what I mean by your being the ruin of me. But if you would return a favourable answer to my offer of myself in marriage, you could draw me to any good – every good – with equal force' (*Chapter 15: Bradley Headstone*).

BOOK THE THIRD: A LONG LANE

It was a foggy day in London, and the fog was heavy and dark. Animate London, with smarting eyes and irritated lungs, was blinking, wheezing, and choking; inanimate London was a sooty spectre, divided in purpose between being visible and invisible, and so being wholly neither. Gaslights flared in the shops with a haggard and unblest air, as knowing themselves to be night-creatures that had no business abroad under the sun; while the sun itself, when it was for a few moments dimly indicated through circling eddies of fog, showed as if it had gone out, and were collapsing flat and cold. Even in the surrounding country it was a foggy day, but there the fog was grey, whereas in London it was, at about the boundary line, dark yellow, and a little within it brown, and then browner, and then browner, until at the heart of the City – which call Saint Mary Axe – it was rusty-black. From any point of the high ridge of land northward, it might have been discerned that the loftiest buildings made an occasional struggle to get their heads above the foggy sea, and especially that the great dome of Saint Paul's seemed to die hard; but this was not perceivable in the streets at their feet, where the whole metropolis was a heap of vapour charged with muffled sound of wheels, and enfolding a gigantic catarrh *(Chapter 1)*.

He is struggling to come back. Now he is almost here, now he is far away again. Now he is struggling harder to get back. And yet – like us all, when we swoon – like us all, every day of our lives when we wake – he is instinctively unwilling to be restored to the consciousness of this existence, and would be left dormant, if he could *(Chapter 3)*.

'And yet, Pa, think how terrible the fascination of money is! I see this, and hate this, and dread this, and don't know but that money might make a much worse change in me. And yet I have money always in my thoughts and my desires; and the whole life I place before myself is money, money, money, and what money can make of life!' *(Chapter 4:* Bella Wilfer*)*.

'Walk in, brother,' said Silas, clapping him on the shoulder, 'and take your seat in my chimney corner; for what says the ballad?

> "No malice to dread, sir,
> And no falsehood to fear,
> But truth to delight me, Mr. Venus,
> And I forgot what to cheer.
> Li toddle dee om dee.
> And something to guide,
> My ain fireside, sir,
> My ain fireside." '
> — *(Chapter 6:* Wegg*)*.

'We'll devote the evening, brother,' exclaimed Wegg, 'to prosecute our friendly move. And arterwards, crushing a flowing wine-cup – which I allude to brewing rum-and-water – we'll pledge one another. For what says the Poet?

> "And you needn't, Mr. Venus, be your black bottle,
> For surely I'll be mine,
> And we'll take a glass with a slice of lemon in it to
>   which you're partial,
> For auld lang syne." '
> — *(Chapter 6)*.

'Rome, brother,' returned Wegg: 'a city which (it may not be generally known) originated in twins and a wolf, and ended in Imperial marble, wasn't built in a day.'

'Did I say it was?' asked Venus.

'No, you did not, brother. Well inquired' *(Chapter 6)*.

'And there you sit, sir,' pursued Wegg with an air of thoughtful admiration, 'as if you had never left off! There you sit, sir, as if you had an unlimited capacity of assimilating the fragrant article! There you sit, sir, in the midst of your works, looking as if you'd been called upon for Home, Sweet Home, and was obleeging the company!

> "A exile from home splendour dazzles in vain,
> O give you your lowly Preparations again,
> The birds stuffed so sweetly that can't be expected to come
>   at your call,
> Give you these with the peace of mind dearer than all.
> Home, Home, Home, sweet Home!"

– Be it ever,' added Mr. Wegg in prose as he glanced about the shop, 'ever so ghastly, all things considered there's no place like it' *(Chapter 7)*.

In those pleasant little towns on Thames, you may hear the fall of the water over the weirs, or even, in still weather, the rustle of the rushes; and from the bridge you may see the young river, dimpled like a young child, playfully gliding away among the trees, unpolluted by the defilements that lie in wait for it on its course, and as yet out of hearing of the deep summons of the sea. It were too much to pretend that Betty Higden made out such thoughts; no; but she heard the tender river whispering to many like herself, 'Come to me, come to me! When the cruel shame and terror you have so long fled from, most beset you, come to me! I am the Relieving Officer appointed by eternal ordinance to do my work; I am not held in estimation according as I shirk it. My breast is softer than the pauper-nurse's; death in my arms is peacefuller than among the pauper-wards. Come to me!' *(Chapter 8)*.

'I wish, Eugene, you would speak a little more soberly and plainly, if it were only out of consideration for my feeling less at ease than you do.'

'Then soberly and plainly, Mortimer, I goad the schoolmaster to madness. I make the schoolmaster so ridiculous, and so aware of being made ridiculous, that I see him chafe and fret at every pore when we cross one another. The amiable occupation has been the solace of my life, since I was baulked in the manner unnecessary to recall. I have derived inexpressible comfort from it. I do it thus: I stroll out after dark, stroll a little way, look in at a window and furtively look out for the schoolmaster. Sooner or later, I perceive the schoolmaster on the watch; sometimes accompanied by his hopeful pupil; oftener pupil-less. Having made sure of his watching me, I tempt him on, all over London. One night I go east, another night north, in a few nights I go all round the compass. Sometimes, I walk; sometimes, I proceed in cabs, draining the pocket of the schoolmaster, who then follows in cabs. I study and get up abstruse No Thoroughfares in the course of the day. With Venetian mystery I seek those No Thoroughfares at night, glide into them by means of dark courts, tempt the schoolmaster to follow, turn suddenly, and catch him before he can retreat. Then we face one another, and I pass him as unaware of his existence, and he undergoes grinding torments. Similarly, I walk at a great pace down a short street, rapidly turn the corner, and, getting out of his view, as rapidly turn back. I catch him coming on post, again pass him as unaware of his existence, and again he undergoes grinding torments. Night after night his disappointment is acute, but hope springs eternal in the scholastic breast, and he follows me again to-morrow. Thus I enjoy the pleasures of the chase, and derive great benefit from the healthful exercise. When I do not enjoy the pleasures of the chase, for anything I know he watches at the Temple gate all night' (*Chapter 10:* Eugene Wrayburn).

'It seems to me,' said Mrs. Lammle, 'that you have had no money at all ever since we have been married.'
'What seems to you,' said Mr. Lammle, 'to have been the case, may possibly have been the case. It doesn't matter.'
Was it the speciality of Mr. and Mrs. Lammle, or does it ever obtain with other loving couples? In these matrimonial dialogues they never addressed each other, but always some invisible presence that appeared to take a station about midway between them. Perhaps the skeleton in the cupboard comes out to be talked to, on such domestic occasions (*Chapter 12*).

'The best wish I can wish you is,' said Bella, returning to the charge, 'that you had not one single farthing in the world. If any true friend and well-wisher could make you a bankrupt, you would be a Duck; but as a man of property you are a Demon!' (*Chapter 15:* Bella Wilfer).

'But we must think of dear Pa,' said Bella; 'I haven't told dear Pa; let us speak to Pa.' Upon which they turned to do so.
'I wish first, my dear,' remarked the cherub faintly, 'that you'd have the kindness to sprinkle me with a little milk, for I feel as if I was – Going' (*Chapter 16:* Bella and Reginald Wilfer).

Bella playfully setting herself about the task, Mrs. Wilfer's impressive countenance followed her with glaring eyes, presenting a combination of the once popular sign of the Saracen's Head, with a piece of Dutch clockwork, and suggesting to an imaginative mind that from the composition of the salad, her daugher might prudently omit the vinegar. But no word issued from the majestic matron's lips. And this was more terrific to her husband (as perhaps she knew) than any flow of eloquence with which she could have edified the company (*Chapter 16*).

'Ma, pray don't sit staring at me in that intensely aggravating manner! If you see a black on my nose, tell me so; if you don't, leave me alone.'
'Do you address Me in those words?' said Mrs. Wilfer. 'Do you presume?'
'Don't talk about presuming, Ma, for goodness' sake. A girl who is old enough to be engaged, is quite old enough to object to be stared at as if she was a Clock.'
'Audacious one!' said Mrs. Wilfer. 'Your grand-mamma, if so addressed by one of her daughters, at any age, would have insisted on her retiring to a dark apartment.'

'My grandmamma,' returned Lavvy, folding her arms and leaning back in her chair, 'wouldn't have sat staring people out of countenance, I think.'
'She would!' said Mrs. Wilfer.
'Then it's a pity she didn't know better,' said Lavvy. 'And if my grandmamma wasn't in her dotage when she took to insisting on people's retiring to dark apartments she ought to have been. A pretty exhibition my grandmamma must have made of herself! I wonder whether she ever insisted on people's retiring into the ball of St. Paul's; and if she did, how she got them there!'
(*Chapter 16:* Lavinia Wilfer and Mrs. Wilfer).

'Listen, sir,' said Bella. 'Your lovely woman was told her fortune to-night on her way home. It won't be a large fortune, because if the lovely woman's In-tended gets a certain appointment that he hopes to get soon, she will marry on a hundred and fifty pounds a year. But that's at first, and even if it should never be more, the lovely woman will make it quite enough. But that's not all, sir. In the fortune there's a certain fair man – a little man, the fortune-teller said – who, it seems, will always find himself near the lovely woman, and will always have kept, expressly for him, such a peaceful corner in the lovely woman's little house as never was. Tell me the name of that man, sir.'
'Is he a Knave in the pack of cards?' inquired the cherub, with a twinkle in his eyes.
'Yes!' cried Bella, in high glee, choking him again. 'He's the Knave of Wilfers! Dear Pa, the lovely woman means to look forward to this fortune that has been told for her, so delightfully, and to cause it to make her a much better lovely woman than she ever has been yet. What the little fair man is expected to do, sir, is to look forward to it also, by saying to himself when he is in danger of being over-worried, "I see land at last!" ' (*Chapter 16:* Bella and Reginald Wilfer).

BOOK THE FOURTH: A TURNING

'Gently, Mr. Wegg, gently,' Venus urged.
'Milk and water-erily you mean, sir,' he returned, with some little thickness of speech, in consequence of the Gum-Ticklers having tickled it. 'I've got him under inspection, and I'll inspect him.

"Along the line the signal ran,
England expects as this present man
Will keep Boffin to his duty."

– Boffin, I'll see you home' (*Chapter 3*).

'Now, darling Pa, give me your hands that I may fold them together, and do you say after me: – My little Bella.'
'My little Bella,' repeated Pa.
'I am very fond of you.'
'I am very fond of you, my darling,' said Pa.
'You mustn't say anything not dictated to you, sir. You daren't do it in your responses at Church, and you mustn't do it in your responses out of Church.'
'I withdraw the darling,' said Pa.
'That's a pious boy! Now again: – You were al-ways –'
'You were always,' repeated Pa.

'A vexatious – '

'No you weren't,' said Pa.

'A vexatious (do you hear, sir?), a vexatious, capricious, thankless, troublesome, Animal; but I hope you'll do better in the time to come, and I bless you and forgive you!' Here, she quite forgot that it was Pa's turn to make the responses, and clung to his neck. 'Dear Pa, if you knew how much I think this morning of what you told me once, about the first time of our seeing old Mr. Harmon, when I stamped and screamed, and beat you with my detestable little bonnet! I feel as if I had been stamping and screaming and beating you with my hateful little bonnet, ever since I was born, darling!'

'Nonsense, my love. And as to your bonnets, they have always been nice bonnets, for they have always become you – or you have become them; perhaps it was that – at every age.'

'Did I hurt you much, poor little Pa?' asked Bella, laughing (notwithstanding her repentance), with fantastic pleasure in the picture, 'when I beat you with my bonnet?'

'No my child. Wouldn't have hurt a fly!' *(Chapter 4)*.

Say, cherubic parent taking the lead, in what direction do we steer first? With some such inquiry in his thoughts, Gruff and Glum, stricken by so sudden an interest that he perked his neck and looked over the intervening people, as if he were trying to stand on tiptoe with his two wooden legs, took an observation of R. W. There was no 'first' in the case, Gruff and Glum made out; the cherubic parent was bearing down and crowding on direct for Greenwich church, to see his relations.

For Gruff and Glum, though most events acted on him simply as tobacco-stoppers, pressing down and condensing the quids within him, might be imagined to trace a family resemblance between the cherubs in the church architecture, and the cherub in the white waistcoat. Some resemblance of old Valentines, wherein a cherub, less appropriately attired for a proverbially uncertain climate, had been seen conducting lovers to the altar, might have been fancied to inflame the ardour of his timber toes. Be it as it might, he gave his moorings the slip, and followed in chase *(Chapter 4)*.

What a dinner! Specimens of all the fishes that swim in the sea, surely had swum their way to it, and if samples of the fishes of divers colours that made a speech in the Arabian Nights (quite a ministerial explanation in respect of cloudiness), and then jumped out of the frying-pan, were not to be recognised, it was only because they had all become of one hue by being cooked in batter among the whitebait. And the dishes being seasoned with Bliss – an article which they are sometimes out of, at Greenwich – were of perfect flavour, and the golden drinks had been bottled in the golden age and hoarding up their sparkles ever since *(Chapter 4)*.

'You remember how we talked about the ships that day, Pa?'

'Yes, my dear.'

'Isn't it strange, now, to think that there was no John in all the ships, Pa?'

'Not at all, my dear.'

'Oh, Pa! Not at all?'

'No, my dear. How can we tell what coming people are aboard the ships that may be sailing to us now from the unknown seas!' *(Chapter 4:* Bella and Reginald Wilfer).

'But you do forgive me that, and everything else; don't you, Pa?'

'Yes, my dearest.'

'And you don't feel solitary or neglected, going away by yourself; do you, Pa?'

'Lord bless you! No, my Life!'

'Good-bye, dearest Pa. Good-bye!'

'Good-bye, my darling! Take her away, my dear John. Take her home!'

So, she leaning on her husband's arm, they turned homeward by a rosy path which the gracious sun struck out for them in its setting. And O there are days in this life, worth life and worth death. And O what a bright old song it is, that O 'tis love, 'tis love, 'tis love, that makes the world go round! *(Chapter 4:* Bella and Reginald Wilfer).

'You shall not be annihilated, George!' cried Miss Lavinia. 'Ma shall destroy me first, and then she'll be contented. Oh, oh, oh! Have I lured George from his happy home to expose him to this! George, dear, be free! Leave me, ever dearest George, to Ma and to my fate. Give my love to your aunt, George dear, and implore her not to curse the viper that has crossed your path and blighted your existence. Oh, oh, oh!' The young lady, who, hysterically speaking, was only just come of age, and had never gone off yet, here fell into a highly creditable crisis, which, regarded as a first performance, was very successful; Mr. Sampson, bending over the body meanwhile, in a state of distraction, which induced him to address Mrs. Wilfer in the inconsistent expressions: 'Demon with the highest respect for you – behold your work!' *(Chapter 5:* Lavinia Wilfer).

John gone to business and Bella returned home, the dress would be laid aside, trim little wrappers and aprons would be substituted, and Bella, putting back her hair with both hands, as if she were making the most business-like arrangements for going dramatically distracted, would enter on the household affairs of the day. Such weighing and mixing and chopping and grating, such dusting and washing and polishing, such snipping and weeding and trowelling and other small gardening, such making and mending and folding and airing, such diverse arrangements, and above all such severe study! For Mrs. J. R., who had never been wont to do too much at home as Miss B. W., was under the constant necessity of referring for advice and support to a sage volume entitled The Complete British Family Housewife, which she would sit consulting, with her elbows on the table and her temples on her hands, like some perplexed enchantress poring over the Black Art. This, principally because the Complete British Housewife, however sound a Briton at heart, was by no means an expert Briton at expressing herself with clearness in the British tongue, and sometimes might have issued her directions to equal purpose in the

Kamskatchan language. In any crisis of this nature, Bella would suddenly exclaim aloud, 'Oh, you ridiculous old thing, what do you mean by that? You must have been drinking!' And having made this marginal note, would try the Housewife again, with all her dimples screwed into an expression of profound research.

There was likewise a coolness on the part of the British Housewife, which Mrs. John Rokesmith found highly exasperating. She would say, 'Take a salamander,' as if a general should command a private to catch a Tartar. Or, she would casually issue the order, 'Throw in a handful – ' of something entirely unattainable. In these, the Housewife's most glaring moments of unreason, Bella would shut her up and knock her on the table, apostrophising her with the compliment, 'Oh, you ARE a stupid old donkey! Where am I to get it, do you think?' *(Chapter 5)*.

It was a Saturday evening, and at such a time the village dogs, always much more interested in the doings of humanity than in the affairs of their own species, were particularly active. At the general shop, at the butcher's and at the public-house, they evinced an inquiring spirit never to be satiated. Their especial interest in the public-house would seem to imply some latent rakishness in the canine character; for little was eaten there, and they, having no taste for beer or tobacco (Mrs. Hubbard's dog is said to have smoked, but proof is wanting), could only have been attracted by sympathy with loose convivial habits. Moreover, a most wretched fiddle played within; a fiddle so unutterably vile, that one lean long-bodied cur, with a better ear than the rest, found himself under compulsion at intervals to go round the corner and howl. Yet, even he returned to the public-house on each occasion with the tenacity of a confirmed drunkard.

Fearful to relate, there was even a sort of little Fair in the village. Some despairing gingerbread that had been vainly trying to dispose of itself all over the country, and had cast a quantity of dust upon its head in its mortification, again appealed to the public from an infirm booth. So did a heap of nuts, long, long exiled from Barcelona, and yet speaking English so indifferently as to call fourteen of themselves a pint. A Peep-show which had originally started with the Battle of Waterloo, and had since made it every other battle of later date by altering the Duke of Wellington's nose, tempted the student of illustrated history. A Fat Lady, perhaps, in part sustained upon postponed pork, her professional associate being a Learned Pig, displayed her life-size picture in a low dress as she appeared when presented at Court, several yards round. All this was a vicious spectacle, as any poor idea of amusement on the part of the rough hewers of wood and drawers of water in this land of England ever is and shall be. They *must not* vary the rheumatism with amusement. They may vary it with fever and ague, or with as many rheumatic variations as they have joints; but positively not with entertainment after their own manner *(Chapter 6)*.

'I was hateful in mine own eyes. I was hateful to myself, in being so hateful to the debtor and to you. But more than that, and worse than that, and to pass out far and broad beyond myself – I reflected that evening, sitting alone in my garden on the housetop, that I was doing dishonour to my ancient faith and race. I reflected – clearly reflected for the first time, that in bending my neck to the yoke I was willing to wear, I bent the unwilling necks of the whole Jewish people. For it is not, in Christian countries, with the Jews as with other peoples. Men say, "This is a bad Greek, but there are good Greeks. This is a bad Turk, but there are good Turks." Not so with the Jews. Men find the bad among us easily enough – among what peoples are the bad not easily found? – but they take the worst of us as samples of the best; they take the lowest of us as presentations of the highest; and they say "All Jews are alike." If, doing what I was content to do here, because I was grateful for the past and have small need of money now, I had been a Christian, I could have done it, compromising no one but my individual self. But doing it as a Jew, I could not choose but compromise the Jews of all conditions and all countries. It is a little hard upon us, but it is the truth. I would that all our people remembered it! Though I have little right to say so, seeing that it came home so late to me' *(Chapter 9:* Riah).

A humble machine, familiar to the conspirators and called by the expressive name of Stretcher, being unavoidably sent for, he was rendered a harmless bundle of torn rags by being strapped down upon it, with voice and consciousness gone out of him, and life fast going. As this machine was borne out at the Temple gate by four men, the poor little dolls' dressmaker and her Jewish friend were coming up the street.

'Let us see what it is,' cried the dressmaker. 'Let us make haste and look, godmother.'

The brisk little crutch-stick was but too brisk. 'Oh, gentlemen, gentlemen, he belongs to me!'

'Belongs to you?' said the head of the party, stopping it.

'Oh yes, dear gentlemen, he's my child, out without leave. My poor bad, bad boy! and he don't know me, he don't know me! Oh, what shall I do,' cried the little creature, wildly beating her hands together, 'when my own child don't know me!'

The head of the party looked (as well he might) to the old man for explanation. He whispered, as the dolls' dressmaker bent over the exhausted form and vainly tried to extract some sign of recognition from it: 'It's her drunken father.'

As the load was put down in the street, Riah drew the head of the party aside, and whispered that he thought the man was dying. 'No, surely not?' returned the other. But he became less confident, on looking, and directed the bearers to 'bring him to the nearest doctor's shop.'

Thither he was brought; the window becoming from within, a wall of faces, deformed into all kinds of shapes through the agency of globular red bottles, green bottles, blue bottles, and other coloured bottles. A ghastly light shining upon him that he didn't need, the beast so furious but a few minutes gone, was quiet enough now, with a strange mysterious writing on his face, reflected from one of the great bottles, as if Death had marked him: 'Mine' *(Chapter 9)*.

When the Reverend Frank had willingly engaged that he and his wife would accompany Lightwood back, he said, as a matter of course; 'We must make haste to get out, Margaretta, my dear, or we shall be descended on by Mrs. Sprodgkin.' To which Mrs. Milvey replied, in her pleasantly emphatic way, 'Oh *yes*, for she *is* such a marplot, Frank, and *does* worry so!' Words that were scarcely uttered when their theme was announced as in faithful attendance below, desiring counsel on a spiritual matter. The points on which Mrs. Sprodgkin sought elucidation being seldom of a pressing nature (as Who begat Whom, or some information concerning the Amorites), Mrs. Milvey on this special occasion resorted to the device of buying her off with a present of tea and sugar, and a loaf and butter. These gifts Mrs. Sprodgkin accepted, but still insisted on dutifully remaining in the hall to curtsey to the Reverend Frank as he came forth. Who, incautiously saying in his genial manner, 'Well, Sally, there you are!' involved himself in a discursive address from Mrs. Sprodgkin, revolving around the result that she regarded tea and sugar in the light of myrrh and frankincense, and considered bread and butter identical with locusts and wild honey. Having communicated this edifying piece of information, Mrs. Sprodgkin was left still un-adjourned in the hall, and Mr. and Mrs. Milvey hurried in a heated condition to the railway station. All of which is here recorded to the honour of that good Christian pair, representatives of hundreds of other good Christian pairs as conscientious and as useful, who merge the smallness of their work in its greatness, and feel in no danger of losing dignity when they adapt themselves to incomprehensible humbugs *(Chapter 11)*.

The train rattled among the house-tops, and among the ragged sides of houses torn down to make way for it, and over the swarming streets, and under the fruitful earth, until it shot across the river: bursting over the quiet surface like a bomb-shell, and gone again as if it had exploded in the rush of smoke and steam and glare. A little more, and again it roared across the river, a great rocket: spurning the watery turnings and doublings with ineffable contempt, and going straight to its end, as Father Time goes to his. To whom it is no matter what living waters run high or low, reflect the heavenly lights and darknesses, produce their little growth of weeds and flowers, turn here, turn there, are noisy or still, are troubled or at rest, for their course has one sure termination, though their sources and devices are many *(Chapter 11)*.

'And talk of Time slipping by you, as if it was an animal at rustic sports with his tail soaped,' said Mr. Inspector (again, a subject which nobody had approached); 'why, well you may. Well you may. How has it slipped by us, since the time when Mr. Job Potterson here present, Mr. Jacob Kibble here present, and an Officer of the Force here present, first came together on a matter of Identification!' *(Chapter 12)*.

'Not caring what she thought of you (and Goodness knows *that* was of no consequence!) you showed her, in yourself, the most detestable sides of wealth, saying in your own mind, "This shallow creature would never work the truth out of her own weak soul, if she had a hundred years to do it in; but a glaring instance kept before her may open even her eyes and set her thinking." That was what you said to yourself; was it, sir?'

'I never said anything of the sort,' Mr. Boffin declared in a state of the highest enjoyment.

'Then you ought to have said it, sir,' returned Bella, giving him two pulls and one kiss, 'for you must have thought and meant it. You saw that good fortune was turning my stupid head and hardening my silly heart – was making me grasping, calculating, insolent, insufferable – and you took the pains to be the dearest and kindest finger-post that ever was set up anywhere, pointing out the road that I was taking and the end it led to. Confess instantly!'

'John,' said Mr. Boffin, one broad piece of sunshine from head to foot, 'I wish you'd help me out of this.'

'You can't be heard by counsel, sir,' returned Bella. 'You must speak for yourself. Confess instantly!'

'Well, my dear,' said Mr. Boffin, 'the truth is, that when we did go in for the little scheme that my old lady has pinted out, I did put it to John, what did he think of going in for some such general scheme as *you* have pinted out? But I didn't in any way so word it, because I didn't in any way mean it. I only said to John, wouldn't it be more consistent, me going in for being a reg'lar brown bear respecting him, to go in as a reg'lar brown bear all round?' *(Chapter 13)*.

'Why, you smell rather comfortable here!' said Wegg, seeming to take it ill, and stopping and sniffing as he entered.

'I *am* rather comfortable, sir,' said Venus.

'You don't use lemon in your business, do you?' asked Wegg, sniffing again.

'No, Mr. Wegg,' said Venus. 'When I use it at all, I mostly use it in cobblers' punch.'

'What do you call cobblers' punch?' demanded Wegg, in a worse humour than before.

'It's difficult to impart the receipt for it, sir,' returned Venus, 'because, however particular you may be in allotting your materials, so much will still depend upon the individual gifts, and there being a feeling thrown into it. But the groundwork is gin' *(Chapter 14)*.

'When is it to come off?' asked Silas.

'Mr. Wegg,' said Venus, with another flush. 'I cannot permit it to be put in the form of a Fight. I must temperately but firmly call upon you, sir, to amend that question.'

'When is the lady,' Wegg reluctantly demanded, constraining his ill-temper in remembrance of the partnership and its stock in trade, 'a-going to give her 'and where she has already given her 'art?'

'Sir,' returned Venus, 'I again accept the altered phrase, and with pleasure. The lady is a-going to give her 'and where she has already given her 'art, next Monday' *(Chapter 14)*.

'I wish to goodness, Ma,' said Lavvy, throwing herself back among the cushions, with her arms crossed, 'that you'd loll a little.'

'How!' repeated Mrs. Wilfer. 'Loll!'

'Yes, Ma.'

'I hope,' said the impressive lady, 'I am incapable of it.'

'I am sure you look so, Ma. But why one should go out to dine with one's own daughter or sister, as if one's under-petticoat was a backboard, I do *not* understand.'

'Neither do I understand,' retorted Mrs. Wilfer, with deep scorn, 'how a young lady can mention the garment in the name in which you have indulged. I blush for you.'

'Thank you, Ma,' said Lavvy, yawning, 'but I can do it for myself, I am obliged to you, when there's any occasion.'

Here, Mr. Sampson, with the view of establishing harmony, which he never under any circumstances succeeded in doing, said with an agreeable smile: 'After all, you know, ma'am, we know it's there.' And immediately felt that he had committed himself (*Chapter 16: Lavinia and Mrs. Wilfer*).

'Dearest Lavinia,' urged Mr. Sampson, pathetically, 'I adore you.'

'Then if you can't do it in a more agreeable manner,' returned the young lady, 'I wish you wouldn't.'

'I also,' pursued Mr. Sampson, 'respect you, ma'am, to an extent which must ever be below your merits, I am well aware, but still up to an uncommon mark. Bear with a wretch, Lavinia, bear with a wretch, ma'am, who feels the noble sacrifices you make for him, but is goaded almost to madness' – Mr. Sampson slapped his forehead – 'when he thinks of competing with the rich and influential.'

'When you have to compete with the rich and influential, it will probably be mentioned to you,' said Miss Lavvy, 'in good time. At least, it will if the case is *my* case.'

Mr. Sampson immediately expressed his fervent opinion that this was 'more than human,' and was brought upon his knees at Miss Lavinia's feet (*Chapter 16*).

Through the whole of the decorations, Mrs. Wilfer led the way with the bearing of a Savage Chief, who would feel himself compromised by manifesting the slightest token of surprise or admiration.

Indeed, the bearing of this impressive woman, throughout the day, was a pattern to all impressive women under similar circumstances. She renewed the acquaintance of Mr. and Mrs. Boffin, as if Mr. and Mrs. Boffin had said of her what she had said of them, and as if Time alone could quite wear her injury out. She regarded every servant who approached her, as her sworn enemy, expressly intending to offer her affronts with the dishes, and to pour forth outrages on her moral feelings from the decanters. She sat erect at table, on the right hand of her son-in-law, as half suspecting poison in the viands, and as bearing up with native force of character against other deadly ambushes. Her

carriage towards Bella was as a carriage towards a young lady of good position whom she had met in society a few years ago. Even when, slightly thawing under the influence of sparkling champagne, she related to her son-in-law some passages of domestic interest concerning her papa, she infused into the narrative such Arctic suggestions of her having been an unappreciated blessing to mankind, since her papa's days, and also of that gentleman's having been a frosty impersonation of a frosty race, as struck cold to the very soles of the feet of the hearers. The Inexhaustible being produced, staring, and evidently intending a weak and washy smile shortly, no sooner beheld her, than it was stricken spasmodic and inconsolable. When she took her leave at last, it would have been hard to say whether it was with the air of going to the scaffold herself, or of leaving the inmates of the house for immediate execution. Yet, John Harmon enjoyed it all merrily, and told his wife, when he and she were alone, that her natural ways had never seemed so dearly natural as beside this foil, and that although he did not dispute her being her father's daughter, he should ever remain steadfast in the faith that she could not be her mother's (*Chapter 16*).

'But, excuse me,' says Podsnap, with his temper and his shirt-collar about equally rumpled; 'was this young woman ever a female waterman?'

'Never. But she sometimes rowed in a boat with her father, I believe.'

General sensation against the young woman. Brewer shakes his head. Boots shakes his head. Buffer shakes his head.

'And now, Mr. Lightwood, was she ever,' pursues Podsnap, with his indignation rising high into those hair-brushes of his, 'a factory girl?'

'Never. But she had some employment in a paper mill, I believe.' General sensation repeated. Brewer says, 'Oh dear!' Boots says, 'Oh dear!' Buffer says, 'Oh dear!' All, in a rumbling tone of protest.

'Then all *I* have to say is,' returns Podsnap, putting the thing away with his right arm, 'that my gorge rises against such a marriage – that it offends and disgusts me – that it makes me sick – and that I desire to know no more about it.'

('Now I wonder,' thinks Mortimer, amused, 'whether *you* are the Voice of Society!')

'Hear, hear, hear!' cries Lady Tippins. 'Your opinion of this *mésalliance,* honourable colleague of the honourable member who has just sat down?'

Mrs. Podsnap is of opinion that in these matters 'there should be an equality of station and fortune, and that a man accustomed to Society should look out for a woman accustomed to Society and capable of bearing her part in it with – an ease and elegance of carriage – that.' Mrs. Podsnap stops there, delicately intimating that every such man should look out for a fine woman as nearly resembling herself as he may hope to discover (*Chapter 17*).

GEORGE SILVERMAN'S EXPLANATION

My parents were in a miserable condition of life, and my infant home was a cellar in Preston. I recollect the sound of father's Lancashire clogs on the street pavement above, as being different in my young hearing from the sound of all other clogs; and I recollect, that, when mother came down the cellar-steps, I used tremblingly to speculate on her feet having a good or an ill-tempered look, – on her knees, – on her waist, – until finally her face came into view, and settled the question. From this it will be seen that I was timid, and that the cellar-steps were steep, and that the doorway was very low.

Mother had the gripe and clutch of poverty upon her face, upon her figure, and not least of all upon her voice. Her sharp and high-pitched words were squeezed out of her, as by the compression of bony fingers on a leathern bag; and she had a way of rolling her eyes about and about the cellar, as she scolded, that was gaunt and hungry. Father, with his shoulders rounded, would sit quiet on a three-legged stool, looking at the empty grate, until she would pluck the stool from under him, and bid him go bring some money home. Then he would dismally ascend the steps; and I, holding my ragged shirt and trousers together with a hand (my only braces), would feint and dodge from mother's pursuing grasp at my hair (*Chapter 3: George Silverman*).

Brother Gimblet came forward, and took (as I knew he would) the text, 'My kingdom is not of this world.' Ah! but whose was, my fellow-sinners? Whose? Why, our brother's here present was. The only kingdom he had an idea of was of this world. ('That's it!' from several of the congregation.) What did the woman do when she lost the piece of money? Went and looked for it. What should our brother do when he lost his way? ('Go and look for it,' from a sister.) Go and look for it, true. But must he look for it in the right direction or in the wrong? ('In the right,' from a brother.) There spake the prophets! He must look for it in the right direction, or he couldn't find it. But he had turned his back upon the right direction, and he wouldn't find it. Now, my fellow-sinners, to show you the difference betwixt worldly-mindedness and unworldly-mindedness, betwixt kingdoms not of this world and kingdoms *of* this world, here was a letter wrote by even our worldly-minded brother unto Brother Hawkyard. Judge, from hearing of it read, whether Brother Hawkyard was the faithful steward that the Lord had in his mind only t'other day, when, in this very place, he drew you the picter of the unfaithful one; for it was him that done it, not me. Don't doubt that!'

Brother Gimblet then groaned and bellowed his way through my composition, and subsequently through an hour. The service closed with a hymn, in which the brothers unanimously roared, and the sisters unanimously shrieked at me, That I by wiles of worldly gain was mocked, and they on waters of sweet love were rocked; that I with mammon struggled in the dark, while they were floating in a second ark.

I went out from all this with an aching heart and a weary spirit: not because I was quite so weak as to consider these narrow creatures interpreters of the Divine Majesty and Wisdom, but because I was weak enough to feel as though it were my hard fortune to be misrepresented and misunderstood, when I most tried to subdue any risings of mere worldliness within me, and when I most hoped that, by dint of trying earnestly, I had succeeded (*Chapter 6: George Silverman*).

HOLIDAY ROMANCE

'Prince,' said Grandmarina, 'I bring you your bride.'

The moment the fairy said those words, Prince Certainpersonio's face left off being sticky, and his jacket and corduroys changed to peach-bloom velvet, and his hair curled, and a cap and feather flew in like a bird and settled on his head. He got into the carriage by the fairy's invitation; and there he renewed his acquaintance with the duchess, whom he had seen before.

In the church were the prince's relations and friends, and the Princess Alicia's relations and friends, and the seventeen princes and princesses, and the baby, and a crowd of the neighbours. The marriage was beautiful beyond expression. The duchess was bridesmaid, and beheld the ceremony from the pulpit, where she was supported by the cushion of the desk.

Grandmarina gave a magnificent wedding-feast afterwards, in which there was everything and more to eat, and everything and more to drink. The wedding-cake was delicately ornamented with white satin ribbons, frosted silver, and white lilies, and was forty-two yards round.

When Grandmarina had drunk her love to the young couple, and Prince Certainpersonio had made a speech, and everybody had cried, Hip, hip, hip, hurrah! Grandmarina announced to the king and queen that in future there would be eight quarter-days in every year, except in leap-year, when there would be ten. She then turned to Certainpersonio and Alicia, and said, 'My dears, you will have thirty-five children, and they will all be good and beautiful. Seventeen of your children will be boys, and eighteen will be girls. The hair of the whole of your children will curl naturally. They will never have the measles, and will have recovered from the whooping-cough before being born.

On hearing such good news, everybody cried out 'Hip, hip, hip, hurrah!' again *(Part 2)*.

'He nears him!' said an elderly seaman, following the captain through his spy-glass.

'He strikes him!' said another seaman, a mere stripling, but also with a spy-glass.

'He tows him towards us!' said another seaman, a man in the full vigour of life, but also with a spy-glass.

In fact the captain was seen approaching, with the huge bulk following. We will not dwell on the deafening cries of 'Boldheart! Boldheart!' with which he was received, when, carelessly leaping on the quarter-deck, he presented his prize to his men. They afterwards made two thousand four hundred and seventeen pound ten and sixpence by it.

Ordering the sails to be braced up, the captain now stood W.N.W. 'The Beauty' flew rather than floated over the dark blue waters. Nothing particular occurred for a fortnight, except taking, with considerable slaughter, four Spanish galleons, and a snow from South America, all richly laden. Inaction began to tell upon the spirits of the men *(Part 3)*.

Capt. Boldheart ... turned to the Latin-grammar master, severely reproaching him with his perfidy, and put it to his crew what they considered that a master who spited a boy deserved.

They answered with one voice, 'Death.'

'It may be so,' said the captain; 'but it shall never be said that Boldheart stained his hour of triumph with the blood of his enemy. Prepare the cutter.'

The cutter was immediately prepared.

'Without taking your life,' said the captain, 'I must yet for ever deprive you of the power of spiting other boys. I shall turn you adrift in this boat. You will find in her two oars, a compass, a bottle of rum, a small cask of water, a piece of pork, a bag of biscuit, and my Latin grammar. Go! and spite the natives, if you can find any' *(Part 3)*.

One day during a gleam of sunshine, and when the weather had moderated, the man at the mast-head – too weak now to touch his hat, besides its having been blown away – called out,

'Savages!'

All was now expectation.

Presently fifteen hundred canoes, each paddled by twenty savages, were seen advancing in excellent order. They were of a light green colour (the savages were), and sang, with great energy, the following strain:

> Choo a choo a choo tooth.
> Muntch, muntch. Nycey!
> Choo a choo a choo tooth.
> Muntch, muntch. Nicey!

As the shades of night were by this time closing in, these expressions were supposed to embody this simple people's views of the evening hymn. But it too soon appeared that the song was a translation of 'For what we are going to receive,' &c. *(Part 3)*.

THE MYSTERY OF EDWIN DROOD

An ancient English Cathedral Tower? How can the ancient English Cathedral tower be here! The well-known massive gray square tower of its old Cathedral? How can that be here! There is no spike of rusty iron in the air, between the eye and it, from any point of the real prospect. What is the spike that intervenes, and who has set it up? Maybe it is set up by the Sultan's orders for the impaling of a horde of Turkish robbers, one by one. It is so, for cymbals clash, and the Sultan goes by to his palace in long procession. Ten thousand scimitars flash in the sunlight, and thrice ten thousand dancing-girls strew flowers. Then, follow white elephants caparisoned in countless gorgeous colours, and infinite in number and attendants. Still the Cathedral Tower rises in the background, where it cannot be, and still no writhing figure is on the grim spike. Stay! Is the spike so low a thing as the rusty spike on the top of a post of an old bedstead that has tumbled all awry? Some vague period of drowsy

laughter must be devoted to the consideration of this possibility *(Chapter 1)*.

Whosoever has observed that sedate and clerical bird, the rook, may perhaps have noticed that when he wings his way homeward towards nightfall, in a sedate and clerical company, two rooks will suddenly detach themselves from the rest, will retrace their flight for some distance, and will convey their poise and linger; conveying to mere men the fancy that it is of some occult importance to the body politic, that this artful couple should pretend to have renounced connection with it.

Similarly, service being over in the old Cathedral with the square tower, and the choir scuffling out again, and divers venerable persons of rook-like aspect dispersing, two of these latter retrace their steps, and walk together in the echoing Close.

Not only is the day waning, but the year. The low sun is fiery and yet cold behind the monastery ruin, and the Virginia creeper on the Cathedral wall has showered half its deep-red leaves down on the pavement. There has been rain this afternoon, and a wintry shudder goes among the little pools on the cracked, uneven flag-stones, and through the giant elm-trees as they shed a gust of tears. Their fallen leaves lie strewn thickly about. Some of these leaves, in a timid rush, seek sanctuary within the low arched Cathedral door; but two men coming out resist them, and cast them forth again with their feet; this done, one of the two locks the door with a goodly key, and the other flits away with a folio music-book *(Chapter 2)*.

They all three look towards an old stone gatehouse crossing the Close, with an arched thoroughfare passing beneath it. Through its latticed window, a fire shines out upon the fast-darkening scene, involving in shadow the pendent masses of ivy and creeper covering the building's front. As the deep Cathedral-bell strikes the hour, a ripple of wind goes through these at their distance, like a ripple of the solemn sound that hums through tomb and tower, broken niche and defaced statue, in the pile close at hand *(Chapter 2)*.

'How does our service sound to you?'

'Beautiful! Quite celestial!'

'It often sounds to me quite devilish. I am so weary of it. The echoes of my own voice among the arches seem to mock me with my daily drudging round. No wretched monk who droned his life away in that gloomy place, before me, can have been more tired of it than I am. He could take for relief (and did take) to carving demons out of the stalls and seats and desks. What shall I do? Must I take to carving them out of my heart?' *(Chapter 2: John Jasper)*.

An ancient city, Cloisterham, and no meet dwelling-place for any one with hankerings after the noisy world. A monotonous, silent city, deriving an earthy flavour throughout from its Cathedral crypt, and so abounding in vestiges of monastic graves, that the Cloisterham children grow small salad in the dust of abbots and abbesses, and make dirt-pies of nuns and friars; while every ploughman in its outlying fields renders to once puissant Lord Treasurers, Arch-bishops, Bishops, and such-like, the attention which the Ogre in the story-book desired to render to his unbidden visitor, and grinds their bones to make his bread *(Chapter 3).*

A city of another and a bygone time is Cloisterham, with its hoarse Cathedral-bell, its hoarse rooks hovering about the Cathedral tower, its hoarser and less distinct rooks in the stalls far beneath. Fragments of old wall, saint's chapel, chapter-house, convent and monastery, have got incongruously or obstructively built into many of its houses and gardens, much as kindred jumbled notions have become incorporated into many of its citizens' minds. All things in it are of the past. Even its single pawnbroker takes in no pledges, nor has he for a long time, but offers vainly an unredeemed stock for sale, of which the costlier articles are dim and pale old watches apparently in a slow perspiration, tarnished sugar-tongs with ineffectual legs, and odd volumes of dismal books. The most abundant and the most agreeable evidences of progressing life in Cloisterham are the evidences of vegetable life in many gardens; even its drooping and despondent little theatre has its poor strip of garden, receiving the foul fiend, when he ducks from its stage into the infernal regions, among scarlet-beans or oyster-shells, according to the season of the year *(Chapter 3).*

'And how did you pass your birthday, Pussy?'
'Delightfully! Everybody gave me a present. And we had a feast. And we had a ball at night.'
'A feast and a ball, eh? These occasions seem to go off tolerably well without me, Pussy.'
'Delightfully!' cries Rosa, in a quite spontaneous manner, and without the least pretence of reserve.
'Hah! and what was the feast?'
'Tarts, oranges, jellies, and shrimps' *(Chapter 3: Edwin Drood and Rosa Bud).*

'I want to go to the Lumps-of-Delight shop.'
'To the – ?'
'A Turkish sweetmeat, sir. My gracious me, don't you understand anything? Call yourself an Engineer, and not know *that*?' *(Chapter 3: Edwin Drood and Rosa Bud).*

'But don't she hate Arabs, and Turks, and Fellahs, and people?'
'Certainly not.' Very firmly.
'At least she *must* hate the Pyramids? Come, Eddy?'
'Why should she be such a little – tall, I mean – goose, as to hate the Pyramids, Rosa?'
'Ah! you should hear Miss Twinkleton,' often nodding her head, and much enjoying the Lumps, 'bore about them, and then you wouldn't ask. Tiresome old burying-grounds! Isises, and Ibises, and Cheopses, and Pharaohses; who cares about them? And then there was Belzoni, or somebody, dragged out by the legs, half-choked with bats and dust. All the girls say: Serve him right, and hope it hurt him, and wish he had been quite choked' *(Chapter 3: Edwin Drood and Rosa Bud).*

'If I have not gone to foreign countries, young man, foreign countries have come to me. They have come to me in the way of business, and I have improved upon my opportunities. Put it that I take an inventory, or make a catalogue. I see a French clock. I never saw him before, in my life, but I instantly lay my finger on him and say "Paris!" I see some cups and saucers of Chinese make, equally strangers to me personally: I put my finger on them, then and there, and I say "Pekin, Nankin, and Canton." It is the same with Japan, with Egypt, and with bamboo and sandal-wood from the East Indies; I put my finger on them all. I have put my finger on the North Pole before now, and said "Spear of Esquimaux make, for half a pint of pale sherry!" ' *(Chapter 4: Mr. Sapsea).*

'Mrs. Sapsea's monument having had full time to settle and dry, let me take your opinion, as a man of taste, on the inscription I have (as I before remarked, not without some little fever of the brow) drawn out for it. Take it in your own hand. The setting out of the lines requires to be followed with the eye, as well as the contents with the mind.'
Mr. Jasper complying, sees and reads as follows:

> ETHELINDA,
> Reverential Wife of
> MR. THOMAS SAPSEA,
> AUCTIONEER, VALUER, ESTATE AGENT,
> &c., OF THIS CITY.
> Whose Knowledge of the World,
> Though somewhat extensive,
> Never brought him acquainted with
> A SPIRIT
> More capable of
> LOOKING UP TO HIM.
> STRANGER, PAUSE
> And ask thyself the Question,
> CANST THOU DO LIKEWISE?
> If Not,
> WITH A BLUSH RETIRE.
> *(Chapter 4:* Sapsea)

Durdles is a stonemason; chiefly in the gravestone, tomb, and monument way, and wholly of their colour from head to foot. No man is better known in Cloisterham. He is the chartered libertine of the place. Fame trumpets him a wonderful workman – which, for aught that anybody knows, he may be (as he never works); and a wonderful sot – which everybody knows he is. With the Cathedral crypt he is better acquainted than any living authority; it may even be than any dead one. It is said that the intimacy of this acquaintance began in his habitually resorting to that secret place, to lock-out the Cloisterham boy-populace, and sleep off the fumes of liquor: he having ready access to the Cathedral, as contractor for rough repairs *(Chapter 4).*

'How are you, Durdles?'
'I've got a touch of the Tombatism on me, Mr. Jasper, but that I must expect.'
'You mean the Rheumatism', says Sapsea, in a sharp tone. (He is nettled by having his composition so mechanically received.)
'No, I don't. I mean, Mr. Sapsea, the Tombatism. It's another sort of Rheumatism. Mr. Jasper knows what Durdles means. You get among them Tombs

afore it's well light on a winter morning, and keep on, as the Catechism says, a-walking in the same all the days of your life, and *you*'ll know what Durdles means' *(Chapter 4)*.

> 'Widdy widdy wen!
> I–ket–ches–Im–out – ar–ter–ten,
> Widdy widdy wy!
> Then–E–don't–go–then–I–shy –
> Widdy Widdy Wake-cock warning!'
> *(Chapter 5:* Deputy)

'Mrs. Sapsea'; introducing the monument of that devoted wife. 'Late Incumbent'; introducing the Reverend Gentleman's broken column. 'Departed Assessed Taxes'; introducing a vase and towel, standing on what might represent the cake of soap. 'Former pastrycook and Muffin-maker, much respected'; introducing gravestone. 'All safe and sound here, sir, and all Durdles's work. Of the common folk, that is merely bundled up in turf and brambles, the less said the better. A poor lot, soon forgot' *(Chapter 5:* Durdles).

'I tap, tap, tap. Solid! I go on tapping. Solid still! Tap again. Holloa! Hollow! Tap again, persevering. Solid in hollow! Tap, tap, tap, to try it better. Solid in hollow; and inside solid, hollow again! There you are! Old 'un crumbled away in stone coffin, in vault!' *(Chapter 5:* Durdles).

A short, squat omnibus, with a disproportionate heap of luggage on the roof – like a little Elephant with infinitely too much Castle *(Chapter 6)*.

'In a last word of reference to my sister, sir (we are twin children), you ought to know, to her honour, that nothing in our misery ever subdued her, though it often cowed me. When we ran away from it (we ran away four times in six years, to be soon brought back and cruelly punished), the flight was always of her planning and leading. Each time she dressed as a boy, and showed the daring of a man. I take it we were seven years old when we first decamped; but I remember, when I lost the pocket-knife with which she was to have cut her hair short, how desperately she tried to tear it out, or bite it off' *(Chapter 7:* Neville Landless).

'You know that he loves you?'

'O, don't, don't, don't!' cried Rosa, dropping on her knees, and clinging to her new resource. 'Don't tell me of it! He terrifies me. He haunts my thoughts, like a dreadful ghost. I feel that I am never safe from him. I feel as if he could pass in through the wall when he is spoken of.' She actually did look round, as if she dreaded to see him standing in the shadow behind her *(Chapter 7:* Helena Landless and Rosa Bud).

Rumour, Ladies, had been represented by that bard – hem! –

> 'who drew
> The celebrated Jew,'

as painted full of tongues. Rumour in Cloisterham (Miss Ferdinand will honour me with her attention) was no exception to the great limner's portrait of Rumour elsewhere. A slight *fracas* between two young gentlemen occurring last night within a hundred miles of these peaceful walls (Miss Ferdinand, being appar-

ently incorrigible, will have the kindness to write out this evening, in the original language, the first four fables of our vivacious neighbour, Monsieur La Fontaine) had been very grossly exaggerated by Rumour's voice. In the first alarm and anxiety arising from our sympathy with a sweet young friend, not wholly to be dissociated from one of the gladiators in the bloodless arena in question (the impropriety of Miss Reynolds's appearing to stab herself in the band with a pin, is far too obvious, and too glaringly unlady-like, to be pointed out), we descended from our maiden elevation to discuss this uncongenial and this unfit theme. Responsible inquiries having assured us that it was but one of those 'airy nothings' pointed at by the Poet (whose name and date of birth Miss Giggles will supply within half an hour), we would now discard the subject, and concentrate our minds upon the grateful labours of the day' *(Chapter 9:* Miss Twinkleton).

'My visits,' said Mr. Grewgious, 'are, like those of the angels – not that I compare myself to an angel.'

'No, sir,' said Rosa.

'Not by any means,' assented Mr. Grewgious. 'I merely refer to my visits, which are few and far between. The angels are, we know very well, upstairs' *(Chapter 9)*.

' "Pounds, shillings, and pence," is my next note. A dry subject for a young lady, but an important subject too. Life is pounds, shillings, and pence. Death is – ' A sudden recollection of the death of her two parents seemed to stop him, and he said in a softer tone, and evidently inserting the negative as an afterthought: 'Death is *not* pounds, shillings, and pence' *(Chapter 9:* 'Mr. Grewgious').

'I am a particularly Angular man,' proceeded Mr. Grewgious, as if it suddenly occurred to him to mention it, 'and I am not used to give anything away. If, for these two reasons, some competent Proxy would give *you* away, I should take it very kindly' *(Chapter 9)*.

'As a particularly Angular man, I do not fit smoothly into the social circle, and consequently I have no other engagement at Christmas-time than to partake, on the twenty-fifth, of a boiled turkey and celery sauce with a – with a particularly Angular clerk I have the good fortune to possess, whose father, being a Norfolk farmer, sends him up (the turkey up), as a present to me, from the neighbourhood of Norwich' *(Chapter 9:* Grewgious).

He descended the stair again, and, crossing the Close, paused at the great western folding-door of the Cathedral, which stood open on the fine and bright, though short-lived, afternoon, for the airing of the place.

'Dear me,' said Mr. Grewgious, peeping in, 'it's like looking down the throat of Old Time.'

Old Time heaved a mouldy sigh from tomb and arch and vault; and gloomy shadows began to deepen in corners; and damps began to rise from green patches of stone; and jewels, cast upon the pavement of the nave from stained glass by the declining sun, began to perish. Within the grill-gate of the chancel, up the steps surmounted loomingly by the fast-darkening organ, white robes could be dimly seen, and one feeble voice, rising. and falling in a cracked, monotonous mutter, could at intervals be faintly heard *(Chapter 9)*.

'God bless them both!'
'God save them both!' cried Jasper.
'I said, bless them' remarked the former, looking back over his shoulder.
'I said, save them,' returned the latter. 'Is there any difference?' *(Chapter 9:* Grewgious and Jasper).

It has been often enough remarked that women have a curious power of divining the characters of men, which would seem to be innate and instinctive; seeing that it is arrived at through no patient process of reasoning, that it can give no satisfactory or sufficient account of itself, and that it pronounces in the most confident manner even against accumulated observation on the part of the other sex. But it has not been quite so often remarked that this power (fallible, like every other human attribute) is for the most part absolutely incapable of self-revision; and that when it has delivered an adverse opinion which by all human lights is subsequently proved to have failed, it is undistinguishable from prejudice, in respect of its determination not to be corrected. Nay, the very possiblity of contradiction or disproof, however remote, communicates to this feminine judgment from the first, in nine cases out of ten, the weakness attendant on the testimony of an interested witness; so personally and strongly does the fair diviner connect herself with her divination *(Chapter 10)*.

As, whenever the Reverend Septimus fell a-musing, his good mother took it to be an infallible sign that he 'wanted support,' the blooming old lady made all haste to the dining-room closet, to produce from it the support embodied in a glass of Constantia and a home-made biscuit. It was a most wonderful closet, worthy of Cloisterham and of Minor Canon Corner. Above it, a portrait of Handel in a flowing wig beamed down at the spectator, with a knowing air of being up to the contents of the closet, and a musical air of intending to combine all its harmonies in one delicious fugue. No common closet with a vulgar door on hinges, openable all at once, and leaving nothing to be disclosed by degrees, this rare closet had a lock in mid-air, where two perpendicular slides met; the one falling down, and the other pushing up. The upper slide, on being pulled down (leaving the lower a double mystery), revealed deep shelves of pickle-jars, jampots, tin canisters, spice-boxes, and agreeably outlandish vessels of blue and white, the luscious lodgings of preserved tamarinds and ginger. Every benevolent inhabitant of this retreat had his name inscribed upon his stomach. The pickles, in a uniform of rich brown double-breasted buttoned coat, and yellow or sombre drab continuations, announced their portly forms, in printed capitals, as Walnut, Gherkin, Onion, Cabbage, Cauliflower, Mixed, and other members of that noble family. The jams, as being of a less masculine temperament, and as wearing curlpapers, announced themselves in feminine caligraphy, like a soft whisper, to be Raspberry, Gooseberry, Apricot, Plum, Damson,

Apple and Peach. The scene closing on these charmers, and the lower slide ascending, oranges were revealed, attended by a mighty japanned sugar-box, to temper their acerbity if unripe. Home-made biscuits waited at the Court of these Powers, accompanied by a goodly fragment of plum-cake, and various slender ladies' fingers, to be dipped into sweet wine and kissed. Lowest of all, a compact leaden vault enshrined the sweet wine and a stock of cordials; whence issued whispers of Seville Orange, Lemon, Almond, and Caraway-seed. There was a crowning air upon this closet of closets, of having been for ages hummed through by the Cathedral bell and organ, until those venerable bees had made sublimated honey of everything in store; and it was always observed that every dipper among the shelves (deep, as has been noticed, and swallowing up head, shoulders, and elbows) came forth again mellow-faced, and seeming to have undergone a saccharine transfiguration *(Chapter 10)*.

Into this herbaceous penitentiary, situated on an upper staircase-landing: a low and narrow whitewashed cell, where bunches of dried leaves hung from rusty hooks in the ceiling, and were spread out upon shelves, in company with portentous bottles: would the Reverend Septimus submissively be led, like the highly popular lamb who has so long and unresistingly been led to the slaughter, and there would he, unlike that lamb, bore nobody but himself *(Chapter 10)*.

Behind the most ancient part of Holborn, London, where certain gabled houses some centuries of age still stand looking on the public way, as if disconsolately looking for the Old Bourne that has long run dry, is a little nook composed of two irregular quadrangles, called Staple Inn. It is one of those nooks, the turning into which out of the clashing street, imparts to the relieved pedestrian the sensation of having put cotton in his ears, and velvet soles on his boots. It is one of those nooks where a few smoky sparrows twitter in smoky trees, as though they called to one another, 'Let us play at country,' and where a few feet of gardenmould and a few yards of gravel enable them to do that refreshing violence to their tiny understandings. Moreover, it is one of those nooks which are legal nooks; and it contains a little Hall, with a little lantern in its roof: to what obstructive purposes devoted, and at whose expense, this history knoweth not *(Chapter 11)*.

Neither wind nor sun ... favoured Staple Inn one December afternoon towards six o'clock, when it was filled with fog, and candles shed murky and blurred rays through the windows of all its then-occupied sets of chambers; notably from a set of chambers in a corner house in the little inner quadrangle, presenting in black and white over its ugly portal the mysterious inscription:

$$P$$
$$J \qquad T$$
$$1747$$

In which set of chambers, never having troubled his head about the inscription, unless to bethink himself at odd times on glancing up at it, that haply it might mean Perhaps John Thomas, or Perhaps Joe Tyler, sat Mr. Grewgious writing by his fire *(Chapter 11)*.

Bazzard returned, accompanied by two waiters – an immovable waiter, and a flying waiter; and the three brought in with them as much fog as gave a new roar to the fire. The flying waiter, who had brought everything on his shoulders, laid the cloth with amazing rapidity and dexterity; while the immovable waiter, who had brought nothing, found fault with him. The flying waiter then highly polished all the glasses he had brought, and the immovable waiter looked through them. The flying waiter then flew across Holborn for the soup, and flew back again, and then took another flight for the made-dish, and flew back again, and then took another flight for the joint and poultry, and flew back again, and between whiles took supplementary flights for a great variety of articles, as it was discovered from time to time that the immovable waiter had forgotten them all. But let the flying waiter cleave the air as he might, he was always reproached on his return by the immovable waiter for bringing fog with him, and being out of breath. At the conclusion of the repast, by which time the flying waiter was severely blown, the immovable waiter gathered up the tablecloth under his arm with a grand air, and having sternly (not to say with indignation) looked on at the flying waiter while he set the clean glasses round, directed a valedictory glance towards Mr. Grewgious, conveying: 'Let it be clearly understood between us that the reward is mine, and that Nil is the claim of this slave,' and pushed the flying waiter before him out of the room *(Chapter 11)*.

The host had gone below to the cellar, and had brought up bottles of ruby, straw-coloured, and golden drinks, which had ripened long ago in lands where no fogs are, and had since lain slumbering in the shade. Sparkling and tingling after so long a nap, they pushed at their corks to help the corkscrew (like prisoners helping rioters to force their gates), and danced out gaily. If P. J. T. in seventeen-forty-seven, or in any other year of his period, drank such wines – then, for a certainty, P. J. T. was Pretty Jolly Too *(Chapter 11)*.

'I hazard the guess that the true lover's mind is completely permeated by the beloved object of his affections. I hazard the guess that her dear name is precious to him, cannot be heard or repeated without emotion, and is preserved sacred. If he has any distinguishing appellation of fondness for her, it is reserved for her, and is not for common ears. A name that it would be a privilege to call her by, being alone with her own bright self, it would be a liberty, a coldness, an insensibility, almost a breach of good faith, to flaunt elsewhere' *(Chapter 11: Grewgious)*.

Repairing to Durdles's unfinished house, or hole in the city wall, and seeing a light within it, he softly picks his course among the gravestones, monuments, and stony lumber of the yard, already touched here and there, sidewise, by the rising moon. The two journeymen have left their two great saws sticking in their blocks of stone; and two skeleton journeymen out of the Dance of Death might be grinning in the

shadow of their sheltering sentry-boxes, about to slash away at cutting out the gravestones of the next two people destined to die in Cloisterham. Likely enough, the two think little of that now, being alive, and perhaps merry. Curious, to make a guess at the two; – or say one of the two! *(Chapter 12)*.

Ask the first hundred citizens of Cloisterham, met at random in the streets at noon, if they believed in Ghosts, they would tell you no; but put them to choose at night between these eerie Precincts and the thoroughfare of shops, and you would find that ninety-nine declared for the longer round and the more frequented way *(Chapter 12)*.

As aëronauts lighten the load they carry, when they wish to rise, similarly Durdles has lightened the wicker bottle in coming up. Snatches of sleep surprise him on his legs, and stop him in his talk. A mild fit of calenture seizes him, in which he deems that the ground so far below, is on a level with the tower, and would as lief walk off the tower into the air as not. Such is his state when they begin to come down. And as aëronauts make themselves heavier when they wish to descend, similarly Durdles charges himself with more liquid from the wicker bottle, that he may come down the better *(Chapter 12)*.

It is not much of a dream, considering the vast extent of the domains of dreamland, and their wonderful productions; it is only remarkable for being unusually restless and unusually real. He dreams of lying there, asleep, and yet counting his companion's footsteps as he walks to and fro. He dreams that the footsteps die away into distance of time and of space, and that something touches him, and that something falls from his hand. Then something clinks and gropes about, and he dreams that he is alone for so long a time, that the lanes of light take new directions as the moon advances in her course. From succeeding unconsciousness he passes into a dream of slow uneasiness from cold; and painfully awakes to a perception of the lanes of light – really changed, much as he had dreamed – and Jasper walking among them, beating his hands and feet *(Chapter 12)*.

Among the mighty store of wonderful chains that are for ever forging, day and night, in the vast iron-works of time and circumstance, there was one chain forged in the moment of that small conclusion, riveted to the foundations of heaven and earth, and gifted with invincible force to hold and drag *(Chapter 12)*.

Christmas Eve in Cloisterham. A few strange faces in the streets; a few other faces, half strange and half familiar, once the faces of Cloisterham children, now the faces of men and women who come back from the outer world at long intervals to find the city wonderfully shrunken in size, as if it had not washed by any means well in the meanwhile. To these, the striking of the Cathedral clock, and the cawing of the rooks from the Cathedral tower, are like voices of their nursery time. To such as these, it has happened in their dying hours afar off, that they have imagined their chamber-floor to be strewn with the autumnal leaves fallen from the elm-trees in the Close: so have the rustling sounds and fresh scents of their earliest impressions revived when the circle of their lives was very nearly traced, and the beginning and the end were drawing close together.

Seasonable tokens are about. Red berries shine here and there in the lattices of Minor Canon Corner; Mr. and Mrs. Tope are daintily sticking sprigs of holly into the carvings and sconces of the Cathedral stalls, as if they were sticking them into the coat-buttonholes of the Dean and Chapter. Lavish profusion is in the shops: particularly in the articles of currants, raisins, spices, candied peel, and moist sugar. An unusual air of gallantry and dissipation is abroad; evinced in an immense bunch of mistletoe hanging in the greengrocer's shop doorway, and a poor little Twelfth Cake, culminating in the figure of a Harlequin – such a very poor little Twelfth Cake, that one would rather call it a Twenty-fourth Cake or a Forty-eighth Cake – to be raffled for at the pastry-cook's, terms one shilling per member. Public amusements are not wanting. The Wax-Work which made so deep an impression on the reflective mind of the Emperor of China is to be seen by particular desire during Christmas Week only, on the premises of the bankrupt livery-stable-keeper up the lane; and a new grand comic Christmas pantomime is to be produced at the Theatre: the latter heralded by the portrait of Signor Jacksonini the clown, saying 'How do you do to-morrow?' quite as large as life, and almost as miserably *(Chapter 14)*.

He has another mile or so, to linger out before the dinner-hour; and, when he walks over the bridge and by the river, the woman's words are in the rising wind, in the angry sky, in the troubled water, in the flickering lights. There is some solemn echo of them even in the Cathedral chime, which strikes a sudden surprise to his heart as he turns in under the archway of the gatehouse.

And so *he* goes up the postern stair *(Chapter 14)*.

Mr. Jasper is in beautiful voice this day. In the pathetic supplication to have his heart inclined to keep this law, he quite astonishes his fellows by his melodious power. He has never sung difficult music with such skill and harmony, as in this day's Anthem. His nervous temperament is occasionally prone to take difficult music a little too quickly; to-day, his time is perfect *(Chapter 14)*.

The Precincts are never particularly well lighted; but the strong blasts of wind blowing out many of the lamps (in some instances shattering the frames too, and bringing the glass rattling to the ground), they are unusually dark to-night. The darkness is augmented and confused, by flying dust from the earth, dry twigs from the trees, and great ragged fragments from the rooks' nests up in the tower. The trees themselves so toss and creak, as this tangible part of the darkness madly whirls about, that they seem in peril of being torn out of the earth: while ever and again a crack, and a rushing fall, denote that some large branch has yielded to the storm.

Not such power of wind has blown for many a winter night. Chimneys topple in the streets, and people hold to posts and corners, and to one another, to keep themselves upon their feet. The violent rushes abate not, but increase in frequency and fury until at midnight, when the streets are empty, the storm goes thundering along them, rattling at all the latches, and tearing at all the shutters, as if warning the people to get up and fly with it, rather than have the roofs brought down upon their brains.

Still, the red light burns steadily. Nothing is steady but the red light *(Chapter 14)*.

Before coming to England he had caused to be whipped to death sundry 'Natives' – nomadic persons, encamping now in Asia, now in Africa, now in the West Indies, and now at the North Pole – vaguely supposed in Cloisterham to be always black, always of great virtue, always calling themselves Me, and everybody else Massa or Missie (according to sex), and always reading tracts of the obscurest meaning, in broken English, but always accurately understanding them in the purest mother tongue *(Chapter 16)*.

'Murder!' proceeded Mr. Honeythunder, in a kind of boisterous reverie, with his platform folding of his arms, and his platform nod of abhorrent reflection after each short sentiment of a word. 'Bloodshed! Abel! Cain! I hold no terms with Cain. I repudiate with a shudder the red hand when it is offered me' *(Chapter 17)*.

There was no more self-assertion in the Minor Canon than in the schoolboy who had stood in the breezy playing-fields keeping a wicket. He was simply and staunchly true to his duty alike in the large case and in the small. So all true souls ever are. So every true soul ever was, ever is, and ever will be. There is nothing little to the really great in spirit *(Chapter 17)*.

His gaze wandered from the windows to the stars, as if he would have read in them something that was hidden from him. Many of us would, if we could; but none of us so much as know our letters in the stars yet – or seem likely to do it, in this state of existence – and few languages can be read until their alphabets are mastered *(Chapter 17)*.

'I was saying something old is what I should prefer, something odd and out of the way; something venerable, architectural, and inconvenient.'

'We have a good choice of inconvenient lodgings in the town, sir, I think,' replied the waiter, with modest confidence in its resources that way; 'indeed, I have no doubt that we could suit you that far, however particular you might be. But a architectural lodging!' That seemed to trouble the waiter's head, and he shook it *(Chapter 18: Dick Datchery)*.

'It is not enough that Justice should be morally certain; she must be immorally certain – legally, that is' *(Chapter 18: Sapsea)*.

'Rosa, even when my dear boy was affianced to you, I loved you madly; even when I thought his happiness in having you for his wife was certain, I loved you madly; even when I strove to make him more ardently devoted to you, I loved you madly; even when he gave me the picture of your lovely face so carelessly traduced by him, which I feigned to hang always in my sight for his sake, but worshipped in torment for years, I loved you madly; in the distasteful work of the day, in the wakeful misery of the night, girded by sordid realities, or wandering through Paradises and Hells of visions into which I rushed, carrying your image in my arms, I loved you madly' (*Chapter 19:* Jasper).

'Hiram Grewgious, Esquire, Staple Inn, London.' This was all Rosa knew of her destination; but it was enough to send her rattling away again in a cab, through deserts of gritty streets, where many people crowded at the corner of courts and byways to get some air, and where many other people walked with a miserably monotonous noise of shuffling of feet on hot paving-stones, and where all the people and all their surroundings were so gritty and so shabby!

There was music playing here and there, but it did not enliven the case. No barrel-organ mended the matter, and no big drum beat dull care away. Like the chapel bells that were also going here and there, they only seemed to evoke echoes from brick surfaces, and dust from everything. As to the flat wind-instruments, they seemed to have cracked their hearts and souls in pining for the country (*Chapter 20*).

> ' "Confound his politics!
> Frustrate his knavish tricks!
> On Thee his hopes to fix?
> Damn him again!" '
> (*Chapter 20:* Grewgious).

'You shall have the prettiest chamber in Furnival's. Your toilet must be provided for, and you shall have everything that an unlimited head chambermaid – by which expression I mean a head chambermaid not limited as to outlay – can procure' (*Chapter 20:* Grewgious).

'If I was under sentence of decapitation, and was about to be instantly decapitated, and an express arrived with a pardon for the condemned convict Grewgious if he wrote a play, I should be under the necessity of resuming the block, and begging the executioner to proceed to extremities, – meaning,' said Mr. Grewgious, passing his hand under his chin, 'the singular number, and this extremity' (*Chapter 20*).

Mr. Tartar's chambers were the neatest, the cleanest, and the best-ordered chambers ever seen under the sun, moon, and stars. The floors were scrubbed to that extent, that you might have supposed the London blacks emancipated for ever, and gone out of the land for good. Every inch of brass-work in Mr. Tartar's possession was polished and burnished, till it shone like a brazen mirror. No speck, nor spot, nor spatter soiled the purity of any of Mr. Tartar's household gods, large, small, or middle-sized. His sitting-room was like the admiral's cabin, his bath-room was like a dairy, his sleeping-chamber, fitted all about with lockers and drawers, was like a seedsman's shop; and his nicely-balanced cot just stirred in the midst, as if it breathed. Everything belonging to Mr. Tartar had quarters of its own assigned to it: his maps and charts had their quarters; his books had theirs; his brushes

had theirs; his boots had theirs; his clothes had theirs; his case-bottles had theirs; his telescopes and other instruments had theirs. Everything was readily accessible. Shelf, bracket, locker, hook, and drawer were equally within reach, and were equally contrived with a view to avoiding waste of room, and providing some snug inches of stowage for something that would have exactly fitted nowhere else. His gleaming little service of plate was so arranged upon his sideboard as that a slack salt-spoon would have instantly betrayed itself; his toilet implements were so arranged upon his dressing-table as that a toothpick of slovenly deportment could have been reported at a glance. So with the curiosities he had brought home from various voyages. Stuffed, dried, repolished, or otherwise preserved, according to their kind; birds, fishes, reptiles, arms, articles of dress, shells, seaweeds, grasses, or memorials of coral reef; each was displayed in its especial place, and each could have been displayed in no better place. Paint and varnish seemed to be kept somewhere out of sight, in constant readiness to obliterate stray finger-marks wherever any might become perceptible in Mr. Tartar's chambers. No man-of-war was ever kept more spick and span from careless touch. On this bright summer day, a neat awning was rigged over Mr. Tartar's flower-garden as only a sailor could rig it; and there was a sea-going air upon the whole effect, so delightfully complete, that the flower-garden might have appertained to stern-windows afloat, and the whole concern might have bowled away gallantly with all on board, if Mr. Tartar had only clapped to his lips the speaking-trumpet that was slung in a corner, and given hoarse orders to heave the anchor up, look alive there, men, and get all sail upon her! (*Chapter 22*).

When a man rides an amiable hobby that shies at nothing and kicks nobody, it is only agreeable to find him riding it with a humorous sense of the droll side of the creature. When the man is a cordial and an earnest man by nature, and withal is perfectly fresh and genuine, it may be doubted whether he is ever seen to greater advantage than at such a time. So Rosa would have naturally thought (even if she hadn't been conducted over the ship with all the homage due to the First Lady of the Admiralty, or First Fairy of the Sea), that it was charming to see and hear Mr. Tartar half laughing at, and half rejoicing in, his various contrivances (*Chapter 22*).

'There is this sitting-room – which, call it what you will, it is the front parlour, Miss, . . . the back parlour being what I cling to and never part with; and there is two bedrooms at the top of the 'ouse with gas laid on. I do not tell you that your bedroom floors is firm, for firm they are not. The gas-fitter himself allowed, that to make a firm job, he must go right under your jistes, and it were not worth the outlay as a yearly tenant so to do. The piping is carried above your jistes, and it is best that it should be made known to you' (*Chapter 22:* Mrs. Billickin).

'Mr. Grewgious, . . . if I was to tell you, sir, that to have nothink above you is to have a floor above you, I should put a deception upon you which I will not do.

No, sir. Your slates WILL rattle loose at that elewation in windy weather, do your utmost, best or worst! I defy you, sir, be you what you may, to keep your slates tight, try how you can.' Here Mrs. Billickin, having been warm with Mr. Grewgious, cooled a little, not to abuse the moral power she held over him. 'Consequent,' proceeded Mrs. Billickin, more mildly, but still firmly in her incorruptible candour: 'consequent it would be worse than of no use for me to trapse and travel up to the top of the 'ouse with you, and for you to say, "Mrs. Billickin, what stain do I notice in the ceiling, for a stain I do consider it?" and for me to answer, "I do not understand you, sir." No, sir, I will not be so underhand. I *do* understand you before you pint it out. It is the wet, sir. It do come in, and it do not come in. You may lay dry there half your lifetime; but the time will come, and it is best that you should know it, when a dripping sop would be no name for you' (*Chapter 22:* Mrs. Billickin).

'It is not Bond Street nor yet St. James's Palace; but it is not pretended that it is. Neither is it attempted to be denied – for why should it? – that the Arching leads to a mews. Mewses must exist. Respecting attendance; two is kep', at liberal wages. Words *has* arisen as to tradesmen, but dirty shoes on fresh hearth-stoning was attributable, and no wish for a commission on your orders. Coals is either *by* the fire, or *per* the scuttle.' She emphasised the prepositions as marking a subtle but immense difference. 'Dogs is not viewed with favour. Besides litter, they gets stole, and sharing suspicions is apt to creep in, and unpleasantness takes place' (*Chapter 22:* Mrs. Billickin).

'Cannot people get through life without gritty stages, I wonder?' (*Chapter 22:* Rosa Bud).

'I will not hide from you, ladies,' said the B., enveloped in the shawl of state, 'for it is not my character to hide neither my motives nor my actions, that I take the liberty to look in upon you to express a 'ope that your dinner was to your liking. Though not Professed but Plain, still her wages should be a sufficient object to her to stimilate to soar above mere roast and biled' (*Chapter 22:* Mrs. Billickin).

'I was put in youth to a very genteel boarding-school, the mistress being no less a lady than yourself, of about your own age or it may be some years younger, and a poorness of blood flowed from the table which has run through my life' (*Chapter 22:* Mrs. Billickin).

'If you was better accustomed to butcher's meat, Miss, you would not entertain the idea of a lamb's fry. Firstly, because lambs has long been sheep, and secondly, because there is such things as killing-days, and there is not. As to roast fowls, Miss, why you must be quite surfeited with roast fowls, letting alone your buying, when you market for yourself, the agedest of poultry with the scaliest of legs, quite as if you was accustomed to picking 'em out for cheapness. Try a little inwention, Miss. Use yourself to 'ousekeeping a bit. Come now, think of somethink else' (*Chapter 22:* Mrs. Billickin).

'I like,' says Mr. Datchery, 'the old tavern way of keeping scores. Illegible except to the scorer. The scorer not committed, the scored debited with what is against him. Hum; ha! A very small score this; a very poor score!' (*Chapter 23*).

A brilliant morning shines on the old city. Its antiquities and ruins are surpassingly beautiful, with a lusty ivy gleaming in the sun, and the rich trees waving in the balmy air. Changes of glorious light from moving boughs, songs of birds, scents from gardens, woods, and fields – or, rather, from the one great garden of the whole cultivated island in its yielding time – penetrate into the Cathedral, subdue its earthy odour, and preach the Resurrection and the Life. The cold stone tombs of centuries ago grow warm; and flecks of brightness dart into the sternest marble corners of the building, fluttering there like wings (*Chapter 23*).

INDEX TO QUOTATIONS

INDEX TO QUOTATIONS

compiled by Ann Hoffmann

THIS Index has been compiled with the sole purpose of assisting the general reader to locate a passage in Dickens's works, bearing in mind that all he may remember of it may be one key-word, one phrase or one character. It is not, therefore, a conventional index to quotations. In addition to key-words and key-phrases, entries will be found for characters who either speak or are spoken of, as well as for subjects which are described in the quotations but which cannot be indexed adequately under a key-word or phrase. Names of places are also included where they form the subject of a quoted passage.

Words are indexed under the spellings in which they appear in the text, except where there is a corresponding key-word—in which case a sub-heading will be found under the key-word and a cross-reference if the entry is of sufficient merit. Contrary to normal indexing practice, a phrase is sometimes entered under the adjective or adverb, where these are more likely to be remembered than the nouns they qualify.

In indexing the names of characters, the same principle has been followed as in THE PEOPLE, whereby male persons without Christian names are indexed by their surname only. This being primarily an index to quotations, the references to characters are *finding references only* and do not, especially in the case of main characters, list every single page on which a person is mentioned. The first and last page references of a sequence are given, and where a character appears on almost every page (but not necessarily every column) the reference is followed by *passim*,

The letters *a* and *b* after the page numbers provide a finding reference to the left- and right-hand columns respectively.

In the sub-headings the initial letter of the key-word is used as an abbreviation, 's' being added for the plural form.

The method of alphabetical arrangement used in the Index to Quotations, and in the Selective Index which follows, is that of word-by-word.

R

garnished and tricked out, 406b–407a

gas
the g. . . . has a haggard and unwilling look, 403b

Gashford, 317a

gate, ferocious strong spiked iron, 456a

Gay, Walter, 342b–343a, 346b–347b, 348b, 349a, 353b–354a

geese
picking her g. pretty hard, 390a

General, Mrs., 433b–434a

generic bore, 386a–b

generosity, [Mr. Turveydrop's] uncommon, 410a

genteel
so exceedingly g., that our scope . . . very limited, 367b

gentleman
g. in small-clothes, 296a–297b, 299a–b
g. with no stomach, 249a
he is a g., . . . has the manners of a g., . . . the appearance of a g., 295a
pale-faced g. with the red head, 243a
powdered-headed old g., 242b
red-faced g. in a white hat, 242b
skin tie g., 263b–264a
the fat g., 254b
the poetical young g., 283b
the single g., 242a
the theatrical young g., 283b

gentlemen
g. . . . kidnapped to pay attention to some person's daughters, 250b
the 'professional g.', 243a

genuine
nothing's g. in the place . . . but the dirt, 366a

Geographical chop-house, 465b

geological hammer, 407b

George, Mr., see Rouncewell, George

geraniums, 370a

gets on
g. finer as she g.o., 410b

ghost
Cock Lane G., 299a, 438b
g. in master B.s room, 395a
G. of Christmas Present, 334a
g. stories, 389a–b
g.s. . . . waiting their dismissal from the desolate shore, 446a
haunted by the g. of a tremendous pie, 391a
Marley's G., 333b
also 304b, 317b, 339a

giant
family of g.s. . . . throwing tea-leaves on the shore, 384b
ill-mannered G., 453a
jolly G., glorious to see, 334a
picter of the G., 392a

Giles, 277a–b

Gills, Solomon, 342b–343a, 354a

Gimblet, Brother, 481a

gin, 270a
g. and water warm, 329a

gin-shops, 247b

gingerbread, despairing, 478a

girl
the Odd G., 394b
the old g., 410b, 412b, 417a–b, 418b

give
a-going to g. her, 479b

giver up, not a, 350a

Glory, 317a

gloves, white kid, 466b

goad the schoolmaster, 475b

Gobler, 249a–b

goblin
conscientious g. of the bull species, 343b
G. of the Bell, 336a

God bless them . . . God save them, 485a

God bless Us, Every One!, 334b

Godfather
G. and godson do credit to one another, 417b
G. to a Bell, 334b

godson, George's, 417b

'goes' [of gin, brandy], 243a

going
always . . . g. to go, and never g., 325a
feel as if I was – G., 476a
g. a fishing, 443b
know that I am G., 326a

'going about', 473a

gold, 284a

gold mine
not for an annual g.m., and found in tea and sugar, 318b

good
he wos wery g. to me, 406a, 416a

good-bye
last g-b. on the list, 427a

Good Let, 396b

good points, 458b

Goodchild, Francis, 436b, 437a–b

goose
never was such a g., 334a

gooseberries
mathematical g., 345a
Mrs. Pipchin acts like early g. upon me, 352b

gore
human g., 315a
two forms . . . steeped in his Goar, 285b

goroo, 360a–b

gout, sovereign cure for the, 258b–259a

Government
G. offices, 420a–b
no G., 414b

Gowan, Mrs., 432b, 433a

Gradgrind, Thomas, 420a–426a passim

Gradgrind, Mrs. Thomas, 420b–421a, 423b, 425a

Gradgrind, Louisa, 421a–423b
see also Bounderby, Mrs. Josiah

Gradgrind, Tom, 422a

graminivorous ruminating quadruped, 420b

grandfather
ancient title of g. . . . long laid dormouse, 305a
boy arter his g.'s own heart, 305b
wery wrong in little boys to make game o' their g.s., 306a

Grandfather, narrator of Old Curiosity Shop, 307a–b

Grandmarina, 481b

grandmother
my mother left me to my g., 421a

grapes, 433a–b

grass
told the famished people that they might eat g., 445b

grave-digging
a good damp, wormy sort of business, 325a

graves
abounding in vestiges of monastic g., 482b

gravitation, moral law of, 316b

gravity
his g. was unusual, portentous and immeasurable, 469a

gravy
dropped . . . upon the stairs, where it remained . . . until it was worn out, 372a–b
more of g. than of grave, 333b
no such passion in human nature, as the passion for g. among commercial gentlemen, 326a
the g. alone is enough to add twenty years to one's age, 326a

SELECTIVE INDEX

SELECTIVE INDEX

compiled by Ann Hoffmann

THIS is an index to the TIME CHART (excluding the *General Events* column) and to information concerning publishers, dates and places of publication contained in the preambles under each title in THE WORKS. Finding references (in bold figures) are also given for all entries in DICKENS AND HIS CIRCLE.

The letters *l* and *c* after a page number refer to the *Life* and *Career* columns of the TIME CHART respectively; *a* and *b* indicate the left- and right-hand columns of pages elsewhere, following the system used in the *Index to Quotations*.

In order to avoid overloading the entry for Charles Dickens, personal sub-headings only have been included there and the rest, together with titles of his works, placed in their alphabetical sequence.

Sub-headings are arranged chronologically rather than alphabetically, except in the case of addresses of Dickens in London, titles of works and theatrical productions.

The following abbreviations of names have been used: CD, for Charles Dickens; D, for Dickens; H, for Hogarth.

Where titles of works by Dickens appear more than once in the same column on the same page of the TIME CHART, one entry only will be found in the index. A series of sub-headings to cover the writing, completion, serialisation and book publication of each work, followed by identical page references, would merely add bulk to the index, and the reader should have no difficulty in locating these references. A similar rule applies where the names of journals, publishers and places occur more than once in the same column.

'Aboard Ship', 25*b*

Agassis, Jean Louis Rodolph, **223a**

Ainsworth, William Harrison, 201*l*, 202*l*, **223a**

Albaro, Italy, 206*l*

All the Year Round, 17*b*, 18*a*, 25*a*, 26*a*, 29*a*, 215*c*, 217*c*, 219*c*; CD chooses title, takes offices for, 214*c*; first number, 23*a*, 215*c*; CD writes last Christmas piece for, 218*c*

Alphington, Devon: Mile End Cottage, 202*l*

amateur theatricals, *see* theatricals, private

America: CD's first visit to, 11*b*, 204*l*–205*l*; second visit to, 218*l*–219*l*

American Notes, 11*b*, 205*c*

Andersen, Hans Christian, **223a**

'Arcadian London', 25*b*

Associated Newspapers, 31*b*

'Astley's', 3*a*

Athenaeum Club: CD elected member of, 202*l*; CD presides at opening of, in Manchester, 205*l*; CD opens, in Glasgow, 208*l*

Atlantic Monthly, 29*a*, 218*c*

Austin, Henry, brother-in-law of CD, **223a**; death, 216*l*

Austin, Mrs. Henry, **223a**; *see also* Dickens, Mary Letitia

Baltimore, U.S.A: CD in, 205*l*; reading in, 218*c*

Barham, Richard Harris, **223a**

Barnaby Rudge, 10*a*, 202*c*, 203*c*, 204*c*

Barrow, Edward, uncle of CD, **223b**

Barrow, Elizabeth, *see* Dickens, Mrs. John

Barrow, John Henry, uncle of CD, 198*c*, **223b**

Barrow, Thomas Culliford, uncle of CD, **223b**

Bath, Somerset: CD at York House Hotel, 203*l*

'Battle of Life, The', 13*a*, 14*a*, 207*c*–208*c*; CD at rehearsals of, 208*l*

'Beadle, The', 3*a*

Beadnell, Anne (later Mrs. Henry Kolle), **223b**

Beadnell, Maria (later Mrs. Henry Winter), 198*l*, 199*l*, 213*l*, **224a**

Beard, Dr. Francis Carr, physician, 219*c*, **224a**

Beard, Thomas, **224a**

Beecher, Ward: reading at chapel of, 218*c*

'Begging-letter Writer, The', 17*b*

Belgium: CD with Catherine and Browne in, 201*l*; *see also* Brussels

Bell's Life in London, 3*a*, 200*c*

Bentley, Richard, 5*b*, 6*b*, 10*b*, 200*c*, **224a**

Bentley & Son, Richard, publishers, 6*a*

Bentley's Miscellany, 6*a*, 6*b*, 10*b*, 201*c*; CD agrees to edit, 200*c*; first number, 201*c*; CD relinquishes editorship, 202*c*; *Tales and Sketches from*, 6*b*

Berwick-upon-Tweed, Northumberland: reading at, 216*c*

'Bill-Sticking', 17*b*

Birmingham: CD in, 203*l*, 211*l*; CD takes chair at Polytechnic Institution at, 206*l*; CD's theatre company at, 209*l*; CD at Twelfth Night Banquet at, 211*l*; readings at, 212*c*, 216*c*

'Birthday Celebrations', 25*b*

'Births: Mrs. Meek, of a Son', 17*b*

'Black Veil, The', 4*a*

Blacking Warehouse, Warren's, 196*l*, 197*l*

Blackmore, Edward, **224a**; *see also* Ellis & Blackmore

Blackwood's Magazine, 21*b*

Bleak House, 19*a*, 211*c*, 212*c*

Blessington, Marguerite, Countess of, 20*b*, **224a**

'Bloomsbury Christening, The', 4*a*

'Boarding-house, The', 3*b*

'Boiled Beef of New England, The', 25*b*

Bologna, Italy, 206*l*

Bonchurch, Isle of Wight, 209*l*; *Copperfield* partly written at, 16*a*

Boston, U.S.A.: 205*l*; CD speaks in, 205*c*; readings in, 218*c*, 219*c*

Boulogne, France: CD and family in, 211*l*, 213*l*; at Château des Moulineaux, 212*l*; CD at Villa Camp de Droite, 212*l*; works written at, 18*b*, 19*a*, 20*b*

'Bound for the Great Salt Lake', 25*b*

Boyle, Mary, **224b**

'Boz', 3*a*, 6*a*; statement on identity of, 201*c*; *see also* Sketches by Boz

Bradbury & Evans, publishers, **224b**; CD leaves Chapman & Hall for, 206*c*; CD quarrels with, 214*c*; editions of CD's works, 5*b*, 13*b*, 14*a*, 14*b*, 16*a*, 18*b*, 19*a*, 20*b*, 21*b*